W9-BJK-669

ECONOMICS

Fourth Edition

Ralph T. Byrns
The University of Colorado at Boulder

Gerald W. Stone
Metropolitan State College

Scott, Foresman and Company
Glenview, Illinois   London

Cover and part opening photos property of Scott, Foresman.

Library of Congress Cataloging-in-Publication Data
Byrns, Ralph T.
  Economics.

  Includes indexes.
  1. Economics. I. Stone, Gerald W. II. Title.
HB171.B99 1989   330   88–26389
ISBN 0–673–38194–3

1 2 3 4 5 6–RRW–93 92 91 90 89 88

TO THE INSTRUCTOR

Our major objective is to ensure that students learn the basic economic principles that provide unique insights into how the world works. Just as one task of any good actor is to keep the audience from yawning, our goal cannot be realized if students find the material so difficult, abstract, or dull that they will not read it—an all-too-common failing.

Good writing and powerful examples can overcome student apathy and a routine failure to link "textbook" economics with highly-publicized, real-world issues. Smooth and logical flow are a product of revision—and more revision. We are pleased that each new edition of *Economics* seems livelier and more polished than its predecessor. Far more than most principles texts, this book applies theory to a rich variety of everyday experiences, historical events, and recent headlines. These intuitively appealing examples help students internalize and apply economic reasoning.

Special Features of this Text

Our conventional organization should make it unnecessary to radically alter your principles syllabus. Each part of *Economics* 4/e opens with a broad introduction indicating how sequential chapters are related, and each chapter begins with a list of Key Terms and an overview of the topics it covers. Numerous other pedagogic aids run through the text:

1. Major points are *italicized*, and

   Key terms and **economic laws** are **bold-faced** when introduced, with *definitions that are set off from the rest of the text.*

2. Analytical graphs are rendered simply, to efficiently convey economic concepts, and attractively, to pique students' interest. Standardized notation in graphs and equations aids student comprehension. Descriptive and historical data are illustrated in a modern style that parallels the graphical techniques used when data are presented by the media—whether in newspapers, in such magazines as *Fortune* or *Time*, or in TV news broadcasts.

3. Boxed Focuses (for example, Will Social Security Absorb our National Debt?, Should We Export Pollution?, and The Costs of Protectionism) and Biographical Sketches are used judiciously to give students a well-rounded introduction to economics.

4. Chapters conclude with (*a*) a comprehensive Chapter Review that covers Key Points, (*b*) Problems for students to work, and (*c*) several Questions for Thought and Discussion.

5. Frequent legal cases reveal the linkages between Law and Economics.

6. Optional Materials on selected analytical concepts (for example, Graphing, the Mathematics of Multipliers, Indifference Curves, and Isoquants) are appended to some chapters for instructors who like more intensive coverage.

7. An extensive Glossary and thorough Indexes at the end of the book provide handy references for students.

Key Changes in the Fourth Edition

A mix of minor and major improvements in content, organization, and flow permeates every page of *Economics* 4/e, but certain key changes may affect how you structure your course if you taught out of our previous edition:

1. Two new chapters cover the causes and effects of mammoth deficits, and the microeconomics of agriculture.

2. International economics receives greater emphasis. Such issues woven throughout the text are: the competitiveness of U.S. business, the consequences of federal deficits for U.S. balances of payments and the exchange rate of the dollar, how increasingly open international markets may affect antitrust policies, and the "dumping" of agricultural products in the context of rising protectionist sentiment. There is also expanded discussion of the many types of gains from trade and the costs of protectionism.

3. The chapter on imperfect competition now includes more material on advertising and such "new industrial organization" tools as game theory. Deregulation and re-regulation is also treated in greater depth.

4. New studies on wage discrimination and comparable worth augment our chapters on labor markets.

5. The Law and Economics sections include more timely cases on such issues as seniority and job security, and the consequences of insider trading in securities markets.

Printed Supplements

Our *Economics* package provides a broader spectrum of teaching supplements than is available for any other set of texts for principles of economics:

1. *Great Ideas for Teaching Economics* now includes roughly 600 analogies, anecdotes, exercises, and general teaching tips, contributed by instructors from across the country.

2. Our *Student Guide for Learning Economics* uses a variety of techniques to facilitate student mastery of economic concepts. Each chapter includes an extensive chapter review, matching problems, true-false questions, fill-in reviews, multiple-choice questions, and problem sets, and some have specialized exercises as well. Answers are keyed to the text, and the logic of the economic reasoning used to solve challenging problems is outlined.

3. The *Instructor's Manual for Teaching Economics* contains chapter outlines, lecture suggestions, answers to end-of-chapter problems and questions, and analyses of the legal cases that conclude many chapters. Some supplementary materials can be reproduced as class hand-outs (e.g., selected legal cases and extra biographical sketches).

4. The *Test Bank for Economics* has grown into *Bank A* and *Bank B*. Our 7,000 question base allows you to alternate test banks between semesters. Software versions of this set of class-tested *Test Banks* are available for IBM and Macintosh compatible microcomputers.

5. The expanded *Hyperinflation Collection* contains brief histories and actual samples of currency and stamps from such hyperinflations as those experienced in Germany in the 1920s, Greece and Hungary in the 1940s, and South America in the 1980s.

6. 120 four-color overhead *Transparencies* of selected important figures and tables from the text are provided.

Software Supplements for Students

Available shrink-wrapped with *Economics* 4/e is an Economics Software Package containing four new or revised programs: *Macrosim, Raiders, Study-Calc,* and the *Graph Tutor*. Students should find the exercises they contain a gratifying and enjoyable way to study parts of this material.

1. *Macrosim,* a computer-based simulation, allows students to manipulate policy instruments (e.g., government spending, tax rates, and the money supply) in attempts to stabilize economic activity and stimulate growth. The new *Student Edition* (with problem sets) uses building blocks, starting with a very simple Keynesian model, so that it can be used step-by-step throughout the macro course. An Instructor's Edition, *Create,* allows instructors to tailor scenarios to reflect virtually any macroeconomic view of how the world works.

2. *Raiders* is a tutorial that students can begin to use by the second week of class. This program sequentially tests students' mastery of simple demand and supply analysis, then elasticity calculations, production and costs, and, ultimately, their ability to maximize profits in a series of progressively more complex product and resource markets. Students who successfully solve this program should understand virtually all fundamental microeconomic principles.

3. *Study-Calc,* a simple spreadsheet and graphics generator, provides students with a "hands-on feel" for the relationships between equations and economics graphs. Exercises for macro and micro are included.

4. *Graph Tutor* is a new program that helps students learn to interpret, understand, and manipulate graphs. Students begin with such fundamentals as constructing graphs by identifying points in Cartesian space. They then shift curves or move along them in response to on-screen queries.

Software Supplements for Instructors

1. *ExamWord* is a new program that converts your favorite word processor into a powerful test generator for IBM compatibles. Draw questions from the 7,000 item Test Banks we've prepared (or write your own with any processor that supports ASCII text), build your exam with *ExamWord,* and then use your own program's familiar routines to print your exams.

2. *ExamScience* extends *ExamWord* to allow automatic printing of complex equations and sophisticated graphics. Ready-to-print graphs are included on the diskettes for our 7,000 item Test Banks, or you can use *ExamScience* (or most standard graphics programs) to build files for your own questions. This versatile program supports over 150 different printers.

3. *TSP*—the Student Version. We provide a data diskette containing dozens of macroeconomic time series (and student exercises) with this statistical analysis program. Many economists have found this version of *TSP* to be a great tool for a wide variety of elementary research.

4. The *Diploma* class management system includes four computer programs for IBM, Apple IIc and IIe, and compatible microcomputers:

(*a*) *Exam* provides question creation and editing features for use in developing, maintaining, and altering test banks. Unlimited questions can be accommodated in four formats: multiple choice, true/false, matching, and short answer/essay. Our *Test Banks* are provided on diskettes for this program.

(*b*) *Gradebook* automatically tracks grade averages for both students and tests and can display letter grades, percentage averages, or points earned.

(*c*) *Proctor* allows students to take tests at a computer. Students can browse, skip hard questions, alter answers, and review responses, as if the test were being taken on paper. Grading is automatic. Our *Guides* software provides drills that use *Proctor* to cover 15 core areas in ways that economics students will remember, and can easily be supplemented.

(*d*) *Calendar* is a free-form scheduling tool that allows instructors to enter several events or messages for any particular day. A transfer feature automatically recycles recurring events without retyping. Messages can be easily entered, edited, saved, displayed, or printed.

5. *Microtest II* is a computer test generator that makes our *Test Banks* run on the Macintosh.

Any principles text is always in process. Suggestions that aid us in making the next edition of *Economics* or its supplements clearer, more topical, or more complete will be deeply appreciated and gratefully acknowledged. Please send your comments to us, c/o Scott, Foresman and Company, 1900 East Lake Avenue, Glenview, Illinois 60025.

Acknowledgements

Many economists and students have made suggestions that have improved this edition of *Economics*. New biographies for George Stigler and Irving Fisher were drafted by Richard Winkelman of Arizona State University. A few ideas from reviewers of this edition were not implemented because of onrushing deadlines and so must await the next revision. Most, however, are reflected in these pages or in our supplements. Several reviewers of this edition have also contributed comments on previous editions. We deeply appreciate the many suggestions provided by:

Jim Alm	*University of Colorado, Boulder*
George Anayiotos	*University of Colorado, Boulder*
Robert E. Arnold, Jr.	*Henry Ford Community College*
John Baden	*Southern Methodist University*
Bill Barber	*Henry Ford Community College*
Carrie Battaglia	*University of North Texas*
Donna M. Bialik	*Indiana University-Purdue University/Fort Wayne*
Brian Binger	*University of Arizona*
Carl Biven	*Georgia Institute of Technology*
Dudley Blair	*Clemson University*
Kenneth Boulding	*University of Colorado, Boulder*
Colleen Cameron	*University of Southern Mississippi*
John P. Cochran	*Metropolitan State College, Denver*
Diane Coogan	*Boston University*
Larry Daellenbach	*University of Wisconsin-La Crosse*
A. Edward Day	*University of Central Florida*
Larry DeBoer	*Purdue University*
Norbert Dorow	*North Dakota State University*
Keith D. Evans	*California State University-Northridge*
Robert Eggleston	*Shippensburg State University*
Gordon Erlandson	*North Dakota State University*
Patricia J. Euzent	*University of Central Florida*
Ronald C. Fisher	*Michigan State University*
David Fractor	*California State University, Northridge*
Fred Glahe	*University of Colorado, Boulder*
Steven Greenlaw	*Mary Washington College*
Robert Gustavson	*Washburn University*
Dan Hagen	*Western Washington University*
Reza G. Hamzaee	*Missouri Western State College*
John S. Henderson	*Georgia State University*
Thor Hertsgaard	*North Dakota State University*
Elizabeth Hoffman	*University of Arizona*
Dave Huddleston	*Lurleen B. Wallace State Junior College*
E. Bruce Hutchinson	*University of Tennessee, Chattanooga*
Hong Hwang	*National Taiwan University*
Nicholas Karatjas	*Indiana University of Pennsylvania*
William Kaempfer	*University of Colorado, Boulder*
Mahmoud Khaboudan	*Penn State University, Allentown*
Gerrit Knaap	*University of Wisconsin, Green Bay*
Jerry J. Knarr	*Hillsborough Community College*
Kishore Kulkarni	*Northeast Louisiana University*
Richard Long	*Georgia State University*

Larry Mack	*North Dakota State University*
Mehrdad Madresehee	*Lycoming College*
Mike McKee	*University of Colorado, Boulder*
Charles E. McLure	*Stanford University and the Hoover Institute*
Patrick H. McMurray	*Missouri Western State College*
Tommy C. Meadows	*Austin Peay State University*
Mostafa Mehdizadeh	*Miami University of Ohio*
Jay Meyer	*Black Hills State College*
Peter Meyer	*University of the Pacific*
Edward Mills	*Clackamas Community College*
Ed Morey	*University of Colorado, Boulder*
Panos Mourdoukoutas	*Long Island University*
Michael Nieswiadomy	*University of North Texas*
Esmail Noori	*Metropolitan State College, Denver*
Neil Pelsue	*University of Vermont*
Tim Petry	*North Dakota State University*
James A. Phillips	*Cypress College*
Hassan Pirasteh	*Southern Oregon State College*
Mark Prell	*California State University-Northridge*
Joseph E. Pluta	*University of Texas at Austin*
Tom Rogers	*Southern Methodist University*
Saroj Sawhney	*Suffolk University*
Richard Schiming	*Mankato State University*
Donald Shadoan	*Eastern Kentucky University*
David Shorow	*Richland College*
Melvin Skold	*Colorado State University*
Gordon Smith	*Rice University*
Richard Spivack	*Bryant College*
Dudley Stewart	*Stephen F. Austin State University*
Tom Teitenberg	*Colby College*
F. Stephen Trimby	*Worcester State University*
Edwin F. Ulveling	*Georgia State University*
Jim Vincent	*University of St. Thomas*
Frank Vorhies	*University of Witwatersrand*
Steve Weiss	*University of Toledo*
Art Welsh	*Pennsylvania State University*
Jonathan Wight	*University of Richmond*
Peter A. Zaleski	*Villanova University*
George Zodrow	*Rice University*

This edition of our books and supplements would have been less timely and complete without the help of Mark Arnold, LaVonne Garcia, Christine Hughes Heckart, Susan Hessmann, Donna Martin, Carla Pacheco, and Mark Young, all of BRG Scientific and the Byrns & Stone Users Group. The editors at Scott, Foresman and Company would jointly deserve an Oscar if they produced films instead of books. Jim Sitlington's faith in our ideas and unwavering support have been a mainstay in both smooth times and rough. This book owes much of its polish and cohesiveness to Bruce Kaplan's skills and ideas, and to Ginny Guerrant's mastery of the editorial craft. Our superb design reflects the aesthetic sense of Kathy Cunningham, and our distinctive artwork was rendered by Precision Graphics.

Once more, we dedicate this book to Sheila, Trish, Mathew, Rachel, Jennifer, and Melissa. We hope that seeing their names in print remains a thrill.

TO THE STUDENT

A 1987 poll of almost 1,600 Americans generated the following list of the ten biggest problems facing the United States:[1] 1. AIDS, 2. illicit drugs, *3. costs of health care, *4. size of the federal deficit, *5. taking care of the homeless, *6. quality of public education, *7. U.S. trade deficit, 8. agreements with the USSR, 9. U.S. involvement in Central America, *10. likelihood of a recession.

The six problems marked with asterisks involve economics directly. The other four—controlling AIDS and drug addiction, and peacefully resolving the cold war with the Soviet Union and civil wars in Central America—are less obviously economic problems, but each has major economic consequences. This list suggests that economics looms large in most major national problems. But how does economics directly affect your life?

The basic economic problem confronting you, if you are typical, is that you would like far more than you can afford. Tuition and books probably absorb much of the income you would like to devote to clothes, cars, and entertainment. You would probably also like more time to study, a more gratifying social life, or more sleep. Your limited budget and time require decisions about how you will spend your hours and money. In a similar way, all societies must choose among alternatives. How individuals and societies choose, and the effects of their choices, are the focal points of economics.

Economics can be as fascinating as anything you will ever study and, if you are diligent, it will seem natural and logical. Understanding economics enables you to systematically address issues ranging from national policies to your professional and personal life. Insights gained from an economic perspective can provide you with advantages that most people lack.

---

[1] *U.S. News & World Report*, 28 December 1987, p. 28.

How to Study Economics _____

Superficial cramming is very unlikely to succeed in an economics course. Keeping up is crucial. Research by educational psychologists indicates that learning is most effective when you are exposed to information and concepts in several ways over a period of time. You will learn more economics and retain it longer if you read, see, hear, communicate, and then apply economic concepts and information. This material is much more than a few facts and glib generalizations; understanding economics requires reflection. Here is one systematic study strategy that many students have found successful in economics, and have adapted for other classes.

Visual Information

Don't let the extensive graphs in economics frighten you. There is a brief review of graphical analysis at the end of chapter 1; our *Student Guide for Learning Economics* also opens with a set of helpful exercises. Avoid the agony of trying to memorize each graph by taking the time to learn how graphs work. Proceed to chapter 2 only after you quell your anxiety a bit. (Be sure that you also understand simple algebra. The algebra used in this book is elementary, and should prove no problem if you have learned the material from a basic course.) As you become familiar with graphs, you may be surprised to find yourself mentally graphing many noneconomic relationships, and even more amazed to find this process enjoyable.

Reading

Schedule ample time to read your assignments, and try to use the same quiet and cool (but not cold) room every day. Avoid drowsiness by sitting in a hard chair in front of a desk or table. Think about the material as you read. Many students spend hours highlighting important points for later study, for which they somehow never find time. Too frequently, busywork substitutes for thinking about economics. Try to skim a chapter; then go back and really focus on five or six pages. Don't touch a pen or pencil except to make margin notes cross-referencing related materials you already know.

Writing

After a healthy dose of serious reading, close your text and outline the important points with a half-page of notes. If you cannot briefly summarize what you just read, put your pen down and re-read the material. You have not yet digested the central ideas. Don't be surprised if some concepts require several readings. Be alert for graphs and tables that recapitulate important areas. When you finish each chapter, read its Chapter Review, work through all Problems, and outline good, but brief, answers to all Questions for Thought and Discussion.

Listening

Most lectures blend your instructor's own insights and examples with materials from the text, but few students conscientiously work through assignments before lectures. You will have a major advantage over most of your classmates if you do, and will be able to take notes selectively. Focus on topics that your instructor stresses but which are not covered in depth in the text. Notes from lectures should supplement, not duplicate, your text.

Teaching

Your instructors know that they learn their subject in greater depth every time they teach it. Teaching exposes you to previously unfamiliar aspects of a topic because you must conceptualize and verbalize ideas so that other people can understand them. Take turns with a classmate in reading the Key Points (in the Chapter Review) to each other. After one person reads a Key Point aloud, the other should explain it in his or her own words. Study groups work well in this way, but you may learn economics even more thoroughly if you simply explain economic concepts to a friend who has never studied it.

Applications

Working through the material from our *Student Guide for Learning Economics* that parallels each chapter of the text will make it easier to comprehend the economic events regularly featured in the news. When this happens, you will be among the minority who truly understand economic and financial news. Use economic reasoning to interpret your day-to-day behavior, and that of your friends and relatives. This will provide unique insights into how people function and how the world works.

Examinations

Following the preceding suggestions should prepare you for minor tests and quizzes. To prepare for major exams and finals:

1. Read the Chapter Reviews for all chapters that will be covered on the examination. Keep a record of each Key Point that you could not explain to an intelligent friend who had never taken economics.
2. Return to each Key Point that you have not grasped adequately. Read the text material that covers it and rework the parallel parts of the accompanying chapter from your *Student Guide*.
3. Discuss any Key Point that is not clear to you with a friend.
4. Skim the Glossary at the end of the text for a last-minute refresher before your final exam. See if this technique works for you.

We know that this is a tall order, but if you conscientiously follow these study tips, we guarantee you an enjoyable and enlightening course.

We hope that you find this text helpful and enjoyable as you study economics. Many valuable suggestions for improvement were provided by students who used earlier versions of this book. If you have any comments, we would like to hear about them. Write us in care of Scott, Foresman and Company, 1900 East Lake Avenue, Glenview, Illinois 60025.

Ralph T. Byrns
Gerald W. Stone, Jr.

CONTENTS

ECONOMICS

CHAPTER 5   Economic Institutions: Households, Firms, and Government   82

MACROECONOMICS

PART 2   Measuring

Economic Performance   99

CHAPTER 6   Unemployment and Inflation   100

CHAPTER 7   Gross National Product (GNP)

PART 4

Money, Monetary Theory,

and Monetary Policy   217

CHAPTER 12   Money and Its Creation   218

CHAPTER 15 Financing Government: Deficits and the Public Debt 279

CHAPTER 18   Limitations of Stabilization Policy   353

MICROECONOMICS

PART 6   **Core Concepts**

of Microeconomics   403

CHAPTER 25 Monopolistic Competition and Oligopoly 522

CHAPTER 26 Antitrust Policy: Reducing Monopoly Power 543

CHAPTER 27   The Role of Government Regulation

CHAPTER 30   Rent, Interest, Profits, and Capitalization   634

PART 9   **The Microeconomics of Government Policy**   655

CHAPTER 31   Market Failures and Public Microeconomics   656

CHAPTER 32   Public Choice   677

CHAPTER 35 Redistribution of Income and Wealth   727

GLOBAL ECONOMICS

PART 10

The International

CHAPTER 38   Capitalism and Its Alternatives

Foundations of Economics

Many people have only fuzzy notions about economics—that it addresses aspects of business and money in some fashion—but for most, distinctions between economics, accounting, and finance are quite blurred. Just as putting a jigsaw puzzle together is easier if you first build its border by connecting the straight-edged pieces, this first part of the book introduces core concepts to provide a framework for understanding economics. We then apply these concepts to a variety of problems so that when you finish this book, you will have a relatively complete picture of the world of economics.

Fundamental economic concepts are the focus in chapter 1. Our first building block is an overview of the fundamental economic problem—*scarcity*—which arises because society's limited capacity to produce goods is exceeded by human desires for goods. We survey various types of productive resources, and whether people can be expected to behave selfishly or as humanitarians.

Scarcity makes decisions necessary and *opportunity costs* unavoidable. Economic analysis is important only because of this basic economic problem. Thus, we will look at methods that economists use to investigate the

way the world works, and the division of economics into *positive* (scientific) versus *normative* (prescriptive) components. We also distinguish *macroeconomics,* which addresses national economic issues, from *microeconomics,* which examines the choices made by individual decision makers. Chapter 1 concludes with discussions of *economic efficiency* and *comparative advantage and exchange.*

This provides a background for our first formal economic model, the *production-possibilities frontier,* introduced in chapter 2. There, too, we examine various mechanisms (such as brute force or the market system) that are used to answer the basic economic questions arising from scarcity. How our attempts to resolve the problem of scarcity affect economic growth and social well-being is interpreted using the production-possibilities frontier model.

A survey of the foundations of capitalism leads us into chapter 3, where *supply and demand* are introduced. Supply and demand analysis provides significant insights into how prices and outputs are determined in a market system; it also allows us to interpret a surprisingly wide range of human behavior. In chapter 4, we apply supply and demand to a variety of public policy topics, ranging from agriculture to wage and price controls. Part 1 concludes with chapter 5, which describes the roles played in a market economy by government and such private institutions as households and business firms.

CHAPTER 1

scarcity

production and resources

labor and wages

land and rent

capital and interest

investment and financial
 capital

entrepreneurship and
 profit

opportunity cost

positive vs. normative
 economics

macroeconomics vs.
 microeconomics

economic efficiency

comparative advantage

Scarcity and Choice

Can American workers and business firms meet growing challenges from foreign competition? Why is the stock market so volatile? Will giant corporations absorb most small firms if merger mania persists? Should massive federal deficits be cured by raising taxes, cutting government spending, or both? Why do the rich few seem to get richer while most people seem caught on a treadmill—going to and from work but never really getting ahead? And why do some poor people seem to lack opportunities to share in the "American Dream"? These and similar questions are just part of the puzzle we face as we try to accomplish the ultimate economic goal—high standards of living for people everywhere.

History books are filled with stories of politicians who lost power partially because they failed to solve major economic problems. President Hoover lost his 1932 reelection bid to President Roosevelt in the midst of the Great Depression. Policies to stabilize the economy and stimulate economic growth have been key issues in every election from 1792 through the 1988 election of President Bush.

Before you get the idea that economics is relevant only for politics or business, we should mention that *economics focuses on* **all** *the choices people make and the personal and social consequences of these choices.* Some choices involve money, but many do not. Thus, even seemingly noneconomic decisions fall within the realm of economics. Most decisions involve attempts to balance costs versus benefits, which may or may not be measurable with money. For example, many costs and benefits are primarily psychological.

Will you continue college? (Potential benefits include higher lifetime income, the joy of learning, or good times and personal contacts; costs include outlays for tuition and books, the drudgery of sitting through dull classes, and the income you could be making right now.) What will be your major area of study? (Will you only take classes in lucrative fields, or will you weigh enjoyment of the subject matter against potential monetary rewards?) Where will you live and work? Should you marry? If so, when? To whom? (Marriage involves both financial and psychological costs and benefits.) Should you have children? If so, how many? How will you spend your limited income? Your decisions about these and other economic choices will shape your life.

Economics looms large in everyday life, but you may know little about it as a field of study. You have probably heard words such as *prices, costs, profit, supply and demand, inflation, unemployment,* and *socialism* bandied about for much of your life. Right now, you may be skeptical about the *models, graphs,* and *theories* that economists use to interpret how the world works. These concepts and many more are woven into the fabric of economics. We believe that when you finish this book you will join us in the view that the economic way of thinking offers valuable insights into our everyday interactions with one another—producing, consuming, voting, and striving for the good life.

Foundations for your study of economics are set in this chapter by looking at bedrock concepts that will help you understand why people make certain choices and avoid others. Some basic economic concepts may seem overly abstract at first glance, but you will learn that many are simply precise descriptions of everyday events. We begin with a survey of scarcity—the basic economic problem—and the interplay between limited resources and relatively unlimited human wants that causes it. Scarcity implies that every decision involves opportunity costs, our second major topic. Then we look at some methods economists use to study human behavior, which leads to the key concept of economic efficiency. Linking these building blocks brings us to our final task in this chapter—describing why people specialize in some types of production and exchange their outputs for goods produced by others.

Scarcity: The Economic Problem

A world in which all human wants were instantly and perfectly fulfilled is hard to imagine. The harsh reality is that productive resources, and hence, production, are limited. Moreover, human wants are virtually unlimited. Combining these facts yields the basic economic problem—scarcity.

> **Scarcity** *occurs because human wants exceed the amounts of production possible with the limited resources that are available.*

The pervasiveness of scarcity means that you cannot have everything you want. You can, however, have some things you want, but must decide among the alternative choices that are available. Thus, scarcity forces us to choose, a fact reflected in a standard definition of economics:

> **Economics** *is the study of how individuals and societies allocate their limited resources to try to satisfy their unlimited wants.*[1]

A **good** (anything that adds to human happiness) is scarce if the amounts people desire are greater than the amounts freely available. Most people are individually or collectively (through taxes) willing to pay a positive price for scarce goods—banana splits, public parks, or apartments are obvious examples, but services such as haircuts or police protection are also goods because they add to our happiness. Garbage, an economic **bad** (anything that detracts from happiness), is not scarce. Most of us are dismayed when trash accumulates. Thus, garbage collection is a scarce good. The few desirable things that are not scarce are called **free goods.** For example, you can have all the seawater you want at zero cost (if you are on the beach), or freely breathe all the air your lungs will hold (accepting the current pollution level), or look at a sunset all you like (if you truly have nothing else to do).

Circumstances make goods either free or scarce. Potable water is nearly free when you camp next to a clean mountain stream, but is very scarce if you are lost in the desert. Even air is scarce for scuba divers, astronauts, and victims of flat tires. The fact that few things that people enjoy are free is reflected in the cliché that "there ain't no such thing as a free lunch (*TANSTAAFL*)." Our insatiable desires for goods are one dimension of scarcity; resource limitations are the other.

---

1. Modified from Lionel C. Robbins, *An Essay on the Nature and Significance of Economic Science* (London: Macmillan, 1935).

Production and Resources

Production occurs when we use knowledge or technology to apply energy to materials in ways that make the materials more valuable.[2] Houses and yo-yos are obviously produced goods, but services also entail production. For example, pouring a cup of coffee is productive—the coffee is more valuable in your cup than it was in the coffee pot. All **productive resources** (or *factors of production*) are limited, and are conventionally categorized as labor, land, capital, and entrepreneurship. These resources provide the knowledge, energy, or materials that make production possible.

Labor **Labor** refers to the physical and mental talents people make available to produce goods and services. Labor resources typically are measured by the time available for work during a given period. Payments for labor services are called **wages.**

Land **Land** includes all natural resources, such as unimproved land, minerals, water, air, climate, forests, and wildlife. Payments per time period for the use of land are called **rent.**

Capital **Capital** refers to improvements made to natural resources, such as buildings, machinery, sidewalks, and utility lines. Economic capital increases our capacity to produce other goods and services.

Investment refers to new capital produced each year. Some of our existing capital wears out each year. *Depreciation* is the term applied to the resulting decline in value and occurs, for example, as a new car becomes worth less as it ages and suffers wear-and-tear. The total amount of investment each year is called *gross investment.* Subtracting depreciation leaves *net investment,* which is the growth or decline in our capital stock. Suppose business buys $120 billion in new equipment, machinery, and other capital goods, but existing capital depreciates by $20 billion. The capital stock grows by $100 billion and society's net investment for the year is $100 billion.

---

2. Technology is the "recipe" used to combine resources so that production occurs. The technology used to grow roses is a simple example. If you know that roses need sunlight and moisture, you find a sunny spot and then apply energy (labor) to a shovel (capital) to dig a hole in the earth (land). Insert a rose bush, add fertilizer, dirt, and water (materials), and, with luck, roses will soon bloom.

Financial capital refers to currency, money in a bank account, or other paper assets (like stocks or bonds) that ultimately permit claims on raw resources or finished products. Thus, financial capital may be a paper claim on economic capital. Many people think that economic capital is the same as financial capital, but the two are very different concepts. Capital is physical; financial capital is normally a document of some sort. The deed to a house is financial capital; the house itself is economic capital. The term *capital* in this text will normally refer to economic capital. Payments for both types of capital services are called **interest.**

Entrepreneurship **Entrepreneurs** are people who combine labor, natural resources, and capital to produce goods and services and who incur risk in their quest for profits. After paying wages, rent, and interest for the use of other resources, entrepreneurs keep any money left over from the sales of the goods and services. The entrepreneur's **profit** is a reward for bearing business risks, organizing productive activities, and introducing innovations that improve our enjoyment of life.

Risk of loss is often enormous when entrepreneurs launch new products or enter new markets. More than half of all firms fail in their first two years. Texas Instruments, Coleco, and Atari were among the many ventures that lost fortunes trying to develop small computers and software in the mid-1980s. And hundreds of small oil companies went bankrupt in the late 1980s when oil prices plummeted. Only prospects of profit can overcome fears of loss. (Note that providers of capital receive interest rather than profit; all profit goes to entrepreneurs.)

Resource constraints are one of two important dimensions of scarcity. The other dimension of scarcity stems from our unlimited wants.

Human Wants and Rational Self-Interest

An economist is a man with an irrational passion for dispassionate rationality.
                                                        —*John Maurice Clark*

You might be able to imagine consuming all the water, steak, or cars that you would ever want if these items were costless. Even though your desires for some goods might be met completely, it is difficult to

Is Self-Interest Immoral or Unavoidable?

If you sliced off your finger tip while buttering your toast only minutes after reading in today's paper that an earthquake had swallowed China and its billion people, which event would dismay you most? In his first book, *Theory of Moral Sentiments* (1759), Adam Smith, the father of economics, argued that the loss of a little finger would keep the average European from sleeping that night, ". . . but, provided he never saw them, he will snore with the most profound security over the loss of millions of his brethren, and the destruction of that immense multitude seems plainly an object less interesting to him than this paltry misfortune of his own."

Smith illustrated the power of self-interest with this example, and suggested that disasters to others elicit sympathy only to the extent that you can imagine yourself in similarly dire straits. Suppose that the catastrophe in China would be prevented if you inserted your little finger into a crack in the space/time continuum of our universe, but that you would lose your finger in the process. Would you?

Smith thought that most of us would, not out of love for humanity, but rather because of " . . . love of what is honourable and noble, of the grandeur, and dignity, and superiority of our own characters." That is, you probably

would not be able to live with yourself if you failed to give up your finger.

Self-interest tends to limit, but not eliminate, charitable acts. Our personal senses of morality yield a spectrum of willingness to sacrifice for others. If you would surrender your pinkie for the lives of a billion anonymous Chinese, would you give up an arm? (Would whether others knew about your sacrifice matter?) Would you sacrifice your life? Only a saint would automatically answer this last question.

imagine being so satisfied that you could think of nothing that would add to your happiness. You will always want more goods and pleasures for as long as you live. (If all wants could be met, economics and economists would be irrelevant because no one would ever be forced to make decisions. But this imaginary world might be very boring; most of us thrive on overcoming a bit of adversity.)

Most economic theory follows the lead of Adam Smith, the father of economics, by assuming that people act purposefully and rationally to maximize their satisfactions, given their limited information, resources, and budgets. This characterization of *homo sapiens* as *homo economicus* (not to be confused with home economists) views all human behavior as self-interested. Why Smith, an eighteenth-century philosopher, advocated this approach is addressed in Focus 1.

Humanitarian or charitable acts are not viewed as exceptions to self-interested behavior: Philanthropists and Good Samaritans act charitably because it makes them feel better. People pick up litter or establish orphanages because they enjoy doing so or seek the public reputation and self-esteem derived from these activities.

You may agree with the many philosophers who deny that human behavior uniformly reflects attempts to maximize pleasure and minimize pain—an idea that seems to reduce motivation to its lowest common denominator. But even those who prefer to ascribe loftier basic motives to people concede that personal interest is an important consideration at the margin. (Otherwise, charities would not be so resistant to the elimination of tax deductions for charitable contributions.) Moreover, self interest need not condemn humanity to a constant state of conflict—

you will learn in chapters 3 and 4 that most econo-mists perceive it as a force that tends to coordinate people's plans and that commonly leads, indirectly, to a broad form of social cooperation.

Theories based on individual "happiness maximi-zation" or "wealth maximization" tend to explain economic activity more accurately than models based on selfless or humanitarian motives. In fact, so-called selfish people and so-called altruists often react to events in similar ways. For example, if the price of fruit falls relative to the prices of other foods, both the selfish person and the altruist may buy more—the selfish person to personally devour the fruit and the altruist to distribute it to needy children.

Scarcity occurs because resource limitations make it impossible to produce all the goods we want. We can have some things we want, but not everything. Prices are important information in choosing among the limited alternatives that are available. This raises the question of what we mean when we say *price* or *cost*. The answer is less obvious than you might think.

Forgone Alternatives: Opportunity Costs

Scarcity forces us to choose, but choosing one thing means that other options are lost. Economists focus on the most valuable option forgone because of a decision as the best measure of its real economic (op-portunity) cost.

Opportunity cost *is the value of the best alter-native surrendered when a choice is made.*

Most people think of costs as the amounts of money paid to produce or acquire goods. Money is a reason-able measure of costs for many purposes, but oppor-tunity cost is ultimately personal. (If costs were basi-cally objective rather than subjective, everyone's deci-sions would be identical in identical situations.)

Have you ever estimated the cost of your educa-tion? Table 1 indicates that these costs extend far beyond payments for tuition and books. How about the value of your time? Instead of studying and attending class, you could be holding a full-time job (or maybe two). You may be giving up a nice car, a

TABLE 1 *The Costs of a College Education*

	National Average (annual)	Your Costs
Tuition	$ 1,000 (public) $ 7,000 (private)	_____
Books (Misc.)	$ 5,530	_____
Forgone Income	$ 6,700 (minimum wage)	_____
Annual Total	$ 8,300 to $14,300	_____
Total for a Four Year Degree	$33,200 to $61,200	_____

Sources: American Council on Education, Education Department Estimates for 1988–89, and author estimates.

comfortable apartment, and fancy food and clothes. The values of these forgone alternatives are the true costs of your education. But suppose you quit school. Then the costs of your nice car, apartment, food, and clothing would be the sacrificed enjoyment of learn-ing and campus life, and the higher future income and consumption your degree may have made pos-sible.

To show how broad the concept of opportunity cost is, consider the example of a lovers' triangle. Suppose that Hortense and Wilhelmina both love Alphonse. Alphonse reciprocates fully; resigned to the indifference of Eudora, his true heartthrob, he loves both Hortense and Wilhelmina. Unfortunately, Hortense is jealous and threatens to find "someone new" if Alphonse does not quit seeing Wilhelmina. While soap opera fans might commiserate with Al-phonse's dilemma, economists view his situation as very similar to that faced by a family that would really like lobster but can afford either small steaks or big hamburgers, but not both. Irrelevant alternatives (such as Eudora and lobster) have no effect on the real costs of the choices at hand—the real cost to Alphonse of a continued relationship with Hortense is giving up Wilhelmina, and vice versa.

Opportunity costs are both crucial for rational decision making and unavoidable. Even if we try to ignore them at times, the alternatives sacrificed when we choose are still very real costs to us, and failing to

Is Life Priceless?

"You can't assign a value to human life" is a cliché frequently voiced in debates about public policies. In reality, however, people constantly and unavoidably assign prices to their own lives and those of others. Some of this is obvious, but some is quite subtle. Here are a few of the countless ways that life is priced.

1. Choosing more dangerous over less dangerous activities. For example, every time you ride in a car without using a seat belt, you (perhaps subconsciously) weigh the inconvenience of buckling up against the increased probability of death or injury. In so doing, you implicitly assign prices to your life and body parts. And parents assign prices for their children when they fail to buckle up their kids. Using tobacco, skydiving, hitchhiking, swimming, or even taking a walk all involve risks that assign prices to life.

2. After adjusting for the training required and the pleasantness of working conditions, higher wages are paid for riskier jobs.*

3. High prospective medical bills cause some people to forgo treatment that would prolong their lives, or the lives of seriously ill relatives.

4. The lives of millions of starving children in famine-plagued countries could be saved for only a few dollars each.

5. Every major war has been fought with draftees, whose lives are implicitly priced by political leaders and military strategists.

6. We could cut murder rates by surer and swifter law enforcement, but choose not to because reforming or expanding our police forces, the judicial system, and prisons seems too costly.

7. The fees of paid killers range from $200 to $500,000.

8. The 1975–86 drop in speed limits on interstate highways from 70 MPH to 55 MPH was estimated to save lives at a cost of from $2–5 million each (based on the value of time lost because travel was slower). Congress responded to widespread calls for more speed by raising the limit to 65 MPH in 1986, suggesting that many people viewed the lives saved by 55 MPH limits as too costly.

*Numerous studies conclude that an annual wage premium of about $2,000 is paid for each additional 0.1 percent probability of dying on the job. This translates into $1–2 million as a value for the life of U.S. workers.

---

consider opportunity costs may be disastrous. People sometimes refer to something as "priceless," implying that its value is so high that trying to specify opportunity cost is a futile exercise. This is generally an exaggeration, as Focus 2 indicates.

Many people feel trapped because they fail to recognize their options: suicidal teenagers who lose "the only one I'll ever love;" workers who lose jobs when plants shut down; high-risk entrepreneurs bankrupted when market conditions change. Numerous alternatives are available in most situations.

We have introduced the concept of scarcity, which makes economic choices necessary and opportunity costs unavoidable. This leads us to the area of economic analysis. After you learn a bit about how economists try to interpret human behavior, we will analyze some basic aspects of typical economic behavior.

The Nature of Economic Analysis

Economics is what economists do.

—*Jacob Viner*

Even Jacob Viner's circular approach barely hints at the full scope of economics. Economic reasoning involves studying and weighing alternatives. Economic analysis is concerned with decision making—the choices we make and the consequences of these choices for ourselves and others.

Economics conventionally has addressed how individuals' choices are coordinated to determine *what* goods a society will produce, *how* resources will be used to produce these goods, and to *whom* these goods will be distributed. Every society must resolve these problems in some fashion because resources are scarce and human wants are relatively unlimited. Should government decide what goods we produce and who gets to enjoy them? Should brute force or tradition prevail? What role, if any, should the marketplace play?

Areas traditionally within the sphere of economics include consumer behavior, business decisions, inflation, taxes, unemployment, international trade, and economic growth and development. More recently, economic analysis has been applied to areas ranging from marriage and the family to explanations for criminal behavior and war; from aspects of our political and legal systems to questions about environmental quality, education, and discrimination. No short description can cover all the varied concerns of economists.[3] One famous economist, John Maynard Keynes, summarized economics as: " . . . a method rather than a doctrine, an apparatus of the mind, a technique of thinking which helps its possessor to draw correct conclusions."

Good economic analysis blends elements of both art and science and borrows freely from the ideas of philosophers, legal scholars, ecologists, and behavioral scientists, all of whom offer alternatives to the economic way of thinking. Economics is an art because it often requires qualitative judgments about apparently contradictory evidence; it is a science because it requires organizing a maze of ideas and phenomena into a coherent whole. Sound theory is the key to the scientific side of economics.

Common Sense and Theory

Everything should be made as simple as possible, but not more so.

—*Albert Einstein*

Theory is often disparaged as impractical. Many people believe that few theorists cope in the "real world," and that most find it hard to walk and chew gum simultaneously. These critics view **common sense** as a practical guide for life. How can we judge the merits of a bit of common sense or theory? Common sense or theory are good if they correctly describe how things work, and bad if they fail to account for how the world works. In other words, we judge both theory and common sense by their accuracy! In fact, most common sense is nothing more than a collection of theories that have been long tested and found useful. Progress occurs when old theories are disproved by new knowledge that causes better theories to be developed and absorbed, albeit slowly, into our common sense. But how do theories develop? And how may new theories become tomorrow's common sense?

The process of theorizing consists, first, of identifying a problem area. Then we collect facts that seem related to the problem. Of course, we cannot gather all the facts because some things cannot be sensed directly. For example, sophisticated equipment may discern microwaves, but subatomic particles cannot be viewed directly with our most advanced technology—their existence is inferred. Moreover, we cannot concentrate on everything that can be sensed. Our senses are selective. (If you live near the tracks, after a while you don't hear the trains.) Finally, gathering all potentially helpful data is prohibitively costly, so we deal with incomplete information.

Once we have some data that seem relevant to our problem area, we try to figure out how they are related. That is, we develop a theory that we can test to see how well it performs in similar situations. If our new theory explains how things work better than existing

---

3. Evidence of the diversity of economics is that only half of all academic Economics Departments are in Schools of Business, with most of the rest being housed with Social Sciences or Liberal Arts.

theories, we replace the old ones with the new. New theory that is tested and found reliable eventually becomes part of our common sense—until even better theories are developed, a pattern illustrated in Figure 1.

The scientific approach contradicts the saying "That's the exception that proves the rule." Exceptions disprove scientific rules. For example, prior to Columbus's voyages, conventional European wisdom viewed our world as flat. Earth's roundness cannot be discerned from casual observation. Viewed from your window, it looks irregular but basically flat. The flat Earth theory was gradually replaced by a better theory when ships began to sail around the world, but there are still people who would call you crazy if you told them that Earth is a sphere. (The British Flat Earth Society still meets regularly.)

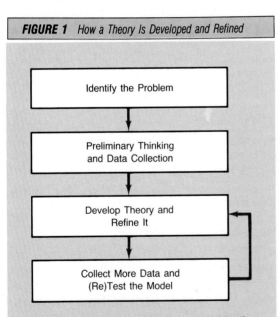

FIGURE 1 *How a Theory Is Developed and Refined*

Identify the Problem

↓

Preliminary Thinking and Data Collection

↓

Develop Theory and Refine It

↓

Collect More Data and (Re)Test the Model

The first step in any scientific theory is to identify the problem to be studied. (Asking the right questions is a sign of genius.) The second step is to collect some data and think about how they are related. Next, we formally develop a theory. Then we test it. This leads into a loop in which the theory is refined, more data are collected, and we test and retest our model. If the theory is an improvement over past theories, it eventually becomes a part of our common sense.

Models are representations of theories. The terms *model* and *theory* are interchangeable for most purposes. Some models are graphical, such as an architect's blueprints for a house or the highway maps you consult on your vacation. Some are physical, such as a watch, which models the passage of time. Others exist as mental images or mathematical equations. Many people are surprised to learn that their heads are filled with models. For example, most single people who ultimately plan to marry have in their minds general models of what their prospective spouses will be like (general appearance, intelligence, sense of humor, etc.).[4]

Many theories are criticized as too complicated. In fact, most scientists subscribe to an idea called **Occam's Razor**, which suggests that the simplest *workable* theories are also the most useful and best. For example, Earth once was thought a fixed point about which the rest of the universe spun. Incredibly complex equations were developed to trace movements of then observable planets and stars. Modern astronomy applies Occam's Razor to explain cosmic activity more simply—all the universe is in motion, and Earth revolves around the Sun, not vice versa.

A good model may be so simple that it is unrealistic except for its intended use. Simple models are usually less costly than complex ones. For example, you can look at intricately detailed metal or plastic models if you want to see how an airplane looks, but buying a cheap balsa glider and tossing it into the air will give you a better understanding of aerodynamics. Watches come in tuning-fork, 21-jewel, quartz-crystal, solar, atomic, and other varieties. Which is best? If all you care about is knowing what time it is, the best one most simply, accurately, and reliably (and cheaply?) reflects the passage of time.

To summarize, a good theory or model predicts as simply as possible how the real world works. Common sense evolves as exceptions to old theories compel acceptance of better theories after they have been tested extensively and appear reliable.

---

4. These examples are drawn from articles by Donald Elliott, Joe Garwood, Regan Whitworth, and Salvatore Schiavo-Campo in Ralph Byrns and Gerald Stone, eds., *Great Ideas for Teaching Economics,* 4/ed. (Glenview, IL: Scott, Foresman/Little, Brown, 1989).

Positive Versus Normative Economics

If you took all of the economists in the country and laid them end to end, they'd never reach a conclusion.
—George Bernard Shaw

Shaw's famous line echoes a popular but erroneous view that economists seldom agree on anything. In fact, 90 percent of economists would probably accept 90 percent of the fundamental theory presented in this book (with only nit-picking differences about which 90 percent of this theory to accept). What explanation is there for the disparity between the fact of widespread agreement and the common perception of disagreement? Part of the answer is that economists may disagree sharply about how even a widely accepted theory applies to a particular situation. The differences among economists about how theory should be translated into policy receive tremendous publicity, while broad areas of agreement are often ignored.

Even if economists agree amongst themselves, politicians often reject advice based on economic theory. For example, most economists favor free international trade but tariff barriers are standard responses to voter pressures when jobs are threatened by imports. Apparent discord also arises when economists in government feel compelled to agree publicly with the politicians who appoint them, while most other economists offer advice that the politicos find unacceptable.

Economists agree most about **positive economics,** which predicts tendencies in economic relationships. Ideally, positive economics is value free and addresses *what is,* while **normative economics** depends on value judgments and addresses *what should be.* Economists tend to disagree most when value judgments are at the core of an economic problem. For example, economists may differ sharply about the normative question of whether government should ever take a life, even that of a murderer, but most economists would agree that quicker, stiffer, and surer penalties deter crime, which is a value-free prediction from positive economics.

Normative issues frequently turn on questions of **equity** (fairness) and generate arguments among economists and the public alike. Policy is inherently more normative than theory, as exemplified by such statements as "We should redistribute wealth from the rich to the poor." This implies a value judgment that the benefits to the poor would exceed the harm done to the rich. There is little reason to suppose that an economist's value judgments about equity are basically superior to those of other people, but economic reasoning can offer unique insights into the effectiveness of alternative policies in achieving specific normative goals.

Normative issues are seldom settled by looking at evidence because value judgments generally involve faith and argument, not scientific proof. Disputes about positive economics ultimately can be settled by evidence, but even economists with shared values may disagree because some areas of positive economics remain unsettled for generations. For example, virtually everyone favors price-level stability and high employment, but economists may disagree about a proper cure for general economic instability. Some disputes remain unresolved because of difficulty in finding the right evidence and then digesting and accurately interpreting it in changing circumstances.

Even though all economic policy hinges on normative issues, if economists try to design policies consistent with goals set by policymakers, then their quest is positive in nature. For example, if minimizing unemployment is a goal, then developing policies to accomplish this goal involves positive economics. We can evaluate policies by how well they accomplish our goals, but positive economics cannot determine whether any goal is good or bad.

Macroeconomics and Microeconomics

Another way to categorize economic analysis is into macroeconomics and microeconomics. The prefixes *macro* and *micro* come from Greek words for "large" and "small," respectively. Thus, macroeconomics is the economic study of the entire society, while microeconomics focuses on the behavior of the individual household, firm, or a specific industry. By analogy, the tools of macroeconomics are telescopes, while those of microeconomics are microscopes. Differences between macroeconomics and microeconomics are, however, more of degree than kind.

Macroeconomics Large, economy-wide *aggregate* variables such as indicators of total economic activity are the focus of **macroeconomics.** Thus, macroeconomic analysis is concerned with our banking and monetary systems and how our national income, unemployment, inflation, and economic growth are determined. Macroeconomic policy analysis considers such things as the effects of changing taxes and government spending, or growth in the money supply. Commonly agreed upon normative goals of macroeconomic policy include:

1. **High employment.** People suffer when many workers cannot find jobs and many manufacturing plants and much machinery sit idle.
2. **Price level stability.** If, on the average, prices rise or fall rapidly, people may become confused about how much their wages will buy, or whether to consume now or invest in hopes of future returns.
3. **Economic growth.** People want to enjoy higher standards of living this year than last and most hope that their children will be even more prosperous than they are.
4. **Economic security.** People want to retain their jobs and the good things they have acquired. Security may be threatened by changes in what society wants (the birth of the auto put buggy-whip braiders out of work) or by such possibilities as nuclear war.

Microeconomics An economy's components are the focus of microeconomic analysis, which is the study of individual decision making, resource allocation, and how prices, production, and the distribution of income are determined. Thus, **microeconomics** focuses on interactions among individual households, firms, and specific government agencies.

Microeconomic policy involves the ways government regulations and taxes affect price and output structures, the numbers of firms in an industry, and the income distribution. Our ability to achieve the macro goals discussed previously depends strongly on micro policy. Beyond ensuring that micro policies are compatible with macro goals, there are three major goals for micro policy. The first is generally accepted; the second and third depend on more controversial value judgments:

1. **Efficiency.** An inefficient economy wastes resources and fails to provide the highest possible standard of living for consumers.
2. **Equity.** Equity is another word for fairness. If disparities between the "haves" and "have nots" are enormous, a few may enjoy great luxury while most people live in misery.
3. **Freedom.** Maximum freedom requires the range of choices available to people to be as wide and deep as possible. As with equity, however, more freedom for some may leave less for others. You may be limited in how wildly you can swing your arms if my nose is in the way.

These goals are sometimes inconsistent. For example, more efficiency may create inequity in the minds of many people. Granting a patent for a cancer cure might be efficient if potential profit would stimulate research to cure the disease. But once a cure was discovered, it might seem unfair not to treat those unable to afford the patented treatment. Alternatively, if one person (a stickup artist) disrupts another's production (operating a gas station), there is a trade-off between freedom and efficiency. Such trade-offs are among the reasons why societies everywhere implement legal systems to govern people's relationships. Acceptably balancing freedom, efficiency, and equity is among society's major challenges.[5]

Most early economists emphasized microeconomics, believing that macroeconomics merely entailed summing micro variables and then tacking in changes in the money supply to account for changes in the price level. Lack of time spent analyzing macro phenomena may have contributed to the boom-bust cycles that culminated in the Great Depression of the 1930s. That slump forced us to realize that one decision maker's actions may yield a far different result than if all decision makers take the same action at once. For example, one person in the bleachers may

---

5. Equity is inescapably normative and a bit nebulous. You will notice frequent conflicts between efficiency and equity in this book. We cannot avoid issues of equity, but focus on efficiency because it is easier to analyze with economic reasoning. This conflict is treated at length in Arthur Okun's *Efficiency vs. Equity: The Big Tradeoff* (Washington, D.C.: Brookings, 1973).

see a ball game better by standing up, but when others also stand (as they will) this advantage is lost. It is now clear that reaching our micro goals depends on achieving our macro goals, and vice versa. Understanding both is essential for an accurate perception of how any economy operates.

Efficiency is the microeconomic goal most easily addressed by economic analysis. Although economic goals sometimes seem in conflict, all economic goals tend to be more easily achieved in an efficient economy. Lack of opportunity for employment is one form of inefficiency. Excessive costs are another. More generally, inefficiency means that resources are wasted that could be used to enhance stability, growth, security, freedom, and equity.

Economic Efficiency _____

Different people may mean very different things when they use the word *efficiency*. For example, engineers or physicists call a system efficient if it minimizes the amount of energy lost in accomplishing some task, and environmentalists may talk about efficiency as the absence of waste in an ecological system. The concept of economic efficiency is a bit different.

> **Economic efficiency** *for society as a whole is achieved when we produce the combination of outputs with the highest attainable total value, given our limited resources.*

Alone, however, this definition offers few guidelines for achieving efficiency. Breaking this concept down into **production** *(technical)* **efficiency** and **consumption efficiency** yields clearer insights for policy.

Production Efficiency

Production (technical) efficiency occurs when:

1. The opportunity cost of a given value of output is minimized, or
2. The value of output produced from given resources is maximized, or

3. The value of output produced for a given cost is maximized.

If you think about these requirements for production efficiency, you will see that if any one condition is attained, the other two must also be met. All three are specified to help you recognize inefficient situations.

Production is technically inefficient whenever production costs are unnecessarily high or if more output could be produced without raising costs or using more resources. For example, the saying that "Too many cooks spoil the broth" implies that too much company in the kitchen causes economic inefficiency. Presumably, more good quality food could be produced at lower cost using fewer resources if some of the cook's helpers left. Government farm programs frequently create technical inefficiency in production. For example, farmers with superior land for growing sugar beets may be forbidden to do so because they lack federal allotments (authorization) for their acreage, while farmers with less suitable land but who have allotments are subsidized to grow sugar beets.

Consumption Efficiency

Efficiency in consumers' purchasing patterns requires that they:

1. maximize the satisfaction attainable from their budgets, or
2. minimize outlays to obtain goods yielding a given total satisfaction.

This means that if you would be happier by changing the mix of goods you now buy for a given cash outlay, you are currently an inefficient consumer. Alternatively, you could cut your total spending and achieve the same satisfaction as when your purchasing pattern was inefficient.

People try to act in ways that are efficient for them. For example, you could always turn off all lights and adjust your thermostat when you leave home to prevent "wasting" electricity or gas. Instead, many of us frequently leave on lights and heat or cool empty buildings. The time consumed to conscientiously quit wasting energy is more valuably used in other ways. Recognition that a current buying pattern is inefficient usually leads to changes in consumption. If you were shocked by an unexpected $700 utility bill, you would probably try harder to conserve energy in the future. Breaking habitual patterns can sometimes be difficult, however, as any ex-smoker will tell you.

An economy-wide state of economic efficiency must conform to certain general rules. Efficiency requires that opportunity costs be minimized for all forms of economic activity. Consumption patterns and the production of goods are both efficient whenever any change from the current situation would unavoidably harm at least one person. This implies that resources are allocated so that they produce the most valuable combination of goods possible—every drop of potential net benefits must be squeezed from the resources available.

Alternatively, economic inefficiency exists if production could be changed or goods could be exchanged so that no one lost and at least one person gained. Thus, whenever we can show potential but unrealized gains to someone entailing losses to none, the current situation is inefficient. Inefficiency means that appropriate corrections would enable society to cope better with scarcity. It is often easier to recognize inefficiency than efficiency. A few moments spent thinking about the following concepts will aid you in distinguishing efficient from inefficient situations.

The current situation is economically *inefficient* whenever:

1. the opportunity cost of a given amount of production exceeds its minimum possible value.

2. less than maximum possible output is produced from the resources available.

3. less than the maximum possible output is produced for a given cost.

4. consumers could gain more satisfaction by changing their purchasing patterns, given their budgets.

5. consumers could change their purchasing patterns and spend less income while still enjoying a given satisfaction level.

6. someone would gain while no one else loses if we made some feasible change.

The gains from the bargains people make represent movements towards greater economic efficiency. All parties to a voluntary transaction expect to gain or else they will not bother. For example, you will not give me an apple for my orange unless you value the orange more than the apple, and vice versa. Thus, a trade of your apple for my orange raises your satisfaction from a given outlay because you now have a subjectively (to you) more valuable orange. I gain by the exchange in a similar fashion. Thus, economic efficiency is enhanced through trade, and a failure to trade when such gains are possible is inefficient. In fact, if only *one* of us would gain by a trade but no other party would be harmed, failure to trade is inefficient.

Comparative Advantage

Among the basic forms of social interaction is trading what we have for things others have. Economic efficiency requires production and exchange according to *comparative advantage*. Imagine how low your standard of living would be if your family had to be totally self-sufficient—no convenience foods, no ready-made clothing, no utilities or machines. You could consume only what you produced yourself, and life would be "nasty, brutish, and short." Specialized production and exchange yield tremendous advantages: the gains to Floridians and Iowans from trading Florida oranges for Iowa wheat are fairly obvious examples, but similar gains can be realized whether we trade with Americans or foreigners.

Specialization occurs when different people produce different things, and should not be confused with the *division of labor,* which entails dividing the work associated with producing a given good. The division of labor allows such gains to occur as when one person on an assembly line puts a bumper on a car, another works on the engine, and a third installs headlights.

Both specialization and the division of labor allow individuals to produce more. Specialization and exchange also makes greater consumption possible. But how should people specialize? Specialization generates the largest gains when you concentrate on doing that which you can do at the lowest cost relative to other people; areas of relative efficiency are

TABLE 2 *Opportunity Costs and Efficiency*

Before Specialization	Hours Worked		Production and Consumption
Alaskan	4		5 fur coats
	4		1 pound of coffee
Brazilian	4		1 fur coat
	4		5 pounds of coffee

After Specialization	Hours Worked	Production	Consumption
Alaskan	8	10 fur coats	5 fur coats
			5 pounds of coffee
Brazilian	8	10 pounds of coffee	5 fur coats
			5 pounds of coffee

known as **comparative advantages.** Brazilians can grow coffee more easily than they can make fur coats, while Alaskans find it difficult to grow coffee but relatively easy to make fur coats, so an exchange of Alaskan fur for Brazilian coffee will definitely yield gains to both trading parties. In this case, Alaskans have a comparative advantage in fur production; the Brazilians, in coffee production.

The critical point is that efficiency requires all resources to be used where they are relatively the most productive. Table 2 shows how both parties to a trade can gain as long as their opportunity costs are not identical. In this case, Alaskans and Brazilians each specialize in their areas of comparative advantage—fur coats and coffee, respectively. If we assume that 1 fur coat trades for, say, 1 pound of coffee, then Alaskans can consume an extra 4 pounds of coffee daily while Brazilians can consume an additional 4 fur coats.

Notice that the Alaskans' opportunity cost of producing 1 pound of coffee is 5 fur coats before trade, while the Brazilians' opportunity cost of 1 pound of coffee is only 1/5 of a fur coat. Thus, opportunity cost guides us to comparative advantage: Nations and individuals gain when they produce goods with relatively low opportunity costs and then exchange their output for goods that others can produce at lower cost. The standards of living of all potential trading partners can be improved enormously through appropriate specialization and exchange.

But what if Alaskans had *absolute advantages* in everything; that is, could do virtually every task faster and easier than Brazilians? You might think that Brazilians could gain from exchange, but that Alaskans must lose if Brazilians gain. Surprisingly, however, both sides can gain. Suppose, for example, that a lawyer whose fees run $100 an hour types twice as fast as her secretary, whose wage is $10 an hour; she has absolute advantages in both typing and legal work. She will still gain by hiring the secretary to do her typing; her time is worth more in the courtroom. Similarly, many professional athletes probably have an absolute advantage in lifting and carrying when compared to furniture movers. Nevertheless, few highly paid athletes move their own furniture when they are traded between teams. Athletes and professional movers both gain by concentrating in their respective areas of comparative advantage.

U.S. exports have been swamped by imports in most recent years. Is this a signal that we are losing all comparative advantages? NO! Being comparatively disadvantaged in all areas is impossible because comparative advantage is based on relative magnitudes. What has been happening is that many other countries are expanding areas of production in which the United States has traditionally enjoyed huge advantages. Focus 3 identifies some continuing areas of comparative advantage for U.S. producers.

The major bedrock concepts developed in this chapter are scarcity and how it makes choices and

Is the United States at a Comparative Disadvantage?

One new car in four bought by Americans is foreign. We now import large quantities of steel, many of our clothes, and most of our shoes. Imports have exceeded exports during much of the 1980s. Such facts are cited by people who believe that we are losing our ability to compete in world markets.

The first and most important of several factors that account for concern that the United States has lost its ability to compete is the internationalization of most major economies. Most countries are both exporting and importing larger shares of their production and income than ever before, so almost every society is gaining an increasingly international flavor. Any growth of foreign influence alarms many Americans.

Second, some countries' exports have grown faster than those of the United States. Other countries have been playing "catch up," but signals are emerging that their rates of gain are slowing down. For example, our average labor productivity grew slower than in Japan and parts of Western Europe during much of 1950–79. This pattern was reversed during the 1980s, but wages in those countries have grown faster than U.S. wages. The result is that U.S. labor costs per unit of output, which were higher on average than those of other major industrial powers, have fallen to roughly average.

Third, the dollar was at post World War II highs in the mid-1980s. This caused foreigners to export more goods to the United States so that they would receive high prices, and discouraged them from buying high priced U.S. exports. We consequently experienced huge deficits in our balance of trade during 1983–87. Combining the recent relative decline in U.S. labor costs per unit of output with the fall in the value of the dollar during 1986–87 will encourage U.S. exports and discourage imports.

The United States was once the world's dominant industrial exporter. The growth of international competition apparently made it easy to forget that the U.S. continues to be the world's largest producer in most major industries, including aircraft, aluminum, computers, and paper. Voracious national consumption may mean, however, that we sometimes import goods at which we excel as producers. For example, we import steel even though the United States is the world's second biggest steelmaker.

Broad areas in which our comparative advantages are overwhelming include advanced technology, entertainment, and agriculture. It may be a surprise for you to learn that the United States remains the world's largest "high-tech" exporter if we lump together such things as aircraft, computers, instruments, petrochemicals, plastics, and semiconductors. We dominate exports of movies and music, and of agricultural products. (The top soil in our farm belt and our agricultural technology is the envy of the rest of the world.) Even our auto industry is the third highest exporter in world markets. If you are in another country and see a new "foreign" car, chances are one in nine that it was Made in the U.S.A.

opportunity costs unavoidable. We have also discussed efficiency, a concept that permits us to evaluate economic circumstances. You will repeatedly encounter these and other "building blocks" from this chapter when we investigate more advanced topics in the rest of this book. In the next chapter, we develop devices called *production-possibilities frontiers* to illustrate how scarcity limits our available choices, and we examine some mechanisms that people use in trying to cope with scarcity.

CHAPTER REVIEW: KEY POINTS

1. *Economics* is concerned with choices and their consequences. It has been described as the study of the ways that individuals and societies allocate their limited resources to satisfy relatively unlimited wants.

2. *Scarcity* occurs because our relatively unlimited wants cannot be completely met from the limited resources available. A good is scarce if people cannot freely get all they want, so that the good commands a positive price.

3. *Production* occurs when knowledge or technology is used to apply energy to materials to make them more valuable.

4. *Resources* (factors of production) include:
- **a.** *Labor*. Productive efforts made available by human beings. Payments for labor services are called *wages*.
- **b.** *Land*. All natural resources such as land, minerals, water, air. Payments for land are called *rents*.
- **c.** *Capital*. Basic improvements that increase the productive potential of other resources. Payments for the use of capital are called *interest*. When economists refer to capital, they mean physical capital rather than financial capital. Financial capital consists of paper claims to goods or resources.
- **d.** *Entrepreneurship*. The organizing, innovating, and risk-taking function that combines other factors to produce goods. Providers of this resource receive *profits*.

5. The *opportunity costs* of the consumption choices you make are measured by the subjective values of alternatives you sacrifice.

6. *Common sense* is theory that has been tested over a long period and found useful. In general, good theory accurately predicts how the real world operates. *Occam's Razor* suggests that the simplest workable theories are the most useful or "best."

7. *Positive economics* is scientifically testable and involves value-free descriptions of economic relationships, dealing with "what is." *Normative economics* involves value judgments about economic relationships and addresses "what should be." Normative theory can be neither scientifically verified nor proven false.

8. *Macroeconomics* is concerned with aggregate (the total levels of) economic phenomena, including such items as Gross National Product, unemployment, and inflation.

9. *Microeconomics* concentrates on individual decision making, resource allocation, and how prices and output are determined.

10. *Economic efficiency* occurs when a given amount of resources produces the most valuable combination of outputs possible. *Production (technical) efficiency* is obtained when a given output is produced at the lowest possible cost. Another way of looking at efficiency is that it occurs when the opportunity cost of obtaining some specific amount of a good is at its lowest. *Consumption efficiency* requires consumers to adjust their purchasing patterns to maximize their satisfactions from given budgets.

11. The concept of *comparative advantage* is a guide to efficient specialization: You should specialize in producing things where your opportunity costs are lowest and trade your production for things other people can produce at lower opportunity cost.

PROBLEM

1. Suppose that Ludwig can compose two symphonies or bake 800 pizzas per year while Gino can write only one symphony or bake 600 pizzas. (We use Occam's Razor to assume, for simplicity, that only these two goods are produced.) How much music is sacrificed for each pizza Ludwig bakes? For each pizza Gino bakes? Assume that each initially devotes half of his time to music and the other half to baking and that they do not trade. What will be their respective consumption patterns? Demonstrate how both Ludwig and Gino can gain through specialization and exchange even though Ludwig has an absolute advantage in both forms of production.

QUESTIONS FOR THOUGHT AND DISCUSSION

1. Why is it probably accurate to believe that you can think of nothing better to do with your time right now than to study this book?

2. Why is class attendance almost always higher on days when examinations are given?

3. Truly free goods are almost inconceivable. Some alternative is nearly always forgone. Why are none of the following goods "free"?
   a. A mother's love.
   b. An all-expense-paid trip to Paris, won on a TV game show.
   c. Free popcorn at a theater.
   d. A free school lunch program for poor children.
   e. Leftovers dug from a fancy restaurant's garbage by a bum.

4. Do you agree with the adage that "You can't get rich working for someone else"? Must successful entrepreneurs serve others to enrich themselves? Can wage earners achieve great wealth without investing? How might you test the correctness of your answers to these questions?

5. Some critics of our economic system contend that self-interested behavior is not intrinsic, but that people are taught to be "selfish" by our society's stress on competition. These critics argue that if we encouraged cooperation as much as we now reward competitive behavior, children would be far less selfish when they became adults. Are people naturally selfish? If you agree with these critics, how might we restructure typical child-rearing practices and our education system to discourage selfish behavior and to foster cooperation? Whether you agree or disagree that selfishness is a learned behavior, would the world be better off if people acted in less self-interested ways? Why, or why not?

6. Modern sociobiologists view perpetuation of one's gene pool as the basic human motive, and offer numerous examples of behavior that apparently conflict with the economist's *homo economicus* assumption: Parents sacrifice their lives for their children, or invest in their kids' college educations so that the next generation will enjoy richer lives. On the other hand, people adopt other people's biological children and some childless people are voluntarily sterilized or join religious orders that require sexual abstinence. To what extent might perpetuation of one's gene pool conflict with self-interested behavior? Which assumptions do you think will more accurately predict human behavior?

7. In an economic sense, can two ever live as cheaply as one? What are the opportunity (alternative) costs of marrying someone you love?

8. Does everything have a price? Can you think of anything you would not do regardless of price? Remember: prices and money are not synonyms; prices may be nonmonetary.

9. Henry Hazlitt, author of *Economics in One Easy Lesson,* claims that "economics is haunted by more fallacies than any other study known to man." He offers the following anecdote to prove his point:

   > A young hoodlum, say, heaves a brick through the window of a baker's shop. The shopkeeper runs out furious, but the boy is gone. A crowd gathers, and begins to stare with quiet satisfaction at the gaping hole in the window and the shattered glass over the bread and pies. After a while the crowd feels the need for philosophic reflection. And several of its members are almost certain to remind each other or the baker that, after all, the misfortune has its bright side. It will make business for some glazier. As they begin to think of this they elaborate upon it. How much does a new plate glass window cost? A hundred dollars? That will be quite a sum. After all, if windows were never broken, what would happen to the glass business? Then, of course, the thing is endless. The glazier will have a hundred dollars more to spend with other merchants, and these in turn will have a hundred dollars more to spend with still other merchants, and so ad infinitum. The smashed window will go on providing money and employment in ever-widening circles. The logical conclusion from all this would be, if the crowd drew it, the little hoodlum who threw the brick, far from being a public menace, was a public benefactor.

   Eliminating the moral question of criminal activity, is the little hoodlum a public benefactor from an economic point of view?

10. Why do people often let water run onto sidewalks and into the street when they water their lawns? Is this wasted water a sign of inefficiency?

11. In what kinds of goods do Americans enjoy comparative advantages over production by foreigners? How is this related to the relative abundance of resources here in the United States compared to abroad?

Does the sight of an equation, figure, or graph strike fear in your heart? Do you still have nightmares about the geometry class you nearly flunked? You may be among the many intelligent and otherwise well-educated people whose palms sweat when they are confronted with elementary mathematical analysis. The biggest problem you have to overcome is "math/graph-phobia."

Try to cast aside your apprehensions and spend an hour or so studying this section. Working through the parallel exercises in our *Student Guide For Learning Economics* should also make it much easier to follow the economic analysis in this course, and may help you in other areas of study.

With the approach of the twenty-first century, mathematics and computer programming vie as useful second languages. Your reaction may be that well-written or properly spoken English is enough for your purposes. The major advantages of mathematical expression reside in its precision and efficiency in relating certain concepts that cannot be expressed easily in words. Graphs and mathematics can simplify many discussions. For example, try to describe in simple English how much you would be paid if you worked 42 1/2 hours in a week at an hourly rate of $4.00 per hour, with time and a half for anything in excess of 40 hours. Isn't $(40 \times \$4) + (2.5 \times \$4 \times 1.5) = (\$160) + (\$15) = \$175$ much easier?

Most economic relationships treated in this book can be described in any of four ways: with English, graphs, tables, or equations. We try to use more than one technique each time we treat an important concept. You need to be able to deal with all four if you want to understand economic reasoning fully. Graphs are visual aids that make analysis easier. In this section, we will show you how to read, interpret, and use simple graphs. Concentrating on the graphical analysis as you proceed through the first few chapters will yield proficiency and confidence in your ability to understand graphical techniques.

Graphical Analysis

Even to students . . . who possess the mathematical tools to handle a more formal approach, there is just no substitute for the [economic] intuition that one acquires with lots of curve bending.

—*James P. Quirk (1976)*

Graphs are little more than snapshots of information. They can be used descriptively, as in maps and charts, or analytically, to gain insights into theory. The simplest and most commonly used descriptive graphs are maps. Almost all road maps use indexed systems of coordinates as guides to locations. These coordinates are then indexed. If you are reading a California map and trying to locate Fresno, you could look up Fresno on the map index. The coordinates provided, *G-9*, guide you to Fresno by directing you to a certain part of the map. Looking at the sides of the map, coordinate *G* tells you how far north or south Fresno is. Glance at the top of the map, and coordinate *9* indicates Fresno's east/west orientation. Thus, *G-9* lets you know where to look for Fresno on the map. Aha!—Fresno! The coordinate systems of maps are examples of **Cartesian coordinates.**

Cartesian Coordinates

Economic graphs are also based on Cartesian coordinate systems. A thorough grasp of this graphing system will aid your understanding and enjoyment of such economic theory as supply and demand analysis.

The Cartesian coordinate system is constructed by drawing two lines (or **axes**) perpendicular to each other. These axes, labeled *x* and *y*, are numbered and normally intersect at their respective zeros. The black lines in Figure 2 are axes for a standard set of Cartesian coordinates.

FIGURE 2 Cartesian Coordinates

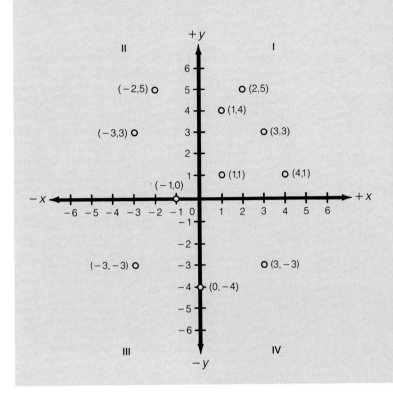

The coordinate system is divided into four areas called *quadrants*; starting from the northeast, they are numbered in a counterclockwise fashion. A point is located numerically by an ordered pair, denoted (x,y). Various ordered pairs are located on the graph. The x value represents a rightward movement from the vertical axis if the number is positive, and vice versa. The second coordinate (y) value is the vertical distance from the horizontal axis (upward movement if y is positive and downward if y is negative).

This coordinate system divides a "space" into four areas called **quadrants.** The quadrants are numbered I through IV, beginning from the northeast area and then moving in a counterclockwise direction. A point in any one of the quadrants is located numerically by an **ordered pair**, denoted (x,y). The first coordinate or number, x, directs rightward movement if x is positive, or leftward movement if x is negative. The second coordinate, y, governs upward movement if y is positive, or downward movement if y is negative. Thus quadrant I contains pairs for which both x and y are positive, quadrant II shows pairs for which x is negative and y is positive, quadrant III shows situations where both x and y are negative, and quadrant IV depicts positive values of x paired with negative values of y.

The following points are placed on the coordinate system in Figure 2: (1,1), (1,4), (3,3), (4,1), (2,5), (-2,5), (-3,3), (-1,0), (-3,-3), (0,-4), and (3,-3). Be sure that you know how to locate these coordinates graphically be-

fore proceeding. Remember, each set of numbers in parentheses gives two pieces of information; left-right for the value of x; then up-down for the value of y. Even though economists consider multidimensional problems, this technique allows us to deal with very complex issues by considering only two dimensions of a problem at a time.

Most economic analysis uses only the first, or positive, quadrant (Quadrant I). Negative values of many economic variables do not make sense; examples of such nonsense include negative prices or negative unemployment rates.

Descriptive Graphs

Economists and other users of business and social data (such as anthropologists, sociologists, and people in the media) have devised some ingenious methods for depicting relationships among numerous variables. The introduction of computer-generated graphics has merely enhanced their ability to present these data in new and interesting ways. Perhaps you have noticed that you are seeing more and more graphs on the network news, in your local newspaper, and in news magazines, and that these graphs are not simple lines on grids. All of us are being asked to develop a certain amount of sophistication about graphs to keep pace with these changes. It will be easier for you to read and understand these graphs if you keep a few basic points in mind. The most important of these is that the same set of data can be presented in a number of different ways. The following discussion should show you what we mean.

Let's begin by examining Figure 3. In this advertisement, **Macron** uses a set of vertical bars to indicate increased sales of their software over the period 1985–89. Is this figure based on a Cartesian coordinate system? The answer is yes, and Figure 4 shows why.

The bars in the Macron advertisement show sales in recent years. Cartesian coordinates for these data are also shown in Panels B and C of Figure 4. Sales are on the vertical axis and are graphed against years on the horizontal axis. Panels B and C are called **bar graphs,** because they use bars to represent sales in each year.

Line graphs are shown in Panels D and E. Rather than using a series of bars, the Cartesian points showing sales data over time are connected by a line. All five panels illustrate the same information. Only five data points are presented in the simple graphs in Panels, A, B, and C. Graphs can be used to present much more complex pictures of data, but reading them is easy if you concentrate on what the graph shows.

FIGURE 3 *An Example of How Economic Data Can Be Graphically Depicted in an Advertisement*

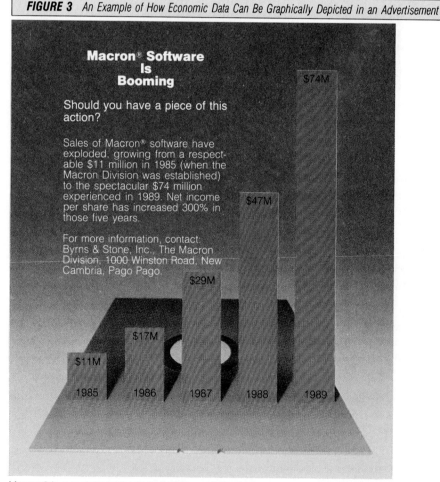

Macron® is a registered trademark of Byrns & Stone, Inc.

FIGURE 4 *Different Ways the Same Data Can Be Depicted*

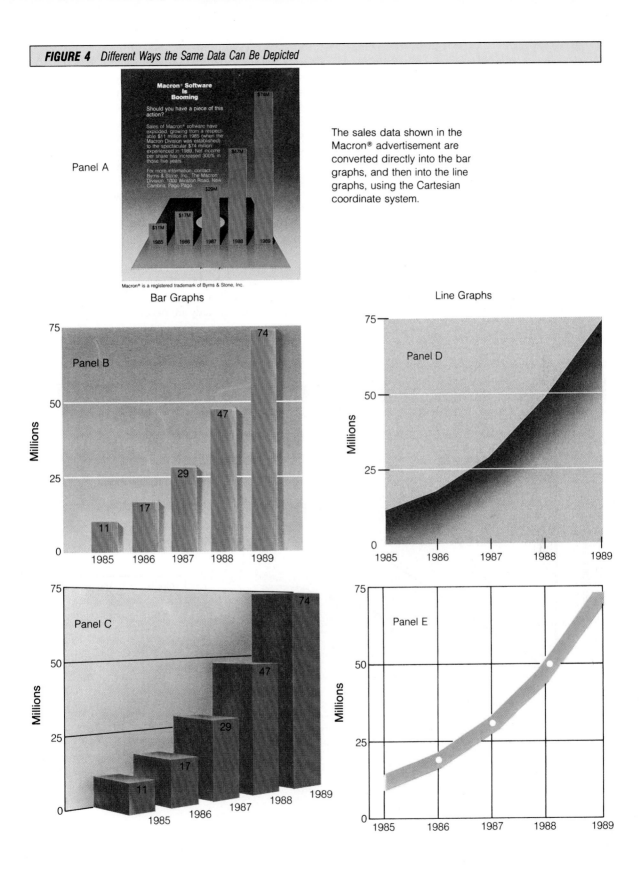

Panel A

The sales data shown in the Macron® advertisement are converted directly into the bar graphs, and then into the line graphs, using the Cartesian coordinate system.

Bar Graphs

Line Graphs

Measuring the Slope of a Line

Many important economic concepts hinge on how much one variable changes in response to changes in another. Graphically, such relationships are equivalent to the **slope** of the line depicting the association between the two variables. Typically, two variables will be positively or negatively related to each other. That is, higher values of *x* will be associated either with higher values of *y* (a **positive relation**) or with lower values of *y* (a **negative relation**).

For example, Figure 5 depicts possible relationships for students with good, typical, and poor study habits between hours spent studying (*x*) and grade point average (*y*). Generally, the more you study, the higher the grade point average. Thus, the relationship is positive. But how much will you have to study to raise your grade point one full grade? The answer is found by determining the slope of the grade point average/study hours

line. You may have heard slope described as "rise over run" (rise/run). In this case, the grade is the rise, measured by the vertical axis; study hours is the run, measured along the horizontal axis. Thus, if you have typical study habits and study each subject for 30 hours a semester, your grade point average will be a 2.0, or C. If you increase your study time to 45 hours per subject, your average will rise to 3.0, or B. Fifteen extra hours of study per subject will raise your grade point average by one full point if the middle line in Figure 5 corresponds to the relationship between your average and the hours you study.

The **slope of a line** is defined as the ratio of the vertical change (rise) to the horizontal change (run) as we move along a line from left to right. In the case of typical study habits, the slope is 1/15. Notice that the slope of each line reflects the efficiency of each individual's study time. For the student with good study habits, only 7.5 hours of study are necessary to raise the aver-

FIGURE 5 *Hypothetical Relationship Between Hours Spent Studying and Cumulative Grade Point Average*

The *slope* of a line is defined as the ratio of the vertical change (rise) to the horizontal change (run). Curve *A* might reflect good study habits; each one-point improvement in your grade point average requires only an extra 7.5 hours of study per course. Curve *B* might depict average study habits; an extra 15 hours of study are required to raise your grade point average by a full point. Curve *C* shows the problem faced by someone with inferior study habits; 30 hours of extra study time are required per course to raise the grade average by one point.

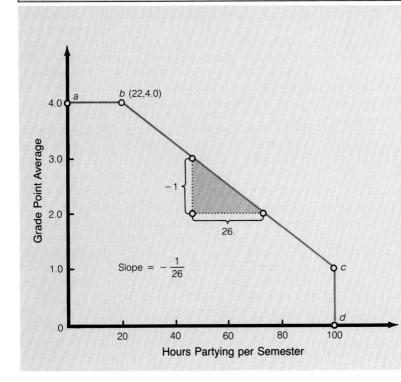

FIGURE 6 Hypothetical Relationship Between Hours of Partying and Grade Point Average

The slope of a line can be negative, zero, or infinite. Between points *a* and *b* the slope is zero, indicating that a little partying will not affect grades. Between points *b* and *c* the slope is −1/26, suggesting that each additonal 26 hours of partying will reduce your grade point average by one point. Between points *c* and *d*, the slope is infinite, which means that a small change in partying may result in a one point or more decline in your grade point average.

age grade by one point, while the person with poor habits must study 30 hours more to achieve the same results. Thus, the slopes showing these relationships are 1/7.5 and 1/30, respectively.

The slope of a line can also be negative. Extensive partying almost invariably results in lower grades. This typically negative relationship is reflected in Figure 6. As the graph suggests, you can party for up to 22 hours with negligible harm to your grade point average (point *b*). After that, for every 26 hours you party, your grade point average falls by one grade point until point *c* is reached (1.0 grade point average and 100 hours of partying). Once you party beyond 100 hours, your grades drop to 0.0, or failing. Thus, between points *a* and *b*, the slope of the curve is zero (change in partying has no effect on grades or, alternatively, the two variables are unrelated). The slope of the line is -1/26 between 22 and 100 hours of party time (between points *b* and *c*). This means that for every 26 hours partied, your grade average falls by one full grade point. The slope is infinite if you party 100 hours (between points *c* and *d*). Any small change

(even as little as five or ten seconds) may result in a full point increase or decrease in your grade point average.

Intercepts

Much of economic analysis is most easily understood if we assume that the relationship studied is **linear,** which means that a graph of the relationship has a constant slope. The only information we need beyond slope to specify a linear relationship completely is the **intercept,** which is the value of the y variable when the x variable has a value of zero.

For example, Figure 7 shows a hypothetical relationship between lumber yields and the annual maintenance per acre of forest to clear debris (reducing fire hazards) and control tree diseases. Even with zero maintenance ($x = 0$) we may harvest some lumber ($y = 10,000$). As maintenance increases, the harvest rate rises. Specifically, for every extra hour of maintenance

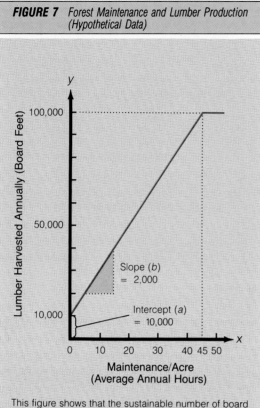

FIGURE 7 Forest Maintenance and Lumber Production (Hypothetical Data)

This figure shows that the sustainable number of board feet of lumber that can be harvested from a forest annually is 10,000 board feet, if no one works to maintain the forest. As the number of hours rises that forestry experts devote to each acre of forest, the forest's yield rises by 2,000 board feet/hour.

per acre, annual lumber yields rise by 2,000 board feet. This continues (given the linear relationship) until the ability to harvest lumber peaks when 45 hours of annual maintenance are devoted to each acre of forest.

In general, linear relationships are written algebraically as: $y = a + bx$, where y and x are the variables considered, b is the slope of the relationship, and a is the intercept. For this forestry example, $a = 10,000$, $b = 2,000$, and the equation is:

$$y = 10,000 + 2,000x,$$

where

y = annual yield of lumber in board feet,
10,000 = the intercept (the value of y, which is

board feet of lumber annually, when x [maintenance] is zero), and

x = hours of maintenance per acre, annually.

To find the harvest rate for each maintenance level, just plug in the value of x, multiply it by 2,000 and add 10,000.

To ensure that you understand how the intercept and slope of a line are influenced by how variables interact, you should construct graphs of $y = a + bx$ where you select values of a and b as if you were blindly drawing them out of a hat.

The Misuse of Graphs

Darrell Huff and Irving Geis wrote a popular book called *How to Lie With Statistics*. They also show how you can be misled by cleverly drawn graphs. You should be alert for several pitfalls when graphs are used to illustrate, support, or prove an analytical point.

First, make sure the time period selected for the graph is typical for the point made by the analysis. For example, during the 1960s, mutual funds and stocks were sold on the basis of booming performance in the previous decade. It seemed that the prices of stocks and shares of mutual funds could only rise. Unfortunately, mutual funds were losers during the 1970s, not even coming close to their average performance in the 1950s and 1960s.

Second, be aware that the appearance of a graph depends on the choice of measurement units. One distortion caused by using different units on the axes is illustrated in Figure 8. Curve *A* appears to have a greater slope than Curve *B*, but both curves accurately portray the same data, so this is impossible. The vertical axes are measured on different scales, accounting for the illusion that they have different slopes.

Finally, the data used should be tightly linked to the analysis. Thus, comparing standards of living between countries cannot be done by simply looking at countries' total production or income; India is much bigger but far less prosperous than Kuwait. Income per person or family is a much closer measure.

As you read through the remainder of this book, you will be confronted with numerous graphs, both analytical and descriptive. We hope this section has helped ease your mind and that you will find the graphs helpful to your understanding of economics. The adage that one picture is worth a thousand words is often especially true in economics.

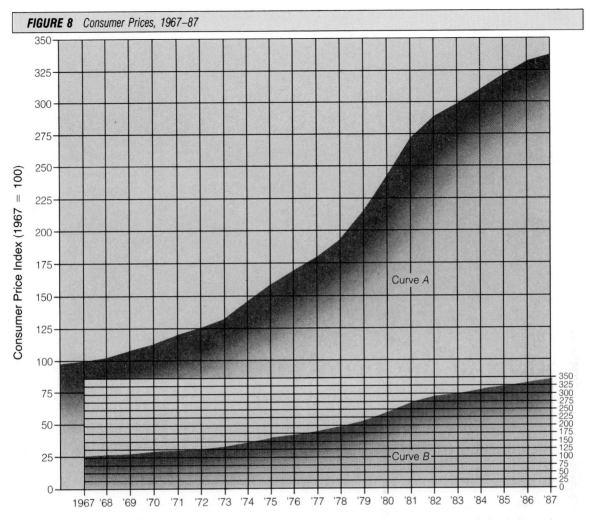

FIGURE 8 Consumer Prices, 1967–87

Consumer Price Index (1967 = 100)

Curve A

Curve B

1967 '68 '69 '70 '71 '72 '73 '74 '75 '76 '77 '78 '79 '80 '81 '82 '83 '84 '85 '86 '87

The unit of measurement on the axes can make the line appear steeper(have a greater slope), even though the slope remains constant. Both curves A and B have the same slope; the units of measurement on the vertical axes have been expanded in curve A.

Source: Bureau of Labor Statistics.

What? How? Who? When?

production-possibilities
   frontier (PPF)

law of diminishing returns

brute force

queuing

random selection

tradition

capitalism and markets

property rights

laissez-faire

socialism

central planning

CHAPTER 2

Resolving the Problem of Scarcity

We need to build a framework for further analysis on the foundations we laid in the preceding chapter. We begin this chapter by examining basic issues that must be addressed whenever people are confronted by scarcity. What will be produced? How will it be produced? Who will get to consume the goods that are available? Second, we outline the boundaries to the alternatives available to answer such questions with our first formal economic model—the production-possibilities frontier. Then we survey some allocative mechanisms that society can use to choose among these limited alternatives: Shall we use brute force, tradition, government, the market system, or some other device to answer basic economic questions? Finally, we look at major differences in the ways capitalism and socialism resolve basic economic issues.

Basic Economic Questions _____

Scarcity confronts every society with four basic economic questions:

1. **What** economic goods will be produced?
2. **How** will resources be used in production?
3. **Who** will get to consume economic goods?
4. **When** will resources or goods be used?

What?

Current resources and technology limit a society to choosing only one combination from the innumerable mixes of goods that could be produced during a given period. How much of each good would we like? Shall we choose more guns and less butter?

More health care and less housing? If production is technically efficient, more of any good means less of another. Ideally, the combination of goods a society chooses will be the one most in accord with its consumers' wants.

How?

Numerous mixes of resources and technologies can be used to produce most goods. For example, excavating a hole for a swimming pool can be done in 1 day with 1 bulldozer and 1 operator, or by 30 people with shovels in 1 week, or in 1 month by 300 people wielding teaspoons. Most agricultural products can be harvested by hand or by machine. Shirts can be carefully cut out and sewn at home or mass-produced in a factory. Selecting the most efficient technology and combination of resources for every form of production enables a society to reach the mix of goods most compatible with the allocatively efficient choices of consumers. When this occurs, there is economic efficiency throughout the society.

Who?

Even if we efficiently produce what consumers want, we still need to address to whom income and wealth will be distributed because these distributions determine, in turn, how large each individual's budget is and whose preferences matter. Every society is inevitably faced with hard questions about equity when it decides for whom to produce. Should the desires of the rich and powerful count more than those of the poor?

When?

Perishables such as ice cream cones or newspapers must be used soon after production or they quickly lose value, but durable goods such as stained glass windows or canned coffee can be stored for years. Similarly, some productive resources are perishable, while others last for centuries. For example, eight hours of labor are lost forever each day that a worker is unemployed, but a vein of copper ore or a barrel of oil can be stored indefinitely. Each generation decides how much capital to accumulate and how many natural resources to leave for use by future generations.

This list of basic questions—what, how, for whom, and when—seems quite simple. Note that each question, however, has more layers than are exposed if you peel an onion. For example, the question "What?" covers not only the specific types of goods to be produced, from a to z (aardvark fodder to zig-zag sewing machines?), but also how much or how many of each good. Different aspects of these basic questions recur throughout economic analysis. We will now look at a simple model that qualitatively portrays potential limits to our attempts to resolve the problem of scarcity.

Production Possibilities

Your budget is limited. Can you afford a flight in a hot air balloon if you already spend all your income each week? Of course, but only by buying less of something else. If you only have $10 to spare, you cannot see a movie, buy a record, fill your gas tank, eat at Burger King, and still get your flat tire fixed. Something has to give! Just as your budget constrains your purchases, scarcity forces society as a whole to make choices about the goods we produce and consume. We represent the limits to what a society can produce by devices called production-possibilities frontiers.

Production-Possibilities Frontiers

A **production-possibilities frontier (PPF)** is among the simplest models of an economy and relies on three critical assumptions:[1]

1. The amounts of the various resources (land, labor, capital, and entrepreneurship) are fixed, but can be allocated among different types of production.
2. Technology, which includes such things as the state of knowledge about production and the qualities of resources, is assumed constant.
3. All scarce resources are fully and efficiently employed.

---

1. If you are disturbed by the lack of realism in these assumptions, remember (from chapter 1) that a model need be no more realistic than is necessary for the purpose at hand. The *PPF* model yields valuable qualitative insights even if it lacks quantitative precision.

Suppose that you live in Ruritania; a mythical empire ruled by the dictator Atilla, who has appointed himself president-for-life and minister of production. He believes that "balanced" production requires all industries to use the same proportional mixes of capital, land, and labor. (In a moment, you will see how dumb this constraint on technology is.) Ruritania contains 1,000 units of each of these resources.

Some production possibilities for Ruritania if it uses Atilla's technology are detailed in Table 1, located in Figure 1. Points *a, b, c, d,* and *e* in the figure designate five of the possible combinations of armaments and bread that can be produced during a given period. (For simplicity, we assume that only two goods are produced.) As resources are shifted from armaments to bread, weaponry output falls and bread output rises. When all resources are used to produce guns, no bread is produced, and vice versa.

Alternatives *a* through *e* are only five from many feasible combinations. Atilla can choose any point on the production-possibilities frontier (*PPF*) graphed when combinations *a* through *e* are connected by a smooth line. The point he chooses will depend on whether he wants Ruritanians to be better fed and less well defended, or vice versa. Would Atilla ever choose a point such as *x*? Not likely, because at point *x* many resources would be either idle or used in wasteful ways. Any inefficiency (e.g., underemployment of resources) could be eliminated by moving from *x* to a point between *c* and *d* so that more of both goods were produced.

Producing 1,250 units of each commodity at point *z* is clearly preferable to all points on the existing frontier. Resources cannot be stretched to attain point *z*, however, in part because of Atilla's neurotic fixation on a "balanced" production technology. Remember that an economy operating on its produc-

FIGURE 1 *A Primitive Production-Possibilities Frontier*

This straight-line *PPF* reflects the availability of resources (1,000 units each of capital, land, and labor) and the crude technology used (Atilla's "balanced" production formula). If production of both arms and bread is exactly proportional to the amounts of resources used and a maximum of 1,000 boxcars of bread (or 1,000 guns) can be produced daily, then total production when all resources are employed will equal 1,000 total units of bread plus weapons. Each gun produced costs 1 boxcar of bread, and vice versa.

Moving from *c* to *d* Entails Losing 250 Guns to Gain 250 Boxcars of Bread

Production Possibilities for Ruritania

TABLE 1 *Production-Possibilities Schedule*

Production Alternative	Arms (Machine Guns per Day)	Bread (Box Cars per Day)
a	1,000	0
b	750	250
c	500	500
d	250	750
e	0	1,000

tion-possibilities frontier is producing efficiently, given the technology available.

What does bread cost in our example? If Ruritanians move from point *c* in Figure 1 to production possibility *d*, they gain 250 boxcars of bread but lose 250 machine guns; the cost of each extra boxcar of bread is one machine gun. The guns that must be sacrificed for extra bread are the opportunity costs (in guns) of producing and consuming more bread, and vice versa.

Diminishing Returns and Increasing Opportunity Costs

You may have heard the phrase "diminishing returns." Here is a very general statement of the law of diminishing returns:

> The **law of diminishing returns** *means that as any activity is extended, it eventually becomes increasingly difficult to pursue the activity further.*[2]

For example, the faster you drive, the harder it is to gain another ten miles per hour and your car's gas mileage drops. Diminishing returns are encountered in physics, biology, and a host of other areas outside of economics. Within economics, this concept has wide and varied applications: Expanding a given form of production eventually becomes ever more difficult. Increasing your total satisfaction from any good ultimately also becomes more difficult the more of the good you have already consumed. Would your enjoyment from eating five candy bars per week quadruple if you ate twenty?

One corollary of the law of diminishing returns is that raising any form of production eventually entails **increasing opportunity costs.** This means that repeatedly increasing production by some set proportion ultimately requires more than proportional increases in resources and costs. For example, the more you study, the better your grades tend to be. It requires more effort to earn a C than a D. But raising

your grade from a B to an A normally requires far more extra work than moving from a D to a C. Thus, there are increasing costs to raising your grade point average. Let's see how this concept applies to the production-possibilities frontier.

Atilla's "balanced" production formula required all types of production to use the same mix of resources. This is a very primitive technology. Suppose Atilla now appoints you minister of production. You might reason that, relative to armaments, efficient bread production requires more land and labor and less capital, while weapons should use capital relatively more intensively. This new knowledge is a technological breakthrough! After experimenting with different mixes of resources until you discover the appropriate technology, you will find that increasing costs are encountered as production of either good is expanded. This yields production-possibilities curves that are concave (bowed away) from the origin. Here is why.

Ruritania's production-possibilities frontier for bread and arms under this new technology is detailed in Figure 2 and Table 2, located in the figure. When bread production is raised from zero to 100 boxcars daily, machine gun output falls only from 1,000 units to 995 daily (from point *a* to point *b*). Why does the first 100 boxcars of bread cost only 5 machine guns? Because the resources first shifted into food production will be those relatively best suited for bread and least suited for arms. Far more land than capital will be transferred to bread production. But as bread output is continually increased, the resources shifted are decreasingly suited for bread production relative to the production of armaments, and the cost of extra bread rises. Thus, moving from point *f* to point *g* results in an extra 100 boxcars of bread per day, but costs 66 machine guns, while moving from point *i* to point *j* also yields 100 extra boxcars of bread, but the cost is higher: 164 machine guns.

When bread output is finally expanded from 900 boxcars to 1,000 boxcars daily (point *j* to point *k*), the last resources shifted from armaments production are very productive for machine guns but ill-suited for producing food. Thus, 436 machine guns are sacrificed for the last 100 boxcars of bread. Less and less land is available for shifting, so more and more cap-

---

2. The occurrence of a law of diminishing *marginal* returns in production is only an example of the broader tendency described here.

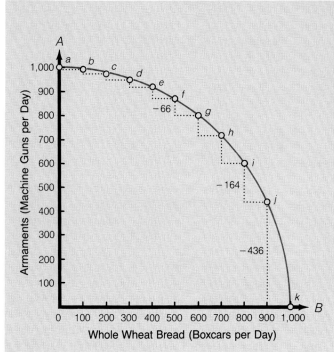

FIGURE 2 *A More Realistic Production-Possibilities Frontier that Reflects Increasing Costs*

If the resources available (1,000 units each of capital, land, and labor) are used in the combinations that best fit the various forms of production, the *PPF* will be concave from the origin. In this example, arms are capital intensive (use more capital relative to land), and bread is land intensive. The differences in the appropriate mixes of capital/labor/land causes a society to encounter diminishing returns (increasing costs) as more and more boxcars of bread (or arms) are produced.

TABLE 2 *Production Possibilities and Increasing Costs*

(1)	(2)	(3)	(4)
	Average Daily Production		Average Opportunity Costs (Average Machine Guns Sacrificed per
Point	Arms	Bread	Extra Boxcar of Bread)
a	1,000	0	—
b	995	100	0.05
c	980	200	0.15
d	954	300	0.26
e	917	400	0.37
f	866	500	0.51
g	800	600	0.66
h	714	700	0.86
i	600	800	1.14
j	436	900	1.64
k	0	1,000	4.36

ital moves into agriculture. The ever-rising cost of extra bread in terms of forgone machine guns, as shown in Column 4 of Table 2, is depicted in Figure 3. You will learn in the next chapter that Figure 3 shows the typical shape of a society's long-run supply curve for bread.

To summarize, the production-possibilities model illustrates three important concepts: scarcity, opportunity costs, and choice. Desires for "more" are boundless but resources are scarce, so only limited amounts of goods can be produced. Scarcity forces every society to choose among competing goods. Finally, the most valued alternative sacrificed to obtain another unit of a given good is its opportunity cost. Opportunity costs eventually rise if we repeatedly expand the production of any good.

Economic Growth

One way for **economic growth** to occur is for resources to be used more efficiently, but growth in an efficient economy requires either that more resources become available or that technology ad-

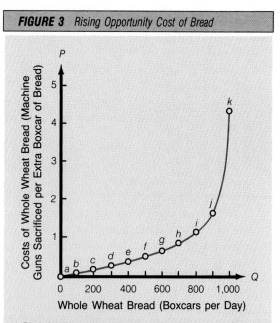

FIGURE 3 *Rising Opportunity Cost of Bread*

Diminishing returns cause the opportunity cost of bread to rise as production is increased. This means that more and more guns must be sacrificed as bread production grows.

vances. An outward shift of a production-possibilities frontier reflects growth because more of both goods can be produced. This is illustrated in Panel A of Figure 4.

Investment in new capital is one source of economic growth. Opening up new land is another possibility, but there is little unexplored land on Earth and settling other planets remains in the realm of science fiction. Expanding the labor force is yet another way to stimulate economic growth. Labor resources can grow in two ways: increases in the number of workers, or improvements in their quality and productivity. Economic growth also occurs if more entrepreneurs are successful when they risk implementing new technologies.

Technological advances occur when given amounts of resources become capable of greater production. Suppose that technology improves only in the clothing industry. It may seem surprising that more of *both* food and clothing can be produced, as illustrated in Panel B of Figure 4, but this breakthrough means that fewer resources are required to produce a given amount of textiles. Resources will be freed for food production. Although point *a* in Panel B remains stationary, most of the curve shifts to the

right, reflecting not only an increase in the potential output of clothing but also increased possibilities for the production of food.

Choices Between the Present and Future We must choose between consumer goods and military goods, among various commodities, and between work and leisure. The basic question *When?* also forces choices between current and future consumption. Inadequate investment may sharply restrict the goods available in the future if perishable goods absorb most production and society builds little machinery and few manufacturing plants. A society can produce investment goods only to the extent that it forgoes potential current consumption.

National income that is not consumed, making resources available for new capital investment, is called **saving.** Rapid investment directly augments productive capacity and updates technology, and it often boosts labor productivity and generates new products as side benefits. But society's productive capacity declines if depreciation exceeds investment. Stagnation inevitably follows if worn-out capital is not replaced. In such cases, the production-possibilities frontier shrinks towards the origin.

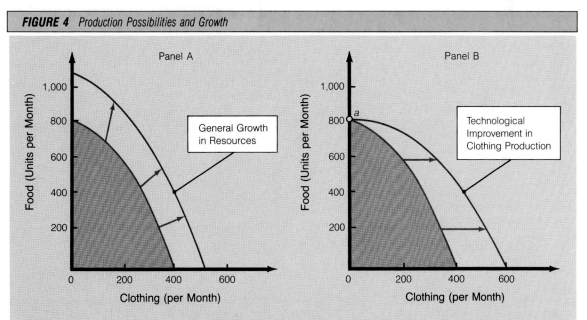

FIGURE 4 Production Possibilities and Growth

Growth in an economy can be generated through a general increase in resources (Panel A) or through technological improvement (Panel B). The entire *PPF* clearly expands when available resources increase. Note that technological improvement, even if only in one commodity, expands production opportunities for both commodities because technological advances make resources available for other uses.

Thus, the choice we make between current consumption and saving (to allow investment) determines our future prosperity, as shown in Figure 5. Panel A indicates some possible choices between consuming and investing in 1990, with point *a* reflecting greater consumption than point *b*, point *b* more consumption than point *c*, and so on. Curves PPF_a through PPF_e in Panel B show the production possibilities in the year 2000 that result from choices of *a*, *b*, *c*, *d*, and *e*, respectively from the year 1990. In sum, more rapid growth in an efficient economy is stimulated by higher investment, which requires more saving (less consumption).

This analysis partially explains why, on average, U.S. economic growth since 1970 has been anemic compared to that in some other countries. Americans have typically saved only about 4–6 percent of their income since 1970, while various nationalities of Europeans saved 8–16 percent of their incomes. During this same period, the Japanese saved over 20 percent of their income, facilitating substantial

new investment in capital goods. The result is that numerous antiquated American industries now try to compete with foreign firms that use newer machinery and more advanced technology. For example, our automobile industry has faltered recently in competition with prosperous Japanese carmakers, who rely much more on industrial robots on their assembly lines.

What is done with people's savings is as important as its level in explaining international differences in growth rates. If savings are channeled into the most productive forms of investment, economic growth is stimulated. But capital accumulation and economic growth may both be hampered if government uses most private savings to fund a war, or if savings are funneled into obsolete and inefficient industry, growth is dampened. For example, between World War II and 1980, most private British saving was used for investment in nationalized industries in which Britain had lost its comparative advantage. The result was that the British economy was stagnant relative to

FIGURE 5 *Consumer Versus Investment Goods Choices and the Production Possibilities of the Future*

Society must make choices between present and future consumption. If, in 1990, this society selects a mix of production that emphasizes consumer goods (point *a* in Panel A) rather than investment (capital) goods (point *e* in Panel A), the 2000 PPF will be relatively smaller. Choice *a* in Panel A yields only enough investment to replace the capital that has depreciated, so PPF_a is the same in both panels. Moving from point *a* to point *b* in Panel A causes capital to grow somewhat, so that in Panel B more of both consumption and investment are possible along PPF_b than on PPF_a. Moving to point *c* in Panel A enables still greater growth yielding PPF_c in Panel B. And so on.

the U.S. economy, in spite of relatively higher rates of saving by the British than by Americans.

One reason for weak economic growth in the United States during the 1980s may be that much of private saving has been absorbed by a string of record U.S. budget deficits—many people and financial institutions bought U.S. government bonds instead of making their savings available to investors. High interest rates and recurring $100 billion or higher annual deficits in our federal budget discouraged investors and caused many to question coupling major cuts in tax rates (1982–84) with vigorous attempts to expand defense spending. This debacle is an example of the dilemma every society faces when it chooses between "guns" and "butter."

Unemployment, Inflation, and National Defense

Production-possibilities analysis highlights some interesting differences between the World War II and Vietnam War eras. Wars unavoidably alter economic activity. At the dawn of World War II, the United States was sluggishly recovering from its deepest depression ever. Unemployment had fallen from its 25 percent peak in 1933 to roughly 15–16 percent by 1939. In reasonably prosperous times, the unemployment rate averages 4–6 percent. Thus, many resources were idle when the United States entered World War II. This initial situation is represented by point *a* in Figure 6.

Some consumer goods (butter) and a few military goods (guns) were being produced, but high unemployment signalled that the economy operated well inside its production-possibilities frontier. When hostilities erupted, mobilizing these idle resources enabled military production to grow rapidly without cutting back outputs of consumer goods. In fact, consumption actually rose in the early 1940s. This drive towards full employment is graphed as a movement from point *a* to point *b*.

The production-possibilities frontier also grew rapidly in the early war years as new technology was introduced, women flocked into the work force to support the defense effort, and patriotism spurred worker productivity. The economy moved from point *b* to point *c* in Figure 6 as production possibilities

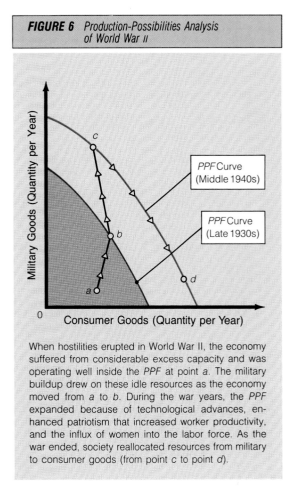

FIGURE 6 Production-Possibilities Analysis of World War II

When hostilities erupted in World War II, the economy suffered from considerable excess capacity and was operating well inside the PPF at point a. The military buildup drew on these idle resources as the economy moved from a to b. During the war years, the PPF expanded because of technological advances, enhanced patriotism that increased worker productivity, and the influx of women into the labor force. As the war ended, society reallocated resources from military to consumer goods (from point c to point d).

expanded. Then, when the war ended, the United States experienced a transition phase as the economy retooled from military hardware to consumer goods, gradually approaching point *d*.

This experience contrasts sharply with what happened during the Vietnam era. The economy was close to full employment in the mid-1960s, with a jobless rate of around 4 percent, corresponding to point *a* in Figure 7. President Johnson strove for "more guns and more butter," and attempted to increase military involvement in Vietnam while expanding domestic programs (e.g., the "War Against Poverty"). His goals required a movement to point *b* in Figure 7, but unfortunately, moving beyond a society's PPF is impossible. The economy experienced moderate growth, moving, say, to point *c* by 1969, but

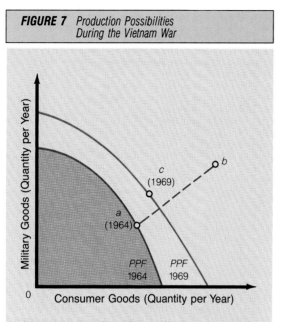

FIGURE 7 *Production Possibilities During the Vietnam War*

Military Goods (Quantity per Year)

Consumer Goods (Quantity per Year)

c
(1969)

a
(1964)

b

PPF
1964

PPF
1969

0

At the beginning of the Vietnam War the economy was roughly at full employment (point *a*). By trying to expand both the Indochina conflict and domestic programs, the government attempted to reach point *b*. However, this was unattainable. Actually, the economy experienced moderate growth, and we achieved point *c*. The result of attempting the unattainable contributed to the inflationary pressures of the early 1970s.

at least part of the persistent double-digit inflation suffered during the 1970s was a hangover from pressures exerted on the U.S. economy by the Vietnam conflict.

A production-possibilities frontier depicts the menu available to a society with fixed resources and technology. Just as every family has a limited budget, a *PPF* represents society's limited budget. But attaining the *PPF* requires technical efficiency in production. Some methods of selecting what and how to produce may be so inherently inefficient that ever reaching true capacity is impossible. (Recall Atilla's formula for "balanced" production.) Even if production is efficient, neither nature nor human industry can provide everything we want; any decision automatically eliminates other options. Some methods of choosing among goods may preclude allocative efficiency in consumption. (Would you like it if all res-

taurants forced you to select food by playing "pin the tail on the donkey" with their menus?) Important insights into issues posed by scarcity and the need to choose are gained by examining various mechanisms used to resolve competition among people for scarce goods.

Allocative Mechanisms

No society has been able to remold people into humanitarians who ignore self-interest when they choose. Self interested behavior combines with scarcity to yield competition for the good things in life. This competition can take many forms. Some of the **allocative mechanisms** used to deal with scarcity yield less satisfactory solutions than others. The mechanisms discussed in this section are all used in some situations and in all countries. This is why societies everywhere have *mixed* economic systems. Although different allocative mechanisms channel competition in different ways, no mechanism eliminates it because people everywhere try to "beat the system," competing to attain their own interests. Each mechanism works well in certain circumstances, but at other times their consequences can be tragic.

The Market System

The **market system** is the major device used in the United States to address economic problems. Private buyers and sellers trade money for resources or goods in our market economy, which some people call the *price system*. Much of this book describes how markets allocate resources and distribute income and production. Before we examine how markets resolve economic issues, however, we will look at some non-market methods of choosing.

Brute Force

Brute force is one way to decide who gets what, when, from whom, and how. You could be threatened with loss of life, limb, or loved ones if you refused to hand over your goods to a neighborhood bully. You may think that brute force sounds like a fine system for people who are inclined to be thugs—but the film *The Untouchables* provides a good example of how violence tends to beget unending cycles of violence. Consider how much waste occurs when goods are allocated through brute force and how little productive activity is likely.

Queuing

Queuing (lining up) is another way to decide who gets what. First-come, first-serve systems operate for staking mining claims or making purchases at bookstores and ice cream parlors. However, if waiting in a queue were the dominant means of allocating resources and goods, so much time would be spent standing in line that little production would occur—and you would be forced to be very selective about which long waiting line you chose. Should production then be oriented towards the goods that have the longest queues? It's hard to say, because what people want may change quickly. Winter coats in July attract few buyers.

Random Selection

Random selection is yet another way to allocate goods and services. All economic questions could be decided by such random means as throwing dice, drawing straws, or other games based on pure luck. Once again, little production is likely. If your job were randomly assigned without regard to your talents, you probably would not be a very motivated worker and the advantages of specialization would be lost as well. Many of us would be round pegs in square holes. Young men are now required to register with the Selective Service. Is a lottery to determine who will serve in the Army fair? Is a draft efficient? Would you want all college educations, new cars, or the tastiest food to be distributed by lottery?

Tradition

Tradition may also be used to resolve basic questions about production and distribution. Feudal European monarchies and the caste system in India operated largely on this basis. In our society, women and minority members have often been pushed into low-paying jobs because tradition has limited their access to better positions. Most of us reject the notion that only senators' children should become senators, or that garbage collectors' kids should necessarily haul tomorrow's trash. Many resources and too much human talent are wasted when tradition alone rules.

Government

Government is the major alternative to the marketplace when fundamental economic issues must be resolved—but how should government decide? Even if we unanimously agreed that a democratic government should make all economic decisions, we would still confront the questions of who should be given what and how to produce the things to be distributed. Among the criteria that government might use to distribute production are equal shares and need.

Equal Shares   An egalitarian approach entitling everyone to *equal shares* might seem a fair way to distribute goods and services, but equal amounts of food may be more than can be eaten by a person weighing 100 pounds, yet a starvation diet for a 250-pound all-pro linebacker. Should we all be issued equal paychecks and identical housing and clothing? Moreover, egalitarianism offers few incentives for production. Why should an American farm family work hard to produce wheat if its share is only 1/240 millionth of the farm's production?

Another difficulty arises because government decision makers are as self-interested as the rest of us. If you had the right to decide what is equal or fair, you would probably give yourself and your relatives and friends every benefit of any doubt. Quite often an egalitarian policy may deteriorate to the state of George Orwell's *Animal Farm:* "All animals are equal, but some animals are more equal than others."

Need   An alternative is for government to distribute goods in accord with *need.* Unfortunately, it is extremely difficult for anyone to judge someone else's needs. Moreover, distribution according to need is costly and likely to be inaccurate. It might cause people to exaggerate their needs. Here is one horrifying example. Beggars in underdeveloped countries sometimes cripple their children so that the children will appear more pathetic to compassionate strangers.

A less brutal example is a 1950s TV game show called "Queen for a Day." Contestants told heartbreaking tales of children needing operations, unemployed husbands, and foreclosed mortgages. The woman who drew the loudest applause from the audience was crowned "Queen for a Day" and awarded a washer and dryer or trip to Las Vegas. If you had been a contestant, would you have stretched the truth a bit? If all goods were distributed on a *needs* basis, the officials making distribution decisions might become calloused to the plights of the truly unfortunate. Do you think even well-intentioned decision makers might become especially sensitive to their own material needs?

Still another difficulty is that distribution according to need causes special interest groups to spend time and effort lobbying to make decision makers aware of their special needs. What better way to make your needs known than through contributions to campaign funds? The potential for graft and corruption is enormous—few politicians can be expected to be Good Samaritans. Finally, only minimal production is likely. How many people would exert themselves to produce things only for redistribution to the "needy"?

Production and Consumption Choices   If government dictated production and consumption in detail, we could count on policymakers' preferences being reflected but should not be surprised if there were only two sizes of everything—too big and too little. Even if government decision makers conscientiously try to mirror the varied desires of millions of consumers, they face an almost unsolvable dilemma. Here is an example to show why even a democratic government is always in a quandary.

Suppose that Xavier, Yolanda, and Zelda are elected to specify our national priorities for the coming years and that each perfectly reflects the sentiments of one-third of the populace. Their rankings of national priorities are shown in the blue rectangles shown in Table 3. If you study this table for a moment, you will conclude that no matter which priorities are finally chosen, at least one-third of all citizens will have their first choice placed last and their last choice ranked first. This example illustrates why it may be impossible for democratic decisions to be consistent with voter preferences.[3]

Now consider the green rectangles in Table 3, which show the committee members' preferences

---

3. A similar example has been offered by Nobel Laureate Kenneth Arrow to illustrate a theorem proving the impossibility of democratic choices being consistent with voter preferences.

TABLE 3 *Choices about National Priorities Versus Choices about Meals*			
	Decision Makers		
	Xavier	**Yolanda**	**Zelda**
First Policy Choice	Stronger National Defense	Cleaner Environment	Controlling Inflation
First Choice of Meal	Ham	Roast Beef	Turkey
Second Policy Choice	Cleaner Environment	Controlling Inflation	Stronger National Defense
Second Choice of Meal	Roast Beef	Turkey	Ham
Third Policy Choice	Controlling Inflation	Stronger National Defense	Cleaner Environment
Third Choice of Meal	Turkey	Ham	Roast Beef

for main courses at a Thanksgiving meal. It might seem that similarly irreconcilable differences exist. In this case, however, we can leave the decisions up to the individuals and their families. Each family can have its first choice because decisions about what to eat can be made individually rather than by democratic vote. The point is that decision making by government is inherently crude relative to the fine tuning made possible through individual choice in a marketplace.

You can probably identify situations in which each of the allocative mechanisms just discussed seems to work well. However, most economic decisions in the United States are made through markets in which prices and productivity are major factors in determining what is produced and who gets it. One important exception is the family, whose decisions are based on varying degrees of command, tradition, and communal sharing, whether equally, by need, or based on some other criterion. The second most important mechanism for decision making in our society is government. In many countries, government is the dominant economic decision maker.

Economic Systems

All societies must address the basic economic questions, but each has a lot of leeway in how it answers *What? How? Who?* and *When?* Brute force, tradition, queuing, and other allocative mechanisms play roles in every society. Economic systems are conventional-

ly classified, however, by who makes decisions and who owns which resources. These questions are critical in determining the importance of government relative to the market system.

Who Decides?

Some economies rely heavily on **decentralized decision making.** This is generally true in the United States. Most decisions about what to produce, how to produce, and who shall get the production are determined by the individual actions of numerous consumers and producers. The other extreme is **centralized decision making,** where most important decisions are made by the government. Elaborate plans for output (production quotas) and distribution to consumers are drawn up and enforced. This type of organization, called a **command economy,** has been epitomized by the Soviet Union.

Who Owns?

Economic systems can also be broken down by whether their pattern of ownership is private or public. The means of production are owned primarily by individual citizens in capitalistic nations. In socialist countries, most productive resources are owned by the state, acting as a collective trustee for its citizens. However, whether resources are privately or publicly owned is not rigidly determined by whether decisions are made in centralized or decentralized fashion. Table 4 summarizes the four basic types of eco-

TABLE 4 Economic Decision Making		
	Decision Making	
	Decentralized	**Centralized**
Private Ownership	**Capitalism** United States Canada Western Europe Australia	**Wartime Capitalism or Fascism** Japan (Tojo) Germany (Hitler) Italy (Mussolini)
Public Ownership	**Decentralized Socialism** Yugoslavia Romania Czechoslovakia (before 1968) China (Deng Xiaoping)	**Communism** USSR East Germany (today) Czechoslovakia (after 1968) China (Mao Tse-tung)

nomic systems and lists some countries where each system has dominated.

In the early 1960s, the Soviet Union began an erratic drive to rely less on centralized decision making. This trend was accelerated in 1986 when Premier Gorbachev launched his policy of *glasnost* (openness) and greater accommodation with the United States and its allies. China began to slowly decentralize economic decisions early in the 1980s. Both of these countries began to rely more on market forces in hopes of matching the economic growth common in western Europe, North America, and Japan. Focus 1 indicates, however, that this can be a rocky road to prosperity.

Coupled with increasing U.S. government controls over economic activity during the past six decades, it appears that "we" are becoming somewhat more like "them" and "they" are becoming somewhat more like "us," although staunch old Soviet bureaucrats and some American politicians try to accentuate our differences. Former President Reagan has been among the American leaders calling for greater reliance on decentralized capitalism.

Foundations of Capitalism

Capitalism is not like it used to be, and never was.
                                                    —*Anonymous*

Capitalism and its ideological foundations are only a few centuries old, but its roots go back to the dawn of history when primitive people first began staking claims to their territory. The hallmarks of "pure" **capitalism** are the institution of private property and laissez-faire policies by government.

Private Property Rights

It is common to refer to something as being "owned" by someone. You probably own textbooks, sports equipment, or perhaps a car. Exactly what does your ownership mean? Generally it means that you have certain rights to use these things in certain ways. **Fee-simple property rights** are the broadest of **private property rights,** and include rights to (*a*) use a good as you choose as long as no one else's rights are violated; (*b*) trade or give these rights to other people; and (*c*) deny use of the good to others.

Most property rights are much more limited than this, however. For example, you cannot shoot people or dogs for trespassing on your land, or burn rubbish in smog-filled cities. You cannot use leaded gas in most new cars. You cannot raise pigs in New York City (or Des Moines, Iowa, for that matter). You cannot abuse your children, burn your house for the insurance money, . . . the list goes on and on. The critical point is that most property rights are circumscribed.

How does a person acquire rights to property? John Locke, a seventeenth-century English philosopher, offered the labor theory of value to justify natural property rights. The *labor theory of value* assumes that all value is created by human labor. According to Locke, mixing your labor with "gifts of nature" makes land and the crops it produces valuable. Thus, he viewed improvements to natural resources as the ethical cornerstones of original property rights, which could then be legally transferred to others.

This view of labor as the basis for property rights raises several moral and practical problems, however. If you are the first to pour a pint of blood into the sea, should the oceans and all their riches be yours? Should those who encounter "gifts of nature" have property rights on a first-come, first-serve basis? What about rules for transferring property? Who should have property rights to things produced by employees? . . . by slaves? Should you own a piece of land, not because of anything you have done, but because you inherited it from your parents who inherited it from their parents who bought it from the family who cleared the land? What if the family who cleared it murdered the previous owners? Should property rights be a matter of convention, so that property rights become ever stronger over time, regardless of whether a transfer of property long ago was legal or illicit? Difficulties posed by these and similar questions for Locke's "natural rights" theory suggest that we need a more practical view of the foundations of property rights.

A system of property rights based on brute force would be violent. If your claims were only valid to the extent that you had the muscle to enforce them, many

Pie Producers vs. Pie Splitters

Extreme socialists (and especially, Marxists) have long viewed the market system with contempt. A proper blend of "need" and "equality" is the only fair criterion for distributing income, according to orthodox socialist doctrine, and extreme inequality is an evil characteristic of capitalism. "Freedom" in capitalist economies has been condemned as a facade: rich capitalists have freedom to hog most consumer goods and to exploit poor workers, who have only the freedom to suffer in silence. Capitalism's alleged economic efficiency has been vilified as an empty shell that masks distortions by advertisers and a general exploitation of workers and consumers.

This overall characterization of capitalist markets was an article of faith among the leaders who led Marxist revolutions and installed communism as official policy in the Soviet Union and the People's Republic of China. In more recent years, however, new groups of leaders (led by Premier Gorbachev in the USSR and Deng Xiaoping in China) have become resigned to the futility of trying to reform centralized bureaucracies created to coordinate economic activity. These leaders have attempted to stimulate greater efficiency in their economies with policies that rely more on market forces.

These limited experiments with markets have succeeded in achieving rapid growth in targeted economic sectors. But some bureaucrats and ideologues who feel threatened by market experiments have counterattacked, focusing on high incomes earned by some would-be entrepreneurs. For example, a report from Beijing cites two cases:* Liu Changfu earned about $11,840 in 1986 by restructuring a marginal metal utensil factory. Local officials refused to pay him, however, because his income would be 30 times what average workers receive. Guan Guangmei, a food store manager, was criticized for making 20 times the income she paid her employees.

Hardliners have proposed narrow limits on income differentials in response to these and similar cases, but China's new leaders are trying to reassure the nervous entrepreneurs who are emerging. Zhao Ziyang, the head of the Communist Party, has stated that ideology and socialist class struggle are now less important than economic development. He has also stressed the need to reward China's most talented and diligent in accord with their productive contributions. Zhao's views are supported by Zhu Yong-ming, a local official: "This is a matter that tests whether the government means what it says. If in the first year, the government goes back on its words, how should the reforms be carried further next year?"

The debates that rage in both China and the Soviet Union over high incomes for new entrepreneurs are evidence that rapid changes wrought by market forces make many people uncomfortable. This seems to be especially true in countries with long histories of official policies to treat almost all market activities as criminal behavior.

*"Big pay can be big pain in China," Chicago Tribune, 30 Dec. 1987, sec. 3.

---

resources would be devoted to aggressively protecting your rights and trying to take from others. Because of this inefficiency, we surrender to government the right to be violent, giving it a near-monopoly on the use of force. Most legal scholars would argue that your property rights are determined by law—what the law says is yours is yours; neither more nor less. Society can be viewed as specifying sets of rights by law and then redefining rights through changes in statutes or legal opinions.

Most of us think of property rights only with respect to tangible goods. Property rights and most legal rights, however, are almost synonymous to many economists. For example, traffic laws define how we may use our cars; zoning ordinances, how we may use our land and buildings; and criminal laws, how we must treat our neighbors. We place ourselves in legal jeopardy if we abuse any of them. You do not have the right to slander your neighbor, litter, or shout "FIRE" in a crowded theater. All laws establish boundaries governing our uses both of our own and our neighbors' property. Laws can be viewed as setting the framework of property rights within which we deal with others, where the concept of property rights is defined very broadly. Naturally, changes in rights occur whenever there are changes in laws. Just as laws create property rights, they can take them away. For example, before 1974, you could go 70 MPH on most freeways. Between 1974 and 1986, your rights were restricted to 55 MPH. Some legal rights of drivers were withdrawn. When 65 MPH speed limits were re-established for many highways in 1986, some of drivers' legal rights were restored.

Thus, government's major role in a capitalist economy is to establish laws that govern who owns what and how ownership rights can be transferred. Government creates property rights and it can also change them—tariffs, entitlement programs, and similar laws help determine who gets what. Beyond this, pure capitalism requires very little of government except reasonable consistency. Frequent legal changes, even those that seem trivial, may create uncertainty and discourage production and investment.

The major challenger of capitalism is **socialism,** which holds that most resources should be owned jointly by all people in society instead of by private individuals. Differences between capitalism and socialism also tend to be very pronounced when we try to specify appropriate roles for government.

Laissez-Faire Policies

That government is best which governs least.
— *Thomas Jefferson*

Feudal monarchs ruled by "divine right," claiming they were chosen by God to lead their countries. Even so, their policies often failed. Vexed by the economic plight of seventeenth-century France, Louis XIV's finance minister asked for advice from a leading industrialist. Without hesitation, the manufacturer responded, *"Laissez-nous faire,"* roughly, "Leave us alone." **Laissez-faire** has ever since been a rallying cry for those who believe that the market system works best with only minimal government.

But what specific roles should government play? Nearly everyone recognizes needs for national defense and police protection. In the economic sphere, a laissez-faire government only specifies property rights and enforces contracts. Under pure capitalism, private individuals own virtually all resources and decide their uses. Market prices determine the range of choices available to us, given our budgets, which are in turn determined by the resources we individually own. Most socialist economies replace the marketplace with government coordination, or **central planning.**

Private property and laissez-faire policies distinguish capitalism from alternative systems. Ideological battles between advocates of capitalism and socialism have raged for centuries. Capitalism's defenders cite many virtues of the price system, but the two most important are freedom and efficiency. Capitalism, it is argued, allows people maximum freedom because it requires only minimal government. A tradition predating the American Revolution views all "Big Brother" governments as enemies of freedom.

All societies blend elements of both capitalism and socialism, so people everywhere live in **mixed economies.** Thus, in the Soviet economy, most fruits, vegetables, and meats are produced for private *kolkhoz* markets. These markets tend to be efficient relative to other aspects of the Soviet economy. In the United States, socialism appears in the form of government-provided education, highways, and medical care for the aged or poor.

There are many aspects of American government which represent political attempts to achieve what some people perceive as a greater equity. Where efficiency is our major goal, we tend to rely on the marketplace. The efficiency of capitalism depends on how well it meets consumer wants, given the resources available. In the next chapter, we examine the forces of supply and demand, which are the devices determining *What? How? Who?* and *When?* in a market system.

CHAPTER REVIEW: KEY POINTS

1. Every society must address four basic economic questions (*a*) *What* goods will be produced? (*b*) *How* will productive resources by used? (*c*) *Who* will get the production? (*d*) *When* will production and consumption occur?

2. A *production-possibilities frontier* (*PPF*) shows the maximum combinations of goods that a society can produce. The *PPF* curve assumes that (*a*) resources are fixed; (*b*) technology is constant; and (*c*) all scarce resources are fully and efficiently employed.

3. Opportunity costs are the values of outputs if resources were switched to their best alternative uses. Opportunity costs are not constant because resources are not equally suited for all types of production. Increasing a particular form of production invariably leads to *diminishing returns* and *increasing opportunity costs,* so the production-possibilities curve is concave (bowed away) from its origin.

4. *Economic growth* occurs when technology advances or when the amounts of resources available for production increase. Economic growth can be shown as an outward shift of the production-possibilities curve; more of all goods can be produced.

5. When technology advances for one good in a production-possibilities model, most of the curve will shift outward and to the right; fewer resources are needed to produce that good and thus are available for producing other goods.

6. The choices a society makes between consumption and investment goods affects its future production-possibilities curve. Lower saving and investment restricts economic growth and *PPF* expansion.

7. Alternative *allocative mechanisms* include the following (*a*) the *market system,* (*b*) *brute force,* (*c*) *queuing,* (*d*) *random selection,* (*e*) *tradition,* and (*f*) *government.*

8. Many different economic systems are used in attempts to resolve the problem of scarcity. They can be classified by who makes the decisions (*centralized* or *decentralized*) and who owns the resources (*public* versus *private*).

9. Property is privately owned under pure *capitalism* and government follows *laissez-faire* (hands-off) policies. Thus, decisions are decentralized and rely on individual choices in a market system. Under *socialism,* government acts as a trustee over the nonhuman resources jointly owned by all citizens, with many socialist economies also relying heavily on centralized production and distribution decisions.

PROBLEM

1. Some health care professionals argue that our system delivers "the best care for the most people," and use this slogan to defend the American medical system against its critics. Suppose that current levels of medical resources (11 percent of the value of our total output nationally in 1987) yield the *PPF* curve going through points *a* and *b* in Figure 8. Complete the following questions and exercises.

   a. Point _____ must be attained to make this slogan true.

   b. Attaining this point would require either more _____ or an advance in _____ .

   c. This *PPF* is concave from below because medical resources _____ in their _____ for different types of medical care.

   d. A *PPF* that would conform to this slogan would be unusual looking because it would _____ . (This question is a bit tricky.)

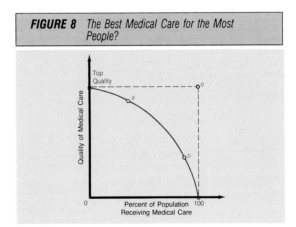

FIGURE 8 *The Best Medical Care for the Most People?*

Source: J. Michael Swint, "Best Medical Care for the Most People Myth," in R. T. Byrns and G. W. Stone, eds., *Great Ideas for Teaching Economics,* 4/ed. (Glenview, IL: Scott, Foresman/Little, Brown, 1989).

QUESTIONS FOR THOUGHT AND DISCUSSION

1. Explain why a family with a fixed budget has a "purchasing possibilities" frontier that is a straight line. But a family's budget is seldom independent of the activities of family members. Suppose that different family members can work for different hourly incomes, and that they differ in their ability to do tasks for the family (e.g., cooking, cleaning, gardening, painting, household repairs). Discuss whether production and the generation of income within the family is characterized by a family production-possibilities frontier that is straight or concave from below.

2. What is the mix of allocative mechanisms used within most American families to decide which family members get what, given limited family income? How are different mechanisms used for different kinds of decisions?

3. One way to illustrate that an economic arrangement is inefficient is to show how, through some rearrangement, some people could gain with no one else losing. Use this approach to evaluate the following situations:

   a. *Brute force.* The Soviet Union and the United States devote valuable resources to national defense because each side fears attack by the other.

   b. *Queuing.* A $100-per-hour lawyer is at the end of a two-hour waiting line to renew a driver's license, and a vacationing college student is at the front of the line.

   c. *Random selection.* A rock star who makes $10 million or more annually is drafted, while an unem-

   ployed 18-year-old high-school dropout who would be willing to join the Army for a $9,000 salary is not drafted and does not enlist because the pay is only $7,000 annually.

   d. *Tradition.* Quota systems once limited the numbers of women, Jews, blacks, and Hispanic Americans admitted to medical school.

   e. *Government.* Procurement procedures sometimes require that imported goods be used to fulfill government contracts only if American-made goods are not available.

4. Use the concept of the opportunity cost of time to explain why our welfare system involves long queues for those who seek food stamps, housing allowances, or aid for dependent children.

5. Suppose that government could perfectly control the rate of interest, the rate of inflation, the level of taxes, and the relative levels of wages and prices. How could the government foster economic growth through low consumer spending and more saving and investment via each of these tools?

6. Evaluate the following argument: Grades and athletic medals should be allocated through a market system. The buyers would be the people who value such awards the most, so this would be more efficient than awarding according to merit. For example, if a C student could buy an A from a more diligent student, both could gain from the exchange without harming anyone else in the process.

CHAPTER 3

Demand and Supply

The tools of supply and demand analysis are as basic to economics as saws and hammers are to carpentry. Models of supply and demand yield profound insights into why prices are what they are, and why prices or sales of goods move in particular directions. Your objective in this chapter is a tall order that requires only a short sentence: Learn how demand and supply interact in markets to determine prices and outputs. We first discuss markets and prices a bit, then look at some fundamentals of demand and supply, and finally, show how these two concepts are linked in markets. After you have worked through this chapter and the next, you should be able to use supply and demand to interpret output and price changes in the markets for oil, gold, food, home computers, air fares, and almost all other goods.

Markets and Prices

Markets enable buyers and sellers to transact business and, thus, allow people to share in the gains made possible through specialization and exchange according to comparative advantage (discussed in chapter 1). Markets range from commodity exchanges where millions of bushels of grain change hands in thousands of daily trades to markets where one huge transaction requires years to complete (major construction contracts). Markets range from geographically limited (kids' lemonade stands) to global (international markets for petroleum engineers). Some deal in a single type of good (brickyards), while others offer thousands of products (shopping centers). Every market is somewhat unique, but all share certain characteristics (*a*) buyers who demand goods or the resources that produce them and (*b*) suppliers who make products or resources available if the price is right.

It is important to distinguish the *relative price* of a good from its **absolute price.** You may have heard of the Consumer Price Index, which was over 350 at the beginning of 1988. It is probably difficult for you to identify a discernible impact of this estimate of the absolute price level on any of your decisions. In fact, whether we use francs, pesos, inflated dimes, or solid gold dollars to measure absolute prices is largely irrelevant for most market decisions. The **relative prices** of goods and resources, however, embody a tremendous amount of information to guide decisions because they reflect opportunity costs. How many sundaes must you sacrifice for a new record album? For a ski vacation to Aspen?

Relative prices are the prices of goods in terms of each other, and are computed by dividing their absolute prices by one another. If hot fudge sundaes are $1, while records are $7 and all-expense-paid ski vacations are $280, then a record costs 7 sundaes and a vacation costs 280 sundaes or 40 records. (7/1 = 7; 280/1 = 280; 280/7 = 40. Test your understanding by computing the relative prices of sundaes and records in terms of vacations.)

Suppose a onetime, fixed-proportional increase occurred in all absolute prices. Relative prices would not change, nor would most rational decisions. Try a mental experiment to prove this point: What would you do if your income, assets, liabilities, and the prices of all goods and resources doubled on a one-time basis? Answer: You would handle twice as many dollars, but otherwise your behavior should not change. Reflect on this for a moment. *Conclusion:* Relative prices are important for *micro*economic decisions; absolute prices are ultimately unimportant for most decisions about the goods we buy or the resources we supply.

This result must be qualified somewhat, however, because inflationary changes in absolute prices are unimportant only if relative prices and the distribution of income are unchanged. Unfortunately, inflation always disrupts both of these, distorting economic activity and creating uncertainty, and so it is a major concern for *macro*economic policymakers. In the following discussion, however, our references are to relative, not absolute, prices.

Demand

Economists view buying a good as casting a vote with money. "Dollar votes" are signals that guide business decisions about how to profitably satisfy consumer wants. Items with the highest prices relative to their production costs earn the greatest profits. Firms compete to provide these items so that the needs consumers perceive as most pressing tend to receive top priority.

You may wonder whether our "needs" can be met with available resources. A real problem arises if we focus on what many view as "necessities." Most suburbanites find a car a "necessity," and many of us go through withdrawal symptoms when deprived of television for only a day or two. In a wealthy society like ours, even much of the food we eat is recreational and unnecessary.

What is truly needed for survival? Two thousand or so calories daily, some vitamins and minerals, and shelter and sufficient clothing to prevent sunstroke or frostbite. What do absolute necessities cost? Well, you can get by on soybean curd and vitamin pills, a shack made of discarded cardboard, and a few clothes from Goodwill Industries. Life could be sustained for $1,000 a year, although most of us would view anyone trying to live on that little as still needy. Economists concentrate on consumer demand because "need" is both ambiguous and very normative.

> **Demands** *are the quantities of various goods that people are willing and able to buy during some period, given the choices available to them.*

Consider a typical consumption choice. Many of us attend concerts, listen to tapes or records, and watch television. These different forms of entertainment have varying prices, with the price of viewing TV being approximately $0, and rock concert tickets ranging from $16 to $100 apiece. (For now, we will ignore pay TV and the value of your time.) If we rank these activities from the cheapest to the most expensive, you probably spend the most time watching TV and the least going to concerts, with listening to a stereo falling somewhere in between. Even though different people choose different combinations, this example suggests that there is a negative relationship between the price of a good and the quantity that consumers purchase.

Consumer decisions are based on two sets of relative prices—market prices and demand prices. **Market prices** are the prices sellers charge for goods whether we buy or not; **demand prices** are the relative values that individuals *subjectively* place on having a bit more or less of a good. You buy chewing gum or pizzas only when they are subjectively worth their market prices to you.

Our budgets help determine whether or not our demand prices are aligned with market prices. Rolls-Royces are worth their market price to those who buy them. The demand prices at which many of us would purchase a new Rolls-Royce are far below the market price. Thus, Rolls-Royces are subjectively "not worth the price" to us, given our budgets, and we drive cheaper cars, if we drive at all.

Substitution and the Law of Demand

When the relative price of a good falls, it is advantageous to substitute it for other goods where possible. Conversely, when a good becomes more expensive, you find substitutes for it. This is known as the **substitution effect** of a change in relative prices, and is the foundation for the law of demand, a basic concept of the economic theory of consumer behavior.

According to the **law of demand,** *all else assumed equal, consumers purchase more of a good during a given time interval the lower its opportunity cost (relative price), and vice versa.*[1]

Most goods have many possible uses. Substituting a good into more uses the lower its price is advantageous. For example, caviar is now a delicacy, but if its price fell to $0.50 per pound, it might replace baloney on sandwiches for children's school lunches. Were it free, we might use caviar for dog food, hog slop, or fertilizer. If diamonds were as cheap as gravel, we would use them as a base material for high-

ways. On the other hand, if gasoline cost $10 a gallon, cities would be more compact and we would rely far more on bicycles, walking, or public transit; few people would waste gasoline on meandering pleasure trips or hit-and-run shopping. If peanut butter were $50 per pound, gourmets might consider it a delicacy to be savored on fancy crackers at posh parties. The critical point is that people substitute for goods that become relatively more costly and find wider uses for goods that become cheaper. Focus 1 indicates how even people's use of water changes as its price varies.

Substitution occurs for several reasons, including a facet of the law of diminishing returns known as the principle of diminishing marginal utility (satisfaction):

According to the **principle of diminishing marginal utility,** *the more you have of any good relative to others, the less you desire and are willing to pay for additional units of that good.*

For example, it is unlikely that you would value a ninth chocolate chip ice cream cone as much as the first you ate on a given day. The same principle holds true for wind surfing, hair transplants, affection from your current heartthrob, or any other good.

Another reason that purchases of a good rise when its price falls is that the purchasing power of your limited income increases, and you can buy more of it while maintaining or even increasing your other purchases. This is known as the **income effect** of a price change, but income effects tend to be less direct and far less important than substitution effects.

The Demand Curve

The law of demand's negative relationship between the price of any good and the quantity consumed yields a negatively-sloped demand curve:

A **demand curve** *depicts the maximum quantities of a good that given individuals will purchase at various prices during a given period, all else assumed equal.*

An alternative perspective yielding different insights but identical demand curves views them as showing

---

[1]Note that all influences on consumption of the good other than price are held constant! Throughout economic analysis, this "all else assumed equal" methodology is used so that we can examine, one at a time, the variables that affect human behavior. The Latin term *ceteris paribus* is used by many economists to refer to the idea that "all other influences" on some **dependent** variable are held constant while examining the effect of changing a single **independent** variable. Thus, the law of demand deals with the independent influence of price on the quantity demanded (the dependent variable), *ceteris paribus.*

Substitution and the Uses of Water as Its Price Changes

The extent of substitution when prices change depends on the options available. If a good has close relatives (cotton and wool are examples), we may switch from one product to another with little inconvenience as their relative prices change. In other situations, substitution is difficult and entails a loss of efficiency or quality (replacing light bulbs with candles, for instance). In extreme cases, adjusting to higher prices may require that we simply do without.

Figure 1 shows how our uses of water might be influenced by different prices. If water were incredibly scarce and costly because you were stranded in the desert, you might sip only a little to avoid feeling parched and trust your camel to make it to the next oasis without a drink. Once there, the subjective value of water decreases and you would find ever broader uses for water— brushing your teeth, washing, and so on. You will see water flowing down streets when people water their lawns only when the price of water is incredibly low.

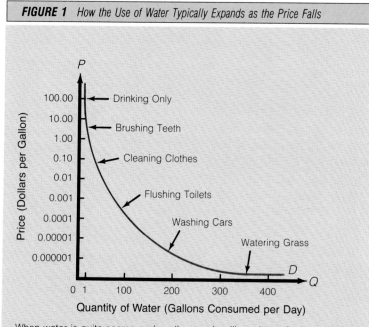

FIGURE 1 How the Use of Water Typically Expands as the Price Falls

When water is quite scarce and costly, people will use it sparingly, confining its uses to those most necessary. As the price falls, more and more uses are considered economical.

the maximum price that people are willing to pay for an *additional* unit of a good, given their current consumption.

Figure 2 uses Arlene's demand for paperbacks to illustrate the law of demand; lower market prices make her willing and able to buy more books. Arlene purchases 30 novels annually when each is $1.75, but only 10 at $3.75 apiece. She buys none if the price rises to $4.75, possibly watching more TV or renewing her public library card instead.

Suppose that Arlene currently buys 14 books at $3.30 apiece. Her demand price (the subjectively

FIGURE 2 An Individual's Demand Curve for Paperback Books

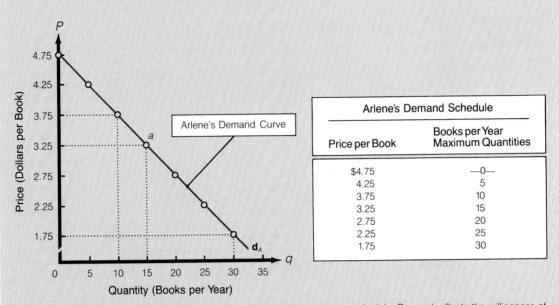

Arlene's demand for paperback books can be shown as a demand curve or schedule. Demand reflects the willingness of an individual to purchase various quantities of a commodity at various prices. The demand curve is negatively sloped, reflecting the *law of demand*–at lower prices individuals will purchase larger quantities of a particular product. In this instance, more paperback books will be purchased at lower prices per book.

determined maximum she would pay) for a fifteenth book is $3.25 (point *a*). Figure 2 also includes Arlene's demand schedule. A *demand schedule* is a table listing the maximum quantities of a good that consumers will purchase at various prices during some period, and summarizes points on a demand curve.

Market Demand Curves

Individual demand curves are interesting from a theoretical standpoint, but market demand curves are far more important and practical for most analytical purposes. Market demands simply sum up all individual demands.

Figure 3 depicts the demand curves of Arlene and Bert, and the market demand curve if they alone bought paperbacks. Below each demand curve is a corresponding demand schedule. *Horizontal summation* of the individual demand curves of all potential buyers yields a **market demand curve.** This means that we sum the quantities per period that

individuals buy at each price. At a price of $3.75, Arlene buys 10 paperbacks annually while Bert buys none. Thus, at $3.75, the quantity demanded in this market is 10 books (10 + 0). At $2.25, Arlene purchases 25 books and Bert buys 15, so the quantity demanded is 40 (25 + 15), and so on.

Actually measuring demand is difficult because markets are dynamic and "all else" is seldom equal. Prices are important, but not alone in influencing market behavior, which has been described as a process of discovery. (Most parents know that what they buy on a given trip to a grocery store depends as much on whether they go alone or have a child in tow as it depends on food prices.) Market fluctuations caused by changes in the many influences on buying and selling yield sketchy price and quantity information. Professional economists who estimate market demands for particular goods must unravel fragmentary market data with sophisticated statistical methods beyond the scope of this book. Nevertheless, most influences on buying patterns are conceptually simple.

FIGURE 3 *Individual and Market Demand for Paperbacks*

Demand Schedule Arlene		+	Demand Schedule Bert		=	Demand Schedule Total Market	
Price	Quantity (q_A)		Price	Quantity (q_B)		Price	Quantity (Q)
$4.75	—0—		$4.75	—0—		$4.75	—0—
4.25	5		4.25	—0—		4.25	5
3.75	10		3.75	—0—		3.75	10
3.25	15		3.25	5		3.25	20
2.75	20		2.75	10		2.75	30
2.25	25		2.25	15		2.25	40
1.75	30		1.75	20		1.75	50

The market demand curve can be derived from a series of individual demands by horizontally summing the individual demand curves. That is, for each price, we add the quantities that each individual will purchase. At a price of $2.25, Arlene is willing to purchase 25 books, while Bert demands 15 books. Thus the quantity demanded in the market at a price of $2.25 is 40 books. To obtain market demand, this process is followed for each price.

Other Influences on Demand

Demand curves reflect how purchases are related to prices, but a good's price does not solely determine the quantity bought during a given period. Other influences tend to fall into one of six categories (*a*) tastes and preferences; (*b*) income and its distribution; (*c*) prices of related goods; (*d*) numbers and ages of buyers; (*e*) expectations about future prices, incomes, or availability; and (*f*) government taxes, subsidies, and regulations.

Tastes and Preferences People's preferences for goods vary because of styling, quality, personal idiosyncrasies, or status characteristics (whether or not our friends or neighbors have them). Cars, clothes, music, and numerous other products are subject to consumers' whims. "Knockoffs" of the latest fashions, the numerous clones of hit TV shows, and the proliferation of brands of wine coolers (largely ignored before 1985) are evidence that business can react quickly to fads. If everyone abandoned rock-and-roll for country music, would it take long for top-40 disc jockeys to cultivate drawls and twangs while announcing the songs of Randy Travis and Dolly Parton?

Demands obviously depend on consumer tastes and preferences, but measuring these precisely is almost as impossible as predicting the next hot trend. You should, however, be able to evaluate whether a given change in preferences will raise or lower demand. For example, if the 1992 Olympics popularize judo as a way for people to stay in shape, what will happen to the demand for gym mats and judo lessons?

Income and Its Distribution

Income also affects consumer demand. As your income rises, your demands for higher quality goods will tend to rise markedly. Goods for which demand is positively related to income are called **normal goods.** Vacations, live entertainment, luxuries such as jewelry and limousines, and most other products and services are normal goods. Demands for luxuries are especially responsive to changes in income.

On the other hand, when a poor family's income rises, its demands for such **inferior goods** as lye soap and pinto beans falls. Clunker cars and peanut butter sandwiches may be inferior goods. When students graduate and get "real" jobs, their incomes typically jump and they buy fewer inferior goods. All else equal, it follows that income redistribution alters the structure of demands: Taking from the rich to provide welfare for the poor causes declines in demands for both inferior goods and luxuries, whereas rising inequality stimulates the demands for both.

Prices of Related Goods

A good's own price is important, but prices of related products also influence demand. Most goods are at least mild **substitutes** for one another. For example, if golf balls climbed to $5 each, you would golf less frequently, but your consumption of such substitute goods as tennis balls and racquets might rise. This is especially true

for duffers who drop at least one golf ball in every water hazard. When coffee prices soared in the 1970s, sales of tea bags also climbed. Like golf and tennis, coffee and tea are *close* substitutes. Other examples include chicken and pizza; phone calls and letters; Acuras and BMWs; or hot tubs, Jacuzzis, and saunas.

Cars, tires, and gasoline are examples of **complementary goods;** they are consumed together. Other sets of *complements* are tuition and textbooks; steak and A–1 sauce; computers and diskettes; or left shoes and right shoes. As the prices of complementary goods rise, the demand for the good in question falls, and vice versa.

Numbers and Ages of Buyers

Population growth raises the number of potential buyers and, hence, market demands for most goods. Age structures of the consuming public are also a factor. Expanding average life spans has swollen demands for retirement communities and medical services. Demands for baby products slumped when birth rates fell in the 1960s, but producers of diapers and formula recovered somewhat when "baby boomers" began their families.

Expectations about Future Prices, Incomes, or Availability

Consumers who expect shortages or sharp price hikes in the coming weeks or months may race to buy storable products now, thus boosting current demands. Many Americans went on buying sprees at the onset of the Korean War because shortages, spiralling prices, and rationing had been common during World War II; memories of the previous war caused people to try to stockpile sugar, flour, appliances, tires, autos, and many other goods. This created shortages and drove up prices. Today, some consumers react to news that killing frosts threaten citrus crops by hoarding frozen orange juice concentrate.

People may also splurge if they expect their incomes to rise substantially in the near future. You might buy a car on credit after accepting a job before you have even received your first paycheck. Many people spend income before they make it and fall deeply in debt.

Expectations about government actions also reshape buying patterns. A Food and Drug Administration proposal to ban saccharine in 1977 because it was suspected as a cause of cancer resulted in shoppers stripping grocers' shelves. These consumers worried more about the health hazards of "fat attacks" than about greater risks from cancer.

Taxes, Subsidies, and Regulations   We have focused on ways that the behavior of private individuals shift demands. But taxes, subsidies, and regulations may also strongly influence demand. From a buyer's perspective, demand is a relationship between the quantity bought and the price *paid.* Sellers, on the other hand, view demand as the relationship between the quantity sold and the price *received.* These approaches normally yield the same results, but taxes or subsidies can drive a wedge between the demand price that buyers are willing to pay and the price the seller receives. Figure 4 illustrates this.

Suppose the government imposes a tax of $1 per paperback novel. Buyers perceive no change in their willingness to purchase, so they view their demand for paperback books as being stable at D_0. They are still willing to buy 200 million books annually at a demand price of $3.75. However, publishers view demand as having declined to D_2 because the after-tax prices they receive are reduced by $1 for each novel sold. They would receive only $2.75 per book if they priced books so that 200 million were bought.

Now suppose the government offered publishers a $1 subsidy per book sold to encourage national literacy. Buyers would view their demand curves as stable at D_0, but from the vantage points of publishers, demand would rise to D_1. They would receive $1 more per paperback at every output level. Regulation may either stifle demand, as it does for narcotics and other illicit activities, or bolster demand, as the effect of compulsory education on the demands for chalk and erasers demonstrates.

To summarize, demand increases if (*a*) consumer preferences change so that people are more inclined to buy a good; (*b*) consumer incomes rise (*fall*) in the case of a normal (*inferior*) good; (*c*) the price of a substitute (*complementary*) good rises (*falls*); (*d*) the number of consumers increases; (*e*) consumers anticipate higher prices or incomes, or expect shortages of the good; or (*f*) favorable regulation is adopted, taxes are reduced, or government subsidizes the good. Decreases in demand would result if the changes were reversed for these influences on demand.

FIGURE 4   *Changes in the Market Demand for Paperback Books*

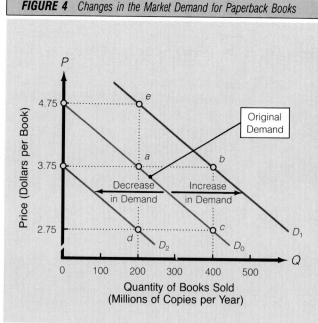

Movements along a demand curve (point *a* to point *c*, or point *b* to point *e*) occur when buyers respond to a change in the price of the good itself. It is important to distinguish such changes in quantity demanded (movements along a single demand curve) from changes in demand—a shift to the right (D_0 to D_1) represents an increase in demand, while a shift to the left (D_0 to D_2) is a decrease in demand. These shifts result from changes in influences other than the product price itself. For example, demand increases for most goods when consumer incomes grow; demand declines if consumers begin viewing a good with distaste.

Changes in Demand

A demand curve shows the negative relationship between the price and quantity of a good demanded during a given interval, holding all other influences constant. But what happens if influences on the demand for a good other than its own price change?

Tastes and preferences may be reshaped by a firm's marketing strategy. Publishers often mail novels to reviewers gratis, hoping to promote a best-seller. When male beer drinkers worried about their weight but viewed light beers as tasteless and un-macho, one brewer's ads featured retired jocks debating whether the beer was "less filling" or "tastes great." And the suds flowed and flowed.

Another marketing technique is to tie products to each other. Producers of kids' lunch boxes, underwear, and toys regularly mirror the latest crazes, from Care Bears to Transformers. Firms commonly link new films and books in their advertising, trying to swell both book and box-office receipts. Figure 4 shows how successful promotion can shift a demand curve to the right (from D_0 to D_1) so that more books are demanded at every price.

If paperbacks are normal goods, demand will increase if income rises. Beginning on D_0 in Figure 4, boosts in income cause consumers to purchase more paperbacks at every price, moving demand to D_1. On the other hand, a drop in income normally causes demand to fall (a shift of the demand curve toward the origin—from D_0 to D_2). Naturally, such effects are reversed if novels are inferior goods.

Now consider changes in the availability or prices of related products. The advent of cable TV, for example, broadens the range of available programs, and some readers might become TV addicts, shrinking the demand for books (again in Figure 4, from D_0 to D_2). Or if ticket prices for movies fell, substitution could cause demands for books to fall. Take a moment to think of examples of how demand would shift if there were changes in the number of buyers or in consumers' expectations.

Thus, *a change in demand means a shift in the demand curve.* Declines in demand cause shifts to the left, while shifts to the right show increases in demand. These shifts result from changes in: tastes and preferences, incomes, related prices, numbers of consumers, expectations, or government policies. Consumers may perceive no changes in their demands with the imposition of taxes or subsidies, but sellers will. Demand rises when consumers become willing to purchase more of a good at every price, or to pay a higher demand price for a given quantity of the good, and vice versa. These relationships are summarized in Figure 5.

Changes in Quantity Demanded Versus Changes in Demand

Distinguishing **changes in demand** from **changes in quantities demanded** is crucial. Changes in the quantity of a good demanded are *movements along a demand curve* and are caused by only one thing—a change in its price. Changes in demand, on the other hand, involve *shifts* of demand curves.

A review of these differences using Figure 4 will help you avoid errors on this point. Suppose 200 million books are currently sold annually at a price of $3.75. How might sales be raised to 400 million paperbacks? The demand curve could grow from D_0 to D_1 so that 400 million would be bought at $3.75 (point *b*); alternatively, 400 million copies would be sold annually if the price were cut to $2.75 (point *c*). Increased income is one of many ways to increase *demand* (to point *b*), while simply reducing price yields an equivalent increase, but in *quantity demanded* (point *c*). Similar differences apply to decreases in demand versus a decrease in quantity demanded. A shift in the entire demand curve as illustrated in Figure 4 from D_0 to D_2 represents a drop in demand. Given demand curve D_0, an increase in price from $2.75 (point *c*) to $3.75 (point *a*) reduces the quantity demanded from 400 to 200 million books.

You will spare yourself a lot of grief if you can clearly distinguish changes in demand from changes in quantity demanded. Changes in demand follow changes in influences on purchases other than a good's own price; a change in the quantity demanded follows changes in the price of the good. Thus, a change in the price of compact disks (CDs) yields a change in the quantity demanded, but changes in the prices of CD players, tapes, or in consumers' incomes will change the demand for compact disks. The importance of this distinction will become clearer

FIGURE 5 Factors Causing Shifts in Demand

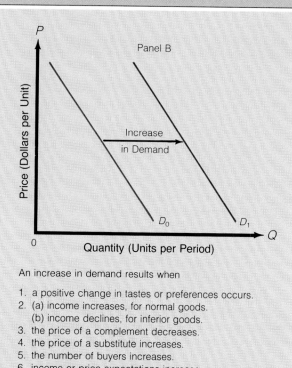

A decrease in demand results when

1. a negative change in tastes or preferences occurs.
2. (a) income declines, for normal goods.
   (b) income rises, for inferior goods.
3. the price of a complement increases.
4. the price of a substitute decreases.
5. the number of buyers decreases.
6. income or price expectations decrease.
7. expected surpluses or expectations of greater product availability occur.
8. the government reduces subsidies or increases taxes.

An increase in demand results when

1. a positive change in tastes or preferences occurs.
2. (a) income increases, for normal goods.
   (b) income declines, for inferior goods.
3. the price of a complement decreases.
4. the price of a substitute increases.
5. the number of buyers increases.
6. income or price expectations increase.
7. expected shortages or expectations of decreased product availability occur.
8. the government increases subsidies or reduces taxes.

after we show how demand and supply are linked in markets.

Supply

Transactions require both buyers and sellers. Thus, demand curves are only one aspect of decisions about prices and the amounts of goods traded; supply curves are another.

Supply *refers to the outputs that sellers provide under certain conditions during a given period.*

One critical condition is that producers must expect to gain by selling their outputs or else they will refuse to incur production costs. This section outlines some influences on firms' decisions to produce and sell.

The Law of Supply

Producers' decisions about the amounts to sell hinge on the law of supply.

According to the **law of supply,** *all else assumed equal, higher prices induce greater production and offers to sell more output; firms provide less during a given period at lower prices.*

One reason is that higher prices provide greater production incentives. More importantly, attempts to expand output ultimately yield diminishing returns; increasing costs occur when returns diminish because, as larger numbers of costly "doses" of resources are applied, output may grow, but less than proportionally. When this happens, higher prices are needed to sustain incentives for suppliers to produce and sell their goods.

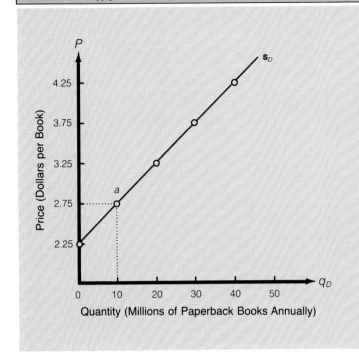

FIGURE 6 Supply Curve of Paperback Books for Dell Publishing Co., Inc.

The supply curve and schedule represent the maximum amounts of a commodity firms are willing to produce and sell during a given period at different prices. The supply curve depicted reflects the *law of supply*—at higher prices, more of the commodity will be offered to the market.

Supply Schedule Dell Publishing Co. Inc.	
Price	Quantity (Millions)
$4.25	40
3.75	30
3.25	20
2.75	10
2.25	—0—

The Supply Curve   Just as the law of demand yields *negatively* sloped demand curves, the law of supply generates *positively* sloped supply curves.

> A **supply curve** *shows the maximum amounts of a good that firms are willing to furnish during a given time period at various prices.*

A different perspective views the same supply curve as showing the minimum prices that will induce specific quantities supplied.

The positive slopes of supply curves reflect eventual increases in costs per unit when output grows because firms (*a*) ultimately encounter diminishing returns; (*b*) may be forced to pay current workers overtime wages for extra hours; or (*c*) successfully attract more labor or other resources only by paying more for them. Working closer to capacity also causes more scheduling errors and equipment breakdowns. Such problems raise costs when firms increase output.

A typical supply curve and schedule are shown in Figure 6. Dell will produce and sell 40 million paperbacks annually at $4.25, but only 10 million books if the price falls to $2.75. A **supply price** is the minimum price that will induce a seller to increase production beyond its current level. For example, if Dell were selling 9 million books annually at a price of $2.70, the market price would have to grow to Dell's supply price of $2.75 (point *a*) before production would be expanded to 10 million books annually.

Just as market demand curves are the horizontal summation of individual demands, computing **market supply curves** requires horizontally summing individual firms' supply curves, as shown in Figure 7, which assumes the paperback market to contain only two firms, Dell and Bantam. At a $2.75 price, Dell will produce and sell 10 million books, and Bantam, 15 million, making the annual quantity supplied 25 million books, and so on. The law of supply asserts that quantities supplied per period are positively related to prices; as the price of a good rises, the quantity supplied grows.

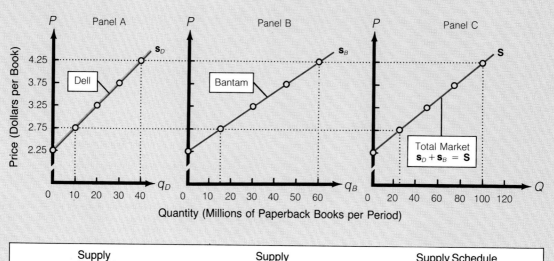

FIGURE 7 *Individual Firm and Market Supply Curves for Paperback Books*

Supply Schedule Dell		+	Supply Schedule Bantam		=	Supply Schedule Total Market (Dell + Bantam)	
Price	Quantity (q_D) (Millions)		Price	Quantity (q_B) (Millions)		Price	Quantity (Q) (Millions)
$4.25	40		$4.25	60		$4.25	100
3.75	30		3.75	45		3.75	75
3.25	20		3.25	30		3.25	50
2.75	10		2.75	15		2.75	25
2.25	—0—		2.25	—0—		2.25	—0—

To obtain market supply, the supplies of all individual producers are added horizontally. For example, at $4.25 per paperback, Dell will furnish 40 million and Bantam 60 million books. Thus, quantity supplied to the market at $4.25 per paperback is 100 million books. The same procedure is followed for all possible prices to obtain the market supply curve.

Other Influences on Supply

Just as there are a number of influences on demand, a number of influences other than the price of the good affect market supply. Thus, a supply curve shows the positive relationship between price and quantity supplied per period, holding constant (*a*) production technology; (*b*) resource costs; (*c*) prices of other producible goods; (*d*) expectations; (*e*) the number of sellers (producers) in the market; and (*f*) taxes, subsidies, and government regulations. Changes in any of these influences can shift the short-run supply curve.

Changes in Supply

Shifts in the supply curve outward and to the right show increases in supply, while movements upward and to the left reflect decreases in supply, as shown in Figure 8. Along S_0, the original supply curve, 50 million paperbacks are supplied at $3.25 per book. If supply grows to S_1, 80 million books are supplied at the same price. If supply falls to S_2, only 30 million books will be offered at $3.25 each. Thus, an increase in supply means that more of the good is offered for sale at every market price; the supply prices required to induce various levels of output fall. On the other hand, decreases in supply cause supply prices (the minimums required per unit to induce extra production) to rise.

Caution: Supply curve movements may seem confusing; the shift from S_0 to S_1 is vertically downward even though supply is rising. Always think of horizontal movements *away* from the price axis as increases, and shifts *towards* the price axis as decreases. This rule also works for shifts of demand curves. Parallels between our development of supply and earlier discussions of demand may correctly have led you to expect that shifts in supply result from changes in one or more of the influences on supply.

Production Technology Technology is a broad term applied to the environment within which resources are transformed into outputs, and it is a major determinant of production costs. It includes such influences on production as the qualities of available resources, the state of knowledge, and such natural phenomena as physical laws (e.g., gravity) and weather.

Costs fall and supply grows when technology advances. Consider the revolution in markets for calculators and computers. Desk-top calculators were $400 to $600 in the 1960s. New technology enabled cheap microchip processors to displace heavy mechanical calculators from the market, and computer capacity that once occupied huge rooms can now be carried in a briefcase. Supplies jumped dramatically and prices fell so that $10 hand-held calculators are now common, and home computers that are more powerful than most business computers of a few years ago are available for $200 and up.

There are occasions when technology regresses, however. Two examples of negative technological changes should shed light on how broad this term is: plagues of locusts or drought might cause agricultural production to plummet, or a nuclear war could blast production technology back to the Stone Age. Technology is very difficult to quantify, but you should be prepared to predict whether a given technological change will boost or inhibit supply.

Resource Costs Supply declines when resource costs rise. Higher wages, rents, or interest rates raise production costs and squeeze profits. Higher prices for raw or semifinished materials do the same. For example, higher prices for coal raise steel companies' costs. Firms have less incentive to produce,

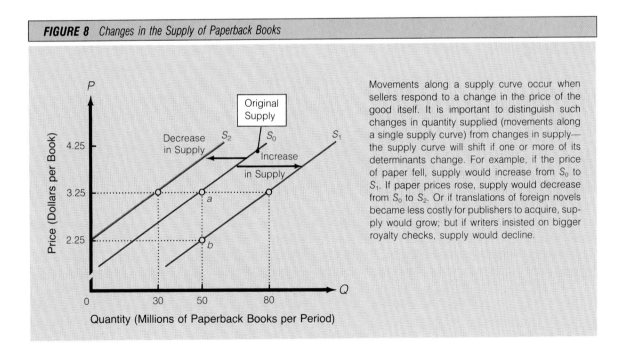

FIGURE 8 *Changes in the Supply of Paperback Books*

Movements along a supply curve occur when sellers respond to a change in the price of the good itself. It is important to distinguish such changes in quantity supplied (movements along a single supply curve) from changes in supply—the supply curve will shift if one or more of its determinants change. For example, if the price of paper fell, supply would increase from S_0 to S_1. If paper prices rose, supply would decrease from S_0 to S_2. Or if translations of foreign novels became less costly for publishers to acquire, supply would grow; but if writers insisted on bigger royalty checks, supply would decline.

causing supply to shrink. Conversely, falling resource prices cause supply to grow. Thus, lower fertilizer prices cause agricultural production to expand.

Prices of Other Goods

Most firms have options to produce a variety of goods, so changes in the prices of other potential outputs can affect the supply of the current good. Price hikes increase the quantity of a good supplied, but shrink the resources available to supply other goods. Shirtmakers, for example, might switch to sewing parachutes if skydiving became more popular and profits from making parachutes grew. The supply of shirts would fall. If corn prices rise, farmers might plant more corn and reduce the soybean supply. These sets of goods are examples of *substitutes in production.* On the other hand, when goods are by-products (beef and leather, for example), an increase in the price of one *joint product* yields an increase in the supply of the other; production is complementary among such goods. For example, hikes in the price of honey will induce a greater quantity of honey supplied, and the supply of beeswax will grow automatically even if the price of beeswax falls.

Expectations of Producers

If a firm expects its output prices to rise in the near future, it may react by boosting output now. Then, because this producer would like larger inventories to sell when prices rise, it may temporarily cut back supplies if its product is easily stored.

These reductions occur regularly in agriculture as farmers attempt to time their sales to obtain the highest prices. For example, ranchers increased breeding but withheld cattle from the market in 1978, temporarily lowering the supply. This drop in beef shipments actually raised 1978 prices, but prices fell by 1980 when these extra cattle were finally marketed. Short-term withholding of products from the market triggers higher prices that, in the longer term, generate larger supplies. Thus, the longer term effect of expectations of rising prices is that supplies of durable goods grow when swollen inventories are sold.

Firms may adjust very differently, however, if building inventories is impossible. For example, if newspaper publishers thought that booming market conditions would soon justify a higher price, they could not store the news but would probably increase supply immediately, partially to justify expanding their capacity to print newspapers and partially to hook more customers into reading the publisher's paper each day.

Other expectations also influence production and sales. For example, a steel company may cut current supplies and try to expand production and inventories if it anticipates a strike. This will enable the firm to serve some customers during the strike. Generalizing about the effects of expectations on supply is somewhat difficult, however, because they vary with the form of expectations and the nature of products and technology.

Number of Sellers

More producers generate more output. Thus, as the number of sellers in a particular market increases, the supply also increases (shifts to the right).

Taxes, Subsidies, and Government Regulation

Government policies affect supply as powerfully as they influence demand. From the sellers' vantage point, supply is the relationship between the prices *received* per unit and the numbers of units produced and sold. Buyers perceive supply as the relationship between the quantities available and the prices *paid.* Again, taxes or subsidies cause these prices to differ. In Figure 8, a subsidy to buyers of $1 per book yields no change in the original supply curve (S_0) from the perspective of sellers. But buyers would perceive an increase in supply from S_0 to S_1, which is the same as a price cut of $1 for every quantity purchased. For example, 50 million paperbacks could now be sold for $2.25 retail price (point b).

The taxes and subsidies we have considered are simple examples of the differences that government policies cause between sellers' and buyers' supply curves. These differences result from taxes, subsidies, and numerous regulations. Regulations either raise or lower supplies, depending on their effects on production costs. For example, policies to control pollution often drive up costs and reduce supplies.

In sum, supply decisions are influenced by numerous factors other than the price of the product. Specifically, the supply of a good grows (the curve will shift to the right) if (a) costs decline because resource prices fall or technology improves; (b) substitute goods that firms can produce decline in price, or the price of a joint product rises; or (c) the number of suppliers increases. Expectations of higher prices normally cause lower supplies in the short term and higher supplies in a longer term if products

FIGURE 9 Factors Causing Shifts in Supply

Panel A

Price (Dollars per Unit)

Decrease in Supply

S_2 S_0

Quantity (Units per Period)

Panel B

Price (Dollars per Unit)

Increase in Supply

S_0 S_1

Quantity (Units per Period)

A decrease in supply results when

1. the number of sellers decreases.
2. technology deteriorates.
3. resource costs increase.
4. the price of production substitutes increases.
5. the price of production by-products decreases.
6. taxes increase, or subsidies decrease.

An increase in supply results when

1. the number of sellers increases.
2. technology improves.
3. resource costs decline.
4. the price of production substitutes decreases.
5. the price of production by-products increases.
6. taxes decrease, or subsidies increase.

can be inventoried, but generate uncertain results for less durable goods. Subsidies tend to expand supply; taxes tend to shrink supply.

Changes in Quantity Supplied Versus Changes in Supply

A *change in supply* occurs only when the supply curve shifts. A *change in the quantity supplied* (a movement along the curve) is caused only by a change in the price of the good in question. Consider an adjustment in quantity supplied caused by a change in the market price. The supply curve stays constant because it is defined by the entire relationship between price and quantity. A change in supply (caused by a change in a nonprice determinant) shifts the supply curve because this price/quantity relationship is altered. (You will learn why this distinction is not trivial after we combine supply and demand curves in a market.) Figure 9 summarizes categories of things that shift supply curves.

Demands, Supplies, and Time

Consumers demand certain amounts of shrimp dinners, surf boards, and bottles of perfume weekly, larger amounts monthly, and still larger amounts annually. A Pizza Hut that sells 827 pizzas on an average day is probably much more profitable than one selling 827 weekly. These examples illustrate that both demand and supply are *flows*; consumer purchases or sales by firms mean little unless time intervals are specified. But this is only one way that time influences demands and supplies.

An interesting effect of time on demand is that as longer time intervals are considered, the quantity demanded responds more to price changes because the range of possible adjustments expands. For example, an increase in the price of gasoline will not cause much reduction in the amount bought in the *very short run* (say, a week or two), and a slightly greater

FIGURE 10 Demands, Supplies, and Time

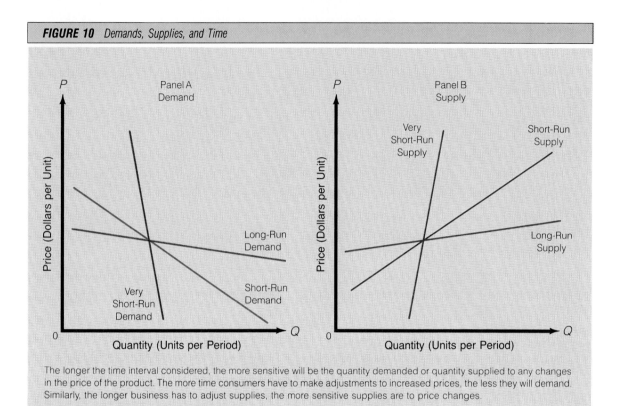

The longer the time interval considered, the more sensitive will be the quantity demanded or quantity supplied to any changes in the price of the product. The more time consumers have to make adjustments to increased prices, the less they will demand. Similarly, the longer business has to adjust supplies, the more sensitive supplies are to price changes.

reduction in gasoline bought in the *short run* (say, six months to a year). People will gradually modify their habitual driving patterns to save gas and thus, will demand a little less. Car pooling is one possible adjustment. However, in the *longer run* (say, two to five years), big gas price hikes cause people to buy smaller cars, get tune-ups more regularly, or to rely more on mass transit. They may even move closer to work, shopping, and so on. The longer the adjustment period, the more consumers will reduce gas consumption in response to any given price increase.

Another interesting influence of time on demand is that some goods require substantial time for consumption. Time limits your enjoyment of food. (Your stomach does not have unlimited capacity.) You can only wear one hat at a time. Vacations are expensive not only because of the money you spend but also because of the income you sacrifice by not working. Airline tickets typically have higher monetary prices than touring by car, but air travel is increasingly popular because of the time it saves.

Time spans also affect supply. Longer periods obviously enable firms to make more of a good available. Less obviously, supplies respond more strongly to price changes as time elapses because the range of possible adjustments grows. For example, if asparagus prices rise, vegetable growers can do little to boost production in a short period, say a month or so. However, a year or so enables a farmer to acquire more seed, plow and fertilize more ground, and put more acreage into asparagus. Figure 10 summarizes these effects of time on supply and demand.

Market Equilibrium _____

It's easy to train economists. Just teach a parrot to say "Supply and Demand."
                                                —*Thomas Carlyle*

Supply and demand go together like diapers and babies or the top and bottom blades of scissors; each seems incomplete without the other. Supply and demand jointly determine prices and quantities so that markets achieve **equilibrium,** a term meaning that all forces for change are balanced.

Buyers and sellers use prices as signals to communicate their wants, and then exchange money for goods or resources, or vice versa. You accept or reject thousands of offers during every trip to a shopping center or perusal of the newspaper. Prices efficiently transmit an incredible amount of information that is relevant for decisions to buy or sell, and makes a lot of other information (or misinformation) irrelevant. For example, during the nineteenth century, peasants in Ghana produced and shipped cocoa to England, believing that the British used it for fuel. Their mistaken impression was not a problem, however, because their decision to produce depended on the price of cocoa, not its final use. The importance of prices has caused many economists to refer to the market system as the *price system.*

Suppose that every potential buyer and seller of a good submitted demand and supply schedules to an auctioneer, who then calculated the price at which the quantities demanded and supplied were equal. All buyers' demand price (the maximum they are willing to pay) equal all sellers' supply price (the minimum they will accept per unit for a given amount), and the market *clears.* This means that the amounts that buyers will purchase exactly equal the amounts that producers are willing to sell, a solution known as the **equilibrium price and quantity.** Let's examine the sense in which this is an equilibrium.

Figure 11 summarizes the market supplies and demands for paperbacks. (Note that there are more buyers and sellers than in earlier examples.) After studying the supply and demand schedules, our auctioneer ascertains that at $3.25 per book, the quantities demanded and supplied both equal 300 million books annually. Sellers will provide exactly as many novels as readers will purchase at this price, so the market clears.

FIGURE 11 Equilibrium in the Paperback Book Market

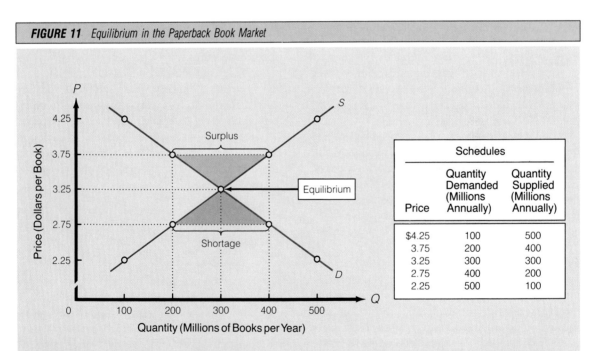

	Schedules	
Price	Quantity Demanded (Millions Annually)	Quantity Supplied (Millions Annually)
$4.25	100	500
3.75	200	400
3.25	300	300
2.75	400	200
2.25	500	100

At a price of $3.75 per paperback, there is a surplus of 200 million books annually. (The *surplus* is the horizontal distance between the demand and supply curves when the price is *above* $3.25.) At a price of $2.75, there is a shortage of 200 million books annually. (The *shortage* is the horizontal distance between the demand and the supply curves when the price is *below* $3.25.) When the price is $3.25, quantity demanded is equal to quantity supplied, and the market is in equilibrium.

But what if the auctioneer set a price of $3.75 per book, or $2.75 per book? First, let us deal with the problem of a price set above equilibrium. A **surplus** is the excess of the quantity supplied over quantity demanded when price is above equilibrium. At $3.75 per book, publishers would print 400 million books annually, but readers would only buy 200 million books. This yields a surplus of 200 million books in Figure 11, which would wind up as surplus inventories in the hands of publishers.

Most firms would cut production as their inventories grew, and some might cut prices, hoping to unload surplus paperbacks on bargain hunters and readers willing to buy more at sale prices. Other firms with unwanted inventories would join in the price war. Prices would fall until all surplus inventories were depleted. As prices fell, some businesses might stop producing temporarily; others might permanently leave the industry.

Just how much the quantity supplied would decline is shown in the table accompanying Figure 11. When the price falls to $3.25 per book, consumers will buy 300 million books annually, and publishers will supply 300 million books—the quantity demanded equals the quantity supplied. The market-clearing price is $3.25 per book. At this **market equilibrium,** any pressures for price or quantity changes are exactly counterbalanced by opposite pressures.

When the quantity of a good supplied is less than the quantity demanded, there is a **shortage** of the product. This occurs when the market price is below equilibrium; this is the flip-side of a surplus. At $2.75 per book, readers demand 400 million books, but publishers only provide 200 million. There is a shortage of 200 million books annually, as depicted in Figure 11. Publishers will try to satisfy unhappy, bookless customers who clamor for the limited quantities available by raising the price until the market clears; then books will be readily available for the people most desperate to buy them. (Clearing occurs because quantity supplied rises as price rises while quantity demanded falls; they become equal at the equilibrium price.)

Achieving equilibrium is not instantaneous. Firms experiment with the prices of their products in a process resembling an auction. Inventories vanishing from store shelves are signals that prices may be too low. Retailers will order more goods and, because the market will bear it, may tend to raise prices. If orders to manufacturers grow rapidly, prices also tend to rise at the wholesale level. This process quickly eliminates most shortages. When shortages appear in a market, people refer to it as a "tight market," or a "sellers' market." Suppliers have no difficulty selling all they produce, so quality may decline somewhat at the same time that sellers raise prices. Many sellers also exercise some favoritism in deciding which customers to serve during shortages.

When prices are above equilibrium, surpluses create "buyers' markets" and force sellers to consider price cuts. This is especially painful if production costs seem immune to downward pressures even though sales drop and inventories swell. (Most workers stubbornly resist wage cuts.) In many cases, firms can shrink inventories and cut costs only by laying off workers and drastically reducing production. The price system ultimately forces prices down if there are continuing surpluses. Huge losses by major oil producers and sluggish economies in energy-producing states during the oil gluts that characterized 1982–87 are testimony that this process may be long and traumatic.

Price hikes eliminate shortages fairly rapidly, and price cuts eventually cure surpluses, but these automatic market adjustments may be uncomfortable for many buyers and sellers. These self-corrections are what Adam Smith described as the *invisible hand* of the marketplace. Long-term shortages or surpluses are, almost without exception, consequences of government price controls. We will discuss price controls and other applications of supply and demand in the next chapter.

Transaction Costs

Differences between market prices and opportunity costs occur because of transaction costs. We often refer to "the price" of a good as if each good had only one price at a given time. But gas prices differ between service stations, and grocery stores commonly charge different prices for what seem to be the same foods. How can this be reconciled with economic models that arrive at a single price? The answer lies in transaction costs.

Transaction costs are the costs associated with gathering *information* about prices and availability, and *mobility,* or transporting goods and people between markets. The value of the time you take reading ads and driving to a store to take advantage of a bargain is one form of transaction costs. Gasoline used and wear and tear on your car in gathering information and locating goods are also transaction costs. Would you drive fifty miles to save $5 by going from store to store, or would you simply go to a department store or shopping mall?

If transaction costs were zero, sellers would always sell at the highest possible price, while buyers would only pay the lowest possible price. Therefore, the highest and lowest possible prices would have to be identical and only one price could exist for identical goods. Thus, transaction costs, in which the value of time plays an important role, account for ranges in the monetary prices of any single good. Paying a higher monetary price is frequently efficient behavior if the transaction cost of acquiring the good at the lower monetary price is high.

Supplies and Demands Are Independent

While specific demands and supplies jointly determine prices and quantities, it is important to realize that they are normally independent of each other, at least in the short run. Many people have difficulty with the idea that demands and supplies are independent. It would seem that demand depends on availability—or that supply depends on demand. The following examples show that supplies and demands are normally independent in the short run.

1. Suppose that non-reusable "teleporter buttons" could instantly transport you anywhere you chose. Your demand price to go on the first, most valuable tour would be quite high, but it would decline steadily for subsequent journeys. Using these buttons for little shopping trips would be economical only if they were very inexpensive. By asking how many teleporter buttons you would buy at various prices, we can construct your demand curve for such devices even though there is no supply.

2. Would you have made more mud pies when you were a kid if your parents had bought them for a penny apiece? At two cents each, might you have hired some of your playmates to help you? If mud pies were worth $1 each today, might you be a mud pie entrepreneur? Our point is that supply curves can be constructed for mud pies even if there is no demand for them.

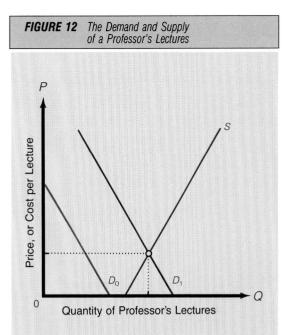

FIGURE 12 The Demand and Supply of a Professor's Lectures

This figure depicts the supply of a professor's lectures and student demand for them (D_0). Without supplementing their demand through lower tuition or other contributions (D_1), this professor would have to lecture for free . . . and, at times, to an empty room (S and D_0 do not intersect at any positive price and quantity.)

3. You might be willing to pay a little to hear some professors' lectures, even if you did not receive college credit for gathering the pearls of wisdom they offer. However, some professors like to talk even more than you like to listen. A set of such demand and supply curves is illustrated in Figure 12. It is fortunate for both you and your professors that your demands for their lectures are supplemented by contributions from taxpayers, alumni, and possibly your parents because only later and upon mature reflection will you realize how valuable those lectures really were!

We hope these examples convince you that specific supplies and demands are largely independent of each other, and that they are relevant for markets only when they intersect at positive prices. Markets establish whether the interests of buyers from the demand side are compatible with the interests of sellers from the supply side, and then coordinate decisions where mutually beneficial exchange is possible. Keep this in mind as you study the applications of supply and demand in the next chapter.

CHAPTER REVIEW: KEY POINTS

1. A *market* is a social institution that enables buyers and sellers to strike bargains and transact. *Absolute (monetary) prices* are far less important for consumer or business decisions than *relative prices,* of which consumers' *demand (subjective) prices* and *market prices* must be in accord before people will purchase goods.

2. *The law of demand.* People buy less of a good per period at high prices than at low prices. *Demand curves* slope downward and to the right, and show the quantities demanded at various prices for a good. Changes in market prices cause changes in quantity demanded.

3. Consumers buy more of a product per period only at lower prices because consuming the additional units ultimately does not yield as much satisfaction as consuming previous units; *diminishing marginal utility* causes demand prices to fall as consumption rises. In addition, a lower price for one product means that the purchasing power of a given income rises (the *income effect*). Most importantly, the cheaper good will be used more ways as it is substituted for higher priced goods (the *substitution effect*).

4. In addition to the price of a good, demand depends on (*a*) tastes and preferences; (*b*) income and its distribution; (*c*) prices of related goods; (*d*) numbers and ages of buyers; (*e*) expectations about future prices, income, or availability; and (*f*) government taxes, subsidies, and regulations. Changes in nonprice variables that influence demand cause shifts in demand curves. Taxes and subsidies shift demand curves from the perspectives of sellers, who are concerned with the price *received* when a good is sold, while buyers focus on the price *paid*. Taxes or subsidies make these two prices differ.

5. *The law of supply.* Higher prices cause sellers to make more of a good available per period. The *supply* curve shows the positive relationship between the price of a good and the quantity supplied. Supply curves generally slope upward and to the right because (*a*) diminishing returns cause opportunity costs to increase; (*b*) to expand output, firms must bid resources away from competing producers or use other methods (such as overtime) that increase cost; and (*c*) profit incentives are greater at higher prices.

6. In addition to the price paid to producers of a good, supply depends on (*a*) the number of sellers; (*b*) technology; (*c*) resource costs; (*d*) prices of other producible goods; (*e*) producer's expectations; and (*f*) specific taxes, subsidies, and governmental regulations. Changes in prices cause *changes in quantities supplied*, while changes in other influences on production or sales of goods cause shifts in supply curves that are termed *changes in supply.*

7. When markets operate without government intervention, prices tend to move towards *market equilibrium* so that quantity supplied equals quantity demanded. At this point, the demand price equals the supply price.

8. When the market price of a good is below the intersection of the supply and demand curves, there will be *shortages* and pressures for increases in price. If price is above the intersection of the supply and demand curves, there will be *surpluses* and pressures for reduction in price.

9. *Transaction costs* arise because information and mobility are costly. This allows the price of a good to vary between markets.

10. Supply and demand are largely independent in the short run.

PROBLEMS

Use scratch paper to draw graphs illustrating the changes in supply or demand described in problems 1–7. If only one curve shifts, assume that the other is stationary.

1. What happens in the market for bananas if the Food and Drug Administration announces research results suggesting that eating five pounds of bananas monthly raises IQ scores by an average of ten points? What would happen in the markets for apples or other fruit?

2. What happens to the demand for college professors in the short run if government raises its funding of graduate school educations? What happens to the supply of college professors over a longer time span? What will happen to their wages during the adjustment periods?

3. What happens if new "miracle" seeds allow grain to be grown in shorter periods and colder climates? If the world population mushrooms because starvation ceases to be so widespread?

4. What happens in the U.S. clothing market if freer trade with the People's Republic of China expands our imports of textiles? If after two years import tariffs and quotas are imposed?

5. Around the middle of every January, the annual crop of mink furs is put on the auction block. How will the following affect the supplies and demands for mink pelts?
   a. More fur-bearing animals are classified as endangered species.
   b. The price of mink food rises.
   c. Extraordinarily mild winters for five years are followed by a long period of severe blizzards.
   d. A worldwide (1929-type) depression occurs.
   e. Higher income tax rates and a new wealth tax are imposed, and the added revenues are used to raise welfare payments.

6. If oil prices suddenly fell after rising rapidly for several years, what might happen to the:
   a. demand for small cars?
   b. demand for luxury sedans?
   c. demand for air travel?
   d. supply of records?
   e. supply of synthetic fabrics?
   f. demand for wool and cotton?
   Hint: Records and synthetic fabrics are made from petroleum products.

7. Use supply and demand curves to show why the monetary price of color TVs declined consistently over the past thirty years in spite of inflation that more than tripled the absolute prices of other goods.

8. Suppose that the absolute price of generic computer diskettes is $1, tuition is $2,200 per semester, compact disks are $15, and movie tickets are each $6. Calculate the relative prices of all these goods so that they can be stated in terms of each other.

QUESTIONS FOR THOUGHT AND DISCUSSION

1. Suppose that the price of a home video rises from $2 per day to $3 per day, while tickets to movies rise from $5 to $7. Which of these forms of entertainment has become relatively less costly?

2. Is the law of demand refuted if snobs are willing to buy more mink coats only at high prices, or if some people buy more high-priced aspirin than low-priced aspirin? Discuss.

3. Imports of oil rose during the 1970s even though prices skyrocketed over the decade. Is this an exception to the law of demand? Why or why not?

4. Is the assertion that "Everyone always buys everything at the lowest possible price" correct? Have you ever paid more than you had to for any good, after allowing for transaction costs? Discuss.

5. The law of demand asserts that the quantity of a good demanded will fall if the price rises because people will find substitute goods or will alter their behavior so that they do with less. Does the law of demand hold for people who rely on certain goods to continue living, such as:
   (a) insulin for a diabetic? (b) kidney dialysis? (c) heart transplants?
   If not, what would happen to most of these sick people if insulin rose to $800 per dose, kidney dialysis to $10,000 per session, and a heart transplant to $1,000,000? Can you think of substitutions that these consumers could make?

6. Why do some people pay premium prices for "brand-name" goods? All else equal, people will pay more for goods that they perceive as higher quality. Some people will pay higher prices for goods in certain stores than in others, even if they know the goods are physically identical. Does knowingly paying higher prices in fancier stores than in discount stores refute the law of demand?

7. How can a production-possibilities curve be transformed into market supply curves for the two goods considered by the *PPF?*

8. Which of the following sets of goods are substitutes in production, and which are either joint products or complementary in production?
   a. wool and cotton
   b. oranges and honey
   c. lumber and paper
   d. eggs and hashbrowns
   e. footballs and ham

9. The text asserts that the demands for both inferior goods and luxury goods will fall if income is redistributed from the rich to the poor. Why is this true? Name some goods for which sales would suffer if income were redistributed. Name other goods for which sales would rise.

invisible hand
middlemen
arbitrage
speculators
price controls
price ceiling
black market
price floor

CHAPTER 4

Markets and Equilibrium

*Every individual endeavors to employ his capital so that its produce may be of greatest value. He generally neither intends to promote the public interest, nor knows how much he is promoting it. He intends only his own security, only his own gain. And he is in this led [as if] by an **invisible hand** to promote an end which was not part of his intention. By pursuing his own interest he frequently promotes that of society more effectually than when he really intends to promote it.*
— *Adam Smith   Wealth of Nations (1776)*

Prices sometimes move slowly and unevenly towards equilibrium. If information were perfect and mobility instantaneous and costless, prices would be driven to their equilibrium values like arrows shot at a bullseye by an expert archer. Instead, prices may resemble basketballs—bouncing up, down, and sideways before finally "reaching equilibrium" by going through the hoop. In this chapter, we explore the ways prices and outputs move when supplies and demands fluctuate and then apply supply and demand analysis to specific social problems.

The Search for Equilibrium _____

Some markets are not very stable because consumers can be fickle, forever changing their minds. Changes in income, expectations, taxes, or the prices of related goods also constantly shift the demands for some goods. On the supply side, the business environment is in constant flux: resource prices vary and technology advances, altering costs and, thus, supplies. Changes in taxes and regulations, producer expectations, or the prices of alternative products also shift supply curves.

Let's examine in a general way how changes in supplies and demands affect prices and quantities. (You should get pencil and paper and duplicate the graphing we do in this section.) We will use the wheat market to explore how Adam Smith's "invisible hand" accommodates changes in both supply and demand.

BIOGRAPHY

Adam Smith (1723–90)

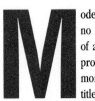

Modern economics is by no means the product of a single mind, but probably no one is more deserving of the title "Father of Economics" than Adam Smith. Smith was a Scottish philosopher of international fame even before he published *An Inquiry into the Nature and Causes of the Wealth of Nations* in 1776. This enduring work attracted widespread attention and helped establish economics as a field of study apart from moral philosophy.

The eccentric Smith was a lifelong bachelor who described himself to a friend as "a beau in nothing but my books." Shortly before his death he burned sixteen large volumes of unpublished manuscripts, but his published remains are literary classics. Smith's *Wealth of Nations* covered the spectrum of the then current knowledge of economics and was the starting point for virtually every major economic treatise until 1850.

This work provided (*a*) an impressive collection of economic data gleaned from Smith's wide reading of history and his keen insights into human affairs; (*b*) an ambitious attempt to detail the nature of economic processes in an individualistic society; and (*c*) a radical critique of existing society and government. Smith advocated replacing government activities with laissez-faire policies in most economic matters.

Laissez-faire ideas were a sharp departure from *mercantilism*, the conventional wisdom of his era. Among other policies, mercantilist doctrines supported (*a*) imperialism in an era when European powers competed to colonize the rest of the world, and (*b*) restrictions on imports because it was erroneously thought that a country grew pow-

erful by exporting goods in exchange for gold. Smith thought such policies were balderdash, arguing that the real "wealth of nations" consisted of the goods available for its people, not shiny metal.

Government restricted competition and created monopolies in Smith's day; he strongly dissented from the interventionist policies prevalent in the eighteenth century, and called for a minimal economic role for government. A major point of his argument is that economic freedom is an efficient way to organize an economy. The model of the marketplace was the centerpiece of Smith's economic inquiry. Decisions freely made by buyers and sellers are coordinated in the marketplace by what he called **the invisible hand** of competition. Competition harmonizes the driving force of self-interest with the public interest, yielding increases in real national wealth.

The freshest idea in Smith's argument is that the public interest is not served best by those who intend (or pretend) to promote it through government regulation, but rather by those who actively seek their own gain in disregard of the public interest. Economic competition compels self-interested merchants to serve consumers' interests better if the merchants are to increase their sales and gain advantage over rival sellers. Monopoly, on the other hand, is destructive of the public interest because it restricts output and forces prices up. Smith thought that unless government promoted and protected monopolies, competition would quickly eradicate monopoly power.

FIGURE 1 The Effects of Increases and Decreases of Supply (American Wheat Market)

Panel A illustrates that increases in supply put downward pressures on prices. When supply increases from S_0 to S_1, prices fall to P_1 and quantities sold rise from Q_0 to Q_1 (equilibrium point a to point b). The opposite is true when supply declines as depicted in Panel B. Supply declines from S_0 to S_2, causing prices to rise and quantity sold to fall (from point a to point c).

Changes in Supply

Suppose that the initial supply and demand for American wheat are S_0 and D_0, respectively, as shown in Figure 1. Equilibrium at point a occurs when Q_0 bushels of wheat sell at price P_0. Suppose that extraordinarily fine weather yields a bumper crop, so that supply grows from S_0 to S_1 in Panel A. The market now clears at point b; price declines from P_0 to P_1, and equilibrium quantity rises from Q_0 to Q_1. We conclude that growing supplies push prices downwards and increase the quantities sold.

Now consider what happens if higher seed or fuel prices raise the costs of farming wheat. Starting at the original equilibrium point a, now shown in Panel B of Figure 1, supply declines from S_0 to S_2. The equilibrium price rises from P_0 to P_2 at point c, while equilibrium quantity falls from Q_0 to Q_2. Thus, decreases in supply exert upward pressures on

prices and decrease the quantities traded in the market.

We have held demand constant while shifting supply. We will now hold supply constant and review how shifts of demand curves affect equilibrium prices and quantities.

Changes in Demand

The original demand D_0 and supply S_0 from Figure 1 are duplicated in Figure 2. Assume that rising oil prices stimulate gasohol production from grain. Demand for wheat would rise to, say, D_1 in Panel A. Equilibrium price will rise to P_1, and quantity to Q_1 (point b). Here we see that increases in demand yield upward pressures on both prices and quantities.

Suppose that new dietary findings recommend replacement of wheat bread by soybran loaf, causing the demand for American wheat to fall from D_0 to D_2

FIGURE 2 *The Effects of Increases and Decreases in Demand (American Wheat Market)*

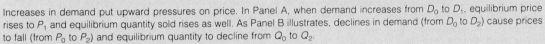

Increases in demand put upward pressures on price. In Panel A, when demand increases from D_0 to D_1, equilibrium price rises to P_1 and equilibrium quantity sold rises as well. As Panel B illustrates, declines in demand (from D_0 to D_2) cause prices to fall (from P_0 to P_2) and equilibrium quantity to decline from Q_0 to Q_2.

in Panel B of Figure 2. The equilibrium price and quantity both fall (point *c*). Thus, decreases in demand exert downward pressures on both prices and quantities.

In chapter 3, we distinguished a change in demand from a change in the quantity demanded, and changes in supply from changes in the quantity supplied: Changes in demand (*supply*) refer to *shifts* of the curve, while changes in the quantity demanded (*supplied*) refer to movements *along* a curve. Review Figures 1 and 2. If you compare equilibrium positions in Figure 1, you will notice that changes in the quantities demanded result from changes in supply. It would be wrong to say that demand changed; it was supply that shifted. Similarly, Figure 2 shows that changes in quantities supplied are caused by changes in demand. Demand shifted; supply did *not* change. This illustrates how failing to keep your terminology straight in this area leads to confusion and error.

If you are still with us, congratulations. If not, please review the preceding material before reading on because now we are going to shift supply and demand curves simultaneously.

Shifts in Supply and Demand

Numerous forces for change are constantly at work in most markets. Technology may advance during periods when consumer preferences are also changing or resource costs are rising. We need to fit each change into our supply/demand framework to determine the net changes in equilibrium price and quantity. As you will see, the net impact on equilibrium price or quantity depends on the relative magnitudes of shifts in supplies and demands.

The wheat market is now shown in Figure 3, allowing us to examine what happens when supply and demand curves shift in the same direction. De-

FIGURE 3 *The Effects of Increases in Both Supply and Demand (American Wheat Market)*

When both supply and demand increase, equilibrium quantity traded will always rise, but the change in price will depend upon the relative magnitudes of the two shifts. When both supply and demand decline, quantity will always fall, and again the price change is uncertain, being dependent upon the relative magnitudes of the two shifts.

mand and supply are originally at D_0 and S_0, respectively, with equilibrium price at P_0 and equilibrium output at Q_0 (point a). Assume that the Soviet Union begins buying more U.S. wheat in a year when we experience a bumper crop. These events increase *both* demand and supply in Figure 3. But this information by itself leaves us unsure whether the price at the new equilibrium (point b) is higher or lower than P_0, but equilibrium quantity (now Q_1) is definitely higher than its old value of Q_0. The lesson here is that when both demand and supply grow, quantity increases but price changes are unknowable without more information.

You may have perceived that whether the new price of wheat will be above or below P_0 depends on the relative magnitudes of the two shifts. For example, if the Soviet Union's new demand was relatively large and drove market demand to D_2, equilibrium price would rise (point c). Symmetric results occur if both demand and supply decrease, say, from D_1 and S_1 to D_0 and S_0: quantity falls, but price changes cannot be predicted without more information.

What happens if supplies and demands move in opposite directions? The wheat market is again initially in equilibrium at point a in Figure 4. Equilibrium moves to point b if population growth boosts demand to D_1 while drought cuts supply to S_1. Price

increases to P_1, but we need more information to be sure whether quantity increases, decreases, or remains constant. In this case, quantity changes depend on the relative magnitudes of the shifts. Thus, if demand rises while supply falls, the price rises but we cannot predict quantity changes without more information.

Similar results occur if demand falls and supply rises. Thus, declines in demand and increases in supply cause prices to fall, but predicting quantity changes requires more data. Figure 5 (on page 70) summarizes these effects of supply and demand changes on prices and quantities.

Price volatility may plague a market economy. If prices are high and profit opportunities abound, existing firms will expand and new firms will enter the market, boosting supply and driving the high price down. Low prices and inadequate profits, on the other hand, cause some firms to exit an industry, while the survivors cut back on output and reduce their hiring. This pushes low prices up. When there are long lags between planning for production and selling output, prices and outputs may swing wildly before they finally settle at equilibrium.

Suppose, for example, that wheat prices rose sharply after a drought devastated a crop. The high price relative to cost could cause wheat farmers to

FIGURE 4 *The Effects of an Increase in Demand and a Decrease in Supply (American Wheat Market)*

When demand and supply curves move in opposite directions, the price change is predictable, but the quantity adjustment is not. When demand increases and supply falls, price will rise, but the change in equilibrium quantity depends on the nature of the two shifts. When demand declines and supply increases, prices will fall, but again the change in quantity is uncertain without further information.

over-produce in the next year, driving the price down. This low price could cause discouraged farmers to cut production back too much in the third year, causing the price to again rise far above production costs. And so on. Similarly cyclical price swings have been observed for engineering wages (it takes four years to get an engineering degree) and in other markets in which training and/or production take a long time.

Middlemen and Speculators _____

People search for bargains only to the extent that they expect the benefits from shopping (price reductions) to exceed the transaction costs they expect to incur. We live in an uncertain world and constantly make decisions based on incomplete or inaccurate information. Acquiring better market information is a costly process, as is moving goods or resources between markets. Firms popularly known as **middlemen** specialize in reducing uncertainty and cutting the transaction costs of conveying goods from the original producers to final users, often transforming the good so that it is more compatible with the ultimate users'

demands. Surprisingly, price swings are moderated by the activities of speculators, who are special types of middlemen.

Speculators and middlemen are standard targets when some people try to identify villains who cause inflation, shortages, or a host of other economic maladies. Middlemen and speculators actually absorb risk and help move prices towards equilibrium. This process reduces transaction costs and aids in getting goods to those who desire them most while boosting the incomes of the original suppliers. In fact, middlemen reduce the opportunity costs of goods to consumers, and speculators tend to reduce both the volatility of prices and the net costs of products.

Middlemen

Have you ever paid more than you had to for anything you bought from a retailer or other middleman? Your answer must be NO if you behave rationally. You might object that, say, buying apples from a grocery store costs more than buying them from an apple grower. But if you bought from a store, it must have charged less than if you had bought the apples directly from the orchard, after considering all infor-

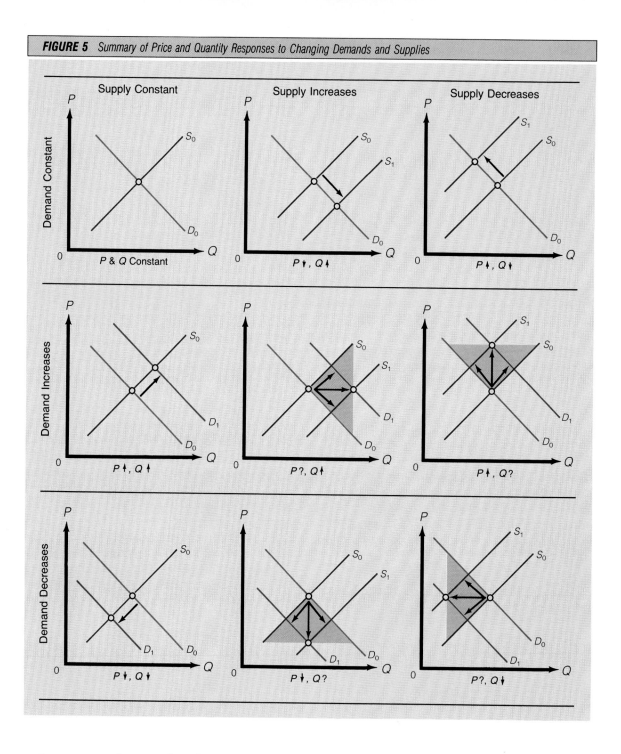

FIGURE 5 Summary of Price and Quantity Responses to Changing Demands and Supplies

mation costs, travel, potential spoilage, and time entailed in going to the orchard. Otherwise, you would have bought directly from the apple grower.

Similarly, the monetary prices you pay at convenience stores are higher than at supermarkets. However, after we adjust for greater accessibility because of the longer hours typical of convenience stores and the frequent extended waits in checkout lanes at supermarkets, the customers of convenience stores must be paying less, or they would buy elsewhere.

One important way that middlemen reduce transaction costs is by absorbing risk. Almost any good is somewhat variable in quality. Apples, for example, range from rotten to those that would win prizes at county fairs. Final consumers would be highly distressed if they bought a few apples to eat fresh, but wound up with fruit suitable only for applesauce. Orchard owners specialize in growing apples, but might not be geared to assuring quality to every consumer of every apple. Another problem is that an individual customer may buy apples only at irregular intervals, while individual orchards have tons of apples available at some times, and none at others. Timing between individual purchases and harvesting at a given orchard may not be synchronous.

Apple wholesalers and grocers, however, purchase such large quantities that they are accustomed to dealing with a mix of good and bad apples. They also sell to so many customers that they do not rely heavily on any single final buyer. This assures apple eaters high quality, and enables orchard owners to ignore timing and concentrate on production. Thus, one specialized service rendered by middlemen is the absorption of risks that ultimate producers and consumers want to avoid.

Time, transportation costs, and risk are only a few of the many dimensions of transaction costs. No matter how hard you think about it, we doubt that you can come up with a single example where you have paid more than the lowest price possible for any good, once you account for all transaction costs.

Arbitrage   Profit is ensured if you can buy low and sell high. **Arbitrage** is the process of buying at a lower price in one market and selling at a higher price in another, where the arbitrager knows both prices and the price differential exceeds transaction costs. For example, if gold is priced at $328 per ounce in London while the New York price is $337 per ounce, an arbitrager can make $9 per ounce (minus transaction costs) by buying in London and selling in New York.

Traders constantly seek opportunities to arbitrage because profits can be made risklessly. When middlemen buy in the market with the lower price, demand is increased, which drives up the price. When they sell in the market with the higher price, the greater supply pushes the price down. Thus, arbitrage reduces transaction costs and forces relative prices toward equality in all markets. This middleman activity promotes economic efficiency by linking markets that are spread geographically, so that goods are moved from areas where they have a relatively low value to markets where the goods are more highly valued.

Speculators

Speculators derive income by buying something at a low price and storing it in the hope of selling it *later* at a higher price. Thus, speculators buy things if they think prices are going to rise and sell them if they expect prices to fall. Speculation is unlike arbitrage because this time delay makes speculation risky. Speculators can make fortunes if they predict correctly; if they are wrong too often they go broke and cease being speculators.

If speculators believe that prices will soon rise, then they expect demands to grow faster than supplies. They respond by buying now, increasing the *current* demand and price, so that they can sell later at a higher price. Do they cause prices to be higher later? NO! If speculators are more often right than wrong, they sell when prices are high and add to the supply at that time. Thus, successful speculation shifts the consumption of a good from a period in which it would have a relatively low value into a period when its value to consumers is higher. Correct speculation reduces price peaks and boosts depressed prices, so successful speculators reduce price swings and, by absorbing some risks to others of doing business, raise the net incomes of the ultimate suppliers. Overall, costs fall because speculators absorb risks and the prices consumers pay are lower and more predictable.

Markets and Public Policy

The level of the sea is not more surely kept than is the equilibrium of value in society by supply and demand; and artifice or legislation punishes itself by reactions, gluts, and bankruptcies.

—*Ralph Waldo Emerson*

No economic system can distribute income and allocate resources to everyone's satisfaction. Our mixed economy relies most on the market system, with government coming in a close second—the list of regulations and governmentally provided goods and services ranges from police and fire protection to dog leash laws and financial regulations; from national defense to education and interstate highways; and on and on. In this section, we look at some policies that alter market solutions. Taxes, one way to finance government activity, can have major effects on market prices and quantities.

Taxes and Subsidies

Taxing a good drives a *wedge* between the price paid by buyers and the price received by sellers. Taxes tend to be shared between buyers and sellers. Supply and demand analysis allows us to see how taxes (or subsidies, which can be thought of as negative taxes) are shared.

The equilibrium in Figure 6 is at point e without taxes, and 16 million video cassettes are sold monthly at a price of $7 each. Suppose that a $2 tax per cassette is imposed so that there is a $2 difference between the price paid by the buyer and the price received by the seller. Graphically, the market demand curve from sellers' perspectives shifts vertically downwards by $2 (distance ac) to D_2 while the supply of cassettes falls from the vantage points of buyers

to S_2. (Although this supply curve "rises" vertically by $2 (distance ac) at each quantity, recall that shifts towards the price axis reflect declines in both supply and demand curves.)

At the new equilibrium, the quantities supplied and demanded must be equal, but the demand price and the supply price differ by the $2 tax. One easy way to identify this new equilibrium is to slide a $2 tax wedge in from the left of the original curves (D_0 and S_0) until the vertical distance between them (ac) just equals the tax. Thus, at the new equilibrium, buyers pay $8 for each of 12 million video cassettes per month, while, net of the $2 tax, suppliers receive $6 per cassette.

The intersection of taxed supplies and demands helps to identify the proportions of the tax borne by buyers and sellers, respectively. In this simple case, each side bears $1 of the tax, but different slopes of the supply and demand curves will yield different proportional burdens. (Vary the slopes of these curves on graph paper to prove this to yourself.) Note that the tax reduces incentives to produce video cassettes, and incentives to buy them as well. This may create inefficiency and is one reason econ-

---

FIGURE 6 *The Effects of Taxes or Subsidies on Equilibrium*

Taxes and subsidies are normally shared by buyers and sellers. A $2 tax shrinks demand from the seller's perspective (from D_0 to D_2), but does not affect demand from the consumer's perspective. Rather, the consumer perceives supply as shrinking from S_0 to S_2 because of the $2 tax, while the sellers view their supply as unchanged. On the other hand, a $2 subsidy expands supply from S_0 to S_1 from the perspective of consumers, but does not change demand in the view of buyers. Sellers, however, view demand as growing from D_0 to D_1, but perceive no changes in their supplies. In this example, the tax burden (or the benefits from subsidies) are split evenly between buyers and sellers, but the tax or subsidy may be quite unevenly split in other situations. The actual split depends on the relative slopes of these curves, as you can discover by drawing your own examples.

omists refer to tax wedges as creating disincentive effects.

Subsidies are the flip side of taxes. If a $2 subsidy were placed on video cassettes, a subsidy wedge can be slid between the original supply and demand curves from the right of the original equilibrium, so that the vertical distance (*bd*) between them reflects this subsidy. This bolsters demand to D_1 from sellers' perspectives, while raising supply to S_1 in the views of buyers. The buyer's (demand) price falls to $6, while the seller's (supply) price rises to $8.

You might think that the enhanced incentives to produce and buy cassettes reflect an efficient strategy. There is a problem, however, because more scarce resources must be diverted from other goods into producing video cassettes, and the other goods not produced are normally more socially valuable than these extra cassettes. If markets are competitive, supply reflects production costs and demand reflects the values consumers place on goods. Taxes or subsidies distort the price signals that lead to efficient exchanges.

Some regulations inefficiently raise costs. If production costs rise by more than the benefits of a regulation, this is another example of an inefficient wedge between buyers and sellers. Let's see how specific laws and regulations may cause inefficiency.

Price Controls

You can't repeal the Laws of Supply and Demand.
—*Anonymous*

Influences on supplies and demands change continuously, so we might expect relative prices to bounce around like ping-pong balls. We all want low prices for the things we buy and high prices for the things we sell. Whenever prices rise or fall, some people gain while others lose. Consequently, a lot of people are angered by volatile prices. There is not much that any individual can do alone to directly control market forces. Special interest groups, however, often act through government to attempt to establish **price controls.**

Price Ceilings   A *maximum* legal price is termed a **price ceiling.** A price ceiling set above the equilibrium price tends to be as irrelevant as a law forbidding joggers to exceed 65 miles per hour. Price ceilings that are below the equilibrium price, however, keep monetary prices but not opportunity costs from rising and, unfortunately, also create shortages. Shortages needlessly absorb resources because when the price mechanism does not operate, less efficient mechanisms will be used to allocate goods. Severe shortages were the major result when President Nixon imposed a wage and price freeze in August 1971. This price freeze initially covered virtually all markets in the United States, although controls were phased out and then largely abandoned by 1976.

Suppose that a price ceiling of $1 per gallon is set in the market for gasoline depicted in Figure 7. The quantity of gasoline demanded will be 75 million gallons daily, but the quantity supplied will be only 30 million gallons. There will be an *excess demand* (or shortage) of 45 million gallons. Who will get gasoline? People who bribe service station attendants, or who are able to persuade government to give them priority access, or those who wait through long lines. Even people who waited several hours in gasoline lines in 1974–75 often went without because the pumps ran dry.

But price ceilings keep prices down, don't they? Unfortunately, the answer is NO! The people who most value the 30 million gallons of gas available daily tend to get it. They are willing to pay at least $2 per gallon for gasoline; that is, an extra dollar per gallon in waiting time, lobbying efforts, bribery, or as a black market premium. (A **black market** is an illegal market where price controls are ignored.) Had the price ceiling not been imposed, the price of a gallon of gasoline would have been around $1.25. Although the monetary price of gasoline is held at $1 per gallon, this price ceiling raises its opportunity cost to $2 per gallon to the average customer.

Ceilings do not hold costs down; they raise them. When ceilings are effective, there will be shortages so that opportunity costs—including money, time wasted in lines, and illegal side payments—unnecessarily exceed free-market prices. Only pump prices are controlled; real costs to average consumers are not.

Price Floors   A *minimum* legal price is termed a **price floor.** A price floor set below equilibrium tends to be as irrelevant as a law requiring pilots on intercontinental flights to fly above sea level. Price

FIGURE 7 *Governmentally Induced Shortages in the Gasoline Market*

Actual Price Paid Including Money (Ceiling) Price Plus Opportunity Costs of Standing in Line and Alternative Means of Payment: Bribery, Black Market Deals, and So On

This figure depicts the effect of a $1-per-gallon ceiling on the price of gasoline. At $1 per gallon, 75 million gallons will be demanded but only 30 million will be supplied. Therefore, shortages will exist, and nonprice methods of allocating the shortages will emerge.

floors that are above equilibrium, however, artificially raise costs and tend to create surpluses. Price floors are most prevalent in labor markets (minimum wage laws) and agriculture, where the government commonly attempts to stabilize or raise farm incomes by maintaining the prices of farm commodities above their equilibrium values. Figure 8 depicts the consequence of price floors in the cotton market.

The equilibrium price and quantity are $0.60 per pound and 4 million bales of cotton annually (point *e*). At a price floor of $0.75 per pound, the quantity supplied is 5 million bales annually, but the quantity demanded is only 3 million bales. There is an *excess supply* (surplus) of 2 million bales annually. The government can ensure the $0.75 price by buying and storing these excess supplies. (Over the years, government warehouses have been filled to their bursting points with surplus wheat, peanuts, soybeans, corn, beet sugar, and cotton.) Alternatively, the government can pay cotton farmers not to produce or forbid a certain amount of planting. (It has done both.)

In any case, these price floors are quite inefficient. In our example, consumers view the 5-millionth bale

as worth only $0.45 per pound, even though this last bale produced cost $0.75 per pound to grow and harvest. Worse than that, people do not get to use the surplus 2 million bales society buys from farmers. Hardly a bargain.

Price ceilings cause shortages and do not hold down the real prices paid by most consumers. Transaction costs during shortages are sometimes outrageous, so the opportunity costs associated with acquiring goods are actually raised by price ceilings. On the other hand, price floors cause surpluses. Production costs of the surplus goods are far greater than their values to consumers.

If price controls are typically counterproductive, why are they so common? In some cases, price ceilings are enacted because the voting public clamors for them, mistakenly perceiving controls as a solution for inflation. Most of the time, however, controls are the result of political pressures from special interest groups.

The beneficiaries of controls are at times obvious: Price floors in agriculture have existed for three generations because of bloc voting by farmers. Even price supports have not prevented recurring crises in agriculture, however, as the widespread foreclosures of family farms during 1981–86 attests. Advances in technology have made it possible for ever smaller numbers of farmers to feed our growing population. Price supports have merely slowed the inevitably painful flow of people from agriculture into other work.

In other instances, however, the beneficiaries of price controls are far less obvious. For example, minimum wage laws establish wage floors that create surpluses of labor. These surplus workers, most of whom are young or unskilled, wind up being unemployed. Why have labor unions long sought high minimum wage laws even though union workers invariably receive wages far above these wage floors? Misguided humanitarianism may play a role, but another reason is that wage floors limit the ability of unskilled workers to compete with skilled union workers. For example, if two unskilled workers willing to work for $3.00 hourly apiece can do the job of a $6.50 per hour skilled worker, a $3.35 minimum wage eliminates their ability to compete.

Yet another problem is that most immediate gainers from controls are very conscious of their ben-efits, while those who lose from the long-run effects of controls may fail to recognize their losses. For example, if controls prevent your current landlord from raising the rent, you might favor rent control. But will you recognize that rent controls are at fault if you later want to relocate and cannot find an apartment because construction has been squelched and many older rental units have turned into slums because landlords quit repairing their property? Shortages of rental property and inadequate maintenance are the predictable consequences of rent controls.

Society as a whole loses from price controls. The winners tend to be special interest groups who lobby for controlled prices, and even their gains are eroded by lobbying costs and related inefficiencies. One lesson from price controls is that government policies may distort supply and demand, yielding unintended and undesirable side effects.

Market forces often thwart policies that, on the surface, seem compatible with certain social goals. Some people are outraged when human desires and actions are viewed from an economic perspective. The following analyses suggest that economic reason-

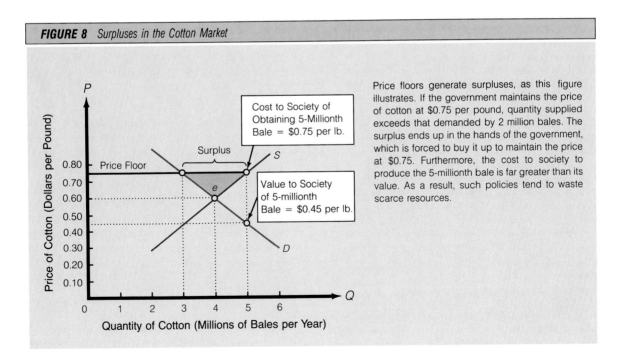

FIGURE 8 Surpluses in the Cotton Market

Cost to Society of Obtaining 5-Millionth Bale = $0.75 per lb.

Value to Society of 5-millionth Bale = $0.45 per lb.

Price floors generate surpluses, as this figure illustrates. If the government maintains the price of cotton at $0.75 per pound, quantity supplied exceeds that demanded by 2 million bales. The surplus ends up in the hands of the government, which is forced to buy it up to maintain the price at $0.75. Furthermore, the cost to society to produce the 5-millionth bale is far greater than its value. As a result, such policies tend to waste scarce resources.

ing may lead to more humane policies for issues ranging from illicit drugs to adoption than policies based on good intentions or "gut feelings."

Heroin Addiction

Drug addiction, once thought confined to the nation's ghettos, has become much more widespread in the past twenty years. Standard approaches to the drug problem have emphasized punishing users somewhat, but pushers much more harshly. This reduces demands for drugs but shrinks their supplies much more. The result is that illicit drug prices are much higher than free-market prices, and addiction poses more problems for the rest of society.

Suppose that S_0 and D_0 in Figure 9 represent the demand and supply of heroin if it were legal. The price of heroin, P_0, would probably fall somewhere between the prices of aspirin and penicillin because its production is not complex nor are presently legal narcotics very expensive. (Some estimates suggest that completely legalized and untaxed marijuana would sell for about $8 a bale—roughly the price of prime hay.)

Penalizing heroin users reduces demand to D_1 while the stiffer punishment of dealers reduces supply to S_1, boosting the price to P_1. This high price permits successful pushers to drive luxury cars and live in plush houses, but many users are pushed into prostitution, mugging, and other street crimes. Thus, higher crime rates are among the social costs of policies that reduce the supply of heroin more than the demand for it.

One alternative approach is complete legalization. The few advocates of allowing heroin to be governed strictly by demand and supply argue that it would be so cheap that few addicts would feel driven to commit crimes against others. Instead, they would spend a lot of time nodding off, bothering people no more than derelict alcoholics. Most people, however, are unwilling to let others waste away their lives in such a fashion.

What policies might reduce heroin usage below Q_0 (the free-market amount in Figure 9) without stimulating addicts to commit crimes? One option is to punish users far more than suppliers. This would reduce demand to, say, D_2 in Figure 9, and would cut the price of heroin, profits for pushers, and rates of addiction (Q_2). Most people, however, are reluctant to impose life sentences or the death penalty to punish drug users, especially when minors or experimenters are involved.

Paradoxically, allowing clinics to give heroin freely to proven addicts while maintaining stiff penalties against pushers may be a workable solution if society wants to suppress both addiction and the crime that it fosters. Such a policy would leave suppliers with only experimenters as potential customers and might, over time, reduce the illicit demand for heroin even below D_2. Pushers would be more vulnerable to undercover police work because they would not know their customers and the illicit supply of heroin should dry up. A similar approach has been followed in England for over two decades and appears to work

FIGURE 9 *The Heroin Market*

Prosecuting pushers reduces supply more than demand, but the resulting hike in price from P_0 to P_1 makes selling heroin very profitable. Severe prosecutions of addicts might reduce demand to D_2, eliminating much of this profit. Alternatively, giving heroin to addicts through government clinics might dry up both the demand and the supply of illegal heroin. Supply would shrink because catching and prosecuting pushers would be easier.

reasonably well. It does not, however, cure those who are addicted, which causes some people to view it as a failure.

The Problem of Adoption

Some social issues require basic value judgments; economics cannot directly address the morality of such controversial issues as capital punishment, euthanasia, or abortion. Once society permits certain behavior, however, economic analysis can help in evaluating alternative allocative mechanisms or policies by identifying their costs, benefits, and consequences.

Whether to allow adoption, for example, is a settled issue. Adoption matches children who have been orphaned, abandoned, or relinquished by their natural parents, with adults who view parenting as a way to add meaning to their lives. The needs of adoptable children and the wants of potential adoptive parents are reflected in supplies and demands, regardless of the mechanism by which adoptive families are matched. Thus, economic analysis may offer valuable insights into alternative mechanisms for adoption.

The Current System of Adoption Laws governing adoption were fairly lax during the Depression and the post-World War II baby boom, when orphans and foundlings outnumbered the families seeking to adopt. In recent years, the number of adoptable children has fallen because of widespread birth control, legalized abortion, and a reduced stigma on unwed mothers who keep their children. Demand, however, has grown rapidly over this period, in part because people now typically wait until they are a bit older before they marry and the incidence of sterility has risen. The result is a highly publicized shortage of adoptable children. As is the case with most lasting shortages, this shortage is a predictable consequence of government policy. Supply and demand in the absence of controls provides a starting point to examine any government policy.

Figure 10 shows the private supply and demand for adoptable children. Some children are available for adoption without compensation to the relinquishing parents; the quantity of these children is Q_0 in Figure 10. The supply curve is positively sloped

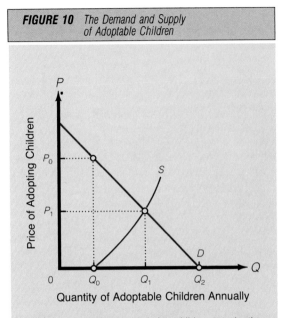

FIGURE 10 *The Demand and Supply of Adoptable Children*

Higher rewards for surrendering children to adoption yield greater numbers available for adoption. Lower prices charged adopting families would result in a greater number of adoptions. Thus, demands and supplies in this market conform to the laws of supply and demand.

because, as the price paid for children is raised, some women may decide not to have abortions and others who might otherwise keep unexpected or unwanted children may relinquish them for a price.

The demand curve in Figure 10 slopes down because people find substitutes as prices rise; you may know people who treat their pets as child surrogates. Other families may abandon the quest for an adoptive child or postpone kids until they can afford them. At the legally permissible explicit price of zero, there will be Q_0 children available for adoption and Q_2 children demanded, leaving a shortage of at least Q_2-Q_0. Does this mean that under the current adoption system Q_0 children are adopted, or that the economic costs to adopting parents are zero? Both answers are no.

Social concern about the well-being of foster and adopted children has generated a large bureaucracy to oversee their care. Applicants for adoption are carefully screened, and extensive efforts are made to match children and adoptive parents. Many questions are asked about such areas as finances and attitudes about sex, religion, race, and discipline. Common grounds for rejecting applicants may seem capricious: obesity, atheism, radical politics, or the desire for a career by the female member of an applying couple are all frequent grounds for rejection. Even when all barriers are hurdled, the process of becoming an "approved home" may take years because social workers lack incentives to act quickly or efficiently. Indeed, persisting through this trying process is viewed as a way for potential adoptive parents to demonstrate their commitment to adoption.

Even approval does not guarantee that a family can adopt. Each child is also screened; children and prospective adoptive parents alike must wait for a "match." Infants are seldom placed in an adoptive home at ages of less than three months; six months is common. Older children or those with severe handicaps remain "hard to place," but the adoption shortage has become so acute that such previously hard-to-place children as those who are racially mixed or mildly handicapped are relatively easily placed. Even so, adoption agencies fail to find homes for many children who are available for adoption (Q_0 in Figure 10) when a zero price is paid to the relinquishing parents.

Is the economic cost of these adoptions zero? Far from it. Long waiting periods for both prospective parents and adoptable children entail substantial costs. Most successful adoptive families are willing to pay a demand price of at least P_0 for the children available for adoption at Q_0. The parents who most desire children pay this price by courting the social workers to prove their commitment to adoption. Prospective adoptive parents, however, are legally forbidden to pay an explicit monetary price greater than zero for a child. The result? Gray and black markets for infants flourish, with high prices being paid to doctors and lawyers who are willing to flirt with prosecution by acting as baby brokers. Many American couples now avoid the U.S. adoption system by adopting children from Asia or South America.

Many children are stranded in foster care for years under the current system because some biological parents run hot and then cold in their concern for their offspring. Some parental indecisiveness about relinquishment might be overcome were these parents simply paid. The price paid for a child need not be monetary, however; in currently legal markets, many biological parents consider payment of medical costs by adoptive parents or reasonable assurances about the treatment of the child to be adequate payment.

In a black market exchange, of course, cold cash changes hands. Infants have been sold for more than $60,000. We should note, however, that the cost per current legal adoption is probably not far from the average of $25,000 or so that children bring on black or gray markets. More than $36,000 in tax revenues were spent per legal adoption in 1981, and the extended periods of waiting that confront both adoptive parents and children must be considered.

A Market Alternative   Many childless couples place values on children that exceed the (re)production costs to some natural parents. (Surrogate motherhood is evidence of this.) Demand prices for children exceed supply prices up to Q_1 adoptable children in Figure 10. Allowing the market to resolve the allocation of adoptable children would allow children who were not especially valued by their natural parents (those whose supply prices range from zero to P_1) to be sold to people who would value them more (those with demand prices of at least P_1).

Drawbacks of a Market Solution   One counterargument against reliance on the market is that only the rich would be able to adopt. Under the current system, however, adoption agencies typically disqualify the childless poor because income weighs heavily when agencies screen applicants for adoption. Many poor people might find adoption easier under a market system. In the absence of other evidence, willingness to pay is a reasonable measure of how much someone values something.

Another objection to the market solution is that explicit prices provide incentives for kidnapping for the market. (Of course, the high hurdles facing couples who want to adopt provide even greater incentives for kidnapping, but, perhaps also, greater hurdles against long-run success from kidnapping.) Birth certificates and footprinting would only partially impede determined thieves, and tattooing (common for valuable pets) is socially unacceptable. It is also possible that a "baby" industry might emerge. This would be morally repugnant to many people. Still another problem is that some people might buy children for such unacceptable reasons as child prostitution. Of course, child protection laws apply to all homes, whether natural or adoptive. Current kiddie-porn stars are often exploited by their natural parents.

Although a market for adoption would have many shortcomings, proposals to change any policy should not be evaluated against perfection, but rather against the current system, warts and all. At the very least, the current system might be modified so that market forces were allowed to play a role wherever this would benefit adoptees, adopters, and relinquishing parents. For example, the government might allow transactions for infants while continuing to monitor children's welfare closely during adoption proceedings.

Do simple solutions exist for such problems as heroin addiction and baby shortages? Should supply and demand operate without controls? The answers probably depend on particular market conditions. Supply and demand exert considerable pressure regardless of which allocative mechanism is used to resolve any problem. We hope that these overviews of the heroin and adoption markets convince you that market forces cannot be ignored when structuring social policies, even in areas that are closely tied to people's views of morality.

You have now had an overview of supply and demand in action. It is time to address how effectively, equitably, and efficiently market mechanisms answer the questions of **What? How? Who?** and **When?.**

The Market in Operation _____

Our analysis of the price system relies on two critical assumptions:

1. *Individuals are self-interested* and try to maximize their personal satisfaction through the goods they consume. If goods add less to your satisfaction (valued in terms of money) than they cost, you will not buy them. Consumer willingness to buy underpins the demands for goods.
2. *Firms attempt to maximize profits.* They do this by selling goods to consumers who are willing to pay

for them. The drive for profit underpins the supply side of the market.

Thus, the price system answers the *What?* question by producing the things consumers demand.

Two things limit a firm's ability to take advantage of consumers. First, competition among sellers keeps prices from straying much above costs for very long because high profits attract new firms, increasing supply so that prices and profits fall. Second, suppliers strive to be efficient because any firm that cuts costs or introduces a successful technology temporarily reaps higher profits. Before long, any firm not using the new technology will be trying to sell outdated products, or its costs will exceed its competitors' prices and it will fail. Competition among producers ensures that price is approximately equal to the opportunity cost (sacrifice to society) entailed in production. Thus, a competitive market system answers the *How?* question by using the least costly method of production.

How are products distributed among consumers? The answer to this *Who?* question is relatively simple. Consumers who hold "dollar votes" and are willing to pay market prices purchase and consume products. Those who do not own many resources cannot buy a lot of goods. It is this distributional side that seems to cause the most problems for critics of the market system. The question of *When?* is automatically answered by the cumulative answers a society gives over time to the questions of *What?, How?,* and *Who?*.

Many people perceive the price system as impersonal and inequitable. However, the market offers some major compensating advantages. Decisions are decentralized; no government agency dictates what everyone must (or cannot) buy or produce. Moreover, markets tend to be efficient. Consumers usually pay prices for goods that roughly reflect the minimal costs of producing these goods. Finally, although markets may not provide perfect stability, the forces that drive markets towards equilibrium tend to yield more stability than most other mechanisms.

As you proceed through this book, you will constantly encounter the supply and demand analysis presented in this and the previous chapter. No tool of economics is more important. Material in the next chapter discusses the institutions within which supply and demand operate in a market economy.

CHAPTER REVIEW: KEY POINTS

1. Increases in supplies or decreases in demands tend to reduce prices. Decreases in supplies or increases in demands tend to increase prices. Increases in either supplies or demands tend to increase quantities. Decreases in either supplies or demands tend to decrease quantities. If both supply and demand shift, the effects on price and quantity may be either reinforcing or at least partially offsetting. (If these points make little sense to you, you need to review this important material.)

2. Prices may not move quickly to their equilibrium values, and can swing up and down as they slowly approach the intersections of demands and supplies.

3. *Middlemen* prosper only if they reduce the transaction costs associated with getting goods from the ultimate producers to the ultimate consumers. *Speculators* aid in movements towards equilibrium because they try to buy when prices are below equilibrium (increasing demand) and sell when prices are above equilibrium (increasing supply). This dampens price swings and reduces the costs and risks to others of doing business.

4. *Arbitrage* involves buying in a market where the price is low and selling in a market where the price is higher. If this price spread is greater than the transaction costs, arbitrage is risklessly profitable. Competition for opportunities to arbitrage dampens profit opportunities and facilitates efficiency by ensuring that price spreads between markets are minimal.

5. Government can set monetary prices at values other than equilibrium price, but *price ceilings* or *price floors* do not "freeze" opportunity costs; instead, these *price controls* create economic inefficiency and either shortages or surpluses, respectively.

6. Taxes and subsidies drive *wedges* into markets so that buyers and sellers have different perceptions about supplies and demands. The slope of supplies and demands determine the proportions of tax burdens borne by buyers and sellers.

PROBLEMS

Draw supply and demand graphs for the relevant markets to show the impact of the following changes on prices and quantities. Be as explicit as possible about the market adjustment mechanisms.

1. There is a major technological breakthrough in producing natural gas from coal. What happens in the market for natural gas? The market for coal?

2. What happens to the world market for coffee if coffee blight destroys three-quarters of the crop in Brazil? The market for tea?

3. Gasoline prices soar. What happens in the markets for big cars? Bicycles? Tune-up shops? Rapid-transit systems?

4. The economy goes sour. What happens to the market for economists?

5. Tomorrow afternoon AT&T announces that oil has been discovered under every telephone pole. What happens to the market for AT&T stock? How rapidly would this occur? Do you think you could get rich buying AT&T stock the next day? (The answer is NO!) Who would get rich from this discovery?

6. A legal maximum price for denim jeans is set at $1 per pair. What happens to quantity? To quality? To opportunity cost? Is the government doing denim-jean wearers any favors?

7. A "miracle seed" for corn is developed. Analyze the markets for corn and wheat.

8. The birthrate suddenly increases enormously. What would happen in the market for baby furniture? The market for babysitters? The market for movies? Are the answers to these questions different in the short run and long run? How?

9. In 1989, the government announces a major renewal of space exploration. In 1997, this program is discontinued. What will happen to the market for aeronautical engineers in 1989–90? Between 1990 and 1997? In 1997–98?

10. There is a radical overhaul and simplification of the income tax system. What happens to the market for accountants? Lawyers? Erasers?

11. The minimum legal wage is raised from $3.35 per hour to $5.00 per hour. What happens in labor markets for teenagers and other unskilled workers?

QUESTIONS FOR THOUGHT AND DISCUSSION

1. Ticket scalpers provide consumers with various services. The latecomer can avoid standing in line for tickets and can wait until the last moment before deciding to attend. Should these services be free? What can promoters of an event do to prevent scalping? Do they really want to prevent scalping? See if you can devise graphs to explain this form of speculation.

2. Financial institutions such as banks act as middlemen. They lend their depositors' savings to ultimate borrowers, charging higher interest to borrowers than they pay to depositors, who are the ultimate providers of loans. How does this reduce the transaction costs incurred in making private savings available to borrowers?

3. Senator Ernest Hollings (D-South Carolina), in advocating wage-price controls, asserts that "most people would prefer shortages to higher prices." Do you think this is true? Why or why not? Do you think advocates of wage-price freezes understand that shortages arise from controls?

4. Casual surveys of our students at the beginning of each semester reveal an amused but overwhelming support for a proposal to raise the legal minimum wages of college graduates to $50,000 per year. (They assume our proposal is facetious.) After covering this chapter, student support for this idea evaporates. How might such a minimum wage law be harmful to most new college graduates?

5. Pharmaceutical companies have recently developed and tested drugs that reverse the influence of alcohol on the brain within a half hour. These pills enable drivers to sober up before driving home, and also tend to reduce the severity of hangovers. In the past few years, many states have imposed stiff mandatory penalties for drunk driving convictions. How do you think these two separate events will interact to influence alcohol consumption?

6. In 1979, President Carter imposed quotas limiting oil imports, using the argument that ". . . we import inflation every time we import another barrel of expensive oil into this country." Do import quotas (on such things as oil, clothes, or cars) drive prices up, or will prices be held down as President Carter suggested?

7. Laws forbid or severely limit free market transactions in atomic bombs, adoptable babies, murder-for-hire, sex, marijuana, surrogate motherhood, pornography, and a host of other activities. At the same time, minimal education and inoculations against communicable diseases are compulsory. Which of these or other illegal or mandatory goods do you think could be allocated more efficiently and equitably through the market system? Are there goods that are now bought and sold freely that you believe the government should control tightly? What are they? Why?

8. Ceilings on rents for apartments and housing are in effect in several U.S. cities, including New York and Santa Monica, California. What effect do such controls have on the incentives of property owners to build residences for rent? To maintain rental property in top shape? Can you identify some groups that may gain from rent controls? Now identify several groups that lose.

CHAPTER 5

Economic Institutions: Households, Firms, and Government

The social structures within which demands and supplies operate determine how well markets perform. This chapter surveys the major social institutions that shape economic behavior: households, firms, and government. Market systems pivot on the decisions of households and business firms, which together are called the *private sector*. In our mixed economy, government, or the *public sector*, takes a back seat only to the marketplace as a dominant allocative mechanism. We will use a simple model of the private economy to set the stage for an examination of public and private relationships.

Circular Flows of Resources, Goods, and Income

Households are centers for consumption and ultimately own all wealth, including resources that they supply to business firms in exchange for income. They are also the firms' ultimate customers, as shown in the **circular flow** diagram in Figure 1. In this model of a purely private economy, households demand food, shelter, and a host of other goods, and own all productive resources. Households supply la-

FIGURE 1 *The Circular Flow of Income, Resources, and Goods*

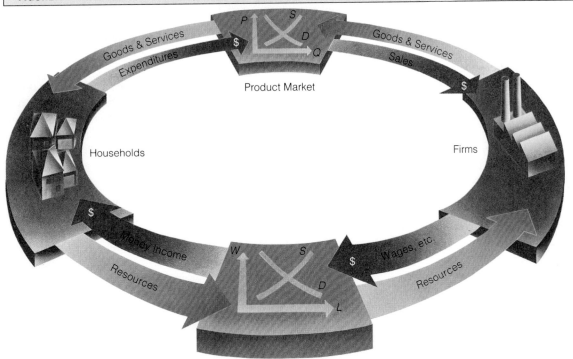

Product Market

Households

Firms

Resource Market

The circular flow of income is a simple model depicting a private economy. Firms provide goods and services to households and receive dollars for these products. Households in turn provide resources (factors) to business in exchange for money income, which is used to purchase goods and services from business.

bor services, land, capital, and entrepreneurial skills to firms, and then spend their incomes for consumer goods.

In turn, firms use sales revenues to pay for the resources that households provide. Firms interpret prices and profits as signals about consumer demands, and use the wage rates paid for specific labor skills, rental rates for land, or rates of return on capital to signal households about the resources demanded for production.

A critical point is that firms are not the final owners of either resources or products. Businesses and all the assets they use are owned by individuals. Thus, firms ultimately do not reap profits; they only relay profits to their owners. Nor can firms bear tax burdens; only their owners, customers, or resource sup-

pliers truly pay taxes. It is common to speak of a firm profiting, changing prices, or introducing a new product, but regularly remind yourself that firms are merely conduits through which individual decisions flow. Activities that matter affect people, not business firms per se.

Households

The catchall term *households* covers a rich variety of economic behavior. By 1988, 247 million Americans lived in more than 87 million households. Sociologists perceive constant upheavals in modern family structures, but the basic economic roles of households change only at a snail's pace.

Sources of Household Income

Circular flow diagrams indicate that households ultimately receive all income. Table 1 shows that rent, interest, and profit provide roughly one fourth of total household income. The rest of income from supplying resources is from *wages*—which include salaries, commissions, and fringe benefits. The major asset of most households is the labor provided by family members.

A century ago, most families relied on income from agriculture. Today, over half of all labor is in white-collar occupations—a category that includes doctors, lawyers, teachers, managers, and sales and clerical workers. Employment in blue collar work (assembly lines and construction are examples) and, especially, farming has declined over the years.

The most dramatic change in labor markets over the past few decades has been the surge of women into the labor force. In the 1950s, only one woman in three worked outside the home; more than half hold jobs today, and 44 percent of all workers are women. Even more remarkable is the threefold increase in working mothers with small children.

Several theories have been advanced to explain these changes. A revolution of rising expectations about living standards propelled many women into the work force who might have been housewives in an earlier era. Legal reforms and changing attitudes about women's work roles has opened doors to careers that were previously closed. The flight from the worst types of household drudgery was facilitated by such innovations as washers and dryers, microwave ovens, and permapress clothing. Options to postpone children and curb family size have been made available by cheap and effective birth control, also increasing women's labor force participation rates.

These changes have not occurred in a vaccuum. The labor force participation rates of men fell slightly over this same period, partially because more young men are going to college, while mature men have typically been retiring at earlier ages.

Household Uses of Income

Household income is totally exhausted by *consumer spending, saving,* and *taxes.* Consumer spending absorbs about 70 percent of national income, and can be used for the services and durable or nondurable goods sold by private firms. **Services** include medical care, haircuts, and education and account for a growing share of total spending. Furniture, appliances, cars, and other **durable goods** normally last more than a year. **Nondurable goods** tend to be used up quickly and include such things as food, clothes, and gasoline.

Spending on food as a proportion of income has fallen over time, reflecting advances in agricultural technology and decreases in the relative prices of food. Five out of six Americans lived and worked on farms in 1800, but fewer than one in thirty now depends primarily on agriculture for income. This small group feeds all of us and many foreigners as

		Percentage of Total Income				
TABLE 1 *Functional Distribution of Income, 1929–87*						
Year	**$ Billions Total Income**	**Compensation of Employees**	**Proprietors' Income**	**Net Rents**	**Corporate Profits**	**Interest**
1929	84.8	60.3	17.6	5.8	10.8	5.5
1933	39.9	73.9	14.5	5.5	−4.3	10.3
1940	79.7	65.4	16.2	3.4	10.9	4.1
1950	236.2	65.5	16.3	3.0	14.3	1.0
1960	412.0	71.6	11.4	3.3	11.3	2.4
1970	798.4	76.3	8.2	2.3	8.5	4.7
1980	2,117.1	75.5	5.7	3.1	8.6	8.9
1987	3,635.9	72.8	9.0	0.8	8.4	9.3

Source: *Economic Report of the President,* 1988.

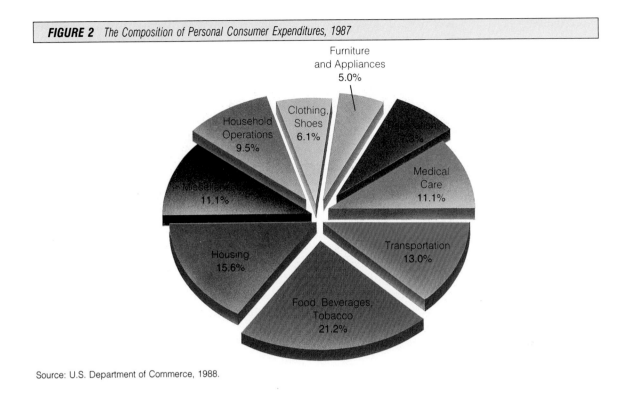

FIGURE 2 The Composition of Personal Consumer Expenditures, 1987

Furniture
and Appliances
5.0%

Clothing,
Shoes
6.1%

Household
Operations
9.5%

Recreation
7.3%

Medical
Care
11.1%

Miscellaneous
11.1%

Housing
15.6%

Transportation
13.0%

Food, Beverages,
Tobacco
21.2%

Source: U.S. Department of Commerce, 1988.

well, but predicted worldwide droughts may soon enlarge the role of food in typical family budgets. The share of income spent on housing fell after the Depression, but recently rose as average home prices climbed past the $100,000 mark.

Consumption expenditures have fallen from 83 percent of income in 1929 to roughly 70 percent today. Over the same interval, net taxes rose from about 12 percent to about 25 percent of income. This reflects persistent growth in demands for government services over the past half century.

Saving has oscillated a bit over the past half century or so, averaging about 4–7 percent of income. Families save only if their income exceeds the spending absorbed by what they view as necessities. In fact, the bulk of personal saving in our society is done by families with annual incomes over $60,000. Figure 2 shows how income is used by typical American households.

We have now looked at the roles of households as resource suppliers to business firms and as customers for the final products of business. This leads to the roles played by the business sector.

The Business Sector

The business of America is business.
— Calvin Coolidge

Over 75 percent of employment and 80 percent of U.S. production flows from the business sector, with most of the rest being accounted for by government. Although business dominates the economic landscape, many people take it for granted. In this section, you should understand what firms do and how they interact with households and government.

Plants, Firms, and Industries

Your favorite pro football team, IBM, and the local phone company are all business **firms.** Firms operate one or more **plants,** which are facilities clumped together at a specific location. Plants manufacture, process, fabricate, assemble, or sell outputs. Firms that operate more than one plant are called *multiplant* firms; if they produce several types of goods, they are *multiproduct* or *diversified* firms. Giant multiproduct firms are termed **conglomerates.**

An **industry** is composed of all firms competing in a given market; for example, tobacco, chemicals, or clothing. **Horizontally integrated** firms operate at a number of sites, each doing essentially the same thing. For example, General Motors produces the same cars in plants in Michigan and Ohio, and McDonald's "golden arches" grace the scenery from Berlin to Singapore. It might seem easy to identify the firms that make up an industry, but consider motor vehicles. Are Lincolns and Chevettes really close substitutes? Should imported cars be included? Vans? Trucks? Is it reasonable to lump all these goods into a single industry?

Another problem in identifying an industry's boundaries is that conglomerates are often major producers in several industries. Even nonconglomerates may operate at different production levels in an industry; these firms are **vertically integrated.** Most steel producers are examples of vertical integration. They operate mines, smelting plants, mills for producing rolled steel, and fabrication plants. Conglomerates, in contrast, operate plants in several different industries. For example, Gulf and Western produces movies, publishes books, and is also involved in electronics and mining. In fact, most large corporations are conglomerates.

Legal Forms of Business

Businesses are operated as sole proprietorships, partnerships, or corporations. Over three fourths of all U.S. firms are sole proprietorships, but they account for less than one third of all profits. At the other extreme, only one firm in seven is incorporated, but corporations generate over 60 percent of total profits in the United States. The message seems to be that a first step towards success is to incorporate. Then why do over 10 million sole proprietorships exist? The answer comes from an examination of the strengths and weaknesses of each type of organization.

Sole Proprietorships   Establishing a **sole proprietorship** requires little more than declaring, "I am in business for myself." You are your own boss, and your profits depend on your skill, hard work, and luck. The major advantages to sole proprietorships are that such firms are (*a*) easy to organize, (*b*) simple to control, (*c*) quite flexible, and (*d*) relatively free from government regulation.

There are, however, some major disadvantages. The firm's size is limited by the proprietor's initial wealth and credit standing and by the profits of the business as time unfolds. Capital accumulation for expansion is difficult. Proprietors normally perform most management functions, and such firms lack permanence because they cannot outlive their owners. The greatest disadvantage, however, is a proprietor's *unlimited liability*. Nearly all a proprietor owns, including possessions unrelated to the business, may be sold to pay a firm's debts if it fails or is held liable for a huge judgment in a lawsuit. Much more is at risk than the owner's investment, although insurance can protect proprietors from some legal hazards.

Partnerships   **Partnerships** are extensions of proprietorships; two or more people combine their resources to form a business, hoping to overcome some financial and managerial disadvantages faced by a sole proprietor. Partnerships are easy to establish, relatively simple to control, allow some specialized management, and are subject to relatively few regulations. Pooled resources in a partnership may make capital accumulation easier than for sole proprietorships.

Partners continue to face unlimited personal liability for the firm's debts, however, and dishonest, incompetent, or accident-prone partners can cost you all your assets. Shared ownership also often creates discord over a firm's policies. Other drawbacks are that resources for growth tend to remain quite limited, and partnerships automatically dissolve upon the withdrawal or death of any partner.

Corporations   **Corporations** are firms sanctioned by state laws and are considered *legal persons* separate and distinct from their owners. Incorporating a firm requires submitting a *charter* to a state government outlining the intended line of business and specifying how the firm will be financed and governed. Once formed, numerous special taxes and regulations hinder corporate operations.

Why then do people incorporate a business? One major reason is that corporations excel at raising financial capital because they can sell **common stocks** (ownership shares in a corporation) and **bonds** (corporate IOUs). Combined with undistributed profits, these funds may permit acquisition of vast amounts of economic (physical) capital. This is partially due to a second corporate advantage: the *limited liability* of stockholders, which means that owners of a corporation cannot lose more than they have paid for stock. Their other assets are not directly jeopardized if the corporation fails.

Other advantages include potential stability and permanence. A stockholder's death does not require terminating a corporation. A final advantage is that large corporations are able to employ highly specialized management. In fact, large corporations are often controlled by their top managers because stock is so widely spread that individual stockholders have very little influence on business policies. This is a gain for corporate managers, but can be a disadvantage for a corporation's stockholders.

Other negative aspects of incorporation are special corporate taxes and regulations. The divorce of ownership from managerial control opens up opportunities for fraud, so strict accounting and reporting requirements govern corporate life and add to business costs. Because corporations are viewed as fruitful sources of tax revenue, corporate profits are subject to double taxation. This *double taxation* occurs because corporations pay taxes on their incomes and then, when some aftertax income is distributed to

stockholders as dividends, they are taxed again at the individual's personal income tax rate. Table 2 summarizes the attributes of the three major forms of business organization.

Although proprietorships, partnerships, and corporations dominate private production, other types of organizations exist. *Producer cooperatives* share the profits from marketing such things as handicrafts or agricultural goods. *Consumer cooperatives* share savings achieved through large scale buying. *Nonprofit corporations* operate hospitals, charities, private schools, and such community services as educational TV. *Closely held corporations* and *limited partnerships* are legal devices to obtain certain tax advantages and limited liability for family-owned businesses or partnerships. Still other minor forms of business organization abound, varying in their particulars according to the state laws that govern them.

Corporate Goals and Control

Some firms fail while others prosper. The market system rewards those who serve the consumer and society, while competitive pressures force inefficient

TABLE 2 Summary of Legal Forms of Business Organization		
Form of Business	**Advantages**	**Disadvantages**
Sole Proprietorship	1. Easy to organize. 2. Simple to control. 3. Freedom of operation. 4. Not subject to much government regulation.	1. Difficult to acquire funds (capital) for expansion. 2. Firm lacks permanence. 3. Unlimited liability. 4. Owner must perform all management functions.
Partnership	1. Easy to organize. 2. Greater specialization of management is possible. 3. Securing financial resources easier than in sole proprietorship (pooling of funds). 4. Subject to limited regulation.	1. Division of ownership may lead to disagreements. 2. Death or withdrawal of one partner automatically ends the organization. 3. Subject to unlimited liability. 4. Financial resources are typically quite limited.
Corporation	1. Capability of raising large amounts of capital through sale of stocks and bonds. 2. Limited liability of stockholders. 3. Stability and permanence: is a legal entity (person) all its own. 4. Employment of specialized management personnel.	1. Subject to considerable government regulation. 2. Taxes and organizing costs for corporations are heavy burdens. 3. Double taxation of corporate income and dividends. 4. Separation of ownership and control.

firms to adapt or exit the market. Many firms vie for the patronage of consumers in competitive markets. Will society derive the same benefits if a few firms dominate a market? Most people think not.

Criticisms of Corporate America

Economist John Kenneth Galbraith and consumer advocate Ralph Nader achieved fame by attacking economic theories that stress competitive markets and the goal of profit maximization. In one of his many books, *The New Industrial State,* Galbraith argued that giant corporations:

1. dominate economic activity because small competitive firms cannot afford the modern technologies required for efficient production.
2. are controlled by corporate managers who seek maximum power and pay for themselves instead of maximum profits for stockholders.
3. tend to corrupt government policies to help consolidate managerial power and achieve managers' goals rather than the public interest.
4. use extensive advertising to avoid meaningful competition.

What evidence supports Galbraith's claims? First, corporations do account for $5 out of $6 of U.S. business revenues, and control a large share of our national resources. The top 2,000 manufacturing corporations have assets exceeding $10 million each, and the largest 200 control roughly 60 percent of all manufacturing assets. There is also an erratic long-term trend towards even greater concentration in the ownership of total manufacturing assets. According to Galbraith, our only hope for a just society is for modern corporate managers to become more *socially responsible,* but he is pessimistic about the prospects for such changes of heart.

Ralph Nader agrees with many of Galbraith's points, but his focus is different. He believes that giant corporations are too profit-oriented and has lobbied long and hard for laws and regulations to limit corporate discretion about pricing, pollution, product safety, and a long list of other areas.

Are Corporate Giants Immune from Market Pressures?

Much of modern economic life seems far removed from competitive models of the economy. Indeed, some corporate giants dwarf the governments of even sizable countries, as Figure 3 indicates. There is, however, evidence that markets serve consumers reasonably well and that size alone does not insulate huge firms from competitive pressures. Giants compete with giants.

Such once dominant retailers as Sears, Montgomery Ward, and J. C. Penney have lost ground to firms like K-Mart, Venture, and Wal-Mart, while Woolco and other giants have collapsed. In the late 1950s, Ford Motor Company lost millions of dollars when it launched the ill-fated Edsel. It more than recouped these losses when it developed the Mustang, a car that passed the test of the marketplace. A shaky economy and competition from foreign automakers imposed billions of dollars in losses on U.S. automakers in the late 1970s, and Chrysler teetered on the brink of bankruptcy. Automakers recovered only when they marketed more fuel efficient and reliable cars. What happened to the giant railroads of a century ago? Most disappeared or were absorbed into Amtrak, a government-subsidized money loser.

Interindustry competition has become increasingly important. Xerox once had a near monopoly on copying equipment, but now competes with IBM and a host of Japanese firms. IBM had a stranglehold on computers in the 1960s, but now must compete with Apple, Radio Shack, Control Data, Wang, NCR, DEC, Xerox, Compaq, AT&T, and hundreds of small electronics firms.

Giants often emerge from nowhere when entrepreneurs perceive a void in the marketplace. A 17-year-old and a 22-year-old launched Apple Computers from a garage in 1978 for under $500, creating a billion-dollar firm within four years after they built the first low-cost personal computer. It is hard to overstate how risky business can be. A boom in personal computer sales and software in the early 1980s made overnight millionaires of hundreds of young workaholics in the "Silicon Valley," an area just south of San Francisco. Gluts on the market quickly appeared, however, and numerous computer firms of all sizes collapsed during 1984–86.

Another type of adjustment occurs when firms headed by inefficient managers are targeted for "hostile" takeovers by "corporate raiders." The absorbed companies generally grow more profitable when new managers steer these firms towards areas more compatible with consumer demands. This often involves closing unprofitable subsidiaries of overly diversified conglomerates, or selling them if more specialized management can run them better. Examples of dynamic competition are almost innumerable. Some firms that have, relatively, lost or gained a lot in

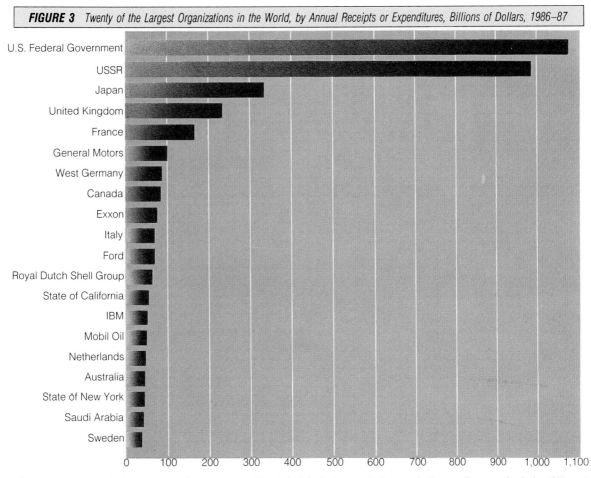

FIGURE 3 *Twenty of the Largest Organizations in the World, by Annual Receipts or Expenditures, Billions of Dollars, 1986–87*

The 20 largest organizations are not all governments. Nearly half, in fact, are private organizations—oil companies being the most numerous. *Note:* Some giants may not be represented because reasonable estimates are not available.

Source: CIA, *The World Factbook 1987, Fortune,* August 23, 1987 and April 25, 1988; *1988 World Almanac.*

the past few years are listed in Table 3, which indicates how the corporate pecking order changes over time.

The key point is that high profits attract aggressive competition, both foreign and domestic, so that consumers' needs are met in a reasonably efficient fashion. Many people remain unhappy with market outcomes, however, and increasingly turn to government to resolve economic problems. The distribution of income as determined in the market is widely perceived as unfair. What can be done about national defense, or such problems as pollution and unemployment? These are among the areas in which government plays an active role in our society.

The Role of Government

Government directly provides some goods, and indirectly channels resources and the production and consumption of other goods via taxes and regulations. As we approach the twenty-first century, our society is much more regulated and taxed than in earlier times when government economic policies were restricted by a more laissez-faire philosophy. Federal, state, and local governments now directly allocate roughly one fifth of national production; another 15 percent is redistributed through transfer payments, with two thirds of all transfers being made

TABLE 3	Turnover among the Top 10 and Top 50 U.S. Corporations, 1977–87	

Dates	Entered the Top 10	Left the Top 10
1987–82	General Electric AT&T Chrysler	Standard Oil of California Gulf Oil Standard Oil (Indiana)
1982–77	DuPont Standard Oil (Indiana)	General Electric Chrysler

Dates	Entered the Top 50		Left the Top 50	
1987–82	BP America Lockheed Unysis Digital Equipment Sara Lee	ConAgra Georgia–Pacific Anheuser–Busch Hewlett–Packard Johnson & Johnson	Standard Oil (Ohio) Western Electric Getty Oil Union Carbide Ashland Oil	General Electric Amerada Hess Monsanto Coca-Cola W. R. Grace
1982–77	Standard Oil (Ohio) Getty Oil Phillip Morris Pepsico General Dynamics	Coca-Cola Allied W. R. Grace McDonnell Douglass	Continental Oil International Harvester RCA Bethlehem Steel Esmark	LTV Firestone Tire and Rubber Cities Service Marathon Oil

Source: *Fortune*, "The Fortune 500: The Largest U.S. Industrial Corporations," May 8, 1978, May 2, 1983, and April 25, 1988.

by the federal government. *Transfer payments* include welfare expenditures, loans to farmers and students, and similar outlays. Figure 4 provides some measures of the size and recent growth of total government activity.

Many people see government action as necessary whenever markets apparently fail to respond to our desires for equity, efficiency, full employment, stable prices, and prosperous growth. Widely accepted economic goals for government in a market economy are to:

1. provide a stable legal environment for business activity;
2. promote and maintain competitive markets;
3. allocate resources to meet public wants efficiently;
4. facilitate equity through redistributions of income: and,
5. ensure full employment, a stable price level, economic security, and a growing standard of living.

Although macroeconomic and microeconomic policies are unavoidably interdependent, goals 1–4 tend to be microeconomic concerns, while goal 5 is the focus of macroeconomic policymaking.

Providing a Stable Legal Environment

A reasonably certain legal environment helps to prevent chaos. Could any economy operate efficiently if ownership rights or the rules of business were uncertain? Private property rights or contracts, if they existed, would be enforced only through brute force or individual persuasion. Primitive trading would occur, but complex financial transactions would be impossible.

The government sets rules establishing legal relationships between parties, regulates public utilities and other vital industries, establishes standards for money and weights and measures, insures bank deposits, and engages in other activities to promote public confidence and health.

Promoting Competition

Competition allows us to enjoy the benefits of efficient markets. Profits signal that consumers want more of certain goods; losses signal that too much is being offered. New technologies that create better and cheaper products force older firms to adapt or

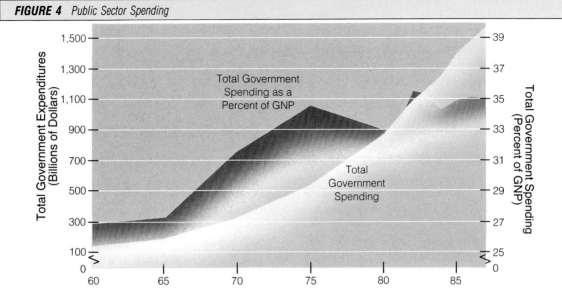

FIGURE 4 Public Sector Spending

Source: *Economic Report of the President*, 1987.

perish. Thus, hand-cranked autos don't clog our highways and motor-driven calculators don't clutter our desks.

Monopoly lies at the opposite end of the spectrum of market structures from competition, and occurs when a single firm dominates a market. **Monopoly power** exists when individual firms significantly influence the supply and price of a good, and may be present even if several firms share a market. Competitive buyers and sellers are so small that, alone, none can noticeably affect total output or prices. Firms with monopoly power boost profits by restricting output and setting higher prices. This is inefficient because equilibrium monopoly prices exceed the opportunity cost to society of additional production.

The basic approach to controlling monopoly power in the United States has been through antitrust laws and regulation. Antitrust laws are attempts to curb unfair business practices and prevent huge firms from absorbing all their competitors. Where competition is impractical, regulation is used to limit the abuse of monopoly power.

Providing for Public Wants

No private firm could sell you a cleaner environment without simultaneously providing it for your neighbors. Nor could a neighbor privately buy national defense without protecting you. Because no individual willingly bears the costs of adequately accommodating everyone's desires for such otherwise desirable goods, price signals emitted by consumers are distorted and firms cannot privately market these goods profitably.

Even if firms operate in a stable and competitive environment, certain market failures may still seem to justify government action. Externalities, of which pollution is one form, can warp price signals so that our demands are not accurately reflected. A second difficulty, called the public goods problem, results when shared consumption is possible but people cannot be denied access to the benefits of a good. National defense is an example.

Externalities **Externalities** occur when some benefits or costs of an activity *spill over* to parties not directly involved in the activity. For example, when farmers spray their crops, some pesticide may eventually wash into nearby lakes or streams. If the pesticide is absorbed by microorganisms and works its way up the ecological chain, your fishing or health may deteriorate so that you partially bear the cost of the use of chemical sprays. Most human activities generate externalities, some trivial and some of major concern. Cooking creates heat and smoke, every car emits noxious fumes, and loud stereos annoy your neighbors. All forms of pollution—chemical, air, noise, and litter—are *negative externalities*.

Producers whose activities generate negative externalities tend to ignore costs imposed on others, and the prices they charge reflect only their private costs. Pollution-generating goods consequently tend to be overproduced and underpriced. The government uses various regulations to control different pollutants because absolutely prohibiting pollution would probably eliminate all production—most human activities, including production, generate at least trivial pollution. There is a trade-off between the cleaner environment most of us would like and the higher level of consumption most of us desire.

Inefficiency may also occur when *positive externalities* spill over from an activity. Immunization against contagious diseases is one such activity. You are less likely to suffer from the flu if you are inoculated, and we who are your neighbors are less likely to catch it as well. But you tend to ignore our benefits when you decide whether or not to be immunized, and so are less likely to get a flu shot than is socially optimal. Thus, private market decisions result in underproduction and overpricing of goods that generate positive externalities because the value to society exceeds the demand price individuals willingly pay when they are uncompensated for external benefits.

Public Goods Prisons are examples of public goods because keeping violent criminals behind bars makes the world safer for the rest of us. **Public goods** are both *nonrival* because people can consume such goods simultaneously, and *nonexclusive,* because denying people access to such goods is prohibitively expensive. Most goods are private goods, however; they are *rival* and *exclusive.* If you eat a corn chip laden with guacamole, no one else can enjoy that particular morsel; food and such goods as raincoats are rival and exclusive. But we need not compete with each other to use public goods once they are produced because our uses of public goods do not involve rivalry.

Most cities would suffer terminal gridlock without traffic lights, which smooth traffic patterns, cut accident rates, and hasten us to our destinations. All drivers benefit simultaneously. Other public goods include weather reports, cancer research, democratic government, and national defense. Once the armed forces are maintained and ready, every person in the United States consumes defense services simultaneously, and we all receive this protection whether we pay (through taxes) or not, and whether we want it or not!

Public goods cannot be privately and profitably marketed to efficiently service our collective demands for them. A few people might contribute funds for a nonrival good from which exclusion was impossible, but not in amounts sufficient for efficient provision. There is little incentive to reveal your demands for police protection, space exploration, spraying against mosquitos, landscaping along a public highway, or maintaining courts and prisons if you will be taxed accordingly. Why not be a "free rider"? Private firms could not adequately market such services, so government provides a variety of public goods and forces us to pay for them through taxes.

Public provision does not, however, require public production. For example, NASA space probes use equipment built by private firms. Alan Shepard, the first American in space, reported that the last thought that flashed through his mind before his rocket was launched was that it was made of millions of parts, ". . . all built by the lowest bidder."

Income Redistribution

Market mechanisms seem impersonal and yield distributions of income and wealth that many people view as inequitable. Goods are channeled to those who own valuable resources, whether they "need" them or not. Most people are distressed by the suffering of those who live in abject poverty and, if they are modestly prosperous, will donate to charities to help starving children or the unfortunate poor. But private charity may be inadequate to fulfill society's collective desire for equity because "curing poverty" is a public good—I may not donate if your charitable contribution makes me more comfortable when thinking about the poor. This leads to such government programs as welfare and disaster relief.

Stabilizing Income, Prices, and Employment

Market mechanisms may lack strong natural mechanisms that consistently yield full employment without inflation. In fact, wide swings in economic activity, called **business cycles,** may be a natural tendency in a market economy. During business cycles, employment and inflation fluctuate, dislocating workers, firms, and consumers, and generally disrupting our social institutions.

Shortly after World War II, Congress stated some general goals in the Employment Act of 1946:

> *The Congress hereby declares that it is the continuing policy and responsibility of the federal government to . . . promote maximum employment, production, and purchasing power.*

The major tools government uses to try to achieve these macroeconomic goals include variations in taxes, government spending, and the supply of money.

The Scope of Government

Now that you know some reasons for government action in a market economy, we will briefly survey the extent of the public sector. Total government spending on goods and services now tops $800 billion annually—over 20 percent of our national production. When we include transfer payments (Social Security, welfare, and other income payments that are not tied to production), government outlays exceed one third of all spending.

Figure 5 breaks down government spending by its major functions. Nearly half of the 1970 federal budget was devoted to national defense; today that figure is less than one third. During the 1970s, outlays on

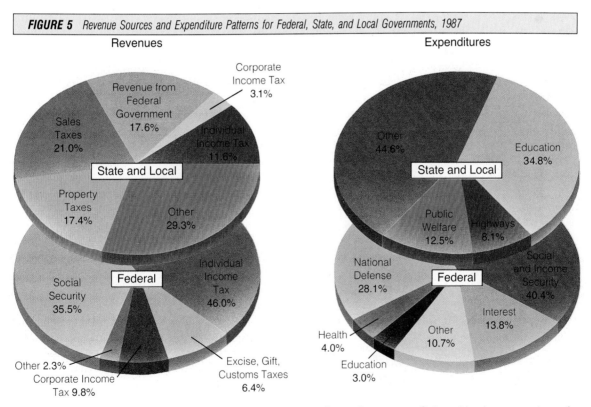

FIGURE 5 *Revenue Sources and Expenditure Patterns for Federal, State, and Local Governments, 1987*

Revenues

Expenditures

State and Local

Revenue from Federal Government 17.6%
Corporate Income Tax 3.1%
Sales Taxes 21.0%
Individual Income Tax 11.6%
Property Taxes 17.4%
Other 29.3%

Federal

Social Security 35.5%
Individual Income Tax 46.0%
Other 2.3%
Corporate Income Tax 9.8%
Excise, Gift, Customs Taxes 6.4%

State and Local

Other 44.6%
Education 34.8%
Public Welfare 12.5%
Highways 8.1%

Federal

National Defense 28.1%
Social and Income Security 40.4%
Interest 13.8%
Other 10.7%
Health 4.0%
Education 3.0%

The federal government relies almost exclusively on income and payroll taxes for revenues. State and local governments, on the other hand, get the bulk of their revenues from property and sales taxes, from user fees, and from the federal government through grants-in-aid. Federal expenditures are focused on those activities that are national in scope (national defense and social security), while state and local expenditures are for services that affect people within limited geographical areas.

Source: *Economic Report of the President,* 1988.

such domestic programs as income security, health, education, natural resources, environmental protection, and energy policy more than absorbed the funds freed by reductions in national defense. The Reagan administration's budgets beginning in 1982 and ending in 1988 may have signaled a reversal of this trend, with renewed emphasis on defense and attempts to slash the growth of welfare and other domestic programs. The "Star Wars" proposal alone is expected to cost over $1 trillion during the next twenty years; this is more than it would cost to replace all existing U.S. schools, streets, and highways.

Federal expenditures tend to focus on activities that have national implications. State and local government spending is directed at services that affect people within limited geographical areas. In contrast to federal outlays, the composition of state and local spending has changed little since the early 1960s, although there has been a relative reduction in highway spending and a rising proportion of outlays for welfare.

Figure 6 also shows that different levels of government rely on different taxes as revenue sources. State and local governments generate roughly two thirds of their revenues from three major sources (a) grants from the federal government, (b) property taxes, and (c) sales taxes. On the other hand, almost 60 percent of federal revenues come from taxes on individual or corporation incomes. When we include the second largest source of federal revenues, Social Security taxes (which are based solely on wage incomes), the figure is over 90 percent. Thus, less than 10 percent of total federal tax revenues rely on sources other than income.

You may have heard our income tax system referred to as *progressive,* which means that the rich pay a greater percentage of their income as taxes than do the poor. There are three basic ways that taxes can be related to income:

1. **Progressive.** A tax is progressive if the percentage tax rate rises as income rises; higher incomes are taxed proportionally higher than lower incomes.

2. **Proportional.** Taxes collected are a fixed percentage of income. The "flat rate" tax proposal would institute a proportional tax.

3. **Regressive.** A tax is regressive when the percentage of income paid as taxes declines as income rises.

The 1986 reform of our federal income tax lowered and flattened tax rates, but it also closed many tax loopholes so that collection is more certain and the resulting pattern of collection is moderately progressive: people with higher incomes tend to pay greater percentages of their incomes as taxes. Social Security taxes totalling roughly 15 percent of the first $50,000 of an individual's wages are collected, and the tax is roughly proportional in the range $0–50,000 of wage income. Fixed-rate sales taxes tend to be regressive because low income individuals commonly spend larger proportions of their income than high income families.

Taxing and spending are only two of the tools that government uses to mold economic activity. Laws and regulations also have very powerful economic effects. Several studies have concluded that compliance with regulation absorbs 5–15 percent of our national income.

In chapter 2 we described some allocative mechanisms people use to resolve economic questions. If the effects of people's choices were perfectly foreseeable and if everyone could as costlessly as possible acquire all the information bearing on every decision, the most useful mechanisms would be fairly obvious. Information is costly and the future, unfortunately, is uncertain. Information for decision making is sought only as long as the benefits expected from acquiring a bit more information exceed the costs. Beyond that point, we as individuals rationally choose to be ignorant. Thus, private decision making is flawed because we are unavoidably somewhat **rationally ignorant** when we choose, and cannot know what the future holds.

One question is whether, in an environment of rational ignorance and pervasive uncertainty, government can make better decisions for us than we would make for ourselves. A part of the answer is that government decision makers also operate in an uncertain environment, and they also have only limited information when they make decisions. There are no perfect mechanisms for decision making. If you were able to vote in the last election, how much did you know about the individual candidates and the important issues? How certain were you about the policies your candidates would support as the future unfolded?

An inequitable distribution of income is one perceived flaw of a market system, and markets tend to be inefficient when firms exercise monopoly power or when property rights are unenforceable or are not clearly specified. At the macroeconomic level, persistent high unemployment, erratic swings of the price level, and unbalanced or sluggish growth may also signal inefficiency.

Much of the rest of this book addresses the operation of a market economy and government policies intended to correct for market failures. This chapter has provided a discussion of the institutions within which the market system operates.

CHAPTER REVIEW: KEY POINTS

1. Households are both consumers of goods and providers of labor and other resources to business. Interactions between business and households are illustrated in *circular flow* models.
2. All household income is spent, saved, or taxed. Three major trends are discernible in U.S. household spending patterns during the past half century:
   a. Consumption expenditures as a percentage of personal income have declined from 90 percent to 80 percent.
   b. Taxes have increased from roughly 3 percent to nearly 14 percent.
   c. Saving has been roughly stable as a percentage of income.
3. Wages and salaries make up approximately three quarters of the income of typical families. During the last two decades, women's rates of participation in the labor force have risen markedly while those of men have fallen slightly. The proportion of families in which both husband and wife are employed has also been climbing.
4. Six businesses out of seven are either *sole proprietorships* or *partnerships,* but *corporations* account for more than 80 percent of all goods and services sold and receive roughly two thirds of all profits in the United States. Compared to corporations, however, sole proprietorships and partnerships are easily formed and less subject to government regulation. The major advantages of corporations are the limited liabilities of stockholders and better access to financial capital markets.
5. An erratic trend towards increased concentration of economic power in America has continued for more than a century—well over half of all manufacturing assets are held by the 200 largest corporations in the United States.
6. Corporate goals of making profits are under attack by people who believe "the new industrial state" is much too powerful, both politically and economically. These critics argue that big business should be "socially responsible."

7. Even though control of much of modern economic life is concentrated in the hands of those who control giant corporations, changing market shares and the growth of various imports are evidence that the processes of competition are still vigorous.
8. Where the price system is incapable of providing certain goods or fails to provide the socially optimal levels, *government* steps in to supplement the private sector in five major ways. It attempts to:
   a. provide a legal, social, and business environment for stable growth;
   b. promote and maintain competitive markets;
   c. redistribute income and wealth equitably;
   d. alter the allocation of resources in an efficient manner where *public goods* or *externalities* are present; and
   e. stabilize income, employment, and prices.
9. If negative externalities (costs) exist, the private market will provide too much of the product and the market price will be too low because full production costs are not being charged to consumers. If positive externalities (benefits) exist, too little of the product will be produced by the private market and the market price will be too high, requiring a government subsidy or government production or provision of the commodity.
10. Once public goods are produced, it is costly to exclude people from their use, and everybody can consume the goods simultaneously with everyone else. The free market will not adequately provide public goods because of the "free rider" problem.
11. Total spending on goods and services by all three levels of government exceeds 20 percent of GNP. State and local governments spend the bulk of their revenues on services that primarily benefit people in their local communities and rely heavily on the property and sales taxes as sources of revenue. Federal government spending is generally aimed at activities that are national in scope. Over 90 percent of federal revenue comes from individual and corporate income taxes plus Social Security and other employment taxes.

QUESTIONS FOR THOUGHT AND DISCUSSION

1. More than 30 million women have entered the labor force since 1970. These women are spending more of their lives working. For example, in 1970, the average 20-year-old woman could expect to spend 21.3 years in paid employment compared with 37.3 years for an average 20-year-old man. By 1985, the average number of working years rose to 27 for typical women and declined to 36.6 for men. During this same period, the earnings gap between men and women narrowed slightly, and the percentage of families with two earners had jumped by over 14 percent. How have these changes affected the following economic activities?
   a. Consumer spending.
   b. Unemployment rates.
   c. Unemployment as a measure of economic hardship.
   d. Productivity growth. (Some commentators argue that the slow growth in productivity of the 1970s was due to large numbers of relatively unskilled women entering the labor market, lowering the overall increase in productivity. Why might this be true?)
   e. Population growth rates.
   f. The demand for such products as:
      (1) day care centers.
      (2) clothes.
      (3) automobiles.
      (4) central city property.
      (5) restaurants.

2. Suppose you were the chief executive officer of a major corporation. Would your primary goal be to maximize profits for stockholders or to maximize your own subjective income via a high salary, friendly subordinates, plush offices, private airplanes, and other "perqs"? What does your answer suggest about the compatibility of maximum corporate profits and the separation of ownership from control? What does this imply for economic efficiency?

3. Since World War II, government transfer payments as percentages of national income have grown sharply, and federal spending on goods and services have fallen relative to state and local spending. What might be some explanations for these changes in patterns of government outlays?

4. Suppose you wanted a measure to estimate the importance of government in the economy over time. Would you use government spending on goods and services alone relative to national income, or would you include transfer payments? Can you think of any way to quantify increases in regulation by government? Are there other dimensions of government activity that should be measured? If so, which ones, and how?

5. Inherent in all policies adopted by political decision makers are some characteristics of public goods. Explain the sense in which the policies themselves are public goods (or public bads).

6. Can you think of ways to induce people to reveal their preferences for certain public goods so that they will not be free riders? Try this for such things as schools, highways, and national defense.

7. "Small firms are less able to comply with stringent government regulations than are large corporations, so regulatory growth has the undesirable effect of strangling competition in our economy." Your reaction?

8. Corporations have traditionally been private institutions that generate profits, create jobs, and accumulate capital—pursuits that Milton Friedman, Nobel Prize winner in economics, thinks they should continue to concentrate upon to promote economic efficiency. Friedman feels that corporations should ignore the "social responsibility" that critics of corporate policies would foist upon them because he sees the job of promoting social goals as belonging to government, not corporate management. These critics, however, want to make corporations accountable to the American public. How might corporations be forced to develop social "consciences"? Would profits and share prices be lower? Who would bear the burden of the changes critics have advocated? Would society benefit? What are the arguments for and against these proposals to make corporations quasi-public institutions?

9. Should most taxes be progressive, proportional, or regressive? Why? Try to use economic reasoning to classify the following current taxes according to whether, as family incomes grow, the proportions of income absorbed by these taxes rise, remain constant, or fall.
   a. Personal income tax.
   b. Corporation income tax.
   c. Social Security tax.
   d. Sales and excise taxes.
   e. Property taxes.
   f. Inheritance taxes.

Macroeconomics

Measuring
Economic Performance

PART 2

High employment, price-level stability, and economic growth are the major macroeconomic goals of all societies. Achieving these goals simultaneously is difficult but not impossible. For example, boosting employment may cause inflation to rise, at least temporarily, while attempts to curb inflationary pressures can push hordes of workers into unemployment lines. We must have reasonably accurate estimates and definitions of such important economic aggregates as employment, inflation, and Gross National Product to discuss these goals, formulate policy, and evaluate the actions of policymakers.

In chapter 6, we investigate how *unemployment* and *inflation* are measured, the shortcomings of these measurement techniques, and the problems policymakers face when using unemployment and inflation as guides to economic policy. We also lay the groundwork for understanding the causes and cures of unemployment and inflation.

One possible cure for excessive rates of both unemployment and inflation is economic growth. Economists attempt to measure economic growth and stagnation by tracing changes over time in the levels of our national income and output. This is the focus of chapter 7. Once you understand the concepts we present in Part 2 you will be ready to begin analyzing macroeconomic theory and policy in greater depth. Over the last two decades, the economy has suffered alternating bouts of high inflation and high unemployment in spite of government's attempts to cure instability. This experience illustrates the major challenge facing policymakers—maintaining steady economic growth.

CHAPTER 6

Unemployment and Inflation

Unemployment and inflation, the major macroeconomic problems of the post-World War II era, have been addressed almost endlessly by politicians, pundits, and editorial writers. Why are so many people concerned about these issues? To answer this question, we must examine what we mean by these terms, how each is measured, and their costs and benefits. (Surprisingly, both offer some benefits.) Only then can we address the questions of how to reduce the level of unemployment and dampen the inflationary pressures that have built up over the past quarter century.

Aggregate Demand and Aggregate Supply

The demand and supply analysis from chapter 4 provides a broad framework useful in explaining not only movements of the prices and quantities of individual goods, but also the movements of broad aggre-

gates such as the price level and national income. The foundations of macroeconomic Aggregate Demand and Aggregate Supply curves (illustrated in Figures 1 and 2) differ from the microeconomic bases of demands and supplies for particular goods.

As the aggregate price level falls, the value of your wealth may increase. Assets such as stocks, bonds, cash, and checking account balances will now buy more; thus, the Aggregate Demand curve slopes downward. The positive slope of the Aggregate Supply curve reflects the fact that as prices rise, cost increases often lag. Delayed cost increases cause rising profits that encourage firms to produce more. More detailed foundations for these curves await you in chapter 15, but for now, examining shifts in Aggregate Demand and Supply curves provides some immediate insights into a number of problems faced by macroeconomic policymakers.

Prior to World War II, all American depressions and recessions were periods when output, employment, and the price level all declined. Note that in

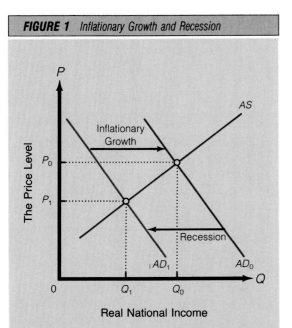

FIGURE 1 Inflationary Growth and Recession

Unemployment, income, and the price level all fall if Aggregate Demand shrinks from AD_0 to AD_1, while Aggregate Supply is stable, and society experiences the hardship of recession. Expansion of Aggregate Demand AD_1 to AD_0, on the other hand, precipitates booming employment and real growth of income accompanied by inflationary pressure.

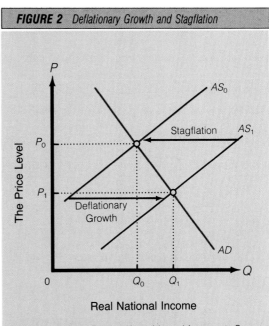

FIGURE 2 Deflationary Growth and Stagflation

When Aggregate Demand is stable and Aggregate Supply increases, the economy experiences deflationary growth as real output rises but prices fall. When Aggregate Supply declines, the economy is hit simultaneously with the twin evils of reduced employment and real output (or higher unemployment) plus inflation. This has been named *stagflation*.

Figure 1, if the Aggregate Demand curve falls from AD_0 to AD_1, the price level and the level of real national income (Q) both decline. Employment is closely tied to national output, so employment also falls and unemployment rates tend to rise. Thus, one explanation for recessions or depressions is a decline in the Aggregate Demand for goods and services.

If Aggregate Demand rises from AD_1 to AD_0, both the price level and real output rise; employment also rises, and all else equal, unemployment falls. Thus, periods such as the 1960s when mild inflation was accompanied by real economic growth and rising employment might be explained as times when Aggregate Demand grows relative to Aggregate Supply.

The period from roughly 1870–1895 was marked by substantial real economic growth, but marred by occasional minor financial crises. Over the same interval, the price level fell fairly consistently. What

movements of Aggregate Demand and Supply are consistent with these changes in prices and outputs? In Figure 2, increases in Aggregate Supply from AS_0 to AS_1 yield a lower price level and a higher level of national income. Thus, growth in Aggregate Supply relative to Aggregate Demand allows both real national income and employment to rise while the price level falls.

During the 1970s, real output grew very slowly; on the average, unemployment rates rose, while the United States experienced its highest rates of fairly consistent inflation since Revolutionary War days. Although the economy as a whole grew, the growth in Aggregate Supply remained below that of Aggregate Demand; the shift from AS_1 to AS_0 in Figure 2 reflects this relative movement. Thus, declines (or slower growth rates) in Aggregate Supply relative to Aggregate Demand may account for poor overall economic performance during the late 1970s and early 1980s.

This Aggregate Demand and Supply framework allows us to illustrate the major goals of macroeconomic policy—full employment, price stability, and economic growth. But before we discuss goals and policy options in detail, we need to examine how both unemployment and inflation are measured.

Unemployment

Friday began like any other morning. The shrill beep-beep-beep of the alarm, the steam rising from the shower, the smell of brewing coffee. Driving to the office provided the usual irritations. Morning conferences and activities seemed standard fare, with most thoughts focused on the upcoming weekend's activities. At 2:00 P.M., the bomb dropped. The plant manager announced that the firm lost a major contract. Layoffs would affect not only assembly-line workers this time but executives as well. Everything was ready; two-weeks' severance pay and accrued vacation were in the final check. Firm handshakes accompanied condolences and sincere wishes for the best of luck. Then, out the door, carrying a cardboard box full of personal effects. The trip home was a nightmare. "My skills are strong; some competitors may need my expertise. But are they hiring now? News reports have been talking recession lately. How will the mortgage be paid? Will I have to move to find work?" The happily anticipated weekend disintegrated into pure gloom.

Every worker faces the possibility of joblessness and most have experienced it at one time or another. Hardships caused by extended periods of massive unemployment led to the Employment Act of 1946, which specified *maintaining maximum employment* as one government goal. Weighing achievement of this goal usually begins with the overall unemployment rate—a statistic heard regularly on the nightly news. But this single measure is only a crude guide to policy because unemployment occurs for several reasons. Each form has different implications for government policies. Before examining the different types of unemployment, however, we must discover who the unemployed are.

The Concept of Unemployment

There are roughly 240 million Americans, of whom about half are in the labor force. Does this mean that roughly half of all Americans are unemployed? Hardly. In fact, if you think that housewives are *not* work-

ing, a short stint on the "home front"—up to your elbows in dish suds, a screaming 2-year-old tugging at your leg, the phone and doorbell both ringing—will quickly change your mind. Adults can elect to be, or not be, members of the labor force. People can be classified as either "employed" or "unemployed" only if they choose to be in the labor force.

Conceptually, **unemployment** *occurs when people are able to work and would willingly accept the prevailing wage paid to someone with their skills but either cannot find or have not yet secured suitable employment.*

Voluntary Versus Involuntary Unemployment

Unemployment can be viewed as either voluntary or involuntary. **Voluntary unemployment** occurs when people could find work quickly but choose to look for what they view as better jobs in terms of pay, location, or working conditions. For example, you would be voluntarily unemployed if you turned down a night job that required a 50-mile round trip each work shift, choosing instead to look for 9-to-5 work or a position closer to your home.

Some people believe that almost all unemployment is voluntary: If you really want a job and are willing to work for "what you're worth," you can find work almost immediately. I am willing to hire you to paint my home, mow my lawn, or babysit as long as you accept a wage equal to what these activities are worth to me. My neighbor would do the same. Hence, if you are unemployed for more than a few hours, it *must* be voluntary.

The counterargument is that people should not be forced to accept just any job. If you are willing to work but there are no jobs presently available at a wage rate acceptable and suitable for a person with your training and skills, you are **involuntarily unemployed.** Human worth is involved, and people should have jobs that do not underemploy their skills. Moreover, this argument continues, there are simply times and places where business conditions are so bad that no jobs are available.

We cannot tell you which position is correct. A precise measure of willingness to work at prevailing wages is impossible, so any measure of involuntary unemployment is only an educated guess. In any event, published unemployment data rely on surveys of people 16 years of age or older and use criteria only loosely related to our conceptual definition of unemployment.

Measuring Unemployment

The U.S. Department of Labor uses the following definitions to classify people as employed, unemployed, and in or out of the labor force.

Employed persons include (*a*) all civilians who worked for pay any time during the week which includes the twelfth day of the month or who worked unpaid for fifteen hours or more in a family-operated enterprise and (*b*) those who were temporarily absent from their regular jobs because of illness, vacation, industrial dispute, or similar reasons. Members of the Armed Forces stationed in the United States are also included in the employed total. Persons working at more than one job are counted only in the job at which they worked the greatest number of hours.

Unemployed persons are those who did not work during the survey week but were available for work except for temporary illness and who had looked for jobs within the preceding four weeks. Persons who did not look for work because they were on layoff or waiting to start new jobs within the next thirty days are also counted among the unemployed.

> The **labor force** consists of all employed or unemployed civilians plus members of the Armed Forces stationed in the United States.

The overall *unemployment rate* represents the number unemployed as a percent of the labor force, including the Armed Forces. The unemployment rate for all civilian workers represents the number unemployed as a percent of the civilian labor force. A *labor force participation rate* is the proportion of a specific population group that is in the labor force. The *employment-population ratio* is total employment as a percent of the population.[1]

Our major source of unemployment statistics in the United States is a monthly Department of Labor survey of about 60,000 households. The survey

(outlined in Focus 1) asks detailed questions to determine the labor force status of each adult family member. This large sample ensures that the statistics collected are reasonably good. Among the reasons for inaccuracy are discouraged workers and dishonest nonworkers.

Flaws in Unemployment Statistics

Some people are so pessimistic about their job prospects that they do not look for work, although they would like jobs. These *discouraged workers* are not counted among the unemployed but should be, under the economic definition of unemployment. Thus, published statistics may understate true unemployment. Figure 3 shows that the discouraged worker syndrome is most pronounced during economic downturns, when many people perceive that job openings are few and far between.

On the other hand, unemployment statistics may be overstated because of the incentives embedded in our unemployment compensation system. Some people have no intention of taking a job, but report that they are available for work so that they can draw unemployment benefits.

The discouraged worker and *dishonest nonworker* syndromes each cause inaccuracy in unemployment statistics, but in opposite directions. Which effect is stronger is a source of continuing debate.

The Sources of Unemployment

There are five major types of unemployment: frictional, structural, seasonal, cyclical, and induced. These are related to the major forces generating unemployment. Each type poses different problems for government policy.

Frictional Unemployment   People enter or reenter the work force, are fired or permanently laid off, or voluntarily quit one position to look for another. Information about job openings and applicants is far from perfect, and mobility (e.g., relocating to get a job) is often quite costly. It takes time for workers to move between jobs and match their skills with the work requirements of business. Finding job openings, interviewing, processing applications, and making hiring decisions all absorb resources. All these activities involve transaction costs, which give rise to

---

1. United States Department of Labor, *Monthly Labor Review*, numerous issues.

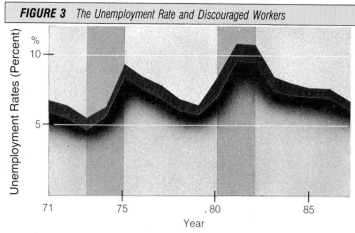

FIGURE 3 *The Unemployment Rate and Discouraged Workers*

Unemployment Rate + Discouraged Workers

Civilian Unemployment Rate

This graph indicates how much failure to include discouraged workers among the unemployed causes the measured unemployment to be understated. More workers become despondent and cease looking for a job during economic downturns. In a similar fashion, dishonest nonworkers may cause the measured unemployment rate to be overstated. Obtaining an accurate count of both discouraged workers and dishonest nonworkers is extremely difficult.

Source: U.S. Department of Labor, Bureau of Labor Statistics, *Handbook of Labor Statistics*, 1985, and *Monthly Labor Review*; U.S. Department of Commerce, *Statistical Abstract of the United States*, 1988; and *Economic Report of the President*, 1988. Updated by authors.

frictional unemployment, an unavoidable by-product of normal economic activity.

There is considerable **turnover** (the term given to workers changing jobs) among both the employed and unemployed. For example, employment in 1988 averaged more than 120 million persons per month, but about 130 million different persons worked at some time during the year. While unemployment averaged around 7 million per month, nearly 25 million people experienced unemployment at some time during those 12 months.

Structural Unemployment *Structural unemployment* occurs when a worker's skills do not mesh with the requirements of virtually any job opening. Some individuals are unable to find work during even the best of times. Their unemployment may be of long duration for a variety of reasons.

First, structural change may displace some workers. For example, a major technological innovation may make certain skills obsolete. Many typesetters found themselves jobless with the introduction of computerized typesetting equipment that does the same job with fewer workers and at less cost. Today, desktop publishing is replacing traditional paste-up

and layout work. Some economists have argued that blue-collar occupations in our primary industries are drying up, which means that unemployment rates for blue-collar workers throughout the 1990s may be higher than in earlier times.

Second, some people have acquired few, if any, job skills. Examples include many high school dropouts, most ex-convicts, and some housewives who decide to work after their children leave home. Firms may find it unprofitable to hire and train workers if they expect their training costs to exceed the benefits to the firm. This is especially a problem if employees commonly find better jobs once trained.

Seasonal Unemployment Some activities are inherently seasonal. For example, from the demand side, weather often determines patterns of employment in agriculture and the construction industry. Department store Santa Clauses may only work a few weeks annually. Beach towns and ski resorts also experience seasonal swings in employment. Seasonal influences emerge on the supply side as well, especially in teenage labor markets. Students' summer vacations are the major cause of seasonality in this market. Teenage unemployment rises in June and

Determining Who Is Unemployed

The unemployment rate is not only a function of how the term is defined but how the Department of Labor questionnaire is administered as well. The interview questions are designed to elicit the most accurate picture of each person's labor force activities. The survey asks one adult to report for all members of the household who are over age 16. The major questions that determine one's employment status are:

1. What was _____ doing most of last week—working, keeping house, going to school, or something else?

For everyone not working and not reported unable to work because of a physical or mental disability, the next question is:

2. Did _____ do any work at all last week, not counting work around the house?

For those who say no, the next question is:

3. Did _____ have a job or business from which _____ was temporarily absent or on layoff last week?

For those who say yes, the next question is:

4. Why was _____ absent from work last week?

If the response to this question indicates that the person is waiting for a new job to begin within thirty days or awaiting recall from layoff, he or she is counted as unemployed. For those who are reported as having no job or business from which they were absent, the next question is:

5. Has _____ been looking for work during the last four weeks?

For those who say yes, the next question is:

6. What has _____ been doing during the last four weeks to find work?

If a specific activity, such as applying directly to an employer, placing or answering ads, registering with either a public or private employment agency, being on a union or professional roll, or checking with friends and relatives is mentioned, the following question is asked:

7. Is there any reason why _____ could not take a job last week?

If there is not a reason, except temporary illness, that the person could not take a job, he or she is considered to be not only looking but also available for work, and he or she is counted as unemployed.

falls in September. These and many other published economic statistics are seasonally adjusted to make the figures comparable over the year.

Cyclical Unemployment   Unemployment resulting from a general business recession is called *cyclical unemployment* because it coincides with downturns in business cycles. As an economy gains momentum, employment and output increase. When output falls, employment and output do too. During a recession, business expansions decline, companies close, and some face bankruptcy. These changes throw people out of work and increase overall rates of unemployment. Figure 4 shows tremendous variations in rates of joblessness over the past century. Most of these swings reflect cyclical unemployment. Reducing this component of unemployment is a major focus of government fiscal and monetary policies.

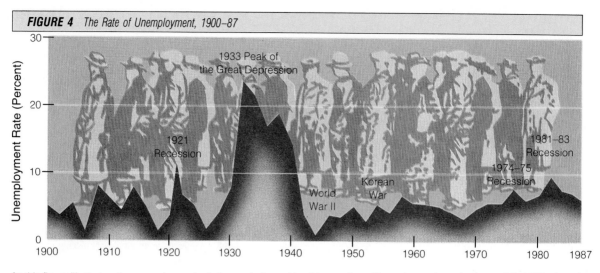

FIGURE 4 The Rate of Unemployment, 1900–87

1933 Peak of
the Great Depression

1921
Recession

1981–83
Recession

1974–75
Recession

World
War II

Korean
War

As this figure illustrates, the unemployment rate has varied considerably over time. Unemployment reached a peak in 1933 when al-most one in four was out of work. Unemployment rtaes dropped to 1.2 percent, an all-time low, during World War II.

Source: 1900–28 derived from Stanley Lebergott, *Manpower in Economic Growth* (New York: McGraw-Hill Book Co., 1964); 1929–87 derived from the Bureau of Labor Statistics and *Economic Report of the President*, 1988.

Not all groups of workers are affected in the same way by a cyclical downturn. Table 1 shows unemployment rates for specific groups during selected periods of high and low employment. Cyclical swings are far less severe in the service sector of our economy than in construction and manufacturing. Professional and technical workers suffer only moderate unemployment compared to blue-collar, service, manufacturing, and construction workers.

Induced Unemployment Finally, some unemployment is induced by certain government policies. The minimum-wage law, for example, limits job opportunities for unskilled and inexperienced workers by overpricing their labor. Unemployment compensation also provides an incentive for people who sincerely desire work to turn down some offers of employment in the hope that, if they keep looking, they will find the perfect jobs. Laws requiring wages

TABLE 1 Percentage of Unemployment by Industry and Occupation (Selected Periods of High and Low Unemployment)

	(1973) Peak Low Unemployment	(1975) Trough High Unemployment	(1981) Peak Low Unemployment	(1982) Trough High Unemployment
Total unemployment	4.9	8.5	7.6	9.8
Professional and technical	2.2	3.2	2.8	3.3
Government	2.7	4.1	4.7	4.9
Blue-collar	6.2	14.7	12.2	17.7
Manufacturing	4.4	10.9	8.3	12.3
Service	5.8	8.6	8.9	10.6
Construction	8.9	18.0	15.6	20.0

Source: U.S. Department of Labor, *Monthly Labor Review*, 1988.

at the union scale on government contract work are another hindrance to full employment—they leave workers unemployed who would be willing to work for less on government contracts.

The Costs and Benefits of Unemployment

Unemployment imposes costs on all of us. Those out of work typically receive unemployment compensation, which reduces their individual burdens from lost wages, but spreads the cost across all workers and employers through unemployment compensation taxes. The aggregate costs of unemployment fall into two categories: lost income and social costs.

Losses in Aggregate Income

The *lost-income costs of unemployment* consist of the value of the output the unemployed individuals could have produced. These costs are not trivial. The recession of 1981–83 has been estimated to have cost nearly $600 billion in lost national income—almost 15 percent of potential annual Gross National Product at that time. Even if the unemployed are partially buffered from losses of income by unemployment compensation, society as a whole suffers because production falls when the jobless rate soars.

Social Costs of Unemployment

The *social and psychic costs of unemployment* may be even more tragic than the financial losses. Table 1 shows that the burdens of unemployment and recessions are not spread equally. Dry statistics sometimes cloud our view of the people behind the numbers. Consider the memories of a woman who was a college student during the Great Depression:

> *When I attended Berkeley in 1936 so many of the kids had actually lost their fathers. They had wandered off in disgrace because they couldn't support their families. Other fathers had killed themselves, so the family could have the insurance. Families had totally broken down. Each father took it as his personal failure . . . so they killed themselves.*
> *It was still the Depression. There were kids who didn't have a place to sleep, huddling under bridges*

on the campus. I had a scholarship, but there were times when I didn't have food. The meals were often three candy bars.[2]

Extended unemployment places tremendous psychological pressure on family structures. Families may plunge deeply into debt after exhausting most of their assets, irrevocably changing their children's futures. Plans for college can go up in smoke. Teenagers experience especially high unemployment rates, and some may acquire criminal records. Table 2 provides estimates of some human costs of unemployment. The shocks imposed by severe long-term unemployment are among the major reasons that the Employment Act of 1946 focused on promoting full employment.

In 1960, both spouses worked full time in only one quarter of all families; today, over 50 percent have two earners. In 1988, in two thirds of all households where the husband was unemployed, another family member held a full-time job. These changes in employment patterns, along with improved unemployment compensation benefits, have reduced the desperation associated with unemployment.

Benefits from Unemployment

The bad press unemployment receives may make it hard to believe that there actually are benefits from some types of unemployment. These break down into allocative benefits and disciplinary benefits.

Allocative Benefits A primary benefit of unemployment is that it is easier for unemployed workers to search for new employment than it is for workers who are holding full-time jobs. At the same time, a pool of unemployed labor affords firms the opportunity to interview more potential employees than would be the case if jobless rates were zero. This process, whereby the unemployed search for work while employers search for suitable help, can be viewed as an *investment in information*. Thus, unemployment yields *allocative benefits* by permitting better match-ups between workers and jobs; better information reduces transaction costs and improves our economy's overall efficiency.

---

2. Studs Terkel, *Working: People Talk About What They Do All Day & How They Feel About What They Do* (New York: Pantheon Books Inc., 1974).

TABLE 2 *Estimates of the Total Effects of a 1 Percent Change in Unemployment Rates Sustained Over a 6-Year Period on the Incidence of Social Trauma*

Measures of Social Trauma	Incidence of Death Related to a 1 Percent Increase in Unemployment (Based on 1980 Population)
Total mortality	41,088
Whites	
Males	13,769
Females	18,418
Nonwhites	
Males	4,266
Females	4,635
Cardiovascular mortality	22,547
Cirrhosis of liver mortality	1,025
Homicide	722
State mental hospital	
First admissions	4,709
Males	3,407
Females	1,302
State prison admissions	3,720

Source: M. Harvey Brenner, "Influence of the Social Environment on Psychopathology: The Historical Perspective," in *Stress and Mental Disorder*, ed., James E. Barrett (New York: Raven Press, 1979).
Note: Estimates represent updates to the 1980 population, as calculated by the authors.

Disciplinary Benefits We all know people who overestimate the worth of their own work and who consequently make demands for wages, vacations, coffee breaks, and other perquisites that far exceed the value of their contributions. There are also workers who do not pull their own weight. Some economists view the possibility of widespread layoffs as a curb to excessive demands for wages and fringe benefits. Threats of unemployment may also reduce "goldbricking" and may be good work incentives for people who respond better to "sticks" than to "carrots." These are the *disciplinary benefits* to firms (and consumers) from having some slack in labor markets. The workers affected naturally do not view pressures for greater work discipline as beneficial.

We have surveyed various aspects of the unemployment problem. Accurate measurement of unemployment is difficult, but it is essential as a guide to macroeconomic policy. The size of the various categories of unemployment help to determine which macro policies will be effective. Finally, keeping unemployment low is a major goal because high unemployment carries high social and economic costs. Now we are ready to take a look at the other great macroeconomic problem—inflation.

Inflation

Whip inflation now.
> —President Gerald Ford, 1975
> (Lost Re-election Bid in 1976)

Inflation is Public Enemy #1.
> —President Jimmy Carter, 1977
> (Lost Re-election Bid in 1980)

Inflation is America's most pressing economic problem.
> —President Ronald Reagan, 1981
> (Won Re-election Bid in 1984)

Beating inflation may be a bit like spanking a child—it hurts you more than it does the child. Politicians have railed against the evils of inflation ever since the Roman Emperor Diocletian tried to combat inflation with price controls (laws prohibiting inflation). In the United States, the political battle against inflation has been on a front burner since World War II, but until the 1980s, each passing decade yielded a higher average rate of price increases.

Some observers think that inflation, like the weather, is something that everyone talks about but that no one can do anything about. They cite failures to achieve political solutions to inflation as evidence that attempts to control it are futile. Most economists view these failures as proof that effective anti-inflationary policies are very costly, either politically—for those who have the power to enact such policies—or economically. The benefits from dampening inflationary trends in our economy may be less than the political costs or the costs in terms of potential damage to the economy.

The Reagan administration's policies reduced inflation but temporarily threw the economy into a severe slump (1981–83). By 1988, unemployment rates had recovered to the levels of the late 1970s, with only modest inflationary pressures. Was defusing inflation worth the national income lost because of this effort? Before we deal with the costs and benefits of inflation, we need to specify what we mean by inflation and how it is measured; we also need to survey some of its possible causes.

The Concept of Inflation

Most people view increases in any of the prices they pay for goods or services as inflationary. For the purpose of macroeconomic analysis, we are concerned with changes in the level of *absolute* prices because these changes represent inflation or deflation.

> **Inflation** *occurs when the average level of prices rises, while* **deflation** *occurs when prices fall on the average.*

An increase in the price of a single good is not necessarily inflationary. For example, a hike in the price of football tickets is not inflationary if it is offset by declines in the prices of domestic wine or long-distance phone calls. Only when the average overall price level rises do we actually have inflation.

Not all economists, however, accept this definition. Some argue that one-shot jumps in average prices should not be viewed as inflation; only continuous and prolonged increases in the price level should be termed inflationary. But even one-shot general price hikes take some time, so it is often hard to distinguish between *continuing* inflation and *one-shot* increases in average prices.

Price Index Numbers

If the prices of houses, straw hats, and candy bars rise while the prices of sweaters, juke boxes, and gasoline fall, how can we tell whether or not we have experienced inflation? Answering this question systematically requires that we deal with price indices. Even the most casual readers of newspapers and magazines frequently encounter indices of one kind or another.

> **Index numbers** *summarize what happens over time to prices (inflation or deflation), productivity, labor market conditions, new construction, or some agglomeration of other items.*

Index numbers compress, sharpen, and simplify information. The ability to understand and interpret these statistics is essential to understanding economic changes. We will begin with a discussion of index numbers and then proceed to the three major indices published as measures of inflation.

An index is a series of numbers, calculated as:

$$\frac{\textbf{value of variable in current period}}{\textbf{value of variable in base period}} \times \textbf{100.}$$

Suppose that you wanted to develop an index for job opportunities in your community. You might count the number of help-wanted ads reported in your local newspaper each month. Then you would need to determine a base period against which all other periods will be compared. Suppose January 1988 was the base period, and 38,510 help-wanted ads appeared in your newspaper over the month. During February 1989, you count 47,230 ads. The February 1989 index of job opportunities (as measured by the number of help-wanted advertisements) would be

$$\frac{47,230}{38,510} \times 100 = 122.6.$$

Looking at the index for February 1989, you can see that job opportunities in the community during February are estimated to be 122.6 percent of those available during January 1988, which indicates that job opportunities have grown 22.6 percent. Interpreting change is much simpler using index numbers than using the original (raw) numbers. Notice that the value of the index for the base period is 100 $[(38,510/38,510) \times 100 = 100]$.

As a track record developed for the job opening index, you might notice that it tends to rise in November and December, reflecting Christmas employment, and to fall each spring. This phenomenon is termed *seasonality* in the data, and refers to those changes that regularly occur over the year. Most indices are seasonally adjusted to show comparable data over time.

With this discussion in mind, we will now examine the three principal measures of inflation (*a*) the Consumer Price Index (*CPI*); (*b*) the Producer Price Index (*PPI*); and (*c*) the Gross National Product Deflator (GNP Deflator).

Measuring Consumer Prices (CPI)

The most widely known of the price indices computed by the Department of Labor is the Consumer Price Index (*CPI*).

> The **Consumer Price Index** *is a statistical measure of changes, over time, in the prices of the goods purchased by typical consumers.*

Revised in 1987, the *CPI* is based on buying patterns for over 80 percent of all households. The *CPI* measures changes in consumer purchasing power by tracking changes in what a sample "market basket" costs over time. This market basket includes most major expenditure categories such as food, housing, apparel, and transportation.

Consumer expenditure surveys help keep the *CPI* up-to-date when consumer patterns change over the years. Each year the Bureau of Labor Statistics (BLS) samples thousands of households in over 1,000 marketing areas to determine typical spending patterns. The 1982–84 Consumer Expenditure Surveys provide information about the relative importance of different categories of goods. The information is used to weight various components of the *CPI*. For example, if typical families spend twice as much on electricity as on natural gas, the weight assigned to electricity rates will be twice that of the weight for natural gas prices.

The prices of over 600 different products and services are sampled each month in nearly 100 different markets. These BLS samples focus on consumer products that make up the bulk of sales at the most popular stores. Table 3 summarizes the methods currently used by the Bureau of Labor Statistics to compile the *CPI*.

How the CPI Is Used

The *CPI* is used to estimate changes in the purchasing power of money and as an escalator in contracts calling for future payments of money. Unfortunately, there are some inherent problems in using the *CPI* or, for that matter, with any other index used for diagnosing the economy and prescribing policy.

Moving from Nominal to Real Values Most values of economic variables are presented in their current dollar, or nominal, values. The **nominal** (or *monetary*) **value** is the dollar amount you receive or pay.

TABLE 3 Summary of the Procedures and Methods Used to Compute the CPI	
Item	**Methods and Procedures**
Title	1. Consumer Price Index for All Urban Consumers (CPI-U) 2. Consumer Price Index for Urban Wage Earners and Clerical Workers (Revised Series) (CPI-W)
Population covered	CPI-U—All urban residents, including salaried workers, self-employed workers, retirees, unemployed persons, and urban wage earners. CPI-W—Urban wage earner and clerical worker families and single individuals living alone. At least one family member must be employed for 37 weeks or more during the year in wage or clerical worker occupations.
Geographic coverage	278 urban areas selected to represent all urban places in the United States, including Alaska and Hawaii.
Sample of items priced	Consumer Expenditure Survey (1982–84) data classified into 68 expenditure classes covering roughly 650 goods.
Sample of stores	A sample of retail stores and other outlets was selected from the results of a Point-of-Purchase Survey covering about 23,000 families across the country.
Number of price quotations obtained	About 650,000 food prices per year. About 70,000 rent charges per year. About 350,000 quotations per year for items other than food, rent, and property taxes. About 28,000 property tax quotations per year.

For example, suppose that your current income is $20,000 annually. How does the purchasing power of that nominal income compare with your $10,000 family income of 10 years ago? Your real income (purchasing power) is your current income ($Y_{current}$) adjusted for inflation or deflation. Real income (Y_{real}) is computed using the following formula:

$$Y_{real} = \frac{Y_{current}}{CPI/100}.$$

You could buy given amounts of goods and services from a family income of $10,000 in 1978. Suppose that by 1988 your income rose to $20,000 but that over the same period all prices in the economy also doubled. Would you be better or worse off? Since all prices doubled, it would take twice as much money in 1988 to buy the same goods that you bought in 1978. Thus, your real income in 1988 would still be $10,000, with 1978 as the base year.

Using the formula, the 1988 CPI would be 200 in terms of 1978 as the base year (prices are assumed to have doubled and 100 is the index for the base year). Thus, compute real 1988 income by dividing your 1988 income by 1 percent of the *CPI* ($20,000/2.00 = $10,000). Table 4 illustrates this conversion process for per capita income during selected years since 1929.

Just as we have adjusted nominal income to account for changes in the price level, we can adjust other nominal variables to see how relative prices are changing. This process is called **deflating.** The general formula for deflating any variable is:

$$\text{real value} = \frac{\text{nominal variable in dollars}}{\text{price index}/100}.$$

For example, the price of oil rose from roughly $3 per barrel in 1967 to around $20 in 1988. How large was the increase in real oil prices? The consumer price index (based on 1967 prices) rose to roughly 300. Therefore, the real 1988 cost of oil (in 1967 prices) was $20/3.00, or around $6.67 per barrel. This means that the relative price (real cost) of oil more than doubled in this 21-year period while the nominal price rose nearly seven times. You can use similar computations to deflate housing prices, wages, or any other nominal variables.

CPI *as an Income/Payment Escalator* The payments received by nearly half of our population are directly tied to the *CPI*. For example, if a union wage contract has an escalator clause, wages and monetary fringe benefits rise by roughly the same percentage that the *CPI* increases. Escalator clauses providing insurance against losses in purchasing power due to inflation are included in collective bargaining contracts covering more than 8.5 million workers. Our income tax system, many pension plans, Social Security retirement benefits, and various welfare payments are also tied to the *CPI* in one way or another.

CPI *as an Economic Indicator* The *CPI* is a major yardstick by which the success of economic policy is measured. Every president since George Washington has promised price level stability. Macroeconomic

Year	Aggregate Monetary Income ($ Billions)	Population (Millions)	Per Capita Money Income (Dollars)	CPI (1967 = 100)	Real per Capita Income (Deflated)
1929	$ 84.9	121.8	$ 697	51.3	$1,359
1933	46.9	124.8	376	38.8	969
1940	77.8	132.6	587	42.0	1,398
1950	226.1	152.3	1,485	72.1	2,060
1960	399.7	180.7	2,212	88.7	2,494
1970	801.3	204.9	3,911	116.3	3,363
1980	2,160.0	222.3	9,717	246.8	3,937
1987	3,635.9	243.8	14,913	340.4	4,381

TABLE 4 *Converting Nominal Income (Before Taxes) to Real Annual Income*

Sources: *Statistical Abstract*, 1987; *Economic Report of the President*, 1988.

policymakers keep a close watch on movements in price indices for indications of their success in controlling inflation. Attempts to shrink the double-digit inflation rates of the mid-1970s and early 1980s were successful by 1983, but led to high unemployment that only recovered to moderate rates in 1986. As inflation seemed to rise and become more persistent, Americans paid more attention to the Consumer Price Index.

Problems with the CPI Estimating changes in consumer prices poses major conceptual and statistical problems for the Bureau of Labor Statistics. How can the BLS adjust the *CPI* to accurately reflect changes in (*a*) consumption patterns, (*b*) the availability of new products, (*c*) the qualities of older goods, and (*d*) the prices of major assets such as homes, which some families bought earlier at lower prices, while others must pay higher current prices if they buy now?

The *CPI* is thoroughly revised about once a decade, with relatively constant consumption patterns being assumed to compute the *CPI* between revisions. The failure of the fixed representative market basket to reflect changes in typical buying patterns reduces the accuracy of the *CPI*. Inflation tends to be overstated because consumers purchase more goods whose prices rise most slowly and to cut back on items where prices rise most rapidly. For example, between 1972 and 1980, average energy prices rose 218 percent, but consumer outlays for energy only rose 140 percent.

To compensate for this problem, the BLS began annual Consumer Expenditure Surveys in 1986 to keep up with changing consumption patterns. Area and item samples are now updated regularly instead of once a decade as was done in the past. Annual surveys and phased updating help to eliminate the fixed market basket limitations of the *CPI*.

Changes in quality may also affect the accuracy of the *CPI*. Quality changes in products *should not* cause changes in the price index because the index ideally measures consumers' costs of purchasing a *constant* market basket. The *CPI* will overstate inflation if prices rise to reflect greater quality and this changing quality is ignored. Suppose, for example, that the movies of 1990 are much better than the movies of 1989. If ticket prices rise only because better production quality costs more money, then the *CPI* might still show some inflation because of these hikes. Ideally, a dollar measure would be obtained

because consumers value the improvement in the quality of products; these values would then be deducted from the increase in price. Similarly, deteriorating quality may result in an understatement of inflation. Inflation occurs even though money prices stay constant, as when, say, the tastiness of restaurant meals declines because soybeans are substituted for ground beef in hamburgers.

Direct measurements of the values consumers place on quality changes are unobtainable, however, so the Bureau uses an indirect method—it estimates the costs of quality changes. When figures are available, the cost differences between new and old features are treated as proxies for the real values of quality changes. This approach poses many problems. For example, does the cost of installing pollution control equipment on cars represent an increase in the quality of an automobile? Maybe what we are actually buying is cleaner air.

Another problem of measuring inflation is that some asset owners gain from higher prices. Thus, if inflationary pressures cause both wages and housing prices to rise, this does not mean that current homeowners who have fixed mortgage payments pay more for housing services. In fact, after adjusting for inflation, "real" mortgage payments fall. For this reason, in 1981 the BLS changed the way the *CPI* measures housing costs. Previously, the Bureau measured the costs of acquiring a house as reflected in the monthly payment, rather than the price of "housing services" consumed. As a result, when mortgage interest rates rose or fell and changed typical monthly payments, the *CPI* reflected these changes as if all families bought new houses each month. The new approach of the BLS is to estimate rental values to represent the cost of shelter. These changes permit the *CPI* to more truly reflect inflation for established American households. Despite these problems, the *CPI* is a reasonable estimate of changes in consumer prices.

Other Price Indices

The *CPI* only tracks changes in the prices consumers pay. Other prices are important as well.

Producer Price Index (PPI) The **Producer Price Index (*PPI*)** measures average price changes for over 2,800 primary products. The *PPI* is a general purpose index for nonretail markets; it covers such intermediate goods as flour, steel, rubber, computers, and office supplies. Most prices used to compute this index are the wholesale selling prices of representative producers, but some prices come from specialized markets such as commodity exchanges. The prices used for imported products (for example, coffee beans) are the prices paid by the original importer (for example, Folger's).

The GNP Implicit Deflator Adjusting Gross National Product (total output in the economy) for price changes is done with an index called the **GNP Deflator.** (We deal with GNP accounting in the next chapter.) The GNP Deflator is based on components drawn from other price indices—primarily the *CPI* and *PPI.* For example, each component of consumer spending is adjusted using the appropriate data from the Consumer Price Index. Business expenditures for such items as capital equipment or raw materials are deflated using the appropriate parts of the Producer Price Index. Components of other indices are used to deflate the prices of items not included in the *CPI* or the *PPI,* such as government services, construction, and agricultural production.

The History of U.S. Inflation

Between 1929 and 1933 prices fell by an average of one-third while wages dropped by roughly one-fourth, so wages after adjustment for deflation actually *rose.* It sounds as though workers gained during this period. Remember, however, that the Great Depression began in 1929. By 1933, the unemployment rate was roughly 25 percent, and average working-class families were not doing well. There have been other periods when we experienced deflation, as you can see in Figure 5. For example, prices fell on average by roughly 40 percent between 1870 and 1895.

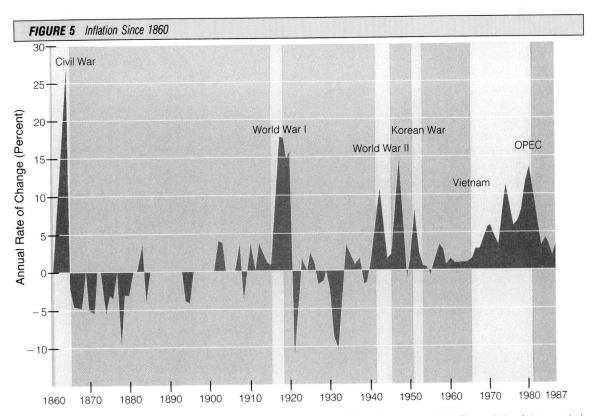

FIGURE 5 *Inflation Since 1860*

This figure highlights the various inflationary periods experienced by the United States since 1860. The majority of these periods have occurred during extended military hostilities; however, although the 1970s and early 1980s were relatively peaceful, the price level crept up briskly.

Source: U.S. Department of Labor, Bureau of Labor Statistics, 1988.

Before we got used to continually creeping inflation in the 1970s, an annual inflation rate of 4 percent seemed outrageous. Nevertheless, Americans became accustomed to annual inflation rates ranging from 6 percent to 14 percent during the 1970s. Today, most of us view 2–4 percent inflation as price-level stability. To some extent, what you are accustomed to determines what you consider moderate or excessive inflation. Many South Americans perceive inflation rates of 40–50 percent as no big deal. Inflation in some of these countries raged at annual rates as high as 400–800 percent at times between 1950 and 1988.

Types of Inflation

One way to categorize inflation is by how rapidly prices rise on average. Other distinctions try to pinpoint the *causes* of inflation. Both approaches are examined in this section.

Creeping Inflation Versus Hyperinflation

The price level may rise for a number of reasons and at different rates over time. When prices rise consistently but at fairly low rates, an economy is said to have a case of *creeping* inflation. Most Americans view double-digit inflation as almost unbearable. Most economists, however, would follow the lead of Phillip Cagan, a specialist in the study of inflation, in defining *galloping* inflation, also known as hyperinflation.

> **Hyperinflation** *occurs when average prices rise by 50 percent or more per month.*

At times, some countries have experienced average rates of price increases that can only be described as astronomical. In 1919, it took only 9 German marks to buy an American dollar. A kilogram of bread cost less than 1 mark. By the end of 1923, an incredible 4.2 trillion German marks were worth only 1 dollar. Between the beginning of World War I and 1923, average prices in Germany rose 1,422,900 million percent. A one inch stack of 5 million mark notes would buy one egg. As remarkable as these numbers seem, even more rapid inflation has occurred. Hungary experienced annual inflation of 3.81 octillion (381 followed by 27 zeros!) percent between

1945 and 1946. Figure 6 depicts twentieth-century episodes of hyperinflation.

Interestingly, studies by Phillip Cagan indicate that a monetary system still works reasonably well as long as inflation stays below 50 percent monthly. This is only one indication of the resilience of market systems. Creeping inflation clearly poses fewer problems for macroeconomic policymakers than does the galloping variety. If inflation "gallops" too rapidly, people quit accepting money. *Barter* takes over when people no longer trust money; goods and resources are only traded for other goods or resources when a monetary system collapses.

Now that we have seen the difference between creeping and galloping inflation, let us go on to look at the causes of inflation.

Demand-Side Inflation

Whenever a given price rises, we know that either (*a*) demand has increased; or (*b*) supply has decreased. Demand-side inflation occurs if Aggregate Demand grows and the economy is near full employment. As illustrated in Figure 7, when Aggregate Demand increases from AD_0 to AD_1, the price level rises from P_0 to P_1. Continued increases in Aggregate Demand will simply be reflected in a higher rate of inflation.

> *If expanding demands cause the average price level to rise, the economy experiences* **demand-pull (demand-side) inflation.**

Economists are nearly unanimous in believing that inflation results whenever our demands for goods and services grow faster than our capacity to produce them. Indeed, a substantial minority of economists insist that this is the only realistic explanation for inflation. Excessive demands ripple through a fully employed economy when the money supply grows too rapidly or government spends far more than it collects in taxes.

Supply-Side Inflation

Most economists agree that some inflation may originate with disturbances to the supply side of the economy. Creeping inflations in many industrialized Western style economies during the 1960s and 1970s were commonly diagnosed at least partially, originating

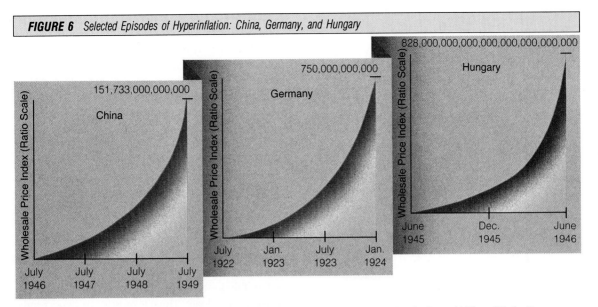

FIGURE 6 Selected Episodes of Hyperinflation: China, Germany, and Hungary

Source: For China: Shun-Hsin Chou, *The Chinese Inflation 1937–1949* (New York: Columbia University Press, 1963), p. 261; for Germany: Fritz K. Ringer, *The German Inflation of 1923 (New York: Oxford University Press, 1969), p. 79; for Hungary: B. Nogaro, "Hungary's Monetary Crises,"* The American Economic Review, XXXVIII (1948), pp. 526–42.

FIGURE 7 Demand-Side Inflation

Real National Income

If the price level increases due to increased demands, the economy experiences demand-side inflation, shown here as the jump in the price level from P_0 to P_1.

with shocks from the supply side. Figure 8 illustrates a supply-side "shock" as a shift in Aggregate Supply from AS_0 to AS_1. Skyrocketing energy costs, worldwide crop failures, growing monopoly power, and disputes between labor unions and management are only a few of the culprits that some people identify as causal factors.

> **Supply-side** *inflation results when Aggregate Supply shrinks (e.g., because of rising resource prices or technological reversals), causing the price level to rise and aggregate output to fall.*

Supply-side shocks can be grouped into the broad categories of *cost-push, administered-price, composition-shift,* and *expectational* explanations for inflation.

Cost-Push Inflation You may have heard people blame inflation on large union wage hikes. This is one example of a **cost-push** theory of inflation. Powerful unions presumably demand wage increases not warranted by increased worker productivity. Increased labor costs are then passed forward to con-

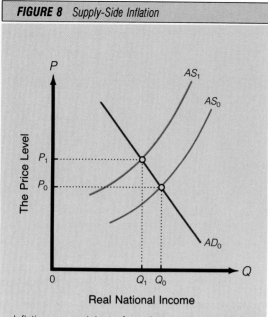

FIGURE 8 Supply-Side Inflation

P — The Price Level (vertical axis)

AS_1, AS_0, AD_0

P_1, P_0

Q_1 Q_0

Real National Income

Q

Inflation may originate from the supply side of the economy; when the Aggregate Supply curve shifts from AS_0 to AS_1, the price level rises from P_0 to P_1.

sumers as "pushed up" prices. This explanation points to unions as the villains causing inflation. Blaming unions is especially popular among some politicians and business leaders. Other cost-push theories point to rising prices for oil or to increases in the prices of imported goods, foods, fibers, ores, or other raw materials.

Administered-Price Inflation Some economists borrow the mechanics of the union-based, cost-push inflation explanation, but turn the theory inside out. According to the **administered-price** theory of inflation, firms with monopoly power may be reluctant to raise prices because they fear adverse publicity, antitrust actions, or similar threats to their domination of a market. They use hikes in wages or other resource costs as excuses to raise prices, generally by more than can be justified by the higher costs. Hence, huge firms do not resist excessive wage demands. This pattern, it is argued, tends to perpetuate inflationary momentum in an economy.

Composition-Shift Inflation The foundation of **composition-shift** inflation theory is the assumption that prices rise more easily than they fall. Thus, if demands increase in one sector of the economy, prices rise. But if there are offsetting decreases in demands in other sectors, prices do *not* fall, at least in the short run. Instead, as sales shrink, firms reduce output and lay workers off. As the composition of demands and supplies changes, there will be pressures for inflation. Growing sectors will typically experience increases in prices, while declining sectors suffer from stagnation and unemployment rather than long-term price cuts.

Expectational Inflation Broad expectations of inflation may cause **expectational** inflation because widespread economic forecasts are at least partially self-fulfilling—we create our own future realities by what we anticipate. Thus, if most of us expect inflation, producers will try to boost production while cutting back on current sales to build their inventories. Why sell now when, if firms just wait a bit, prices will be higher? The reduction of current sales is accomplished by immediately raising prices and temporarily lowering supplies.

If, at the same time, buyers expect inflation, they will try to accumulate their own inventories of durable goods. This bolsters their current demands as they attempt to avoid the higher prices expected later. Thus, inflationary expectations quickly cause price hikes because such expectations lead to reduced supplies and increased demands. These adjustments explain why inflation may develop incredible momentum. Inflation causes expectations of inflation, which stimulates more inflation, and so forth. You may have heard people refer to the "wage-price inflationary spiral" or to the "vicious circle of inflation." Expectations of inflation are important in explaining why inflation is so difficult to suppress.

These are only some of possible explanations of inflation. They are not mutually exclusive; many inflations are caused or intensified by combinations of forces. An accurate portrait of any given episode of inflation normally requires that we consider forces from both the supply side and the demand side. For example, all European hyperinflations following World Wars I and II were triggered by political turmoil and supply-side disturbances, that were followed by incredibly rapid growths of these countries' money supplies. Bolivian inflation in the 1980s was caused by government policy that financed 15 percent of its spending by taxation and printed money to cover the remaining 85 percent. When the money supply grows faster than real output, there is inflationary pressure from the demand side. When we explore these sources of inflation in detail in chapters 12 through 18, you will learn why inflation cannot be sustained for long without growth of the money supply.

Inflation's Costs and Benefits _____

You now have some ideas about how price indices are calculated and about various types of inflation. We need to examine some effects of inflation. You may be surprised to learn that it brings both gains and losses and that there are people with vested interests in rising prices.

Losses from Inflation

There are two major sources of losses arising from inflation. First, inflation may cause reductions in our capacity to produce or losses of efficiency in production and distribution. In either case, there will be declines in standards of living. These are the **real-income costs of inflation.** Second, inflation fractures the implicit and explicit agreements that bind people together. These are the **social costs of inflation.**

Unanticipated inflation is generally far more harmful than inflation that people have learned to expect. If you accurately forecast the rate of inflation, you can buffer yourself against its costs. For example, you can invest in commodities that are "hedges" against inflation. If most people accurately anticipate inflation, the social costs of inflation are minimal.

Real-Income Costs of Inflation

How might inflation cause declines in our real incomes?

Repricing (Menu) Costs One real cost of inflation is that resources that could have been used productively elsewhere are used to reprice goods. Some repricing occurs because relative prices change even when the price level is stable. During an inflationary period, however, it is not unusual to find that most items in your grocery cart have been marked up since they were first put on the shelf. Restaurant menus and airline and bus ticket schedules must be reprinted with higher prices. Candy and cold drink machines must be adjusted to accept different denominations of coins. Where prices are regulated by government (for example, utility rates or bus fares), considerable time and effort may be expended in redesigning rate schedules. All these expenses of repricing are collectively known as the **repricing (*menu*) costs of inflation.**

Distortions Costs Another and even more important cost arises from the fact that inflation may stimulate feelings of uncertainty among savers and investors. Saving and investing reflect our faith in the future. The uncertainty caused by inflation may dampen the incentive to save.

Reduced incentives to save coupled with widespread uncertainty may cause rates of capital accumulation to fall and hamper growth of our national productive capacity. Funds that would normally flow into new capital may be diverted into real estate or inventories, so that growth and technological advances sputter well below the levels needed for a healthy economy. Firms may also mark up their prices to compensate for the increased risks they perceive. If so, the quantity of goods available over the long run may be reduced because of inflation.

Some economists argue that distortions in relative prices that occur because prices rise at different rates during inflationary episodes are another major cost of inflation. These price distortions cause inefficient decisions about production and consumption. For example, in the early 1980s, many people signed enormous obligations for mortgages that required monthly payments that they could not afford. By 1985–86, there was an epidemic of bankruptcies and foreclosures. These people would have waited to buy homes were it not for their fear that "if we don't buy now, housing prices will rise by so much that we won't ever be able to afford one." This is only one way that inflation warps efficient decision making. These sorts of responses are known collectively as **distortions costs.**

Social Costs of Inflation

When markets are out of equilibrium and prices are unstable, there is far more strife than normal between buyers (who want low prices maintained) and sellers (who want prices raised to reflect rising production costs). Conflicts among consumers, producers, and regulatory agencies are accentuated during inflationary episodes. Ignoring menu and distortions costs for a moment, inflation is roughly what mathematicians call a *zero sum game.* For every loser during inflation (someone who must pay more for a given good), there is a winner (someone who receives a greater price for the things sold.) The somewhat arbitrary income redistributions caused by inflation are a major source of inflation's *social cost.* Even though losses to some are offset by gains to others, the process erodes the trust we have in each other.

You gain during inflation if the prices of things you sell go up faster than the prices of things you buy. Generally, inflation is most advantageous to you the more accurately you anticipate it. And, since the gains from inflation going to one party almost exactly offset the losses to some other party, the biggest losers are normally those who do not correctly anticipate inflation. Some people lose when their incomes do not keep pace with the average prices of the goods they buy. Why all the furor over inflation if the gains and losses are roughly in balance? There are several reasons. One is that major gains from recent inflation went to people who sell petroleum—many of whom are foreigners.

A basic problem is that inflation is blamed for many unfavorable circumstances that would have arisen because of shifts in *uninflated* demands and supplies. Most of us feel that increases in our paychecks are much-deserved rewards for hard work. Have you ever considered that your raise is an increase in the price of your services and that it can be seen as inflation by purchasers of the services or the goods you produce? If your neighbor's pay rises faster than your own, supply and demand may be at work, not inflation.

Even recognizing that our income may have risen, we find that the value of money we have saved falls during inflation. A past irritant was that the progressivity of our tax system allowed inflation to bump us into higher tax brackets, a process called *bracket creep.* Congress indexed tax rates to inflation beginning in 1985, virtually eliminating bracket creep. On the other hand, the prices of physical assets such as land and housing often rise even more rapidly than the rate of inflation. Homeowners gain during inflation; first-time home buyers lose.

One important group that gains from inflation is borrowers. Homeowners with huge mortgages are prime examples. Repaying loans gets easier and easier if both incomes and the price level rise. Of course, borrowers' gains are almost exactly offset by losses in the real wealth of lenders. Government, business firms, farmers, and young families are often net debtor/borrowers, and they may gain from unexpected inflation.

Established households and older people anticipating retirement are generally savers and lose from inflation. (The ultimate lender is the person with bank deposits, not the banker.) Another major problem with inflation is that this redistributional effect of rewarding borrowing and penalizing saving provides substantial incentives for the use of credit. It is probably undesirable for most of us to become even more debt-ridden than we already are.

Still another consideration is that some people live on fixed incomes—their pensions or wage contracts are not adjusted for changes in the cost of living. The growing numbers of contracts containing escalator clauses illustrates how people adjust to inflation over time. Even so, there are people whose incomes are at least partially fixed; those living on life insurance annuities or who long ago contracted for long-term fixed-dollar payments to take care of their old age are examples. Many senior citizens are harmed by inflation to the extent that some portions of their incomes are fixed.

Government also tends to gain from inflation because it is a major debtor, and because bracket creep formerly bumped people into higher tax brackets. Holders of U.S. Treasury bonds and taxpayers are the losers in this exchange of wealth.

Redistributions caused by inflation are commonly seen as unfair and capricious, but many social ills blamed on it actually result from other forces. You may have seen news programs indicating that low-income people suffer most from inflation, a charge contrary to most studies of this problem. The difficulties faced by the poor result from poverty, not inflation per se. Joseph Minarik analyzed census data on income and concluded that the sustained but moderate inflation of the 1970s harmed people at the top proportionally far more than it did people at the lower end of the income spectrum.[3]

The income redistribution aspects of inflation generally do not affect the real level of national production, which Adam Smith (in 1776) rightly termed the *wealth of nations*. Rather, the redistributive properties of inflation are part of the larger problem of achieving and maintaining an equitable distribution of our real national income.

Benefits of Inflation

The major possible benefit of inflation is that needed changes in relative prices may be accomplished more easily if there is a little inflationary pressure in the economy. This is especially true if price reductions are resisted more vigorously than price increases. For example, in the 1970s the demand for college professors fell due to declines in enrollment, but the supply of professors increased. Market pressures to reduce professors' real wages were accommodated fairly easily by allowing their salaries' purchasing power to decline because of inflation. This process would have been far more traumatic if colleges had been forced to negotiate lower money wages for faculty, which might have been necessary had the price level been stable.

Inflation's effects on capital accumulation and economic growth are also positive at times. If managers believe that equipment costs less now than it will in the future, firms may boost investment in capital equipment, thereby raising the real supplies of goods available for purchase. Such planning may backfire, however; some investment decisions made because of inflationary expectations may prove premature and disastrous for the investors.

---

3. Joseph J. Minarik, "Who Wins, Who Loses from Inflation," *The Brookings Bulletin,* 15, 1 (1980): 6.

A third possible benefit (questioned by many) from inflation is that it may ease expanding government spending relative to private spending. Political leaders may use inflation to finance rising government spending in preference to an inequitable or inefficient tax system—spending can grow without paying for it directly via taxes. For example, inflationary pressures were allowed to build during World War II. Tax hikes sufficient to finance the war in a noninflationary way might have posed severe disincentives for production. Of course, many people would argue that under most circumstances, inflationary growth of government is a cost, not a benefit, of inflation. This issue will be treated in more detail in chapters 12, 18, and 19.

The Discomfort Index

Arthur Okun, chairman of President Lyndon Johnson's Council of Economic Advisors, developed an economic discomfort index as a way to summarize the general state of the economy.

> The economic **discomfort index** *equals the inflation rate plus the overall unemployment rate.*

In 1976, Jimmy Carter renamed this the **misery index** and used it to brand President Ford's economic policies as failures. Ronald Reagan resurrected the misery index to condemn economic performance during Carter's administration. The index was also featured in the 1984 political campaign.

The index for 4-year presidential terms (averaged to smooth short-run fluctuations) since 1950 is presented in Table 5. The index showed remarkable stability during the 1950s and 1960s but took a big leap upward during the 1970s and early 1980s. By 1985, however, the discomfort index had returned to levels accepted as normal before 1970.

Macroeconomic policies focus on the goals of full employment, price level stability, and economic growth. Implementing appropriate policies requires relatively accurate measures of unemployment and inflation. You should keep the various costs and benefits of unemployment and inflation in mind, as well as data limitations, as you study the material in the next few chapters.

TABLE 5 The Discomfort (Misery) Index

Term	President	Average Inflation Rate	Average Unemployment Rate	Discomfort Index
1949–52	Truman	2.8	4.4	7.2
1953–56	Eisenhower	1.4	4.2	5.6
1957–60	Eisenhower	1.7	5.5	7.2
1961–64	Kennedy-Johnson	1.2	5.8	7.0
1965–68	Johnson	3.2	3.9	7.1
1969–72	Nixon	4.6	5.0	9.6
1973–76	Nixon-Ford	8.2	6.7	14.9
1977–80	Carter	10.6	6.5	17.1
1981–84	Reagan	5.2	8.6	13.8
1985–88	Reagan	3.4	6.4	9.8

Source: *Economic Report of the President,* 1988. Author estimates for 1988.

CHAPTER REVIEW: KEY POINTS

1. Major macroeconomic goals include full employment, price stability, and economic growth. Economic security is also an important goal.

2. People are *unemployed* if they are able to work and are willing to accept prevailing wage rates for people with their skills and experience, but cannot find work or have not yet secured suitable employment.

3. Unemployed people who are so discouraged about job prospects that they do not look for work are not counted in unemployment statistics. Some people who are not truly out of work indicate that they are in order to maintain eligibility for unemployment compensation. Thus, unemployment statistics may either understate the true unemployment rate because of *discouraged workers* or overstate it because of *dishonest nonworkers.*

4. Unemployment arises in five major ways (*a*) frictional, (*b*) structural, (*c*) seasonal, (*d*) cyclical, and (*e*) induced. *Frictional unemployment* arises because of transaction costs and is a by-product of normal entry and exit from the labor market, voluntary job changes, or layoffs or firings. *Structural unemployment* results from mismatches between workers and jobs because of changes in the skill require-

ments of job openings or individuals' lack of marketable skills. *Seasonal unemployment* arises from the annually recurring influences of weather, vacations, and the like on labor markets. *Cyclical unemployment* results from downturns in overall economic activity (recessions). Government policies that reduce work incentives cause *induced unemployment.*

5. Unemployment causes both *economic* and *social costs.* Society as a whole suffers because of lost output that unemployed individuals could have produced. Personal losses are cushioned by such programs as unemployment compensation. Individuals and their families suffer socially and psychologically when they are unemployed for exceptionally long periods.

6. Unemployment is not distributed equally across all groups. Workers in manufacturing and construction are hit harder by cyclical unemployment during recessions than employees in most other lines of work.

7. *Index numbers* are used to compare particular variables over time. The *Consumer Price Index* (*CPI*) measures average price changes for a given bundle of consumer goods over time. The *CPI* is based on

typical consumer patterns for approximately 80 percent of the urban population.

8. The *CPI* is used extensively as an escalator clause (cost-of-living adjustment) in many contracts. It is also an economic indicator and is used to convert nominal values to real values. *Deflating* nominal variables means dividing their monetary values by (1 percent of) a price index.

9. Among the major difficulties in computing the *CPI* are the problems inherent in adjusting the index for (*a*) new products; (*b*) changes in the qualities of existing products; (*c*) changes in the composition of consumer expenditures; and, (*d*) already owned consumer durables such as housing.

10. The *Producer Price Index* (*PPI*) measures the changes in the prices of goods in other than retail markets. The *GNP implicit Deflator* is used to adjust the *GNP* for changes in prices. It is composed of relevant portions of the *CPI* and the *PPI,* plus some additional prices covered by neither.

11. Relative prices and economic decision making are distorted by *inflation,* and incentives to save are depressed. Capital accumulation may or may not be hampered by inflation, depending on business expectations and the availability of funds for investment. These are the *distortions costs of inflation.* Inflation causes resources that could be used productively elsewhere to be used for repricing. These are the *repricing (menu) costs of inflation.*

12. There are *social costs of inflation* because people feel greater uncertainty during inflationary periods. People living on fixed incomes are hurt by inflation, but many of today's transfer payments and wage contracts have escalator clauses that adjust payments for price level changes. Borrowers tend to gain from unexpected inflation, while the ultimate lender loses. When inflation boosts income, meeting a fixed mortgage payment becomes easier, so heavily mortgaged homeowners tend to gain.

13. The *discomfort (misery) index* is the sum of the inflation rate and the unemployment rate. It averaged 6–7 percent during the 1950s and 1960s. During the late 1970s and early 1980s, the index ranged from 13 to more than 20 percent. By the late 1980s, economic growth had pushed the index below 10 percent.

PROBLEMS

1. Table 6 lists aggregate personal income in current dollars for selected years since 1929 and the *CPI* for the same years.
   a. Compute real personal income in 1972 dollars for each year.
   b. How much did real income increase between 1929 and 1987?
   c. Convert the *CPI* to a base year of 1987=100. Adjust current dollar personal income to 1987 dollars.
   d. What percent did prices fall between 1929 and 1933?
   e. If between 1988 and 1989, nominal personal income grew 7 percent and the inflation rate was 4 percent, by how much did real personal income grow? What was the percentage growth?

2. In 1987, the total labor force (including the Armed Forces) was 121,602,000, the civilian labor force was 119,865,000, and civilian employment was 112,440,000. Compute the following:

TABLE 6 Personal Income (Billions of Dollars)		
Year	**Current $B**	**CPI (1972 = 100)**
1929	85.0	37.0
1933	47.0	27.7
1960	402.3	82.2
1972	810.3	100.0
1980	2165.2	212.0
1985	3294.2	249.7
1987	3745.8	271.7

a. Total unemployment rate (including the military).
b. Civilian unemployment rate.
c. Why is the total unemployment rate lower than that for civilians?

QUESTIONS FOR THOUGHT AND DISCUSSION

1. In October of 1982, the Reagan administration faced political embarrassment: the unemployment rate had soared into the double-digit range (10.1 percent) for the first time since the 1930s. The White House implemented a proposal, advocated by numerous politicians in the past—to base unemployment rates on the total (civilian plus military) labor force instead of on the civilian labor force alone. Our military force is between 2 and 3 million people. What effect did this change have on published unemployment rates? Why did several previous presidents favor this change?

2. Some critics believe that unemployment statistics tremendously underestimate unemployment because so many potential workers have become discouraged. Other critics suggest that the published unemployment rate "measures with considerable lack of reliability the number of people in the labor force of this country who, if the pay were right and the hours were right, might be available for a little work once in a while." Which position do you think is correct?

3. Changes in the Consumer Price Index are the most quoted measures of inflation, but the way the index is computed often has perverse consequences for public policy. For example, the index includes property, sales, and Social Security taxes, but not income taxes. If elected officials wanted to lower taxes and "cut" inflation at the same time, which tax rates would they prefer to cut? Does this method make any sense, or would we simply be the victims of a political con?

4. The *CPI* traditionally used fixed consumer budgets (expenditure categories) that were updated every few years. But when the price of one good rises relative to another, consumers do not wait to change their buying patterns. What kinds of adjustments will consumers make? Did the *CPI* consequently overstate or understate the true inflation rate? What was the effect of this over- or understatement on contracts containing cost-of-living adjustments? Could this inaccuracy fuel the fires of inflation? How was the *CPI* altered to remedy such problems? Do you think implementing these changes was very costly?

CHAPTER 7

Key Terms

Gross National Product (GNP)

consumption (C)

investment (I)

government purchases (G)

net exports (X − M)

National Income (NI)

depreciation

Net National Product (NNP)

Personal Income (PI)

Disposable Personal Income (DPI)

Measure of Economic Welfare (MEW)

Gross National Product (GNP)

Statisticians commonly are regarded as even duller people than economists, and sometimes they deserve the reputation.

—John Lewis and Robert Turner

Feature articles in news magazines regularly discuss the latest figures for unemployment, inflation, and Gross National Product (GNP). You now know a bit about unemployment and inflation, but what is Gross National Product? When the Commerce Department unveils its estimates of GNP, Wall Street gurus and economic analysts pore over these figures the way fortune-tellers read tea leaves or tarot cards for signals about the future. How accurate are the available data? Do you feel better if GNP rose last month? This chapter provides an understanding of what GNP estimates represent and suggests some of the problems with GNP accounting.

Gross National Product (GNP) _____

Accounting problems cause published estimates of Gross National Product (GNP) to differ somewhat from GNP as an economic concept:

> *Conceptually,* **Gross National Product (GNP)** *is the total market value of all production during some period, usually one year.*

Other conceptual definitions of GNP exist, but each has flaws. For example, some describe GNP as the total market value of all final goods and services produced annually. This definition is acceptable only if the many intermediate commodities produced and held as inventories at the end of the accounting year are viewed as final goods. We will return to this point a bit later.

GNP as an Economic Indicator

A major reason for measuring Gross National Product is to provide regular and continuing gauges of total economic activity that are comparable over time. Experience has taught us that when production drops, many people are laid off and have difficulty finding jobs. Forecasting GNP helps government policymakers determine when to take corrective policy actions, and measures of GNP allow us to assess the success or failure of specific policies. The level of economic performance is also important to business managers who must constantly review their plans about employment, production, sales, and investment in new plants and equipment.

GNP and Economic Well-Being

Measures of Gross National Product also provide us with a crude yardstick to estimate national well-being. Employment and income are related to aggregate production, so our individual incomes and spending tend to rise or fall with aggregate economic activity. A rough measure of well-being is obtained if we divide real GNP by the population. Per capita GNP can be used to estimate how well-off the average American is now compared with previous periods or with average people in other countries. Measures such as per capita GNP are also used to compare growth rates among various countries around the world.

FIGURE 1 The Circular Flow and National Income Accounting

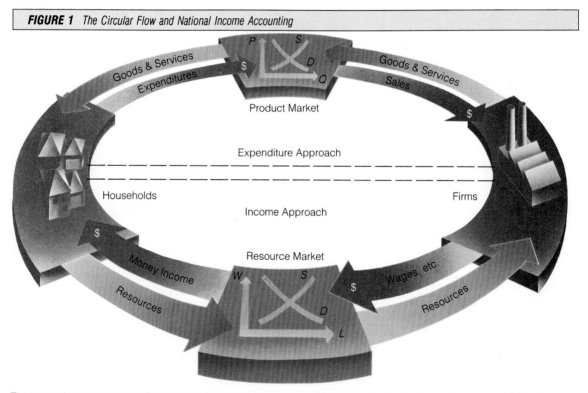

The two major approaches to GNP accounting are illustrated in this figure using the circular flow of income model. In this simple model, all goods are traded in the product market, and total expenditures equal the total value of output. Similarly, income is paid to owners of resources, and summing all of these payments will provide an estimate of GNP. Note that all expenditures on goods and services must necessarily equal all of the payments to resource owners to produce the output. That is, what is bought must have been sold. (*Note:* Clockwise arrows show money flow; counterclockwise arrows show flow of goods and resources.)

The uses of GNP as a measure of total production *and* as a measure of economic well-being is sometimes inconsistent. Some numbers that should be included in GNP to measure economic welfare cause inaccuracies when we measure production, and vice versa. For example, if we produce more atomic weapons because the Soviet Union is doing so, are we better-off than people in countries with lower per capita GNP who do not have to engage in extensive defense spending? Most of the choices made have favored accurate measurement of production. This is why we include such things as business investments, inventory accumulation, and exports in the GNP calculation.

Measuring GNP

There are two conceptually different ways of measuring Gross National Product (*a*) the *expenditure* approach and (*b*) the *income* approach. Neither is perfect. Figure 1 illustrates the income and expenditure approaches with a version of the circular flow diagram you studied earlier. This shows that everything

bought (expenditures) is *sold* by someone who receives income from the sale. As you read about these approaches, keep in mind that each approach only approximates true economic GNP. Most data used to measure GNP are initially recorded for accounting purposes and are only roughly suitable for economic analysis. Naturally, there are many different categories of both income and expenditures. The proportions making up some important categories of income and expenditure are shown in Figure 2.

The Expenditure Approach

The *expenditure approach* to measuring Gross National Product leads us to the final users of our output. All production in our economy is ultimately bought by (*a*) consumers, (*b*) business investors, (*c*) government, or (*d*) foreigners. Figure 2 illustrates this division of the national pie into consumption (C), investment (I), government purchases (G), and net exports—exports $-$ imports ($X - M$). Naturally, foreigners also provide goods that we may consume, invest, or use for government provided goods and services. We will clarify why foreign buyers are

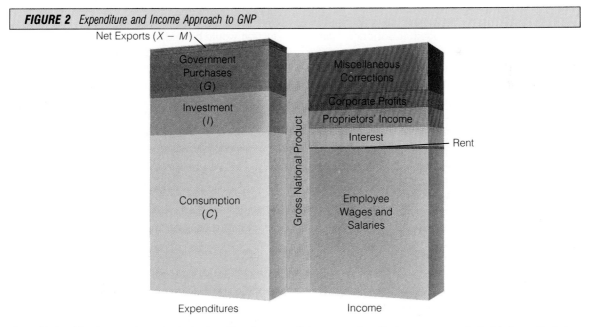

FIGURE 2 *Expenditure and Income Approach to GNP*

Net Exports ($X - M$)

Government Purchases (G)

Investment (I)

Consumption (C)

Gross National Product

Miscellaneous Corrections

Corporate Profits

Proprietors' Income

Interest

Rent

Employee Wages and Salaries

Expenditures

Income

Gross National Product can be estimated using either the expenditure approach or the income approach. As this figure illustrates, the sum of factor incomes approximately equals the totality of spending in the economy.

shown as having such a small share of our GNP after examining spending by domestic purchasers in more detail.

Personal Consumption Expenditures (C)

Household outlays include spending for *nondurable* goods (food and clothing), *durable* goods (appliances, cars, and televisions), and *services* (such as medical care, legal assistance, and automobile repairs).

> *Personal* **consumption** *expenditures (C) are the values of all commodities and services that households and individuals buy.*

This category is familiar because we all engage in consumption every day.

Business Spending on Capital Goods (I)

Remember that investment (I), as economists use the term, does not refer to the flows of money or documents that we term *financial investment.*

> **Economic investment** *refers to acquisition of physical capital.*

All business spending for physical assets is technically referred to in the GNP accounts as *Gross Private Domestic Investment,* or *GPDI.* The word *gross* means that all purchases of *new* buildings, equipment, and the like are included. It does not matter whether or not investment is intended to replace obsolete or worn-out capital. *Private* means that government investment is not counted in this category. *Domestic* means that the new capital is put to use in the United States. We exclude foreign investments by American firms, but investment by foreign companies in the United States is part of our GPDI. The major components of investment spending are (a) all final purchases of new equipment (e.g., machinery and tools), (b) all new construction, and (c) changes in inventories.

The first of these items, capital equipment, enhances the productive capacities of firms and clearly fits the category of investment. But what about purchases of stocks and bonds? These are *financial* rather than *economic* investments. Financial investment may facilitate spending on economic capital, but buying and selling securities merely transfers ownership from sellers of stock to buyers; our productive capability is not directly enhanced. For this reason, transactions in financial instruments are not economic investments.

In our GNP accounts, all new construction is considered investment. New production facilities, apartment buildings, and office space seem to fit the definition of investment, but why not treat construction of residential dwellings as consumer spending? One reason is that housing can be bought for rental purposes. In addition, the useful life of residential housing is quite long relative to most consumer goods. Consequently, housing is regarded as a capital good, and newly constructed housing is included in investment. The rental value of owner-occupied housing is considered consumption because housing produces the service of providing shelter year after year.

Inventory growth is considered investment as well. Declines in inventories are **disinvestments.** Inventories include (a) raw materials or intermediate goods that firms buy to use as productive inputs, and (b) finished goods held in stock to rapidly meet customers' demands. Your customers would soon buy from other firms if they constantly had difficulty getting prompt delivery.

Adjustments for inventory changes are needed since we use sales data to estimate production. If we excluded growth of inventories from GNP, total production would be understated. Goods held as inventories should be counted in GNP in the year produced rather than the year sold. Since inventories vary from year to year, changes in inventories must be estimated to consistently measure total production and keep our national income accounts straight. Increases in inventories *add to* investment, and decreases *reduce* investment.

Government Purchases (G)

We consume commodities and services both as private individuals and collectively, through government. When the government provides goods, it may either buy them in finished form from private firms, or it may buy resources or intermediate products and use them to produce the goods it provides. The most important resource government buys is the labor of its employees. *Government purchases of goods and services (G)* are then provided at zero or minimal prices to the

TABLE 1 Components of Gross National Product: Expenditure Approach (1987 Billions of Dollars)

Component	$ Billions
Personal consumption expenditures (C)	$2,966.0
Gross private domestic investment (I)	716.4
Government purchases of goods and services (G)	923.8
Net exports of goods and services (X − M)	− 119.9
Gross National Product (GNP)	$4,486.2

Source: Economic Report of the President, 1988.

people who use them. Because these items are seldom sold in markets, we do not know their value with any precision. Thus, all government goods enter the GNP accounts at the prices government pays for them. This means that, for GNP accounting purposes, government is assumed to add nothing to the value of the labor and other resources it uses.

An important point to remember is that transfer payments are excluded from government purchases. Transfer payments (welfare payments, Social Security, and others) are simply shifts in income from one set of households to another set and are not connected with production.

Net Exports (X − M) Net exports are defined as exports (X) minus imports (M). *Exports* are goods manufactured in this country and bought by foreigners. We obviously need to include exports in GNP as a measure of the value of all production in a year. But what about imports? *Imports* are produced in foreign countries and consumed or invested in the United States. Do imports reflect American production? The answer is clearly no.

A Hyundai purchased in the United States is part of Korean production (and adds to Korean consumption when the owners of the resources that produce the car spend their pay). When Americans buy a Korean auto, this spending must be subtracted from U.S. consumption or it will appear that the car was produced in the United States. Similarly, if an American investor buys Swiss machinery, the purchase appears in the U.S. investment category and should be subtracted. Thus, imports are subtracted from exports to

arrive at the net effect of foreign trade on GNP in our economy.

To summarize briefly: Using the expenditure approach, Gross National Product is the sum of consumer spending (C), business investment (I), government spending for goods and services (G), and net exports (X − M):

$$C + I + G + (X - M) = \text{GNP.}$$

Table 1 shows these expenditures. Measurement of GNP by these categories was developed by Simon Kuznets, a Nobel prize winner (see his Biography).

The Income Approach

The second approach to measuring GNP is the income approach.

Adding together all the payments to resource owners—wages and salaries, rents, interest, and profits—yields **National Income (NI).**

The Components of National Income (NI) Conceptually, National Income is the sum of all income—wages, interest, rent, and profit—received by owners of the various resources (labor, capital, land, and entrepreneurship). In fact, however, limitations of accounting data cause NI to be measured as the sum of five slightly different categories (a) wages and salaries, (b) noncorporate proprietors' income, (c) corporate profits before taxes, (d) rental income, and (e) interest. Table 2 presents the proportions and trends in these income payments for selected years.

TABLE 2 *National Income: Income Approach to GNP (Selected Years 1929–87)*

Category	1929 Billions $	%	1933 Billions $	%	1960 Billions $	%	1980 Billions $	%	1987 Billions $	%
Wages and salaries	51.1	58.9	29.5	73.1	294.2	71.0	1,598.6	75.5	2,647.5	72.8
Proprietors' income	15.2	17.5	5.9	14.6	46.2	11.2	116.3	5.5	327.8	9.0
Corporate profits	10.5	12.0	−1.2	−3.0	49.9	12.0	181.6	8.6	305.3	8.4
Rental income	5.4	6.2	2.0	5.1	15.8	3.8	32.9	1.5	18.6	.5
Interest	4.7	5.4	4.1	10.2	8.4	2.0	187.7	8.9	336.7	9.3
National income	86.8	100.0	40.3	100.0	414.1	100.0	2,117.1	100.0	3,635.9	100.0

Source: U.S. Department of Commerce, *Economic Report of the President*, 1988.
Note: The declining share of rental income is misleading because rapid depreciation schedules (tax breaks) cause rental income to be severely understated in recent years. Rounding may cause each total to be slightly different from the sum of each column.

Wages and Salaries   This accounting category includes not only employees' wages and salaries, but also the monetary values of fringe benefits, tips, bonuses, stock option plans, paid vacations, and firms' contributions to Social Security. As you can see from Table 2, wages and salaries constitute by far the largest single category in National Income. Throughout this century, wages and salaries have increased as a percentage of National Income, growing from less than half in 1900 to roughly three-fourths today.

Proprietors' Income   National Income accountants separate accounting profit into two categories: proprietors' net income and corporate profits. *Proprietors' incomes* are the incomes received by sole proprietorships, partnerships, professional associations, and (unincorporated) farms. Included in farm income is an estimate of the value of food grown and consumed on farms—although it is not marketed, this clearly represents production.

Much of this income category represents wages, interest, or rent that proprietors would have earned if they had not been operating these firms personally. Dividing this category according to purely economic concepts (to distinguish opportunity costs) is not possible, however, given the limitations of the accounting data available. Thus, here we will follow accounting conventions and label it as profit.

Over the last few decades, proprietors' income has declined relative to National Income, falling from 17.5 percent in 1929 to around 9 percent today.

(Could a recent reversal of this trend be signalling the onset of a new era for entrepreneurs?) Part of the reason for shrinkage in proprietors' incomes and the growth in wages and salaries is that many people whose families once owned small farms have sold these farms and moved to urban areas where they could realize greater incomes through wages and salaries.

Corporate Profit   Corporations use their accounting profit in three ways. First, they *must* pay corporate income taxes. Second, they *may* pay dividends to stockholders from what is left after taxes. Finally, remaining profits are kept in the firm to help finance expansion, to be used as working capital, or for other purposes. Economists call the corporate profits kept within the firm *undistributed corporate profits;* to accountants they are *retained earnings.*

Much of the accounting category called *corporate profit* actually represents interest stockholders could have made had they bought bonds instead of stock. Again, because the data are difficult to divide, it is conventional to lump this figure in with corporate profits.

Proprietors' income has fallen as a percentage of National Income, so you might expect that the share accruing to corporate profit would be rising. A glance at Table 2, however, reveals that corporate profit as a percentage of National Income was falling prior to the 1980s. What accounts for the increase in wages and salaries and the erratic declines in both corpo-

BIOGRAPHY

Simon Kuznets (1901–85)

Russian-born but American-educated, Simon Kuznets received his Ph.D. at Columbia University in 1926 and began an association with the National Bureau of Economic Research that lasted for a half century. Kuznets developed and refined the concepts and measurements used in GNP accounting. When he began estimating economic aggregates, empirical data for many aspects of economic life were either crude or nonexistent. The concept of national income could be traced to Francois Quesnay, an eighteenth-century Frenchman, but techniques to estimate national income remained primitive.

Kuznets changed all that by pioneering modern estimation techniques that sum expenditures by different classes of purchases over different classes of goods. Thus, he was responsible for providing the statistical foundations for modern studies of the relationships

among income, consumption, and investment, and well deserved the title, "Father of GNP." Without his work, quantitative methods to evaluate the Keynesian revolution in economic thought would have been impossible. This realization prompted one economist to declare that "we live in the age of Keynes and Kuznets." For his monumental achievements in empirical economics, Kuznets won a Nobel prize in 1971.

His almost single-handed construction of the national income accounts made him keenly aware of GNP's deficiencies as a measure of well-being. GNP ignores working conditions (e.g., stress and strain) and most nonmarket activities, so Kuznets strongly opposed reliance on national income data as sole indicators of economic performance. Nevertheless, GNP is generally accepted today by economists, businesspeople, and politicians as a barometer of macroeconomic performance.

---

rate and proprietors' entrepreneurial profits? The explanation lies partially in the fact that government outlays as a percentage of total output has risen markedly since the Great Depression. The bulk of government provided services require substantial labor, so wages and salaries have been growing steadily.

Rental Income   Rental income is derived from leasing various resources. Accounting rents are usually associated with the leasing of real property (such as land, houses, offices), but can be obtained from renting any asset. Determining what part conforms to the economic definition of rent is impossible, so again we use the accounting classification. As you can see in Table 2, rental income is the smallest category in our National Income accounts.

Interest   Interest is also rather self-explanatory. Accountants include the payments made for the use of borrowed capital (usually, financial capital). These payments are made to or by banks, or to holders of

bonds. In the 1970s, rising interest rates caused interest income to be the most rapidly growing component of National Income. Inexplicably, national income accounting conventions treat interest paid to holders of government bonds as a transfer payment and exclude it from the interest component of National Income. If interest on government bonds were included, interest would have been roughly 13 percent of National Income in 1987.

Reconciling GNP and NI

Gross Private Domestic Investment (GPDI) overstates the growth of the nation's stock of capital because some capital wears out each year.

> *Accountants refer to the decline in value of capital because of wear and tear or obsolescence as* **depreciation.**

Accounting estimates of depreciation reflect rapid write-offs because of advantageous tax treatment. To economists, accounting depreciation is known as the *capital consumption allowance.*

Subtracting the capital consumption allowance from Gross Private Domestic Investment yields *Net Private Domestic Investment,* which is an estimate of growth in the nation's capital stock over the year. All else equal, depreciation reduces the wealth and income of capital owners. Consequently, one step in reconciling GNP and NI requires subtracting the capital consumption allowance from GNP, which yields Net National Product, or *NNP.*

Conceptually, Net National Product is an estimate of how much we could consume in a given year and still have the same amount of capital available for production at the beginning of the next year.

Net National Product (NNP) *is the net value of annual output in the economy after adjustment for depreciation.*

Failing to consider depreciation would cause overstatement of the net value of our production. In a sense, depreciation represents a "death rate of capital" that must be subtracted from the "birth rate of capital" (GPDI) to arrive at net capital formation.

There is one more adjustment to our Gross National Product before it equals National Income. The amounts you pay for products and the amounts received by firms are not equal. There is the matter of sales and excise taxes to consider. These are called *indirect business taxes,* and they drive wedges between what consumers or investors spend and the amounts received by sellers. For example, sales and excise taxes must be subtracted from the buyer's payment for a new car before we arrive at the amount that auto workers or manufacturers will receive as income. Consequently, indirect business taxes must be subtracted from Net National Product. We will obtain National Income only after these and other miscellaneous adjustments and allowances have been made. Table 3 shows the adjustments necessary to reconcile GNP and NI.

The Value-Added Technique What are the mechanics of computing GNP? Government statisticians could wait for households to file their income taxes. Calculating GNP would require summing all declared incomes and then adding indirect business taxes and depreciation, but this strategy depends crucially on people's honesty. Worse yet, revised figures would only be available in May or June, which would make

them five or six months old since the income tax returns due on April 15 are for the preceding year. For these reasons and more, National Income is calculated primarily as a double check on GNP figures.

An alternative is to collect all sales figures for a year. Most firms are subject to sales and income taxes and to other government controls requiring extensive reporting, so sales figures are available on a regular and continuing basis. But what then? If we just total all sales figures, there will be a lot of *double counting.* For example, if U.S. Steel's sales are added to General Motors' sales, we count steel output twice—once when it is sold to GM and again when GM sells the steel in, say, a new Chevette to the final customer.

For this reason, National Income statisticians use the **value-added technique.** A firm's purchases of intermediate goods from other firms are subtracted from its sales, leaving only the value of its own production—its *value added.* Summing the values added by all firms in an economy generates reasonably accurate GNP figures, after adjusting for such things as changes in inventories, the imputed (estimated) rental values of owner-occupied housing, and the imputed values of food grown and consumed on the farm.

Consider the following example. While wandering in a forest one weekend, you find an interesting piece of weathered wood. You backpack it home and show it to an artist friend. Your friend wants to carve a figure from the piece of wood and offers you $20 for it. When you accept, GNP has grown by $20. Your friend carves the wood and sells the finished sculpture to a gift shop for $100, which then sells the carving to a customer for $150.

Has GNP increased by $270 ($20 + $100 + $150)? The answer is no. If we were to sum all these transactions, your original sale of the wood for $20 would be counted three times—in the original sale, in the sale to the shop, and then in the final sale to the customer. During the first two sales, the piece of wood is an *intermediate good*—something used in the production of another good. The sale to the customer is the final sale, and the carving sold by the shop is the *final good.*

The value-added approach sums the value added at each stage of production. In the example of the wood carving, $20 in value was added by you in finding and selling the piece of wood to your friend, who

TABLE 3 *Reconciling the Income and Expenditure Approaches to GNP (1987 Billions of Dollars)*

Expenditure Approach	$ Billions
Gross National Product (GNP)	$4,486.2
minus: Capital consumption allowance (depreciation)	− 479.4
equals: Net National Product (NNP)	$4,006.8
minus: Indirect Business Taxes (IBT) and misc.	− 370.9
equals: National Income (NI)	$3,635.9

Income Approach	$ Billions
Wages and salaries	$2,647.5
plus: Proprietors' income (business, professional, farm)	327.8
plus: Corporate profits before taxes	305.3
plus: Rental income	18.6
plus: Interest	336.7
equals: National Income (NI)	$3,635.9

Source: U.S. Department of Commerce, 1988.

generated $80 in value added by sculpting the wood. Then the store created a value added of $50 by putting the carving in the hands of the final buyer.

Moving from GNP to Disposable Personal Income

We models we use to explain how national income is determined largely ignore the differences among GNP, National Income (NI), Net National Product (NNP), Personal Income (PI), and Disposable Personal Income (DPI). We already know that capital consumption allowances (depreciation) must be subtracted from GNP to compute Net National Product (NNP). Subtracting indirect business taxes from our NNP yields the total income earned by the suppliers of productive resources, which is known as National Income (NI).

More adjustments are needed, however, before arriving at household income before taxes (*Personal Income,* or *PI*) and the income households actually have left to spend after taxes (*Disposable Personal Income,* or *DPI*).

From NI to Personal Income (PI)
National Income includes wages, interest, rent, proprietors' income, and corporate profit. Firms often act as tax collection

points; in fact some households never see parts of the income attributed to them. For example, corporate taxes must be paid before stockholders have claims on corporate incomes, so that these taxes must be subtracted from National Income. Stockholders' dividends are parts of their Personal Income, but undistributed corporate profits must also be subtracted from National Income. Also, business firms are legally obligated to match employees' Social Security contributions. National Income accounts subtract both employer and employee Social Security taxes from NI on this journey towards Personal Income.

Personal Income (PI) *is the money income received by households before they pay their personal taxes.*

In addition to household income that is earned but not received, two forms of income are *received* but *not earned.* A growing share of our National Income is devoted to government transfer payments (e.g., welfare payments). Many firms also engage in charitable activities. Funds transferred through either government or business to private individuals must be added to National Income. At this point, we have finally arrived at the total amount of personal money income that households receive.

From PI to Disposable Personal Income (DPI) You might think that Personal Income is the amount available for personal consumption and saving, but direct taxes on individuals must be paid out of your Personal Income.

> **Disposable Personal Income (DPI)** *is income households can consume or save as they choose after subtracting federal, state, and local income taxes from their Personal Income.*

Table 4 provides a detailed summary of the breakdown from GNP to DPI for selected years.

Some Limitations of GNP Accounting

How well do estimates of GNP and National Income measure economic performance? Although the National Income accounts are fine for some purposes, they suffer from certain limitations. These limitations fall into three categories (*a*) accuracy, (*b*) inclusion of only "legal" market transactions, and (*c*) measurement of government output. Among the most ardent critics of the accuracy of GNP data was the late Oskar Morgenstern (see his Biography).

TABLE 4 Gross National Product and Related Data (Billions of Dollars)			
	1929	**1950**	**1987**
Gross National Product (GNP)	$103.1	$284.8	$4,486.2
minus: Capital consumption allowance (depreciation)	−7.9	−18.3	−479.4
equals: Net National Product (NNP)	$ 95.2	$266.5	$4,006.8
minus: Indirect business taxes	−3.4	−14.1	−370.9
equals: National Income (NI)	$ 86.8	$241.1	$3,635.9
minus: Corporate profits with inventory evaluation adjustment	−10.5	−37.7	−305.3
Contributions for social insurance	−.2	−6.9	−394.4
Net interest	−4.7	−3.0	−336.7
plus: Government transfer payments	0.9	14.3	519.8
Personal interest income	2.5	7.2	515.8
Dividends	5.8	8.8	87.5
Business transfer payments	0.6	0.8	22.3
equals: Personal Income (PI)	$ 85.9	$227.6	$3,745.8
minus: Personal taxes	−2.6	−20.7	−564.7
equals: Disposable Personal Income (DPI)	$ 83.3	$206.9	$3,181.1
minus: Consumer interest and personal transfer payments to foreigners	−1.9	−2.8	−95.0
Consumption expenditures	−77.2	−191.0	−2,966.0
equals: Personal saving	$ 4.2	$ 13.1	$ 120.2

Source: U.S. Department of Commerce and *Economic Report of the President*, 1988.
Note: Totals may not add due to rounding.

BIOGRAPHY

Oskar Morgenstern (1902–77)

Born in Silesia and educated in Germany, the aristocratic Oskar Morgenstern fled to America after the Nazi invasion of Austria. Among his many accomplishments was codevelopment with the mathematician Jon von Neumann (another German emigré) of *game theory*, which aids analysts in modeling a wide range of situations involving conflict and cooperation; e.g., competition among large firms, labor negotiation, or war strategy. Morgenstern was also skeptic about the accuracy and usefulness of much economic data that many social scientists take as gospel in their analyses.

Simon Kuznets had conscientiously warned of the incompleteness of National Income data, but Morgenstern went much further, persistently criticizing the accuracy of economic reporting. He was convinced that the results of statistical analyses are no better than the raw material on which they are based and believed that the maxim "Garbage In, Garbage Out (GIGO)" applied to GNP accounting.

Many economists have striven for the reasonably precise empirical validations of theory possible in some physical sciences. Morgenstern argued that there are several reasons why data problems in the social sciences are essentially different from data problems in the physical sciences. Incentives often exist for collectors of aggregate data to fabricate statistics and for those who give the data to report incorrect figures.

"Disguised" or inaccurate data may be reported to avoid or evade taxes, to throw competitors off the track, or to guard trade secrets. Estimates of many highly aggregated variables, moreover, are little better than guesses because they require data for parts of the economy about which there is little precise and reliable information. For example, should old machinery that has been idle for years be considered when we estimate capacity utilization rates? Growth of the underground economy compounds problems of this type.

Accuracy is extremely important in gathering national income data, according to Morgenstern, because errors that creep into the data at different levels of collection have a way of compounding. He asserted that "national income is a total of composites which differ in reliability from sector to sector and year to year, and hence the error of the composite is a complex amalgam of errors in the parts whose magnitude is not easily determined." In a speech in 1975, Morgenstern argued that the data errors that enter calculations of GNP are larger than the fluctuations of GNP that most economists consider significant. If Morgenstern was correct, this seriously undermines the reliance usually placed on GNP as a predictor of booms and recessions.

Accuracy of GNP Figures

There is a tendency toward specious accuracy, a pretense that things have been counted more precisely than they can be—e.g., the U.S. Army published enemy casualties for the Korean war to 1/1000 of 1 percent, at a time when our own losses were not well known even to the thousands of men! The classic case is, of course, that of the story in which a man, asked about the age of a river, states that it is 3,000,021 years old. Asked how he could give such accurate information, the answer was that twenty-one years ago the river's age was given as three million years. There is a fair amount of this in economic (and other social) statistics.

—Oskar Morgenstern
("Qui Numerare Incipit Errore Incipit")

Just how accurate must GNP accounts be to be useful to economic planners, business forecasters, and others concerned with the health of our economy? There is reason to believe that there are biases in the data. For example, many people systematically understate the incomes they report on their tax forms. Statisticians commonly assume that errors of measurement are offsetting. We have a bridge to sell anyone who thinks that as many people overreport, as underreport it so that estimation errors for income are unbiased.

Another problem is that many of our social accounts are reported to the exact dollar. For example, per capita personal income for California in 1980 was reported as $6,114. Numbers like these are disclosed each month by various data-gathering agencies and firms. Would it be just as useful (and less misleading) to know that personal income in California in 1980 was something over $6,000? Social and economic statistics need be no more accurate than their use dictates. Further, social scientists should not report results from studying these numbers in a fashion that creates a false sense of precision.

Exclusion of Nonmarket Transactions

GNP is the total value of all production during a year, so it should cover all outputs. Our national accounts focus on market transactions because dollar sales figures are reasonably available, but not all productive activity goes through the marketplace. Some nonmarket transactions are included in GNP because estimates of their values are available (e.g., estimated rents for owner-occupied housing and estimates of the value of food produced and consumed on farms). But the values of housewives' services are excluded from GNP because of the difficulty of generating even crude estimates. This leads to the ludicrous situation where a maid hired to clean your home causes GNP to rise, while the same work done by a family member does not enter our GNP accounts. The same is true of homemade haircuts, mowing your own lawn rather than hiring your neighbor's kid, and many other nonmarket activities.

Government cannot estimate accurately the values of unrecorded activities (such as cash or barter transactions) and generally excludes them as well as all illegal activities (see Focus 1). Should legalization of gambling or marijuana lead to growth in measured GNP figures even if there were no changes in people's behavior? Under the current accounting system, it would. Such problems mean that comparisons of GNP over time or among countries must be tempered by recognition that GNP accounts are affected by the relative importance of do-it-yourself production, by the frequency of barter, and by differences in laws and regulations.

In addition to these problems, some items seem misclassified. For example, individual investment in education is treated as personal consumption spending. Football games, parties, many other collegiate social activities, and a number of frivolous courses are consumption activities. But time and effort spent studying will increase your future productivity and should be considered investment, not consumption. (Should the deterioration of your body as you age be considered "depreciation"?) Government investments in research and development, transportation, flood control, and so on are treated in similar fashion. These investments are reported as government spending rather than as investment. Classification in this way tends to understate the extent to which present consumption is diverted to activities that should enhance our future productivity, output, growth, and well-being.

Measuring Government Output

Measuring the value of government output poses special problems. Few government services are directly charged to final users, so there is considerable difficulty in valuing government output. Consequently, government accountants use the next best estimate—the cost of the inputs (primarily, government workers) used to produce the output.

Problems with GNP accounting cause some critics to assert that the GNP and NI figures are worthless. It may be that parts of our measures of GNP and some of its relatives are a bit like the following example.

Imagine that all the members of your class are transported back in time to around 1803. Each is assigned by President Thomas Jefferson the task of traveling to various parts of North America and then returning to Washington, D.C. with estimates of the distances between certain points. To standardize measurements, everyone is to pace the distances.

People pacing the distance to Philadelphia, New York, or Boston would cross-check each other, making sure estimates of these short distances were fairly accurate.

But some people would differ in the length of their strides, some people would just wander in circles, and others might guess at the distance while they rode on horses or in wagons. Still others might not even go to faraway destinations but would fill in travel vouchers as though they had. The mishmash of distance estimates turned in to President Jefferson might be a lot like parts of GNP accounting—far from precise, but still better than no data at all.

GNP and Social Welfare

GNP accounts were created to measure economic performance. These accounts may be abused when they are used to make comparisons about the well-being of citizens in various countries. This is especially true if the relative amounts of self-production, barter, or the underground economy varies much among countries.

When our government reports that per capita GNP rose by 1 percent last month, this need not imply that your personal quality of life improved by 1 percent. There may be some correlation between the growth of GNP and growth in your income, but the relationship is far from perfect.

How GNP Differs from Well-Being

If you decided to take a year off to see the world, our GNP would fall if your present activities add to GNP. You might gain subjectively from this decision, but the GNP accounts would not reflect your enjoyment of added travel and leisure. One of the most important recent changes in our economy that reflects an improvement in the quality of life is the increased leisure time that most of us enjoy. The GNP accounts ignore the value of leisure.

This accounting system also fails to deduct for many negative aspects of economic growth, particularly environmental degradation. Greater outlays on packaging for products boost measured GNP, but the accounting process fails to deduct the accompanying destruction of national forests. GNP does include the costs of removing litter and of increased medical care caused by pollution or auto accidents, but do injurious wrecks increase our welfare? Are we better off if a disastrous leak from a nuclear reactor necessitates a billion-dollar cleanup? Some people argue that we need an index that measures economic well-being rather than economic production.

A Measure of Economic Welfare (MEW)

Work in this direction has been done by William Nordhaus and James Tobin. They attempted to adjust GNP to account for some of the deficiencies we have described. Their statistic is called a Measure of Economic Welfare.

> The **Measure of Economic Welfare (MEW)** *adjusts GNP by deducting items that do not contribute to economic welfare and adding items that do but that are not now counted in GNP.*

Major items deducted from GNP include (*a*) household spending that does not add to a better life—for example, police protection, costs of commuting, and national defense and (*b*) losses associated with pollution, urban congestion, and so on. The major additions are estimates for (*a*) values of goods that do not pass through the market and (*b*) increased leisure.

The crude MEW estimates done by Nordhaus and Tobin suggest that our welfare has grown more slowly than has GNP. One important question society must answer is, How much growth in GNP might we be willing to sacrifice to improve our quality of life (as measured by MEW growth)? Even these MEW accounts leave many questions unanswered. For example, if water prices rise because of drought, should we rejoice because the value of water consumed as measured by our water bills has risen?

Despite the many difficulties associated with accurately measuring GNP and its related subcomponents, GNP remains the best measure of aggregate economic activity available today. In the discussions of macroeconomic theory and policy that follow, we will use GNP (both real and nominal) and the rates of unemployment and inflation to judge present and past policymaking. While making these evaluations, however, you should keep in mind the limitations described in this chapter.

The Underground Economy

We all know people who cheat on their taxes by understating their income. The waiter who reports only half of his tips, the plumber who gives customers a break if they pay cash, and the gambler who keeps no records are all part of the growing "underground economy." Estimates of its size range from a conservative 3 percent to an astounding 20 percent of GNP, which means that our official 1987 GNP of $4.5 trillion could have been as high as $5.4 trillion if ev-

eryone had reported all their income. Moreover, it means that underground participants may now cheat the U.S. Treasury out of as much as $250 billion in taxes annually. Figure 3 presents one set of estimates of the size of the underground economy.

Although researchers disagree on the size of the subterranean economy, all agree that it is growing roughly twice as fast as GNP. Why is this happening? One part of the answer is that economic

growth and inflation have driven many Americans into high tax brackets, so there is a greater incentive to cheat. Another aspect of this problem is the falling probability of an Internal Revenue Service audit. About 3 percent of all tax returns were audited in the late 1960s; the proportion is now around 1.5 percent. Finally, tax evasion has become respectable in the eyes of some, who excuse their behavior with the argument that "everybody does it."

Cataloging all the ways that people have discovered to cheat on their taxes would generate a book as thick as a New York City telephone directory. Legitimate business people may not report cash income or may overstate their tax deductions and, thus, understate their incomes. If you falsely claim that new drapes in your home are a business expense, you are involved in the underground economy. Barter is perfectly legitimate but is a major avenue for tax evasion. When a dentist trades a root canal for brickwork on a backyard fireplace, both the dentist and the bricklayer should report as income the value of what they received.

Nearly 70 percent of the underground economy consists of income that, if reported, would be legitimate; 30 percent or so of the income flowing through untaxed channels is derived from criminal activities. Bank robbers, shoplifters, drug dealers, prostitutes, and loan sharks understandably try to minimize their contact with the Internal Revenue Service. Failure of the IRS to collect taxes is important because those

FIGURE 3 *Sources of Underground Income, 1987*

Unreported Income from Illegal Sources (Billions of Dollars)

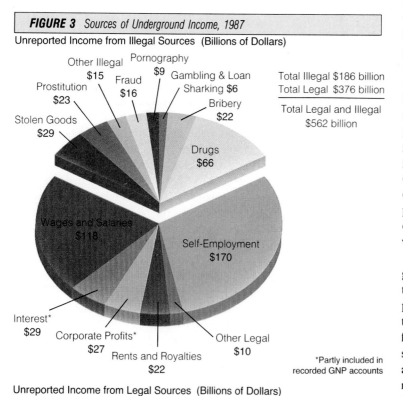

Other Illegal $15 — Pornography $9 — Fraud $16 — Gambling & Loan Sharking $6 — Prostitution $23 — Bribery $22 — Stolen Goods $29 — Drugs $66 — Wages and Salaries $118 — Self-Employment $170 — Interest* $29 — Corporate Profits* $27 — Rents and Royalties $22 — Other Legal $10

Total Illegal $186 billion
Total Legal $376 billion

Total Legal and Illegal $562 billion

*Partly included in recorded GNP accounts

Unreported Income from Legal Sources (Billions of Dollars)

Source: Carl R. Simon and Ann D. Witte, *Beating the System: The Underground Economy* (Boston, Mass: Auburn House Publishing Co., 1981); updated by authors.

of us who scrupulously pay our taxes suffer from higher tax rates.

Growth of self employment in almost all economies during the past decade may be evidence of an international surge in entrepreneurial instincts, but it also signals growth of underground economies in countries ranging from the United States to Sweden to Taiwan to the Soviet Union.* Tax evasion is far easier for the self-employed than for most other people.

What are the implications of the underground economy for economic statistics and public policy? For one thing, the slowdown of GNP growth during the 1970s may have been overstated to the extent that unreported income grew in importance nationally. In January 1986, the Department of Commerce improved its adjustments to the GNP accounts to try to account for misreporting on tax returns. These adjustments totaled more than $200 billion for 1987.

Another consideration is that unemployment statistics may be overstated (or labor force participation understated) if underground activity is not taken into account. Still another is that, if poor people participate in cash or barter transactions proportionally more than do high-income individuals, the degree of income inequality and the need for welfare programs may be overstated; conversely, if high-dollar, white-collar crime is rampant, income may be even less evenly distributed than we think. This list of reasons for the importance of accounting for underground transactions could be extended considerably.

We can wish that compliance with tax laws was more widespread among Americans but, at the same time, we can be grateful that we do not suffer from the underreporting that appears common in parts of Europe. As Figure 4 shows, the underground economy is estimated to run as high as one-third of Italian GNP.**

***

**"Lies, Damned Lies, and Italy's GDP," *The Economist,* 27 Feb. 1988, 4–9.

FIGURE 4 *Estimates of the Size of the Underground Economy in Selected Countries*

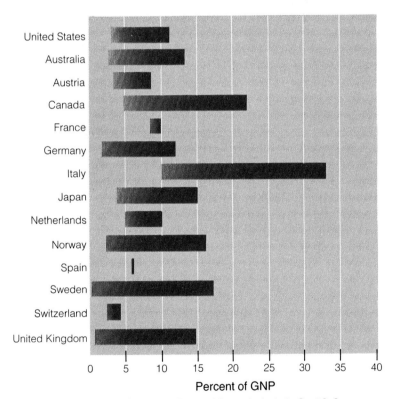

Source: U.S. Department of Commerce, Bureau of Economic Analysis; Carol S. Carson, "The Underground Economy: An Introduction," *Survey of Current Business,* May 1984, p. 33.

Note: The estimates are from many sources; when a range is shown, the high and low estimates for a country may bracket one or more estimates. Both among countries and for a particular country, the estimates vary in the scope of the underground economy measured, the methodology used, and the time period covered.

---

*"The Shadow Economy: Grossly Deceptive Product." *The Economist,* 19 Sept. 1987, 25–28.

CHAPTER REVIEW: KEY POINTS

1. *GNP* is the total market value of a nation's annual production. GNP measures estimate the economic performance of an economy and are important for government policy and business decisions.
2. The *expenditures* approach to GNP sums *consumption* spending (C), business *investment* spending (I), *government purchases* of good goods or services (G), and *net exports* ($X - M$):

$$GNP = C + I + G + (X - M).$$

3. *Gross Private Domestic Investment* (*GPDI*) is the economic term for business spending. To arrive at net investment, we need to subtract depreciation from GPDI.
4. Government purchases (G) do not include *transfer* (welfare) *payments,* which are treated as flows of income from some households to others.
5. The *income* approach to GNP sums wages, interest, rent, and profits. We use the figures available, which are (*a*) wages and salaries, (*b*) proprietors' income, (*c*) corporate profits, (*d*) rental income, and (*e*) interest. The sum of these figures is *National Income* (*NI*). Addition of *indirect business taxes,* which is not anyone's income, yields *Net National Product* (*NNP*). The *capital consumption allowance* (*depreciation*) is the difference between GNP and NNP.
6. The *value-added* approach to GNP sums the sales of all firms and subtracts their purchases of intermediate products, which are goods bought by one firm from another for further processing. Failure to exclude purchases of intermediate goods from GNP figures would result in substantial *double counting* of production.
7. GNP figures should be used cautiously in any discussions of economic welfare. One problem is that they may be systematically biased and are often presented in an artificially precise fashion. Another problem is that they ignore most nonmarket production (for example, housewives' services, do-it-yourself projects, and the like). GNP accounts include as production many disproducts (for instance, pollution abatement equipment is added to GNP, while environmental decay is not subtracted).
8. A *Measure of Economic Welfare* (*MEW*), which attempts to correct for some of these flaws in GNP accounts, shows much less rapid growth than GNP.

PROBLEMS

1. Suppose a car dealer sells a new car in September 1989 for $10,400, but allows a trade-in of $3,800 for a car that turns out to be a clunker. After $600 worth of repairs, the clunker is sold for $2,900. The new car cost the dealer $9,000. How will each phase of these transactions affect the GNP accounts? What were the values added at each step?
2. Use the following data to calculate:
   a. Gross National Product.
   b. Net National Product.
   c. Personal saving.

	$ billions
Gross Private Domestic Investment	666.1
Exports	363.2
Personal Tax Payments	498.2
State and Local Government Purchases	467.7
Capital Consumption Allowance	441.4
Imports	451.0
Personal Consumption Expenditures	2,606.1
Federal Government Purchases	364.8
Personal Income	3,298.5

3. You own a company that has annual sales of $500,000. The value added of your company's production (your addition to GNP) is estimated to be $250,000. Is your company making a profit of $250,000? If not, how is the difference between your firm's sales and your firm's addition to GNP explained?
4. If you start your own business and use $23,000 of your savings to buy used equipment from a dealer, is the $23,000 considered economic investment? Will any part of the $23,000 add to GNP? Explain.

QUESTIONS FOR THOUGHT AND DISCUSSION

1. National Income accounting values government services at the costs of the inputs government uses. Why does the government value its output in this manner? Do you feel that this understates or overstates the value of government? How would you measure the value of government services?

2. Should the purchase of education be viewed as consumption or investment expenditure? Why? What would happen to the National Income accounts if purchases of education, medical care, and dental care were counted as investment and not consumption?

3. Why is NNP a more appropriate measure of true economic productivity than GNP? As they are currently constructed, which do you think is the best measure of economic welfare on a per capita basis (*a*) GNP, (*b*) NNP, (*c*) NI, (*d*) PI, (*e*) DPI, or (*f*) consumption? What makes the category you selected preferable to each of the others?

4. What would be the effect on GNP accounting if marijuana, prostitution, and gambling were legalized nationwide? What do you think would happen to economic well-being? Why?

5. Suppose that all homeowners in America decided to move into their next-door neighbor's house and pay that neighbor rent. What would happen to GNP? Would your answer be the same if GNP estimates did not include an estimate of the rental value of owner-occupied housing? How would it differ?

6. Suppose one fourth of all young women workers take a maternity leave and then, after their children are born, decide to stay home permanently. What will happen to our GNP accounts? As we defined GNP conceptually, what happens to actual GNP relative to measured GNP? Measured GNP relative to economic welfare?

7. The government has gone to great lengths to compile and distribute measurements of aggregate economic activity. Some critics would say, "This information is not all that useful, and collecting it is just a method to employ a sizeable portion of the federal bureaucracy." Your reaction?

8. What is the effect of arson on estimates of GNP? What should it be?

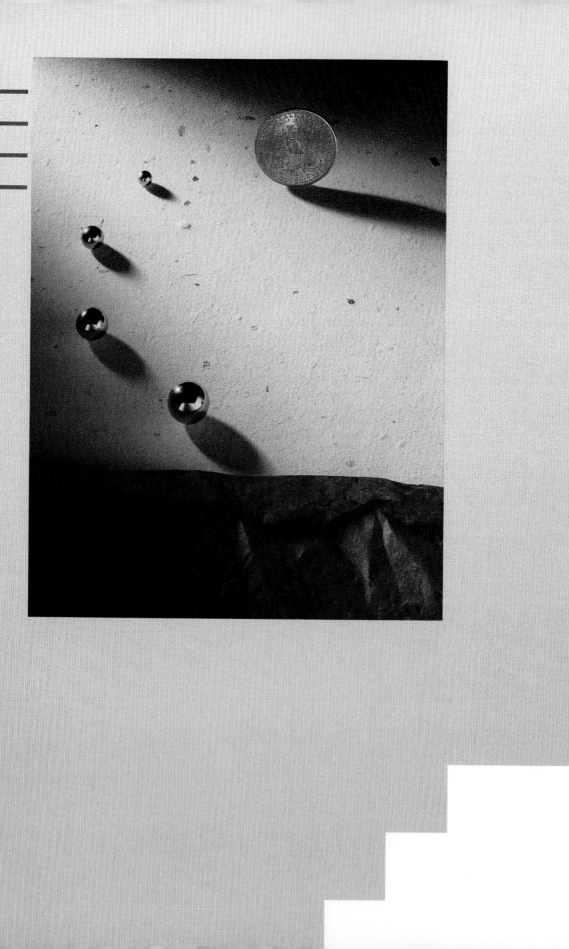

Keynesian Macroeconomics

PART 3

Isaac Newton's theories of gravity and mechanics suggest that the laws of nature sustain a natural harmony throughout the universe. Adam Smith extended Newton's view into the realm of economics with the idea that an "invisible hand" governs the marketplace. Smith's theory of markets, expressed in his *Wealth of Nations* (1776), led to *laissez-faire* policy prescriptions—ideas that were compatible with the hostility towards powerful government expressed in the American Declaration of Independence—which also appeared in 1776. The political climate and Smith's theories merged to shape an American economy that, with few exceptions, was dominated by this free market perspective until the worldwide Great Depression of the 1930s.

In chapter 8, we review several early macroeconomic theories; the classical economics that grew from Smith's "invisible hand" approach concludes that simple market economies naturally and quickly gravitate to full employment. From roughly 1790 until 1930, however, economies in Western Europe and North America evolved beyond their agricultural roots, becoming largely industrialized. Economic theories adapted very slowly to these changes.

Frequent booms and busts did not shake most economists' faith in laissez-faire policies until the 1930s depression launched the *Keynesian Revolution* in economic theory. Keynesian theory is the centerpiece of chapters 9 and 10, and is blended with Keynesian policy in chapter 11. This Keynesian approach to macroeconomics suggests that the government budget (taxing and spending) must be manipulated for a market economy to be stable.

Part 4 of this book revisits a classical macroeconomic perspective in which money plays an important role. Part 5 combines Keynesian and classical analytics in a more sophisticated model of the economy that explains movements of both unemployment and inflation and provides the background necessary to understand modern macroeconomic problems.

CHAPTER 8

Macroeconomics Before Keynes

Business activity has been plagued by booms and busts since the onset of industrialization, sporadically displacing workers from their jobs, pressing firms into bankruptcy, and bouncing politicians from office. Most early macroeconomic theories initially addressed business cycles and financial panics, but gradually evolved into general theories of aggregate economics.

This chapter begins with overviews of how business cycles are measured and early theories of business cycles, ranging from a "sunspot" theory to the Marxist approach. Our attention then turns to a historical overview of business cycles in the United States. Finally, we explore how the classical theory of markets dismissed the possibility of severe business cycles. This theory set the stage for the Keynesian analysis discussed in the next few chapters. The

Keynesian revolution in economic theory occurred in the 1930s, but even today, major macroeconomic debates range between modern Keynesians and those who have resurrected the classical tradition.

Business Cycles

"Boom-bust" patterns have been a persistent feature of economic history.

> The **business cycle** *consists of alternating periods of expansion and contraction in economic activity.*

Nevertheless, some economists are not convinced that cycles are inevitable. In the early 1960s, most economists viewed business cycles as obsolete. Although extensive studies of business cycle activity in both Western capitalist and socialist countries suggest that severe cycles leading to deep depressions may be less likely than in earlier times, less traumatic economic disruptions continue to nag societies everywhere.

A Typical Business Cycle

Business cycles are typically divided into two basic alternating periods—expansion and contraction. It can be useful to subdivide the cycle into (a) **peak,** (b) **contraction,** (c) **trough,** and (d) **expansion.** These four phases are illustrated in the insert of Figure 1. Some prefer the terms *boom, recession, depression,* and *recovery,* respectively, to describe cyclical activity. These sets of terms are used interchangeably in the remainder of this book.

The insert in Figure 1 depicts a relatively smooth cycle. As you can see, however, fluctuations are seldom this regular. Expansion phases last from as little as 10 months to as long as 105 months, while contraction phases range from 7 to 65 months in length. Notice that long contractions may be associated with short expansions, or vice versa.

NBER Classification System The *National Bureau of Economic Research* (*NBER*) was founded in 1920 by Wesley C. Mitchell, an early student of U.S. business cycles. Business cycle analysis is based on over 5,000 series of economic data, many of which have been collected by the NBER on a monthly basis since the early 1920s. These series cover such data as unemployment rates, the Dow-Jones stock index, new capital orders, rates of inventory accumulation, and new car sales.

These data are used to "date" business cycles. Troughs of the cycle occur when most measures of business activity are at their low points; peaks are dated when most data are at their high points. The turning points used to date peaks and troughs are unofficial until the next peak or trough has been reached and passed. For example, the latest trough, tentatively dated as November 1982, will not be official until after the end of the 1983 expansion.

The U.S. Department of Commerce now uses the NBER system to classify data by timing and economic process. *Timing* considers a series' performance during historical peaks and troughs that have been established as reference points. Data series that appear synchronized with overall economic activity are called business cycle *indicators.* **Leading indicators** reach their respective highs and lows before the cyclic peak and trough. **Coincident indicators** move almost simultaneously with aggregate economic activity. Finally, **lagging indicators** reach their respective highs and lows after the economy has peaked or troughed. The relationships between them are shown in Figure 2. Table 1 lists examples of these three types of indicators.

Social Aspects of the Business Cycle

The roller coaster effects of booms and depressions may disrupt individuals' plans so much that the effects reverberate for generations. Business cycles strongly affect general mental and physical health and can stimulate the breakdown of families, suicide, alcoholism, prostitution, illegitimacy, and crime. Some analysts focus too much on losses of production during recessions and ignore the high costs of severe social problems.

Interestingly, both marriage and divorce are positively related to economic swings. Hard times cause many couples to delay marriage. Rates of illegitimate births soar, and unhappy couples postpone divorce. Changes in marital status seem to be "luxuries" that are demanded when income is secure. Would you be as prone to marry if you feared losing your job? Would couples with young children be as apt to divorce during hard times?

Such stress-related diseases as heart attacks, strokes, and mental illness become more common during protracted economic downturns. Suicide rates were 60–70 percent above normal during the depths of the Great Depression, reflecting the gloom that arises when people suffer severe losses of income and forced idleness. One study indicates that roughly 240 more males aged 20 to 60 commit suicide annually with each 1 percent hike in the unemployment rate.

Jails also tend to fill during periods of widespread unemployment. Crime in general tends to be inversely related to the business cycle. Prosperity typically

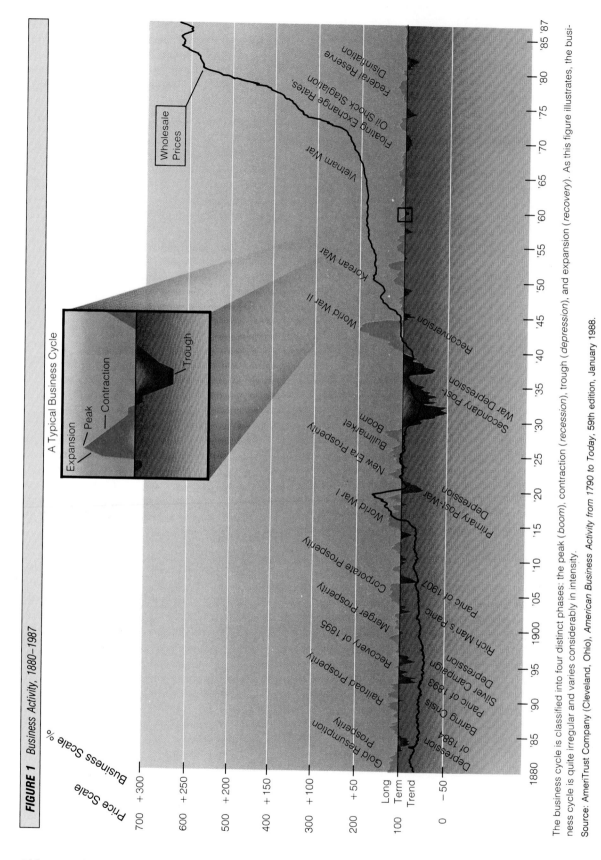

FIGURE 1 *Business Activity, 1880–1987*

A Typical Business Cycle

Expansion
Peak
Contraction
Trough

Wholesale Prices

Price Scale
Business Scale %

700 +300
600 +250
500 +200
400 +150
300 +100
200 +50
100 Long Term Trend
0   −50

'85 '87
'80
'75
'70
'65
'60
'55
'50
'45
'40
'35
'30
'25
'20
'15
'10
'05
1900
'95
'90
'85
1880

Disinflation
Federal Reserve
Oil Shock Stagflation
Floating Exchange Rates,
Vietnam War
Korean War
World War II
Reconversion
Secondary Post-War Depression
New Era Prosperity
Bullmarket Boom
Primary Post-War Depression
World War I
Corporate Prosperity
Merger Prosperity
Recovery of 1895
Railroad Prosperity
Gold Resumption Prosperity
Rich Man's panic
panic of 1907
Silver Campaign Depression
Panic of 1893
Baring Crisis
Depression of 1884

The business cycle is classified into four distinct phases: the peak (*boom*), contraction (*recession*), trough (*depression*), and expansion (*recovery*). As this figure illustrates, the business cycle is quite irregular and varies considerably in intensity.

Source: AmeriTrust Company (Cleveland, Ohio), *American Business Activity from 1790 to Today*, 59th edition, January 1988.

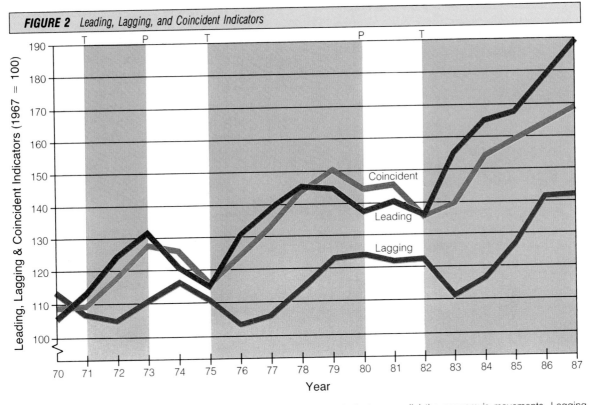

FIGURE 2 Leading, Lagging, and Coincident Indicators

Leading indicators turn up or down ahead of the economy. Coincident indicators parallel the economy's movements. Lagging indicators follow the movements of the economy.

Source: *Business Conditions Digest*, April, 1988.

abates crime rates while crime waves rise during recessions. Although violent crimes rise somewhat during slumps, property crime tends to rise dramatically. More individuals slip into illegal activities when legitimate income-earning opportunities shrink.

The ugly repercussions of business cycle downturns prod policymakers to try to steady the economy. If there were only mild swings around a trend of sustained growth, the social effects of business cycles would be muted. In the abyss of the Great Depression, policymakers enacted Social Security, unem-

TABLE 1 Selected Leading, Lagging, and Coincident Indicators

Leading	Coincident	Lagging
Average workweek for production workers	Real Personal Income less transfers	Average duration of unemployment
Index of net business formation	Index of industrial production	Labor cost per unit of production
New building permits (housing)	Employees on nonagricultural payrolls	Average prime rate charged by banks
Index of stock prices (500 common)	Manufacturing and trade sales	Commercial and industrial loans

Source: *Business Conditions Digest*, 1988.

ployment compensation, and other relief systems for those hit hardest by economic collapse. More recent economic reversals have done less harm than in the past, but the social maladies of business cycles have not vanished.

The American Business Cycle

The next nine chapters provide extensive discussions of the macroeconomy and of ways the federal government and monetary authorities might reduce the severity of business cycles. This section reviews business cycles in the last six decades to help prepare you for this material. Our discussion begins with the 1920s because the events of that decade and of the 1930s significantly changed the ways many of us think about capitalism.

The Prosperous 1920s   The 1920s were prosperous by any yardstick. A minor dip in business activity followed World War I, and then the United States enjoyed a boom that lasted until 1929. This prosperity was attributable to (*a*) rapid growth of technology and productive capacity; (*b*) development and wide distribution of such new and important goods as radios, autos, and telephones; (*c*) the electrification of most homes and industries; (*d*) significantly enhanced labor productivity; and (*e*) a wave of optimism lasting until the end of the decade.

Rising auto production spurred oil production and subsidiary industries such as tire manufacturing and service stations. Nationwide electrification also stimulated demands for business capital equipment and consumer goods. These key ingredients yielded record growth. Rapid technological advances allowed growth without inflation because growth in Aggregate Supply kept pace with growing Aggregate Demand. But the prosperity of the majority of urbanized Americans bypassed most rural areas of our country because agricultural prices were falling. This background of growth caused the severity of the 1930s Depression to unpleasantly surprise most people.

The Depressed 1930s   The year 1929 began with widespread expectations of a continued boom. By October, however, a business slump was clearly under way. Almost everyone was shocked when the economy collapsed, not to recover fully until the eve of World War II.

Statistical evidence of the severity of the Great Depression is provided in Table 2. Real disposable income fell by more than 26 percent, while unemployment rates soared from 3.2 percent in 1929 to nearly 25 percent in 1933. One person was out of a job for every three employed. Skimpy public welfare and unemployment compensation programs imposed most of the burden of economic relief on private charities. Donations to these were sparse because times were harsh. Family incomes and assets melted away when breadwinners lost their jobs. Even though consumption spending fell sharply, years of

TABLE 2   *The Severity of the Great Depression*

Measure	1929 High	1933 Low	Percentage Change
GNP (billions, 1972 dollars)	$314.6	$215.6	−31.5%
Gross private domestic investment (billions, 1972 dollars)	55.9	8.4	−85.0
Disposable income (billions, 1972 dollars)	229.8	169.7	−26.2
Total new construction (billions, current dollars)	10.8	2.9	−73.1
Producer prices (1926 = 100)	98.0	59.8	−40.0
Consumer prices (1967 = 100)	51.3	38.8	−24.4
Stock prices (1935–39 = 100)	238.0	36.0	−84.9
Unemployment rate (percentage)	3.2%	24.9%	+678.1

Sources: *Economic Report of the President*, 1988.

accumulated savings were eroded. Investment was insignificant.

Many families were evicted when they were unable to pay rent. The lucky ones would then move to another dwelling, or live with friends or relatives for as long as possible. It was as if a large segment of the population had stepped through doors into the distant past. Entire families spent their days as hunter-gatherers, prowling streets and garbage dumps looking for scraps of food and clothing with which to keep warm and alive.

Landlords were caught in the middle because paying their mortgages required rent revenue. When they failed to meet their mortgages, their buildings were often sold for less than the mortgage due. Landlords' own homes might then be sold to make up the deficit, leaving them out in the street, trapped in the same cycle that had ensnared their former tenants.

The 1940s: War and Its Aftermath

The economy began to recover falteringly after the trough of 1933, but unemployment hovered at 15 percent in 1940. Massive defense spending during World War II snapped the economy out of the Depression in the early 1940s. The war effort quickly moved the economy to full employment and brought both a new age of prosperity and knowledge about how to deal with recessions. John Maynard Keynes wrote *The General Theory of Employment, Interest, and Money* during 1935; its publication in 1936 reshaped subsequent economic thought. The magnitude of government spending during World War II seemed to confirm his theory of how to pull an economy out of a depression.

The economy has weathered several business cycles since World War II, but these downturns were less intense than the Great Depression because:

1. Widespread bank failures in the 1930s caused reforms to be enacted that now buffer the banking community against a severe collapse. These include the deposit insurance program (FDIC) and a strengthened role for the Federal Reserve System.
2. The Depression was so hard on so many families that lawmakers enacted several relief programs that act as "automatic stabilizers." For example, unemployment compensation slows declines in disposable income when individuals lose their jobs. This buoys consumer spending and fortifies a sick economy. Conversely, when the economy is

booming, few are unemployed, and the outlays for such programs fall.
3. Government spending grew during World War II and permanently became a larger part of Gross National Product. These relatively stable expenditures may help dampen business fluctuations. Furthermore, the U.S. government is now legally obligated by the Employment Act of 1946 to follow policies to maintain maximum employment.

There are other reasons why recent downturns have been less severe than the Great Depression, but these are the main forces dampening cyclical slumps.

Inflationary pressure built during the war, and the government imposed rationing and price controls to divert the bulk of output to the war effort. After World War II, many consumers had amassed huge savings because there was little to buy—many consumer goods were either tightly rationed or not produced at all. The price level jumped about 10 percent in 1946 after the war ended and price controls were lifted. Consumers had done without for years and would not be denied. Their favorite targets during this spending binge were automobiles and appliances because the plants where these products were made had been restricted to war goods.

The Sluggish 1950s

The 1950s were a period of modest growth, with occasional mild doses of creeping inflation. The most notable economic event of those years was a short-term jump in inflation at the beginning of the Korean conflict. Many consumers, remembering the problems associated with rationing and price controls during World War II, attempted to stockpile commodities that they expected to be rationed. This panic buying caused prices for numerous goods to soar temporarily. Over the rest of the decade the price level was relatively stable, rising at an average rate of only 1–2 percent annually. A mild recession followed the Korean War and another ended the decade.

The Booming 1960s

John F. Kennedy really introduced the country to activist policies based on macroeconomic theory. For the first time, expansionary policies were proposed when the economy was not in a deep depression. Lyndon Johnson's supporters used tax cuts in 1964 and 1965 to drive the economy to full employment. The experiment worked, and the nation heralded an era of prosperity and growth under the guiding hands of Washington economists. A minor trade-off between unemployment and inflation seemed to exist; policymakers could apparently choose a combination of the two that the country could endure. Escalation of the Vietnam War pushed the economy closer to full employment, but it ultimately overheated our economic engine. Nevertheless, the last time the federal budget was balanced was in 1969.

The Stagnant 1970s   Escalation of the Vietnam War without tax hikes to finance it yielded inflationary pressures that lasted into the 1970s. These demand-induced inflationary forces caused President Nixon to introduce peacetime wage and price controls on August 15, 1971. The mid-1970s saw our first brush with serious supply-side inflation. Lagging productivity growth and rising prices for energy and other raw materials erupted in high inflation and unemployment during 1974–76. Attempts by the Carter administration to solve the unemployment problem of the late 1970s generated double-digit inflation.

The Erratic 1980s   The Reagan administration's attempts to shrink inflation and high interest rates resulted in the deepest slump since the 1930s, with double-digit civilian unemployment in 1982. "Supply-side" tax cuts, enacted in 1981, eventually stimulated both Aggregate Demand and economic growth. By the mid-1980s, inflation and unemployment were both relatively low, but federal deficits continued to mushroom into the late 1980s. The national debt, which had tripled during the 1970s, tripled again between 1980 and 1989.

The international competitiveness of American business became an important issue during this period. The dollar was in danger of losing its status as the world's premier currency and U.S. balances of payments and trade persistently experienced huge deficits. Curing these three deficits and adapting to the growing internationalization of economies everywhere in the world may be as formidable a task as curing the Depression seemed in 1933.

Early Business Cycle Theories

Scholars have attempted to explain periodic fluctuations in economic activity since the dawn of commercial transactions. Accurately foreseeing the next boom or bust offers substantial strategic advantages

to business firms and can be an easy path to riches for individuals. (Perhaps you thought fortune-tellers were used only for romantic forecasts).

Early economists were limited to impressionistic theorizing about changing levels of economic activity. Today's methods are more precise. First, intricate models are used to forecast each sector of the economy. Then a simultaneous forecast of the macroeconomy is made using computers and sophisticated statistical techniques. Some early theories of business cycles seem ludicrous from the vantage point of modern knowledge of business activity.

Sunspot Theory

The absence of elaborate macroeconomic models drove many early business cycle theories to focus on **external forces** as sources of instability. An external force theory known as the **sunspot theory** was developed in 1875 by W. Stanley Jevons, a prominent economist. Sunspots are storms on the sun's surface caused by violent nuclear explosions. Jevons hypothesized that variations in sunspots cause fluctuations in economic activity. He reasoned that sunspots affect weather and, hence, agricultural yields. Since economies of his time were heavily dependent upon agriculture, sunspots supposedly caused swings in agriculture that reverberated throughout the economy. (If we ever depend heavily on solar energy, a new sunspot theory may be developed.)

Other early theorists also concentrated on swings in agriculture as a source of business instability. Many analysts watched weather cycles to predict general business conditions. Today, weather is still watched closely because agriculture remains important throughout the international economy. For example, a severe drought in the U.S. farm belt in the summer of 1988 drove up food prices around the world. Higher food prices limit the availability of national income for industrial development.

Population Dynamic Theories

Two hundred years ago, Adam Smith, Thomas Malthus, and their colleagues pondered the long-term effects on human history of such things as plagues, wars, famines, natural disasters, and the opening of new territory. They were convinced that increases in natural resource supplies normally generate drops in infant mortality and increases in longevity. From this assumption, they developed long-run business cycle theories based on how population adjusts to the congeniality of its habitat and to the state of international conflict.

According to the **population dynamics approach,** biological urges make birth rates almost constant, but survival rates depend on prosperity. When circumstances favor more production, the resulting booms cause population to explode; death rates fall for both infants and adults. As human population presses against available resources, strife over resources results in drops in both economic activity and population. Adjustments to adverse changes naturally follow a reverse pattern. Booms and then busts in economic activity, according to this line of reasoning, should alternate across generations.

These early economists failed to anticipate technological advances and birth control programs, so their speculations apply more to primitive economies than to today's industrial giants. Indeed, even now one of the first results of growth in less developed countries is often a population explosion.

Marxian "Capitalistic Crises"

Contrary to many perceptions of Karl Marx, he was in awe of economic progress under capitalism. In the *Communist Manifesto* (1848), he marveled that capitalism

> . . . *has created more massive and more colossal forces than have all preceding generations together.* . . . *It has accomplished wonders far surpassing Egyptian pyramids, Roman aqueducts, and Gothic cathedrals; it has conducted expeditions that put in the shade all former migrations of nations and crusades.*

Nevertheless, Marx declared himself the enemy of the market system as pitting man against man, with the rich and powerful exploiting workers.[1] Describ-

ing his views as scientific socialism, he predicted that capitalism would move spasmodically through expansions and contractions, with each peak higher than its predecessor and each successive crash deeper than the last. Ultimately, the working class would overthrow its exploiters, the spark of a communist takeover igniting during the deep abyss of a depression.

The driving forces behind Marxian business cycles are ever greater concentrations of wealth and power in the hands of capitalists. Briefly, rapid investment and growth are assumed to result in increasingly unfair distributions of income. Poor workers lack income to buy the goods they produce, resulting in overproduction (or underconsumption). Because capitalists lack markets, capitalism plunges into depressions or imperialistic wars. Then wars, the openings of new markets, or the discoveries of new raw materials result in an upswing. The next downswing then emerges, and so on. Marx's views of **capitalist crises** are treated more completely in later chapters.

Innovations

In 1911, Joseph Schumpeter (See his Biography.) developed a **long-wave theory of business cycles.** This theory suggests that development is propelled by **innovations,** including (*a*) new discoveries of raw materials, (*b*) introduction of a new good or new quality in a familiar product, (*c*) technological advances, (*d*) opening of new markets, and (*e*) major reorganizations of industries.

Major innovations generate **spin-offs**—other new inventions, mimicry of the original innovation, and the rise of new industries. The space program, for example, yielded such advances as microelectronic circuitry and Teflon. An economy grows but ultimately peaks as society adapts to a major innovation; entrepreneurs quit innovating when markets for closely related goods become saturated. Markets will not sustain further increases of supplies or emulation of technology. Retrenchment occurs while firms reevaluate their roles, and the economy slumps while awaiting another wave of innovation. The long-wave process begins anew when another major innovation appears. Of course, less significant innovations might explain shorter cycles.

---

1. One of the oldest jokes floating around communist countries is that, "Under capitalism, man exploits man. Under socialism, it's vice versa."

BIOGRAPHY

Joseph A. Schumpeter (1883–1950)

As a young man, Joseph Schumpeter expressed three life ambitions: to be the world's greatest economist, lover, and horseman. He joked that he had achieved two of the three, confessing in his wry way that he never was much of an equestrian. The issue of his ambitions aside, he was unquestionably a man of extraordinary energy and accomplishment.

Widely versed in economics, mathematics, statistics, history, and social philosophy, Schumpeter was both a scholarly observer and a major participant in the world of affairs. At one time or another he was lawyer, banker, teacher, and public official, serving a stint as finance minister in his native Austria. Two books on economics, both published before he was 30 years old, are still highly regarded. In 1932, he became a professor of economics at Harvard University, where he taught until his death eighteen years later.

Schumpeter's writings contain concepts of the whole economic process: equilibrium, business cycles, and the survival prospects of capitalism. He viewed competition as a learning process and an ordering force. Somewhat paradoxically, he considered business cycles essential to economic progress.

Cycles occur because equilibrium is destroyed by innovations, but since innovations improve the economic conditions of society, this destruction of equilibrium is "creative."

Schumpeter considered certain institutional features essential to the continued vitality of an economy. First, there must be broad scope for the operation of entrepreneurs (Schumpeter's innovators). Second, it must be possible for new entrepreneurs to break into the system. This second condition requires well-developed credit markets that allow entrepreneurs to capture income streams and use them in production even before actually contributing anything to national income.

Schumpeter distinguished three types of business cycles, naming the cycles for earlier pioneers in business cycle theory. The length of each depends on the kind of disturbance that causes it. The shortest (*Kitchin*) cycle is associated with inventory changes and usually lasts about 3 years. An intermediate (*Juglar*) cycle depends on fairly small innovations, such as microwave ovens or electronic calculators, and runs its course in 8–11 years. The long (*Kondratieff*) cycle lasts 40–60 years and is caused by sweeping innovations such as electrification or jet flight.

Schumpeter used railroads as an example of a major innovation.[2] Cars and airplanes also significantly shaped U.S. economic development. More recent-

ly, the computer has enabled some industries to grow to sizes that were impossible when information processing was more primitive. An important innovative spin-off is miniaturization using microchips. "High-tech" now allows hand-held calculators and minicomputers to do what required rooms full of equipment a few years ago. Perhaps the most underrated innovation of our time is the supermarket. Supermarkets reduce transaction costs for an incredible variety of goods and provide outlets for specialized firms that would have been denied shelf space in an old-fashioned general store.

---

2. He noted: "Expenditures on, and the opening of, a new line has some immediate effects on business in general, on competing means of transport, and on the relative position of centers of production. It requires more time to bring into use the opportunities of production newly created by the railroad and to annihilate others. And it takes still longer for population to shift, cities to decay, and, generally, the new face of the country to take a shape that is adapted to the environment as altered by railroadization." Joseph A. Schumpeter, *Business Cycles: A Theoretical, Historical, and Statistical Analysis of the Capitalist Process* (New York: McGraw-Hill Book Company, Inc., 1939).

Kondratieff Long Waves

Another theory of long waves in economic activity was developed in the 1920s by the Russian economist Nikolai Kondratieff. After studying many economic aggregates over the period 1780–1920, he identified two complete long waves (40–60 years each) and the beginning of a third. Kondratieff hypothesized that the world economy would boom and then bust every 40–60 years. The third wave began its decline in the early 1920s, culminating in the "Crash of '29."

Kondratieff's theory predicts a serious worldwide depression during the 1980s or 1990s. Studies of business cycles, however, have found no convincing evidence that **Kondratieff long waves** are anything but a statistical accident, so most economists are skeptical that the world economy will collapse in the near future. Believers remain convinced that the fourth Kondratieff wave will begin in the next few years, reaching its trough around the year 2,000 (see Figure 3). Some observers felt the 1982 recession was the beginning of this decline, but steady growth from 1983 to 1988 was contrary to this prediction.

Will the Bottom Drop Out in the 1990s? Gloom and doom forecasts have found receptive audiences for generations. Some analysts perceive a danger that policy mistakes that contributed to the onset and severity of the Great Depression will be mirrored in policies adopted in the late 1980s. One group blames the Great Depression on a trade war that was set off by the Smoot-Hawley tariff of 1930. According to this group, the stock market crashed in 1929 when it became apparent that Smoot-Hawley would be en-

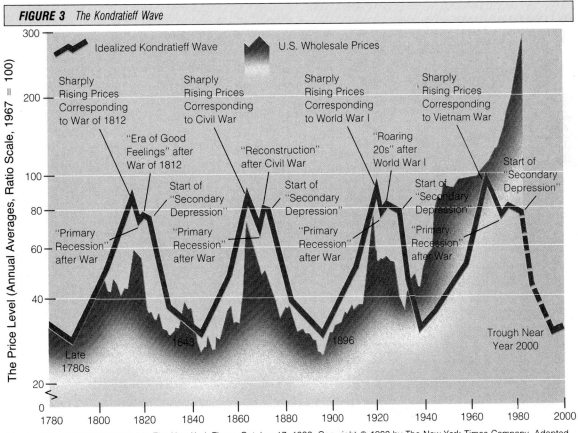

FIGURE 3 The Kondratieff Wave

Source: "The Kondratieff Wave," in *The New York Times*, October 17, 1982. Copyright © 1982 by The New York Times Company. Adapted by permission.

acted.[3] The ensuing of international trade then precipitated a worldwide depression. This group views growing sentiment for protectionist measures that reduce international trade as a threat that could cause the collapse of both world trade and economies everywhere. This group, however, does not rely on cyclic regularity for its pessimistic forecasts.

A more formal long-wave theory of business activity was recently introduced by Ravi Batra, an eminent scholar in the area of international economics.[4] His 1985 book, *The Great Depression of 1990,* became a bestseller after the "Black Monday" stock market crash in October 1987.

Batra echoes Kondratieff's 60 year cycles and argues that a recent trend towards greater income inequality will create underconsumption (an idea borrowed from Marx and Malthus). Other signs of impending doom cited by Batra include rampant speculation, deficits in our international payments and trade and in the federal budget, and year-by-year parallels between the 1920s and the 1980s. He predicts that the 1990s will be even more depressed than the 1930s. Most economists view differences between these periods as far more important than their similarities, but his ideas have gained a coterie of followers. If Batra's predictions prove accurate, it may be because widespread belief about a dismal economic future can become a self-fulfilling prophecy.

Psychological Theories

Psychological theories of the business cycle usually focus on how human herd instincts result in prolonged periods of optimism or pessimism. This approach recognizes that people are swayed by both psychological and economic factors. Psychological theories of business cycles explain the momentum of booms or busts initiated by real changes in such things as agricultural yields, the profitability of investments, or natural resource availability.

Once some "real" disturbance occurs, decision makers' reactions cause secondary shock waves—the psychological part of the cycle. Most decisions rely on educated guesses (much as you sometimes answer multiple-choice questions on exams) because information is limited and costly. Most business managers operate from the same information bases, which include government and market research data. There is a general reluctance to go it alone. It is not surprising, therefore, that many firms often move in the same direction.

Business cycles originate when many firms develop similar new expectations about economic expansion or contraction and adjust their investment and production plans accordingly. Waves of pessimism or optimism, once set off, seem to have a life of their own. Economic recoveries commence when business becomes optimistic and begins to expand production. This requires that more workers be hired, which tends to bolster household optimism and spending, creating more employment, and so on. A wave of pessimism can operate in just the opposite way. (With psychology involved, is there any wonder at the term *depression?*)

Psychological theories illustrate why a recovery or downturn is a cumulative process, but do not help us predict swings in economic activity. For this reason, economists have devoted most of their research to discovering more fundamental causes of ups and downs in business cycles.

Most early business cycle theories use broad brush strokes to paint impressionistic images of an economy in motion. Early theories of capitalism known as *classical theory* dominated economics from the early nineteenth century until the Great Depression. Learning this theory will enable you to tie together some strands of analysis that help explain how the world works.

Classical Theory

Not the creation of a single economist, classical theory is a mix of theories arising from studies of how markets operate. Many economists view the modern re-emergence of classical analysis as the major force advancing the frontiers of modern economics.

> **Classical economics** *is not a theory of business cycles per se, but it suggests that aggregate supply and demand adjust naturally to offset pressures for long-term unemployment or substantial economic inefficiency. Thus, classical macroeconomics shows how the negative effects of the business cycle are automatically overcome by market forces.*

---

3. "The Trade Bill Fluffs its Feathers," *The Economist,* 19 March 1988, 21–22.

4. Ravi Batra, *The Great Depression of 1990* (New York: Simon and Schuster, 1987). Batra privately published his book in 1985.

Classical reasoning offers stabilizing mechanisms that resemble biological processes called *homeostasis*. Here is an example of biological homeostasis: you break into a sweat if your temperature rises above 98.6°. Your body cools as your perspiration evaporates. A low temperature causes shivering and your teeth to chatter; friction in your muscle tissues then generates heat, raising your temperature towards 98.6°. Just as homeostasis automatically moves your body toward health, classical economics suggests that an idea known as *Say's Law* will ensure full employment and economic health if combined with flexible prices, wages, and interest rates.

Say's Law

Say's Law is named after the nineteenth-century French economist Jean Baptiste Say, who believed that the very act of production creates an equivalent amount of demand.

> **Say's Law** *asserts that supply creates its own demand.*

He based his law on the idea that people work, not for the sake of working, but only to obtain income to spend on goods they want. People produce (*supply*) roller skates or biscuits only so that they can buy (*demand*) cars or fur coats. Similarly, investors do not seek income per se. Rather, they seek what their income will buy. Thus, the act of producing requires that resources be hired and paid, which in turn leads to the resource owners' incomes being spent on other goods.

Say conceded that there might be sporadic gluts of some goods, but reasoned that surpluses in any market must be offset by shortages in another; economy-wide gluts of most goods are impossible. Surpluses and shortages in specific markets are remedied in the long run because prices and production both fall if there are surpluses, or both rise to cure shortages.

Flexible Interest Rates and Underconsumption

Challengers of Say's Law point out that most people do not spend all their earnings, and that saving might result in a deficiency of Aggregate Demand. If consumers do not spend all of their incomes, firms may find inventories rising, causing employment to fall when firms adjust to insufficient demand. Classical economists respond that all consumer saving is invested by business.

Early classical reasoning argued that people save only to facilitate higher future consumption. In a monetary economy, saving is translated into funds available for loans. Stocks and bonds are financial investments representing saving. According to classical reasoning, interest payments are required to encourage consumers to forgo present consumption. Higher interest rates paid by borrowers encourage more saving. Thus the amount of saving is positively related to the interest rate, as shown in Figure 4.

The other side of the saving/investment market is business demands for loans for capital investments. Lower interest rates stimulate more investment. This occurs because firms rank potential opportunities to invest from those with the highest expected rates of return, after adjusting for risk, to those with the lowest. Individual firms then try to borrow funds to

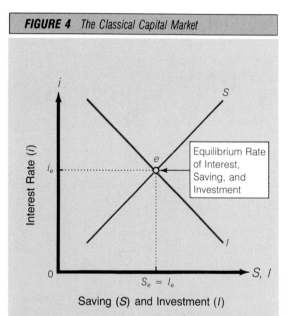

FIGURE 4 *The Classical Capital Market*

Saving (*S*) and Investment (*I*)

Classical economists argued that flexible interest rates would equate saving and investment in the capital market. Savers elected to postpone current consumption, and interest was their reward. A higher reward (higher interest) would encourage more saving. Business would demand more loans at lower interest rates. Thus, flexible interest rates would equate saving and investment at $S_e = I_e$ when the interest rate was i_e.

invest in activities for which the expected rate of return is greater than the interest they must pay. Thus, saving is positively related to interest rates, while investment is negatively related to interest rates, as shown in Figure 4.

Flexible interest rates tend to equalize the amounts of saving and investment. If interest rates were below i_e in Figure 4, there would be pressure for interest rates to rise as firms sought more financial capital for investment than savers willingly provided. Savers who were unable to loan funds at current interest rates would bid them down if they exceeded i_e. It follows that interest rates respond to changes in the demands and supplies of loanable funds that facilitate investment; this balances aggregate saving with investment. Any deficiency in consumption demand caused by saving is matched in equilibrium by business demands for financial capital to invest.

Flexible Wages and Prices

Classical economists went a step farther, arguing that if the capital market failed to reach equilibrium, **flexible wages and prices** would still ensure full employment. Wages and prices are like readings on an automatic thermostat. If saving exceeds investment, then Aggregate Supply exceeds Aggregate Demand. This deficiency of demand presses prices down as firms accumulate unwanted inventories, resulting in layoffs and causing temporary surpluses in labor markets. If wages and prices fall, the quantities of goods and labor demanded will rise, restoring the economy to full employment. On the other hand, excess demands would cause the thermostat of price adjustments to generate wage hikes and price increases. You should note that much of classical economics just applies supply and demand analysis to macroeconomics.

Suppose that the average wage rate is $10 per hour, as shown in Figure 5. One hundred million people are willing to work at $10 per hour, but firms are only willing to hire 80 million people, so there will be 20 million unemployed. But will this unemployment persist? Classical reasoning answers NO to this question, arguing that when this labor surplus causes average wages to drop to $8 per hour, the 90 million people willing to work at this wage will be employed. What about the other 10 million? They

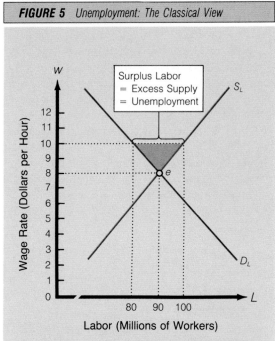

FIGURE 5 Unemployment: The Classical View

Surplus Labor
= Excess Supply
= Unemployment

Unemployment occurs, according to classical reasoning, primarily because wages are too high. The economy will self-correct for this problem when workers bid wages down to get jobs. This is what has happened at point e. The 90 million people who are willing to work have found employment at an hourly wage of $8. This fails to occur only if unions or legal minimum wages prevent wages from falling. Without legal wage floors, most who are unemployed must be so voluntarily. They could cure their own unemployment by accepting lower pay.

would drop out of the work force because they are unwilling to work at an $8 hourly wage.

Thus, flexible wages and prices are another safety valve. This returns us to the topic of voluntary and involuntary unemployment from chapter 6. In the classical view, anyone who is unemployed for long in a pure market economy is *voluntarily* unemployed because they are offering their labor only at higher than equilibrium wages. People willing to work at sufficiently low wages can always find jobs. The unemployed are simply exercising preferences for leisure over working for the going wage or a bit less. Thus, unemployment is not a social problem. In large measure, classical economists use intuition and logic to define away the problem of involuntary unemployment.

Classical Theory and the Price Level

Extended involuntary unemployment is impossible according to classical reasoning. Unstable price levels remain as potential major macroeconomic problems. Classical economists believed that Aggregate Demand is closely tied to the amounts of money available for people to spend. (We will delve into exactly why this is so in chapters 13–15.)

Say's Law, coupled with flexible interest rates, prices, and wages would, according to classical theory, keep workers fully employed. Essentially, classical reasoning views the Aggregate Supply curve as vertical at full employment. Figure 6 illustrates this concept, assuming an initial equilibrium level of national output of Q_f at point a with an initial price level of P_0.

Suppose private spending fell because of a drop in the money supply or increased desires to save (the underconsumption problem discussed previously). This would cause Aggregate Demand to fall from AD_0 to AD_1. Excess supplies would result in layoffs, reduced output, and rising inventories (point b). According to classical economics, the economy would move to point c relatively quickly as prices and wages fell, restoring full employment. If the pressures were reversed (Aggregate Demand rises to AD_2), the economy would expand along a path like ade, restoring full employment at Q_f with higher price level P_2. There might be short-run deviations from full employment, but the economy would self-correct rapidly without government intervention. This is consistent with the laissez-faire political atmosphere of earlier times.

Classical analysis teaches that the price level is directly related to aggregate spending, which in turn depends strictly on the money supply. Thus, a stable money supply is the key to solving price level instability. Some people who believe fervently in laissez-faire policies advocate a gold standard. They believe that the supply of gold is inherently stable, so that policies requiring all money to be backed 100 percent by gold would preclude rapid changes in the value of money and prevent significant inflation or deflation.

In summary, classical economics depends on Say's Law and flexible interest rates, prices, and wages to ensure full employment. This theory suggests that price level stability depends only on a stable money supply so that aggregate spending is relatively steady. Some modern economists of the classical school believe a gold standard would guarantee a stable money supply.

The Great Depression: Classical Theory at Bay

Until the Great Depression, classical economists smugly believed that laissez-faire capitalism automatically gravitates towards full employment. The (short-run?) decline of classical macroeconomics commenced on October 24, 1929, when the New York Stock Exchange crashed. Dana Thomas recalled that day, known since as "Black Friday," with the following story:

The newspapers recounted the plight of a jury that before the crash had been sworn in for the trial of a former State Banking Superintendent indicted on charges of bribery. Several jurors had heavy commitments in the stock market. They were under strict

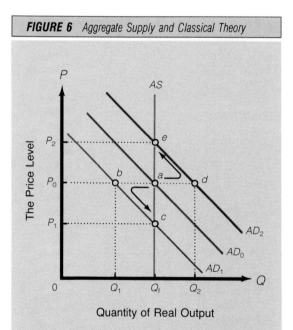

FIGURE 6 *Aggregate Supply and Classical Theory*

Unexpected expansions of Aggregate Demand (from AD_0 to AD_2) result in a temporary boom (movement of the economy along a path like *ade*). Unexpected contractions of Aggregate Demand (from AD_0 to AD_1) would cause the economy to suffer a temporary recession (movement along a path like *abc*).

orders from the judge not to read newspapers or engage in any conversation with outsiders. Nevertheless, news of the debacle in Wall Street had leaked in to them and they pleaded with court attendants to let them contact their brokers to find out how they stood. But there was nothing that could be done. One juror, while he sat in a sweat listening to courtroom testimony, lost $80,000.[5]

Between 1929 and 1933 the ranks of the unemployed grew from about 3 percent to around 25 percent of the labor force. While the unemployment rolls swelled, investment spending collapsed even though the interest rate dropped to around 1.5 percent. Many people were willing to work for almost nothing; for them, the classical economists' promise of employment opportunities seemed a mirage. The September 1932 issue of *Fortune* noted:

Dull mornings last winter the sheriff of Miami, Florida, used to fill a truck with homeless men and run them up to the county line. Where the sheriff of Fort Lauderdale used to meet them and load them into a second truck and run them up to his county line. Where the sheriff of Saint Lucie's would meet them and load them into a third truck and run them up to

his county line. Where the sheriff of Brevard County would not meet them. And whence they would trickle back down the roads to Miami. To repeat.

The classical view that the people described in this passage were "voluntarily unemployed" seems callous and unrealistic. They were willing to work for considerably less than prevailing wages, but were unable to find jobs.

A Prelude to Modern Macroeconomic Theory

The persistence of worldwide 15 to 25 percent unemployment rates throughout the 1930s led John Maynard Keynes to scrutinize the traditional assumptions about the economy and precipitated the **Keynesian Revolution.** He offered several reasons why the capitalistic system might neither automatically nor quickly rebound from a depression. In the next three chapters, we examine the macroeconomic model developed by Keynes and his followers during the Great Depression. The knowledge gained in studying this model will aid you in analyzing current macroeconomic problems that confront policymakers and analysts. As you can see in Figure 7, the growth rate of

---

5. Dana L. Thomas, *The Plungers and the Peacocks* (New York: G. P. Putnam's Sons, 1967), 211.

FIGURE 7 *Changes in Real GNP, 1910–87*

Our Gross National Product has grown at a 2–3 percent average rate over the past century, but was quite erratic prior to 1950. Negative growth has occurred at times since then, but the overall upward trend has been smoother over the past 35 years or so.

Source: *Business Conditions Digest,* January 1988 and *Economic Report of the President,* 1988.

GNP appears to have become more stable since 1950. A large part of this reduced instability over the last few decades must be attributed to the work of Keynes.

Keynes's writings are a starting point for modern business cycle theory. The paradox for classical theory presented by the Great Depression set the stage for the development of a theory to explain involuntary unemployment. Classical economics, which assumed mechanisms of flexible interest rates, wages, and prices, had apparently broken down. We begin with a very simple Keynesian model. As you might suspect, Keynes's original model has been refined and integrated with classical reasoning into a more complete theory. This more sophisticated amalgam of Keynesian and classical models is developed further in chapters 16–19. But first, you will need to master the simple Keynesian macroeconomic model.

CHAPTER REVIEW: KEY POINTS

1. *Business cycles* consist of alternating periods of economic expansion and contraction. From World War II into the early 1960s, many economists felt that the business cycle was obsolete because government could fine-tune the economy with monetary and fiscal policy. This optimistic point of view is no longer widely held.

2. The business cycle is typically broken down into four phases (*a*) *peak* (boom), (*b*) *contraction* (recession or downturn), (*c*) *trough* (depression), and (*d*) *expansion* (recovery or upturn). Business cycles are measured from peak to peak and have averaged roughly 4 years. Some have been as short as 18 months, while others have lasted a decade.

3. Business cycles are dated and analyzed by the *National Bureau of Economic Research (NBER)*. Reference dates are established by a detailed examination of data from past cycles.

4. The NBER has examined thousands of individual data series and classified those that seem systematically related to cycles into three groups (*a*) *leading indicators* reach their respective highs and lows before the general cycle peak and trough; (*b*) *coincident indicators* tend to turn roughly with the general business cycle; and (*c*) *lagging indicators* reach their respective peaks and troughs after the general business cycle.

5. Business cycles leave their mark on people and families in many ways besides loss of income. Such things as mental and physical health problems, marital tensions, divorces, suicides, alcoholism, prostitution, illegitimacy, and both personal and property crime are closely related to changes in business conditions. Marriages and divorces alike tend to be positively related to the business cycle. Mental disorders and some physical diseases, suicides, crimes, and illegitimate births appear inversely related to business conditions. That is, they all rise when the economy turns down. Declines in income and the negative social effects of business slumps together have prompted policymakers to look for ways to keep the economy on a steady path.

6. Prosperity in the 1920s was caused primarily by the rapid growth of the automobile industry and the spread of such innovations as electricity, radio, and the telephone. A wave of optimism lasted through much of the period.

7. The Great Depression of the 1930s was the most severe in U.S. history. At its trough, a fourth of the labor force was unemployed and real disposable personal income had fallen by about 26 percent. Many were left homeless and hungry. The devastation of the Depression led to new economic theories and to numerous reforms in banking and social welfare programs.

8. World War II rapidly lifted the country out of the Depression. Massive government spending to fight the war brought unemployment down from 15 percent in 1940 to less than 3 percent during 1944–45. Inflation became a major problem after World War II as the federal government focused its policies on achieving full employment.

9. The 1960s were prosperous, consistent with the government's perceived ability to "fine-tune" the economy using the latest techniques of macroeconomic policy. President Johnson's decision to expand both domestic programs and the Vietnam conflict generally overheated the economy in the late 1960s and early 1970s.

10. In 1971, wage and price controls were used by President Nixon to slow the rate of inflation. In the middle 1970s, the economy was battered with large doses of both unemployment and inflation—a combination generally called stagflation. The economy remained sluggish, with substantial amounts of both unemployment and inflation lingering into the

early 1980s. Attempts by the Reagan administration to reduce both inflation and interest rates resulted in high unemployment in 1982, but a sustained recovery brought unemployment back down by the mid-1980s.

11. Many early business cycle theories were *external force theories,* focusing on events outside the economic system. The *sunspot theory* and other external force theories were based on changing weather conditions and wars as sources of instability.

12. *Joseph Schumpeter* developed a business cycle theory around major innovations that may partially explain major long-term business fluctuations. He cited the developments of railroads, automobiles, and similar innovations as generating significant investment leading to tremendous economic growth for a period of time.

13. *N. D. Kondratieff* suggested that long waves of economic activity (40–60 years) underlie the minor reverberations that occur roughly every 4 to 8 years. This *long-wave theory* has not been especially convincing to economists, being widely viewed as a statistical coincidence.

14. *Psychological theories* of the business cycle use people's herd instincts to explain the effects of extended periods of optimism or pessimism. These theories may partially account for the cumulative nature of business cycle downturns or recoveries, but provide little insight into the reasons for turning points.

15. *Classical theory* is not a business cycle theory per se, but a systematic examination of how the economy operates. Classical theory is a conglomeration of the thoughts of many economic thinkers dating back to Adam Smith.

16. Classical economists based their theory on *Say's Law: Supply creates its own demand.* Coupled with assumptions that wages, prices, and interest rates are all perfectly flexible, Say's Law drives the economy towards full employment. All unemployment is considered voluntary—simply a refusal to work at the equilibrium wage. The protracted unemployment of the early 1930s diluted acceptance of classical theory and led to the development of the radically different Keynesian theory.

PROBLEM

1. Use Aggregate Demand and Aggregate Supply curves to show the circumstances under which lower unemployment means higher inflation, and vice versa—the circumstances when unemployment and inflation would rise or fall together.

QUESTIONS FOR THOUGHT AND DISCUSSION

1. The word "recession" replaced "depression," which was called "panic" a century ago. Why do you think the terms for economic downturns change over time?

2. Most people alive today had not been born before the Great Depression of the 1930s. Those who remember the Depression have a different perception of the effect of the business cycle on economic well-being than those whose memories span only the 1950s, 1960s, 1970s, or 1980s. How do you think the perception of economic cycles differs between generations?

3. Some people are convinced economic catastrophe is just around the corner, while others are optimistic about the economic trends in the United States. Do you think economic cycles are inevitable? Of the theories of business cycles presented in this chapter, which do you find most believable?

4. Are the classical writers correct in asserting that all unemployment is voluntary? Can you conceive of circumstances under which people willing to work for the wages paid other people with similar skills and experience would be involuntarily employed?

5. Productivity grew very slowly, if at all, through the 1970s. Can you think of a number of reasons why labor productivity grew comparatively slowly during this period?

CHAPTER 9

Aggregate Expenditures: Consumption, Investment, Government, and Foreign Spending

Classical macroeconomics stresses the stability of a market system and has as its central goals (*a*) expanding Aggregate Supply—our productive capacity, and (*b*) limiting growth of Aggregate Demand to keep inflation muzzled. According to Say's Law, *supply creates its own demand,* so classical theory suggests that severe unemployment is unlikely and certainly cannot persist. Thus, most economists of the 1930s were baffled by the Great Depression. A reassessment of economic theory seemed in order.

The first major economist to challenge the classical stress on supply was John Maynard Keynes (see his Biography). Keynes's *The General Theory of Employment, Interest, and Money* (1936) turned Say's Law upside down. Keynesian theory assumes that "demand creates its own supply." The Keynesian model is essentially a *depression* model. To some degree, its wide acceptance in more prosperous times stems from the appeal to politicians of its major policy prescriptions—lower taxes and increased government spending.

In this and the next two chapters, we will develop the Keynesian model one step at a time. In chapters 10 and 11, we will look in more detail at the interactions of Aggregate Expenditures and national output, and will explore adjustments that move an economy to a macroeconomic equilibrium. Learning the anatomy of Aggregate Expenditures is a necessary first step; it will be the focus of our attention for the remainder of this chapter.

BIOGRAPHY

John Maynard Keynes (1883–1946)

Bernard Baruch once put an end to an economist's badgering with the question, "If you're so smart, why aren't you rich?" John Maynard Keynes would not have been daunted by such a question. A keen observer of economic and human affairs, Keynes amassed a private fortune by speculating in commodities, foreign currencies, and stock market securities. He was equally successful in the social, political, and academic arenas.

Keynes married a world famous Russian ballerina and was a shining light in the illustrious Bloomsbury group, England's foremost intellectual set. He served as a treasury official and major representative of the British government during important negotiations following both World Wars. Nevertheless, he will be remembered longest as a leading figure in economics. Only the works of Smith and Marx rival Keynesian theories and policies in their impact on economic thought and practice in the twentieth century.

Much of modern macroeconomics is based on Keynes's 1936 treatise, *The General Theory of Employment, Interest, and Money,* his reaction to contradictions between classical economic theory and the worldwide Great Depression. This work challenged the conventional view that *aggregate equilibrium* is synonymous with *full employment.* Keynes reconstructed economic theory to explain persistent and high unemployment throughout market-oriented economies. He concluded that, far from being inconsistent with aggregate equilibrium, unemployment might be a consequence of it.

In brief, Keynes argued that a capitalist economy might experience high unemployment as a permanent situation unless some external force were used to reduce it. For practical and political reasons, he thought that this external force must come from government and should take the form of large expenditures on public works projects capable of mobilizing idle labor. Therefore, Keynes turned away from the long tradition of laissez-faire economic thought, which held that any government intervention in the economy is misguided and harmful.

There is generally a long lag between ideas and actions. In the United States in the early 1960s, the Kennedy administration ushered in our major experiments with Keynesian economic policies. Keynesianism cut across party lines and continued to dominate economic policy until the election of Ronald Reagan. But two decades of activist Keynesian economic policies in this country yielded mixed results. Because the specter of deep depression largely gave way to persistent inflation in the 1960s and 1970s, Keynesian economics has been under fire from many quarters.

Former President Reagan's "supply-side" economic policies represented an attempt to turn back the Keynesian clock in favor of classical economic remedies. Many observers, however, attributed the strong recovery of 1983–88 to powerful Keynesian policies—tax cuts, expanded government outlays, and huge deficits—that were based on a "supply-side" approach only in political oratory.

Keynesian Focus on Aggregate Spending

Keynes's major concern was ensuring that Aggregate Demand is adequate for full employment of all resources. Keynes and his early followers demoted expansion of productive capacity and maintenance of price level stability to secondary goals, to be pursued only *after* an economy reaches full employment. Keynes argued that although classical theory may apply in a fully employed economy, Aggregate Demand alone determines output and employment when an economy is in the midst of a depression.

Keynes's reasons for ignoring the price level and focusing primarily on Aggregate Demand can be seen in Panel B of Figure l, which shows real GNP and the price level during the Great Depression. Real output began to grow after the Depression bottomed out in 1933. This recovery occurred when Aggregate Demand grew without stimulating major hikes in the price level.

Keynes assumed that idle productive capacity makes Aggregate Supply almost flat during depressed times, as shown in Panel A of Figure 1; production and income stretch to conform to growth in Aggregate Demand without spawning serious inflationary pressure. Real output grew more than 60 percent during the seven years after the Depression reached its trough, while the price level rose less than 12 percent.

Keynesian Aggregate Expenditures

Certain terminology has become conventional in macroeconomics, largely following Keynes's lead.

> **Aggregate Expenditures (AE)**—*also known as* **Aggregate Spending**—*is the total value of spending on domestic production annually. An* **Aggregate Expenditures curve** *is the relationship between total spending and national income.*

Spending generally rises when income grows, so there is a positive relationship between Aggregate Expenditures and income.

Components of Aggregate Spending

In chapter 7, you learned that Gross National Product (GNP) consists of consumer goods (C), capital investment (I), government purchases of goods and ser-

FIGURE 1 The Keynesian Focus on Aggregate Demand

Panel A
Aggregate Supply and Demand

Panel B
Real GNP and the Price Level
During the Great Depression

Keynes believed that increased aggregate spending would stimulate hikes in employment and output in a depressed economy without raising the specter of inflation. This idea is illustrated in Panel A by a flat Aggregate Supply curve in the region where Aggregate Demand grows from AD_0 to AD_f. Panel B indicates that Keynes's notions were borne out during the recovery from the trough of the Great Depression. The economy increased its real annual output by roughly $100 billion between 1933 and 1940 without a significant increase in the price level. For this and other reasons, Keynes argued that Aggregate Demand alone determined the level of real output in a severely depressed economy.

Source: U.S. Department of Commerce.

vices (*G*), and net exports (*X − M*). These are useful categories for examining the structure of Aggregate Expenditures. A glance at Figure 2 shows that consumption absorbs almost two thirds of GNP, with investment and government spending comprising most of the rest. Exports are part of Aggregate Expenditures, while imports add to the goods and services available; hence, imports contribute to Aggregate Supply. By convention, only the net influence of foreign trade (*X − M*) is considered.

Consumption and Saving

What determines total consumer spending? You may be able to identify other things that influence your family's spending, but the single most important factor is probably your family's current income. In his *General Theory* (1936), John Maynard Keynes asserted:

> The **fundamental psychological law,** *upon which we are entitled to depend with great confidence both a priori from our knowledge of human nature and from the detailed facts of experience is that men are disposed, as a rule and on the average, to increase their consumption as their income increases, but not by as much as the increase in their income.* (p. 96)

This insight, which today seems obvious, reflected a drastic change in the thrust of economic reasoning. Classical economists had recognized earlier that consumer spending is affected by income. They believed, however, that national income automatically moves to a full employment level. Their focus on Aggregate Supply—stimulating economic growth and development—caused the division of a given full employment level of income into consumption and saving to seem far more vital than how consumption and income are related. They viewed this division as determined primarily by the interest rate.

Consumption and Saving Schedules

Classical theory emphasizes interest as a reward for saving. Higher interest rates foster higher saving and lower consumption out of a given income. As you will see in the following chapters, Keynes's *fundamental*

FIGURE 2 Components of Gross National Product

The four major components of GNP, from the vantage point of Aggregate Demand, are consumption, investment, net exports, and government spending. Consumer spending is rather stable at roughly two thirds of the total. Investment and government spending constitute the bulk of the remainder. Net exports are a relatively minor proportion of the total.

Source: *Economic Report of the President*, 1988.

FIGURE 3 Income and Consumption in the United States, 1929–87

Keynes stressed the relationship between income and saving or consumption. The 45° line represents income plotted against itself. Since disposable income is either consumed or saved, the 45° line is labelled $Y_d = C + S$. The darkened area represents saving (or dissaving). During the Great Depression, saving was negative (dissaving), while during World War II, saving was over 20 percent of disposable income.

Source: *Economic Report of the President*, 1988.

psychological law of consumption barely hints at the totally different orientation of Keynesian analysis. Figure 3 provides evidence that supports Keynes's observation.

The 45° line in Figure 3 reflects points mapped if consumption exactly equalled disposable income. (Any variable plotted against an equal variable is a 45° line.) If consumption points for all years were located on this reference line, then consumption would always equal disposable income. How can you use your after-tax (disposable) income? By definition, anything not consumed is saved ($S = Y_d - C$). Thus, the 45° line may be labeled $Y_d = C + S$; your disposable income is absorbed by what you consume and save.

Notice that saving was relatively high during World War II, while many families spent more than their income during the Great Depression. Spending more than income is called **dissaving;** it requires borrowing or dipping into past savings. Aggregate consumption and saving absorb relatively stable shares of aggregate disposable income. Until recently, saving averaged roughly 7 percent of disposable

income except during World War II and the Great Depression. Even though saving slipped a bit in the past decade, consumption has consistently been the most stable component of Aggregate Expenditures.

Consumption occurs when goods are used up to satisfy our wants. Many durable goods provide services and satisfaction for years. Ideally, only their drop in value during a year should count as consumption. For example, if you invest in a new house, the consumption is the rental value of the house while you enjoy it during the time you occupy it. Similarly, only about 1/10th of a television set with an expected ten year life is used up in a single year. (Unfortunately, GNP accounts do not divide consumer durables, other than housing, into consumption and investment components.)

Saving is not necessarily the amount of money you put in a financial institution during some income period. Saving is the amount your wealth changes—the amount of your unconsumed income.

Saving *is the change in total wealth over some period of time.*

Your wealth is the **stock of savings** accumulated out of past saving periods. But what if there is a loss of wealth?

> **Dissaving** *occurs when people spend more on consumption than they make in income during a year. It is financed by borrowing, or by spending out of past savings.*

Figure 3 indicates how consumption is related to aggregate disposable income.

Consumption falls into five main categories: food, housing, clothing, transportation, and medical expenses. Low income families often dissave because they spend everything and then some on bare necessities. As gross incomes rise, growing shares of income are allocated to taxes, transportation, housing services, and various luxuries.

Autonomous and Induced Consumption and Saving

Keynes asserted that as income grows, so does planned consumption—but by less than income. People must consume something to live, however, even if they have zero income. This part of consumption is independent of income.

> **Autonomous consumption (C_a)** *is consumer spending that is unrelated to income.*

People tend to spend more on consumer goods if they receive more income.

> *Consumption that occurs because people have income to spend is called* **induced consumption.**

Thus, consumption includes both autonomous and induced elements.

Consider Table 1. At zero income, autonomous consumption requires dissaving equal to spending, which is $1,600 in this example. Thus, autonomous saving is minus $1,600. At low disposable income, planned consumption exceeds income; there is planned dissaving. In Table 1, dissaving occurs at all income levels below $8,000. When income is $8,000, planned consumption equals $8,000 and planned saving is zero. This is sometimes referred to as a break-even point. When income exceeds $8,000, plans for positive saving result.

Data from Table 1 are used to construct Figure 4. Autonomous consumption causes the intercept in Panel A to equal $1,600; induced consumption equals the vertical rise in consumption as income grows. The vertical distance between the 45° reference line (blue) and the consumption line (red) is saving or dissaving. Panel B plots the amount of planned saving associated with the levels of planned consumption from Panel A. For example, when disposable income is $12,000, saving is $800.

Average Propensities to Consume and Save

Keynes asserted that consumption grows as income grows but by less than income rises. We will now examine what happens to spending as income rises, both on average and at the margin. Remember that disposable income can be either consumed or saved. We need to develop these relationships further by

TABLE 1 *Representative Annual Consumption and Savings Schedules*						
(1) Annual Disposable Income	**(2)** Annual Planned Consumption	**(3)** Annual Planned Saving (1) − (2)	**(4)** Average Propensity to Consume (2)/(1)	**(5)** Average Propensity to Save (3)/(1)	**(6)** Marginal Propensity to Consume (Δ2)/(Δ1)	**(7)** Marginal Propensity to Save (Δ3)/(Δ1)
0	$ 1,600	−$1,600	—	—	—	—
$ 2,000	3,200	−1,200	1.60	−.60	.80	.20
4,000	4,800	−800	1.20	−.20	.80	.20
6,000	6,400	−400	1.07	−.07	.80	.20
8,000	8,000	0	1.00	0	.80	.20
10,000	9,600	400	.96	.04	.80	.20
12,000	11,200	800	.93	.07	.80	.20

FIGURE 4 *Consumption and Saving Schedules*

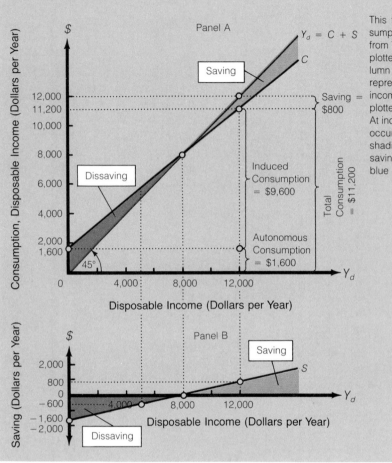

This figure graphically depicts the consumption (C) and saving (S) schedules from Table 1. Consumption (column 2) is plotted against disposable income (column 1) in Panel A. Again, the 45° line represents $Y_d = C + S$. When disposable income is $8,000, saving is zero and is plotted on the horizontal axis in Panel B. At income levels below $8,000, dissaving occurs, and this is reflected by the red shading in both panels. Above $8,000, saving occurs and is represented by the blue shading in both panels.

examining the average and marginal propensities to consume and save.

*The **average propensity to consume (apc)** is the fraction of disposable income consumed.*

Arithmetically:

$$apc = \frac{\text{consumption}}{\text{disposable income}} = \frac{C}{Y_d}.$$

Thus, your *apc* = 0.8 if you spend 80 percent of your income. In Table 1, the average propensity to consume is (*a*) more than 1 at income below $8,000, (*b*) exactly 1 at an $8,000 income, and (*c*) below 1 when income exceeds $8,000.

*The **average propensity to save (aps)** is the fraction of disposable income that is saved.*

$$aps = \frac{\text{saving}}{\text{disposable income}} = \frac{S}{Y_d}.$$

Like the *apc*, it varies with the level of income. Because the *apc* falls as income grows, the *aps* becomes larger as income grows.

Since $C + S = Y_d$, we can divide both sides of this equation by Y_d and find that:

$$\frac{C}{Y_d} + \frac{S}{Y_d} = \frac{Y_d}{Y_d} = 1,$$

so the *apc* + *aps* = 1. This means that the *aps* = 1 − *apc*. Thus, if you spend 80 percent of your income (*apc* = 0.8), then you save 20 percent (*aps* = 0.2). The national *apc* has varied slightly over time, averaging approximately 93 percent. The *aps* has averaged roughly 6–7 percent of disposable income.

Marginal Propensities to Consume and Save

Average propensities to consume and save indicate the shares of total income spent and saved, but not how an *additional* dollar of disposable income will be divided between consumption and saving. It is easier for policymakers to affect disposable income a little (through, e.g., taxes) than to directly control total income. What you will do with a bit more or less income is crucial.

> The **marginal propensity to consume (*mpc*)** *is the relative change in consumption induced by a small change in disposable income.*

Throughout this book, we will use Δ (the Greek letter delta) to represent a change in a variable. Arithmetically, the *mpc* is written:

$$mpc = \frac{\text{change in planned consumption}}{\text{change in disposable income}} = \frac{\Delta C}{\Delta Y_d}.$$

The marginal propensity to consume in the example in Table 1 is 0.8. For every dollar increase (*decrease*) in disposable income, consumption increases (*decreases*) by $0.80. For example, when disposable income rises from $8,000 to $10,000 (by $2,000), planned consumption rises from $8,000 to $9,600 (by $1,600). Thus, the marginal propensity to consume is: $1,600/$2,000 = 0.8.

A geometric treatment of the *mpc* is shown in Panel A of Figure 5. In an appendix to chapter 1, slope is defined as *rise over run*. The change in planned consumption is measured by the vertical increase (*rise*) on the graph of consumption and is labeled Δ*C*. The change in disposable income is measured along the horizontal axis (*run*) and is labeled Δ*Y_d*. Thus, the slope of the consumption function is Δ*C*/Δ*Y_d*, which equals the *mpc*.

What do people do with an extra dollar of income if they don't spend it? They save it.

> The **marginal propensity to save (*mps*)** *is the relative change in saving induced by a change in disposable income.*

Arithmetically:

$$mps = \frac{\text{change in planned saving}}{\text{change in disposable income}} = \frac{\Delta S}{\Delta Y_d}.$$

For example, in Table 1, as disposable income rises from $8,000 to $10,000, planned saving increases by $400 and the *mps* equals 400/2,000, or 0.2.

You may already see that the sum of the *mpc* and the *mps* equals 1. From $C + S = Y_d$, it follows that any change in disposable income (ΔY_d) must result in changes in consumption (ΔC) or changes in saving (ΔS). Thus, $\Delta C + \Delta S = \Delta Y_d$. Dividing both sides of this equation by ΔY_d yields

$$\frac{\Delta C}{\Delta Y_d} + \frac{\Delta S}{\Delta Y_d} = \frac{\Delta Y_d}{\Delta Y_d} = 1$$

so $mpc + mps = 1$; any change in disposable income is divided between changes in consumption and saving. A graphic representation of the *mps* is shown in Panel B of Figure 5.

The consumption function in Figure 5 portrays Aggregate Expenditures by consumers. The major determinant of this demand is aggregate disposable income (Y_d). Other influences on consumption determine the level of autonomous consumption. When they change, the entire consumption/income relationship is shifted up or down. These shift variables tend to change fairly slowly, however, so the relationship between consumption and disposable income has been fairly stable over time.

Other Determinants of Consumption and Saving

There are five major determinants of consumption and saving other than current income. They are (*a*) wealth and expectations about lifetime income, (*b*) average size and age consumption of households, (*c*) stocks of consumer goods on hand, (*d*) household balance sheets, and (*e*) consumer expectations about the prices and availability of products. These influences, in concert with customary standards of living and habitual purchasing patterns, determine autonomous spending. Current disposable income alone determines induced consumption in the simple Keynesian model we are developing here.

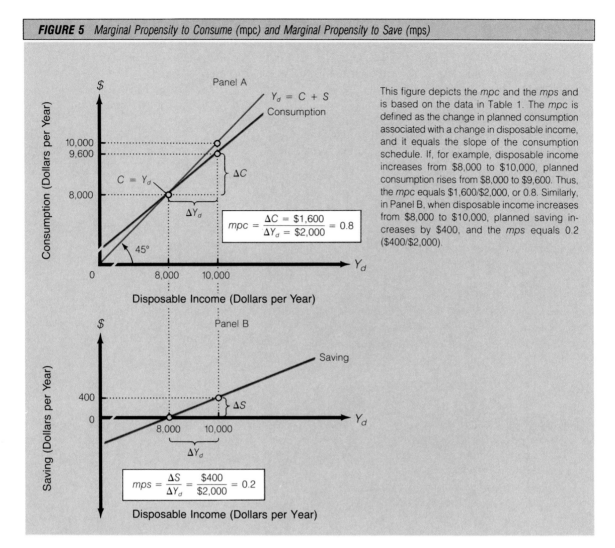

FIGURE 5 *Marginal Propensity to Consume (mpc) and Marginal Propensity to Save (mps)*

This figure depicts the *mpc* and the *mps* and is based on the data in Table 1. The *mpc* is defined as the change in planned consumption associated with a change in disposable income, and it equals the slope of the consumption schedule. If, for example, disposable income increases from $8,000 to $10,000, planned consumption rises from $8,000 to $9,600. Thus, the *mpc* equals $1,600/$2,000, or 0.8. Similarly, in Panel B, when disposable income increases from $8,000 to $10,000, planned saving increases by $400, and the *mps* equals 0.2 ($400/$2,000).

Wealth and Lifetime Income   Suppose a computer science major and a philosophy major will each graduate from the same college this year. Who is more likely to buy a new car before graduating? The computer science major is because of an expectation of higher income upon graduation. Now consider the relative spending patterns of a wealthy retired tycoon and a retired postal employee. Even if the retired tycoon has a bad year on the stock market and suffers losses, the tycoon is still likely to be the bigger spender by a huge margin. These examples suggest that

wealthy people or those who expect high income in the near future typically consume more than other people who have identical current incomes.

Household Size and Age Composition   Young families initially acquiring consumer durables (house, washer, dryer, refrigerator, car, and so on) generally have higher consumption demands than established families who already own these goods, who only buy replacements as their older household goods become obsolete or break down. Bigger families usually have higher average propensities to consume than smaller families. (That should come as no surprise.) Thus, societies full of young or large families will have higher average propensities to consume and lower rates of saving than societies comprised of older or smaller families.

Stocks of Goods on Hand   At the end of World War II, Americans had powerful pent-up demands. There had been war-time shortages of numerous consumer goods; many were rationed or did not exist at all; consumers had long "wish lists" and they went on spending binges. Just the opposite occurs when consumers have been on lengthy buying sprees recently—large stocks of new durable goods alleviate the necessity to purchase more.

Household Balance Sheet   Financially secure families tend to spend more of their current income. A family deeply in debt tends not to incur more debt. All else equal, as their debts grow, consumers defer spending so they can pay off existing debt. Conversely, shrinking indebtedness may result in binges of spending.

Consumer Expectations   If a wave of inflationary expectations hits consumers, they may either (*a*) buy now to avoid high prices in the future, or (*b*) lose confidence, causing them to buy less.

Consumer debt may climb when buyers try to buffer themselves against future inflation, or their confidence may be shaken and their use of credit may fall. In the late 1970s, many young people bought houses because soaring prices made them afraid they would never be able to buy homes if they waited. This panic buying pushed up housing prices even faster. In 1974, a rumor circulated about a "toilet paper shortage." Shoppers responded by stripping the stocks from supermarket shelves. The source of the rumor was traced to a Johnny Carson quip on the "Tonight Show." When people expect widespread shortages, they buy and hoard almost anything that can be stored.

Consumption and Aggregate Expenditures

Consumption spending is the major component of total spending, representing about two thirds of Aggregate Expenditures. Three other components must be added to consumption to reach Aggregate Expenditures: investment, government spending, and net exports. We turn now to a discussion of investment and its determinants. Then we briefly consider government spending (a more detailed discussion is left to chapter 11), and look at the foreign component of Aggregate Expenditures.

Investment

In chapter 7, you learned that Gross Private Domestic Investment (GPDI) is an important component of GNP. If we subtract capital depreciation from GPDI, the result is net investment; Net National Product (NNP) is GNP adjusted for depreciation. We indicated that consumption is the most stable component of GNP and Aggregate Expenditures; investment is the most volatile (least stable). According to Keynesian theory, investment instability may be the root cause of most business cycles.

Types of Investment

People commonly talk about investing in stocks or bonds or existing real estate. Remember that these are what economists call financial investments; economic investment entails buying new physical capital (buildings, machinery, tools, equipment, and the like) that can be used in the future to produce other goods and services. Some financial investments facilitate economic investment (for instance, purchases of newly issued stocks or bonds, which are just forms of saving); others do not (e.g., speculative purchases of land).

Our discussion in chapter 7 classifies economic investment into three basic groups (*a*) new construction, which includes such things as office buildings, manufacturing plants, warehouses, hotels, retail stores, and private homes; (*b*) new machinery and equipment, including tools and office equipment and furnishings; and (*c*) inventory accumulation. The composition of investment is illustrated in Figure 6.

You may already know that construction of residential and office buildings, manufacturing facilities, and such are extremely cyclical. Business investment in new machinery and equipment is also very sensitive to the ups and downs in economic activity. But the least stable component of investment is inventory

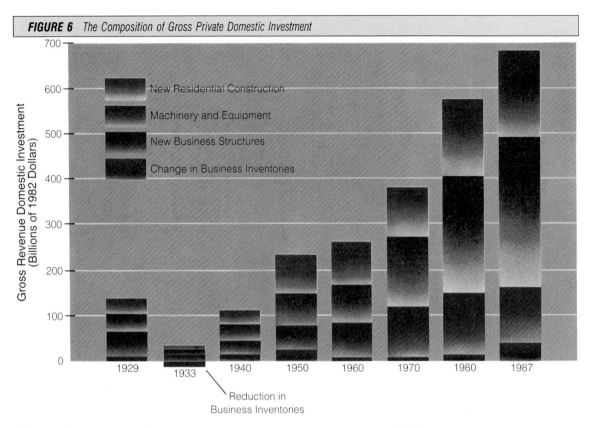

FIGURE 6 *The Composition of Gross Private Domestic Investment*

Gross Revenue Domestic Investment (Billions of 1982 Dollars)

- New Residential Construction
- Machinery and Equipment
- New Business Structures
- Change in Business Inventories

1929 1933 1940 1950 1960 1970 1980 1987

Reduction in Business Inventories

This figure details the composition of investment spending, the least stable component of GNP.

Source: *Economic Report of the President,* 1987.

accumulation (see Figure 7). One important reason for this volatility in inventories is that business firms only have partial control over inventory accumulation or shrinkage. Customers frequently fail to buy according to business forecasts.

Firms maintain inventories because they cannot predict their sales accurately on a week-to-week, month-to-month, or even year-to-year basis. If they knew exactly when (or if) sales were going to occur, their merchandise could arrive for sale simultaneously with their customers and inventories would be minuscule or unnecessary. Firms (sometimes intuitively) forecast their sales and calculate the inventories they think they need to maintain.

If sales are below the levels forecast, inventories grow and businesses unintentionally invest in new inventories. If sales are unexpectedly high, inventories dwindle and there is unintentional disinvestment. Unexpected changes in inventories are signals to businesses either to raise or lower orders from their suppliers. In the next chapter, you will see how

inventory adjustments are used to bring aggregate spending and production into balance.

The reasons people consume are fairly obvious—they are trying to maximize their individual satisfactions. Why people invest, and under what circumstances, is less obvious.

Expected Returns from Investment

A simple explanation for firms' investment in new capital goods is that they expect to profit. If the stream of income is expected to exceed the opportunity costs of a given investment, it will be made.

The annual percentage by which assets will grow if the profits from an investment are continually reinvested is known as the **rate of return** *on investment.*

This rate is quite similar to a percentage interest rate. We will discuss factors that influence the expected returns from investment before delving into some of the intricacies of the costs of investment.

FIGURE 7 Changes in Business Inventories (1982 Dollars)

Changes in Business Inventories (1982 Dollars)

Inventory changes are by far the most volatile component of investment, which, in turn, is the most erratic part of GNP. Inventories decline sharply when business sales unexpectedly boom or when business firms become very pessimistic in forecasting future sales. Inventories mushroom when business anticipates sharp increases in sales or when customers unexpectedly quit buying.

Source: *Economic Report of the President*, 1988.

Expectations about the Business Environment

New capital goods are expected to generate extra output which, if sold, means extra revenue for the firm. Confidence that there will be demand for more production is necessary before businesses will make new investments. When consumer spending is expected to grow and existing capital is already pressed to capacity, the stream of new investment will be very high. Conversely, if consumer demands are expected to be weak, or if there is substantial excess capacity in existing production facilities, businesses will not invest very much.

A major problem for business investors is the long lag that is common between placing orders for new investment goods and actually achieving the greater capacity made possible by these investments. Time is required to acquire the appropriate building or to produce new equipment and to comply with laws and regulations that control new facilities. Another lag arises between production from the new capital and final sales of the output. These lags make it necessary to forecast consumer demand far into the future. Risks involved in long-range projections make firms leery of many investments.

Difficulties in predicting swings in a firm's sales and economic activity are only one source of risk for investors. Expected changes in governmental policies may either encourage or squelch investment. For example, when the New Jersey government was expected to legalize gambling, there was a flurry of investment in Atlantic City as people readied casinos and "tourist traps." Similarly, the prospect of huge defense budgets result in massive investment by defense contractors. On the other hand, if policies restricting foreign trade are expected to be adopted, firms that rely on exports or imports might postpone investment plans indefinitely.

Changes in business expectations that affect investment may be contagious. If most other investors become bearish (pessimistic), might it be wise for you to reconsider some of your riskier ventures? If they become bullish (optimistic), might you be more willing to take a plunge? One possible reason for investment volatility is a tendency for expectations about business conditions to move simultaneously. But there are other explanations.

Technological Innovations

Many firms and government agencies are extensively involved in research and development (R & D). Methods are developed to produce new or better goods, or less costly ways of making existing products are found. New technologies tend to arrive erratically and in waves. Consequently, investment to implement technological breakthroughs is clustered over time. Some economists attribute much of investment volatility to the bunching of new technologies. For example, the space program refined the computer, gave birth to solid-state electronics, and generated a host of other technological innovations.

Stocks of Capital Relative to Total Production

Just as consumption is affected by the consumer durables households already possess relative to their incomes, the stock of physical capital relative to GNP influences the level of investment. If near-peak levels of economic activity press against capital capacity, there will be strong incentives for new capital investment. On the other hand, if economic activity fades so that substantial amounts of capital are idle, purchases of new capital will decline.

The Equilibrium Rate of Investment

Firms will buy machinery, construct buildings, or attempt to increase inventories whenever they expect the gross returns on these investments to exceed the total opportunity costs of acquiring them. Let us see how expectations and costs interact to determine the level of investment.

Diminishing Returns to Investment   Suppose that most economic forecasts point up, reflecting substantial business optimism. Many potential investors probably know of a few investments that could be expected to generate healthy rates of return (r) of, say 30–40 percent—a new hamburger franchise, an apartment complex, or a plant to manufacture solar cells might be examples. Once these investments were made, only less profitable investments would be available—a fried chicken outlet, a duplex, or a new laundromat might be expected to yield annual rates of return of 20–30 percent. Once these investments were made, still less profitable investments would be the only options available—a hot dog franchise, renovation of a seedy motel, or a used-book

store might be anticipated to return 10–20 percent on investment.

We are now at rock-bottom—a shovel-sharpening shop or greasy spoon franchise might generate near zero rates of return, plus or minus 10 percent. The point is, for a given mood among investors, the higher the level of investment in the economy, the lower the expected rate of return on additional investment. Changes in business expectations shift the investment demand schedule. Expected rate of return schedules when investors are optimistic and when they are pessimistic are shown in Figure 8.

Costs of Investment   New capital costs are important for investment decisions. All else equal, rate of return schedules like those shown in Figure 8 rise (shift to the right) when capital prices fall and shrink (move leftward) when these costs rise. Demand for new capital tends to rise during prosperity, causing capital prices to rise and thus, chokes off surges in investment. Conversely, investor pessimism during downturns reduces the demand for new capital goods. Capital suppliers accumulate what they view as excessive inventories. New equipment prices fall

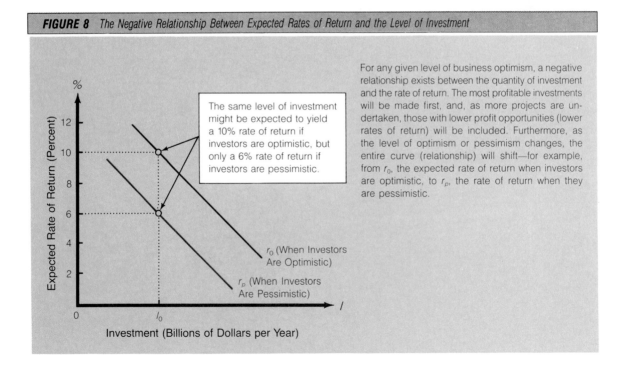

FIGURE 8   *The Negative Relationship Between Expected Rates of Return and the Level of Investment*

The same level of investment might be expected to yield a 10% rate of return if investors are optimistic, but only a 6% rate of return if investors are pessimistic.

r_0 (When Investors Are Optimistic)

r_p (When Investors Are Pessimistic)

For any given level of business optimism, a negative relationship exists between the quantity of investment and the rate of return. The most profitable investments will be made first, and, as more projects are undertaken, those with lower profit opportunities (lower rates of return) will be included. Furthermore, as the level of optimism or pessimism changes, the entire curve (relationship) will shift—for example, from r_0, the expected rate of return when investors are optimistic, to r_p, the rate of return when they are pessimistic.

as they liquidate inventories, slightly dampening drops in investment.

Taxes on investment income are another cost consideration. For example, higher corporate income taxes cause the (after-tax) rate of return curve to fall. Investment tax credits, on the other hand, may boost demands for investment goods.

One of the most important costs from investors' perspectives is the interest rate. When it rises, investors' opportunity costs rise. If investors have money, they might make loans instead of buying investment goods. If most investors borrow to invest, then a hike in the interest rate makes investment less attractive. Interest rates (i) and rates of return (r) are both expressed as annual percentages, making it possible to put both on the vertical axis of Figure 9. Changes in interest rates involve movements *along* rate of return curves. Any other changes generate shifts in these curves.

Ignoring transaction costs and risk for simplicity's sake, investment will occur as long as the expected rate of return is at least as great as the interest rate. Here is an example that explains why. If you can borrow money at 11 percent interest and expect an 11.5 percent rate of return from some investment, you probably will make the investment. If not, then someone else will go after this profit. It is just like trading

11 cents for 11.5 cents. How many times will you go for a deal like this? If you can do it infinitely, you will become infinitely rich. Any investment expected to yield a rate of return greater than the interest rate will be profitable and will be undertaken. Those yielding returns lower than interest rates will not be profitable and will not be made. This is why investment will move to $100 billion in Figure 9 if the interest rate is 8 percent and the expected rate of return is reflected in curve r_p.

In summary, the expected rate of return schedule increases when GNP rises and investors become optimistic or when the price of capital declines. Pessimistic economic forecasts or jumps in capital prices shrink expected rates of return and investment. For a given expected rate of return, higher interest rates discourage investment (this is a movement along a rate of return curve) while falling interest rates foster investment and economic growth. Interest rate changes induce movements along a rate of return curve.

Our inability to perfectly predict the future leads to unexpected changes in inventories. When these are coupled with the effects of herdlike changes in investors' expectations and wide swings in interest rates, no wonder investment is the most volatile component of GNP. The example in Figure 9 suggests that

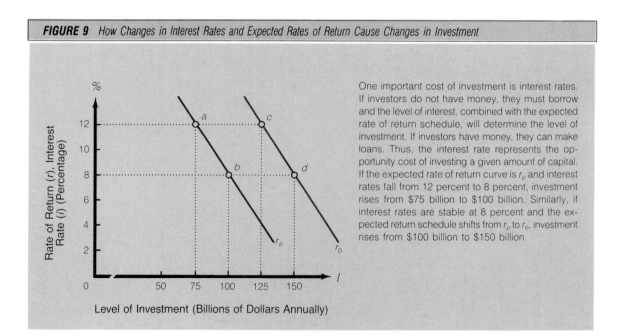

FIGURE 9 *How Changes in Interest Rates and Expected Rates of Return Cause Changes in Investment*

One important cost of investment is interest rates. If investors do not have money, they must borrow and the level of interest, combined with the expected rate of return schedule, will determine the level of investment. If investors have money, they can make loans. Thus, the interest rate represents the opportunity cost of investing a given amount of capital. If the expected rate of return curve is r_p and interest rates fall from 12 percent to 8 percent, investment rises from $75 billion to $100 billion. Similarly, if interest rates are stable at 8 percent and the expected return schedule shifts from r_p to r_o, investment rises from $100 billion to $150 billion.

annual investment would grow from $75 billion (point *a*) to $100 billion (point *b*) if the interest rate fell from 12 to 8 percent but investors were somewhat pessimistic (movement along the r_p curve).

A similar decline in interest rates will cause investment to rise from $125 billion annually to $150 billion annually if investors are more optimistic (along the r_0 curve from point *c* to point *d*). For every interest rate, shifts from optimistic to pessimistic outlooks (shifts in the curves), or vice versa, mean annual changes in investment of $50 billion. Thus, in this example, swings in investors' moods and interest rates may mean that investment is doubled or halved. The real-world volatility of investment is probably attributable to changes both in expectations and in interest rates.

Investment and Aggregate Expenditures

We know that investment is affected by the level of national income because the state of the economy is a major influence on investors' expectations. An economic boom raises business profits and gives corporations greater opportunities to retain earnings for investment purposes. Nevertheless, for simplicity the simple Keynesian model treats investment as autonomous.

Autonomous investment *is independent of income in the simple Keynesian model.*

Figure 10 shows the level of autonomous investment (I_a) to be determined by expected rates of return and the market rate of interest. It also shows how this

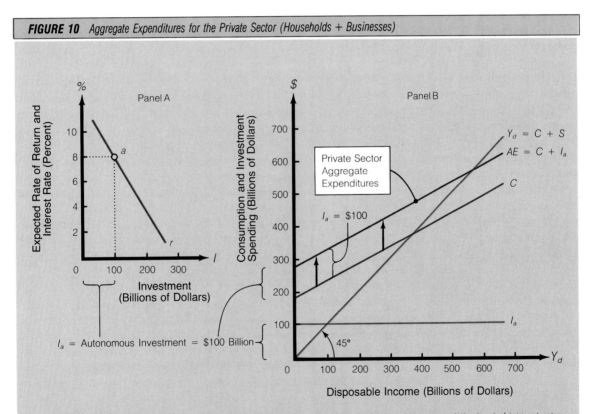

FIGURE 10 Aggregate Expenditures for the Private Sector (Households + Businesses)

In Panel A, the level of investment is determined by the intersection of the rate of return (*r*) curve and the level of interest rates (*i*). This capital-market-determined level of investment (I_a = $100 billion) is then included on the Aggregate Expenditure (AE) curve in Panel B. If the interest rate is 8 percent, autonomous investment (I_a) will be $100 billion (point a, Panel A). Adding this level of investment to the consumption line (C) in Panel B results in the Aggregate Expenditure curve labeled $AE = C + I_a$. Notice that the Aggregate Expenditure curve is equal to consumption plus investment ($AE = C + I_a$) when the economy consists only of households and businesses. Finally, note that the 45° reference line is equal to $Y_d = C + S$.

externally determined level of investment affects Aggregate Expenditures. In Panel A, an interest rate of 8 percent yields autonomous investment of $100 billion. In Panel B, the $100 billion of autonomous investment is added to the consumption curve to obtain the private sector Aggregate Expenditures curve ($AE = C + I_a$).

Optimism joined with low interest rates creates high levels of autonomous investment. Pessimism or high interest rates cause autonomous investment to be very low. In fact, Keynesians believe that pessimism may so overwhelm even very low interest rates that investment will be trivial.

Government Purchases

Some government purchases resemble private investment in that they yield benefits over time. Highways, flood control projects, and education are examples. Other purchases resemble private consumption by immediately exhausting resources; e.g., police and fire protection, school lunch programs, and Medicare payments. Both consumption and investment types of government purchases exert direct demands on national output and so are parts of Aggregate Expenditures. Some government outlays, however, do not entail direct spending. For example, cash transfer payments are only translated into Aggregate Expenditures when the recipients spend these funds on consumer goods. Thus, these outlays are not lumped into government purchases.

The percentage of GNP absorbed by government purchases has grown substantially, but erratically, over the past two centuries. This growth has been greatest at the onset of wars. The Civil War, World Wars I and II, the Korean conflict, and the Vietnam War were high points of government demands. Following these high levels of wartime spending, government purchases have tended to fall—but not to prewar levels.

One possible explanation for the upward trend of government spending is that rising standards of living make people willing, through their votes, to devote ever larger shares of their income to publicly provided goods such as education, public parks, or highways. Nevertheless, while government purchases

seem to be related to income, they are even more affected by the state of international relations. For these reasons and, more importantly, to keep our analysis of Aggregate Expenditures simple, we will assume that government purchases are independent of income.

Autonomous government purchases (G_a) *are independent of income.*

The Foreign Sector

Exports (X) reflect foreign demands for American goods. Thus, they add to Aggregate Expenditures. Imports (M) are goods produced by foreigners but available for use by American consumers, investors, or government. In fact, the accounting categories of consumption, investment, and government spending include goods produced abroad. These imports are a part of Aggregate Supply. In a sense, however, they reduce Aggregate Expenditures on domestically produced goods because, presumably, imports may replace some purchases of domestic output. This is one reason cries for protection from foreign competition are loudest when an industry is in a downturn. The pleas from the auto, clothing, and steel industries during 1981–84 are examples.

It is conventional to look only at the net effect of the foreign sector on Aggregate Expenditures, so that $AE = C + I + G + (X - M)$. The level of our national income undoubtedly influences our imports. When times are prosperous domestically we import more Toyota and Mercedes-Benz cars and more Minolta and Nikon cameras; our vacations and booming industrial production require more foreign oil. On the other hand, our exports depend primarily on economic conditions abroad, which may be in the doldrums even if the American economy is prosperous. International economic interdependence is, however, accurately characterized by a cliché that "When America sneezes, the rest of the world catches a cold."

Although the foreign sector is vital for the strength and health of our economy, its net effect on Aggregate Expenditures is relatively small. Exports and imports each *average* around 10 percent of GNP, so net exports $(X - M)$ are usually plus or minus roughly 2 percent of aggregate spending. Sophisticated Keynesian models take interdependencies between nations into account explicitly. For the purposes of the Keynesian model of Aggregate Expenditures we are building here, however, we will treat net exports as independent of income.

Net exports $(X_a - M_a)$ *are treated as* **autonomous** *in the simple Keynesian model.*

Aggregate Expenditures _____

Some of our national product is consumed in the year it is produced (C), some is invested (I_a), some is bought by foreigners $(X_a - M_a)$, and the rest is purchased by government (G_a). In the simple Keynesian model used in the next two chapters, we assume that

income is the major influence on consumption, while private investment, net exports, and government spending are not affected by income. Aggregate Expenditures (AE) is the sum of all autonomous demands $(C_a + I_a + G_a + [X_a - M_a])$ **plus** consumption induced by having positive levels of income. Induced consumption $= mpc(Y)$ in a simple linear model, so

$$AE = C_a + mpc(Y) + I_a + G_a + (X_a - M_a).$$

Suppose we assume that: (a) autonomous investment (I_a) is \$100 billion, (b) autonomous net exports $(X_a - M_a)$ is \$25 billion, (c) autonomous government purchases (G_a) is \$150 billion, (d) autonomous consumption (C_a) is \$175 billion, and (e) the marginal propensity to consume (mpc) is 0.5. Figure 11 depicts the resulting relationship between national income (Y) and Aggregate Expenditures. The autonomous components of Aggregate Expenditures total

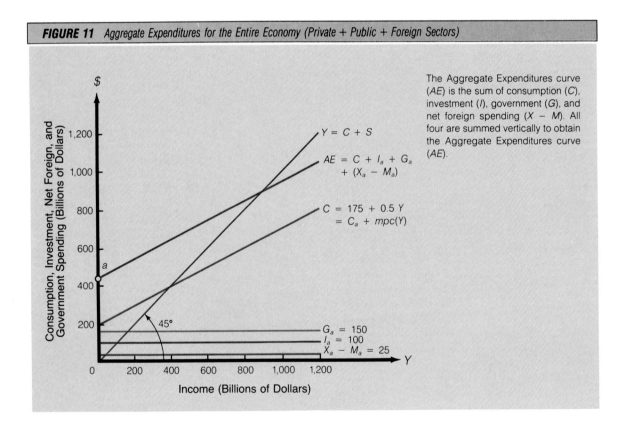

FIGURE 11 *Aggregate Expenditures for the Entire Economy (Private + Public + Foreign Sectors)*

The Aggregate Expenditures curve (AE) is the sum of consumption (C), investment (I), government (G), and net foreign spending $(X - M)$. All four are summed vertically to obtain the Aggregate Expenditures curve (AE).

to \$450 billion, which corresponds to point a in Figure 11. $[C_a + I_a + G_a + (X_a - M_a) = \$450$ billion.] We still must consider induced consumption, which equals the *mpc* times income, or $0.5Y$. Thus, total Aggregate Expenditures rises by one half of any increase in income as income rises, and vice versa.

Note (a) that these categories of spending are all summed vertically to arrive at Aggregate Expenditures, and (b) that this Keynesian depression model assumes a fixed price level. In the next chapter, we explore how equilibrium in National Income and product is determined by Aggregate Expenditures. After you have been thoroughly exposed to this Keynesian model, we will introduce you to a slightly different model of Aggregate Demand and Supply which incorporates price level flexibility.

CHAPTER REVIEW: KEY POINTS

1. Keynesian analysis focuses on Aggregate Demand. During the Great Depression, the economy had considerable excess productive capacity. During a slow recovery from 1933 to 1940, real output expanded by more than 60 percent with only slight increases in the price level. Keynesian economics assumes that Aggregate Supply is flat in a depressed economy so that the price level can be ignored; it is primarily concerned with maintaining Aggregate Demand consistent with full employment.

2. *Aggregate Expenditures* (*AE*) is total spending on domestic output during a year. Aggregate Expenditures has four components (a) *personal consumption expenditures,* (b) gross private domestic investment, (c) government purchases of goods and services, and (d) net exports of goods and services.

3. The single most important determinant of consumer spending is disposable income through its influence on *induced consumption.* Consumer spending is related directly to disposable income and is a stable component of Aggregate Expenditures. Other important determinants of consumption and saving include (a) wealth and expectations of future income, (b) the average size and age composition of typical households, (c) the stocks of consumer goods on hand, (d) the level of household assets and debts, (e) consumer expectations regarding prices and availability of products. These determine the level of *autonomous consumption* (C_a).

4. The *average propensity to consume* (*apc*) is the share of total disposable income that is consumed (C/Y_d). The *average propensity to save* (*aps*) is the fraction of total disposable income that is saved (S/Y_d). In addition, $apc + aps = 1$. Until recently, the average propensities to consume and to save were relatively constant over time, at roughly 93 percent and 7 percent,

respectively. The *aps* has only averaged 4–5 percent during the past decade.

5. The *marginal propensity to consume* (*mpc*) is the change in planned consumption associated with a given small change in disposable income; it tells us how much of an additional dollar of income will be consumed. Similarly, the *marginal propensity to save* (*mps*) is how much of an additional dollar in income will be saved. Furthermore, $mpc + mps = 1$.

6. Capital investment refers to purchases of new output that can be used in the future to produce other goods and services. There are three major components of investment (a) new business and residential structures, (b) machinery and equipment, and (c) inventory accumulation.

7. The primary factors determining the quantity of investment are (a) expected returns from investment, (b) expectations about the business environment, (c) rates of technological change and innovation, (d) the level of existing stocks of business capital relative to total production, and (e) the costs of investment, including the interest rate. In simple Keynesian models, investment is treated as *autonomous* (I_a).

8. While government spending is probably influenced by changes in income, it is even more strongly affected by the state of international relations and domestic politics. Thus government spending as a component of Aggregate Expenditures is also treated as autonomous.

9. Exports and imports are reasonably balanced, so net exports $(X - M)$ make a comparatively small contribution to Aggregate Expenditures. The foreign sector is, however, very important to the strength and vitality of our economy by providing markets for our production and imported goods that would be much more costly if produced only domestically. Simple Keynesian models treat net exports as autonomous.

PROBLEMS

1. Construct a graph showing the Aggregate Expenditures curve based on the following relationships.

   Consumption = $500 + .6 (Income)
   Autonomous government spending = $400
   Autonomous investment spending = $200
   Autonomous exports = $300
   Autonomous imports = $200

   Plot the new Aggregate Expenditures curve if the consumption relationship changes to consumption = $800 + .75(Income).
2. Use the values for Disposable Income and Planned Consumption to complete Table 2.

TABLE 2

Disposable Income	Planned Consumption	Planned Saving	aps	mpc	mps
$ 0	$ 500	____	____	____	____
500	800	____	____	____	____
1,000	1,100	____	____	____	____
1,500	1,400	____	____	____	____
2,000	1,700	____	____	____	____
2,500	2,000	____	____	____	____

QUESTIONS FOR THOUGHT AND DISCUSSION

1. Saving was negative for the economy as a whole during part of the Great Depression of the 1930s. How did this occur? What were the long-term effects of this negative rate of saving?
2. People have no difficulty in rapidly raising their consumption to accommodate any increases in their incomes, but adjusting to sharp declines in income tends to be a slow and painful process. What implications does this have for swings in consumption over the business cycle?
3. Do you think people's consumption depends most on their current income or on their expectations of income over the future? What does this imply about the stability of Keynes's *consumption function?* Why?
4. How might the psychological theory of the business cycle (described in chapter 8) account for huge swings in investment over the cycle?
5. We are treating investment, government spending, and net exports as autonomous. To what extent do you think each of these spending categories is influenced by national income? Why are we treating them as autonomous here if they are all influenced by income in fairly consistent ways?

CHAPTER 10

disequilibrium

saving = investment (S = I)

withdrawals

injections

multiplier effect

*autonomous spending
   multiplier*

paradox of thrift

potential GNP

GNP gap

recessionary gap

inflationary gap

Equilibrium Output, Employment, and Income

The market forces of supply and demand yield an equilibrium when the quantity demanded of a specific good equals the quantity supplied at the current price. All forces are in balance, so there are no net pressures for prices, outputs, or purchases to change. The concept of macroeconomic equilibrium is similar. John Maynard Keynes and his followers, however, differ sharply with adherents of classical economic reasoning in their perceptions of exactly what constitutes equilibrium.

Classical macroeconomics (introduced in chapter 8) takes a long-run view that a market economy will hover around full employment if it is allowed to adjust to shocks. Keynes countered that "in the long run, we are all dead," and dismissed the pressures that classical writers counted on to drive economies to full employment as weak or nonexistent. Keynes compared continuous economic changes to an

ocean's waves—waiting for a long-run classical equilibrium is like waiting for the ocean to become flat. Consequently, Keynes focused on short-run problems and described how the economy might be stuck in a short-run equilibrium with substantial idle capital and unemployed labor.

How purchases by consumers, investors, government, and foreigners are summed to form an Aggregate Expenditures curve (sometimes called a *Keynesian cross*) was explored in chapter 9. In this chapter, we inspect Keynes's view that macroeconomic equilibrium might occur at less than full employment. For now, we will focus this discussion exclusively on private sector activities. In chapter 11, government spending and taxes are brought into the picture so that we can examine and try to understand what policymakers might do to correct for excessive inflation or unemployment.

Aggregate Expenditures and Equilibrium

We will assume initially that there are no taxes, depreciation, transfer payments, government expenditures, or undistributed corporate profits. This simplification blurs distinctions among GNP, NNP, and disposable income and permits us to use the term *income* (Y) to refer to all three.

Labor is required to produce the output, which, if sold, translates into National Income and maintains employment and income. If output is unsalable at prices that cover costs, some workers will lose their jobs. Thus, when we say that National Income is rising, employment will also rise. Higher employment usually means lower unemployment, and vice versa; thus, growth in National Income or product tends to cause unemployment to fall, while downturns in National Income signify rising unemployment rates. Aggregate Spending interacts with National Output to yield a macroeconomic equilibrium.

National Output

Table 1 presents hypothetical data for income, employment, and output. The relationships among these aggregates illustrates how an economy approaches macroequilibrium. Column 1 shows the employment required to produce the levels of National Output (column 2) that producers are willing to offer at current prices if they are confident that it will be sold. You might think of the National Output schedule as reflecting a Keynesian Aggregate Supply curve because firms willingly produce whatever is demanded. For example, firms will employ 85 million workers and produce $2,750 billion in output and income *only* if they expect to be able to sell the output for $2,750 billion. Remember, *demand creates its own supply* in Keynesian analysis.

In Figure 1, National Output is graphed as a 45° ray from the origin because, in Keynesian analysis, Aggregate Supply (output) adjusts passively to Aggregate Demand (expenditures). Equilibrium requires that Aggregate Output and Income (on the horizontal axis) just equal Aggregate Expenditures (on the vertical axis). This occurs when the Aggregate Expenditures curve intersects the 45° line. (Any variable plotted against an equal variable is on this 45° line.) Following convention, Y (on the horizontal axis) denotes real National Income and is measured against Aggregate Expenditures (on the vertical axis).

Aggregate Expenditures

You learned in the last chapter that Aggregate Expenditures is the sum of consumer spending, investment, government purchases, and net foreign spending. The basic Keynesian model we are building here ignores government and the foreign sector to simpli-

	TABLE 1	Levels of Income, Employment, and Output (Billions of Dollars)						
(1) Employment (Millions of Workers)	**(2)** National Output & Income	**(3)** Planned Consumption	**(4)** Planned Savings	**(5)** Planned Investment	**(6)** Unplanned Inventory Changes	**(7)** Aggregate Expenditures (*AE*) (Columns 3 + 5)		
70	$2,000	$2,100	$−100	$100	$−200	$2,200	Tendency for income to rise
75	2,250	2,300	−50	100	−150	2,400	
80	2,500	2,500	0	100	−100	2,600	
85	2,750	2,700	50	100	−50	2,800	
90	3,000	2,900	100	100	0	3,000	Equilibrium
95	3,250	3,100	150	100	+50	3,200	Tendency for income to fall
100	3,500	3,300	200	100	+100	3,400	
105	3,750	3,500	250	100	+150	3,600	

FIGURE 1 *Consumption, Investment, and Income*

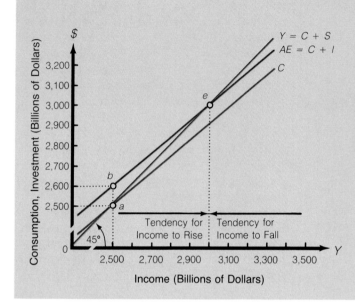

Equilibrium income (point *e*) is found where National Output is just equal to Aggregate Expenditures. Whenever the system is not in equilibrium, pressures will exist to move the economy to an equilibrium income level of $3,000 billion. If National Output is $2,500 billion, Aggregate Expenditures will equal $2,600 billion. This excess Aggregate Demand generates expansionary pressures in the form of declining inventories moving the economy upward to point *e*. When income exceeds $3,000 billion, pressures mount to move the economy back to equilibrium. Note: This figure is based on the data in Table 1.

fy our analysis, so column 7 in Table 1 reflects Aggregate Expenditures (*AE*) as the sum of planned consumption (column 3) and planned investment (column 5). Thus, *AE = C + I* indicates planned levels of Aggregate Spending for each level of output and income.

Keynesian Equilibrium

Classical economics suggests that a deviation from full employment represents disequilibrium that is, at most, a short-run phenomenon that will be quickly remedied by Say's Law and flexibility of interest rates, wages, and prices. The Keynesian perception of a short-run disequilibrium is very different.

Disequilibrium *occurs whenever Aggregate Spending differs from Aggregate Income and Output.*

What pushes an economy back to equilibrium? Classical reasoning suggests that *supply creates its own demand*—Aggregate Spending automatically rises to accommodate the full employment level of output. Keynesians respond that **demand creates its own supply**—that supply passively adjusts to demand. In

this context, *spending* and *demand* are synonymous. We will now scrutinize Keynesian adjustment processes—in situations of disequilibrium, National Output adjusts to the level of Aggregate Spending.

Eight possible levels of National Output and Aggregate Expenditures are listed in Table 1. What level of income and output will bring the economy into equilibrium? Consider for a moment employment of 75 million with National Output equal to $2,250 billion. Aggregate Expenditures equal $2,400 billion and so exceed the $2,250 billion National Output. What adjustments will yield an equilibrium such that National Output equals Aggregate Spending?

In this situation, there will not be enough output to enable most firms to maintain sufficient inventories to meet the demands of their customers—consumers and other firms. When firms' inventories fall below desired levels, they respond by expanding employment and output. This causes income to grow. Suppose employment grows from 75 to 80 million. Even at employment of 80 million workers, the problem remains—Aggregate Expenditures—now $2,600 billion—still exceed National Output—now $2,500 billion. Employment, output, and income will continue to climb until 90 million people are working.

Aggregate Expenditures and National Output both equal $3,000 billion at this employment level. Any further pressures to expand output are countered by offsetting pressures to contract output because firms are able to maintain the inventories needed to meet their customer's demands.

Pressures to move the economy to equilibrium are shown in Figure 1. For example, if National Output is only $2,500 billion (point *a*), then planned Aggregate Expenditures is $2,600 billion (point *b*). Excess Aggregate Spending ($100 billion = *b* − *a*) shrinks inventories and generates expansionary pressures that push the economy rightward from both *a* and *b* up the 45° reference line (National Output) to equilibrium at point *e* ($3,000 billion).

What happens if National Output exceeds planned *AE?* Suppose that most firms were overly optimistic in forecasting consumer and investor demands and produced $3,750 billion worth of goods and services. Firms would find their inventories of unsold goods swelling. Businesses cannot precisely regulate their inventories because customers may buy either more or less than firms expect. In this case, firms would reduce inventories and output by cutting back production, necessitating layoffs of employees. As output fell to point *e* in Figure 1, business inventories would shrink to the planned levels. This economy settles at an equilibrium income of $3,000 billion.

Both Table 1 and Figure 1 indicate that National Income will expand when output is less than $3,000 billion because spending exceeds production. When income or output exceeds $3,000 billion, income falls because production exceeds spending. Only when National Output is *exactly* $3,000 billion are all decision makers content to continue operating at existing levels of production, consumption, and investment. All forces are balanced and there are no net pressures for the economy to shrink or grow from this short-run equilibrium.

Price Versus Quantity Adjustments

In chapter 3, we suggested that price adjustments are part of the cure for disparities between the quantities of individual goods demanded and supplied. Price rises in individual markets if quantity demanded exceeds quantity supplied; if quantity supplied exceeds quantity demanded, price falls. You may wonder why such price adjustments are absent in this example.

The reason is that Keynesian analysis assumes that only **quantity adjustments** occur in situations of high unemployment and excess capacity.

The price level is constant because the simple Keynesian depression model assumes that capacity poses no problem. Expanding output in an economy with many idle workers does not require higher wage or price incentives. Classical analysis presumes severe capacity constraints because the economy is thought to hover close to full employment. Thus, a classical model would use **price-level adjustments** to solve the problem we have described. This part of the book focuses on the Keynesian model so we will ignore price movements for now, but they will be treated in detail in chapters 14–19.

Keynesian Saving = Investment Approach to Equilibrium

Closer scrutiny of Table 1 and Figure 1 reveals that the planned levels of saving and investment must be equal before the economy is in a stable equilibrium. Moreover, the plans of households and firms must be realized.

A requirement for macroequilibrium is that actual and planned saving and investment are all equal ($S = I$).

Investigating the relationships between investment and saving provides another view of the way the levels of National Income and Output are determined.

Planned Saving and Investment

Study columns 4 and 5 in Table 1, which are also graphed in Figure 2. In our simple Keynesian model, firms plan to invest $100 billion regardless of the level of income, while consumers' plans to save are tied to income. Suppose income were $3,500 billion. Consumers would try to save $200 billion (point *f* in Figure 2), but investment plans are for only $100 billion (point *g* in Figure 2). What will be the result?

Saving is the act of not consuming. Because income saved is money not spent, saving is a withdrawal of funds from the system.

Withdrawals *occur when income is not spent on domestic output.*

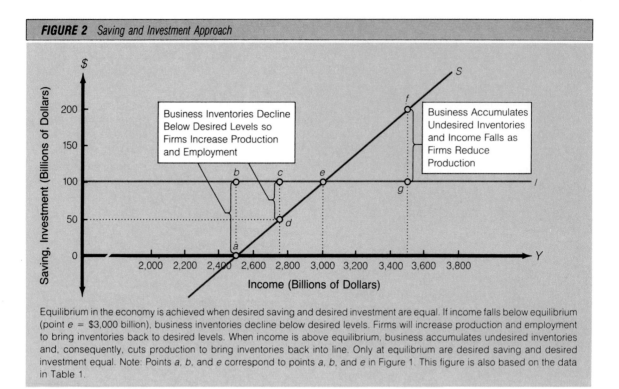

FIGURE 2 *Saving and Investment Approach*

Equilibrium in the economy is achieved when desired saving and desired investment are equal. If income falls below equilibrium (point *e* = $3,000 billion), business inventories decline below desired levels. Firms will increase production and employment to bring inventories back to desired levels. When income is above equilibrium, business accumulates undesired inventories and, consequently, cuts production to bring inventories back into line. Only at equilibrium are desired saving and desired investment equal. Note: Points *a*, *b*, and *e* correspond to points *a*, *b*, and *e* in Figure 1. This figure is also based on the data in Table 1.

In addition to saving, withdrawals include taxes (income paid to the government) and imports (most foreign income is spent in the recipients' own countries). Because spending is perceived to drive a capitalist system, withdrawals tend to suppress income generation in a Keynesian model.

Injections are the reverse of withdrawals; they reflect spending introduced into the economy.

> *Autonomous spending (regardless of source) represents an **injection** into the Keynesian spending stream.*

We will discuss the effects of injections on national income after we consider the consequences of such withdrawals as household saving.

Withdrawal because of excess saving causes firms to accumulate unwanted inventories because output exceeds sales. (This discussion parallels our previous description of adjustments to excess supply.) Firms will find total consumer and business spending (*C* + *I*) insufficient to clear new output from the market. Production and employment will fall because firms do not desire these investments in inventory. Income

drops as the economy moves back from points *f* and *g* toward equilibrium at point *e*, where planned saving and planned investment are equal. Planned and realized saving and investment are all equated and income stops falling when the economy approaches equilibrium.

This adjustment process works in the opposite direction when National Output and Income are below the equilibrium level of $3,000 billion. For example, when National Output is $2,750 billion, consumers desire to save $50 billion and consume $2,700 billion, while business plans to invest $100 billion; Aggregate Expenditures (*C* + *I*) are $2,800 billion. The $50 billion shortfall of goods required to satisfy consumer and investor demands causes inventories to shrink. Firms unintentionally disinvest in inventories, which fall by $50 billion in each period. Business will adjust by boosting production to raise inventories back to desired levels. Output and income rise to $3,000 billion (from *c* and *d* to point *e* in Figure 2) before planned inventories can be maintained; planned saving and investment are equal at $100 billion. Thus, equilibrium requires that planned saving equals planned investment (*S* = *I*).

Balancing Planned and Actual Saving and Investment

You can see that inventories are vital in movements from disequilibrium to equilibrium. Unintended inventory changes ensure that actual saving and investment are equal at all times. Firms use inventory changes as barometers. If inventories drop, there is an unintended disinvestment in inventories and firms boost their production. If inventories unexpectedly rise, firms view this unplanned investment as a signal to cut production and employment. Thus, changes in inventories resolve any differences between planned saving and planned investment.

Fluctuating inventories provide signals to raise or lower output so that planned saving equals planned investment, but other mechanisms also aid in equilibration. Consumers sometimes are unable to buy all the goods they demand; people often wait in lines during shortages. Queues and shortages signal firms to expand their production facilities or, perhaps, to raise prices.

Since Keynesian models generally assume excess production capacity, equilibration takes the form of changes in quantities—real National Income and employment adjust to eliminate disparities between Aggregate Spending and National Output. Classical reasoning assumes full employment so that all adjustments take the form of wage and price changes. The differing economic conditions that generate quantity adjustments instead of price adjustments are treated toward the end of this chapter.

In sum, only when planned investment exactly equals planned saving will the economy stay in equilibrium. When households' plans to save and business investment plans are both realized, firms' sales will just maintain equilibrium output and there will be no net tendency for the economy to move.

The Multiplier Effect

If there were no investment in the simple example shown in Figure 1, Aggregate Expenditures would consist only of consumption (C), and equilibrium income would be $2,500 billion (point a). When autonomous investment of $100 billion is injected, however, its effect is multiplied so that equilibrium

income rises to $3,000 billion (point e). The total change in income is five times the initial increase in autonomous spending!

You may wonder why a relatively small injection of investment ($100 billion) so powerfully expands equilibrium income ($500 billion). The answer rests in a concept called the multiplier.

> The **multiplier effect** *occurs when one person's spending becomes someone else's income, and some of the second person's income is subsequently spent, becoming the income of a third person, and so on.*

But at what level of income does this multiple spending→income→spending cycle stop? The answer requires a bit of arithmetic.

> The **autonomous spending multiplier** *is the total change in income generated divided by the change in autonomous spending that triggered the spending→income→spending sequence.*

When the new autonomous spending is investment, this ratio is:

$\Delta Y/\Delta I.$

The example in Table 1 and Figures 1 and 2 is based on a marginal propensity to consume (*mpc*) of 0.8. Suppose we begin with zero investment. Table 1 suggests that equilibrium income will be $2,500 billion because only at that level do planned saving and planned investment both equal zero. If firms decide to invest $100 billion on new capital goods, the workers and owners of firms producing capital goods receive $100 billion in additional income.

How will the workers and owners of firms who produce capital goods respond? Their *mpc* is 0.8 in their roles as consumers, so these producers can be expected to spend $80 billion of this new income on consumer goods and save $20 billion. When they spend the $80 billion, this second round of spending adds $80 billion to Aggregate Expenditures; National Output must increase by $80 billion, which becomes new income to the firms providing these consumer goods and to their employees. In turn, they will spend 80 percent of the $80 billion, or $64 billion, and so on throughout the system.

This round-by-round spending is illustrated in Table 2 and Figure 3. The cumulative effect of an auton-

TABLE 2 *A Tabular Example of the Multiplier*

Round	Increases in Expenditures (Billions of Dollars)	Increases in Saving (Billions of Dollars)
Initial Increase	$100	
Round 2	80	$ 20
Round 3	64	16
Round 4	51	13
Round 5	41	10
Round 6	33	8
Round 7	26	7
Round 8	21	5
Round 9	17	4
Round 10	13	3
Sum of First 10 Rounds	$446	$ 86
Sum of All Other Rounds	54	14
Total Increase in Spending (Income)	$500	
Total Increase in Saving		$100

Note: Data in the table are from Table 1. The *mpc* is 0.8 and the *mps* is 0.2. Figures after Round 3 are rounded off to the nearest dollar.

FIGURE 3 *The Multiplier Effect*

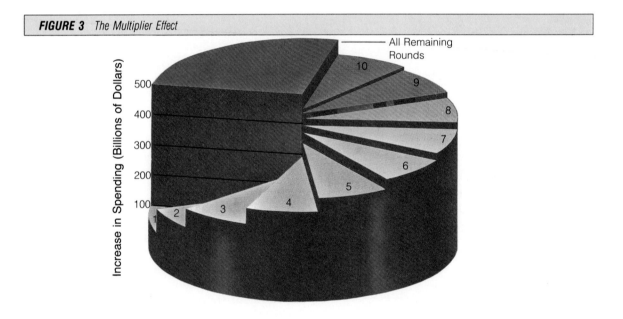

The round-by-round cumulative spending effect is illustrated in this figure. An additional $100 billion in spending in Round 1 is multiplied throughout the economy and results in a total increase in income of $500 billion when the *mpc* = 0.8. Each increase in spending in each round, when multiplied by the *mpc*, is the increase in spending for the subsequent round. When this infinite series is cumulated, aggregate income grows by $500 billion from an initial new injection of $100 billion.

omous investment injection of $100 billion is also illustrated in Figure 4, which is based on the data from Table 1. As we noted earlier, the *mpc* is 0.8, so the *mps* is 0.2 and the multiplier for our example is 5. It is no coincidence that the multiplier is the reciprocal of the *mps*: $1/mps = 1/.2 = 5$. In fact, any change in *injections* (for example, either autonomous consumption or investment) divided by the marginal propensity to save yields the total multiplied effect on National Output and Income.

In our highly simplified model, the only withdrawal is saving, so the multiplier is $1/mps$. (A higher *mps* yields a faster rate of withdrawal and a smaller multiplier.) Alternatively, the multiplier is the change in income divided by the change in autonomous injections; so:

$$\frac{\Delta Y}{\Delta I} = \frac{1}{mps}.$$

Since the *mpc* + *mps* = 1, the *mps* = 1 − *mpc* and the multiplier may also be written as $1/(1 - mpc)$. If we consider withdrawals other than saving:

**autonomous   = 1/(withdrawal
spending multiplier   fraction per
                spending round)
       = 1/(1 − fraction
                re-spent),**

and

**total changes = amount of injection
in income   × multiplier.**

A mathematical derivation of this autonomous spending multiplier is provided in the optional material at the end of this chapter.

Our highly simplified model may seem to suggest that the multiplier effect will be enormous—the marginal propensity to save is, historically, about 7 per-

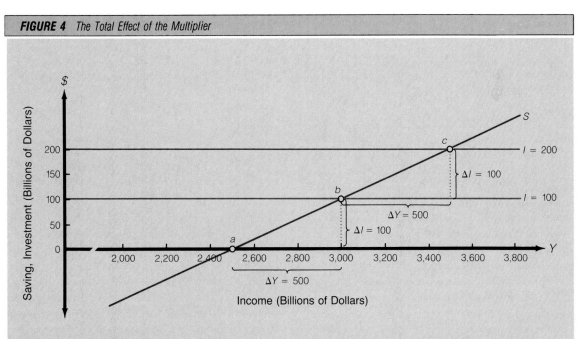

FIGURE 4   *The Total Effect of the Multiplier*

The effect on total income from a spending injection is equal to the injection times the autonomous spending multiplier. When the *mpc* = 0.8, this multiplier is 5. Therefore, an increase in investment (an injection) of $100 billion results in a total increase in income of $500 billion. This simple multiplier is $\Delta Y/\Delta I = 1/mps = 1/(1 - mpc)$.

cent, which suggests a multiplier of between 14 and 15. The linkages between spending rounds are much looser in the real world, however, than in this model. More sophisticated models consider other withdrawals of funds from the American spending→income→spending sequence.

Withdrawals include taxes (roughly 30 percent) and other "leakages" such as imports—a case where the funds we spend go into the hands of foreign suppliers. Moreover, the full multiplier effect is felt only after all spending rounds have been completed. Realistically, only the first four or five rounds of spending will be completed in the year in which an injection occurs. For all these reasons and more, prudent statistical estimates of the value of the autonomous spending multiplier place its maximum effective value at around 2. The Depression is a prime case of the multiplier at work.

The Great Depression: The Multiplier in Action

Brother, can you spare a dime?
—A Hit Song from the 1930s

No one alive in the early 1930s escaped the effects of the Great Depression. The labor force was roughly at full employment in 1929; unemployment was only 3.2 percent. By 1933, unemployment had soared to 25 percent—one worker in four was unemployed. Soup kitchens were inadequate to deal with widespread hunger. Windows along Wall Street became diving boards for those who saw defenestration as a cure for bankruptcy. A wave of failures threatened to make U.S. banks fall like a line of dominoes. Unfortunately for the people of that era, programs such as unemployment compensation and Social Security were not available to provide temporary replacement incomes. Economically, these were the hardest times this country has ever experienced.

Figure 5 uses a Keynesian framework to illustrate the first four years of the Great Depression (1929–33). This portrayal of the Great Depression seems fairly accurate and rather simple by today's standards, but it was not understood at all during the early 1930s.

The actual data for the four components of Aggregate Expenditures ($C, I, G, X - M$) show that changes in net foreign spending and government purchases were quite small and largely offset each other during this period. The huge decline in Gross Private Domestic Investment (I in Figure 5) between 1929 and 1933 can be viewed as the root cause of most of the collapse in Aggregate Spending. During this period, investment fell from $55.9 billion to only $8.4 billion, and "induced consumption" plummeted almost $45 billion. This $47.5 billion decline in investment spending was accompanied by a $92.6 billion drop in income (from $314.7 billion in 1929 to $222.1 billion in 1933). The multiplier is the change in income divided by the change in injections, which in this case is roughly $\Delta Y/\Delta I$. Thus, our highly simplified model suggests a multiplier during this period of 1.95 ($-92.6/-47.5 = 1.95$).

In future chapters, we detail possible macroeconomic effects of government monetary and fiscal policies. Could such a collapse occur again? Most economists think not. How do you think the government might have prevented this collapse or, at least, cushioned its effects? In chapters 11–19, we examine the tools government can use to combat both recessions and inflations.

The Paradox of Thrift

What happens if we as a society try to save more? The classical analysis in chapter 8 suggests that saving facilitates investment and economic growth. There is, however, a potential problem known as the paradox of thrift.

*Keynesian theory suggests that widespread attempts to save more may cause income to fall so that actual saving shrinks, a problem known as the **paradox of thrift.***

Most of us consider thrift a virtue. Ben Franklin's adage, "A penny saved is a penny earned," haunts many of our psyches when we shop, and we think we might be better off if we saved more. The term *paradox* correctly reflects, however, Keynesians' belief that Ben's adage is inappropriate for the general economy. Keynesian analysis indicates that if we *all* try to save more, we may *all* wind up worse off and actually save less.

Showing how the desire to save more may cause actual saving to fall requires a slight, but temporary, change in the assumptions used to build a simple Keynesian model. We have assumed that investment is autonomous, or unaffected by income. A more

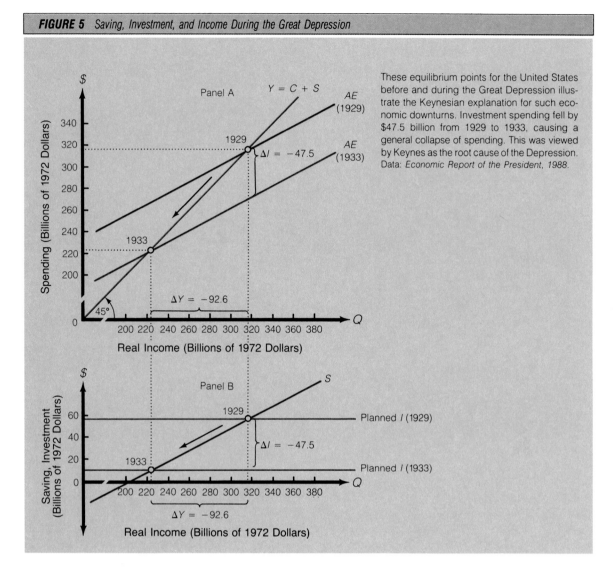

FIGURE 5 *Saving, Investment, and Income During the Great Depression*

Panel A $Y = C + S$

AE (1929)

1929

$\Delta I = -47.5$

AE (1933)

1933

$\Delta Y = -92.6$

45°

Spending (Billions of 1972 Dollars)

Real Income (Billions of 1972 Dollars)

Panel B S

1929

Planned I (1929)

$\Delta I = -47.5$

1933

Planned I (1933)

$\Delta Y = -92.6$

Saving, Investment (Billions of 1972 Dollars)

Real Income (Billions of 1972 Dollars)

These equilibrium points for the United States before and during the Great Depression illustrate the Keynesian explanation for such economic downturns. Investment spending fell by $47.5 billion from 1929 to 1933, causing a general collapse of spending. This was viewed by Keynes as the root cause of the Depression. Data: *Economic Report of the President, 1988.*

realistic assumption is that as income rises, firms become more optimistic about the profit prospects for new investment. Hence, for the moment we will assume that investment rises as income rises.

The paradox of thrift is illustrated in Figure 6, which shows households initially saving and firms initially investing $100 billion. National Income is $600 billion, with equilibrium at point *a* on curves S_0 and *I*. Suppose consumers decide to save more (consume less) at each level of income, causing the saving curve to rise from S_0 to S_1. The average propensity to save (*aps*) rises, but note that the marginal propensity

to save (*mps*) is constant at 20 percent. With the increased desire to save, people want to set aside $110 billion (point *c*) if total National Income is $600 billion, and $50 billion (point *d*) if National Income is $300 billion. What happens as the economy adjusts to this increased desire to save?

Consumption falls when households attempt to save more. Firms will counter declining sales and rising inventories with cutbacks in production, employment, and investment. As employment falls, so does income. Does this sound familiar? The economy moves from the original equilibrium income and

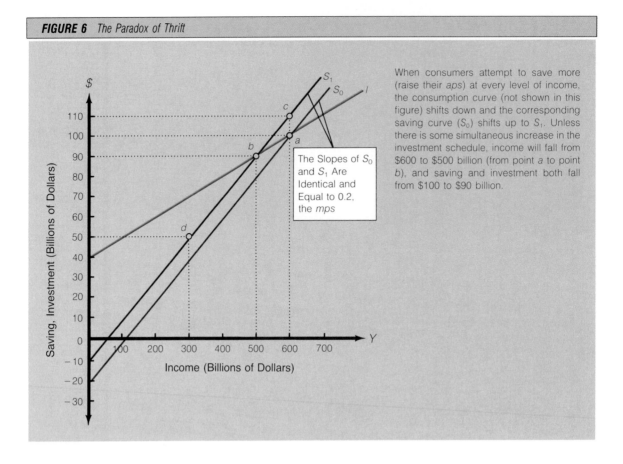

FIGURE 6 The Paradox of Thrift

When consumers attempt to save more (raise their *aps*) at every level of income, the consumption curve (not shown in this figure) shifts down and the corresponding saving curve (S_0) shifts up to S_1. Unless there is some simultaneous increase in the investment schedule, income will fall from $600 to $500 billion (from point *a* to point *b*), and saving and investment both fall from $100 to $90 billion.

The Slopes of S_0 and S_1 Are Identical and Equal to 0.2, the *mps*

output of $600 billion (point *a*), to a new equilibrium position at $500 billion (point *b*). Notice that saving actually declines by $10 billion, to a level of $90 billion. Why? Because actual saving and investment and planned saving and investment all must be equal in equilibrium; at point *b*, consumers want to save $90 billion because income is $500 billion and investors want to invest $90 billion at this new lower level of income.

But observe that consumption has fallen from $500 billion (600 − 100) to $410 billion (500 − 90). Thus, this Keynesian model suggests that increased desires to save may lead to cuts in actual consumption, investment, saving, and income—and to a declining standard of living. This line of reasoning certainly poses a paradox for those of us who think that more saving is always good for the economy.

Unfortunately, increased saving may be a typical household response at the worst possible time, when the economy begins slipping into a recession. If families fear that breadwinners will lose their jobs, they may begin saving a little more each payday, trying to build nest eggs to cover expenses should income cease. If growing numbers of households adopt this strategy, they increase the likelihood of a recession and compound the task of policymakers who are trying to restore the economy to full employment.

The paradox of saving may not be a problem if the economy is close to capacity. Classical reasoning reveals that increased desires to save may cause interest rates to fall, which may result in increases in investment and, thus, may yield the dividend of bolstering economic growth. President Reagan and his advisors relied on classical economics when, in 1981, they launched "supply-side" policies to stimulate saving and investment and reduce inflation.

Shortly thereafter, the economy tumbled into its deepest recession since the 1930s, but inflation subsided and interest rates began to fall. Between 1980 and 1985, Gross Private Saving (saving by households plus business saving) as a percent of National Income remained roughly constant at around 20 percent. Although "supply-side" policies may have helped cut inflation and interest rates while promoting economic growth, they (along with free-spending politicians) were credited with causing enormous budget deficits. In chapter 19, we will explore how successful policies that raise saving enhance economic growth.

The Investment Accelerator

The multiplier process relies on the fact that any increase in autonomous spending creates income, which generates further consumer spending, creating more income, and so on. The pressure to generate new income because rising consumption also causes new capital investment is known as the **investment accelerator.** (More sophisticated Keynesian models than any we consider in depth in this book describe interaction between aggregate output and investment by interweaving investment accelera-

tors with the multiplier process.) New autonomous spending causes investment to accelerate, so that Aggregate Expenditures are both *multiplied* by induced consumption and *accelerated* by induced investment. The effects on equilibrium income of this interaction of the multiplier and accelerator are summarized in Figure 7.

Potential Income Versus Equilibrium Income

We now turn to the most important conclusion of Keynesian analysis. Keynes was the first internationally prominent mainstream economist to argue that the mechanisms that push a market economy towards full employment may be very weak. Keynesian analysis was an important challenge to the classical economists of the 1930s, most of whom believed that flexible wages and prices automatically restore an economy to full employment. The Great Depression taught us that mechanisms that automatically stabilize capitalistic economies sometimes operate very slowly at best. Unemployment rose sharply between 1929 and 1933, and the economy showed few signs of automatic recovery prior to World War II.

FIGURE 7 *Integrating an Investment Accelerator into a Keynesian System*

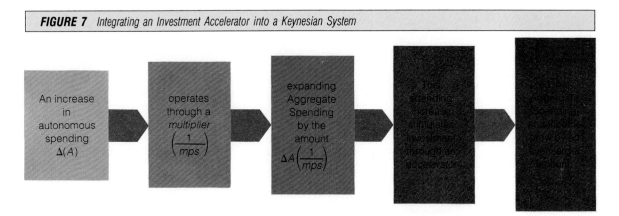

Investment is stimulated by a change in autonomous spending (ΔA) through the accelerator principle. This change in autonomous spending magnifies Aggregate Expenditures even more than is suggested by the multiplier process, but it also makes Aggregate Spending highly volatile.

Potential GNP

Potential GNP and *full-employment GNP* (or income) are rough synonyms.

> **Potential GNP** *is an estimate of what the economy could produce at high rates of utilization of our available resources, especially full employment of labor.*

Estimates of potential GNP reflect trends in productivity, the size and composition of the labor force, and other influences on our capacity to produce. Estimates of potential GNP for 1960–1987 are illustrated in Figure 8.

The GNP Gap

National output often falls far below potential GNP.

> *The* **GNP gap** *is the difference between potential and actual GNP.*

In the simple Keynesian model described by Table 1 and graphed in Figure 9, equilibrium income is $3,000 billion along expenditure curve AE_0. Suppose that potential GNP at full employment is $3,250 billion, so that a *GNP gap* exists of $250 billion. Would market pressures quickly move the economy above its original equilibrium of $3,000 billion? Keynesians believe the answer is NO. How might this $250-billion GNP gap be filled to achieve equilibrium income and output of $3,250 billion? The Keynesian answer is to increase Aggregate Spending from AE_0 to AE_1. How much of an increase in autonomous spending is required?

The Recessionary Gap

Given that the multiplier in our example is 5, an increase in autonomous investment spending of $50 billion will raise Aggregate Spending and output by $250 billion, filling the GNP gap and moving the economy to full employment.

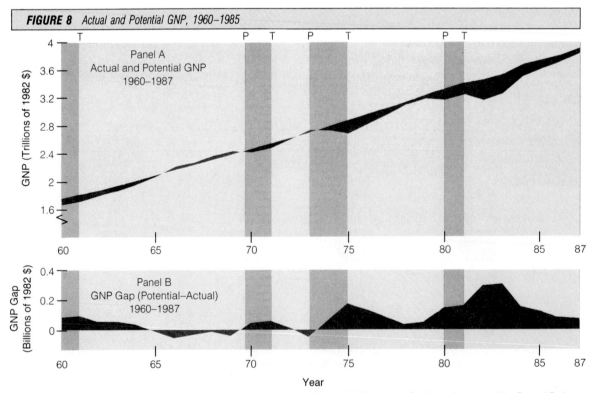

FIGURE 8 *Actual and Potential GNP, 1960–1985*

Source: *Economic Report of the President*, 1988, and Frank de Leeuw and Thomas M. Holloway, "Cyclical Adjustment of the Federal Budget and the Federal Debt," *Survey of Current Business*, December 1983. Updates by authors.

FIGURE 9 Inflationary and Recessionary Gaps

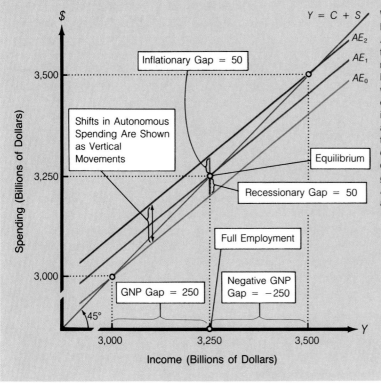

With full employment income of $3,250 billion and Aggregate Expenditures of AE_0, output will not automatically expand to reach full employment. Given that the multiplier in this example is 5, a $50-billion increase in autonomous spending will cause the economy to expand to full employment. This $50-billion deficiency in autonomous spending is referred to as the *recessionary gap*. Whenever autonomous spending exceeds that necessary to achieve a full employment level of Aggregate Spending, an *inflationary gap* exists. With Aggregate Spending of AE_2, the inflationary gap is $50 billion, and there is a *negative GNP gap* of −$250 billion.

The **recessionary gap** *measures the amount by which autonomous spending falls short of that needed to bring equilibrium income to full employment.*

The recessionary gap is measured along the vertical axis in Figure 9. This means that the gap is defined by any shortfall in autonomous spending and *not* by the amount by which equilibrium income falls short of full employment income (measured along the horizontal axis). This shortfall is the GNP gap and equals the recessionary gap times the autonomous spending multiplier:

GNP gap = recessionary gap × multiplier.

The Inflationary Gap

An inflationary gap is the reverse of the recessionary gap.

An **inflationary gap** *is the amount by which autonomous spending exceeds that needed to achieve full employment equilibrium.*

Graphically, it is the vertical distance between AE_1 and AE_2 in Figure 9. The inflationary gap is $50 billion if Aggregate Spending is AE_2. Since the economy can only produce $3,250 billion in output, this additional demand will result in upward pressures on prices when potential buyers compete for this limited real output.

Keynesian Equilibrium and the Price Level

National Income (Y) is a monetary value and can be thought of as the product of the price level (P) and the level of real output (Q). Thus, $Y = PQ$. In our example, real income and output (Q) cannot exceed the $3,250-billion full employment level. The $50 billion inflationary gap is expanded through the multiplier, which equals 5, so that equilibrium monetary income (Y) equals $3,500 billion. Equilibration requires that $3,500 billion = $P \times $3,250 billion, which means that the price level must rise to 3,500/3,250, or roughly 1.077. (A price index would rise from 100 to more than 107.) Thus, this $50-billion inflationary gap will cause the price level to rise almost 8 percent. Preventing this inflationary adjustment to excessive Aggregate Spending entails cutting the autonomous spending of either consumers, investors, government, or foreigners. Some methods government might use to reduce these inflationary pressures are presented in the next chapter.

Keynesian analysis largely focuses on achieving full employment if the economy is operating below its potential; it generally ignores the inflation that might emerge if Aggregate Demand is excessive. The price level is sensitive, however, to total spending by both consumers and investors, and vice versa. Let us see why.

Simple Keynesian theory views production decisions as being based strictly on expected sales; prices are assumed fixed. This is implicit in the idea that "demand creates its own supply." Thus, the Aggregate Supply curve compatible with Keynesian analysis of a recession is horizontal until a full employment level of output is reached. Then, just like the classical Aggregate Supply curve (discussed in chapter 8), this Aggregate Supply curve becomes vertical, as shown in Figure 10. Once the economy reaches full employment, further growth of spending would result in pure price increases.

If Aggregrate Demand is AD_0 in Figure 10, equilibrium output will be Q_0 at a price level of P_0 (point a). There is substantial excess capacity and unemployment in this equilibrium, and the GNP gap = $Q_f - Q_0$. The Keynesian prescription is to increase Aggregate Spending so that Aggregate Demand increases to AD_1, and the economy achieves full employment with price-level stability at point b. The growth in output from Q_0 to Q_f to fill the GNP gap can be accomplished by increases in autonomous spending equal to the recessionary gap described earlier. If Aggregate Spending increases more than the difference between Q_f and Q_0 and Aggregate Demand shifts to AD_2, the economy will suffer inflation as prices rise to P_2 from P_0 (point c). The vertical distance $P_2 - P_0$ reflects inflation caused by excessive

---

FIGURE 10 *A Simple Keynesian Relationship Between Output and the Price Level*

Simple Keynesian theory operates as though "demand creates its own supply" since prices are assumed fixed. As a result, the Aggregate Supply curve is horizontal until full employment is reached. If Aggregate Demand is AD_0, the GNP gap is $Q_f - Q_0$, which is equal to the recessionary gap times the multiplier. Once full employment is reached (Q_f), the Aggregate Supply curve (AS) becomes vertical. Thus, if Aggregate Demand rises from AD_1 to AD_2, the price level will rise from P_0 to P_2 due to excessive autonomous spending and the inflationary gap just described.

autonomous spending, in accord with the inflationary gap we described earlier.

The central topic in the next chapter is how government fiscal policy (spending and taxing) can eliminate inflationary or recessionary gaps so that GNP moves to a non-inflationary full employment level. A word of caution is in order. You have acquired considerable insight into the workings of our economy by studying the model developed in this chapter. When Keynes wrote *The General Theory of Employment, Interest, and Money* in 1936, he was primarily concerned with filling a huge recessionary gap and suggested massive government spending as the best way to increase Aggregate Expenditures sufficiently to pull an economy out of a depression.

Policies to shrink inflationary or recessionary gaps require accurate estimates of these gaps and then timely and appropriate actions to achieve full employment with price-level stability. This is actually an incredibly difficult task, obscured by the crude over-simplification of our model. This analysis will, however, help you to understand and formulate solutions to problems that we encounter in the next chapter. The model presented there is slightly more complex, making it possible to consider a broader range of stabilization problems and policies.

CHAPTER REVIEW: KEY POINTS

1. Keynesian theory suggests that erratic changes in *business investment spending* (especially inventories) play a major role in causing fluctuations in aggregate income and employment.

2. Equilibrium income and employment occur at the output level at which *Aggregate Spending equals National Output;* firms desire to produce and sell exactly the amounts consumers and investors want to purchase. Any deviation from equilibrium income sets forces in motion to drive the economy towards a new equilibrium.

3. When *planned saving equals planned investment* ($S = I$), the economy will be in *equilibrium.* Actual saving and investment are equal at all times because inventory adjustments and similar mechanisms ensure this balance.

4. When *autonomous spending* in the economy increases by $1, income rises by an amount equal to the *autonomous spending multiplier* times the original $1. The multiplier exists because the original $1 in new spending becomes $1 in new income, parts of which are then spent by successive consumers and businesses. The simple autonomous spending multiplier equals:

$$\frac{\Delta Y}{\Delta A} = \frac{1}{mps} = \frac{1}{(1 - mpc)},$$

where A represents some form of autonomous spending. More generally, the multiplier equals 1/(withdrawal fraction per spending round).

5. Investment spending dropped precipitously during the 1929–33 period. This decline reduced equilibrium income sharply, and it may have been a principal cause of the Great Depression.

6. The *paradox of thrift* appears to be an important challenge to our conventional wisdom. If more consumers decide to increase their saving, the result might be declining income, consumption, and saving.

7. *Potential GNP* is an estimate of the output the economy could produce at full employment. The *GNP gap* is the difference between potential and actual GNP.

8. The *recessionary gap* is the amount by which autonomous spending falls short of that necessary to achieve a full employment level of income; it is measured on the vertical axis. An *inflationary gap* is the amount that autonomous spending exceeds what is necessary for a full employment equilibrium and is a measure of upward pressure on the price level.

9. Keynes felt that in a depression, increases in output with no increase in the price level could be stimulated by raising demand. Simple Keynesian theory suggests that the Aggregate Supply curve is horizontal up to the point of full employment. Once full employment and the economy's capacity to produce are reached, the economy conforms to classical reasoning. The Aggregate Supply curve becomes vertical because higher prices cannot generate extra production. When the economy is at full employment, any increase in Aggregate Demand simply bids up prices and results in inflation.

PROBLEMS

1. A simple way to calculate an autonomous spending multiplier is to invert (turn upside-down) the fraction representing the *mps*. For example, if *mps* = 1/6, this multiplier equals 6. Compute the *mps* and the autonomous spending multiplier for the following values of the *mpc*: 1/2, 3/5, 2/3, 3/4, 4/5, 5/6, 6/7, 7/8, 8/9, and 9/10.

2. Use the consumption relationship described in Table 3 to answer the following questions.
   a. If autonomous investment is 200, what is equilibrium income?
   b. Assume that full employment income is $4,000. What is the GNP gap?
   c. How much is the inflationary gap?
   d. How much is the autonomous spending multiplier?
   e. If extreme pessimism caused investment spending to fall by −$600, what would the equilibrium income be? What would the recessionary gap equal?

TABLE 3	
National Output and Income	**Planned Consumption**
$ 0	$1,000
1,000	1,800
2,000	2,600
3,000	3,400
4,000	4,200
5,000	5,000
6,000	5,800
7,000	6,600

QUESTIONS FOR THOUGHT AND DISCUSSION

1. What are the similarities and the differences between equilibrium for Aggregate Expenditures and National Output curves and equilibrium for Aggregate Demand and Supply when the price level is a consideration? How do these macroeconomic equilibria compare with the equilibria in markets for individual goods and services?

2. In the simple Keynesian model presented in this chapter, the only forms of injection considered are autonomous investment and the only withdrawal is saving. What are other possible injections? Or other possible withdrawals? How might exports and imports be incorporated to make this model a more complete picture of the way the world really works?

3. Do you think prices will fall in response to declines in Aggregate Demand, as classical economists suggest? Or will quantities decline, as Keynesians believe? What bearing does your answer have for designing policies to combat inflationary pressures? If the economy has considerable excess capacity, will expanding Aggregate Expenditures cause output to grow, or will the price level simply rise?

4. What are the alternatives available to a retailer whose inventories are growing because sales are not as large as planned? Will the alternative most retailers select be important in determining National Income? How? How will the strategies chosen by retailers with excess inventories vary over the business cycle? Why is this important?

OPTIONAL MATERIAL: MATHEMATICS OF THE KEYNESIAN AUTONOMOUS SPENDING MULTIPLIER

A more rigorous treatment of our hypothetical model will help you understand why income changes by some multiple of any change in autonomous spending. (We use delta (Δ) to signify change. Thus, ΔY is read "change in income.") How large will be the total change in income (ΔY) from a given change in, say, autonomous investment spending (ΔI)? This ratio ($\Delta Y/\Delta I$) is known as the **autonomous spending multiplier.**

We have assumed that consumption is related to income and that changes in income will cause consumption to change by a value equal to the *mpc* times the change in income. Since we know that:

$$Y = C + I \qquad \text{Equation 1}$$

(output is either consumed or invested), then:

$$\Delta Y = \Delta C + \Delta I \qquad \text{Equation 2}$$

(changes in output reflect changes in consumption and/or investment). We assume that consumption spending is related to income by the *mpc*, so:

$$\Delta C = mpc \times \Delta Y \qquad \text{Equation 3}$$

(this is the change in induced consumption). The change in consumption is equal to the change in income times the proportion of the change you intend to spend.

Substituting Equation 2 into Equation 3 yields:

$$\Delta Y = mpc\Delta Y + \Delta I. \qquad \text{Equation 4}$$

Now we need to move all income (Y) terms to one side. This is accomplished by subtracting $mpc\Delta Y$ from each side of Equation 4, so:

$$\Delta Y - mpc\Delta Y = \Delta I \qquad \text{Equation 5}$$

Factoring the ΔY terms on the left side of Equation 5 leaves:

$$\Delta Y(1 - mpc) = \Delta I, \qquad \text{Equation 6}$$

and dividing both sides by $(1 - mpc)$ yields:

$$\Delta Y = \frac{\Delta I}{(1 - mpc)} \; or$$

$$\Delta Y = \Delta I \times \frac{1}{(1 - mpc)} \qquad \text{Equation 7}$$

The term $1/(1 - mpc)$ is the **autonomous spending multiplier.** Since $mpc + mps = 1$ so that the $mps = 1 - mpc$, another way to write the autonomous spending multiplier is $1/mps$.

We have used investment to show how hikes in autonomous spending yield increases in income via the multiplier. Mathematically identical effects occur if autonomous consumption, government spending, or exports are raised. Economists often use A to stand for all forms of autonomous spending when writing formulas for multipliers. Thus, the following are all equivalent ways to write the autonomous spending multiplier:

$$\frac{\Delta Y}{\Delta A} = \frac{1}{1 - mpc} = \frac{1}{mps} \qquad \text{Equation 8}$$

If the marginal propensity to consume is 0.8, the autonomous spending multiplier will be 5 because $[1/(1 - 0.8) = 1/0.2 = 5]$. Calculate the multipliers for alternative values of *mpc* (e.g., 9/10, 6/7, 5/6, 4/5, 3/4, 2/3, and 3/5). Observe what happens to multipliers as *mpc* rises and *mps* falls. Naturally, reversed multiplier effects follow cuts in autonomous spending. Some multipliers that are appropriate for government purchases and taxes are treated in the optional material following chapter 11.

CHAPTER 11

Fiscal Policy: Government Taxing and Spending

Keynesians perceive variations in government tax and spending policies as tools that policymakers can use to smother cyclical fluctuations in output, income, and employment. Many Keynesians believe that proper fiscal policy can "fine-tune" Aggregate Expenditures so that people are shielded from violent swings in their incomes and economic well-being.

Fiscal policy **is the use of government spending and tax policies to stimulate or contract macroeconomic activity.**

Classical economics has been reborn as "supply-side" economics. In this view, Aggregate Supply is far more significant than Aggregate Demand. Supply-siders stress the advantages of low tax rates and generally advocate minimal government. They emphasize market incentives for private work effort and believe that high saving rates promote private investment in new capital goods. Supply-side analysis suggests that government outlays may "crowd-out" private investment and consumption and that high taxes may so discourage productive efforts that incomes fall and that total tax revenues actually shrink. We will examine both approaches to fiscal policy in this chapter. Many Americans foresee chaos unless government starts balancing its budget.

The federal government operates a **balanced budget** *when its tax revenues and outlays of funds are equal, a* **budget deficit** *when its outlays are greater than revenues, and a* **budget surplus** *if tax revenues exceed outlays.*

We touch on the wisdom of balancing the federal budget and the prospect of eventual bankruptcy in this chapter; chapter 15 treats these issues in depth.

Fiscal Policy: The Demand Side

Changes in federal taxes and outlays fall into two policy categories: discretionary and automatic. The next section examines how some fiscal policy structures automatically change spending and taxes so that new legislation is not always required to adjust to changing economic conditions. But first we will consider the federal government's discretion to enact new tax laws or to alter its spending or transfer programs.

Discretionary fiscal policy *involves deliberate legislative changes in government outlays or taxes to alter Aggregate Demand (AD) and stabilize the economy.*

What is the Keynesian view of the effects of fiscal policy on Aggregate Expenditures? We will initially assume, for simplicity, that (*a*) government spending (*G*) is autonomous and affects neither the consumption nor the investment schedules; (*b*) investment (*I*) is also autonomous—at a constant level that is independent of income; and (*c*) taxes (*T*) are also autonomous—unaffected by income. These restrictive assumptions will be relaxed a bit after you are more comfortable with our expanded model.

Discretionary Spending and Equilibrium

The numerical Keynesian model built in chapter 10 is expanded to consider government in Table 1. These data are graphed in Figure 1. Without government, the private sector yields equilibrium spending and income of $3,000 billion (point *a*). But if full-employment income is $3,250 billion, there is a GNP gap of $250 billion. Keynesian analysis perceives any forces pushing the economy toward full employment as weak, so there is a recessionary gap of $50 billion that will not be remedied quickly through private action.

TABLE 1 Curing a Recessionary Gap with the Keynesian Remedy of Government Spending (Billions of Dollars)

	Private Sector Only						Addition of Government Sector		
(1) Employ-ment (Millions)	(2) National Output	(3) C	(4) S	(5) I	(6) Aggregate Expenditures Without Government (AE₀)	(7) Pressures on Income & Output	(8) G	(9) Aggregate Expenditures With Government (AE₁)	(10) Pressures on Income & Output
70	2,000	2,100	−100	100	2,200	Tendency	50	2,250	Tendency
75	2,250	2,300	−50	100	2,400	for	50	2,450	for
80	2,500	2,500	0	100	2,600	income to	50	2,650	income to
85	2,750	2,700	50	100	2,800	increase	50	2,850	increase
90	3,000	2,900	100	100	3,000	Equilibrium	50	3,050	
95	3,250	3,100	150	100	3,200		50	3,250	Full employment equilibrium
						Tendency			Tendency
100	3,500	3,300	200	100	3,400	for	50	3,450	for
105	3,750	3,500	250	100	3,600	income to decrease	50	3,650	income to decrease

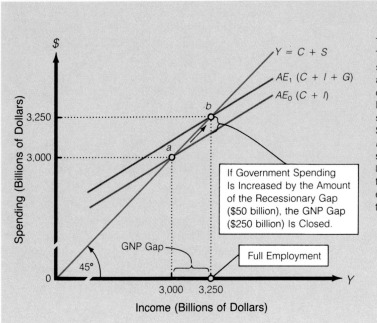

FIGURE 1 Using Fiscal Policy to Achieve Full-Employment Equilibrium Income

This figure graphically depicts the data in Table 1. Equilibrium without government spending is $3,000 billion (point *a*) and a GNP gap of $250 billion exists. The economy can be brought to full employment by adding $50 billion to government spending. This increases Aggregate Spending from AE_0 ($C + I$) to AE_1 ($C + I + G$). The $50 billion in government spending is subject to the multiplier just like private autonomous spending. Thus, the $50 billion times the multiplier (5 in this example) closes the GNP gap and moves the economy to full employment.

Note that $50 billion in new autonomous spending will close the $250 billion GNP gap because the multiplier is 5. The economy would achieve its potential GNP if this recessionary gap were somehow closed. One way to fill this recessionary gap is for the government to add $50 billion to autonomous spending (column 8 in Table 1). When Aggregate Expenditures shift from AE_0 to AE_1 in Figure 1 because government spending rises from zero to $50 billion, equilibrium moves from point *a* to full employment at point *b*.

Notice that autonomous government spending and autonomous private spending are subject to the multiplier in the same way. The multiplier was originally described in terms of investment ($\Delta Y / \Delta I =$ **autonomous spending multiplier**), but all macroeconomic injections and withdrawals are subject to the multiplier principle. Government spending is simply another form of injection, so it should not be surprising that, dollar for dollar, it is as powerful as investment spending in increasing Aggregate Expenditures. For example, a new federal contract places new income in the hands of government contractors and their employees. Some of their new income is saved, but most will be spent. This spending in turn

becomes new income for those from whom they buy and is then spent or saved. And so on.[1]

The effect of a hike in government purchases can be described in a manner parallel to the planned savings-equal-investment approach outlined in chapter 10. Saving and taxes are both withdrawals, while investment and government purchases are both injections. *Planned injections must equal planned withdrawals at equilibrium.*[2]

Figure 2 illustrates the planned-injections-equal-planned-withdrawals approach, which parallels the savings-equals-investment approach we developed when only private spending was considered. Households would save $150 billion if income were $3,250

---

1. You may wonder how the government can spend more without raising taxes. One possibility is for the government to borrow the money by selling Treasury bonds. Alternatively, the budget deficit can be financed by printing more money. The ability to print money certainly distinguishes the federal government from the rest of us. (We address the specific mechanisms used by the Federal Reserve System (FED) in chapter 13. The FED is the arm of government empowered to print and regulate money. The process of printing money to cover a deficit is a bit more complex than we suggest here.)

2. Algebraically, since $C + I + G = C + S + T = Y$ in equilibrium, then $I + G = S + T$ is an equilibrium condition.

FIGURE 2 Injections-Equals-Withdrawals Approach to Equilibrium National Income (I + G = S + T)

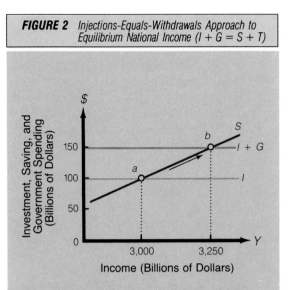

This figure examines the effect of an increase in government spending on equilibrium income using the injection-equals-withdrawals approach. Without government, the private economy will reach equilibrium at $3,000 billion (point *a*). Introducing $50 billion in government spending into the system increases income by $250 billion, so the economy moves to equilibrium at $3,250 (point *b*). Total injections (*I + G*) are $150 billion and are equal to total withdrawals (*S + T*) at the new equilibrium. Note that in this example, since *T* = 0, *S* = *I + G*.

billion. The introduction of $50 billion in new government spending boosts total injections ($I + G$) to $150 billion. Planned saving ($100 billion in planned withdrawals) at the initial equilibrium of $3,000 billion is less than planned investment and government spending ($150 billion in planned injections), so output will rise until injections equal withdrawals. Equilibrium is reached only when output has risen to $3,250 billion.

Taxes and Equilibrium

Now that we know how raising government spending affects equilibrium, we now introduce taxes (T) into our model. The **autonomous tax multiplier** can be expressed much like the autonomous expenditures multiplier.

> The **autonomous tax multiplier** *is the proportional change in income caused by a given change in autonomous taxes, and is written as:* $\Delta Y/\Delta T$.

Taxes, like saving, are withdrawals that pull down spending and income. Thus, the autonomous tax multiplier is a *negative* number.

Suppose an inflationary psychology becomes so contagious that people start spending their income almost as soon as they receive it. Table 2 reflects

TABLE 2 Curing an Inflationary Gap with Taxes

(1) Employment (Millions)	(2) National Output & Income (Y)	(3) C	(4) S	(5) I	(6) Spending Without Taxes (C + I)	(7) T	(8) Y_d	(9) C_t	(10) S_t	(11) Aggregate Spending ($C_t + I$)	(12) Net Pressure on Output
90	3,000	3,150	−150	100	3,250	250	2,750	2,950	−200	3,050	Tendency for income to rise
95	3,250	3,350	−100	100	3,450	250	3,000	3,150	−150	3,250	0
100	3,500	3,550	−50	100	3,650	250	3,250	3,350	−100	3,450	Tendency for income to fall
105	3,750	3,750	0	100	3,850	250	3,500	3,550	−50	3,650	
110	4,000	3,950	50	100	4,050	250	3,750	3,750	0	3,850	
115	4,250*	4,150	100	100	4,250*	250	4,000	3,950	50	4,050	
120	4,500	4,350	150	100	4,450	250	4,250	4,150	100	4,250	

*Note: Equilibrium without taxes equals 4,250 (Y = C + I = 4,150 + 100 = 4,250).

these inflationary expectations by showing planned consumption (column 3) at $250 billion higher and planned saving at $250 billion lower (column 4) for each income level than in Table 1.

With no government involvement, equilibrium income (where column 2 equals column 6) is $4,250 billion; so Aggregate Spending is $1,000 billion too high for a fully employed economy with price-level stability. This occurs only at $3,250 billion in output. There is a negative GNP gap of $1,000 billion ($3,250 billion - $4,250 billion). Given the autonomous spending multiplier of 5 ($mpc = 0.8$), this GNP gap implies an inflationary gap of $200 billion in this situation, which means that autonomous spending is $200 billion too high. Alternatively, autonomous saving is $200 billion too low (distance bc in Figure 3). This model lacks government spending, so raising taxes to boost withdrawals is the only way government can reduce Aggregate Expenditures.

Suppose autonomous taxes of $250 billion are now imposed (column 7). How will this $250 billion in taxes affect Aggregate Spending? Consumer decisions about spending depend on disposable income (Y_d) instead of aggregate income (Y) because households alone ultimately bear all tax burdens. Subtracting taxes (column 7) from National Income (column 2) yields the disposable income ($Y - T = Y_d$) shown in column 8 of Table 2. Note that this relationship between disposable income and consumption is identical to the one between income and consumption from Table 1 when we ignored taxes.

How much of this $250 billion in taxes will come from consumption and how much from saving? With an mpc of 80 percent and an mps of 20 percent, consumption will initially fall 0.8 times the $250 billion in taxes, for a total of $200 billion. This shifts consumption in the Aggregate Expenditures schedule down by $200 billion for every level of gross (before tax)

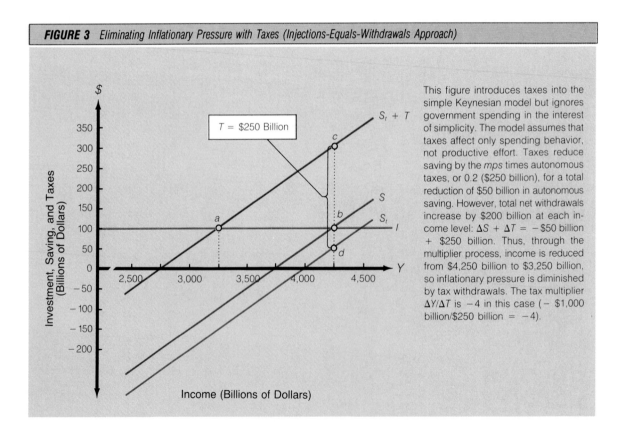

FIGURE 3 Eliminating Inflationary Pressure with Taxes (Injections-Equals-Withdrawals Approach)

This figure introduces taxes into the simple Keynesian model but ignores government spending in the interest of simplicity. The model assumes that taxes affect only spending behavior, not productive effort. Taxes reduce saving by the mps times autonomous taxes, or 0.2 ($250 billion), for a total reduction of $50 billion in autonomous saving. However, total net withdrawals increase by $200 billion at each income level: $\Delta S + \Delta T = -$50 billion + $250 billion. Thus, through the multiplier process, income is reduced from $4,250 billion to $3,250 billion, so inflationary pressure is diminished by tax withdrawals. The tax multiplier $\Delta Y / \Delta T$ is -4 in this case ($-$1,000 billion/$250 billion $= -4$).

TABLE 3 Round-by-Round Effects of $100 Billion Increases in Spending, Taxing, and the Balanced Budget (in Billions of Dollars)

Effect	(1) $100 Billion Extra Government Purchases	+	(2) $100 Billion Extra Autonomous Taxation	=	(3) $100 Billion Extra Taxing and Purchases
Round 1: Initial effect of change on income	$100		0		$100
Round 2: induced spending	80		$ −80		0
Round 3: induced spending	64		−64		0
Round 4: through all subsequent rounds	256		−256		0
TOTAL CHANGE	$500		$−400		$100
MULTIPLIER ($mpc = 0.8$)	5		−4		1

Note: Each $1 increase in government purchases creates $1 in new income in Round 1, but each $1 in new taxes does not influence first-round income. In Round 2, each $1 in new government purchases has caused the person whose income was increased to spend $0.80, but this is offset by the reduced spending of $0.80 caused by each $1 in new taxes. Moreover, the effects of the new spending and taxing offset each other in all subsequent rounds. Thus, only Round 1 spending has any net effect on income, and the balanced-budget multiplier equals one.

income. Similarly, the saving schedule falls $50 billion at all income levels.

The new saving curve S_t (savings after taxes are imposed) is exactly $50 billion lower (measured on the vertical axis) than the original saving curve S in Figure 3. (Remember, a drop in saving is shown as a shift of the saving curve to the right because consumers will now save less at each income level.) Let's look at this using the injections-equal-withdrawals approach.

Withdrawals in the form of after-tax saving are now shown as S_t. Taxes of $250 billion are withdrawn from the economy as well. Consequently, total withdrawals = $S_t + T$. This combined withdrawal function is $S_t + T$ in Figure 3 and is exactly $250 billion above S_t (distance cd); thus, it is $200 billion above the original S curve for each income level.

On the other side of the ledger, business investment of $100 billion is still the only injection in this economy. Equilibrium requires total leakages (another term for withdrawals) to equal total injections, so $S_t + T = I$ (point a in Figure 3). Equilibrium National Income (determined now by Aggregate Spending of $C_t + I$, where C_t reflects after-tax consumption) falls from $4,250 billion to $3,250 billion. The autonomous tax multiplier ($\Delta Y / \Delta T_a$) equals

−$1,000/$250, so it is −4. In this example, inflationary expectations cause saving to be −$150 billion in equilibrium; therefore, taxes (withdrawals) of $250 billion just offset investment injections ($100 billion) and dissaving ($150 billion) to keep this economy at full employment without inflation.

The Tax Multiplier

In our example, the autonomous spending multiplier ($\Delta Y / \Delta A$, where A equals the sum of all forms of autonomous spending) is 5 because the marginal propensity to consume is 0.8. Our calculations indicate that the autonomous tax multiplier ($\Delta Y / \Delta T_a$) is −4 in this case. Notice the relationship: one minus the autonomous spending multiplier equals the tax multiplier $[1 − 1/mps = \Delta Y / \Delta T; \ 1 − 5 = −4]$. The form of this simple tax multiplier is **−mpc/mps**.[3] The *autonomous tax multiplier* is the negative value of one less than the spending multiplier. An example of why this is so is shown in Table 3.

---

3. We know that $mpc + mps = 1$. Substitute this into part of $1 − (1/mps)$, and we get $1 − [(mpc + mps)/mps]$. Factoring, we have $1 − [(mpc/mps) + (mps/mps)]$, which simplifies to $1 − (mpc/mps) − 1$, which equals $− mpc/mps$. This is the value of the autonomous tax multiplier.

Table 3 traces the effects on spending of $100-billion increases in government purchases and taxes, both individually and together, through a few rounds of transactions, assuming that the $mpc = 0.8$. In column 1, 80 percent of each extra dollar income is spent and becomes someone else's income. Thus, a new injection of $100 billion in government spending (Round 1) means that $80 billion in consumer spending is induced in the second round. The people whose incomes rise by this $80 billion then spend $64 billion, which becomes other people's extra income. And so on. The autonomous spending multiplier is 5, indicated at the end of column 1.

The effect that new autonomous taxes of $100 billion have on spending and income is shown in column 2 of Table 3. Note that in Round 1, this tax has no effect on gross (pre-tax) incomes. The $100-billion tax hike may be viewed by taxpayers as a cut in disposable income, but it does not initially reduce production or National Income. It is when this decline in disposable income is translated into lower spending that National Income is reduced. Thus, new government purchases have an initial effect on Aggregate Spending; in Round 1, new taxes do not. Subsequent rounds cancel, so the tax multiplier is a negative value equal to one minus the spending multiplier.

The Balanced-Budget Multiplier

You may have noticed something startling in Table 3. Expanding both government spending (column 1) and autonomous taxes (column 2) by $100 billion causes equilibrium income to rise, on balance, by exactly $100 billion (end of column 3). The reasoning is actually straightforward: The spending multiplier $(1/mps)$ plus the tax multiplier $(-mpc/mps)$ equals $(1 - mpc)/mps$. Since $1 - mpc = mps$, the ratio $(1 - mpc)/mps$ equals 1. This bit of algebra suggests that the **balanced-budget multiplier** in a simple Keynesian model is exactly one. The conclusion is that equal increases (*decreases*) in government spending and taxes will raise (*lower*) equilibrium National Income by an identical amount. Table 3 should help you discern the fiscal mechanisms at work when either spending or taxing is changed. The autonomous spending and tax multipliers and the balanced-budget multiplier are described in the optional material at the end of this chapter.

Let us summarize the discretionary fiscal policies Keynesians prescribe to remedy specific economic ills. Inflationary pressures can be relieved through tax hikes or cuts in government purchases, or both. Both tax increases and government spending cuts will drive the government budget towards surplus (or reduce deficits) during inflationary periods. If excessive unemployment is the major problem, then tax cuts or increases in governmental purchases will temporarily move the budget into a deficit (or reduce a surplus) and cause expansions of output, income, and employment.

This analysis suggests that budgetary deficits are the right medicine to cure a recession and that budgetary surpluses are a remedy when the economy suffers from inflation. Most political decision makers enjoy granting the tax cuts and new government spending projects that are appropriate to combat recession because such measures are popular with voters. But the tax hikes and slashed budgets needed to fight inflation are unpopular with the public and, consequently, are an anathema to many political leaders. Explicit political actions to create surpluses during inflation, fortunately, are not always necessary. There are certain features of our tax system and some government spending programs that automatically push budgets towards surpluses during inflationary periods and into deficits during economic downturns.

Automatic Stabilizers

Discretionary variations in spending and taxes require congressional action. Fortunately, they are not the only fiscal instruments available to help us achieve full employment and price-level stability. Keynesians count on several built-in mechanisms to dampen swings in Aggregate Spending and economic activity. Until now, we have unrealistically assumed that neither taxes nor government spending depend on income. The fact that both are sensitive to changes in National Income lends an automatic resilience to the economy.

Tax structures and government spending programs that cause budget deficits to grow automatically during recessions, or surpluses to grow during episodes of inflation, are known as **automatic stabilizers.**

Automatic stabilizers are sometimes called *nondiscretionary* fiscal policy because no overt government action is required.

Automatic Tax Adjustments

Personal and corporate income taxes are both closely tied to income. When prosperity boosts National Income, federal revenues from progressive corporate and personal income taxes rise more than proportionally. Corporate profit is the most sensitive of all incomes to swings in economic activity. A 10 percent decline in National Income might totally wipe out corporate profit, while 10 percent growth may cause aggregate profit to double or even triple, as illustrated in Figure 4. Thus, tax revenue from corporate income is highly cyclical.

Our progressive personal income tax structure is the main reason why tax collections rise or fall proportionally faster than income. This process acts as an automatic stabilizer during inflationary episodes because as income rises, tax collections rise even faster and the overall rate of withdrawal from the economy

increases. Inflationary growth of nominal income is slowed as withdrawals rise. This effect is partially offset today because Congress indexed personal income tax *rates* to inflation beginning in 1985. Just the opposite occurs when the economy enters a recession. Tax revenues tumble even faster than gross income falls, swelling budget deficits. Figure 4 shows how deficits tend to grow as the economy enters a recession and shrink or (rarely) become surpluses when the economy turns up.

Automatic Changes in Spending

Transfer payments rise during recessions and bolster Aggregate Spending by keeping consumption up because disposable income does not fall as fast as gross income. More people are eligible for welfare payments during hard times. People retire earlier during recessions and later during booms. Consequently,

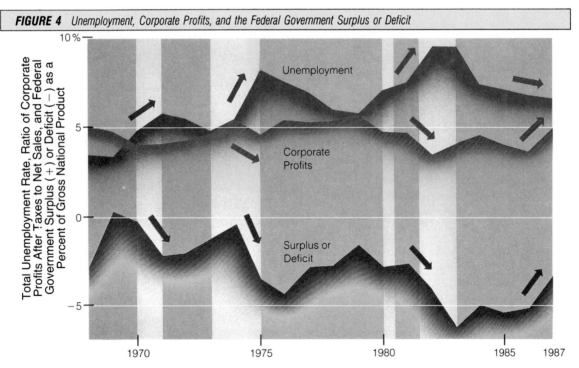

FIGURE 4 *Unemployment, Corporate Profits, and the Federal Government Surplus or Deficit*

This figure illustrates the effect of automatic tax adjustments when unemployment increases or the economy enters a recession. A downturn in economic activity causes unemployment to rise, which causes personal income and corporate profits to decline (or their rates of growth to decline). Our progressive tax structure then causes tax revenues to decline more than proportionally. This, coupled with the expansion of government transfer payments, results in rising budget deficits. In this figure, recessions are shaded with a white background. Note the long recovery from 1983 through 1987.

Source: *Economic Report of the President,* 1988.

Social Security payments buffer the economy against both downturns and inflationary expansion. Unemployment compensation is another automatic stabilizer because workers' incomes do not drop to zero when they are laid off. Comsumption by unemployed workers' families would plummet during widespread layoffs without unemployment compensation, and economic downturns would be worse than they are. The Great Depression would probably have been far less severe had our modern automatic stabilizers been in effect.

Falling tax collections and rising transfer payments during downturns help consumers maintain their customary consumption levels. The easier it is for households to maintain consumption, the less will be the momentum of any decline in gross income. Just how powerful are the automatic stabilizers in our economy? Although inadequate to completely offset strong pressures for a recession, they do tend to slow abrupt changes in the economy and give policymakers more time to formulate discretionary policy. Some studies suggest that declines in income during recent recessions would have been from one-third to one-half more severe in the absence of automatic stabilizers. Unfortunately, automatic stabilizers may be a mixed blessing.

Fiscal Drag

When potential income is growing rapidly, our built-in stabilizers may retard actual economic growth, a problem Keynesians refer to as fiscal drag.

> **Fiscal drag** *occurs with any growth of* GNP *because rising income boosts tax revenue and may shrink needs for transfer programs.*

Suppose all resources are fully employed and the budget is balanced. Technological advance, capital accumulation, and labor force growth all contribute to growth of potential GNP. Without bigger government outlays or lower tax rates, economic growth boosts tax revenues; a budget surplus may even emerge. This potential surplus hinders growth in disposable income and Aggregate Spending; withdrawals grow but injections do not. This may retard economic growth. Raising government spending or lowering tax rates may unshackle the economy. Both approaches are politically popular, so Congress quickly enacts Keynesian policies to counter potential recessions.

You may have wondered why government spending and deficits seem to grow each year. One reason may be the desire of dedicated politicians to overcome fiscal drag. It is easy for Congress or any president to find worthy projects. Most of us can think of areas where we would like to see the government spend more money or where we would like to cut taxes.

The Full Employment Budget _____

To this point, we have treated government surpluses or deficits as inconsequential in themselves, having importance ony to the extent that they stimulate or dampen Aggregate Spending. The suggestion that the federal budget be balanced annually does, however, receive a lot of popular support and has been proposed as a constitutional amendment. Imbedded in this appealing notion are some serious pitfalls. A surplus or deficit in the federal budget may be more a symptom of economic distress than a result of discretionary fiscal policy. As we just discussed, automatic stabilizers could create budgetary surpluses if unsustainable and inflationary growth mushroomed. Conversely, tax revenues fall and government spending rises during economic downturns, resulting in mounting budgetary deficits.

Does the Actual Budget Reflect the Thrust of Policy?

If the economy slides into a recession, should taxes be raised and government spending cut to balance the budget? If inflation looms, should we cut taxes or raise spending to balance the budget? The government deficit or surplus is affected by the level of GNP as well as by discretionary fiscal policy, so we cannot judge the appropriateness of policy merely by observing an actual budget deficit or surplus.

Economists who were perplexed by this problem developed the concept of the **full employment budget.** The question addressed is, "If our economy were approximately at full employment, what would the budget surplus or deficit be, given current tax structures and governmental spending programs?" If the economy is well below full employment, answering this question entails adding the extra tax revenues that would be collected if the economy moved to full employment and then subtracting the current outlays on unemployment benefits and other transfers caused by cyclical unemployment.

Government transfer payments can be treated as negative taxes (*negative* because the government pays people), which decline in importance as National Income rises. Figure 5 illustrates various possible relationships between **net taxes** (tax revenues minus transfer payments) and government purchases under three alternative tax structures. Notice that the tax functions are all positively sloped; net taxes rise as income rises. We will assume that the noninflationary

FIGURE 5 The Full Employment Budget

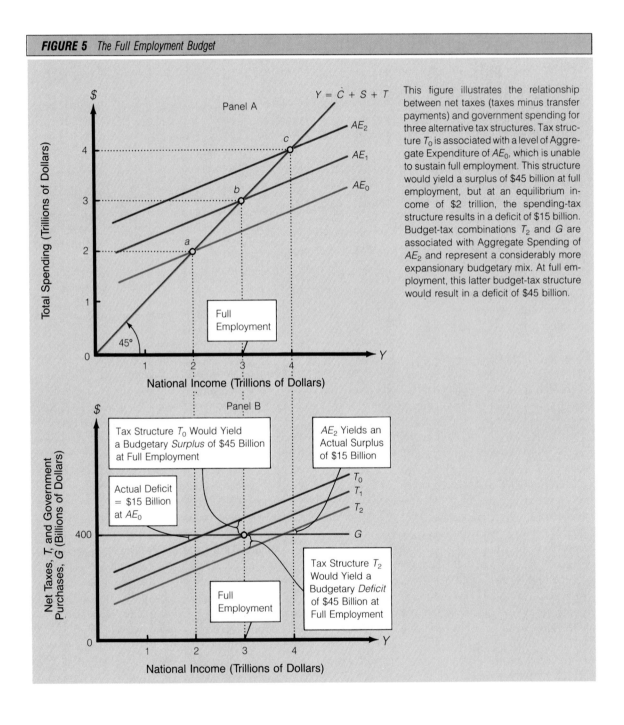

This figure illustrates the relationship between net taxes (taxes minus transfer payments) and government spending for three alternative tax structures. Tax structure T_0 is associated with a level of Aggregate Expenditure of AE_0, which is unable to sustain full employment. This structure would yield a surplus of $45 billion at full employment, but at an equilibrium income of $2 trillion, the spending-tax structure results in a deficit of $15 billion. Budget-tax combinations T_2 and G are associated with Aggregate Spending of AE_2 and represent a considerably more expansionary budgetary mix. At full employment, this latter budget-tax structure would result in a deficit of $45 billion.

Panel A: $Y = \dot{C} + S + T$, AE_2, AE_1, AE_0, points a, b, c, 45°, Full Employment. Total Spending (Trillions of Dollars) vs National Income (Trillions of Dollars).

Panel B: Tax Structure T_0 Would Yield a Budgetary *Surplus* of $45 Billion at Full Employment. AE_2 Yields an Actual Surplus of $15 Billion. Actual Deficit = $15 Billion at AE_0. T_0, T_1, T_2, G, Full Employment. Tax Structure T_2 Would Yield a Budgetary *Deficit* of $45 Billion at Full Employment. Net Taxes, T, and Government Purchases, G (Billions of Dollars) vs National Income (Trillions of Dollars).

full employment level of income is $3 trillion and that government purchases of goods and services (G) are independent of income.

Very high tax rates may be associated with a level of Aggregate Spending that is inadequate for full employment. This is the case with tax structure T_0 and Aggregate Expenditures AE_0, which together yield equilibrium at point a in Panel A of Figure 5. Because tax rates are high, the full employment budget is in surplus to the tune of $45 billion; however, the actual budget at equilibrium ($2 trillion income) is $15 billion in deficit in this example.

Contrast this with the budgetary mix of G and tax structure T_2. Simultaneous inflationary pressures and budgetary surpluses coexist if Aggregate Spending is AE_2 and the tax schedule is T_2; there is equilibrium at point c, and a realized budgetary surplus of $15 billion. This budget combination yields a deficit of $45 billion at full employment (ignoring inflationary pressure). The full employment budget is in deficit and is considerably more expansionary than that represented by G and T_0. Finally, a budget combination that will result in a full employment balanced budget is represented by the tax schedule T_1, which yields Aggregate Expenditures AE_1. Deficits result below full employment, while surpluses are generated above full employment.

Suppose Aggregate Spending is excessive because tax rates are quite low. If the Aggregate Expenditures curve is AE_2 and the tax curve is T_2, there is a substantial budget surplus. If we follow a rule of perpetually balancing the budget, we would cut taxes and raise spending. This is a bad policy, certain to accelerate any inflationary tendencies. Fiscal policy of either raising tax rates or cutting spending can cure this inflation by temporarily creating a budget surplus.

During inflation, however, many voters react harshly to any proposal that "the cost of government, in addition to other prices, should be raised." On the other hand, the beneficiaries of public programs, including those whose livelihoods depend on government contracts, vigorously fight budget cuts because they perceive inflation as shrinking their real income. In fact, political opposition to spending cuts or tax hikes is now so intense that we need not worry about simultaneous inflation and actual surpluses.

The reverse situation is a budget structure yielding a full employment surplus but an actual budget deficit because tax rates are so high that the economy is stuck well below full employment; fiscal drag is quite powerful. Some analysts have suggested that the sluggish American economy of the late 1950s and the early 1980s suffered from this malady.

The critical point in this section is that huge deficits do not imply a very expansionary tilt to fiscal policy, nor are large surpluses evidence of contractionary policies. Deficits may arise because high tax rates produce a sick economy. Congress can only set tax *rates;* it cannot dictate the resulting tax *revenues.*

Structural and Cyclical Deficits

The concept of a full employment budget can help us split the actual budget deficit into two distinct components that reflect different reasons for it. The structural deficit arises directly from current tax and spending laws.

> A **structural deficit** (*a synonym for a full employment deficit*) *is the deficit that would have resulted if the economy were at full employment, given existing tax and spending structures.*

As economic conditions deteriorate, the cyclical (and actual) budget deficit worsens and vice versa.

> A **cyclical deficit** *occurs if our economy has excessive idle capacity.*

The composition of the actual budget deficit is illustrated in Figure 6. Suppose that government spending and net taxes are G_0 and T_0, respectively, and that the economy is currently at a full employment equilibrium real income of $1,500 billion. The structural deficit is $100 billion ($300–$200 billion, or distance ab in Figure 6). If the economy went into a slump without any change in federal policy and real output fell to $1,400 billion, the deficit would increase to $150 billion (distance cd). Of this, $100 billion would be structural (distance ed) and $50 billion would be cyclical (distance ce).

Similarly, if the economy moved to $1,600 billion, the resulting deficit would be $50 billion less than the structural deficit of $100 billion because economic growth boosted tax revenue by $50 billion. Given the existing tax and spending structure, a balanced budget would require an equilibrium income of $1,700 billion. Finally, if Congress reduced tax rates (illustrated by a shift from T_0 to T_1), the structural deficit would grow to $125 billion (distance fb). Recent esti-

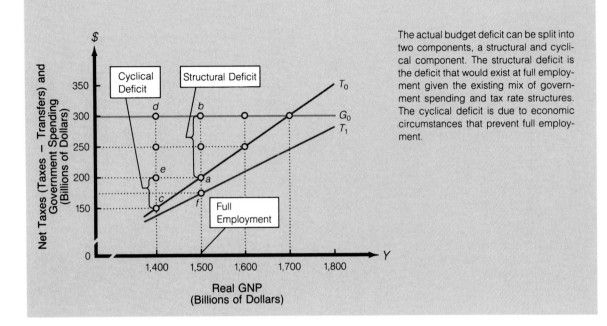

FIGURE 6 The Structural Deficit and the Cyclical Deficit

The actual budget deficit can be split into two components, a structural and cyclical component. The structural deficit is the deficit that would exist at full employment given the existing mix of government spending and tax rate structures. The cyclical deficit is due to economic circumstances that prevent full employment.

mates place the structural deficit at nearly two thirds of the actual deficit and growing.[4]

In summary, the actual deficit is determined by the fiscal policy mix of the federal government and the state of the economy. Expansionary fiscal policy creates structural deficits, and depressed economic conditions create cyclical deficits.[5]

Fiscal Policy and Supply-Side Economics

Keynesian analysis recognizes the possibility that high tax rates may stifle an economy because they reduce disposable income and spending. Classical economics, under the modern name of **supply-side economics,** points to another way high tax rates may be harmful.

---

4. William Beeman, Jacob Dreyer, and Paul Van de Water, "Dimensions of the Deficit Problem," in Phillip Cagan ed., *Essays in Contemporary Economic Problems, 1985: The Economy in Deficit* (Washington, D.C.: American Enterprise Institute, 1985).

5. The rising structural deficit of the 1970s and 1980s was not totally independent of changing economic conditions. Beeman et al. suggests that the reduced rate of productivity growth in the last two decades has added to rising structural deficits.

The Laffer Curve

There is a danger that very high tax rates may result in severe disincentives against work effort and private investment, causing actual GNP and tax revenues to fall. This idea has been traced back to a financial advisor to an Egyptian pharaoh. Arthur Laffer, a celebrated supply-sider, explained this concept to a journalist after dinner at a restaurant in Washington D.C.—illustrating his point with what is now known as the Laffer curve.

> The **Laffer curve** *suggests that very low tax rates might be raised to generate increases in tax revenues, but continually raising tax rates will eventually cause a heavily tax-burdened population to decide that the extra effort necessary to generate extra taxable income is not worth it, so tax revenue will fall.*

If Uncle Sam's bite is too fierce, many taxpayers will choose leisure over additional work and will consume immediately from income instead of saving and investing. Tax evasion may divert some productive effort into the underground economy. A modified Laffer curve is shown in Figure 7.

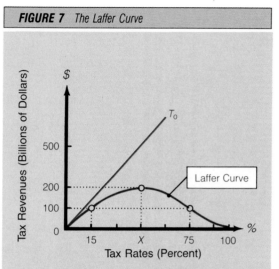

FIGURE 7 The Laffer Curve

If the tax base were unaffected by the tax rate, tax revenues would be exactly proportional to tax rates and could be graphed as a straight line, such as T_0. Declines in the tax base that result when people legally avoid taxed behavior or illegally evade taxes cause the base to erode, so that tax revenues actually reach a peak and then decline.

Supply-siders argue that high tax rates erode incentives to work and to invest, so that income shrinks as tax rates climb. This means that given tax revenues might be generated by both a high tax rate and a low one. In Figure 7, marginal tax rates (the percentage taxes paid on small amounts of extra income) that average either 15 percent or 75 percent yield tax revenues of $100 billion, while a marginal tax rate that averages X percent yields $200 billion to the tax collector. Any increase in marginal tax rates over X percent actually causes tax collections to fall.

What will people do if high marginal income tax rates reduce the advantages of working and of saving to invest? Like classical economists, many supply-side economists see little difference between saving and investing. Keynes argued that, in a modern monetary economy, savers and investors are very distinct groups with very different motives. Savers seek security, while investors bear risks and seek profits. As a result, savings may not necessarily be invested.

Potential workers may respond to high tax rates by engaging in many more nonmarket activities, such as do-it-yourself projects. Potential savers and investors will realize less interest income and profit if marginal tax rates are high; therefore, they will consume more currently, forgoing future consumption. Evidence of this sort of behavior was provided when wealthy people in Britain went on shopping sprees in the 1970s, buying fur coats and Rolls-Royces. Investing was not worthwhile because of high inflation and high British tax rates on investment income. The British economy stagnated while areas of London where high society gathered abounded with conspicuous consumption of luxury goods.

Some economists believe the United States has been in the outer region of the Laffer curve and advocate reductions in taxes to eliminate major impediments to work effort and investment. They believe reduced tax rates will simultaneously stimulate economic growth and generate higher tax revenues. This idea picked up a lot of converts in the past decade, including Ronald Reagan. Congress enacted a 5 percent tax cut in 1981, an additional 10 percent cut in 1982, and another 10 percent cut in 1983. Between 1980 and 1988, federal revenues rose over 65 percent, but government outlays grew 70 percent, resulting in record budget deficits. This occurred partly because Congress and the Reagan administration were unwilling to reduce the growth of federal spending.[6]

Notice that Keynesians may accept the general form of the Laffer curve, while perceiving different behavior as its basic cause. Supply-siders blame declines in tax revenues as tax rates rise on reduced incentives to supply goods and services. Keynesians perceive high tax rates and fiscal drag as smothering Aggregate Spending. Admitting that high tax rates also inhibit supply incentives, Keynesians still perceive most macroeconomic problems as originating from the demand side, while supply-siders see high tax rate disincentives as more powerful on the supply side.

---

6. In *The Triumph of Politics: Why the Reagan Revolution Failed* (New York: Harper & Row, 1986), former Budget Director David Stockman documents political reluctance to slash any government spending programs. Even politicians who constantly attack "big government" appear to fear the backlash from voters whose pet programs are cut.

Government Purchases and Transfers: The Supply Side

Keynesians view government purchases as direct sources of Aggregate Spending and transfer payments as quickly translated by recipients into new consumer spending. Supply-siders sense that this focus on demand is shortsighted and worry about the incentive effects of government programs. Their reasoning goes like this: Modern government provides school lunch programs, public parks and highways, medical care for the poor and the aged, and a host of other goods. There is less incentive to sacrifice our time by working and less net gain from investing if the government guarantees us a reasonably comfortable life by providing many necessities.

Transfer payments are viewed as a problem for two reasons. First, incentives to work and invest are reduced for those who work and invest, and who then pay taxes that government channels to welfare recipients. Second, those who receive transfer payments also suffer disincentives against work or saving. (Would you work as hard if you were forced to give your neighbors 20 percent of your income? Would your neighbors?) According to some supply-siders, extensive government purchases and transfer payments trap low-income individuals in a rut; they are discouraged from work effort and from trying to improve their economic status.

In conclusion, **supply-side fiscal policy** focuses on the long run and views high tax rates and massive government spending as embodying disincentives that dampen Aggregate Supply; Keynesians focus on curing short-run problems and see activist fiscal policy as being needed to augment Aggregate Demand. Specific differences between these schools of thought are summarized in Table 4. Now we will review a little of the history of fiscal policy.

TABLE 4 *Keynesian Versus Supply-Side Views of Fiscal Policy*

Policy Change	Keynesian (Short-Run) View of Effect	Classical Supply-Sider (Long-Run) View of Effect
Tax policy Increase (*decrease*) tax revenues	Reduces (*increases*) Aggregate Spending via a tax multiplier because consumers have less (*more*) disposable income.	Reduces (*raises*) Aggregate Supply because workers and investors have fewer (*more*) incentives to produce.
Raise (*lower*) tax rates	Generates more (*less*) revenue for government unless fiscal drag smothers Aggregate Spending, in which case, higher (*lower*) tax rates may generate less (*more*) revenues. If an economy is in a recession, higher tax rates may also worsen the state of the economy and actually reduce tax revenues because high taxes dampen consumer spending.	Reduces (*raises*) Aggregate Supply because of incentive effects. Disincentives from very high tax rates may cut Aggregate Supply so much that tax revenues fall, a possibility shown in the upper region of a Laffer curve.
Government purchases Raise (*lower*)	Raises (*lowers*) Aggregate Spending and income both directly and through a multiplier effect. (Demand creates its own supply.)	Reduces (*expands*) Aggregate Supply because people have fewer (*more*) incentives to produce and generate income if the government does more (*less*) for them. (Supply creates its own demand.)
Transfer payments Raise (*lower*)	Increases (*reduces*) Aggregate Spending and income by the multiplier process. Transfer payments can be thought of as negative taxes, to which the tax multiplier ($-mpc/mps$) can be applied.	Reduces (*raises*) the incentives of both transfer (tax) payers and transfer receivers, so Aggregate Supply is diminished (*raised*).

Fiscal Policy in Action

For almost half a century, changes in tax rates and spending by government have been viewed by Keynesians as cures for macroeconomics problems. The conventional wisdom before the Keynesian Revolution was that taxation and spending should be adjusted to balance the actual budget at all times. Then the economy would automatically adjust to a noninflationary full employment equilibrium. A problem with putting this idea into practice is that higher tax rates may yield lower tax revenues, and vice versa, because of the influence of tax rates on our major tax base—income. Failure to understand this led President Hoover and the Congress to raise tax rates in 1932, exacerbating the economic collapse of 1929–33. The success of expansionary fiscal policy in the mid-1960s also hinged on this relationship between tax rates and tax revenues.

The Tax Increase of 1932

Keynesians and modern "supply-siders" argue that a fetish for balancing the budget was one reason why the economy, following what should have been a minor recession in 1929, continued tumbling downward until 1933. Their explanation for the intensity and duration of the Great Depression is that President Hoover and the Congress reacted to a minor recession-caused deficit (like the $15 billion for AE_0 and T_0 in Figure 5) by raising tax rates. This caused National Income and tax revenues to fall further, which resulted in still higher tax rates in attempts to balance the budget, and so on.

Figure 8 presents the actual relationships between expenditures and net tax revenues (after subtracting transfers) to real Gross National Product for 1929–33. We have superimposed curves showing government spending and taxes before and after the tax rate increase of 1932. This tax increase was designed to generate roughly one-third more revenue in fiscal 1932 than in 1931. Policymakers failed to realize that higher tax rates could force GNP down. Keynesians interpret Figure 8 as evidence that the massive withdrawal of funds arising from these higher tax rates led to much of the severity of the Great Depression. Some modern supply-siders see this as proof that, even in the 1930s, high tax rates stifled Aggregate Supply.

The Tax Cut of 1964–65

Keynesians recommend tax rate cuts or increased government purchases when a recession causes even a slight cyclical budget deficit. In the example illus-

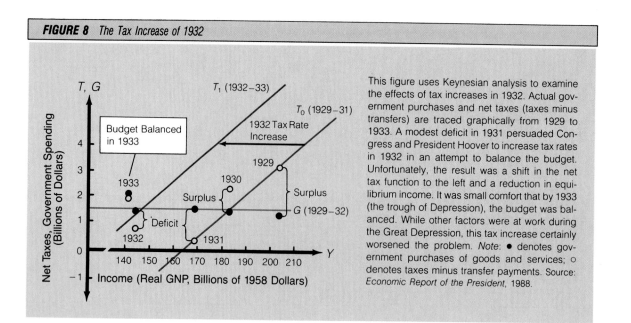

FIGURE 8 *The Tax Increase of 1932*

This figure uses Keynesian analysis to examine the effects of tax increases in 1932. Actual government purchases and net taxes (taxes minus transfers) are traced graphically from 1929 to 1933. A modest deficit in 1931 persuaded Congress and President Hoover to increase tax rates in 1932 in an attempt to balance the budget. Unfortunately, the result was a shift in the net tax function to the left and a reduction in equilibrium income. It was small comfort that by 1933 (the trough of Depression), the budget was balanced. While other factors were at work during the Great Depression, this tax increase certainly worsened the problem. *Note:* ● denotes government purchases of goods and services; ○ denotes taxes minus transfer payments. Source: *Economic Report of the President,* 1988.

FIGURE 9 The 1964–65 Tax Cut

In 1964–65, tax rates were cut substantially, shifting the net tax schedule from T_0 to T_1. Income, employment, and tax revenues rose, converting a deficit in 1964 into a small surplus in 1965. Source: *Economic Report of the President*, 1988.

trated in Figure 5, cutting tax rates from T_0 to T_1 raises Aggregate Spending to AE_1, tax revenues increase to $400 billion at an income level of $3 trillion, and the federal budget is balanced. Notice that tax collections actually increase in response to cuts in tax rates.

The idea that cutting tax rates might stimulate Aggregate Spending so that both National Income and tax revenues would rise first gained wide acceptance in the early 1960s. President Kennedy's economic advisors perceived the 1950s as a period of slow economic growth and stagnation caused by high tax rates that created severe fiscal drag. They argued that substantial reductions in tax rates would stimulate substantial growth, reduce unemployment and poverty, and generate higher tax revenues. In 1964, a massive tax cut engineered by President Kennedy and enacted during the Johnson administration supported these predictions. These tax cuts were sold politically largely based on Keynesian (demand-side) reasoning, although Arthur Laffer has pointed out that supply-side arguments were also used.

The 1964–65 tax cuts were broad-based reductions in income tax rates. Personal income tax rates were reduced from brackets of 18–91 percent to 14–70 percent. Corporate taxes for corporate incomes over $25,000 were cut from 52 to 48 percent. The results of this experiment with broad-based cuts in tax rates are shown in Figure 9. The economy, and

hence, the tax base, expanded so rapidly that the 1964 deficit actually gave way to a small surplus in 1965. Supply-siders naturally interpret the success of these policies as evidence that the economy was on the wrong side of the Laffer curve and that tax revenue was stimulated as Aggregate Supply grew.

These examples have shown that putting fiscal policy to work is more complex than our simple theory suggests. Whether changes in tax rates will reduce budget deficits often depends on the state of the economy and the initial level of tax rates. Tax rate cuts may stimulate economic growth but, in the short run, revenues may not grow sufficiently. This can result in soaring budget deficits, as President Reagan discovered in the early 1980s. The Kennedy round of tax cuts suggests that if the economy is poised for growth, tax cuts may simultaneously stimulate growth and reduce deficits.

The Budget Deficits of the 1980s ___

The American economy followed a rocky path through the 1970s, with budget deficits at new record levels almost each year. (Our most recent budget surplus was experienced in fiscal year 1968–69.) By the late 1970s, discomfort with the growth of federal spending had reached epidemic levels. Congress and Ronald Reagan tried numerous measures to reduce the impact of government in the economy. It proved, however, far harder for Congress to restrain spending growth than revenue growth. The result has been persistent deficits ranging from $120 billion to $220 billion that have been forecasted to persist through the early 1990s.

Budget Deficits and the Reagan Administration

Many observers blamed Keynesian fiscal policies for the rising deficits, inflation, and unemployment of the 1970s and saw classical (supply-side) economics as the remedy. Former President Reagan sought, and the Congress passed, a 25 percent tax cut in 1981, phased in over three years. At the same time, eligibility for transfer payments was tightened, and nonmilitary government spending was slowed sharply. Advocates of these policies hoped to stimulate Aggregate Supply so much that inflation and unemployment would fall quickly. They also hoped that tax revenues would be so responsive to economic growth that persistent budget deficits would abate.

This approach, illustrated in Figure 10, yielded income far below the optimistic predictions that had accompanied the adoption of supply-side policies. Restrictive monetary policy sharply reduced inflation in 1981–83 but, as a result, unemployment rose and the economy did not begin to recover until 1983. Federal budget deficits hovered around the $200 billion mark, and forecasts were for continued high deficits through the 1990s. Figure 10 suggests that the 1981–83 tax cuts may have shifted the net tax function downward and to the right, increasing the structural deficit. Problems posed by these persistent deficits and some possible solutions are treated in depth in chapter 15.

This chapter has examined government spending and tax policies from both Keynesian and supply-side perspectives. We have seen that the structure of government spending and taxation play an important role for achieving economic growth and price stability. Our next task is to examine the macroeconomic role of monetary policy. Take a moment, however, to read Focus 1, which discusses how the new President views the issues of taxing and spending.

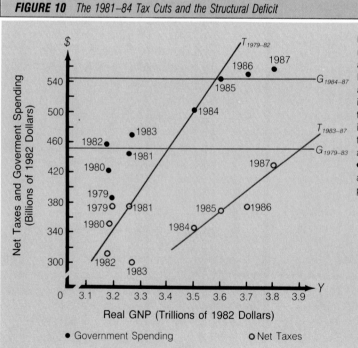

FIGURE 10 The 1981–84 Tax Cuts and the Structural Deficit

President Reagan sought and received tax rate reductions between 1981 and 1983 that appear to have increased the structural deficit. Increased goverment spending coupled with a flatter net tax function ($T_{1983-87}$), has resulted in swelling deficits. Tax reform in 1986 flattened the progressivity of income taxes, but it was "revenue neutral" and so was not intended to cure persistent huge deficits, which are projected to continue into the 1990s. *Note:* ● denotes government purchases of goods and services; ○ denotes taxes minus transfer payments.

Source: *Economic Report of the President,* 1988.

New Directions for Fiscal Policy?

President Bush's 1988 victory over Michael Dukakis was based in part on some differences about fiscal policy.

Dukakis argued that incentive-based supply-side policies are major sources of inequity and root causes of massive federal deficits. To remedy rising inequity, he proposed major new programs for health care, housing, and education. Several of his advisors favored more emphasis on government planning, with a moderate "Industrial Policy" aimed at stimulating certain "key" industries by (*a*) redirecting flows of investment funds, (*b*) favorable tax treatment, and (*c*) favorable trade policies (i.e., subsidies for exports and protection against imports). Dukakis also advocated reducing budget deficits by reinstituting higher personal tax rates on high incomes and by cutting spending on national defense.

President Bush's platform promised to extend the incentive-based "supply side" approach begun in the early 1980s. For example, the net effect of the 1986 Tax Reform was that corporate tax liabilities were raised, and special low rates were rescinded for investors who realized long-term capital gains. Bush viewed these hikes in effective tax rates as severe disincentives that endan-

ger the investment that is vital for healthy economic growth, ultimately yielding more tax revenue to shrink federal budget deficits. Thus, Bush proposed reducing both corporate tax liabilities and personal income tax rates on income that qualifies as a capital gain.

President Bush has stressed his opposition to any new taxes, arguing that vigorous growth and cuts in wasteful social spending can shrink federal deficits. His election probably signaled a continued reemphasis of the market forces upon which recent policy-making has relied to drive our economy.

||||||||||||||||||||||||||||||||||||||||||||||||||||||||||||||||||||||||||||||||||||||||||

CHAPTER REVIEW: KEY POINTS

1. *Keynesian fiscal policy* is the use of federal spending and tax policies to stimulate or contract Aggregate Spending and economic activity to offset cyclical fluctuations. *Classical (supply-side) fiscal policies* rely on low tax rates and minimal government spending to allow Aggregate Supply to grow.

2. *Discretionary fiscal policy* consists of deliberate changes in federal government spending and taxation for stabilization purposes. Without congressional action *automatic stabilizers* such as corporate and personal income taxes and various transfer programs cause changes in spending and taxation as economic conditions change.

3. Increases in *government spending* increase Aggregate Expenditures and National Income through the multiplier process in the same way as changes in investment or autonomous consumer spending.

4. Changes in *net tax revenues* (tax revenues minus transfer payments) affect Aggregate Spending differently than changes in government spending. Changes in net taxes directly affect disposable income and, therefore, saving. These effects are transmitted into spending through the *autonomous tax*

multiplier ($\Delta Y/\Delta T = 1 - 1/mps$), which is weaker than the spending multiplier.

5. In a Keynesian depression, the *balanced-budget multiplier* equals one, suggesting that equal increases (*decreases*) in government spending and taxes will increase (*decrease*) Aggregate Spending and equilibrium income by an equal amount. This result follows from the fact that the autonomous tax multiplier ($-mpc/mps$) is one minus the autonomous spending multiplier.

6. *Automatic stabilizers* tend to cushion the economy. When income falls, automatic stabilizers keep the level of disposable income from falling as rapidly as income. Our progressive income tax causes tax collections to fall proportionally faster when income is falling and to increase proportionally faster when income is rising.

7. These built-in stabilizers can become a problem. When potential income is rising, automatic stabilizers brake the economy and slow the rate of growth. This problem is referred to as *fiscal drag*.

8. The *full employment budget* is the amount of surplus or deficit that would be generated at full

employment with the existing tax and expenditure structure. The full employment budget is a way of estimating the expansionary or contractionary influence of any tax and expenditure mix.

9. The *Laffer curve* indicates that high tax rates may impose such large disincentives to productive effort

that Aggregate Supply and tax revenues are both restricted.

10. Structural deficits result directly from a mix of spending and tax policies. The cyclical deficit is attributable to business conditions. As unemployment grows, the cyclical deficit grows, and vice versa.

PROBLEMS

We know that multipliers are difficult. We also know that economics students are often tested extensively over autonomous spending and tax multipliers and equilibrium income.

1. Calculate the autonomous spending multiplier, the autonomous tax multiplier, and the balanced-budget multiplier for values of the *mpc* equal to 1/2, 3/5, 2/3, 3/4, 4/5, 5/6, 6/7, 7/8, 8/9, and 9/10.

2. Compute National Income with these different values of multipliers when taxes equal $100 billion, govern-

ment spending equals $200 billion, investment spending equals $150 billion, and autonomous consumption equals $400 billion. Now try other values for each of these autonomous components of Aggregate Spending. Work examples until you get these sorts of calculations down pat. Be sure you understand the meaning of these computations for determination of the equilibrium levels of National Income.

QUESTIONS FOR THOUGHT AND DISCUSSION

1. Do you think cuts in tax rates stimulate Aggregate Supply more than Aggregate Spending? Why or why not? Why is the answer to this question important in explaining what will happen to the price level?

2. Professional football teams sometimes trade their future draft choices for veteran players. In what sense is this like government financing current purchases through deficits? What are the crucial differences, if any, between the two situations in terms of future production?

3. The Kemp-Roth Bill cut federal income tax rates by 25 percent in stages over the three years following its enactment in 1981. What happened to budget deficits over this period? By roughly what percentage would

National Income need to have grown in order to have generated more revenues than would have occurred without the tax cut? Do you think it likely that National Income would ever grow at such a rate?

4. Explain the sense in which federal taxes determine how much each of us will help control inflation. If you could print money, would you ever try to remove any from circulation as long as there were trees and green ink? Why? Then why does the federal government bother to collect taxes?

5. What are the similarities and differences between taxes and savings? Are these differences important for the purposes of determining National Income? Why or why not?

OPTIONAL MATERIAL: MORE MATHEMATICS OF KEYNESIAN MULTIPLIERS

In our simple model of fiscal policy and equilibrium income, equal increases in government spending or cuts in taxes will have different effects on National Income and employment. Let us briefly review tax multipliers, balanced-budget multipliers, and autonomous

spending multipliers. Then you will have a better perspective when you try to understand what the president and Congress are trying to do the next time a policy change is under consideration. You may benefit from trying to graph some of the discussion that follows.

The Autonomous Spending and Tax Multipliers

A recessionary gap can be erased (or an inflationary gap might be created) through increased autonomous spending. This will occur regardless of whether it comes from more government spending, expanded investment, higher autonomous consumption, or more autonomous exports. The autonomous spending multiplier applies to all new injections of spending; they are perfect substitutes for one another in their impacts on equilibrium income. Alternatively, tax cuts can be used to encourage economic growth. The autonomous tax multiplier equals one minus the autonomous spending multiplier. To see why, we will look at it algebraically.

Income is the sum of consumption, investment, government spending, and net exports:

$$Y = C + I + G + (X - M).$$

We assume that taxes (T_a), investment (I_a), government purchases (G_a), net exports $(X_a - M_a)$ and part of consumption (C_a) are autonomous and that $mpc(Y - T_a)$ is induced consumption (the mpc is based on disposable income). Then:

$$Y = C_a + mpc(Y - T_a) + I_a + G_a + (X_a - M_a)$$

We can define total autonomous spending as $A = C_a + I_a + G_a + (X_a - M_a)$. This leaves us with the equations $Y = A + mpc(Y - T_a)$ or $Y = A + mpcY - mpcT_a$. Subtracting $mpcY$ from both sides leaves the equation $Y - mpcY = A - mpcT_a$. Simplifying by factoring Y out of the left side yields $Y(1 - mpc) = A - mpcT_a$. Dividing both sides by $1 - mpc$ gives the results we seek:

$$Y = A\left(\frac{1}{1 - mpc}\right) + T_a\left(\frac{-mpc}{1 - mpc}\right).$$

Translated into English, this equation means that aggregate income (Y) equals autonomous spending $[C_a + I_a + G_a + (X_a - M_a) = A]$ times the autonomous spending multiplier $[1/(1 - mpc)]$, plus the level of taxes (T_a) times the autonomous tax multiplier $[-mpc/(1 - mpc)]$. The autonomous tax multiplier $[-mpc/(1 - mpc)]$ can be rewritten $(-mpc/mps)$. Thus, if the spending multiplier is 5, the tax multiplier is -4; if the spending multiplier is 4, the tax multiplier is -3; and so on.

The Balanced-Budget Multiplier

All else equal, any changes in national income can be traced to changes in autonomous spending or taxes:

$$\Delta Y = \Delta A\left(\frac{1}{1 - mpc}\right) + \Delta T_a\left(\frac{-mpc}{1 - mpc}\right).$$

If the mpc equals 0.8, the spending multiplier equals 5 and the tax multiplier equals -4. Thus: $\Delta Y = \Delta A(5) + \Delta T_a(-4)$. If government spending and taxes each rise by $20 billion, total income also increases by $20 billion: $20 billion times (5) plus $20 billion times (-4) equals $20 billion. We can generalize: Equal changes in autonomous government spending and taxes cause income to change in the same direction and by the same amount. The applicable multiplier is termed the *balanced-budget multiplier* and always equals one.

Why don't equal increases in government spending and taxes exactly offset each other? The change in income from such a policy results because the first-round effect of a $1 increase in government spending is to increase income by $1. The autonomous spending multiplier then applies. While the first-round effect of the $1 increase in taxes is to cut disposable income by $1, gross pretax income is not affected. Hence, the multiplied effect does not apply to income until the next round, when the taxpayers' spending falls by $1(0.8) = $0.80. This example suggests that if both government purchases and taxes are increased by $1, then, because the balanced-budget multiplier equals one, equilibrium income will rise by exactly $1. The balanced-budget multiplier equals one because it reflects the numerical sum of the autonomous spending and tax multipliers:

$$\frac{1}{1 - mpc} + \frac{-mpc}{1 - mpc} = \frac{1 - mpc}{1 - mpc} = 1.$$

Much more realistic assumptions than the ones used in this chapter are the bases for the econometric models used to forecast national economic activity. For example, the effects of income on investment, government purchases, and taxes are recognized. Even though these forecasting models are much more complex than those we have considered, the approaches are similar. Assumptions are made about the behavior of various economic agents; these assumptions generate predictions regarding National Income.

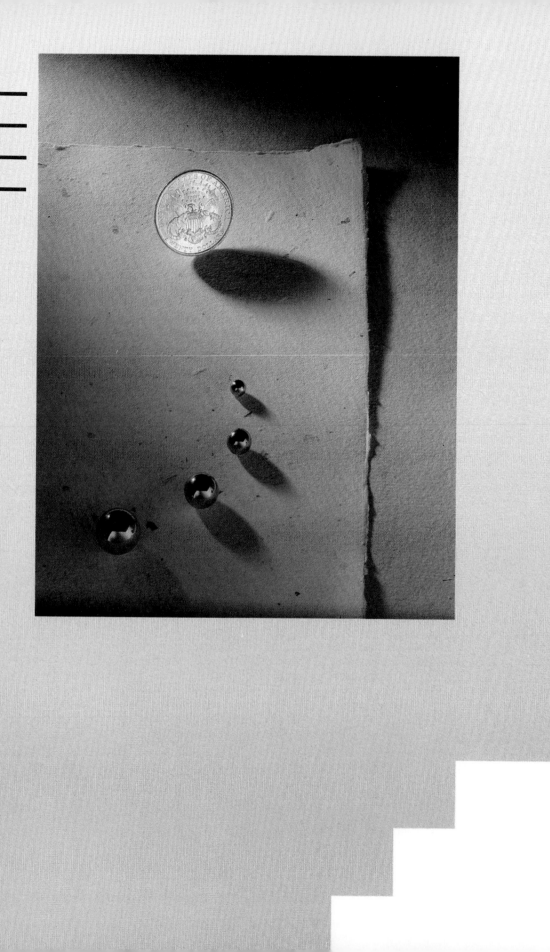

Money, Monetary Theory, and Monetary Policy

PART 4

Keynesians believe that income is the major determinant of spending. Classical economists typically join with modern monetarists in the view that the amount of money available is the major influence on Aggregate Expenditures. To understand the reasons for these areas of agreement and disagreement among Keynesians and classical economists, you need to know more about the monetary economy. What money is, what services it performs, and how money is created are the questions addressed in chapter 12. Then, chapter 13 provides an overview of the Federal Reserve System and the tools it uses to regulate our financial system and to determine the money supply.

Chapter 14 looks at the demand for money and how the supply and demand for money jointly determine the price level, the rate of inflation, aggregate output, and the rate of interest. We also examine how monetary and fiscal policy interact and the Keynesian-Monetarist debate regarding the effectiveness of monetary versus fiscal policy. In chapter 15, we survey alternative ways to finance government outlays, look at how monetary and fiscal policy are linked in a government budget equation, and discuss the ramifications of persistent deficits and soaring national debt.

To this point we have developed the Keynesian model of Aggregate Demand focusing primarily on fiscal policy—government spending and taxation. This part builds the monetarist model, focusing on the effects of money on Aggregate Demand. In Part 5, we integrate the two models and introduce a more formal model of Aggregate Supply. This synthesis provides a more sophisticated view of the economy and a more satisfactory perspective on recent macroeconomic problems.

CHAPTER 12

Money and Its Creation

The love of money as a possession—as distinguished from the love of money as a means to the enjoyment and realities of life—will be recognized for what it is, a somewhat disgusting morbidity, one of those semi-criminal, semi-pathological propensities which one hands over with a shudder to the specialists in mental disease. . . .
                                      —*John Maynard Keynes*

Any list of inventions that shaped the development of civilization would include the wedge, the wheel—and *MONEY*. Suppose a cultural anthropologist from Venus visited Earth. Scientific journals on Venus would report many curiosities, but one of the biggest puzzles for Venusians might be trying to understand why Earthlings work, invest, lie, cheat, steal, or commit murder for stones, beads, dirty pieces of paper, bits of metal, or bookkeeping entries in computers in buildings called "banks." It would probably take the Venusians a long time to understand the important roles played by money—unless they had a monetary system themselves. And, of course, they would.

Barter: Exchange Without Money

You may have heard some pundit predicting "a cashless society" in which all transactions will be executed via computer. But can you imagine a moneyless society? Our ancestors used some forms of money at least as early as the seventh century B.C., but we know that our earliest ancestors had no money. Anthropologists have recorded occasional cases of primitive tribes who lived without monetary systems before the encroachment of modern civilization. The 1976 discovery of the Tasadays in the Philippines is an example.

If you lived in a society without money, you would be limited to producing or stealing everything you used or engaging in barter.

Barter *occurs when people directly exchange their goods for someone else's goods.*

One drawback of barter is that you must find someone who has what you want *and* who wants what you have before any exchange occurs. This requirement is called the *double coincidence of wants*. Even having a double coincidence of wants, however, might not be enough for trade to occur. For example, you might have a spare horse and want a loaf of bread, and a baker with a lot of bread might be in need of a horse. You still might not strike a bargain—making change without money is nearly impossible.

The costs of securing information about potentially profitable bargains are huge in a barter economy. Few transactions occur because exchange tends to be very costly. As a result, most people tend to be largely self-sufficient producers/consumers. Few advantages of specialization of labor will be realized, which explains in part why standards of living tend to be low in moneyless economies. Small wonder that money is often rated with the wheel as an invention crucial to the development of the modern world.

What Is Money?

I measure everything I do by the size of a silver dollar. If it don't come up to that standard then I know it's no good.

—Thomas A. Edison

What money is may seem obvious. But if you were asked how much money you have, you might respond in a number of ways. You could count only the bills and coins in your purse or pocket. More likely, you would extend this to "money" you keep in checking accounts or savings accounts. You could include deposits at a savings and loan association or credit union or even the total value of any U.S. Savings Bonds or corporate stocks or bonds you might own. But why stop there? Most of your possessions are worth money. You might include the values of all your assets—a car, a house, clothes, books, a ping-pong table, and whatever else you own. Just how much money do you have? Ambiguities in this question arise from failure to differentiate between wealth and money. Your **wealth** is the difference between the value of your assets and the value of your liabilities. In addition to being an asset itself, money has the unique characteristic of being the unit by which other assets or liabilities are measured.

Functions of Money

Money performs certain functions in all but the most primitive societies. These functions provide a descriptive definition of money.

> **Money** is (a) a medium of exchange, (b) a measure of value or standard unit of account, (c) a store of value, and (d) a standard of deferred payment.

Memorizing this list might help you a little on an exam, but money will be more understandable if you consider what each part of this description implies. You may even be able to anticipate the operational definitions of money used by modern monetary analysts.

Medium of Exchange

Money makes the world go around. . . .

—Unknown

Money finesses the necessity for exchange of a double coincidence of wants imposed by barter.

> *Money is used as a **medium of exchange** when it is used to execute transactions.*

Money as a *medium of exchange* is its most important and most easily understood function. If you have assets for sale (for example, labor services), you normally expect to be paid in the form of cash or a check, although you may be willing to trade your assets for other assets. Also, when you want something, you generally expect to shell out cash or a check, although you may choose to use a credit card or take out a loan. *Credit* is simply an extension of money.

The prominent economist Robert Clower has characterized monetary economies as societies in which "money is traded for goods, and goods are traded for money, but goods are not traded for goods." We might qualify his statement by paraphrasing it: Goods *seldom* trade for goods in a monetary economy. Even barter organizations that spring up to avoid or evade taxes have bookkeeping "credits" that serve as a medium of exchange. Credits are really a form of money. A carpenter who gets credits for framing a house and trades them for a shar-pei puppy is using these credits as money.

Measure of Value

Money is an elastic yardstick.

—Unknown

Suppose that we did not use money to measure relative prices. The values of bearskin rugs might be stated in terms of bath brushes or Butterfingers, which in turn might be stated in terms of shirts or shoelaces.

> *Money performs as a* **measure of value** *or* **standard unit of account** *when it is used as a common denominator by which to state the relative prices of goods.*

Use of money as a *standard unit of account* substantially reduces the information we need to make sound market decisions. Measuring the values of all goods in terms of all other goods would be tedious, involving enormous transaction costs, because the relative prices between goods increase faster than the number of goods considered.

For example, suppose apples (*a*) and burritos (*b*) are the only two goods in an economy. In this case, there is only one relative price to consider. If you know how many apples must be traded to get a burrito, you automatically know how many burritos must be traded for an apple. Introducing a third good, carrots (*c*), complicates things. You still need to know the rates of exchange between apples and burritos, but it is now also necessary to know the price of carrots in terms of both burritos and apples. There are three relative prices to worry about now: P_a/P_b, P_a/P_c, and P_b/P_c. Addition of a fourth good, doughnuts (*d*), means that there are six relative prices. Focus 1 should help you understand why the number of relative prices expands faster than does the number of goods exchanged.

The invention of money permitted people in 100-good economies to worry about only 100 prices instead of 4,950. Use of money as a unit of account permits a tremendous reduction in the information costs associated with exchange. Because acquiring information requires time and effort, using money increases the efficiency of the market system. Because exchange costs are reduced, more exchange occurs. And because monetary exchange makes greater specialization feasible, small groups can re-

duce reliance on self-production. Much greater production will occur as people specialize in producing things in which they have a comparative advantage.

Store of Value

Money . . . lulls our disquietude.

—John Maynard Keynes

People hold money not only for the transactions they anticipate but also because money is normally a relatively riskless way of holding wealth.

> *Money performs as a* **store of value** *when people prefer it as an asset because it is relatively less risky, or because they view the transaction costs of conversion into other assets as too high.*

You do not have to pay brokerage fees to hold money as an asset, but you would incur such costs if you held stocks, bonds, capital equipment, or real estate. The values of these other assets also tend to be much more volatile than the purchasing power of money in most economies. There is some risk, however, because money may lose its value during inflationary periods, but bonds, for example, do also.

Another way risk enters the picture emerges from *diversification*. If you hold wealth in a number of different forms, it is unlikely that the value of each will be influenced in the same ways by the same things. For example, if you own both a new-car dealership and a junkyard, a recession will kill new-car sales but your junkyard will do very well. In chapter 6, you learned that the purchasing power of a dollar is $1/P$, where P is (1/100th of) the price level: if the price level doubles, the value of the dollar is cut in half. Since World War II, inflation has pushed the price level up. Even so, the old admonition "Don't put all of your eggs in one basket" suggests that it would be wise for many people to include some money in their portfolios of assets.

Prior to the Depression-era writings of John Maynard Keynes, orthodox economists did not accept the idea that you would want money for other than reasonably immediate purchases. Since then, money has played an integral role in the development of modern "portfolio" theory, which is an important part of modern financial analysis in American business.

Relative Prices in a Four-Good Economy

In our four-good economy, each good is priced in terms of every other good. Follow the horizontal "Apples" column across the table until you hit the vertical "Burritos" column. That fraction, P_b/P_a, represents the price of burritos in terms of apples. We might find, for example, that it takes 4 apples to buy 1 burrito. Thus, the price of 1 apple is 1/4 burrito. Notice the fractions P_a/P_a, P_b/P_b, P_c/P_c, and P_d/P_d are shaded. These elements are items priced in terms of themselves (1 apple/1 apple = 1) and, thus, can be ignored. Moreover, each price in the area below the shaded diagonal is the reciprocal of a price above this diagonal. Thus, information is duplicated and these prices below this diagonal also can be ignored. The formula for determining the number of ba-

sic relative prices in an n-good economy (where n equals the number of goods) is $[n(n-1)]/2$, where n can be any number. For our example, the

formula becomes $[4(4-1)]/2 = 6$ prices.

Good Used to Price	Good to Be Priced			
	Apples	Burritos	Carrots	Doughnuts
Apples	$\dfrac{P_a}{P_a} = 1$	$\dfrac{P_b}{P_a}$	$\dfrac{P_c}{P_a}$	$\dfrac{P_d}{P_a}$
Burritos	$\dfrac{P_a}{P_b}$	$\dfrac{P_b}{P_b} = 1$	$\dfrac{P_c}{P_b}$	$\dfrac{P_d}{P_b}$
Carrots	$\dfrac{P_a}{P_c}$	$\dfrac{P_b}{P_c}$	$\dfrac{P_c}{P_c} = 1$	$\dfrac{P_d}{P_c}$
Doughnuts	$\dfrac{P_a}{P_d}$	$\dfrac{P_b}{P_d}$	$\dfrac{P_c}{P_d}$	$\dfrac{P_d}{P_d} = 1$

Standard of Deferred Payment

Money is a contract with parties unknown for the future delivery of pleasures undecided upon.
— David Bazelon
The Paper Economy (1965)

Money as a standard of deferred payment is implicit in the other three functions of money, but it is worth discussing to illustrate the relationship between time and money.

> *Money performs as a* **standard of deferred payment** *because it allows intertemporal contracts.*

Money is a link between the past, present, and future.

Many contracts, such as military or construction, call for production that requires time for completion and that would not be done without a contract. Naturally, these contracts call for future payments of money. Other exchanges occur so continuously that it is more efficient if only one contract is used for many present and future transactions. Labor contracts are examples. Still other deals are negotiated for immediate delivery of a good with delayed payment for the buyer's convenience. For example, you may be borrowing money to finance your education.

When you sign a credit contract, you agree to make later payment of the money you borrow—plus interest. All these contracts are measured in money.

Liquidity and Money

One important aspect of any asset is its **liquidity,** which depends on the cost of converting the asset into cash. Many people think that liquidity is defined only by the time required for the conversion, but any asset can be converted into cash almost immediately. If you are willing to accept $10 for your stereo system, I will buy it right now. *Time required to sell* is one aspect of asset liquidity. *Certainty regarding price* is another important dimension of liquidity. Both time and certainty are inextricably tied together in transaction costs.

> **Liquidity** *is negatively related to the proportion of the transaction costs incurred in purchase or sale of an asset.*

One way to rank assets in terms of liquidity is to estimate the percentage you would lose if you had to sell them immediately. Houses are relatively *illiquid* assets. You must pay realtor fees, closing costs, several special finance charges, and various other transaction costs when you sell one house and buy another. On the other hand, savings accounts tend to be very liquid. You can go to your bank, close one savings account and open another, losing virtually no interest or principal in the process—just your time.

Types of Money

An incredible diversity of items has served as money at various times and places, but all can be classified as either commodity money or fiat money.

> **Commodity money** *has substantial value apart from what it will buy, but* **fiat money** *is valuable only because of its use as money.*

Use of fiat money is ultimately based on faith—faith in its purchasing power, its general acceptability, and in the stability of the government that issues it.

Commodity Monies

Rubber balls of various sizes were once used as money in the Amazon jungles. On the Pacific island of Yap, sculptured stones weighing as much as three tons have served as money. From the beginning of the sixteenth century until the end of the nineteenth, most American Plains Indians had no money as such, but measured their wealth in horses. Throughout Europe, Africa, and the Americas, beads, stone spearheads, and arrowheads once were used as money. Focus 2 describes one well-known transaction from American history.

What caused these forms of money to fall into disuse? For any commodity to be widely accepted as money over a long period, several attributes are necessary:

1. durability;
2. divisibility;
3. homogeneity (uniformity or standardization);
4. portability (high value-to-weight and value-to-volume ratios);
5. relative stability of supply; and
6. optimal scarcity.

These characteristics are reasonably self-explanatory. Ice cream will not do for money—it is not durable (it melts). Diamonds are insufficiently homogeneous—there are good diamonds, and then there are "diamonds" that some shifty-eyed rascal tries to sell you in a parking lot. Water and elephants are insufficiently portable, and elephants are indivisible. (If divided, they are not durable.) The wheat supply is too volatile—if the supply of money (wheat) grew too rapidly, its value would plummet; if this supply shrank precipitously, a severe recession or depression might occur. The state of the economy would be too closely tied to good and bad wheat harvests, something that is often out of our control. *Optimal scarcity* means that any commodity used as money cannot be common. Sand, bricks, or two-by-fours are insufficiently scarce.

Historically, the only commodities that seem to combine most of the desirable characteristics for use as money are rare metals, especially gold and silver. Standardization was achieved by making small ingots

Wampum

You probably learned in a history course that the Manhattan Indians sold their island to the Dutch in the seventeenth century for $24 worth of beads, hatchets, knives, and firewater. History books generally give the impression that the Dutch took advantage of the unsophisticated Indians in this deal, although some estimates suggest that, at 6 percent interest, the $24 could now repurchase Manhattan.

Suppose that you were offered a box containing ten thousand $100 bills in exchange for everything you own (that's $1 million). You would probably count yourself very fortunate to be able to walk away from your house, car, stereo, and clothes with all that green stuff, even though you would be temporarily naked. If seventeenth-century Indians viewed the transaction, however, they would think you had been swindled.

The two situations are really very similar because the Indians used strings of beads (wampum) for money and thought themselves rich because they had received so much money for a pitiful little island. In effect, the Dutch were counterfeiters; the Indians could not have predicted that Europeans would "counterfeit" so much wampum that it soon would become almost worthless as anything other than ornamentation. In effect, the Indians experienced hyperinflation in wampum.

---

or coins of these precious metals and stamping "face values" on them. The earliest known metal coins date back to Imperial Rome in the sixth century B.C. Governments soon discovered that the face values of coins had to exceed substantially the values of the metal in the coins; otherwise, small increases in the values of these metals would cause people to melt the coins down.

The profit government makes when it coins or prints currencies whose face values exceed their commodity values is known as **seignorage.**

Some advocates of laissez-faire capitalism vehemently oppose government discretion in printing money. They often favor a return to the gold standard because the amount of money in circulation would then be controlled by the forces of supply and demand. These "gold bugs" are willing to accept the inefficiency of the costly process of producing money through mining and then burying this base for money in a place like Fort Knox in order to limit government control over the money supply.

When the world relied almost exclusively on gold and silver coins for money, kings and queens often found royal treasuries inadequate for the palaces, ornate finery, and large armies and navies they thought due them. One common solution was to launch a war to secure foreign treasures. This solution was seldom successful. (War is a *negative-sum game,* which means that the total losses to all participants outweigh the gains to the "winners," if any.) An alternative for semi-impoverished (by their standards) heads of state was to *debase* the coinage so that profits from seignorage rose. This means that the government mint melted down relatively pure gold and silver coins and "stretched" these precious metals by adding generous portions of nickel, copper, zinc, or lead before restamping coins. (You may have wondered where the people who put soybeans and

Gresham's Law

In the 1950s, it was very common to use silver coins minted 40–60 years earlier. What happened to all the gold and silver coins minted in the United States prior to 1964? Sir Thomas Gresham, a sixteenth-century financial adviser to Queen Elizabeth, may have had the answer. He observed that debased coins remained in circulation while relatively pure coins disappeared rapidly after debasement. This led him to state a famous economic doctrine that has stood the test of time: *"Bad money drives out good."* This idea is known as **Gresham's Law**. People will spend coins that contain far less valuable metal than their face values and hoard (save) coins that contain close to or more than the face values. This explains why almost all our current dimes, quarters, half dollars, and "silver" dollars are relatively recently minted cupronickel "sandwiches."

||||||||||||||||||||||||||||||||||||||||||||||||||||||||||||||||||||||||||||||||||||||||||||||||

sawdust into hamburgers got the idea.) Focus 3 explores a predictable consequence of *debasement*.

Paper money dates back to the Ming Dynasty in China, from 1368 to 1399 A.D. Until recently, many paper monies could have been classified as "pseudo-commodity" money because governments would convert the paper money into specified amounts of gold or silver on demand. The United States was the last country in the world to abandon the gold and silver standards; it was not until 1933 that this country went off the gold standard domestically. From 1933 until 1974, foreign bankers and governments could proffer $35 and get an ounce of gold from the United States Treasury, but it was illegal for American citizens to hold gold coins or ingots. American dollars were, however, redeemable for silver until the late 1960s.

Fiat Money

Many Americans still believe that currency is "backed by gold in Fort Knox."

Paper money and coins are collectively called **currency.**

Take a dollar bill from your purse or wallet. You will see "Federal Reserve Note" above George Washington's picture, but nowhere will you find any statement about the worth of the bill in gold or silver. Now look at any of your "silver" coins. These coins are "sandwiches" of cupronickel (not silver) around copper—the face value of the coin is about fifteen to forty times the total value of the metal. What makes this paper and these bits of metal valuable if they are not "backed" by gold or silver? One hint lies just to the left of George's picture: *This Note is Legal Tender for All Debts, Public and Private.* The government declares that the pieces of paper printed by the Federal Reserve System and the bits of metal issued by the United States Mint are money by fiat. (**Fiat** can be interpreted to mean: "Because we say so.")

Now that you know the secret that our money has no gold or silver backing, should your behavior change in any way? NO! Even if you are convinced that the government perpetrates fraud in issuing coins and bills, you can buy just about anything for which you have the money, so you will continue to try to get money in the same ways as previously. The real foundation for fiat money is the *faith* we have that it can be used to buy goods and services. In other words, our money is "backed" by loaves of bread, Chevrolets, stereo systems, college educations, and also by government's ability and willingness to maintain money at a relatively stable value by controlling the money supply.

The major advantages of fiat money are (*a*) that its supply can be controlled fairly precisely by government; (*b*) that it is much less costly to produce than commodity money, and, therefore, its use is comparatively efficient; and (*c*) that if monetary policymakers do a good job, fiat money possesses all of the characteristics required of a good commodity money.

The Supply of Money

You may be surprised to learn that the purchasing power of money and the cost of credit (interest rates) are determined by supply and demand in much the same manner that prices are determined for such goods as wheat, paperback novels, or fudge. In the remainder of this chapter, we will describe the assets that make up the United States money supply and examine the role of financial institutions in determining the money supply. This sets the stage for a look at how the demand and supply of money jointly determine the price level, the rate of inflation, and the rate of interest.

The functions of money discussed earlier in this chapter provide us with a descriptive definition: Money is a medium of exchange, a measure of value, a store of value, and a standard of deferred payment. This definition guides us into operational definitions of money. Be aware, however, that just as no measure of unemployment conforms precisely to the economic concept of unemployment, no measure of the money supply is in perfect accord with the concept of money.

Narrowly Defined Money (M1)

Currency (paper coins and bills) is probably the most easily identified component of the money supply because (*a*) it may be used for virtually all transactions (*b*) it is used to price goods and services, and (*c*) it counts as an asset. The only other assets that perform all monetary functions are demand deposits.

Demand deposits *are funds in checking accounts in commercial banks, savings and loans, or credit unions.*

These funds (which include such minor accounts as travelers' checks for the purpose of measuring the money supply) are legally required to be available to depositors *on demand.* Together, currency and demand deposits are the narrowly defined money supply, which is known as *M*1:

$$M1 = currency + demand\ deposits\ in\ financial\ institutions.$$

We do need to qualify this a bit. Only currency held by the nonbanking public is included in the money supply. We would be "double counting" if we included both the currency you deposit in your checking account and your demand deposits. We also ignore the deposits of the federal government since the government, via the Federal Reserve System, can print money at will. Moreover, since the federal government's spending is not constrained by the money it has in banks, inclusion of federal deposits would not aid in predicting Aggregate Expenditures using money supply data.

"But," you might object, "credit cards can be used to pay for just about everything. Aren't credit cards money? And how about my savings account?" Unfortunately, a credit card is simply an easy way to get into debt; a credit card is not a store of value, so credit cards are not money. Standard savings accounts are not money because spending funds from a savings account first requires converting your savings account "money" into currency or a demand deposit. Just try to pay for your next meal out by presenting your savings passbook to a waiter—you will be washing dishes in no time!

Federal laws formerly prohibited banks from paying interest on checking accounts. These laws began to be phased out in 1980. Savings and loan associations and credit unions now also offer checking account services where depositors receive interest on some checking accounts. These changes in legal constraints effectively make these thrift institutions into banks and some of their deposits into checking accounts. In most of the discussion in the next few chapters, we include all bank-like institutions when we say "banks" and consider all checkable accounts when we refer to "checks."

Only checking accounts or currency are assets that are both mediums of exchange and widely accepted as money. We admit that parking meters do not accept checks, that few cab drivers will change a $100 bill for a $3 fare, and that you cannot present 10 million loose pennies to a bank and expect them to settle a $100,000 mortgage. But checks and currency are assets that can be used for most transactions much more easily than can other assets.

Near-Monies (M2 and M3)

Some economists do count certain highly liquid assets, such as savings accounts in commercial banks (*time deposits*), as parts of the money supply. The economists who use broader definitions of the money supply than $M1$ believe that people's spending levels are more predictable by monetary data if we include the liquid assets that are highly interchangeable with currency and demand deposits.

One such broader definition is **M2**, which currently adds such assets as noninstitutional money market funds and savings and small time deposits in commercial banks and thrift institutions to $M1$:

> $M2 = M1 + miscellaneous\ short\text{-}term\ time$
> *deposits.*
> $= currency + demand\ deposits + small$
> *time deposits.*

Other monetary theorists expand the definition of money to $M3$, which includes such items as large time deposits and institutional money market mutual funds:

> $M3 = M2 + institutional\ money\ market\ mutual$
> *funds + large time deposits.*

There is one even broader official definition of the money supply, *L*, which adds such liquid assets as short-term government bonds and commercial paper to $M3$. Exactly which definition of the money supply is most useful will depend on why we want to measure money. Throughout this book when we say *money,* we mean *currency plus any funds available by writing checks* ($M1$). How various measures of the money supply have grown is shown in Figure 1.

All these measures of the money supply have grown substantially over the years, as have GNP and the cost of living (*CPI*). How should we interpret these positive correlations? Does monetary growth cause inflation? Does it cause GNP to grow, or does economic growth cause the money supply to expand? How does monetary growth affect the total output of goods, and vice versa? These questions are at the heart of a continuing controversy between monetarists and Keynesians, and they are examined in the next few chapters.

Banks and the Creation of Money

Where does money come from? We know that U.S. currency is printed by the Federal Reserve System (bills) or minted by the Treasury (coins). But demand deposits (checking accounts) are the largest

FIGURE 1 *The Various Measures of the Money Supply*

The money supply is composed of various aggregates, depending on how broadly you define it. *M1* is the narrowest definition, while *L* is the most expansive.

Source: *Economic Report of the President,* 1988.

component of our money supply. Currency is little more than convenience money (less than 30 percent of $M1$). How or where do demand deposits originate?

The Origin of Fractional Reserve Banking

Several centuries ago, almost all money was in the form of gold coins. Wealthy people found the quantities of gold they accumulated quite heavy. (Gold is only semiportable.) An even bigger disadvantage of gold is that it is difficult to discourage thieves from taking it; stolen gold pieces (or modern coins for that matter) are rarely identified. Looking around for safe places to store their gold, people in medieval Europe thought of goldsmiths. Goldsmiths made jewelry, gold statues, and other precious goods—they also generally had some excess space in their heavily guarded vaults.

Goldsmiths were generally willing to store other people's money for a small fee and issued receipts for the gold deposited with them. Buyers found it convenient to exchange these receipts instead of physically getting the gold, and sellers were happy to take these receipts because they knew they could redeem them for gold from the goldsmith whenever they wished. As you may have guessed, this was the beginning of checking accounts—the receipts issued by the goldsmiths were effectively demand deposits.

Goldsmiths observed that they stored nearly all of a community's coins and that the amounts of gold in their vaults did not fluctuate very much. When a buyer paid for a purchase with a gold receipt, the seller was typically content to leave the gold with the goldsmith. After all, the receipt could be used for purchases just like gold. One depositor's withdrawal was just another customer's deposit. The goldsmiths began lending some of the gold on deposit to borrowers who would pay interest. In fact, it was not even necessary to relinquish physical control of the gold—just like depositors, borrowers generally preferred a receipt to the actual gold. This was the origin of modern fractional reserve banking.

Money Creation: Demand Deposit Expansion

Some people occasionally would physically withdraw gold, so the goldsmith was limited in the total amount of receipts he could write as loans. He would maintain reserves in the vault to meet withdrawals of deposits.

> *Banks keep **reserves** on hand to meet withdrawals by depositors.*

Suppose a goldsmith observed that even though deposits and withdrawals were sporadic, the total amounts of gold in his vault did not vary more than 10 percent a year. How much might the goldsmith be able to loan from a given amount of gold deposits?

To keep the analysis simple, we assume that the goldsmith is a monopolist who has the only local bank vault. We will examine a multibank world in a bit. The goldsmith prudently stops making loans when the value of receipts (demand deposits) issued is five times as large as the amount of gold on deposit. That is, the goldsmith keeps reserves equal to 20 percent of deposits; reserves are twice as much as the variations in current deposits (10 percent) that the goldsmith has observed, so this level is good insurance against a large number of people simultaneously wanting to withdraw gold.

> *Fractional reserve banking* refers to a system in which financial institutions can legally hold less than 100 percent of their deposits as currency in their vaults.

We also assume the goldsmith already has many deposits and loans outstanding prior to the transactions we will be considering and views himself as "fully loaned up" (reserves equal 20 percent of earlier deposits).[1] Finally, we initially assume that no one actually withdraws any gold during the period we are considering; receipts for gold are perfectly acceptable as money.

Suppose Allen, a gold miner, deposits $1,000 worth of newly mined gold into Goldsmith's bank. This deposit and issuance of a receipt are written in the bank's "T-account" statement shown in Table 1. These T-accounts represent partial balance sheets for the bank. The left-hand and right-hand side entries must be equal, and they reflect only the changes in the bank's accounts following the new $1,000 depos-

---

1. When we introduce the Federal Reserve System in the next chapter, you will learn that banks legally are required to keep certain proportions of deposits in reserves. The process of money creation is essentially the same analytically, regardless of whether banks plan to hold reserves in the interest of prudence or because the FED requires them to do so.

it. The $1,000 recorded on the right side (credit) represents a liability or debt of the bank—Goldsmith owes Allen $1,000 on demand. The left side (debit) shows an increase of $1,000 in the bank's reserves, which is Goldsmith's new asset.

When Bob, a local customer, wants to borrow money, Goldsmith is happy to accommodate him with as much as $800. How did we arrive at $800? Goldsmith calculates 20 percent times $1,000 equals $200, which is planned for reserves (RR). Actual reserves of $1,000 minus $200 in planned reserves equals $800 in excess reserves ($XR$) that are available for the loan. When Bob borrows the full $800, the bank deposits $800 to Bob's account, and the bank's accounts change as shown in the T-account of Table 2. When you borrow money from a bank, the standard practice is to credit your account instead of giving you cash. The bank's assets are increased by an $800 IOU from Bob; its new liability is Bob's demand deposit for $800.

Suppose Bob writes Carol a check for $800—he did intend to spend the money he borrowed. Table 3 shows the bank's view of this exchange. Bob's $800 demand deposit simply becomes Carol's demand deposit. In fact, since all deposits stay in the bank, we can ignore further transactions between the bank's customers. Such transactions are irrelevant for the bank's asset/liability position and for the amount of money in circulation. Notice that the $1,000 in gold reserves now "backs" $1,800 in demand deposit money. This may sound like a magician's trick, but it is the way banks operate.

When Deirdre wants to borrow money, Goldsmith can still lend up to $640 because actual reserves of $[\$1,000 - 0.20 \times (\$1,000 + \$800)] = \$640$ (excess reserves available to lend her). Alternatively, 80 percent of Carol's deposit ($0.80 \times \$800$) is $640. Her IOU and the loan that is deposited to her account are shown in the T-account in Table 4.

When Ed comes in to borrow money, Goldsmith offers a loan of as much as $512 because $1,000 $- [0.20 \times (\$1,000 + \$800 + \$640)] = \$512$. Again, 80 percent of Deirdre's $640 deposit is $512 and is available to loan. Table 5 depicts this loan and demand deposit (DD).

At this point, the $1,000 the bank holds as reserves supports $2,952 in demand deposits ($1,000 + $800 + $640 + $512). How much longer can this

---

TABLE 1 Initial Deposit of $1,000 in a New Account in Goldsmith's Bank

Assets (Debits)	Liabilities (Credits)
+$1,000 Reserves (Gold) 　$200 Planned reserves (*RR*) 　$800 Excess reserves (*XR*)	+$1,000 (Demand Deposit–Allen)

TABLE 2 First-Round Lending: Changes in Accounts in Goldsmith's Bank

Assets (Debits)	Liabilities (Credits)
+$800 (IOU–Bob)	+$800 (Demand Deposit–Bob)

TABLE 3 Transaction Between Customers of the Bank: Changes in Accounts in Goldsmith's Bank

Assets (Debits)	Liabilities (Credits)
(No change)	−$800 (Demand Deposit–Bob) +$800 (Demand Deposit–Carol)

TABLE 4 Second-Round Lending: Changes in Accounts in Goldsmith's Bank

Assets (Debits)	Liabilities (Credits)
+$640 (IOU–Deirdre)	+$640 (Demand Deposit–Deirdre)

TABLE 5 Third-Round Lending: Changes in Accounts in Goldsmith's Bank

Assets (Debits)	Liabilities (Credits)
+$512 (IOU–Ed)	+$512 (Demand Deposit–Ed)

TABLE 6 All Remaining Rounds: Changes in Accounts in Goldsmith's Bank

Assets (Debits)	Liabilities (Credits)
+$2,048 (IOU–All others)	+$2,048 (Demand Deposit–All others)

process continue? The answer is that the bank can make more loans as long as 20 percent times all demand deposits is less than the $1,000 held in reserve. To spare you further agony, we have summarized all possible subsequent loans and demand deposits (*DD*) in Table 6.

How did we know how large this entry would be? We know the bank will continue to make loans until: 0.20(*DD*) = $1,000. If both sides of this equation are multiplied by five, we get: *DD* = 5($1,000) = $5,000.

The $1,000 held in bank reserves will support up to $5,000 in *DD*, regardless of whether these *DD*s are based on loans or not. In fact, the original $1,000 in new money deposited by Allen allowed the creation of an additional $4,000 in demand deposits generated as loans. Table 7 summarizes all these transactions.

It is not absolutely necessary for Goldsmith, as a monopoly banker, to go through all these lending rounds. After experimenting a bit, he would learn that Allen's $1,000 deposit could be translated direct-

TABLE 7 Summary of Transactions: Accounts in Goldsmith's Bank

Entry (Assets) (Debits)	(Liabilities) (Credits)
1 +$1,000 Reserves	+$1,000 (Demand Deposit–Allen)
2 +800 (IOU–Bob)	+800 (Demand Deposit–Bob)
3 No change	−800 (Demand Deposit–Bob)
	+800 (Demand Deposit–Carol)
4 +640 (IOU–Deirdre)	+640 (Demand Deposit–Deirdre)
5 +512 (IOU–Ed)	+512 (Demand Deposit–Ed)
6 +2,048 (IOU–All others)	+2,048 (Demand Deposit–All others)
Total +$5,000 ($1,000 gold reserves) ($4,000 IOUs)	+$5,000 (Total new Demand Deposits)

ly into a $4,000 loan to Bob. We have gone through several steps of this **loan-money creation process** because of its relevance for a multiple-bank financial system.

The Potential Money Multiplier (m_p)

You may have noticed that the multiplier by which the money supply is expanded (5) is the reciprocal of the percentage Goldsmith plans as reserves against demand deposits (1/5 or 0.20).

> The **potential money multiplier ($m_p = 1/rr$)** indicates the amount in demand deposits that can be generated from a new deposit of $1 in a banking system that is "fully loaned up" if people keep all their currency (gold, in our example) in the bank and no one keeps any cash on hand.

The arithmetic parallels that used to compute the autonomous spending multiplier, described at the end of chapter 10. The autonomous spending multiplier is $1/mps$ (the marginal propensity to save), while the potential money multiplier is $1/rr$, where rr is the reserve ratio or percentage of demand deposits (DD) held as reserves. If we denote total planned reserves as RR, the proof is simple: Since $rr(DD) = RR$, then $DD = (1/rr) \times (RR)$.

The Actual Money Multiplier (m_a)

Actually, banks are seldom fully loaned up, and most people do hold some currency as a convenience for small transactions. These leakages from the deposit → loan → deposit stream cause the actual money multiplier to fall far below its potential value. Let us see why.

When banks hold reserves in excess of the planned (or legally required) amounts, these reserves are available for loans. These available funds, or *excess reserves* (XR), can be expressed as a proportion of the bank's total deposits: $XR/DD = $ **xr**. Thus, the actual money multiplier (m_a) could be as high as $1/(rr + xr)$, but *only* if there are no other drains on the value of the money multiplier. In reality, people keep some of their money as cash, and firms hold some currency. These currency drains from the banking system are a major reason why the actual money multiplier never reaches its potential

value. The Federal Reserve Bank of St. Louis estimates the historical average real money multiplier (which we label m_a) at 2.6.

It is possible to express this "real world" multiplier through a very complex formula that accounts for every form of withdrawal of cash from the banking system. The critical thing for you to remember is that the actual money multiplier (m_a) never reaches its potential value ($1/rr = m_p > m_a$) because of these and other drains of cash.

> The **actual money multiplier (m_a)** expresses the relationship between the money supply and currency in circulation or in bank vaults.

The simplest algebraic expression of the actual multiplier (m_a) is:

$$m_a = MS/MB,$$

where MS is the money supply and MB is the gold, currency, or whatever else serves as reserves for banks. MB is known as the *monetary base*, or *high-powered money;* it is the base on which the money multiplier operates in the money creation process. In the United States, the "monetary base" now equals currency in the hands of the nonbanking public plus all bank reserves.

A Multibank Model

When there are many banks in a community, each bank expects most checks written by its customers to be deposited in the banks of the payees. Does this mean that the total amount of deposits in any single bank is likely to be highly volatile? Not really. Most banks find that even though their customers' individual accounts vary tremendously over the month, the average daily amount in a given account is fairly stable on a month-to-month basis over the year. This occurs because most people have reasonably stable patterns of income and spending and seldom let their accounts drop below some comfortable minimum value (or they fear losing their "free" checking accounts).

Flows of deposits among banks do not affect the total amounts of reserves in the banking system but will cause individual banks to hold slightly higher percentages of excess reserves (xr) than would be the case for a monopoly banker. This reduces the size of the real world money multiplier. Other than this, the process of money creation follows the pattern

TABLE 8 Transaction with Another Bank Account in First National Bank

Entry (Assets)	(Liabilities)
1 +$1,000,000 Reserves	+$1,000,000 (Demand Deposit–IBM)
2a +800,000 (IOU–U.S. Steel)	+800,000 (Demand Deposit–U.S. Steel)
2b −800,000 Reserves	−800,000 (Demand Deposit–U.S. Steel)

Reserve Position after Transaction	

(Assets)	(Liabilities)
$ 200,000 Reserves 800,000 Loan (IOU–U.S. Steel)	$1,000,000 (Demand Deposit–IBM)
Total $1,000,000	$1,000,000 (Total Demand Deposits)

outlined in the preceding section, which assumed a monopoly bank.

Let us look at an example in which IBM sells a $1 million computer system to an oil firm in Venezuela. The payment is from a Venezuelan bank, and so represents new money to the American banking system. IBM deposits this $1 million in new money in the First National Bank, which enables First National to create $800,000 by giving U.S. Steel a loan. The two entries in First National's accounts are shown in Table 8. U.S. Steel borrowed the money to buy smelting equipment; it writes a check for $800,000 to American Smelting. Unfortunately for First National, American Smelting banks with Pittsburgh National

Bank. When Pittsburgh National takes American Smelting's deposit of U.S. Steel's check and demands $800,000 from First National, First National loses $800,000 in reserves and reduces U.S. Steel's account by $800,000. This is shown as entry 2b in Table 8. Notice that First National still has U.S. Steel's IOU for $800,000 plus $200,000 on reserve in the event that IBM wants to withdraw some money.

When American Smelting deposits U.S. Steel's check and Pittsburgh National collects the check from First National, Pittsburgh's accounts change per entry 1 in Table 9. Pittsburgh can loan $640,000 to Security Life Insurance if it regards anything greater than 20 percent as excessive reserves, shown as entry 2. (First

TABLE 9 Second-Round Transactions Accounts in Pittsburgh National Bank

Entry (Assets)	(Liabilities)
1 +$800,000 Reserves	+$800,000 (Demand Deposit–American Smelting)
2 +640,000 (IOU–Security Life)	+640,000 (Demand Deposit–Security Life)
3 −640,000 Reserves	−640,000 (Demand Deposit–Security Life)

Reserve Position after Transaction	

(Assets)	(Liabilities)
$160,000 Reserves (Cash) 640,000 Loan (IOU–Security Life)	$800,000 (Demand Deposit–American Smelting)
Total $800,000	$800,000 (Total Demand Deposits)

National had to turn down Security Life's loan application—they had no excess reserves to spare.) If Security Life writes a check to Xerox, which banks with New York's City Bank, Pittsburgh loses $640,000 in reserves and Security Life's account falls to its original balance (entry 3). Pittsburgh, however, still has $160,000 in reserves plus Security Life's IOU for $640,000.

City Bank's accounts now change as in entry 1 of Table 10. It can lend Sony $512,000 (neither First National nor Pittsburgh has excess reserves available). When Sony takes the loan, City Bank makes entry 2 in their books. The multiple expansion process can be continued from customer to customer as reserves flow between banks until an additional total of $4,000,000 in newly created money in the form of demand deposits is generated through loans. The money creation process for an entire banking system parallels that for a single monopoly bank.

You may have some nagging feelings that something is wrong because new money seems to have appeared out of thin air. If so, you are not alone in being a bit mystified by bankers' juggling acts. Still, the fractional reserve process of money creation is very old and is widely accepted as compatible with sound banking practices.

You may be concerned that there is not enough money in bank vaults to meet withdrawals of deposits. Suppose IBM tries to withdraw its $1,000,000 from First National. Will this system fall like a house of cards? One part of the answer is that we have only covered the changes in bank accounts as $1 million in new reserves was used to create an original demand deposit of $1 million and an additional $4 million in demand deposits based on loans. The reserves backing other deposits in First National are available to cover IBM's withdrawal. Another option is that First National might sell U.S. Steel's $800,000 IOU to another bank. This is effectively what has happened if you have ever borrowed money from one lender for, say, a car, and then received a request that you pay a different lender. Your paper IOU was sold (or *factored*, as it is known in banking circles).

The "Money Destruction" Process

The reverse of the money creation process is *money destruction*. There generally are adequate funds so that IBM can withdraw its $1,000,000 from First National because all banks hold substantial reserves. Suppose that IBM withdraws its $1,000,000 and keeps it in the corporate vault. First National will feel uncomfortably short of reserves, to the tune of $800,000. Remember, First National was holding $200,000 in reserves against the $1,000,000 deposit, so its loses $800,000 in reserves that backed other accounts ($1,000,000 − $200,000 = $800,000). When U.S. Steel's $800,000 loan is due, First National will not renew the loan, nor will First National make new loans when U.S. Steel repays its loan. U.S. Steel's repayment must come from existing bank reserves. Ultimately, Pittsburgh National Bank will reduce outstanding loans by Security Life's $640,000, City Bank will reduce loans by Sony's $512,000, and so on.

TABLE 10 *Third-Round Transactions Accounts in City Bank of New York*

Entry (Assets)	(Liabilities)
1 +$640,000 Reserves	+$640,000 (Demand Deposit–Xerox)
2 +512,000 (IOU–Sony)	+512,000 (Demand Deposit–Sony)
3 −512,000 Reserves	−512,000 (Demand Deposit–Sony)
Reserve Position after Transaction	
(Assets)	**(Liabilities)**
$128,000 Reserves (Cash) 512,000 Loan (IOU–Sony)	$640,000 (Demand Deposit–Xerox)
Total $640,000	$640,000 (Total Demand Deposits)

IBM's withdrawal of $1,000,000 from the reserves of the banking system will cause a $4,000,000 decline in demand deposit money, originally created by expansionary lending. IBM's $1,000,000 demand deposit will also be lost, so demand deposits will drop by a total of $5,000,000. IBM, however, will have $1,000,000 in currency, which was not included in the money supply while it was held as bank reserves. Thus, there is a net $4,000,000 reduction in the money supply caused by IBM's decision to hoard $1,000,000 in its own vault.

If individual banks hold 20 percent of all deposits in reserves, then there will be no problem unless they rapidly lose 20 percent or more of their deposits. Has this ever happened? Yes. Does this mean that such banks are insolvent? NO! When only a few banks are short of reserves, other financial institutions will buy (at a discount) the IOUs from the loans these banks have made. Alternatively, banks that are short

of reserves might just borrow funds from institutions that have excess reserves available.

> Banks borrow and lend from each other through a private banking network called the **federal funds market.**

These mechanisms normally enable banks that have inadequate reserves to replenish their reserves and honor all their demand deposit liabilities.

Unfortunately, there have been times when there were inadequate reserves in the financial system as a whole, and there were a lot more loans for sale than there were buyers. The "runs on banks" and financial panics that resulted finally caused the Congress to establish a "banker's bank" with the enactment of the Federal Reserve Act of 1913. In the next chapter, we will examine the powers of the Federal Reserve System.

CHAPTER REVIEW: KEY POINTS

1. *Barter* requires a *double coincidence of wants*—trade can only occur if each party has what the other wants and if divisibility poses no problems.
2. *Money* ensures this double coincidence of wants—the seller will accept money because of what it will buy, while the buyer is willing to exchange money (and, thus, all else it will buy) for the good or service in question.
3. Money facilitates specialization and exchange by decreasing transaction costs. The more sophisticated the financial system, the greater the level of production and consumption and the higher the standard of living.
4. Money is a *medium of exchange*. It is used for most transactions in monetary economies.
5. Money is a *measure of value*. Used as a standard unit of account, it is the common denominator for pricing goods and services.
6. Money is a *store of value*. It is among the most nominally secure of all assets people can use to hold their wealth.
7. Money is a *standard of deferred payment*. Serving as a link between the past, present, and future, it is used as a measure of *credit* to execute contracts calling for future payments.
8. *Liquidity* is negatively related to the transaction costs incurred in exchanges of assets. *Time, certain-*

ty regarding price, and the *quality of information in a market* are all dimensions of liquidity. Assets are liquid if transaction costs are low, *illiquid* if transaction costs are high.
9. *Commodity monies* (precious metals, stones, or arrowheads) have values that are independent of what they will buy. *Fiat money* (paper currency) is valuable only because it is money; its use is based on *faith*.
10. The profit governments make from printing money or stamping coins is called *seignorage*.
11. According to *Gresham's Law*, "Bad money drives out good."
12. The very narrowly defined money supply ($M1$) is the total of (*a*) *currency* (coins and bills) in the hands of the nonbanking public, plus (*b*) *demand deposits* (checking accounts of private individuals, firms, and nonfederal government units in financial institutions).
13. Some highly liquid assets are viewed as near-monies and are included in broader definitions of the money supply ($M2$ and $M3$) by monetary analysts who believe the spending of the public can be predicted better if these assets are included. Examples of such highly liquid assets include short-term *time deposits* (savings accounts) or *certificates of deposit* (*CDs*). The assets included in "money supplies"

defined more broadly than *M*1 are judgmental because these assets are not mediums of exchange.

14. Banks and some thrift institutions *"create"* money through loan-based expansions of demand deposits (checking account money). They make loans based on currency they hold as reserves, and these loans take the form of new demand deposit money.

15. Banks hold *reserves* that are far less than their deposit liabilities. The larger the proportion of deposits held as either excess or required reserves, the smaller are the money multiplier and resulting money supply, given some fixed total amount of reserves.

16. The *potential money multiplier* (m_p) equals $1/rr$, where *rr* is the banking system's planned or legally required reserves as a percentage of deposits. The *actual money multiplier* (m_p) is much smaller because (*a*) households and firms hold currency that could be used as a base for the money creation process were this currency held in bank vaults as reserves against deposits; and (*b*) banks hold excess reserves to meet withdrawals of deposits. The actual money multiplier equals *MS/MB*, where *MS* is the money supply and *MB* is the *monetary base*, or high-powered money.

PROBLEMS

1. How many relative prices are relevant for market decisions if 50 goods are traded in a society that does not use money? How many relative prices would people keep track of if money were introduced into this society?

2. Calculate potential money multipliers for reserve-requirement ratios (*rr*) equal to: 1/10, 1/9, 1/8, 1/7, 1/6, 1/5, and 1/4.

3. How large might the money supply be for each value you calculated in the preceding question if there is $1 million in bank reserves and $1 million in currency in circulation? What will be the actual money multiplier for each reserve-requirement ratio in the preceding question if banks hold no excess reserves? If banks hold an extra 10 percent in reserve for each reserve-requirement ratio listed?

QUESTIONS FOR THOUGHT AND DISCUSSION

1. Explain how the introduction of money permits society to better realize the advantages of specialization of labor. Would you expect to find a sophisticated division of labor in a barter economy? Explain why the standards of living tend to be very low in moneyless economies.

2. Explain what is meant by the phrase: "Money is a link between the past, present, and future." Can you explain how the use of money makes the economy operate more smoothly through time?

3. How would you define *money*? Do you feel that the degree of liquidity is important in determining what things are money and what things are not? List the following items according to their degree of liquidity, from least liquid to most liquid (*a*) dollar bill, (*b*) U.S. government bond, (*c*) house, (*d*) car, (*e*) pedigreed dog, (*f*) television set, (*g*) savings account, and (*h*) human skills.

4. The functions of money include (*a*) a medium of exchange, (*b*) a unit of account or measure of value,

(*c*) a store of value, and (*d*) a standard of deferred payment. There are items that perform some, but not all, of these functions. Which functions do credit cards (Visa, Master Card, Discover) serve? Which are not served? How about time deposits? Gold or silver? Stocks and bonds?

5. What problems might confront people who live in different societies with different monetary systems and who wish to trade with one another? Would it be advantageous if the entire world used a common currency? What do you think are some of the reasons we do not have a world currency?

6. In 1933, Adolph Hitler decreed that the old German deutsche mark was worthless and could be exchanged at a fixed rate for new reichsmarks. The British redeemed their old currency in the late 1960s, replacing it with a "metric" style currency. What circumstances might make it appropriate to completely withdraw one currency from circulation and replace it with a new currency?

CHAPTER 13

Federal Reserve System
(FED)

reserve-requirement ratio
(rr)

federal-funds market

open-market operations
(OMO)

discount rate (d)

margin requirements

financial intermediation

usury laws

The Federal Reserve System and Financial Institutions

Whoever controls the volume of money in any country is absolute master of all industry and commerce.
—President James A. Garfield

The owners and managers of the institutions we trust with our money have enormous potential for fraud and general abuse. Thus, it is not surprising that financial institutions are more closely regulated than any other U.S. industry except, perhaps, secret weapons research or atomic energy.

*The **Federal Reserve System (FED)** regulates our banking system.*

The FED is among the most powerful of government agencies because it regulates the volume of money in circulation; it is also among the least accountable and most independent.[1] During hearings on the FED's

policies, one senator compared getting an answer out of the chairman of the FED's Board of Governors to "nailing a chocolate cream pie to a wall."

The structure of the FED and the tools it uses to control the money supply and shape financial conditions are examined in this chapter. We also survey different types of financial institutions, the goals of regulation, and the consequences of certain policies intended to alter economic activity.

Early Experiments with Central Banks

Our country's founders feared central government abuse and saw the American Revolution as a triumph over parasitic coalitions of economic and political power. When our Constitution was ratified, the federal government, the various states, and many private banks all issued different currencies. But there were

---

1. Representative Jack Kemp (R-NY), on being asked whether he would run for president in 1988, replied that he wanted to hold the most powerful position in the world: Chairman of the FED. He ran for president anyway, but was clobbered in the primaries by George Bush.

problems—"Not worth a continental" crept into our language after money issued by the Continental Congress to fight the Revolution became worthless. Alexander Hamilton's political skills were taxed to the limit to establish a central bank. The dollar became a sound currency only after the First Bank of the United States honored federal war debts.

The Bank of the United States was privately owned and operated, but it was also the government's bank because it (*a*) stored tax revenues, (*b*) arranged for loans to and from the government, and (*c*) paid the government's obligations. The Bank's power provoked immense opposition among Westerners and farmers, who felt it served only the rich and the "Eastern Establishment." Hamilton's death and the ascendancy of his rival, Thomas Jefferson, led to the end of our first experiment with central banking in 1811.

The Second Bank of the United States was chartered in 1816 under the direction of Nicholas Biddle, a member of a prominent Philadelphia family. The Bank's foes triumphed, however, when, in 1832, President Andrew Jackson vetoed its recharter. When the original charter expired in 1836, Nicholas Biddle was disgraced by a financial scandal; the Bank's collapse precipitated the financial crash of 1837. For the next 75 years, the American economy experienced substantial but erratic growth without a central bank.

The Federal Reserve System

The American economy thrived from the American Revolution until the Great Depression even though it suffered major financial panics roughly every 20 to 25 years. These crises usually set off depressions. A wave of bank failures in 1906 led to the passage of the Federal Reserve Act in 1913, which established a third central bank, the **Federal Reserve System.** One major objective of the FED is to act as a "lender of last resort." This means that the FED lends money to inherently sound banks so that they can survive financial panics.

The seven members of the **Board of Governors** of the Federal Reserve System are appointed to staggered fourteen-year terms because Congress feared the instability of a highly politicized central bank. Each president and Congress has limited power over the FED because they only appoint one new member of the Board of Governors every other year. The majority of Board members traditionally have been bankers, causing some people to question how diligent they are as public "watchdogs." Recently, however, presidents have nominated increasing numbers of governors from the general public, including more than a few economists.

The FED (in concert with the Comptroller of the Currency, the Federal Deposit Insurance Corporation, and various state government agencies) is responsible for regulating banks. It audits the books of federally chartered banks to prevent fraud and to ensure compliance with numerous regulations. Other FED services to the banking community include processing checks drawn on one bank and deposited elsewhere. The key macroeconomic role of the FED, however, is conducting monetary policy. Before we survey monetary policymaking, it is helpful to know a bit more about the FED's structure.

Federal Reserve Bank Districts

There are 12 regional districts in the Federal Reserve System, each having a primary bank, with the major districts having branch offices. Figure 1 shows the locations of these primary and branch banks and outlines their boundaries. If you check the money in your billfold or purse, you will probably find that many of the bills have travelled far from their points of issue.

Federal Reserve Banks and branches do not directly serve the general public. They are "bankers' banks" that lend to member banks, help them clear checks drawn on other banks, and otherwise facilitate financial efficiency. The FED operates under the fiction that it is privately "owned" by federally chartered private banks, but it is actually an arm of government created by an act of Congress. The FED's rulings have the force of law, and annual returns on investment exceeding 6 percent must be paid to the U.S. Treasury.

Member Banks   There are almost 15,000 privately owned and managed commercial banks in the United States. About 5,000 of these are national banks chartered by the Comptroller of the Currency. The remaining 9,000 or so are state banks chartered by state governments. *National banks* must be members

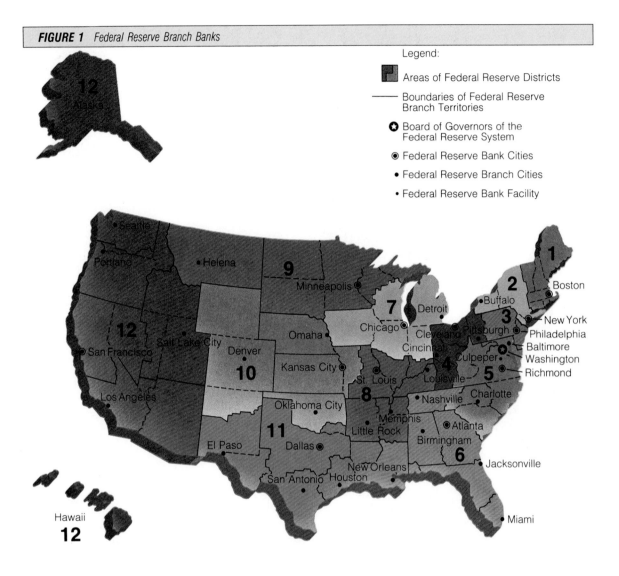

FIGURE 1 *Federal Reserve Branch Banks*

Legend:

▨ Areas of Federal Reserve Districts

— Boundaries of Federal Reserve Branch Territories

✪ Board of Governors of the Federal Reserve System

◉ Federal Reserve Bank Cities

• Federal Reserve Branch Cities

• Federal Reserve Bank Facility

The Federal Reserve System consists of 12 districts. Each district has a Federal Reserve Bank; some of the larger districts also have branch banks. This figure depicts the locations of these primary and branch banks and outlines their boundaries.

Source: Federal Reserve Bulletin.

of the Federal Reserve System; *state banks* have the option (upon approval) of becoming *member banks*. More than 70 percent of all deposits are in member banks, and the FED, since 1980, has set legal reserve requirements on all checkable deposits in *all* financial institutions since 1980. As a result, the FED has immense direct power over most of the financial system in the United States.

The Organization of the FED

The formal structure of the Federal Reserve System is shown in Figure 2. The chairman of the Board of Governors is supposedly only a "first among equals." Like the Supreme Court's chief justice, the chair has only one vote in any decisions made. In reality, however, the chair has disproportionate power within the

FIGURE 2 The Formal Organization of the Federal Reserve System

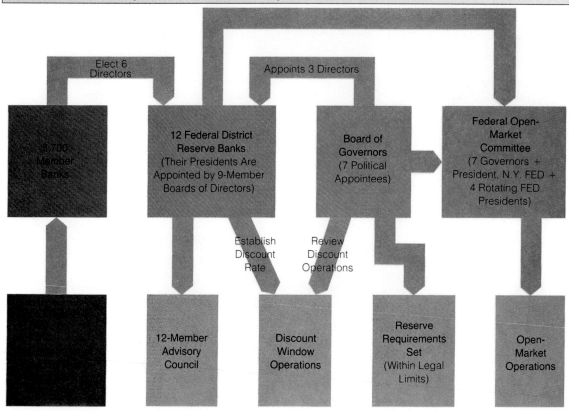

Board of Governors. Naturally, the chair's control of monetary policy depends on personality and on the dynamics among all the governors.

Concerned that political shenanigans might distort financial regulation and stabilization activities, Congress tried to shield the FED from politics by making it a pseudo-private organization. As a "private" organization, the FED's member banks elect six of the nine directors of each District Bank; the other three are selected by the Board of Governors. These directors appoint the presidents of their District Banks, who are free to orate about policy but whose jobs are primarily concerned with administration, not policymaking.

Real power in the FED is exercised through the **Federal Open Market Committee (FOMC),** which is composed of all seven members of the Board of Governors plus the president of the New York District Bank. Four other District Bank presidents rotate on the committee. The FOMC conducts monetary policy and so has enormous control over our financial system and the general economy. Committee members' terms of office and votes leave the real clout within the FOMC to the Board of Governors, especially the chair. Figure 3 portrays the actual channels of power within the FED.

Economists focus on incentives. Should the FED maximize profit? Should monetary policymakers be subjected to political pressures in our democracy? Before we tackle these problems, let's see why the answers to these questions are important.

The Tools of the FED _____

The Federal Reserve System uses several tools to control the money supply and financial conditions. The FED's major tools are (*a*) reserve requirements, (*b*) open-market operations, and (*c*) discounting operations. Secondary tools of the FED include controls over stock market credit and "jawboning." Day in and day out, the FED actively uses open-market operations to implement its policies. Reserve requirements and discounting operations are important, though generally passive, monetary policy instruments.

Reserve Requirements (rr)

Bank reserves can be kept in bank vaults or on deposit at Federal Reserve banks.

The Federal Reserve System sets the **reserve-requirement ratio (rr)**—*a legal floor on the percentage of a bank's deposits that must be held in reserves.*

Suppose the reserve-requirement ratio is 1/6 or 16.7 percent. For the actual money multiplier (m_a) to reach 6 and, thus, equal the potential money multiplier $(m_p = 1/rr = 1/.167 = 6)$, banks need to be "fully loaned up" (no excess reserves), and no currency can be held outside of banks. Only then are the actual (m_a) and potential $(m_p = 1/rr)$ money multipliers equal.

Banks cannot survive for long if reserves sink to the legal minimum; they need excess reserves to accommodate any outflows of funds. Otherwise, they would be unable to meet any demands for withdrawals of deposits without being in trouble with the FED. The overall system usually operates with few excess reserves, however, because banks lend and borrow money from each other daily through the privately operated **federal-funds market.**

The total amount of legal reserves held by a bank can be divided into required reserves $[RR = rr(DD)]$ and excess reserves (XR):

$$\text{legal reserves} = \text{required reserves} + \text{excess reserves.}$$

Notice that the reserves available to meet the FED's reserve requirements are called *legal reserves* and that they include *excess reserves,* which differentiates them from *required reserves.*

Is There Any "Real" Money in Banks?
If *real money* is interpreted as meaning bills and coins, the answer to the above question is "Not much." Banks

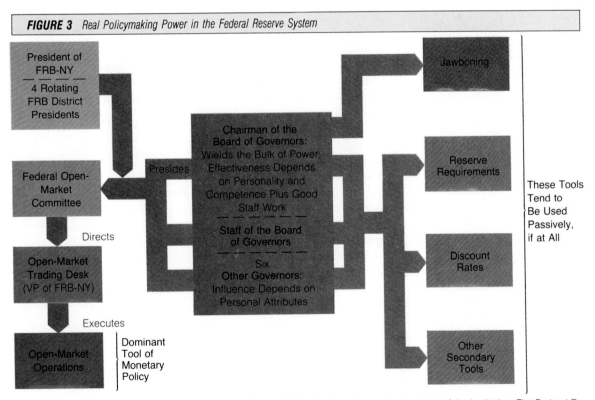

FIGURE 3 Real Policymaking Power in the Federal Reserve System

President of FRB-NY

4 Rotating FRB District Presidents

Federal Open-Market Committee

Directs

Open-Market Trading Desk (VP of FRB-NY)

Executes

Open-Market Operations

Dominant Tool of Monetary Policy

Presides

Chairman of the Board of Governors: Wields the Bulk of Power; Effectiveness Depends on Personality and Competence Plus Good Staff Work

Staff of the Board of Governors

Six Other Governors: Influence Depends on Personal Attributes

Jawboning

Reserve Requirements

Discount Rates

Other Secondary Tools

These Tools Tend to Be Used Passively, if at All

In many organizations, the real policymaking power does not follow the formal organization chart of the institution. The Federal Reserve System is no exception. This figure depicts the flow of real policymaking power within the FED.

keep enough currency on hand to meet their customers' demands for cash, and that is about it.

Since average banks have deposits of well over $10 million, where do they store our money? You learned in chapter 12 that in a fractional reserve banking system, banks only hold about 15–30 percent of deposits as reserves. However, a $10-million bank will not keep $1.5 to $3 million on hand in cash—keeping track of the inventory might be a problem, and there is no sense in tempting thieves. Consequently, banks keep most of their reserves on deposit with Federal Reserve Branch or District Banks.

Even these FED banks do not hold your bank's deposits as cash. To do so would mean storing literally tons of the green stuff. You have probably figured out that your bank account is simply a few electronic impulses stored in the bank's computer. The FED does the same thing with the reserves that banks keep on deposit at Branch or District Banks—it is all in the computer. Roughly two thirds of the nation's money supply exists only in computers.

Reserve Requirements and the Money Multiplier

One way the Federal Reserve System can vary the money supply is through changes in the reserve-requirement ratio (rr). If the FED *raises* the reserve-requirement ratio, then $1/rr$ falls. The smaller potential money multiplier (m_p) means the total reserves in the banking system will support only smaller potential totals of loan-based demand deposits. Conversely, a *cut* in the reserve-requirement ratio enables banks to increase the money supply through expansion of demand deposit-based loans.

Most banks try to maintain roughly the same percentage of excess reserves against demand deposits no matter what happens to the reserve-requirement ratio because the percentage fluctuations of bank deposits depend on people's behavior rather than on the FED's reserve requirements. (You may need to review the section on monetary expansion in chapter 12 if this is not clear.) Notice that the reserve-requirement ratio does not influence the amount of reserves in the banking system. Instead, it affects the potential money multiplier m_p. Naturally, whenever the m_p changes, the actual money multiplier (m_a) moves in the same direction.

The amounts of excess reserves held by banks will depend on (*a*) the expected profitability of lending any excess reserves, and (*b*) the expected costs of acquiring reserves should borrowing be necessary to meet the FED's reserve requirements. In other words, the percentage of deposits held as excess reserves will be *negatively* related to the difference between the interest rates banks can charge borrowers and the interest rates banks themselves must pay to borrow reserves from other banks or the FED.

The reserve-requirement ratio (rr) is the FED's most powerful tool. Suppose that the rr was increased from 1/6 (16.7 percent) to 1/5 (20 percent)—a change of 3.3 percentage points. The potential money supply would fall by roughly 1/6 (m_p falls from 6 to 5). Curiously, this powerful tool is seldom used; reserve-requirement ratios have been changed only about two dozen times since the Great Depression. Why? The very power of changes in rr makes it difficult to predict the magnitude of their effect.

An analogy may help you understand why. Imagine that you were scheduled for brain surgery. Would you want the surgeon to use the most powerful tool available—a chainsaw? Or would you prefer that the surgery be done with more finesse, using a tool such as a scalpel? A second tool of the FED, open-market operations, is the best tool available for the conduct of monetary policy. It is the FED's scalpel.

Open-Market Operations (OMO)

The FED's most important tool, open-market operations, links monetary policy with bonds issued by the U.S. Treasury to finance federal budget deficits.

> **Open-market operations (OMO)** *entail buying and selling securities issued by the U.S. Treasury and are used to vary the size of the monetary base.*

Recall (from chapter 12) that the monetary base equals currency held by the nonbanking public plus bank reserves: MB = currency + bank reserves. Thus, the monetary base underpins our money supply because the money creation process depends on the amounts of reserves in the banking system.

The FED's Open Market Committee (FOMC) directly alters the monetary base through *open-market* purchases or sales of U.S. Treasury securities. When the FOMC decides to increase the money supply by expanding the monetary base, the "open-market desk" buys Treasury bonds, primarily from commercial banks. (A significant amount of the "lending" done by banks is simply purchases of government securities.) If the FOMC sells bonds, the monetary base is reduced.

Banks are not the only buyers of bonds from the FED or sellers of bonds to the FED. Private individuals or firms can also be the FED's trading partners. The funds paid by the FED invariably are deposited in banks by private sellers, however, and so end up as bank reserves. Similarly, private buyers of bonds withdraw funds held in banks to pay for their purchases. Thus, the effects on total bank reserves and the money supply is similar regardless of with whom the FED deals.

When the FED buys bonds, bank reserves rise and the banking system will increase loan-based demand deposits in accord with the money creation process discussed previously. You may wonder where the FED gets the money to buy the bonds. Answer: The FED can print new currency, or it can simply credit the reserve accounts of the private banks via computer at one of the Federal Reserve District Banks.

"T-account" entries for a typical expansionary open-market transaction are shown in Table 1. When the FOMC buys $1,000 in Treasury bonds from Bank A, the Federal Reserve Bank's liabilities are increased by $1,000 in reserves held for Bank A; its assets rise by $1,000 in Treasury bonds. Bank A's assets change from $1,000 in Treasury bonds to $1,000 in new reserves. Bank A views the sale of the bond to the FED in the same way that it would the payback of a loan by a private borrower. Note, however, that this "payoff" creates new reserves for the banking system as a whole, while payment of a private loan does not. These new reserves can then be loaned to private borrowers, creating new demand deposit money via the expansionary money multiplier process.

The FED sells bonds to commercial banks to reduce the money supply. This sops up excess reserves and may even threaten to cut into banks' required reserves. As banks attempt to rebuild their reserves to desired levels, they turn down applications for new loans or renewals of old ones and the amount of loan-based demand deposits falls. The "money destruction" process that results from FED sale of Treasury bonds is exactly the opposite of the money creation process. If the positive numbers in Table 1 were negative, and vice versa, it would illustrate a *contractionary* open-market operation.

You may wonder why private individuals or banks sell bonds when the FED conducts expansionary open-market operations. Focus 1 illustrates the bidding process; the sellers are those who offer desired amounts of bonds at the lowest prices. No matter how high the bond prices are, the FED buys. The FED can shrink the money supply by selling some of the Treasury bonds in its portfolio; this withdraws reserves from the banking system. The FED takes the highest bids for bonds it sells, no matter how low the bids are.

Actually, the open-market desk of the FOMC both buys and sells bonds every business day.

1. If the FED buys more bonds than it sells, total bank reserves are increased and the money creation process leads to growth of the money supply.
2. When the FED sells more bonds than it buys, reserves fall and the money destruction process causes a contraction of the money supply.

TABLE 1 T-Account Changes for a Typical Open-Market Transaction	
Federal Reserve Bank	
Assets	**Liabilities**
+ $1,000 Treasury bonds	+ $1,000 Reserves held for Bank A
Member Bank A	
Assets	**Liabilities**
− $1,000 Treasury bonds + $1,000 Loanable reserves	No change

The "Go-Around"

It is an early Thursday afternoon in June. The scene is the trading room on the eighth floor of the Federal Reserve Bank of New York. The manager of the Open Market Account for Domestic Operations gathers with his trading room officers to reaffirm a decision to buy roughly $1¼ billion of Treasury bills. The banking system needs additional reserves to meet the increased public demand for currency and deposits expected as the end of the quarter and July 4 approach. The markets for bank reserves and Treasury securities are functioning normally with prices moving narrowly. After a brief discussion, the manager gives final approval to the operation.

The officer-in-charge at the FED's Trading Desk turns to the ten officers and securities traders who sit before telephone consoles linking them to three dozen primary dealers in U.S. government securities. "We're going to ask for offerings of all bills for regular delivery," she says. Each trader knows this means delivery and payment will take place the next day. Each picks up the vertical strips on which the offerings will be recorded for the four dealers he will call.

One officer, Bill, presses a button on his telephone console, buzzing the corresponding console of a government securities dealer. "John," Bill says, "we are looking for offerings of bills for regular delivery." John replies, "I'll be right back." He turns and yells, "The

FED is in, asking for all bills for delivery tomorrow." Moments later information screens around the country and abroad flash the news. Salesmen begin ringing customers to see if they have bills they want to offer. Meanwhile, John checks with the trading manager of his firm to see how aggressive he should be in pricing the firm's own securities.

Twenty minutes later John rings back. "Bill, I can offer you $15 million of bills maturing August 9 at 9.20 percent, $40 million September 13 bills at 9.42, $25 million of September 20's at 9.46 and another 25 at 9.44. I'll sell $75 million December 13's at 10.12 and another 100 at 10.09. I can offer $20 million of March 21's at 10.25 and 50 May 16's at 10.28. All for delivery tomorrow."

Bill reads back each offering to double check, then asks, "Can I have those firm?"

"Sure."

Within ten or fifteen minutes each trader has written the offerings obtained from his calls on preprinted strips. The officer-in-charge arrays the individual dealer strips on an inclined board placed atop a stand-up counter. A quick tally shows that dealers have offered $7.8 billion of bills for regular delivery on Friday.

The officer and a colleague compare rates across the different maturities, seeking those that are high in relation to adjoining issues. She circles any special bargains with a red pencil. With an

eye on heavy existing holdings, she circles other propositions that offer yields on or above a yield curve she draws mentally through the more heavily offered issues. Her associate keeps a running total of the amounts being bought. When the desired volume has been circled and cross-checked, the individual strips are returned to the traders, who quickly ring up the dealers.

Bill says, "John, we'll take the $25 million of September 20's at 9.46, the 75 of December 13's at 10.12, and the 50 of May 16's at 10.28 for regular delivery. A total of $150 million. No thanks on the others."

Forty-five minutes after the initial entry, all follow-up calls have been completed. The Trading Desk has bought $1,304 million of Treasury bills. Only the paperwork remains. The traders write up tickets, which authorize the accounting section to instruct the Reserve Bank's Government Bond Department to receive and pay for the specific Treasury bills bought.

Source: From Open Market Operations *by Paul Meek. Reprinted by permission of the Federal Reserve Bank of New York.*

Open-market operations ultimately affect the money supply *only* through changes in the amounts of reserves in the banking system, *not* through changes in the money multiplier. The maximum possible value of the multiplier (m_p) is determined by the reserve-requirement ratio (rr). The FED's discounting operations affect both the size of the monetary base (MB) and the value of the actual money multiplier (m_a).

Discounting Operations

When commercial banks have insufficient reserves to meet the FED's reserve requirements or want to increase their reserves, they can borrow money from the *discount windows* of the FED's District or Branch banks; the FED is a bankers' bank. Loans to banks from the discount window become part of bank reserves and, hence, cause the monetary base to grow.

The interest rate the FED charges bankers is called the **discount rate (d).**

Most bank borrowing from the FED is to cover temporary deficiencies. The likelihood that banks will have inadequate reserves, however, depends strongly on the discount rate. When the discount rate (d) is much less than market interest rates (i), the monetary base grows; bankers will borrow from the FED to expand their loans and demand deposits. They do so because the interest rate the bank pays is less than the interest rate it charges on loans. (It's a bit like trading nickels for dimes.) On the other hand, if the discount rate is substantially higher than the market interest rate, it penalizes bankers who are forced to borrow from the FED because of unforeseen withdrawals of deposits. Consequently, banks try to avoid any need to borrow by holding greater excess reserves. Thus the actual multiplier m_a shrinks as the difference between the discount rate and the market interest rate grows.

All else equal,

1. when the FED hikes the discount rate, banks borrow less, reducing total reserves or limiting their growth. Banks also lend less, so individual banks' excess reserves grow and the actual money multiplier and money supply fall.
2. when the FED cuts the discount rate, banks borrow more from the FED and cut holdings of excess reserves; this results in increases in the actual money multiplier and money supply.

The FED's Secondary Tools

The reserve-requirement ratio, open-market operations, and the discount rate are the major mechanisms at the FED's disposal, but other devices in the FED's toolbox also help it control financial markets and economic activity:

1. The FED sets margin requirements to control stock-market credit.
2. The FED "jawbones," or rages at people or institutions who do things it does not like.

Until recently, the FED could also (*a*) regulate credit to consumers and business firms during wars or crises, and (*b*) set the maximum interest rate that could be paid on bank deposits. Congress rescinded both these FED powers during a continuing wave of economic deregulation in the 1980s.

Margin Requirements   Many people blamed overspeculation for the Stock Market Crash of 1929 and the Great Depression. People could buy stock in the 1920s with a down payment of as little as 10 percent. This is called "buying on margin."

The FED sets the **margin requirement** *(the percentage down payment required) for purchases of securities.*

Some 1920s investors used almost all their assets for down payments. Then, when stock prices fell, they were wiped out. In the aftermath of the Crash, the Federal Reserve System was granted power to set *margin requirements,* which have hovered around 50 percent for the past three decades. Presumably, higher margin requirements squelch speculation and lower margin requirements stimulate speculation.

There is, however, little evidence that margin requirements significantly influence the average level of stock prices. Indeed, a powerful economic theory suggests that even if low margin requirements cause some individuals to speculate, their behavior will be offset by adjustments on the parts of more prudent financial investors. Suppose that financial investors expected a 10 percent return on stocks but a 12 percent return on equally risky real estate. Funds would flow into real estate from the stock market. The stock market would fall a bit, and real estate prices would rise until the returns were equalized at, say, 11 percent. This is precisely the type of adjustment that, presumably, would follow even minor overspeculation in stocks. When low margin requirements encourage speculation so that stock prices rise slightly, the expected returns (dividends, etc.) per dollar of financial investment in stocks decline. This result makes real estate or other investments comparatively more attractive to prudent investors, so money will flow from the stock market until expected returns on all investments are equated. Overspeculation in stocks due to low margin requirements is eliminated automatically.

Nevertheless, the 1987 Stock Market crash has been attributed to overspeculation and **program trading** (computer assisted transactions.) This has resulted in some political sentiment for tighter regulation of securities trading by the FED and the Securities and Exchange Commission (SEC).

Jawboning   Self-restraints on union wage increases or business price hikes are commonly advocated by political leaders seeking to contain inflation.

> **Jawboning** *is oratory used by policymakers who want people or institutions to act against their individual interests (or to see their interests in a different light).*

The FED occasionally has tried to use jawboning to persuade banks either to expand or contract credit. Economists tend to be skeptical of the effectiveness of appeals to public-spiritedness. The FED's jawboning may have some effect, however, because it is backed up by the power to audit and otherwise harass banks. A major problem is that the effects of jawboning are less predictable than those of virtually any other tool. Because the FED has learned this lesson, few recent chairmen have spent time exhorting bankers to do something other than maximize their banks' profits.

Which Tools Are Used?

The FED strongly influences the money supply, but lacks precise and direct control. We have identified the actual money multiplier (m_a) as the relationship between the money supply and the monetary base, $m_a = MS/MB$. This equation implies that the money supply is the product of the money multiplier and the monetary base:

$$MS = m_a(MB).$$

The FED can change either the discount rate or reserve-requirement ratios to try to manipulate the value of the actual money multiplier and, thus,

change the money supply. Alternatively, it can use open-market operations (and, to a lesser extent, discount operations) to vary the monetary base to alter the money supply. Table 2 summarizes how the tools of the FED affect the money supply by altering the behavior of banks and the public.

If the FED does not independently determine the money supply, then what other groups have influence, and how? The FED directly, and with some precision, controls the monetary base through open-market operations. The nonbanking public can affect the money multiplier through its holding of cash. As private stores of cash rise, currency held as bank reserves falls; the actual money multiplier and the money supply fall because the money expansion process only applies to currency in bank vaults. Independently of FED policies, banks may unintentionally influence the actual money multiplier through variations in the percentage of total demand deposits held as excess reserves. The greater the excess reserves held by banks, the smaller will be the actual money multiplier and, hence, the money supply.

If private activities can alter the actual money multiplier and thwart FED attempts to change the money supply, then which tools are most effective in accomplishing the FED's objectives? Any versatile do-it-yourselfer accumulates a number of tools that rust because they are seldom, if ever, used. Similarly, changes in stock-market margin requirements and jawboning are used only rarely. Reserve-requirement ratios are seldom varied, and then only slightly. They are too powerful to be very useful.

Since roughly 1967, the discount rate has been "pegged" slightly above interest rates in the federal-funds market. This encourages banks to borrow from each other and discourages them from borrowing reserves from the FED. At times, however, the discount rate and market interest rates have been inconsistent because the FED historically viewed it as undignified to change the discount rate more than two or three times a year to reflect changes in interest rates in the federal-funds market. Changes in the discount rate normally are not intended to affect the money supply directly because the FED would like the actual money multiplier to be stable. Thus, discount rate changes are used primarily to keep constant the percentage of deposits held as excess reserves.

Open-market operations are the best tool to control the money supply. It took a long time for the FED

TABLE 2 FED Tools and Effects

Tool Used	Potential Money Multiplier ($m_p = 1/rr$)	Excess Reserves Ratio ($xr = XR/DD$)	Actual Money Multiplier ($m_a = MS/MB$)	Monetary Base (MB)	Currency NBP[a]	Bank Reserves	Loans, Demand Deposits, and Money Supply ($M1$)
Reserve-requirement ratios (rr)							
Raise rr	Lower	No change	Lower	No change	No change	No change	Lower
Lower rr	Higher	No change	Higher	No change	No change	No change	Higher
Open-market operations (OMC)							
Buys bonds	No change	No change	No change	Higher	Higher	Higher	Higher
Sells bonds	No change	No change	No change	Lower	Lower	Lower	Lower
Discounting operations							
Lower rate	No change	Lower	Higher	Higher	Higher	Higher	Higher
Raise rate	No change	Higher	Lower	Lower	Lower	Lower	Lower
Jawboning							
No change		Ambiguous		No change		Ambiguous	
Stock market margin requirements	Lower margin requirements presumably cause more stock market speculation while higher margin requirements presumably discourage speculation. There is, however, little statistical support for this proposition and a powerful theory to refute the idea.						

[a]Note: Unless interest rates paid on deposits change, households and firms are assumed to keep stable proportions of their money holdings in the forms of cash and demand deposits, respectively.

to understand this, but open-market operations are now the dominant discretionary tool used actively by the Federal Reserve System. Open-market operations directly alter the reserves in the banking system. In the long run, open-market operations have no effect on the money multiplier. Active use of changes in reserve-requirement ratios or the discount rate operate primarily through changes in the actual money multiplier. The results of policy-caused changes in the actual multiplier have been erratic and unsatisfactory when used.

Financial Institutions and Regulations

Among our more important financial institutions are commercial banks, savings and loan associations, credit unions, insurance companies, and the various stock exchanges.

Financial Intermediation

Households allocate their after-tax incomes between consumption and saving. If you do not intend to use your savings for a while, you should be willing to let other people use them if they pay you interest so that you ultimately receive more than they borrowed. Financial institutions find borrowers willing to pay higher interest rates than must be paid to savers.

Differences between the interest paid by borrowers and that paid to savers provide income to the owners of financial institutions. You can imagine how chaotic it would be if all savers had to seek out their own investors or borrowers, and vice versa. Transaction costs would be enormous. Financial institutions serve economic efficiency by cutting transaction costs.

Financial intermediation *occurs when financial institutions make the savings of households whose incomes exceed their spending available* *to investors or to other households that wish to spend more on consumer goods than their incomes allow.*

This is the most crucial economic function of financial institutions. Other important roles of financial institutions are (*a*) to provide secure places for savers to keep their deposits, and (*b*) to facilitate flows and payments of funds. For example, most payments are made through checking accounts.

The Diversity of Financial Institutions

Different financial institutions use different methods to secure the savings of individuals, which then can be either loaned or invested directly. Since people have different ideas about the best way to save (or borrow) and firms differ in the types of debt they are willing to incur, it seems natural that various types of financial intermediaries have developed to meet these diverse needs. A second reason for the diversity of financial institutions is the mix of federal and state laws and regulations governing them. Many of these institutions, however, are growing less distinct because of major banking deregulation that began in 1980.

Commercial Banks "Full service" **commercial banks** provide more services to their customers than checking and savings accounts. Most banks offer a variety of personal and commercial loan services, issue bank credit cards such as MasterCard and Visa, and have trust departments available to administer wills and estates.

Thrift Institutions Savings and loan associations, mutual savings banks, and credit unions are all called **thrift institutions.** A major revision of our banking laws in 1980 made it possible for thrift institutions to offer accounts that are almost identical to bank checking accounts. Most loans made by savings and loan associations and mutual savings banks are used to finance housing. Membership in a credit union is normally limited to the employees of a particular firm or members of a particular labor union or profession, although in some rural areas a geographic boundary determines eligibility for membership.

Insurance Companies Many people will bet small amounts on the outcome of the flip of a coin, but only a few high rollers are willing to bet thousands of dollars with no better than even odds of winning. Most of us want risky activities to favor us substantially or we just won't play. This widespread characteristic, called *risk aversion,* provides insurance companies with profit opportunities.

Since most of us are willing to pay money to avoid some of the financial consequences of taking risks, **insurance companies** can sell us a guarantee against risk for a fee that is large enough to cover their claims and operating costs and still permit a profit. No one can predict whose house will burn down next—yours or your neighbor's. Thus, all insurance policy buyers make small contributions toward a fund that can be used to compensate the person whose house goes up in flames.

Insurance companies can provide this service and expect to make profits as long as the fee (premium) is greater than the amount they might have to pay multiplied by the probability of payment. Vast amounts of money are paid to insurance companies as premiums for life, auto, and health insurance, or as contributions to pension funds, many of which are administered by insurance companies. These funds are made available for loans to business firms or are invested directly by the insurance companies.

Securities Markets Brokers, through whom securities are bought and sold, also provide financial intermediation.

> **Securities** *include paper assets such as stocks and bonds. A* **bond** *is simply an IOU issued by a corporation or government agency that pays interest to the lender. A* **share of stock** *is a claim to partial ownership of a corporation.*

Most corporations and government agencies do not solicit you directly for funds that you might be willing to lend or invest. Instead, they typically leave this specialized sort of solicitation to brokers, who communicate offers to buy or sell securities through stock exchanges. Although the New York Stock Exchange (also known as *Wall Street*) is the best known, there are a number of lesser and regional stock exchanges.

The Evolution of Financial Institutions

Table 3 summarizes the major roles played by various types of financial intermediaries, but you should be aware that the differences between these institutions are increasingly blurred, in large measure because of recent deregulation of the financial sector of our economy.

During the 1970s, international inflation, the dollar's decline from complete dominance in world money markets, and a host of other factors generated pressures for changes in the financial sector. Major deregulation occurred in 1980, but many reforms were phased in gradually. As inflation subsided in the 1980s, further pressures for deregulation abated but there are still many inefficient financial regulations.

The FED's Independence Under Attack

The Great Depression of the 1930s caused a widespread loss of faith in monetary policy. The Keynesian Revolution, from 1936 into the late 1960s, convinced most economists that fiscal policy is the best way to stabilize the economy. Since the 1970s, however, monetary policy has made a strong comeback, and few economists today believe that "money doesn't matter."

The gradual reaffirmation of the importance of monetary policy began in the late 1950s. At that time, the FED's policy of slow monetary growth was widely attacked as hindering the economy from achieving its potential. In the early 1960s, William McChesney Martin, Jr., was the chairman of the Board of Governors. He was roundly condemned by Keynesians for following contractionary monetary policies that partially

TABLE 3 Financial Intermediaries

| | Commercial Banks | Thrift Institutions | | Insurance Companies | Securities Markets |
		Savings and Loans Mutual Savings Banks	Credit Unions		

Primary sources of funds (liabilities)	Deposits
	  Checking accounts
	  Savings accounts
		Deposits
		  Shares (savings)
		  Checking accounts
		  Other
			Deposits
			  Shares
			  Checking accounts
				Insurance policies	Sales of stocks and bonds are accomplished primarily through stockbrokers and investment bankers who charge brokerage fees for getting savers (purchasers) together with business firms that do the direct economic investment with the funds made available

Primary uses of funds (assets)	Business loans
	Consumer loans
	  Automobiles
	  Home equity loans
	  Furniture and
	    appliances
	  Education
	  Personal
		Home mortgages
		Home equity loans
		  and improvements
			Consumer loans
			  Autos, etc.
				Business loans
				Real estate
				Direct financial investment	

Notes	Banks "create" money by crediting your account when they extend a loan to you	Major function is to finance housing (not business construction)	Focus on consumer loans for members only	Insurance company premiums exceed their expected payouts; people buy insurance because they are risk averse	

Monetary Targets and Stop-and-Go FED Policies: 1976–87

FIGURE 4 Rate of Change in M1 and GNP (Current Dollars, Quarterly Percentage Change)

In 1979, the FED announced it would target and control the rate of growth of *M1*. Since then, both *M1* and GNP have risen for a few quarters, then fallen the next few. Targeting *M1* in the 1980s has proven so difficult for the FED that it recently broadened the targeted rate of growth for *M1* to an annual rate anywhere between 3–8 percent.

Source: *Business Conditions Digest,* January 1988.

offset the expansionary fiscal policies adopted by the Kennedy and Johnson administrations. The failure of a 1968 tax surcharge to slow inflation was blamed by some on too rapid monetary growth during 1968–69. In the 1970s, "stop-go" monetary policies were partially blamed for stagflation and the reemergence of the business cycle. Then, in the early 1980s under the chairmanship of Paul Volcker, the FED was blamed by many for following restrictive monetary policies that caused a severe slump in business activity. Most observers conceded, however, that these restrictive

policies did much to reduce inflation and interest rates.

One consequence of the renewed recognition of the power of monetary policy is pressure for the FED to be "politically accountable." Many regulatory agencies are thought to be controlled by the industries they are supposed to oversee. Is the FED a captive of banking interests? Does it follow monetary policies to benefit bankers without regard for the public interest? A recent proposed reform is for the four-year term of the chairman of the Board of Governors to

Abrupt changes in monetary policy can cause economic chaos. Monetary growth was erratic in the 1970s and 1980s. Indeed, many observers lay the full blame for a deep recession in 1981–83 at the FED's doorstep. Supply-side economists blame restrictive monetary policies for keeping the full effects of Reagan's tax cuts from taking effect in the early 1980s. Other critics perceive the FED as to blame for swings in the international value of the dollar during 1985–88.

Uneven but growing inflation plagued the 1970s. Money supply growth accelerated, and monetarists believed it to be the root cause of this erosion of the dollar's purchasing power. Keynesians tended to point to other causes, such as the huge OPEC oil price hikes of 1974 and 1979–80.

Paul Volcker, then Chairman of the FED, believed the monetarist prescription that lowering the growth rate of money was the key to curbing inflation. His policies to decelerate inflation were successful in 1980. Because the side effects (high unemployment and high real rates of interest) of the rapid cuts in monetary growth were politically unpalatable, monetary restrictiveness was loosened in late 1982 and early 1983.

Figure 4 shows that achieving a stable growth rate of 2–4 percent annually is a painful process when people are accustomed to more rapid monetary growth. The economy has followed a jerky path since World War II. The disruptions of the Vietnam War or other shocks to our economy may be partial explanations, but most monetarists believe that attempts to fine-tune the economy were doomed to failure.

Attempts at monetary fine-tuning are illustrated in Figure 4. In 1979, the FED announced it would target $M1$ and control its rate of growth. Since then, as the figure illustrates, monetary growth and GNP growth have been on a roller coaster—up for a few quarters and then down the next few. The FED announces targets in one period, then adjusts them later when economic conditions warrant it. Milton Friedman, a leading monetary economist, compares the FED to the farmer who used his barn door for target shooting. "A visitor was astounded to find that each of the numerous targets on the door has a bullet hole precisely in the center of the bull's-eye. He later discovered the secret of such remarkable accuracy. Unobserved, he saw the farmer first shoot at the door and then paint the target." * He contends that the FED "simply repaints the target" to cover its discretionary policymaking.

---

*Milton Friedman, "The FED Hasn't Changed Its Ways," *The Wall Street Journal*, 20 Aug. 1985.

begin and end in the presidential election years. A new president could ensure that the chairman would conduct monetary policy compatible with "the people's choice." Opponents of this reform argue for close checks on presidential power over both monetary and fiscal policies.

A recent congressional resolution is intended to eliminate shocks to the economy arising from erratic and unexpected changes in monetary policy. It prescribes that the FED try to limit monetary growth to a range of 2–6 percent annually and that it announce its targets for growth well in advance so that businesses and financial institutions can adjust. Focus 2 illustrates why critics of the FED characterize recent FED policies as following an erratic "stop-go" pattern that exacerbates macroeconomic instability.

The FED has mounted a multifaceted defense of its independence and discretion over policy. The fear of politicization is a central issue. The FED argues that it should be free to follow what it perceives to be the best monetary policies possible, not policies based on political considerations.

What incentives do the governors of the FED have to follow policies most beneficial for the economic well-being of the American people? The banks that "invest" in the FED are limited to a 6 percent rate of return, and there are no strong political checks on FED governors. The FED responds that its officers and administrators are public-spirited people who simply want the satisfaction of knowing that they are doing the best job they can for the American public. This answer is not very satisfying to economists, who believe that the most powerful of human motivations is self-interest. Subjecting the FED to political pressure, however, is not an especially appealing alternative to relying on the FED management's interest in the public welfare. Will the role of the FED change? Should it? If so, how should it change? Only time will tell.

The Purposes of Financial Regulations

The purpose of any financial system is to channel saving to its most productive uses. The major goals in regulating financial institutions are (*a*) protection of savers, (*b*) stabilization of the economy, and (*c*) promotion of efficiency. The government traditionally has been willing to forgo some efficiency in the financial system in order to achieve other objectives.

Financial institutions are not lenders per se, but only act as intermediaries between savers and borrowers. In this context, **financial efficiency** means minimizing the costs of intermediation, or the bankers' "spread"—the differences between the costs of loans to borrowers and the interest incomes received by ultimate lenders. This is the financial equivalent of the principle that efficiency requires all services to be produced at the lowest possible opportunity cost. Unfortunately, protecting people's savings and ensuring economic stability are often in conflict with efficiency in financial intermediation.

Recent trends in deregulation have allowed many financial institutions to become "money supermarkets" capable of providing virtually all financial services. Many firms in other lines of business have been expanding into the financial sector. Sears, for example, has issued its Discover card and is soliciting deposits into Discover accounts. Increasing competition tends to facilitate efficiency. Some regulations, however, are still financially inefficient.

Usury Laws and Credit Rationing

The economic distortions associated with price controls have long been recognized and are discussed in chapters 4 and 17. Controls on interest rates are no exception to this principle. Most states and several federal agencies impose ceilings on interest.

> **Usury laws** *limit the maximum interest rates that can be charged to borrowers.*

For example, agencies that guarantee home mortgages set maximum permissible interest rates for many home loans. Whenever market interest rates exceed these ceilings, funds are not available for mortgages. Usury laws and regulations undoubtedly account for more of the volatility of commercial and residential construction than does any other single factor. In addition, usury laws may cause interstate money (credit) flows.

When ceilings on interest rates apply, credit is rationed on some other basis—quite often credit worthiness. The extent of **credit rationing** varies considerably over the business cycle, and the bulk of the distortive impacts of the numerous "credit crunches" over the past two decades can be attributed directly to interest-rate ceilings.

Another reason to eliminate usury laws is that they are inequitable. Poor people often cannot borrow at rates allowed by law because of lack of "credit worthiness," while wealthier borrowers pay lower interest rates because the competition for loanable funds is reduced when low-income borrowers are *rationed out* of the market. Loan applications from poor people who wish to borrow are rejected in favor of extending loans to people who are less risky. If usury ceilings were eliminated, flows of credit to poor people would grow, and the interest rates paid by those who are better off would rise a bit.

In this chapter, we have outlined the most heavily regulated major industry in America. These regulations stem from the disasters of the Great Depression and a recognition that controlling monetary aggregates is necessary to control aggregate economic activity. The FED uses three main tools to alter the money supply: reserve requirements, open-market operations, and discounting operations. How monetary policy is used to control inflation or avert a recession is the focal point of the next chapter.

CHAPTER REVIEW: KEY POINTS

1. Fractional reserve banking makes it impossible for all banks to pay all demand deposits simultaneously, so resolutions of monetary crises may require intervention by a *central bank*, or "bankers' bank." Our central bank is the *Federal Reserve System* (*FED*).

2. The potential money multiplier (m_p) is the inverse of the *reserve-requirement ratio* ($1/rr$). Excess reserves in the financial system and cash holdings by the public are drains on the potential multiplier. The actual multiplier (m_a) is the money supply (MS) divided by the amount of currency and bank reserves (MB) issued by the FED: $m_a = MS/MB$.

3. The FED's most powerful but least used primary tool is its power to change reserve requirements (rr). Increases in rr reduce the money multiplier and money supply, and vice versa.

4. The most useful tool of the FED is *open-market operations* (*OMO*). After all adjustments, open-market operations affect the monetary base, not the money multiplier. When the FED sells government bonds, bank reserves are reduced and the money supply declines. FED purchases of bonds increase bank reserves and the money supply.

5. The *discount rate* (*d*) is the interest rate the FED charges member banks. When the discount rate is low relative to market interest rates, banks hold few excess reserves and will borrow funds from the FED. Consequently, the money supply increases. High discount rates relative to market interest rates cause banks to borrow less from the FED and provide incentives for larger holdings of excess reserves. The actual money multiplier and total bank reserves fall, and the money supply falls. Most interbank borrowing, however, is through the privately operated *federal funds market*.

6. The FED's other tools include *margin requirements* to limit stock-market credit and *jawboning*.

7. *Financial institutions* facilitate flows and payments of funds and provide secure places for savers' deposits. Their most important economic function is to channel funds from savers to financial investors and other borrowers through a process called *financial intermediation*. Commercial banks, savings and loan associations, mutual savings banks, credit unions, insurance companies, and stock exchanges are all financial intermediaries.

8. *Usury laws* reduce the availability of credit to the poor because *credit rationing* channels loanable funds to superior credit risks.

PROBLEM

1. Draw supply and demand curves for loanable funds so that the market clearing rate of interest for a home mortgage would be 12 percent. Suppose that state laws and federal housing regulations forbid charging more than 10 percent annual interest on mortgages. Show this in your graph. Will there be a surplus or a shortage of mortgage funding? What types of households will be able to secure mortgage loans? What types will experience adverse credit rationing? Which groups lose because of these usury ceilings?

QUESTIONS FOR THOUGHT AND DISCUSSION

1. How will a million-dollar bank robbery affect the money supply in the short run? Over a longer period? What happens to the monetary base and money supply if you accidently wash some clothes with bills in a pocket and destroy this currency in the process?

2. Until 1980, the reserve-requirement ratios for state-chartered banks were generally lower than for na-

tional banks. How might this partially explain the growth in state banks relative to national banks during the preceding sixty years? What effects would this have on the FED's ability to control the money supply? On pressures for the FED to reduce reserve-requirement ratios for national banks? How might you test to see whether your answers to these questions are correct?

3. Banks have been forbidden to establish branches across state borders, and many states absolutely forbid branch banking. Bank "holding companies" have finessed those laws in some places, and there is now substantial political pressure to relax these laws. What potential gains and losses do you perceive from allowing nationwide branch banking?

4. Should opening a financial institution be more complicated than starting a business as a florist? What special controls, if any, should the government exercise over financial institutions?

5. Since most bank deposits are insured for up to $100,000 by the Federal Deposit Insurance Corpora-

tion (FDIC), do reserve requirements add to the safety of depositors? If not, what is the purpose of requiring banks to hold reserves?

6. Would it matter if the FED eliminated the discount rate entirely and abolished bank borrowing from the Federal Reserve? One of the original roles played by discounting operations was averting panics touched off by the withdrawal of currency from banks in response to the fear of bank insolvency. Is this role still valid today? What benefits are derived from current discounting operations?

7. Standard rationales for reserve requirements are that they preserve the liquidity and solvency of banks and protect the public from bank failures. Critics of reserve requirements argue that these requirements are nothing more than an "interest free" loan to the government or a "tax on banking." Suppose that reserve requirements were eliminated. What would be the effect on (a) bank solvency, and (b) ability of the FED to control the money supply? Would banks continue to hold reserves? Why or why not?

CHAPTER 14

Monetary Theory and Policy

Money is but a symbol of all that is worth having. Its possession in quantity can be a blessing to the virtuous individual, but a curse to masses afflicted by gluttony. Prudent coiners of a society's money gain for their country a stable prosperity, but profligate masters of money can visit ruin on their nation and all its neighbors.   *—Attributed to Daniel Webster*

Money is important to each of us. You would gain if the amount of money you have now were doubled. But how important is the total quantity of money in circulation? If everyone's money holdings were doubled, would you benefit? Would the average person?

Controversy raged over questions like these even before the conquistadors shipped enormous amounts of stolen gold from the "New World" to sixteenth-century Spain and created a wave of inflation throughout Europe. The Depression-era work of John Maynard Keynes rekindled the fires surrounding these issues. They are still far from resolved.

Just as markets for goods are in equilibrium only if the quantities supplied and demanded are equal at current prices, the quantities of money supplied and demanded must be equal to balance money markets. In this chapter, you will learn that money markets must be in equilibrium before national income, the price level, and the market rate of interest will be stable.

The Demand for Money

I have all the money I need for the rest of my life—provided I die by 4 o'clock this afternoon.
                                        —Henny Youngman

"NO" is a standard response to the question "Do you have enough money?" As with "What is money?," the answer seems obvious. Your behavior, however, indicates that at times you have too much money, so you spend it; at other times you try to acquire more money because you have too little. Ambiguity arises because people often use *money, income,* and *wealth* interchangeably. If asked if you had enough income or wealth, you could undoubtedly justify an answer of no. But money is identical to neither income nor wealth—although it is related to both. Money is the device used to buy goods or resources and by which we measure our incomes, wealth, and the prices we pay.

Most people spend in predictable ways and receive money at regular intervals. If you act to secure more money income by selling your time or your goods, or by saving more money out of your income, you must have temporary shortages of money relative to your time or these goods. But when you spend money, you see your purchases as more desirable than the money they cost; relative to these goods, you have temporary surpluses of money.

Individual demands for money are fairly complex. It would be fruitless to break up our demand for cars into "vacation," "work," "commuter," or "shopping" motives. Some economists, however, have found it useful to compartmentalize the reasons we hold money instead of consuming more or investing in other assets. The functions money performs were addressed in chapter 12: money is a medium of exchange, a unit of account, a store of value, and a standard of deferred payment. One trivial way of explaining your demand for money is to say that you desire money for the functions it performs. You can gain deeper insights into the way money works by looking at three categories of motives for holding money.

Transactions Demands

Before the Great Depression, classical reasoning focused on spending plans as the sole rational motive for holding money. This is called the transactions demand for money.

> The **transactions demand for money** arises because people anticipate spending it.

This is usually the dominant reason for holding money. You can predict many if not most transactions fairly accurately. You know how much your monthly rent and car payment will be, and roughly how much you will spend on utilities, gasoline, and meals. You probably also have a good idea about how much money you will receive in the near future. Most workers receive their paychecks regularly—either daily, weekly, biweekly, or monthly. Students may receive money monthly or once or twice a semester.

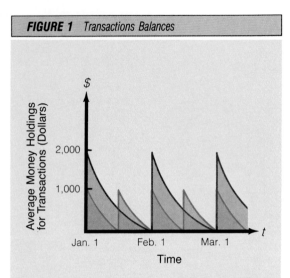

FIGURE 1 Transactions Balances

The same income per year will result in average holdings of money that are inversely related to the frequency of receipts of income. All else equal, a person paid twice a month will hold only half the average money balances held by someone paid once a month. Our spending patterns ensure that most of us will have far less money on hand at the end of a pay period than at the beginning because we use money to make transactions.

Predictable transaction flows of money to and from an individual who is paid $2,000 monthly are reflected in the blue line in Figure 1. The vertical rise ot the area shaded in red shows money-holding patterns for someone with an identical $2,000 monthly income, but who is paid $1,000 at the middle and again at the end of each month. Notice that this person's average holdings of money are much lower than for the individual paid monthly. We have shown more rapid declines in money holdings right after a payday than toward the end of the pay period. You are typical if you write a lot of checks right after you get paid, and then find yourself almost broke before you are paid again.

Precautionary Demands

Even people who hold enough money to cover their planned spending feel very uncomfortable if they have no extra money in reserve. There always seem to be little—and sometimes big—emergencies that require money. For example, you may have the hard luck of a flat tire or lost textbooks, or you may pleasantly discover that the "Blue Light Special" at a department store is a record you want. You hold precautionary balances to ensure that you will have money on hand to meet unexpected expenditures.

The **precautionary demand for money** *arises because people know that unanticipated spending is required at times.*

The major difference between the transactions and precautionary demands for money lies in the degree of predictability about future spending. Both motives, however, suggest that your average money balances held will be positively related to your income—you probably hold more money now than when you were ten years old, and far less than you will hold when you put your student days behind you and find a good job. Figure 2 stacks the precautionary demand for money on top of the transactions demand to show how the total of these two demands are related to income. One of Keynes's innovations in monetary theory is the idea of the precautionary motive. While earlier classical writers ignored this motive in their writings on money, they would have had little difficulty accepting this idea because, like transactions balances, precautionary balances of money are closely related to income.

Asset Demands

Keynes's major innovation in monetary theory is the concept of an asset demand for money, an idea that clashes with early classical theory.

The **asset demand for money** *arises because people sometimes want to hold part of their wealth in the form of money.*

Early theorists argued that no one will hold money as an asset because they could earn interest on stocks or bonds if they made these financial investments instead. The desire to hold some wealth in the form of money originates from (*a*) expectations that the prices of stocks or bonds will fall in the near future,

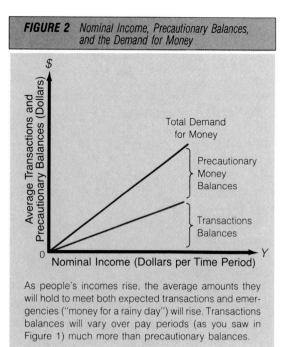

FIGURE 2 *Nominal Income, Precautionary Balances, and the Demand for Money*

As people's incomes rise, the average amounts they will hold to meet both expected transactions and emergencies ("money for a rainy day") will rise. Transactions balances will vary over pay periods (as you saw in Figure 1) much more than precautionary balances.

(*b*) reluctance to hold only assets that tend to swing widely in value, or (*c*) a belief that transactions costs are higher than any expected return from investments in stocks or bonds.

Speculative Balances Suppose that you have saved some of your income and plan to buy stocks, bonds, or real estate. If you expect the prices of these financial investments to fall in the near future, you will postpone their purchase until prices are down, holding money as an asset in the interim.

People hold **speculative money balances** *if they expect the prices of alternative assets to fall in the near future.*

Bond Prices and Interest Rates Rising interest rates cause bond prices to fall and lower interest rates mean higher bond prices. Suppose you were offered a chance to buy a government bond that offered the following terms:

> The bearer of this bond will be paid $100 on January 31 of each year, forever.

If it required a 10 percent return to persuade you to buy this bond, you would be willing to pay $1,000 for it because 10 percent times $1,000 equals $100, which is the annual payment. If you required a 20 percent return on your financial investment, the bond would be worth only $500 to you [0.20($500) = $100]. Thus, higher interest rates imply lower bond prices (20 percent > 10 percent, and $500 < $1,000).

A general formula for this type of bond (called a *perpetuity*) is:

$$\text{present value} = \frac{\textbf{annual payment}}{\textbf{interest rate}}.$$

Remember that higher interest rates mean lower bond prices, while falling interest rates drive bond prices up. If you and other potential bond buyers believe that interest rates will rise soon, you would speculate against bonds and hold money while waiting for bond prices to fall.

Risk Avoidance   Keynes emphasized the speculative aspect of the asset demand for money. Other economists have developed other reasons individuals may hold money as an asset. Assets that yield high average rates of return tend to be very risky. Most people are *risk averse*, so they buy various kinds of insurance. We invest only if the assets we buy with money are expected to yield returns that compensate us for our reduced liquidity *and* the increased risk of loss. Some people are so risk averse that they hold (hoard) money because they view the expected rates of return on any other asset as too low to overcome the associated risks.

Transaction Costs   Money is the most liquid of all assets. If you have so little wealth that transaction costs overshadow any potential gains, you will hold money instead of investing. For example, if you have only $50 to invest and expect a $50 share of stock to generate a $5 profit, it is better to hold money if the stockbroker's fee is more than $5.

All these reasons for people to hold money as an asset lead to the conclusion that their money holdings will be negatively related to the interest rate. Transactions demands are related to time, as suggest-

ed in Figure 1. But there is little reason to believe that either precautionary or asset demands for money are systematically related to time. It is impossible to isolate precise chunks of money into handy compartments, but the transactions, precautionary, and asset motives are reasonable explanations for why most of us keep positive balances of money handy. Typical total money holdings for a person paid $2,000 once a month are shown in Figure 3.

The Costs of Holding Money

As with other goods, the quantity of money demanded will depend on its opportunity cost. Most goods or resources can be bought with money, so it might seem difficult to specify the sacrifice associated with money holdings. These sacrifices, however, take the form of either interest forgone from income-earning assets not held (the Keynesian view) or forgone consumer goods and services (the classical view).

The Classical View   The subjective value of a dollar in exchange for consumer goods from the vantage point of the typical consumer is roughly the reciprocal of the price level ($1/P$). This occurs because the greater the cost of living, the lower the consumption sacrificed by holding a dollar. Each dollar will buy fewer goods. Thus, the higher the price level, the more dollars you need to hold for expected transactions. This relationship between the quantity of money demanded and the reciprocal of the price level is at the root of classical monetary theory.

But the relationship between the cost of living and the quantity of money demanded is not quite this simple. Suppose that we have experienced inflation for a substantial period of time and that you expect inflation to continue. Fearing the decline in value of money, you will want to *reduce* your dollar holdings and purchase more goods since those dollars buy more today than you expect them to in the future. Consequently, there tends to be a negative relationship between the expected rate of inflation and the demand for money. We know that this is a bit sketchy at the moment, but these relationships are explored in more detail when we examine modern monetarism later in this chapter.

The Keynesian View   Keynesians perceive the interest rate as the cost of holding money because they view stocks or bonds that pay interest as the closest

FIGURE 3 *Typical Patterns of Money Holdings*

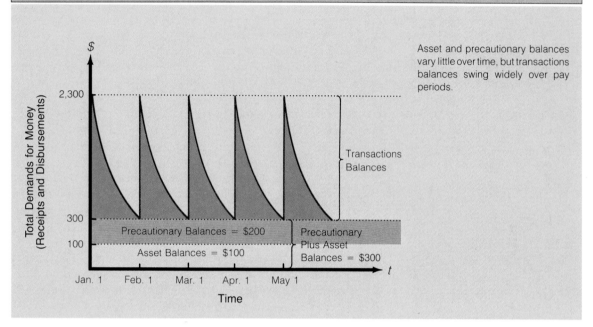

Asset and precautionary balances vary little over time, but transactions balances swing widely over pay periods.

alternatives to money as an asset. You receive no interest on cash holdings and relatively low interest rates on demand deposits. If interest rates are relatively high on nonmonetary assets, you are more likely to hold your wealth in stocks or bonds than if interest rates are low; money is then a more attractive asset. This differs sharply from the classical view that the costs of holding money are the goods that might be enjoyed were the money spent.

Classical Monetary Theory

Before Adam Smith cleared the air with his *Wealth of Nations* in 1776, the economic policies of most European monarchs were grounded in **mercantilism,** a doctrine based on a misunderstanding of the difference between money and wealth. Gold and silver were thought to be real wealth, so England, Spain, and other European countries engaged in colonial expansion to find gold or silver and fought numerous wars in the process. The losers were invariably forced to pay the winners out of their national treasuries. Aztec gold and Inca silver poured into Spain. Monarchs often debased national currencies to fi-

nance wars in the Old World and colonization of the New World.

Whether debasement or foreign conquest enriched the royal coffers, the amount of money in circulation grew. Several early economic thinkers noted that inflation always seemed to follow rapid monetary growth.

Quantity theories of money *indicate that the money supply is the primary determinant of nominal spending and, ultimately, the price level.*

Earlier quantity theories of money were formalized about a century ago by some British economists at Cambridge University and by Irving Fisher of Yale University. Fisher's analysis began with the equation of exchange.[1]

---

1. Fisher, whose biography appears in chapter 17, focused his version of the equation of exchange on total transactions (T) in an economy rather than real national income (Q). Transactions differ from GNP because of sales of things not produced in the relevant year such as used goods or land, and because of transactions involving intermediate goods, which would be double-counted compared to the income version of the equation. Thus, Fisher's equation of exchange is $MV = PT$ rather than the $MV = PQ$ that we discuss later, and V stands for *transactions* velocity instead of income velocity.

The Equation of Exchange

Gross National Product can be written as PQ because GNP has price level (P) and "real" output (Q) components. Just how is the supply of money (M) related to our GNP? One crucial consideration is the average number of times that money changes hands annually for purchases of final output. For example, GNP in 1987 was roughly $4.5 trillion, while the money supply ($M1$) was about $753 billion (or $0.75 trillion)—the average dollar was used about six times for purchases of output produced in 1987.

> *The average number of times a unit of money is used annually is called the* **income velocity (V)** *of money.*

Velocity is computed by dividing GNP by the money supply: $V \equiv PQ/M$.

Multiplying both sides of $V \equiv PQ/M$ by M, yields $MV \equiv PQ$, a result called the equation of exchange.

> *The* **equation of exchange** *is written as* $(M \times V \equiv P \times Q)$.

This equation is definitionally true given our computation of velocity and is interpreted: The quantity of money times its velocity is equal to the price level times real output, which equals GNP. Note that this equation suggests that the *velocity* of money is just as important as the quantity of money in circulation.

A proximate corollary is that *the percentage change in the money supply* **plus** *the percentage change in velocity* **equals** *the percentage change in the price level* **plus** *the percentage change in real output:*[2]

$$\frac{\Delta M}{M} + \frac{\Delta V}{V} = \frac{\Delta P}{P} + \frac{\Delta Q}{Q}.$$

Focus on the right-hand side of this equation for a moment. Does it make sense that if the price of, say, oranges rose 1 percent and you cut your purchases 2 percent, your spending on oranges would fall 1 percent? Intuitively, the percentage change in price plus the percentage change in quantity equals the percentage change in spending. Now examine the equation

once more. Suppose output grew 3 percent, that velocity did not change, and that the money supply rose 7 percent. Average prices would rise 4 percent (7 percent + 0 percent = 4 percent + 3 percent). Learning these relationships will help you comprehend arguments between classical monetary theorists and their detractors.

The Crude Quantity Theory of Money

From certain assumptions about the variables in the equation of exchange (M, V, P, and Q), classical economists (including Fisher) conclude that, in equilibrium, the price level (P) is exactly proportional to the money supply (M). Let us see how they arrived at this conclusion.

Constancy of Velocity Classical economic reasoning views the income velocity (V) of money as determined solely by institutional factors, such as the organizational structure and efficiency of banking and credit, and by people's habitual patterns of spending money after receiving income. Velocity is thought to be constant, at least in the short run, because changes tend to occur slowly in (*a*) the technologies of financial institutions (the ways checks clear or loans are granted or repaid); and (*b*) in the inflows and outflows of individuals' money (frequencies of receipts of incomes and the habits that people have about spending their money). Thus, we see a central assumption of the classical quantity theory: $\Delta V/V = 0$. Focus 1 reveals, however, that this assumption may not always hold.

But why does classical economics view velocity ($\overline{V}$) as unaffected by the price level (P), the real level of output (Q), or the money supply (M)?[3] The answer lies in why people demand money. Classical macroeconomic models assume that people want to hold money only to consummate transactions and that people's spendings are fixed proportions of their incomes. Our previous discussion of the transactions motive is basically classical. Since national income is approximately GNP (or $P \times Q$), then the demand for money M_d (a transactions demand) can be written:

$$M_d = \overline{k}PQ,$$

---

2. For math purists only: this is roughly equivalent to taking the time derivative of this equation in its logs and ignoring the cross partials.

3. Bars over variables indicate constancy.

Velocity in the 1980s

The results postulated by monetarism and the quantity theory of money depend heavily on the relative constancy of velocity. If velocity is constant, then a more rapid rate of monetary growth would mean higher inflation. But what happens if the public desires more money as the FED expands the money supply? Income velocity falls and the inflationary effects forecasted by monetarists may not be forthcoming.

Velocity fell substantially in most Western countries during the first half of the 1980s, as shown in Figure 4. The inflationary effects of increased monetary growth were partially offset by declining velocity. High real interest rates attracted saving into interest-bearing accounts, and these accounts now constitute a large fraction of all monetary aggregates. The deregulation of financial markets in the 1980s generated dozens of new instruments and virtually eliminated the boundaries between different types of financial institutions. Monetarists would argue that the early 1980s were unique and that once people have thoroughly adjusted to deregulation, velocity will regain its relative stability and the classical relationship between the rate of change of the money supply and inflation will resume.

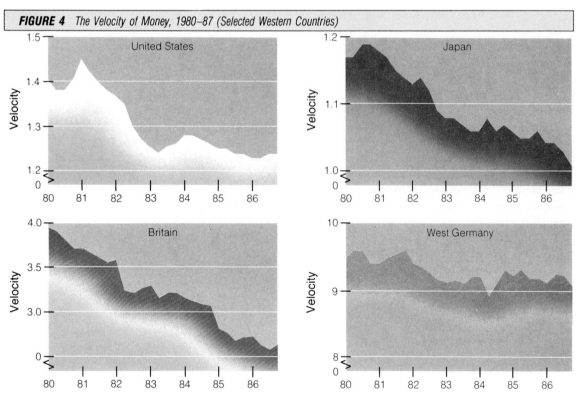

FIGURE 4 *The Velocity of Money, 1980–87 (Selected Western Countries)*

The velocity of money is nominal GNP divided by the money supply. The measure of the money supply used for the United States is $M3$; for Britain, £$M3$; for Japan, $M2$ + CDs; and for West Germany, Central Bank Money (CBM).

Source: From "Deciphering the Writing on the Wall" in *The Economist,* July 27, 1985. Copyright ©1985 by the Economist Newspaper Ltd. Reprinted by permission with updates by authors.

where $\bar{k}$ is the constant proportion of income that would be held in monetary balances.[4] For example, if each family habitually held one fifth of its average annual income of $10,000 in the form of money, then the average quantity of money each family would demand would be $M_d = 0.20(\$10,000) = \$2,000$. The quantity of money demanded in the entire economy would be $2,000 times the number of families.

Constancy of Real Output

Classical theory also assumes that real output (Q) does not depend on the other variables (M, V, and P) in the equation of exchange. Classical economists believe that the natural state of the economy is full employment, so real output is influenced solely by the state of technology and by the amounts of resources available. Full employment is ensured by Say's Law if prices, wages, and interest rates are perfectly flexible. Moreover, both the amounts of resources available and the state of technology are thought to change slowly, if at all, in the short run. Thus, real output (Q) is assumed to be approximately constant and $\Delta Q/Q = 0$. This may seem like a very strong assertion, but the intuitive appeal of the argument that real output is independent of the quantity of money (M), its velocity (V), or the price level (P), is convincing to both classical monetary theorists and to the modern supply-side economists who have updated the classical tradition.

The idea that the amount of paper currency or coins issued by the government has virtually no effect on the economy's productive capacity seems reasonable. Similarly, the velocity of money should not influence capacity. But what about the price level? After all, the law of supply suggests that the quantities of individual goods and services supplied will be greater the higher the market prices are. Shouldn't the nation's output increase if the price level rises? Classical economists say NO! Here is why.

A Crude Monetary Theory of the Price Level

Suppose that your income and the values of all your assets exactly double. (That's the good news.) Suppose that the prices of everything you buy and all your debts also precisely double. (That's the bad news.) Should your behavior change in any way? Your intuition should suggest not. Using similar logic, classical economists conclude that, in the long run, neither real output nor any other aspect of "real" economic behavior is systematically affected by changes in the price level. Economic behavior is shaped by relative prices, not the absolute price level.

Recall that the percentage changes in the money supply and velocity roughly equal the percentage changes in the levels of prices and real output. If velocity is constant and output is stable at a full employment level in the short run, then $\Delta V/V = \Delta Q/Q = 0$. Classical economists are left with a fixed relationship between the money supply (M) and the price level (P): In equilibrium, the rate of inflation is exactly the same as the percentage rate of growth in the money supply ($\Delta M/M = \Delta P/P$). Thus, any increase in the rate of monetary growth would not affect real output, just inflation.

The Classical View of Investment

Firms will buy machinery, construct buildings, or attempt to increase inventories whenever they expect the gross returns on these investments to exceed the total costs of acquiring them. Classical economists assume relatively stable and predictable economies, so they focus on the costs of acquiring investment goods; business investors' expectations of profits are assumed realized, and the costs of new capital goods are presumed stable.

Equilibrium investment occurs when the expected rate of return on investment equals the interest rate. Since the prices of capital equipment are fairly stable, any changes in the costs of acquiring capital are primarily the result of changes in interest rates. [Investors are effectively trading dimes for dollars as long as the cost of borrowing (the interest rate) is less than the return from investments made possible by borrowing.] Naturally, business people will not invest unless they expect a return at least as high as they would receive if they simply lent their own money out at interest.

---

4. We know that the equation of exchange relates the supply of money to national income through velocity: $MV \equiv PQ$. Let us divide both sides by V:

$M = PQ/V$.

Since the quantities of money supplied and demanded must be equal in equilibrium ($M = M_d$), $\bar{k}$ must be equal to $1/\bar{V}$, both $\bar{k}$ and $\bar{V}$ being constants. As a result, classical monetarists discerned a fixed relationship between $\bar{k}$ (the proportion of annual income people want to hold as money) and $\bar{V}$ (the velocity of money).

FIGURE 5 The Classical View of Investment

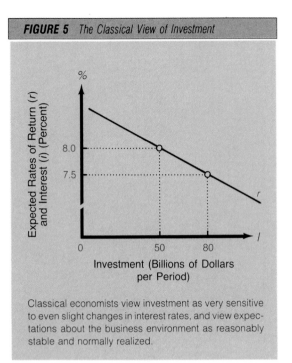

Classical economists view investment as very sensitive to even slight changes in interest rates, and view expectations about the business environment as reasonably stable and normally realized.

Classical writers believe that investment is very sensitive to the interest rate and that large swings in the level of investment occur because of minute changes in interest rates. The expected rate of return (r) curve in Figure 5 is relatively sensitive, or flat. In this example, a decline in interest of 1/2 percent (from 8 percent to 7.5 percent) will cause a 60 percent increase in investment [$(80 - 50)/50 = 30/50 = 0.60$]. Flexible interest rates and a highly sensitive investment (rate of return) schedule easily equate planned saving and investment, stabilizing the economy at full employment.

The Classical Monetary Transmission Mechanism

Monetarists believe that the linkage between the money supply and national income is not only strong, but direct. This **classical monetary transmission mechanism** (how money enters the economy) is shown in Figure 6. Panel A reflects the effects of monetary changes on nominal income and Panel B translates these changes into effects on real output.

If the money supply is initially \$2 trillion (M_{s0}), nominal income in Panel A will be \$4 trillion (point a). Note that $M\bar{V} = P\bar{Q}$, and thus $M = \bar{k}P\bar{Q}_f$ where $\bar{k} = 1/\bar{V}$. This figure initially assumes that $\bar{V} = 2$ and, thus, $\bar{k} = 0.5$. This \$4-trillion nominal income ($Y = P_0\bar{Q}_f$) is equal in Panel B to 4 trillion units of real output (point a) at an average price level P_0 of 100 ($M\bar{V} = P\bar{Q}_f \rightarrow 2 \times 2 = 1 \times 4$). Money supply growth to \$3 trillion (M_{s1}) boosts nominal income to \$6 trillion (point b in Panel A). Output is fixed at full employment ($\bar{Q}_f$) and velocity is constant at 2, so introducing this extra money into the economy pushes the price level to 150 (point b in Panel B where $M\bar{V} = P\bar{Q}_f \rightarrow 3 \times 2 = 1.5 \times 4$). Thus, in a classical world, monetary policy will have only price effects, not quantity effects.

Summary: The Crude Quantity Theory of Money

Summarizing the foundations of the early *crude quantity theory of money,* we know that the equation of exchange is a truism because of the way velocity is computed: $MV \equiv PQ$. It follows that:

$$\frac{\Delta M}{M} + \frac{\Delta V}{V} = \frac{\Delta P}{P} + \frac{\Delta Q}{Q}.$$

If velocity is assumed constant (written $\bar{V}$) and real output is fixed at a full employment level (written $\bar{Q}_f$), then $\Delta V/V = 0$, and $\Delta Q/Q = 0$. Moreover, $\Delta M/M = \Delta P/P$: Any changes in the money supply will be reflected in proportional changes in the price level. This is the major result of the crude quantity theory of money:

$$M\bar{V} = P\bar{Q}_f.$$

Another conclusion is that real output (or any other "real" economic behavior) is unaffected in the long run by either the money supply or the price level. These early versions of the quantity theory of money are clearly misnamed—they should be called *monetary theories of the price level.*

Classical theorists concluded by saying "Money is a veil." By this they meant that money, inflation, or deflation may temporarily disguise the real world, but in the long run, money affects only the price level, with virtually no effect on such real variables as production, employment, labor force participation, unemployment, or relative prices. Even though classical theorists vehemently opposed large expansions

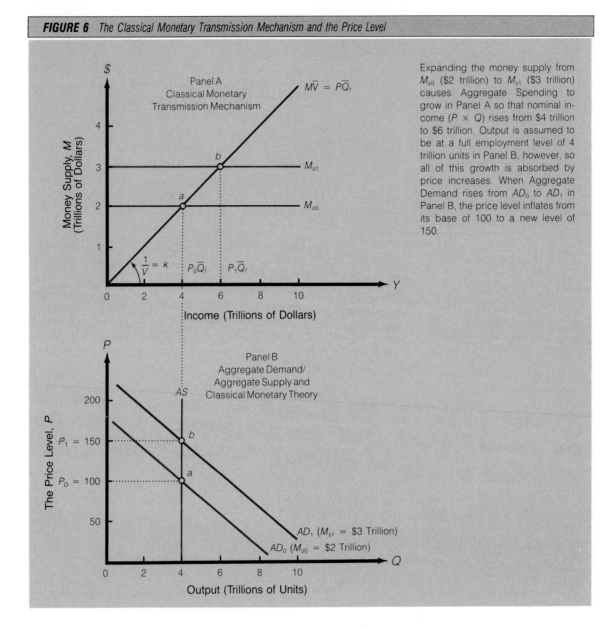

Expanding the money supply from M_{s0} ($2 trillion) to M_{s1} ($3 trillion) causes Aggregate Spending to grow in Panel A so that nominal income ($P \times Q$) rises from $4 trillion to $6 trillion. Output is assumed to be at a full employment level of 4 trillion units in Panel B, however, so all of this growth is absorbed by price increases. When Aggregate Demand rises from AD_0 to AD_1 in Panel B, the price level inflates from its base of 100 to a new level of 150.

of the money supply because of fear that inflation temporarily distorts behavior, it is probably fair to say that classical monetary theory leads to the conclusion that in the long run, "money does not matter." It does not affect production, consumption, investment, or any other "real" economic behavior. When we deal graphically with the demand and supply of money in later sections, we will resurrect some of these classical propositions to see what they contribute to modern monetary theory.

Keynesian Monetary Theory _____

The brunt of Keynes's attack on the classical quantity theory of money was directed at its conclusions that (*a*) velocity is a constant, and (*b*) full employment is the natural state of a market economy.

Early classical economists believed that money balances are held only for transactions purposes and that the transactions anyone engages in are roughly proportional to that individual's nominal income. Thus, planned money balances were assumed roughly proportional to nominal income. "Why," they asked, "would people want to hold money unless they intend to spend it? Virtually any other asset yields a positive rate of return—and money holdings do not. No one holds more money than they need for transactions. They hold income-earning assets instead of money whenever possible." Keynes responded by adding the precautionary and asset (speculative) motives to the transactions motive for holding money.

Remember that people adjust their money balances until what they demand equals what they have. If you have more money than you demand, you spend or invest more, reducing your money balances. If you demand more money than you presently hold, you acquire more by cutting back on your spending out of income, liquidating some of your assets, or selling more of your time. Keynes emphasized financial investments (stocks or bonds) as the major way to reduce one's money holdings.

The Asset Demand for Money

One major difference between the classical model and Keynes's model is that classical economists view the world as a reasonably certain place, while Keynesian reasoning emphasizes uncertainty and describes how our expectations about uncertain futures might affect the economy. Rising uncertainty is a major reason for growth of the asset demand for money.

Suppose you are working on an assembly line when the economy nose-dives. Many of your co-workers are laid off. You would probably start saving more because you could be the next one to find a "pink slip" in your pay envelope. As your savings mount, assets in the form of money balances grow. What happens to the velocity of money? *Velocity falls as saving increases.* Why not invest these funds in a stock or bond that pays interest or some positive rate of return? You must be kidding! The economy is in a tailspin—a depression may be approaching rapidly. The crucial point here is that when people expect hard times, the velocity of money falls when people convert money from transactions balances to precautionary or asset balances. Conversely, money balances are increasingly held for transactions purposes

when prosperity seems just around the corner. This causes velocity to rise.

Let us see what all this means within the context of the equation of exchange. Since the percentage changes in the money supply plus velocity are equal to the percentage changes in the price level plus the real level of output, a 5 percent decline in velocity (money supply assumed constant) will cause nominal GNP to fall by 5 percent. If prices do not fall fairly rapidly, output and employment will decline by about 5 percent. (One of the rules of economics is that *if circumstances change and prices do not adjust, quantities will.*) The economy may settle in equilibrium at less than full employment.

Keynes and his followers assumed that prices adjust slowly, especially on the down side, and that people's expectations are volatile. This implies that the velocity of money may vary considerably over time and that the real economy may adjust only slowly, if at all, to these variations.

The Liquidity Trap

Classical economists viewed the interest rate as an incentive for saving—you are rewarded for postponing consumption. Keynes's rebuttal was that interest is a reward for sacrificing liquidity. According to Keynes, how much you save is determined by your income and will be affected very little by interest rates. Interest rates are important, however, in deciding the form your saving takes. You will hold money unless offered some incentive to hold a less liquid asset. Interest is such an inducement. Higher interest rates will induce you to relinquish money and hold more illiquid assets.

Keynes believed that very high interest rates cause people to hold little, if any, money in asset balances—the demand for money consists almost exclusively of transactions and precautionary balances. But low interest rates result in large asset balances of money. Just as we horizontally sum individual demands for goods to arrive at market demands, we can sum the transactions, precautionary, and asset demands for money to obtain the total demand for money. This demand curve for money is shown in Figure 7.

Note that at a very low interest rate, the demand for money becomes flat. This part of the demand curve for money is called the liquidity trap.

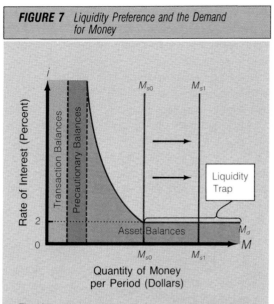

FIGURE 7 Liquidity Preference and the Demand for Money

The Keynesian total demand for money is the horizontal summation of transactions, precautionary, and asset demands for money. At very low interest rates, Keynesian theory predicts a *liquidity trap,* in which increases in the supply of money result in no spending and no declines in interest rates. In a liquidity trap, extra money is simply absorbed through hoarding into idle cash balances.

A **liquidity trap** *occurs if people will absorb any extra money into idle balances because they are extremely pessimistic or risk averse, view transaction costs as prohibitive, or expect the prices of nonmonetary assets to fall in the near future.*

It implies that if the money supply grew (say, from M_{s0} to M_{s1}), any extra money you received would not be spent, but hoarded; that is, absorbed into idle cash balances. Monetary growth would increase Aggregate Spending very little, if at all. Expectations about economic conditions might become so pessimistic that people would hoard every cent they could "for a rainy day," an instance of the liquidity trap. Alternatively, historically low interest rates might persuade nearly everyone that interest rates will soon rise. You would not want to hold bonds because rising interest rates would reduce bond prices and you would suffer a capital loss—you and many other investors would hold money while waiting for interest rates to rise and bond prices to fall.

Even though Keynes was writing during the Depression, he suggested that no economy had ever been in a perfect liquidity trap. At the trough of the Great Depression, however, the interest rate hovered around 1.5 percent and we may have been in a "near"-liquidity trap. Severe depressions may cause near-liquidity traps because (*a*) banks pile up huge excess reserves when nominal interest rates are very low because the returns from lending are small; (*b*) bankers fear that all loans are very risky, even those that normally would pose no problem of repayment; and (*c*) private individuals hoard their own funds, fearing that neither their job prospects nor investment opportunities are very bright.

Keynes rejected classical theory in his thinking about the demand for money, broadening the earlier perspective to consider precautionary and asset demands for money. Keynes thought that interest rates are determined solely by the demand and supply of money. His classical predecessors viewed interest rates as being determined in the market for capital goods. Thus, Keynesian and classical economists differ sharply in their perceptions of investment.

The Keynesian View of Investment

The capital stock consists of all improvements that make natural resources more productive than they are in their raw states—equipment, buildings, inventories, and so forth. Economic investment is the growth of the capital stock during a period. Classical and Keynesian theories differ about how variations in the money supply affect investment. Over a business cycle, investment fluctuates proportionally more than either consumption or government purchases. Inventory accumulation is especially unstable.

Keynes and his followers focused on investors' volatile moods: optimism and expectations of large returns generate high levels of investment, while pessimism stifles investment. Both Keynesian and classical writers agree that greater investment eventually leads to lower rates of return.

Keynesian analysis takes the position that the interest rate, which is the major opportunity cost of investment, is only one aspect of investment planning and is not the overwhelming influence posited by classical economists. This perspective emphasizes changes in investors' expectations about future economic conditions as far more important in explaining changes in investment. Figure 8 shows why.

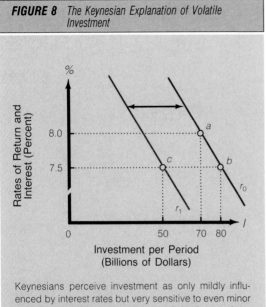

FIGURE 8 The Keynesian Explanation of Volatile Investment

Keynesians perceive investment as only mildly influenced by interest rates but very sensitive to even minor changes in business perceptions of the future of the economy. Pessimism causes investment to plummet, while optimism causes sudden, and perhaps unsustainable, surges in investment.

Suppose that the initial investment curve is r_0 and that equilibrium investment is $70 billion (point a) at an 8 percent interest rate. Note that the rate of return curves are relatively steep in this Keynesian view of the world. A drop in interest to 7.5 percent moves the equilibrium from point a to point b, causing investment to grow only slightly, from $70 billion to $80 billion.

Now suppose that investors become skeptical about future economic conditions so that the expected rate of return schedule shifts leftward from r_0 to r_1. Equilibrium shifts from point b to point c, and investment falls sharply to $50 billion. If investors' herdlike mentality (Keynes described them as possessed of "animal spirits") then caused them to begin bubbling with optimism, the schedule shifts rightward, moving equilibrium from c back to b, so that investment rises back to $80 billion. Keynesians argue that investment is not very responsive to small changes in interest rates but that investment demand responds strongly to changing expectations.

Summarizing, both Keynesian and classical economists agree that equilibrium investment requires the expected rate of return on investment to equal the rate of interest. Keynesians, however, attribute cyclical swings of investment to changes in investors' expectations of future returns. They believe that investment is as influenced by changes in interest rates as it is by the unpredictable expectations of investors. Classical economists perceive investors' expectations about returns as quite stable and explain large variations in investment as responses to small changes in interest rates.

The Keynesian Monetary Transmission Mechanism

The demand and supply of money determine the nominal rate of interest in financial markets, as shown in Panel A of Figure 9. Keynesian theory suggests that during recessions, changes in the interest rate (Panel A) may cause small changes in the level of investment (Panel B) and thus, in national income (Panel C). The demand for money, however, is thought to be fairly sensitive with respect to the interest rate, especially during economic downturns. Hence, interest rates may not decrease (*increase*) very much as the money supply is increased (*decreased*.) Even if expansionary monetary policies do reduce interest rates a bit, Keynesians believe that investment is relatively insensitive to the interest rate, and so income is hardly affected by monetary policies.

Keynesians argue that changes in the money supply do not affect consumer spending directly, but only indirectly through the

money → interest rate → investment → income

sequence. Even then, the effects of monetary policy are thought to be slight and erratic because the linkages are perceived to be weak. This view of the chain of events emanating from a change in the money supply is called the **Keynesian monetary transmission mechanism.** If the money supply is increased from $400 billion to $500 billion (a 20 percent increase) in Panel A of Figure 9, the interest rate falls from 8 percent to 7 percent and investment grows slightly from $100 billion to $110 billion (a 10 percent increase). Total output grows via the multiplier effect from $2 trillion to $2.02 trillion (only a 1 percent increase). This suggests that monetary policy will be weak compared to fiscal policy. Note that the Keynesian view assumes that the economy is slack, and so the adjustment to monetary expansion is purely a quantity change; the price level is unaffected.

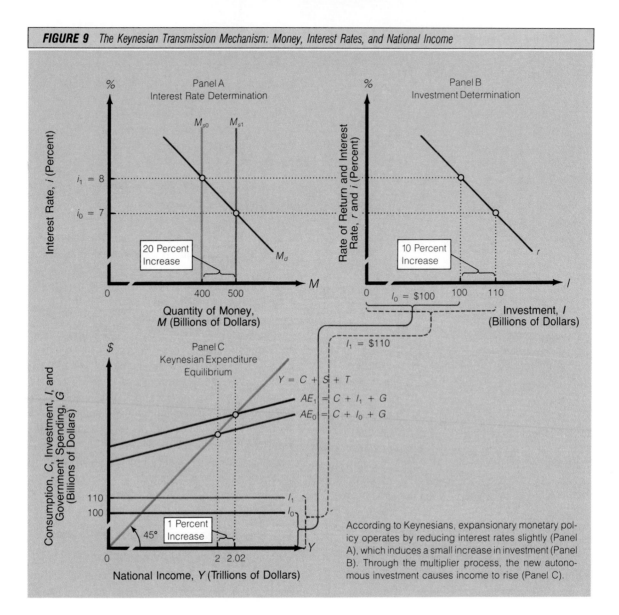

FIGURE 9 *The Keynesian Transmission Mechanism: Money, Interest Rates, and National Income*

According to Keynesians, expansionary monetary policy operates by reducing interest rates slightly (Panel A), which induces a small increase in investment (Panel B). Through the multiplier process, the new autonomous investment causes income to rise (Panel C).

Keynesian Analyses of Depressions and Inflations

The differences between classical and Keynesian predictions are the greatest during depressions. Classical economists and modern supply-siders generally advocate laissez-faire policies because they believe that the natural long-run state of the economy is full employment equilibrium. If pressed, however, classical economists would assert that expansionary monetary policies increase Aggregate Spending enough to rapidly boost the economy out of any depression if it had lasted a bit too long. Classical reasoning also suggests that restrictive monetary policies are the only lasting cure for inflation.

Most Keynesians agree that monetary restraint dampens inflationary pressures, but they disagree with the notion that monetary expansion will cure a depression. During a depression people are generally pessimistic and interest rates tend to plummet.

Consequently, Keynesians suggest that expansionary monetary policies will not bring the economy out of a recession because any extra money people receive is seldom spent but is hoarded. This is another way of saying that the velocity of money falls to offset monetary growth. Keynesians compare money to a string—you can pull on it to restrain inflation, but trying to push the economy out of the doldrums through expansionary monetary policy is like "pushing on a string." Expansionary monetary policy is viewed as stringlike both because banks may not lend out their reserves if their view of the economic horizon is pessimistic and because people may simply hoard rather than spend most of any extra money that comes their way.

Early Keynesians recommended massive government spending and tax cuts to cure recessions. They emphasized fiscal policy because of a widespread (though mistaken) belief that central banks throughout the world attempted to push their respective nations out of the Depression with expansionary monetary policies. Only long after the Depression did researchers discover that although the U.S. monetary base rose slightly between 1929 and 1933, the money multiplier shrank and the money supply fell sharply. Remember that good information is costly; the economic data of the time were awful.

Modern Monetarism

The Keynesian Revolution soon stirred a counterrevolution by **modern monetarists,** who recognize some holes in classical theory but reject any need for massive government intervention to stabilize an economy. Their counterattack, led by Milton Friedman, began with a reformulation of the demand for money. (See his Biography.)

The Demand for Money Revisited

Modern monetarists concede that money might be demanded for reasons other than anticipated transactions, but they see no reason to compartmentalize the demand for money as Keynesians have. Instead, they have identified certain variables that influence the amounts of money demanded. Milton Friedman has arrived at the most widely accepted formulation of the *new quantity theory of money.* Fried-

man distinguishes the nominal money people hold from their "real" money holdings. *Real money* is the purchasing power of the money a person holds. It can be computed by dividing the face values of money assets by the price level (M/P). As the price level rises, the face amount of money needed to buy a particular bundle of goods rises proportionally.

Variables Positively Related to Money Demand

According to Friedman, the variables (besides the price level) that will be *positively* related to the quantity of money demanded are (*a*) people's total real wealth (including the value of their labor), (*b*) the interest rate, if any, paid on money holdings, and (*c*) the illiquidity of nonmonetary assets.

Wealth (or Permanent Income)   Classical economists (and Keynesians, to a lesser extent) relate the demand for money to current income. Friedman suggests that expected lifetime income better explains both a person's patterns of consumption and money holdings. Take two twenty-five-year-olds—one, a recent college graduate in accounting and the other, a manager of a convenience store. Each has a current annual income of $23,000. The consumption level of the young accountant is likely to be higher than that of the convenience store manager because of a greater possibility of borrowing money; thus, the accountant will hold more money for transactions purposes.

The Interest Rate on Money   You do not receive interest on cash you hold and only relatively low interest on your demand deposits. Banks do, however, offer free checking accounts and other incentives for depositors who keep certain minimum balances in their accounts. Most people would probably maintain higher checking account balances if the interest rates paid to depositors were increased.

The Illiquidity of Nonmonetary Assets   Most college students are not poor, they are just broke. That is, they have highly marketable skills. Another way of saying this is that they have substantial wealth in the form of human capital but not many other assets. According to Friedman, if most of your assets are very illiquid, you will want higher money holdings than

BIOGRAPHY

Milton Friedman 1912–

ilton Friedman is among the most publicly visible of modern economists. He has won respect of both his followers and those economists who disagree strongly with his views. Few significant honors in economics have not come Friedman's way. He was president of the American Economic Association in 1967 and in 1976 received the Nobel prize in economics. Looking very much like everyone's "favorite uncle," Friedman often disarms his adversaries with a wink and a gentle smile, but those who have argued with him find him a formidable debater. He is able to express complicated ideas in simple terms understandable by those untrained in formal economic theory. This makes him popular with the media and keeps Friedman in touch with a wide audience.

Friedman has been a vital force in attacking the orthodoxy of the "new" (Keynesian) economics. He has done this in a way that combines his argumentative talents with solid, empirical research and a desire not merely to tear down existing economic theory but to restructure it. Friedman's most notable research has involved monetary theory, but, as with all master economists, his thoughts have touched many areas of economics. In the monetary field, Friedman has reconstructed the quantity theory of money, reemphasized the importance and significance of monetary policy, questioned the Keynesian interpretation of the Great Depression, and developed his own prescriptions for preventing future economic catastrophe.

Friedman has also made major contributions in such areas as risk and insurance (answering why people simultaneously gamble and buy insurance) and has developed a theory of consumption based on wealth, as opposed to the Keynesian view that consumption depends only on current income.

Along the way, he has attempted to restate the classical liberal philosophy of Adam Smith in terms pertinent to the modern era. (Friedman's admiration of Adam Smith is virtually unbounded—he has a necktie patterned with cameos of Smith that he wears during public appearances.) Friedman has offered many ideas about replacing the influence of government with market solutions. For example, he argues that government could eliminate public schools and give the parents of students vouchers (grants) so that all children could attend private schools tailored to their individual needs. He also argues that cash grants to poor people make more sense because these grants would leave more choices in the hands of the poor as well as require fewer tax dollars.

Friedman's restatement of the quantity theory of money is important because it made the theory statistically testable, something the old theory was not. His restatement is essentially a theory of the demand for money, whereas the original version was a theory of the price level. Friedman's analyses of the statistical evidence indicate that the demand for money is stable over the long run and conclude that large changes in the supply of money cause undesirable fluctuations in employment and in the price level. His disenchantment with fiscal policy is due in large measure to the fact that government deficits are most often financed by inflationary expansions of the supply of money and credit. Finally, Friedman has been critical of the performance of the Board of Governors of the Federal Reserve System because he sees the FED as either following the wrong policy (trying to control interest rates instead of the money supply) or yielding to political pressure rather than sound economic logic.

will people who have similar amounts of wealth but whose major assets are more liquid. His reasoning is that some liquidity is desired to meet emergencies, and people with large amounts of human capital may not be able to liquidate their major assets (themselves) very easily. Selling yourself into bondage or slavery is illegal, and marketing your skills takes time. Consequently, Friedman expects that you will probably hold more cash than similarly "wealthy" people who are not in college. (Our memory is that when we were students, we were flat broke most of the time).

Variables Negatively Related to Money Demand

Friedman also identifies some variables that should be *negatively* related to the real (purchasing power) amounts of money people will hold (*a*) the interest rate on bonds, (*b*) the rate of return on physical capital, and (*c*) the expected rate of inflation.

Interest Rates on Bonds and Rates of Return on Investment

The major alternatives to holding money are spending it on consumer goods *or* buying stocks, bonds, or capital goods. While modern monetarists emphasize the value of consumption as the alternative cost of holding money ($1/P$), they also recognize either direct investment or purchases of stocks or bonds as possibilities. If such activities are your best alternatives to holding money, then the prices you pay for holding money are the interest (i) that could be received from a bond or the rate of return (r) you might expect from buying stocks or investing directly in physical capital.

Friedman accepts a negative relationship between the interest rate or rate of return on capital and the quantity of money demanded, but his studies conclude that the demand for money is relatively insensitive to the interest rate. He absolutely rejects any hint that a liquidity trap has ever existed.

Expected Rates of Inflation

You may have heard that to "get rich," you should "buy low and sell high." This advice implies that if you expect inflation, then you should get rid of your money while it has a high value and buy durable assets instead. During inflation, money becomes a hot potato because expectations of inflation cause people to reduce their money holdings. The greater the expected inflation, the more rapid the velocity of money.

The Stability of the Demand for Money

While modern monetarists are willing to accept the idea that the demand for money is influenced by variables other than income, they contend that these are very stable relationships. Moreover, they believe that most influences on the demand for money are relatively constant because they are the outcomes of an inherently stable market system. Table 1 summarizes these influences on the demand for money. Monetarists believe that the bulk of any instability in a market economy arises because of erratic government policy —the Federal Reserve System is the main villain in their scenario. Before investigating why the FED is perceived as the culprit, we need to examine the modern monetarist monetary transmission mechanism.

The Modern Monetarist Monetary Transmission Mechanism

Modern monetarists, like their classical predecessors, believe that the linkage between the money supply and national income is strong and direct. Monetarists think that the demand for money is stable, so an expansion in the money supply is viewed as putting more money in the hands of both consumers and investors who will quickly spend these surpluses.

Classical economics stresses Aggregate Supply, viewing Aggregate Demand as adjusting quickly and automatically when supply conditions change. (Sup-

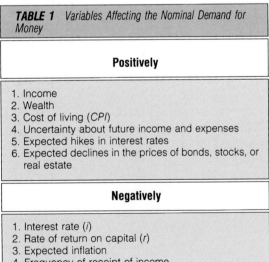

TABLE 1 *Variables Affecting the Nominal Demand for Money*

Positively
1. Income
2. Wealth
3. Cost of living (*CPI*)
4. Uncertainty about future income and expenses
5. Expected hikes in interest rates
6. Expected declines in the prices of bonds, stocks, or real estate

Negatively
1. Interest rate (*i*)
2. Rate of return on capital (*r*)
3. Expected inflation
4. Frequency of receipt of income

ply creates its own demand). Recognizing the importance of Aggregate Demand in the short run because the economy may falter occasionally, most monetarists believe that money supply growth can boost spending and drive a slumping economy toward full employment.

Much like classical theorists, modern monetarists perceive the market system as inherently stable and think that the economy will seldom deviate for long from full employment. Modern monetarists consequently predict that, in the long run, growth in the money supply will be translated strictly into higher prices, even if monetary expansion occurs during a recession. Expansionary macroeconomic policies will, however, induce greater output quicker in the midst of a recession. In other words, the Aggregate Supply curve described by Keynesians may accurately represent a recessionary economy, but only in the very short run. This view of the world is portrayed in Figure 10.

Suppose the money supply is initially at $400 billion and the price level is 100. The economy is temporarily producing at point *a*, which is half a trillion units of real GNP below capacity, because full employment income is 4 trillion units. If the money supply and Aggregate Demand were held constant, then prices and wages would eventually fall so that a long-run equilibrium at point *b* would be achieved. Full employment would be realized when the price level fell to 80. If the money supply were expanded to $500 billion, Aggregate Demand would grow and full employment output of 4 trillion units would be realized more rapidly (point *c*). The price level is higher in this long-run equilibrium, being maintained at 100.

Most modern monetarists oppose active monetary policy to combat recessions. They view long-run adjustments as fairly rapid, believing instead that deflation will quickly restore an economy to full employment. An even greater concern is their fear that discretionary monetary policy might "overshoot," causing recession to move into inflation. This is shown in Figure 10 by too rapid growth of Aggregate Demand when the money supply is increased to $600 billion. In this case, the consequence of policy to combat recession is a 20 percent increase in the price level (point *d*). According to this monetarist line of thinking, overly aggressive monetary expansion can eliminate recession and unemployment more quickly than "do-nothing" policies, but only at the risk of sparking inflation.

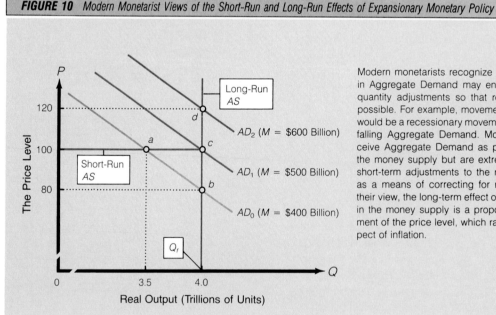

FIGURE 10 Modern Monetarist Views of the Short-Run and Long-Run Effects of Expansionary Monetary Policy

Modern monetarists recognize that variations in Aggregate Demand may entail short-term quantity adjustments so that recessions are possible. For example, movement from *c* to *a* would be a recessionary movement caused by falling Aggregate Demand. Monetarists perceive Aggregate Demand as proportional to the money supply but are extremely leery of short-term adjustments to the money supply as a means of correcting for recessions. In their view, the long-term effect of any increase in the money supply is a proportional movement of the price level, which raises the prospect of inflation.

Summary: Keynesian Versus Modern Monetary Theory

The monetary theories of classical economists, Keynesians, and modern monetarists are outlined in Table 2. The major differences in these schools of thought are found in (*a*) the nature of the demand for money, (*b*) the nature of the investment relationship, (*c*) the monetary transmission mechanism, and (*d*) assumptions about the velocity of money.

Assumptions about the creation of money and, thus, the effectiveness of monetary policy are crucial differences between Keynesians and monetarists. Most monetarist models ignore the institutional mechanisms used to create money (for example, that the FED might buy government bonds from banks, thereby increasing excess reserves that are multiplied into new loan-based demand deposits). Re-

member, however, that the FED directly controls the monetary base, not the money supply. Monetarists often simply assume that increases in the money supply become money in the hand of the consuming/investing public. A common monetarist analogy is that a helicopter dumps money into the economy. They then argue, not unreasonably, that if sufficient new money is given to the public, people will feel wealthier, quit worrying about "bad times," and spend it. This part of the monetarist scenario dispenses with theoretical difficulties like liquidity traps.

Modern Keynesians describe not only consumer/investor liquidity traps, but bank liquidity traps as well. Here is their story. Suppose that an economic downturn is under way and interest rates have plummeted. The FED buys government bonds from banks to counteract the recession. Will the banks' new excess reserves be translated into borrowing, in-

TABLE 2 *Summary of the Important Differences Between Classical, Keynesian, and Modern Monetarist Monetary Theories*

	Classical	Keynesian	Modern Monetarist
Demand for money	For transaction purposes only	Money demanded for: Transactions Precautionary purposes Asset purposes Speculative Risk aversion Transaction costs	Money demand is *stable*, but influenced by: Wealth (or permanent income) Interest rates Liquidity of other assets Expected rate of inflation
Money and investment	Investment is very sensitive to the interest rate	Investment is related to interest rate but is insensitive; related primarily to business expectations	Investment is very sensitive to the interest rate
Monetary transmission mechanism	Direct: $MV \equiv PQ$ $$\dfrac{\Delta M}{M} = \dfrac{\Delta P}{P}$$ Velocity (V) is constant; output (Q) is fixed at full employment	Indirect: ΔM (money) $\rightarrow \Delta i$ (interest rates) $\rightarrow \Delta I$ (investment) $\rightarrow \Delta AE$ (expenditures) $\rightarrow \Delta Y$ (income) $\rightarrow \Delta Q$ (output) Money is transmitted through interest rates to investment to Aggregate Spending to income and output	Direct: $\Delta M \rightarrow \Delta C$ or $\rightarrow \Delta I$ $\rightarrow \Delta Y$ $\rightarrow \Delta P$ or ΔQ Money is transmitted directly through changing real balances that result directly in altering spending or investment; these changes then cause changes in income, output, or the price level
Velocity	Constant	Volatile	Relatively stable

creased demand deposits, and then spending? (This is necessary for the monetarist transmission mechanism to work). Keynesians think not.

If you were a banker and the economy was depressed, would you want to reduce already low interest rates in order to attract new borrowers, many of whom look like deadbeats? Would the small declines in interest that are feasible be sufficiently attractive to prudent borrowers to induce them to apply for new loans? Keynesians answer NO to both questions. They suggest that the banks will simply accumulate more and more vault cash if the FED tries to counter recessionary tendencies through open-market operations. This is just another aspect of the argument that money (and monetary policy) is a string that is useless for pushing the economy out of the doldrums.

The Relative Potency of Monetary and Fiscal Policies

Classical economics and supply-side approaches lead to the conclusion that Aggregate Demand matters little, if at all, in the long run. Keynesians and monetarists alike, however, focus on Aggregate Demand. Modern monetarists and contemporary Keynesians clearly have different views on some things, but this should not cloud their common areas of agreement. Their differences lie in different views of how important monetary policy is relative to fiscal policy, and not that one alone matters to the total exclusion of the other.

FIGURE 11   *Monetary Versus Fiscal Policy: The Keynesian View*

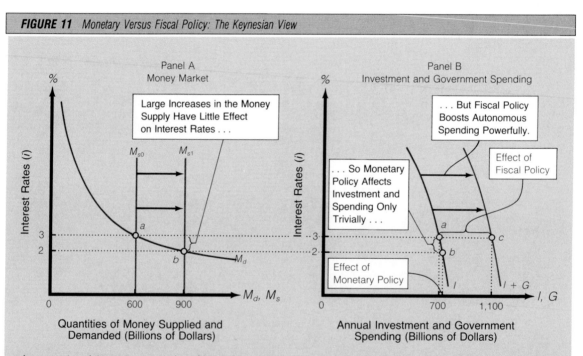

An expansion of the money supply from $600 to $900 billion reduces interest rates by only 1 percent in a Keynesian slump (Panel A). This small decline in interest rates only raises investment by $50 billion in Panel B because investment is insensitive to interest rates in the Keynesian view. Fiscal policy, on the other hand, is very effective in a Keynesian slump because it is, dollar for dollar, just as powerful as new investment in inducing further income through the multiplier process. New government spending of $400 billion ($c - a$) in Panel B expands autonomous spending far more powerfully than did the 50 percent monetary growth depicted in Panel A.

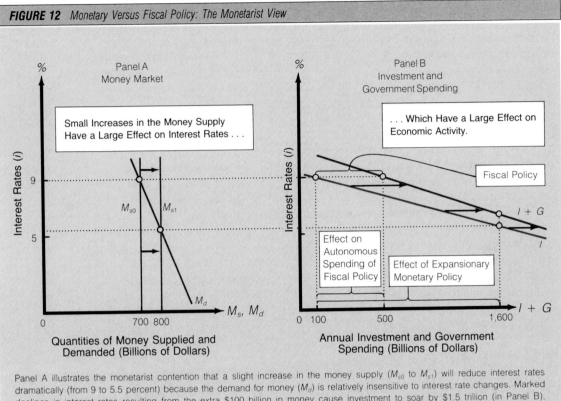

FIGURE 12 Monetary Versus Fiscal Policy: The Monetarist View

Panel A illustrates the monetarist contention that a slight increase in the money supply (M_{s0} to M_{s1}) will reduce interest rates dramatically (from 9 to 5.5 percent) because the demand for money (M_d) is relatively insensitive to interest rate changes. Marked declines in interest rates resulting from the extra $100 billion in money cause investment to soar by $1.5 trillion (in Panel B), stimulating autonomous spending far more than even a massive dose ($400 billion) of new government spending.

The Ineffectiveness Argument

Keynesians and monetarists agree that money matters, but differ as to *how much* it matters. Keynesians argue that monetary growth will not raise spending or cut interest rates very much in a slump. Figure 11 shows why. Keynesians view investment as relatively insensitive to interest rates, depending instead primarily upon business expectations. This suggests that slight drops in interest rates when the money supply grows (Panel A) will affect investment and output very little (Panel B). Fiscal policy, on the other hand, is extremely powerful in a slump. Adding government purchases to investment in Panel B boosts autonomous spending and, via the multiplier, massively raises national production and income.

Monetarists see the demand for money as relatively insensitive to interest rates but perceive investment

as highly dependent on interest. Even a small increase in the money supply drives interest rates down sharply in the monetarist view (Panel A in Figure 12), which in turn strongly stimulates investment (Panel B). Monetarists also see expansionary monetary policy as bolstering consumer spending, both because extra money "burns holes" in people's pockets and because lower interest rates make buying on credit easier and cheaper. Thus, modern monetarists view money as a powerful tool.

Fiscal policy has only a negligible effect, according to monetarist reasoning, because new government spending does not raise injections ($I+G$) nearly as much as does even a small decline in interest rates. Moreover, monetarists object that government spending may "crowd out" investment. Careful study of Figures 11 and 12 will enable you to understand the fundamental reasons why Keynesians advocate fiscal policy to regulate Aggregate Spending, while monetarists prefer monetary policy.

Keynesians and modern monetarists agree that when an economy is at full employment, growth of Aggregate Demand results in a rising price level. When an economy is in a severe slump, both would agree that increases in Aggregate Demand will restore full employment. They would, however, disagree on the appropriate way to expand Aggregate Demand. Monetarists favor expansionary monetary policy to increase private consumption and investment, while Keynesians view that approach as ineffective because of widespread pessimism on the parts of workers, consumers, and business firms. Keynesians, therefore, favor expansionary fiscal policy.

We have examined the theoretical arguments that explain why Keynesians prefer fiscal policy and why monetarists prefer monetary policy to stabilize the economy. Just how convincing are these positions when applied to the art of policymaking? And how frequently should policy be changed?

Rules Versus Discretionary Policies

Most modern monetarists believe that designing discretionary monetary and fiscal policies to buffer business cycles is an impossible task. They favor doing away with all discretion in policymaking and adopting stable and permanent monetary and fiscal rules. These critics believe that the market system is inherently stable and that severe swings in business activity inevitably follow ill-advised discretionary policies. One mechanism to eliminate discretion in monetary policymaking is a monetary growth rule.

> A **monetary growth rule** *would dictate that the money supply be increased at a rate compatible with historical growth of GNP, say 3 percent annually.*

Suppose you are driving a high-powered car on a fairly straight highway that is banked slightly along the edges to keep you on the road. Someone has blackened the front and side windows—you cannot see where you are or what lies ahead. To make matters worse, your gas pedal sticks at times, the steering wheel is loose, and your brakes alternate between mush and grabbing sharply. You can vaguely see where you have been through a fogged-over rearview mirror. What is your best strategy?

If you press the gas pedal too hard, you may go so fast that the curbs at the edge of the road will fail to keep you on course. If you try to steer, you may guide yourself over the side. Your best strategy will be to carefully adjust the accelerator to maintain a slow but steady speed and let the car steer itself away from the road's edges.

The economists who blame cyclical swings on erratic monetary or fiscal policies perceive macroeconomic policymakers as being in our economy's "driver's seat." Attempts to fine-tune the economy through discretionary policies are viewed as the fumblings of people who barely deserve learners' permits playing with the controls of an Indianapolis 500 racer. They tend to oversteer and to jump back and forth from the accelerator to the brake. The resulting stop-and-go economic pattern might resemble your path when you were learning to drive—and, unlike policymakers, you knew what you were passing and could see what lay ahead. We also hope that the steering, braking, and acceleration of the car you drove responded more precisely than the cumbersome tools available to monetary and fiscal policymakers.

In addition to a monetary growth rule, most economists opposed to discretion in policymaking advocate certain fiscal rules:

1. Government spending should be set at the amounts of government goods and services that the public would demand if the economy were at full employment; no "make work" projects should be permitted.
2. Tax rates should then be structured so that the federal budget would be roughly in balance if the economy were at full employment.

Although monetarists perceive some problems emerging from improper spending and tax policies (e.g., Hoover's tax hike in 1930–1932, Johnson's simultaneous wars on poverty and in Vietnam, and the enormous budget deficits of the Reagan years), they cast central bankers (the FED) as the major villains in their explanations of cyclical chaos in market economies.

The Culpability of the FED

Modern monetarists view the market system as largely self-stabilizing and predictable; they perceive erratic government policies as the leading cause of business cycles. Monetarists believe that rapid inflation is explained by excessive monetary growth, which results in "too much money chasing too few goods." Alternatively, severe deflations, recessions, or depressions result when the money supply grows too slowly (or even falls), resulting in "too little money chasing too many goods." Government can prevent macroeconomic convulsions by simply holding the rate of growth of the money supply roughly in line with our (slow growing) capacity to produce.

Monetarists view income (or wealth) as the major determinant of the demand for money. Recall the equation of exchange: $MV \equiv PQ$. If the money supply (M) grows at the same rate as our ability to produce (Q), and if velocity (V) is constant, then the price level (P) will be stable. Given that

$$\frac{\Delta M}{M} + \frac{\Delta V}{V} = \frac{\Delta P}{P} + \frac{\Delta Q}{Q},$$

then, if $\Delta M/M = \Delta Q/Q$, and if $\Delta V/V = 0$, it follows that $\Delta P/P = 0$.

This sounds fairly easy. Why has government not learned these simple monetary facts of life and followed policies to achieve a stable price level and facilitate smooth economic growth? The monetarist answer to this question is that no one is able to predict precisely what will happen to our productive capacity in the near future. Moreover, instituting policies and having them take effect requires time. (We discuss time lag problems in chapter 18). Monetarists also believe that the FED tries too hard to control the economy. Finally, political considerations too often dominate sound policymaking. The solution, according to many monetarists, is to follow a rule of expanding the money supply at a fixed annual rate in the 2–4 percent range compatible with historical growth of our productive capacity.

The Failure of Discretionary Fine-Tuning

Many economists view the Great Depression and the Kennedy years as evidence that only Keynesian engineering can keep the economy stable. Discretionary changes in taxes and spending are the fiscal tools Keynesians recommend. Others argue that the FED can keep the economy on track by expanding or con-

tracting the money supply as needed. Fiscal and monetary policies both have been frequently changed to try to fine-tune the economy so that Aggregate Demand and Aggregate Supply are balanced.

Tax rates were cut and the money supply was expanded to stimulate a previously sluggish economy during the early 1960s. Then, monetary restraint was applied in 1966 to curb mounting inflationary pressures. A temporary tax surcharge was imposed in 1969. The money supply grew rapidly in the early 1970s, screeched to a halt causing a short collapse in 1975–1976, accelerated from 1977 to 1979, and then slowed sharply in the early 1980s. Cuts in tax rates from 1981 to 1983 were coupled with a monetary slowdown to yield mixed results.

Keynes believed that central banks tried to follow expansionary policies but failed to curve the Great Depression. That is, in part, why Keynes and his followers sought to replace passive monetary policy with aggressive discretionary fiscal policies. Milton Friedman and other monetarists question the widely held belief that the Great Depression occurred despite highly expansionary monetary policies. Collecting and reviewing monetary data for the United States for the past century, they discovered that the money supply fell considerably just before and during the Depression. Their interpretation is that the Federal Reserve System caused the Depression because (perhaps unwittingly) it followed contractionary policies.

In fact, most monetarists believe that the business cycle is largely a consequence of improper monetary policy—when the money supply grows too slowly, economic downturns and stagnation soon follow; when the money supply mushrooms, increases in the price level are inevitable. These difficulties are the major reasons for monetarists' advocacy of stable monetary growth rates. The crucial differences between fiscal and monetary policies, according to the theories of Keynesians, monetarists, and classically oriented supply-siders are summarized in Table 3.

We will look at various ways to finance government activity in the next chapter; monetary and fiscal policies are linked through the government budget equation. We will also examine the effects of the growth of government debt caused by persistent federal deficits. Then, in chapters 16–18, we will examine several macroeconomic issues from the perspectives of both Keynesians and modern monetarists.

TABLE 3 *Alternative Views of Monetary and Fiscal Policies*

Keynesians	Monetarists	Supply-Siders
1. Fiscal policy is very powerful.	1. Fiscal policy is relatively unimportant due to *crowding out.*	1. High tax rates and vast government spending both reduce the incentives for people to be productive.
2. Monetary policy is not very powerful or important during economic slumps.	2. Erratic monetary policy is the major cause of business cycles. Money is important at all times.	2. Erratic fiscal policy confuses investors and workers, reducing incentives for productivity. Erratic monetary policy diverts resources from production into hedges against inflation or deflation.
3. Monetary policy affects spending through changes in interest rates and investments.	3. Monetary policy affects spending in all markets simultaneously (MV = PQ).	3. Money is a veil.
4. Discretionary policies are necessary to offset the economy's inherent instability.	4. Smooth growth of the money supply is crucial. Rules should replace discretion in policy. Economy is inherently stable.	4. Steady monetary policy enhances the quality of information about economic decisions.
5. Velocity is erratic; it rises during inflation but falls sharply during recessions.	5. Velocity is relatively stable.	5. Velocity is stable if monetary policy is stable.
6. During deep depressions, fear causes velocity to plummet, resulting in *liquidity traps.*	6. Liquidity traps are highly implausible and have never actually occurred.	6. Liquidity traps are irrelevant to the real world.

CHAPTER REVIEW: KEY POINTS

1. You increase your *spending* when you have "too much" money; your rate of *saving* increases when you have "too little" money.

2. People hold money for predictable spending (*transactions demands*) with a cushion for uncertain outlays or income receipts (*precautionary demands*). People also have *asset demands* for money because (*a*) money is relatively riskless, (*b*) transaction costs associated with less liquid assets may exceed expected returns, or (*c*) people speculate by holding money when they expect the prices of alternative assets (e.g., stock, bonds, or real estate) to fall.

3. According to classical monetary theory, the sole rational motive for holding money is to consummate *transactions.*

4. Interest rates and bond prices are *inversely related.* Bond prices fall if interest rates rise, and vice versa.

5. The costs of holding nominal amounts of money are (*a*) *the reciprocal of the price level* (1/P) if the choice is between saving money or buying consumer goods; or (*b*) *the interest rate,* if money is viewed as an asset substitutable for some highly liquid income-generating asset, say a bond. *Inflation* also imposes costs on holdings of money.

6. The *income velocity* (V) of some money equals GNP (PQ) divided by the money supply (M).

7. The *equation of exchange,* a truism, is written MV=PQ. Therefore, the percentage change in the money supply plus the percentage change in velocity roughly equals the percentage change in the price level plus the percentage change in real output:

$$\frac{\Delta M}{M} + \frac{\Delta V}{V} = \frac{\Delta P}{P} + \frac{\Delta Q}{Q}.$$

8. Classical economics assumes that *velocity* (*V*) and *output* (*Q*) are reasonably constant and independent of the money supply (*M*) and the price level (*P*). Classical economists believe that changes in the money supply result in proportional changes in the price level and expressed this belief in early versions of the *quantity theory of money*. The quantity theory of money is more accurately a *monetary theory of the price level*.

9. Keynes's attack on the quantity theory disputes the assumptions that (*a*) the natural state of the economy is full employment, (*b*) the velocity of money is inherently stable, and (*c*) the only rational motive for holding money is for transactions purposes.

10. Modern monetarists perceive a direct link between the money supply and national income. Since the demand for money is relatively stable, growth of the money supply puts excess money balances in the hands of consumers and investors who, in turn, spend this surplus money on goods and services. Monetary growth may expand output in the short run, but modern monetarists conclude that in the long run, higher prices will result.

11. The difficulties confronting monetary and fiscal policymakers have caused many economists to favor putting the economy on "automatic pilot." The advocates of replacing *discretionary policy* with *monetary growth rules* would replace the Federal Open-Market Committee with a couple of reliable but unimaginative clerks. Their job would be to increase the money supply by a fixed small (3 percent?) increase annually, and the federal budget would be set to balance at full employment.

PROBLEMS

1. Suppose the money supply grows by 12 percent and real output grows by 3 percent, but the income velocity of money is constant. What happens to the price level?

2. If potential output grows 2 percent while velocity falls 3 percent, what rate of monetary growth should keep the price level stable?

3. If average prices are rising 20 percent annually while monetary growth is 12 percent in a stagnant economy, what is happening to velocity? Has anything like this occurred in the U.S. economy? When?

4. If both velocity and the price level fall 8 percent while real output drops a startling 15 percent, what must be happening to the money supply? Has anything like this ever happened in the U.S. economy? When?

QUESTIONS FOR THOUGHT AND DISCUSSION

1. According to monetarists, expanding the money supply inevitably causes higher prices. In what ways do Keynesians disagree and why?

2. Do you think most people want to balance illiquid assets against highly liquid assets, such as money? Why? How does your line of reasoning lead to the demand for money? Does your answer suggest that the demand for money will be sensitive to interest rates? To the cost of living? How, and why or why not?

3. Describe the differences between Keynesian and monetarist monetary transmission mechanisms. Why are these differences important? In what way does Keynesian fiscal policy short-circuit the difficulties they perceive in transforming new money into new spending?

4. If the economy took a tailspin into a depression, would you expect any (short-run) liquidity trap to emerge more from the banking sector or from the behavior of the nonbanking public?

5. According to Keynesians, interest is a reward for sacrificing liquidity. Classical and modern monetarists describe interest as a reward for postponing consumption or as a return on investment. Which of these explanations seem most plausible to you? Is either approach totally false?

6. As people expect more inflation, they may begin treating money as a "hot potato"; average money holdings may fall, with the result that velocity increases. On the other hand, increased inflation may generate more uncertainty, which may cause people to *increase* their money holdings. People who anticipate higher inflation and want to accumulate a given real amount of saving before retirement, but who are leery of most financial investments, may try to build their holdings of money. On average, do you think the inflation of the past twenty years has caused real money balances per capita to rise or fall? How would you test this hypothesis? To what extent can inflation be considered a tax on money balances?

7. Do you think the evidence better supports the Keynesian view that velocity is erratic or the monetarist position that velocity is stable? What economic forces are you aware of that may explain trends and fluctuations in velocity?

8. In late 1979, the Federal Reserve announced that it would focus its attention primarily on rates of monetary growth instead of interest rates. While this action has often been urged by monetarists, the monetarist camp received the announcement with less than full enthusiasm. Many monetarists would like the FED to concentrate on the monetary base, citing statistical studies that suggest a reasonably stable and predictable relationship between the base and GNP. The FED does not yet seem ready to adopt such a simple approach.

   What is necessary for the monetary base and money supply to be tightly linked? Is it possible for the FED to maintain money supply or monetary base growth rate goals in the face of political pressures if interest rates rise to levels that are perceived to be too high? Can both targets (money supply growth rates and reasonable interest rates) be controlled simultaneously? How? Numerous economists are skeptical because the FED has made similar announcements in the past, but policies did not change. What makes a monetary growth approach so hard for the FED to implement?

9. Keynesian theory suggests that the relevant substitutes for money are securities, while monetarists argue for a broader range of substitutes that include consumer and investment goods. How important is this difference in explaining the impact of money on economic activity? Why?

10. Suppose a rule of 3 percent annual monetary growth were imposed. How long should policy-makers doggedly follow such a policy if inflation soared to more than 20 percent or unemployment hovered around 15 percent?

11. Paul Volcker, then chair of the FED, testified before Congress in 1986 that NOW and other interest-bearing demand deposit accounts, disinflation, and falling interest rates have (at least in the short run) altered the basic relationship between the rate of change in $M1$ and inflation. Accordingly, given the greater uncertainty associated with the relationship between $M1$ and economic activity, the FED adopted a broader range for its $M1$ growth rate. Thus, if velocity continues to fall, $M1$ growth can be near the upper end of the target range and vice versa. Does Volcker's testimony of a wider $M1$ range confirm Milton Friedman's argument (made in Focus 2 of chapter 13) that the FED simply adjusts its target to cover its discretionary policymaking? What would be the effect on the economy of a fixed (3 percent) rule for $M1$ growth if velocity is falling?

CHAPTER 15

Financing Government: Deficits and Public Debt

Unemployment and inflation are macroeconomic problems with obvious relevance to our lives, but few Americans can identify ways that huge federal budget deficits and an enormous public debt affect them personally. Nevertheless, many people are upset because our federal budget has been awash in red ink. Budget deficits during the Reagan years exceeded those piled up by all presidents from George Washington through Jimmy Carter; national debt held by the public more than doubled, surpassing $2 trillion in 1988. But what do the terms "budget deficit" and "national debt" mean?

> The federal **budget deficit** *is the difference between federal government outlays and receipts (G − T) during a year.* **National (public) debt** *results from cumulated federal deficits.*

Critics of astronomical deficits and soaring debt often assert that any organization that spends more than its receipts is doomed and argue that government should be run "more like a business." Many politicians at least pay lip service to their message. When the Dow-Jones stock market average plunged over 500 points on October 19, 1987—all time records, both absolutely and relatively—Congress and the Reagan administration, believing that huge deficits were responsible for the crash, hurriedly reached an overnight budget compromise to reduce the deficit. Was the basic problem our huge budget deficit? Or are deficits and the debt just political issues used to lambast incumbent office holders around election time?

In this chapter, we will address a number of issues about deficits and the national debt: Are budget deficits, government spending, and the national debt out of control? How are budget deficits financed? What macroeconomic consequences follow binges of deficit spending? When, if ever, is a deficit desirable? Do budget deficits contribute to deficits in our international trade? If so, have budget deficits caused us to sell U.S. resources to foreigners wholesale? Are future generations destined for lives of poverty?

Recent Growth of Deficits and Debt

Since World War II, the federal budget has been in deficit 80 percent of the time. Our most recent budget surplus was experienced in 1969. Federal budget deficits over the past three decades are shown in Panel B of Figure 1. Deficits were relatively small until the mid-1970s. Under the Ford, Carter and Reagan administrations, huge budget deficits became the norm. Persistent deficits have pushed the public debt over $2 trillion (Panel A).

Every modern president has expressed concern about these deficits. Political battles over the budget, however, have normally pivoted on spending priorities instead of balancing the budget. Whose programs will be sacrificed? For example, Presidents Ford and Reagan both sought to build up national defense and urged cuts in transfer programs to reduce deficits. Congress, however, resisted cuts in transfer payments. The result was that both defense and transfers grew, swelling both deficits and debt.

The rapid growth of public debt shown in Panel A of Figure 1 concerns many people. Our analysis in earlier chapters, however, suggested that during a recession, deficit spending to stabilize the economy may be necessary—Herbert Hoover's attempts to balance the budget when the Great Depression began contributed to rapid economic decay. We will now examine the various arguments for and against budget deficits.

Functional Finance Versus Balanced Budgets

Should the federal budget be balanced continuously or only over the business cycle? Or is balancing the budget irrelevant? Each of these positions finds some

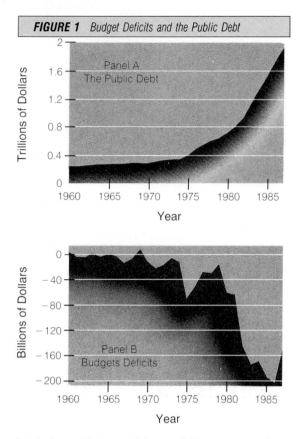

FIGURE 1 Budget Deficits and the Public Debt

Relatively small budget deficits were fairly persistent until the 1970s, when they began to grow sharply, as shown in Panel B. Enormous deficits plagued the 1980s so that the national debt (shown in Panel A) more than doubled during President Reagan's two terms of office.

adherents among politicians, economists, and the public at large. We will examine the economic logic of these positions on balancing the budget or running deficits.

Balancing Budgets Annually

Many people who want less government also advocate continually balancing the budget for political reasons. Their rationale is that less government will unchain market forces and stimulate economic growth. This group sees government as so intrusive that many favor a constitutional amendment requiring an annually balanced budget. Their view is that a Constitutional requirement of balanced budgets would force Congress to limit its spending.

Even if you agree that government should be limited, however, you should recognize that a balanced-budget amendment would open up some dangerous possibilities. We might find ourselves confronted with Herbert Hoover's dilemma—curing deficits may worsen unemployment. If National Income began falling, tax revenues would fall. At the same time, rising unemployment would mandate higher outlays for unemployment compensation and other public assistance programs.

How might we balance the budget when massive deficits loom? Raising tax rates would result in substantial declines in both Aggregate Supply and Aggregate Demand and might cause tax revenues to fall. Attempts to slash government spending might even cause National Income to fall so much that tax revenues would fall even more than the spending reduction, worsening any deficit. Few economists are convinced that fiscal policy has absolutely no effect on National Income, and even fewer advocate rigidly balanced budgets. Focus 1, however, describes a recent revival of an ancient view that total government spending matters, but how the budget is financed is irrelevant.

Balanced Budgets Over the Business Cycle

A more sophisticated view admits that annually balanced budgets may foster instability. This proposal is to balance the budget *over the business cycle*. Its advocates realize that we should not raise taxes or cut spending to cover cyclical deficits caused by recessions, nor should we liquidate inflation-caused surpluses through tax cuts or hikes in spending. This group contends that cyclical deficits should be offset by surpluses collected during prosperity. Thus, over a complete business cycle, there would be no net growth in national debt.

A major problem with this approach is that prosperity may not last long enough or be strong enough to permit the generation of surpluses sufficient to off-

set deficits, especially if recessions tend to be either extended or especially severe. Our economy might equilibrate around a lower average level of income than might otherwise be sustainable.

Functional Finance

Most Keynesian economists favor "activist" fiscal policies. They argue that we need to balance the economy at full employment and that the effect on the national debt of balancing or not balancing the budget is irrelevant. In this view, injections (investment plus government spending plus exports) need to be set so that, at a high rate of capacity utilization, they equal withdrawals (saving plus taxes plus imports). The best mix should be used; taxes and government outlays never need to balance precisely.[1]

> The **functional finance** *approach to the government budget emphasizes that taxation is only one way to finance government outlays. How best to pay for government depends on which policies are least costly under existing economic conditions.*

Taxation to cover new government spending is the least expansionary of all alternatives and is most appropriate when the economy is close to full employment. If the Treasury borrows to cover a deficit, the people who buy government bonds may reduce their spending. This is more expansionary than taxation as a way to finance government outlays. The most expansionary method of all is creating a more monetary base to cover a deficit.

Any of these ways to cover new spending can be disastrous. In the early 1980s, Bolivia financed about 15 percent of its government budget with taxes and 85 percent with new money. The result? Annual inflation exceeded 500 percent. Accelerating inflation caused the Bolivian economy to collapse until a severe austerity program finally slowed galloping inflation to a trot.

1. Abba P. Lerner, "Functional Finance and the Federal Debt," in Richard Fink and Jack High, eds., *A Nation in Debt: Economists Debate the Federal Budget Deficit*, 1987.

Ricardian Equivalence

The debate about how to finance government dates back for centuries. The great classical economist David Ricardo's analysis of public debt and deficits treated public debt as if people regarded it as a private burden similar to private debt. The Ricardian equivalence theorem as he elaborated it stated:

When for the expenses of a year's war, twenty millions are raised by means of a loan, it is the twenty millions which are withdrawn from the productive capital of the nation. . . . Government might at once have required the twenty millions in the shape of taxes; in which case it would not have been necessary to raise annual taxes to the amount of a million. This, however, would not have changed the nature of the transaction. An individual instead of being called upon to pay £100 per annum, might have been obliged to pay £2000 once and for all.*

A modern economist, Robert Barro,** has resurrected Ricardo's argument that

loans (public debt) and taxes are equivalent. According to Barro, if government borrows more today, all taxpayers recognize that future tax bills will rise, so our current saving rates should rise as we bank funds to pay these future tax bills.

Barro's version of Ricardian equivalence essentially treats the burden of paying for government spending as unaffected by the mode of finance—citizens adjust to taxes, public debt, or new monetary base as mechanisms that simply transfer parts of gross private saving to use by the public sector. Ultimately, nominal variables such as the price level or the monetary rate of saving or interest might be affected by how government budgets are financed, but real macroeconomic variables—employment, output, and national income—would be unaffected. Thus, we gain nothing by piling up public debt or issuing monetary base instead of financing government through taxes. We might as well balance the budget annually.

One important assumption of Barro's model is that taxpayers have an infinite time horizon. This seems unlikely. Moreover, predictions based on Ricardian equivalence have not been borne out. The tax cuts and rising deficits of the early 1980s did not yield higher saving rates. In fact, saving rates fell. Rising saving during 1985–88 might seem

to support Barro, but his model is inconsistent with such lags. This recent rise in saving is, however, consistent with Keynesian theory (rising income during the 1983–88 recovery stimulated saving) or with demographic changes (baby boomers are outgrowing the high consumption period of young family formation and are beginning to save for retirement).

---

*David Ricardo, "Principles of Political Economy and Taxation," *Works and correspondence*, Vol. 1, Cambridge, 1951 (reprint).

**Robert Barro, "Are Government Bonds Net Wealth?," *Journal of Political Economy*, December 1974.

Private Versus Public Finance

What mechanisms enable individuals and governments to run deficits? Many people draw an incorrect analogy between government finance and business or private household budgeting because they fail to understand the different spending constraints facing the private and the public sectors.

Private Budget Constraints

The availability of funds limits the spending of households, proprietorships, and partnerships. Funds are made available through (*a*) sales of current assets, (*b*) current income (including gifts or inheritance), and (*c*) potential borrowing against current assets or expected future income. You know how tightly credit is rationed to fund these types of private spending if you have ever exceeded your MasterCard or Visa credit limit. Even young people with great potential future income have problems borrowing. This is one reason that most student loans are guaranteed by the government. Big corporations tend to have fewer problems in securing funds.

Corporations Most corporations borrow by issuing bonds. Their bonds tend to be more salable than the IOUs of households, proprietorships, or partnerships because most large corporations are superior credit risks. Corporations have an additional source of purchasing power available to neither households nor to noncorporate firms: they can sell stock to finance spending. The ability to sell bonds and to offer ownership shares (stock) makes corporations more flexible and powerful than other firms in securing funds to cover operating expenses or new investments in plant and equipment.

Local Government Budget Constraints

States, counties, cities, school districts, and other local government units face slightly different constraints on their spending. Like proprietorships or partnerships, they can use revenues from the sale of assets or the goods and services they provide to finance current spending. Like corporations, they may issue bonds to obtain purchasing power, but government does not sell ownership shares.

Taxes Another major difference between private and government organizations is that government can enact *taxes* to finance its spending, which gives government tremendous power to use resources as it wishes. Even the power to tax allows only limited command over resources. Excessive spending by the governments of New York City and Cleveland, for example, almost forced them into bankruptcy in the 1970s. Local governments sometimes default on their loans. Some hobbyists collect defunct municipal bonds the way others collect stamps. They have little hope that these bonds will ever be redeemed; rarity and appearance alone determines their values.

Confiscation or Regulation Government can also channel the allocation of resources through *confiscation* or *regulation*. For example, regulation now forces car owners to buy emission-controlling exhaust systems and limits firms' pollution levels. Through such regulations, the government buys a cleaner environment for all of us and makes us pay for it without explicit tax increases. You may think that direct confiscation is not used by governments in the United States. The right of eminent domain, however, can be and is used by all levels of government to secure land for such things as highway rights-of-way or areas for dams or parks. When the government exercises *eminent domain,* those who are forced to surrender their property to government are typically paid a fair-market value. Although the military draft is not used at present, it is another example of government confiscating resources.

Federal Budget Constraints

A national government has one more major mechanism in its toolbox: it can print money to pay for the goods it provides; this printing creates additional *monetary base.* (Recall that the monetary base equals currency plus the reserves in the banking system.) The separate identities of the Federal Reserve System (FED) and the Department of the Treasury disguises this means of financing spending somewhat.[2] In an accounting sense, the Treasury "borrows" the money from the FED, which actually creates new money.

In summary, government can secure resources to provide us with goods and services through (*a*) sales of its current assets or production; (*b*) borrowing from U.S. citizens, corporations, foreign citizens or governments, or commercial banks; (*c*) taxation; (*d*) confiscation; or (*e*) expansion of the monetary base (currency in circulation plus bank reserves).

Confiscation can be regarded as taxation in kind, so central government outlays are characterized by a government budget constraint:

> The **government budget constraint** *specifies the financing options open to the federal government and is defined as:*

$$G = T + \Delta B + \Delta MB.$$

where,

G = total government outlays,

T = total governmental revenues from taxes, charges, and sales,

ΔB = change in the national debt,

ΔMB = change in the monetary base (currency in circulation plus bank reserves).

This makes it possible to express the federal deficit as $G - T = \Delta B + \Delta MB$. If the federal government spends more than it collects ($G - T > 0$), it must either borrow ($\Delta B > 0$) or create (print) the monetary difference ($\Delta MB > 0$). If the government collects more than it spends ($G - T < 0$), it can either retire some existing debt ($\Delta B < 0$) or retire some money it has previously created ($\Delta MB < 0$). Budget deficits cause growth in the national debt or in the money supply, while government surpluses make it possible to pay off some national debt and/or remove some money from circulation.

Borrowing money or selling current assets to secure purchasing power are common to both private and government decision makers. But private citizens cannot legally tax, confiscate, or create (print) more monetary base. The money expansion process— bankers lend out their new reserves—then applies to this increase in the monetary base, as described in chapter 12.

Are there limits to a government's command over resources? The ultimate limit is people's faith that government will survive, honor its contracts, and maintain reasonable stability in the value of the money it issues. The worthlessness of bonds issued by Russian czars, Chinese warlords, and other dictators overthrown by military coups or revolutions attests that this faith is not always justified. Fiscal mismanagement has been the problem as frequently as political oppression or widespread corruption.

Crowding Out and Trade Imbalances

Most critics of Keynesian policies do not believe that extra government purchases cause much growth of GNP because government spending tends to replace or "crowd out" private economic activity. They point out that *gross private saving* (total production minus private consumption) is absorbed by government purchases regardless of whether government taxes (T), borrows (ΔB), or inflates the money supply (ΔMB) to finance its outlays: $G = T + \Delta B + \Delta MB$. Nevertheless, how government is financed strongly affects the impact of government purchases. The FED is the government's banker and, with the Treasury, determines how deficits and surpluses are financed. This resolution is crucial in determining the levels of prices, interest rates, trade balances, income, and output. We will examine these issues in detail.

Crowding Out

What the government gives it must first take away.
—*John S. Coleman*

Crowding out and paying for government are closely related.

---

2. The U.S. government uses a roundabout method to finance a deficit by creating new monetary base. The Treasury first issues new bonds to cover its deficit. The FED then uses expansionary open-market operations to buy these bonds. This expands bank reserves, which are then transformed into new money through the money multiplier process. The bonds bought by the FED are considered, for accounting purposes, to be part of our national debt. It is nonsense, however, to suggest that our national debt is enlarged because one government agency (the Treasury) owes another (the FED). Thus, in what follows, we ignore Treasury bonds held by the FED when we count the national debt.

Crowding out *is the idea that increases in government purchases inevitably cause reductions in private consumption or investment.*[3]

Government outlays may crowd out private activities through (*a*) less leisure for workers, (*b*) less consumer purchasing power (caused by inflation or tax hikes), or (*c*) fewer profits for investors (because of higher interest rates). Keep in mind, however, that the goods government provides may be more valuable than the crowded-out activity.

Government's Costs When Resources Are Idle

The alternatives individuals lose when government acquires more resources determine who really pays for government. Suppose that our economy is in a recession with massive unemployment of land, labor, and capital. Government might boost output by drafting (confiscating) idle resources, or it could secure money to pay for them through taxes, growth of the monetary base, or borrowing. If these resources would have been completely unproductive in the absence of government action, the opportunity costs of the extra output are zero; the additional government services would not cost anyone anything.

The production-possibilities frontier in Figure 2 allows us to examine an increase in government spending and the resulting induced consumption. If many resources are idle and the economy is initially at point *a*, raising government spending from G_0 to G_1 closes the recessionary gap in this idealized case. Consumption induced through the Keynesian multiplier process will drive total consumption from C_0 to C_1. This completes the closure of the GNP gap so that the path to full employment is $a \rightarrow b \rightarrow c$.

Does this seem an exception to the *TANSTAAFL* rule that "There ain't no such thing as a free lunch"? It is not. Few resources are ever totally without valuable uses "in the absence of government action." For example, idle labor produces leisure; most of us prefer no work to work with no pay. To induce idle labor

3. Early "crowding-out" hypotheses focused only on how government deficits drive interest rates up and, consequently, reduce investments. Our treatment follows a more recent convention that crowding out encompasses all reductions in private activities caused when government programs grow.

FIGURE 2 *The Costs of Additional Government: Crowding Out*

The general problem of government spending crowding out private activity is illustrated in this figure. Beginning from a point of considerable unemployment (*a*), government can increase spending from G_0 to G_1; new consumption equal to $C_1 - C_0$ will be induced through the multiplier. The opportunity costs of such increases are the value of the private uses to which the ΔG would have been put, including the leisure forgone by the newly employed. Once the economy has achieved full employment (point *c*), increased government spending to G_2 (point *d*) necessarily causes a reduction in private spending from C_1 to C_0.

to work voluntarily, government must pay a wage that offsets the value of the leisure lost in producing the extra output; increases in employment come at the cost of forgone leisure.

Government might use simple confiscation to impose on the owners of idle resources the full cost of providing extra government goods; drafting unemployed labor for armies of conservation workers or highway repair crews would be examples. (Siberian salt mines developed under the Russian czars continue today under the Soviet regime.) If tax revenues are used to pay the owners of the newly employed resources, the burden falls largely on taxpayers. If government creates money to pay for these resources, then the higher incomes of the owners of previously idle resources may be partially offset by inflationary reductions in the purchasing power of other citizens.

Suppose the government issues bonds to buy the resources used to produce extra government goods. The consequences are illustrated in Figure 3. Bond prices fall when more Treasury bonds are issued,

FIGURE 3 *The Crowding-Out Effect: Investment*

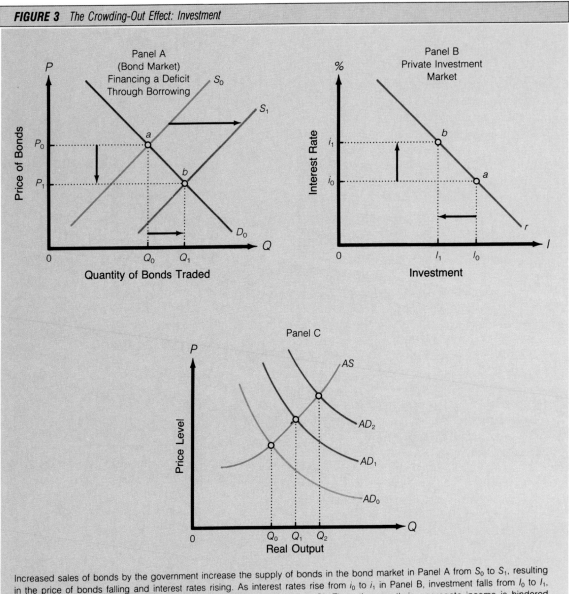

Increased sales of bonds by the government increase the supply of bonds in the bond market in Panel A from S_0 to S_1, resulting in the price of bonds falling and interest rates rising. As interest rates rise from i_0 to i_1 in Panel B, investment falls from I_0 to I_1, diminishing the increase in Aggregate Demand by $AD_2 - AD_1$ (Panel C). Thus, the growth in aggregate income is hindered because of crowding out.

raising the supply of bonds from S_0 to S_1 (in Panel A). The falling price of bonds causes interest rates to climb from i_0 to i_1 (from points a to b in Panel B). Successful borrowers pay higher interest rates and some private investment is crowded out. This dampens the growth in Aggregate Demand, which rises only from AD_0 to AD_1—not to AD_2—in Panel C, as would occur without crowding out.

Borrowers and potential borrowers pay the short-run burden of more government spending when a budget deficit is financed by sales of new government bonds. Figure 4 illustrates how closely real interest rates have paralleled recent record deficits. In the longer run, consumers will pay higher prices because investment shrinks, adding less to the stock of capital. With less capital growth, real wages and output will not rise as fast.

When the economy is at less than full employment, the degree of crowding out depends in part on the interest sensitivity of demands for loans by investors and consumers. During severe recessions, induced Keynesian growth of income can overwhelm

any losses in purchasing power caused by crowding out. But crowding out always restricts the power of the Keynesian multiplier process to boost real income—especially in a fully employed economy.

Government's Costs During Full Employment

We have assumed that some resources were idle when government purchases grew. Expanded government spending is a standard Keynesian prescription when the economy is in a slump. Who pays for government growth if the economy is fully employed? Either private consumption, investment, or exports must fall if government purchases are raised when there is efficient and full employment of all resources. Refer back to Figure 2. If the economy were initially fully employed at point c, boosting government purchases from G_1 to G_2 would move the economy to point d and shrink the sum of private consumption and investment from $C_1 + I_0$ to $C_0 + I_0$.

Government can achieve the necessary crowding out through tax hikes, confiscation, inflation, or through higher interest rates. Excessive reliance on

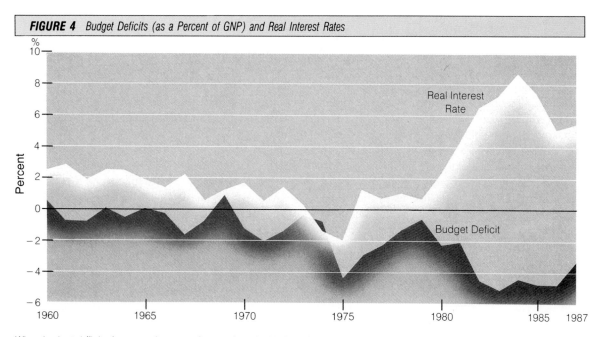

FIGURE 4 Budget Deficits (as a Percent of GNP) and Real Interest Rates

When budget deficits (measured as negative numbers in this figure) have grown relative to our GNP, real interest rates (money rates of interest adjusted for inflation) have also tended to rise.

any single mechanism may cause political turmoil and significantly reduce some resource owners' incentives to be productive; therefore, government commonly chooses a mix of these ways to cover new government spending.

For example, President Johnson realized that tax increases to pay for the War in Vietnam and the "War on Poverty" would encounter tremendous political resistance in the late 1960s. In spite of advice from his Council of Economic Advisors that tax increases were necessary to avoid inflationary pressures, President Johnson chose to run budgetary deficits. What choices were available? Because $G - T = \Delta B + \Delta MB$, the alternatives were either to borrow the money or print it.

The Treasury initially covered the deficits by issuing new bonds. A large proportion of the loanable funds available at that time would have been absorbed if these bonds had been purchased solely by the public; interest rates would have soared, leaving little funding available for private investment. The Federal Reserve Board elected to buy many of the new bonds issued by the Treasury. This expanded the monetary base and caused the money supply to rise, preventing the full brunt of financing the Vietnam War from falling exclusively on private investment. Inflation caused prices and nominal income to swell so that total tax revenues increased.

The overall result was that crowding out spread the costs of the War on Poverty and the Vietnam War across four groups (a) investors, who paid higher interest rates; (b) consumers, who paid higher prices; (c) taxpayers, who paid higher taxes; and (d) Selective Service draftees—being drafted was a form of confiscation of your labor to pay for the Vietnam War. This example correctly suggests that the mix of policies government uses to finance its spending has important implications for the distribution of income; each method of reducing private activity imposes burdens on different groups.

The Government Budget and Foreign Trade

The government budget equation ($G - T = \Delta M + \Delta MB$) reveals that government deficits can be funded through expansionary open-market operations by the FED or by having the Treasury borrow via the issuance of new bonds. If the FED does not monetize the deficit by buying Treasury bonds, national debt that is privately held by Americans or foreigners grows.

Government spending not covered by taxes ($G - T > 0$) represents production saved by households but unavailable for investment. This saving may be voluntary (private purchases of Treasury bonds) or involuntary (newly printed money creates inflationary pressure that has been called "the cruelest tax"). This private but uninvested saving may be made available to government by domestic entities or by foreigners.

Trade Deficits   Foreigners make parts of their gross saving (production minus consumption) available by exporting more to us than we export to them; we experience a *trade deficit* in which imports exceed exports. Thus, if we separately consider the foreign sector when we build a government budget equation, it can be expressed as:

$$G - T = (S - I) + (M - X) = \Delta B + \Delta MB,$$

where S = domestic savings; I = domestic investment; M = imports; and X = exports.

Adding the international sector explicitly into the government budget constraint suggests that federal deficits must equal the domestic savings surplus (saving minus investment) plus the trade deficit (imports minus exports). For example, in 1980 the budget deficit was $61.3 billion, the savings surplus was $93.4 billion, and the U.S. ran a trade surplus of $32.1 billion [61.3 = (93.4) + (−32.1)]. By 1987, the budget deficit had grown to $152.6 billion and the domestic saving surplus had shrunk to $32.7 billion, balanced by a trade deficit of $119.9 billion [(152.6 = (32.7) + (119.9)].

Thus, federal deficits can be financed by increasing domestic saving or by securing the savings of foreigners. Alternatively, the deficit can be financed by reductions in domestic investment or in our exports of goods and services. In effect, a trade deficit represents net funds that the United States borrows from abroad. Finally, note that for a given budget deficit, increased domestic investment (saving held con-

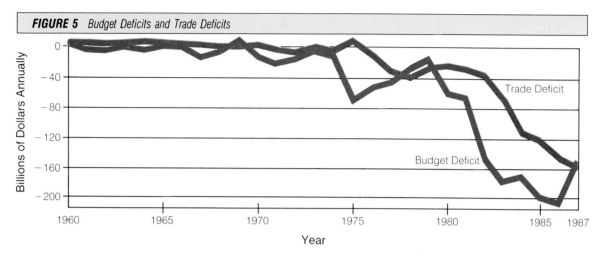

FIGURE 5 Budget Deficits and Trade Deficits

Large shares of the massive federal budget deficits of the 1980s have been financed by foreigners. Thus, U.S. trade deficits have paralleled our budget deficits.

stant) must ultimately be financed by a worsening trade deficit.

In summary, with aggregate saving fixed, rising budget deficits will inevitably result in growing trade deficits or a reduction in domestic investment. Figure 5 illustrates what Gary Stern has called "the unpleasant arithmetic of budget and trade deficits".[4] As deficits in the 1980s mushroomed, trade deficits widened as well. The persistent budget deficits of the 1980s were paralleled by mounting trade deficits. Thus, foreigners financed much of the federal budget deficit—a problem that will probably not be resolved until our federal budget deficit shrinks.

Some people are alarmed by huge U.S. deficits in international trade, and have proposed high tariff walls and restrictive import quotas. This might prevent a flood of imports from competing with U.S. output, but the expanded government budget deficit $[G - T = (S - I) + (M - X)]$ reveals that protectionist policies would also shift the brunt of the budget deficit into greater crowding out of private investment. The only option would be to reduce the budget

deficit by raising taxes or cutting government outlays. The Laffer curve described in chapter 11 depicts one of many constraints on government's ability to slash a deficit by raising taxes. Reducing the budget deficit through spending cuts is also very difficult because large parts of federal outlays are mandated by law.

The Ability to Control Government Spending

[These tax cut bills represent] a turnaround of almost a half a century of a course this country has been on . . . and marks an end to the excessive growth in government bureaucracy and government spending and government taxing.

—Ronald Reagan, August 13, 1981

Despite these brave words, Ronald Reagan found that cutting the federal budget was an overwhelming task. Doing so quickly seems virtually impossible.

Relatively uncontrollable outlays *cannot be changed without changes in major federal laws. They are often beyond administrative control and involve contractual obligations of government.*

---

4. Gary H. Stern, "The Unpleasant Arithmetic of Budget and Trade Deficits," Federal Reserve Bank of Minneapolis, 1986 Annual Report.

An example would be transfer payments that beneficiaries are entitled to by law.

Many enormous items in the federal budget are continuing programs that Congress is legally obligated to fund. For example, Social Security payments are legally guaranteed to recipients, commitments for Medicare funding were made by the Congress years ago, and contracts for some transportation or defense systems take years to complete. Moreover, the government's legal obligations to provide public assistance, to operate the Post Office, to regulate pollution and industrial safety—the list seems to go on forever—are long-term commitments that simply cannot be abandoned during short periods of time. Estimates by the Conference Board, a research organization, indicate that roughly 60 percent of all outlays were relatively uncontrollable in the 1960s. That number has now grown to nearly 75 percent.

Panel A of Figure 6 shows the growth of real federal outlays and tax revenue. Despite sweeping polit-

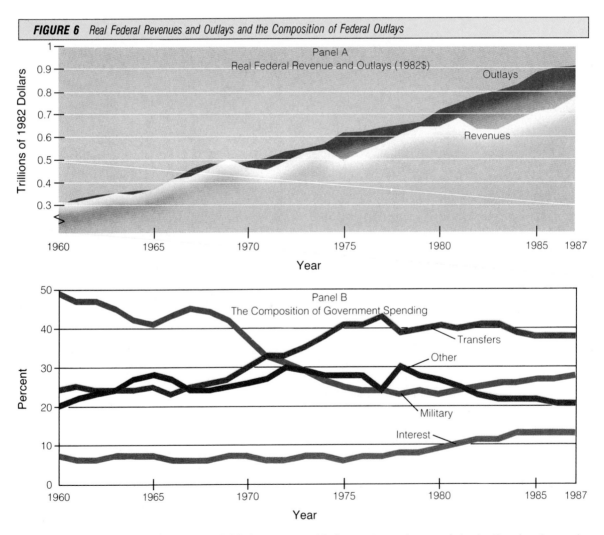

FIGURE 6 Real Federal Revenues and Outlays and the Composition of Federal Outlays

Deficits have been enormous and the national debt has grown rapidly in recent years because federal outlays (purchases plus transfer payments) have grown much faster than federal tax revenues (Panel A). Growing shares of government outlays are absorbed by transfer payments and interest on the national debt (Panel B), while the military budget, which had been declining relative to other types of spending from 1968 through 1977, recovered somewhat during the 1980s.

ical rhetoric in the 1980s about reducing the size of government, growth in real outlays has grown steadily. Where has this growth in expenditures originated? Panel B shows the composition of federal expenditures. Major increases in spending shares since the 1960s have been in interest on the public debt and transfer payments. Major declines have been in purchases of goods and services (both military and nonmilitary).

The Gramm-Rudman-Hollings Balanced-Budget Law

In 1985, Congress adopted a new strategy in an attempt to control soaring deficits: the Gramm-Rudman-Hollings Deficit Reduction Act set specific deficit reduction targets. If these targets were not met, "across-the-board" cuts in spending were mandated. In effect, Congress is like a dieter who puts a lock on the refrigerator, and gives the key to someone else. Critics of Gramm-Rudman charge that it makes federal spending a captive of some deficit target instead of making the deficit the result of congressionally determined spending. But how effective will this approach be? Many parts of the budget were excluded from the across-the-board cuts, including most in the categories labeled relatively uncontrollable. Cold comfort, indeed, for those who would like to reduce the size of government!

Gramm-Rudman limited the fiscal year 1986 deficit to $171.9 billion and the 1987 deficit to only $144 billion. In each of the four fiscal years after 1987, the targeted federal deficit is reduced by $36 billion until it is zero in 1991. The law sets up specific processes to enable agreement between Congress and the administration on a deficit-reduction package. If Congress and the president are unable to reach agreement, there are automatic selective spending cuts. The budget processes and timeline outlined in the Gramm-Rudman Act are detailed in Table 1.

Whether Gramm-Rudman will survive is a question. Some parts of this law have been found unconstitutional, and others face further legal challenge. Many critics view Gramm-Rudman as a symptom of

---

TABLE 1 *The Gramm-Rudman Budget Process (1987–91)*

The Gramm-Rudman Act established budgeting deadlines that overlap traditional Congressional budget processes.

First Monday after January 3	President submits budget for next fiscal year (begins October 1). Cost-of-living increases are deferred until it is determined that automatic spending cuts are unnecessary.
April 15	Congress completes action on the budget resolution for the next fiscal year.
June 15	Congress reconciles appropriations with targets set by the budget resolution.
June 30	The House finishes the annual appropriations bills for the next fiscal year. (There is no deadline for action by the Senate.)
August 20	The Congressional Budget Office (CBO) and the Office of Management and Budget (OMB) submit the joint deficit estimate to the Government Accounting Office (GAO).
August 25	If the deficit ceiling is exceeded, the GAO issues a report to the president detailing the automatic spending cuts necessary to comply with the law.
September 1	President issues automatic spending cut order.
October 1	Fiscal year begins. Automatic spending cuts take effect unless Congress and the president have reached an alternative budget that meets the Gramm-Rudman deficit target.
October 5	The OMB and CBO issue their final deficit projection to the GAO.
October 10	The GAO revised report is sent to the president.
October 15	The president issues the final order for automatic spending cuts.

Source: *Facts on File*, February 5, 1986.

general hysteria about budget deficits, and argue that the official estimates of the deficit should be adjusted downward to reflect the impact of inflation on the national debt. Critics also contend that much of the deficit is the result of capital spending, not spending on current services. These critics conclude that the federal government uses an outdated accounting practice long abandoned by business, and that this causes overstatement of the real budget deficit.

Other critics argue that reducing the deficit rapidly could lead to a disastrous recession, putting further pressures on the deficit that may require further spending cuts and so on. Herbert Hoover attempted to balance the budget in 1931 by raising taxes, plunging the economy further into the Depression. Still others argue that a balanced budget is unduly restrictive, and urge a compromise that would limit the deficit so that our public debt could not grow faster than GNP.

The Public Debt

Prophets of doom who cite growth of public debt as a sign of impending collapse and urge government to operate more like a business just aren't paying attention. Although the federal debt is enormous and growing, private debt has grown even faster. Part of this is household debt, but most private debt is corporate. Although substantial corporate debt is accounted for by recent "merger mania," successful corporations that are not involved in mergers invariably owe more with each passing decade.

You may have heard someone say that the United States teeters on the verge of bankruptcy. Doomsayers fail to consider (*a*) the ability of government to tax and to create money to cover budget deficits or to pay off the national debt, (*b*) the basic differences between internal and external debts, and (*c*) the relative versus absolute size of the debt.

External Versus Internal Debt

The major difference between private and public debt is that all private debt is held externally—the borrowers owe other people—whereas public debt

is primarily held internally—we owe most of our *national debt* to Americans. That is, we owe it to ourselves. (Do you own any U.S. Savings Bonds?)

External debt *is owed to outsiders;* **internal debt** *is owed to those who, at least in part, are obligated to pay the debt.*

Borrowing from internal sources does not change the total current amount that may be spent. When our government issues new bonds, the purchasing power temporarily surrendered by U.S. bond buyers just offsets the government's gain in purchasing power. People in the United States as a whole neither gain nor lose immediately through such transactions, although the uses of these funds may affect future American purchasing power. If borrowed funds are used for a government investment in, say, a hydroelectric dam, then real future income may be increased because more and cheaper electricity may be available over the productive life of the facility.

On the other hand, if government borrows to pay for such current operating costs as police protection or transfers and this diverts funds from private investments, then future purchasing power may fall. For example, if a war is financed by bonds, lower rates of domestic capital formation may hinder standards of living for generations. Just as borrowing funds internally does not change total current purchasing power, repayment of internal debt does not reduce total American purchasing power at the time of repayment. People who cash their bonds receive purchasing power exactly equal to the loss of purchasing power to taxpayers or the government sector.

When private households or firms borrow externally, they immediately gain the purchasing power that lenders temporarily sacrifice. Similarly, when the government sells bonds to foreign governments or investors, the United States as a whole temporarily gains purchasing power. But external borrowing normally entails eventual repayment to the external sources of funds. If the borrowed funds were used for investment goods that were sufficiently productive to cover the principal borrowed plus interest charges, the borrowers still would be ahead after repayment. If, on the other hand, the loans were used to finance consumption, then repayment to external lenders could entail net losses of purchasing power.

This case requires curtailing future consumption because higher consumption is enjoyed today.

Table 2 indicates that the proportion of the national debt held by foreigners grew markedly in the 1970s. Before 1975, foreign holdings of U.S. government debt were negligible. As real interest rates rose, foreigners bought greater quantities of our debt. When foreigners buy U.S. bonds, we experience gains in purchasing power. It is possible that future generations of Americans may lose purchasing power when these bonds are redeemed and will bear the burdens of paying the interest on externally held debt.

Figure 7 illustrates how real interest rates, inflation, and deficits as a percent of Gross Domestic Product (*GDP*) compare among developed nations. This figure indexes all countries to the United States (U.S. = 100). Big budget deficits are usually associat-

TABLE 2 *Percentage of the Public Debt Held by Foreigners*

Year	Percentage of Public Debt Owned by Foreigners
1939	.5
1946	.8
1965	5.2
1970	5.3
1975	11.5
1978	17.5
1980	16.3
1987	15.9

Source: Board of Governors of the Federal Reserve System, *Federal Reserve Bulletin*, October 1985; and *Economic Report of the President*, 1988.

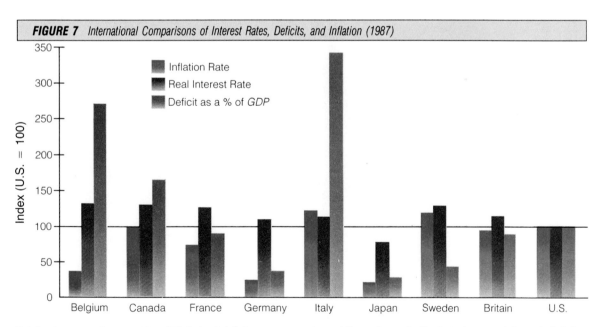

FIGURE 7 *International Comparisons of Interest Rates, Deficits, and Inflation (1987)*

Relative to many other countries, U.S. federal deficits as a percentage of Gross Domestic Product, the rate of domestic inflation, and real interest rates (monetary interest adjusted for inflation) were not out of line in 1987. Note however, the consistently superior position of the Japanese economy.

ed with high real rates of interest. The relatively high U.S. interest rates shown in Figure 7 partially explains why Japanese investors have been major buyers of U.S. government bonds, companies, and real estate in the late 1980s.

Interest on Public Debt

Until recently, the national debt held by the public was declining as a proportion of Gross National Product (see Figure 8). Beginning in 1982, rising deficits and relatively high interest rates caused total public debt and interest payments—as percentages of GNP—to grow. Interest rates fell in 1986, so this trend in rising interest costs may reverse as old debt is rolled over and new debt is financed at lower real rates.

Debt roll-over *occurs if, when any given bond issue comes due, the debt is refinanced.*

Government and corporations typically go deeper and deeper into debt as time passes. (Most large corporations also roll over their debts.) Investors who buy government bonds, however, must have confidence in the continued existence and taxing power of the government.

Politically unstable countries find it difficult to borrow because investors fear that the current government may fall. New regimes commonly disavow the debt of overthrown governments, rendering it worthless. For example, owners of bonds issued by czarist Russia, post World War I Germany, and many South American countries experienced this misfortune. The discounts at which the debts of some countries are sold are shown in Table 3. The amount of the

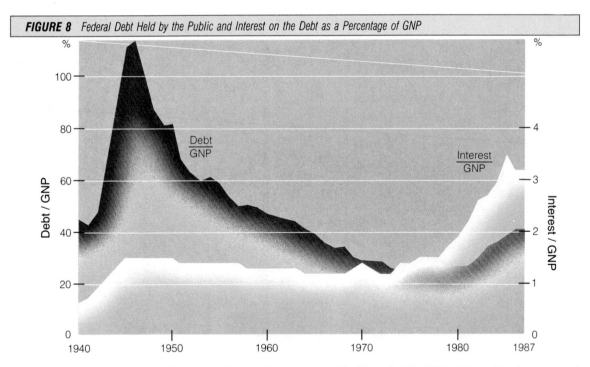

FIGURE 8 *Federal Debt Held by the Public and Interest on the Debt as a Percentage of GNP*

The public debt as a percentage of GNP was declining until relatively recently. Right after World War II, the public debt exceeded GNP; today, the ratio is nearly 40 percent. When greater public debt has been financed, interest rates have risen. New debt and old debt that was rolled over have had to be floated at these higher rates of interest. The result is that interest paid on public debt as a percentage of GNP rose during the early 1980s. Quite recently, however, interest rates have fallen, and as debt is refinanced, interest costs should fall both absolutely and as a percentage of GNP.

discount is roughly proportional to the difficulties faced when one of these countries tries to borrow or to refinance (roll over) its debt. Debt can be floated almost perpetually, however, as long as the government of a country is reasonably stable and maintains its credit.

An often ignored aspect of federal debt is that the FED acquires large chunks of national debt when it buys bonds during expansionary open-market operations. Other government agencies (e.g., the Social Security Administration) also buy bonds when they run temporary surpluses. Accountants count these organizations' bond holdings as national debt, but this is a lot like saying that your right pocket owes your left pocket when you shift spare change from one pocket to another.

If taxes are raised to pay the interest on federal debt, incentives to work and invest may wither. In 1987, the interest cost of the national debt was nearly $150 billion, or about 16 percent of all federal outlays. When the federal government finances a huge deficit by selling debt securities, real interest rates climb or remain high, and considerable private borrowing for investment may be crowded out. The exact effect will depend on the state of the economy and private saving rates. If the economy is especially sluggish, increased deficits may not crowd out much investment. If savings rates rise, large deficits may not raise interest rates. In general, large deficits put upward pressure on interest rates. The end result is that future generations may inherit a smaller capital stock and, hence, reduced production possibilities—one real burden of the public debt.

The Burden of Public Debt on Future Generations

Does national debt burden future generations? As we discussed previously, if newly incurred debt diverts funds from investment to satisfy present consumption, then future generations lose the investment income that might have been generated. But future generations do not lose because of national debt per se. Rather, they lose because the current generation opts for more consumption and less investment out of today's income.

Future generations may bear higher taxes to pay interest on the national debt. Of course, members of future generations also receive the interest payments as bondholders, so the burden nets out as long as the national debt is held internally—that is, as long as we owe it to ourselves. Future generations can lose, however, if foreigners decide to reduce their holdings of U.S. bonds. It is not obvious that they will, or that the national debt will ever be retired, or that it would be desirable for us to retire it.

Must the National Debt Be Repaid?

What would happen if we retired the national debt? Would the government be ruined? Suppose government raised income taxes enormously to repay the outstanding debt. People who hold the existing public debt tend to be individuals in high-income categories, so they would be paying a lot of the higher taxes and then would receive the payments—a transfer to themselves. Alternatively, the value of all Treasury bonds could be taxed 100 percent. Goodbye national debt. (This is not a likely option.)

Some critics of national debt policies argue that if the government can issue unlimited debt, it will continually overspend. These critics argue that Congress often mistreats the ability to issue debt and is unwilling to exercise fiscal restraint. Persistent increases in both government debt and spending tend to support their line of argument. It may be easier to increase the national debt (and the debt ceiling) than to say no to projects supported by powerful special-interest groups. Focus 2 suggests that a growing national debt may be the natural (but undersirable) result of democratic processes.

Some Benefits of Public Debt

The national debt would not exist without a benefit side. Stabilization policy depends heavily on the ability of the federal government to deficit spend and pay for this spending with bonds. Annually balancing the budget could prove disastrous during recessionary periods. President Herbert Hoover attempted to balance the budget by raising taxes when faced with rapidly growing deficits between 1929 and 1932. This policy accelerated a trend into the economy's deepest depression ever. Additionally, the national debt provides a relatively risk-free asset (government bonds) for individuals who need to protect their financial capital. (Of course, there is the risk of inflation.) You should realize by now that manipulation of the public debt is crucial for the most effective instrument of monetary policy—open-market operations. The FED buys bonds from banks when it wants to expand the money supply and sells bonds to restrict the money supply.

One recent development is potentially explosive growth of surpluses in the Social Security trust fund. These surpluses legally must be invested in federal debt and, as Focus 3 indicates, may make growth of debt a moot issue.

Remeasuring Public Debt and Budget Deficits

The deficit and debt statistics reported earlier in Figure 1 reflect a federal budget that began moving severely out of balance in the early 1970s. These data are reported by the government and the media to the public. There are, however, a growing number of economists who dispute these figures. They suggest that we would have been better off had we totally ignored these data instead of adopting incorrect policies based on these numbers.[5]

Correcting alleged flaws in budget deficit and debt data requires (a) converting the nominal budget to real values, (b) adjusting public debt for interest rate changes (converting the value of the debt from par value to market value), and (c) revising the budget so that reported values conform to generally accepted accounting principles.

For the same reasons that nominal GNP is adjusted for inflation to yield real GNP, the nominal budget deficit and public debt should be deflated to reflect changes in the price level. Real national debt remains constant if it doubles while the price level also doubles. In the same way that inflation wipes out the value of money, it also reduces the value of the national debt.

Similarly, if interest rates rise, all bond prices fall—and the national debt issued previously becomes less burdensome. The reported public debt is the par value of government bonds in the hands of the public or foreigners. Par value means that if a government bond is issued for $100,000 in 1970, the public debt grows $100,000. Public debt statistics are not adjusted to reflect changing market values if interest rates later change so that the market value of this bond changes. The par value of a bond remains constant, but the market value of the debt changes as interest rates fluctuate. Consequently, to measure national debt accurately, published government statistics should be adjusted for changes in interest rates.

---

5. Robert Eisner, *How Real is the Federal Deficit?*, (New York: The Free Press), 1986.

Is There a "Moral Dimension" to Debt and Deficits?

The outcry against large deficits and the growing national debt continues to mount. Both candidates for the presidency campaigned in 1988 against the deficits of the 1980s. Why would an economy so seemingly united against deficits and an escalating public debt do so little to reverse the trend? As Nobel prize winner James Buchanan has asked: Why do we choose to "eat-up" our national capital through debt-financed current consumption?*

The answer may lie in recent research by Alex Cukierman and Allan Meltzer that analyzes the reasons for issuing public debt.** Their analysis is based on the simple but powerful premise that rising deficits and national debt in a democracy are the result of the desires of the majority. Given the inequality in the distribution of income and wealth in the United States, one legitimate role of government may be to redistribute income between generations.

Their analysis uses an intergenerational model introduced by David Ricardo and recently refined by Robert Barro.*** Since poor individuals are *bequest constrained*—they cannot leave negative bequests (debts) to their offspring—and since some of their children will be wealthy, they can relax this constraint and increase consumption now by voting for deficits and higher public debt. Similarly, individuals with substantial nonhuman wealth may gain as rising debt increases real interest rates and their return. The authors also find that as longevity rises, the number of people bequest constrained rises. In summary, the very poor, very rich, and retired people tend to benefit from rising public debt that finances current consumption.

Alternatively, individuals with significant human wealth (Yuppies) who are highly productive lose. Real wages decline as public debt and deficits crowd out investment and reduce the rate of growth of capital. A reduced future capital stock means that real wages do not rise as rapidly and productivity growth is diminished.

This analysis suggests that the growing national debt may simply reflect the will of the voting majority. The current uproar about the present generation burdening future generations may not only be true, but what the majority desires. In many ways, financing current consumption with deficits is akin to the destructive exploitation of the environment that this society elected to protect many years ago by creating national parks and wilderness areas.

James Buchanan attributes this change in attitude about deficits and debt to a marked change in moral norms that is a result of the Keynesian Revolution in macroeconomic policy. This moral dimension of fiscal policy, in Buchanan's opinion, argues forcefully for a constitutional amendment to balance the federal budget. In his view, this is the only way the current generation can be prevented from "eating-up" the capital stock of future generations.

*James M. Buchanan, "The Moral Dimension of Debt Financing." *Economic Inquiry,* January 1985.

**Alex Cukierman and Allan H. Meltzer, "A Political Theory of Government Debt," a paper presented at the American Economic Association meetings, December 1987.

***Robert Barro, "Are Government Bonds Net Wealth?," *Journal of Political Economy,* December 1974. For an alternative point of view, see Olivier Blanchard, "Debt, Deficits, and Finite Horizons," *Journal of Political Economy,* April 1985.

Will Social Security Absorb Our National Debt?

The 1930s ushered in an era in which federal budget surpluses have been tiny, rare, and cumulatively swamped by deficits that have driven the national debt towards the stratosphere. Explosive growth of government debt has been dwarfed by growth of private debt, with U.S. saving rates being relatively low compared to many other industrialized countries.

In part, private saving rates were depressed by family formation among "baby-boomers," many of whom borrowed heavily to acquire the houses and other amenities that have become the norm for those who pursue the American Dream. By the 1980s, private domestic saving fell far short of the funds needed to finance (*a*) adequate domestic investment and (*b*) record federal deficits. The result was that U.S. federal deficits were covered by imports that allowed foreigners to invest heavily in the United States.

Many people are concerned that our deficits have effectively "sold our country to foreigners at cut-rate prices." Others worry that some future day of reckoning will usher in financial catastrophe and economic collapse. Are there natural economic limits to the size of our national debt? Do any natural forces exist to offset our national momentum towards infinite debt? One surprising force that soon may relieve swollen deficits and rising debt is the projected growth of the Social Security Trust Fund.

The Social Security system ran large deficits from the 1970s into the early 1980s. During this era, each retiree was supported by about four active workers. These deficits spelled potential bankruptcy for the Social Security Trust Fund when post-World War II "baby-boomers" begin retiring in around 2010. Demographers predicted that by 2030, each retiree would be backed up by only about two active workers. A "blue-ribbon" panel was appointed to find a solution to this problem.

This panel based its recommendations on relatively pessimistic forecasts of economic growth; it wanted to ensure that another crisis would not arise from a temporary "band-aid" solution to the problem. The resulting 1983 reform of the Federal Insurance Contribution Act (FICA) more than doubled the FICA tax. Consequently, FICA revenues exceeded Social Security benefit payments by a healthy $40 billion in 1988, with even heftier surpluses on the horizon.

Social Security surpluses are legally required to be placed in "reserves" that are based on "investments" in long-term U.S. Treasury bonds. This seems, on the surface, to be both prudent policy and a good way to ensure a healthy market for government securities. Figure A reflects recent Social Security Administration long-term forecasts of its expected outlays (benefit payments), income (FICA tax revenues), and reserves (holdings of U.S. Treasury bonds). Social Security taxes will soon exceed personal income taxes as sources of federal revenue. In fact, the Social Security Trust Fund Reserve, based on expected cumulative surpluses, is anticipated to mount to roughly $12 *trillion* by 2030. A wave of "boomer" retirements should begin in about 2008, however, and last until about 2030. Reserves will gradually be dissipated until, by 2050, they are completely exhausted.

The enormity of the financial flows into and out of the Social Security Trust Fund will require major macroeconomic adjustments based on careful planning. The $12 trillion in total reserves expected by 2030, for example, is about 10 times as large as the level of privately held federal debt in 1988.

One effect of the imminent surge of FICA revenues may be a powerful reversal of federal deficits and national debt. Every dollar of surplus in the Social Security system will slash the federal deficit by a dollar. If the Social Security system's surpluses are, as expected, larger than the rest of the U.S. Treasury's deficits, then the federal government will run a net surplus. Anticipated Social Security surpluses will undoubtedly absorb all outstanding national debt by the upcoming turn of the century.

All national debt (and more) will soon be owned by the Social Security system. Once the national debt has been absorbed, a new law must be passed to either allow the Social Security Administration to buy other assets, or to view FICA as a pure tax. Our entire financial system will be reshaped by this massive change:

1. The FED will not be able to alter its holdings of Treasury bonds. This means that Open-Market Operations will be impossible unless the law is changed so that some national debt is available for this purpose. Without such a change, the FED will lose its most valuable tool for controlling the money supply.
2. The portfolios of many individuals and financial institutions rely on Treasury bonds as the most riskless of all financial assets. As privately held national debt disappears, either (*a*) most portfolios will be somewhat more risky (raising the possibility of macro-financial instability) or (*b*) new instruments that are relatively riskless must be developed.

In a sense, public saving (through the Social Security Administration) may become so enormous that real interest rates in private financial markets will plummet. This should facilitate both domestic investment by U.S. companies and substantial investment abroad. If these developments occur as expected, the United States, which moved from being the world's largest creditor nation in 1980 to being its greatest debtor by 1985, could easily revert to being the world's largest supplier of investment funds.

The Social Security surpluses expected over the next 40 years are, in a sense, a nest egg that could, if invested properly, support our retirement system permanently. A major issue is: Into what should these funds be invested? Even if our national debt were to double by 1995, it would only amount to $2.5 trillion—and total reserve funds are expected to mount to $12 trillion. As you might expect, answers from all over the political spectrum have been offered to the question of how these retirement funds should be used.

Some critics argue that the expected Social Security surpluses justify huge current expenditures to fix our roads, enrich our educational system, or cure poverty everywhere. Others want to defend Social Security from any spending binge. Rep. Andrew Jacobs of the House Social Security Subcommittee has characterized this task: "It'll be like walking through a bad neighborhood with a diamond ring."

Others assert that this public saving (Social Security) is just a distortive shift away from what should be decisions by private individuals. According to this line of reasoning, FICA taxes should be slashed so that private individuals could choose their own retirement plans. A variant of this approach would be to allow individuals to specify for themselves the types of investments into which their taxes would be placed. This approach has been described as "privatization."

The "baby-boomers" were a tidal wave that engulfed our educational system in the 1950s and 1960s and flooded the labor market in the 1970s and 1980s. The depressed savings rate of the 1970s and 1980s reflected their attempts to borrow huge amounts so that they could buy their way into the good life. It is predictable that the aging and then retirement of this bubble of humanity will have profound social and economic consequences. A burst of saving (albeit public saving) for retirement by this group will probably transform persistent federal deficits into surpluses and national debt into national "credit." The precise ways that this occurs will be determined by how macroeconomic policymakers choose to cope with the issues addressed in this chapter.

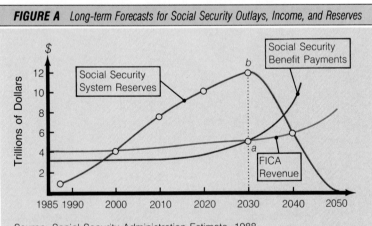

FIGURE A *Long-term Forecasts for Social Security Outlays, Income, and Reserves*

Source: Social Security Administration Estimate, 1988.
Note: When FICA revenue exceeds benefit payments (up to point *a*), total FICA reserves grow (up to point *b*). Thereafter, payments exceed revenue, so total FICA reserves decline.

Finally, the government has a large stock of tangible assets, including land, buildings, and equipment. Annually adjusting our public debt data in the same way as corporations would to obtain net worth tells a different story. Figure 9 shows the budget deficit and public debt adjusted for inflation, its market values, and changing values of assets and liabilities since 1960. Interestingly, there are years in which the government reported a deficit and this adjusted budget indicates a surplus.

The reported "official" deficit may provide misleading signals for macroeconomic policy. In years when policymakers think there is a deficit and the budget is really in surplus, contractionary measures to balance a budget would be counterproductive. Even after all adjustments are made, however, there is still a striking move toward a government in deficit in recent years. While U.S. policymakers fight rising deficits, how do our levels of debt and deficits compare to those of other industrialized countries?

International Comparisons of Debt

Until recently, national debt as a percent of U.S. GNP was declining. Figure 10 shows budget deficits, gross public debt, and household savings rates as a percent of Gross Domestic Product (*GDP*) for thirteen developed countries in 1986. (*GDP* excludes the foreign sector.) The lines across the figure are averages for these thirteen countries. Most ran deficits and most had large public debts in proportion to their *GDP*s. The United States currently has an average deficit, below average debt ratio, and below average saving rate. U.S. debt and deficits are large absolutely, but don't appear disastrous relative to those in many other developed countries.

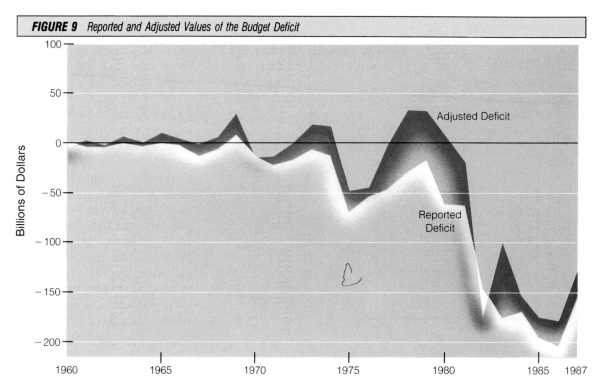

FIGURE 9 Reported and Adjusted Values of the Budget Deficit

Robest Eisner has dragged the antiquated accounting system used by the federal government for its budgeting into closer conformity with modern corporate accounting standards. His estimates suggest that recent federal deficits have not been as terrible as the official data indicate.

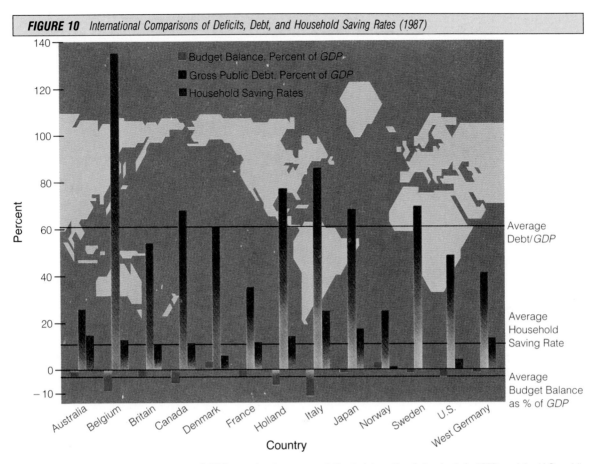

FIGURE 10 *International Comparisons of Deficits, Debt, and Household Saving Rates (1987)*

The U.S. budget deficit as a percentage of *GDP* was about average relative to international standards in 1987, and the U.S. public debt was relatively lower than in most countries, but Americans typically save smaller shares of their personal incomes than do average people elsewhere.

One area worthy of major concern is the net international investment position of the United States. Figure 11 traces our path as we deteriorated from the world's largest net international investor in 1981 to its biggest net creditor by 1986. Large parts of recent federal deficits were financed by foreign investment in the United States.

What can we conclude about the current state of public debt in the United States? Clearly, both debt and deficits, no matter how measured, have been growing in recent years. Any deficit must be financed with bonds or new monetary base and rising deficits have predictable impacts on our international accounts.

To the extent that added debt is used for public investment, future generations may gain, but they will bear the burden if debt and deficits are used to finance consumption for the current generation. Large deficits and debts can increase real interest rates that may soak up additional government resources in the future. Reducing government spending appears impossible since so many federal outlays are relatively uncontrollable.

Finally, when we compare our national debt and deficits to other developed countries, the United States shows up rather well. All in all, the growing debt and deficits in our country are a cause for concern and need to be addressed over the long haul. They do not, however, appear to be the crisis situation that so may politicians and pundits would have us believe.

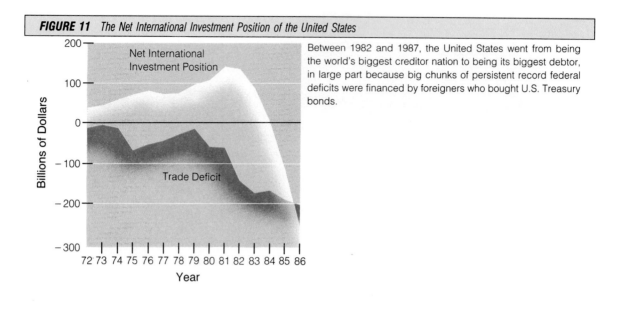

FIGURE 11 *The Net International Investment Position of the United States*

Net International Investment Position

Trade Deficit

Billions of Dollars

200

100

0

−100

−200

−300

72 73 74 75 76 77 78 79 80 81 82 83 84 85 86

Year

Between 1982 and 1987, the United States went from being the world's biggest creditor nation to being its biggest debtor, in large part because big chunks of persistent record federal deficits were financed by foreigners who bought U.S. Treasury bonds.

CHAPTER REVIEW: KEY POINTS

1. The *budget deficit* equals annual government outlays minus receipts. The *public debt* is total federal indebtedness resulting from current and past deficits.

2. *Balancing the budget annually* might result in incorrect fiscal actions to combat either inflation or recession. Some have suggested balancing the budget *over the business cycle.* This would entail running deficits during recessions and surpluses over the boom. Unfortunately, business cycles are not symmetric, and the budget may not be easy to balance over the cycle without hampering prosperity. Advocates of *functional finance* believe that the size of the public debt is unimportant. They suggest that we ignore the problem of balancing the budget and focus on balancing the economy instead.

3. The federal government can finance *public spending* by collecting taxes, printing money, selling government securities, or through confiscation. All of these techniques are drains on *gross private saving* (production minus private consumption) that can crowd out private economic activities. *Ricardian equivalence* suggests that whether government spending is financed by taxes or borrowing is irrelevant.

4. The *crowding-out hypothesis* states that increases in government purchases inevitably reduces private consumption, investment, or leisure.

5. Federal deficits can be financed by increasing domestic saving, securing the savings of foreigners, or by reducing domestic investment or exports. All else constant, a growing budget deficit will cause growth of a trade deficit.

6. Some government spending is uncontrollable (roughly three quarters today). These programs are long-range or are committed by law each and every year. Reducing these expenditures is virtually impossible.

7. A major difference between private and public debt is that *private debt* is entirely owned by persons *external* to the issuing institution, while the bulk of *public debt* is *internal,* being owed to ourselves. Private debt has grown faster than public debt since the early 1950s and is currently over twice as big.

8. The *real burden of the national debt* stems from the federal government "crowding out" private investment as it drives interest rates up when competing with the private sector for loanable funds. As a result, future generations may inherit a smaller capital stock and a smaller production-possibilities frontier.

9. Among the major benefits of the public debt are its use as a *stabilization instrument* and as a *risk-free asset* for savers.

QUESTIONS FOR THOUGHT AND DISCUSSION

1. What are the potential advantages and disadvantages if the Constitution were amended to require that the federal outlays and receipts be balanced each time the Earth circles the sun?

2. Explain the sense in which federal taxes determine how much each of us will help control inflation. If you could print money, would you ever try to remove any from circulation as long as there were trees and green ink? Why? Why does the federal government bother to collect taxes?

3. Government spending can be financed by taxation, borrowing, or by creating new money. Rank these from least expansionary to most expansionary and explain your ranking system.

4. What mechanisms cause the Federal Reserve System to experience pressure to expand the money supply when the Treasury runs a huge deficit? When the FED yields to this pressure, does this add or detract from the goal of achieving macroeconomic stability? Why?

5. Why do foreigners willingly hold Treasury bonds that represent so much of our national debt? Is it desirable from our vantage point for them to do so? What are the long-term consequences of these loans?

Challenges to
Macroeconomic Policy-making

PART 5

You now have some ideas about how fiscal policy works (from Part 3) and how money affects economic activity (from Part 4). This part of the book extends our previous macroeconomic models to consider how different policies may operate under varying economic conditions.

The foundations of Aggregate Demand and Aggregate Supply curves are featured in chapter 16. We use these curves to investigate some of the reasons for the prosperity of the 1960s, the "stagflation" of the erratic 1970s, and the economic crunch, disinflation, and then recovery of the 1980s.

Problems faced by policymakers who try to achieve full employment, price level stability, and healthy economic growth are the focus of chapter 17. We deal in depth with the *Phillips curve,* which suggests that there may be a

trade-off between unemployment and inflation. Also discussed is the theory of *rational expectations,* which implies that private adjustments to discretionary macroeconomic policy will thwart its effectiveness.

We hope that our earlier descriptions of monetary and fiscal policy have not convinced you that macroeconomic problems are easily solved. We survey such alternative approaches to policy as price controls and industrial policy in chapter 18. We also deal with major impediments to macroeconomic tinkering: such problems as poor timing, erratic lags, and improper doses of policies.

This part of the book concludes with chapter 19, where we examine the challenge of achieving long-run economic growth and development. It would be hard to overestimate the hurdles confronted in countries plagued by inadequate natural resources, high rates of population growth, and insufficient capital as people attempt to improve their standards of living.

stagflation

Aggregate Demand curve

Aggregate Supply curve

demand-side
(demand-pull) inflation

supply-side (cost-push)
inflation

disinflation

CHAPTER 16

Aggregate Demand and Supply

Conventional monetarist or Keynesian approaches offer little insight into why high rates of inflation and unemployment might occur simultaneously. A major reason is that these models focus on variations in Aggregate Demand while, in the 1970s, Aggregate Supply was battered. Most economists had ignored possible supply-side shocks, so the failure of demand-side models to explain the events of the 1970s seemed an enigma. More recent macroeconomic models have begun to address problems posed by changes in Aggregate Supply.

High unemployment and inflation first occurred simultaneously in 1974–75, giving rise to "stagflation"—a contraction of stagnation and inflation.

Stagflation *is the simultaneous occurrence of high rates of inflation and unemployment.*

This malady proved persistent. Inflation and unemployment remained well above historical norms for a full decade. Attempts to knock inflation down from the double-digit range during 1979–81 had partially

succeeded by 1982, but temporarily drove unemployment above 10 percent. By 1988, inflation had settled in at around 3 percent, while unemployment fell below 6 percent.

Double-digit inflation with high unemployment (or double-digit unemployment with rapid hikes in price levels) was thought so unlikely that these possibilities were ignored during the 1950s and 1960s. Policymakers familiar with Keynesian theory believed that low unemployment rates might stimulate rapid inflation, and vice versa, but faith in government's ability to fine-tune Aggregate Demand to produce continuous growth and a reasonably stable price level was commonplace. By the end of the 1970s, however, many economists had become skeptical about government's ability to fine-tune the economy by manipulating Aggregate Demand. In the early 1980s, the Reagan administration turned its attention to expanding Aggregate Supply.

The time paths of employment, inflation, national output and income, and unemployment can be explained by relative shifts in Aggregate Demand and Aggregate Supply. But why is Aggregate Demand positively sloped, while Aggregate Supply is negatively sloped? And what causes these curves to shift?

The Aggregate Demand Curve

Keynesian policy analysis is largely a prescription for achieving full employment if the economy is operating below its potential, but it generally ignores the inflation that might emerge if Aggregate Demand is excessive. On the other hand, total spending by both consumers and investors is sensitive to the price level, and vice versa. Let us see why.

The market demand curve for a specific good is negatively sloped because consumers substitute towards other goods when its price rises. Rationalizing a negative slope for the economy's Aggregate Demand curve is more difficult.

> The **Aggregate Demand curve** *reflects a negative relationship between the price level (P) and the quantity demanded (Q) of national output.*

If the general price level rises, toward what goods will consumers move? Substitution remains important but it shows up in a different guise when we consider the economy as a whole.

Slope of the Aggregate Demand Curve

All else equal, planned spending on American products falls when higher domestic prices cause:

1. higher interest rates that reduce planned investment, Aggregate Expenditures, and ultimately, output.
2. the purchasing power of assets stated in money terms to fall, causing wealth to decline.
3. American and foreign consumers to substitute goods produced elsewhere for American-made goods.
4. investors to find foreign investment relatively more profitable than U.S. investment.

Let us examine each of these relationships briefly. You will see that each effect operates by reducing the Aggregate Expenditures schedule. For simplicity, we will temporarily assume that all domestic prices—including wages and rents—increase by the same proportion.

Interest Rate/Investment Adjustments   A major reason for the negative slope of the Aggregate Demand curve is the effect that higher prices have on the chain reaction from interest rates to investment to Aggregate Spending, and then to income and output. These adjustments closely parallel the Keynesian monetary transmission mechanism you saw earlier.

When prices rise, the real purchasing power of a fixed money supply (M/P) falls. Consider Figure 1. Raising the price level from P_0 to P_1 (Panel D) has the following effect in Panel A: The nominal money supply is assumed constant at M_{s0}; so the real supply of money shifts from M_{s0}/P_0 to M_{s0}/P_1. Equilibrium interest rates rise from i_0 (point a) to i_1 (point b). Rising interest rates result in equilibrium moving from point a to point b in Panel B; thus, planned investment falls from I_0 to I_1. This reduction in planned investment shifts the Aggregate Expenditures schedule in Panel C from AE_0 to AE_1, resulting in a reduction in real national income from Y_0 (point a) to Y_1 (point b). Finally, this reduced national income at higher prices means real output must fall from Q_0 (point a) to Q_1 (point b), as shown in Panel D. Duplicating this same process for every possible price level results in the negatively sloped Aggregate Demand curve illustrated in Panel D. The higher interest rates that result from higher prices squeeze both government spending at the local and state levels (especially that which is bond financed) and consumer credit, in addition to crowding-out private investment. Thus, higher interest rates reduce all these sources of Aggregate Spending.

The Wealth Effect   Another reason for the negative slope of the Aggregate Demand curve is termed the *wealth effect*. Most of us hold some of our wealth in such assets as cash or savings accounts. Changes in the price level alter the purchasing power of these assets and, hence, our wealth. As our wealth rises, we tend to spend more for both consumption and investment goods, and vice versa.

Suppose the price level fell sharply. To the extent that your wealth rises because of the increased purchasing power of your assets held as money, you will

FIGURE 1 Interest Rates, Investment, and the Negatively Sloped Aggregate Demand Curve

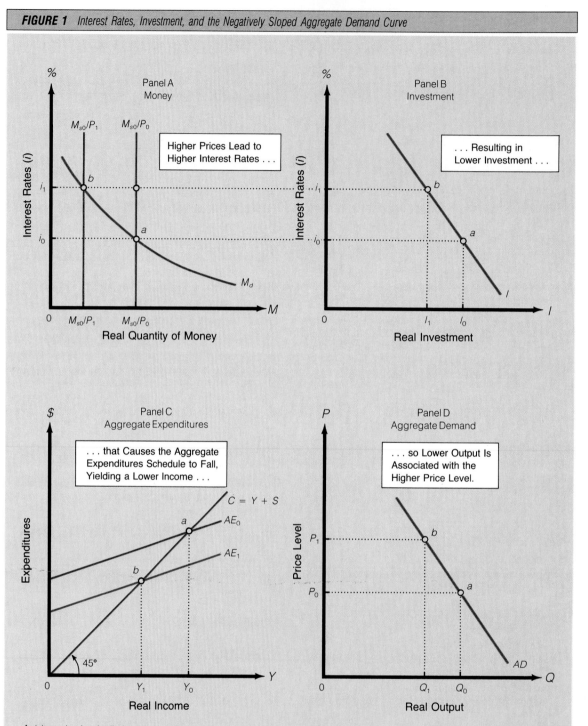

A rising price level, all else equal, reduces the real supply of money (Panel A), which increases interest rates, reducing investment (Panel B) and Aggregate Expenditures and income (Panel C). Reduced income at higher prices means real output has fallen (Panel D). Repeating this process for all possible price levels produces a negatively sloped Aggregate Demand curve.

be able to buy more goods and services and so you will spend more. Conversely, even if your monetary income keeps pace with the price level during an inflationary episode, you will lose to the extent that your wealth is stored as cash or in bank accounts and you will reduce your spending.

Another adjustment occurs because most of us want to maintain fairly stable amounts of liquid assets relative to our income. Thus, even if your income rises at the same rate as the price level, you may temporarily reduce the proportion of income devoted to consumption so that the purchasing power of your liquid assets is restored through a short-term higher rate of saving. Because consumption declines as the price level climbs due to the wealth effect, Aggregate Spending also falls in a manner similar to that described for interest rate/investment adjustments and shown in Figure 1.

Exports and Imports We import goods when foreigners can produce them at lower costs and export goods when American production costs are lower than those in other countries. (International trade is addressed in detail in a later chapter.) If the prices of American goods rise, you will buy more imported goods than previously because they will be relatively cheaper. At the same time, foreign consumers will reduce their purchases of now higher priced American goods. Thus, inflation causes imports to increase and exports to decrease, resulting in reduced Aggregate Expenditures and National Income and Output.

Foreign Investment Increases in American prices usually are accompanied by higher U.S. costs of production. Higher wages and increased costs for land and machinery in the United States make it profitable for investors (both domestic and foreign) to reduce investment in the United States and substitute foreign investment, which reinforces the decline in Aggregate Spending as the price level rises from P_0 to P_1 in Figure 1.

To summarize, higher prices cause lower quantities of Aggregate Demand because (*a*) rising prices result in higher interest rates that reduce investment and purchases of consumer durables; (*b*) rising prices reduce the real value of assets stated in monetary terms (the wealth effect); (*c*) imports grow and exports fall; and (*d*) domestic investment declines and foreign investment by U.S. firms flourishes.

Shifts in Aggregate Demand

Any changes in planned Aggregate Expenditures (vertical shifts in Keynesian cross diagrams) are paralleled by shifts of the Aggregate Demand curve. Thus, spending plans ultimately determine the magnitude of Aggregate Demand. Movements of the Aggregate Demand curve are caused by changes in monetary or fiscal policies or by changes in planned consumption, investment, or foreign spending. How changes in the various influences that affect spending plans will cause the Aggregate Demand curve to shift are summarized in the chart below Figure 2.

How expanded spending plans shift Aggregate Demand to the right is shown in Panel B of Figure 2. Plans to spend more originate in tax cuts, increases in government purchases or transfer payments, or more optimistic expectations by consumers and investors. Expansionary monetary policies such as open-market purchases of bonds or reductions in either reserve requirements or the discount rate also cause growth of Aggregate Demand. Symmetrically, when the government pursues contractionary monetary or fiscal policies, the Aggregate Demand curve shifts to the left. This is shown as the movement from AD_0 to AD_1 in Panel A of Figure 2.

The Aggregate Supply Curve _____

Classical theory concludes that market forces will quickly and automatically drive an economy to full employment. Thus, it predicts a vertical long-run Aggregate Supply curve. Keynesian theory, on the other hand, deals with depressed economies plagued by so many idle resources that the Aggregate Supply curve is horizontal. An intermediate position is that Aggregate Supply is positively sloped.

> The **Aggregate Supply curve** *reflects a positive relationship between the price level and the real quantity of national output.*

Slope of the Aggregate Supply Curve

The general law of diminishing returns partially accounts for the upward slope of supply curves for individual firms and for market supply curves. Additional production eventually becomes ever more costly as the level of production grows. Producers' costs rise

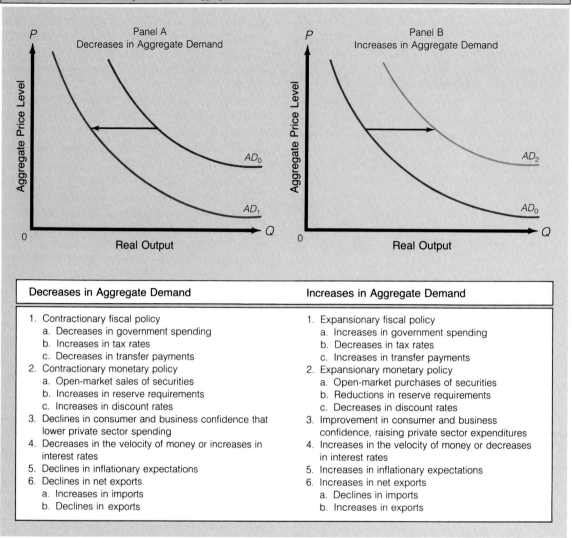

FIGURE 2 *Factors Causing Shifts in the Aggregate Demand Curve*

Panel A
Decreases in Aggregate Demand

Aggregate Price Level / P

Real Output / Q

AD_0

AD_1

Panel B
Increases in Aggregate Demand

Aggregate Price Level / P

Real Output / Q

AD_2

AD_0

Decreases in Aggregate Demand	Increases in Aggregate Demand
1. Contractionary fiscal policy a. Decreases in government spending b. Increases in tax rates c. Decreases in transfer payments 2. Contractionary monetary policy a. Open-market sales of securities b. Increases in reserve requirements c. Increases in discount rates 3. Declines in consumer and business confidence that lower private sector spending 4. Decreases in the velocity of money or increases in interest rates 5. Declines in inflationary expectations 6. Declines in net exports a. Increases in imports b. Declines in exports	1. Expansionary fiscal policy a. Increases in government spending b. Decreases in tax rates c. Increases in transfer payments 2. Expansionary monetary policy a. Open-market purchases of securities b. Reductions in reserve requirements c. Decreases in discount rates 3. Improvement in consumer and business confidence, raising private sector expenditures 4. Increases in the velocity of money or decreases in interest rates 5. Increases in inflationary expectations 6. Increases in net exports a. Declines in imports b. Increases in exports

with output. Thus, firms may require higher prices to justify expanding their outputs. Moreover, higher prices embody greater incentives for firms to produce more output because of the enhanced opportunities for profits. A similar logic applies for the economy as a whole.

Capacity and Price/Cost Dynamics The availability of idle resources shrinks when higher employment presses against society's productive capacity. If Aggregate Demand grows, however, the resource costs of a

firm tend to rise less rapidly than the prices it can charge. Thus, profit per unit of output grows during a business upturn. Business firms naturally respond by producing and selling more goods. But prices tend to fall faster than costs when business slows down. Profit per unit of output may even become negative. Declining profit margins cause firms to drastically cut back on their orders and to lay off workers.

For example, if demand expands for food and sundries from your local grocery store, the manager will order more goods and quickly mark up prices. Grocers will also hire more workers. Employees' wages and other costs will rise, but much less rapidly than prices, so that total profits swell. What happens if demand collapses? The prices the grocer charges will fall much faster than wages or other production costs. Profit plummets, so many grocery workers will lose their jobs.

Conclusion? Production costs per unit are much slower to adjust to changes in Aggregate Demand than are the prices of output. This is the major reason why a short-run Aggregate Supply curve is positively sloped.

An Aggregate Supply curve is shown in Figure 3. Note that if much of our capacity is idle, as Keynes suggested, so that output is less than Q_0, output can increase in the short run without significant increases in the price level. But when the classical prediction of full employment is approached, even small increases in output above Q_1 necessitate huge increases in the price level. Between output levels Q_0 and Q_1, moderate increases in output result in moderate price hikes.

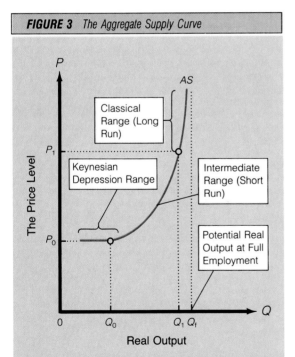

FIGURE 3 *The Aggregate Supply Curve*

The Aggregate Supply curve, like the market supply curve, is positively sloped. This suggests that increases in National Output normally entail increases in the price level.

National Output and the Work Force

National output expands as increasing numbers of workers are employed productively. At some point, however, each additional worker adds less and less to total output because of diminishing returns. The labor market operates on the basis of supply and demand much like the other markets we have studied. Higher wages may induce greater effort (e.g., overtime work), attract more people into the labor force, or cause unemployed workers to take jobs sooner without extended shopping for better jobs. Thus, unless the economy is extremely slack, labor's supply curve has a positive slope.

Increases in the total demand for labor generate pressure for higher employment and output levels and for hikes in wages and prices as well. Conversely, declines in the economywide demand for labor create pressure for lower employment, output, wages, and prices. There are, however, differences between short-run and long-run adjustments. Understanding Aggregate Supply requires an appreciation of these differences.

Labor Market Adjustments: The Short Run   Let us begin our discussion of short-run adjustments by re-examining the Keynesian depression model. In a severe depression like that of the 1930s, Keynes believed that business could fill any vacant positions at the going wage. Suppose that Aggregate Demand grew slightly. There would be no need to increase wages to attract additional labor because so much of the labor force would be out of work. This part of labor's supply curve is assumed to be flat because growing business demands for labor could be met at the prevailing market wage. Large quantities of idle capital also prevent diminishing returns from posing a problem. Thus, if the demand for labor grows during a depression, employment and output rise but wages and prices may not. Consequently, Keynesian analysis assumes a horizontal *Aggregate Supply curve* (see the Keynesian depression range in Figure 3). Remember that from Keynes's point of view, Say's Law was backwards and should have read "Demand creates its own supply."

Keynes's assumptions about depressed labor markets are drawn from the 1930s experience of an extended and severe depression. Labor's supply curve normally has a positive slope, reflecting the fact that drawing more workers into the labor force requires higher wages; rising wages also enable un-employed workers to more rapidly find jobs they perceive as suitable. As firms pay higher wages to attract additional employees, wages rise for all workers. This results in a moderately positive slope in the Aggregate Supply curve, shown as the intermediate range in Figure 3.

Workers recognize that increases in the price level will lower their real wages, but there is a time lag between a given inflationary reduction in real wages and labor's comprehension of this loss. Workers may temporarily be fooled by hikes in money wages that are less than the inflation rate so that more labor services may be offered even though real wages decline. Firms hire more labor to produce more output if they can sell that output at higher prices. They do so because they perceive new profit opportunities from selling their products at higher prices and because real wages have declined. In the short run, workers fail to revise their expectations about changes in the price level and are fooled because they believe the original price level will prevail. Workers may suffer from inflation illusion in the very short run, but their misconceptions are unlikely to persist.

Labor Market Adjustments: The Longer Run   In the longer run, workers will recognize price increases as reducing their real wages (w/P) and will react by reducing the real supply of labor. Suppose Aggregate Demand grows even though the economy is close to full employment. Higher money wages may temporarily lure more workers into the labor force if they expect the price level to remain constant. Workers try to base decisions about their work loads on real wages, not on nominal money wages. People work for what their earnings will buy, not for the money itself. Once workers recognize that prices have risen, they will demand commensurate raises, resulting in a vertical long-run Aggregate Supply curve similar to the classical range shown in Figure 3.

This analysis represents the polar extreme from Keynesian analysis, being derived from the classical reasoning we have described previously. Classical economics assumes that workers react to changes in real wages almost instantly, keeping the economy close to full employment. At the very least, there can be no involuntary unemployment.

In reality, workers do not react quickly to changes in real earnings. Focus 1 indicates that firms may have

better access to information about inflation while needing less of it than workers do to react to changes in the price level. Workers also respond relatively slowly because (*a*) most long-term union contracts set nominal wages for the lives of these agreements; (*b*) many nonunion wages are adjusted only at scheduled intervals; and (*c*) changing jobs often entails considerable "search time" and lost income.

Shifts in Aggregate Supply

Labor is just one of the resources used to produce goods; other resources also shape the Aggregate Supply curve through their effects on productive capacity and costs. In addition, regulations and technology affect the relationships between resource inputs and production.

We begin our discussion of Aggregate Supply curve shifts with a quick review of the influences on individual market supply curves facing buyers, already detailed in chapter 3. In addition to price, the major determinants are (*a*) resource costs, (*b*) production technology, (*c*) expectations, (*d*) taxes or subsidies or regulations on producers, (*e*) prices of other producible goods, and (*f*) number of producers in the market. Changes in influences other than its own price cause market supplies of a good to shift.

We are dealing with the Aggregate Supply curve for the economy, however, which encompasses all production and all producers. Substitutions between domestic production of different goods tend to cancel each other out, so we will ignore the changes in the prices of other producible goods. We are left with changes in the quantities and costs of available resources, technology, expectations, and regulations and government policy as the four major shifters of the Aggregate Supply curve.

You may be getting tired of this curve bending, but we urge you to bear with us for a few more moments. You nearly have the tools necessary for understanding and formulating solutions to the greatest economic problem of the 1970s and early 1980s—solving the stagflation dilemma; disruptive shocks to Aggregate Supply are the ultimate explanation of stagflation.

Shocks Arising in the Labor Market   Labor supplies depend on individual preferences for income from labor versus personal enjoyment of leisure. As our

Why John Smith, but Not General Motors, May Be Fooled by Inflation

There are at least a couple of reasons why workers may be more easily fooled by inflation than are the firms that employ them. First, firms devote more resources to forecasts of inflation. Second, a firm only needs to estimate how much extra revenue will be generated if extra workers are hired to know how much of a monetary wage (w) it can profitably afford to pay. This calculation requires only estimates of the worker's physical productivity and a forecast of the price (P_i) at which the firm will be able to sell its own product.

Thus, the real wage paid a worker from the vantage point of the firm is w/P_i. Workers, on the other hand, must have forecasts of all the prices of all goods they expect to buy (e.g., the *CPI*) before they can estimate the purchasing power of their monetary wages. The real wage from the point of view of a typical worker equals w/CPI. Thus, firms may need less information about future prices (only P_i) to make profitable decisions than workers need (forecasts of most prices in the *CPI*) in order to make personally beneficial decisions.

economy has matured, there seem to be strong tendencies for shorter workweeks, more part-time employment, and for other forms of work sharing that allow people more leisure time. Increases in labor's preference for leisure over work cause the labor supply curve to shift to the left, reducing total labor supplies. This reduction in labor supply shifts Aggregate Supply to the left, as illustrated in Panel A of Figure 4 by the shift from AS_0 to AS_1. Alternatively, if more people chose to work or began working longer hours, Aggregate Supply might shift from AS_0 to AS_2, as shown in Panel B.

Work-leisure choices for many people are strongly influenced by taxes and social welfare policies. For example, if personal income tax rates rise, fewer people may work or those who do may work fewer hours. Increases in Social Security taxes accomplished by boosting either the tax rate or the maximum amount of income covered will probably also shrink the supply of labor. These leftward shifts of the labor supply curve occur because higher taxes make earning additional income worth less. Workers base work-leisure decisions on take-home pay, not gross wages.

Unemployment compensation or welfare payments also affect the supply of labor. If unemployment compensation payments are raised or extended for longer periods, the labor supply will shrink because more people will draw these benefits. You may have heard stories like the one about the Michigan golf pro who works summers in Michigan and spends winters in Florida. Competition from other migratory Northern golf pros is so severe that he draws unemployment compensation in Florida each winter while he practices putting. This behavior occurs because people often qualify for unemployment compensation payments unless they are offered and subsequently decline "comparable" positions.

Analysis of this type was at the heart of the 25 percent cut in income tax rates phased in during 1981–83 and also was partially responsible for vigorous attempts to cut growth in government transfer payments and other social programs. The Reagan administration hoped that revitalization of incentives to produce would raise Aggregate Supply more than these tax cuts raised Aggregate Demand, so that substantial growth would offset any emerging inflationary pressure.

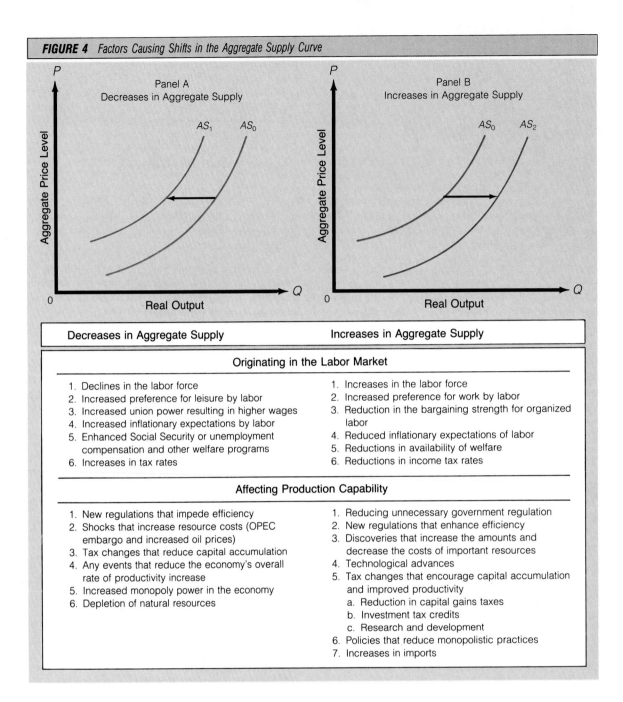

FIGURE 4 Factors Causing Shifts in the Aggregate Supply Curve

Panel A
Decreases in Aggregate Supply

Panel B
Increases in Aggregate Supply

Decreases in Aggregate Supply	Increases in Aggregate Supply
Originating in the Labor Market	
1. Declines in the labor force 2. Increased preference for leisure by labor 3. Increased union power resulting in higher wages 4. Increased inflationary expectations by labor 5. Enhanced Social Security or unemployment compensation and other welfare programs 6. Increases in tax rates	1. Increases in the labor force 2. Increased preference for work by labor 3. Reduction in the bargaining strength for organized labor 4. Reduced inflationary expectations of labor 5. Reductions in availability of welfare 6. Reductions in income tax rates
Affecting Production Capability	

1. New regulations that impede efficiency
2. Shocks that increase resource costs (OPEC embargo and increased oil prices)
3. Tax changes that reduce capital accumulation
4. Any events that reduce the economy's overall rate of productivity increase
5. Increased monopoly power in the economy
6. Depletion of natural resources
	1. Reducing unnecessary government regulation
	2. New regulations that enhance efficiency
	3. Discoveries that increase the amounts and decrease the costs of important resources
	4. Technological advances
	5. Tax changes that encourage capital accumulation and improved productivity
	   a. Reduction in capital gains taxes
	   b. Investment tax credits
	   c. Research and development
	6. Policies that reduce monopolistic practices
	7. Increases in imports

A second type of labor market disturbance would occur if unions grew more powerful and organized labor commanded higher wages; the Aggregate Supply curve would decline. Wage hikes raise production costs and push up prices. A third source of disruption would be any rise in the inflation rate expected by labor. Inflationary expectations continuously shift the supply of labor curve leftward as workers try to protect the real purchasing power of their earnings. Naturally, decreases in inflationary expectations or in union power will shift the labor supply and Aggregate Supply curves toward the right.

Incomes Policies   Incomes policies might be used to reduce labor's inflationary expectations. The term **incomes policy** refers to a variety of measures designed to curb inflation without reducing Aggregate Demand. These methods include such practices as jawboning, wage-and-price guidelines, and wage-price controls. The most extreme of these is a *wage-price freeze* of the type imposed by President Nixon in 1971. It was hoped that this freeze would reduce the anticipated inflation rate to zero and stop continuous shrinkage of Aggregate Supply. Ideally, it might even increase the supplies of labor and output, shown as the shift of the Aggregate Supply curve from AS_0 to AS_2 in Figure 4.

Incomes policies, unfortunately, may have perverse effects on both inflationary expectations and Aggregate Supply. If workers and firms share a belief that prices will soar as soon as wage or price controls are lifted, they may withhold production from the market now in hopes of realizing higher wages or prices later. For example, suppose you have the following choices (*a*) you could work during a period when wages are frozen and save money to cover your college expenses, or (*b*) you could borrow to go to college during a freeze and then repay the loan from money you earn after the lid is removed from wage hikes. You will be like a lot of other people if you delay working until after the freeze. There is also a problem that relative price adjustments are hampered by incomes policies; in chapter 18 we detail how the resulting distortions in economic behavior retard Aggregate Supply.

Other Shocks Affecting Our Productive Capacity

Labor is only one of many influences on our national productive capacity. Many people argue that massive growth of government regulation causes inefficiency. Some recent estimates suggest that between 5 and 10 percent of GNP is absorbed in complying with federal regulations.[1]

If new regulations smother the private business sector, the resulting inefficiency shifts the Aggregate Supply curve to the left (a movement from AS_0 to AS_1 in Figure 4). Elimination of burdensome federal regulation in turn shifts the Aggregate Supply curve rightward. For example, airline deregulation in 1978 resulted in sharp declines in fares and the emergence of several new airlines; passenger volume almost doubled in the decade that followed.[2] New regulations that facilitate efficiency increase the Aggregate Supply curve. For example, the supplies of professional services were enhanced by Federal Trade Commission orders forbidding the American Medical Association and American Bar Association from setting medical or legal fees or prohibiting advertising by doctors and lawyers.

Increased concentration of economic power also shrinks Aggregate Supply. Firms with monopoly power extract high prices and profits by reducing their output. Consumers become, in a sense, more desperate for these goods, so they pay higher prices. Alternatively, competition may intensify for a number of reasons, including other firms' quests for shares of monopolists' profits, technological breakthroughs, vigorous antitrust action, or the invasion of a market by imports. Events that enhance competition cause Aggregate Supply to grow.

Government policies that reduce incentives to accumulate capital or to introduce new technologies hamper economic growth. If policies impede investment and technological advances, the economy declines (or fails to grow as fast as it could), and the Aggregate Supply curve shifts to the left (or is held back). Government policy encouraging capital accumulation (for example, reduced capital gains taxation) or speeding the introduction of modern equipment (investment tax credits) shift the Aggregate Supply curve to the right.

From the mid-1970s onward, drives to deregulate many sectors of our economy were directed at removing inefficiency and bolstering Aggregate Supply. Deregulation was a major feature of the Reagan administration's supply-side policies. Substantial cuts in corporate taxes, favorable tax treatments for savers, investment tax credits, and accelerated depreciation allowances were all directed at expanding Aggregate Supply.

---

1. See Murray L. Weidenbaum and Robert DeFina, *The Rising Cost of Government Regulation* (St. Louis, Mo.: Center for the Study of American Business, 31 January 1977).

2. U.S. Aviation Safety Commission, April 18, 1988.

Politicians who favored these policies conceded that they would be most advantageous to upper income groups, but argued that the benefits of expanding Aggregate Supply would accrue to workers and the poor as well. Opponents, fearing that the benefits to the rich would far outweigh those to the poor, labeled this "trickle-down" economics. The 1986 Tax Reform Act, however, was intended to close tax loopholes so that investment would be less influenced by taxes and more by market forces. Loophole closure should enhance equity and stimulate growth of Aggregate Supply.

External shocks to the economy that increase the cost of imports or resources cause Aggregate Supply to shrink. Drastic shocks to the U.S. economy occurred when OPEC coalesced in 1973 and world oil prices quadrupled. The United States and other industrialized countries endured painful leftward shifts in their Aggregate Supply curves. Rightward shifts occur when new resources are discovered. For example, Great Britain and Mexico, respectively, were aided by Britain's North Sea oil finds and the discoveries of huge pools of Mexican oil during the late 1970s. Gluts of oil on world markets and the relative instability of OPEC drove prices down; energy costs fell in the mid-1980s, boosting our Aggregate Supply curve to the right.

Influences that shift Aggregate Supply are listed in the chart below Figure 4. Be sure that you understand why each factor moves Aggregate Supply as it does. Grasping these concepts is essential to understanding stagflation. Now that you have been exposed to the foundations of both the Aggregate Supply and Aggregate Demand curves, we can turn to the interesting problems of demand-side and supply-side inflation.

Supply-Side and Demand-Side Inflation _____

Equilibrium prices rise only if demands increase or supplies decrease. Inflation that originates on the *demand side* is referred to as "demand-pull inflation," while *supply-side* inflation is commonly termed "cost-push inflation."

You may have heard people complain, "If those #@*%! unions were less greedy and powerful, we would not suffer from inflation." Others blame all inflation on overly expansionary monetary policies. Still others cite government deficits as causing inflation: "Inflation would disappear if the federal budget ever balanced." Then there are those who blame wars or foreigners for our problems. What have been the basic sources of inflation in the last few decades? We will explore the expected equilibrium paths during both supply-side and demand-side inflation to begin to answer this complex question. Then we can compare these results with recent U.S. experience.

Demand-Side Inflation

Growth of Aggregate Demand in an economy operating below capacity causes employment, output, income, and, perhaps, the price level to grow. End of the Keynesian story. But suppose an economy is in a noninflationary equilibrium at full employment, such as that labeled point a in Figure 5: full employment GNP equals Q_f, and the price level is P_0. "Full employment" includes an allowance for frictional unemployment caused by flows of workers between jobs and in and out of the work force. Labor supplies reflect no expectations of inflation, which, along with other institutional characteristics and aggregate productive capacity, results in an Aggregate Supply curve of AS_0.

Now assume that Aggregate Demand rises from AD_0 to AD_1 because government spending grows, moving the economy towards a new short-run equilibrium at point b. We assumed that the economy started at full employment, but employment can exceed a full employment level if frictional unemployment falls and if business can be induced to employ the extra workers. If firms can pass the costs of hiring these workers forward to consumers, they will hire beyond the full employment point. The price level rises to P_1 with this swollen Aggregate Demand.

But what happens to the real wages of the workers? Money wages do not rise as quickly as prices rise, so real wages (w/P) fall. When labor eventually demands higher money wages to correct for this reduction in their purchasing power, the Aggregate

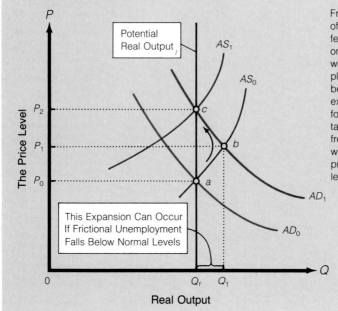

FIGURE 5 Demal-Side Inflation

Frictional unemployment, a normal by-product of economic activity, is represented by the difference between Q_1, which assumes that everyone who wants to work is employed, and Q_f, which makes allowances for frictional unemployment. Frictional unemployment may artificially be reduced below normal levels ($Q_1 - Q_f$) if expansions of Aggregate Demand temporarily fool some frictionally unemployed workers into taking jobs that pay low real wages (movement from a to b). In the long run, however, workers will adjust their wage demands to reflect higher prices, and unemployment will rise back to normal levels (movement from b to c).

Supply curve shifts leftward toward AS_1. Along the equilibrium path between points b and c, labor finds that although it receives higher money wages, these wages are partially eroded by continuing growth of the price level. How long will this process continue? Labor repeatedly reacts to price hikes by demanding higher wages until equilibrium at point c is reached. At this point, real wages have regained their original values and the economy is back to full employment with the aggregate price level equal to P_2, which is just equivalent to labor's expectations about the price level.

Price level increases initiated when the Aggregate Demand curve expands (shifts to the right) are called **demand-side** *or (demand-pull)* **inflation.**

Prices continue to rise when labor's inflationary expectations adjust and so might be thought of as supply-side inflation, but this is simply the second phase of a demand-side cycle—the original inflationary impetus came from increased demand. The forces that set this inflationary spiral in motion shift the Aggregate Demand curve to the right. Notice that as labor reacts to the inflationary spiral, the economy's equilibrium path runs from point a to b to c, following a *counterclockwise path.*

In the Keynesian discussion in chapter 10, we indicated that pressure for inflation builds when there is an inflationary gap, such as that reflected by $Q_1 - Q_f$ in Figure 5. In a sense, this is a "negative" GNP gap. As you can see, there are natural pressures that reduce output down from *overfull employment* towards full-employment levels. Overfull employment occurs because frictional unemployment is artificially driven down by expansions of Aggregate Demand. These adjustments are not instantaneous. The economy depicted in Figure 5 first moves from a to point b. When workers eventually discover that they have been fooled the labor supply falls, returning the system to full employment at point c—but at a higher price level. Remember that (a) we initially assumed a full employment economy, with allowances only for normal frictional unemployment, and (b) if the economy is initially plagued by excess capacity, that only the first phase of this cycle needs to occur—growing demand can yield much more output with only slightly higher prices.

Supply-Side Inflation

What happens if workers simply demand higher wages and their demands are not responses to inflation? This situation might occur if unions became stronger, if legislation making it easier to organize labor were enacted, or if hard bargaining by existing unions became the norm in key industries.

The effect of such actions by workers is illustrated in Figure 6. Their demands for higher wages will shift Aggregate Supply to the left. Suppose that the economy is originally in equilibrium at point d. As the Aggregate Supply curve shrinks from AS_0 to AS_1, equilibrium moves from point d to e. Business will

demand less labor at the higher wages because these higher costs can only partially be passed on to consumers as higher prices. Unless something happens to raise Aggregate Demand, less real output is demanded at the new price level P_1, and real output and employment are reduced to Q_1. For incumbent politicians, this is the worst of all worlds: rising prices and unemployment and declining real incomes and output.

As the economy moves to point e, policymakers may begin to worry about voters' reactions to recession. Policymakers may also perceive a duty to maintain full employment under the Employment Act of 1946 and the Full-Employment and Balanced Growth Act of 1978 (the Humphrey-Hawkins Act). The movement from point d to point e portrays an economy moving into a recession, and political pressures will mount to launch expansionary policies.

Alternatives to expanding Aggregate Demand would be policies to restore Aggregate Supply from AS_1 to AS_0. More output and employment would be generated at lower prices. This is a time-consuming process, so the federal government has historically tended to be demand-management oriented. President Reagan and his supporters were frustrated in the early 1980s because considerable time was required for supply-side policies to operate. Supply-side policies are aimed at increasing our productive capacity, a task not accomplished overnight. (Return to Figure 4 if you want to review policies that shift the Aggregate Supply curve to the right.)

Stimulating Aggregate Demand is a relatively quick and easy process; government cuts tax rates or boosts its outlays for goods and services or transfer payments, or the FED increases monetary growth. The president's party tends to lose voter support when unemployment begins to soar. Many have attributed President Ford's election loss to Jimmy Carter in 1976 to the joint occurrence of double-digit inflation and mounting unemployment during 1974 and 1975. Carter faced similar problems and lost the 1980 election. The sharp recession of 1981–83 reinforced Republican losses in the 1982 congressional elections. Many observers credited the 1984 Reagan landslide to a strong economic recovery that began in 1983. Focus 2 discusses the effect of economic conditions on the 1988 election.

FIGURE 6 *Supply-Side Inflation*

Shocks to the supply side cause prices to rise while output and employment fall (movement from point d to e). If policymakers follow expansionary policies to counter unemployment, prices will rise further (from point e to f). If, on the other hand, they fight inflation by reducing Aggregate Demand, the price level will remain at the P_0 level, but output and employment will shrink dramatically (from point d to g).

Macroeconomics and the 1988 Election

Many social commentators have criticized political campaigns as increasingly resembling beauty contests—looks, personality, and images created by public relations specialists are viewed as dominating recent political contests. But there is a growing body of evidence that economic circumstances have powerful effects on the outcomes of major elections.

Prosperity favors the prospects of political incumbents, and, apparently, the candidates of the party of the previous president. Ray Fair, a Yale economist, has developed a simple statistical equation based on three macroeconomic variables—unemployment, inflation, and growth of per capita real income—that "picked" the winner in all but two of the presidential elections held between 1948 and 1984 (and his equation predicted both of those elections to be close).

Fair's prediction for 1988? George Bush, by about 51 percent to 48 percent. President Bush's margin of victory in the election suggests that he may have received considerable support from voters because of the prolonged economic upswing that began in 1983.

Republican President Hoover did not stand a chance of reelection in 1932; the Great Depression that began late in 1929 (the year he took office) continued to worsen until 1933. Democrat Franklin D. Roosevelt's reelection in 1936 occurred during recovery, as did his reelection in 1940—the economy had faltered again in 1937, recovering during 1938-46. World War II yielded high levels of patriotic fervor and eco-

nomic prosperity, ensuring his reelection for an unprecedented fourth term in 1944. President Truman was reelected in November 1948—the month a business cycle reached its peak. Republican Dwight Eisenhower (a popular hero from World War II) defied the odds in besting Adlai Stevenson in 1952 when the economy was expanding, but his victory in 1956 occurred in the middle of an economic recovery from a 1954 recession, though the economy weakened again in 1957.

Richard Nixon blamed his narrow loss to Democrat John F. Kennedy on a minor recession in 1960. President Lyndon Johnson was reelected by a landslide in 1964 in the middle of the longest economic recovery since World War II. His vice-president, Hubert Humphrey, lost a close election to Richard Nixon in 1968 even though the U.S. economy was relatively strong. Fair's equation picked Humphrey as the winner by a slim margin. Humphrey's loss appears primarily to have resulted from dissension over the way Johnson conducted the unpopular Vietnam War. Nixon was determined to be reelected by a landslide in 1972; per capita income soared in that election year, and his wish (the same as most other incumbents) was granted.

President Ford, who succeeded Nixon after Nixon resigned because of the Watergate scandal, lost his 1976 bid for reelection to Jimmy Carter; the economy was still weak from the "energy crisis" and a severe recession in 1975. The economy recovered somewhat during 1976-78, but double digit inflation and

growing unemployment in 1979-80 doomed President Carter to his loss to Ronald Reagan.

President Reagan's intention to stimulate rapid economic growth through incentive-based supply-side policies was frustrated when the FED followed disinflationary policies in the early 1980s; the period 1982-83 was the deepest economic downturn that the United States had experienced since the Great Depression. A strong recovery that began late in 1983, however, swept Reagan into another four-year term of office.

This recovery continued through the 1988 election, which pitted George Bush against Michael Dukakis. Between 1983 and 1988, unemployment fell steadily, finally reaching a 5.5 percent rate—the lowest rate in nearly two decades. Inflation, which was at double digit rates in 1981, had stabilized by 1988 to a rate that most people perceived as tolerable. Economic growth continued a path of moderate recovery. Given this background, it seemed that George Bush, as the nominee of the incumbent party, should have won the election handily.

Why didn't Bush swamp Dukakis? By late 1988, most business economists predicted that a downturn was on the horizon. The 1987 collapse of the Stock Market convinced many voters that it was "time for a change." We will see in 1992 whether President Bush's policies secured the prosperity to enable him to serve another term of office, or whether he, like many of his predecessors, will suffer political defeat because of economic malaise.

In any event, government commonly counters shrinkage of Aggregate Supply by increasing Aggregate Demand, shown by a shift from AD_0 to AD_1 in Figure 6. With demand management, the economy will move along the equilibrium path described by the arrow from point e to f. Employment ultimately returns to a full employment level, but at a higher price level. Notice that the long-term equilibrium path for supply-side inflation is from point d to e to f, a *clockwise pattern*. (Remember, a demand-side inflationary cycle follows a counterclockwise pattern.)

Supply-side inflation *is initiated when the Aggregate Supply curve shifts to the left and the price level rises as output falls.*

A few qualifications should be noted at this point. First, shifts in the Aggregate Supply curve from AS_0 to AS_1 originate in a multitude of ways, summarized previously under Figure 4. Second, the federal government need not increase government spending to shift the Aggregate Demand curve from AD_0 to AD_1. For example, monetary authorities might stimulate rapid monetary growth in attempts to push the economy out of a recession.

U.S. Inflation: Demand-Side or Supply-Side?

We are now prepared to examine the inflationary experiences of the 1960s and 1970s.[3] The previous sections suggest that demand-side inflations cause the economy to equilibrate in a counterclockwise fashion, while supply-side inflations cause the economy to follow a clockwise pattern.

The inflations of the 1960s and 1970s are graphed in Figure 7. The most significant difference between this and previous graphs is that we have altered the axes slightly to accommodate the data. The GNP

FIGURE 7 Supply-Side and Demand-Side Inflations in the United States, 1962–80

When inflation originates from excessive growth in Aggregate Demand, the adjustment path follows a counterclockwise pattern, as was true of the 1960s. The clockwise pattern shows up for supply-side inflations, like that of the 1970s. Source: Adapted from the *Economic Report of the President*, 1988.

---

3. For an extended discussion of this issue, see Robert J. Gordon, *Macroeconomics*, 4th ed. (Glenview: Scott, Foresman and Company, 1987), especially Part IV. Our discussion owes much to Gordon's pioneering efforts.

deflator (described in chapter 6) is still measured on the vertical axis, but each period starts out at a base of 100. We also have converted the horizontal axis to real GNP divided by potential GNP so that we adjust for growth in our productive capacity. Potential GNP grows because of technological advances, capital accumulation, or growth of the labor force.

The demand-pull inflation of the 1960s resulted primarily from increased government spending for domestic programs, the space program, the escalation of the Vietnam conflict, stimulation from the 1964 tax cut, and rising monetary growth. As you can see in Panel A, the equilibrium process followed a counterclockwise path.

Contrast the 1960s inflation with that of the middle 1970s, which may have been triggered by rising prices for oil and other imported goods. A second major external shock was a worldwide drought and agricultural shortage, leading to price hikes in the United States as substantial domestic farm production found its way into the world market. The Arab oil embargo and ensuing OPEC price increases contributed strongly to the inflationary pressures of this period. Many economists would include the 1971–73 price controls as a shock to the supply side. Panel B of Figure 7 shows that the system equilibrated in a clockwise fashion, although price controls disguised inflationary pressure during 1971–73. This figure indicates that inflation in the 1970s derived primarily from supply-side pressures.

Prosperity in the 1960s

The economy was recovering from a modest recession when John F. Kennedy took office in 1961. President Kennedy used small doses of fiscal spending to support expansion and, in 1962, proposed cuts in tax rates to stimulate the economy and to reduce the government deficit as well. Appealing somewhat to "supply-side" arguments, he relied primarily on Keynesian multiplier analysis. Together, these approaches suggest that cuts in tax rates might increase both Aggregate Demand and Aggregate Supply (and, hence, GNP and income) sufficiently that tax revenues would actually rise rather than fall.

The 1960s were an era of increasing fiscal stimulus unmarred by serious supply-side shocks. The path of the American economy from 1961 to 1970 is depicted in Panel A of Figure 8 and is based on the actual data

for real GNP and the GNP deflator.[4] According to the model we have developed, this path appears to result from expansionary monetary and fiscal policies that accommodated the growth in potential GNP as the post–World War II baby boom began to enter the work force.

In Panel B of Figure 8, a set of curves representing Aggregate Demands and Supplies is superimposed over the equilibrium path shown in Panel A. The smooth rightward shifts in Aggregate Supply (Panel B) reflect regularity in the growth of potential output (full employment real GNP) each year. The vertical portion of the curve represents potential GNP in 1969. This figure reveals that the slightly more rapid growth of Aggregate Demand than Aggregate Supply during 1960–1969 did not trigger much inflation. Generally, there is considerable excess productive capacity in the early stages of a recovery, which was the case between 1961 and 1964. As the economy recovered and approached full employment, further increases in demand brought forth ever greater increases in prices and smaller increases in output.

As the United States escalated its role in Vietnam and domestic spending accelerated, the economy experienced mild but increasing inflation. This can be seen in Panel A of Figure 8 by looking at the economy's path from 1966 to 1970. The events of 1969–70 are especially interesting. The economy reached full employment and there was a slight surplus in the government budget for fiscal year 1969. Still, government spending continued to increase.

By 1971, the rate of inflation had become a matter of widespread concern, compounded because real output grew very little. Federal tax receipts fell 6 percent short of budget outlays, the prelude to a series of then record-breaking deficits—deficits that seem small by today's standards. As workers began to recognize erosion in the purchasing power of their wages, the shrinking supply phase of that demand-side cycle of inflation was activated. Rapid price increases unaccompanied by growth of real output

---

4. This figure does not incorporate the adjustment of GNP by potential GNP, which was used to depict clockwise and counterclockwise patterns in Figure 7.

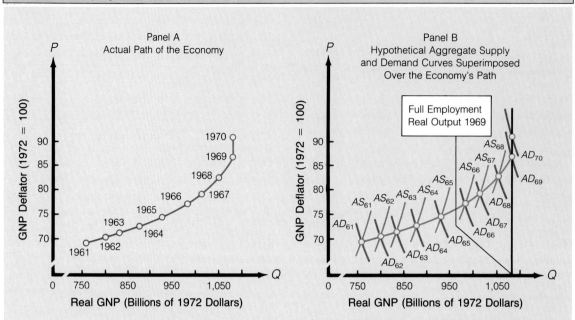

FIGURE 8 Prosperity of the 1960s

Panel A
Actual Path of the Economy

Panel B
Hypothetical Aggregate Supply
and Demand Curves Superimposed
Over the Economy's Path

Aggregate Supply grew smoothly in the 1960s; Aggregate Demand grew even faster, but relatively smoothly as well, causing the price level to rise somewhat while unemployment rates fell a bit. Inflation was a minor but growing problem by the end of the decade. The Aggregate Supply and Aggregate Demand curves in Panel B are simply suggestive of the path of the economy; you should not infer from Panel B that the economy was perpetually in equilibrium because symptoms of disequilibrium did occur from time to time. Source: *Economic Report of the President, 1988.*

between 1969 and 1970 prompted President Nixon to impose a wage-price freeze in August 1971, even though inflation had begun to subside. The *CPI* grew at annual rates of 6.2 percent in 1969 and 5.2 percent in 1970, but inflation had fallen to 4.2 percent by the first half of 1971. As you will see, the freeze had only a temporary and artificial effect in holding down inflation, which seems to have been subsiding anyway.

Stagflation in the 1970s

Lingering effects of the demand-side inflation of the 1960s caused President Nixon and his advisors to fear that inflationary expectations would provide momen-

tum for further inflation and lead to economic havoc. Although the Vietnam War was gradually winding down, the war effort still absorbed hefty spending. Concern about the political repercussions of tax hikes necessitated federal deficits that further fueled inflation.

Under pressure from Congress and the general public, President Nixon took an unusual step for an avowed conservative: on August 15, 1971, he announced a 90-day wage-price freeze. Less stringent price controls were phased in when this freeze expired. As you can see in Panel A of Figure 9, these controls seemed partially effective in that nominal inflation abated during the 1971–73 period. In reality, inflationary pressures continued to build throughout the period, only being disguised by price controls. In fact, some people argue that the public anticipated substantial inflation when Nixon's temporary controls were scheduled to end, so controls may actually have increased inflationary momentum.

The economy suffered substantial stagflation (high rates of both inflation and unemployment) for the first time ever as price controls were relaxed between 1973 and 1975. This "stagflationary" recession was, at that time, the most severe since the Great Depression of the 1930s. There were numerous reasons for the downturn, the bulk of which were supply shocks: worldwide agricultural shortages, depreciation of the dollar relative to most foreign currencies (which caused import prices to soar), and the Arab

oil embargo, which was followed immediately by an initial OPEC decision to raise oil prices from $2.50 to more than $10.00 per barrel. The economy went into a tailspin, with inflation of more than 12 percent and unemployment soaring to above 9 percent of the labor force during 1975. In the period from 1975 to 1978, the economy followed a path of fairly steady recovery. Inflation remained high but stayed below the double-digit range until 1979. Fiscal policy was aimed at continuing the economic recovery from supply shocks with the hope of avoiding a resurgence of inflation, although politicians spun a lot of rhetoric about balancing the budget.

In Panel B of Figure 9, we have superimposed the Aggregate Supply/Aggregate Demand model over the actual data from Panel A, showing only the most important changes. The period from 1971 to 1973

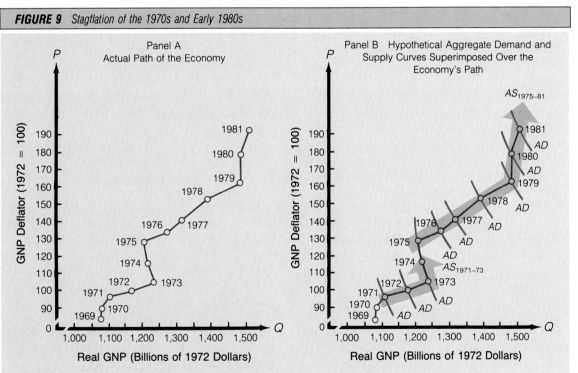

FIGURE 9 *Stagflation of the 1970s and Early 1980s*

The economy suffered from stagflation during 1973–75 when the Aggregate Supply curve shifted to the left. The shift in the Aggregate Supply curve was due to: (*a*) rising oil prices, (*b*) agricultural shortages, (*c*) a 20 percent depreciation of the dollar raised import prices, and (*d*) rising inflationary expectations. Source: *Economic Report of the President*, 1986.

was characterized by shifts in Aggregate Demand that moved the economy up along the supply curve labeled $AS_{1971-73}$. The supply shocks of 1973–75 shrank Aggregate Supply, resulting in equilibration along the 1973–75 demand curves. The stagflation of the 1973–75 period might be traceable in part to the lifting of price controls. Both workers and businesses attempted to recoup their precontrol positions by boosting wages and prices. By late 1975, Aggregate Supply appears to have become relatively stable, and the economy resumed its equilibrating movement along the supply curve labeled $AS_{1975-81}$. Although the federal government used demand-management policies in trying to steer the economy to a smooth and steady recovery, policies to reduce unemployment toward the full employment level fostered the reemergence of inflationary pressures.

Disinflation in the 1980s

Restrictive monetary policies that were intended to offset growing inflationary pressures left over from the 1970s pushed the economy into a severe slump during 1981–83. But inflation continued at high rates. Interest rates skyrocketed in 1979 and again in 1981. Tighter monetary policies than had been followed in over a decade finally caused both inflation and interest rates to begin drifting down in 1982. One side effect, however, was that in 1983, unemployment rose to its highest rate since the Great Depression. Some economists viewed the 1981–83 slump as castor oil required to cure earlier policy excesses.

Panel A of Figure 10 uses our Aggregate Demand and Aggregate Supply framework to illustrate these general movements. Several years of growing demand and high inflation had boosted inflationary expectations, causing the Aggregate Supply curve to shrink. This is shown as the shift from AS_0 to AS_1. To slow this inflationary spiral, the Federal Reserve Board tightened the screws during 1981–82, shifting Aggregate Demand from AD_0 to AD_1. This dampened inflationary expectations and, coupled with tax cuts that kicked in during 1982–83, helped stabilize the Aggregate Supply curve at AS_1. The resumption of mildly expansionary fiscal and monetary policies in 1983 allowed Aggregate Demand to drift back toward

AD_0. The net result was disinflation and falling real output between points a and b (1980–1983), and then steady growth along AS_1 with significantly lower inflation (1983–87).

The clockwise equilibration path is reflected in the actual equilibrium path for the economy illustrated in Panel B of Figure 10. The path of the economy between 1979 and 1987 indicates that Aggregate Supply continued to shrink and that tight monetary policies during this period decompressed inflation, but only by precipitating a severe recession. The growth in the economy between 1983 and 1987 points to an economy moving along a flatter and more stable Aggregate Supply curve.

Decompressing inflation did not come cheaply. In the early 1980s, the economy slipped below its previous growth trend to a lower path. Through 1987, cumulative losses of real income in 1987 dollars were between $2–3 trillion, due in large part to policies designed to offset the accelerating inflation in the 1970s.

Disinflation *is a significant reduction in the rate of inflation.*

Disinflation has caused many problems for both business and consumers. Many people who had expected inflation to continue through the 1980s had invested heavily in real estate and other inflation "hedges." Inflation abated and these debtors found themselves stuck paying high real rates of interest. When inflation faltered and failed to reduce the real value of future mortgage payments, many investors were clobbered by huge losses. Many houses that had cost $75,000 in 1975 had shot up to over $100,000 by 1980. Disinflation drove down asset prices that had swollen because of inflationary expectations, and simultaneously disrupted the declines in real mortgage payments that many had relied upon as a way of reducing their real debt burdens. Real estate foreclosures reached record highs by the mid-1980s. A similar outcome befell farmers and the rural banks that supported them. Farmers who had borrowed to purchase high-priced land faced bankruptcy as both farm incomes and land values plummeted.

Firms had grown accustomed to price increases as cures for even major problems. When disinflation made price hikes unwise, firms were forced to find other ways to boost sales and profits. During disinfla-

FIGURE 10 *Disinflation in the 1980s*

Panel A
The Disinflation Process

Panel A illustrates the disinflation process after a number of years of an inflationary spiral. Leftward shifts of the Aggregate Supply curve (due to rising inflationary expectations) are combined with reduced Aggregate Demand to produce a recession and quash inflation. Disinflation occurs between points *a* and *b*. Once the inflationary psychology is removed from the economy, rising Aggregate Demand allows growth without rising inflation. Panel B shows the actual equilibrium values for the economy during the 1980s.
Source: *Economic Report of the President*, 1988.

Panel B
The Economy's Equilibrium Path (1979–87)

tionary times, productivity growth and new products are keys to business success because prices cannot be raised. New products typically yield higher profits and facilitate growth. Another solution to the problems posed by disinflation is to cut labor costs. Disinflation causes firms to bargain harder and workers, sensing reduced inflation, tend to be more receptive to lower wage increases.

Pressures to raise productivity during disinflation cause changes in firms' investment patterns. First, more investment is directed toward productivity-enhancing plant and equipment, and less is aimed at expanding capacity. Second, more investment is financed internally as firms attempt to limit their debt burdens. Finally, the acquisition binge that some firms undertake during inflationary periods is reversed when debt consolidation requires the selling off of subsidiaries.

You should now have some appreciation for how difficult it is to predict and then deal with stagflation. Demand-management policy cannot completely re-solve the problems posed by supply-side distur-bances. As we have seen, disinflation can be an extremely painful cure. The next chapter turns to a discussion of some other possible ways to overcome the problems posed by inflation and stagflation.

CHAPTER REVIEW: KEY POINTS

1. *Stagflation,* a contraction of the terms *stagnation* and *inflation,* is the simultaneous occurrence of high rates of both unemployment and inflation.

2. Decreases in the Aggregate Supply curve cause *sup-ply-side inflation* and declines in real incomes and output. Excessive increases in the Aggregate Demand curve cause *demand-side inflation,* which initially is accompanied by increased incomes and output.

3. If Aggregate Demand grows excessively in a fully employed economy, the first phase of the *demand-side cycle* entails rising prices, outputs, employment, and incomes. In the second phase, supply-side adjust-ments to the demand-originated disturbances cause prices to continue to rise, but total employment, pro-duction, and income fall. *Demand-side* inflation in-duces a *counterclockwise adjustment* path of infla-tion versus real output. If the economy starts at less than full employment, only the first phase necessarily occurs when Aggregate Demand is increased.

4. Supply-side inflation generates a *clockwise adjust-ment* pattern. During the first phase of a *supply-side* (cost-push) *cycle,* prices rise while real output and incomes fall. If the government attempts to correct for the resulting inflationary recession by increasing Aggregate Demand, the second phase occurs—prices continue to rise, but real output and income rise as well.

5. Mild but increasing demand-side inflation accompa-nied the prosperity of the 1960s. From the mid-1970s into the early 1980s, stagflation took over with a ven-geance. Whether this stagflation was the supply-adjustment phase of the earlier demand-pull cycle or originated solely from supply-related shocks cannot be established conclusively. It seems likely, however, that even if the economy had been stable when the *supply shocks* listed previously emerged, consider-able supply-side inflation would have plagued the American economy from 1973 to 1980.

6. *Disinflation* is a significant reduction in the rate of inflation. Most people adjust their behavior if they expect inflation. Their expectations cause disinflation to entail losses in real income before it restores the economy to a relatively stable growth path. Thus, the 1981–83 recession was especially severe.

QUESTIONS FOR THOUGHT AND DISCUSSION

1. If you were a fiscal policymaker, would you rather face the problem of a recession or inflation? Which set of fiscal policies would be most popular with vot-ers? Now suppose you were confronted by stagfla-tion—both recession and inflation. Should you fight inflation, fight unemployment, or do nothing? What course of action do you think politicians would fol-low? What are the long-term effects of such poli-cies?

2. Do you think that fiscal and monetary policies differ in their effectiveness in dealing with high unemploy-ment and high inflation, respectively? From a politi-cal perspective, against which is monetary policy most likely to be used? Fiscal policy? Does this seem appropriate?

3. How might wage-price controls increase Aggregate Supply or at least prevent it from falling? How might wage-price controls actually cause Aggregate Supply to fall? Do you think it more likely that incomes pol-icy would cause increases or decreases in Aggregate Supply? If your answer is "It depends," on what does it depend?

4. How might certain social programs in the United States cause Aggregate Demand to rise and Aggregate Supply to decline? Do you think that growth of these programs is important in explaining why the economy has experienced high rates of both unemployment and inflation?

5. Suppose your friends asked how they might protect themselves from inflation. What advice would you give them? Suppose they then asked how to protect themselves from an economic slump. Would your advice to them be consistent with your previous sug-gestions? Can people buffer themselves from the risks of stagflation?

6. Paul Samuelson has argued that "democracies have a persistent inflationary bias." A look at inflation data since the Great Depression supports this statement. Why do you suppose this might be true? We know that disinflation involves costs. What would be some major problems with deflation (an actual reduction in the price level)? What level of unemployment would you expect the economy to experience during deflation? What would this level depend upon?

CHAPTER 17

The Policymaker's Dilemma

Demand-side and supply-side inflation are the two dominant categories of general price hikes, but most inflationary episodes involve elements of both. Curing high unemployment by stimulating Aggregate Demand may set off inflation and similarly, reducing inflation may mean rising unemployment. Political leaders face a policy dilemma because high rates of unemployment and inflation each create economic stress and are unpopular with voters.

This chapter focuses on trade-offs between inflation and unemployment and explanations for why these trade-offs may worsen to yield stagflation. Our discussion centers on how equilibrium output and inflation are related. Aggregate output is positively related to employment and tends to be negatively related to unemployment—which provides a basis for a relationship between unemployment and inflation. Another issue addressed is why inflation and interest rates seem positively related. Finally, we introduce the theories of efficient markets and rational expectations, which are the core of a growing school of thought call the *new classical macroeconomics.*

Phillips Curves: Trade-Offs Between Inflation and Unemployment

We all, or nearly all, consent,
when wages rise by ten percent,
it leaves the choice before the nation,
of unemployment or inflation.
—Kenneth Boulding (1967)

Boosting Aggregate Demand raises real output and employment in an economy with excess capacity, but ever greater upward pressures on prices and wages emerge as excess capacity disappears. Output growth cannot be sustained in the long run once an economy reaches its productive capacity; further increases in Aggregate Demand only cause inflation. Our general Aggregate Demand/Aggregate Supply framework in the previous chapter hinted at a possible inverse relationship between unemployment and inflation.

This chapter explores this trade-off in more detail. More than three decades ago, A. W. Phillips compared plotted data for wage inflation and unemployment rates for the preceding century in Great Britain. Curves that seem to fit such data have become known as Phillips curves.

> The **Phillips curve** *is an inverse statistical relationship between the rate of inflation and the unemployment rate.*

Phillips's original work examined wage inflation, but subsequent researchers focused on trade-offs between unemployment and price inflation.

Wage Increases, Productivity, and Inflation

A fairly tight relationship linking nominal wage inflation, price inflation, and productivity can be expressed as:

$$\text{percentage } \Delta \text{ prices} = \text{percentage } \Delta \text{ wages} - \text{percentage } \Delta \text{ in productivity.}$$

For example, if typical workers can produce 5 percent more this year than last, then wages can rise by 5 percent before maintaining firms' profit margins requires raising prices. The relationship is illustrated in Figure 1. A 2 percent annual rate of productivity gain is assumed and is reflected by shifting the scale for price inflation ($\dot{p}$) down by 2 percent relative to wage inflation. Thus, 4 percent wage hikes combined with

a 2 percent productivity gain only imposes pressures for prices to rise by 2 percent. But if productivity gains for the economy are nil and workers successfully demand higher wages, the net result is likely to be price inflation.

American Phillips Curves

Figure 1 superimposes a Phillips curve over U.S. data for the 1960s. Because Aggregate Supply was thought relatively stable, the Phillips curve was thought to be so; monetary and fiscal policymakers could manage Aggregate Demand to achieve the least harmful combination of unemployment and inflation. The dilemma seemed clear: if high inflation is associated with low unemployment, and vice versa; the Phillips curve is a "menu" showing the trade-off available to policymakers who seek to minimize our economic woes.[1]

The Phillips curve shown in Figure 1 was thought roughly reflective of a trade-off confronting American policymakers. If they insisted on zero price inflation, American workers would suffer roughly 6–8 percent unemployment. Unemployment rates as low as 3–4 percent were thought feasible only with inflation of

---

1. Recall (from chapter 6) that the misery index is the sum of the rates of unemployment and inflation. High interest rates, low rates of investment and productivity growth, and a variety of other difficulties are also sources of macroeconomic distress.

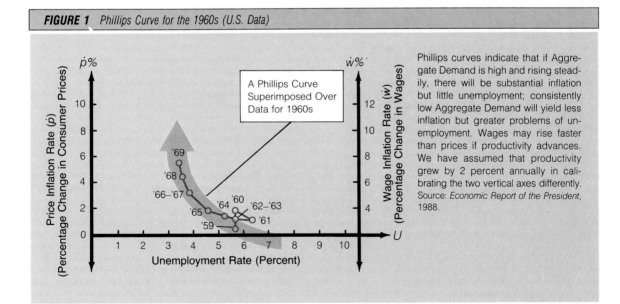

FIGURE 1 *Phillips Curve for the 1960s (U.S. Data)*

A Phillips Curve Superimposed Over Data for 1960s

Phillips curves indicate that if Aggregate Demand is high and rising steadily, there will be substantial inflation but little unemployment; consistently low Aggregate Demand will yield less inflation but greater problems of unemployment. Wages may rise faster than prices if productivity advances. We have assumed that productivity grew by 2 percent annually in calibrating the two vertical axes differently.
Source: *Economic Report of the President*, 1988.

4–6 percent. Policymakers would have preferred less of each, but Phillips curve analysis suggested that this was impossible.

Shifts in Aggregate Demand and the Stable Phillips Curve

National output and income are positively related to employment. In turn, there is a close negative relationship between employment and unemployment: higher employment generally means lower unemployment, and vice versa. But changes in the size or composition of the labor force may obscure this relationship. For example, rapidly rising labor force participation rates may cause frictional unemployment to rise even if real output and employment are growing.

An Aggregate Supply curve is a positive relationship between the level of output and the price level, while a typical Phillips curve depicts an inverse correlation between unemployment and inflation. Thus, Phillips curves roughly mirror Aggregate Supply curves, as shown in Figure 2. Points $a, b, \ldots g$ in Panel A roughly correspond to points $a, b, \ldots g$ in Panel B. Expanding Aggregate Demand from AD_a to AD_b in Panel A moves the economy from point a to point b in Panel B. Keeping the economy at point b requires raising Aggregate Demand by the same proportion in each subsequent period. Similarly, expanding Aggregate Demand from AD_a to AD_c moves the economy to point c in Panel B; staying at point c would require continuous similar expansions of Aggregate Demand. And so on, for points $d, e, f,$ and $g.$[2]

---

2. Readers familiar with differential equations will recognize this discussion as a description of moving from static analysis of price level changes to a more dynamic analysis of sustained inflation.

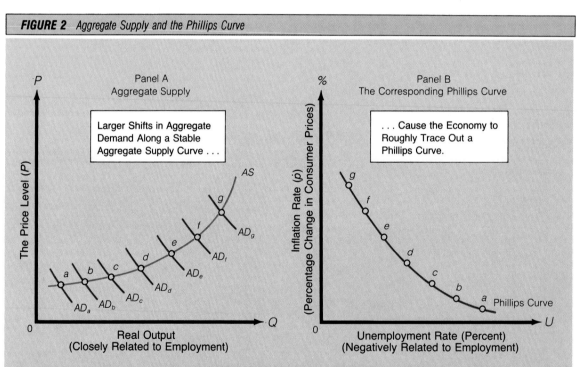

FIGURE 2   *Aggregate Supply and the Phillips Curve*

Panel A
Aggregate Supply

Larger Shifts in Aggregate Demand Along a Stable Aggregate Supply Curve . . .

The Price Level (P)

Real Output
(Closely Related to Employment)

Panel B
The Corresponding Phillips Curve

. . . Cause the Economy to Roughly Trace Out a Phillips Curve.

Inflation Rate (ṗ)
(Percentage Change in Consumer Prices)

Unemployment Rate (Percent)
(Negatively Related to Employment)

Ever larger sustained increases in Aggregate Demand in Panel A along a stable Aggregate Supply curve would trace out a series of equilibria like a, b, . . . g in Panel A as employment and output increased. The unemployment rate would fall during these movements, but prices would rise, tracing a pattern roughly like a, b, . . . g along the stable Phillips curve in Panel B.

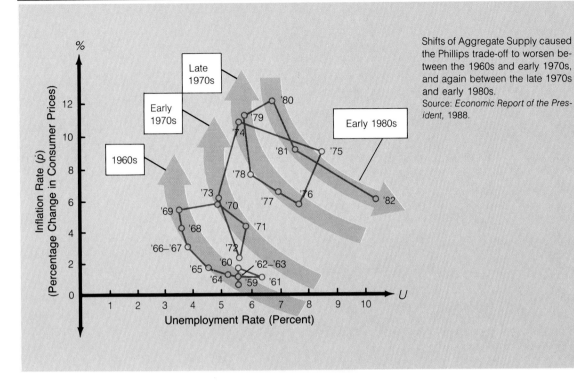

FIGURE 3 The Shifting Phillips Curve Relationship

Shifts of Aggregate Supply caused the Phillips trade-off to worsen between the 1960s and early 1970s, and again between the late 1970s and early 1980s.
Source: *Economic Report of the President*, 1988.

The Stagflation of the 1970s: Stable Phillips Curves at Bay?

The early 1970s saw the trade-off between inflation and unemployment worsen. Ever greater sacrifices of inflation appeared necessary to keep unemployment rates in the 5–6 percent range. The worsening trade-off is shown in Figure 3. We have superimposed four Phillips curves over the data. What happened in the 1970s to cause the Phillips curve to worsen?

Shifts in Aggregate Supply and Shifting Phillips Curves

Continually expanding the growth rate of Aggregate Demand while Aggregate Supply remains stable results in upward movements along a stable Phillips curve, as in Figure 2. The 1960s seemed to provide evidence of a roughly stable Phillips curve, but bouts

of stagflation in the 1970s betrayed the naiveté of this view. Shocks to Aggregate Supply apparently worsened the short-run trade-off between unemployment and inflation, as shown in Figure 4. Suppose that Aggregate Supply begins to shrink, declining from AS_0 to AS_1 to AS_2, and so on in Panel A. Output and employment fall while the price level rises (stagflation), so that policymakers are presented with worse short-run options such as curves PC_0, PC_1, PC_2, and so on in Panel B. As Phillips curves move to the right, achieving a given level of unemployment requires suffering more rapid inflation.

Recent Keynesian and modern classical economic reasoning offer alternative explanations for the existence of Phillips curves. In the following section, we examine these alternative theories and, more importantly for economic policy, explore the different interpretations of why Phillips curves shifted so that the economy experienced stagflation during the 1970s.

FIGURE 4 Shifting the Phillips Curve

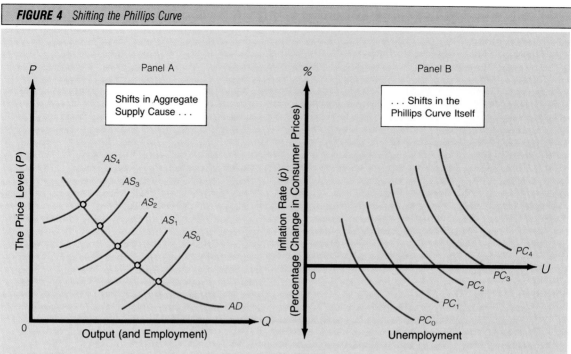

Shifts in Aggregate Supply, as shown in Panel A, cause shifts in Phillips curves (*PC*), as shown in Panel B, and account for the stagflation of the 1970s and 1980s.

Aggregate Equilibrium and the Rate of Inflation

Almost from its inception, the Phillips curve hypothesis has been in the eye of a stormy controversy about macroeconomic theory and policy. Keynesians view Phillips's discovery of a negative statistical relationship between unemployment and inflation as a reflection of a trade-off confronting policymakers. Economists of a classical persuasion, including modern monetarists, view the Phillips relationship as a short-run artifact and argue that policymakers who attempt to trade inflation for lower unemployment will soon find that the Phillips curve is a mirage. These theorists perceive no permanent connection between unemployment and inflation. They reason that money is a veil in the long run and that nominal things, such as the price level, are determined by the money supply and will not be related to any aspect of real behavior, such as unemployment.

In this section, we explore the views of classically oriented economists and monetarists. Their theory of the Phillips curve as transitory is widely known as *natural rate theory.* This theory concludes that the Aggregate Supply and Phillips curves shift persistently only because of changing inflationary expectations. Next, we will examine the Keynesian view of the Phillips curve. Modern Keynesians recognize that Aggregate Supply will decline if inflationary expectations build, but they also consider other disruptions as important in explaining stagflation and the apparent deterioration of the Phillips curve in the 1970s.

The Natural Rate of Unemployment

Would it be good if unemployment were always exactly zero? "Yes, of course" seems an easy answer. But keeping the unemployment rate at zero would require people who were unhappy with their jobs to stay in them until they found new ones—or else they would be unemployed. Moreover, there would be pressures on firms to immediately hire anyone who applied for work. And if you were not in the labor force and then decided to look for a job, you would be forced to take the first job offered—otherwise you would be unemployed. Zero unemployment is not as attractive a goal as it sounds.

Wage Adjustments: The Natural Rate Approach

Economists who believe in natural rate theory view nearly all unemployment as voluntary, the sole exception being unskilled people who are unemployed because minimum-wage legislation prevents employers from hiring these workers at the low wages commensurate with their productivity. Natural rate theorists view all other unemployment as the result of friction—it takes people time to find what they regard as suitable employment and while they are looking for work, they are unemployed by choice. Individuals can presumably get jobs almost instantly if they are willing to take the wage they are worth to the first employer willing to hire them. Frictional unemployment can be viewed as a cost of investment in labor market information and mobility. Table 1 presents estimates of the natural rate of frictional unemployment for a number of developed economies.

Expansionary macroeconomic policy reduces frictional unemployment, according to natural rate theory, only because workers are fooled by unanticipated inflation into thinking that the higher wages offered by employers represent real increases in the purchasing power of their earnings. Anyone who is unemployed can get a seemingly "suitable" high-paying job quickly during expansionary periods, when the pool of frictionally unemployed workers is small. In the natural rate view, these artificial declines in frictional unemployment reflect cyclical overemployment that is a consequence of inadequate investment in labor market information. But why do employers offer higher wages when expansionary policies are followed? Expansionary policies cause business firms to forecast booming sales that will enable them to raise the prices of their products. After workers recognize that their wages do not buy as much as expected because prices are also rising, many will become dissatisfied and quit to look for more lucrative work.

The eventual result is that frictional unemployment will rise back to its "natural rate" when workers cease being fooled. The natural rate of unemployment is the rate that exists before expansionary policy is initiated; it is achieved when all economic transactors have accurate expectations about inflation. If expansionary policies are continued, workers will learn to expect inflation and will begin to demand wages that rise continuously to compensate for inflation. This means that Aggregate Supply will shrink continuously.

Wage Adjustments to Inflation

Consider next Figure 5. A starting point for the natural rate explanation for Phillips curves is to assume a macroeconomic equilibrium with no inflation at points a in both panels. The price index is 100 (point a in Panel A) and unemployment is at a level compatible with potential real output (point a in panel B). Inflation is initially zero, and the natural rate of unemployment, U_n, is between 5 and 7 percent. The shaded parts of Figure 5 represent output below and unemployment above the natural rate.

Now assume that overly expansionary monetary policy drives Aggregate Demand up to AD_1. Real output will rise to Q_1 (point b), but the adjustment pro-

TABLE 1 Unemployment Rates Required to Keep Inflation Stable (%)		
	1971-1975	**1981-1983**
United States	6	6½
Japan	1	2
West Germany	1½	8
France	3½	8
Britain	4	9
Italy	7	6½
Canada	7	7½
Holland	4	10½

Sources: OECD, Layard and Nickell, 1984, from *The Economist*, 14 May 1988, p. 69.

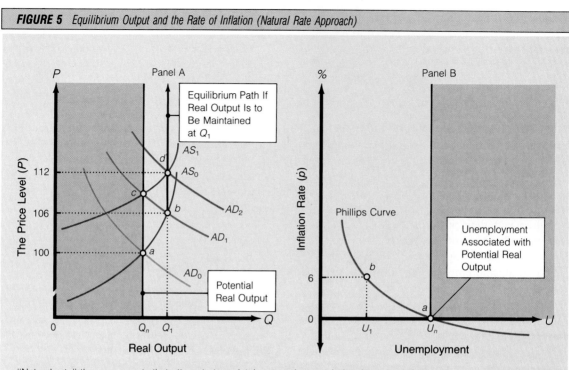

"Natural rate" theory suggests that attempts to maintain unemployment below its normal, frictional rate require continuous expansions of Aggregate Demand, raising the possibility of accelerating inflation.

cess entails 6 percent inflation and the price level rises from 100 to 106. We suggested in the previous chapter that this equilibrium will not be maintained for long. Workers will find their real wages falling, precipitating attempts to catch up. As they do so, the Aggregate Supply curve shifts leftward to AS_1 and the economy moves toward point c in Panel A. If policymakers try to preserve real output at Q_1 and unemployment at U_1 by shifting Aggregate Demand to AD_2, this unleashes another inflationary round equal to roughly 6 percent as the economy moves to equilibrium at point d in Panel A. The equilibrium path for the economy is denoted by the arrow.

Notice that if policymakers want to maintain unemployment U_1, continual 6 percent inflation is required. The model to this point naively supposes that workers always expect inflation to be zero and only seek wage adjustments after the price level has risen. If workers begin to anticipate inflation, policymakers are confronted with additional problems.

The Long-Run Phillips Curve This natural rate extension of classical reasoning suggests that Phillips curves do not present policymakers with stable frontiers along which inflation can be "traded off" against unemployment.

> **Natural rate theory** *implies that each Phillips curve is associated with a particular rate of expected inflation. If workers foresee higher rates of inflation, the Phillips curve worsens by shifting outward.*

Panel A of Figure 6 illustrates how this occurs. Suppose that the economy is at point a initially; there is frictional unemployment equal to U_n, with zero inflation and zero inflation expected; $E(\dot p)$ indicates the inflation rate that workers expect. What happens if policymakers view an unemployment rate of U_n as unacceptably high and follow expansionary policies? Growth of Aggregate Demand yields increased sales for business firms, so they offer higher wages to

FIGURE 6 *Natural Rate Theory and the Shifting Phillips Curve*

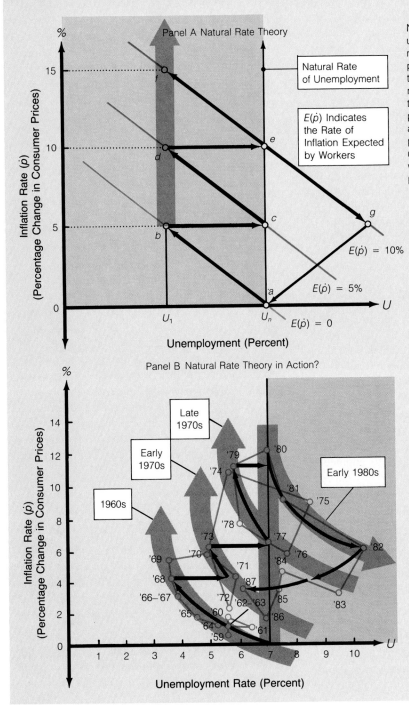

Panel A Natural Rate Theory

Natural Rate of Unemployment

$E(\dot{p})$ Indicates the Rate of Inflation Expected by Workers

$E(\dot{p}) = 10\%$

$E(\dot{p}) = 5\%$

$E(\dot{p}) = 0$

Natural rate theory suggests that unemployment will be *less* than the natural rate (U_n) only if workers expect less inflation than occurs and that it will be *more than* the natural rate if workers expect more inflation than results from macroeconomic policy. In the long run, workers will adjust perfectly to any changes in price levels so that normal, frictional unemployment will be maintained, which is totally independent of the price level or inflation.

Panel B Natural Rate Theory in Action?

Late 1970s

Early 1970s

Early 1980s

1960s

attract new workers to accommodate the higher demands for their products. Workers who are frictionally unemployed will have little difficulty finding what they perceive as good, high-paying jobs. Thus, expansionary policies push the economy along the $E(\dot{p})=0$ Phillips curve from point a towards point b.

The fly in this ointment is that higher demands for goods encourage firms to increase prices. As workers learn to expect 5 percent price hikes, the Phillips curve shifts rightward and the economy moves to point c at the old natural rate of unemployment U_n. This occurs because workers will demand wage increases of 10 percent: 5 percent to cover the past inflation plus 5 percent for expected inflation. But firms forecast only a 5 percent growth in the nominal demands for their products and will refuse to meet these demands for 10 percent wage increases. Frictional unemployment rises as workers hit the pavement looking for better jobs.

If policymakers again view unemployment (U_n) as unacceptably high, they might follow even more expansionary policies. If so, the economy initially will move from point c to d, but then ultimately to e as workers again cease being fooled. All that policymakers will have achieved is 10 percent inflation with no long-term reduction in unemployment. If policymakers were undaunted by their failures, they might even proceed to f.

If they had learned their lessons, however, they would find moving directly and quickly back from e to a almost impossible. The build up of inflationary momentum may force policymakers to engineer a recession to point g to dampen inflationary expectations. An extended recession may be required before the economy will return to point a. Similar adjustments may explain why a severe recession occurred in 1981–83 when deflationary monetary policies brought inflation under control. Panel B of Figure 6 shows data for 1960–1987 suggesting that natural rate theory explains the stagflation of the last two decades reasonably well.

Pure natural rate theorists view rising expectations of inflation as the only explanation for any worsening of any short-term relationship between inflation and unemployment. There is a family of short-run Phillips curves; each depends on different expectations of inflation by labor. Unemployment will gravitate back to its natural rate in the long run. Thus, there is no long-run trade-off between inflation and unemployment. In Figure 6, the long-run Phillips "curve" is the vertical path ace. According to natural rate analysis, if policymakers attempt to maintain unemployment below the natural rate, the short-run Phillips curve trade-off worsens. Accelerating bouts of inflation (up the vertical arrow in Panel A) are inevitable until policymakers accept the futility of trying to hold unemployment below its natural rate.

Keynesian Phillips Curves: Sticky Wages and Prices

The major Keynesian explanation for Phillips curves' shapes hinges on two key ideas (a) shocks to demands and supplies continually bombard all economies and (b) wages and prices are assumed downwardly "sticky." That is, wages and prices rise more easily than they fall. At any moment in time the composition of demands—both private and public—is changing. These are shocks to the economy. As new products are developed or national priorities change, the demands for some goods rise while those for others fall.

Output growth in sectors where demand grows is limited in the short run by existing plant, equipment, and trained labor. Thus, wage and price hikes are the primary adjustments to stronger demand. In sectors where demand shrinks the norm is production cutbacks and layoffs—not price reductions. Workers are reluctant to accept wage cuts, so firms find layoffs the easiest way to cut wage costs. Some temporary price cuts (e.g., automobile rebates) may be used to liquidate unwanted inventories, but these price cuts will be accompanied by declining output and rising unemployment.

Suppose that Aggregate Demand is constant but that the composition of demand changes. Prices in growing sectors rise faster than outputs, but prices fall slowly if at all in declining sectors, while outputs plummet. The net result is a higher price level, more unemployment, and less total output.

Compositional shocks *to the economy cause Aggregate Supply to fall temporarily because of friction encountered in moving resources from declining to growing sectors.*

How this modern Keynesian analysis is consistent with Phillips curves is shown in Figure 7.

FIGURE 7 Full Employment Output, Shocks, and the Rate of Inflation: The Modern Keynesian Approach

A modern Keynesian approach suggests that constant shocks to the supplies and demands in individual markets may create excessive unemployment that can only be overcome by expansionary policies that lend a natural bias for inflation to the economy. This theory is elaborated in James Tobin's article, "Inflation and Unemployment," *The American Economic Review*, 62, No. 1 (March 1972), pp. 1–18.

At our initial equilibrium at both points *a*, the price level is stable at 100. Assume that Aggregate Demand remains constant at AD_0 but that its composition changes, causing dislocations to labor and other resources so that Aggregate Supply shrinks from AS_0 to AS_1. Equilibrium moves from point *a* to point *b*. Given the downward wage-price stickiness in declining markets, compositional changes cause the price level to rise. Again, if policymakers desire to maintain output at Q_f and unemployment at U_f, expansionary policies are necessary so that Aggregate Demand grows from AD_0 to AD_2. These expansionary policies will move the economy from point *b* to point *c* in both panels of Figure 6. Thus, adopting policies to maintain unemployment at U_f will result in an annual inflation rate of 3 percent if compositional changes of the same magnitudes and frequencies continually recur.

This result suggests that our economy has a "natural" *inflationary bias* caused by continuous changes

in the structure of economic activity. If policymakers chose to suppress this natural inflation, they might reduce Aggregate Demand to AD_1 (point *d* in Panel A), but unemployment would rise to U_1 in Panel B. Thus, policymakers can reduce either the unemployment or the inflation caused by compositional changes in economic activity, but not both. Less inflation means more unemployment, and vice versa.

The Keynesian Structuralist Approach

Another Keynesian explanation for the Phillips curves—the *structuralist* approach—goes like this: As unemployment falls and full employment is approached, it becomes increasingly costly to produce extra output. One reason is that as more and more firms and industries operate nearer their capacities, their costs rise and are passed on to consumers as higher prices.

Another reason costs rise as unemployment falls is increasingly vigorous competition among firms for the best workers. Even when unemployment is high, most of the best labor is employed. The majority of those remaining in the unemployed labor pool in prosperous times are, for the most part, nearly unemployable. These workers lack the skills required for jobs during hard times; many other workers' skills may have depreciated during extended periods of joblessness. Employers begin "pirating" qualified workers from other firms when unemployment rates are low by offering higher wages. This competition drives up costs, prices, and so on.

The Keynesian structuralist and "shock" theories explain the existence of Phillips curves, but we need to probe a bit deeper to see how these approaches illuminate the rocky path of our economy over the past two decades.

A Modern Keynesian View of Stagflation

Natural rate theorists believe that mounting expectations of inflation sustained by overly expansionary macroeconomic policies are the only reason for leftward shifts of the Aggregate Supply curve and worsening Phillips curves. Modern Keynesians accept inflationary expectations as only one of many destabilizing influences on Phillips curves. Other causes can be classified under four broad headings (*a*) external shocks, (*b*) labor market disturbances, (*c*) compositional changes in product markets, and (*d*) disruptions emerging in the public sector. Let us examine each, remembering that Aggregate Supply and the Phillips relationship can shift in either direction.

Shocks to the System   Any event that reduces Aggregate Supply (shifts it to the left) causes supply-side inflation and tends to worsen the trade-off between unemployment and inflation. During 1974–81, recurrent oil price hikes and the subsequent jumps in firms' energy costs reduced Aggregate Supply and eroded the short-run Phillips curve. This is shown in Figure 7. Wars, bad weather that reduces crop yields, or other natural disasters will have similar effects. On the other hand, discoveries of new resources, significant technological advances, prolonged periods of economic stability, or reductions in international tensions may improve the Phillips trade-off.

Labor Market Changes   Natural rate theory pivots on changing inflationary expectations to explain instability in the Phillips relationship. Incentive structures that encourage or discourage work effort also play roles. Unemployment compensation, Social Security, and other transfer programs all affect the labor-leisure choices of workers. For example, raising unemployment compensation payments will encourage greater unemployment and will intensify inflationary pressure. Unemployment compensation has been found to encourage temporary layoffs by firms because it eases the distress felt by firms' workers when slack demand causes orders for output to drop; it also appears to extend the average duration of unemployment. Social Security currently encourages many older workers to take an early retirement. Increases in the sizes of payments under most welfare programs also worsen the trade-off between unemployment and inflation.

Some recent reforms are intended to reverse the negative effects of these programs. For example, welfare recipients who work can use subsidized day-care facilities for their children, the government now supports job training for the "hard-core" unemployed, and the penalties exacted from Social Security recipients who earn income have been reduced. All these reforms may reduce the severity of the inflation/unemployment trade-off by increasing work effort and Aggregate Supply. Policies to enhance job mobility and improve matches between workers and available job openings also improve the Phillips trade-off, as will programs to reduce discrimination so that productivity becomes the primary criterion for employment.

Demographic changes also affect the relationship between inflation and unemployment. The post-World War II baby boom provided a growing pool of labor in the 1960s. But younger workers tend to bounce from job to job and are unemployed more often, worsening the Phillips relationship. As this group becomes older, the changing age structure of the population should reduce the severity of this trade-off. Women's labor force participation rates grew markedly from the late 1950s onward. Even though this influx of labor bolstered Aggregate Supply, it also seems to have worsened the Phillips curve because women's unemployment rates are typically higher than those of males.

Collective bargaining may also affect the Phillips curve. If growth of union power enables them to obtain contracts with inflationary wage hikes, or if strike activities intensify, the trade-off between inflation and unemployment will deteriorate.

Product Market Composition Changes   One explanation for the shape and existence of Phillips curves is drawn from continuous changes in the composition of demands for goods, combined with wage and price stickiness and a policy of trying to maintain full employment. The menu of choices between unemployment and inflation worsens if external shocks become stronger or if compositional changes occur more rapidly. If consumer tastes and preferences or investors' perceptions of the economic outlook change markedly, the composition of output may also change drastically. Of course, this trade-off is more favorable the slower or less extreme these changes are during a given interval.

Changes in laws governing foreign trade become more important as our economy becomes more internationally oriented. Hikes in tariffs or cuts in import quotas raise the prices of imported goods and worsen the dilemma posed by the Phillips curve. Competition is also reduced. Similarly, growth of domestic monopoly power and the resulting drives for greater profits will worsen the inflation/unemployment trade-off.

Public Sector Changes   Just as erratic disruptions to the composition of private demands can shift the Phillips curve, so can changes in the composition of public sector demands for goods and services. Changes in tax structures, subsidies, and transfer payments will also influence the trade-off. Major revisions of such government regulations as those policed by the Occupational Safety and Health Administration (OSHA), minimum-wage laws, environmental protection regulations, leasing policies for mineral exploration on public lands, or changes in property rights structures may all shift the Phillips curve relationship. The direction of the shift depends on whether a particular regulatory change enhances or encumbers economic efficiency.

For modern Keynesians, an explanation for the stagflation of the 1970s goes something like this: Rising inflationary expectations and disruptions associated with the Vietnam War caused the first shift in the Phillips curve in the early 1970s. The increase in world oil prices in 1974 caused the second shift. Even higher oil prices in 1979 and 1981, coupled with a worldwide crop shortage, caused the shift of the Phillips curve in the early 1980s. And relative cessation of shocks to the economy in the mid-1980s resulted in improvement of the Phillips curve trade-off.

Supply-Side Policies

Short-run trade-offs between unemployment and inflation can be improved by stimulating Aggregate Supply. As we indicated previously, expanding Aggregate Supply yields a multitude of economic blessings—output, job opportunities, and employment all grow. This, in turn, reduces unemployment, dampens inflation, and raises standards of living.

President Reagan's *supply-side* economic package was launched in 1981 amid glowing promises that prosperity was just around the corner. The cornerstones of his policies included (*a*) cuts in the growth of domestic social programs, (*b*) cuts in individual and corporate income tax rates, (*c*) accelerated depreciation allowances, (*d*) investment tax credits, and (*e*) special tax incentives for savers.

Cuts in the Growth of Domestic Social Programs

Most welfare programs were privately funded before the Great Depression. Social Security, unemployment compensation, and several other programs launched in the 1930s were intended to ease the misery common among the aged, unemployed, and poor. Then, in 1965, President Lyndon Johnson declared a *War on Poverty* to raise poor Americans' minimum standard of living. The result was an explosion of outlays that made transfer payments grow faster than any other major component of the federal budget. The cause of equity may have been served, but many critics felt that too many welfare recipients who were capable of providing for their families chose not to do so.

President Reagan and his advisors were convinced that more labor effort would be forthcoming if many people who relied on transfer payments had to provide for themselves. Their reasoning: If you must give me some of your income because I don't work and you do, neither of us is as likely to work as much. Thus, cuts in transfer payments should enhance Aggregate Supply because we will both work harder. Although Reagan failed to cut transfer payments and other social programs in absolute dollar amounts, his administration succeeded in cutting the growth rate of social spending.

Cuts in Personal Income Tax Rates

Key officials in the Reagan administration believed strongly that work and investment incentives were severely hampered by high marginal tax rates—so much so that they felt the economy might be operating in the upper range of the Laffer curve (described in chapter 11). By cutting personal income tax rates 25 percent over three years, they expected to stimulate substantially greater effort from workers and more rapid investment, increasing Aggregate Supply. They also expected higher tax revenues. In addition, by reducing tax rates, the Reagan administration expected money to be moved out of tax shelters and into more productive investments.

Cuts in Corporate Income Tax Rates

The corporate income tax rate was 46 percent from the 1960s until 1986. This meant that a corporate investment had to generate almost twice as much pretax profit as a noncorporate investment to yield the same after-tax rate of return to an individual investor. Some analysts point to this special tax penalty on corporate investments as a major cause for the low rates of investment in the United States compared to other industrialized nations. Among other problems, it appears that faltering labor productivity growth may be attributable to our failure to accumulate sufficient new capital.

The Reagan administration's attempts to reduce corporate tax rates were part of a broader strategy to stimulate investment while simultaneously reducing what it saw as unfair burdens on corporations. Economists from across the political spectrum are generally opposed to the corporate income tax, some for these reasons and others because they are convinced that the tax is forward-shifted, falling most heavily on the poor. As percentages of their incomes, the poor are most prone to buy the standardized goods manufactured in the corporate sector. Thus, these economists consider corporate taxes to be hidden and regressive. The corporate income tax is politically popular, however, because most people see it as a tax on big business. Nevertheless, corporate tax rates were reduced sharply (to 34 percent) as part of the Tax Reform Act of 1986.

Incentives for Saving

Investment requires corresponding amounts of saving. President Reagan's supply-side policies included special tax incentives to persuade Americans to save more. Individual Retirement Accounts (IRAs) were one such program. Individuals could set aside up to $2,000 annually and could deduct this amount from their taxable income. Penalty-free withdrawals from IRA accounts were permitted only at age 59. These withdrawals would then be taxable, but most people would be taxed at lower rates because they would be past their peak earning years. Moreover, they would have the advantage of postponing their taxes. The interest you can draw almost always makes it advantageous to delay paying a given dollar amount in taxes as long as possible. IRAs were only one of several programs intended as incentives for saving. The Tax Reform Act of 1986, however, dramatically reduced the availability of IRA deductions, depending on your income level and whether or not you are covered by an employer-sponsored retirement plan.

Another facet of the attempt to bolster saving was the attack on inflation spearheaded by the FED. The FED had begun reducing the rate of monetary growth in 1979. Unanticipated inflation rewards borrowers who pay back their debts in less valuable dollars, but it penalizes savers because it erodes the purchasing power of their savings. Thus, the FED's policy of squelching growth in Aggregate Demand was seen as a necessary step along the path toward long-term growth of Aggregate Supply.

The thrust of supply-side economics was to offer incentives to middle- and upper-income workers and investors while reducing transfer payments so that welfare recipients would lose less by working. These policies began to be instituted in 1981. The supply-siders' response to accusations that this approach was grossly inequitable was that poor people would ultimately gain the most from long-run expansion of Aggregate Supply; to supply-siders, the best antipoverty program is a strong and growing economy. Most supply-siders expected the economy to respond immediately to the stimulus to Aggregate Supply that began in 1981.

A strong economic recovery did begin, but not until 1983. Why were the desirable effects predicted from supply-side policies delayed? Part of the explanation is that the FED followed anti-inflationary policies while these policies were being enacted. In addition, federal deficits skyrocketed; defense spending was expanded to absorb most of the anticipated reduction in growth in transfer payments. Unfortunately, cuts in transfer payments did not materialize until the economy began its recovery from the recession of 1981–83, which required massive outlays for unemployment compensation and other welfare programs. Output did not grow quickly, nor did supply-side policies stimulate an immediate investment boom. Thus, the expected surge in Aggregate Supply did not swell tax revenues (see Figure 8). Why?

A key to this puzzle was high interest rates. Tight monetary policies and fears that inflation might revive combined with enormous deficits to keep real interest rates high. But what are real interest rates, and why did they remain so high that investment was retarded during the 1981–83 recession? The natural rate approach also addresses the rate of interest.

The Natural Rate of Interest _____

Natural rate theory views attempts to achieve lower unemployment rates or interest rates than are consistent with people's individual decisions as ultimately self-defeating. We will now examine the natural real rate of interest hypothesis and discover why the interest rate may not be an appropriate target for monetary authorities.

The Natural "Real" Rate of Interest Hypothesis

Just as there are any number of wage rates or prices in the economy, there are also any number of interest rates. The interest rates paid by borrowers to lenders reflect, among other considerations (*a*) risk, (*b*) length of time to maturity of the note or bond, (*c*) the availability of credit, and (*d*) legal constraints. For simplicity, however, we will assume that there is only one interest rate for borrowing.

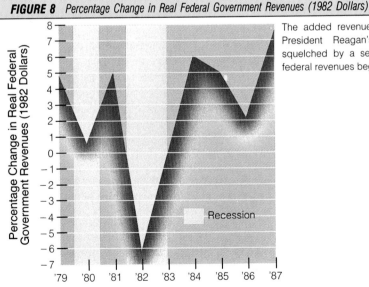

FIGURE 8 *Percentage Change in Real Federal Government Revenues (1982 Dollars)*

The added revenue expected from the growth dividend of President Reagan's supply-side tax cuts were totally squelched by a severe recession. Only recently have real federal revenues begun to grow.

Source: *Economic Report of the President,* 1988.

When people discuss "the" interest rate, they usually mean the average annual percentage monetary premium paid for the use of money. Economists refer to this percentage monetary premium as the **nominal rate** of interest.

> The **real rate of interest** *is the annual percentage of purchasing power paid by a borrower to a lender for the use of money.*

Estimating the realized real rate of interest (r) is simple—the nominal interest rate (i) minus the percentage rate of inflation ($\dot{p}$) yields the percentage purchasing power premium, or real interest rate (r), paid over the life of a note or bond:

$$r = i - \dot{p} \qquad \text{(real interest rate)}.$$

For example, if the nominal interest rate is 12 percent and the price level rises 15 percent annually, the real rate of interest is −3 percent and lenders lose 3 percent of purchasing power in each such year.

Workers bargain for higher nominal wages in order to protect their real wages when they anticipate inflation. Naturally, people whose incomes are based on interest will react similarly. The natural real rate of interest hypothesis suggests that borrowers and lenders adjust nominal interest to expected inflation $E(\dot{p})$, so that the nominal rate of interest charged for borrowing money reflects lenders' desires and borrowers' willingness to pay purchasing power premiums (desired real interest, r_d) for the use of money. Thus, when a note or bond is issued:

$$i = r_d + E(\dot{p}) \qquad \text{(nominal cost of borrowing)}.$$

If inflation is expected, lenders try to charge higher interest to ensure that they will not lose purchasing power, but why will borrowers be willing to pay such "high" interest rates? To understand this essential point, consider the housing market during the late 1970s, during which housing prices increased from 10 to 30 percent annually in some regions.

Suppose that you expect housing prices in your area to increase by 15 percent annually. To keep it simple, we will assume that you can borrow money at a nominal interest rate of 10 percent. If you are able to repay the loan with dollars that have depreciated in value by 15 percent annually, this situation is similar to being paid 5 percent of the price of your house annually to live in your own home. Negative real rent sounds pretty good to most of us, which explains, in part, the 1970s boom in housing prices.

The **natural real interest rate hypothesis** suggests that the desired real rate of interest (r_d) reflects (*a*) the real (purchasing power) premium necessary to induce savers to delay gratification—most people value having goods today more than having goods tomorrow; (*b*) the premiums necessary to induce people to hold their wealth in less liquid forms; and (*c*) the expected productivity of capital, which yields extra goods in the future. The real interest rate is the percentage of extra goods that can be enjoyed if consumption is delayed so that extra capital is available for production.

Keynes and Fisher Effects

According to the natural real interest rate hypothesis, expansionary monetary policy might temporarily reduce nominal interest rates, but in the long run, overly expansionary policies cause nominal interest rates to climb, not fall. Figure 9 shows why by relating the supply and demand for loanable funds to nominal interest rates. The supply and demand for loanable funds is linked closely to the supply and demand for money discussed in chapter 14. Changes in real interest rates will cause these supplies and demands to shift.

Suppose that monetary policymakers view the nominal interest rate of 6 percent (given by the intersection of D_0 and S_0 at point *a*) as too high—they perceive it as inhibiting investment and spending. If they follow expansionary open-market operations, the supply of loanable funds initially rises to S_1 and the nominal interest rate falls to 4 percent (point *b*). This temporary decline in nominal interest rates caused by expansionary policies will result in even larger declines in real interest rates since natural rate theory predicts that overly expansionary policies cause inflation.

> The **Keynes effect** *predicts declines in interest rates following expansionary monetary policy, and vice versa.*

If expansionary policies cause the price level to rise by 4 percent annually, the real rate of interest is zero ($r = i - \dot{p} = 4$ percent − 4 percent = 0 percent). Borrowers eventually will increase their real demands for funds to, say, D_1 because borrowing seems so cheap; since they repay these loans in depreciated dollars. Lenders will reduce supplies to S_2 because they gained no real purchasing power at a

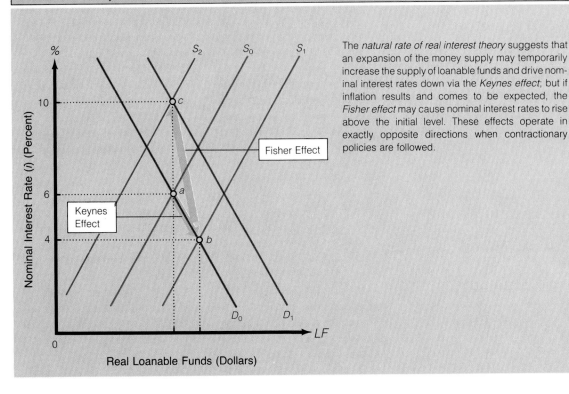

FIGURE 9 *The Keynes and Fisher Effects in the Market for Real Loanable Funds*

The *natural rate of real interest theory* suggests that an expansion of the money supply may temporarily increase the supply of loanable funds and drive nominal interest rates down via the *Keynes effect*; but if inflation results and comes to be expected, the *Fisher effect* may cause nominal interest rates to rise above the initial level. These effects operate in exactly opposite directions when contractionary policies are followed.

real interest rate of zero. In the long run, the nominal interest rate will rise to 10 percent (point *c* in Figure 9). These types of adjustments were addressed systematically by Irving Fisher, the first prominent American monetary theorist (see his Biography).

> The **Fisher effect** *predicts upwards adjustment in nominal interest rates as borrowers and lenders compensate for expected inflation, and downwards shifts if deflation is expected.*

Contractionary monetary policies tend to reduce the availability of credit in the short run; thus, in such cases the Keynes effect drives nominal interest rates up. After borrowers and lenders have learned to expect the deflationary pressures resulting from contractionary policies, however, the Fisher effect brings nominal interest rates down. Focus 1 provides an example of both Keynes and Fisher effects in recent years.

Overall, natural rate analysis suggests that discretionary macroeconomic policies are futile in the long run; they cannot permanently reduce either real interest rates or unemployment below their natural rates. The advocates of a *fixed monetary growth rule* believe that discretionary policies work temporarily only if people suffer from *money illusion*. Even temporary reductions of interest and unemployment are harmful because they are achieved only by thwarting people's desires; everyone eventually compensates for having been fooled by policymakers. But can policymakers consistently fool people? A recent theory answers NO.

New Classical Macroeconomics ___

You can fool some of the people all of the time, and all of the people some of the time, but you can't fool all of the people all of the time.
—Abe Lincoln

You can fool some of the people all of the time, and all of the people some of the time, and them's pretty good odds.
—Motto of Brett Maverick, a Gambler/Con Man Played by James Garner in the TV Western Maverick

BIOGRAPHY

Irving Fisher (1867–1947)

rving Fisher was the premier American economic theorist of the early twentieth century. His best known works address monetary economics and theories of capital and interest. He was also a pioneer in the explicit use of mathematics as a major tool of economic theory and cofounded the Econometric Society. Though Fisher was a theoretical economist, his objective was not only to develop theories with great explanatory power, but to develop them in operational terms—he tried to base his theories on measurable variables that permitted his hypotheses to be tested.

Let us look at Fisher's Equation of Exchange as an example of his work. He stated that $MV + M'V' = PT$, where M is the quantity of currency, V is the velocity of currency as it circulates, M' represents the quantity of demand deposit dollars, V' is the velocity of demand deposits, P is the price level, and T is the number of transactions in the economy. Modern quantity theorists have reduced this equation to $MV = PT$ by adding together the two forms of money. In this equation M, P, and T are directly observable and measurable. Hence the equation can be solved for V. (Most quantity theorists now use the $MV = PQ$ formula discussed in chapter 14.) The equation of exchange plays a very important role in current macroeconomic theory and policy disputes.

Fisher was impressed by the power of money and strongly advocated policies of monetary stability, an important theme in two of his major works, *The Purchasing Power of Money* and *The Theory of Interest*. In the latter, Fisher also distinguished between the real rate of interest and the nominal rate of interest. The nominal rate consists of the real rate, based on the real productivity of new capital investments, plus a premium for anticipated inflation on the part of lenders. The nominal rate, then, is the stated or contractual rate of interest observed in the market. The premium for expected inflation generates the Fisher effect: $i = r + E(\dot{p})$.

In addition to teaching and research, Fisher was a successful inventor who patented scores of devices. Among other items, he invented a folding chair and the Rolodex (wheels used in most offices today to hold business cards and addresses). Income from his inventions enabled him to invest. He was very interested in public health issues and put time and money into the temperance movement. He also invested heavily in health food companies.

Few of the reform movements Fisher supported ultimately achieved their goals. For example, the Constitutional amendment that prohibited alcoholic beverages was repealed after it ushered in an era of lawlessness. Some health food firms he invested in—Kellogg's and Post—now produce such sugary cereals as "Coco-Puffs" and "Sugar Pops," which says something about where the profit motive can lead even the most well-intentioned of reforms. (In all fairness, each does produce healthy cereals.) Nevertheless, Fisher was an active participant in the social and economic debates of his time. His life was one of accomplished scholarship and useful invention. Fisher's ideas live on. Growing numbers of modern economists now echo his call for monetary stability.

Keynes and Fisher Effects in Action—1978–82

The Federal Reserve Board eased monetary policy in 1978, reducing real rates of interest (the Keynes effect). During most of 1978–80, real rates of interest were actually negative or nearly zero. By 1981, real and nominal interest rates began to soar as financial markets adjusted to higher expected inflation (the Fisher effect). Figure 10 illustrates the Keynes and Fisher effects as they occurred during 1978–82.

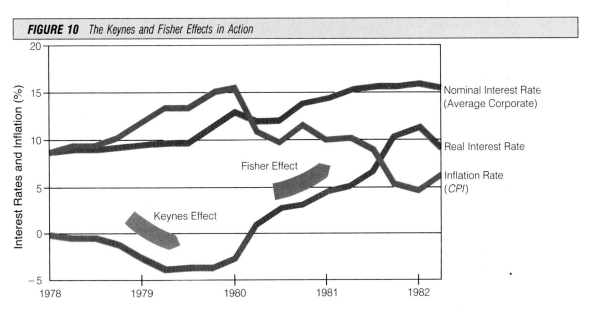

FIGURE 10 *The Keynes and Fisher Effects in Action*

Expansionary money policies in 1978 drove real interest rates down via the Keynes effect as inflation exceeded nominal interest in 1979. Nominal interest rates rose to compensate for unexpected inflation in 1980–1981, even though inflation was falling; this was the Fisher effect in action.

Sources: *Moody's Bond Record* and *Business Conditions Digest.*

The strongest of recent challenges to discretionary demand-management policies has been issued by economists who question whether either monetary or fiscal policies will work consistently. Much of their pessimism about active policy is based on assumptions drawn from classical theories about the operations of competitive markets. Thus, this analysis has become known as the *new classical macroeconomics.*

Competitive Markets

The theory of competitive markets is predicated on a number of assumptions. The most important of these for analyzing macroeconomic policy are:

1. All economic behavior is based on perfect information among market participants.

2. Transportation costs are zero, so all goods and resources can move freely and instantaneously between markets.
3. Buyers try to maximize their satisfactions; sellers, their profits; and workers, their net well-being.
4. All prices are perfectly flexible.

A logical consequence of these assumptions is that any profitmaking opportunities or opportunities for workers and consumers to increase their welfare will be exploited instantly. Thus, the economy will operate efficiently at all times. The problem posed for demand-management policy-making is that fiscal and monetary policies based on Keynesian analysis only work if the economy is inefficiently operating inside its production-possibilities frontier. If the economy is efficient and at its capacity, then there can be no quantity adjustments to policy (changes in output and employment), only price adjustments (inflation or deflation).

Equally critical is the fact that fiscal and monetary policies will have different effects in the short run than in the long run only if people are ignorant either about policies' thrusts or their long-run effects. We discussed in the previous section how expansionary or contractionary policies might have different effects in the short run than in the long run. Let us see why perfectly efficient competitive markets might cause long-run adjustments to occur instantly when demand-management policies are used.

Efficient Markets

Efficient markets theories suggest that discretionary policymakers try to fool people in the fashion of riverboat gamblers, but these policies do not work because Lincoln was a better observer of human nature than was the scriptwriter who contributed Maverick's famous line. In fact, these modern classically oriented theorists go beyond Lincoln, asserting that you can't fool all of the people *any* of the time.

Markets will operate efficiently if substantial information about profitable opportunities is widely available.

> The **efficient markets** *theory is based on the idea that there is vigorous competition for any ideas or information that might prove profitable. Competition causes any predictable abnormal gain from an investment to be exploited almost instantly.*

Profits that might reasonably be expected from some activity will draw alert profit seekers like garbage trucks draw flies. Thus, easily anticipated economic profits will evaporate because of competition. When an attractive investment becomes public knowledge, the cost of investing will be bid up so that only normal returns can be realized. Only above-normal profits that reasonable people would not anticipate remain as possibilities. Thus, extraordinarily high returns from an investment are largely a matter of luck.

Rational Expectations

A close relative of efficient markets theory is the theory of rational expectations. If people's expectations are formed rationally, they will learn to identify the variables that shape the circumstances affecting their lives.

> The theory of **rational expectations** *suggests that after policymakers pursue either expansionary or contractionary policies a few times, people learn how to predict changes in policies. Consumers and investors then will behave in ways that prevent predictable policies from having the desired results.*

Accordingly, adherents of the rational expectations approach believe that policy goals cannot be achieved, even in the short run, unless the effects of demand-management policies come as complete surprises to the public. Rational expectations theorists believe that predictable policies cannot consistently fool the public. This is a modern extension of the idea that inflation illusion is never permanent.

Natural rate theory is an important cornerstone for rational expectations theory. The concepts of natural rates of interest and unemployment are starting points in exploring the view that demand-management policy is impotent even in the short run.

Consider Figure 11. Suppose that a heavy short-run dose of expansionary monetary policy shifts Aggregate Demand from AD_0 to AD_1 causing prices and real output to rise to P_1 and Q_1 respectively (point b). This drives down unemployment rates and both nominal and real interest rates. When people eventually begin to anticipate inflation, then output, unemployment, and the real rate of interest return to their original values, while prices and nominal interest rates increase (point c). After this cycle occurs once

FIGURE 11 *Rational Expectations and Equilibrium Output and the Price Level*

Expansionary monetary or fiscal policy shifts the Aggregate Demand curve from AD_0 to AD_1. As both output and the price level rise, people begin to anticipate inflation and take steps to counter the effects of inflation and federal policy-making. Simple natural rate theory would predict a path for the economy of $a \rightarrow b \rightarrow c$, while rational expectation theorists would expect the economy to move directly from $a \rightarrow c$ as individuals instantly take countermeasures to expansionary policies.

or twice, most people learn to anticipate it and try to turn this ability to "predict the future" to their advantage.

Suppose that you are one of those who have observed this cycle and begin following the FED's policies closely. If increases in the prices of bonds and declines in interest rates invariably follow expansionary monetary policies within a few weeks, then you should make some money if you buy bonds the instant that monetary expansion begins. Since you will be holding bonds when interest rates fall, the increase in bond prices should profit you immensely. (Recall the inverse relationship between bond prices and interest rates.) As you and other "money-watchers" try to put this strategy into practice, the demand for bonds, and hence, their prices, would begin to rise just as soon as expansionary monetary policies are adopted. The short-run lag between expansionary

policies and the declining interest rate will collapse to zero—the adjustment becomes instantaneous. In Figure 11, as individuals anticipate the effects of policy, the economy will move directly from point a to point c and aggregate output will not change.

This is not, however, the end of the story. In the long run, nominal interest rates presumably rise to reflect inflationary expectations. Therefore, you and all the other people who watch the FED's actions will want to sell all your bonds before interest rates increase. Because the short run is now extremely short, the time to sell bonds is the instant you discern an expansionary policy. Since you will only be one among many unloading bonds when the money supply increases, the almost immediate result of an expansionary monetary policy will be to drive bond prices down and interest rates up in anticipation of inflation. But the story goes on.

If you expect inflation, you (and just about everyone else who is paying attention) will want to spend your money on goods and services while they are still cheap. (Remember, *buy low.*) If you manage a firm, you will immediately raise prices when monetary expansion begins; higher prices might help you build inventories that will be worth more money if you just wait a bit before you sell. Thus, inflationary policies will cause almost immediate increases in nominal demands for goods and reductions in their nominal supplies.

If you are unemployed, your inflationary expectations will adjust quickly to expansionary policies, and you will be unwilling to accept a job at lower real wages. Therefore, unemployment will not fall below the natural rate as a consequence of expansionary policy. The end of this rational expectations story is that unless the government disguises its policies, an expansionary policy will almost instantly drive up the price level and nominal interest rates, with little or no effect on employment and output. A reversal of this story can be told for contractionary policies (see Focus 2).

Note that one essential difference between the simple natural rate theory and rational expectations theory is the speed with which accurate expectations are assumed to be realized. Simple natural rate analysis would predict a path like $a \rightarrow b \rightarrow c$ in Figure 11, while rational expectationists would expect a direct movement from point a to point c, with no temporary increases in output and employment.

Rational Expectations and Hyperinflation

[Rational expectationists] are optimistic that inflation can be wiped out with little pain if only the government makes credible its determination to do so.

—Paul Samuelson

Hyperinflation—inflation of at least 50 percent per month—tends to cause monetary systems to collapse so that barter takes over. Most modern analyses of inflationary spirals suggest that halting inflation requires protracted high unemployment; presumably, the more rapid the inflation, the more severe the adjustment process. Surprisingly, several hyperinflations have been stopped almost over night with minimal increased unemployment.

Figure 12 provides data for major hyperinflations in Austria, Hungary, Poland, and Germany right after World War I. In each country, the abruptness of the halt in inflation was as spectacular as the rise itself. How did policymakers gain control of their monetary

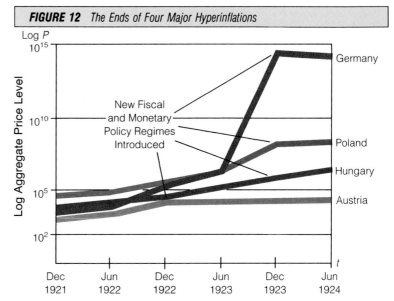

FIGURE 12 *The Ends of Four Major Hyperinflations*

Source: Thomas J. Sargent, *Rational Expectations and Inflation* (New York: Harper & Row, Publishers), 1986.

systems to end hyperinflation? The answer lies in the events preceding the hyperinflations and the actions taken to

end them. Paul Samuelson's observation (above) provides a clue to the solution, but first let's examine the causes.

Limitations of Rational Expectations Theory

Just how realistic is rational expectations theory? You and most of the population may ignore monetary and fiscal policies. There are a number of economic institutions, however, that devote considerable resources

to studying government in the hopes of predicting future economic policies so that they can get the jump on their competition or buffer themselves from hardship. Examples include banks, major corporations, unions, trade groups, and foreign governments. These groups do have substantial resources that can be shifted rapidly whenever the direction of

In commenting on inflationary finance, John Maynard Keynes noted:

It is common to speak as though, when a government pays its way by inflation, the people of the country avoid taxation. We have seen this is not so. What is raised by printing notes is just as much taken from the public as is beer-duty or an income-tax. What a government spends the public pays for. There is no such thing as an uncovered deficit. But in some countries it seems possible to please and content the public, for a time at least, by giving them, in return for the taxes they pay, finely engraved acknowledgments on watermarked paper. The income tax receipts which we in England receive from the surveyor, we throw into the wastepaper basket; in Germany they call them bank-notes and put them into their pocketbooks; in France they are termed Rentes and are locked up in the family safe.*

After World War I, Austria, Germany, Hungary, and Poland all faced severe hardships and financed massive budget deficits by printing fiat money; all except Poland owed sizable war reparations. Their currencies depreciated at alarming rates and inflation had a momentum that appeared unstoppable. But in Thomas Sargent's view,

. . . inflation only seems to have a momentum of its own; it is actually the long-term government policy of persistently running large deficits and creating money at high rates that imparts the momentum to the inflation rate.**

One rational expectations perspective is that stopping inflation, especially hyperinflation, requires more than just temporary adjustments in monetary and fiscal policy; the entire policy regime must be altered. Government finance must change in a *credible* way so that

the public *believes* that government is committed to eliminating the abuses that caused hyperinflation. Such measures ended hyperinflation in all four countries.

First, all four governments created independent central banks that were prohibited from issuing unsecured credit. Second, all four committed to relatively balanced budgets and agreed to cover government debt strictly through bond financing. Finally, the debtor countries renegotiated war reparations. Thus, by altering the "rules of the game," these governments literally stopped hyperinflation in its tracks.

Argentina recently went through a similar experience. Throughout the 1970s and early 1980s, inflation in Argentina rose until it exceeded 500 percent per year. In 1985, a new government instituted austerity measures, a new currency, and the will to stop hyperinflation. By early 1986, relative normalcy had returned to Argentina. It appears that policies that worked after World War I in Europe continue to work today.

---

*John Maynard Keynes, *Monetary Reform* (New York: Harcourt Brace Jovanovich), 1924, pp. 68–69.

**Thomas J. Sargent, *Rational Expectations and Inflation* (New York: Harper & Row, Publishers), 1986. This book discusses how these four and several modern hyperinflations were ended.

---

policy appears likely to change. For example, price hikes are common adjustments whenever the imposition of wage and price controls seems imminent.

Other factors, however, may limit the potential impact of rational expectations adjustments. First, rational expectations analysis assumes that people are able to accurately forecast government policy-making

when often it seems the government is unable to do this itself. Information about government policies is unavoidably expensive and imprecise. As a result, many people remain "rationally ignorant." Critics contend that, in the short run at least, government policy may push employment, prices, and interest rates away from their natural levels.

Second, public policy may alter the composition of output. For example, the Reagan administration increased defense spending in the 1980s, changing the composition of aggregate output. Similarly, expansionary monetary policy may reduce interest rates in the short run, resulting in rising investment which may alter the long-run production possibilities for the economy.

Finally, rational expectations theory assumes that wages and prices are perfectly flexible and adjust instantaneously to market forces. Union contracts, certain laws and regulations, long-term business contracts, and numerous other obstacles all keep wages and prices from adjusting immediately to changes in Aggregate Demand and Supply. It takes time for private investors and households to (*a*) recognize that policies and situations have changed, (*b*) implement plans to reflect new circumstances, and (*c*) have their new plans take effect. Government policymakers face parallel recognition, administrative, and impact lags. (These policy lags are discussed in more depth in chapter 18.) All of these reasons cause critics of the new classical macroeconomics to believe that short-run macroeconomic movements can be controlled by appropriate policies.

The new classical macroeconomics is a critique of discretionary macro policy. To this point in the book, we have addressed monetary and fiscal policy instruments and a few of their limitations. In the next chapter, we tackle other objections to discretionary macroeconomic policies, and introduce some alternative approaches to policy.

CHAPTER REVIEW: KEY POINTS

1. The *Phillips curve* depicts a trade-off for policymakers between unemployment and inflation. Lower unemployment rates presumably might be purchased through higher inflation, or vice versa; it is up to policymakers to choose the least harmful mix of evils. The Phillips curve appeared to be relatively stable through the 1960s, but it shifted sharply in the 1970s and early 1980s so that much higher rates of unemployment appeared necessary to dampen inflationary pressures. The reasons for the instability of the Phillips curve are the subject of a continuing debate within the economics profession.

2. The *natural rate theory* of the instability in the Phillips trade-off focuses on expectations of inflation. As labor begins to anticipate inflation, greater increases in wages are required for a given level of real output. Thus, accelerating inflation is required if policymakers desire to hold unemployment below its "natural rate," but even this policy will not work forever.

3. Modern Keynesian analysis suggests that several factors in addition to inflationary expectations can cause stagflation and instability in the Phillips curve. A critical assumption is that wages and prices are "sticky," especially in a downward direction. Unexpected shocks to the supply side, rapid compositional changes in demand or output, changes in labor institutions that generate disincentives for work, and changes in public regulatory policies all are capable of shifting the Phillips curve. The Keynesian *structuralist* approach emphasizes production "bottlenecks" as foundations for the Phillips curve.

4. If interest rate targets or unemployment rate objectives are set below their "natural rates," expansionary policies may ultimately cause *nominal interest rates* to rise, not fall. *Natural rate* theorists believe that only temporary reductions in interest rates or unemployment can be obtained through expansionary policies, and even in the short run, only by "fooling" lenders or workers.

5. The *Keynes effect* predicts that monetary growth will decrease interest rates, and vice versa. The *Fisher effect* is the upwards adjustment of nominal interest rates when transactors begin expecting inflation.

6. The *new classical macroeconomics* is based on the model of perfect competition, or *efficient markets,* which suggests that even in the short run, macropolicy only works when the economy is operating inefficiently and that this does not occur.

7. The theory of *rational expectations* suggests that people eventually figure out how a given change in policy affects the economy and learn to predict how policymakers react to swings in economic activity. Thereafter, people focus on what policymakers are doing and make adjustments that prevent the policies from accomplishing their objectives.

PROBLEMS

1. What is the realized real rate of interest in the following situations?
  a. $i = 8$ percent, $\dot{p} = 8$ percent.
  b. $i = 12$ percent, $\dot{p} = 15$ percent.
  c. $i = 2$ percent, $\dot{p} = -10$ percent.

2. After a full Fisher effect has been made, what will be the nominal interest rate in the following situations?
  a. $r_d = 8$ percent, $E(\dot{p}) = 8$ percent.
  b. $r_d = 5$ percent, $E(\dot{p}) = -3$ percent.
  c. $r_d = 6$ percent, $E(\dot{p}) = 18$ percent.

QUESTIONS FOR THOUGHT AND DISCUSSION

1. When double-digit inflation erupted in the United States during the middle 1970s, many economists became advocates of *indexing:* putting cost-of-living adjustment (COLA) clauses into all contracts calling for future monetary payments. They argued that indexing wages and other incomes such as rents, pensions, and interest payments would help fight inflation and, more importantly, would offset its negative effects. The theory was that indexation would make it impossible for policymakers to use inflation to fool workers into reducing their voluntary frictional unemployment, eliminate arbitrary redistributions of income, and so on. If the federal government used contractionary monetary and fiscal policies to fight inflation, indexation of income shares would cause the rates of growth of resource costs to slow automatically, making the process relatively painless. In theory, indexing some or all sectors could help slow inflation or at least cushion its impact.

Trace the effects of indexing if demand-side inflation is the problem. Some economists hold that indexing factor incomes may make controlling an inflationary spiral more difficult. How could this be true? How would supply-side shocks such as OPEC oil price increases work their way through an indexed economy? Through an economy without indexation? Would politicians have incentives to introduce inflationary or contractionary monetary and fiscal policies if all incomes were indexed? Why or why not?

2. If indexation is used for such retirement programs as Social Security, should pensions be adjusted using average changes in take-home salaries so that retirees share in the gains and losses of workers, or should cost-of-living adjustments be used to ensure pension-

ers a constant purchasing power income? What are the advantages and disadvantages of each approach?

3. Keynes argued during the Great Depression that the way to put unemployed workers back on payrolls and get machinery humming again was to increase the demand for goods and services by putting more money in people's pockets. His main argument concerned insufficient demand. If Aggregate Demand were increased, the economy would climb out of any recession or depression. Many economists believe that the Keynesian method for resolving the problems of recession may not produce the desired results in an era of stagflation. Why do most economists now believe that Keynesian demand management is effective only for problems like those of a depression era and cannot remedy the multitude of problems facing the economy today?

4. The 1979 Annual Report of the Joint Economic Committee of Congress states that stagflation is the result of policies that have stimulated demand while retarding supply. In other words, our national economic policies have concentrated on the economics of demand while neglecting the economics of supply. Would you agree with this diagnosis? What policies during the 1960s and 1970s may have inhibited the growth of Aggregate Supply?

5. Policies that enhance competition and economic efficiency tend to reduce inflation, unemployment, or both. Can you think of changes from current American policies in the following areas that would move the Phillips curve leftward and down? Try to do at least three or four areas (*a*) labor markets; (*b*) international trade; (*c*) transportation; (*d*) communications; (*e*) welfare; (*f*) housing; (*g*) government procurement; (*h*) big, highly concentrated industries; (*i*) education; and (*j*) finance. How or why would your policies be preferable to the current system?

6. Some economists argue that the Smoot-Hawley Tariffs enacted in 1930 were a major cause of the collapse in the stock market and the resulting Great Depression. Rational expectations analysis suggests that the impact of future events will be rapidly capitalized into stock prices. One political sage recently suggested that the Gramm-Rudman Act pointed to a new fiscal policy regime, accounting for the stock market's record performance in 1985–87. What argument could you make that passage of Gramm-Rudman would be beneficial for the stock market? Are there other factors that might account for the stock market's sustained rise in 1985–87?

CHAPTER 18

Limitations of Stabilization Policy

You may now be convinced that economic stabilization is a reasonably straightforward process: decide which goals to pursue in price-level stability, employment, and economic growth, and then translate these goals into an appropriate mix of fiscal and monetary policies. There may be hard choices about macroeconomic goals, but it seems that fault for any failure to achieve reasonable macrostability can be laid at the doors of policymakers who are just "too dumb" to apply a few simple principles of economics.

In the preceding chapter, however, you learned that new classical macroeconomics suggests that the reactions to policy by private individuals and firms may stifle the seemingly desirable effects of some countercyclical measures. There is growing acceptance of the somewhat broader notion that political actions are more often a cause than a cure for macroeconomic problems. Adam Smith's doubts about government are mirrored in modern monetarism and supply-side economics, which have borrowed much from the *Austrian* school, a group of thinkers typified by Ludwig Von Mises and Friedrich Hayek. (See their Biography.)

In this chapter, you will learn more about obstacles that make it difficult to properly design and implement discretionary countercyclical policies. Frankly, macroeconomic policy-making is as much an art as it is a science. Common difficulties facing policymakers include problems of timing and imperfect information, imperfect monetary and fiscal policy-making institutions, and imperfect politicians who adopt specific policies to maximize their prospects for reelection. These problems severely limit discretionary policy-making and stand as arguments for following macropolicy rules.

Lags, Doses, and Stabilization ___

Stabilization policy suffers from fits and starts because of lags in recognition, administration, and impact. Suppose that discretionary monetary and fiscal policies are equally powerful and have equally harmful side effects. There is still a question of whether monetary or fiscal policy is preferable because of the different timing lags that characterize each.

BIOGRAPHY

Ludwig Von Mises (1881–1973) and Friedrich A. Hayek 1899–

Ludwig Von Mises was born in Austria and taught at the University of Vienna before migrating to America to escape Hitler's invasion. As a youth he was fond of tennis, but when someone remarked that he was not very good at it, he replied: "The fate of the ball does not interest me very much." What did interest him was the whole range of human action. Von Mises's system of thought focused on the supremacy of the individual as a purposeful decision maker, constantly adjusting price, production, and consumption in order to live better and enjoy maximum personal freedom. In a free marketplace, *economic calculation* provides prices and profits as signals that motivate business to adjust production to the demands of consumers. But in a government-directed economy, agencies have no economic measure comparable to profits by which their operations can be evaluated.

Von Mises also rejected the Keynesian idea that a nation can solve the problems of inflation and unemployment by *countercyclical* fiscal policy. Such an idea ignores the fact that politicians have a strong propensity to spend in good times as well as bad. Von Mises added the conviction that government managers are always fumbling in the dark because they cannot possibly know all the data needed to make "correct" macroeconomic adjustments. He concluded that the likely outcome of *budget management* is inflation, followed by price controls, and, ultimately, stagnation.

Friedrich Hayek is one of Von Mises's many brilliant former students who later achieved prominence. This elder statesman of the Austrian school of economics became a Nobel Laureate in 1974. While Keynes advocated a very active role for government in controlling the economy, Hayek argues that the extension of government control is the enemy of freedom. He denounces a growing government role as "the road to serfdom."

Hayek decries constructivism more than anything else, calling it "the pretense of knowledge" and "the illusion of human omnipotence." *Constructivism* is the idea that enlightened leaders can remake society in the current fashionable image. Hayek believes that culture and civilization are not consequences of deliberate human design but are instead the products of the survival of society's successful groups. Hence, civilization depends on rules of behavior, not on goals. A couple of examples of constructivism in action follow. In the early 1980s Iran's theocratic dictator, the Ayatollah Khomeini, wanted his people to be more zealous in following the precepts of Islam. His regime killed thousands in order to reconstruct society to his design. Hitler, too, was a constructivist, as was Stalin.

Hayek believes that Keynesianism is a much less virulent strain of the constructivism disease. Keynes's message is very seductive: Through simple manipulation of total spending, a government can control the twin problems of unemployment and unstable prices. Keynes's comforting message has not been lost on many politicians, who no longer consider themselves to be helpless before the convulsions of a business cycle nor limited in what they can deliver to voters. Keynesian policy analysis looks like an instruction manual for running the economy as a well-oiled machine.

The trouble, says Hayek, is that the economy is an organism, not a machine. Individual behavior and economic interactions are so complex that they cannot be manipulated in the ways many modern macroeconomists suppose. In vain attempts to maintain very low unemployment, government may feel compelled to spend faster and faster, so that prices wind up rising faster and faster as well. This kind of artificial stimulant, says Hayek, distorts the price signals that indicate genuine scarcities in the marketplace when intervention is absent.

Recognition Lags

Our perceptions of the present are clouded, and our predictions about the future emerge only from more or less educated guesswork.

The time required for policymakers to realize that macroeconomic conditions have changed is the **recognition lag.**

Monetary and fiscal policymakers are equally affected. It takes time and effort to gather, compile, process, and interpret economic data so that we have some feel for macroeconomic trends. Even then, the data may be sketchy, contradictory, or misleading. Of course, if 25 percent of the work force were laid off tomorrow, policymakers would know by next weekend that we (and they) were in deep trouble. But our economy moves sluggishly, making it difficult for policymakers to determine exactly how hard and in which direction they should be steering.

Administrative Lags

After macroeconomic change is identified, it still takes time to institute proper countercyclical policies.

The time required to implement new policies is called the **administrative lag.**

If recession seems to be on the horizon, monetary policymakers could print more monetary base and buy bonds (open-market operations), or they might lower the discount rate or reserve requirements. (You should remember these from chapter 13.) Reversed measures would be appropriate if inflationary pressures were picking up steam. Changes in monetary policy can be implemented quickly by the FED's Open Market Committee. Consequently, administrative lags pose only trivial problems for monetary policy-making.

Fiscal policy-making, however, does encounter major administrative lags because discretionary changes in taxation or government outlays require legal changes. New legislation can take years to process so that minor crises may become catastrophic before (*a*) new laws are drafted, (*b*) congressional committees finish wrestling with questions about whose taxes to cut or raise or whose pork-barrel legislation to pass or kill, (*c*) both the House and Senate pass some compromise bill, (*d*) the president signs the bill, and finally (*e*) any legal challenges clear the courts.

This long administrative lag for fiscal policy might suggest a strong preference for monetary policy, which exhibits only short administrative lags. Some advocates of fiscal policy, however, suggest that this lag could be finessed if the president were granted discretionary power to raise or lower tax rates within narrow limits—say, 10 percent. Alternatively, the president might be given the discretion to impound funds for certain public works projects to fight inflation or to authorize preselected projects if recession threatens. One major difficulty with this proposal is that Congress and the voters seem loathe to give any president this much new power.

Impact Lags

It also takes time for any change in policy to affect the economy.

The time required for new policies to affect the economy is known as the **impact lag.**

Our $5-trillion economy can develop a lot of momentum—changing its direction through fiscal and monetary policies might be compared to using a rowboat oar to steer an ocean liner against a strong tide.

Even after legislation is passed, changes in most government outlays have long impact lags because it takes time for old government contracts to lapse or for new contracts to be awarded and then begun. The personal income tax system, however, is the major fiscal policy tool for altering consumer spending via the multiplier process. Consumers quickly learn about changes in tax rates because their paychecks almost immediately reflect higher or lower withholdings. People rapidly translate tax cuts that increase their take-home pay into new cars, video recorders, clothes, or more frequent chocolate chip ice cream cones. Adjusting to tax increases may be painful, but most consumers do so fairly rapidly because they must. The impact lag for fiscal policy may be long for changes in government purchases, but it is comparatively short when tax rates are changed.

In contrast, monetary impact lags may be relatively long and variable. When expansionary open-market operations are used, banks' excess reserves quickly grow. But bankers may "hoard" these funds if their confidence is down so that the lending → spending → lending sequence is squelched. Nevertheless, the loanable funds available generally rise and interest rates drop. While consumers may view this as an inducement to buy more durable goods, a decline in interest rates does not generally have nearly as large or immediate an effect on consumer spending as does a healthy cut in tax rates.

Lower interest rates will boost business investment, but investors may take some time to respond. Decisions about new capacity involve extensive deliberations in the major corporations that do the bulk of investment in our economy. Corporate planning is so complex that most major investments require heavy commitments of funds years before additional capacity comes on line. This extended investment

process is countercyclical in itself since changes in economic activity may have little effect on these decisions in the short run. The impact of monetary expansion on consumption and investment spending is positive, but it may be both slow and erratic. While estimates of the effect of monetary policy on spending place the beginnings of the new spending at as soon as two or three months, the full effects of monetary expansion or contraction appear to take up to seven years.

Discretionary monetary policy is like an automatic baseball pitching machine that randomly selects its pitches. The first pitch a batter faces may take five minutes to float over home plate belt-high, while the second pitch whistles by low and outside. (If all pitches were identical, batters' problems would be over.) Just as the batter tires of waiting for the third

TABLE 1 *A Summary of Approximate Lags, Timing of Major Effects, and Uses of Selected Specific Fiscal and Monetary Policies*

Policy	Administrative Lag	Impact Lag	Major Effects: Short-Run Versus Long-Run	Major Use
Fiscal Policies				
Change in taxes	L*	S	LR	Private to public transfers, and vice versa
Change in investment tax credits	L	L	LR	Stimulate investment, capital formation, and economic growth
Change in government purchases	L	L	SR	Countercyclical fiscal policy, pork barrel, etc.
Change in regulations	S	S	LR	Increase regulation to curb abuses and "cutthroat" competition; reduce regulations to improve efficiency in the market
Change in composition of government purchases	L	S	LR	Change the distribution of government spending—guns versus butter
Monetary Policies				
Change in discount rate	S	L	SR	Encourage or discourage borrowing (signals to market)
Change in reserve requirements	S	L	LR	Change the potential money multiplier
Open-market operations	S	L	SR	Week-to-week control of the money supply and interest rates

*The recognition lag is equal for both types of policy-making. The letter L stands for a relatively long lag, while S means that the lag is relatively short. The major effects of policies occur roughly in the short run, SR (1–3 years), or they occur in the long run, LR (4 years and over).

pitch and starts across home plate for the dugout, the ball suddenly arrives. This analogy suggests that a variable lag is just as dangerous as a long lag. Baseball pitchers vary their speed or placement on purpose to frustrate batters. The variable impact lags of discretionary monetary policy are unintentional, but they similarly frustrate decision making in the private sector.

Thus, although fiscal policy exhibits a longer administrative lag than monetary policy, this may be offset by the shorter and more certain impact lag of revisions in tax rates. Prolonged discussion of the need for tax reform or higher tax rates to eliminate ballooning deficits have, according to critics of discretionary fiscal policy, introduced greater uncertainty for investment decision making. And the long and variable impact lag of monetary policy is a major shortcoming of discretionary policy in the eyes of proponents of monetary growth rules. Table 1 summarizes lags, effects, and major uses of several specific fiscal policies and the three main monetary policies. The table provides a glimpse of the complexity involved in choosing a policy mix.

Destabilizing Effects of Policy Lags

Critics of discretionary policies contend that recognition, administrative, and impact lags make fine-tuned macropolicies an oxymoron. Suppose that the economy is self-stabilizing but that it does have a natural cyclical pattern as shown in Figure 1. The story of the effect of these lags may go like this.

Suppose the economy begins to heat up at the beginning of 1990. Policymakers recognize the emergence of inflationary pressures by the end of the first quarter of 1990 and implement contractionary policies by midyear. The braking effect of the engineered reduction in Aggregate Demand begins just as the economy would have begun to cool down by itself (point b). The effect of this seemingly correct policy is to cause a deeper recession than would have occurred normally in the latter half of 1991 (point c). Lags lead to a timing problem, making the cycle more severe.

The recognition, administrative, and impact lags consume nine months before proper expansionary policies to counteract this recession are felt in the economy—again, just as self-correction mechanisms would have brought the economy out of the recession. Mistiming means that expansionary policies are too powerful and that the inflationary pressure of mid-1992 is accelerated (point d). And so on.

Figure 1 portrays the worsening of a business cycle by correct, but poorly timed, policies. This example suggests that active countercyclical policy may be self-defeating, actually making the business cycle worse than it would be with a fixed monetary

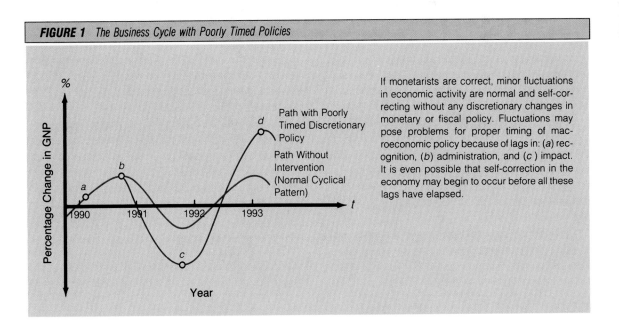

FIGURE 1 The Business Cycle with Poorly Timed Policies

If monetarists are correct, minor fluctuations in economic activity are normal and self-correcting without any discretionary changes in monetary or fiscal policy. Fluctuations may pose problems for proper timing of macroeconomic policy because of lags in: (a) recognition, (b) administration, and (c) impact. It is even possible that self-correction in the economy may begin to occur before all these lags have elapsed.

growth rule and fixed tax and government outlay structures. For instance, you can stabilize "waves" in a water bed if you push down on a wave at just the right time and with just the right pressure, but if your timing or pressure is off, you may synchronize with the waves and amplify them substantially. In a similar fashion, mistimed or incorrect policies may create chaos out of minor economic fluctuations.

Overdosing or Undermedicating a Sick Economy

Inflationary and recessionary gaps are, respectively, the decreases or increases in autonomous spending needed to decompress inflationary pressure or to push the economy out of a recession by filling the GNP gap. Unfortunately, these gaps cannot be measured precisely because we never know the exact limits of our productive capacity, nor do we know in advance the precise sizes of autonomous spending or tax multipliers. As we'll see later in Focus 1, monetary policymakers are plagued with similar ignorance about capacity, and the values of either the money multiplier or its velocity may vary. (Recall that velocity (V) helps us measure how a stock of money is translated into spending: $V = PQ/M$.) Another problem for monetary authorities is that the growth rates of $M1$, $M2$, and $M3$ may vary substantially. Which of these measures should policymakers try to control? Of course, this is also a hurdle for establishing a monetary growth rule.

These difficulties make it nearly impossible for policymakers to know how much stimulus to inject or withdraw. At times, as with Franklin Roosevelt's first two administrations during the Great Depression (1933–39), discretionary policies may be "too little, too late." In the eyes of critics who advocate putting the economy on automatic pilot, policymakers more commonly administer too much medicine. Lags in discretionary policies make it easy to overdose the economy with stimulants so that recessions lead into periods of hyperactivity and inflation. The American economy began to exhibit these symptoms in 1968 under President Johnson.

Alternatively, excessive doses of sedatives may cause an overstimulated economy to crash into a deep depression. Opponents of fine-tuning cite the economic nosedives of 1974–75 and 1981–83 as evidence of the harm done by abrupt reductions in monetary growth after extended inflationary growth. In situations where occasional aspirin would cure our economic headaches, the FED may administer uppers and downers in a cyclical fashion. The result is that the economy follows a snakelike stop-go path, with demand-side inflationary cycles causing supply-side cycles, causing demand-side cycles, and so on, as shown in Figure 2.

Financial Insulation to Counter Monetary Policy-making

Some modern Keynesians, most notably Hyman Minsky, also refute the idea that countercyclical monetary policy can be consistently effective. Their objection is based on a belief that technological changes in financial institutions are induced by *tight money* or *easy money* policies.

> **Financial insulation** *occurs when organizations develop new technologies that allow them to use money more efficiently so that more transactions can be supported from a given amount of monetary base.*

Among other effects, financial insulation tends to raise the income velocity of money (V). Here is one example of ways the financial system adjusts to tight money policies and, in the process, reduces the power of the FED.

Suppose monetary authorities try to combat inflationary pressures with contractionary policies. Excess reserves throughout the banking system fall, and credit availability throughout the economy is diminished. Especially when interest rates are high, any single bank's profits are enhanced if it finds new ways to support more loans from given total reserves.

In the 1960s, bank officials found that they could conserve on reserves by pooling their excess reserves. If one bank needed funds temporarily to meet its reserve requirements, it would borrow some excess reserves from another bank at a lower interest rate than the FED's discount rate. The *federal funds market* (a market for excess reserves) that grew out of this effort is now available to bankers across the country. Because of this financial insulation, banks can literally lend or borrow millions of dollars for as

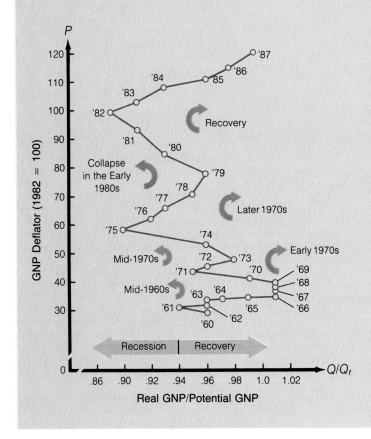

FIGURE 2 *The Economy's Snakelike Path*

Critics of discretionary policies attribute booms (rightward movements) and busts (leftward movements) of the economy to both mistimed policies and the tendencies of policymakers to administer overdoses. Keynesians argue that the economy would be far less erratic of policy were fine-tuned to cure our economic woes.
Source: *Economic Report of the President,* 1988; Frank deLeeuw and Thomas M. Holloway, "Cyclical Adjustment of the Federal Budget and the Federal Debt," *Survey of Current Business,* December 1983. Updates by authors.

little as one or two days at comparatively low interest rates.

Many institutions learn how to shield themselves from tight credit conditions. Other financial intermediaries, major corporations, accountants, and stockbrokers, among others, develop new techniques for minimizing money balances when a credit crunch hits. This is a "creative response" of the financial system. Discoveries of ways to dampen the effects of contractionary policy increase both velocity and the money multiplier and reduce the power of the FED. As Focus 1 illustrates, the FED's tools do not work as well when banks take steps to insulate themselves from the effects of FED policies.

Discretionary monetary policy can be compared to a pesticide, with firms being a variety of insects. Just as initial doses of a new pesticide wipe out a lot of bugs, contractionary monetary policies may reduce the availability of credit, causing marginal firms to succumb. And just as the insects that survive repeated doses of the pesticide become immune to it after a few generations, the firms that have learned to adjust to credit crunches become immune to contractionary monetary policies. Moreover, these surviving firms have a profitable advantage: many competitors will have collapsed during periods of tight money. Thus, adjustments by financial institutions to FED policies further limit the power of discretionary policies.

Money, Prices, and Financial Insulation

Figure 3 illustrates how financial institutions may adjust to counter monetary policy. The growth rates of M1 (lagged eight quarters), real GNP, and the GNP deflator are graphed. Both real GNP and the GNP deflator track M1 growth during the 1970s. Beginning in 1982, price changes and M1 growth uncharacteristi-cally diverged while real GNP continued on track. More recently, high rates of money growth have not translated into price increases because velocity has fallen. Many factors may account for velocity's decline including financial inventiveness, monetary deregulation, disinflation, and declining interest rates.* Basic departures from past relationships make implementing monetary policy much more difficult.

*For a detailed discussion of these issues, see J. A. Cacy, "Recent M1 Growth and Its Implications," Economic Review, Federal Reserve Bank of Kansas City, December 1985, pp. 18–23.

FIGURE 3   *Growth of Rates of M1 (Lagged Eight Quarters), GNP Deflator, and Real GNP*

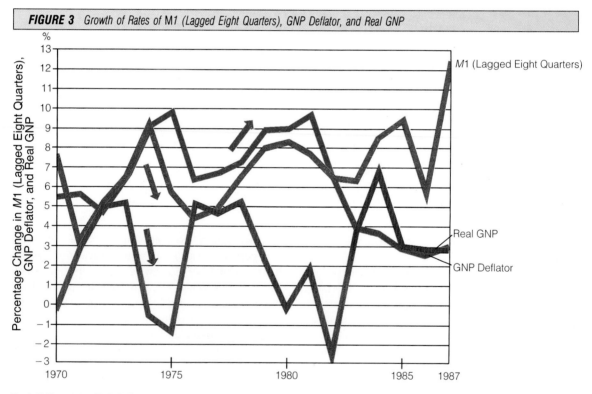

Real GNP and the GNP Deflator generally tracked the rate of growth of M1 until the 1980s. During the 1980s, the velocity of money has fallen due to financial inventiveness, monetary deregulation, disinflation, and declining interest rates.

Source: *Economic Report of the President,* 1988.

Political Dimensions of Macropolicy

Every recovery is hailed by an incumbent president as the result of his own wise policies, while every recession is condemned by him as the result of the mistaken policies of his predecessor.

—*Gardner Ackley*

We have described how macropolicy should be conducted if policymakers, for all their limitations, were selfless people interested only in the economic welfare of the entire populace. But you should never overlook the fundamental truth that fiscal and monetary policymakers are either politicians or their appointees. Both Keynesian and monetarist theories suggest that, in the short run, macropolicymakers can use expansionary policies to move the economy towards full employment. Through contractionary policies, they can combat inflationary pressures. Might these policies be affected by political goals?

Political Business Cycles

Macropolicy has occasionally been compared to alcohol. Alcohol can be medicinal; a little can loosen you up and allow you to have more fun. At least in the short run, expansionary policies stimulate employment, investment, and new sales for business firms. Everything looks rosy. But just as a mild buzz is often followed by a hangover, a binge of expansionary policies may be followed by a period of drying out. Unemployment and inflation soar, and business activity slumps.

The idea that political tactics cause economic instability is reasonably straightforward. Incumbent politicians who seek reelection may hope for spillovers into the ballot box from the short-lived pre-election upswings that follow tax cuts and a shot of new government spending. If monetary authorities are in cahoots with incumbents, they can help out with a chaser of expansionary monetary policy. Incumbents do well in elections during prosperity, but are turned out of office in droves when the economy sours.

After the election, the inflation that emerges from politically motivated expansionary policies can be dealt with by a strong dose of tax hikes, cuts in government pork-barrel projects, and monetary restraint. Thus, democracies may be plagued by political business cycles.

> **Political business cycles** *may occur if incumbent policymakers manipulate macroeconomic policies to enhance their reelection prospects.*

Politicians who adopt policies to influence voting patterns obviously hope that voters have short memories. Several studies indicate that the success of incumbents seeking to retain their offices is closely related to how fast disposable income grows during the year immediately preceding elections.

With these incentives for politicians to pursue policies leading to booms prior to elections and then to slowdowns immediately after the voting, what does the U.S. record show? Table 2 shows that between 1952 and 1988, our real disposable income typically grew at higher average rates during election years than in off-election years. The relationship is not perfect, but disposable income generally grew faster in presidential election years.

In chapter 13, we dealt with the issue of the FED's independence. Recall that the FED contends that it can do a better job if it is independent from political

TABLE 2 *Annual Percentage Change in Real Disposable Personal Income*

President(s)	Election Years	Off-Election Years
Eisenhower (1953–56)	2.7	1.0
Eisenhower (1957–60)	5.9	1.1
Kennedy/Johnson (1961–64)	4.1	4.2
Johnson (1965–68)	3.3	4.9
Nixon (1969–72)	4.1	4.0
Nixon/Ford (1973–76)	3.7	−.08
Carter (1977–80)	2.0	4.4
Reagan (1981–84)	3.1	.08
Reagan (1985–88)	7.3	2.1
Average	4.0	2.5

Source: *Economic Report of the President,* 1988.

pressures. Figure 4, which relates monetary growth to recent presidential election years, shows that monetary growth has generally been higher than average immediately before presidential elections.

Political business cycles are not unique to the United States. Among the more striking foreign examples is the case of Israel. There were six major elections during the period 1952–73. In every instance, the period immediately preceding an Israeli election was more prosperous than the period immediately after the election. After reviewing 1961–72 data for 90 elections in 27 countries, an American political scientist found that for 19 of the 27 countries, "real disposable income accelerated in 77 percent of election years compared with 46 percent of years without election."[1]

In 1943, Michael Kalecki, a Polish economist, suggested that after World War II, cycles caused by business instability would be supplanted by political business cycles in modern democracies. The evidence seems to support his contention that when politicians have a working knowledge of fiscal and monetary tools, they try to use these tools for their own ends.

Has Keynesian Theory Induced Government Growth?

A final criticism of activist policies is that as politicians use these tools, the government sector will grow larger relative to the private sector. Opponents of large government have lost most battles in the past fifty years; government's role has expanded in most of the world's economies. Many of these critics identify Keynesian fiscal policy as the culprit.

---

1. E. Tufte, *Political Control of the Economy* (Princeton, N.J.: Princeton University Press, 1978), p. 11.

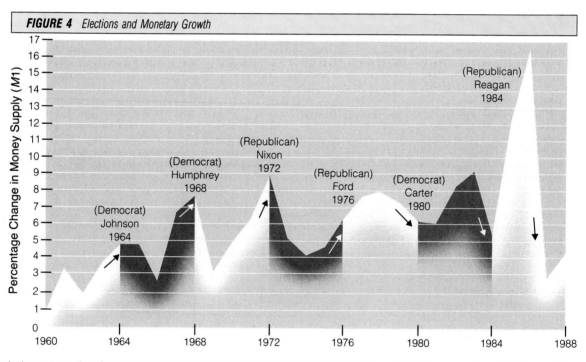

FIGURE 4   *Elections and Monetary Growth*

In the past two decades, monetary growth has generally been higher than average immediately before presidential elections. *Note:* The incumbent party and its candidate are shown for election years.

Source: *Economic Report of the President*, 1988.

Keynesian theory originated amid attempts to end a massive worldwide depression caused by inadequate demand during the 1930s. The Keynesian prescription? Spend your way into prosperity; ignore budget deficits and fight unemployment by boosting government spending and cutting taxes. Although largely ignored, the Keynesian cure for inflation is a healthy budget surplus. In fact, we sustained greater total deficits during the inflationary period from 1970 to 1976 than in the previous 200 years. (The deficits during the Reagan years made even these previous record deficits seem trivial.)

Many conservative politicians and economists continued into the 1960s to preach the old-time religion of cyclically balanced budgets, but the Keynesian approach gained increasing acceptance from 1936 into the 1970s. Critics of Keynesian policies have argued that government spending inevitably mushrooms once politicians learn that governmentally provided goods and services need not be paid for by politically unpopular tax increases.

Immense deficits during the Reagan administration produced the Gramm-Rudman Act, an attempt by Congress to force itself to bite the bullet. Eliminating programs and cutting budgets has proved to be a difficult task for both the administration and Congress. Critics see huge deficits, a $2-trillion national debt, and $1-trillion federal budgets as evidence that Keynesian theory promotes governmental growth.

In the post-World War II period, government spending and transfer payments as percentages of GNP have grown substantially in most democratic countries. This growth may be the result of the respectability of Keynesian policies. Until recently, deficits were not viewed with much alarm, even during inflationary periods. To the extent that deficits cause inflation, inflation should be viewed as a hidden tax. But if poorly informed voters blame government-generated inflation on unions or businesses, then politicians are encouraged to hand out "free lunches"—popular new government programs without unpopular tax hikes. Many voters are very aware of the direct benefits of deficit-financed special interest spending, but fail to recognize the inflation indirectly caused by such deficits.

During depressions, the deficits caused by higher government spending and lower taxes have beneficial effects—output and employment grow—but government also grows. Government outlays are seldom cut during inflationary periods, and proposals to raise taxes can be political suicide. Few politicians are willing to be accused of "raising the price of government" by raising tax rates. The net result is that government grows during economic downturns but does not shrink during inflationary periods as proper fiscal policy would dictate. According to critics of Keynesian policies, this occurs because the inflationary effects of high and rising government spending are disguised.

In summary, macroeconomic policies may be misused by politicians who cut taxes and increase government spending (*a*) shortly before elections, anticipating a short-lived prosperity that will aid them in reelection; and (*b*) during economic slumps, without offsetting increases in taxes or cuts in government spending during prosperity or inflation. The former leads to political business cycles; the latter, to expansion of the government and declining reliance on the private acts of individual households and firms.

The argument that political considerations upwardly bias the growth of government might seem to suggest that incumbent politicians will do almost anything to avoid a recession. There are times, however, when inflationary pressure may overwhelm politicians' preferences.

Engineered Recessions to Decompress Inflation

Curbing Aggregate Demand may lessen inflation. A mild recession can defuse inflationary pressure caused by excessive demand. Hair-raising depressions may emerge, however, if contractionary demand-management policies are used to combat severe supply-side inflation. If, as Figure 5 illustrates, Aggregate Supply is shifting leftward from AS_0 to AS_1, equilibrium output will fall to Q_1. But if contractionary demand-management policies are used to keep prices stable, a severe recession (or worse) will result as output falls to Q_2. Mild supply-side inflations already bear the seeds of recession.

Labor markets tighten and firms scurry to fill their labor needs as a boom caused by excessive demand

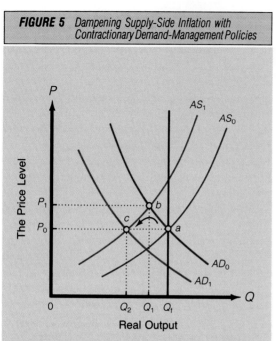

FIGURE 5 *Dampening Supply-Side Inflation with Contractionary Demand-Management Policies*

Dampening supply-side inflation with contractionary demand-management policies may diffuse inflationary pressures, but it is sure to generate a severe recession. If the Aggregate Supply curve shifts from AS_0 to AS_1, output falls to Q_1 but prices rise to P_1. If Aggregate Demand is reduced to AD_1, inflation is halted, but the economy suffers a serious recession.

unemployment will bring workers' expectations about wages, fringe benefits, and other job conditions into line with the real value of their production and firms' desires for higher profits. This is a minority view, unpalatable to most economists and policymakers, but the idea contains some kernels of truth.

Among the major benefits of recessions are the opportunities afforded firms to clear out "deadwood" and to boost labor productivity. Workers know that finding other jobs is more difficult during recessions, and that substantial disposable income may be lost if they quit their present jobs. Therefore, they work harder and complain less. The natural long-run result of a recession is that profits rise and owners and managers of firms are again happy. The recurrence of this process led one radical economist, David Gordon, to entitle an article, "Recession Is Capitalism as Usual."

Policymakers' Abhorrence of Recessions

Policymakers dislike using recessions to reduce inflationary pressure. High unemployment creates political discontent and can lead to changes of the guard at the White House and in Congress. Business downturns create pressures to restore full employment via expansionary policies that may rekindle inflationary pressures. While some radical economists argue that recession is capitalism's way of restoring labor market equilibrium, such an approach is pursued only reluctantly. To some degree, however, the slumps of 1969–70, 1973–75, 1980 and 1981–83 all resulted from such policies.

proceeds. Wages begin to rise, flattening profits. Hence, prices are pushed up because many firms seem to mark up costs by a fixed percentage to set their prices, a method known as **cost-plus** (or *markup*) **pricing.** Labor unions become more militant, strikes for higher pay and benefits become more common, and labor productivity falls as more workers with lower skill levels find jobs during prosperity. Consequently, labor cost per unit of output rises, intensifying upward pressures on prices.

Recessions to Discipline Labor

Some observers argue that a long period of prosperity may necessitate a recession to dampen inflationary expectations and "discipline labor" so that workers will work harder and accept less. Only a bout of high

Incomes Policies to Combat Inflation

Monetary and fiscal policies have been our government's favorite macroeconomic tools, followed closely by more direct forms of economic regulation.

Incomes policies *include such strategies as wage and price controls, wage and price guideposts or guidelines, and presidential jawboning.*

Seven of the nine presidents following Herbert Hoover used some form of *incomes policy*. Wartime wage and price controls were abandoned at the end of World War II. For roughly five years, there were no explicit controls, but the onset of the Korean War prompted Truman to reinstate some curbs. Both sets of wartime restraints were mandatory, having the force of law. The Eisenhower era, from 1953 to 1961, was free of controls.

Guideposts were introduced under President Kennedy in 1962 and stiffened by President Johnson, who accompanied these efforts with considerable jawboning. These voluntary guideposts lost their bite as inflationary pressures mounted in the late 1960s when both domestic spending and outlays for the Vietnam conflict escalated. President Nixon instituted full-fledged price controls, beginning with a 90-day price freeze in August 1971. In 1979, President Carter resorted to jawboning (with threatened losses of government contracts) to make his "voluntary" wage and price guidelines more effective.

Incomes policies are designed to reduce inflationary pressures without actually changing government spending, taxing, or monetary policy. If successful, the Phillips curve would shift to the left, making the feasible combination of unemployment and inflation less severe. A wage and price freeze is the most restrictive form of incomes policy, followed by wage and price controls, guidelines and guideposts, and finally, jawboning. Let us examine each a little more closely.

Mandatory Wage-Price Controls

Mandatory and wide-ranging **wage-price controls** normally have been associated only with war. President Nixon, however, introduced Americans to peacetime controls with his announcement of a 90-day freeze on wages and prices in August 1971. The freeze was followed by several phases that provided legal ceilings for increases in specific prices and wages.

These mandatory controls were intended to suppress inflationary pressures that had built up during the Vietnam War. Mandatory controls are legally enforceable price ceilings that carry penalties for noncompliance. Enforcement costs are high because the government is heavily involved in monitoring compliance by both business and labor. For example, in 1983, the government was still prosecuting violations of oil price ceilings, nearly a decade after the ceilings had been rescinded. (This point is also illustrated by the legal case at the end of this chapter.)

Voluntary Wage-Price Guideposts/Guidelines

Voluntary **price guidelines** and **wage guideposts** have traditionally been tied to the growth of labor productivity. The theory behind wage guideposts is that wages can increase by amounts equal to increases in productivity without forcing manufacturers to raise prices. Thus, if average wage increases equal only average increases in productivity, inflation (average price increases) can be held to zero. During the Kennedy administration, the wage guideposts were set to allow for a small, but tolerable, amount of wage inflation.

On the price side, the same logic was used to set the guidelines. Prices were expected to be stable in industries with average growth in productivity. Industries experiencing more rapid than average productivity growth were expected to lower their prices. Finally, in those industries where productivity growth was below the national average, permissible prices rose by the difference between productivity growth and the national average.

Evaluation of Incomes Policies

Incomes policies, like many other government policies, have both friends and foes. Supporters of wage-price policies point principally to their impression that many important U.S. markets are so concentrated that their pricing decisions are "monopolistic." Properly administered controls presumably will make the behavior of these firms more compatible with the interests of society. Monopolistic attempts to expand profits are thought to cause price hikes that translate into supply-side inflation.

Unions or firms that dominate a market may unilaterally raise prices, fueling inflationary pressures. Many primary product industries (steel, oil, and lumber, among others) exhibit these characteristics, so their price increases tend to ripple through the economy. Proponents also argue that when the principal underlying cause of continuing inflation is the inflationary expectations of workers and firms, controls can simultaneously reduce these expectations and reduce the basic rate of inflation.

Opponents cite the results of the 1971–73 wage and price controls as evidence that controls do not work. The evidence is diagrammed in Figure 6. The rate of inflation was actually declining just prior to President Nixon's announcement of a wage-price freeze. Throughout the freeze and during Phase II when wage and price increases were strictly controlled, the inflation rate began soaring. Inflation continued even after controls were lifted in 1973 and it

took a severe recession in 1975–76 to temporarily slow the inflationary spiral. Figure 6 also shows that President Carter's guidelines had little effect on inflation in the late 1970s.

Critics have pointed to this evidence to counter the view that controls reduce the inflationary expectations of workers and businesses. These opponents contend that controls actually create the worst kind of expectation—the expectation that when the controls are lifted, prices will rise more rapidly than before the restraints were instituted.

Further, critics maintain that artificial wage and price restraints warp market signals and lead to widespread shortages. Long-term controls breed corruption in government as bribery for the right to raise prices becomes common. Black markets emerge

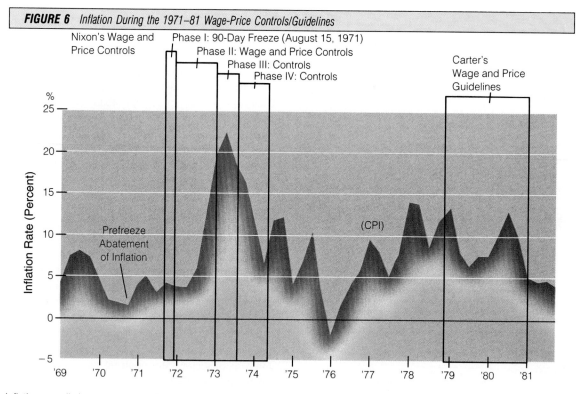

FIGURE 6 *Inflation During the 1971–81 Wage-Price Controls/Guidelines*

Inflation actually increased during President Nixon's four phases of wage and price controls, and intensified, erratically, throughout the 1970s.

Source: *Business Conditions Digest*, January 1986.

when people seek shortcuts around shortages. Distortions are greater the tighter controls are or the longer they are in effect. Price signals to reallocate production from less desired to more desired items get lost in the shuffle because they are masked by controls. These problems might be handled by granting exceptions to the controls, but each exception precipitates numerous applications for other exceptions. The complexity of regulations and monitoring tend to escalate, and eventually the economy may suffer from terminal red tape.

Guideline or guidepost policies without any legal muscle rely on appeals to patriotism. The battle is already lost if unions and managements of vital industries do not respond to the call. Most presidents have recognized this fact and have coupled voluntary controls with moral suasion or jawboning. Business and labor leaders are invited to the White House for little chats about antitrust investigations, public admonition, or various forms of regulatory harassment. Such confrontations with business and labor seldom achieve more than surface compliance and public relations rhetoric. Firms commonly learn to announce even higher price hikes than they desire so that, when faced with political heat, they can roll back the prices a bit. In this way, business leaders and politicians can each claim victory.

A crucial question about incomes policies is whether such schemes, without appropriately restrictive monetary and fiscal policies, would actually solve the inflationary dilemma. An incomes policy could be seen as a panacea by policymakers who might then feel free to follow expansionary monetary or fiscal policy if that suited their whims. Incomes policies are, at best, temporarily effective when expansionary monetary and fiscal policies are pursued; incomes policies will fail to hold the economy together for any longer than the very short run.

National Economic Planning _____

The basic guide to national economic policy from World War II until 1978 was the Employment Act of 1946, which established the Council of Economic Advisors and set full employment with price stability as national economic priorities. The *Humphrey-Hawkins Full Employment and Balanced Growth Act of 1978* augments the Employment Act of 1946 in several important ways. The Humphrey-Hawkins Act (*a*) identifies several specific economic priorities and objectives; (*b*) directs the president to establish goals based on those priorities and objectives (Congress is to review these goals periodically); and (*c*) creates procedures to improve coordination and development of economic policy by the president, Congress, and the Federal Reserve System.

Section 206 of the act, which provides standby public employment powers to the president, ignites most of the controversy that surrounds this "economic planning act." The president must ensure, however, that no workers from private employment are drawn into public employment projects. Second, the jobs made available must be productive and in the lower range of skills and pay. Third, the administration must identify target areas of high unemployment and focus on the structurally unemployed—those whose skills are obsolete or absent.

Critics of the act assert that the lack of coordinated economic planning is not the major cause of our economic ills. In fact, they see government actions as the major problem—not the solution. They assert that misdirected federal programs have created disincentives to invest in the private sector; counterproductive tax and regulatory policies also hinder the efficiency of the marketplace that they consider vital to a healthy economy.

National Industrial Policy

Many interpreted the stagflation of the 1970s as evidence of profound structural changes in our economy. The U.S. economy appeared to move away from its traditional strength in basic industries (steel, autos, and manufacturing) toward expanding new service-oriented sectors. Productivity grew only about a third as fast as in previous decades and real wages (after taxes) declined somewhat during the decade.

Some policymakers have called for a **national industrial policy** to counteract these changes. The concept of industrial policy or **reindustrialization** (which calls for a second industrial revolution) re-

Did Japan's Industrial Policy Sink Our Steel Industry?

Japan's rapid emergence as a massive exporter of steel in the '60s and '70s is still the most widely cited example of successful industrial policy. The decline of the U.S. industry is correspondingly held up as an example of the adverse consequences of the lack of a U.S. response.

To understand the dynamics of competition in the steel industry requires an appreciation of four factors: the "maturity" of steelmaking technology, the internationalization of raw material supply, the persistent differential between U.S. and Japanese employment costs, and the unexpectedly slow growth in demand after 1973. These factors, more than industrial policy, determined the basic outline of shifting market positions.

The technology of making steel is a mature one. That is, it is fairly standardized and not changing too rapidly. As a result, the most advanced nations do not have a significant technological advantage over only moderately advanced countries. From the 1950s on, new steel plants in Japan, Europe, and the U.S. have all been roughly comparable in their labor and materials efficiency. More recently, advanced developing countries such as Korea have also shown their ability to borrow this technology.

It should be noted, however, that while new plants have been roughly comparable in different countries, there is a strong vintage effect: new plants have higher labor productivity than older plants. This is important in explaining relative U.S. and Japanese productivity performance.

There was a time when the world distribution of steelmaking was largely determined by the location of raw materials. Steel production was located on top of coalfields which were not too far from sources of iron ore. By 1960, however, the advantages of traditional locations had evaporated. On one hand, traditional raw material sources were becoming increasingly worked out. On the other hand, falling ocean transportation costs made it possible to exploit new sources, such as Brazilian ore and Australian coal. The result was to turn steel into a "footloose" industry: any decent coastal location with a good har-

quires government support of targeted industries. Industrial policy offers a sophisticated rationale for certain pork barrel legislation and enjoys some support in Congress from both ends of the political spectrum. The fact that the specifics of an industrial policy are yet to be defined may account for some of its support.

The means used to target industries for supportive government policies and subsidies are extremely important to the success of any plan. Proponents of industrial policies argue that resources should be directed to industries where (*a*) productivity is the highest, (*b*) linkages to the rest of the economy are high, (*c*) future competitiveness is important, and (*d*) foreign governments target their resources. Proponents argue that shifting resources to high productivity industries will generate higher real national income and, thus, higher aggregate income per capita. Industries like steel, autos, or semiconductors that have extended linkages (or multipliers) to the rest of the economy would be targets for industrial policies, regardless of specific rates of productivity growth.

bor would be adequate. The critical factor became the cost of capital and labor.

In spite of the rapid rise in real wages in Japan over the past twenty years, the compensation of U.S. steelworkers has consistently been far higher than those of their Japanese counterparts. In the mid-1960s U.S. steelworkers received wages and benefits about six times those of Japanese workers; in 1981 they still received about twice as much. During the 1960s the major reason for this differential was the higher level of U.S. wages in general, which in turn reflected general U.S. economic advantages: superiority in high technology industries, a higher level of capital per worker, and greater self sufficiency in natural resources. As these advantages have narrowed, the differential in the steel industry has been sustained through a sharp rise in the wages of U.S. steelworkers relative to the U.S. manufacturing average, from 38 percent

above the average in 1967 to a 71 percent premium in 1977.

Finally, the state of the steel industry in all countries has been powerfully conditioned by the slow growth in consumption since 1973. From 1968 to 1973, world steel output grew at an annual rate of 5.7 percent, but after 1973 the combination of higher energy prices and slower growth in industrial countries brought a sharp slowdown, even before the 1981–83 worldwide recession. From 1973 to 1978, world output of steel rose at an annual rate of only 0.5 percent.

By the early 1960s the Japanese steel industry would have had a competitive advantage over the U.S. industry even if the Japanese government had kept hands off. The same technological "book of blueprints" was available to both countries, access to raw materials was no longer a crucial factor, and labor costs were much higher in the U.S. Capital was becoming steadily more

available in Japan, thanks to a high saving rate. Quite independent of industrial targeting, Japan was gaining a comparative advantage in steel while the U.S. was losing one.

Source: Paul R. Krugman, "Targeted Industrial Policies: Theory and Evidence," in Industrial Change and Public Policy: A Symposium sponsored by the Federal Reserve Bank of Kansas City, *1983, pp. 141–44.*

This is seen as especially important where the federal tax code, OPEC, labor unions, or other factors are perceived as distorting efficient market operations.

Almost two centuries ago, Alexander Hamilton suggested that "infant industries" were appropriate for government support. Today, some proponents of industrial policies would limit their support to industries that would eventually be internationally competitive. Others suggest that the United States should fight fire with fire by targeting industries that other foreign governments support. (Focus 2 addresses se-

lective support of industry in Japan.) They believe that this will enable U.S. industries to compete in international markets and re-establish a balance of international trade.

Opponents argue that reallocating workers into high productivity sectors may not increase national income. High productivity industries tend to be capital intensive; a given investment in these industries will employ fewer workers relative to less capital intensive industries. As employment growth declines, unemployment will rise, putting downward pressure on real wages, and there will be overbuilding in capital intensive industries.

Opponents also argue that the market provides the right level of investment for industries with extended "linkages" to the rest of the economy. They contend that it is almost impossible to forecast which industry may, at some time in the future, be internationally competitive. And finally, letting our industrial policy be dictated by that of foreign governments means that we might ignore market forces within our economy. Opponents stress that industrial policy will, for political reasons, be directed toward "troubled high wage, unionized, politically powerful traditional heavy industries" or emerging high-tech industries. Finally, market forces are often so powerful that industrial policies may be ineffective.

The idea of a national industrial policy is an offshoot of national economic planning, but on a smaller scale. A form of industrial policy has existed since the Great Depression. For example, in the 1950s we stimulated oil and mineral production with the depletion allowance; in the 1960s we underwrote the high-tech space program; in the 1970s we encouraged solar energy development using tax credits; and in the 1980s we returned to high tech with massive military spending on the Strategic Defense Initiative ("Star Wars") program.

What proponents of a national industrial policy want is a coherent set of long-run policies to promote economic growth and international competitiveness of U.S. industries. For example, Robert Reich has suggested a program to "create a dynamic economy" and speed the movement of capital into higher-valued productivity.[2] His plan includes such proposals as (a) use of employment vouchers for on-the-job training; (b) a human capital tax credit and community tax deduction for firms that retrain older workers and remain in their communities; (c) regional development banks to extend low interest loans to targeted industries; (d) applied research centers where firms could join together with a regional university to fund research; (e) replacing the current income tax with a progressive consumption tax to encourage savings; and (f) a national industrial board to monitor all government programs that allocate capital in the economy.

For industrial policy to succeed, restructuring of industry (promoting high productivity industries) will require employment opportunities to be available in other sectors. Industrial policy without sound macroeconomic policy to promote full employment will be virtually worthless. Ironically, good macroeconomic policy to promote full employment may mitigate the need for a national industrial policy.

A Brief Evaluation of Policy Rules Versus Discretion

Many of the ideas in this chapter address the shortcomings of discretionary policy. Advocates of stable macroeconomic policy rules continue to mount powerful and often persuasive arguments that discretionary policies do not work as intended. But their assertions are at times contradictory. Can discretionary policies be perverse because of inefficiencies caused by lags, incorrect doses, improper targets, or venal politicians, and simultaneously impotent because markets operate efficiently or because of rational expectations? In combination, these arguments are logically inconsistent.

Advocates of discretionary policies also offer persuasive arguments, many of which were presented in chapters 9–15. At times, discretionary policies have performed as advertised. The economic boom following the 1964 tax cut is one example of successful discretionary policy. On the other hand, the abysmal policy failures during the 1970s are testimony to the folly of fighting supply-side disturbances with demand-management techniques.

Whether discretionary policies or rules work better depends in part on the circumstances and on the people who control policies. But the central questions remain (a) Is the economy inherently stable, or is the market system unstable? (b) Can changes in spending, taxes, and monetary policies lend greater stability to a market economy, or are erratic government policies major sources of business cycles and instability? These questions cannot be answered definitively at this point.

Just as generals are sometimes accused of always fighting the last war, economic policymakers in the 1970s used the demand-management tools that were developed to solve the demand-side problems of earlier decades. Table 3 summarizes various theories

---

2. Robert B. Reich, "Industrial Policy," *The New Republic,* 31 March 1982, pp. 28–32.

TABLE 3 A Summary of Theories about Demand-Management Policies

	Critical Assumptions	Discretionary Monetary Policy	Discretionary Fiscal Policy	Monetary Growth Rules
Classical (old-style pre-Keynesian)	Flexible wages, prices, and interest rates ensure full employment. *Supply creates its own demand.*	Only the price level is affected, and then in precise proportion to the money supply.	Irrelevent except to the extent that the size of government relative to the private sector is changed.	Might prevent price level declines in a growing economy, but largely irrelevant. Money is a veil, not affecting real variables.
Keynesian	Wages and prices are downwardly sticky but upwardly flexible. Interest rates will not fall below the level of interest of the liquidity trap. *Demand creates its own supply.*	Ineffectual in a liquidity trap. Only influences Aggregate Demand through any decreases in interest rates causing increases in autonomous investment, which expands demand through the multiplier process.	Immediately increases Aggregate Demand via the multiplier process.	Irrelevant except to the extent that the interest rate is affected, and hence investment and Aggregate Demand are also affected.
Post-Keynesian monetarists	Keynesian analysis may be correct for the very short run in its Aggregate Demand orientation, but classical assumptions are correct for the long run. Velocity and the demand for money are stable.	Nominal GNP will be proportional to the money supply. Discretionary policy causes business cycles. The Depression was a consequence of contractionary policies; inflation is the result of overly expansionary policies.	Affects the size of government relative to the private sector and may pose problems because of political pressures to print money to cover government deficits. Otherwise, irrelevant for macroeconomics, although crowding out may be a severe problem if government spending grows. Modern supply siders also argue that potential GNP is shrunk because of disincentives when tax rates are high.	Permits the private sector to anticipate policy and facilitates noninflationary growth without raising the possibility of contractionary policies causing severe recessions. A monetary growth rule will eliminate swings in real output because of changes in policies. Prices will rise only slightly if economic growth falls below monetary growth, and prices will fall if economic growth exceeds monetary growth.
Natural rate theory	There are "natural" rates of frictional unemployment and natural real rates of interest. Differences between natural rates and actual rates occur only when people inaccurately forecast changes in price levels.	Unemployment and real interest rates will decline below their natural rates only if people are fooled by overly expansionary policies. This can happen only in the short run; in the long run, everyone catches on.		
New classical macroeconomics	Markets are efficient. Rational expectations theory suggests that inflationary expectations will reflect predictable changes in policies quickly.	People will not be fooled by predictable policies, even in the short run, so expansionary policies will be immediately translated into higher prices and higher nominal interest rates.		

about demand-management policies and should help in organizing your thoughts about these issues.

The wave of supply-side problems that has plagued the world economy for the past two decades requires development of policy tools that address the supply side. The next chapter focuses on some aspects of the supply side that enhance economic growth and development.

CHAPTER REVIEW: KEY POINTS

1. Macroeconomic policy-making is at least as much art as it is a science. A multitude of problems preclude perfect analysis and policy.

2. A *recognition lag* occurs because it takes time to get even a modestly accurate picture of changes in the state of the economy. An *administrative* (implementation) *lag* exists because it takes a while to get the tax and monetary machinery in gear even when policymakers' plans are made. An *impact lag* confounds the proper timing of policy; the economy budges only stubbornly to the prods of the policymakers' tools. These lags, which may be long and variable, may cause discretionary policy to be more destabilizing than stabilizing.

3. Lack of precise knowledge about recessionary gaps, inflationary gaps, and GNP gaps, as well as uncertainty about multipliers and velocity, mean that estimating the correct doses of monetary and fiscal medicine is extremely difficult.

4. Some modern Keynesians challenge the long-term effectiveness of monetary policy, arguing that adjustments in financial technologies will ultimately *insulate financial institutions* and make monetary tools inoperative.

5. Incumbents' prospects for return to office improve as per capita disposable income grows immediately prior to elections. There is some evidence that policymakers try to manipulate Aggregate Demand to enhance their positions in the eyes of voters, which induces *political business cycles*.

6. Some critics of Keynesian fiscal policies also suggest that the government grows relative to the private sector when policymakers increase spending and cut taxes during downturns. Policymakers neither cut spending nor restore taxes, however, during periods of prosperity or inflation.

7. *Intentional recessions* can decompress accumulated inflationary pressures and inflationary expectations. Recessions, however, tend to be very hard on political incumbents, so many politicians favor incomes policies of various sorts.

8. *Incomes policies* (mandatory wage-price freezes or controls, voluntary guidelines, or "jawboning") muzzle the effectiveness of the price system, creating shortages and widespread misallocations of resources.

9. The *Humphrey-Hawkins Full Employment and Balanced Growth Act of 1978* makes government the "employer of last resort" and requires that the administration submit continuous five-year plans for achieving various macroeconomic objectives. It also encourages coordination of government macroeconomic policies.

10. *National industrial policy* involves government policies designed to support targeted industries. Proponents argue that a coherent industrial policy is needed to increase economic growth, enhance U.S. industrial competitiveness, and counteract industrial policies of foreign governments. Opponents maintain that free markets will provide the appropriate investment in various industries and that an industrial policy will misallocate resources to politically powerful unionized industries.

QUESTIONS FOR THOUGHT AND DISCUSSION

1. Evaluate the proposal of granting the president discretionary power to raise or lower taxes 10 percent in order to overcome the administration lag that plagues fiscal policy. If there are substantial differences between this proposal and the power the FED now has over the money supply, what are they? If such a presidential power were enacted, would the president or the FED have more discretionary power to control economic activity? Why?

2. If you were the president and were intent on having "four more years," what new laws would you like enacted to ensure a booming economic climate around election time? What might be the longer term consequences of these policies?

3. Interest rates skyrocketed in late 1979, with the prime rate exceeding 20 percent, but they then plummeted even more rapidly than they had risen. Interest rates then soared again in 1981 but dropped afterward. From today's perspective, which parts of these violent fluctuations represented the Keynes effect and which parts the Fisher effect? (See Optional Material.)

OPTIONAL MATERIAL: A NATURAL RATE EXPLANATION FOR UNEMPLOYMENT AND INTEREST RATE MOVEMENTS OVER AN INFLATIONARY CYCLE

In this section, we follow interest rates and unemployment through a typical demand-side inflationary episode. By tracing through this rather intricate example, you should gain considerable insight into the nature of a business cycle that occurs because of overly expansionary policies.

Suppose that the natural real rate of interest is 6 percent, that the natural rate of unemployment is 5 percent, and that stable prices have been experienced for quite

some time. What will happen if policymakers are unhappy with this situation and pursue policies that cause Aggregate Demand to grow 4 percent faster than Aggregate Supply? In the next page or two, we will graphically trace short-run and long-run adjustments to this expansionary policy.

Figure 7 shows that the values of both the nominal and real interest rates equal 6 percent during the initial period (Time 0 to Time 1). Nominal and real interest

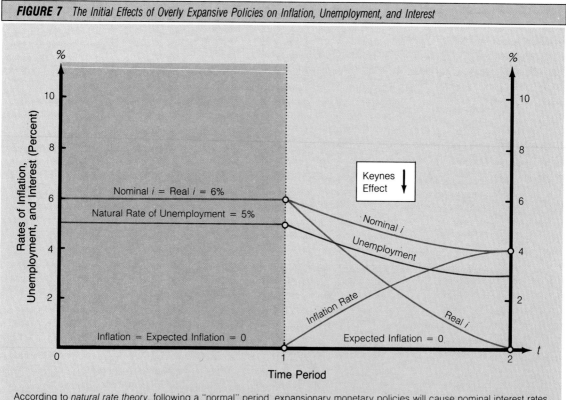

FIGURE 7   The Initial Effects of Overly Expansive Policies on Inflation, Unemployment, and Interest

According to *natural rate theory*, following a "normal" period, expansionary monetary policies will cause nominal interest rates to fall because of the Keynes Effect, the unemployment rate to fall because workers suffer from inflation illusion, and the real rate of interest to fall even faster than the nominal rate because inflation is not anticipated.

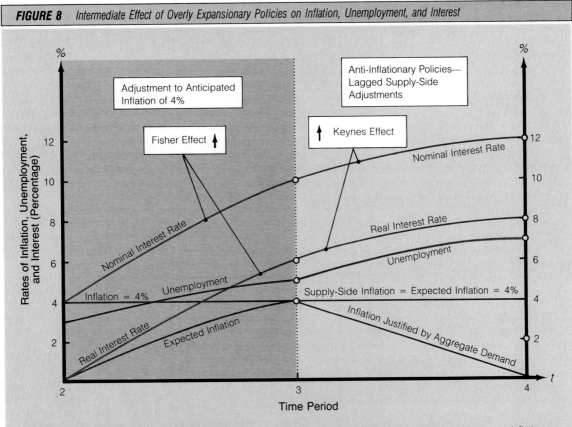

FIGURE 8 *Intermediate Effect of Overly Expansionary Policies on Inflation, Unemployment, and Interest*

The Fisher Effect causes both nominal and real interest rates to rise as borrowers and lenders learn to expect inflation; as workers adjust to inflation of 4 percent, unemployment also rises. If government then follows deflationary policies, the Keynes Effect causes both nominal and real interest rates to rise because both borrowers and lenders expect more inflation than will occur. Similarly, unemployment will climb because workers will insist on pay increases that overcompensate for inflation.

rates are equal because there is no inflation and none is expected. The unemployment rate is 5 percent because of the frictional, seasonal, and structural forces at work. At Time 1, suppose that the money supply begins to grow 4 percent faster than potential real output. Between Times 1 and 2, the supply of loanable funds increases and the nominal interest rate declines, say, from 6 to 4 percent because of the Keynes effect. Simultaneously, spending and employment increase, and unemployment declines, say, from 5 to 3 percent. This excessive rate of monetary growth causes the price level to rise 4 percent; so real wages fall and real interest rates dip to zero percent.

Eventually people become accustomed to this overly expansionary policy. The paths of interest and unemployment rates as lenders, borrowers, and workers adjust to 4 percent inflation are shown on Figure 8 between Times 2 and 3. Unemployment rates rise to the "natural" 5 percent rate, the Fisher effect kicks the nominal interest rate up to 10 percent, and the real interest rate climbs back to the "natural" 6 percent rate.

Suppose (naively?) that policymakers have quickly learned their lesson and decide to fight inflation. Beginning at Time 3, the rate of monetary expansion is reduced to the same rate as real growth of potential output. Unfortunately, this disinflation is contractionary because of people's inflationary expectations. In chapter 17, we described the lagged supply adjustment phase of demand-side inflationary cycles. This phase kicks in during the period between Times 3 and 4, and prices continue to rise at 4 percent annually. This will be a period of stagflation because the reduced growth of spending will cause unemployment to exceed its natural rate, rising to, say, 7 percent. The Keynes effect of the *contractionary* policy will cause the nominal interest rate to jump to, say, 12 percent, while the real rate climbs to above normal at 8 percent.

Figure 9 portrays adjustments as inflation finally subsides during the period from Time 4 to Time 5. Unemployment rates begin to trickle back toward the natural rate, but the real rate of interest skyrockets to 12 percent. Neither lenders nor borrowers anticipated the abatement of inflation; thus the nominal rate continues at 12 percent ($r = i - P = 12$ percent $- 0$ percent $= 12$ percent). During the period from Time 5 to Time 6, people adjust to zero inflation, so the unemployment rate settles toward 5 percent and the Fisher effect causes drops in both the nominal and the real interest rate to 6 percent. Finally, at Time 6, all adjustments to expansionary and contractionary policies are complete, and the economy has stabilized to the natural state that existed before policymakers started tinkering. The various effects of this complete inflationary episode are summarized in Figure 10.

FIGURE 9 *Final Decompression from Overly Expansionary Policies*

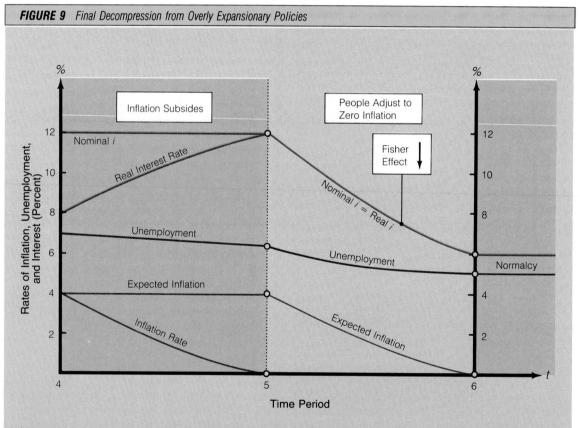

As inflation subsides, nominal interest rates initially remain high, while real interest rates climb. Then, as expectations of inflation gradually decline, the rate of unemployment slowly gravitates back to its natural rate, and the Fisher Effect causes both nominal and real interest rates to fall to the natural rate.

FIGURE 10 Keynes and Fisher Effects (The Complete Cycle)

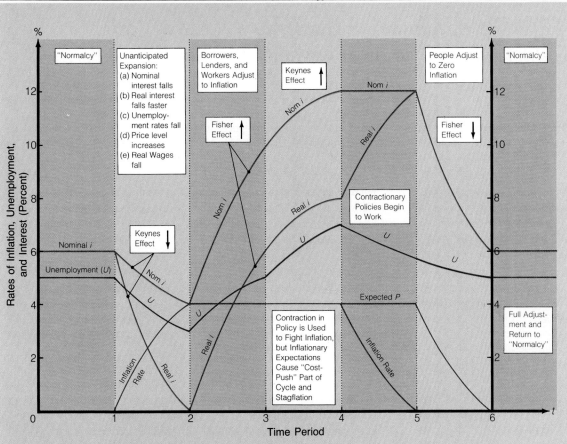

This figure summarizes the changes that natural rate theory predicts for a full (but simple) demand-side inflationary cycle.

University of Southern California v. Cost of Living Council and Office of Emergency Preparedness (1972)

Some government agency must develop and promulgate definitions, rules, and regulations whenever wage and price guidelines are imposed. These are invariably complex, and some groups are bound to be harmed in some manner. The University of Southern California found itself inadvertently in violation of the 1971 wage-price freeze. This case points out only some of the controversies that inevitably accompany incomes policies.

The University of Southern California (USC) seeks a ruling that its prices for tickets to its 1971 football games were not in violation of the Phase I "price freeze" signed by the President on 15 August 1971.

The Presidential Executive Order decreed that for a period of ninety days prices were to be stabilized "at levels not greater than the highest of those pertaining to a substantial volume of actual transactions by each firm during the thirty-day period in which transactions did occur."

On 28 January 1971, USC set the prices of reserved seats for each of its home football games in 1971 at fifty cents above those charged during the 1970 football season. On 30 April 1971, USC distributed brochures that announced the 1971 football schedule and solicited the purchase of tickets for re-

served seats, at the increased price, on a season-ticket basis or for individual games. Before 16 July 1971 (the beginning of the thirty-day base period established by the executive order), USC had received payment for about 125,000 tickets to the six home games on a season basis and several thousand additional tickets to individual games. During the thirty-day base period (16 July to 14 August), USC sold about 5,000 more tickets. Five of the six home games were played during the ninety-day "freeze" established by the executive order; the last game was played on 20 November 1971.

On 5 October 1971, the Cost of Living Council (CLC) notified USC that the price increase was in violation of the freeze and demanded that refunds of fifty cents per ticket be made.

The obvious purpose of the executive order was to stabilize prices as of 15 August 1971, and to prohibit sellers from increasing their prices beyond those charged prior to that date. There is no suggestion in the order that such controls would have a retroactive effect and require refunds of prices charged in transactions that preceded the executive order.

The CLC insists, however, that their demand is not retroactive. They contend that the "transactions" affected by the order were not the sales of tickets but, instead, were the playing of the games.

According to the CLC, inasmuch as there were no such "transactions" during the base period (16 July to 14 August 1971 inclusive), the 1971 prices could not exceed those of the 1970 football season, which was the "nearest preceding thirty-day period in which transactions did occur," required in the executive order.

The university asserts that a tackle on the USC Varsity would be surprised to hear that his performance in a game is in fulfillment of his employment to provide a service for the spectators as his customers or clients, comparable to services rendered by an electrician or a lawyer. The goal of a college football player is to represent his school as a member of the team and to help win games and perhaps a championship. The ticket holders are incidental; and the game presumably would be played with comparable motivation whether or not there were spectators in attendance. It is relevant to note that many intercollegiate athletic contests are held and earnestly fought virtually without paying spectators.

The university points out that purchasers of season tickets, rather than contracting for future services, are completing a transaction in which they give and receive value. They obtain the right to view the games from reserved seats, and their names are put on a preference list that accords them the availability of progressively better seats in successive seasons. In return, they pay the full purchase price without any right to a refund, and the games are played whether or not the ticket holders are present.

Questions

1. How would you decide the case? Why?
2. Do you feel the playing of a football game constitutes a service as suggested by the CLC? Why or why not? Does selling tickets constitute a service?
3. For this price-freeze regulation, what constitutes a "transaction"? Which is the most important for determining violations of the "freeze": transactions or services?
4. What are the practical problems in a case like this if you (the judge) decide for the council? If you decide for the University of Southern California?
5. What are some of the difficulties inherent in implementing wage and price controls that are illustrated by this case?

economic growth
economic development
Rule of 72
capital widening
capital deepening
technological change
infrastructure

CHAPTER 19

Economic Growth and Development

Most people expect a higher standard of living than their parents or grandparents enjoyed. For almost two centuries, such progress has been common throughout much of the world. Before the industrial revolution, however, each generation lived much like their immediate ancestors. Identifying the changes in the human condition that make rapid growth and development possible has been a challenge that has occupied economists and social philosophers for centuries.

One central macroeconomic goal is a healthy rate of economic growth. People in the United States have a stake in more vigorous international economic growth because growth is a mutually reinforcing process that links our economic fate with that of people everywhere. For example, when the United States recovers from a recession, the world economy often rebounds. Similarly, sluggish foreign economies can retard growth in our economy because of weak demands for our exports.

From the end of World War II into the 1960s, communist countries competed intensely with countries that rely primarily on the market system to see which would grow faster. Former Premier Khruschev's prediction, "We will bury you," referred as much to economic rivalry between the United States and Soviet Union as to anything else. During this earlier era, economic growth (at least our own) was regarded as unambiguously good. More recently, mounting concern about the environment and recognition that the world's resources are finite have caused many to ask "Economic growth for what?"

Economic Growth

Most of us applaud economic development that enriches the quality of our lives, but is all economic growth necessarily good? If a population explosion increased the size of the work force and caused growth in our GNP, it might simultaneously reduce our average standard of living. Do we want maximum income? Maximum income per capita? And what about pollution and other economic bads that often accompany economic growth?

Connections Between Growth and Development

How are economic growth and development related? People become bigger as they emerge from the shelter of the womb and proceed through infancy and childhood into adulthood. But infants differ from adults both quantitatively and qualitatively. Similarly, it is important to ask if economies also mature as they grow. Economic growth has only a *quantitative* dimension, while economic development refers to *qualitative* advances in an economy.

> **Economic growth** *occurs when more goods may be produced;* **economic development** *entails improvements in the quality of life, in the qualities of goods available, or in the ways production is organized.*

Describing economic progress requires both concepts. Focus 1 discusses the Rule of 72, which is a handy technique for calculating economic growth and several other quantitative variables.

Aggregate Demand, Aggregate Supply, and Economic Growth

What causes increases in potential Gross National Product? Before we confront the problem of growth in real per capita income or GNP, we need to explore the circumstances and events that cause potential real income itself to grow. The macroeconomic theory covered in chapters 9–18 suggests that increases in Aggregate Demand during economic slumps can boost GNP toward full employment levels of output.

While management of Aggregate Demand through monetary and fiscal policies may cause GNP to increase, this is not what we mean here by economic growth. Management of Aggregate Demand is basically a short-term concept. Modifying dosages of Aggregate Demand is similar to administering food and medicine to a malnourished child.

Growth and development as an area of study focuses on enlarging potential real GNP. This is a long-run concept, so we ignore demand to look at expanding the limits of Aggregate Supply. Just as the malnourished child whom we have fed and medicated may remain developmentally impaired, so, too, proper Aggregate Demand policies do not ensure that a disabled economy will exhibit healthy economic growth. In this chapter, we will assume that monetary and fiscal policies are used to ensure that Aggregate Demand accommodates economic growth. Potential Aggregate Supply depends on the state of technology and the qualities and quantities of resources available for productive activities during some time period. All labor is not identical, nor are other resources homogeneous: land, capital, or entrepreneurship.

How does growth in potential real GNP occur? Potential output rises through technological advances, increases in the amounts of land available, new discoveries of resources, capital accumulation, or through increases in the size or quality of the labor force. Although the land available to a given populace might be expanded by space exploration or imperialism, these strategies are so risky and expensive that in the long run, they are more likely to fail than to succeed. Growth, however, may be stimulated by a more efficient use of existing land or land reclamation. New discoveries of resources are so sporadic that we cannot rely on them. This reduces the feasible sources of economic growth to (*a*) increases in population and the labor force, (*b*) capital accumulation, or (*c*) technological advances. Let us examine aspects of each of these sources of growth.

Population and Labor Force Changes

Population growth per se may not yield economic growth. More people mean nothing for production unless the labor force grows, and the labor force

Growth and the Rule of 72

Many people are bewildered by all the concern over whether the economy grows at rates of 2 percent, 3 percent, 4 percent, or whatever the small number happens to be. U.S. policymakers and economists concern themselves with these small numbers because each 1 percent growth represents extra production of roughly $50-billion worth of 1989 output—hardly small change. Because continuous growth is compounded over the years, a 1 percent difference in the annual growth rate would mean a total difference of approximately $500 billion in production between 1989 and 1997.

Growth is a cumulative process analogous to compound interest. If you are paid 10 percent interest on $100 compounded annually, then at the end of the first year your $100 stake is worth $110. At the end of two years you have interest on both the principal plus the accumulated interest, so your original $100 is now $121: [$1.10 \times (\$100 + \$10) = \$121$]. And so on.

Compounding calculations can be simplified by using the Rule of 72.

*The **Rule of 72** is a "rule of thumb" whereby the time required for any variable to double is calculated by dividing its percentage rate of growth into 72.*

This rule works because growth or decline is compounded. Thus, if the annual interest rate is 10 percent, financial investments will double in about 7.2 years, not 10 years. A country's population will double in 36 years if population growth is 2 percent annually, but it will require only 18 years to double at a 4 percent annual rate of increase.

---

drawn from a given population can vary. We will treat this relationship first and then describe the interactions between population and national income.

Population and the Work Force   Population growth expands the size of the potential work force. All else being equal, if the work force increases proportionally as population grows, per capita GNP will decline. Why? Additional labor reduces the capital and land per worker, so labor productivity and per capita GNP will decline. This is one more example of the law of diminishing returns rearing its ugly head.

Consider Figure 1. Suppose that with 100 workers, 100 machines, and 1,000 acres of land we can produce 100 computers, 100 units of food, or any other combination on the production-possibilities frontier labeled PPF_1. We assume that the use of labor is relatively more intensive in computer production, while capital and land are most intensively used in agriculture. If all these resources were exactly doubled, we would expect potential output to double. Feasible outputs are shown as the combinations along PPF_3, which is a radial expansion of (that is, it approximately parallels) PPF_1.

Now suppose we held capital at 100 machines, land at 1,000 acres, and doubled labor alone to 200 workers. The production-possibilities frontier expands from PPF_1 to PPF_2: maximum food output only

FIGURE 1 Increasing Population and Diminishing Returns

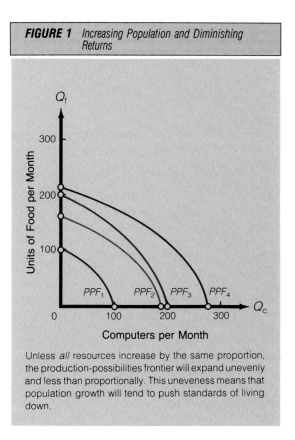

Unless *all* resources increase by the same proportion, the production-possibilities frontier will expand unevenly and less than proportionally. This unevenness means that population growth will tend to push standards of living down.

grows to 160 units and only 190 computers can be produced. The *PPF* does not expand to *PPF*₃ as labor doubles because we have not doubled land and capital inputs. Similarly, if labor were quadrupled to 400 units, diminishing returns would prevent the potential outputs of computers or food from also quadrupling. Using 400 workers, 100 machines, and 1,000 acres of land yields *PPF*₄, with maximums of only 205 units of food or 275 computers per month.

In a densely populated country such as India, needs for more housing, roads, and schools could cause standards of living to fall even if the labor force grew faster than population. Extra workers add to total output in all but the most heavily populated regions, however, so per capita GNP normally rises when the ratio of the work force to a given population increases.

The labor force as a percentage of the population is known as the *labor force participation rate*. Labor

force participation rates are also calculated for such subpopulations as working women between the ages of 25 and 35 as a percentage of all women in that age group. Just what determines labor force participation rates? Certainly social customs and mores play a role. For example, the "Protestant work ethic" creates certain expectations so that roughly 80 percent of all American males between the ages of 25 and 55 are in the work force. Wage rates are also clearly important. High wage rates raise the cost of not working and encourage labor force participation.

Another important determinant of the work force relative to population is the rate of population growth. Variations in population growth rates may cause a society to have high proportions of young and dependent members during one decade and large numbers of old and dependent members six or seven decades later. Of course, this is only one of many possibilities.

Suppose that birth rates have been declining for some time. Labor force participation rates will first rise as the number of children in the population falls and more women are free to enter the labor force if custom permits. Then the work force will gradually decline relative to population as fewer young people enter the work force and the number of retirees rises relative to population. Finally, labor force participation will stabilize. Can you outline some of the short- and long-term economic effects of the post-World War II "baby boom"? Couple the high birth rates of the late 1940s and 1950s with the recent declines in birth rates and the gradually lengthening life span in the United States. What will happen to the number of dependents per worker over time? What are the implications for our Social Security system? For the health-care industry? Other groups?

Subsistence and Population S Curves

Biologists have developed a theory of animal populations that goes something like this. Beginning at Time 0 in Figure 2, we have given amounts of land, vegetation, water, and other requirements for life along with a very small number of rabbits. With a substantial amount of space and food available per pair of rabbits, the rabbit population grows at an increasing rate for some time. When this population ultimately becomes congested, however, there will be ever in-

FIGURE 2 *An S Curve for a Rabbit Population*

Biological Equilibrium

Rabbit Population

0

Time

If resources are plentiful, population will grow quite rapidly. However, growth slows markedly as the resources available to sustain a population approach full utilization.

that the passion between the sexes is necessary, and will remain nearly in its present state. . . . These two laws ever since we have had any knowledge of mankind, appear to have been fixed laws of our nature. . . . Assuming, then my postulata as granted, I say that the power of population is indefinitely greater than the power in the earth to produce subsistence for man. . . .

Population, when unchecked, increases in a geometrical ratio. Subsistence only increases in an arithmetical ratio. *A slight acquaintance with numbers will show the immensity of the first power in comparison of the second. . . .*[1]

Reverend Malthus meant that food output might grow in a sequence like 1, 2, 3, 4, 5, 6, ... But if there were enough food, space, and other necessities, then human population would grow like 1, 2, 4, 8, 16, 32, . . . (much like rabbits). Population would be kept in check, however, by disease, starvation, or war, to grow only at the same pace as food: 1, 2, 3, 4, ... This theory may draw a grim picture of how human population is naturally regulated, but such a fate seemed inevitable to Malthus.

A corollary of this theory is that population will be constantly pressing on the means of subsistence. The theory provides for a number of limits that Malthus classified as either positive (things that increase deaths) or preventive (things that reduce births). Each possible limit to population was seen as being derived from limited food supply; starvation constitutes the ultimate check in Malthus's theory. In this way, Malthus introduced the notion of a physiological "standard of living" that regulates population.

The second edition of Malthus's *Essay on the Principle of Population* (1st edition, 1798) allowed habits to influence the minimal standard of living—a notion designed to explain the fact that laboring classes in several countries during Malthus's era lived at levels considerably above subsistence. Malthus nevertheless felt that almost insurmountable difficulties block permanent improvement of the condition of the working classes. His theory states that changes in economic conditions ultimately yield no change in the average quality of life, only a decrease or increase of

creasing competition for food and territory. A parallel population explosion among rabbit predators and the emergence of malnutrition will cause a gradual drop in the growth of the rabbit population. Pressure for "survival of the fittest" will mount. Finally, many rabbits will fail to secure territory and the specter of starvation will loom. Even if rabbits continue to reproduce at the same rate as previously, a sufficient number of their young will die and the average life span of the population will decline so that an equilibrium population will be achieved. This sequence is called a *population S curve.*

Early economists using similar reasoning concluded that human life would almost continuously be at only a subsistence level. Technological advances or an extended period of favorable weather for agriculture would simply result in higher wages, then population growth, and, ultimately, the misery of an even larger number of people. In the oft-quoted words of the Reverend Thomas Malthus, written in 1798:

I think I may fairly make two postulata. First, that food is necessary to the existence of man. Secondly,

---

1. Rev. Thomas Malthus, *Essay on the Principle of Population,* 1st ed. (London: 1798), privately published (Malthus's emphasis).

people living at this constant standard. Malthus preached that only through sexual continence could we avoid his grim predictions, but he was so pessimistic about the prospects for worldwide chastity that, to him, a razor's edge existence for the bulk of humanity seemed inevitable.

Malthusian population theory, influential and popular throughout much of the nineteenth century, lost favor rapidly once scholars recognized that Malthus had underestimated the rate of technological change. The most pertinent technological advances include several efficient birth control techniques and machinery and knowledge that have allowed food supplies to grow rapidly during the past century. Modern critics of Malthus's theory point out that humans, unlike rabbits, possess the ability to innovate and alter the carrying capacity of their environment. Prophets of doom and eternal optimists share an inability to predict the direction technological advances will take. For example, someone in the late 1800s might have predicted that the United States would "never sustain 240 million people because there wouldn't be enough land to pasture each person's horse." Our imaginations tend to be limited to the here and now, prisoners of current technologies.

Problems in underdeveloped countries have reawakened interest in Malthus's ideas in recent years. Many emerging countries have the worst of both worlds: the high birth rates of a typical agrarian economy and the low death rates of a modern industrialized economy. Barring major progress in the near future, these countries may face the unsavory choice of limiting the sizes of families—in opposition to widespread social values and religious beliefs—or the Malthusian checks of famine and disease that stem from limited food supply. Small wonder that the historian Thomas Carlyle, a contemporary of Malthus, characterized economics as "the dismal science."

It is unclear whether overpopulation causes underdevelopment or whether economic development will cure overpopulation. In most advanced societies, children seem to be regarded as "inferior goods." That is, as per capita income rises in these countries, there is a tendency to substitute a higher standard of living and more leisure for more children, despite the fact that more children can be afforded at the higher income levels.

The idea that equilibrium occurs at subsistence levels of income may seem naive to people in advanced industrial nations. The widespread misery and hardship experienced throughout much of Africa, Asia, and South America, however, at least partially confirms long-term economic forecasts made more than 180 years ago by Malthus and some of his colleagues.

How have the people of Western Europe, Japan, and North America escaped this fate? Their production and incomes have grown faster than their populations, which in some advanced nations have recently seemed at a standstill. In fact, as Table 1 indicates, population in many developed countries tends to be relatively stable or even declining, while primitive and less developed nations continue to experience explosive population growth.

But why has population growth in highly developed societies not responded to economic growth, driving per capita income down to subsistence levels? A partial answer to this question lies in the recent availability of low cost, effective birth control devices—a development that Malthus would have regarded as immoral. More critically, rapid technological advances and the accumulation of both physical and human capital have caused income in developed nations to grow more rapidly than population. Hence, although war has been all too common, we have not had to endure the starvation and plagues that Malthus viewed as the other natural checks on population.

Savings, Investment, and Capital Formation

Potential real output will grow with increases in the labor force, but per capita income will grow only when the quality and/or quantities of the resources we work with expands. Let us take a bird's-eye view at how the capital stock grows so that you can appreciate the difficulty of traveling this route to the good life.

Recall that investment is a major component of GNP and that production and income (and, consequently, investment) are flow variables. How is the flow of investment translated into a newer and bigger

TABLE 1 *Percentage Annual Population Growth for Selected Countries (Average Rates for 1980–87)*

Developed Countries		Less Developed Countries	
Country	**Percent**	**Country**	**Percent**
Austria	0.0	Algeria	3.0
Belgium	0.0	Bangladesh	2.8
Canada	1.0	Brazil	2.5
Czechoslovakia	0.3	China	1.3
France	0.5	Ecuador	2.9
East Germany	−0.1	Ghana	3.6
West Germany	−0.1	Honduras	3.5
Italy	0.2	India	2.1
Japan	0.6	Iran	3.6
Norway	0.3	Jordon	3.5
Sweden	0.1	Mexico	2.2
U.S.A.	1.0	Pakistan	2.9
USSR	0.9	Uganda	3.1
		Zambia	3.7
Average	0.3		2.9

Source: U.S. Department of Commerce, Bureau of the Census, *Statistical Abstract of the United States,* 1988.

capital stock (K)? Well, gross investment minus depreciation is net investment (I), which equals net *capital accumulation* during a given time period (t). That is, $\Delta K / \Delta t = I$. Omitting both government and the foreign sector for now, investment during any period will equal saving: $C + S = C + I$.

Thus, $S = I$. This familiar equation reveals that rates of saving must be high to achieve the high levels of investment necessary for rapid capital formation. Figure 3 indicates that if we choose to consume much and invest little of our national income (point a on PPF_{1989}), economic growth will proceed slowly. On the other hand, if our society chooses to sacrifice substantial potential consumption (point b), we will be able to produce and consume at higher levels in the future because of the extra capital accumulation that lower current consumption permits.

The share of national output devoted to capital goods instead of consumer goods may reflect individual decisions alone, or it may result from collective choice through government. When this decision is left to individuals, there is *voluntary saving.* When governments follow policies that force consumption down to allow capital accumulation, we describe the process as *involuntary saving.*

FIGURE 3 *The Effects of Consumption/Savings Choices on Economic Growth*

Societies that invest more by consuming less will experience greater economic growth and expanded potential consumption in the future. High rates of investment require high rates of saving.

Voluntary Saving

The act of saving can be viewed as a decision to delay consumption. Just what factors influence the choice between consuming now and postponing consumption so that we can enjoy more later? Although there are a number of considerations, two important influences on individuals' consumption/saving choices are the interest rates paid to savers and the level of income. A third significant influence may be the distribution of income.

Interest Rates The Keynesian Revolution ushered in a deemphasis on the importance of interest rates in determining rates of saving, suggesting that income is the major determinant of the level of saving. There has been a recent resurgence in the classical belief that the interest rate paid savers is critical in determining the saving/investment decision. The argument runs along the following lines.

An increase in the interest rate received by savers (who are the ultimate lenders) raises the relative price of consumption today versus consumption tomorrow. Thus, higher interest rates cause people to postpone consumption. Increases in interest rates will also discourage people who are marginal borrowers and who would use their borrowings for consumer purchases. This means that the quantity of funds supplied to investors will grow as interest rates rise, facilitating investment.

Must higher interest rates paid to savers discourage investment? Not necessarily. After-tax interest income is the concern of savers, and high after-tax rates of return are the goals of investors. A variety of government policies can be manipulated so that the net interest rates received by savers rise, while the interest costs of investors fall. For example, many of President Reagan's advisers believed that saving and investment in the United States had plummeted relative to national income throughout the 1970s. They felt that this was caused by the combination of very high tax rates on investment and interest incomes coupled with very low ceilings on the interest rates that could be paid to depositors by financial institutions.

Exempting interest incomes from taxation through such devices as *Individual Retirement Accounts* (*IRAs*) might increase saving from S_0 to S_1 in Figure 4 if savers view an untaxed 6 percent interest rate (on S_1) as equal to a taxed interest rate of 10 percent (on S_0). In this example, savers had been receiving and investors had been paying a taxable 8 percent interest rate on $50 billion. After interest is exempted from taxes, investors have $70 billion available to invest at an annual interest cost of 6 percent.

Other policies to simultaneously increase after-tax interest payments to savers and after-tax rates of return to investors include general reductions in marginal tax rates, rapid depreciation allowances, or investment tax credits. Direct government subsidies to investors would also automatically reward savers as the demand for investment grew. Taxes on consumption rather than income would stimulate saving and facilitate investment; saving would be deducted from taxable income if this proposal were enacted.

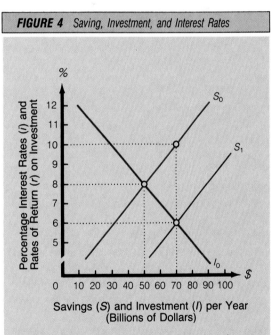

FIGURE 4 *Saving, Investment, and Interest Rates*

Savings (S) and Investment (I) per Year (Billions of Dollars)

Saving can be encouraged by raising the after-tax interest rates paid to savers; some supply-side policies will also encourage investment because the interest cost to investors falls.

This line of attack is increasingly popular. For example, after suffering a serious recession in 1985, Singapore's Economic Committee recommended a strong supply-side approach to revive Singapore's sagging economic growth rate. The proposals included (*a*) sharply reduced corporate and personal income tax rates, (*b*) tax breaks for firms engaged in research and development, (*c*) cuts in compulsory pension fund payments (similar to our Social Security taxes), and (*d*) pressure on Singapore's government to stabilize laws and regulations and reduce the uncertainty encountered in business planning. These examples of supply-side policies are seen as the road to economic growth.

Income   The Keynesian idea that income (*Y*) largely determines saving (*S*) was developed in chapter 9. The relationship between the average propensity to save (*S/Y*) and income is important in understanding barriers that limit economic growth in impoverished countries. If you are poor, you face the hard alternatives of consuming at low levels forever or reducing already low levels of consumption now to finance investments that might pay off in the future. You faced a similar choice when you decided to invest in your education; you probably could be consuming more if you were not in school. Hardships encountered in this saving/consumption decision are less of a burden for wealthy people or wealthy countries. Widespread poverty, on the other hand, inhibits saving and capital accumulation.

Inequality of Income   Impoverished countries tend to have less equal income distributions than highly developed nations. One way to accumulate capital is to rely on high saving rates by the wealthy and to hope that current deprivation of the masses will pay off in higher incomes for future generations. This idea is called the *trickle-down theory*. The wealthy may not save in ways that foster domestic growth, however; instead, they might buy foreign stocks or bonds or consume imported luxury goods. Foes of income redistribution programs often assert that saving and investment will fall if money is transferred from the rich to the poor. They argue that recent declines in American saving relative to GNP are consequences of rapid expansion of social programs.

Involuntary Saving

Governments do have some alternatives to voluntary saving if, for whatever reasons, they view voluntary saving and capital accumulation as inadequate for the rate of growth they desire. The trick is to force consumption down relative to total production so that the difference can be put into the production of new capital goods.

Central Planning and Confiscation   In a centrally planned economy such as the Soviet Union, the government sets wages and prices. Under the five-year plans initiated in 1929 by Joseph Stalin and still used today, wages have been low relative to individual production, and the prices of consumer goods have been set very high. People have no choice but to "save"; their consumption has been held far below their production. As a result of this forced saving, the Soviet Union experienced enormous industrial growth and rapidly attained the status of a world power. The costs of this growth were declines in already low standards of living—and millions of deaths.

The Marxist term *surplus value* refers to gaps between what people are paid and the average value of their total output. They contend that capitalists exploit workers by seizing surplus values. It is ironic that societies governed by Marxists are historically among the most exploitative. Although Stalin was succeeded by Khruschev, Brezhnev, and now Gorbachev—each seemingly more moderate than his predecessor—the USSR has only gradually reduced its "expropriation" of surplus value to generate rapid economic growth.

This sort of exploitation is just one way a government can confiscate resources to use them for capital accumulation and economic growth. Revolutionary "land reform" programs are another confiscation method: large estates are seized and allocated to peasants. Revolutionary governments also rely on direct confiscation of the factories or financial assets of deposed wealthy elites as sources for "social" capital accumulation.

The comparatively rapid evolution of the Soviet Union from "sleeping giant" to industrial power during 1930–1970 seemed a model of success for the leaders of many underdeveloped countries to follow.

Result? Their countries suffered from the inefficiency inherent in central planning. Moreover, the Soviet economy was relatively stagnant during 1970–1985. To remedy recent slowdowns in the USSR, Premier Gorbachev's new economic policy (*perestroika*) calls for heavier reliance on market forces. This policy sharply reduces forced savings through central planning. There are, however, other ways to force higher saving in democratic, market-oriented economies: inflation and taxation.

Inflation   A government can issue contracts for schools, highways, or industrial facilities and then pay the contractors with freshly printed money. If the economy is initially at full employment, inflation will crowd out private consumption. This has been a very popular form of forced saving in a number of countries, most notably Brazil. Throughout the 1950s, 1960s, and 1970s, Brazil experienced high rates of real economic growth despite high inflation.

Taxation   High rates of taxation may also be used to reduce private purchasing power and consumption and to increase rates of government investment. But the Laffer curve described in chapter 11 points to the danger that very high tax rates may result in severe disincentives for work effort and private investment, actually causing GNP to fall so much that tax revenues shrink.

Capital Widening and Capital Deepening

The rate at which the capital stock grows is crucial for economic growth, and determines the relative capital/labor mix in the economy.

> **Capital widening** *occurs if the capital stock grows, but only at or below the percentage growth rate of the labor force.*

Let us assume that the labor force is a fixed percentage of population. Capital widening (even if population and capital grow at identical rates) will not even stabilize per capita GNP because the increased doses of capital and labor relative to land result in diminishing returns. Since land resources cannot grow, it is likely that even if the growth of the capital stock does keep pace with population, standards of living will fall.

> **Capital deepening** *occurs when the capital stock grows faster than population.*

The cumulative effect of high rates of saving and investment (capital deepening) over an extended period is a higher ratio of capital to labor (the K/L ratio). This tends to raise labor productivity and yield higher levels of real per capita income. However, the fixity of land yields diminishing returns in the enhanced labor productivity that occurs as the capital stock grows. Thus, the higher a country's capital to labor ratio, the harder it is to use new capital formation as a source of additional economic growth.

Recently, the growth rates of the "four tigers"— South Korea, Taiwan, Hong Kong, and Singapore— slowed down. Earlier double-digit real growth was based on the simple formula of labor intensive exports. But wage rates rose faster than productivity as these economies grew. Slower growth in the 1980s caused policymakers in all four countries to try to expand their capital-labor ratios by channeling investment into capital intensive, high-tech industries.

South Korea's and Singapore's solutions involved tax breaks, credits for private groups, government public works projects, and higher wage floors to discourage labor intensive investment. The results have been disappointing. Capital deepening has not produced growth rates that exceed those in Hong Kong and Taiwan, whose governments did nothing to make one industry more attractive than another.

The preceding analysis suggests that even though rich countries with high capital-to-labor ratios may find it easier than poor countries to finance capital accumulation through saving, capital deepening is less likely to be effective in fostering growth in rich countries than in poor ones. It is crucial, however, that saving be channeled to the most productive investments—a task that seems to be done better by unregulated financial markets than by government planners. Nevertheless, many analysts who recognize that U.S. growth rates may have been lower than those experienced in parts of Western Europe and along the Pacific rim (Taiwan, South Korea, Singapore, Hong Kong, Japan, and parts of China) predict that growth rates elsewhere in the world will slow down as other countries attain our levels of per capita GNP.

Saving to facilitate capital formation can be voluntary or governments can use various tactics to compel greater saving. Voluntary saving is encouraged by attractive interest rates and high per capita income. Centrally planned economies can force consumption below production, thus creating forced savings. Several Far Eastern countries have recently discovered that as a country's capital-to-labor ratio grows, the generation of further growth through capital deepening faces diminishing returns.

Finally, critics of the traditional capital formation → economic development sequence point out that added capital may not help for several reasons. First, housing construction typically is a sizable chunk of total investment (over 30 percent in the U.S. in 1987). This spending, critics argue, might be better classified as spending on consumer durables. Second, much investment is often public investment for social/political reasons where rates of return may be quite low. Third, investment that yields excess capacity and underutilization of plants and equipment is useless. The British steel industry spent huge sums on plant modernization in the 1970s. But their new plants have been underutilized and, therefore, have added little to national income. These critics argue that real long-term economic growth is the result of technological advances, changes in habits, and advances in education. We will now examine one widely accepted ingredient of growth—technological change.

Technological Advances

Given amounts of resources, if used efficiently, will produce specific levels of output over a stated time interval. At a later time it may be possible to produce more output with the same resources. This is not magic.

> **Technological change** *is the process that permits us to produce more from a given resource bundle, or the same output with fewer resources.*

Subcategories of technological change include (*a*) greater efficiency in market processes, (*b*) improved knowledge about how to combine resources, (*c*) totally new production processes, (*d*) improvements in the qualities of human and nonhuman resources, and (*e*) new inventions and innovations. The idea of "progress" is inextricably bound up in the process of technological change.

Technological change can be viewed in two ways. In one sense it is embodied in new forms of capital; in another, technical changes or innovations encourage substantial investment and thus increase the capital stock. The emergence of money, electricity, automobiles, supermarkets, and computer chips are examples. Joseph Schumpeter (discussed in chapter 8) saw major technological breakthroughs as avenues for increased profits for capitalists and as the major source of progress for society.

Technological change can be stimulated by research and development. Innovative entrepreneurs such as Thomas Edison, Alexander Graham Bell, and Henry Ford were responsible for much of the early technological progress in the United States. Government can foster technological advances by directly funding research and development projects or through tax incentives to innovators. Less developed countries may stimulate growth and progress by importing new technologies. Another possibility is to import capital goods from more advanced countries. A slightly different method of securing technology is followed by countries that send some of their most promising young people to more advanced countries to study at colleges and universities. This is one popular way to build the foundations for economic growth.

Social Foundations: The Infrastructure

The path to economic growth in some societies rests on rich lodes of natural resources. The world beats paths to the doors of oil-rich sheikdoms and mineral-rich feudal societies, strewing money left and right that can be used as developmental "seed" money. Other primitive economies have tougher rows to hoe—they must build the foundations of economic development carefully.

*The **social overhead capital** or **infrastructure** of a country includes institutions such as a well-organized financial system, efficient communication and transportation networks, and a well-educated and disciplined work force.*

Any smooth-running economy needs a well-organized and sophisticated financial system. Without such a system, existing firms and industries must rely on internally generated funds (retained earnings) or on foreign sources to finance capital expansion. The same is true for other types of social overhead capital like communication and transportation networks. Methods for selling their products nationwide or worldwide are needed because most firms exhibit some range of production over which average production costs fall as output increases. Well-developed communication and transport systems aid firms in exploiting these declining costs.

Finally, no country grows very rapidly or experiences industrialization without a capable labor force. This includes not only a well-educated population but a healthy one as well. Thus, a nation must set high priorities in the areas of health and education if its economy is to sustain a high level of growth. Edward S. Denison, an expert in this area, attributes nearly 20 percent of U.S. growth between 1929 and 1982 to improved education.[2]

Economic Development and the Unfolding of History

Many historians and social philosophers have attempted to chart the progress of civilizations in broader terms than we have been discussing. Economic events often play central roles on the stage of history. Are there long-term patterns of growth and development common to the economic advances of all societies? Many observers believe so. Does growth ultimately bring stagnation? Most of us hope not, but some students of civilization believe it does.

---

2. Edward F. Denison, *Trends in American Economic Growth, 1929–1982* (Washington D.C.: The Brookings Institution), 1985, p. 30.

Development According to Marx

One of the most influential thinkers of the last century was Karl Marx, who suggested an unabated course of progress and development. (Some who are optimistic about the prospects for humankind hope he was wrong about the specifics.) Marx's prognosis was that every society goes through six major stages of history, culminating in an ideal state.

1. *Prehistory.* Prior to the dawn of civilization, humankind consisted largely of self-sufficient but nomadic hunters/scavengers/foragers. Gradually, these random groups evolved into a

2. *Primitive culture.* Extended families and tribes emerged during this period. Agriculture began to bind small groups to specific territories, but animal herding and hunting continued to be important. As claims to exclusive territories grew in importance, some families were more successful than others in establishing their rights to land, resulting in a system known as

3. *Feudalism.* The offspring of successful warlords became wealthy landholders, who were titled but most of whom owed their ability to protect their turf to a sovereign or king. Kings typically extracted "protection" tributes from lesser royalty; however, the actual production on the manors held by the minor lords and barons was done by peasants, who owned no land and paid a share of their crops to the titled landowners. (The sharecropping system continues to this day in many regions.) This chain of exploitation governed the social and economic behavior of all members of society from the highest born prince to the humblest peasant. Industrialization and the gradual evolution of shopkeepers into powerful merchants slowly eroded the powers of feudal royalty, although some merchants and feudal lords became industrial magnates during the transition to

4. *Capitalism.* The Industrial Revolution and growth in commerce were facilitated by urbanization. Dispossessed peasants streamed into the cities. They owned no resources except their own labor because their income was held at subsistence levels. According to Marx, capitalists accumulated enormous wealth during this period through the expropriation of a *surplus value* which equals the difference between the total value of production and the subsistence wages paid to workers. In Marxist jargon, all rents, interest payments, and profits are surplus values. Marx predicted that ever growing disparities between the wealth of

capitalists and the impoverishment of labor would generate class conflict and the triumph of a workers' revolution. The successful revolution would lead to a transition period called the

5. *Dictatorship of the proletariat.* During this period, all basic industries and productive resources would be *nationalized,* which means that revolutionary governments would seize them from capitalists and hold them in trust for the workers, or proletariat. Each worker would receive compensation only for his or her own production to ensure an absence of capitalistic exploitation. There would be a highly progressive income tax and a confiscatory inheritance tax. Gradually, all material wants would be satisfied, and the need for government would fade—leading to the ultimate state of

6. *Communism or socialism.* In this highest stage of economic development, basic human needs and wants would be met according to the Marxist principle, "From each according to his ability to produce, to each according to need." And everyone would live happily ever after.

Stages of Economic Growth

There have been many non-Marxist theories of the stages of economic development. Among the most noteworthy is one offered by Walt W. Rostow, who is concerned with transitions from a primitive economy to a fully developed and mature industrial economy. Rostow identified certain stages on the path of growth and development to economic maturity:

1. *Traditional society.* Traditional societies are based on agrarian economies that employ primitive technology.

2. *Preconditions for growth.* The traditional economy begins to change, with rapid increases in agricultural productivity. Growing agricultural surpluses free workers for industry and allow investment in capital goods. At this point, entrepreneurship begins to blossom.

3. *Take-off.* High saving rates during this period permit rapid expansion of productive capacity.

4. *Drive to maturity.* Output and income from industrialization grow rapidly.

5. *High mass consumption.* During this stage, services become very important, and consumer goods are abundant for all members of society.

Marxist and non-Marxist models are both highly abstract, and fail to provide less developed countries

with adequate guides about starting and sustaining economic development. Many countries seem caught in an almost insurmountable maze of problems.

The Problems of Developing Nations

Underdeveloped countries often seem caught in what has been called the *trap of underdevelopment.* For these countries, there appears to be no workable solution to poverty and despair, with most families living on the razor's edge of subsistence. The trap of underdevelopment is illustrated in Figure 5.

The Trap of Underdevelopment

Less developed countries typically experience high rates of population growth that result in low per capita incomes. These meager incomes leave families so little extra that saving per worker is very low, resulting in low national capital-to-labor ratios. Further, low incomes require families to spend most of their earnings on rather primitive products. Finally, low saving rates and little capital per worker lead to scant productivity on the supply side. This again translates into poor wages and, thus, low per capita income. No matter where you begin in Figure 5, the story is the same. How do countries escape from this vicious circle of poverty?

Breaking the Bonds of Underdevelopment

Impediments to development include (*a*) explosive population growth and lack of education and job skills, (*b*) little capital per worker, (*c*) primitive technology, (*d*) cultural norms that are hostile to commercial ventures, (*e*) few domestic natural resources, and (*f*) unstable political systems. How can countries suffering from such barriers break the bonds of underdevelopment?

Economic development does not happen overnight, but less developed countries (*LDCs*) can do several things to facilitate development. They can

FIGURE 5 *The Trap of Underdevelopment*

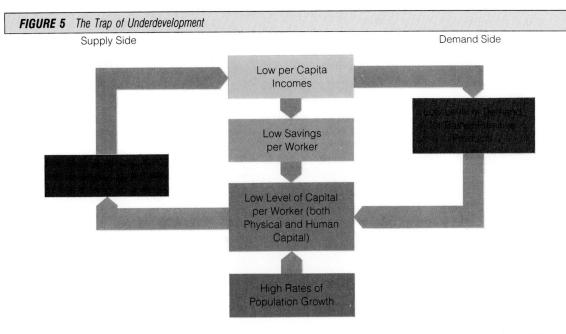

Supply Side   Demand Side

In many less developed countries, high rates of population growth lead to little physical or human capital per worker, which results in low productivity and income, which leads to low levels of saving and Aggregate Demand. This in turn leads to little capital per worker, and so on. Such a cycle makes it extremely difficult for primitive economies to escape the trap of underdevelopment and achieve economic growth.

Source: Ragnar Nurkse, *Problems of Capital Formation in Underdeveloped Countries* (New York: Oxford University Press, 1953); and adapted from Frances Steward, "Technology and Employment in LDC's" *Employment in Developing Nations: Report on a Ford Foundation Study,* Edgar O. Edwards, ed. (New York: Columbia University Press, 1974), p. 92.

eliminate and streamline government impediments to business activity, encourage the adoption of modern agricultural technology, improve the country's infrastructure so that the labor force can use modern agricultural and industrial technologies efficiently, and institute policies to reduce population growth and increase saving.

This is a tall order for any country. Consider the task of reducing population growth. Providing free birth control programs is barely more successful than exhorting people to abstain from sex. Many people in underdeveloped lands view children as old-age insurance and measure their own success by how many of their children attain adulthood. Better medical care or increases in national income are quickly translated into population growth. One example is the recent population explosion in Mexico following major discoveries of oil and other natural resources.

Some countries consider population growth to be such a desperate problem that they have resorted to involuntary programs. Mrs. Gandhi's government in India lost power for a period in the 1970s when her oldest son, Sanjay, directed the army to grab men off the streets in rural areas and sterilize them. In 1981, China passed laws limiting rural couples to two children, while urban couples were prohibited from having more than one child. Press releases periodically reveal that thousands of infant girls have been killed by Chinese parents who want male children. This is further evidence that government policies may have unforeseen and undesirable (or even tragic) side effects, and that devising policies to accomplish growth and development may be an overwhelming task.

The effect of policies that overcome the bonds of underdevelopment is diagrammed in Figure 6. Re-

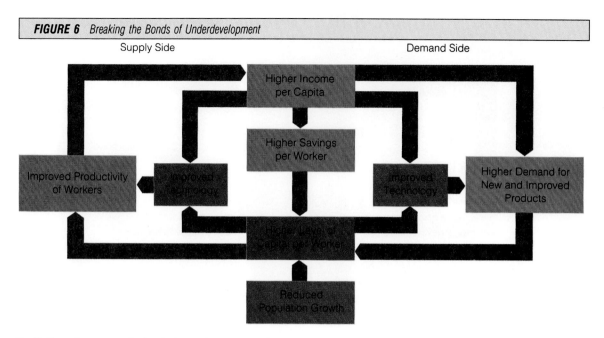

FIGURE 6 *Breaking the Bonds of Underdevelopment*

Supply Side   Demand Side

Higher Income per Capita

Higher Savings per Worker

Improved Productivity of Workers

Improved Technology

Improved Technology

Higher Demand for New and Improved Products

Higher Level of Capital per Worker

Reduced Population Growth

Facilitating advancement in developing nations may require reducing population growth, improving technology, and increasing the saving rate—all very difficult tasks.

Source: Adapted from Frances Stewart, "Technology and Employment in LDC's," *Employment in Developing Nations: Report on a Ford Foundation Study,* Edgar O. Edwards, ed. (New York: Columbia University Press, 1974), p. 92.

ducing population growth, increasing capital per worker, and implementing improved technology produces self-reinforcing benefits. (Some alternative development strategies are discussed in Focus 2.) As per capita incomes rise, saving per worker and consumer demands for new and improved products also rise. As more capital per worker is acquired, worker productivity will rise, resulting in greater wages and income. The circle begins again, this time for the better. It is generally very difficult, however, for any country to begin the development process on its own. Start-up capital often comes from foreign, more highly developed countries.

Is There Really a Trap of Underdevelopment?

The vicious circle of underdevelopment suggests that breaking the bonds of poverty requires domestic sacrifices supplemented by aid from abroad. Growth may depend on the rate of capital formation (investment) which in turn is a function of saving which is determined by income. Low income levels prevent the saving necessary for sufficient investment to fuel economic growth.

Critics of the trap of underdevelopment thesis point out that it is refuted by the very existence of developed countries. These countries all started out poor with low levels of capital; if the vicious circle of poverty thesis were true, developed countries would not exist today.

For example, in the early 1800s Hong Kong was a barren rock; by 1900 it was a substantial port. Hong Kong has little land and may be the most densely populated country on Earth. It has few natural resources and must import most of its raw materials. Today, Hong Kong is a major manufacturing, trading, and banking center. In fact, the Hong Kong experience is so successful that India is now considering turning the Andaman Islands in the Bay of Bengal into a free port and huge export processing zone. Critics ask, "How can all of this be true if the trap of underdevelopment thesis is true?"

Critics of this thesis further argue that development is based on factors other than natural resources, capital accumulation, and reduced population

Two Paths to Development in the Far East

The stage is set as two of Asia's most dynamic economies test competing development theories.* South Korea and Taiwan are taking strikingly different paths in their development strategies. Taiwan is the land of "mom and pop" enterprises with nearly 60,000 registered trading companies where profit rules supreme. In South Korea, less than 7,000 trading companies and a few large corporations dominate commerce. Unlike Taiwan, the South Korean government is heavily involved in industrial policy and South Korean corporations focus more on building international markets.

Much of the differences in their approach to development stem from cul-

*From "South Korea and Taiwan: Two Strategies" by James R. Schiffman and Maria Shao in The Wall Street Journal, May 1, 1986. Copyright © 1986 by Dow Jones & Company, Inc. All Rights Reserved. Reprinted by permission.

tural differences between the Koreans and the Chinese of Taiwan. The Koreans are viewed as aggressive (or even reckless) spenders, while the Chinese are more conservative and cautious, with a tendency to save. Korean companies are borrowing heavily to finance massive factories in capital-intensive industries like steel, appliances, automobiles, and semiconductors. Taiwan's focus is on development of high-tech research and development to suit specific market niches.

Per capita GNP in Taiwan is currently 50 percent greater than in Korea, and Taiwan runs a trade surplus while Korea still has a deficit. South Korean exchange reserves are low and its international debt is much larger than that of Taiwan. If Korea's large investment pays off in the future, however, these positions could be reversed.

The different development strategies represented by both Taiwan and Korea illustrate that there may be "more than

one way to skin a cat." Heavy government intervention and large corporate organizations in Korea are consistent with the Korean culture, which subordinates personal interest to national interests. The Chinese tend to be more entrepreneurial and want to "be their own boss," making development of large organizations more difficult and less efficient. The approach that will ultimately prove to be better is still unknown. What seems clear is that each country has chosen a route that best suits its people, and in the end, this may be more important than anything.

---

growth. They argue that successful development hinges on such factors as human aptitudes and attitudes, social and political institutions, external contacts, market opportunities, and natural resources (to a lesser extent). Development is not just a matter of capital accumulation, and saving; it is vitally related to individuals (entrepreneurs) being able to perceive opportunities and then to take advantage of them. Growth is, of course, conditioned by the opportunities offered by the environment—like natural resources and social institutions—but the pace and pattern of growth will depend on the quality of the entrepreneurial talent in the economy.

These critics point to Hong Kong, Taiwan, and Singapore as counterexamples to the traditional capital accumulation theory of growth and development. Only when free trade and unrestricted entrepreneurial activity are available as springboards to economic

On the Brink in Mexico

The external debts of Latin America had mounted to roughly $400 billion by 1988. Some of these countries (e.g., Brazil) defaulted on payments of interest and principal, and most of the rest teetered on the brink of default. But nowhere was the crisis more severe than in Mexico. The Mexican government owed foreign bankers over $100 billion dollars in 1986. There was $1,250 of foreign debt for each of Mexico's 80 million citizens, and scheduled interest payments alone absorbed one sixth of Mexico's national income.

The major problem is that ambitious development programs were financed with foreign debt during the 1970s. Mexico's oil reserves tripled between 1976 and 1982, making it a major oil

exporter. The government expected rapid economic growth and went on a borrowing binge, expecting rising oil revenues to enable easy debt repayment. Mexican economic planners had assumed that world oil prices would be $60–$90 per barrel by 1985, but oil peaked at roughly $34 per barrel in 1981–82. By 1986, oil prices had fallen to the $10–$14 range, and Mexico's export earnings were only 10 percent of its forecasts. One result was that Mexico was devastated by *triple*-digit inflation and massive unemployment.

In common with most developing nations, Mexico's income distribution is traditionally very unequal; the few rich families are envied and resented by masses of destitute peasants and urban

slum dwellers. An emerging middle class depended on the success of Mexico's development programs, but the state-controlled industries that devoured so much development money have been plagued by red tape and massive corruption. Middle class dreams were crushed by falling oil prices and the stagnation of government industries.

Mexico's problems were worsened by international adjustments to its plight. In 1982 alone, the number of pesos required to buy $1 rose from 22 to 150, increasing external (dollar-denominated) debt from the Mexican perspective by 700 percent. Fear of continuing declines in peso exchange rates (relative prices of currencies) caused middle class and wealthy Mexicans to pour

growth will injections of foreign capital be helpful since, as P. T. Bauer has noted, "A society which cannot develop without external gifts is altogether unlikely to do so with them."

What Developed Countries Can Do to Aid Less Developed Nations ____

The case for foreign aid is regarded as axiomatic, so that either progress or lack of progress can be used to argue for more aid. Progress is evidence of success, and lack of progress as evidence that more must be done.
— *P. T. Bauer*

Many people perceive the most pressing needs of developing nations to be enormous injections of capital, introduction of new technology, and substantial education and job training programs. Developed nations are often in a good position to provide physical capital since many have an abundance and their investors are looking for profitable places to invest. Similarly, the educational systems of developed countries can train technically qualified people for developing industries. Moreover, industrialized countries can provide the technology needed to raise the productivity of workers in less developed countries.

their financial assets into dollar deposits in U.S. banks. A dollar would buy 600 pesos by 1986. Between 1976 and 1985, roughly $53 billion in private financial capital left Mexico; even small banks in Texas border towns grew by as much as $1 billion in new deposits. This *capital flight* has been a huge obstacle to financing economic growth internally, and has increased Mexico's dependence on foreign banks.

Debt repayment as originally scheduled would have required drastic measures but the Partido Revolucionario Institucional (PRI), which has ruled Mexico for six decades, depends on a fragile coalition that limits it to conservative policy changes. An austerity program cost one third of government workers their jobs but did little to cure the basic problem. Selling government industries to private firms might enable Mexico to staunch the flight of private capital and repay more of its debts, but opposition by the bureaucrats who run these industries probably makes this approach politically impossible.

Any quick solution to Mexico's problems would be destabilizing. These problems have been partially exported. Falling incomes and high unemployment rates have increased illegal immigration. The United States, however, has been trying to tighten control over its border. This might close one safety valve that has helped keep Mexico's social and economic problems from erupting.

Even policies necessary to pay the interest on Mexico's external debt threaten to topple the government. Some analysts compare Mexico's debt to the burden of war reparations imposed on Germany following World War I. The German economy was crippled for over a decade and governments fell left and right. Recovery began only when Hitler's Nazis abandoned repayment of Germany's external debt.

Mexico may be forced to operate like a U.S. firm that has filed Chapter 11 bankruptcy—a procedure that allows continued operation and holds creditors at bay. Debt repayment by Mexico has been rescheduled to a slower rate. Further rescheduling is likely because there would be havoc in international banking circles if Mexico disavowed its debts. (Some analysts suggest that defaults on all shaky Latin American loans would leave 90 percent of the top 100 U.S. banks insolvent.) Final resolution of Mexico's problems will take decades, and will require repeated renegotiation between U.S. lenders, our two governments, and international financial agencies.

||||||||||||||||||||||||||||||||||||||||||||||||||||||||||||||||||||||||||||||||||||||||||||||||||||

The Role of International Credit

International capital flows permit countries with more attractive investment opportunities than their domestic savings can finance to obtain resources from countries with excess saving. Countries experiencing temporary economic problems might borrow from world capital markets rather than suffer sharp contractionary policies that restrict consumption and investment. Countries such as Hong Kong, Taiwan, Malaysia, and Israel, to name a few, have benefitted from foreign capital infusions. From World War II until the 1980s, the United States was a net supplier of capital to the rest of the world, primarily through direct investment by private firms in foreign countries. Before World War I, the United States financed domestic investments with loans from Great Britain and other European countries.

During the 1980s, enormous U.S. federal budget deficits have been financed by balance of trade deficits. This net inflow to the United States drains funds that might have financed development in less developed countries. In general, however, international capital flows move into countries with good growth and profit opportunities. Focus 3 indicates, however, that *capital flight* (outflow) can be a major problem when development plans are not instituted in a proper manner.

New capital may also be provided in the form of foreign aid—either grants or loans. The United States has provided billions of dollars in aid each year, administered through the Agency for International Development (AID). Another source of funds for less developed countries is the World Bank, funded by highly developed member nations, which arranges huge loans for social investments such as dams, education, communications, and transportation systems. Most investment flows between countries, however, are private and are channeled through multinational corporations. These companies must perceive substantial potential profits before they invest, and seek opportunities where there are abundant natural resources, a ready (and cheap) labor force, and a favorable political climate.

One problem that arises when development is financed by long-term loans from more mature economies is that regular payments must be made for a less developed country to maintain an acceptable credit rating. A worldwide recession such as the 1981–83 slump reveals how much financial juggling this can entail. Hundreds of billions of dollars in development loans were due for repayment to major American banks. These banks had primarily loaned out the deposits of OPEC countries, and many of the OPEC countries wanted to withdraw funds because of declining oil revenues. The worldwide recession, high nominal and real interest rates, the strengthening of the U.S. dollar until 1985, and the fall in the prices of many commodities exported by developing countries put incredible strains on debtor countries' ability to service their external debt. Some analysts warned that the entire international financial system teetered on the brink of collapse. Refinancing (or rescheduling) of the debt payments, collapsing oil prices, and the sustained economic recovery of the mid-1980s have reduced the financial pressures on many developing nations that do not rely too much on oil revenues.

The world's industrialized nations are not totally philanthropic in contributing to the growth and development of less developed countries. Facing diminishing returns to more capital within their own borders, these countries seek outlets for their internally generated technological advances and capital growth, sources of raw materials and cheap labor, and markets for their finished products. Viewing our world as a self-enclosed "Spaceship Earth" emphasizes the international scope of our interdependencies. As the entire world matures economically, disparities in living standards between countries should decrease. Many have argued that developed countries have a moral responsibility to aid less developed countries in their search for the good life. For whatever reason, most observers believe that the fortunes of the developed nations and their less developed neighbors are inextricably intertwined.

CHAPTER REVIEW: KEY POINTS

1. *Economic growth* refers to quantitative changes in the capacity to produce goods and services in a country. It occurs through expanding capital or labor resources, discoveries of new sources of raw materials, or development of more productive technologies. *Economic development* refers to improving the qualitative aspects of economic growth, including changes in the quality of life.

2. The *Rule of 72* is a rule of thumb for estimating how long it takes for a variable to double in value given some percentage growth rate. Simply divide 72 by the growth rate. For example, if growth in GNP is occurring at 6 percent per year, GNP will double in approximately 12 years (72/6 = 12).

3. *Diminishing returns* because of the fixity of land cause output to grow more slowly, even if labor and capital increase in fixed proportions.

4. *Population S curves* are theories of the growth paths of populations as they approach their biological limits. Reverend Thomas Malthus and other nineteenth-century economists theorized that equilibrium is attained when bare subsistence is common to all.

5. *Population growth* tends to slow as a country develops. The least developed countries of the world tend to have the highest rates of population growth.

6. *Capital formation* requires high saving rates. If *voluntary saving* is used to finance development, greater incomes, higher interest rates paid to savers, and (perhaps) less equal income distributions will lead to higher rates of investment. *Involuntary saving* may be used to free investment resources through confiscation, taxation, or inflation.

7. *Capital widening* occurs when the capital stock grows, but not more rapidly than the labor force. *Capital deepening* requires the capital stock to grow faster than the labor force.

8. *Technological advances* occur when the same amounts of resources acquire greater productive capacity.

9. Rapid development requires a strong *social infrastructure*—education, communications, transportation, and other networks that facilitate production.

PROBLEMS

1. How long will it take the following variables to double?
   a. Your savings account, if the bank pays annual interest of 4 percent?
   b. GNP, if economic growth proceeds at 2 percent annually?
   c. Housing prices, if they grow 6 percent annually?
   d. Population, if the annual population growth rate is 1.5 percent?

2. How long will it take for the value of money to fall by one half if the annual inflation rate is:
   a. 2 percent?
   b. 12 percent?
   c. 24 percent?

3. How long will it take for the *CPI* to move from 100 to 400 if inflation is 1 percent annually?

QUESTIONS FOR THOUGHT AND DISCUSSION

1. The U.S. saving rate is now about 5 percent of national income. This compares to rates of 20 percent in Japan, 15 percent in West Germany, and 13 percent in Great Britain. Why is saving so small in the United States? What effect does this low saving rate have on future economic growth in the United States? How might the federal government encourage greater voluntary saving? Involuntary saving? Are the two sets of policies compatible?

2. In spite of relatively low saving rates in the United States, we have typically grown faster than many countries with higher rates of saving (e.g., England). What does this say about the importance of the structure of investment relative to its level?

3. If all taxes on saving were eliminated, the average saver's return would be increased by roughly 30 percent. Increased incentives to save would add $30–$40 billion to annual savings. Would such a policy increase productivity? Long-term growth? The real earnings of workers? Reduce inflation? Reduce unemployment? Would different groups gain in the short run than in the long run? Is such a policy politically feasible?

4. If you were the leader of an impoverished and densely populated country, what policies might you adopt to foster economic growth and development? To what extent would you encourage private entrepreneurs and for which kinds of projects? What role should your government play in developing social infrastructure?

5. How do people in wealthy countries gain through foreign aid to impoverished countries? Do you think the costs to us exceed the benefits? Should foreign aid programs be shrunk or expanded? Why?

6. Why do many highly trained people from developing nations seek employment in advanced countries? Why are these highly educated people apparently more productive and highly paid in these advanced countries than in their home countries?

7. P. T. Bauer, a critic of foreign aid, has argued that "development depends on personal and social factors, not on handouts." He further asserts that "foreign aid means at most some capital is cheaper than if it had been raised independently at market rates." He then goes on to argue that this is different from say-ing that foreign aid is indispensable for progress. Do you agree with him? Why or why not?

8. Is foreign aid nothing more than a conscience-appeasing payment from rich to poor nations? Is there something wrong with developed countries seeking greater economic growth even if it means that the gap between rich and poor nations may grow wider? Would we in the United States accept greater unemployment for the long run if it meant a greater rate of growth for some developing countries? Are development questions really questions of income distribution on an international scale?

Microeconomics

PART 6

Core Concepts of Microeconomics

Macroeconomic issues were the central concern of Parts 2 to 5 of this book. Our next task is to look at micro-economic theory and policy, which is the focus of Parts 6 to 9. We concentrate on the private decisions of households and business firms for the next six chapters, and will then introduce, in stages, the microeconomic role of government.

You may breathe a sigh of relief upon reading that the tools you learned in macroeconomics should aid you in mastering the concepts and issues you will study in the coming weeks. For example, you have seen that supply and demand are useful in analyzing problems ranging from the price of molasses to the quandary posed for policymakers by stagflation. Supply and demand analysis also provides important insights into microeconomic decision making. This part of the book allows you to explore in greater detail exactly why supply curves are positively sloped while demand curves are negatively sloped.

Two important tools are introduced in chapter 20: marginalism and elasticity. *Marginal analysis* provides guideposts for efficient decision making and pressure for movements towards equilibrium; *elasticity* computations enable a more precise use of supply and demand analysis in predicting how market prices and quantities change as circumstances evolve. Then, in chapter 21, we analyze consumer choice more fully and develop the underpinnings of consumer demand curves. Chapter 22 delves into the nature of production— how inputs are transformed into outputs and how technology shapes the production costs of a firm. You need to understand both of these foundations for firms' decisions in the next part of this book; firms decide which goods to produce and sell and what prices to charge by balancing consumer demands against production costs.

CHAPTER 20

price-elasticity of demand

inelastic demand

elastic demand

unitary elasticity

income-elasticity of demand

cross-elasticity of demand

price-elasticity of supply

tax incidence

law of equal marginal advantage

Elasticity and Marginalism

Firms that raise their prices know that less of their products will be sold because buyers' demand curves slope downwards. But how much less? Buyers who offer high prices know that more will be available because supply curves are positively sloped. But how much more? This chapter introduces the concept of elasticity, a tool used to provide estimates that answer these and similar questions.

Elasticity can be a very useful guide to the consequences of decisions. Predictions about the costs and benefits of the alternatives available are necessary before people can make informed choices. What people do with information about costs and benefits is at the heart of marginal analysis, the second major topic of this chapter. Marginal analysis offers some operating rules for how members of households try to maximize their satisfaction and how business decision makers try to maximize the profits of their firms.

Elasticity

Suppose that you are the chief executive officer (CEO) of United Bullmoose Enterprises (UBE) and are concerned because profit seems below what you think possible. Your economic consultant assures you that the demand curves for all UBE products are negatively sloped, so that if you raise the price of plastic mooseheads (UBE's big novelty seller), annual sales will slip below the million you currently sell. Total production costs will fall, but will sales revenues rise? . . . fall? . . . remain constant?

Suppose each moosehead costs $10 to produce. It would be disastrous if you raised the price from $20 to $25 and lost half of your customers, but if only 50,000 out of UBE's million annual sales of mooseheads were lost, profits would rise by $4.25 million.

(Why?) How should UBE deal with this dilemma? The problem you are wrestling with is the price-elasticity of the demand for mooseheads.

The general concept of *elasticity* provides a technique to estimate the response of one variable to changes in some other variable and has applications not only in economics, but throughout the behavioral sciences and in physics and engineering as well.

The Price-Elasticity of Demand

Price-elasticity of demand *is a measure of the proportional decline* (increase) *in units purchased when price is increased* (cut) *by a given small proportion.*

If both changes are quite small, this roughly equals the percentage change in quantity divided by the percentage change in price. Price-elasticity can be written:

$$e_p = \frac{change\ in\ Q}{Q} \Big/ \frac{change\ in\ P}{P} = \frac{\Delta Q}{Q} \Big/ \frac{\Delta P}{P}$$

$$\cong \frac{percentage\ change\ in\ Q}{percentage\ change\ in\ P} = \frac{\%\Delta Q}{\%\Delta P}$$

Such calculations always yield negative numbers because if price is increased, quantity demanded falls, and vice versa. To simplify things, economists conventionally use the *absolute value* of price-elasticity, eliminating the need to deal with negative numbers.

The Problem of Bases

Suppose that the price of plastic mooseheads is dropped from $20 to $12, and annual sales surge from 1 million units to 5 million. The price-elasticity is 10 if we use the percentage formula:

$$e_p \cong \frac{\%\Delta Q}{\%\Delta P} = \frac{5-1}{1} \Big/ \frac{12-20}{20} = \frac{400\%}{-40\%}$$

$$= -10.\ (\text{Absolute value} = 10.)$$

Now watch what happens if we turn this example around. An increase in price from $12 to $20 per moosehead causes sales to dip from 5 million to 1 million units, and the percentage formula yields:

$$e_p \Big/ \frac{\%\Delta Q}{\%\Delta P} \cong \frac{1-5}{5} \Big/ \frac{20-12}{12} = \frac{-80\%}{66.7\%}$$

$$= -1.2.\ (\text{Absolute value} = 1.2.)$$

The disparity of the elasticity estimates in this example (10 if price is cut, 1.2 if price is raised) demonstrates that the percentage formula is inconsistent because it depends on whether prices rise or fall. We need to discuss this inconsistency before we provide a cure for it.

The basic problem results from the standard practice in mathematics courses of using the initial value as the base when computing percentage changes. Percentage changes computed in this way may create substantial ambiguity. For example, suppose that the annual profit of UBE's subsidiary, United Bullmoose Oil, jumps from $200 million to $1 billion. The media report the 400 percent increase and imply that UBE's profits are somehow responsible for inflation. The next year, profit drops to $150 million, and the media dutifully report an 85 percent decline. John Q. Public is likely to think that UBE is still way ahead because a 400 percent gain would seem to overpower an 85 percent decline, but it does not . . . $200M $\rightarrow$ $1,000M $\rightarrow$ $150M. Although UBE had one very good year, its profit is now less than it was initially.

Using Midpoints as Bases

Elasticity estimates computed by standard percentage changes may be only trivially inconsistent if prices and quantities change very litte, but inconsistency poses major problems when prices or quantities change drastically. Such problems with percentages as normally computed have led economists to compute elasticity using as bases the *midpoints* of changes in prices and quantities:

$$e_p = \frac{Q_n - Q_o}{(Q_n + Q_o)/2} \Big/ \frac{P_n - P_o}{(P_n + P_o)/2}.$$

The subscript o refers to the original price and quantity and the subscript n refers to the new price and quantity. [1] Naturally, the 2s in both denominators can be canceled out, but we will use them here to provide consistency.

Returning to our example of prices of $12 and $20 for plastic mooseheads generating sales of 5 million

---

1. The formula for elasticity can be manipulated in ways that some students find easier to calculate. One example is:

$$e_p = \frac{change\ in\ Q}{change\ in\ P} \times \frac{sum\ of\ P}{sum\ of\ Q}.$$

and 1 million units, respectively, we now get the same elasticity estimate, 2.67, regardless of whether the price is raised or lowered:

$$e_p = \frac{1 - 5}{(1 + 5)/2} \bigg/ \frac{20 - 12}{(20 + 12)/2}$$

$$= \frac{-(4/3)}{8/16} = -2.67,$$

and

$$e_p = \frac{5 - 1}{(1 + 5)/2} \bigg/ \frac{12 - 20}{(12 + 20)/2}$$

$$= \frac{4/3}{-(8/16)} = -2.67.$$

(Absolute value = 2.67)

Thus, using **midpoint bases** to calculate price-elasticity clears up the ambiguity arising with percentage measurements.

Ranges of Elasticity
Price-elasticity of demand is a measure of the relative responsiveness of quantity demanded to given price changes.

*An **inelastic** demand is where the elasticity coefficient (the absolute value of the ratio of proportional changes) is less than 1.0, and price changes are proportionally greater than the resulting quantity changes.*

Inelastically demanded goods include what people tend to consider "necessities"—the quantities you demand are somewhat immune to changes in price, and the share of your income absorbed by such items grows if prices rise, or falls if prices decline. For example, if the price of dog food doubled, would people put their pets on half rations? No. Many people view their pets, and consequently pet food, as necessities.

Curve D_0 in Figure 1 depicts a demand curve that is **relatively inelastic** at a price of $2. When the price rises from $2 to $2.50, quantity demanded only falls from 100 to 98—not much of a change. Compare this to demand curve D_1, where a change in price from $2 to $2.50 results in quantity demanded falling from 100 to 40. Quantity demanded is very responsive to a change in price. Thus, D_1 depicts a product with a **relatively elastic** demand.

*Elastic **demand** occurs when the elasticity coefficient is greater than 1.0, and many consumers are willing to do without the good if the price*

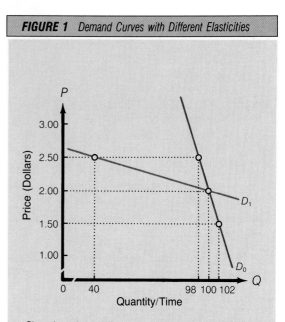

FIGURE 1 *Demand Curves with Different Elasticities*

Slope is, at best, only a very crude indicator of elasticity. As you will see in a few pages, all negatively sloped linear demand curves have elasticities that range from 0 to infinity. In this figure, the D_1 demand curve is more elastic at every given quantity than is the D_0 demand curve.

rises significantly, a sign that the product may have numerous close substitutes.

Examples of goods that exhibit relatively elastic demand curves include Volkswagens, Häagen-Dazs ice cream, McDonald's hamburgers, or Salem cigarettes. Note that total cigarette consumption is probably very unresponsive to price changes, while the demand for a particular brand is likely to be extremely sensitive to price changes because numerous substitutes are available.

Elasticity and Total Revenue
Price-elasticities of demand are guides to what will happen to *total revenue* (the dollar sales of firms) if prices change slightly. The total revenue of a firm equals the price charged times the quantity sold ($TR = P \times Q$). For example, a hamburger stand will generate $1 million in total revenue if it sells a million burgers at $1 apiece (or 1 burger at $1 million). Naturally, firms'

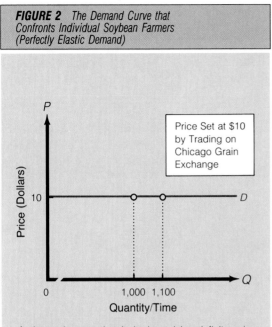

FIGURE 2 *The Demand Curve that Confronts Individual Soybean Farmers (Perfectly Elastic Demand)*

Price Set at $10 by Trading on Chicago Grain Exchange

A demand curve that is horizontal has infinite price elasticity ($e_p = \infty$). Because total revenue equals $P \times Q$ and the price does not change with output, total revenue is exactly proportional to output.

FIGURE 3 *A Perfectly Inelastic Demand*

Vertical demand curves have price elasticity of zero ($e_p = 0$). Although such perfectly inelastic demand curves are impossible, this figure shows that total revenue will be exactly proportional to price. This example is useful because it represents the opposite end of the spectrum from the perfectly elastic demand shown in the previous figure.

total revenues equal total spending by consumers. We will use two extreme cases to illustrate how total revenue and price-elasticity are related.

Firms producing outputs that have perfect substitutes in the eyes of buyers confront horizontal demand curves. Any attempt to raise the price even slightly above the market price causes all potential buyers to switch towards the substitutes. For example, one soybean farmer's product is the same as another's. Because even the largest soybean farmers produce only a small part of total world supplies, no single farm's output has a distinguishable impact on world soybean prices. This means that the soybean farmer represented in Figure 2 faces a horizontal demand curve, and any price above $10 per bushel will generate zero sales. At $10, the farmer can sell all the farm can produce, and so would never charge less than $10. Since price will not vary from $10 per bushel, the farm's *total revenue will be exactly proportional to its output*. For example, if the farm initially produces 1,000 bushels of soybeans annually and then expands output by 10 percent to 1,100 bush-

els, revenue also increases by 10 percent, rising from $10,000 to $11,000. These horizontal demand curves have price elasticities of infinity and are called **perfectly elastic demands.**[2]

The other extreme case would occur if a demand curve were vertical, as in Figure 3. The elasticity of a vertical demand curve is zero because quantity is unaffected by price changes; such curves are termed **perfectly inelastic**. If such cases existed, the firm's *total revenue would be exactly proportional to the price charged.*

Perfectly inelastic demand curves are nonsensical; one is shown here only to aid you in understanding elasticity. Zero price-elasticity implies not only a total lack of substitutes for the good, but also that consumers could and would pay any price to receive a specific quantity of it. A profit-maximizing manager of a firm faced with a perfectly inelastic demand would

---

2. Note for those who are mathematically adept: As the slope of the demand curve approaches zero, the elasticity of demand approaches infinity.

charge an infinitely high price for the product. Any such good would be essential for life, but we could not afford it because our budgets are limited.

You might think that the prices of insulin for diabetics or dialysis for people with defective kidneys would not affect the quantities demanded by patients who needed them. The cruel facts are that if the prices of these medical necessities were raised, more diabetics would try to control their disease with diet therapy. If prices were raised sufficiently, poorer patients would die and the quantities of insulin or dialysis demanded would fall. Every year millions of people die because they cannot afford medical treatment.

An interesting case when demand curves are neither perfectly elastic nor perfectly inelastic occurs when the total amount of money spent on a product does not vary with the price charged. An example is provided by the farmer who observes that revenues from peach sales are about the same regardless of whether there is a bumper harvest or whether blight wipes out most of a peach crop. If a 1 percent decrease in the peach harvest causes the price of peaches to rise by 1 percent, total spending on peaches is virtually unchanged and the price-elasticity of demand equals one. Such demand curves have unitary elasticity.

A **unitarily elastic** *demand curve occurs when the elasticity coefficient equals one and the amount of money spent on a product does not vary with the price charged.*

Examples of unitarily elastic demands occur when a person budgets a certain amount of money for, say, meat or magazines and will not deviate from that figure regardless of price. A representative unitary elastic demand curve is shown in Figure 4.

If the price-elasticity of demand for a product is greater than zero but less than one, the demand curve is *relatively inelastic*. Economists sometimes shorten this to *inelastic*. If the price elasticity is greater than one but less than infinity, the demand for the product is *relatively elastic,* or *elastic.*

Price-elasticities of demand are obviously important to firms because they indicate what will happen to sales revenues when prices are raised or lowered. Price-elasticities of demand are also important to consumers since they reflect how desperately buyers want particular goods and how the composition of consumer budgets will change as relative prices

FIGURE 4 *A Demand Curve with Unitary Elasticity*

The total revenue ($P \times Q$) is unaffected by price or quantity if demand is unitarily elastic. Unitarily elastic demand curves ($e_p = 1$) are rectangular hyperbolas, which have the characteristic that all rectangles drawn from the curve to the axes have exactly the same geometric area ($P \times Q$). You will see more rectangular hyperbolas as we proceed further in economics.

change. Table 1 summarizes how the firm's total revenue (and consumers' total spending) for a good changes as prices change.

Demand curves rarely have constant elasticities along the full range of possible prices and quantities, but Table 2 presents some estimates of the elasticities of demand for a number of products within the range of prices that you would roughly expect each to have. If you will spend a few moments studying this table, you will notice that the elasticities of demand tend to be larger:

1. the more substitutes there are for a good;
2. the more an item absorbs as a share of typical budgets;
3. the less "necessary" (more of a "luxury") a particular good is; and
4. the longer the time interval considered.

The number of substitutes available is by far the most important determinant of price-elasticity of demand. Rising prices drive consumers towards substi-

TABLE 1 *Price Changes, Elasticities, and Total Revenues/Expenditures*

Price Elasticity of Demand	How Total Revenues Change	
	Price Increases	Price Decreases
Inelastic 0 < e < 1	TR increases	TR decreases
Unitarily Elastic e = 1	No change in TR	No change in TR
Elastic ∞ > e > 1	TR decreases	TR increases

tutes; falling prices are incentives to find more uses for a good. For example, the demand for Campbell's pork and beans is very price-elastic because slight price hikes will cause consumers to substitute other brands and slight price cuts will raise Campbell's sales at the expense of competing brands. On the other hand, the demand for local telephone services is relatively inelastic because few substitutes are available.

Another important determinant of price-elasticity is the period allowed for adjustments to price changes. Elasticity rises as longer intervals are considered because as time elapses, more substitutes become feasible. Elasticities are measured for a specified period for this reason. For example, Table 2

indicates that the demand for gasoline is relatively inelastic in the short run, but relatively elastic in the long run. Increases in gasoline prices eventually induce some people to buy smaller cars, get more frequent tune-ups, use mass transit, or relocate closer to their schools or jobs.

If a firm faces a demand curve with a price-elasticity of less than one, it will always find it profitable to raise the product's price since revenue will increase and, as output and units sold fall, total production costs will decline. (Profit must rise if revenue increases and total costs fall.) As the price is increased, growing numbers of consumers will buy substitutes for the good; those who cannot find substitutes ultimately will be forced to do without.

TABLE 2 *Price-Elasticities of Demand for Selected Goods and Services*

Good or Service	Price-Elasticity of Demand
Marijuana	1.51
Automobiles	1.35
Beer	1.13
Housing	1.00
Alcohol	0.92
Hospital and physician services	0.05 to 0.15
Gasoline (transportation only)	
short run	0.1 to 0.3
long run	1.50
Electricity	
long-run residential	
and commercial usage	0.88
short-run residential	0.13

Sources: Marijuana—T. C. Misket and F. Vakil, "Some Estimates of Price and Expenditure Elasticities among UCLA Students," *Review of Economics and Statistics,* November 1972. Automobiles—Gregory C. Chow, *Demand for Automobiles in the United States* (Amsterdam: North-Holland Publishing Company, 1957). Beer—T. F. Hogarty and K. G. Elzinga, "The Demand for Beer," *The Review of Economics and Statistics,* May 1972. Housing—Richard F. Muth, "The Demand for Non-Farm Housing," *The Demand for Durable Goods,* Arnold C. Harberger, ed. (Chicago: University of Chicago Press, 1960). Alcohol—H. S. Houthakker and Lester D. Taylor, *Consumer Demand in the United States,* 2/e (Cambridge: Harvard University Press, 1970). Hospital and physician services—Joseph P. Newhouse and Charles E. Phelps, "New Estimates of Price and Income Elasticities of Medical Care Services," *The Role of Health Insurance in the Health Services Sector,* Richard N. Rosett, ed. (New York: National Bureau of Economic Research, 1976). Gasoline and electricity—J. M. Griffin, *Energy Conservation in the OECD,* 1980–2000 (Cambridge, MA: Ballinger, 1979).

Elasticity Along a Demand Curve We have indicated that price-elasticity varies along most demand curves. You might think that the linear demand curve in Panel A of Figure 5 would have a constant price-elasticity. Not so. The rectangle we have drawn at point *a* represents the highest revenue available with this demand curve. That is, $P \times Q$ is at its maximum possible value. Whether we raise or lower the price from $10, revenue falls, as shown in the table and in Panel B. This demand curve is price-elastic above point *a* because any price increase causes revenue to decline; e_p is greater than one. Symmetrically, price decreases from $10 cause revenue to fall, so below

point *a* the demand curve is price-inelastic; e_p is less than one. At point *a*, demand is unitarily elastic; e_p equals one.

The conclusion is that the price-elasticity of demand tends to rise as we charge higher and higher prices. Slope alone is not a good indicator of elasticity because the price and quantity bases used to compute proportions change continuously. In fact, other than vertical or horizontal demand curves, every linear demand curve has elasticities that range from zero to infinity. Refer back to Figure 1 for a moment and note that both D_0 and D_1, if extended, would have elasticities ranging from 0 to infinity, even

FIGURE 5 *Varying Price Elasticities along a Linear Demand Curve*

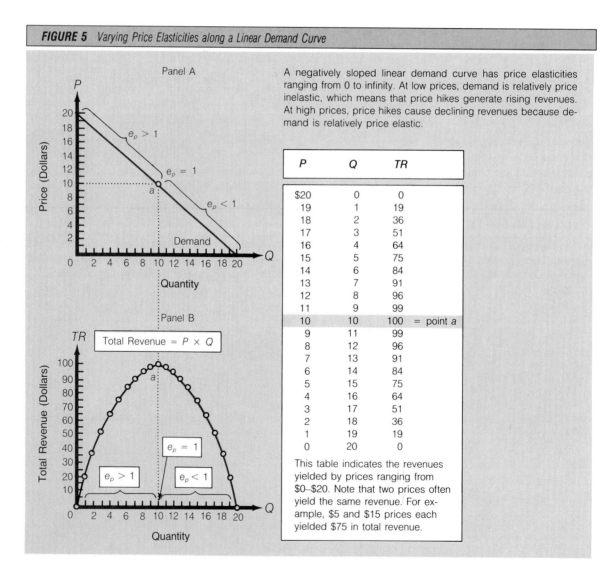

A negatively sloped linear demand curve has price elasticities ranging from 0 to infinity. At low prices, demand is relatively price inelastic, which means that price hikes generate rising revenues. At high prices, price hikes cause declining revenues because demand is relatively price elastic.

P	Q	TR
$20	0	0
19	1	19
18	2	36
17	3	51
16	4	64
15	5	75
14	6	84
13	7	91
12	8	96
11	9	99
10	10	100 = point a
9	11	99
8	12	96
7	13	91
6	14	84
5	15	75
4	16	64
3	17	51
2	18	36
1	19	19
0	20	0

This table indicates the revenues yielded by prices ranging from $0–$20. Note that two prices often yield the same revenue. For example, $5 and $15 prices each yielded $75 in total revenue.

TABLE 3 Income-Elasticities of Demand for Selected Goods and Services

Good or Service	Income-Elasticity of Demand
Automobiles	3.00
Housing	1.15
Beer	0.93
Charitable donations	0.70
Hospital and physician services	0.09

Sources: Automobiles—Gregory C. Chow, *Demand for Automobiles in the United States* (Amsterdam: North-Holland Publishing Company, 1957). Housing—Richard F. Muth, *Cities and Housing: The Spatial Pattern of Urban Residential Land Use* (Chicago: The University of Chicago Press, 1969). Beer—T. F. Hogarty and K. G. Elzinga, "The Demand for Beer," *Review of Economics and Statistics,* May 1972. Charitable donations—M. Feldstein and A. Taylor, "The Income Tax and Charitable Contributions," *Econometrica,* November 1976. Hospital and physician services—Joseph P. Newhouse and Charles E. Phelps, "New Estimates of Price and Income Elasticities of Medical Care Service," in *The Role of Health Insurance in the Health Services Sector,* Richard N. Rosett, ed. (New York: National Bureau of Economic Research, 1976).

though D_1 is more elastic than D_0 for each possible shared price or quantity. Slope is only a crude indicator of elasticity and may mislead you about the elasticity of a given curve.

Other Elasticities

Later in this chapter, we will examine how price-elasticity of demand interacts with price-elasticity of supply to determine such things as who bears the burdens of specific types of taxes. Before we address such questions, however, we will look at other important types of elasticities.

Income-Elasticity of Demand   Rich people do not just buy more goods; the things they buy also differ from the purchases of poor people.

> The **income-elasticity of demand** *for a good measures the proportional change in the amount demanded resulting from a given small proportional change in income.*

For simplicity, you might think of income-elasticity as the ratio of percentage changes in the amount of a good demanded relative to income. For reasons that parallel the rationale for midpoint-based computations of price-elasticities, we actually compute income-elasticity as:

$$e_y = \frac{Q_n - Q_o}{(Q_n + Q_o)/2} \bigg/ \frac{Y_n - Y_o}{(Y_n + Y_o)/2}$$

Again, subscript n refers to new values while subscript o represents old values, and both 2s could be dropped from the denominators without affecting this calculation.

Such goods as scuba lessons or limousines are *income-elastic* because each 1 percent rise in income causes the amounts sold to rise by more than 1 percent. If income increases by 1 percent and the amount of a good demanded rises somewhat, but by less than 1 percent, demand is *income-inelastic.* As long as increases in income stimulate more purchases of a good, it is a **normal good.**[3] Income-elasticity is negative and goods are **inferior goods** if purchases of a good decline as income rises. Lard, pinto beans, and used tires are examples.

Why are these numbers important for, among other things, business decision making? As the CEO of United Bullmoose Enterprises, would you want to know the implications of a recession for plastic moosehead sales? For oil and gasoline? For used auto part sales from your United Bullmoose Junkyards subsidiary? Of course! Would the manager of your travel trailer subsidiary be optimistic about sales prospects if an economic boom were predicted, and downcast if a recession hit? Clearly yes, if the demand for trailers is income-elastic. Estimates of the income-elasticities of demand for particular goods help firms forecast sales and plan production, employment, and investment. Income-elasticities of demand for some broad product categories are displayed in Table 3.

---

3. Sometimes data for the prices or quantities of goods are not available, but sales data ($P \times Q$) are. In such cases, economists approximate income elasticities by:

$$\frac{\text{percent change in expenditures}}{\text{percent change in income}}.$$

If the result exceeds (*is less than*) one, demand is presumed to be income elastic (*inelastic*).

Cross-Elasticity of Demand   Another important measure of consumer behavior is the cross-elasticity of demand.

The **cross-elasticity of demand** *estimates the proportional changes in units sold when the prices of related goods are changed slightly.*

Formally, cross-elasticity can be calculated as:

$$e_{xy} = \frac{(Q_{xn} - Q_{xo})}{(Q_{xn} + Q_{xo})/2} \Big/ \frac{(P_{yn} - P_{yo})}{(P_{yn} + P_{yo})/2},$$

where Q_{xo} (old) and Q_{xn} (new) are the quantities of good x bought before and after price changes for good y (P_{yo} and P_{yn}, respectively). Again, the 2s could be dropped from the equation.

Consider the sales of American cars (Brand X) after U.S. import restrictions in the 1980s drove up the prices of Japanese cars (Brand Y). All else constant, we would expect American car sales to grow when imported cars became higher priced. Thus, we would expect a positive relationship between the prices of imported cars and the quantities of American cars sold domestically; the price cross-elasticity of demand (e_{xy}) should be positive. When price cross-elasticities of demand are *positive,* the items in question are **substitute goods.** Other sets of substitutes are artificial turf and natural grass, golf clubs and tennis racquets, and vans and travel trailers. In fact, broad competition for consumers' dollars causes most goods to be at least weak substitutes for each other.

When the price cross-elasticity of demand is *negative,* the goods in question are **complementary goods.** For example, as the price of hand-held calculators has declined, the demand for alkaline batteries has jumped markedly. Other examples of complementary goods include ham and eggs, cameras and film, suits and ties, and pretzels and beer.

The Price-Elasticity of Supply   The price-elasticity of supply is typically positive because supply curves slope up.

The **price-elasticity of supply** *measures the responsiveness of quantity supplied in the market to price changes.*

The formula to calculate this elasticity is the same as for computing demand price-elasticity:

$$e_s = \frac{(Q_n - Q_o)}{(Q_n + Q_o)/2} \Big/ \frac{(P_n - P_o)}{(P_n + P_o)/2}.$$

If extending the supply curve of a good would result in an intersection with the vertical (price) axis, the amount of the good supplied is highly responsive to its price. In such cases as S_0 and S_1 in Figure 6, the elasticity of supply exceeds one and the supply curve is described as *relatively elastic.* If a supply curve is horizontal, such as S_∞ in Figure 6, then the elasticity of supply is infinity and the supply is *perfectly price-elastic.* Buyers can demand any amount of these goods without affecting the price at all. Examples of goods having perfectly elastic supplies include such things as a family's groceries—no matter how many cans of tuna your family personally consumes, your purchases will not affect the price you pay. Thus, the supply of tuna to you is perfectly elastic even though the market supply of tuna is positively sloped. Similarly, a single baker who buys flour in bulk is faced with a perfectly elastic supply of flour. In these and similar cases, individual demands determine the amounts people buy, but not the prices they pay.

If extending the supply curve would result in intersection with the quantity axis, the amount of a

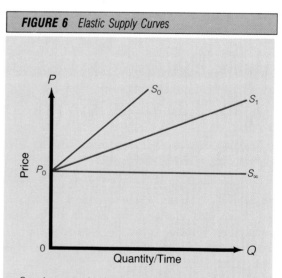

FIGURE 6   *Elastic Supply Curves*

Supply curves that intersect the price axis are relatively elastic ($e_s > 1$). A horizontal supply curve is perfectly price elastic ($e_s = \infty$). In such cases, total revenue or expenditures ($P \times Q$) will be exactly proportional to the quantity demanded.

FIGURE 7 Inelastic Supply Curves

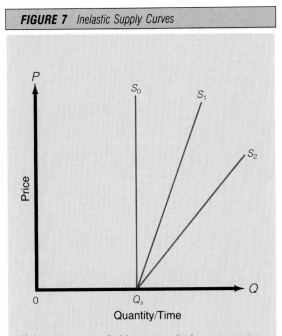

If the amount supplied is comparatively unresponsive to price, supply is relatively inelastic and intersects the quantity axis. A vertical supply curve is perfectly price inelastic ($e_s = 0$). Although rare, such supplies do exist. Land sites are an example. In such cases, total spending (revenue) is exactly proportional to price.

good supplied is comparatively unresponsive to its price. Supply curves such as S_1 and S_2 in Figure 7 are examples of *relatively inelastic supplies*. In the extreme situation where the quantity supplied is totally unresponsive to price, the supply curve is vertical (S_0 in Figure 7) and the elasticity of supply is zero ($e_s = 0$). Examples of these *perfectly inelastic supplies* include land (the fixed amount available is unaffected by price) and other highly specialized items or resources—Rembrandt paintings, Stradivarius violins, and the comedy of Eddie Murphy are each unique. When supplies are fixed, demand alone determines a good's price or person's wage, but the quantity exchanged is not related to the price paid.

You may have noticed that perfectly inelastic supplies look just like perfectly inelastic demands, and that perfectly elastic demands and supplies also appear to be identical. How about *unitarily elastic* supply curves ($e_s = 1$)? Do they resemble unitarily elastic demand curves? Not at all. For e_s to equal one, the

quantity supplied must change in fixed proportion with price. All supply curves that are straight lines through the origin have this characteristic, as shown in Figure 8.

We can summarize the concept of elasticity: Elasticity measures the proportional response of one variable with respect to another. If X influences Y, then the elasticity of Y with respect to X equals:

$$\frac{\Delta Y}{Y} \Big/ \frac{\Delta X}{X}.$$

Elasticity, as a summary measure of responsiveness, is used in many other ways. For example, measures of elasticity have been developed to address the following problems:

1. If wage rates increase relative to the costs of capital, then firms will find it profitable to substitute some capital for labor. How much substitution occurs as relative resource prices change?
2. People's expectations of inflation are related to prior inflation. How does past inflation influence how much inflation people expect?

All supply curves that are straight lines from the origin are unitarily elastic ($e_s = 1$). Along both curves shown here, $\Delta P/P = \Delta Q/Q$, so $e_s = 1$. This is another proof that slope can mislead you about elasticity.

Being able to specify how elasticity would be calculated for these examples is unimportant at this point, but it is important for you to realize that the concept of elasticity may be useful whenever variables are systematically related.

Elasticity and Tax Burdens

One of the most pressing issues facing the United States is tax reform. The phrase *tax reform* is just empty rhetoric unless we know who bears the burden of various taxes. Elasticity plays a major role in answering the question of who bears the tax burden.

Tax Incidence

The *legal incidence* of a tax falls on the individual or firm responsible for writing the check for taxes to government.

> The **economic incidence** of taxation (or tax burden) falls on the person who suffers reduced purchasing power because of the tax.

Tax burdens are often avoided by the party bearing the legal incidence through *tax-shifting*. If the tax is passed on to the consumer in the form of higher prices, we say the tax is *forward-shifted*. Taxes are *backward-shifted* if the tax burden is transferred to workers in the form of lower take-home wages, or to other resource suppliers in the form of lower factor payments. Considering extreme elasticities allows us to develop some general principles.

Inelastic Supply

They ain't makin' any more of the stuff.
—*An Unknown Land Promoter*

The supply of land is perfectly inelastic. The rental price paid for land reflects the demand for land, and renters do not care whether the rent is kept by the landlord or split between the owner and his Uncle Sam. Figure 9 illustrates the effects of taxes on the demand and supply of land. The annual rental value of the land is $100 per acre when demand is D_0 and supply is S_0. (If landowners do not rent their land out,

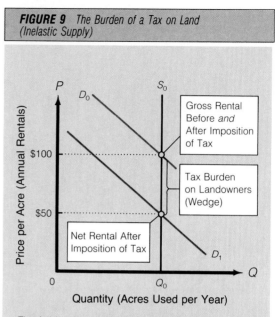

FIGURE 9 *The Burden of a Tax on Land (Inelastic Supply)*

The full burden of a tax on anything that is perfectly inelastically supplied is borne by the current owner or seller. Attempts to forward-shift such taxes cause excess supplies and downward pressures on prices.

we might treat them as their own tenants; the opportunity cost of not renting is $100 per acre per year.)

Suppose that a 50 percent tax on land rents was imposed. If landlords tried to recoup the $50-per-acre tax by raising rents to above $100, there would be a surplus of rentable land. As landlords with vacant land tried to attract renters, the gross rental price of land will fall back to $100. The owners cannot avoid the $50 tax burden per acre by selling because any buyer would base the value of land on the $50 net rent per acre it yields, not the initial $100. Thus, land prices would be halved because of the 50 percent land rent tax; landowners bear both the legal and the economic incidence of the land tax because the supply of land is perfectly inelastic.[4]

---

4. An issue addressed later in this book is the "single tax movement," whose advocates like the idea that landowners fully bear any tax on land.

Inelastic Demand The demand for common table salt is among the least price-elastic of all regular household purchases. Recognizing the inelasticity of this demand, the early Romans enacted a tax on salt in order to ensure that the tax burden fell on the consumer. Let us see why you as a consumer would bear nearly the full burden of a salt tax. Suppose that your annual demand for salt is shown in Figure 10. Because spending on salt absorbs so little of your budget and because of an absence of substitutes, even a 300 or 400 percent increase in the price probably would not noticeably affect the amount you use on your eggs or the rest of your food. You will consume roughly four pounds of salt annually, whether salt is free, costs $0.30 a pound, or $1 a pound.

Initially, competition among salt producers permits you to buy almost any amount you would like without affecting the market price of $0.30 a pound. If a tax of $0.20 a pound were imposed, suppliers could easily forward-shift the tax by raising the price to $0.50 a pound, at which there is neither an excess

supply nor excess demand. The conclusion is that if demand is perfectly inelastic, the consumer will bear the full burden of any taxes.

We stated earlier that demands are never perfectly inelastic. This salt example is intended only to show that if demand were very inelastic, the burden of a tax will fall primarily on the consumer. Would people reduce the salt in their diets if it rose to $100 per pound? Of course. Would salt be used on snowy roads or icy sidewalks at such prices? Of course not.

Elasticities of demand reflect buyers' desperation for goods because of the availability or lack of substitutes. Similarly, supply curves mirror the urgency of sellers' needs for customers because of the availability or the lack of good options for their resources. The more desperate buyers or sellers are, the less elastic their respective demands or supplies and the more difficult it is for them to alter their behavior to avoid a tax. This makes it easier to stick them with the burdens of taxes.

Our analyses of land and salt show why governments are fond of taxes on inelastically demanded goods (tobacco) or inelastically supplied resources: it maximizes government revenue. The story is a bit different when elastic demands or supplies are taxed.

Elastic Demand You and most other people do not care whether the paper clips you use are produced domestically or imported; imported paper clips and domestic paper clips are perfect substitutes. Suppose, therefore, that the demand for imported paper clips is perfectly elastic at the current market price.

If a Bornean paper clip producer is somewhat dependent on the American market, this firm's supply curve slopes upward, as in Figure 11; before any tariff, the Bornean producer sells 121 million paper clips per year in the United States at a price of $0.50 per thousand. If our government imposes a tariff of $0.12 per thousand on imported paper clips, the Borneans cannot forward-shift this tax to consumers in the form of higher prices.

At any price greater than $0.50 per thousand, Americans who have been using Bornean paper clips will completely switch over to American-made paper clips. The Borneans must absorb this tariff and will

FIGURE 10 *The Burden of a Tax on Salt (Inelastic Demand)*

If demand were ever perfectly inelastic (and it cannot be), the full burden of the tax would be borne by the consumer.

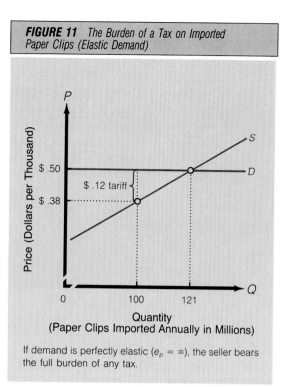

FIGURE 11 *The Burden of a Tax on Imported Paper Clips (Elastic Demand)*

If demand is perfectly elastic ($e_p = \infty$), the seller bears the full burden of any tax.

are both 120 million tons annually. The conclusion is that taxes will be 100 percent forward-shifted if supplies are perfectly elastic.

Summary: Taxes and Elasticity Taxes will be 100 percent forward-shifted (borne by consumers) if either (*a*) demand is perfectly inelastic (salt) or (*b*) supply is perfectly elastic (aluminum). Taxes will be backward-shifted completely (borne by suppliers) if either (*a*) supply is perfectly inelastic (land), or (*b*) demand is perfectly elastic (paper clips). You may believe that these extreme cases of elasticities seldom occur in the "real world." Three chapters hence, you will learn that competition makes perfectly elastic supplies and demands reasonably common.

Although the great majority of products have demands and supplies that are neither perfectly inelastic nor perfectly elastic, our results do suggest a workable general principle: The greater the elasticity of demand relative to the elasticity of supply, the greater the backward-shifting of any tax burden. The smaller the ratio (*elasticity of demand*)/(*elasticity of supply*), the greater the forward-shifting of the tax burden.

You will encounter numerous applications of elasticity in the coming chapters. A tool that is even more pervasive is marginal analysis. Indeed, the "economic way of thinking" is almost synonymous with "thinking at the margin."

wind up with a net price received of $0.38 per thousand. In this case, the tax is completely backward-shifted to the Bornean factory's resource suppliers. Their wages, profits, rents, or receipts of interest will suffer. Whenever demand for a product is perfectly elastic, suppliers will bear the full burden of any taxes.

Elastic Supply The supply curve of the aluminum industry has been estimated to be roughly perfectly elastic because average production costs are constant, no matter how much or how little aluminum is produced. Many materials are substitutes for aluminum in some uses, but none are close substitutes in all uses. Thus, Figure 12 shows a perfectly elastic supply of aluminum and a less elastic demand for it.

Without taxation, 140 million tons of aluminum will be sold annually for $500 a ton. Suppose that a tax of $100 a ton were levied on aluminum producers. They would be unable to cover production costs unless they received at least $600 per ton from consumers, who would cut back purchases to 120 million tons annually at this higher price. (As an exercise, compute the price-elasticity of demand.) Notice that at $600 a ton, there are neither excess supplies nor excess demands. Production and consumption

FIGURE 12 *The Burden of a Tax on Aluminum (Elastic Supply)*

If supply is perfectly elastic ($e_s = \infty$), consumers pay 100 percent of any taxes in the form of higher prices.

Totals, Averages, and Marginals

All decision making is at the margin.

　　　　　　　　　　　　　　—Unknown

Rational decision making is an **incremental** or **marginal** process. For example, you generally do not decide whether you are going to have three brownies before you begin eating dessert; instead, your hunger after finishing your first determines whether you will eat another, and then, having finished your second, whether you will have a third. Similarly, most firm managers decide whether to expand or contract their operations a bit (*marginally*) rather than whether to close a plant's doors or hire 10,000 workers. **Marginalism** exists in most everyday activities. A journey of 1,000 miles begins with a single step. And then another. And yet another.

In microeconomics you will constantly encounter relationships between **total, average,** and **incremental** (or **marginal**) units. You probably know what total and average mean, but marginal may be a mystery. Just as the margin of a piece of paper refers to its boundaries, margin refers to "the edge," or the last few bits one way or another of something. If you pass an exam *marginally,* you are close to failing. A *marginal* firm teeters on the brink of bankruptcy.[5]

Economists often refer to the marginal unit of some thing as the *last* or *extra* unit, and at times students think that this requires the marginal unit to be identifiable as a particular unit. This is not generally the case. For example, if there are 30 students in your class, who is the thirtieth? If any one of you had not enrolled, or if any of you drops the course, there would only be 29 students in the class. Thus, each of you is the thirtieth (marginal) student. (Does that make you uneasy?) Similarly, there is no way to ascertain which is the sixth (marginal) slice out of a cherry pie until the other five are eaten. Nor can we identify a particular individual as the last (marginal) soldier in an army of 3 million, or the marginal worker employed by General Motors. In a sense, every unit of any grouping is the marginal unit. Keep this in mind in the next few chapters and you will avoid a lot of confusion and grief.

Most marginals in economics refer to the ratios of the changes in one thing in response to small changes in another. For example, the *marginal utility* of a brownie is the extra satisfaction derived from the consumption of an extra piece, and the *marginal physical product of labor* refers to the extra output generated by the last worker added to a production process.

The two rules governing how marginals influence totals or averages are:

1. If the marginal unit is positive (*negative*), the total will rise (*fall*). If the marginal unit equals zero, the total is unaffected.

2. If the marginal exceeds (*is less than*) an average, the average rises (*falls*). The average is unchanged if marginal equals average.

For example, an obese dieter does not lose 100 pounds or more instantly, but rather, incrementally—a pound at a time. If, in the next few (marginal) days, the dieter eats only a little lean meat and fresh vegetables (generating *negative* marginal pounds), total weight will drop a bit. Cheating with some hot fudge sundaes will yield *positive* marginal pounds and a jump in total weight. Similarly, if your next few (marginal) grades are above your average, your GPA will rise, but it will fall if your marginal grades are below your previous average.

Geometry and Marginal Units

This section builds on the graphical analysis provided at the beginning of this book. Most functions used in economic analysis involve curved lines. Recall that slope is defined as rise/run. For short segments of curved lines, on the average, slope equals:

　　(change in rise) ÷ *(change in run).*

Thus, dividing the change in the variable on the y-axis by the corresponding small change in the variable on the x-axis yields the slope of a function at a particular point. This slope is the ratio of the marginal units of these variables.

As we increase output along the x-axis in Panel A of Figure 13 from Q_a to Q_b to Q_c to Q_d, profit (on the y-axis) grows from π_a to π_b to π_c, and then falls to π_d. The *marginal profit* as this firm produces slightly larger amounts of output equals the slope of this profit curve at these points, and is graphed in Panel B.

---

5. Several of these examples are drawn from "The Relevance of Marginal Analysis," by Michael Behr, in Ralph Byrns and Gerald Stone, eds., *Great Ideas for Teaching Economics,* 4/ed. (Glenview, IL: Scott, Foresman/Little, Brown, 1989).

Notice that average profit per unit rises whenever it is less than the extra profit made on extra units of output, and falls when the marginal profit is below the average profit.

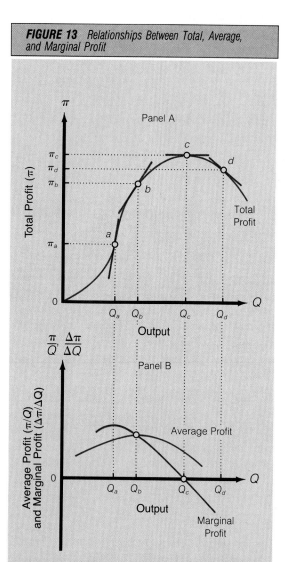

FIGURE 13 Relationships Between Total, Average, and Marginal Profit

Panel A

Panel B

Total profit in Panel A rises as output is expanded until output level Q_c is reached; thereafter, it declines. Maximum average profit occurs in Panel B at output level Q_b, the point at which marginal and average profit are equal. At outputs below Q_b, marginal profits exceeds average profit, "pulling" average profit up. Beyond Q_b, marginal profit is less than average profit, pulling average profit down. When total profit is at its maximum (Panel A), marginal profit is zero and it is negative as output is expanded beyond Q_c in Panel B.

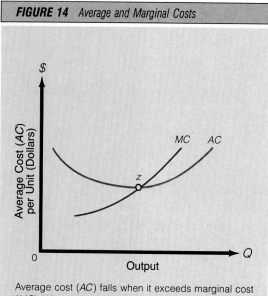

FIGURE 14 Average and Marginal Costs

Average cost (AC) falls when it exceeds marginal cost (MC). When marginal cost is greater than average cost, the average cost will rise. Thus, average cost is at its minimum at point z, where $AC = MC$.

Firms seek maximum profits, which in this case occur at output level Q_c. Notice that the slope of the profit function is zero where the profit function is at its *maximum*. Similarly, if the marginal cost of output starts below the average cost per unit of output and then rises, average costs are minimized where the marginal cost equals the average cost, as at point z in Figure 14. This is the *minimum* point of this average cost curve.

The Law of Equal Marginal Advantage

The goal of economic efficiency is attained only if equivalent goods or similar resources are allocated in equally advantageous ways at the margin. This idea is known as the **law of equal marginal advantage.**

For example, if the last dollar you spend on gasoline fails to yield the added pleasure you would receive if it were spent on an extra milkshake, you will gain by spending less on gasoline and more on milkshakes.

People generally change their patterns of consumption or production whenever resources (in this example, the command over resources represented by your last few dollars) are inefficiently allocated.

Thus, you would gain by drinking an extra milkshake and burning a bit less gasoline, and undoubtedly make these sorts of adjustments with very little conscious thought. You settle into a stable consumption pattern only when the last cent you spend on any single good yields satisfaction equal to that gained from the last cent spent on any other good.

Similar *marginal adjustments* span the realm of economic decision making. Here is an example drawn from choices about work. Suppose that you and your identical twin are equally strong, experienced, and intelligent. If your twin works an eight-hour day and produces $64 worth of mowed lawns while you generate $48 worth of cleaned windows with similar effort, something is wrong. You will (and should) shift into mowing lawns so that your labor resources are allocated equally advantageously, at $8 per hour instead of the $6 per hour you have been earning.

Whenever equivalent resources are not used to equal advantage, there is economic inefficiency. Other applications of the dictate that efficiency requires similar resources to be allocated in equally advantageous ways at the margin include the notions that:

1. People's time must be divided between work and leisure so that the gain from the last hour an individual works (the individual's wage) just equals the subjective value of the last hour of leisure enjoyed.

2. The last dollar a firm pays for labor must generate the same amount of extra production (and profit) as the last dollar spent on capital, land, or energy inputs.

3. The dollar value to a consumer of the right to consume a particular good must equal the value of other production that society sacrifices in making that marginal unit of the good available to that consumer.

Do not worry if these applications of the law of equal marginal advantage seem a bit murky at this juncture. As you continue through this book, you will constantly encounter its corollaries and will see that competitive processes tend to drive a market system so that this requirement for economic efficiency is met.

This chapter has described two tools that you will use extensively in the coming chapters: *elasticity* and thinking on the *margin*. These concepts are vital for understanding the decisions of consumers and suppliers. If you feel befuddled at times when you encounter an application of elasticity, or when you are in the midst of reading about such things as marginal utility, average physical product, or total, average, and marginal costs, don't give up in despair. Refer back to this material to help you with terminology and then keep plugging forward. We promise that many people far less intelligent than you are have mastered these concepts by diligent study and a bit of reflection.

CHAPTER REVIEW: KEY POINTS

1. The *price-elasticity of demand* is a measure of the responsiveness of the amount demanded to small price changes and is defined as:

$$e_p = \frac{\text{relative change in quantity demanded}}{\text{relative change in price}}$$

$$\cong \frac{\%\Delta Q}{\%\Delta P}.$$

2. Problems result when calculating elasticity if initial prices and quantities are used as bases. As a result, economists typically use *midpoint bases*. The price-elasticity of demand is negative but, for convenience, we use absolute values to avoid the negative sign.

3. If price elasticity is less than one, then demand is relatively unresponsive to changes in price and is said to be *inelastic*. If elasticity is greater than one, the demand is very responsive to price changes and is *elastic*. Demand is *unitarily elastic* if the elasticity coefficient equals one.

4. Elasticity, price changes, and total revenues (expenditures) are related in the following manner: If demand is inelastic (*elastic*) and price increases (*falls*), total revenue will rise. If demand is elastic (*inelastic*) and price rises (*falls*), total revenue (expenditures) will fall. If demand is unitarily elastic ($e_p = 1$), total revenue will be unaffected by price changes.

5. Along any negatively sloped linear demand curve, parts of the curve will be elastic, unitarily elastic,

and inelastic. The price-elasticity of demand rises as the price rises.

6. *Income-elasticity of demand* is the proportional change in the amount of a good demanded divided by a given proportionate change in income. Normal goods have income-elasticities above zero, while inferior goods have negative income-elasticities.

7. *Cross-elasticity of demand* measures the responsiveness of the quantity demanded of one good to price changes in a related good. That is, price cross-elasticity is the proportional change in the quantity of good X (Chevrolets) divided by a given proportional change in the price of good Y (Fords). If the cross-elasticity of demand is positive (*negative*), the goods are *substitutes* (*complements*).

8. The *price-elasticity of supply* measures the responsiveness of suppliers to changes in prices, and is defined to parallel that for the price-elasticity of demand: the proportional change in the amount supplied divided by a given proportional change in price. The price-elasticity of supply is typically positive, reflecting the positive slope of the supply curve.

9. The individual who actually loses purchasing power because of a tax is said to bear the tax's *economic incidence* (*tax burden*). This may be quite different from the individual who is legally responsible for the tax, who bears its *legal incidence*. When these individuals differ, the tax has been shifted. A tax can be *forward-shifted* (to consumers) or *backward-shifted* (to labor or other resource owners).

10. If demand is perfectly inelastic or supply is perfectly elastic, a tax will be completely forward-shifted. If supply is perfectly inelastic or demand is perfectly elastic, the tax will be completely backward-shifted.

11. *Incremental* or *marginal* changes direct rational decision making. If a marginal unit of something is positive (*negative*), its total will rise (*fall*). If the marginal unit is zero, the total is unaffected. If the marginal exceeds (*is less than*) an average, the average rises (*falls*). The average is unchanged if marginal equals average.

12. The *law of equal marginal advantage* dictates that similar resources be used in equally valuable ways to achieve efficiency.

PROBLEMS

1. Compute the elasticities in the following situations.

   a. The Jukes family buys 360 lollipops annually at a price of $0.20 each but would consume 480 per year if the price dropped to $0.16. Their price elasticity of demand is _____.

   b. The U.S. Air Force purchased 170 ashtrays for their latest jets when the price was $875 each, but ordered only 130 when the defense contractor raised the price to $1,125. The Air Force's price-elasticity of demand for ashtrays is _____.

   c. If American drivers burned 185 million gallons of gasoline on average when the price was $1.15 per gallon, but cut back to 155 million gallons weekly when the pump price rose to $1.35 per gallon, the price-elasticity of the market demand for gasoline equals _____.

   d. If a $5.98 sale on regular $8.99 cassettes raises a store's sales from 600 to 6,000 per week, the

   price-elasticity of the demand faced by the store is roughly _____.

   e. If a boom raises national income from $4.0 trillion to $4.4 trillion and macadamia nut sales jump from 3 to 5 million pounds annually, the income-elasticity of demand for the nuts is _____

   f. If each 1 percent hike in the price of mousetraps causes a 2 percent decline in the quantity of cheese sold, the price cross-elasticity of demand for these complementary goods is roughly _____

   g. When the Kallikak family can sell Shar-Pei puppies for $1,800 each, they offer 60 to the market annually, but when the price falls to $600 apiece, they are willing to sell only 12 each year. The price-elasticity of their supply is _____.

   h. When the temperature drops from 34°F to 18°F, average attendance at Cincinnati Bengals football games dips from 56,000 fans down to 28,000 diehards. During cold spells, the temperature elasticity of the demand for Bengals' tickets is

_____.

i. When 200,000 gallons of water are applied per acre, 4 tons of jelly beans are harvested from each acre annually, but cutting back to 140,000 gallons causes the crop per acre to fall to 2 tons annually. The water elasticity of jelly bean production is _____.

j. If doubling your consumption of pasta to 6 pounds per week causes you to blossom from a svelte 125 pounds to a rotund 175 pounds, your pasta elasticity of blubber is _____.

2. The concepts of average and marginal occur in many areas other than economics. Describe the effects on averages of the following marginal events:

a. What happens to your average for this class if your score on the next (marginal) test is above your current average? Suppose that you do not do quite as well on the final exam as on the next test. How is it possible for your average to rise even though the marginal test score is falling?

b. Manute Bol, a 7′ 7″ center for the Golden State Warriors basketball team, walks into your class. What happens to the average height of people in your classroom? The average income?

c. Fill in Table 4 to show what happens to the average temperature in Denver in February if, as the month progresses, the following high temperatures are recorded. (Use a hand calculator.)

Is there a consistent relationship between changes in the marginal (observed) temperature for sequential days and the average? (NO!) What is the simple relation between the marginal (observed) temperature and the average for the month?

d. Explain how an increase in the rate of inflation might still reduce the average rate of inflation over a decade.

e. Can you specify a simple mathematical law governing the relations between marginals and averages, and identify five situations outside of economics where this law is important?

3. The *Globe and Mail* (a British publication) reported that in 1981, England drastically increased taxes on cigarettes:

"In an austere March budget, the conservative Government slapped an extra 30 cents on the tax for a pack of 20. It followed with another increase in July, sending the tax up 30 percent [44 cent total increase in taxes] in six months and the average price of a pack to the equivalent of about $2.50."

Taxes grew to absorb roughly 75 percent of the total price of a pack of cigarettes; one industry expert estimated that cigarette sales would decline to 107 billion packs from the 121.5 billion sold in 1980.

a. Compute the price elasticity of demand for cigarettes using the expert's forecast of industry sales. Is the demand for cigarettes relatively elas-

TABLE 4 High Temperatures for the Month of February in Denver

Date	Temperature	Average	Date	Temperature	Average
Feb. 1	16°	_____	Feb. 15	31°	_____
2	18°	_____	16	16°	_____
3	23°	_____	17	15°	_____
4	23°	_____	18	23°	_____
5	20°	_____	19	42°	_____
6	26°	_____	20	34°	_____
7	29°	_____	21	14°	_____
8	37°	_____	22	24°	_____
9	24°	_____	23	24°	_____
10	14°	_____	24	48°	_____
11	12°	_____	25	50°	_____
12	22°	_____	26	39°	_____
13	35°	_____	27	40°	_____
14	30°	_____	28	55°	_____

tic or inelastic? Does your answer conform to your intuition about the nature of the demand for cigarettes?

b. How much added tax revenue could the British government expect to collect? How much sales revenue (after taxes) could the tobacco companies expect to lose?

c. Approximately how much would the tobacco companies have had to increase prices to keep their revenues from falling?

4. The prices of precious metals are set on worldwide commodity exchanges and are affected by such factors as the value of various major currencies, investor's inflationary expectations, and the state of international relations. These price changes clearly affect the quantities of gold and silver ingots sold, as well as the amounts sold of jewelry and other artistic products that use precious metals as an input. Gold is also used extensively by dentists for bridges, inlays, and crowns. The *Wall Street Journal* reported that when gold prices jumped from $415 to $875 per ounce in the late 1970s, gold consumption by dentists fell from 706,000 ounces to 341,000. Compute the price-elasticity of demand for gold as used by dentists for bridges, inlays and crowns.

5. Suppose you are the State Tax Commissioner, and your state legislature decides to raise $120 million in annual tax revenues by imposing a $1 tax per case of beer. They have looked at the figures, and 10 million cases of beer are sold monthly at $3 per case in your state. If you were called to testify before the Legislative Tax Committee, what would you have to say about their prospects for $120 million in new revenues? Suppose that you estimate that the price-elasticity of the demand for beer equals one. How high would the tax need to be to yield the desired revenues?

QUESTIONS FOR THOUGHT AND DISCUSSION

1. Some sports fans support the home team regardless of how well the team does; others only buy tickets if the team is a winner. Demand grows as a team's record improves. Would you expect the price-elasticity of demand to rise or fall as a result of a winning season? That is, would you expect season ticket prices to rise more than proportionally relative to other tickets as a team's record improved, or less than proportionally? Is the elasticity of supply of tickets to sporting events zero, or is it positive over the long run? Why?

2. Revenues from oil exported by members of the Organization of Petroleum Exporting Countries (OPEC) rose each year until 1981 after the price of oil began to rise in the early 1970s. What does this suggest about the short run price-elasticity of the international demand for oil? Even though oil prices rose, worldwide consumption of oil also rose. What does this suggest about the income-elasticity of the demand for oil?

3. What would happen to the elasticity of demand for oil from the perspective of OPEC countries if all countries that import oil imposed sliding tariffs just equal to any future increases in OPEC's oil prices?

4. Suppose you calculate that the price-elasticity of demand for your firm's product is 0.7. Your firm's policies should be changed immediately to increase profits. What policies should be changed? How do you know this?

5. Prices for small, gas-efficient imported cars rose even faster than the prices of American gas hogs during the 1970s, but these imports cornered a growing share of the American market. Rising gas prices were a key to this puzzle. What does this suggest about how demands for gasoline, imported cars, and full-sized Detroit products are related? Analyze pairs as complements or substitutes for all possible pairs.

CHAPTER 21

The Foundations of Consumer Choice

Economics relies on some concepts of human behavior that are closely akin to psychology in explaining the choices consumers make as they try to maximize their satisfactions, either individually or as family units. The microeconomic tools introduced in the preceding chapter were a bit mechanical, but in this chapter you will see that marginal analysis provides a logical view of consumer choices, which often seem dominated by fads and whims. The consumer behavior studied in this chapter is vital information for business decision making, which you will study in the next few chapters.

This chapter begins by categorizing things that satisfy or displease people and how people react to price changes. Its focus then turns to utility analysis, which offers a psychological interpretation of con-

sumer behavior. The issue of consumer sovereignty versus consumer regulation is then discussed. Optional material on indifference analysis concludes this chapter. All these concepts should provide many insights into your own behavior and the behavior of others in their everyday living and consuming.

Goods and Bads

A **good** is anything that adds to human happiness; a **bad** detracts from the enjoyment of life. *Consumption goods* directly add to our happiness and include most ordinary objects of everyday use: food, clothing, or cars. *Capital goods* include the machines and other resources that add to our happiness less directly, through the consumer goods they generate. Distinguishing between these types of goods may require looking at use. For example, identical cars are consumer goods when used by households, but capital goods when used by business. Oversupplies may convert some goods into bads: many home gardeners are inundated with more zucchini than they or their neighbors can eat, and much of it winds up in the trash.

Commodities are produced goods that can be owned—television sets, cowboy boots, and garden hoses are examples. We can purchase **services** without necessarily buying the items or agents that produce them: tuition gives you access to classes, but you own neither your chair nor your instructor. Other services include car repair, television broadcasts, police protection, and medical care.

It is important to note, however, that all goods are ultimately reducible to services. For example, different foods service various parts of our bodies. Bicycles transport us. Houses protect us from foul weather and clothes warm and adorn us. Machines transform materials to create commodities that are enjoyed when they generate services. In fact, virtually every economic activity has value only to the extent that it generates useful services. Capital goods, land, and commodities simply embody streams of services.

Market systems permit ownership of most service-producing goods, but you cannot legally own slaves, nuclear weapons, or certain illegal substances. Curiously, you do not even legally own yourself. But most goods and resources have prices that fluctuate to signal changes in costs or in our desires for goods. How consumers adjust when prices change is next on our agenda.

Effects of Price Changes _____

You will buy less of any good that rises in price, substituting for it goods that decline in relative price. Another effect when the price of a good rises is that the purchasing power of your income shrinks. This drop in purchasing power reduces your total ability to buy consumer goods and services. How purchasing patterns respond when the prices of goods change can be decomposed into substitution effects and income effects.

Substitution Effects

Substitution is the primary cause of negative slopes along demand curves.

The **substitution effect** *is that portion of the change in quantity demanded due solely to a change in relative prices.*[1]

Most goods have numerous possible uses. When the price of a good is reduced, it will be advantageous to devote the good to more of these uses.

For example, buses now provide low-priced transportation for many of us. Rides would be economical for far more people if fares were $0, and the homeless might sleep on warm buses instead of in cold alleys or under bridges. A $15 bus fare would induce most of us to walk, drive cars, or hire taxis. When ballpoint pens were introduced in the 1940s, they were refillable, cost about $25 each, and were a status symbol for business executives. They currently cost about a quarter, are used by almost everyone, and are discarded when the ink runs dry. Expensive ink pens are a rarity, and pencils are less commonly used than they would be if ballpoints still cost $25.

These examples suggest that we substitute some uses of some goods for similar uses of related goods as relative prices change. The critical point is that it is always advantageous to substitute away from goods that become relatively more expensive and to expand the uses of goods that become cheaper. The substitution effect is the major underpinning for the law of demand: *quantity demanded falls as price increases, and vice versa.*

The substitution effect is the change in purchasing patterns caused by changes in relative prices alone, artificially assuming that total purchasing power is constant. But price changes do alter the purchasing power of your income. We need to deal separately with how such changes in real income alter purchasing patterns.

---

1. Mathematically, the substitution effect of a change in the price of a good is always negative. This means that an increase in the price ($\Delta P > 0$) of some good (coffee, for example) will result in a substitution effect (toward tea?) that decreases the amount of coffee consumed ($\Delta Q < 0$). Thus, $\Delta Q / \Delta P$ is negative. Conversely, the substitution effect means that a decrease ($\Delta P < 0$) in the relative price of a good (say, ham) will cause increases ($\Delta Q > 0$) in the quantity consumed (and substitution away from beef). Again, $\Delta Q / \Delta P$ is negative.

Income Effects

If prices rise, the purchasing power of your dollars fall; if prices fall, a dollar will purchase more consumer goods.

Income effects *are the adjustments people make because the purchasing power of a given income is altered when prices change.*[2]

Suppose that tuition was $400 per semester hour and absorbed so much of your paltry budget that at first you could afford to take classes only part-time. If you were then awarded a 90 percent reduction in tuition because of your stellar performance, you could afford everything you had been buying previously and might simply pocket the $360 per semester hour covered by your scholarship. Instead, you would probably enroll for more courses, in part because of your substitution in response to this change in the relative cost of your education, but also because of the now greater purchasing power of your income. This income effect would enable you to enroll in even more courses, or you might buy more books, a better calculator, a few new clothes, tastier food, or more frequent concert tickets.

A slightly different type of income effect (only recently explored by economists) occurs when your money income is affected by changes in prices. If growth of demand causes prices to rise, some seller's income must increase. Suppose that you are the resident manager of an apartment building you also own. If rental rates in your area rise, there is an increase in the opportunity cost of living in your own apartment instead of renting it out, but you now have higher wealth and income because of the higher rent

you can charge for your other apartments. You might move into a smaller apartment because of the substitution effect, but if you are typical, you will opt for more luxurious accommodations. This explains why some wildcat drillers who strike oil drive bigger gas guzzlers longer distances when oil prices rise.

Utility

Digging deeper into consumer behavior leads us into a bit of history. Nineteenth-century economists were fascinated by utilitarianism, a school of thought founded by an eccentric English philosopher named Jeremy Bentham.

Utilitarianism *is the idea that the pain or pleasure from any activity respectively adds or detracts from a person's utility, or satisfaction.*

Utilitarians proposed a variety of social reforms in hopes of achieving their central goal, *the greatest happiness for the greatest number*. Utilitarians assumed that individual pleasure can be measured and then summed, each person being weighted equally, to calculate aggregate social welfare.

Imagine that people were born with forehead gauges that recorded satisfaction in *utils,* an imaginary measurement, much as your electric meter measures kilowatts. Over lunch your head registers: 1 burger = 73 utils; 17 french fries = 31 utils; a small cola = 24 utils; fried cherry pie = 38 utils; heartburn = -18 utils; Alka-Seltzer = 9 utils . . . net gain = 157 utils. Measuring the subjective value of national income would be a snap; simply sum everyone's gains in total utility. A utilitarian goal would boil economic policy down to doing whatever was necessary to maximize the total utility score.

The appealing goal of achieving the "greatest happiness for the greatest number" remains a basis for policies advocated by many politicians and economists, but raises some profound normative issues. The author Dostoyevski confounded utilitarians with his anguished question: "What if eternal happiness for the rest of humanity could be bought with the horrible death by torture of an innocent babe?" Policies that *unambiguously* maximize social utility in an ethical manner could not be formulated even if "utilometers" existed.

---

2. The income effect may be either negative, positive, or zero. All else being equal, when the price of a good rises, your purchasing power falls. For most goods, the income effect (ΔY) is positive. For example, a decrease in the price of gasoline (G) increases the purchasing power of your income ($\Delta Y > 0$). This alone results in higher levels of gas purchases ($\Delta G > 0$). Thus $\Delta G / \Delta Y$ is positive. However, the income effect is negative for inferior goods such as lard, potatoes, lye soap, or black-eyed peas. For example, if a large part of your diet consists of potatoes because you are poor and they are cheap, your purchasing power increases if the price of potatoes falls ($\Delta Y > 0$) and you can afford to buy tastier foods to secure your daily caloric needs. Even though you may buy more potatoes because of the substitution effect, the independent effect of your higher real income is to reduce potato consumption. ΔPotato < 0 so ΔPotatoes$/\Delta Y$ is negative.

BIOGRAPHY

Jeremy Bentham (1748–1832)

Jeremy Bentham—lawyer, philosopher, and social reformer—was hardly an economist, although his influence on subsequent economic thought was immense. He admired the ideas of Adam Smith but rejected Smith's view that people's interests are smoothly reconciled through the *invisible hand* of competitive markets. Bentham focused on conflicts between private and public interests, especially as manifested in illegal activities. He saw Smith's "harmony of interests" as desirable but not as a natural consequence of human behavior. Thus, Bentham devoted his long life to designing institutions that would bring about the harmony of interests Smith took for granted.

Bentham tried to integrate law, economics, politics, and education into a unified science of behavior. His theory identified pleasure and pain as the forces controlling human actions. The goal of Bentham's hedonistic philosophy was the attainment of "the greatest good," or *maximum utility*.

Bentham's most conspicuous successes were in law and judicial procedure. He applied the principles of utility and "felicific calculation" to crime and punishment, suggesting that the evil of a crime is proportionate to the number of people hurt by it. It follows, therefore, that punishment of crimes should not be based on mere motive, but on the amount of social pain caused by a felony. Properly speaking, Bentham viewed law and law enforcement from the economic perspective of incentives. He theorized that stiffer punishments would raise the "cost" of crime, compelling self-interested individuals to commit fewer misdeeds, and the public interest would be served.

Bentham was notably eccentric. His pet pig roamed freely through his mansion, and he once petitioned the London City Council for permission to line his driveway with mummified human cadavers, which he thought "far more aesthetic than flowers." At the age of 32, Bentham immodestly "dreamt the other night that I was a founder of a sect; of course a personage of great sanctity and importance. It was the sect of the utilitarians."

In spite of his personal eccentricities, Bentham's dream proved prophetic. His ideas attracted a loyal group of disciples, including the philosophers James Mill and his son John Stuart Mill, and his proposals for social reforms were widely translated into action. Benthamite principles were among the intellectual wellsprings of many nineteenth-century social reforms. Possibly the secret of Bentham's success is that he instilled in his disciples not only specific ideals but provided concrete plans to achieve them.

Bentham also dreamed of immortality. His sizable estate was left to the University of London on the condition that his body be embalmed in a certain way, stuffed and dressed in his own suit of clothes, and that it attend all meetings of the University's trustees. In this way, Bentham hoped to be "present" whenever utilitarian principles were discussed at "his" university. Bentham's wishes were carried out. (Minutes of all trustees' meetings record him as "present but not voting.") Over 150 years later, the dauntless utilitarian still resides in his glass closet in a corridor at University College, the University of London.

Modern economics rejects direct measurement of utility because (*a*) most of us cannot specify our preferences more precisely than by a rank order (first, second, third, and so on) of possible bundles of goods, and (*b*) satisfaction is not scientifically comparable between individuals. People differ in the intensity of their preferences and there is no way to ascertain exactly how much anyone likes candy (or anything else) relative to someone else's enjoyment of candy. This has led economists to develop *indifference analysis,* a more scientific technique explored at the end of this chapter. Even so, utility analysis offers some rich insights into human behavior.

Marginal Utility

Constructing any aggregate measure of utility remains a futile dream, but marginal utility analysis does offer insights into how people use resources to maximize their individual satisfaction.

> **Marginal utility (*MU*)** *is the gain in satisfaction derived through the consumption of some small additional amount of a good.*

Your marginal utilities from different goods reflect your subjective preferences. Although the subjective gains from a dollar's worth of goods may vary substantially among individuals, the following section shows how we can approximate the relative satisfactions from various goods to a given individual by looking at marginal utility in monetary terms.

The Law of Diminishing Marginal Utility

Suppose that you enjoy quenching your thirst on hot days with fresh lemonade; frozen or artificial will not do. If we measure utility in dollar terms, then MU_L is roughly the amount you would willingly pay for an extra lemonade. After three sets of tennis on a 90-degree afternoon, you stroll into your town's only air-conditioned lemonade stand where the server, an old friend, informs you that icy, fresh lemonade is now $1 per glass. Your throat parched, you decide that one glass is barely worth $1. As you finish it and rise to leave, the ade-tender offers you a break: a sec-

ond lemonade for only $0.85. "All right," you say, "just one more." After gulping it down, you are already off your stool when the ade-tender asks, "How about another for $0.60?" Sitting back down, you put your money on the counter. After your third lemonade, she asks, "How about a fourth at the old price of $0.50?" Somewhat befuddled, you nod your head. The four lemonades have cost you $2.95 ($1.00 + $0.85 + $0.60 + $0.50), as shown in Panel A of Figure 1. At the old price of $0.50, you would have paid a total of only $2.00.

After the fourth lemonade you are ready to face the heat outside but the ade-tender offers you still another, and for only $0.25. You cannot pass up the bargain. Then she says, "A good customer like you deserves a sixth lemonade on the house." It is 90 degrees in the shade, so you assent. Feeling a bit water-logged, you turn down the offer of a seventh even though it is free. "Tell you what," she says, "will you drink it if I pay you $0.50?" Being an impoverished student, you agree. You also drink an eighth, for which you are paid $1. Ultimately, however, you approach your capacity. You offer to drink the ninth for the $3 she offers, but only if you can wait a half hour. Since "It's now or never," you decide to pass. (You would drink the ninth for $25, but she will not offer that much.)

Panel B of Figure 1 shows how the marginal utilities in dollars are related to your total satisfaction from lemonade (Panel A). The points on both curves are connected as if the server had offered these deals by sips rather than glassfuls. Study the relationship between total utility and marginal utility. The accumulated area under the marginal utility curve (note the expanded vertical axis) equals the height of the total utility curve.

The declining marginal utility from lemonade as you drink more and more during a given time interval occurs with virtually all goods and all people. Observing that similar reactions were common, classical economists have generalized this behavior into the following law.

> *The* **law of diminishing marginal utility** *states that the marginal utility associated with consuming equal successive units of a good will eventually decline as the amount consumed increases.*

FIGURE 1 Total and Marginal Utility of Lemonade

Total Utility from Lemonade Estimated in Dollars

$1.00 + .85 = 1.85
$1.00 + .85 + .60 = $2.45
$1.00 + .85 + .60 + .50 + = $2.95
$1.00 + .85 + .60 + .50 + .25 = $3.20
$1.00 + .85 + .60 + .50 + .25 = $3.20
$1.00 + .85 + .60 + .50 + .25 − .50 = $2.70
$1.00 + .85 + .60 + .50 + .25 − .50 − 1.00 = $1.70

Because the total value you place on consuming a good initially increases but at a decreasing rate (from 0 to 6 lemonades in Panel A), the marginal utility of the good is positive but diminishing (Panel B). Eventually, you may reach a point of satiation where the total satisfaction from consuming a good is maximized (6 lemonades in Panel A). At this point the marginal utility of the good is zero (6 lemonades in Panel B); thereafter, marginal utility is negative as the good becomes, in a sense, a bad (more than 6 lemonades in Panel B).

The word *eventually* is important. Horror movie fanciers might enjoy their first movie of the week immensely, and their second film even more. They almost certainly will not enjoy their sixteenth movie of the week as much as their third. Benjamin Franklin's observation in *Poor Richard's Almanac,* "Fish and visitors stink in three days," says far more about the diminishing marginal utility of visitors than about the deterioration of fish.

Consumer Equilibrium and Demand

You may have noticed that the marginal utility curve in Panel B of Figure 1 contains all the information required for a demand curve for lemonade. This is correct because consumers will buy an *extra* unit of a good only if its marginal utility is at least as great as its price. Thus, according to this demand curve, you would buy only one lemonade if the price was $1, two at $0.85, three at $0.60, four at $0.50, five at $0.25, and would drink six lemonades only if they were free. This example illustrates why early economists explained the negative slopes of all demand curves by the law of diminishing marginal utility.

Maximizing Utility

We have asserted that satisfaction can be approximated by looking at utility in terms of money. While we cannot compare different people's utilities from consuming goods, we may be fairly sure that their individual marginal utilities from particular goods are roughly proportional to the prices of the goods. The reason for this is that people will change their spending patterns whenever relative prices and marginal utilities are not in balance. The following example shows why. For convenience, this example assumes that $1 buys 1 util at the margin in the initial equilibrium.

Suppose that you love ice cream and buy an average of six $1 cones per week: three rocky roads (r) and three chocolates (c). Each extra cone initially yields 1 util of satisfaction ($MU_r = MU_c = 1$). This occurs at point x in each panel of Figure 2. If you begin to tire of rocky road and increasingly like plain chocolate, the marginal utility of chocolate cones relative to rocky road rises. Say, $MU_r = 0.75$, while $MU_c = 1.25$, a movement from points x to y in each panel. MU_c/P_c is simply the marginal utility (in utils) you get from the last cent you spend on chocolate ice cream; MU_r/P_r is the marginal utility derived from the last cent spent on rocky road. At point y in both panels, MU_c/P_c exceeds MU_r/P_r, given your current snacking habits. You will start buying more chocolate cones and less rocky road weekly, initially gaining 1.25 utils for each extra $1 spent on chocolate while losing only 0.75 utils for each rocky road cone sacrificed.

Balancing Marginal Utilities

However, the law of diminishing marginal utility comes into play and the marginal utility of chocolate will fall while the marginal utility of rocky road rises. This movement is from point y to z in each panel. All cones cost $1, so your purchases stabilize when:

$$MU_c/P_c = MU_r/P_r = 1/\$1 = 1.$$

FIGURE 2 Realigning Marginal Utilities Through Changes in Consumption Patterns

A decline in the marginal utility of rocky road ice cream results in lower consumption, while a rise in the marginal utility of plain chocolate ice cream causes greater purchases. In equilibrium, $MU_r/P_r = MU_c/P_c$.

Similar adjustments occur whenever an individual's marginal utilities for all goods purchased are not proportional to their market prices; you will be in equilibrium only when:

$$\frac{MU_a}{P_a} = \frac{MU_b}{P_b} = \cdots \frac{MU_z}{P_z},$$

where $a, b, \ldots, z$ are the various goods you buy.

> *This* **consumer equilibrium** *equation can be interpreted to mean that a consumer maximizes utility when the last cent spent on each good yields the same satisfaction as the last cent spent on any other good.*

Identical resources will be equally advantageously allocated at the margin, so that each dollar is allocated in equally advantageous ways to a consumer. This application of the law of equal advantage to consumer behavior is known as the *principle of equal marginal utilities per dollar. Dollar* is used as an arbitrary small denomination of money. In a complete equilibrium, the last *cent* spent on ice cream yields the same satisfaction as the last *cent* spent on lemonade, clothes, books, or housing. A little reflection should suggest that this is roughly true of your own spending pattern.

Let's use this format to describe how quantities demanded change as relative prices change. Figure 3 supposes that your family's purchases of apples (a) and bananas (b) is initially in equilibrium when you consume 6 pounds of apples and 4 pounds of bananas monthly if they cost the same amount per pound (point x). Pounds of the fruit originally exchange one-for-one, and at point x in Panels A and B, $MU_a/P_a = MU_b/P_b$. If the price of apples rises relative to the price of bananas so that a pound of apples now costs as much as 1.25 pounds of bananas, then a pound of bananas costs only as much as 0.8 pounds of apples and MU_a/P_a is less than MU_b/P_b; you will adapt by buying more bananas and fewer apples (point y in each panel). As you consume fewer apples the MU_a will rise, while the MU_b falls as you eat more bananas.

FIGURE 3 *Price Adjustments and Marginal Utility*

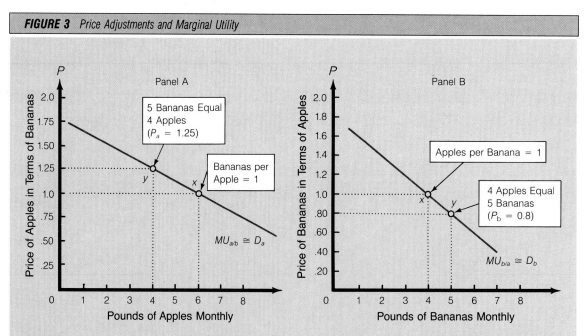

If the price of apples is the same as that of bananas, in equilibrium the two will yield the same marginal utility, which occurs at point x in each panel. A hike in the price of apples relative to bananas (so that 5 bananas are needed to "buy" 4 apples) causes lower consumption and higher marginal utility of apples. As a result, each apple is subjectively more valuable. At the same time, rising consumption of bananas reduces their marginal utility. These changes occur as your family moves from point x to point y in each panel.

Experimenting with other changes in relative prices and the resulting adjustments in your consumption pattern trace out demand curves for apples and bananas. Thus, in equilibrium, the higher-priced goods you purchase uniformly generate more marginal utility than lower-priced goods. The more you pay for a good, the more it is worth to you at the margin. Ultimately, the last dollar you spend on any good, including your holdings of cash, yields the same satisfaction as the last dollar spent on any other good.

Market prices and the subjective demand prices discussed in chapter 3 are different ways of viewing opportunity costs. Demand prices can be thought of as the ratios of the marginal utilities of various goods. Only if market prices and demand prices are in accord will you buy. In equilibrium, your subjective price ratios will be equal to the relative market prices of all the goods you choose to purchase. That is, MU_a/MU_b equals P_a/P_b for any two goods we choose to label a and b, respectively.[3]

---

3. The reason this equation is compatible with the principle of equal marginal utilities per dollar is that in equilibrium, MU_a/P_a equals MU_b/P_b; if we multiply each side of the equation by P_a/MU_b and then simplify, we obtain the result that MU_a/MU_b equals P_a/P_b.

Consumer Surplus _____

We can look at an individual's demand curve for some good from two different perspectives:

1. Most of the time we see demand curves as answers to the question, "How much will be bought at each possible price?" The quantity demanded depends on the price.
2. Alternatively, we might view demand curves as graphing answers to the question, "If people have certain amounts of good X, what is the most that they would be willing to pay for an extra unit of X ?"

Here, price is viewed as depending on quantity. Both approaches yield the same demand curves.

The view that a good's marginal value depends on the amount available to us provides a key to specifying in monetary terms the satisfaction gained from being able to buy at a single market price. Using our original lemonade example (see Figure 4), you paid a total of $2.95 for the first four glasses of lemonade, but only $0.50 for the fourth (last) glass. But if lemonade sold for a flat price of $0.50 per glass, you would spend $2 to drink four lemonades, thereby

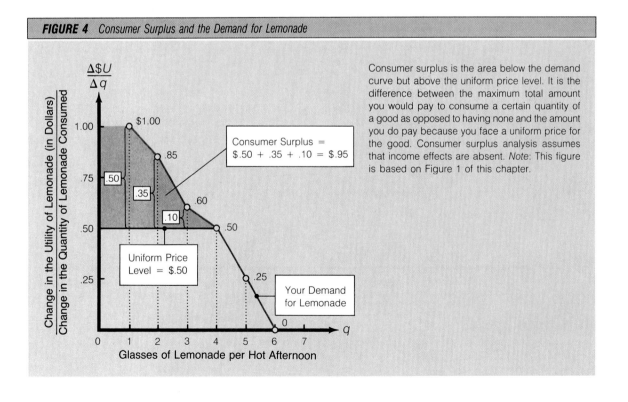

FIGURE 4 Consumer Surplus and the Demand for Lemonade

Consumer surplus is the area below the demand curve but above the uniform price level. It is the difference between the maximum total amount you would pay to consume a certain quantity of a good as opposed to having none and the amount you do pay because you face a uniform price for the good. Consumer surplus analysis assumes that income effects are absent. *Note:* This figure is based on Figure 1 of this chapter.

gaining $0.95 worth of utility. This gain represents consumer surplus.

Consumer surplus *is the difference between the amounts people would willingly pay for various amounts of specific goods and the amounts they do pay at market prices; this is roughly the area below the demand curve but above the price line, assuming that income effects are trivial.*

Even though consumer surplus cannot be measured quantitatively, among its applications is that consumer surplus permits qualitative assessments of the efficiency of many government policies.

The Paradox of Value
Two hundred years ago, economists were stumped by an apparent paradox.

The **paradox of value** *addressed why absolute necessities such as water are valued (priced) so cheaply, while frivolities like diamonds are highly valued and command outrageous prices.*

Questions about the paradox of value were used to stump Ph.D. candidates in economics for generations. This paradox arises from difficulties in distinguishing between total utility and marginal utility.

Suppose that Panel A in Figure 5 depicts your family's demand for water. If you are typical, water is so cheap that you treat drinking water as if it were free: You drink water until an extra glass would actually detract from your well-being—the marginal utility is zero. However, because you know that your water bill (which averages $20 monthly) reflects total use, you are probably somewhat careful about watering your lawn, washing your car, or running bath water.

But suppose you were offered an all-or-nothing choice: 100 gallons of water for $500 monthly or no water at all. If you could afford it, you would willingly pay at least $500 per month for water, and you would limit your use of water to drinking, preparing food, and sponge baths. Your lawn and plants would die, your car would go dirty, and you would forget about

FIGURE 5   *The Paradox of Value*

Water is extremely valuable, but, because of its low price, it generates a substantial consumer surplus. On the other hand, diamonds have a very high price and generate far less consumer surplus.

washing machines and flush toilets. (Do you think this might explain why desert prospectors smell ripe after a few days?) If you had to, you would pay considerably more for the 10,000 gallons of water you use each month than the $20 you do pay, so water yields an enormous consumer surplus.

The total utility of water is substantially higher than its marginal utility and price, while the total utility of diamonds is close to their marginal utility and price. We have shaded the areas representing consumer surpluses in Figure 5. This analysis should help you understand why diamonds, which are not nearly as necessary to life as water, are valued and priced much higher than water. The total utility, marginal utility, and price of diamonds are nearly identical for those of us who own, at most, a few of the baubles.

Goods as Bundles of Attributes   The theory of consumption has been expanded recently to consider each individual good as embodying a variety of utility-relevant characteristics or *attributes*. Cigarettes provide oral gratification and give smokers "something to do with my hands"; they are also carcinogenic, generate hostility from non-smokers, and waste time. Similarly, Sugar Smacks have a certain texture and taste and loads of calories. Rice and potatoes have very similar attributes and are thus substitutes; each is also quite complementary with steak.

The Problem of Rational Choice

Many observers are dubious that people are as rational as economic theory presumes. If you asked typical shoppers in a grocery store if their buying patterns caused their marginal utilities for various goods to be in fixed proportions to the prices of these goods, they would think you were off your rocker. Suppose instead that you asked them why they do not buy more or less of particular goods than they do, or why they reject other items. They would probably begin talking about some things being "good buys," while referring to others as "too high," or "not worth it to me."

Most people seem to behave as economic models of demand suggest, even if they find incomprehensible the economic jargon used to describe their

behavior. There is, however, far from unanimity that people really act in very rational or calculating ways. Take a moment to read the biographical sketch of Thorstein Veblen, a founder of the view known as institutionalism, which largely rejects the kind of reasoning we have described.

Uncertainty and Imperfect Information

We make decisions in an imperfect world rife with uncertainty. You can never be 100 percent certain of the attributes of a specific unit of any good, no matter how familiar. You may buy a moldy loaf of your favorite bread or be injured by an exploding cigarette lighter. There is even less certainty about unfamiliar goods that are bought only once or twice in a lifetime. No one who undergoes surgery can ever be certain in advance about the outcome of an operation. Nor, for that matter, can any surgeon. Uncertainty exists because we have only imperfect information about the present and no crystal ball to predict the future.

Information is costly. Acquiring full information might be incredibly expensive, and the value of some information may be trivial. The result is that decisions are made in an environment of rational ignorance.

> **Rational ignorance** *occurs because consumers search for information only as long as the expected benefit from search exceeds its expected cost. Thus, consumers may choose to be rationally ignorant of much information.*

For example, most standard items people buy are available at a wide range of monetary prices, and most people pay more than the lowest price at which a good is available at a given point in time. Searching until you were sure that you were paying the least amount possible for a good, however, would probably absorb more time and effort than any resulting monetary saving was worth. Similarly, you might spend a lifetime trying to identify the perfect spouse for you from the population of single people of the opposite sex. The costliness of the search, however, probably accounts for findings that propinquity (geographical closeness) is a major determinant of whom one marries. But broadening the options available in any decision-making situation can be costly and pose unforeseen problems.

BIOGRAPHY

Thorstein B. Veblen (1857–1929)

The economic characterization of human behavior as the rational calculation of benefits and costs seemed ludicrous to Thorstein Veblen, one of the great iconoclasts and tragicomic figures of economics. Veblen was trained in philosophy but concentrated on economics because of what he perceived as deficiencies in economic analysis. A first-generation American of Norwegian stock, Veblen viewed capitalism and the American scene as if he were a newcomer to the planet. He found the institutions and behavior of Americans more than a bit strange—exotic and bizarre are probably more appropriate terms. His intellectual work consists primarily of "cultural analysis," the high-water mark of which is pungent criticism. A good example of his satire is contained in this attack on the marginal utility principle:

The hedonistic conception of man is that of a lightning calculator of pleasures and pains, who oscillates like a homogeneous globule of desire . . . under the impulse of stimuli that shift him about the area but leave him intact. . . . He is an isolated, definitive human datum, in stable equilibrium except for the buffets of the impinging forces that displace him in one direction or another. . . . When the force of the impact is spent, he comes to rest, a self-contained globule of desire as before.

Veblen believed that human behavior is best analyzed as interactions of instincts and habits and that many social processes can be interpreted as results of cultural lags. In his doctrine of *conspicuous consumption* (status competition), Veblen explained how the desire to "keep up with the Joneses" motivates people to buy goods in a way that is culturally determined, not price determined. In a more general sense, Veblen insisted on studying the origin and nature of economic institutions. He was especially critical of the *leisure class* and businessmen, whom he viewed as parasites. He argued that conventional economics fails to consider social and economic institutions, artificially reducing human nature to a matter of rational calculation.

As eccentric as Bentham, Veblen washed his dishes in a rain barrel and seldom bathed. Though grubby and quite homely, he was a "lady killer" and lost several academic positions because he had a bad habit of seducing the wives of colleagues and administrators. He was still an assistant professor when he died at age 72.

Veblen's criticisms of economic theory were largely based on anti-rationalist premises and were certainly not the first of their kind. Veblen's savage humor and great erudition made him a formidable critic of the business system. He originated a distinctively American line of inquiry into economics, *institutionalism*, which continues to find proponents to this day.

Bewildering Arrays of Choices

Each year, thousands of products fade into oblivion, but even more thousands are launched in the marketplace. Ever widening ranges of choice become available as firms attempt to attract customer bases sufficient to make their product lines profitable. This is often held up as a major advantage of the market system: even eccentric tastes and preferences may be accommodated when almost innumerable different goods are available. Typical grocery stores now carry over 15,000 different items; together, the stores in a large shopping mall often offer five times as many.

One result of having many choices and constant flux in markets is that the additional information required for wise consumer decisions is costly.[4] One example of this occurs when firms modify products slightly in hopes of getting non-customers to sample their goods: "Try our new, improved _____." You might become agitated if you searched high and low for a familiar red box of your favorite cereal, concluded that the store was out, and then, on a later shopping trip, discovered that the maker had switched to a blue box.

More serious levels of confusion arise when choices are wider. A few happily married couples may swear that they are perfectly matched, but most singles who want to marry agonize over ever finding the right person. A gourmet may dither for hours over a lengthy menu at a posh restaurant. Some people spend days trying to find the perfect gift for a friend or the perfect suit for a job interview. Selecting goods would be a simpler process if fewer options were available. You may know people who would have few problems in finding a TV program to watch if fewer channels were available, but who can't stop pushing the changer when a cable system offers fifty or sixty choices.

An emigré from the Soviet Union to the United States remarked that the biggest culture shock was choosing from among the millions of options our society offers. Might some people who are uncomfortable with decision making feel less pressured in more regimented societies? For example, the arranged marriages common in traditional societies might reduce the anxiety many people experience when less rigid mating rituals prevail. Career choices might be far less traumatic for some people if they were simply assigned jobs. There are, however, social institutions that lessen the need for people to choose. Private schools that require uniforms eliminate any quandary about what a child will wear. A military career limits the scope of individual choice. At the extreme, few choices are required of prison inmates. Indeed, some convicts become so "institutionalized" that they cannot bear life outside prison walls.

Most of us, however, enjoy the wide range of options in a market system, and many of us view the cars, houses, or clothes we purchase as expressions of our individuality. We are accustomed to the inconvenience and confusion of shopping or sorting out the activities we want to do. These are parts of the transaction costs and uncertainty that cause the total price paid by a consumer to exceed the revenue received by a seller.

An even greater problem for any type of decision making is that *rational ignorance* may yield decisions that seem wrong in retrospect. People try to maximize by equating *expected* marginal benefits (e.g., marginal utilities or marginal revenues) and *expected* marginal costs. Some expectations may prove too pessimistic; a dreaded blind date set up by your mother may turn out to be the person you've dreamed about. If people form their expectations reasonably, however, the probability of a pleasant surprise should, on average, be balanced by the probability of a disappointing outcome. This partially explains hangovers, high divorce rates, food poisoning, the spread of venereal diseases, fatal accidents, and why some people suffering serious illness may be stuck with incompetent quacks and die for lack of information about specialists who might have cured their disease.[5]

Moral Hazard

Expectations about costs and benefits from a transaction that requires future performance may be confounded because such arrangements create incentives for inefficient behavior, a problem known as *moral hazard.* Lack of information allowing perfect forecasts of the future is a key to this problem. For example, if you paid for knee surgery in advance, might a surgeon do sloppier work than if you will pay only if the knee responds satisfactorily? On the other hand, after your knee was repaired would you have an incentive to delay payment and haggle about the surgeon's charges?

> A **moral hazard** *occurs when an arrangement provides incentives for one party to engage in behavior that unexpectedly raises the costs or lowers the benefits of the other party.*

---

4. Product differentiation may also drive up production costs, and hence, prices—a process we describe later in this book.

5. Some of these examples are drawn from Gary Galles' "The Best Choice May Be the Wrong One," in Ralph Byrns and Gerald Stone, eds., *Great Ideas for Teaching Economics,* 4/ed. (Glenview, IL: Scott, Foresman/Little, Brown, 1989).

Moral hazards arise because choices tend to reflect personal costs and benefits, with the effects on others being, at most, secondary considerations. No contract can cover every possible contingency so most transactions entailing future performance rely heavily on the good faith of the bargaining parties. Time tends to blur promises to diligently consider the interests of the other party to a bargain.

Suppose that your instructors agreed to enter an A in their grade books right now for every student who promised to work hard this semester. Would most students follow through and study diligently? Do you think that professional athletes with guaranteed contracts might be less careful about diet and physical conditioning than players whose pay is tightly linked to performance? Might ignoring the effects on the people paying a guaranteed contract cause athletes to engage in riskier outside activities—e.g., skiing or hang gliding? Is there a moral hazard when parents provide Visa cards "for emergencies" to college bound students? Might drivers who always removed ignition keys when parking their uninsured vehicles tend to forget to lock up their cars if insurance covers losses due to theft or vandalism?

Opportunistic behavior after an arrangement is made creates the problem of moral hazard, and is most severe if parties to a contract do not anticipate its renewal. Moral hazard is less important if both parties expect to extend or renew an arrangement; unexpectedly imposing costs or reducing the benefits of the other party causes it to rely less on good faith when a subsequent contract is negotiated. This reluctance will increase the bargaining costs of both parties. If either party does not expect "repeat business," a related problem known as *adverse selection* may also arise.

Adverse Selection

Estimates of expected costs and benefits from a contract tend to be unbiased if each party shares fully all the information available before reaching a final agreement. Frequently, however, one side will conceal or distort information to strengthen its bargaining position. This distortion often verges on fraud. For example, a used car lot may advertise a "cream puff" while knowing that a car's odometer has been rewound and that it is on its way to the junkyard.

Adverse selection *occurs when one bargaining party ultimately suffers an unexpected disadvantage because the other party has distorted or concealed information prior to a contract.*

You may have heard of pensioners who have been bilked of their life savings by "con artists"; confidence games are extreme examples of the problem of adverse selection. Operators of fly-by-night businesses often guarantee faulty goods, knowing that the guarantees are worthless. Some deadbeats try to build up records of paying small bills so that they can secure credit that will allow them to run up indebtedness that they never intend to pay. Similarly, a babysitter who wants a job may try to project a nurturing image, never revealing a personal history as a child abuser.

The economic inefficiency caused by such problems as moral hazard and adverse selection have created pressure for government to expand its role in the regulation of consumer behavior.

Caveat Emptor, Caveat Venditor, and Government Edict

Can consumers make appropriate choices for themselves? **Caveat emptor** ("let the buyer beware") is an ancient legal doctrine that buyers are the best judges of whether or not they receive full value and so should bear the consequences of their own decisions. But the doctrine of **caveat venditor** ("let the seller beware") also has a long history, reflected in prohibitions against fraud and in imposing on sellers legal liability for damages if unknown dangers lurk within a product. Society increasingly makes firms responsible for the safety and reliability of their products. Naturally, these regulatory costs are passed forward as higher prices, forcing us to buy "built-in" insurance policies on some goods we purchase.

The strongest trend, however, is toward outright government edict, either to prohibit or mandate certain activities. A century ago, one could legally purchase any available drug. Today, many drugs are absolutely banned (LSD and heroin are examples); others require a doctor's prescription. It is no longer legal to produce automobiles without a laundry list of safety equipment (never mind that most car passengers fail to buckle up).

Cyclamate (an artificial sweetener) was withdrawn from the market in the late 1960s. This may have caused some folks to die of "fat attacks" until NutraSweet appeared in 1983. During this interval, the incidence of heart disease may have been artificially high because heavy people could not choose to trade the risk of heart attack from obesity for the risk of cancer associated with certain diet foods. This list could be extended substantially.

We know that people's ideas cannot be pigeonholed precisely. Those who favor market solutions over government regulation, however, generally have faith in the ability of people to choose for themselves. They reason that if the consumer's problem is a lack of information, government can either provide the information or leave it to organizations such as the Consumer's Union. On the other hand are those who distrust the market system and have little faith in the ability of the average person to choose.

The positions you take on such issues depend on whether you view individuals themselves or govern-ment experts to be better judges of a person's well-being. Both groups will suffer from uncertainty and rational ignorance. Should using a seat belt be mandatory? Should AIDS patients be denied access to potentially beneficial drugs until the Food and Drug Administration has approved them? Should hang-gliding be prohibited? If you are certain to die of cancer if you drink a case of artificially sweetened cola every day for 127 years and you want to do it anyway, should the government let you? These and similar questions about the role of government reg-ulation are addressed in a later chapter.

Some consumer issues and the basis of demand theory have been our focus in this chapter; in the next, you will study the nature of a firm's production and costs. These foundations of demand and supply will be blended in the next part of this book to explain pricing and output decisions of firms under a variety of market situations.

CHAPTER REVIEW: KEY POINTS

1. *Substitution effects* are the changes in consumer purchasing patterns that emerge if relative prices change, artificially assuming that the purchasing power of income is constant.

2. *Income effects* are changes in buying patterns that occur solely because the purchasing power of one's income changes when the prices of individual goods rise or fall.

3. *Utilitarianism* proposes that the best society is the one that provides the greatest happiness for the greatest number of people.

4. *Marginal utility* is the extra satisfaction gained from consuming a bit more of a good. The *law of diminishing marginal utility* states: The marginal utility of any good eventually declines as the amount consumed increases.

5. Measured in dollars, the declining portion of a marginal utility curve translates into a demand curve.

6. Maximum consumer satisfaction (*consumer equilibrium*) requires that the last cent spent on any good yields the same gain in satisfaction as the last cent spent on any other good: $MU_a/P_a = MU_b/P_b = \ldots = MU_z/P_z$. This is known as the *principle of equal marginal utilities per dollar*.

7. *Consumer surplus* is the area above the price line and below the demand curve. It is a consumer's gain from buying at a uniform price instead of paying prices equal to the marginal utility of each unit.

8. We are seldom certain about the *attributes* of any unit of a good. Information is costly and its marginal benefits may be trivial. Thus, our decisions are based on less than full information; we are *rationally ignorant* because we pursue information only as long as its expected benefit exceeds its expected cost.

9. *Moral hazard* occurs when a contract creates an incentive for opportunistic behavior that raises the costs or lowers the benefits to the other party. *Adverse selection* occurs when a party to a contract has been deceived about the qualities it expects to receive from a transaction. Rational ignorance, moral hazard, and adverse selection are all reasons why our effective consumer demands may not maximize our satisfaction.

10. There is an increasing tendency towards government edict as a means of overcoming transaction costs or solving the problems of rational ignorance and uncertainty. Do government experts know better than you do what things are good for you and what things will harm you?

PROBLEMS

TABLE 1 Mabel's Utilities from Pies and Novels					
Apple Pies	**Total Utility**	**Marginal Utility**	**Detective Novels**	**Total Utility**	**Marginal Utility**
0	0	‒‒‒	0	0	‒‒‒
1	200	‒‒‒	1	250	‒‒‒
2	290	‒‒‒	2	295	‒‒‒
3	370	‒‒‒	3	335	‒‒‒
4	440	‒‒‒	4	370	‒‒‒
5	500	‒‒‒	5	400	‒‒‒
6	550	‒‒‒	6	425	‒‒‒
7	590	‒‒‒	7	445	‒‒‒
8	620	‒‒‒	8	460	‒‒‒
9	640	‒‒‒	9	470	‒‒‒
10	650	‒‒‒	10	475	‒‒‒

1. Table 1 illustrates Mabel's total utilities from apple pies and detective novels.
   a. Fill in the columns with Mabel's marginal utilities from these goods.
   b. Does Mabel's response to both goods obey the law of diminishing marginal utility? Why or why not?
   c. Plot Mabel's total and marginal utilities from both goods on a separate sheet of graph paper.
   d. Suppose Mabel has $36.00 to spend on apple pies and detective novels; each pie is $6.00 and each novel is $3.00. How much of each will Mabel purchase in equilibrium?
   e. Suppose the prices of pies and novels both drop to $1 because of a bumper crop of green apples and the advent of a cheap printing process, while at the same time, Mabel's budget shrinks to $10. How much of both goods will she purchase in equilibrium?

2. Table 2 lists Mabel's demand for apple pies.

TABLE 2 Mabel's Demand for Apple Pies	
Quantity	**Price ($)**
1	10.00
2	8.00
3	6.00
4	3.00
5	2.00

   a. Compute Mabel's consumer surplus from pies if the price is $3.00 apiece.
   b. What happens to Mabel's consumer surplus if the pie supply is perfectly elastic at $3.00 per pie and the government levies a tax of $3.00 per pie?

QUESTIONS FOR THOUGHT AND DISCUSSION

1. Would the substitution effect or the income effect be more useful in explaining why many students flock out of classes taught by professors who have reputations for being hard into courses taught by instructors who have reputations for easy grading?

2. Leisure is a good. When wages increase, the cost of leisure rises because you sacrifice more if you don't

work. Thus, the substitution effect of a wage hike is to reduce leisure. How does the income effect of an increase in the wage rate affect the decisions about work if leisure is an inferior good, a normal good, or an extreme luxury good?

3. What are your thoughts on the following examples of ethical dilemmas for a utilitarian approach?

   a. A hospital has just enough medicine to cure ten 20-year-old college students or one 70-year-old derelict. Failure to administer the medicine to a patient will result in the patient's immediate death. Who should get the medicine? Would your answer change if the 70-year-old owned the medicine?

   b. Allowing a corporation to build a shopping center will create traffic congestion and reduce property values in a middle-class suburb. Should the shopping mall be built? Would your answer change if you knew that the corporation would donate all profit to build houses for homeless poor people?

   c. A convicted murderer is scheduled for execution on Friday. She is the only inmate in a jail scheduled for demolition next month. An enormous fire breaks out. Should $100,000 of taxpayer's money be spent to rescue this prisoner?

4. Why do marginal utilities diminish more rapidly as consumption of a good is increased during short periods (a day) as opposed to longer periods (a year)?

5. What concept in this chapter helps explain why a joke is seldom as funny the second or third time you hear it?

6. The law of equal marginal utilities suggests that the last cent spent on any good yields the same gain in satisfaction as the last cent spent on any other good. Do your spending patterns conform to this idea? Are there ever barriers that prevent people from achieving this equilibrium for consumption?

7. Some reliable companies state that their policy is "Satisfaction guaranteed or your money will be cheerfully refunded." Are there some goods for which such guarantees by retailers do not alleviate a need for government regulation? If so, what are they?

8. Which of the following problems are consequences of simple rational ignorance, and which arise from moral hazard or adverse selection?

   a. Your new car turns out to be a lemon.

   b. You get an A in a course by turning in a plagiarized term paper.

   c. Balmy weather ruins your ski vacation.

   d. After saving your money for years, your spouse dies. You then marry a murderous fortune hunter and change your will so that your new spouse will inherit your fortune.

   e. You were laid off because you goofed around on the job after you worked long enough to become eligible for unemployment compensation.

   f. You pay a brilliant friend $100 to write a term paper, and your former friend does a sloppy job that causes you to fail a course.

   g. Soon after your silver anniversary, you become embroiled in a nasty divorce because of irreconcilable differences.

   h. A sluggish housing market keeps you from selling, so you hire an arsonist and "sell" your house to the insurance company.

9. What are some attributes that distinguish goods whose regulation we can leave to the marketplace from those for which government regulation of consumer purchases seems appropriate? What criteria might be appropriate to differentiate between people who should be allowed to make their own choices from people who "need to be looked after"? Society does allow some people to make some choices that are denied others. Can you name some instances?

OPTIONAL MATERIAL: INDIFFERENCE CURVE ANALYSIS

The impossibility of measuring utility by a more objective unit than in mythical "utils" vexed economists until early in this century, when a new approach, *indifference analysis,* finally allowed them to side step this difficulty. This modern approach to consumer choice begins with a look at individual budget constraints.

Budget Lines

Human society cannot maintain consumption beyond a production-possibility frontier constructed for the world. Recall that the production-possibility frontier is concave (bowed out) from the origin because significant changes in patterns of production cause diminishing returns to be encountered. Each individual family is similarly constrained by its income in choosing among consumption alternatives. Because the purchasing pattern a family chooses generally will not affect market prices, the consumer's budget line is straight. **Budget lines** depict the choices available to consumers who face constant prices and who have given levels of income. Figure 6 shows budget lines for two levels of income using the assumption that asparagus (A) and a proxy for all other goods, called shmoo, (B) each costs $1 per pound. Any point in the AB space represents a specific combination of asparagus and shmoos—and would require a certain level of income.

We can write the family's budget constraint as equal to:

$$Y = P_aA + P_bB. \qquad \text{(Equation 1)}$$

All family income (Y) is spent on either asparagus (A) or shmoos (B). Since income is limited, asparagus can be traded for shmoos as long as the family stays within its income constraint (Equation 1). Subtracting P_aA from each side yields:

$$P_bB = Y - P_aA. \qquad \text{(Equation 2)}$$

Finally, we can solve for the amounts of B, given certain purchases of A, if we divide Equation 2 by P_b:

$$B = Y/P_b - P_aA/P_b. \qquad \text{(Equation 3)}$$

Equation 3 defines the budget constraint for the family in Figure 6.

Because both asparagus and shmoos cost $1 per pound ($P_a = P_b$), point v represents the situation where the family has $600 per week, all of which is spent on shmoos. Note that $Y/P_b = \$600/\$1 = 600$ pounds of shmoos. Point z represents just the opposite: all income is spent on asparagus, nothing is spent on shmoos.

The slope of the budget line equals $(-P_a/P_b)$ and is equal to -1 since the prices of shmoos and asparagus are the same. Thus, as income changes, the family's budget line moves in or out, but as long as the ratio of the two prices remains the same, the slope of the budget constraint will not change.

The budget line pivots if the price of asparagus doubles to $2 a pound. A consumer with a $600 weekly income would now be able to buy a maximum of only 300 pounds of asparagus but could still buy as much as 600 pounds of shmoo. Alternatively, if the price of asparagus fell to 50 cents a pound, up to 1,200 pounds of asparagus might be purchased from a $600 income. Budget lines reflecting various possible prices for asparagus, with the price of shmoos still at $1 a pound and with a $600 weekly budget, are shown in Figure 7.

The Nature of Indifference Curves

Suppose that we picked two arbitrary combinations of shmoos and asparagus, bundle x and bundle y shown in Figure 8. Indifference analysis assumes that you always prefer more of each good to less, and that you either (a) prefer bundle x to y, (b) prefer y to x, or (c) are indifferent (don't care) between bundle x or bundle y.[6] Suppose that you prefer x to y. Now let us create a new bundle z by adding small amounts of asparagus or

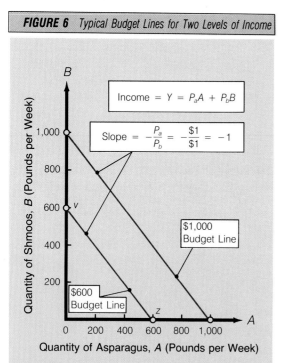

FIGURE 6 Typical Budget Lines for Two Levels of Income

Quantity of Shmoos, B (Pounds per Week)

Income = $Y = P_aA + P_bB$

Slope = $-\dfrac{P_a}{P_b} = -\dfrac{\$1}{\$1} = -1$

$1,000 Budget Line

$600 Budget Line

Quantity of Asparagus, A (Pounds per Week)

Budget lines depict the maximum possible combinations of goods available to consumers with given incomes and faced with specific prices. The slopes of budget lines reflect the relative prices of goods and higher incomes yield higher budget lines. The budget line facing a consumer is analogous to the production-possibilities frontier facing society.

6. Steven Plaut argues that the assumptions of indifference analysis are so unrestrictive that his cat is a rational consumer: it choses between bundles (tuna, milk, dry food) in an orderly way and suffers from diminishing marginal utility. See his "Illustrating the Rationality Assumption" in Ralph Byrns and Gerald Stone, eds., *Great Ideas for Teaching Economics,* 4/ed. (Glenview, IL: Scott, Foresman/Little, Brown, 1989).

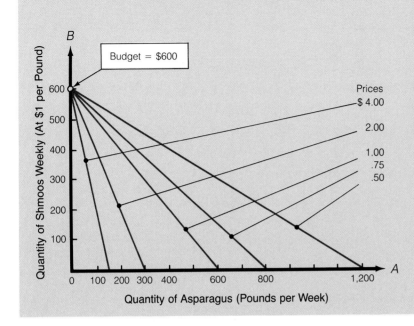

FIGURE 7 Budget Lines for $600 Income with Various Prices for Good A

Prices
$ 4.00
2.00
1.00
.75
.50

Budget = $600

All else being equal, as the price of asparagus falls, the budget line expands and becomes less and less steep. This reflects the declining price of asparagus relative to its alternatives. Alternatively, as the price of asparagus declines, more and more can be purchased if the entire budget is spent on asparagus.

shmoo or both to combination *y* until you are indifferent between *x* and the new bundle *z*. These bundles are shown in Figure 8.

Indifference curves reflect a consumer's preferences and connect all bundles of goods between which the consumer is indifferent. In Figure 8 we have connected the points representing the combinations where you are indifferent between *x*, *z*, and similarly desirable bundles. This is an **indifference curve.** Indifference curves have the following properties:

1. Every possible combination of goods is on some indifference curve.
2. Indifference curves are negatively sloped since you will have to get more of one good in order to maintain your level of satisfaction when you give up some of the other good.
3. Indifference curves that are further from the origin are preferable because they represent larger bundles of goods.
4. Indifference curves never intersect.
5. The slope of an indifference curve reflects the *relative* subjective prices (marginal utilities) of the goods, $-MU_a/MU_b$.
6. Indifference curves are convex (bowed in toward the origin).

FIGURE 8 Typical Indifference Curves

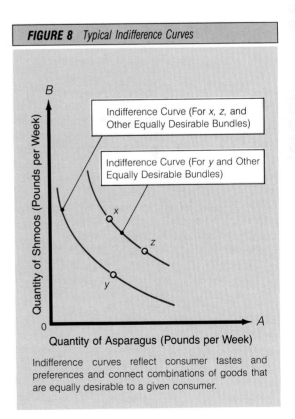

Indifference Curve (For *x, z,* and Other Equally Desirable Bundles)

Indifference Curve (For *y* and Other Equally Desirable Bundles)

Indifference curves reflect consumer tastes and preferences and connect combinations of goods that are equally desirable to a given consumer.

The first five of these properties should be fairly obvious. The sixth is predicated on diminishing relative marginal utilities. In this context, this means that consumers prefer variety to monotony. The following example asks you to use your intuition to show why.

Suppose that steak is your favorite meat and that you almost despise chicken. What would happen if your meat intake were restricted to steak for a solid year? We would bet that you would sacrifice a few steaks for a box of fried chicken. The more you have of a single thing, the more you are willing to give it up to have a given larger amount of something else. This preference for variety over sameness causes indifference curves to be bowed toward the origin (convex). You should try to prove this to yourself, using a graph before proceeding.

Consumer Equilibrium

Figure 9 shows a $600 weekly budget line when the prices of shmoos and asparagus are both equal to $1 a pound, as well as various indifference curves for one consumer. Indifference curve I_2 represents the highest level of satisfaction this consumer can attain, given her level of income. Any other indifference curve that is on or below the budget line (for instance, I_0 or I_1) represents a lower level of satisfaction than I_2. Indifference curves such as I_3 would be preferable to I_2, but are not feasible since they lie beyond the consumer's budgetary constraint.

Indifference curve I_2 is tangent to the budget line at point z. The amounts of asparagus and shmoos associated with point z (A_0 and B_0) represent this consumer's best choices for consumption, given current prices and income. Notice that at point z the slopes of the budget line and I_2 are equal. This means that relative market prices (the slope of the budget line) equal relative marginal utilities (the slope of the indifference curve).

Thus the slope of indifference curve I_2 at point z is $-MU_a/MU_b$ and the slope of the budget line at point z is $-P_a/P_b$. Since both are equal at point z, then

$$\frac{-MU_a}{MU_b} = \frac{-P_a}{P_b}$$

(Equation 4)

or, in equilibrium,

$$\frac{MU_a}{P_a} = \frac{MU_b}{P_b}$$

(Equation 5)

Notice that indifference curve analysis yields the same condition for *consumer equilibrium* as the principle of *equal marginal utilities per dollar*, but we do not have to assume that consumers have "utilometers" and accurately measure utility for each product.

FIGURE 9 *A Consumer's Equilibrium*

An individual's satisfaction is maximized by consuming the bundle of goods that occurs where an indifference curve is just tangent to his or her budget line. Any other affordable bundle is less satisfying; any more desirable bundle (than z, in this case) cannot be afforded.

Deriving Individual Demand Curves

We will keep this person's income at $600 weekly and look at changes in the consumer's equilibrium as the prices of asparagus vary. This permits us to extract the information necessary to graph a demand curve for asparagus.

Panel A of Figure 10 superimposes a set of indifference curves on the budget lines from Figure 7 for a person with $600 weekly income who faces various possible monetary prices for asparagus. We have connected the equilibria for these different prices of asparagus with a **price-consumption curve.** Each point on this curve represents a different price for asparagus on its corresponding $600 budget line. At these points of tangency, indifference curves reflect consumer preferences and budget lines reflect income constraints. Each tangency point represents maximum satisfaction given the constraints of this consumer's income and the relative market prices of the two goods. We can find the quantity of asparagus associated with each price by dropping a line from the price-consumption line to the horizontal (asparagus) axis. Voila! We have the information needed to build a demand schedule and draw a demand curve, as in Panel B of Figure 10. Points a through e in the two panels correspond.

FIGURE 10   Consumer Equilibria and the Price Consumption Curve

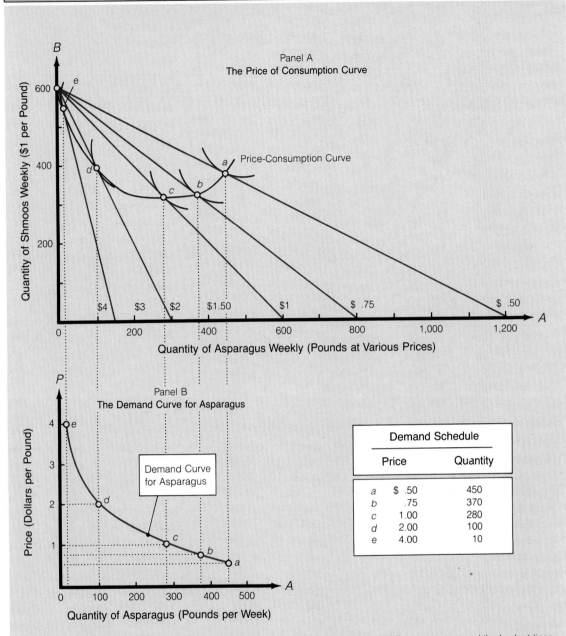

The price-consumption curve is traced out by the successive tangencies between indifference curves and the budget lines representing alternative prices for asparagus. In Panel A, points a through e show declining consumption of asparagus as its price rises. Points a through e from the price-consumption curve in Panel A translate into points a through e on the demand curve in Panel B.

CHAPTER 22

Foundations of Producer Decision Making

economic costs of
production

production

short run

long run

production functions

average physical product
of labor

marginal physical product
of labor

law of diminishing
marginal returns

fixed costs

variable costs

average costs

marginal cost

least cost production

economies of scale

technological change

Underpinnings for consumer demands were discussed in the previous chapter, but supply has been addressed only intuitively. In this chapter we explore how production relationships link inputs and outputs to determine costs and shape managerial decisions about how much to produce and which technology to use. Then, in the next few chapters, we investigate how competition for consumers' dollars differ in intensity across industries and interacts with production costs to determine prices, output, and consumer purchases.

First, however, we need to examine production and costs in detail. We begin by distinguishing economic costs from accounting costs. Then we survey economic facets of typical production processes. This leads to a detailed discussion of various production costs in both the short run and the long run and finally, to a brief overview of the mysteries of technological change.

Economic Costs of Production

You have learned that the value of the best alternative forgone is the economic cost of anything from lard to romance. One way to break down production costs is to view them as either explicit or implicit costs.

Explicit Costs and Implicit Costs

Explicit costs require outlays of money. For example, wages paid employees, rent payments, and utility bills all involve explicit outlays of funds. **Implicit costs** are the opportunity costs of resources the firm's owner makes available for production with no direct cash outlays. Examples include the value of an entrepreneur's labor and the interest that could be earned were the owner's assets not partially tied up in the business. Both implicit and explicit costs bear heavily on rational business decision making.

Economic costs of production *include both explicit and implicit costs.*

Bookkeeping is a mechanical exercise focused only on explicit costs; it primarily records flows of funds and provides a base for computing taxes. Accounting requires evaluation of data for decision making—a purpose not well served by many common bookkeeping practices. Fortunately, accounting standards increasingly conform to the economic view of cost. Let us look at some problems that may emerge if implicit costs are overlooked.

Economic and accounting definitions of profit seem identical:

Profit *is a firm's total revenue minus its total cost.*

Economists, however, include explicit and implicit costs when they think of *total* (opportunity) *cost,* while bookkeepers often fail to include in total cost many implicit costs incurred by the owners of a business.

Here is an example of how **economic profits** and **accounting profits** differ. Imagine that two years after receiving your college degree your annual salary as a stockbroker is $23,000, you own a building that rents for $10,000 yearly, and your financial assets generate $3,000 per year in interest. On New Year's Day, after deciding to be your own boss, you quit your job, evict your tenants, and use your financial assets to establish a health food restaurant and pogo-stick shop.

At the end of the year, your books tell the following story:

Sales of food	$ 18,000
Sales of pogo sticks	112,000
TOTAL SALES REVENUE	**$130,000**

Cost of food	$ 23,000
Cost of pogo sticks	62,000
Employees' wages	20,000
Utilities	5,000
Taxes	5,000
Advertising expenses	10,000
TOTAL (Explicit) COSTS (subtract from revenue)	**−$125,000**

"Congratulations," your bookkeeper pipes up, "you made a
NET (accounting) PROFIT of .... **$ 5,000!"**

"Hold it just a moment," you say, "I have studied economics. You forgot to subtract my *implicit* costs. Being in this business caused me to lose as income:

Salary	$ −23,000
Rent	−10,000
Interest	−3,000
TOTAL IMPLICIT COSTS	**$ −36,000."**

"Therefore, I've had an economic profit that's negative, a
LOSS of .... **$ −31,000**

Even a dolt should recognize that this hare-brained business is a loser!"

If, however, you enjoy operating the restaurant and pogo-stick shop more than your best alternative (being a stockbroker), your higher job satisfaction is called psychic income. *Psychic income* refers to nonmonetary satisfaction gained from an activity and is an implicit revenue. Bookkeeping profit usually overstates economic profit because psychic income rarely exceeds an entrepreneur's implicit costs.

The explicit cost data used to compute accounting profit for tax purposes are more accessible than the additional implicit cost data needed to estimate economic profits or losses. Thus, taxes and national income accounts are based on accounting data. Business decisions tend to be rational, however, and so are most frequently based on expected economic costs and profits.

Good accountants recognize that conventional bookkeeping costs and profits are inadequate; after calculating taxable profits, they subtract implicit costs from bookkeeping profit. This provides managers with a better picture of a firm's track record. Many firms experience positive accounting profits but economic losses; they fail even though bookkeepers view them as "profitable."

Normal Profits as Production Costs

One lesson in this example is that "normal" profit should be considered a production cost. If a firm's accounting profit is less than that normally received by firms with comparable levels of investment and risks, in the long run its owners will move their resources into ventures where at least normal profits are expected. Chronic subnormal accounting profit ultimately forces a firm to adapt or fail.

Economic profit occurs only when a firm's revenue exceeds *all* production costs; **economic loss** is a parallel concept that occurs when revenue fails to cover all economic costs of production. The two concepts differ only by sign. In a competitive market, economic profits and losses will be zero in the long run because profits attract new sellers like picnics attract ants; persistent economic losses (negative profits) cause firms to exit the market or perish. Economic profits or losses persist only when barriers limit entry into or exit from an industry. Profits spur competition and the growth of market supply, while losses are signals that society wants resources shifted elsewhere.

Production _____

Natural forces or accidents may make goods or resources more valuable for human use. For example, geothermal heat and pressure convert lumps of coal into diamonds, and the life processes of generations of flora and fauna make soil more fertile. Reliance on nature or luck would, however, yield goods sufficient to sustain only a slim human population, most of which would live a razor's edge existence. People's productive activities also enhance value.

> **Production** *occurs when goods are transformed to make them more valuable in form, place, possession, or time, and normally involves using knowledge to apply energy to transform materials.*

By "more valuable," we mean that the goods ultimately generate greater consumer utility.

Altering *form* entails reshaping the structures of materials; crude oil is less valuable than gasoline. Augmenting *place* utilities requires movement; a lobster is worth far more in a restaurant's glass tank than in the ocean. *Possession* utilities arise by shifting ownership rights from people who value goods less to those who value them more; realtors match home buyers who are moving into an area with sellers who are moving out. *Time* utilities are created when goods are made available when they are wanted most; speculators buy newly harvested wheat and store it to sell when wheat output is nil. Firms survive and prosper only by making goods more convenient in form, place, or time, or by making them the possessions of people who value them more highly.

Inputs and Outputs

Things that enter a production process are known as **inputs;** the transformed materials are **outputs.** Inputs include machine or labor hours, physical space (e.g., acres used yearly), raw materials, and partially processed (intermediate) products bought from other firms. A firm's output may be purchased by consumers, other firms, or government. Note that inputs and outputs are both *flow* concepts—they are measured per unit of time.

The Short Run and the Long Run

People often talk about the short-run versus the long-run consequences of an event. For example, in the short run, winning a pie-eating contest may give you a bellyache. If you repeatedly win pie-eating tournaments, in the long run you'll be able to get a job in a sideshow as Fatty _____ (fill in your last name). Short and long runs in economics (and pie-eating contests) refer to the completeness of adjustment rather than to time periods per se. Relatively fewer options are available to firms in the short run.

> *The* **short run** *is a period during which the amount of at least one resource is fixed and firms can neither enter nor exit a market.*

In the long run, however, a firm can completely adjust the amounts of all resources and can either enter or leave industries.

> *The* **long run** *is a period of sufficient duration for all feasible resource adjustments to any event to be completed.*

The specific time intervals required for different firms to achieve long-run adjustment differ markedly. Some firms could liquidate all their assets in days; others may take years. A child's lemonade stand may go out of business when it rains, but building a nuclear power plant can take decades. We will focus on short-run managerial decisions before considering longer planning horizons.

Production in the Short Run

Linkages between inputs and outputs are formalized for analytical purposes.

Production functions *summarize relationships between combinations of inputs and the maximum outputs that each combination can produce.*

Output = f(*inputs*) is an example of a production function, and is read as "output is a function f of inputs." The function f summarizes the current state of technology and specifies the amounts of output that can be produced from various combinations of inputs. In this context, technology encompasses current knowledge about production techniques, as well as such things as government regulations, weather, and the laws of physics and chemistry.

Production functions are commonly written $q = f(K, L)$ where q equals output, K equals capital services, and L equals labor services used per production period. (We will ignore land and entrepreneurship for now.) Suppose that our production engineers indicate that 1,000 swimsuits could be produced daily using 600 machine hours (75 sewing machines in continuous use per 8-hour shift) and 800 labor hours (100 workers during the 8-hour shift). The function f summarizes a given production relationship of this type. A technological advance raising productivity by 50 percent would require a switch from the f production function to, say, g. Now, $q = g(K, L)$, and 600 machine hours plus 800 labor hours now yields 1,500 swimsuits.

Imagine that five years after you finish your degree you are in the sand and gravel business. Most firms can vary labor more easily than any other basic resource. Thus, to keep things simple for now, we will assume that your nonlabor resources are all fixed in the short run because you have long-term leases on fixed amounts of capital equipment (trucks and bulldozers) and land, but that you control the amount of labor you hire.

If no one works in your business, production and revenue obviously will both be zero. Working alone, you might excavate and sell 10 tons of earth material daily. Suppose that you hire an assistant and find that production increases to 22 tons daily. Production more than doubled while labor inputs only doubled.

Does this mean your assistant is the better worker? Not at all.

Working alone, you must run the truck, handle all marketing, operate the bulldozer, keep the books—the list goes on and on. The cliché "Chief Cook and Bottlewasher" fits too closely for comfort. After hiring an assistant, you can drive the truck while your helper excavates, keep the books while your employee runs the bulldozer, and so on.

You are able to produce much more as a team than as separate individuals because of the gains from the specialization and *division of labor.* As you hire even more workers, you might find that specialization enables production to continue to rise more than proportionally for the first few extra workers. Eventually, however, the advantages of specialization will be overwhelmed as the law of diminishing marginal returns comes into play, and each extra worker adds less than the preceding worker did to total production.

Marginal and Average Physical Products of Labor

Suppose that you have hired several employees, and your work force is so specialized that you spend all your time pushing a pencil. Table 1 shows how you might apply some economic concepts you learned in college. If you know what total output is for each level of labor hired (columns 1 and 2), you can calculate output per worker by dividing total output (q) by labor (L). Output per worker (q/L) is called the average physical product of labor, or APP_L.

The **average physical product of labor** *equals total output divided by labor.*

These figures are entered in column 3 of the table.

You will also be interested in how much each extra worker adds to total output, a concept known as the marginal physical product of labor, or MPP_L.

The **marginal physical product of labor** *is the additional output produced by an additional unit of labor; computed by dividing the change in total output (Δq) by the change in labor (ΔL):$\Delta q/\Delta L$.*

Hiring decisions intended to maximize profit hinge on labor's marginal physical product. Extra

TABLE 1 *Total Output and the Average and Marginal Physical Products of Labor (Sand and Gravel Operation)*

(1) Workers per 8-hr. Shift (L)	(2) Tons of Sand and Gravel Removed Daily (q)	(3) Average Physical Product of Labor (q/L)	(4) Marginal Physical Product of Labor ($\Delta q/\Delta L$)
0	0	0	0
1	10	10.00	10
2	22	11.00	12
3	36	12.00	14
4	52	13.00	16
5	70	14.00	18
6	86	14.33	16
7	100	14.28	14
8	112	14.00	12
9	122	13.55	10
10	130	13.00	8
11	137	12.45	7
12	143	11.92	6
13	148	11.38	5
14	152	10.85	4
15	155	10.33	3
16	157	9.81	2
17	158	9.29	1
18	158	8.78	0
19	157	8.26	−1

workers will not be hired unless the extra revenue from their marginal physical products would exceed the extra costs incurred in hiring them. Only workers who generate at least as much revenue as it costs to hire them will be employed, a decision we detail in a coming chapter. In most cases each worker's productivity (the MPP_L) will be higher as the amounts of other resources employed rise—a worker operating a bulldozer used on a section of dry river bed will produce more sand and gravel than a shovel wielder digging on a city lot.

The MPP_L is calculated by looking at small differences in the amounts of labor used and the resulting changes in production. With large numbers of workers (as at a steel mill), we would divide a given change in the amount of labor (ΔL) into the resulting change in output (Δq) to approximate the MPP_L. ΔL equals one worker for a small firm like your sand and gravel operation. The marginal physical products of labor ($\Delta q/\Delta L$) for your firm are reported in column 4 of Table 1.

The **total product curve** for your sand and gravel operation, as graphed in Panel A of Figure 1, relates

production and various levels of labor inputs, holding other resources constant.[1] Panel B shows the corresponding marginal and average physical products of labor.

The Short-Run Law of Diminishing Marginal Returns
A problem of congestion emerges as your organization grows. Your dump trucks' passenger compartments become crowded and more time is wasted at the excavation site waiting to load trucks that arrived earlier. A second challenge emerges from coordinating increased work effort: ensuring that the left hand knows what the right hand is doing, limiting coffee breaks to thirty minutes, and so on. Table 1 and Figure 1 indicate that congestion and loss of coordina-

---

1. Note that total product curves and production functions are not the same things. A production function allows all inputs to vary, while the total product curve assumes that only one input changes. We are using labor as the variable input, but had we held labor constant and varied capital (or land), the analysis would be quite similar, although the specific curves would differ.

tion eventually become so severe that the seventeenth worker adds only one ton of material per day, the eighteenth's contribution is nil, and hiring the nineteenth worker actually yields a loss of output.

The decline in extra output as extra workers are employed might seem a consequence of hiring better workers first and then hiring mediocre or inferior workers. This is unnecessary to explain diminishing

As more and more labor is employed, total output (Panel A) initially increases at an increasing rate because of the advantages of labor specialization. In this range, the marginal and average physical products of labor both grow (Panel B). As congestion begins to emerge, total output continues to grow, but at a falling rate. In this range, average physical product continues to climb, but marginal productivity diminishes. Once marginal physical product falls below average physical product, average physical product begins to fall. However, the total product continues to rise until the marginal physical product is zero. This occurs when congestion or other problems are so severe that further labor inputs cause declines in output.

marginal returns. In fact, we might assume that all workers were clones from a robot factory. Every worker is then the last or marginal worker because if you fired any one of them, you would have one less employee. Declining amounts of capital, land, and supervision per worker cause marginal physical products to diminish as the number of workers grows, and this occurs regardless of the qualities of the individual workers.

The **law of diminishing marginal returns** *occurs when successive equal increases of variable resources (e.g., labor) are added to some fixed factor influencing production (such as capital or land); although productivity may rise initially, marginal physical products must eventually decline.*

In the short run, diminishing marginal returns are encountered because at least one resource is fixed. It is impossible to increase all resources proportionally; capital and land per worker fall as more workers are hired, inevitably leading to diminishing additions of output as extra labor is hired. This basic economic law is without exception. Were it not for diminishing returns, enough food might be grown in a flower pot to feed the world.

Table 1 and Figure 1 reflect the outputs produced if various numbers of workers put in 8-hour days. The advantages of specialization enable each of the first five workers to add more than the preceding worker to total output, but the forces that compel marginal productivity to diminish overwhelm any gains from further specialization for the sixth and subsequent workers.

Short-Run Production Costs _____

Production is tightly linked to the costs that shape business decisions. Now that we have studied production, we turn to the process that translates the total, average, and marginal physical products of labor into production costs. We have divided production costs into explicit and implicit costs. A different grouping is into components called fixed costs and variable costs. All production costs fall within these two categories, so total costs (*TC*) equal total fixed costs (*TFC*) plus total variable costs (*TVC*), or

$$TC = TFC + TVC.$$

Business people commonly refer to fixed costs as *overhead,* while variable costs are often called *direct costs* or *operating costs.*

Fixed Costs

History is bunk.
　—Henry Ford

Sunk costs are sunk.
　—Anonymous

Every firm has at least one resource that is fixed in the short run, which implies that its short-run cost cannot be varied; this is a fixed cost. Most implicit costs are fixed costs. Since they were previously incurred, fixed costs are also known as *historical* or *sunk costs.*

Fixed costs *are the sum of all short-run costs that are not related to the level of production.*

For your sand and gravel operation, fixed costs would include such things as business licenses, the value of your time, rent you are obligated by a lease to pay, principal and interest on leases for trucks or other equipment, utility hookup charges, and franchise fees. You might be required to make payments during each period, but these fixed costs are unaffected by your firm's output.

Fixed Costs and Decision Making Suppose that you bought an extravagant imported bicycle and were dismayed when its price was slashed two weeks later. Then a broken leg persuaded you to sell the bike to cover the unexpected medical bills. What is *least* relevant to the price you should charge (*a*) the price you paid, (*b*) the current sales price, (*c*) storage costs, (*d*) expected enjoyment from riding after you get out of your cast, or (*e*) the current prices of similar used bikes?

If you chose answer (*a*) to this question, you may intuitively understand the irrelevancy of fixed cost for rational decision making, a point illustrated in Focus 1. Many people are astounded when told that fixed costs have no bearing on rational decisions about how much to produce, how much to charge for your output, and so on.

Sunk Costs in Stud Poker

In the following example, intended to help you see why fixed costs are irrelevant, all you need to know about stud poker is that any hand with four similar cards (four 7s) beats any hand with three identical cards (three queens and two 10s, for example).

Suppose that a notoriously poor player is dealing five-card stud, and deals four players plus himself one card each in the hole (face down), then one card each face up. Both you and the player to your left have aces showing. With **? A,** she bets $10,000 (we might as well fantasize a bit). You peek at your hole card and discover that you have a second ace—**A A**—so you call.

The dealer, showing **? 3** is the only other player who calls. (We told you he was a bad player.) The dealer rolls the player on your left a seven—**? A 7,** you another ace—**A A A,** and himself another three—**? 3 3.** Having three aces yourself, you hope the dealer has three 3s and you bet $25,000. The dealer calls, but the other player folds her hand. You are then dealt a king—**A A A K,** and the dealer rolls a third three for himself—**? 3 3 3.** Afraid that the dealer (a wild man) has four 3s, you reluctantly call his $50,000 bet. Now the dealer deals you a second king. You have **A A A K K:** a full house with aces up! He blithely rolls another 3, so he is

sitting with **? 3 3 3 3.** (The lunatic probably has something like a 6 in the hole.) He bets a dime. *The Big Question:* Should you call the bet? *The Answer:* If you are rational, absolutely NOT. No matter what the dealer has in the hole, you lose, because a hand with four of a kind beats a full house. Why should you lose another dime? The $85,000 you put in the pot is no longer yours. It is a sunk cost and, so, is irrelevant to your rational decision.

Fixed costs are meaningful only to the extent that, like history or archaeology, we can learn from them. Since they are fixed, there is a sense in which no alternative exists so that the opportunity costs of fixed resources are zero, at least in the short run. Therefore, the only costs that should affect production decisions are those that vary with output because there are alternatives to incurring these costs.

Variable Costs

Such expenses as labor costs, gasoline, truck maintenance, and office supplies will be positively related to the amount of business your sand and gravel operation does.

Variable costs *are costs incurred when a firm produces and vary with the level of production.*

Any costs incurred only when a firm produces are variable costs. If variable costs were exactly proportional to the number of tons of earth processed, the relationships between output and fixed, variable, and total costs would be as depicted in Figure 2. Total fixed costs (*TFC*) are unaffected by production. In the figure, total variable costs (*TVC*) are assumed to be exactly proportional to output. Thus, the constant slope of the total variable cost curve equals the variable cost incurred per ton processed. The total cost (*TC*) curve is the vertical summation of the fixed plus variable cost curves.

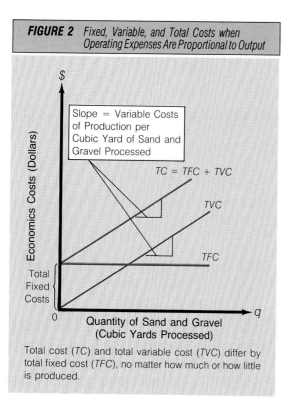

FIGURE 2 *Fixed, Variable, and Total Costs when Operating Expenses Are Proportional to Output*

Slope = Variable Costs of Production per Cubic Yard of Sand and Gravel Processed

$TC = TFC + TVC$

TVC

TFC

Economics Costs (Dollars)

Total Fixed Costs

Quantity of Sand and Gravel (Cubic Yards Processed)

Total cost (*TC*) and total variable cost (*TVC*) differ by total fixed cost (*TFC*), no matter how much or how little is produced.

After you understand this simple linear model, we can consider more realistic cost situations, as represented in Table 2 and Figure 3 by the data for your sand and gravel business. Labor is assumed to be the only variable resource in the short run and the supply of workers is perfectly elastic at $50 per 8-hour shift. You may hire as many workers as you wish from this horizontal labor supply curve. All other resources and costs are assumed constant, and total fixed cost is assumed to be $100 per day.

The total physical product curve (*TPP*) in Figure 1 shows the amounts of labor (*L*) required to produce varying levels of output. When we multiply the horizontal (labor) axis of Figure 1 by the wage rate (*w*) it becomes the total wage bill ($w \times L$) incurred for each level of labor you might hire. (Basic relationships are unchanged when any function is multiplied by a constant.) Wages are the only variable costs of production, so this wage bill equals total variable cost (*TVC*—column 4 in Table 2). Thus, the relationship between the quantity of output and total variable costs is the *TVC* curve in Figure 3.

When total fixed costs (*TFC*) are added vertically to the *TVC* (wage bill) curve, we have a picture of

TABLE 2 *Total Output, Total Costs, and Fixed and Variable Costs (Sand and Gravel Example)*

(1) Workers per 8-hr. Shift (L)	(2) Tons of Sand & Gravel Removed Daily (q)	(3) Wages per Worker (8 hrs. Daily) (w)	(4) Total Variable Cost (w × L) (TVC)	(5) Total Fixed Cost (TFC)	(6) Total Costs (TVC + TFC = TC)
0	0	$50	0	$100	$ 100
1	10	50	$ 50	100	150
2	22	50	100	100	200
3	36	50	150	100	250
4	52	50	200	100	300
5	70	50	250	100	350
6	86	50	300	100	400
7	100	50	350	100	450
8	112	50	400	100	500
9	122	50	450	100	550
10	130	50	500	100	600
11	137	50	550	100	650
12	143	50	600	100	700
13	148	50	650	100	750
14	152	50	700	100	800
15	155	50	750	100	850
16	157	50	800	100	900
17	158	50	850	100	950
18	158	50	900	100	1,000
19	157	50	950	100	1,050

FIGURE 3 Total Costs, Total Fixed Costs, and Total Variable Costs (Sand and Gravel Example)

The total cost (TC) and total variable cost (TVC) curves are "parallel" because the difference between them is total fixed cost (TFC), which is constant. Both first increase at a decreasing rate, because total product (from Figure 1) initially increases at an increasing rate. Then, as total product continues to rise, but at a decreasing rate, TC and TVC rise at increasing rates.

how your total costs (TC) vary with output. We need to explore costs a bit more, however, before we launch into decision making. Notice that if you turn Figure 3 sideways, it "mirrors" Panel A in Figure 1. Variable costs reflect wages and labor inputs, and labor inputs determine the amounts of output, so there is a natural, close relationship between total cost, production, and the amount of labor employed. Now we will explore other costs that are closely related to the average and marginal products of labor.

Average Costs

Some definitions will enable us to examine costs more completely.

Average costs *equal total costs divided by output.*

Average total cost (ATC) is the total cost incurred per unit of output, and is sometimes termed *unit cost,* or simplified to *average cost* and is equal to TC/q. *Average fixed cost* (AFC) is the fixed cost per unit of output or TFC/q. *Average variable cost* (AVC) is the variable cost per unit of output or TVC/q. Table 3 lists these costs for your sand and gravel operation.

You have analyzed the total costs of excavating various amounts of earth, so computing average costs only requires dividing these totals by the output level. Total costs are comprised of fixed and variable costs, so average total cost (ATC) equals average fixed cost (AFC) plus average variable cost (AVC). Proof? Total cost = total fixed cost + total variable cost, so

$$TC = TFC + TVC.$$

Dividing both sides by output (q) yields,

$$\frac{TC}{q} = \frac{TFC}{q} + \frac{TVC}{q}$$

and thus,

$$ATC = AFC + AVC.$$

We will develop graphs of these averages to show you how they are typically related to production.

Average Fixed Costs Just because total fixed costs do not vary with output does not mean that the AFC curve is horizontal. AFC = TFC/q, where TFC is constant. Figure 4 shows how the AFC is related to the output of your excavation operation, calculated in column 6 of Table 3. Total fixed costs are a constant amount so that, as output increases, fixed costs per unit of output decline—a process that many managers describe as spreading overhead through high volume.[2]

Marginal Cost

Graphs for ATC and AVC will be easier to understand if we first introduce marginal cost, which is the most important cost concept for decision making.

---

2. Notice that if we arbitrarily select any two points on the AFC curve (say, *a* and *b*), the rectangles formed by dropping horizontal and vertical lines to the axes have identical areas ($100). (Since AFC = TFC/q, multiplication of AFC by q yields TFC: TFC/q × q = TFC, which is constant.) Thus, the AFC curve is a rectangular hyperbola. Recall that unitary elastic demand curves are rectangular hyperbolas.

TABLE 3 *Average Total Costs, Average Fixed Costs, Average Variable Costs, and Marginal Cost*

(1) Workers per 8-hr. Shift (L)	(2) Tons of Sand and Gravel Removed Daily (q)	(3) Total Variable Cost (w × L) (TVC)	(4) Total Fixed Cost (TFC)	(5) Average Variable Cost (3)/(2) (AVC)	(6) Average Fixed Cost (4)/(2) (AFC)	(7) Average Total Cost (5) + (6) (ATC)	(8) Marginal Cost (Δ3)/(Δ2) (MC)
0	0	0	$100	—	—	—	—
1	10	$ 50	100	$5.00	$10.00	$15.00	$ 5.00
2	22	100	100	4.54	4.55	9.09	4.17
3	36	150	100	4.17	2.78	6.95	3.57
4	52	200	100	3.85	1.92	5.77	3.13
5	70	250	100	3.57	1.43	5.00	2.78
6	86	300	100	3.49	1.16	4.65	3.13
7	100	350	100	3.50	1.00	4.50	3.57
8	112	400	100	3.57	0.89	4.46	4.17
9	122	450	100	3.69	0.82	4.51	5.00
10	130	500	100	3.85	0.77	4.62	6.25
11	137	550	100	4.01	0.73	4.74	7.14
12	143	600	100	4.20	0.70	4.90	8.33
13	148	650	100	4.39	0.68	5.07	10.00
14	152	700	100	4.60	0.66	5.26	12.50
15	155	750	100	4.84	0.65	5.49	16.67
16	157	800	100	5.10	0.64	5.74	25.00
17	158	850	100	5.38	0.63	6.01	50.00
18	158	900	100	5.69	0.63	6.32	—
19	157	950	100	6.05	0.64	6.69	—

FIGURE 4 *Average Fixed Costs*

Quantity of Sand and
Gravel (Cubic Yards per Day)

Since total fixed costs (TFC) do not vary with output (q), increases in output cause average fixed costs (AFC = TFC/q) to decline. Business people refer to this as "spreading their overhead."

Marginal cost (MC) *is the change in total cost associated with producing an additional unit of output.*

Since $TC = TFC + TVC$, any change in total cost necessarily emerges from changes in either fixed or variable costs:

$$\Delta TC = \Delta TFC + \Delta TVC.$$

Dividing this equation by a small change in output (Δq) reveals that

$$MC = \frac{\Delta TC}{\Delta q} = \frac{\Delta TFC}{\Delta q} + \frac{\Delta TVC}{\Delta q}.$$

But output does not affect fixed costs, so $\Delta TFC/\Delta q = 0$ and

$$\boldsymbol{MC = \frac{\Delta TC}{\Delta q} = \frac{\Delta TVC}{\Delta q}.}$$

Thus, marginal cost equals the changes in either the total cost or the total variable cost incurred in producing an additional unit of output; changes in fixed cost are definitionally zero. Marginal cost for your firm is listed in column 8 of Table 3.

Figure 5 shows how average variable cost (AVC) and marginal cost (MC) change as you processed var-

FIGURE 5 Marginal Cost and Average Variable Cost

Average Variable Cost (AVC) and Marginal Cost (MC)

$

6.00

4.00

2.00

0

50 100 150

q

Quantity of Sand and Gravel
(Cubic Yards per Day)

MC

AVC

The average variable cost curve falls when marginal cost is below it, and rises when marginal cost exceeds average variable cost. Average variable cost is at its minimum when $AVC = MC$. Both curves are U-shaped because, initially, gains from specialization push AVC and MC down. However, as output is expanded, diminishing returns are encountered and the MC and AVC rise.

ious amounts of earth. Why are these cost curves **U**-shaped? Recall that the marginal physical product of labor (MPP_L) initially rose as you hired more workers but then fell when diminishing marginal returns were encountered. This means that the labor costs of additional output (its MC, in this case) initially decline, but diminishing returns ultimately cause marginal costs to rise as more workers produce higher outputs. Similarly, the average physical product of labor (APP_L) initially rose, but eventually declined as more workers were employed. This causes the **U**-shape of average variable cost curves. In a moment we will detail these relationships between production levels and costs.

Graphically Summing Average Costs   In Figure 6 we tack an average fixed cost (AFC) curve onto a graph with typical **U**-shaped marginal cost (MC) and average variable cost (AVC) curves. Summing verti-

cally the AVC and AFC associated with each output level yields the average total cost (ATC) curve depicted. Notice that as output increases, differences between the AVC and ATC curves shrink. This convergence of ATC and AVC occurs because their vertical differences equal AFC, which falls as output rises. We now take a look at how costs relate to production.

Relating Costs to Production

Comparing Figures 1 and 3 allows you to see one way that total costs are related to total physical product. Before we use graphs to show the connections between average physical product and average costs and between marginal physical product and marginal cost, we will outline the relationships with a little algebra.

Recall the simplifying assumption for your sand and gravel firm that all nonlabor resources were fixed. Therefore, total variable cost (TVC) equals the wage bill ($w \times L$), and average variable costs ($AVC = TVC/q$) equal wL/q. Since the average physical product of labor (APP_L) is q/L, if we invert APP_L (it is then $1/(q/L) = L/q$) and multiply by the wage (a constant, w), we have calculated the average variable costs of production ($w/(q/L) = w/APP_L$). Algebraically,

$$AVC = TVC/q = wL/q$$
$$= w(L/q) = w(1/APP_L) = w/APP_L.$$

Only labor costs change as you process more tons of earth, so marginal costs ($MC = \Delta TC/\Delta q$) are simply the changes in the total wage bill associated with higher production: $MC = \Delta(wL)/\Delta q$. The wage rate is constant, so $MC = \Delta(wL)/\Delta q = w\Delta L/\Delta q$. Since the marginal physcial product of labor (MPP_L) equals $\Delta q/\Delta L$, we can invert the MPP_L, multiply by w, and arrive at the marginal cost of production. Again, the algebraic sequence is

$$MC = \Delta TVC/\Delta q$$
$$= \Delta(wL)/\Delta q = w\Delta L/\Delta q = w(\Delta L/\Delta q)$$
$$= w(1/MPP_L) = w/MPP_L.$$

Table 4 replicates the total, average, and marginal physical products of labor for your sand and gravel firm from Table 1. Using this data, you can now calculate average variable costs and marginal costs, reported in columns 6 and 7, respectively. You then calculate average fixed costs (column 8) by dividing fixed costs by the various possible output levels. Adding the AFC to the AVC then yields figures for the ATC of production (column 9).

FIGURE 6 Short-Run Costs of Production

As long as marginal cost (MC) is below average total cost (ATC) or average variable cost (AVC), then ATC and AVC, respectively, will fall when output is increased. When MC exceeds AVC or ATC, then AVC and ATC will rise as output is expanded. The ATC and AVC curves are generally **U**-shaped. Gains from specialization eventually are overcome by diminishing returns, so the ATC, AVC, and MC curves are all **U**-shaped. Higher levels of output spread a firm's overhead, so the AFC curve declines continuously. Notice that the MC curve intersects the AVC and ATC curves at their minimum values.

TABLE 4 Relating Production and Costs (Sand and Gravel Example)

(1) L	(2) Q	(3) (q/L) APP	(4) (Δq/ΔL) MPP	(5) w	(6) (w/APP) AVC	(7) (w/MPP) MC	(8) AFC	(9) ATC
0	0	—	—	$50	—	—	—	—
1	10	10.00	10	50	$5.00	$ 5.00	$10.00	$15.00
2	22	11.00	12	50	4.54	4.17	4.55	9.09
3	36	12.00	14	50	4.17	3.57	2.78	6.95
4	52	13.00	16	50	3.85	3.13	1.92	5.77
5	70	14.00	18	50	3.57	2.78	1.43	5.00
6	86	14.33	16	50	3.49	3.13	1.16	4.65
7	100	14.28	14	50	3.50	3.57	1.00	4.50
8	112	14.00	12	50	3.57	4.17	0.89	4.46
9	122	13.55	10	50	3.69	5.00	0.82	4.51
10	130	13.00	8	50	3.85	6.25	0.77	4.62
11	137	12.45	7	50	4.01	7.14	0.73	4.74
12	143	11.92	6	50	4.20	8.33	0.70	4.90
13	148	11.38	5	50	4.39	10.00	0.68	5.07
14	152	10.85	4	50	4.60	12.50	0.66	5.26
15	155	10.33	3	50	4.84	16.67	0.65	5.49
16	157	9.81	2	50	5.10	25.00	0.64	5.74
17	158	9.29	1	50	5.38	50.00	0.63	6.01

Average Product and Average Variable Cost   Figure 7 shows that when six workers are on the job (points *b*), average product is at its maximum (14.33 tons) and average variable cost is at its minimum value ($3.49). Because workers receive a constant wage, we can calculate the amount spent on labor when

AVC (which is wL/q) is at its lowest value. Symmetrically, from this wage bill, you can infer the amount of labor hired when average variable cost is minimized. This result can also be seen in Table 4.

Let us get away from technical descriptions for a moment and look at the intuitive result of this analy-

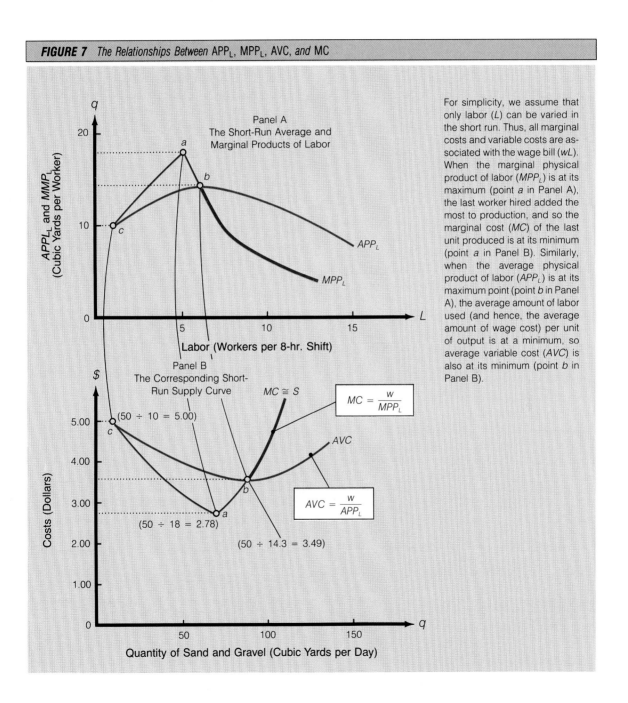

FIGURE 7   *The Relationships Between* APP$_L$, MPP$_L$, AVC, *and* MC

For simplicity, we assume that only labor (L) can be varied in the short run. Thus, all marginal costs and variable costs are associated with the wage bill (wL). When the marginal physical product of labor (MPP_L) is at its maximum (point *a* in Panel A), the last worker hired added the most to production, and so the marginal cost (MC) of the last unit produced is at its minimum (point *a* in Panel B). Similarly, when the average physical product of labor (APP_L) is at its maximum point (point *b* in Panel A), the average amount of labor used (and hence, the average amount of wage cost) per unit of output is at a minimum, so average variable cost (AVC) is also at its minimum (point *b* in Panel B).

sis. If the average amount produced per worker (APP_L) is at its highest value (point b in Panel A), then the average amount spent on labor per unit of output (AVC) logically must be at its lowest value (point b in Panel B).

Marginal Product and Marginal Cost   The marginal physical product of labor for your sand and gravel firm is drawn in Panel A of Figure 7; the corresponding marginal cost curve is in Panel B. These curves parallel the data in Table 4 and, thus, are reflections of each other. Marginal product is at its maximum (18 tons daily) and marginal cost is at its minimum ($2.78) if five workers are hired. Clearly, if the last worker hired produced the most (maximum MPP_L at point a in Panel A), then the last few tons of gravel processed cost the least (minimum MC at point a in Panel B). Some exercises at the end of this chapter will help you understand the tight relationship between various aspects of production and costs.

The relationship between production and costs is critical for the supply decisions of firms. Of course, production costs are only one dimension of a firm's decision matrix. The other side is demand. In the next few chapters, demand-originated constraints on firms facing various degrees of competition will be dealt with at length.

To simplify our analysis of short-run production and costs, only labor has been allowed to vary. The results are substantially unchanged, however, if we allow all resources but one to vary. Long-run production costs must be approached in a slightly different way because all of a firm's resources are variable. Technology is assumed constant in the long run, however, in part because most resources may be varied more quickly than technology is likely to change, and in part because technological changes tend to be somewhat unpredictable. We will deal with technological change later in this chapter.

Costs in the Long Run

The long run is a period sufficient for a firm to completely vary all resources and costs. No resource is fixed in the long run, so fixed costs become variable in the long run. Just when do fixed costs become variable? In the long run, you might sell previously fixed resources to other firms and rid yourself of obligations to meet fixed payments. The original obligation, however, remains a sunk cost—you cannot change history. Alternatively, you might obligate your firm to pay for more machinery, another short-run fixed cost. Until your name is on the dotted line for a new building or machine or to renew a franchise or lease, these are variable costs. Then they become fixed costs, but only for the short run.

In the long run, a firm may enter or leave an industry and either expand or contract the scope of any operation. More land, buildings, or new machinery can be acquired. Alternatively, landholdings can be reduced through sale or by allowing leases to lapse; old equipment can either be sold or fully depreciated and scrapped.

Least Cost Production

We allowed only labor to vary when we analyzed the short run, but all resources may vary in the long run. This allows managers who seek maximum profit to achieve technical efficiency in production by altering the resource mix so that the production cost for any given amount of output is minimized. Equivalently, they try to maximize the output produced for a given total cost.

Efficiency requires conformity with the law of equal advantage, which, applied to consumer behavior, yields the principle of equal marginal utilities per dollar we described in the preceding chapter. In a parallel way, the **principle of equal marginal productivities per dollar** applies the law of equal advantage to production: the marginal physical products of resources must be proportional to the prices of the resources. This means that

$$\frac{MPP_L}{w} = \frac{MPP_K}{i} = \frac{MPP_N}{r} = \cdots,$$

where MPP_K equals the marginal physical product of capital, MPP_N equals the marginal physical product of land, i equals the interest rate, and r equals the rent rate for land. To see why this equation works, suppose that the last $1 you paid in wages generated 1 ton of sand while the last $1 you spent on capital yielded 2 tons of sand. You would gain an extra ton of sand to sell if you shifted $1 away from labor towards capital.

Similar gains of output (or reductions in cost) are possible any time the marginal productivities of resources are not proportional to resource prices.

Least cost production *in the long run entails adjustments until this principle of equal marginal productivities per dollar is met.*

This principle suggests that relatively higher wages will induce a firm to *substitute* capital for labor. This has occurred in the auto industry in recent years as high labor costs have caused an army of industrial robots to invade the assembly line. Symmetrically, higher capital costs induce substitution towards la-

bor. When interest rates are high, investment in new capital falls and labor is substituted for capital. This should not give you the impression, however, that resources are only substitutes for one another. Resources may also be *complements* in production.

Labor productivity, for example, tends to be positively related to the capital and land with which labor has to work. Increases in nonlabor resources tend to raise labor's total, average, and marginal physical product curves, as shown in Figure 8. The close short-

---

FIGURE 8 *Total Product, Marginal Product, and Average Product Labor with Different Amounts of Land and Capital*

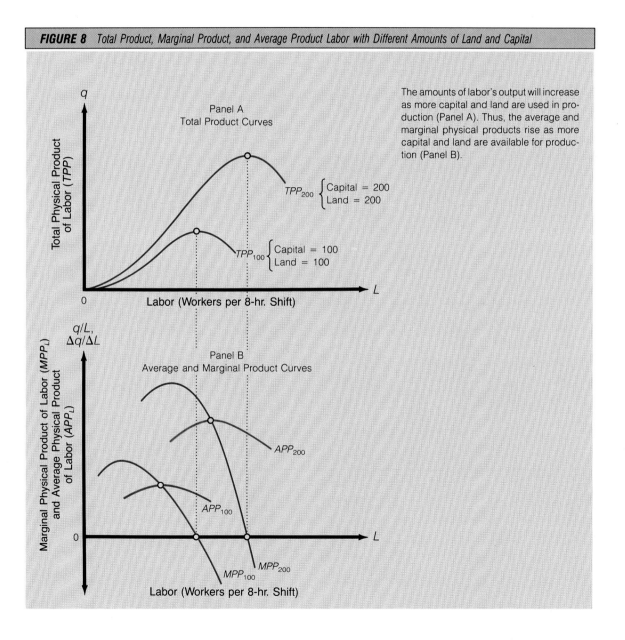

The amounts of labor's output will increase as more capital and land are used in production (Panel A). Thus, the average and marginal physical products rise as more capital and land are available for production (Panel B).

run relationships between production and costs (total, average, and marginal products and costs) suggest that in the long run, average and marginal costs will be influenced by all the resources used.

Possible changes in the short-run marginal costs and average total costs of a garment manufacturer with (*a*) 100, (*b*) 200, or (*c*) 300 sewing machines are highlighted in Figure 9. Other average cost curves associated with other plant sizes are also graphed. Under these short-run cost curves, we have placed an *envelope curve*, which reflects the plant sizes associated with the minimum average costs of producing each level of output. This envelope is the long-run average cost (*LRAC*) curve for the firm. Only a plant in which 200 machines are used to produce 4,000 garments per day yields the absolute minimum long-run average cost of production.

Economies and Diseconomies of Scale

Notice that the long-run average cost (*LRAC*) curve falls as output rises and then increases as output rises further.

Economies of scale *exist when long-run average costs decline as output rises, and larger firms will be more efficient than smaller firms.* **Diseconomies of scale** *occur in the range where average costs rise with increases in output.*

When diseconomies are encountered, reducing the scale of operations is efficient because it allows production at lower average costs.

It might seem that if all resources were expanded by some fixed proportion, output would necessarily expand by that same proportion. The advantages of specialization, however, may cause output to expand more than proportionally as the scale of operation initially grows from some small level. These advantages give rise to economies of scale, causing average production costs to fall.

On the other end of the spectrum, diseconomies of scale emerge because of the application for the long run of the law of diminishing returns. The firm can decide how much capital, land, or labor to use, but diminishing returns remain pervasive, even in

---

FIGURE 9 *The Long-Run Average Cost Curve*

Short-run costs depend on the fixed amounts of capital and land used in concert with labor, which, for convenience, we have assumed is the only variable factor of production in the short run. The long-run average cost (*LRAC*) curve is an envelope of short-run average cost (*SRAC*) curves. There are economies of scale if expanding land and capital result in declining average costs. Diseconomies of scale are present when average costs rise as capacity grows.

the long run, because it is impossible for a firm to vary all technological influences on production proportionally and simultaneously. For example, even in the long run, powerful firms cannot precisely tailor laws or regulations that influence production costs to suit themselves. Moreover, such influences on production as weather and gravity and the laws of physics and chemistry are totally beyond our control, and technology is assumed constant in the long run. Kenneth Boulding has been credited with a variant of the following example of diseconomies of scale that should drive the problem of long-run diminishing returns home to you.

Imagine that the Empire State Building shrinks until a high-jumping flea could hop over it. Now, increase the heights of both the flea and the Empire State Building proportionally until this sky-scraper is back to normal size. The flea would be bigger and heavier than an elephant. Can you imagine what strength would be required for it to make this leap now? Move over, Clark Kent.

One reason giant firms encounter diseconomies of scale is that managerial control deteriorates as more and more layers are added to any hierarchical organization. The mass of information that must be digested and then acted on grows, so that coordinating the activities of ever larger numbers of people becomes an ever more formidable task. Another problem is that huge vertical hierarchies require decision making at many different levels, and not all these decision makers will single-mindedly focus on doing everything with maximum efficiency to realize maximum profits. Like dinosaurs, organizations may become so large and clumsy that extinction becomes a real possibility.

Measuring Long-Run Average Costs

Any firm that fails to exploit economies of scale will have higher average costs than those of competing firms who do; firms that are too small for efficient operation must either grow or fail. Many people think that bigger firms can almost always produce at lower costs than smaller firms. While it is true that, in the long run, a firm must be large enough to exploit all feasible economies of scale, bigger plants may encounter diseconomies of scale and be forced to reduce the scope of their operations or sink.

Studies of Portugal's decline as a world power during 1400–1600 indicate that its wooden sailing ships were built too large for then-current technology. A large part of Portuguese shipping sank in bad weather, in part because of huge cargos. The U.K./French *Concorde* suffered such great cost disadvantages that it caused financial nosedives by the government sponsors of these bigger and faster passenger jets. How large do you think the optimal convenience store or gas station should be? How about atomic power plants or oil refineries? In the 1930s, the world's largest automobile assembly plant was Ford's River Rouge plant. It was never fully utilized, and today much of it has been torn down.

The ranges where economies or diseconomies of scale are actually encountered vary substantially among industries. Engineering estimates and the few statistical studies of cost functions that are available indicate that there are typically substantial ranges of output for which average costs are roughly constant, as shown in the middle of the *LRAC* curve in Figure 10.

An idea known as the *survival principle* suggests that clustering within an industry of firms or plants of a particular size is conclusive evidence about the effi-

FIGURE 10 *Typical "Real World" Average Cost Curves*

Although normal long-run average cost curves are **U**-shaped, there is typically a large range of production where average costs are constant and there are neither economies nor diseconomies of scale.

cient scale of operations. Some economists have tried to apply this principle to specific industries. Detractors, however, argue that survival depends on a multitude of factors (luck, monopoly power, business acumen, growth or decline of an industry, and so on) and thus, that some inefficient firms may survive, while some efficient firms fail. Measuring long-run costs is unavoidably imprecise, but the concept is still useful in analyzing industry adjustments to changes in demands, resource prices, or other events.

Firms and industries grow in response to profit opportunities or wither when economic losses persist. Long-run adjustments allow firms to enter an industry and grow infinitely or to shrink to zero and leave an industry; a firm can perfectly adjust its purchases of resources but, by assumption, we hold technology constant. We need to consider the possibility, however, that research and development may respond strongly to profit opportunities.

Technological Change _____

Much human progress arises from incremental improvements in the methods available to satisfy our wants.

> **Technological change** *increases output from a given set of resources, or allows distribution of previously unknown goods.*

Technological change takes two basic forms (*a*) improvements to nonhuman resources or (*b*) new knowledge about how to combine resources. New capital equipment that cuts production costs or a new strain of seed that boosts crop yields are examples of technological advances in nonhuman resources. New plowing methods that conserve topsoil or medical procedures that reduce a transplant patient's recovery time would be examples of new knowledge that represents technological progress.

Major technological breakthroughs tend to arrive in waves that influence numerous industries or forms of production. Predicting the direction of such sweeping technological advances is impossible. In a few instances, however, profit incentives within a specific industry cause the direction of technological change to be reasonably predictable.

Consider, for example, adjustments to higher energy costs. Most industries had adapted to low-cost, abundant energy sources during 1900–1973. Oil drove much of our technology. Then oil prices quadrupled in 1974–75 alone. Car buyers' demands for more mileage were echoed in many industries when firms scuffled to find energy-efficient technologies. New types of insulation were developed, as were production processes that recycled or used less heat.

Profit opportunities may induce new technologies that change outputs and production techniques or improve resources, and ultimately drive down costs. Some technological changes occur as quickly as a creative mind can solve a new problem. At other times, refining a technology is never ending. Whether technological advances will absorb less time than the short run for a firm or more time than the long run for production is uncertain. It is also uncertain whether giant or small enterprises are systematically favored by technological advance. Some new technologies enhance economies of scale; others work best when an operation is small. We can be sure, however, that technological advances make options available that reduce average production costs.

Table 5 summarizes recent estimates of the sources of U.S. economic growth. These estimates

TABLE 5 Contributions to the Growth Rate of Potential National Income (1929–1982)			
Growth Rate (national income)			3.20
Factor inputs (total)		2.03	
Labor	1.49		
Capital	.54		
Productivity (output/unit of input)		1.17	
Technological change	.68		
Reallocation of labor from farming	.25		
Economies of scale from growth of national and international markets	.27		
Miscellaneous factors	−.03		

Source: From "Contributions to 1929–82 growth rates," *Trends in American Economic Growth, 1929–82* by Edward F. Dennison. Copyright © 1985 The Brookings Institution. Reprinted by permission.

illustrate the impact of technological change on economic growth and productivity. Second only to growth in the labor force, technological change has accounted for over 20 percent of long-term economic growth and over half of our productivity gains during the last half century.

Predicting the precise duration and effect of technological change is impossible, so we usually consider only the long-run adjustments of entry and exit into an industry, or the shrinkage or growth of a firm as we examine the economic responses to changing circumstances in the next few chapters.

This chapter concludes this part of the book. You have used marginal concepts to examine both utility analysis (a foundation for demand) and production and costs (the foundations of supply). You will find all these concepts, and elasticity analysis as well, linked in the coming chapters as we examine business decisions about what prices to charge for output and how much to produce.

CHAPTER REVIEW: KEY POINTS

1. Economic costs include both explicit and implicit costs. *Explicit costs* involve outlays of money for goods or resources. *Implicit costs* are the opportunity costs of resources provided by a firm's owner. Payments for rent, electricity, and wages are explicit costs, whereas the values of the owner's labor and capital are implicit costs.

2. Bookkeeping rarely considers implicit costs, while both implicit and explicit costs are included in economic costs. Consequently, *accounting profits* often overstate the economic profitability of an enterprise because the opportunity costs of owner-provided resources are ignored.

3. A *production function* expresses a relationship between inputs and output. Production transforms goods to make them more valuable in form, place, time, or possession. A *total physical product curve* shows how output is affected as the amount of only one input changes.

4. The *short run* is a period in which at least one resource and one cost are fixed. In the *long run* all resources can be varied, but technology is assumed constant. These periods, therefore, are not defined by time, but rather by the nature of the adjustment process.

5. The *average physical product of labor* (APP_L) equals q/L. The *marginal physical product of labor* (MPP_L) equals $\Delta q/\Delta L$, and is the output generated by an additional unit of labor.

6. When increasing amounts of a variable resource are applied to a fixed resource, although the marginal physical product of the variable factor may initially rise, beyond some point its marginal product inevitably falls according to the *law of diminishing marginal returns*.

7. A firm's total costs can be separated into *fixed costs* (or *overhead*) and *variable* (or *operating*) *costs*. Fixed costs do not vary with output and do not alter rational decisions. Leases, utility hookup charges, opportunity costs of an owner's resources, and other overhead expenses are fixed costs in the short run. Wages paid employees, bills for raw materials, and other costs that change when output is changed are variable costs.

8. When total fixed costs and total variable costs are each divided by output, *average fixed costs* (AFC) and *average variable costs* (AVC) are obtained, respectively. Summing the two yields *average total cost* (ATC). *Marginal cost* (MC) is defined as the additional cost of producing one more unit of a good and equals $\Delta TC/\Delta q$.

9. Firms can enter or leave an industry in the long run because all resources are variable. The *long-run average cost curve* (LRAC) is an *envelope curve* under all short-run average cost curves (different-sized plants). It shows the minimum long-run average costs for each output level. Long-run average cost curves typically have *economies of scale* (LRAC falling) over some portion of the curve, but eventually exhibit *diseconomies of scale* (LRAC rising).

10. Measuring long-run costs is a complex and difficult problem. One method is to examine the size (and cost structure) of firms that have been successful and have "survived" in an industry over a long period of time, but reasons other than efficiency may explain why one firm survives while another fails.

11. *Technological progress* increases output from given resources. New technology resides in new knowledge or improved nonhuman resources, and results in new products or lower costs. Technological improvements account for much of our long-term economic growth and rising productivity.

PROBLEMS

1. Your microcomputer firm's labor requirements for various levels of output are described in Table 6.
   a. Fill in the columns for APP_L and MPP_L.
   b. Use graph paper to plot curves for the total, average, and marginal physical products of labor.
   c. Assume that wages are the only variable costs, and that each employee is paid $10,000 annually. Fill in this table for average variable costs (AVC) for each level of labor. (Note: average variable costs are measured per unit of output.) Now compute marginal costs for each level of labor employed.
   d. What happens to average and marginal costs as production is expanded?
2. A weekly total product schedule for your car wash is listed in Table 7. Plant and overhead (fixed) costs are $2,000 and the weekly wage is $300.
   a. Complete the table.
   b. Does this table describe the short-run or long-run? Why?

FIGURE 11 Solving for Total Costs, Total Fixed Costs, and Total Variable Costs

c. If fixed costs rise to $4,000 per week, does the output where ATC is the lowest rise or fall?
3. Use Figure 11 to compute values for the following variables.
   a. Total costs (TC) when 40,000 and 80,000 units are produced.
   b. Total fixed costs (TFC).
   c. Total variable costs (TVC) when 40,000 and 60,000 units are produced.
4. Table 8 illustrates four short-run average cost schedules (curves).
   a. Use graph paper to plot all four short-run average cost curves and plot the envelope long-run average cost curve.

TABLE 6 Labor Requirements for a Microcomputer Firm

Labor	Output	APP_L	MPP_L	AVC	MC
0	0	—	—	—	—
1	30	—	—	—	—
2	70	—	—	—	—
3	120	—	—	—	—
4	200	—	—	—	—
5	260	—	—	—	—
6	300	—	—	—	—
7	335	—	—	—	—
8	350	—	—	—	—

TABLE 7 Car Wash Total Product Schedule

Labor	Output	TVC	TC	AFC	AVC	ATC	MC
0	0	—	—	—	—	—	—
1	82	—	—	—	—	—	—
2	230	—	—	—	—	—	—
3	450	—	—	—	—	—	—
4	700	—	—	—	—	—	—
5	900	—	—	—	—	—	—
6	1,050	—	—	—	—	—	—
7	1,130	—	—	—	—	—	—
8	1,180	—	—	—	—	—	—
9	1,185	—	—	—	—	—	—

TABLE 8 Four Short-Run Average Cost Schedules

q(000)	SRAC_A	SRAC_B	SRAC_C	SRAC_D
0	—	—	—	—
1	7.50	—	—	—
2	5.40	6.00	—	—
3	5.00	4.50	5.50	—
4	5.30	4.30	4.30	—
5	6.00	4.75	3.85	4.50
6	—	5.70	3.50	4.10
7	—	—	4.00	3.80
8	—	—	4.80	4.00
9	—	—	6.00	4.75
10	—	—	—	6.00

b. Long-run minimum costs are reached at what level of output?

c. If government regulations limit output to 5,000 units, which plant size would you build?

d. Does the envelope curve touch each short-run average cost curve at its minimum point? Why or why not?

EXERCISES

The following exercises will show you how closely production is related to costs.[3] Carefully noting how inflection points and maximums and minimums are related between these curves will pay off in deeper understanding of the material in this chapter.

1. If labor is the only variable input in the short run, and the wage rate (w) is fixed, then the total product curve can be converted into a TVC curve by multiplying the labor (L) axis by w. Draw a total product curve on a clean sheet of paper (as shown in Figure A), then turn the page over and rotate it 90 degrees clockwise. Hold it up to the light and you will see a TVC curve, assuming that $w = \$1$. Adding a constant amount equal to fixed cost to the bottom of the vertical axis results in a mapping of total cost, with quantity (q) on the horizontal axis.

---

3. These exercises were suggested by J. M. Swint in "Transitions from Production to Costs," in Ralph Byrns and Gerald Stone, eds., *Great Ideas for Teaching Economics,* 4/ed. (Glenview, IL: Scott, Foresman/Little, Brown, 1989).

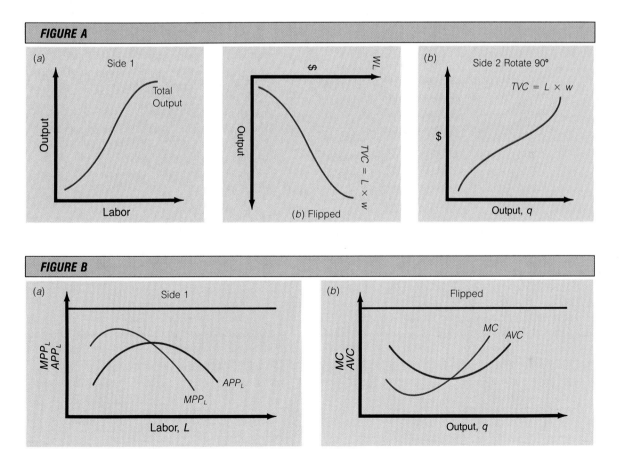

FIGURE A

FIGURE B

2. As shown in Figure B, when labor is the only variable resource, short-run marginal cost equals w/MPP_L and average variable cost equals w/APP_L. If you draw typical marginal physical product (MPP_L) and average physical product (APP_L) curves on a clean sheet of paper and then turn it upside down and backwards, against a light you can see that the relationship between MPP_L and APP_L is mirrored in what appear to be marginal cost (MC) and average variable cost (AVC) curves. This impression is basically correct. However, MC and AVC curves are mapped with quantity (q) on the horizontal axis, while the MPP_L and APP_L curves have labor (L) on the horizontal axis. Since labor input (L) and output (q) are positively related throughout the relevant range of production, this "mirrored" relation is only slightly warped—the maximum MPP_L and minimum MC correspond precisely, as does the maximum APP_L with the minimum AVC.

QUESTIONS FOR THOUGHT AND DISCUSSION

1. Suppose that you offered to buy pizza and cold drinks to bribe your friends to help you move into a new apartment and were deluged with offers of help. What problems would you encounter if too few actually showed up? How would this affect your "average cost" per box or stick of furniture moved? What are some possible "fixed factors" that would decrease the efficiency of your move and drive up its cost if too many people volunteered to help? How would this raise the cost of your move? How many big strong friends do you think would be the ideal number to accomplish this task?

2. Why does marginal cost decline if output increases at an increasing rate when additional workers are hired? Why does average variable cost decline as long as the marginal physical product of labor is greater than the average physical product of labor?

3. The average productivity of labor rises as long as labor's marginal productivity exceeds the average. We call this range of production Zone 1. Do you think firms would knowingly choose to operate in Zone 1, where hiring additional workers raises average productivity? Why, or why not? Would a firm ever operate in Zone 2, the range of output where the marginal returns from labor were positive but diminishing? Would they operate in Zone 3, where the marginal physical productivity of labor is negative? In what zone will firms operate? (A colleague once described another professor as a "Zone 3 personality." What do you suppose was meant by this remark? Have you ever worked with such a person?) Draw a typical total product curve and include average and marginal physical products. Identify these production zones. *Note:* Firms always try to operate in one of these zones, but most firms will avoid operating in the others.

4. Describe the forces that, as more and more labor is hired, cause output to rise at an increasing rate and then at a decreasing rate and that may ultimately cause output to fall as more labor is employed. How do these forces affect marginal and average costs in a similarly systematic fashion? Why? Can you think of any production processes that would not operate in accord with these general principles? What are they?

5. What are the similarities and differences between the ways the general law of diminishing returns (described in chapter 2) applies to consumption and to production?

6. Can you construct a total product curve for "knowledge of economics," with your study time as the variable (labor) input? How might this curve shift with variations in time with tutors, reference books, reading the *Wall Street Journal,* studying only when you are too tired to party, and so on. (Hint: review Figure 8.) At what point would the law of diminishing marginal returns come into play? Should you cease studying at the onset of diminishing returns? You may have heard people suggest that "when you reach the point of diminishing returns, it's time to quit." Are they using this term correctly?

OPTIONAL MATERIAL:
THE GEOMETRY OF TOTAL, AVERAGE, AND MARGINAL PRODUCTS

You have previously encountered the *rise/run* formula for calculating slope. We can use this formula to show geometrically just how total, average, and marginal physical products are related.

Pick any point on the total product curve (TPP_L) in Panel A of Figure 12. Now, using a straightedge (you can make one by folding a piece of paper), connect that point with the origin. The slope of this line is q/L, so if

---

FIGURE 12 *The Total, Marginal, and Average Physical Products of Labor*

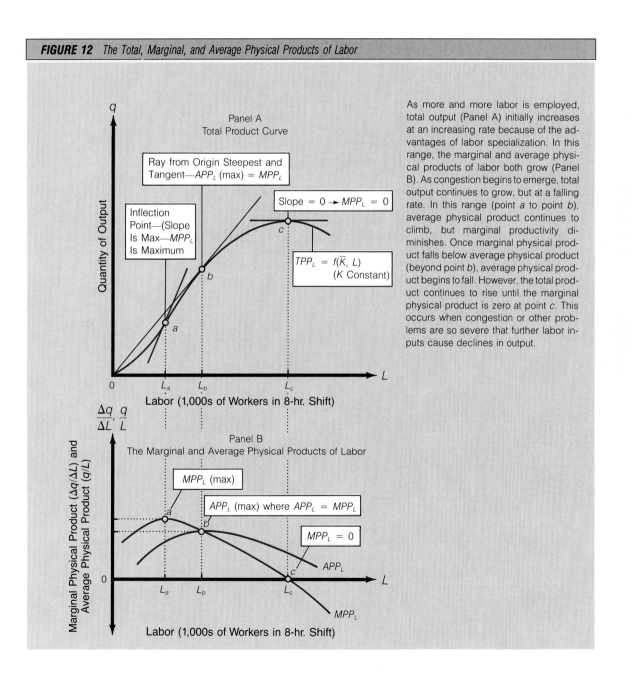

As more and more labor is employed, total output (Panel A) initially increases at an increasing rate because of the advantages of labor specialization. In this range, the marginal and average physical products of labor both grow (Panel B). As congestion begins to emerge, total output continues to grow, but at a falling rate. In this range (point *a* to point *b*), average physical product continues to climb, but marginal productivity diminishes. Once marginal physical product falls below average physical product (beyond point *b*), average physical product begins to fall. However, the total product continues to rise until the marginal physical product is zero at point *c*. This occurs when congestion or other problems are so severe that further labor inputs cause declines in output.

you construct bar graphs of all slopes of rays from the origin to all points on the total product curve, you would get a graph of the average physical product of labor. Since no ray from the origin to the total product curve is steeper than the one that is just tangent (touches) at point b, the amount of labor associated with b (on the horizontal axis) has the maximum value of the average product of labor (measured on the vertical axis of Panel B). Every point other than b on the total product curve lies on a ray with less slope than the one to point b. Therefore, the APP_L curve increases up to L_b, and declines thereafter.

We can use similar analyses of slope to derive geometrically the MPP_L curve. Let us start with an easy point, that at which the total product curve achieves its maximum value. A tangent to the total product curve at c has a slope of zero. The marginal physical product of labor is zero at c. A little more or less labor will not influence output appreciably. Tangents to the total product curve have a slope equal to $\Delta q/\Delta L$, which is the MPP_L. The MPP_L at L_c is zero. Let us look at some other points. At point b (labor = L_b), we know that the APP_L is at its maximum. Moreover, the ray from the origin to point b is just tangent to the total product curve. The APP_L is just equal to the MPP_L where the APP_L is maximized. If you now take your straightedge and place it tangent to the total product curve just below point b, you will see that it is steeper than the ray from the origin to point b. Implication? The MPP_L is greater than the APP_L at lower levels of labor usage than L_b. Now move the straightedge to a tangent point just to the right of point b. It will be less steep than the ray from the origin to point b. Thus, the MPP_L is below the APP_L if more than L_b labor is employed.

If you now move your straightedge so that it is tangent to the total product curve, and then keep it tangent to the TPP curve as we add more labor (move to the right), you will see that the straightedge lies below the TPP curve, and that the slope (MPP_L) increases up to point a. Thereafter, the straightedge tangent lies above the TPP curve, but its slope (the MPP_L) decreases. Conclusion? The MPP_L has its maximum value at point a (labor = L_a). Point a is known as an **inflection point.** Below point a, the TPP curve is increasing at an increasing rate; above point a the TPP continues to increase, but at a decreasing rate.

Let us summarize our findings about the MPP_L and APP_L:

1. The MPP_L equals zero when the TPP curve is at its highest value (point c).
2. The MPP_L equals the APP_L when the APP_L is maximized (point b).
3. The MPP_L is above the APP_L as we consider levels of labor where the APP_L is increasing (points left of b); the MPP_L is below the APP_L where the APP_L is falling (points to the right of b).
4. The MPP_L is maximized at the TPP curve's inflection point, which occurs at a level of labor below that where the APP_L is maximized (point a).

OPTIONAL MATERIAL: ISOQUANTS AND PRODUCTION

How the resource mix is varied in the long-run to maximize a firm's profit was touched on in our discussion of the principle of equal marginal productivities per dollar. Now we will address these long-run adjustments using slightly more sophisticated tools.

Isoquants

Producing any given amount of output can be accomplished with numerous combinations of inputs. For example, suppose you own a firm that packages and sells "Birdhouse" gourd seeds to home gardeners who grow houses for their feathered friends. You estimate that you can wholesale 10,000 cases of packaged seeds at $2 per case over the course of a season. Five of the many different possible combinations of capital (machines) and labor (workers) that will accomplish the job are listed in Table 9. These combinations run the gamut from a few machines with many workers hand-counting and stuffing the packages to production processes using numerous automated machines and very few workers to load seeds and watch the machines work. As you might expect, the process you would eventually gravitate to will be the one with the lowest cost. The last column of Table 9 depicts the total costs of packaging 10,000 cases of seeds if labor and capital each cost $1,000 per unit. To minimize the costs of producing 10,000 packages, you would employ three machines and three workers. The information in Table 9 is graphed in Figure 13; a smoothly curved line connects the five combinations from Table 9. This curve represents all possible mixtures of labor and capital that can produce 10,000 cases, and is referred to as an **isoquant.**

Isoquants are similar to the consumer indifference curves discussed in the optional material at the end of the preceding chapter, but with one major difference. Isoquants show constant levels of output, which is measurable; indifference curves show constant levels of satisfaction, which cannot be measured with precision. Just as the slope of an indifference curve reflects the relative subjective desirability of the two goods considered ($-MU_a/MU_b$), isoquants reflect the relative marginal productivities of the two resources ($-MPP_L/MPP_K$). We will develop this point more in a moment.

Isocost Curves

Superimposed on the isoquant for 10,000 cases of seeds in Figure 13 is a set of isocost curves. **Isocosts** represent different levels of expenditures by your firm for various combinations of labor and capital when the price of labor is $1,000 per unit and the price of capital is $1,000 per unit. These isocosts are close relatives of the consumer budget lines described in the optional material in the previous chapter. Just as the slope of the budget line reflects the prices of the two goods considered ($-P_a/P_b$), the slopes of isocosts reflect the prices of the resources considered ($-w/r$, where w is the wage rate and r is the unit cost of capital). Notice that production process a ($L = 9$, $K = 1$) results in total costs of $10,000, which lies on the $TC = $10,000$ isocost curve. As Figure 13 illustrates, 10,000 cases of seeds can be packaged at a minimum cost of $6,000 using three workers and three machines (point c). Graphically, costs are minimized for a given level of output where the isocost curve is just tangent to the isoquant, representing an output level of 10,000 packages. At this point, $MPP_L/MPP_K = w/r$. This is similar to the tangency between consumer indifference curves and budget lines in which maximum satisfaction is attained for a given bud-

TABLE 9 The Various Combinations of Labor and Capital that Will Package 10,000 Cases of "Birdhouse" Gourd Seeds

Point	Units of Capital (K)	Units of Labor (L)	Output: Cases of Gourd Seeds (q)	Total Cost if w = $1,000, r = $1,000 (TC)
a	1	9	10,000	$10,000
b	2	5	10,000	7,000
c	3	3	10,000	6,000
d	5	2	10,000	7,000
e	9	1	10,000	10,000

FIGURE 13 *Equal Output Curve (Isoquant) for Bird Seed*

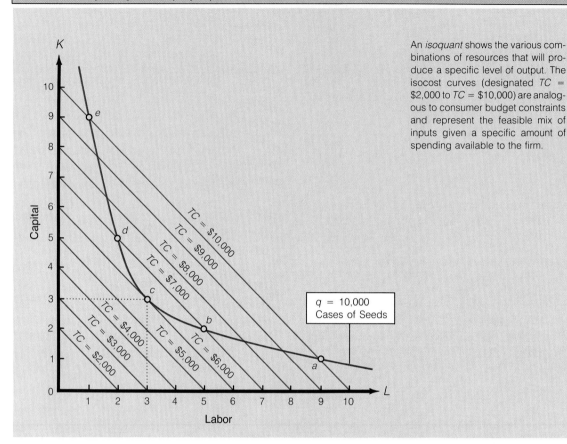

An *isoquant* shows the various combinations of resources that will produce a specific level of output. The isocost curves (designated TC = $2,000 to TC = $10,000) are analogous to consumer budget constraints and represent the feasible mix of inputs given a specific amount of spending available to the firm.

get. Recall (from the preceding chapter) that this point conformed to the principle of equal marginal utilities per dollar: $MU_a/MU_b = P_a/P_b$. Thus, in accord with the principle of equal marginal productivities per dollar, our result that $MPP_L/MPP_K = w/r$ means that maximizing profit requires the marginal payments to resource owners to be in accord with the resources' contributions to production.

One final note: Just as there are numerous isocost curves that represent different levels of cost, there are also numerous isoquants for production levels other than 10,000 packages. We have simplified the analysis by assuming that you expected 10,000 packages of seeds per season to be the most profitable level of output.

Substituting One Resource for Another

Let us take a moment to examine what happens to the marginal products of labor and capital relative to each other when we substitute labor for capital or vice versa.

When we change from production process c to production process b (move from point c to point b in Figure 13), we "give up" one unit of capital; to keep production constant, we must hire two units of labor, which suggests that the third machine does the work of two workers. When we move from point b to point a (giving up another machine), how many workers must be hired to keep production constant? The answer is four, suggesting that the productivity of four workers is required to replace that lost from the second machine. As we substitute more and more labor for capital (move down and to the right on the isoquant in Figure 13), ever-increasing amounts of labor are necessary to keep production constant. Alternatively, the marginal product of labor declines relative to that of capital. The opposite is true when capital is substituted for labor (movements to the left on the isoquant). Thus, the law of diminishing marginal productivity is reflected in the shapes of isoquants, which are convex (bowed in) from the origin.

Diminishing Marginal Product

The analysis in this chapter assumes that the typical production process eventually is subject to diminishing returns to the variable input. The same principle applies to production analysis using isoquants. Figure 14 illustrates the diminishing marginal physical product of labor when the amounts of other resources are held constant. In Panel A of Figure 14, capital is held constant at 3 units. Points *a* through *b* represent the amounts of labor needed to produce output levels ranging from 2,000 to 20,500 units. In Panel B, the total product curve is derived from Panel A when capital is fixed at 3 units, and shows diminishing returns to labor. As we add more labor to a fixed stock of capital, the increased output from hiring additional labor eventually falls.

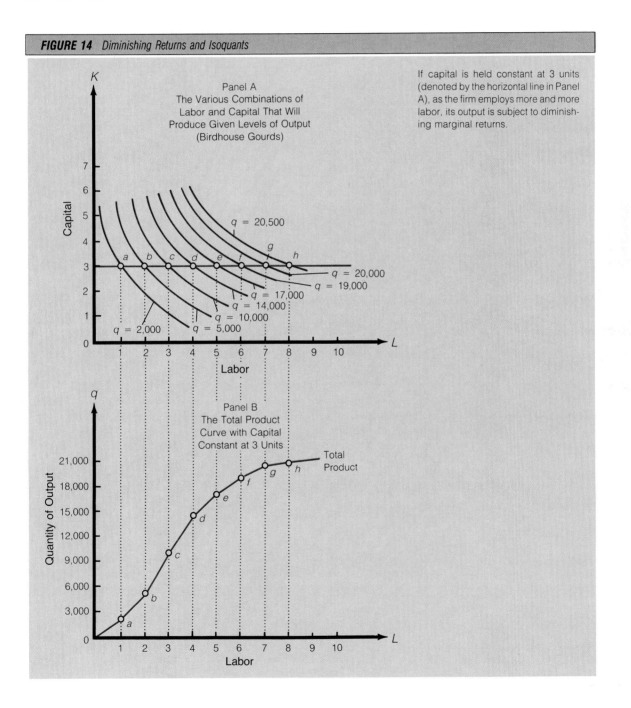

FIGURE 14 Diminishing Returns and Isoquants

Panel A
The Various Combinations of
Labor and Capital That Will
Produce Given Levels of Output
(Birdhouse Gourds)

If capital is held constant at 3 units (denoted by the horizontal line in Panel A), as the firm employs more and more labor, its output is subject to diminishing marginal returns.

Panel B
The Total Product
Curve with Capital
Constant at 3 Units

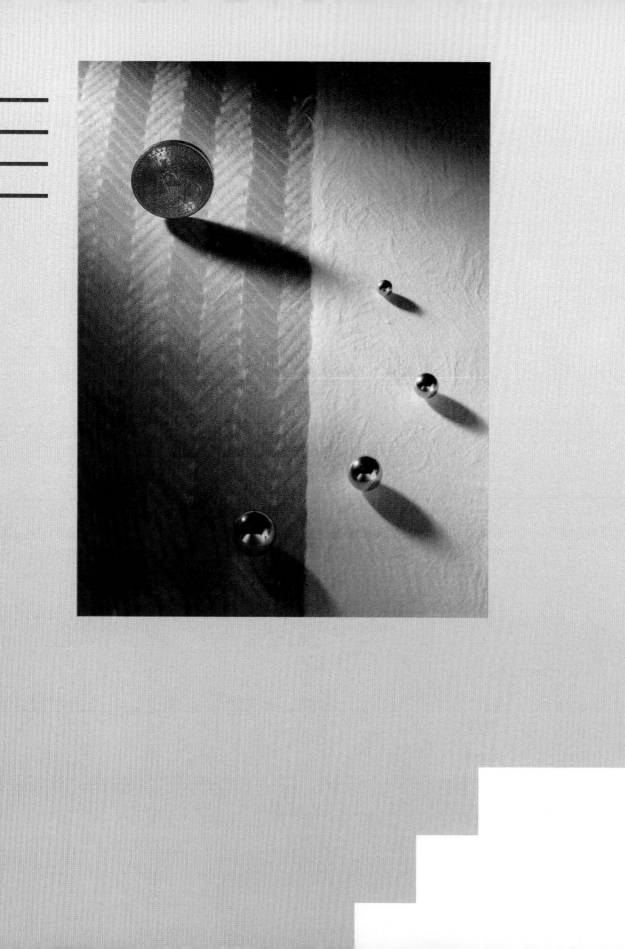

Vigorous competition is the norm for most landscapers, retailers, and home-builders. Other firms only broadly compete for customers: your local phone company may vie with book stores or travel agents for shares of your budget. Some firms specialize in such standard goods as lumber; others focus on such unique goods as organ transplants. A tiny town may support only one gas station, while high capital costs create monopolies in bigger markets: one giant firm, COMSAT operates most communications satellites.

The range of market structures shown in the figure indicates that several factors shape the extent of competition in an industry. We begin by analyzing pure competition in chapter 23. Then, in chapter 24, problems caused by monopolies are contrasted with the results of pure competition. Having dis-

cussed these extremes, we then survey the intermediate situations of monopolistic competition and oligopoly in chapter 25. Part 7 concludes with discussions of antitrust policies in chapter 26 and the regulation of business in chapter 27. Government antitrust actions and regulations are attempts to direct market allocations of resources and incomes in ways thought to be more economically efficient or socially preferable.

We need to discuss the power to set prices, or lack of it, before we study different output market structures. As the figure shows, purely competitive buyers and sellers have no choice but to accept the going price; their only real choices lie in the quantities they buy or sell. These buyers and sellers are called *price takers,* or *quantity adjusters.* For example, you are a quantity adjuster when buying food. You can buy as much or as little as you like, but you have very little leverage with which to dicker over the price.

Weak competition in some markets enables sellers to set prices, at least within some range. Because the demand curves that face them slope down, these *price makers* can manipulate prices only by simultaneously limiting the quantities produced and sold. For example, the international OPEC oil cartel was able to boost oil prices during the 1970s, but only by restricting output through maximum production quotas for each member country.

Any price-making firm is said to possess *monopoly power.* A firm need not be a monopoly per se to possess monopoly power. All it requires is some power as a price maker. Exactly where an industry is on the continuum of market structures can change dramatically over time. For example, the increasing intensity of international competition in recent years is one major reason why many firms that once had substantial power as price makers have lost much of their monopoly power. Before dealing with price makers, we will examine the behavior of price takers in a world of pure competition.

Monopoly	Oligopoly	Monopolistic Competition	Pure Competition
1. One-firm industry	1. Few firms	1. Numerous potential firms and buyers	1. Numerous potential firms and buyers
2. No close substitutes for products	2. Decision making is mutually interdependent	2. Differentiated products	2. Similar products
3. Substantial and effective barriers to entry	3. Major barriers to entry	3. No entry or exit barriers	3. No entry or exit barriers

Highly Concentrated Markets

Competitive Markets with Low Concentration

CHAPTER 23

The Competitive Ideal

Conscious rivalry among giant firms is not addressed by the model of pure competition, which focuses instead on an idealized market structure containing so many small competitors that any single firm's behavior is irrelevant to its competitors. In this fiercely competitive climate, firms lack any discretion about pricing and must be efficient merely to survive. This chapter opens with some requirements for a purely competitive market structure. Short-run pricing and output decisions are then explored, followed by a look at some long-run effects of competitive entry and exit. These results are evaluated and provide a benchmark for efficiency when evaluating other markets.

The World of Pure Competition ___

Certain structural conditions in purely competitive markets enable us to predict how prices and output are determined, or how they will change if circumstances change. A market is **purely competitive** if:

1. There are large numbers of potential buyers and sellers.

2. Firms in the industry produce a homogeneous (standardized) good.

3. Each buyer or firm is so small relative to the market that any one firm's decisions about its purchases or output will appreciably affect neither the total demand or supply of the good, nor its price.

4. Barriers to entry or exit are insignificant. This means that new firms can easily enter the industry if doing so appears profitable. Conversely, existing firms can leave the industry if they anticipate losses.

Generic office supplies, hair cuts, most agricultural products, floppy diskettes, and some other relatively homogeneous goods and services are produced in highly competitive markets. Each buyer or seller is too insignificant to affect the total demand or supply of the product single-handedly, leaving buyers and sellers in competitive markets as *quantity adjusting* **price takers;** they have no choice but to accept the price set by the market. This means that individual competitive buyers view the supply curves facing them as perfectly elastic (horizontal) at the going market price. Similarly, competitive sellers perceive the demand curves they confront as horizontal at the current market price.

Competition Versus Competing

Competition generally connotes rivalry among individuals or groups. We all grow up competing for grades, merit badges, positions on teams, and dates. Iowa farmers compete with other farmers. How do they set the prices for their corn, wheat, pigs, or soybeans? Do they argue that their products are superior and so should command a premium price? Obviously not. Nor do farmers compete by offering coupons or "instant winner bingo" to buyers.

Competitive price setting occurs for basic farm products (from eggs to sugar to orange juice concentrate), raw materials (coal or crude oil), and primary products (steel or lumber) on more than 240 business days each year at commodity exchanges spread across the globe. International markets cause most of these commodities to be traded in a climate approaching pure competition. Market prices are set in an auction environment for hundreds of goods by the bids and offers of thousands of buyers and sellers or their broker representatives.

Commodity exchanges seem chaotic to casual visitors. (There were examples of this in the movies *Trading Places* and *Wall Street.*) Most trading is by "public outcry." Wild-eyed traders angle various numbers of fingers over their heads and scream bids and offers on a huge crowded *trading floor*. The din rivals that during the opening kickoff at the Super Bowl. No single buyer or seller can sway prices as bids and offers are accepted or rejected. A trader may buy cotton for a Tokyo customer one minute and sell Georgia peanuts the next, but most traders are narrowly specialized.

Small farmers often sell their entire crop at the going market price in a single transaction. Farmers are examples of price takers.

Price takers *are buyers or sellers who are so small relative to a market that the effects of their individual transactions are inconsequential for total demands, supplies, or prices.*

Markets for precious metals also are so competitive that no single buyer or seller has much economic clout. If you struck gold at your sand-and-gravel site, you could sell all the gold you mined at the price fixed on the commodity exchange. This is shown in Figure 1. The demand curve facing a purely competitive firm is a horizontal line (**d**) at the market price (P_e). Competitive firms decide the quantities of output to produce and sell at current prices. Even firms mining hundreds of claims and using millions of dollars worth of equipment can sell gold only at the going price. This is why competitive firms are price takers. Purely competitive firms compete in one dimension—efficient production.

The stress on quantity decisions by pure competitors contrasts sharply with competition among carmakers, for example. It is difficult and costly for a new firm to enter the auto market. Cars are not standardized, and the pricing and output decisions of any of the big three U.S. automakers or their foreign counterparts clearly affect the sales of other producers. Advertising, styling, and aggressive marketing are as important as pricing strategy. These firms are rivals, but unlike purely competitive firms, they do not compete solely on the basis of efficient production of output at a market determined price.

Freedom of entry and exit is probably the most crucial ingredient in maintaining competition over time.[1]

Freedom of entry and exit *means that in the long run firms can enter an industry with no cost disadvantages relative to established firms, and old firms can costlessly transfer their resources to other industries.*

Entry and exit is relatively unfettered in many types of agriculture. Existing farms responded quickly to unusual profits in 1973–74 by expanding, and new farmers entered agriculture, causing gluts of many farm products. Then farm prices plummeted and entry faded. During 1977–85, many farmers went bankrupt or were haunted by the prospect of financial catastrophe.

---

1. *Contestable markets theory* contends that potent threats of entry alone yield the same results as pure competition regardless of how few firms are currently in an industry. The next three chapters deal more with this view.

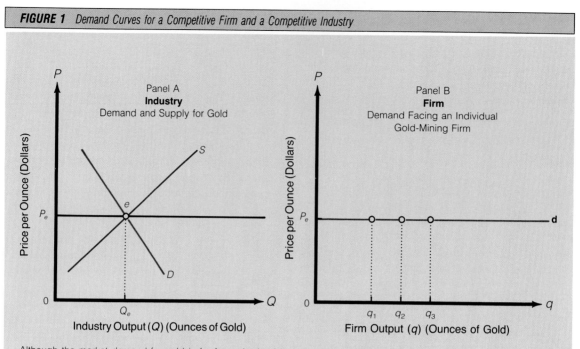

FIGURE 1 *Demand Curves for a Competitive Firm and a Competitive Industry*

Panel A
Industry
Demand and Supply for Gold

Price per Ounce (Dollars)

P_e

e

S

D

0

Q_e

Q

Industry Output (Q) (Ounces of Gold)

Panel B
Firm
Demand Facing an Individual
Gold-Mining Firm

Price per Ounce (Dollars)

P_e

d

0

q_1 q_2 q_3

q

Firm Output (q) (Ounces of Gold)

Although the market demand for gold is far from elastic, the demand curve facing an individual miner is perfectly elastic (horizontal). Competition forces small firms producing undifferentiated products to be *price takers*.

Few industries match all the assumptions of pure competition. But remember that a model should be no more complex than is required for the purpose at hand. (Models are judged by predictive accuracy and not by realism of assumptions.) Pure competition may be uncommon, but vigorous growth of international trade has made many markets more competitive in recent years.

You will learn that pure competition tends to be more efficient and seems more equitable than other market structures. For these reasons, pure competition has become a normative yardstick we use to judge other market structures. More importantly, many results from simple competitive models apply to markets that deviate in major ways from pure competition. For example, the competitive model underpins supply and demand analysis, which enables us to predict qualitatively the effects of certain events on prices and outputs. Understanding competitive reactions to changed circumstances allows us to use supply and demand analysis to explain everyday changes in prices and outputs. Not surprisingly, the range of potential adjustments differs markedly when we consider different time frames.

Supply Responses and Time _____

All decision makers gain flexibility as their time horizons expand. Industry responses to shifts in demand depend in part on how long firms have to adjust. Alfred Marshall, an eminent British economist, designed a way for economists to treat time systematically. Responses are classified as occurring in the **market** (immediate) **period,** the *short run* (*SR*), or the *long run* (*LR*). In general, the more time an industry has to adapt to changes in demands, the greater the impact on quantities and the less the effect on prices. Thus, the market elasticity of supply is positively related to the time allowed for an industry to adjust. In the market period, supply is perfectly inelastic because we assume, for simplicity, that inventories cannot be adjusted. Supplies are somewhat elastic in the short run and much more elastic in the long run.

This relationship is shown in Figure 2. Suppose that the original demand for gold is D_0, price is $600, and quantity sold is Q_0. If demand rises to D_1, existing gold stocks would rise to $850 per ounce during the market period to reflect mining firms' temporary inability to boost output. If the higher demand persists, the mines might boost output by hiring new workers, by paying overtime wages, or by using other short-run devices. The resulting hike in the quantity supplied by existing firms yields a short-run price of $725, which is below the $850 price per ounce immediately after demand rose to D_1. But prospectors will ultimately find more gold; as new gold mine owners respond to higher profitability, supplies will rise further and the long-run equilibrium price will fall to $650. In the long run, quantity changes will always be greater and price changes will be less for a given change in demand than in the market period or the short run. This occurs because potential adjustments in an industry expand when firms have more time to adapt.

Firms cannot modify production during a single market period to minimize losses or to exploit new profit opportunities when demands change. Firms can only partially adjust in the short run because at least one resource is fixed. Only in the long run are all resources variable so that firms can enter or leave markets as their owners choose. Given sufficient time, technology may even improve as miners seek new ways to exploit the higher market demand and price of gold. We will now study the short-run decisions of purely competitive firms before turning our attention to the long run.

Short-Run Competitive Pricing and Output

All firms are assumed to maximize profit, a process that can be described in several ways. The simplest explanation of short-run profit maximization is the total revenue minus total cost ($TR - TC$) approach.

*The **total revenue minus total cost approach** maximizes profit by maximizing total revenue minus total cost.*

FIGURE 2 *Industry Supply Response and the Market Period*

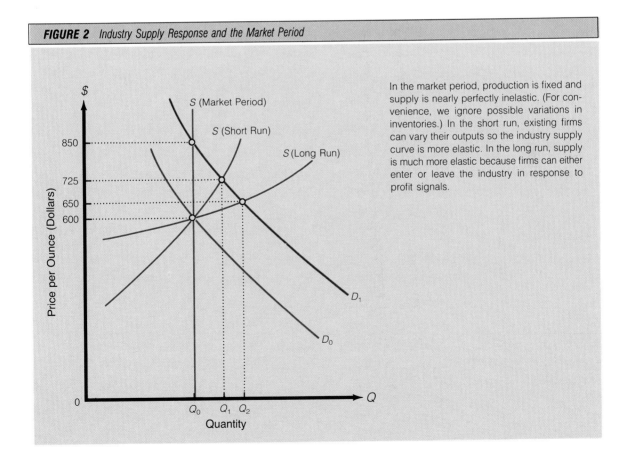

In the market period, production is fixed and supply is nearly perfectly inelastic. (For convenience, we ignore possible variations in inventories.) In the short run, existing firms can vary their outputs so the industry supply curve is more elastic. In the long run, supply is much more elastic because firms can either enter or leave the industry in response to profit signals.

Total Revenue Minus Total Cost Approach

A purely competitive firm is a price taker, so how much to produce (quantity adjustment) is its major decision.[2] Will producing and selling as much as possible maximize profits? The example outlined in Table 1 leads us to the answer. Suppose you can mine weekly gold output levels ranging from nothing to twelve ounces and that the market dictates a price of $600 per ounce. Whether you sell one ounce of gold or twelve, each ounce sells for $600 this week. The total revenue curve in Panel A of Figure 3 shows how revenue grows as output rises; its slope is constant at $600 per ounce of gold. If fixed costs are $570 weekly, the production costs associated with each level of output are shown in column 4 of Table 1 and graphed in Panel A as *TC*.

Subtracting total costs from total revenue is a straightforward way to estimate the amount of gold that maximizes profit. You can mine the amount where this difference—profit (π)—is the largest. Look at column 5 in Table 1; producing seven ounces of gold yields maximum profit—$1,200. In Panel A of

Figure 3, profit is maximized where the vertical distance between total revenue and total costs is greatest; in Panel B, profit is maximized where the vertical distance between the profit curve and the horizontal axis is greatest. The profit-maximizing level of output in this example occurs at seven ounces.

The chief lesson is that there are at least two sides to profit maximization, regardless of market structure. First consider the demand side (total revenue and price), then the supply side (production costs). Each must be taken into account to arrive at appropriate output and/or pricing decisions.

Notice also that two break-even levels of output are shown in both Table 1 and Panel A of Figure 3. *Break-even points* occur where total revenue equals total cost and economic profit is zero; these points are critical for decisions about entering risky lines of business. You would naturally like any risky activity to potentially break even at low levels of output and sales.

The total revenue minus total cost approach is easily understood. A more fruitful approach for operational decision rules, however, is the *marginal cost equals marginal revenue* (*MC = MR*) approach. The total revenue minus total cost (*TR − TC*) and the marginal revenue equals marginal cost (*MR = MC*) approaches yield mathematically equivalent results but arrive at profit maximization by different routes and provide different insights.

---

2. There are choices about what technology to use, or what kind and how much labor to employ. For simplicity, we lump all these as parts of the output decision, postponing our study of resource markets until later chapters.

TABLE 1 Hypothetical Cost Data for a Competitive Gold Miner

(1) Weekly Output in Ounces (q)	(2) Price per Ounce (P)	(3) Weekly Total Revenue (TR)	(4) Weekly Total Cost (TC)	(5) Weekly Profit (3) − (4) (π)
0	$600	0	$ 570	$ −570
1	600	$ 600	810	−210
2	600	1,200	1,000	200
3	600	1,800	1,240	560
4	600	2,400	1,530	870
5	600	3,000	1,920	1,080
6	600	3,600	2,410	1,190
7	600	4,200	3,000	1,200
8	600	4,800	3,690	1,110
9	600	5,400	4,480	920
10	600	6,000	5,370	630
11	600	6,600	6,360	240
12	600	7,200	7,450	−450

FIGURE 3 TR − TC Approach to Finding Maximum Profits

Panel A
Total Revenue, Total Costs, and Profit

- Break-Even Point
- Losses
- Profits = $1,200
- Losses
- Break-Even Point
- Maximum Profits Are Earned by Selling 7 Ounces of Gold

For a competitor who is a price taker, total revenue (TR = PQ) is exactly proportional to output. Diminishing returns imply that total costs (TC) rise at an increasing rate as output expands. Profit maximization entails producing where the difference between total revenue and total cost is *the greatest* (TR − TC = π).
Source: Table 1.

Panel B
Profits

- Break-Even Point
- Profits = $1,200
- Break-Even Point
- Losses
- π (Profit)

Weekly Output (Ounces)

Marginal Revenue Equals Marginal Cost Approach

In the preceding chapter, we spent a lot of time studying marginal cost. Now we need to analyze marginal revenue before turning to a discussion of how firms link these concepts to determine the most profitable output levels.

Marginal Revenue Marginal cost is the addition to total cost associated with the production of one more unit.

BIOGRAPHY

Alfred Marshall (1842–1924)

Few economists extend knowledge in any but their narrow areas of specialization. A handful of master economists, however, have broadly expanded the frontiers of economic analysis. Their names and ideas are scattered across these pages. Adam Smith, David Ricardo, John Maynard Keynes, Karl Marx, and, in our own time, Paul Samuelson have covered the gamut of economic theory. Alfred Marshall also belongs in this elite group.

Born in a middle-class London suburb, Marshall was destined for the ministry, according to his stern, evangelical father. An independent sort, Marshall refused a classics scholarship at Oxford and instead studied math at Cambridge. His exposure to philosophy led to Marshall's lifelong concern with poverty and other social problems that plagued industrial England. This concern led him to study economics, in which he excelled. Marshall's most famous student, John Maynard Keynes, referred to Marshall as the greatest economist of the nineteenth century.

Marshall was a careful writer who tried to avoid controversy. Many ideas that eventually appeared in his *Principles of Economics* (1890) were developed much earlier, but Marshall's patience and diligence paid huge and lasting dividends. Despite the many changes in economics since his death, large parts of economic theory remain distinctly Marshallian. His major contributions include the concepts of both short- and long-run *competitive equilibria, price elasticity of demand, internal* and *external economies of scale, increasing* and *decreasing cost industries, quasi-rent,* and *consumer surplus.*

Perhaps Marshall's greatest contribution was the way he worked time into economic analysis, bequeathing to subsequent generations of economists not only a valuable analytical tool, but also rules for its effective use. Marshall handled continuous economic change by invoking conditional clauses that he grouped under the term *ceteris paribus. Ceteris paribus* allows analysts to study the issue at hand narrowly and precisely by temporarily ignoring other sources of disturbance. This step-by-step approach facilitates treatment of broader issues that contain the narrow one; each bit of new knowledge allows more and more restrictions to be relaxed.

This method is illustrated in Marshall's treatment of demand, in which the number of consumers, their tastes, expectations, money incomes, and the prices of other goods are assumed constant when studying how equilibrium price and quantity are determined. As things change over time, however, each restrictive assumption may be relaxed in turn so that the analysis proceeds to a new equilibrium. Marshall also applied this approach with fruitful results to the theories of value and production. In so doing, he developed an analytical technique used to this day.

Marginal revenue *is defined as the increase in total revenue associated with the sale of one more unit of output.*

Consider your gold mine. The price of gold is set in the international commodity market for precious metals centered in New York, London, and Zurich, so mining firms are price takers. If the going rate for gold is $600 per ounce, a firm's marginal revenue is $600 per ounce sold, regardless of how many ounces individual firms sell. Remember that each gold mine is too small to affect the total market price or output.

Return for a moment to Figure 2. Individual mine operators perceive the demand curves that face them as horizontal at the $600 price. Each firm's perception of demand curves as perfectly elastic means that each mine operator expects total revenues to be exactly proportional to output because price is fixed and total revenue equals price times quantity ($P \times Q$). Thus, because the price is unaffected by the amounts sold by any firm, each ounce of gold is expected to generate marginal revenue equal to $600.

Look again at the data in Table 1. Column 2 reveals the market price to be $600 per ounce. Marginal revenue is the change in total revenue associated with the sale of one more unit, so as we go from five ounces to six ounces of gold sold, total revenue jumps from $3,000 to $3,600 weekly for a net change of $600. *Marginal revenue equals the price* (MR = P) *of the commodity in competitive markets.* Our next order of business is ascertaining how competitive firms use this price and cost information to maximize profits.

Profit Maximization

Suppose you have information about the marginal cost and the price of each unit of output. How much should be produced and sold? One rule of thumb for any firm (regardless of industry structure) might be: Do anything that brings in at least as much money as it takes away. This translates into economic jargon as the marginal revenue equals marginal cost rule.

The **marginal revenue equals marginal cost rule** *states that all profit-maximizing firms produce and sell anything for which marginal revenue is at least as great as marginal cost.*

Your revenue from selling one more unit of gold (from Table 2) is graphed in Figure 4 as the demand curve **d** ($P = MR = 600). Marginal cost from your cost data (column 7 in Table 2) is graphed as the *MC* curve in Figure 4. Consider what happens when you

TABLE 2	Cost Data for Your Competitive Gold Mine								
(1) Weekly Output in Ounces (q)	(2) Total Fixed Cost (TFC)	(3) Total Variable Cost (TVC)	(4) Total Cost (TFC + TVC) (TC)	(5) Average Variable Cost (TVC/Q) (AVC)	(6) Average Total Cost (TC/Q) (ATC)	(7) Marginal Cost ($\Delta TC/\Delta Q$) (MC)	(8) Price Equals Marginal Revenue (P = MR)	(9) Total Revenue (TR = PQ)	(10) Profit (π)
0	$570	0	$ 570	0	—	—	$600	0	$-570
1	570	240	810	$240.00	$810.00	$ 240	600	600	-210
2	570	430	1,000	215.00	500.00	190	600	1,200	200
3	570	670	1,240	223.33	413.33	240	600	1,800	560
4	570	960	1,530	240.00	382.50	290	600	2,400	870
5	570	1,350	1,920	270.00	380.00	390	600	3,000	1,080
6	570	1,840	2,410	306.67	401.67	490	600	3,600	1,190
7	570	2,430	3,000	347.14	428.58	590	600	4,200	1,200
8	570	3,120	3,690	390.00	461.25	690	600	4,800	1,110
9	570	3,910	4,480	434.44	497.78	790	600	5,400	920
10	570	4,800	5,370	480.00	537.00	890	600	6,000	630
11	570	5,790	6,360	526.33	578.19	990	600	6,600	240
12	570	6,880	7,450	573.33	620.83	1,090	600	7,200	-450

FIGURE 4 MR = MC *Approach to Finding Maximum Profits*

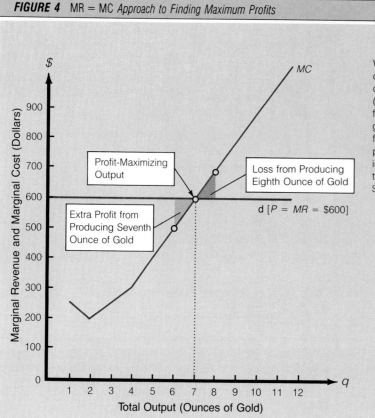

Whenever marginal revenue (*MR*) exceeds marginal cost (*MC*), a firm can increase its profit by expanding output. (Marginal revenue and price are identical for price-taker firms.) If marginal cost is greater than marginal revenue, then the firm is losing money on the last few units produced and will expand profit by reducing output. Thus, maximum profits require that *MR* = *MC*.
Source: Tables 1 and 2.

produce and sell the seventh ounce of gold. The extra revenue to your firm is $600, but the seventh ounce of gold only costs $590 to produce. Thus, extra profit from the sale of this seventh unit is $10. In fact, you will increase total profit by the shaded triangle below the demand curve as you increase output from six to seven ounces.

What would happen to profit if you produced the eighth ounce? You would receive only $600 for it, but its production costs are $690. You will lose $90 on the eighth ounce if you produce and sell it. Your profit will fall by the area of the shaded triangle above the demand curve as output rises from seven to eight ounces. Conclusion? Price and marginal revenue are identical in pure competition, so a profit-maximizing competitive firm produces until marginal cost equals price: $P = MR = MC$ for maximum profits, which, in this example, occurs at seven ounces. This analysis leads to a profit maximization rule that holds for firms ranging from pure competition to pure mono-

poly: all profit-maximizing firms produce and sell until marginal cost just equals the marginal revenue (*MR* = *MC*) derived from the sale of the good.

Marginal revenue and marginal cost data for your gold mine (from Table 2) are graphed in Figure 5, along with average total cost. The marginal revenue equals marginal cost approach reveals that seven ounces is still the profit-maximizing output level (point *e*). The *TR* − *TC* approach provides one way to compute total profit. Total revenue equals price times quantity; for seven ounces of gold at $600 per ounce, this is $4,200. Geometrically, this is the area bordered by 0*dec* in Figure 5. But how much is total cost? Since average total cost for seven ounces is $428.58 for each ounce (point *a*), the total cost for all seven ounces is $3,000 ($428.58 × 7 = $3,000). The area 0*bac* geometrically represents total cost (average cost times quantity). Thus, total weekly profit is $1,200 ($4,200 − $3,000), which is the shaded area *bdea* in Figure 5.

An alternative way to calculate total profit is to multiply average profit per unit times output. Price minus average total cost ($P - ATC$) equals average profit per unit, so average profit per unit when seven ounces are produced is the distance *ae* in Figure 5, which is $171.42 ($600 − $428.58). Thus, total weekly profit is still $1,200 ($171.42 × 7—the shaded area *bdea*, which also equals $TR - TC$). We cannot overemphasize that whether we maximize total revenue minus total cost or use the marginal revenue equals marginal cost approach, the solution is the same for the firm's profit-maximizing decision.

Figure 5 also shows what happens if the price of gold falls sharply. At roughly $385 per ounce, marginal revenue equals marginal cost at point *f,* or an output level of roughly five ounces. Average total cost, however, is in the $380 range, so the firm barely breaks even at a $385 price per ounce of gold. The break-even price in a competitive industry occurs

when the demand curve facing each individual firm (the price line) is tangent to the minimum point of the firm's average total cost curve. Typical firms will neither incur economic losses nor enjoy economic profits at such a price, so there will be no net tendencies for the industry to shrink or grow because of entry and exit. In a moment you will see that this break-even situation characterizes firms in purely competitive industries in long-run equilibrium.

Measuring profits may seem a precise process, but decisions must be made even though managers never perfectly predict the profit yielded by any major decision. What is important is the direction of change—will profit rise or fall if a firm adopts a certain policy? Expected marginal benefits (revenues) and costs are crucial for all types of decisions. For example, when public policy decisions are made about, e.g., tax structures, incentive systems, or various rules or regulations, the same kinds of questions

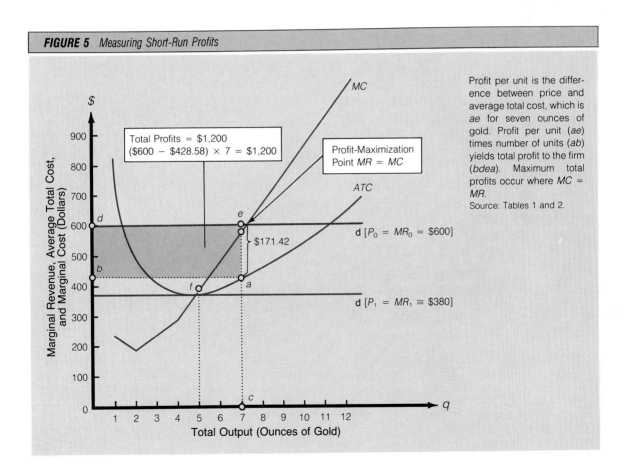

FIGURE 5 *Measuring Short-Run Profits*

Total Profits = $1,200
($600 − $428.58) × 7 = $1,200

Profit-Maximization Point $MR = MC$

$171.42

d [$P_0 = MR_0 = 600]

d [$P_1 = MR_1 \cong 380]

Profit per unit is the difference between price and average total cost, which is *ae* for seven ounces of gold. Profit per unit (*ae*) times number of units (*ab*) yields total profit to the firm (*bdea*). Maximum total profits occur where $MC = MR$.

Source: Tables 1 and 2.

arise: If a specific policy was altered, in what direction would social welfare, net consumer satisfaction, or business profits change? If decision makers know this, they can adjust towards an optimal output level.

Loss Minimization and Plant Shutdown
Alas, business is not always profitable. One of two choices must be made if sales revenues cannot cover costs. The firm will experience losses if it elects to produce and sell output. If the firm shuts the plant down, however, it will incur losses equal to fixed costs. Which decision will yield the smallest loss?

Assume that the demand for gold collapses and the price drops to $300 per ounce, as shown in Figure 6. Should you try to mine any gold? Our rule that a firm maximizes profit or minimizes losses by equating marginal revenue and marginal cost seems to indicate that optimal weekly output in this instance will be four ounces (point *a*). At this level of output, total revenue ($1,200) fails to cover total costs

($1,530) yielding a loss ($330 weekly). The result is the same if we apply an average revenue minus average cost approach to this situation. In Figure 6, average revenue (price) is $300 and average cost is $382.50. Thus, the average loss per unit of output of $82.50 times four ounces yields a total loss of $330 (the colored area *efca* in Figure 6).

If you close the mine rather than sell gold below its average total cost, losses would equal fixed costs, or $570 in our example. Remember that fixed costs are incurred whether or not any output is produced. These include such expenses as rent payments, utility charges (for minimum service), administrative overhead, and insurance. Fixed (sunk) costs are not opportunity costs in the short run because there is no alternative to incurring them.

Variable costs are the opportunity costs a firm incurs for production. Average variable costs of $240 (point *b* in Figure 6) are incurred in wages, materials, and other variable expenses when four ounces of

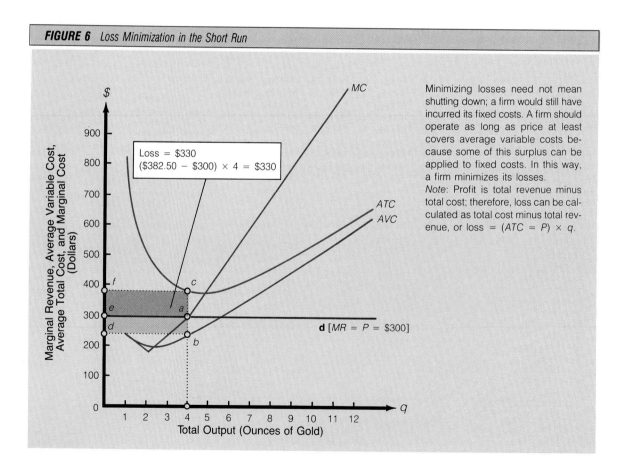

FIGURE 6 Loss Minimization in the Short Run

Loss = $330
($382.50 − $300) × 4 = $330

d [MR = P = $300]

Minimizing losses need not mean shutting down; a firm would still have incurred its fixed costs. A firm should operate as long as price at least covers average variable costs because some of this surplus can be applied to fixed costs. In this way, a firm minimizes its losses.
Note: Profit is total revenue minus total cost; therefore, loss can be calculated as total cost minus total revenue, or loss = (ATC = P) × q.

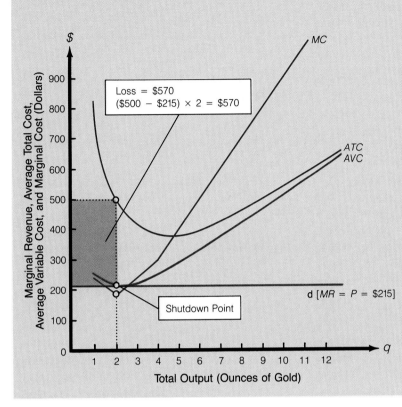

FIGURE 7 Short-Run Shutdown Point

Loss = $570
($500 − $215) × 2 = $570

MC

ATC
AVC

d [MR = P = $215]

Shutdown Point

$

Marginal Revenue, Average Total Cost, Average Variable Cost, and Marginal Cost (Dollars)

900
800
700
600
500
400
300
200
100
0

1 2 3 4 5 6 7 8 9 10 11 12

Total Output (Ounces of Gold)

q

The short-run shutdown point is at a price of $215 per ounce and an output of two ounces per week. At any price below $215, the firm's losses would be larger if it continued to produce. At prices below $215, variable costs of production will not be covered. Thus, at prices below $215, the firm will close its doors to minimize losses.
Source: Tables 1 and 2.

gold are mined. Consequently, average variable costs will be covered as long as the mine can sell the gold for more than $240 per ounce. As the mine operator, you could allocate the difference between price ($300) and average variable costs ($240) to a fund to cover fixed costs. Even if all your fixed costs are not covered, at least some can be. Suffering a loss of $330 is better than suffering a loss equal to the fixed cost of $570. Notice that the critical costs to cover are variable costs, not fixed costs. As the saying goes, sunk costs are *sunk*.

When will it pay the firm to shut down? The answer is that a firm will do as well or better by closing its doors if the price of a good fails to cover its average variable costs. This is shown in Figure 7. When the price falls below $215 per ounce of gold, which is the minimum value of the average variable cost curve, you should close the mine. At a price of $215, the mine just recoups its variable costs from the sale of two ounces of gold weekly since variable costs are $215 per unit for labor, materials, and so forth.

Consequently, total losses are $570 whether or not two ounces of gold are produced and then sold for $215; nothing is contributed to fixed costs from the production and sale of these units.

What happens if gold falls below $215 per ounce—to, say $200? If the mine continues to produce two ounces of gold, in addition to $570 in fixed costs, you will lose at least $15 more per ounce, resulting in total losses of $600 [$570 + ($15 × 2)]. Producing at all would be a bad decision if you were trying to minimize losses. The best decision if the price falls below $215 is to abandon the mine, at least temporarily. Thus, a $215 price corresponds to the shutdown point for your mine. It is the lowest price that will induce you to operate, and you will never attempt to mine less than two ounces of gold.

The **shutdown point** *is encountered by profit-maximizing (and loss-minimizing) firms whenever the market price drops below the minimum point of the average variable cost curve.*

Take a moment to compare Figures 5, 6, and 7. Note that, regardless of market structure, profit should be realized whenever the demand curve facing a firm intersects its *ATC* curve. Similarly, short-run losses are unavoidable if the *ATC* curve lies above the demand curve at all output levels. You will see in a moment that the best a firm can do is break even if the demand curve is exactly tangent to its *ATC* curve.

Short-Run Supply Curves of Purely Competitive Firms

You may have deduced that a competitive firm's marginal cost curve is also its short-run supply curve as long as price exceeds the minimum point of the average variable cost curve. These points along a marginal cost curve reflect the profit-maximizing outputs corresponding to various market prices for the good. If price falls below minimum average variable costs (*AVC*), marginal costs and marginal revenue become irrelevant; the firm's best move is to close its plant and suffer losses equal to fixed costs. However, whenever the price exceeds the shutdown point (the minimum *AVC*), the firm minimizes losses or maximizes profit by supplying the amount of output where $P = MR = MC$. This is a firm's short-run supply response.

> A purely competitive firm's **short-run supply curve** *is the segment of the marginal cost curve that lies above the minimum point of the firm's average variable cost curve.*

This is shown in Figure 8. When price and marginal revenue equal P_0, the firm supplies only q_0. As the price rises, the firm increases the quantity it supplies to maximize profit or minimize loss by equating that price with marginal costs, so if price increases to P_1 and P_2, the firm will supply q_1 and q_2 respectively. Now let us see how individual firms' supply curves are combined to form an industry supply curve.

The Short-Run Industry Supply Curve

A purely competitive industry contains a large number of firms, so there is a predictably tight relationship between the industry supply curve and firm supply curves. Consider, for simplicity, an industry comprised of two firms with individual supply curves as shown in Panel A of Figure 9. When the market price is $1, the first firm is willing to supply 10 units and the second firm is willing to supply 30 units. Together, they supply 40 units at the $1 price, as plotted in Panel B. You should remember from chapter 3 that this process is called *horizontal summation*.

> The **short-run industry supply curve** *is the horizontal sum of the supply curves of all firms in a purely competitive industry.*

We simply add the quantities produced by each firm at each possible price to arrive at the *industry short-run supply curve*. You can verify this graphically by adding together the quantities that each firm will turn out at various prices, and you will also see that these total quantities supplied conform to those plotted in Panel B.

We have now related individual and market supplies. The output decisions of individual firms sum to determine the market supply schedule. This market supply, in conjunction with consumers' demands for a good, determines its market clearing price. The industry is in equilibrium when firms supply all they

FIGURE 8 *The Firm's Short-Run Supply Curve*

A competitive firm's short-run supply curve is its marginal cost curve, as long as the point where the price equals marginal cost ($P = MC$) occurs above the minimum of the average variable cost curve. If price cannot cover average variable cost, the firm will shut down.

FIGURE 9 *The Industry Supply Curve*

The industry supply curve (Panel B) is the horizontal summation of the supply curves of individual firms (Panel A).

are willing to at the going price and consumers are able to buy all they desire at that price. All firms maximize profit by producing where $MR = MC$. If price falls below AVC, firms minimize losses by closing their doors.

Are markets stuck in a short-run equilibrium? What role does profit play in the longer run? What happens if new firms enter an industry? If technological breakthroughs substantially reduce production costs? These and other issues are examined in the following section as we step from short-run to long-run adjustments in purely competitive industries.

Long-Run Adjustments in Competitive Industries

The number of firms in any industry is fixed in the short run but, in the long run, the most important characteristic of competition is freedom of entry and exit. The number of firms in an industry may rise with entry, or fall as existing firms fail or move into different product lines. Entry into prospering industries

and exit from those that are faltering is basic to the smooth operation of a market economy. Economic profit attracts new firms to an industry, while economic losses signal owners to liquidate existing firms or to look for new product lines.

Economic Profits as Market Signals

Recall (from the preceding chapter) that economic profits are a surplus after all implicit and explicit costs of production are subtracted from total revenue. Thus, average total costs include allowances for the opportunity costs of capital and the entrepreneurial talents used by the firm, among other things. Normal accounting rates of return to these resources must be earned. A firm's owners will move their resources into other activities if they suffer economic losses. On the other hand, if revenues exceed all production costs, the firm may try to expand in an attempt to capture as much economic profit as possible. In a sense, however, profit ultimately "self-destructs" by attracting new competitors into the industry.

Suppose that markets for statues and for potted houseplants are both in equilibrium and that both are homogeneous products. Neither economic profits nor losses are experienced by the firms in either industry. Then the demand for indoor plants plummets as interior decorators unite to convince people that plants are passé and that no corner in any room is complete without an imitation early Greek statue. Statue makers are deluged with new orders, while florists and garden shops throughout the country watch their sales fall. Specials and discounts become the order of the day in the houseplant industry, and short-run economic losses occur as prices, outputs, and total revenues decline. On the other hand, the prices and outputs of the imitation Greek statues soar and economic profits are widespread in the short run.

In the long run, resources migrate from the houseplant industry. New investment declines and florists train for other work as flower shops fold. Investment gravitates into statuary making as new firms flock to the industry in search of profits, and more workers become statue makers. Thus, over the long run, competition eliminates both economic losses in the plant industry and economic profits in statuary; plant prices recover from their depressed state, and statue prices fall from their short-run peaks.

Let us discuss market adjustments in more detail. The long run allows all resources (including capital) to enter or leave an industry. New firms move into growing industries, while existing firms wither or die in declining industries. Thus, we expect resources to flow from less profitable towards more profitable industries. Entry and exit from highly competitive industries can be accomplished with ease. Many "hit-and-run" competitors jump into profitable markets and leave as soon as other markets appear more profitable. This hit-and-run pattern is socially beneficial because it ensures that even erratic consumer demands are accommodated quickly.

Social gains from competition depend heavily on freedom to enter or exit markets as firms seek profit or try to evade persistent loss. Focus 1 indicates that firms are increasingly losing flexibility in shutting down inefficient plants so that they can shift capital to more profitable industries.

The Process of Competition

If typical firms make *zero economic profits,* then (all else equal) there will be no long-run changes in the number of firms in the industry, the amount of output supplied, or the price of the good.[3]

> **Zero economic profit** *is a long-run equilibrium condition for firms in a competitive industry. The output, price, and number of firms in the industry will all be stable.*

But if most firms in an industry experience economic profits, competitive pressures tend to eliminate these profits over time because prices will fall or costs will increase. Conversely, economic losses tend to cause prices to climb or costs to decline, or both.

Price Changes Eliminate Economic Profits or Losses
If firms in an industry begin to earn positive economic profits, existing firms will try to capture greater profits by expanding their capacities and production. There are also incentives for entrepreneurs outside the industry to enter profitable markets. Both types of adjustments increase the industry's output. This drives down prices because consumers will buy more than they were buying only if prices decline.

On the other hand, if most firms in an industry experience economic losses, then some will cut their production and, in the long run, the firms with the highest opportunity costs (best alternative uses of their resources) will leave the industry. Thus, the long-run effects of economic losses are that the industry's supply will decline and prices will rise.

How Profits or Losses Affect Costs Competition will grow for the resources used by a profitable industry. If supplies are perfectly elastic for all resources used by an industry, production can expand without driving up average production costs. Resource costs will rise as production in an industry rises, however, to the extent that some resources are

---

3. Recall that normal returns to capital owners and entrepreneurial talent are economic costs. Zero economic profits mean that all costs are covered; i.e., the firm's resources cannot be used more advantageously elsewhere.

Competition in Jeopardy: Exit Restrictions

Licenses and taxes have always restricted entry somewhat, but until recently, exit was largely unfettered. Mounting pressure to limit how quickly firms can close unprofitable plants now threatens business flexibility in responding to shifts in production costs or consumer demands.

Many union contracts now contain "no plant closing" provisions. Laws enacted in several states and more than a few cities now require either ninety day notices of closings or exit penalties and severance pay for workers who lose their jobs. In 1988, Congress passed a major bill requiring ninety day notices prior to plant closings, but former President Reagan vetoed this law.

Plant closings increasingly draw legal fire. Workers laid off by Atari in 1983 filed a class action suit charging that they received no prior warnings that their jobs were in jeopardy. In 1988, the state Attorney General filed suit against Chrysler after it absorbed American Motors and attempted to close an 86-year-old assembly plant in Kenosha, Wisconsin.

Proponents of "plant closing laws" argue that restrictions are needed to buffer the local economic disruption that occurs when a major employer shuts down. Prenotification allows employees to locate alternative work, and communities time to attract new firms to an area. Moreover, the benefits of

competition are not enhanced by secrecy that makes it difficult for people to forecast and adjust to changing circumstances.

Opponents of limits on plant closings contend, however, that exit restrictions hinder the ability of competitive firms and industries to react to changing market conditions. They also argue that plant closing penalties will make it difficult for a region to attract new employers; firms considering relocation must consider the financial consequences if their plans prove overly optimistic. Thus, exit restrictions may also hinder entry.

---

especially suited for certain industries and not others. For example, what do you think happens to the costs of acquiring oil drilling rights as the price of oil balloons? What happens to the prices of agricultural land when food prices soar? Costs rise to reduce profits in both cases.

Here is another example of how rising costs eliminate profits. Suppose that your firm enjoyed extremely high profits because it hired an exceptionally efficient management team. Might some competitor try to hire members of this team? What would happen to their salaries?

The market forces that cause costs to rise in an industry in which most firms make economic profits

also cause costs to fall in instances where most firms incur losses. Both average costs and marginal costs rise in profitable industries and shrink when economic losses are the norm. To simplify the analysis in the following discussion, we focus only on price (not cost) adjustments. Remember, however, that changes in either prices or costs will eliminate economic profits or losses in competitive markets in the long run. Moreover, we assume in the following discussion that prices adjust smoothly towards long-run equilibrium. You should recognize that some firms may over-react in unison to economic profits or losses, so that prices may swing somewhat before ultimately converging on their equilibrium values.

FIGURE 10 Entry and Exit and Long-Run Price, Output, and Profit

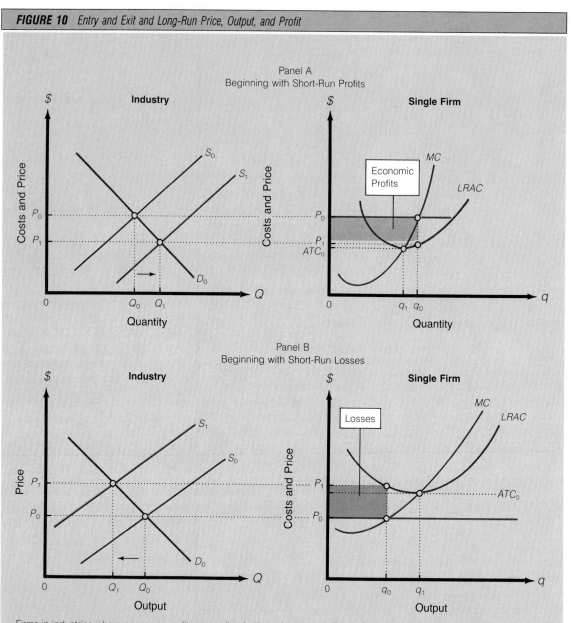

Firms in industries where economic profits are realized will produce where $P = MC$ and output is greater than that associated with minimum average cost. However, the entry of new competitors will cause industry supply to grow and price to fall. As this occurs, existing firms reduce output until $P = MC = LRAC$. LRAC is at its minimum and there are no economic profits when competitive firms are in long-run equilibrium.

If most firms in an industry are suffering economic losses, they will restrict production below the minimum point of their LRAC curves. As some firms leave the industry, the market supply falls and price increases. As the price rises, existing firms will expand their production to the level of output where long-run average cost is minimized. At this point, $P = MC = LRAC$, and neither economic profits nor economic losses are experienced.

Long-Run Equilibrium in a Competitive Industry

Firms run close to capacity in profitable industries, but they produce far less than capacity when business conditions go sour. Consider the industry shown in Figure 10. This industry is in the short-run equilibrium described in Panel A before the entry of new firms. Industry demand and supply are D_0 and S_0, respectively, with industry output equal to Q_0; each firm produces an output of q_0 where $P = MR = MC$. Typical firms in this competitive industry make short-run economic profits equal to the darkened area, causing firms to willingly incur higher-than-minimal costs as they produce extra output to exploit profit opportunities.

Pure competition allows easy entry, so this is a short-run situation because entrepreneurs outside the industry will seek shares of these profits. After new firms enter, industry supply increases to S_1, with a correspondingly higher output Q_1 and a lower equilibrium price, P_1. But observe what has happened to the individual firms. As prices decline, each firm adjusts to a new profit maximization output (q_1), which is lower than the original level (q_0). Consequently, our industry is now composed of more firms, but the absence of economic profit means that each produces less than before.

What has happened to profit? Each established firm in the industry was previously earning positive economic profit. After entry occurs, the lower prices and lower outputs that result have driven economic profits back to "normal" levels; that is, zero economic profits are realized. Product price has fallen to the minimum of long-run average costs (*LRAC*). Remember that the resources provided by the firm's owners have opportunity costs that are included in average costs. Accounting profits are not zero in the industry; they are simply at normal levels—being just high enough so the owners earn as much in this industry as in their next best option.

You may wonder whether symmetric exit adjustments occur in unprofitable situations. Such adjustments are illustrated in Panel B of Figure 10, which shows individual firms initially encountering short-run losses. Price is originally at P_0, which is below average total cost (*ATC*) but above average variable

costs (not shown in the figure) since firms are continuing to operate. Losses are equal to the darkened area. The least efficient firms incur the largest losses and will fold or move into a different activity. Industry supply will shrink as these firms leave the industry, so the price will rise and losses will be eliminated. Profits might temporarily re-appear if enough firms leave, curtailing the exodus of firms. Ultimately, however, price rises to P_1 and profits return to "normal" levels. Notice that this is just the opposite of the adjustment process described in the profitable situation above. Industry output falls, but individual firm outputs grow as the price recovers to normal levels when some firms exit the industry.

At the ends of periods with economic losses or profits, why does profit settle at "normal" levels (zero economic profits)? A moment's reflection should provide the answer. Competitive theory presumes that entry and exit are virtually costless, so the logical stopping point occurs when each firm in the industry earns only normal profits. All opportunity costs are covered, so the owners of existing firms know of no opportunities for their resources that are more profitable. Nor do entrepreneurs outside the industry perceive profit opportunities in the industry. Only then will there be no net incentives for firms to enter or leave the industry.

Another important result of long-run competitive adjustments is that all firms in the industry are forced to adopt the most efficient technology available. This is shown in Figure 11. Long-run pressures will force the price of the product to P_{LR} because competition forces each firm to the lowest point on the *LRAC* curve. Any firm not adopting the technology and amounts of capital that yield the lowest minimum short-run average cost curve (*SRAC*) will earn less than normal accounting profits and will founder in the long run. No firm stays in any industry if it suffers sustained economic losses. Since $P = MC = ATC$ in the long run, the ultimate equilibrium point is the lowest point on the *LRAC* curve, which is also the lowest point on the relevant *SRAC* curve. This means that outputs in competitive markets will be produced at the lowest possible long-run average cost. Hence, competition yields economic efficiency. As you will see later, this result has profound implications for maintaining competition in a free-market economy.

FIGURE 11   Long-Run Equilibrium for the Competitive Firm

In the long run, a firm in a competitive industry will produce where $P = MR = MC = SRAC = LRAC$, and the size of the plant will minimize the average costs of production. Neither economic profits nor economic losses will be realized; the firm's total revenues will just cover all its costs, including normal accounting profits to compensate owners for the resources they provide.

Long-Run Industry Supply Curves

Now that you have some ideas about competitive adjustment processes, we can examine the long-run supply curve for the competitive industry as a whole. The horizontal summation of existing firms' short-run supply curves yields the short-run industry supply curve. The **long-run industry supply curve** reflects the effects on output as entry and exit occur in response to changes in demand. The industry is in long-run equilibrium only after all desired entries and exits have occurred so that active firms realize only normal profits.

Changing demands, technologies, and products cause erratic swings in many industries. The economy continually gropes towards equilibrium, but full equilibrium may never be attained in most industries. Even so, short-run and long-run equilibria remain valuable concepts because of their analytical

convenience and their predictive power. Without these notions, we have analytical mush—no reference points from which to compare other periods, nor to predict the eventual trends of outputs and prices. Long-run industry supply curves can take three general forms (*a*) constant costs, (*b*) increasing costs, and (*c*) decreasing costs. We will examine each of these.

Constant-Cost Industries   Figure 12 illustrates the long-run supply curve (*LRS*) of a constant-cost industry.

> *In a **constant-cost industry,** average production costs are unaffected if the market demand shifts and the number of firms in the industry changes.*

FIGURE 12   Long-Run Supply (Constant-Cost Industry)

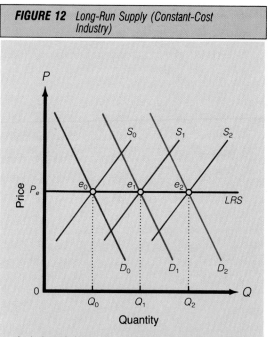

An industry's long-run supply curve is perfectly elastic (horizontal) if the resource costs of individual firms are unaffected by the number of firms in the industry. Industries that use only small percentages of highly specialized resources in an economy will operate under constant costs.

As demand grows from D_0 to D_1 to D_2, long-run responses are increases in short-run supplies from S_0 to S_1 and S_2, respectively, as the number of firms in the industry grows proportionally with demand. As entry occurs, long-run average costs are the same for new entrants as for established firms. All cost curves for individual firms are identical; the number of firms in the industry adjusts proportionally as demand changes. Thus, the long-run supply curve for a constant-cost industry is perfectly elastic. An industry can expand with constant equilibrium price and costs only if technology and the costs of the resources it uses are not affected.[4]

Increasing-Cost Industries

Industries deviate from the constant-cost model for several reasons. The requirement that input prices not rise as an industry's output rises is especially difficult for industries that rely on limited supplies of specialized resources; larger amounts of these resources can be made available only at ever higher costs. This characterizes increasing-cost industries.

> **Increasing-cost industry** *are cases where average production costs rise as market demand and the number of firms in the industry grow.*

In an increasing-cost industry, growth of market demand pulls up resource costs. The average total cost and marginal cost curves for each firm in the industry rise because all firms experience these resource price hikes. Thus, demand growth shifts up the long-run break-even points for each firm as minimal long-run average costs rise. This is illustrated in Figure 13.

If industry demand grows from D_0 to D_1, the industry expands as new firms enter. As a result, the competition for resources drives the short-run supply curve to S_1, resulting in an equilibrium price of P_1. These rising equilibrium costs and prices result in

FIGURE 13 Long-Run Supply for an Increasing-Cost Industry

The long-run supply curve of an increasing cost industry will be positively sloped because the prices of the specialized resources it uses rise as industry output expands. This effect will be stronger the larger the industry is relative to national output and the more specialized resources are. This effect is common and yields production-possibilities frontiers that are "bowed out" from below, as described in chapter 2.

---

4. Were all industries subject to constant cost, the production-possibilities frontier would be a straight line. You might review the material in chapter 2 if you are unsure why this is true.

a positively-sloped long-run supply (*LRS*) curve. For the industry to supply greater quantities to the market, only higher prices can cover higher resource costs. Moreover, these higher costs will cause fewer firms to enter the industry than would enter constant-cost industries that experienced similar growth of demand.

Regardless of the extent of competition, in the long run most industries are characterized by increasing costs. For example, our domestic oil industry faces increasing costs as it attempts to boost petroleum production. Most readily accessible crude oil has been depleted. Higher oil prices induce landowners to charge more for drilling rights. Future oil supplies will be drawn from high cost off-shore drilling or from deeper wells. Alternatively, Americans may try other energy sources, most of which are much more costly than oil.

Decreasing-Cost Industries

One industry's growth may stimulate efficiencies in complementary industries. For example, mass production in the auto industry early in this century stimulated a flock of support industries. As these support industries grew, firms implemented new technology and moved down their long-run average cost curves, supplying intermediate products (tires, batteries, and the like) to the auto industry at lower prices. Car prices dropped.

> **Decreasing-cost industry** *are cases where average production costs fall as market demand and the number of firms in the industry grow.*

Thus, in a decreasing-cost industry, growing demand yields lower equilibrium prices as an industry's output expands, as shown in Figure 14.

In rare circumstances a few industries might experience decreasing costs, but most industries encounter constant or increasing costs. As a result, growing demand tends to yield higher prices in the long run. The possibility that technological advances may be spurred by the search for profits, however, means that some industries may experience decreasing costs in the long run. This seems to be true of many high tech products today.

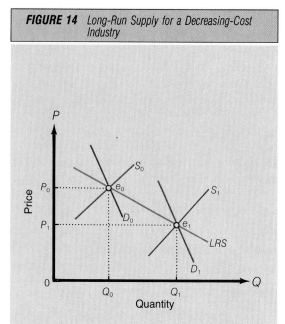

FIGURE 14 Long-Run Supply for a Decreasing-Cost Industry

Decreasing-cost industries generate negatively sloped long-run supply curves, and are extremely uncommon because such decreasing costs rely on either substantial economies of scale or positive externalities within the industry or in the support industries that supply them with intermediate goods. In fact, many economists argue that this is only a theoretical possibility, never encountered in the actual world of production.

The concepts of constant, increasing, or decreasing costs apply *only* for the long run. Decreasing-cost industries do not seem so implausible, however, if we consider the possibility of technological advances.

Evaluating Competitive Markets

Some important points in this chapter are useful in evaluating competition:

1. Pure competition is characterized by freedom of entry and exit by firms that are *price takers* and *quantity adjusters*.

2. A purely competitive firm maximizes its profit or minimizes its loss by producing the level of output that equates price and marginal cost ($P = MR = MC$).

3. In the long run, pure competitors use the most efficient technology available, and $LRMC = P$.[5] This will also be the minimum point on the $LRAC$ curve because the long-run dynamics of entry and exit drive economic profits to zero regardless of whether the industry is characterized by constant, increasing, or decreasing costs. Accounting profits will be at "normal" levels.

In the long run,

$$P = MR = SRMC = SRAC = LRMC = LRAC.$$

---

5. Technical differences between short-run and long-run marginal costs are not considered here. Courses in intermediate microeconomics deal with these differences.

Economic Efficiency

In a purely competitive market, firms employ resources until the marginal cost to them of producing the last unit of a good just equals its price. In the absence of external costs (e.g., pollution) or external benefits (e.g., education, inoculations), the opportunity cost to society of using these resources equals the marginal cost of the resources to producers. If there are no externalities (discussed in depth in a later chapter), these resource costs equal their *marginal social costs* (*MSC*). Competition through freedom of entry and exit ensures that this is at the lowest possible average cost of production and that there is no waste in production. A purely competitive economy is an efficient economy because one aspect of economic efficiency is that all goods must be produced at their lowest possible opportunity cost.

Social Welfare

Does competition also serve society well? Efficiency may be cold comfort if it makes people suffer. You will see in the coming chapters covering other output market structures and resource markets that competition tends to yield greater equality in income distribution than other market structures. While more equal, the distribution of income that might be generated even if the economy were perfectly competitive may still be viewed by many as unfair.

Positive economic analysis cannot directly address the fairest way to divide the pie. If we assume, however, that the proper distribution of income is a normative problem best settled in the political arena and that the resulting political outcome is viewed as acceptable, then the competitive market system not only is efficient, it also maximizes social welfare. Here is why.

Your demand curve for any good is based on the marginal benefits (utility) that you would receive from consuming various possible amounts of the good, as we discussed in a previous chapter. Our assumptions imply that the marginal utility you receive from consuming is also the marginal benefit society receives. That is, your gain is also society's gain because you are a member of society. When we sum all consumer demands, we derive the market demand curve for an industry's product, which is also the *marginal social benefit* (*MSB*) to all of society from having a bit more of the good.

With consumer benefits and producer costs in mind, we can refer to the industry supply and demand curves, respectively, as the marginal social cost (*MSC*) and marginal social benefit (*MSB*) curves. When a purely competitive industry is in long-run equilibrium, *marginal social cost equals marginal social benefit* (*MSC* = *MSB*): the industry is producing where the marginal social benefit from the last unit produced is just equal to the marginal social cost of the resources needed to produce that unit of product. This concept is illustrated in Figure 15.

The *MSB* = *MSC* condition is optimal from society's point of view. Since the opportunity costs of resources represent alternatives for all of society, we want our resources to be used as efficiently as possible. If production were inefficient, then it would be possible for some people to gain without imposing losses on others.

Consider output level Q_0 in Figure 15. The social benefit from a bit more output than Q_0 is P_0, which

FIGURE 15 *Economic Efficiency and Competition*

If there are no externalities in production or consumption, then purely competitive markets generate solutions that are efficient. If, in addition, the distribution of income is deemed equitable, the competitive market equilibrium maximizes social welfare.

BIOGRAPHY

Leon Walras
(1834–1910)
and
Vilfredo Pareto
(1848–1923)

Leon Walras has been described as an architect rather than a builder of economics, meaning that he designed a general system of analytical principles rather than laid in the bricks and mortar of economic theory. Walras tackled the complex problem of the interdependence of all sectors of the economy and represented this complexity in a system of simultaneous equations.

This great architect of economics was descended from a Dutch journey-

man tailor who migrated to the south of France in 1749. His father was a classmate of Cournot (discussed in the next chapter) in Paris and, like Cournot, was a school administrator. The young Walras learned from Cournot the meaning of functional relations between variables. However, concerns about the limits of Cournot's demand curve for a single good led Walras to seek a wider framework within which to express the demand for a good as a function not only of its own price, but of a host of prices of related goods. This was the point of departure for his *general equilibrium model* of an economy.

Most economic writers before Walras followed the lead of Alfred Marshall and employed a convention in dealing with particular markets called *partial equilibrium analysis*. This still common and useful convention calls for ignoring some determinants of demand and supply in order to concentrate on the more direct causes of equilibrium price and quantity. Walras departed from this practice by insisting on recognizing the interdependencies that exist between markets because the process of price determination necessarily occurs in all markets simultaneously. To isolate one market for study without regard to the others was no more appropriate, in Walras's view, than studying the position of the earth in the solar system without regard to other planets. His *architectonics* consequently was an elaborate but highly abstract system of mathematical equations that painstakingly detailed the economic conditions for simultaneous equilibrium in every economic market. Walras's general equilibrium approach to economics did not win favor with the reigning academic hierarchy in France, forcing him to take a teaching position in Switzerland at the University of Lausanne, where he labored until he was replaced in 1893 by Vilfredo Pareto.

Pareto, born of a Genoese father and French mother, was trained as an engineer. At 45, he accepted the chair at Lausanne. Pareto's system of thought and his vision of social processes differed from Walras's, but Pareto cast his pure theory of economics in much the same mold, extending and refining Walras's general equilibrium system. Moreover, Pareto did what Walras had not been able to do: he founded a full-blown school of thought. His disciples cooperated in theoretical research, cultivated personal contacts, and defended one another in controversy. The school, reflecting Pareto's own heritage, was primarily Italian.

Two of Pareto's contributions to economics are especially noteworthy. First, he identified a situation of maximum efficiency for a society as one in which it is impossible to increase the happiness of one individual without decreasing that of someone else. Today all the conditions specifying economic efficiency are referred to as "Pareto optimal." Second, Pareto proved that a state of maximum efficiency and social welfare are identical with equilibrium under perfect competition. This led him to conclude that the problems in reaching a position of maximum efficiency, as well as their solutions, were the same for a collectivist economy as for an economy founded on private property.

Pareto's work spilled over into the field of sociology. His chief objective was to develop general equilibrium models covering the whole spectrum of social phenomena. Both he and Walras were aware that their equations could not be solved due to the lack of data and the large number of variables involved. Nevertheless, theirs was a great achievement from the standpoint of logical clarity, and the impact of their thoughts on modern economic theory ranks them both among the dozen most influential economists of all time.

greatly exceeds the cost (P_1) of the resources required to produce a little more of the good, so society as a whole could gain if more resources were used to produce more of this good. In a competitive industry they will be. If Q_0 were initially produced and sold at price P_0, existing firms in a competitive industry would enjoy economic profit. This would cause the industry to grow until equilibrium output Q_e is reached at a price and (average and marginal) production cost of P_e. The adjustment process is just reversed if industry output exceeds Q_e. Competitive markets tend to squeeze the last bit of gain possible from the resources available.

Decentralized Decisions and Freedom

The ideas of Adam Smith and other early advocates of capitalism were forged during a period of revolt against the dictatorial decisions of monarchs. Isaac Newton had observed movements of the planets and stars and concluded that natural forces generate a stable and orderly universe. Smith perceived that the invisible hand of the marketplace had similarly beneficial economic effects and that the iron fist of government was exercised far too often.

Leon Walras elaborated with mathematical precision Smith's ideas about how peoples' wants are accommodated in a competitive market system, and Vilfredo Pareto developed a concept of economic welfare that still dominates economic analysis. Pareto also proved that a purely competitive equilibrium is efficient, and that other equilibria fail to maximize social welfare.

Most advocates of the market system point to the economic efficiency of competition as a major virtue but prize even more the absence of any need for a central economic authority. In a truly competitive market system, each household and firm make decisions, that in large measure, affect only themselves. This diffusion of market power means that individuals cannot be controlled by other individuals. According to proponents of relying on the marketplace rather than government, this diffusion of coercive power allows the maximum possible personal freedom for everyone.

Efficiency, equity, and the absence of centralized coercion are all reasons why a purely competitive market is the ideal against which we measure indus-trial performance. From society's point of view, it might seem desirable that all industries be competitive so that Adam Smith's invisible hand would yield the results we have described. As you will see in the next chapter, however, competition and access to markets may be very limited if technology dictates that large firms, relative to market demand, will be most efficient.

Some economists who believe strongly in competition as an effective and desirable allocative mechanism are convinced that the model of pure competition grossly *under*states the virtues of the market system. Their views on this topic are sketched in Focus 2.

Some Shortcomings of Market Economics

Many industries are far from competitive—in some, competition is impractical. We examine the behavior of firms that have varying degrees of monopoly power in the next two chapters. In some cases, this power emerges naturally because of technology; in others, it is a consequence of illegal collusion or government policies to protect other goals (patents, licensing, to protect the public health, and so on). In the last two chapters of this part of the book, we scrutinize government attempts to regulate business and to limit monopolistic practices through antitrust actions.

Even if the economy were quite competitive, there might still be problems of fraud, inequity in the distributions of income and wealth, or externalities that the market would not resolve in ways society deems appropriate. Moreover, certain goods will not be provided optimally by a private market system. Atomic bombs, police services, and legal decisions are examples of items no society would want to see sold only to the highest bidder.

Some economists also argue that research and development require bigness; such efforts might be less than optimal if left to small competitive firms. Finally, there are questions about what social restrictions, if any, should be imposed on trade between people in different countries. The tools you have learned to use in the last few chapters will help clarify the remainder of this book as we examine the outcome of private market behavior and assess corrective government policies for these problems.

Dynamic Entrepreneurs vs. Pure Competition

The model of pure competition is largely rejected by the *Austrian* school of thought. ("Austrian" refers to the national origin of most of this school's founders, but its ideas have spread to some economists spread across the world.) Here is an Austrian perspective of competition:

Pure competition focuses on trivia: short- and long-run adjustments among firms that use the same technology to produce a homogeneous good are described accurately, but these are not crucial features of competition. This analysis fails to address a major source of disequilibrium—the entrepreneur. What really matters is how competition affects human progress. Entrepreneurial innovation is the dynamic force that drives the growth and decline of industries in a competitive market system.

The key to entrepreneurial success is finding creative new ways to serve human wants by implementing new technologies or marketing new products better, faster, and at less cost. This can mean producing existing goods at lower costs or enhancing their quality, or it may mean creating markets for entirely new goods.

For example, the U.S. Post Office was an uncontested government monopoly until United Parcel Service was launched by entrepreneurs who thought that people would pay handsomely to have small packages delivered faster and more conveniently. UPS prospered when shippers found it faster and more cost

efficient to have packages delivered by this private firm. Then the founder of Federal Express put competitive heat on both UPS and the Post Office after he risked all he owned and successfully tested the market demand for overnight delivery.

This dynamic form of competition creates new industries and causes old ones to experience disequilibrium. Thus, competition as a source of disequilibrium is more important in the Austrian view than the equilibrating entry and exit of firms stressed by conventional theory. Austrians share conventional notions about pressures for competitors to adopt cost-saving technology or to mimic successful product lines. Extending our previous example, the market for overnight delivery service created by Federal Express has been invaded by UPS, the Postal Service, Flying Tiger, Emery, ... Conventional theory stresses the effects of this second wave of competition; the Austrian school emphasizes the initial entry by Federal Express.

Austrian economists offer countless examples of competition as a robust process, and not as the stagnant set of equilibrium conditions specified by the model of perfect competition: Gutenburg destroyed hand-written book publishing with his moveable type; Thomas Edison's electric light changed our way of life; Henry Ford's assembly line made cars available for the masses. More recently, markets for desk calculators were displaced when two kids working

out of a garage launched Apple Computer and marketed the first personal computers. The original designers of computerized spreadsheets changed the way accountants work. Members of the Austrian school stress the dynamic competition among entrepreneurs rather than the imitative behavior of firms now scrutinized in the model of pure competition.

A further Austrian criticism is that the model of pure competition assumes a large number of similar firms to be vital for vigorous competition. This emphasis on numbers of competitors is accused of leading to bizarre antitrust laws and business regulations that strangle much truly competitive behavior among entrepreneurs. Numbers of competitive firms are far less important, in this view, than the qualities of the goods and the rate of technological advance in an industry.

CHAPTER REVIEW: KEY POINTS

1. Freedom of *entry and exit* is the hallmark of competition. A *purely competitive* market is comprised of numerous potential buyers and sellers of a homogeneous product, none of whom controls its price or is considered a *price maker*.

2. A competitive buyer faces a perfectly elastic supply curve, while competitive sellers face perfectly elastic demand curves. In competition, all are *price takers* or *quantity adjusters*.

3. We assume that no firm can adjust output in the *market period*, so total supply is perfectly inelastic. In the *short run* (*SR*), existing firms in an industry can vary output, but at least one productive factor is fixed and entry and exit cannot occur. Total supply is at least somewhat elastic. Supply is much more elastic in the *long run* (*LR*), because all factors of production are variable and firms may enter or leave the industry.

4. The competitive firm maximizes profits by producing output up to the point where *total revenues minus total costs* (*TR* − *TC*) is maximized, which also occurs when *marginal revenue equals marginal cost* (*MR* = *MC*). Price must be greater than the minimum of the average variable cost curve, however, which is the *shutdown point*. Because competitive firms face perfectly elastic demands, price and marginal revenue are identical. *Break-even points* are the quantities at which total revenue and total cost are equal.

5. A competitive firm's *short-run supply curve* is its marginal cost curve above the minimum of its average variable costs. Horizontally summing the marginal costs from existing firms yields the *short-run industry supply curve*.

6. Competition erases *economic profits* through entry of new firms in the long run, and economic losses are eradicated by exit from the industry. Thus, competitive firms receive exactly enough revenue over the long run to pay the opportunity costs of resources used and realize only *zero economic profit*.

7. Short-run economic profits are ultimately eliminated because either output will be expanded by both existing and new firms in a competitive industry or increased competition for profitable inputs will drive up resource costs. The long-run adjustments that eliminate short-run losses follow precisely reversed patterns.

8. In the long run, firms are forced by competitive pressures to adopt the most efficient (least costly) plant size and technologies. They operate at output levels where

$$P = MR = SRAC = SRMC = LRAC = LRMC.$$

9. For *constant-cost industries,* the minimum *LRAC* for firms is the same no matter how many firms are in the industry. Costs increase for each firm as firms enter increasing-cost industries, and decrease for decreasing-cost industries. Thus, the *long-run industry supply curve* is positively sloped for *increasing cost industries,* horizontal for *constant-cost industries,* and negatively sloped for *decreasing-cost industries.*

10. A purely competitive market is efficient in the sense that goods are produced at the lowest possible opportunity cost. Every feasible bit of net gain is squeezed from the resources available; *marginal social benefits* and *marginal social costs* are equated by competitive forces of supply and demand (*MSB* = *MSC*), assuming the absence of externalities. This will be socially optimal and maximize social welfare if the distribution of income is deemed appropriate. A market system does not require that decision-making power be vested in a central authority. This permits substantial personal freedom and the absence of coercion.

PROBLEMS

1. Cost and output data for a purely competitive firm are provided in the following table. Assume that fixed costs are equal to $40 and that the market price facing the firm is $30 per unit.

Quantity	1	2	3	4	5	6	7	8
TVC	30	55	75	90	110	135	165	200

What is the profit-maximizing rate of output? What does maximum profit equal? At what price will the firm close its doors? What output would this firm produce in the long run if the price remains constant?

2. Suppose your firm has a contract requiring delivery of 1,000 videocameras for $1,000 each, and your aver-

FIGURE 16 *The Market for Eye Tattoos*

age total cost is $800. Why would it be an error to fill a special rush order for one more at a price of $1,500 if producing the extra camera would boost your average total cost to $801? How much would your profit fall if you filled this special order?

3. Some women now use tattoos to give the effect of permanent cosmetic eye liner. The current industry demand (D_0) and supply (S_0) and representative individual firm demand and cost curves for "eye tattoos" are illustrated in Figure 16, which also shows another potential market supply curve (S_1). How many firms comprise the industry in the short run? How many firms will be in the industry in the long run? What will ultimately happen to the price of eye tattoos?

QUESTIONS FOR THOUGHT AND DISCUSSION

1. Are there any differences between the pure competition described in this chapter and the *cut-throat* competition despised by many business executives?

2. The stock market is viewed by some critics of capitalism as the epitome of monopoly power. Are most people who buy or sell stock price makers or price takers? Do you think stock and commodity markets basically meet the requirements for competitive markets? Why or why not?

3. Would you expect someone who selected stocks by throwing darts at stock market reports in the *Wall Street Journal* to experience systematically different economic profits than an expert financial analyst who spent hours every day studying the stock market? If not, what might explain systematically different rates of return reported by their bookkeepers?

4. Is a big city economy more competitive than one in a small town? How? Do you think your grocer has monopoly power? How much? Can you cite recent market entry and exit among firms located within five miles of your home? What industries have been involved? Do you know of any giant firms that have

emerged, almost from oblivion, in the past five years? Any that have failed? Is our economy basically competitive or noncompetitive?

5. A *Wall Street Journal* editorialist noted, "As everyone knows, competition is vital to the preservation of a healthy, efficient market economy. But competition sometimes seems to have few friends." What did this writer mean?

6. In 1978–79, the Hunt brothers (Texas billionaires) allegedly attempted to corner the silver market. What happened to the price of silver during this period? Was their effort successful? What obstacles are faced by anyone who tries to monopolize a previously competitive industry?

7. A theory called perfect competition is more restrictive than the theory of pure competition. It adds perfect (costless and instantaneous) information about goods and resources and perfect (costless) mobility of resources and goods in the long run to the assumptions that underpin the purely competitive model. Which type of competitive model can be used to address the transaction costs that are encountered in real world production and exchange?

monopoly
monopoly power
barrier to entry
artificial barriers to entry
natural barriers to entry
natural monopoly
contestable markets theory
price discrimination
monopolistic inefficiency

CHAPTER 24

Monopoly

Monopoly rekindles memories of a game involving Boardwalk, Park Place, and the B & O Railroad, in which the ultimate winner owns all the property and money. More generally, monopoly seems a sinister term; many social pundits, politicians, and the media equate monopoly with concentrations of economic power and control and blame monopoly power for such evils as inflation and poverty. Business owners and managers sometimes strive to eliminate their competition so that they will enjoy a monopoly position, a situation they view as ideal. Marxists perceive widespread monopoly capitalism as a natural consequence of a competitive market system and as the final stage before capitalism succumbs to a communist revolution.

Monopolies raise the specters of concentrated power, inequitable income distributions, and economic inefficiency. But what exactly is a monopoly?

*A **monopoly** is a firm that is the lone producer of a good for which there are no close substitutes.*

Every producer confronts some competition. Even your local electric power company faces competition from solar cells and gasoline- or diesel-based electric generating systems. But it is doubtful that these substitutes for electric services are sufficiently close that they pose threats to the abilities of power companies to retain their customers. Public utilities are currently the purest forms of monopoly in the United States.

This chapter focuses on the theory of pure, unregulated monopoly, even though very few pure monopolies exist, and even fewer are not regulated by some government agency. This theory provides a rationale for regulation. Moreover, comparisons of monopoly and competitive models point out major differences

BIOGRAPHY

Antoine Augustin Cournot (1801–77)

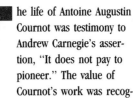

The life of Antoine Augustin Cournot was testimony to Andrew Carnegie's assertion, "It does not pay to pioneer." The value of Cournot's work was recognized only after his death. His life was characterized by anonymity and tragedy. This genius of economics and philosophy was born into a family of French farmers who had tilled the same lands for almost 300 years. He spent most of his life as a school superintendent and even that job was secured only through the influence of his friend Poisson, the famous French physicist and statistician. Cournot is remembered best in his homeland as a philosopher; in the English-speaking world he is hailed as a brilliant pioneer in economics.

Only Cournot's first and most influential book was ever translated into English. It fairly bristles with originality; Cournot formally introduced demand and supply curves; he derived, mathematically, the marginal revenue equals marginal cost rule for profit maximization, and also specified equilibrium conditions for monopolists, interdependent oligopolists, and firms operating under perfect competition.

Cournot's analysis of monopolistic profit maximization contains the kernel of his theory of the firm. As an example, Cournot considered a monopolist who could *costlessly* supply water from a mineral spring with uniquely healthful qualities. Sale of a single liter of water might bring an extremely high price, but Cournot demonstrated that a monopoly will not charge the highest price the market will bear. Rather, it will adjust its price to maximize total receipts; since costs are zero, this is equivalent to maximizing profit.

Cournot demonstrated that this is accomplished when marginal revenue (derived from the demand curve) equals marginal cost ($MR = MC$). Cournot's procedure seems commonplace today, but before 1838 there simply was no formal theory of profit maximization. Virtually every fundamental axiom in the economic theory of the firm stems from Cournot's trailblazing analysis.

Cournot's demeanor was solitary and melancholy, traits that intruded into his writing. His austere books are crowded with facts and rigorous mathematical proofs. He confessed to a fellow French economist that he was unpopular with his publishers because none of his books sold enough to be profitable until years after their first appearance.

Cournot's work was hampered by other economists' discomfort with mathematics and because his most productive years were absorbed by his duties as a school administrator. In addition, gradual deterioration of his eyesight impaired the accuracy of his mathematical notation. For their part, the prejudice and shortsightedness of his contemporaries blinded them to his advances in economic theory, which were not widely recognized until more than two decades after his death.

between the pricing and output decisions of firms having considerable market power as compared to those without such power.

The first systematic analysis of monopoly was pursued more than a century ago by a French economist, Antoine Augustin Cournot. One central concern of Cournot and of economists today is the inefficiency that may result from monopoly. Why might monopolies be economically inefficient? These and related questions are the focus of this chapter.

Monopoly Markets

The definition of monopoly raises several questions. How does a firm become a monopoly? Monopolies in some goods may enrich the firms' owners at the expense of the rest of society, but does a monopoly position guarantee riches? How does a monopoly prevent entry into an industry by other firms? How narrowly are the terms *good* and *close substitutes* defined?

You can probably think of many goods for which there is only one producer or seller. Does this mean that these sellers are monopolists? Not necessarily. For example, Scott, Foresman and Company has the exclusive right to publish this text. Is our publisher a monopolist? No, because there are several close, albeit imperfect, substitutes for this text. Not only is a monopolist the only seller of a given product, but the good itself must lack close substitutes. This means that a monopolist's control of a market must encompass any reasonably close substitutes for the product, a task easier said than done.

Consider the market for cameras producing instant snapshots. Polaroid is now the only producer of cameras that provide finished pictures in sixty seconds or less. Are regular cameras really close substitutes for instant picture cameras? Should the appropriate market for ascertaining whether or not Polaroid has a monopoly be the market for the "instant picture" camera rather than for cameras as a whole? When you consider the closeness of substitutes, a publishers' exclusive right to sell a particular book is clearly inferior to Polaroid's monopoly for instant cameras.

Monopoly Pricing and Output

A purely competitive firm faces a horizontal demand curve and can sell all it chooses to produce at the going market price. Therefore, a competitive firm's marginal revenue (its extra revenue derived from selling an additional unit of output) equals the market price. That is, each unit produced and sold adds the going price to total revenue, regardless of how many it sells. Purely competitive firms are price takers and can only select the *quantities* they will produce and sell.

Many firms that supply goods with close but imperfect substitutes are not true monopolists, but they possess *monopoly power* because they have some discretion about pricing. Any firm with monopoly power is a price maker.

Monopoly power *is a firm's ability to alter the price of its output because of inadequate competition or a lack of perfect substitutes for its products.*

A true monopolist faces the entire market demand curve because it is the only source of a good that lacks close substitutes. It completely controls the supply side of the market and so must select a *price and output combination* from the market demand curve. This flexibility distinguishes monopolistic pricing from that established in purely competitive markets. What price maximizes a monopolist's profits? Is it the price willingly paid by the most desperate buyer? That which maximizes its total revenue? Or the price that maximizes the amount of output sold? What price will a monopolist charge?

Monopoly Power and Demand

The law of demand implies that the demand curve facing a monopolist slopes down; price will be inversely related to quantity demanded. Any firm with monopoly power must lower its price to produce and sell more if it can only charge one price at a time for its output. The differences between the marginal revenues for pure competitors and for firms with monopoly power are illustrated in Figure 1.

Whenever a firm has monopoly power, selling extra output requires lowering the price because consumers are unwilling to purchase additional units at the previous price. Most monopolists can sell extra output only by cutting its price for all units sold. For example, if Polaroid wanted to sell more cameras next year, it could not just lower the price for the few extra customers who required discounts to buy over the next year; Polaroid would be forced to lower the price of its camera to virtually all customers. Thus, marginal revenue will equal the price a monopolist receives from selling an extra unit minus the revenue lost because prices must be reduced on all other units sold.

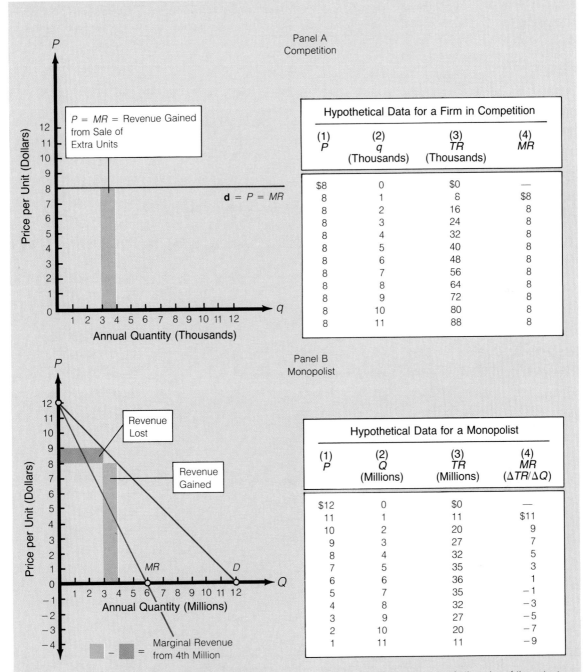

FIGURE 1 Marginal Revenue for Competition and Monopoly

Panel A
Competition

P = MR = Revenue Gained from Sale of Extra Units

d = P = MR

Hypothetical Data for a Firm in Competition

(1) P	(2) q (Thousands)	(3) TR (Thousands)	(4) MR
$8	0	$0	—
8	1	8	$8
8	2	16	8
8	3	24	8
8	4	32	8
8	5	40	8
8	6	48	8
8	7	56	8
8	8	64	8
8	9	72	8
8	10	80	8
8	11	88	8

Panel B
Monopolist

Revenue Lost

Revenue Gained

MR   D

Annual Quantity (Millions)

▢ − ▪ = Marginal Revenue from 4th Million

Hypothetical Data for a Monopolist

(1) P	(2) Q (Millions)	(3) TR (Millions)	(4) MR ($\Delta TR / \Delta Q$)
$12	0	$0	—
11	1	11	$11
10	2	20	9
9	3	27	7
8	4	32	5
7	5	35	3
6	6	36	1
5	7	35	−1
4	8	32	−3
3	9	27	−5
2	10	20	−7
1	11	11	−9

The revenue gained by a perfectly competitive firm when it sells an additional unit of output equals the price of the output (MR = P) because demand for the firm's product is perfectly elastic (Panel A). A firm with monopoly power must reduce price in order to sell extra output, so marginal revenue is always less than price (P > MR). In Panel B, a monopolist can sell 3 million units at $9 each ($27 million) or 4 million units at $8 ($32 million). Thus, the fourth million only adds $5 per unit, on the average, in revenue ($32 million − $27 million = $5 million).

The demand curve facing the monopolist in Panel B of Figure 1 is D and is based on the data next to the figure. Note that D is the industry's demand curve because the monopolist controls the entire industry. Total revenue (TR) equals the price per unit (P) times the amount sold—(Q)—and is listed in column 3. If

the firm set its price at $9, it could sell 3 million units annually and total revenue would be $27 million. The firm would sell 4 million if it lowered its price to $8, annual total revenue would rise from $27 million to $32 million for an extra $5 million. Why would total revenue fail to rise by $8 million—the full price of

FIGURE 2 Relationship Between Demand, Marginal Revenue, Total Revenue, and Elasticity (ε)

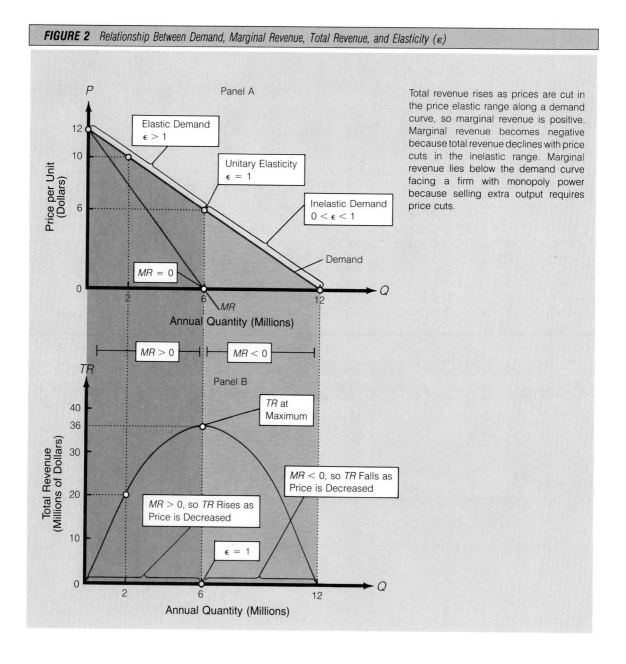

Total revenue rises as prices are cut in the price elastic range along a demand curve, so marginal revenue is positive. Marginal revenue becomes negative because total revenue declines with price cuts in the inelastic range. Marginal revenue lies below the demand curve facing a firm with monopoly power because selling extra output requires price cuts.

the million units sold? The answer is that the firm received $8 for each of the additional 1 million units sold, but it lost $1 per unit on the first 3 million units sold, resulting in an average increase in total revenue of only $5 for each of the last million units sold (8 − 3 = 5).

Numerical values for marginal revenue are listed in column 4 of the data next to Figure 1. Marginal revenue equals $\Delta TR/\Delta Q$ and is labeled *MR* in the figure. Notice that when quantity sold exceeds 6 million units and price is reduced below $6, marginal revenue is actually negative. This means that total revenue falls when extra units are sold and the price is lowered.

Total Revenue, Marginal Revenue, and Elasticity

Recall (from the chapter on elasticity) that there are close relationships between elasticity, price, and total revenue. For example, if expanding output requires such large price reductions that total revenue falls, the demand curve is price inelastic and marginal revenue is negative. How demand, marginal revenue, price, total revenue, and price elasticity are related is graphed in Figure 2, which reflects the data used in Panel B of Figure 1.

When quantity is less than 6 million units and the price is above $6, the demand is price elastic. The price cuts associated with increasing output are proportionately smaller than are the increases in output. Thus, when output is raised and prices are lowered, total revenue rises. This means that marginal revenue is positive when the price is above $6. Whenever marginal revenue is positive, demand is elastic. Conversely, total revenues fall as the price is reduced below $6, and demand is inelastic. Thus, when marginal revenue is negative, we are in the inelastic range of the demand curve. If price is changed slightly and total revenue does not change, marginal revenue is zero and demand is in the unitary elastic range. Let us now examine how the monopolist sets prices and output to maximize profits in the short run. As you will see, the concept of marginal revenue is vital to this decision.

Profit-Maximizing Price and Output

Profit maximization is probably the dominant goal of all firms; in the parlance of accounting, "The bottom line is what counts." Keep in mind that you need information about both revenues (demand) and costs (supply) to determine the profit-maximizing price and output. Like any firm, a monopolist will produce and sell extra output as long as each additional unit adds to total revenue at least as much as it adds to production cost. This is just another way of saying that the firm will continue to produce and sell as long as marginal revenue is greater than or equal to marginal cost ($MR \geq MC$).

In Figure 3 we have added data for costs of production to the revenue data in our previous example. The firm will produce and sell 4 million units at a price of $8 each, receiving total revenues of $32 million. Average total costs are $6 per unit, so $24 million is absorbed in total costs, leaving a total profit of $8 million. Looking at Panel A of the figure, total profit is the shaded rectangle *bcde* and equals price ($8) minus average total cost ($6) times the number of units sold (4 million), for total profits of $8 million.

Why does the firm sell 4 million units? Why not 3 million or 5 million? Maximizing profits requires the firm to produce and sell an extra unit any time the money brought in from an extra sale (*MR*) at least covers its costs of production (*MC*). If only 3 million units were sold, this monopoly firm would forgo profits equal to the shaded triangle to the left of point *a* in Panel A. Whenever marginal costs exceed marginal revenues, a firm will lose by producing extra output. If 5 million units were sold, the last million would add costs that exceed revenues by the amount of the shaded triangle to the right of point *a* (where $MR = MC$).

The rule for profit maximization is that the firm should produce output up to the point where $MR = MC$. A mathematically equivalent alternative rule is that the firm should maximize profits by producing where the difference between total revenue and total costs is greatest, as shown in Panel B. The data from our example are shown as "Total Revenues" and "Total Costs" in Panel B of Figure 3.

Loss-Minimizing Price and Output

One common myth is that monopolists always make profits. Monopolists can control the prices they charge for their products, so it seems natural that they will earn eco-

FIGURE 3   Profit Maximization and the Monopolist

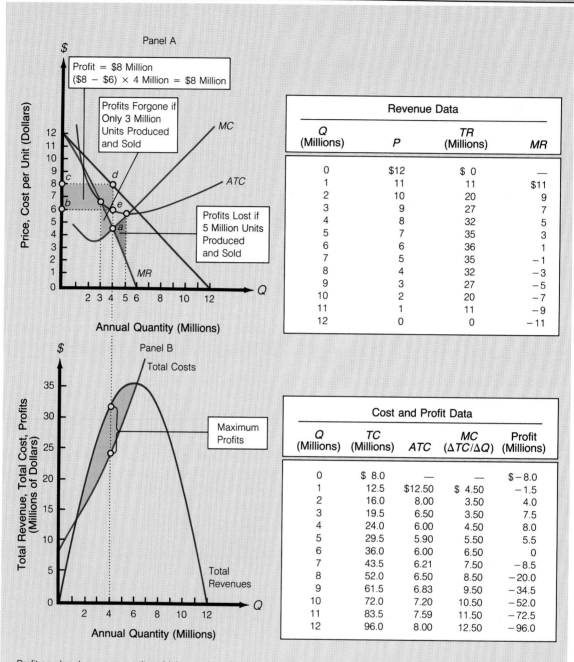

Panel A

Profit = $8 Million
($8 − $6) × 4 Million = $8 Million

Profits Forgone if Only 3 Million Units Produced and Sold

Profits Lost if 5 Million Units Produced and Sold

Revenue Data			
Q (Millions)	P	TR (Millions)	MR
0	$12	$ 0	—
1	11	11	$11
2	10	20	9
3	9	27	7
4	8	32	5
5	7	35	3
6	6	36	1
7	5	35	−1
8	4	32	−3
9	3	27	−5
10	2	20	−7
11	1	11	−9
12	0	0	−11

Panel B

Total Costs

Maximum Profits

Total Revenues

Cost and Profit Data				
Q (Millions)	TC (Millions)	ATC	MC (ΔTC/ΔQ)	Profit (Millions)
0	$ 8.0	—	—	$−8.0
1	12.5	$12.50	$ 4.50	−1.5
2	16.0	8.00	3.50	4.0
3	19.5	6.50	3.50	7.5
4	24.0	6.00	4.50	8.0
5	29.5	5.90	5.50	5.5
6	36.0	6.00	6.50	0
7	43.5	6.21	7.50	−8.5
8	52.0	6.50	8.50	−20.0
9	61.5	6.83	9.50	−34.5
10	72.0	7.20	10.50	−52.0
11	83.5	7.59	11.50	−72.5
12	96.0	8.00	12.50	−96.0

Profit can be shown as quantity sold times price minus average total cost [$\pi = Q(P - ATC)$], as in Panel A, or as the vertical difference between total revenue and total cost ($\pi = PQ - TC$), as in Panel B. Maximum profits are realized only if marginal revenue equals marginal cost ($MR = MC$).

nomic profits. Figure 4 depicts an instance where a monopolist would actually suffer losses if the good or service were produced. There are literally thousands of patented products for which demand is insufficient to justify production. The cost structures associated with these products are so high that there never is a price and output combination where the monopolist can make a profit. For example, you probably could not profit from monopolies on machines that re-weave "runs" in pantyhose, winders for string collec-tors, or disposable razor blade resharpeners. De-mands would be trivial relative to their costs.

Even if a monopolized good initially passes the market test, rising costs or shrinking demand may cause failure. In the short run, if P_e is above average variable costs, a firm would continue to produce despite losses. But what about the long run? This monopolist has two options: leave the industry and put its capital to more profitable use, or try to bolster demand sufficiently to lift its operations into the black, perhaps through aggressive marketing. No firm will tolerate persistent losses; in the long run, the firm will move its resources into a more lucrative line of business.

Is There a Long Run for Monopolists?   In compet-itive markets, short-run economic profits are signals for other firms to enter the industry and try to share in any profits, driving economic profits to zero in the long run. Will this be the case in an industry con-trolled by one firm? It depends on how difficult it is to prevent new firms from entering the market and exploiting potential profit opportunities.

If new competitors can somehow be prevented from entering the industry, the monopolist may ad-just its productive capacity along its long-run average cost curve to most profitably accommodate long-term variations in demand, as shown in Panel A of Figure 5. Alternatively, the owners or managers of a monopoly that is protected from the discipline of competition may allow the firm to operate very inefficiently. Why not hire your lazy relatives and friends at high salaries if a monopoly position ensures that you will have a high income anyway? Why bother to work hard or try to control costs? Why worry about quality and con-sumer satisfaction? Any customers who are going to buy the monopolized product must buy from your company.

If those who control a monopoly choose "the good life," inefficiency may drive up fixed costs, absorbing much of potential monopoly profit. This sort of adjustment is shown in Panel B of Figure 5. Of course, in the long run an inefficient monopoly is a natural target for takeover by profit seekers (corpo-rate raiders) who will manage the firm efficiently, so the previous owners can retire to loaf on the beach. These two prospects—long-term economic profits or a comfortable life with a high income—are good reasons for a monopolist to fear market entry by new competitors.

Maintaining Monopoly Power: Barriers to Entry

Maintaining a profitable monopoly position requires keeping other firms out of the industry.

> A **barrier to entry** is any obstacle that makes it unprofitable or impossible for new firms to enter an industry.

Entry can be thwarted in several ways. Some barriers to entry are artificial; others are technological or "nat-ural." We will discuss both types.

FIGURE 4 Loss-Minimizing Output for a Monopolist

The $MR = MC$ rule minimizes the losses of any firm, including a monopoly, as long as variable costs are covered by revenues.

FIGURE 5 Long-Run Adjustments by Monopoly Firms

Panel A
The Monopolist May Maximize Profits
by Accommodating Variations in Demand . . .

Panel B
. . . or a Monopoly May Operate Inefficiently
and Still be Profitable Because of the
Absence of Competition

If demand were D_0 in Panel A, a profit-maximizing monopoly firm would have a small plant, charge a high price, and earn profits equal to area $bdef$. If demand grew to D_1, the monopolist would expand its production facilities and realize greater profits equal to area $acgh$. Thus, in the long run, a monopolist may accommodate variations in demand through growth or contraction. However, a monopoly whose management was not threatened by competition might make the long-run adjustment of operating inefficiently, as long as it realized satisfactory profits. Panel B assumes that such sloppy management is a fixed cost. (Of course, in the long run, even sloppy managers die.)

Artificial Barriers to Entry **Artificial barriers to entry** can be legally permissible (e.g., annual style changes, excessive national advertising) or established by law (e.g., patents). Some barriers may be beyond the control of the monopolist (e.g., certain government regulations). Other barriers are clearly illegal. Monopolists are ingenious in trying to keep competitors out of a market. Where key natural resources are involved, one firm may attempt to corner the market, precluding other firms from entering the industry.

The most obvious legal barrier is government exclusion of competition. The U.S. Postal Service tries to maintain its monopoly position with laws that prohibit most competition for profitable first-class mail carrying. For example, its competitors cannot deliver to mailboxes. Without these constraints, competition for first-class mail delivery might parallel that for parcel-post deliveries from United Parcel Service and other package handlers. But even these statutes fail to discourage some entrepreneurs. A few firms have entered the first-class mail business by putting the "mail" into plastic bags and hanging it on the doorknobs of recipients. Federal Express now offers one-day hand delivery between many major cities.

Other important legal barriers to entry include patents and copyrights. Patent and copyright monopolies may be justified as incentives for research and development leading to technological progress and cultural enrichment. The granting of a patent monopoly provides expectations of monopoly profit to inventors, potentially allowing them to earn high returns on their risky inventive efforts. However, patents and copyrights are licenses for monopoly; patents bar competitive production for a period of seventeen years, and may be renewed. Patents were the principal barrier to entry protecting the Polaroid Company for years, giving the firm a monopoly in the market for "instant picture" cameras. At times, however, unethical firms "pirate" patented or copyrighted products, as discussed in Focus 1.

Government licenses and bonding restrictions ostensibly protect consumers from fraud or shoddy practices, but may actually be disguised entry barriers. Elaborate regulations may bar smaller firms from competing effectively. For example, there is evidence that the Food and Drug Administration's stringent regulation of the pharmaceutical industry reduced research and development efforts by big drug companies and drove most small firms completely out of that market. Many regulations may be worthwhile, but barriers preventing competition by smaller firms are among the social costs of regulation.

Natural Barriers to Entry
Not all barriers to entry result from the efforts of existing firms. Barriers may also emerge from the nature of a good or the cost structures inherent in some types of production. Nat-

ural gas is one product that leads to a single firm in any service area because of **natural barriers to entry.** Imagine the nuisance and inconvenience if twenty gas companies serviced your neighborhood and consumers did not collude to use gas from only one company. How often would the streets be torn up to install new gas pipe lines? How many pipes would run down every alley? How many firms might you need to contact before planting a tree or digging a drainage ditch? Installing a new storm sewer system would entail incredible expense.

A **natural monopoly** *emerges if economies of scale are substantial relative to the market demand for the product.*

Figure 6 illustrates a situation of *natural monopoly* arising from a production process. An unregulated monopoly could charge P_3 for Q_2 amount of output, reaping profits equal to the shaded area. This production process is characterized by high fixed costs and relatively low variable costs. Economies of scale are tremendous because average costs decline when overhead costs are spread across large amounts of output.

Here is why competition collapses and a monopoly takes over in such markets. Suppose that four firms were initially in the market, each breaking even by producing Q_0 at price P_3, where $Q_0 = Q_2/4$. Each firm would try to expand its output because if it can wrest customers from competitors, its marginal costs of serving new buyers would be far below its marginal revenues. But as industry output expands, price falls much faster than average total costs fall. Suppose, for example, that each firm doubles output. Since the industry output will be Q_3, price will be P_0. If all firms are the same size (Q_1), average total cost will be P_2, and every firm will lose P_2-P_0 on each unit produced. Eventually, three of the firms must leave the market, leaving the fourth to collect the full monopoly profits (the shaded area in Figure 6).

Such natural monopolies as utility companies are regulated in attempts to ensure that consumers enjoy the benefits of economies of scale. Unregulated natural monopolies could generate monstrous profits and tend to be very inefficient from society's vantage point. In later chapters we will consider illegal barriers to competition when there are artificial attempts to monopolize, and investigate potential regulatory benefits when technology makes monopoly a natural outcome of the marketplace.

FIGURE 6 A Natural Monopoly Market

Competitive processes in markets where economies of scale cause average costs to decline across the full range of market demand will ultimately evolve into a natural monopoly. Economies of scale are so significant that local natural monopolies are almost inevitable for electricity, natural gas, water and sewer facilities, and telephone service.

Contestable Markets

No firm with monopoly power can reap sustained economic profits unless competitors are precluded from entry.

> **Contestable markets theory** *suggests that easy market entry can force even firms that are the sole current sellers of goods to produce the same output levels and set the same prices as would firms in pure competition.*[1]

The doctrine of contestable markets pivots on the idea that competitive vigor is *less* related to the number of firms currently in an industry than to the *ease of market access* by other firms if prospects for economic profit exist.

Conventional industrial analysis assumes that the number of firms in an industry determines the extent of monopoly power and, thus, the price charged for output. Contestable markets theory turns this as-

sumption on its head, presuming that the prices buyers are willing to pay for given amounts of goods determine the numbers of firms in an industry if outsiders can always freely enter the market. One conclusion is that even when a single firm is the sole supplier in a market, the firm is forced to behave as if it were in competition if that market is "contestable." This theory has important implications for the antitrust policies we consider two chapters hence.

Price Discrimination

Monopoly power implies some control over price. We have shown how a monopoly maximizes profit if it can charge only one price for its product. In an earlier chapter, we discussed consumer surplus and noted that it was the difference between the amounts people would willingly pay for various amounts of specific goods and the amounts they do pay at market prices. But if the monopolist is able to isolate buyers into separate submarkets and has control over price, different groups of customers can be charged different prices and the monopolist can appropriate the consumer surplus.

---

1. The doctrine of contestable markets is described in W. Baumol, J. Panzar, and R. Willig, *Contestable Markets and the Theory of Industry Structure* (New York: Harcourt Brace Jovanovich, Inc., 1982).

Patents, Trademarks, Copyrights, and Counterfeit Goods

Obtaining patents, trademarks or copyrights is a costly endeavor that imparts monopoly rights on inventions, business identities, and intellectual property.

Inventions like the telephone and the electric light have revolutionized our lives and brought riches to their inventors. Research is pouring into gene splicing, faster computer microchips, and more attractive consumer products. Public and private research and development outlays exceeded $110 billion in 1987, and employed over a million scientists and engineers.

Trademarks also reserve monopoly power for firms. Several million dollars were spent developing the EXXON name. Hundreds of countries were checked to ensure that the name was not trademarked earlier and would not offend any consumers anywhere. Then millions more dollars were spent helping the public remember the new trademark. Firms like Gucci, Cartier, and Chanel invest heavily in their tradenames. Chanel, for example, spends over $1 million a year on tradename security alone.

Copyrights protect intellectual property in books, records, video tapes, and computer software, as well as product designs (e.g., Cabbage Patch Kids). Software developers have formed an organization to fight unauthorized duplication, and record producers use ASCAP and BMI to pressure businesses to license music for commercial purposes. ASCAP and BMI employ agents to see if businesses play background music to entertain customers. If, for example, a firm plays a radio, the owner is asked to purchase a license to play the music. A lawsuit immediately follows refusal. The law is clear—playing unlicensed music for commercial purposes without a license is illegal. ASCAP and BMI prorate their revenue to the music's copyright holders.

Today, counterfeit goods are threatening all these forms of monopoly power. Most imitations are inferior in quality. Replicas of aircraft parts and bogus "high-strengh" fasteners have appeared in civilian and military planes. The U.S. Department of Commerce estimates that almost a million jobs are lost to product "knock-offs," the industry's term for counterfeited goods.

Interestingly, both sides of this problem abhor publicity. Counterfeiters want secrecy so they can sell knock-offs; legitimate firms are reluctant to admit that their product line has been reproduced. Publicity may encourage further copying, or consumers may become wary of their brand names. In any event, counterfeiting increasingly erodes the monopoly power derived from patents, trademarks, and copyrights.

Price discrimination *occurs when a good or service is sold at different prices that do not reflect differences in production costs.*

This practice allows the monetary value of consumer surplus to be transferred from consumers to the producer.

People who think "discrimination" is always illegal may be amazed at the frequency of price discrimination. Have you ever paid a higher price to see a movie than the person who sat next to you did? Theaters often have different prices for children, students, adults, and senior citizens. Does it cost the theater more to seat a 32-year-old at a given show than a senior citizen? Clearly not. Doctors often argue that they render charity by charging their richer patients more than their poorer patients pay for the same service. (Might they charge whatever the market will bear in both cases?) Airlines ticket prices vary widely for roughly the same service (depending on early reservations and special promotions). The family in front of you in a grocery checkout line may pay much less for the same food than you do if it uses coupons and you don't. These are all examples of price discrimination.

Why do firms charge different customers different prices? Is price discrimination beneficial to society or harmful? What conditions make price discrimination possible?

Requirements for Price Discrimination

Price discrimination requires a firm to have monopoly power. The firm need not be a monopoly. Any seller that is a price maker rather than a price taker possesses monopoly power. This occurs whenever the demand curve facing an enterprise has negative slope. In this sense, your local florist has monopoly power even if it is not a monopolist.[2]

A second condition required for price discrimination is that customers with different demand elasticities be separable into submarkets. Different demand elasticities may arise from disparities of income, tastes and preferences, locations, and so on. Once a firm's customers are separated into two or more groups, it must be able to prevent arbitrage. *Arbitrage* occurs if buyers who pay the lower price can turn around and sell to customers charged the higher price. Medical treatment is one area where price discrimination abounds because arbitrage is impossible. One patient cannot sell another a gall bladder operation or an inoculation against polio or measles. Another interesting example of arbitrage is described in Focus 2. Price-discrimination schemes are short-lived when firms cannot prevent arbitrage.

In summary, the firm must have some monopoly power and must be able to separate the market into different groups with different elasticities of demand. Once this is accomplished, the firm must also prevent the lower-price users from selling to higher-price users. We will now look at the effects of two types of price discrimination on monopoly profits.

Profit Maximization and Price Discrimination

Different customers are charged different prices only if this increases a firm's profits. In the extreme case, a firm practicing **perfect price discrimination** extracts from all consumers their demand prices for every unit of a good it sells. These demand prices are the maximum payments each individual would willingly make rather than do without.

This case is illustrated in Figure 7, where we consider a monopolist who markets a tonic that cures baldness. To keep the graph simple, we assume that marginal costs are constant at $200 per bottle.[3] If this

---

3. Note that whenever marginal costs are constant, they also equal average variable costs. Take a the time to make sure you know why.

FIGURE 7 Monopoly Profits and Perfect Price Discrimination

Perfect price discrimination allows this patent-medicine monopolist to charge everything consumers will pay to have hair rather than do without. All potential consumer surpluses are converted into revenues for the perfectly price-discriminating firm.

---

2. Pure competitors would find it difficult to charge different prices for a homogeneous product because the demand curves they confront are horizontal. If one pure competitor raised its price, its customers would simply go elsewhere and their business would be lost to the firm. A competitive firm could (if it were altruistic) sell its product below the prevailing market price to a given group but would lose some of its normal profits in the process.

Arbitrage and Price Discrimination

In Cartels in Action *(New York: Twentieth Century Fund, 1946, pp. 402–4), George Stocking and Myron Watkins reported a classic case of arbitrage:*

Rohm & Haas of Philadelphia and Du-Pont [were] the only American producers of methyl-methacrylate plastics. They marketed methyl-methacrylate in the form of molding powders, for a variety of industrial uses, at $0.85 a pound. To licensed dental laboratories they supplied, at more than $22 a pound, prepared mixtures consisting of methyl-methacrylate powder (polymer) and liq-uid (monomer), both essential to the manufacture of dentures. At the same time they refused to sell the monomer in any other form to any other buyer. In this way they apparently planned to force the dental trade to rely exclusively upon them for supplies. The enormous price spread attracted "bootleggers" who found that they could "crack" the commercial powders back to the liquid, and sell the polymer and monomer together at a profit to the dental trade. To combat this practice, at the suggestion of a licensee, Rohm & Haas considered adulterating the cheap commercial pow-ders so that, for use in dentures, they would come under the ban of the Pure [sic] Food and Drug Administration. The licensee suggested that:

A millionth of one percent of arsenic or lead might cause them to confis-cate every bootleg unit in the country. There ought to be a trace of some-thing that would make them rear up.

Although Rohm & Haas thought this was a "very fine" suggestion, there is no evi-dence that they put it into effect.

monopolist set a single profit-maximizing price, it would charge $500 per bottle of tonic and sell 6,000 units. Total profit would be $1,800,000 [($500 − $200) × 6,000 = $1,800,000]. But this firm can profit more through price discrimination. For the firm to fully extract its customers' consumer surpluses, it must sell the first several hundred for between $800 and $799, the next several hundred for between $799 and $798, and so on, until the last bottle is sold for only a fraction of a cent over $200.

Perfect price discrimination allows this firm to appropriate all consumer surplus above a price of $200. This form of price discrimination allows the tonic bottler to boost its profit from the $1,800,000 (represented by the rectangular area) associated with normal monopoly pricing to $3,600,000 (the area of the entire shaded triangle above marginal costs). Perfect price discrimination would enable a monopolist to literally charge everything the market will bear. But no firm can determine the precise maximum that each individual is willing to pay for each unit of a good. At best, a firm might segment the buying public into a few distinct groups for whom arbitrage is impossible and whose elasticities of demand differ.

How even imperfect market segmentation can be profitable is depicted in Figure 8, which illustrates the demands of two groups of consumers. Fixed costs are zero and marginal cost is a constant $2. This firm charges $5 per unit in Market A and profit is $18,000; the lower price ($3.75) in Market B yields profit of $12,250. Total profit is $30,250. If this firm charged a single monopoly price, it would sell 13,000 units at $4.25 and make a total profit of $29,250. Price dis-crimination generates an extra $1,000 more per month than regular monopoly profits.

This second form of price discrimination is com-mon, and includes grocery coupons, special airline fares, senior citizens' discounts, and student rates for movie tickets or bus rides. Other types of price dis-crimination are more subtle. Private party phones cost less than business phones and long-distance rates historically generated higher rates of profit than

FIGURE 8 Group Price Discrimination and Firm Profitability

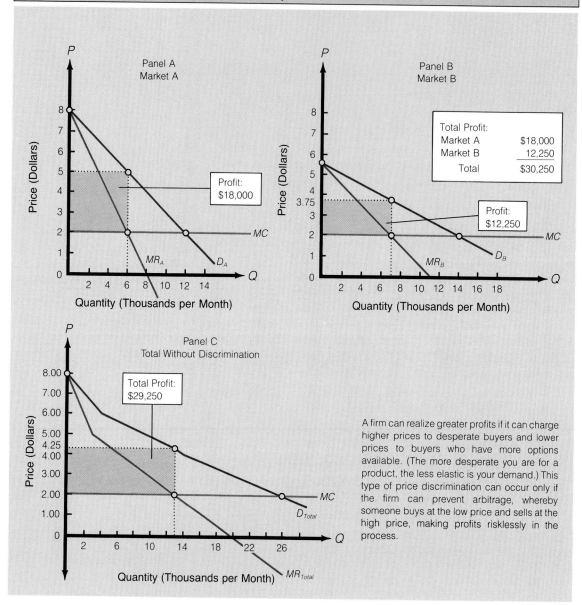

A firm can realize greater profits if it can charge higher prices to desperate buyers and lower prices to buyers who have more options available. (The more desperate you are for a product, the less elastic is your demand.) This type of price discrimination can occur only if the firm can prevent arbitrage, whereby someone buys at the low price and sells at the high price, making profits risklessly in the process.

local services. These gaps were far greater than any cost differentials. (Reorganization of the Bell system in January 1983 has, however, somewhat ameliorated this situation.)

We need to point out why some apparent price discrimination is illusory. It may seem price discriminatory that downtown parking lots charge lower monthly rates than weekly rates, which are lower

than daily, which, in turn, are lower than hourly rates. However, wage costs for parking lot attendants fall as the bulk of parking moves from short-term to long-term. Similarly, quantity discounts granted major purchasers of goods commonly reflect transaction-cost savings. Lower rates for weekend parking or off-peak long-distance telephone calls also reflect lower opportunity costs, not strictly differences in the desperation of buyers. Weekend parking or off-hour phone calls are not the same goods as spaces or calls during business hours. Price discrimination is not present whenever differences in opportunity costs are reflected in prices of similar goods.

Comparing Competitive and Monopoly Markets

We showed in the previous chapter that pure competition yields efficient prices and outputs. Prices are higher when firms exercise monopoly power, and output is less than would be produced were the industry competitive. Is the exercise of monopoly power, therefore, economically inefficient from a social point of view? In almost every instance, the answer is yes. Monopoly power may also cause what many people perceive as inequity in the distribution of income.

Differences in Prices and Outputs

A purely competitive market equilibrium is shown in Panel A of Figure 9. At point a, industry output equals Q_c and price equals P_c. The competitive market supply curve is the sum of the marginal cost curves (above $AVCs$) of all firms in the industry. Contrast these results with those for an unregulated but nondiscriminating monopolist, described in Panel B of the figure. Industry demand for the product is the same, and the marginal cost curve for the monopolist is assumed to be the same as that which collectively characterizes firms in the competitive industry. Equilibrium price and output will be P_m and Q_m, respectively. Not only is the monopoly price higher, but the monopoly output is lower than for a competitive industry.

Take special note of the fact that in Panel B, the monopolist's marginal cost curve is not the industry supply curve. Price is not a given for firms with

FIGURE 9 *Competition Versus Nondiscriminating Monopoly*

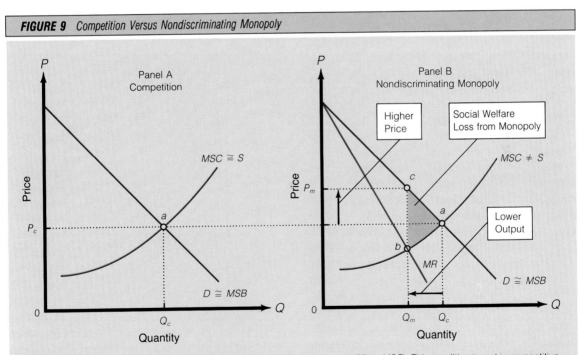

Efficiency requires that marginal social benefit equal marginal social cost ($MSB = MSC$). This condition is met in competitive markets where supply equals demand (Panel A). Because price is greater than marginal cost in equilibrium for a nondiscriminating monopoly (Panel B), some could gain without losses to anyone if output were increased, as long as the monopolist's additional costs were covered.

monopoly power. Since the monopolist is able to select the price that maximizes profit, the marginal cost curve is not the supply curve. We have denoted this as $MSC \neq S$. In fact, the quantities supplied by a firm with monopoly power cannot be ascertained from price alone; such firms first want to know how desperate buyers are (How elastic are their demand curves?) before selecting both price and production. There is no supply curve per se.

The Inefficiency of Monopoly

In the preceding chapter, we showed that the demand curve for any industry's product is roughly society's marginal benefit curve for that product. Thus, the marginal social benefit of the good is roughly its price ($P \cong MSB$). Pure competition forces each manufacturer to use the least-costly production technology, so the marginal social costs of production are reflected in competitive supplies. This is shown in the competitive panel of Figure 9 with the notation that *marginal social cost* approximates supply ($MSC \cong S$). The purely competitive market equilibrium at point *a* equates society's marginal (opportunity) cost of producing this good with the marginal benefits as: $MSB \cong P = MC \cong MSC$. Maximum benefits from available resources are realized only if the price equals the cost for the last unit produced and sold ($P = MC$). This is the reason purely competitive markets set standards for efficiency by which all other market structures are judged.

At the equilibrium for a nondiscriminating monopoly, price (marginal social benefit) exceeds marginal social cost; society would benefit more from extra units of the good than it would cost to produce them. That is, $P > MSC$. At first glance, this might seem desirable; society seems to get more from the marginal unit than it sacrifices. Actually, this situation is not desirable. Society would like more of its resources devoted to the production of any good for which marginal benefits exceed marginal costs. Resources are not allocated efficiently because the monopolist produces too little and charges too much. The potential gains to consumers from extra production exceed the costs of production. Therefore, so **monopolistic inefficiency** causes losses of social welfare equal to area *abc* in Panel B.[4]

Although price discrimination might sound as nasty as other forms of discrimination, it may remedy some of the inefficiency associated with monopoly power.

Price Discrimination and Efficiency

Surprisingly, price discrimination may overcome some of the inefficiency associated with unregulated monopoly power. In Figure 10, a nondiscriminating monopolist will charge a price of P_m for output equal to Q_m, yielding profit of $Q_m \times (P_m - P_c)$, which is area $P_c P_m ba$.

If this monopolist could price discriminate perfectly, profits would expand to the entire shaded area $P_c ec$ in Figure 10. Note that the price charged for the last unit sold, Q_c, will be P_c, which is identical to the constant unit price that would emerge if this market were purely competitive. In addition, the marginal

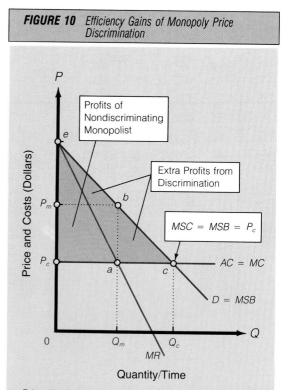

FIGURE 10 *Efficiency Gains of Monopoly Price Discrimination*

Price discrimination by a monopolist results in improvements in efficiency but raises problems for equity because efficiency gains tend to be realized by the discriminating firm and not by consumers.

---

4. This is known as a welfare loss triangle.

social costs and marginal social benefit will both equal the price of that last unit. Thus, price discrimination can lead to the economic efficiency we associate with pure competition. Price discrimination, however, is typically far from perfect (even at the margin). Moreover, under pure competition, the bulk of the net social benefits of the marketplace represent consumer surplus, while these benefits are appropriated by the owners of firms with monopoly power if they can price discriminate. Price discrimination may enhance efficiency, but many people think any exercise of monopoly power tends to distort the income distribution in an unfair way.

Monopoly and Inequity

Their ability to charge prices far in excess of opportunity costs delights monopolists. Most of us, however, view monopoly pricing as a means of gouging the public to provide high incomes for a few people. Their outsized earnings are achieved at the expense of the general public because (a) the inefficiency associated with nondiscriminating monopoly behavior causes real national income to fall below its potential, and (b) the purchasing power of nonmonopoly incomes is eroded. The total value of the national pie is reduced so that nondiscriminating monopolists can have more pie. Monopolistic price discrimination may overcome some inefficiency, but

the distribution of income will tend to be made even less equal and, perhaps, even less equitable.

In summary, the unregulated exercise of monopoly power causes economic inefficiency ($P > MC$), which implies that national income will be below its potential. The lack of competitive pressure may permit some monopolists to operate in a slack and wasteful fashion, worsening the problem. Moreover, monopoly power may pose problems of inequity in the distribution of income, a problem we address in more detail in a later chapter.

Ideally, all industries would be competitive. Unfortunately, this is impossible because certain technologies embody enormous economies of scale and lead to natural monopolies or certain firms are able to erect significant barriers to entry. Even if one firm is the sole supplier in a market, if that market is "contestable," the firm may not enjoy monopoly profits.

Natural monopolies are typically regulated in an attempt to ensure optimal and efficient operation. The government uses antitrust laws to try to make other industries behave as if they were competitive, or it may split some industries into smaller firms to ensure competition. In the next chapter we examine monopolistic competition and oligopoly—the part of the spectrum between monopoly and competition. After we discuss these market structures, the chapters that follow consider regulation of industry and antitrust policy, which represent government attempts to reach the competitive ideal.

CHAPTER REVIEW: KEY POINTS

1. An unregulated *monopoly* controls the output and price of a good for which there are no close substitutes.
2. Few monopolies are unregulated, but all firms with any ability to control prices have *monopoly power*. Models of pure monopoly provide insights into the behavior of the many firms with this power.
3. Monopoly power is maintained through *barriers to entry*. Barriers may be *artificial*, such as government patents or licenses, excessive model changes, and so on. Other entry barriers may be "*natural*"—the result of extreme economies of scale, where average costs decline over a large range of output. A natural monopoly emerges if market demand falls within such ranges.

4. A nondiscriminating monopolist's *marginal revenue* is less than its price. Marginal revenue equals the price the monopolist receives from the sale of the additional unit minus the revenue lost because prices must be reduced on all other units sold. Monopoly power causes the marginal revenue curve to lie below the demand curve.
5. The demand for a good is elastic when output is below the quantity where marginal revenue is zero. Demand is unitarily elastic when marginal revenue is zero. Demand is inelastic for outputs above the point where marginal revenue is zero.
6. A monopolist maximizes profit (or minimizes loss) by selling that output where marginal revenue equals marginal cost. The price charged corre-

sponds to the maximum price from the demand curve at this $MR=MC$ output level.

7. Monopolists' profit-maximizing (or loss-minimizing) levels of output do not normally occur at the minimum points on average cost curves. This level of output can either be less or more than the minimum average cost output.

8. If a monopolist is able to maintain its monopoly position in the long run, then pricing, output, and economic profit will reflect variations in demand. A monopolist may also choose inefficient, but comfortable, policies.

9. *Price discrimination* entails sales of essentially the same good at different prices when these differences are not justified by variations in costs. Price discrimination occurs in airline fares, theater ticket prices, charges for medical and dental services, and in many other areas.

10. Effective price discrimination requires a firm to have some monopoly power and the ability to separate customers into groups with different price elasticities of demand for the good. Further, it must prevent *arbitrage*—the selling of the good to high-price customers by low-price customers.

11. Price discrimination boosts a firm's total profit. *Perfect* price discrimination allows a firm to reap as profit all the consumer surplus that could be derived from the product.

12. A nondiscriminating monopoly is less economically efficient from society's point of view than are competitive industries. A monopolist typically produces less than if the industry were purely competitive and sells at a higher price. Price discrimination may reduce this inefficiency but it intensifies questions about equity in the distribution of income.

PROBLEMS

1. Table 1 lists the demand schedule and total variable costs for a monopolist. Assume that fixed costs are equal to 30. Graph the demand, marginal revenue, average total cost, and marginal cost curves. What is the profit-maximizing rate of output for the nondiscriminating monopolist? What will be the profit-maximizing rate of output if the monopolist can perfectly price discriminate? What is the profit differential between the two?

2. Suppose that materials and labor to duplicate audio tapes absorb marginal cost and average total cost at a constant $2, and that fans will buy 1,000,000 recordings by the hot music group *Chipped Beef on Toast* at $10 per tape. The producer's only other costs are the group's 20 percent royalties on total sales revenue. Suppose further that each 1 cent cut in price boosts sales by 5,000 tapes (e.g., $9 yields 1,500,000 sales, $8 yields 2,000,000 sales, . . .).

   a. How many tapes will the company want to produce and sell? How much profit would the firm realize? What is the elasticity of demand for this tape at this point? How much will the group realize in royalties?

   b. *Chipped Beef* will predictably argue that this price is excessive. What price and quantity would the group want the publisher to charge? How

Output	1	2	3	4	5	6	7	8	9	10
Price	100	90	80	75	70	65	60	50	40	30
TVC	100	175	225	265	300	330	365	410	475	575

TABLE 1 The Demand Schedule and Total Variable Costs for a Monopolist

much profit would the firm receive? What is the price elasticity of demand at this point? How much extra income would *Chipped Beef* realize if it could dictate the price the company charged?

   c. Now suppose royalties are a flat $1 per tape, with the proviso that the group's royalties cannot exceed the company's total revenue. What price will the firm charge, and for what quantity? How much profit would the firm receive? What is the price elasticity of demand at this point? What price would *Chipped Beef* want charged for its tapes? If the firm agreed, how many tapes would it sell? How much profit (or loss) would the firm realize? What is the price elasticity of demand at this point?

QUESTIONS FOR THOUGHT AND DISCUSSION

1. If one person recognizes that she or he is the sole supplier of affection to another, can the first person act like a monopolist to extract pay-offs from the second person? Ignoring monetary transactions, what kinds of payments can be extracted? Is this behavior common?

2. Price discrimination occurs when the price differentials charged for a good do not reflect differences in cost. Suppose that there are substantial differences in costs in serving different customers but a uniform price is charged. In what sense is this also price discrimination?

3. What, if anything, limits the power of the following suppliers to price discriminate? Do typical members of any of these groups attempt perfect price discrimination? Rank these groups according to how much price discrimination you think they typically exercise.
   a. The only bank in a small farming community.
   b. A car dealer.
   c. A grocery store.
   d. A sole supplier of affection to someone who is head-over-heels in love.
   e. A private college with a large endowment fund for scholarships.

4. Some observers of the American business scene think that monopoly power is so common that most giant firms do not maximize profits; they seek only satisfactory profits. Once these have been secured, management tries to maximize sales or growth, or to ensure comfortable, plush personal lives for management personnel. Pursuing the soft life is easy to understand, but how would modern corporate managers gain by maximizing growth or total sales? Do you think these commentators are right?

5. College students in some areas have access to only one institution. In other locations, numerous private or public colleges and universities are available. Since higher education is generally nonprofit, how do these institutions exercise their differing levels of monopoly power? Would you expect treatment of students to differ between private and tax-supported schools? If so, how? Do you think schools behave differently when demand is growing, as in the 1960s, than when it is falling, as in the early 1980s? How?

6. Government has a legal monopoly on most forms of violence outside of athletics. National defense, police services, prisons, and the like are all inherently violent. Do you think violence is lower because of government's monopoly power? Would a society without government be less violent, as anarchist philosophers suggest? Can you apply the analysis of this chapter to this question?

7. Suppose you are the owner-operator of three of the four downhill ski slopes in Aspen, Colorado. Your competitor suggests that you jointly offer four-mountain, 6- or 7-day discount tickets that would permit visitors to ski any mountain on any day of their visit. Revenue would be split based on where skiers actually used the lift tickets included in the booklet.
   a. Who stands to benefit most from this proposal?
   b. For what reasons might you not want to accept this proposal?
   c. Does your control of three of Aspen's four ski slopes constitute a monopoly? Do you have significant monopoly power?
   d. If you decided to offer a three-mountain, 6- or 7-day special coupon booklet yourself, do you think it would sell? What would that do to your competitor? What could your competitor do to combat this threat?
   e. Would it be *economically efficient* if the courts forced you to agree to the four-mountain, 6- or 7-day package? Would it be *fair*?

CHAPTER 25

oligopoly

monopolistic competition

product differentiation

conscious interdependence

concentration ratios

merger

kinked demand curve

limit pricing

cartels

joint profit maximization

game theory

Monopolistic Competition and Oligopoly

The top 200 American firms control roughly 60 percent of U.S. manufacturing assets and are responsible for the bulk of our production. These firms are in industries that lie between the extremes of pure competition and pure monopoly. None is a price taker; all have some monopoly power.

Many major industries are dominated by a few giant corporations. These *oligopolistic* firms individually do not have the discretion available to unregulated monopolists because they must consider other firm's reactions as they make decisions about prices, production, and marketing strategy.

Oligopolies *are industries dominated by a few firms whose decisions are inextricably and consciously linked.*

Models of pure competition and monopoly provide insights into the behavior of oligopolists, but neither pure competitors nor monopolists base their decisions on the expected reactions of other firms. Hence, theories of oligopoly cannot just blend theories of competition and monopoly.

Oligopoly models must qualitatively account for interdependence in decision making. Theories of oligopoly abound because the dynamics of interdependence differ markedly from one industry to another. Just as proper play in poker depends as much on your opponents' characteristics as it does on the cards you are dealt, oligopolists' strategies depend on their individual positions relative to those of current competitors and potential rivals who might enter their industry. Consequently, no single model is sufficiently general to cover all oligopoly markets. In this chapter, we present some representative models that attempt to explain oligopolistic pricing and output.

Oligopoly is closer to monopoly than to pure competition. Firms in a slightly more competitive mode engage in monopolistic competition.

> **Monopolistic competition** *requires easy entry and exit into industries in which many potential suppliers compete vigorously with makers of close, but not perfect, substitutes for their "brand name" products.*

Monopolistic competitors do not base decisions on the anticipated individual reactions of their many competitors, so they are not mutually interdependent in the way oligopolists are. They are not pure competitors, however, because product differentiation gives them some power to set prices.

The continuum from pure competition to monopolistic competition through oligopoly to pure monopoly is not very smooth. Ascertaining where a given industry fits is not easy, and these classifications may change over time. For example, thirty years ago automaking was clearly an oligopoly; General Motors, Ford, and Chrysler sold roughly 95 percent of all cars in the United States. American Motors, Studebaker, DeLorean, and Packard have died, but international competition from BMW, Fiat, Honda, Hyundai, Isuzu, Mazda, Mercedes, Nissan, Saab, Sterling, Subaru, Toyota, Volkswagen, Volvo, Yugo, and others seems to have moved automaking into a monopolistically competitive mode.

Most firms are clearly neither pure competitors nor pure monopolists, but few models of firm behavior occupied this vast middle ground until the 1930s. The works of Joan Robinson and E. H. Chamberlin made earlier models seem incredibly naive. Indeed, many economists argue that this area remains analytically fuzzy and that we need general models about how firms that have incomplete monopoly power make decisions about output and prices.

Which theory of market structure best fits a particular industry may be difficult to determine, but each model can be useful in analyzing some policies of specific firms. Economists have never claimed that one or two simple models explain all business decisions. Your study of this chapter should, however, provide insights into how business operates between the polar extremes of pure competition and unregulated monopoly.

Product Differentiation

The model of pure competition assumes that large numbers of firms produce identical products. This assumption may fit farming and parts of a few other industries, but most firms sell products that differ from those of their rivals.

> **Product differentiation** *is the process of altering goods that serve almost identical purposes so that they differ in minor ways.*

Differentiated products may be normal when our tastes and preferences are still in flux and may signal competition in process. Homogeneity, on the other hand, may occur as a consequence of orders from some central authority. For example, covered wagons in Western movies are all quite similar because the film industry created an image and has them built to order. Most pioneers did not load their belongings into picturesque prairie schooners during the real migration to the Old West. They rode, instead, in a motley assortment of whatever wagons were available; two men reportedly moved their gear from St. Louis to Denver in a wheelbarrow in 1867.

Nevertheless, many firms accentuate product differences to try to make us value their products more than those from rival firms. Some people might argue that gasoline is gasoline, but big oil companies clearly feel that promotion and advertising will make customers perceive differences. Another example is soap. Are Tide, All and Cheer meaningfully different laundry detergents? Soap makers spend millions each year to persuade us that they are. Ford, GM, Chrysler, and numerous foreign producers all sell automobiles that provide the same basic transportation services. Despite the fact that automobiles are similar in many ways, most of us prefer certain cars based on advertising, styling, the reputed frequency of repair, or our past experience.

Advertising

Some critics believe that marketing puffery persuades consumers to buy useless items or creates an image that a particular brand product is unique when in reality it has many close substitutes. Can you

BIOGRAPHY

E. H. Chamberlin (1899–1967) and Joan Robinson (1903–83)

Until Edward Hastings Chamberlin attempted to fuse the theories of monopoly and competition, the case of many sellers offering differentiated products had been overlooked. Earlier mainstream economists concentrated on the theory of pure competition, which assumes many sellers of homogeneous products. Chamberlin instead saw close competitors in nearly every market trying to gain monopoly power by differentiating their products. For example, a firm might allege the superiority of its product over "Brand X."

Born in La Conner, Washington, Chamberlin revised his Harvard Ph.D. dissertation and published *The Theory of Monopolistic Competition* in 1933. His was among the few dissertations to ever profoundly alter economic theory. The central feature of Chamberlin's analysis is that it portrays the demand curves facing firms with differentiated products as being negatively sloped. In other words, firms that compete on the basis of product differences could raise prices without losing all their customers, but they would sell less output. This fact introduces elements of monopoly. Competition tends to lower this negatively sloped demand curve, however, to a point of tangency with the firm's average total cost curve, so that no monopoly profits are realized in the long run. Chamberlin's theory combined with Joan Robinson's ideas to spark numerous studies of industrial markets in the 1940s and 1950s.

I don't know much math, so I have to think.

—*Joan Robinson*

The iconoclastic British economist Joan Robinson was a combatant in virtually every major controversy in economic theory and policy between 1930 and 1983. Her foes joined her friends, however, in admiring the innovative quality of her ideas and research. She married E. A. G. Robinson (another distinguished British economist) after completing her formal studies in economics and was among the small group of Cambridge University economists who aided John Maynard Keynes in launching the Keynesian revolution.

An avowed radical and Marxist, her writings blended the insights of Keynes, Marx, and neoclassical reasoning in a manner uniquely her own. Robinson's work bridged capital theory, the theories of value and distribution, macroeconomics, and the economics of policy-making, but her contributions in the area of imperfect competition were her most noteworthy feat. At almost exactly the same time that Chamberlin issued his theory of monopolistic competition from Cambridge, Massachusetts, Joan Robinson launched a parallel theory from Cambridge, England in her *The Economics of Imperfect Competition.* However, Robinson's "imperfect competition" stresses oligopolistic interdependence and views competition and monopoly as mutually exclusive, while Chamberlin identified modern business as a blending of the two. Robinson refined the theory of price discrimination, introduced the concept of *monopsony power* (that is, the ability of powerful buyers to control prices), and separated average revenue (demand) and marginal revenue curves. These analytical feats have provided useful insights into numerous market situations. In Robinson's phrase, she and Chamberlin introduced a "box of tools" sharper and more generally applicable than those that preceded their works.

remember the worst advertisement you ever saw or heard? If so, the advertiser partially accomplished its goal by making an unforgettable impression.[1]

Most economists agree that informative advertising enables consumers to make more satisfactory choices. *Informative advertising* conserves resources and enhances economic efficiency because it reduces transaction costs. Examples include information about prices, availability, and meaningful differences in products. *Persuasive advertising,* on the other hand, focuses on slogans and imagery. Most beer commercials, for example, feature a bunch of people having a good time, but convey little real information. An advertiser whose commercials dwell on images but say little about price or meaningful features is probably selling a product that lacks much in the way of real differences.

Product differences can be real or illusory. Differentiation only requires that consumers perceive differences. An example of a differentiated product that is physically homogeneous is liquid bleach. All standard liquid bleach is chemically identical, but most people buy nationally advertised brands rather than cheaper generic substitutes. Why? Because marketing programs create imaginary differences among brands.

Meaningless differences are also found in aspirin-based pain relievers that advertisements claim contain "the ingredient that doctors recommend most." We seldom hear that the ingredient is aspirin, and that generic brands are as potent as Bayer. Some folks seem convinced that "the more you pay, the more it's worth." Of course, product differentiation may also be real. Cars, for example, may be quite different in durability, styling, or service.

How firms gain from marketing that differentiates products is obvious. Purely competitive firms are price takers that sell identical products. Firms try to use product differentiation to boost the demands for their products and shrink their price elasticities. Successful product differentiation provides a firm with some degree of monopoly power; they become price makers. This enables the firm to sell more product even if it raises the price.

In Figure 1, we show that product differentiation gives firms some control over price. Without this control, firms can only adjust output levels to maximize profits—the demand curve facing a pure competitor is perfectly elastic. Successful product differentiation expands the demand curve and makes it less elastic. One important result is that the marginal revenue curve now lies below the demand curve, much like that of the monopolist described in the previous chapter. Another result is that the prices charged vary among the firms in an industry in which differentiation is rampant.

The demands facing oligopolists or monopolistic competitors are more elastic than the industry (monopoly) demand since there are substitutes for each

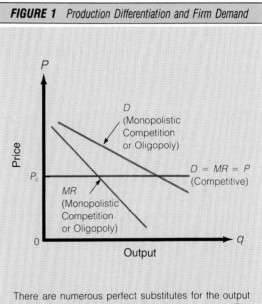

FIGURE 1 *Production Differentiation and Firm Demand*

There are numerous perfect substitutes for the output of competitive firms, so demand is perfectly elastic. The absence of perfect substitutes makes the demand for the output of a monopolistically competitive firm less than perfectly elastic. Because of this small amount of monopoly power, the marginal revenue curve for a monopolistically competitive firm is always below the price of the output. The fewness of competitors similarly causes oligopolists to possess monopoly power so that the demand curve exceeds the marginal revenue curve.

1. This point is made by Robert M. Kenney, "Emphasizing the Effect of Advertising on Consumer Choice," in Ralph Byrns and Gerald Stone, eds., *Great Ideas for Teaching Economics,* 4/ed. (Glenview, IL: Scott, Foresman/Little, Brown, 1989).

firms' products. Still, these firms can increase prices and not lose all their customers. Some of us will continue to eat Wheaties even if the price is raised a bit, but if General Mills boosts the price too much relative to other cereals' prices, our loyalty fades and we feed our faces a bit differently.

Monopolistic Competition _____

Monopolistic competition resembles pure competition in allowing many competitors easy entry or exit, but differs because each firm in the industry produces a differentiated good. Monopolistically competitive industries have

1. large numbers of potential suppliers,
2. each firm producing a slightly differentiated product, and
3. relative ease of entry or exit.

Each monopolistic competitor can act a little like a monopoly because product differentiation creates monopoly power by increasing the magnitude and decreasing the elasticity of the demand curve the firm faces.

Short-Run Pricing and Output

A monopolistic competitor's profit-maximizing short-run price and output combination is illustrated in Figure 2. Regardless of market structure, all firms maximize profits by selling that output where marginal revenue equals marginal cost. This is point a in Figure 2; output q_0 is sold at a price P_0. In the short run, this successful firm's economic profit equals the shaded area.

Monopolistic competitors may suffer short-run losses; if a firm's average cost curve was always above the demand curve, profits would be impossible. Like all firms, a monopolistic competitor would minimize losses by selling that output where marginal revenue equals marginal cost, as long as the price it could set (average revenue) exceeded average variable costs.

Long-Run Adjustments

Monopolistic competitors differentiate products to exploit short-run profit opportunities, and would like these profits to persist and grow. Their wishes are usually frustrated because typical monopolistic com-

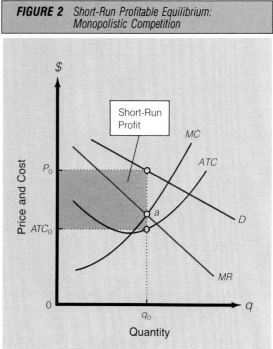

FIGURE 2 *Short-Run Profitable Equilibrium: Monopolistic Competition*

The *MR = MC* cost rule for maximum profits applies to all firms, including those in monopolistically competitive industries. Monopolistically competitive firms can make economic profits in the short run.

petitors earn only normal profits in the long run. Economic profits could be sustained only if other firms could be barred from the profitable industry; but entry cannot be prevented, so the long-run industry adjustments parallel those of pure competition. As new firms enter and try to share profits, prices fall and costs may rise, so that any economic profits disappear. Prices must fall when new competitors expand output and try to take customers from existing firms.

This shrinks demands for successful firms' products, ultimately leaving them in an equilibrium of the sort shown in Figure 3. Marginal revenue equals marginal cost at point a, and the long-run average total cost curve (*LRAC*) is just tangent to the demand curve at point b. This tangency allows the firm to sell its output at a price just equal to average cost ($P_e = ATC_e$), yielding only normal profits in the long run. Price exceeds marginal cost, however, ($P_e = ATC_e > MC$). Product differentiation causes the prices of comparable goods to vary in monopolistic competition, but only within a narrow range.

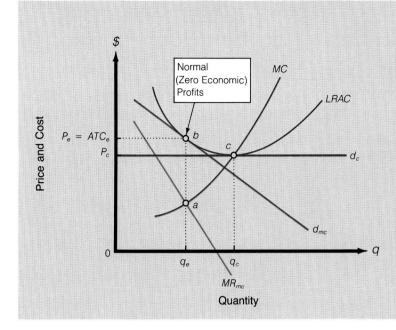

FIGURE 3 *Monopolistic Competition: Long-Run Equilibrium and Efficiency*

In the long run, entry and exit from the industry will prevent the monopolistically competitive firm from experiencing either economic profits or losses. Economic profits would be possible if the demand curve exceeded average costs over any range of output; economic losses would be unavoidable if the average cost was above demand at all output levels. Thus, competition yields an equilibrium where demand is just tangent to the average cost curve, and price equals average cost ($P = AC$). For the competitive firm in the long run, $P = MR = MC = ATC$, so there is economic efficiency. The long-run equilibrium for the monopolistically competitive firm is such that $P > MR$ and $MR = MC$. Even though $P = AC$, $P > MC$ suggests that there is economic inefficiency.

Compare this long-run equilibrium with a purely competitive equilibrium. If this firm were in a purely competitive industry, equilibrium would be at point c and the firm would be producing more and selling at a lower price ($P_c = min\ LRAC = MC$). Does this mean that society as a whole loses because monopolistic competition is inefficient? The answer is MAYBE.

Resource Allocation and Efficiency

Both pure competitors and monopolistic competitors earn only normal profits in the long run, so how can monopolistic competition be inefficient? The answer lies in the costs and benefits of product differentiation to consumers.

The price paid by consumers exceeds the marginal cost of production for the monopolistically competitive firm. Our analyses in the two preceding chapters suggested that pure competition is efficient because marginal social benefit equals marginal social cost ($P = MSC$) in a purely competitive equilibrium, but that a nondiscriminating unregulated firm with monopoly power is inefficient because in equilibrium the marginal social benefit exceeds the marginal social cost ($P > MSC$) of production. The price (marginal social benefit) charged by any monopolistic

competitor exceeds its marginal cost, so it appears that monopolistic competition is economically inefficient.

Some economists rebut this conclusion by arguing that any minor inefficiencies are more than offset by the greater range of choices available. If you view product diversity as worthless and are unwilling to suffer from this type of economic inefficiency, a solution is to buy only generic or unbranded goods. Alternatively, government could set specifications for various products and forbid firms to deviate from government formulas. You could buy any color Model T Ford you wanted—as long as it was black.

The other side of the coin is that product differentiation may have little to do with truly unique features or real differences. The economic inefficiency apparent whenever price exceeds marginal cost may arise, in monopolistic competition, from wasteful advertising and promotion.

Persuasive advertising (slogans and image puffery) is clearly wasteful, as indicated in Figure 3. A purely competitive market yields a market price of P_c and each firm produces q_c units in the long run. Contrast this situation with the long-run output for monopolistic competition in this figure, in which we assume that misleading advertising persuades consumers that physically identical goods differ in desirability so that they develop "brand loyalty." The price is higher (P_e) and each firm sells less (q_e).

Note that relative to the pure competitor, the monopolistic competitor has a higher average total cost curve. At the minimum point, the pure competitor could produce for P_c per unit; advertising and other costs of artificial differentiation drive up the monopolistic competitor's minimum average cost to P_e. Monopolistic competition causes resource misallocation because costs, and thus prices, are higher and each firm's output is less. This equilibrium resembles unregulated monopoly, but inefficiency is less severe.

Is product differentiation desirable because consumers gain a greater range of choice, or is most differentiation an artificial and worthless consequence of misleading advertising? Your answer to this question indicates whether or not you think monopolistic competition is economically efficient. Your answer may easily vary from one industry to the next.

Oligopoly

Less competitive than monopolistic competition, oligopoly lies towards the monopoly end of the spectrum of market structures. Oligopolistic markets are dominated by so few firms that each is cognizant of its rivals' marketing strategies; their behavior is consciously interdependent.

> **Conscious interdependence** *exists when firms consider the reactions of their rivals when they adjust their prices, outputs, or product lines.*

Industries are **pure oligopolies** if firms produce homogeneous outputs. Examples include the steel and aluminum industries. Industries are **impure oligopolies** if the various firms' production is slightly differentiated. Tire makers and tobacco firms are impure oligopolists.

Dominance by a Few Firms

A market shared by two firms is certainly an oligopoly, but would ten or twenty sellers still be considered few? The answer is not clear-cut. What matters is whether or not a handful of large *interdependent*

companies consciously dominate an industry. If so, it is concentrated and oligopolistic. The term *concentration* is often used to identify oligopolistic industries.

> **Concentration ratios** *are the percentages of domestic sales by the largest four (or eight) domestic companies in an industry.*

Figure 4 provides examples of relatively concentrated industries—automobiles, tires, aircraft, and cigarettes seem highly concentrated. In the aircraft industry, for example, the four largest firms generate 66 percent of total industry sales; the eight top firms account for 86 percent of the industry.

Be wary, however, of relying on concentration ratios alone to identify monopoly power. Nor do stable concentration ratios necessarily indicate a lack of competition. First, these ratios consider only U.S. sales by American firms. Imports may offer robust competition. Second, markets containing few firms may be contestable if entry is relatively easy. The international automobile market is an example of an increasingly competitive and contestable industry, but concentration ratios ignore the recent wave of foreign entrants into this market. Nevertheless, industries toward the right in Figure 4 appear to be among the more oligopolistic in the United States.

How Oligopoly Arises

There are three major causes of oligopoly (*a*) economies of scale, (*b*) other substantial barriers to entry, and (*c*) merger.

Economies of Scale Technical efficiency sometimes requires enormous plants and massive equipment. Economies of scale cause an industry to gravitate into a natural monopoly when only a single firm of considerable size relative to market demand is able to produce at a low cost. An industry tends toward the oligopoly mold if economies of scale are less formidable.

Joe Bain's pioneering study of economies of scale concluded that efficient production of copper, typewriters, and tractors each required plants that could supply more than 10 percent of these markets. Ten or fewer firms might be expected to comprise these industries. While Bain's study focused on manufactur-

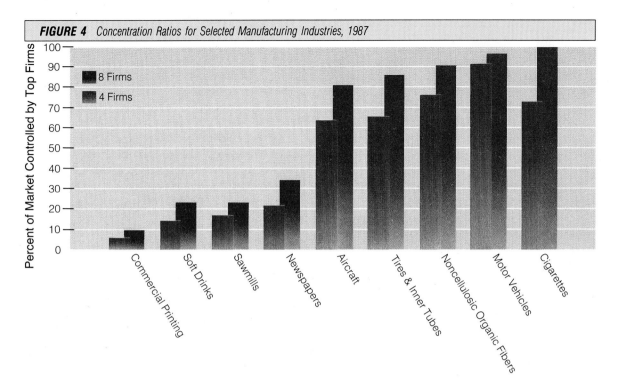

FIGURE 4 Concentration Ratios for Selected Manufacturing Industries, 1987

The shares of sales by the largest four and largest eight firms in an industry indicate little concentration in those industries toward the left side of this figure (e.g., commercial printing, soft drinks) but substantial concentration in those toward the right side (motor vehicles, cigarettes). These numbers must be taken with a grain of salt, however, because only the sales of domestic firms are considered. For example, inclusion of imports would cause a much lower concentration ratio for the automobile industry.

Source: *Statistical Abstract of the United States, 1982–88.*

ing economies of scale, in some industries (automobiles, for example) there may be economies of scale in distribution that determine the optimal sizes of firms. Bain concluded, however, that overall concentration in American industry was not generally justified by economies of scale.

Studies of efficient plant sizes are important, but technology may change so rapidly that some industry studies are obsolete shortly after they are written. For example, Bain's typewriter study is now moot because printers hooked up to personal computers are rapidly replacing these machines in most offices.

An offshoot of technological advance in the last century was pressure for ever larger plants (e.g., steel, railroads). Substantial entry barriers may exist if new technology (e.g., robotics) mandates huge operations. Existing firms with established product lines may be able to activate new technologies so rapidly that new firms cannot get a toehold in the industry. It

is possible, however, for large amounts of old capital to be an anchor that keeps established firms from keeping pace with upstarts that adopt the latest technology. For example, U.S. steelmakers have had problems in recent years because most American steel plants are ancient, while their competitors in Japan, Korea, and Germany operate modern equipment in newer facilities.

Most recent technological advances (e.g., electronics) have probably been relatively less favorable to huge firms than to smaller ones. For example, cable television has diluted the oligopolistic power of the major networks (ABC, CBS, and NBC), and small computer firms have gained on traditional computer giants. Some disadvantages of large firms may have been partially offset by computerization and improved communications, but U.S. employment growth has been most rapid among small firms in new industries.

Artificial Barriers to Entry Substantial economies of scale may impede entry into a profitable oligopoly, but artificial barriers also play a role. For example, existing firms frequently change models or undertake excessive selling and/or advertising expenses. Extravagant marketing may intimidate potential entrants with tight financial constraints. Alternatively, existing firms may market numerous versions of a basic good (differentiated cereals, cigarettes, or over-the-counter drugs), leaving little shelf space in retail outlets for potential rivals. Another strategy to bar entry occurs when mature (senile?) industries and their unions lobby to erect legal import quotas and tariff walls against foreign competition. Textiles, apparel, automobiles, and steel are all industries that have received protection from foreign competition.

Merger Oligopolies also arise through **merger**—the absorption of one firm by another. Merger may be a less rocky path for expansion than using retained earnings, sales of new stock, or borrowing. If the easier route of merger has the added benefit of eliminating a direct competitor, it is called a *horizontal merger*.

Recent *takeovers* by *corporate raiders* illustrate two aspects of mergers. Most top managers of takeover targets fear for their own job security and the jobs of other employees. Communities often become embroiled in these battles when a target company provides a town's economic lifeblood. Focus 1 examines some issues surrounding "corporate raiding."

Conscious Interdependence

When entry is restricted and a few firms dominate an industry, each firm recognizes that any action it takes will be countered by others. For example, when Chrysler introduced big rebates in the late 1970s, Ford and GM quickly responded with similar rebates, denying Chrysler its hoped-for advantage. After "Dallas" became a popular nighttime soap opera, other producers quickly launched "Knot's Landing," "Falcon Crest," "Hotel," . . . . Any successful competitive technique is rapidly imitated by other firms as they attempt to maintain or expand their own market shares.

Consciousness of rivals' expected reactions to policy changes arises primarily from the fewness of firms in an oligopoly. Success often depends on assessing rivals' responses. Failure to predict rivals' reactions may result in bad news on the bottom line of an oligopolist's annual report. Pressures for predictability often lead oligopolists to cooperate; this cooperation is generally not in the interest of society as a whole. You will see that a stable oligopolistic equilibrium presents a surface appearance quite similar to that of pure or monopolistic competition in the long run; prices are stable and there is no net entry or exit in the industry. This requires each oligopolist to behave predictably so that rivals know what to expect from each other.

Oligopolistic Decision Making

Oligopolistic interdependence creates complex problems for any analysis because rival firms may interact in many ways. An obvious strategy is for oligopolists to try to unite and share both the market and monopoly profits. This is known as forming a *cartel*. Another tactic is to allow one firm to set prices for the entire industry. *Price leadership* models leave pricing decisions to the largest firms or to the one with the lowest cost structure.

Many other assumptions can describe cooperation and competition among the few, but models of oligopolistic scheming are generally either *collusive* (formal) or *noncollusive* (informal). Noncollusive pricing may emerge naturally if each firm acts cooperatively because each realizes that others will offset any strategy aimed at boosting market share and profit. Alternatively, the industry may contain a single dominant firm that sets price and output policies that other firms follow without overt agreement. We will investigate only three of many possible oligopoly models. The kinked demand curve and most limit-pricing models are noncollusive, while cartels depend on collusion. More complex oligopoly models are the topics of more advanced courses.

The Kinked Demand Curve

Prices in highly concentrated industries were once commonly thought to be unresponsive to changes in costs or demands. The famous kinked demand curve model of oligopoly pricing sought to explain this "stickiness" of prices in oligopolistic industries as the natural result of noncollusive behavior.[2]

According to **kinked demand curve models,** *other firms maintain current prices if any firm raises its prices, but all firms match any price reductions by any single firm.*

The consequences of these expectations about pricing strategy are shown in Figure 5. At point *a,* the price is currently P_e and q_e units of the product are

---

2. In his Nobel Prize acceptance address, George Stigler discouraged the use of kinked demand curves because of insufficient empirical support for sticky prices predicted by the model. Nevertheless, the kinked demand curve model is the *best* model to illustrate oligopolistic interdependencies.

sold by each firm in this pure oligopoly. Demand curve D_0 represents the highly elastic demand curve facing a firm if no other firms follow its price changes. If the firm were alone in lowering its price, its sales would soar (a movement along D_0 to the right of q_e), but if it raises its price and the others do not follow, its sales plummet (movement along D_0 to the left of q_e). When one firm raises its prices and others do not, the competitors' products become better substitutes for consumers.

If rivals match all price changes, however, demand curve D_1 reflects the firm's less elastic options. If it slashes prices and all other firms do the same, the firm's sales grow only slightly. The firm's sales fall little if both it and its rivals boost prices. Along D_1 the firm would lose few sales to other firms because their

FIGURE 5 *Price Stability and Cost Changes under Oligopoly (Kinked Demand Curve Model)*

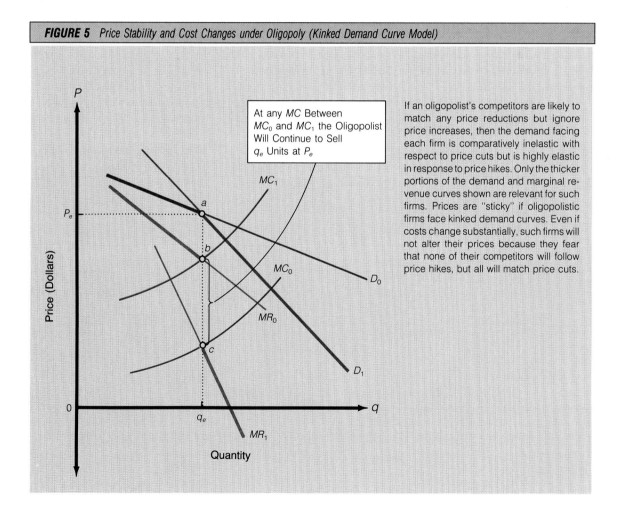

At any MC Between MC_0 and MC_1 the Oligopolist Will Continue to Sell q_e Units at P_e

If an oligopolist's competitors are likely to match any price reductions but ignore price increases, then the demand facing each firm is comparatively inelastic with respect to price cuts but is highly elastic in response to price hikes. Only the thicker portions of the demand and marginal revenue curves shown are relevant for such firms. Prices are "sticky" if oligopolistic firms face kinked demand curves. Even if costs change substantially, such firms will not alter their prices because they fear that none of their competitors will follow price hikes, but all will match price cuts.

Lollipops, Poison Pills, and Corporate Raiders

The next time you hear someone refer to a "hostile takeover," ask them two questions: One, "would you view someone's making you a great offer on, say, your house, as a hostile act?" Two, "who owns companies—managers or shareholders?" If they think an offer to buy is a hostile act, they've got emotional problems. If they think managers own firms, they haven't been to high school. If they answer both questions correctly, ask them not to embarrass themselves in the future by referring to "hostile takeovers."

—*James C. Miller III, Director**
Office of Management and the Budget

---

*Wall Street Journal, 26 Oct. 1987, p. 22.

The 1980s have witnessed dramatic mergers and corporate takeover activity. Students of corporate finance have been forced to learn a new vocabulary. Words like *greenmail, poison pills, lollipops, junk bonds, white knights* and *cash cows* have swollen the vocabulary of heretofore staid Wall Street financiers. Proponents of corporate raiding (acquiring undervalued corporations by purchasing controlling interest through creative financial techniques) argue that raiding is simply the process of competition at work. Opponents charge that corporate takeovers increase concentration and encourage managers to focus on short-term performance at the expense of long-term growth.

First a quick vocabulary lesson. Corporate raiding (or "leveraged take-

overs") typically involve the following: A raider sets up a new corporation on paper. Investment bankers package a block of "junk bonds" (risky bonds with low credit ratings) to be issued by the paper corporation once it gains control through a stock tender offer (an offer to purchase a given percent of stock in the target company for a premium price). The investment bankers then obtain advance commitments from investors (pension funds and other institutional investors) to buy the junk bonds. Once in control, raiders raise cash by selling off pieces of the acquired company. In the words of one investment banker, "We take a minnow, identify a whale, then look to its assets to finance the transaction." In this way many small companies have acquired

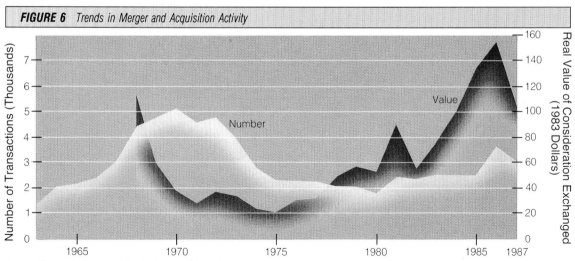

FIGURE 6 *Trends in Merger and Acquisition Activity*

Source: *Economic Report of the President,* 1988. Earlier data reprinted by permission of W. T. Grimm and Company. Data measure only publicly announced transactions and include transfers of ownership of 10 percent or more of a company's assets or equity, provided the value of the transaction is at least $500,000.00. Data for 1986–87 from *Mergers and Acquisitions,* April 1988.

much larger corporations. Attractive "whales" (also known as "cash cows") are firms whose stocks are undervalued by the market and generate massive cash flows.

Managers of targeted firms are not defenseless. They have used (a) "greenmail"; buying the raider's stock back at a premium, (b) "poison pills"; requirements to force the acquirer to sell stock in the merged entity at half price to shareholders of the target company, (c) "lollipops"; offering to buy a large proportion of its own stock for a huge premium with notes, but excluding the raider from the offer, and (d) finding a "White Knight"; locating a buyer that the company prefers to the raider.

Figure 7 summarizes a study of 429 tender offers. It concluded that opposition by the target management was greater when the incumbent management owned less stock. As managements' stock holdings rise, the average potential wealth gain to managers increases and is reflected in a greater likelihood of a friendly response.

Figure 6 illustrates the current merger and acquisition trend. Since the mid-1970s, the number of mergers and acquisitions appears stable. There has been, however, a constant upward trend in their value, indicating larger dollar volumes of merger and acquisition activity. During 1981–1983 five industries—oil and gas, banking and finance, insurance, mining and minerals, and food processing—accounted for over half of total mergers. The FTC concluded that petroleum mergers were attributable to changes in underlying market conditions such as (a) a wider use of

enhanced oil recovery techniques, (b) different expectations about oil price, (c) phased decontrol of crude oil, and (d) capacity consolidation caused by recent declines in oil prices.

Public policy toward the activity of raiders should depend on whether takeovers benefit the economy. Proponents of takeover activity point to the following sources of gain from takeovers (a) firms in related industries can gain production and distribution economies, (b) merging may promote technology transfers, (c) companies with larger market shares may have lower per unit costs, (d) shifting assets to higher valued uses, and (e) improved management. The Council of Economic Advisors concluded that "The evidence is strong that takeovers generate aggregate net benefits to the economy."

Opponents of hostile corporate takeovers base their arguments on feelings that corporate managements are not only responsible to stockholders, but to other *stakeholders* including employees, customers, suppliers and the communities in which they operate. Opponents appeal to the idea that social welfare is a major consideration of American corporations.

Congress has considered increased regulation of takeover activities, but backed away when the stock market began to rise in 1985. As the stock market re-evaluated underpriced companies, the incentive for profitable takeovers declined. To most people, takeovers have become part of what Joseph Schumpeter labled the process of creative destruction.

Source: "The Market For Corporate Control," Economic Report of the President, *1985, Chapter 6.*

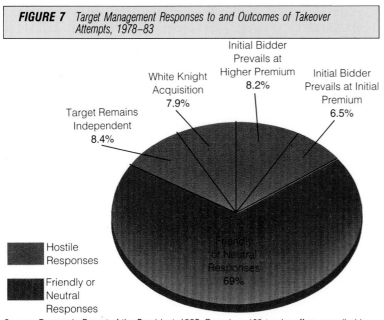

FIGURE 7 Target Management Responses to and Outcomes of Takeover Attempts, 1978–83

Initial Bidder Prevails at Higher Premium 8.2%

White Knight Acquisition 7.9%

Initial Bidder Prevails at Initial Premium 6.5%

Target Remains Independent 8.4%

Friendly or Neutral Responses 69%

Hostile Responses

Friendly or Neutral Responses

Source: *Economic Report of the President*, 1985. Based on 429 tender offers compiled by W. T. Grimm and Company. Reprinted by permission of W. T. Grimm and Company.

relative prices are constant. All firms merely gain or lose sales based on the elasticity of the industry's total demand. The respective marginal revenue curves for D_0 and D_1 are labeled MR_0 and MR_1.

The assumptions that underlie this model imply that only part of each curve is relevant: price cuts will be matched by rivals, but price hikes will not. On balance, the demand curve facing the firm is the thicker portion of the D_0 curve for outputs less than q_e, and the thicker portion of D_1 for outputs above q_e. The corresponding portions of the marginal revenue curves are emphasized similarly. Note that the relevant marginal revenue curve has a gap at output q_e between points b and c, which corresponds to the "kink" in the firm's demand curve; hence, the name kinked demand curve.

The importance of the kink in the demand curve and the gap in the firm's marginal revenue curve is shown in Figure 7. Maximum profit requires producing where marginal revenue equals marginal cost, so q_e output is sold at a price of P_e as long as the marginal cost curve stays between MC_0 and MC_1. Thus, this model explains why prices might be relatively sticky in oligopolistic industries even if production costs change. Marginal cost can rise from point c to point b without any change in price.

The assumptions of kinked demand models seem reasonable, but critics point to some defects. First, price rigidity may be no more frequent in oligopolies than other industries.[3] Concentrated industries appear to quickly pass along cost increases as they occur. After all, advertising, quality, and new product development may raise costs without significantly expanding market demand. If only one firm's profit is squeezed, it may be forced to maintain its current price. But if profit for all firms in an oligopoly shrink, all might follow a price hike; this yields a new kink at the higher price.

Second, kinked demand models fail to explain (*a*) why entry does not occur, (*b*) how oligopoly emerges, (*c*) how the equilibrium price, P_e, is initially established, nor (*d*) how prices change. These problems have caused the model to be used sparing-

ly by researchers. The major advantage of the kinked demand model is its simplicity in conveying the flavor of strategic business behavior when few firms compete in a market.

Limit Pricing to Deter Entry

Kinked demand models fail to explain how oligopolies set prices, how prices change, and how oligopoly is sustained over the long run. Outside firms would seek shares in an industry's profits. Entry would swell market supplies over time and create excess capacities at existing market prices, forcing prices down. This should ultimately shrivel profits in the industry.

Limit-pricing models attempt to rectify these failings of kinked demand curve models. A critical assumption is that high fixed costs yield substantial economies of scale so that small firms suffer significant cost disadvantages relative to large ones.

According to **limit-pricing models,** *established firms in an oligopoly may set a price below the short-run profit-maximizing price to make it unprofitable for new firms to enter the industry.*

Existing firms earn less profit in the short run, but setting lower prices and producing more to discourage entry can shield long-run economic profits.

Will established oligopolists use a limit-pricing strategy, or will they collude to set the monopoly price in the near term, knowing that high prices and profits will encourage entry and thereby erode profits in the long run? The answer depends on how low the limit price must be to deter entry and on comparisons of the profitability from taking monopoly profits now versus barring entry. If companies emphasize profit today and discount future profit heavily, higher short-run prices that attract more competition will result. The answer may depend on the size of the individual firms. Larger firms may be more worried than smaller firms about long run profits since the smaller firms may view short-run profits as sources for potential growth.

Maintaining the entry-deterring price may require established firms to illegally collude. Whether collusion is required is related closely to the number of firms in an industry. The more firms there are, the more likely that collusion is necessary for successful

---

3. This was the finding of George Stigler, reported in "The Kinky Oligopoly Demand Curve and Rigid Prices," *Journal of Political Economy,* October 1947, pp. 432–49.

limit pricing. The sparseness of current evidence of collusion in the United States has prevented widespread application of collusive limit-pricing models.

Cartels

Most Americans would not have recognized the term "cartel" before 1973–1974, when OPEC (Organization of Petroleum Exporting Countries), the best known cartel, became a household word.

> A **cartel** *is an organization through which members jointly make decisions about prices and production.*

Cartels generally require outright collusion. If the industry is sufficiently concentrated, however, (two or three firms), tacit collusion is possible. Collusive price-fixing agreements for most manufactured products are illegal in the United States but are quite legal in many international markets.

Cartels operate primarily in natural resource markets, and control most sales in international markets for such basic materials as copper, tin, bauxite (used to produce aluminum), diamonds, chrome, phosphate, petroleum, coffee, and bananas. Most successful cartels are coordinated by the governments of the major producing countries. Markets were formerly cartelized for sugar, rubber, nitrates, steel, radium, magnesium, and electric lights. Why do cartels seem to come and go? How do cartels set prices and production?

Cartel Requirements
A successful cartel requires control over the bulk of output by a small group of producers who are cartel members. Cartels cannot maintain high prices if many fringe competitors are not members. A small group will be more likely than a large group to agree about pricing and output strategies because the members of any group will have different goals and objectives.

The good must also be rather homogeneous; numerous differentiated substitutes would require agreements on an extensive array of prices. Once a cartel price is established, sales territories or production quotas must be set. Doing this for multiple goods and prices would be extremely difficult. Mature technology is also important for cartel success. If technol-

ogy is advancing rapidly, constant changes in costs make it difficult for members to agree on prices. Moreover, the incentive to cheat on a cartel arrangement may be overwhelming if a firm discovers a new way to cut production costs.

Cartelization will be facilitated the less elastic the total demand for the good. A cartel's ability to raise both price and total revenue requires an inelastic market demand for its product. Less elastic demand also makes excess capacity less of a problem as the price is increased. Finally, some method is needed to monitor member compliance and prevent cheating.

Cartel Pricing Policies
A cartel's members must jointly decide what price to charge and how much to sell. Most cartels try to price like a monopolist and sell the monopoly output. This is known as a **joint-profit maximization** approach and is diagrammed in Panel A of Figure 8. The cartel sets price at P_0 and restricts its members' combined output to Q_0. The largest possible monopoly profit (shaded) is obtained, but a crucial issue remains: sharing the industry's output and profit among cartel members.

How to allocate production depends on the product and the market. In some cases exclusive territories are assigned; each firm agrees to service only its own territory. Where this approach is unworkable, output quotas may be established for each firm. OPEC uses this approach; every member country agrees to limit its crude oil sales to the quota set by the cartel leadership. Nevertheless, a major reason for the breakdown of OPEC in the 1980s was rampant cheating by OPEC members.

Cheating
Each cartel member has strong incentives to cheat. Suppose that you are one of ten members of the cartel shown in Panel A of Figure 8 and are currently selling your equal share ($q_0 = Q_0/10$) of the total output Q_0 at the cartel price P_0. Your firm's marginal cost is shown in Panel B of Figure 8. At q_0 output, your profits equal C_0P_0xy in Panel B, which also equals C_0P_0xy in Panel A after adjusting for differences in scale between Panels A and B.

If you persuade your competitors to maintain the cartel price (P_0) but secretly offer a discounted price P_d to selected customers, your profits will grow from: (*a*) pirating some of their customers; and (*b*) servicing some of the demand that is unmet at this higher

FIGURE 8 *Cartels and the Incentive to Cheat*

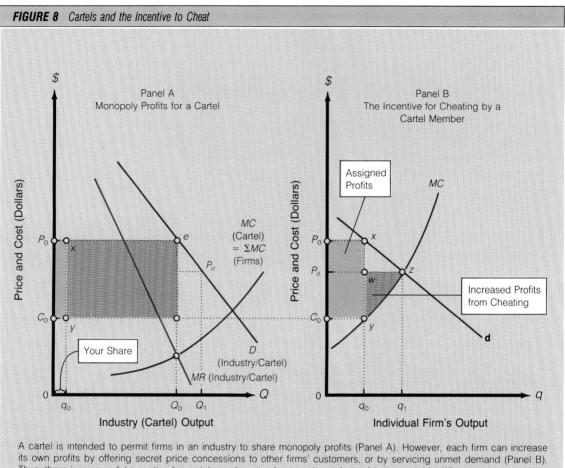

FIGURE 8 *Cartels and the Incentive to Cheat*

A cartel is intended to permit firms in an industry to share monopoly profits (Panel A). However, each firm can increase its own profits by offering secret price concessions to other firms' customers, or by servicing unmet demand (Panel B). Thus, there is a powerful incentive for cartel members to cheat, and cartels tend to be unstable. When governments help in establishing or perpetuating cartels, however, any cheating is easier to control, so moderately stable cartels may result.

cartel price. The marginal revenue to you from cheating exceeds your marginal cost. Your profits will rise because (*a*) you are not giving price cuts to your assigned customers; (*b*) your competitors do not give price cuts to the customers they retain; and (*c*) you can sell to more buyers—the customers who will not buy at a cartel price of P_0, but who are willing to pay P_d for $Q_1 - Q_0$ amounts of output. Your profits will rise by the area *ywz* in Panel B, which is the difference between your marginal cost of producing extra output $q_1 - q_0$ and the price P_d you receive for each extra unit of production.

Instability   Cheating on a cartel agreement can be profitable, but only if it is undetected. Cartel agreements collapse if widespread cheating is uncovered;

most members will cut prices and behave in a fairly competitive fashion, with the result that the profits that originally motivated formation of the cartel vanish. The fact that undetected cheating offers the prospect of great profits is one of the greatest threats to the stability of a cartel. Is cheating likely to go unnoticed? Nobel Prize-winning economist George Stigler has noted that:

The detection of secret price-cutting will of course be as difficult as interested people can make it. The price cutter will certainly protest his innocence, or, if this would tax credulity beyond its taxable capacity, blame a disobedient subordinate. The price cut will often take the indirect form of modifying some non-price dimension of the transaction. The customer may, and often will, divulge price reductions, in order to have them matched by others, but he will learn from experience if each disclosure is followed by the withdrawal of the lower price offer. Indeed the buyer will frequently fabricate wholly fictitious price offers to test the rivals. Policing the collusion sounds very much like the subtle and complex problem presented in a good detective story.[4]

Cheating is only one hazard to cartel stability. There are incentives to try to retain customer loyalty by granting price concessions where sales to individual buyers are large and infrequent. Huge economies of scale and high fixed costs may create irresistible pressure to slash prices during periods of slack demand so that overhead costs can be spread across larger output and sales. For example, cracks in OPEC's effectiveness appeared during the international recession of 1981–83; worldwide consumption shrank, and an oil glut emerged. OPEC members routinely exceeded their quotas, offering crude oil at big discounts below the official $34-per-barrel price. The price had fallen to $10 by 1986, although it recovered to roughly $20 by 1988.

Perhaps the greatest threat to a cartel is that high prices and profits will attract new competitors to enter the industry or to develop substitutes for the cartel's products. From World War II into the 1970s, for example, the Brazilian government restricted coffee exports to bolster its price. Result? Brazilian coffee lost much of its share of the world market when coffee plantations in Africa and Central America were started by profit seekers.

Profits in most industries would soar if competitors were free to collude about prices, enforce output quotas or territories, and bar the entry of potential rivals. Consequently, history is rich with attempts at cartelization that misfired because of cheating, inability to deter entry, or government prosecution. Focus 2 indicates that the breakdown of OPEC took quite a while. All long-term successful cartels have depended on laws, regulations, and intergovernmental cooperation to prevent cheating and deter entry. (It seems almost an economic law that only government-sanctioned cartels last more than two weeks.) However, OPEC and cartels in diamonds, coffee, and bananas are evidence that short-run success is a possibility.

Most cartels violate the antitrust laws covered in our next chapter. But even in the United States, laws against cartels largely exempt agricultural cooperatives, athletic groups, labor unions, such professional bodies as the American Medical Association, and export associations. Farmer organizations, the AFL-CIO, the AMA, and similar cartels all try to restrict output and hold prices up, primarily by limiting entry. The National Collegiate Athletic Association (NCAA) is a legal buyers' cartel that prohibits paying workers (college athletes) more than room, board, and tuition. But every year, several schools are penalized by the NCAA for cartel violations.

Successful collusion requires a stable environment, but business conditions are unlikely to be stable. When products are significantly differentiated, or resource costs are volatile, or demands are fickle, or entry is easy, or competitors are numerous, or technology advances rapidly, or policing a cartel agreement is excessively costly, then the quiet cooperation that oligopolists would like may be replaced by strategic behavior as intense as championship chess and as hostile as war.

Game Theory

The absense of overt or tacit collusion leads to rivalrous behavior that business leaders think of as competition. Pure competition is an impersonal process in which firms adjust their outputs to a market determined price. Oligopolists who compete in a noncooperative fashion have many more weapons at their disposal, including adjustments of prices, outputs, product lines, and advertising. The diversity of possible strategies among oligopolists led to the development of game theory in 1944 by the mathematician John von Neumann and the economist Oskar Morgenstern.

> **Game theory** *is the study of strategic interactions among interdependent decision makers.*

Game theory has been extended beyond oligopolistic behavior and is now applied to such areas as poker, courtship, athletic competition, collective bargaining, and national defense. A "game" requires that the costs and benefits of all possible strategies by one participant be paired with all possible strategies adopted by an opponent. Then each set of possible outcomes is analyzed to ascertain which is the most likely. Gains typically exceed losses in *positive-sum games;* exchange according to comparative advantage is an example. The gains of winners exactly offset

---

4. George J. Stigler, *The Organization of Industry* (Homewood, IL: Richard D. Irwin, Inc., 1968), p. 44.

The Rise and Fall of OPEC

Crude oil prices ranged between $1.80 and $4.00 per barrel from World War II until the 1970s, while gasoline ranged from $0.22 to $0.35 per gallon, including taxes. The Organization of Petroleum Exporting Countries (OPEC), formed late in the 1960s, was a sleeping giant that exercised little economic clout until 1974–75. Figure 9 shows that when this giant cartel finally awoke, it did so with a vengeance.

During 1974–75 alone, OPEC raised the price of crude oil from $4 to $10 per barrel. Output quotas were assigned to OPEC members and, with only limited cheating, these production limits were honored for a brief period. Price hikes continued, with a barrel of oil hitting the $20 mark by 1977, $30 in 1980, and finally peaking at an official price of $34 per barrel in 1982–83. By 1987,

however, the spot price of oil had fallen about $10 per barrel, and gasoline had fallen from its high of $1.45 in 1981 to around $0.70 per gallon. After adjusting for inflation, the real prices of petroleum products were close to pre-OPEC levels. What happened?

Part of the answer is the demand side. The long-term growth of world oil consumption dropped sharply throughout this era. Most industrialized nations are oil importers and skyrocketing oil prices slowed the rate of economic growth and precipitated high unemployment and substantial inflation in much of the world from 1974–83. Growth in the demand for oil also shriveled because its high price stimulated energy conservation: more insulation was put into private residences, office buildings, and manufacturing facilities; cars and

planes were modified to achieve greater fuel efficiency; and industry adopted less energy-intensive technology.

The other key to the collapse of OPEC's high prices came from the supply side. The late 1970s were an era of feverish exploration for new sources of energy. Vast pools of oil were developed in such areas as Mexico, Alaska, and in the North Sea. Coupled with the decline in world energy demand, swelling supplies from non-OPEC members caused OPEC countries to boost output because they relied heavily on oil exports for national income.

Cheating by OPEC members who exceeded their assigned quotas was relatively minor in the 1970s, but so many members were violating the OPEC agreements that by 1984 the spot price of oil was $4 to $8 below the official $34

the losers' losses in such *zero-sum games* as poker. Violence is generally a *negative-sum game;* the victim of a mugging often suffers bodily damage in addition to monetary loss, while the mugger only gains the money.

A Classic: Prisoners' Dilemma

A negative-sum game known as the prisoners' dilemma has been applied to many cases of business competition, and is often used to explain why cartel arrangements break down. Suppose that two armed robbers are jailed separately and cannot communicate. Each is told that if neither confesses, both will go free. If only one confesses and helps to convict the other, the squealer

will serve one year while the silent party serves ten. If both confess, however, both will be sentenced to two-year terms. The usual result of this game is that both suspects get two years of jail time.

How does the prisoners' dilemma apply to oligopoly? Consider a cartel. Every member will enjoy reasonable profit if no firm cheats, but a lone cheater will gain even more profit. If cheating is rampant, however, the profits of all cartel members suffer. The power of the prisoners' dilemma game is reflected in the gradual collapse of OPEC. Fortunately, there is a bright side to this story. The prisoners' dilemma faced by OPEC members generated competition that ultimately brought down the cost of energy.

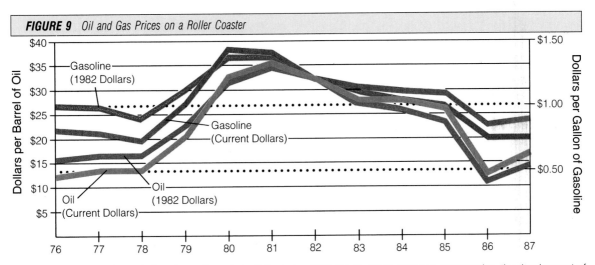

FIGURE 9 Oil and Gas Prices on a Roller Coaster

OPEC drove up the prices of oil and gasoline substantially during 1974–81. By 1986, however, conservation, the development of non-OPEC sources of energy, and the growth of cheating on limits to production by OPEC members appeared to have doomed the success of this oil cartel.

price. Oil flooded the world market, and the price plummeted. Although OPEC had enjoyed substantial success for almost a decade, the growth of external supplies and cheating had seriously undermined the OPEC cartel by 1986.

OPEC drove up the prices of oil and gasoline substantially during 1974–81. From 1983 through 1988, however, conservation, the development of non-OPEC sources of energy, and the growth of cheating on limits to production by OPEC members appeared to

have doomed the success of this oil cartel.

Source: U.S. Department of Commerce, Bureau of the Census, Statistical Abstract of the United States, 1987, and Economic Report of the President, *1988.*

Gains from Randomness   Suppose that you play poker and become enraged whenever another player wins a pot by bluffing. You can curb bluffing by your opponents by calling all bets, but you will soon find yourself only facing good poker hands and you will lose consistently. A good poker player tends to stay in hands with good cards, but will also bluff occasionally so that people will not automatically fold whenever the good player bets or raises. This is one example of how participants in games can gain by being a bit unpredictable. Similarly, police patrols that follow fixed routines will seldom be as effective in capturing criminals as somewhat random patrols would be. Oligopolists may also gain at times by keeping rivals

off balance. An unexpected new product or price cut can prevent rivals from following a strategy that harms a completely predictable firm.

Oligopolistic strategies are as diverse as the personalities of business leaders. The many possible tactics that oligopolists might follow depend on specific circumstances in particular markets. If you have ever played chess, bridge, poker, or Risk, you may have some sense of how volatile business coalitions can be, and how frequently the course of business history turns on personality. Some players like to bluff; some pursue conservative strategies; others are adventurous and explore options with both great potential risk of loss and great potential pay-offs.

Evaluating Oligopoly

How do oligopolies compare with more competitive industries? Firms in oligopolistic industries have considerable monopoly power, yielding economic inefficiency similar to that described for monopoly. In equilibrium, the marginal social benefit (price) of their products exceeds the marginal social cost. Compared with purely or even monopolistically competitive industries, output will tend to be less and prices to consumers will be higher.

If oligopoly arises from economies of scale, however, it is possible that consumers pay lower prices than were the market competitive. Furthermore, if research and development (R&D) leading to technological change requires massive outlays, small competitive firms may be unable to finance adequate innovation. Some economists suggest that society gains over the long run when short-run profits reaped by oligopolistic firms are plowed back into the development and innovation of newer and better products.

Evidence on the effects of oligopolies is mixed. Economies of scale are clearly responsible for the oligopolistic nature of some industries. In other instances, however, satisfactory economies of scale can be realized by smaller firms, and oligopoly is sustained by artificial barriers to entry. Finally, the evidence does not support the idea that large firms are especially responsible for new inventions and technological advances in our economy. If anything, it appears that the desire for increased monopoly power has been the driving force behind the creation of most oligopolies.

CHAPTER REVIEW: KEY POINTS

1. Most U.S. markets fit neither the purely competitive nor the monopoly molds. Most industries are *monopolistically competitive* or *oligopolistic*.

2. *Product differentiation* refers to differences that consumers perceive in goods that are close substitutes. These differences can be real or imagined. They are created by such things as advertising and promotion and/or by differences in the actual goods. Product differentiation is intended to expand the demand for a firm's output and make demand less elastic.

3. *Monopolistic competition* occurs when entry into an industry is easy and there are large numbers of suppliers of slightly differentiated products. Demands for a pure competitor's products are perfectly elastic (horizontal at the market price), but the demands facing monopolistic competitors are negatively sloped but still highly elastic.

4. Monopolistically competitive firms produce and sell levels of output that equate marginal revenue and marginal cost. The price is then determined by demand. This is similar to pure monopoly, but the level of short-run profits derived from monopoly power is generally lower, given that numerous other firms sell close substitutes.

5. Entry is relatively easy in monopolistic competition, so accounting profits are reduced to normal levels (zero economic profits) in the long run. Equilibrium output will be less and prices will be higher, however, under monopolistic competition than in purely competitive markets. Higher prices and lower levels of output are the costs of product differentiation.

6. An *oligopoly* is an industry comprised of a few sellers who recognize their mutual interdependence. Competitive strategies by one firm in the industry will normally be countered by the other sellers.

7. Economies of scale are one of several reasons for oligopoly. Some goods require substantial plant and equipment so that efficient production requires servicing a considerable portion of the total industry demand. Mergers also facilitate the creation of oligopolies by joining competitors into single firms. Finally, oligopolies may exist because of legal or other artificial barriers to entry that deter new firms from entering the industry.

8. There are hundreds of oligopoly pricing models, but they break down into two major categories: *collusive* and *noncollusive*. The *kinked demand curve model* assumes that if one firm raises its prices, other firms will ignore the increase, while other firms in the industry will match any price cuts. The result is a demand curve for the firm that is kinked at the current equilibrium price. This irregularity leads to a discontinuity (gap) in the marginal revenue curve. Consequently, changes in costs may not lead to

changes in prices. This theory forecasts "sticky" prices in oligopolistic industries, but price stickiness is not confirmed empirically. Kinked demand curve models also fail to explain how the original equilibrium price is established, how prices change, or how entry by new rivals is deterred.

9. *Limit pricing* is a model of how oligopolists maintain market power by deterring entry. Oligopolists may establish a low price, making it unprofitable for new firms to enter the industry. Existing firms then accept lower short-run profits to preserve economic profits over the long run.

10. A *cartel* is an effort by firms in an industry to collude, setting prices and limiting output for all its members. Cartels must be concentrated in the hands of a few firms that control significant proportions of an industry's output. The product needs to be reasonably homogeneous, since agreements regarding heterogeneous products would be complex and difficult to enforce.

11. Cartels try to *maximize joint profits* and then allocate territories or industry output quotas. The stability of any cartel is threatened by the profitability associated with undetected price cuts, or "cheating"; by potential new entrants who seek to share in profits; and by adverse legal action. Collusion is illegal in most markets in the United States.

12. *Game theory* is an attempt to model strategic behavior. It requires pairing each possible option open to each participant with the options available to other participants, and then ascertaining the most likely sets of options.

13. Industry output will be less and prices will be higher under oligopoly than in pure or monopolistic competition. Some economists argue that monopoly profits for large firms are necessary to finance extensive research and development activities and facilitate technological advance. The evidence does not confirm this hypothesis.

PROBLEM

1. Calculate concentration ratios for the four largest (*CR*4) and eight largest (*CR*8) firms in the following industries. Rank these industries from most to least concentrated. Are these *CR*s consistent?

   a. The plate glass industry has annual sales of $4 billion. The ten largest glass producers had 1988 sales (in millions of dollars) equal to: Able = $725, Baker = $380, Charlie = $145, Darwin = $710, Eden = $68, Foxtrot = $110, Gulf = $350, Hurricane = $911, India = $168, and Joker = $319.

   b. Annual pencil sales are $600 million, shared (in millions of dollars) among all pencil makers as follows: Smudge = $13, Taxman = $243, Utmost = $122, Vexation = $114, Wax = $78, Xenon = $12, Zebra = $18.

   c. Annual sales of printing equipment total $7 billion, shared (in millions of dollars) as follows: 15 small specialty firms average $40, Korabi = $1,215, Lommox = $642, Mongo = $222, Nota = $98, Oryx = $789, Pogo = $2,130, Quzer = $166, Rastafa = $87, and 291 tiny firms split the remaining sales.

QUESTIONS FOR THOUGHT AND DISCUSSION

1. Are the following examples of persuasive or informative advertising?

   a. Newspaper want ads.
   b. "Coke's the one."
   c. "Merrill Lynch is 'bullish' on America."
   d. "Del Monte now offers more than twenty Mexican food products."
   e. "Symphony Homes—spacious mountainview living for as little as $59,950."
   f. "Allstate—the 'good hands' people."
   g. Coupons for new products in grocery store advertisements.
   h. "You could drive to the moon and back before the gas you'd save with a Toyota would be worth more than the money you'd save buying a Pontiac."
   i. "Buy a new Dodge before May 1 and get a $500 rebate from Chrysler."
   j. "Use Hoarse, the cough medicine more doctors recommend."

2. What factors enabled the OPEC cartel to raise prices so dramatically during the 1970s? What factors contributed to the difficulties experienced by OPEC in the 1980s?

3. The term *invention* covers the research and development of a product or technique. *Innovation* means implementing an invention into production. Can you cite three major inventions made by organizations that were small at the time? Three major innovations by firms with oligopoly power?

4. Until the 1960s, IBM had a stranglehold in the computer industry, Xerox had a near monopoly in copying equipment, and Polaroid was the only maker of "instant picture" cameras. What has happened in these markets since then?

5. One oligopoly model suggests that firms will attempt to capture as large a market share as possible by locating in the center of the market. This model suggests that people will not be served if they want substantially different products than the majority of people. According to the developer of this model, Harold Hotelling, this accounts for such things as parallel programming by television networks, the middle-of-the-road images sought by politicians, the homogeneity of apple cider, the similarities between Protestant churches, and the phenomenon of four gas stations at the corners of busy intersections, among other things. How do you think his view that there is too little product differentiation stacks up against the view that monopolistic competition causes too much artificial product differentiation?

6. How do price takers and price makers differ? Is the difference in the monopoly power held by IBM and the corner grocer more quantitative than qualitative? What are the qualitative differences between these firms?

7. What evidence might you look for to discover whether or not some concentrated industry was contestable, and thus vulnerable to competition?

8. In the 1950s teenagers sometimes played a game called "chicken." Drivers initially half a mile apart would drive their cars at each other at high speed. The first driver who turned to avoid a crash was castigated as a "chicken." What do you think was the most common result of this game? How does this game resemble the nuclear weapons races that sometimes characterize relationships between the United States and the Soviet Union?

9. Suppose that your instructor guarantees that the student with the highest score at the end of this course will receive an A+. A classmate proposes that all students hand in blank paper for all written work, give answer "c" to all multiple choice questions, and answer "T" for all true/false questions. All students will have the same "highest" grade and everyone will get an A+. Why would you expect this scheme to backfire even if all students agreed to this strategy?

10. Standard models predict that if firms wield monopoly power, price will exceed marginal cost and, thus, that there will be inefficiency in equilibrium. These models assume that every good has only a single price, but the reality is that quantity discounts, coupons, and other marketing promotions create tremendous disparities in prices at all times. Does the pervasiveness of price discrimination counter much of the argument that monopolistically competitive or oligopolistic markets are inherently inefficient? Why or why not?

CHAPTER 26

Lerner index of monopoly
   power (LMP)

Herfindahl-Hirschman
   index (HHI)

promotional profits

Sherman Antitrust Act

Clayton Act

Federal Trade
   Commission (FTC) Act

Robinson-Patman Act

Celler-Kefauver
   Antimerger Act

rule of reason

per se doctrine

conscious parallelism of
   action

Antitrust Policy: Reducing Monopoly Power

People of the same trade seldom meet together, even for merriment and diversion, but the conversation ends in a conspiracy against the public, or in some contrivance to raise prices.
    —Adam Smith, The Wealth of Nations, *1776*

Adam Smith and other classical economists loathed attempts to monopolize. Smith also recognized that firms commonly conspire to "sink the wages of labor."[1] These early economists expected that only government support would prevent business conspiracies from succumbing to competitive pressures. The history of trusts and monopolies over the past two centuries suggests that attempts to gain monopoly positions and raise prices succeed more often than early economists might have predicted. An example of groups in revolt against exorbitant prices would be farmer uprisings of a century ago, spurred

by feelings that railroads exploited the farmers' reliance on rail transportation.

The preceding three chapters focused on the unfettered consequences of the four main market structures. Pure competition yields the greatest economic efficiency and unregulated monopoly the least. Many people also believe monopoly power causes inequity in the division of income. This chapter centers on how government might prevent monopolistic abuses in a market economy and concludes with an evaluation of the effectiveness of these methods. Before we consider them, we will take a quick look at industry's current structure and discuss the inferences for the economic performance of the hundreds of thousands of firms in our economy.

In the absence of easy entry, as the average size of the largest firms in an industry grows relative to the entire market, the industry approaches a monopolistic structure. Many people equate *size* with *monopoly power* but if an industry is huge, it may contain many

---

1. Adam Smith, *An Inquiry Into the Nature and Causes of the Wealth of Nations,* 1776, Book I.

large firms, none of which has significant monopoly power. Giants sometimes compete. Big firms often arise because of technology, economies of scale, or the nature of the product.

Measuring Market Power

How can we tell if monopoly power is significant in a particular market? We might rely on hunches, but a more scientific approach is to develop quantitative estimates of the market power concentrated in the hands of a few firms in a given industry.

The Lerner Index of Monopoly Power

The theory presented in the last three chapters suggests that monopoly power creates a widening gap between marginal cost and price. This led Abba Lerner to propose the Lerner index of monopoly power (*LMP*), which is:

$$LMP = \frac{\text{price} - \text{marginal cost}}{\text{price}}.$$

The Lerner index equals zero for a purely competitive industry because price equals marginal cost. Exercising monopoly power causes the Lerner index to grow because the equilibrium gap between price and marginal cost rises.

A major hurdle for calculating a Lerner index is that accounting data seldom estimate marginal costs. Some researchers tried to build Lerner indices using average cost rather than marginal cost data, but this approach has major drawbacks (*a*) pure competitors that temporarily enjoy economic profits are interpreted as monopolistic, (*b*) established firms may restrict prices to inhibit entry (limit pricing), and *LMP* would interpret such cuts in price relative to marginal or average costs as diminished market power.

Market Concentration Ratios

Concentration ratios (discussed in the prior chapter) may also estimate market power. A **concentration ratio** is the percentage of total industry sales, assets, employment, value-added, or output accounted for by an industry's biggest four or eight firms, although

TABLE 1 Concentration Ratios: Commercial Printing and Aircraft, 1982

Number of Firms	Percent of Industry Shipments (Sales)	
	Commercial Printing	Aircraft
Largest 4	6	64
Largest 8	10	81
Largest 20	17	98
Largest 50	24	99+

Source: U.S. Department of Commerce, Bureau of the Census, MC 82–5–7, 1982 Census of Manufacturers (Washington, D.C.: U.S. Government Printing Office, April 1986.)
Note: These data are only collected once every five years, and are published roughly four years later. Thus, the most recent data available are unavoidably up to a decade old.

any number of firms could be used. Table 1 indicates concentration in commercial printing and the aircraft industry.

The largest four and the largest eight commercial printers are all about the same size and control 6 and 10 percent, respectively, of total printing sales; the aircraft industry is much more concentrated. Alone, these data are inconclusive, but, coupled with other data, this information might help explain differences in pricing and output behavior between the two industries.

Table 2 presents the four-firm and eight-firm concentration ratios (*CRs*) for 24 industries in the United States. As you move down from the top of the table, concentration (*CR*8 for 1982) declines. Changing industry concentration can be interpreted from data for changes in concentration ratios and for the number of firms in the industry. For example, market power among firms producing electronic computing equipment appears to have fallen sharply. Not only has its concentration ratio declined, but the computer industry had five times as many firms in 1982 as in 1967. This undoubtedly reflects technological advances that are still taking place in that industry.

In general, however, concentration ratios for most industries did not change significantly between 1967 and 1982. Although the number of firms in many industries increased, the largest firms normally retained their market shares. Relative stability of our

TABLE 2 Concentration Ratios for Selected Industries, 1967–82

Industry	Four Largest Firms 1967	1982	Eight Largest Firms 1967	1982	Total Number of Firms 1967	1982
Motor vehicles and car bodies	92	92	98	97	107	284
Cigarettes	81	(D)	100	(D)	8	8
Telephone, telegraph apparatus	92	76	96	83	82	259
Organic fibers, noncellulosic	84	77	94	91	22	44
Tires and inner tubes	70	66	89	86	119	108
Aircraft	69	64	89	81	91	139
Photographic equipment	69	74	81	86	505	723
Soap and other detergents	70	60	78	73	599	642
Motor vehicle parts and accessories	60	61	68	69	1,424	2,000
Blast furnaces and steel mills	48	42	66	64	200	211
Electronic computing equipment	66	40	83	57	134	685
Farm machinery and equipment	44	53	56	62	1,526	1,787
Petroleum refining	33	28	57	48	276	282
Construction machinery	41	42	53	52	578	817
Pharmaceutical preparations	24	26	40	42	791	584
Paper mills	26	22	43	40	203	135
Bread, cake, and related products	26	34	38	47	3,445	1,869
Periodicals	24	20	37	31	2,430	3,143
Radio & TV communications equipment	22	22	37	35	1,111	2,083
Newspapers	16	22	25	34	7,589	7,520
Sawmills and planing mills	11	17	15	23	10,016	5,810
Bottled and canned soft drinks	13	14	20	23	3,057	1,236
Commercial printing, letterpress	14	14	21	19	11,955	10,211
Commercial printing, lithographic	5	6	8	10	6,718	17,332

Source: U.S. Department of Commerce, Bureau of the Census, MC 82–5–7, 1982 Census of Manufacturers, April 1986.
Note: (D): Withheld to avoid disclosure. See also the note in Table 1.

industrial structure is supported by the data in Table 2. Conglomerate mergers, however, have aided the largest 100 U.S. firms in slowly acquiring a growing share of all manufacturing assets over the past half century. As Figure 1 illustrates, the top 200 firms (0.1 percent of all manufacturing corporations) control nearly 70 percent of all manufacturing assets, and this percentage has crept up slowly over the last half century. Huge corporate takeovers and mergers have recently accelerated this trend. Virtually all these huge organizations operate in a number of industries, and nearly all operate across national boundaries. Thus, although concentration within specific industries has basically stabilized, giant multinationals are increasingly important players on the international economic scene. In addition to their huge shares of manufacturing assets (capital), these corpo-rations also account for growing proportions of employment, sales, and profits.

There is a major debate about whether bigness and badness are synonymous in the case of a conglomerate. Giant conglomerates may not have as much monopoly power as big firms that operate in only one industry, but they do have substantial economic clout and may exercise their power in the political arena. Multinational firms are of special concern because of their interest in international politics, but even giants are not immune to market forces. Many of our 100 or 200 largest firms seem firmly entrenched at the top, but there has been some turnover among these huge organizations.

Substantial economies of scale and high capital requirements may make concentration unavoidable in some industries. High capital costs naturally im-

FIGURE 1 Proportion of Manufacturing Assets Held by the 100 and 200 Largest Corporations, 1950–87

100 Largest Corporations

200 Largest Corporations

The share of manufacturing assets held by the 100 and 200 largest firms has been growing since the Great Depression. These figures suggest a trend toward greater concentration in the ownership of manufacturing assets in our economy.

Source: *Statistical Abstract of the United States*, 1987.

pose substantial entry barriers to new competition if profits are uncertain. Table 3 shows the real values of capital per worker in several industries from 1950 through 1980. The three most capital-intensive major industries in the United States are utilities, petroleum, and communications. The remaining industries employ significantly less capital. Sales per employee roughly parallel the pattern of capital per employee. High capital requirements do pose considerable barriers to entry, although wildcat oil operations are evidence that the prospect of profits can sometimes overcome high capital costs.

Firms with heavy capital requirements incur large fixed costs. Where economies of scale are substantial, average costs fall across a wide range of output. In the short run, average variable costs may reach their minimum (the shutdown point) at very low prices. These economies of scale incite cutthroat competition during periods of slack demand. A price war often shrinks the numbers of firms in an industry when losers go bankrupt. Price wars also generate pressures for collusive price-fixing agreements, or for cries from the industry for government "bail outs" and protective regulations and controls.

One of the greatest deficiencies of concentration ratios lies in identifying industry categories properly.

Firms must be classified into industry groups whose products are easily substituted by consumers. Distinguishing between close and distant substitutes is difficult. One solution might be to examine the cross-elasticities of demand between products. Unfortunately, the data required to estimate cross-elasticities are rarely available.

Alone, even information on substitutability by consumers might be inadequate to define an industry; production substitutability must be considered as well. Markets are *contestable* if a number of firms use roughly the same types of plant and equipment to manufacture different products, and if switching from one product line to another is easy. Firms that can easily cross industry boundaries should be grouped as potential competitors.

Although Standard Industry Classification (SIC) codes attempt to classify industries, SIC codes are frequently overly inclusive. Many patented products with no close substitutes are lumped with goods that are only roughly similar. For example, a decade ago photocopying machines were not separated from other copying equipment. Xerox dominated photocopying equipment at that time. Are mimeographs, ditto machines, and printing presses really close substitutes for Xerox equipment? Perhaps the major de-

TABLE 3 *Capital Stock per Hour Worked, 1950–80 (Reflects Capital/Labor Ratios, in 1972 Dollars)*

Industry	1950	1980	Percentage Change 1950–80
Public utilities	$69.49	$170.20	144.9
Petroleum	34.25	73.11	113.5
Communications	21.14	69.81	230.2
Tobacco	17.21	37.51	117.9
Transportation	34.56	36.09	4.4
Chemicals	15.10	31.19	106.6
Primary metals	13.99	31.04	121.8
Mining	21.02	23.89	13.7
Paper	14.07	22.41	59.3
Food	8.95	19.29	115.5
Transportation equipment	6.84	15.62	128.4
Nonelectric machinery	6.78	12.23	80.4
Finance and insurance	5.15	10.61	106.0
Textiles	3.64	9.63	164.6
Services	5.80	9.13	57.4
Printing and publishing	6.01	7.11	18.3
Furniture	4.24	5.11	20.5
Construction	1.98	3.40	71.7
Apparel	1.88	3.01	60.1

Source: The Conference Board, New York, N.Y., *Economic Road Maps.*

fect of SIC codes is that they consider only domestic sales by U.S. producers. Growing foreign competition is ignored, causing the extent of competition to be understated. Even recognizing such difficulties, however, concentration ratios provide crude snapshots of concentrations of market power.

The Herfindahl-Hirschman Index

Traditional economic theory suggests that economic profits are more likely to be earned in concentrated industries, using concentration ratios as the measuring rod for economic concentration and monopoly power. A Federal Trade Commission study discovered, however, that a single company's market share quite often is the best predictor of economic profits, regardless of whether or not it is in a concentrated industry.[2] The study concluded that, on the average, a 10 percent increase in market share results in a 2 percent increase in profitability.

This evidence recently caused the Antitrust Division of the Justice Department to begin to rely

on the Herfindahl-Hirschman index. The Herfindahl-Hirschman Index, (*HHI*), which estimates industry concentration by emphasizing the firms with the largest market shares, is measured by the following formula:

$$HHI = \sum_{i=1}^{n} S_i^2,$$

where S_i is the market share of the *i*th firm. The *HHI* places the greatest weight on the largest firms by squaring market shares. When the industry is a pure monopoly ($S_i = 100 = 100\%$), then $HHI = 10,000$. If, on the other hand, 100 firms each control one percent of sales, then the *HHI* would be 100. Thus, the *HHI* falls as the number of firms in an industry rises or the firms become more uniform in size.

Consider one market where four firms have 20 percent each and 20 firms have 1 percent each, and a second market where one firm has 77 percent and the remaining 33 firms each have 1 percent. In both markets the four-firm concentration ratio would be 80 percent, but the *HHI* would be quite different; 1,620 and 5,962, respectively. The differences in concentration hidden by four-firm concentration ratios are captured by the *HHI*.

---

2. "Attacking the Test that Curbs so Many Mergers," *Business Week,* 16 Nov. 1981, 151.

Operationally, the *HHI* and price-elasticity measures are now used by the Antitrust Division to screen proposed mergers. Beginning in 1982, the Antitrust Division has used merger guidelines that consider both the postmerger concentration (as measured by the *HHI*) and the increase in concentration resulting from the merger. The Justice Department ignores mergers where the resulting *HHI* (after merger) would remain below 1,800. If the resulting value of the *HHI* after merger is above 1,800, the Justice Department carefully reviews the merger—and might be inclined to disapprove.

The Reagan administration virtually immunized mergers in relatively unconcentrated industries from challenge. Many mergers in concentrated industries were also permitted, including GE/RCA, Chevron/Gulf, Chrysler/AMC, British Petroleum/Standard Oil of Ohio, and Texaco/Getty Oil (in which a $3.5 billion suit settlement may contribute to Texaco's bankruptcy). Allowing such mergers was a radical shift from earlier periods when almost all major merger proposals were rejected. (The Von's Grocery court decision in Focus 1 later in this chapter epitomizes previous policies.)

Mergers and Monopoly Power

If major competitors merge, industry concentration must rise, whether measured by concentration ratios or the Herfindahl-Hirschman index. If an industry is already concentrated and the firms are among its leaders, the market power gained through merger may be both substantial and socially undesirable. On the other hand, merger of small firms into one viable competitor in an industry with relatively high concentration can be beneficial to society if the merged firm is better able to compete with established giants. The tough task, of course, is to develop a coherent public policy that prohibits all harmful mergers, but only them.

The Urge to Merge

There are several possible motives for merger. One obvious goal is to consolidate market power by eliminating a competitor. Sometimes managers of firms with a lot of cash on hand buy a firm having cash-flow problems; this tactic can make the firm with a lot of cash on hand a less attractive target for a hostile takeover. Firms also merge to exploit cost savings arising from economies of information, marketing, advertising, production, or financial aspects of the business, or to pool complementary technologies or patents.

For example, when several firms recently merged to form Hal Roach Studios, the new management moved to exploit a revolutionary technique that adds color to old black and white films. The merged firms included one holding the rights to a "classics" library, another with independent television stations across the nation, and a third that held movie and television distribution agreements worldwide. The earnings potential for this vertically-integrated firm vastly exceeded that of the sum of the individual firms.

Promotional profits *are the rewards received by those who engineer mergers that benefit the final merged company.*

If a merger enhances the expected future profitability of the surviving firm, for example, the price of the stock of the surviving firm will rise, making its value greater than that of the total stock in the previous firms. A higher price for a firm's stock is how the stock market reflects any increased monopoly power or cost savings and expected higher profits. Potential promotional profits to holders of large blocks of stock (often the promoters of merger) provide substantial incentives to merge competing firms.

Major Merger Movements

There have been three important merger movements in the United States in the last century. The data reflected in Figure 2 suggests that a fourth wave may be developing. Each of these major waves of mergers has arisen from the economic conditions and legal restrictions of the times.

The First Wave: Horizontal Acquisition The first merger wave was late in the nineteenth and early in the twentieth centuries. Many early mergers were engineered by tycoons of that era: John D. Rockefeller, Andrew Carnegie, Cornelius Vanderbilt, Jay Gould, Jim Fisk, and J. P. Morgan. They and other "robber barons" aggressively consolidated their control over oil, steel, sugar, railroads, banking, and other industries. Corporate holding companies known as **trusts** permitted these men to gain control of vast

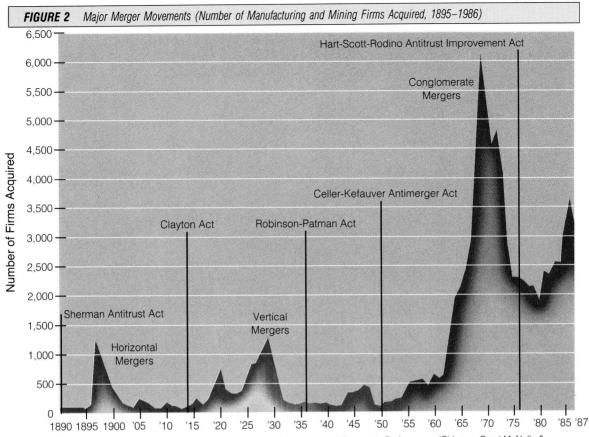

FIGURE 2 Major Merger Movements (Number of Manufacturing and Mining Firms Acquired, 1895–1986)

Sources: Data for 1895–1968 from F. M. Scherer, *Industrial Market Structure and Economic Performance* (Chicago: Rand McNally & Company, 1980), p. 120. Scherer cites the following sources for the data: Ralph L. Nelson, *Merger Movements in American Industry, 1895–1956* (Princeton: Princeton University Press, 1959), p. 37; U.S. House of Representatives, Select Committee on Small Business, Staff Report, *Mergers and Superconcentration* (Washington, D.C., 1962), pp. 10, 266; and U.S. Federal Trade Commission, *Current Trends in Merger Activity*, 1968 (Washington, D.C., March 1969). Data for 1963–1984 from *Economic Report of the President*, 1985. Data for 1986–87 from *Mergers and Acquisitions*, Vol. 22, April 1988.

amounts of capital. History is filled with colorful stories about the chicanery they used to acquire the assets of their competitors.

John D. Rockefeller, for one, was accused of using cutthroat predatory pricing to eliminate smaller rivals. Reformers claimed his Standard Oil trust reduced oil and gas prices in one area below cost and, when rivals were bankrupted, it then purchased their assets at distress prices. Once Standard Oil's competitors were vanquished, Rockefeller allegedly would raise prices to compensate for past losses, thereby reaping monopoly profits. The evidence is mixed, however, that this sequence of events ever occurred.

The vast majority of mergers and acquisitions during this period were **horizontal mergers**—absorbing direct competitors is a relatively quick way for a

firm to gain market dominance. Such giants as U. S. Steel, General Electric, and Standard Oil were formed during this period. Once market dominance was obtained, abuse of market power appeared routine. Perceived offenses by these major companies fomented a general outcry for restrictions on trusts, leading to the passage of the Sherman Antitrust Act in 1890, which attempted to forbid horizontal mergers. Ironically, horizontal mergers mushroomed until loopholes were tightened by the Clayton Act in 1914.

The Second Wave: Vertical Acquisition   A second irony is that the second merger wave followed on the heels of passage of the Clayton Act, only ending when the Great Depression caused most corporate profits to evaporate. Most mergers during this period were vertical. **Vertical mergers** entail gaining control over various stages of production ranging from raw materials to finished manufacturing. Because the Sherman and Clayton Antitrust Acts squelched most horizontal mergers through specific prohibitions on "monopolization or attempts to monopolize," firms desiring to grow via merger were channeled towards vertical mergers. Some horizontal mergers did occur, but only trivially compared with the boom of monopolization that occurred during the first great merger wave.

The Third Wave: Conglomerates

The Great Depression devastated momentum for mergers. Potential promotional profits were evaporated by the stock market collapse of 1929, and slack demands for output curtailed mergers based on economies of scale. Figure 2 shows that the merger rate fell drastically and remained low throughout the Depression. Some merger agreements were reached following World War II, but the third big wave did not appear until late in the 1950s, again, ironically, on the heels of major antitrust legislation—the Celler Kefauver Act of 1950. This third wave lasted into the early 1970s.

The vast majority of the mergers during this period were of the conglomerate form. A **conglomerate merger** combines two or more firms from unrelated industries. For example, DuPont's (a chemical company) 1982 acquisition of Conoco Oil was a conglomerate merger. One of the most famous conglomerates is International Telephone and Telegraph (ITT), which mushroomed in 1960. ITT's assets grew from roughly $900 million in 1960 to over $6 billion in 1970. About two-thirds of this 700 percent growth occurred through mergers with companies in unrelated industries.

A Fourth Merger Wave?

The 1970s were a quiet era for merger activity, but the perception that the Reagan administration was sympathetic to big business in general, and to "corporate raiders" in particular, renewed interest in mergers. Permissive antitrust guidelines announced in the early 1980s fostered conglomerate mergers, and also seemed to allow horizontal or vertical mergers that would have been challenged by earlier administrations. Horizontal mergers among giant oil companies were common in the mid-1980s. Whether the current boom of merger activity will continue depends (*a*) on whether the new administration reverses the policies established during the Reagan administration, and (*b*) on general business conditions.

The Urge to Purge

Mergers and acquisitions do not always produce happy and successful marriages. Successful mergers tend to share certain features (*a*) they involve companies in closely related businesses (horizontal mergers), (*b*) the price paid by the acquiring firms is not excessive, (*c*) the acquisition is financed with stock swaps or cash rather than debt (bond financing), and (*d*) managers of the acquired firm continue to operate it.[3]

A common problem with mergers is that good executive skills in one business may not easily transfer to another. Conflicting corporate "cultures" can make an acquisition worthless, as Exxon discovered when, in 1975, it attempted to expand into office automation. Over the next decade, Exxon poured over $2 billion into its QYX office products division. Exxon executives, accustomed to three to five year planning horizons in the oil business, could not make decisions quickly enough to keep pace with the rapidly changing technology associated with office automation. Exxon finally sold its office products division at a loss in 1985.

The 1980s have seen both mergers and its flip side, "voluntary restructuring," the jettisoning of bad acquisitions. Many conglomerates are scaling back to "do what they do best." For example, ITT disposed of nearly 100 subsidiaries in the first half of the 1980s. Beatrice, another giant conglomerate, went through a spasm of "demerger" during 1987–88. The relaxed merger rules of the Reagan administration have allowed firms to more freely swap assets.

Moreover, *corporate raiding* has pressured management to see if undervalued plums can be disposed of at prices higher than those reflected in the price of the company's stock. Firms unable to milk their assets for the highest possible return are prime targets for corporate raiders and other disposal experts. Whether corporate divorces will continue as a strong trend is uncertain, but restructuring was encouraged during the Reagan administration.

---

3. "Do Mergers Really Work?", *Business Week*, 3 June, 1985, 88–100.

Public Policy Toward Business

Government policies about industrial structure have been directed along two broad lines. The first, regulation, has existed since the adoption of the U.S. Constitution: Article I, Section 8 gives Congress the power "To regulate Commerce with foreign Nations, and among the several States . . . ." Any federal law might be considered regulation, but in the next chapter we focus on instances where some government body sets comprehensive rules for a market about prices, outputs, or operating and managerial procedures. In such situations, government substitutes regulation for the forces of competition.

The second general approach to dealing with industry structure has been through antitrust policies. Several federal laws have amended the Sherman Antitrust Act of 1890. In general, the antitrust approach is to restructure industry so that it conforms as much as possible to the assumptions of pure or monopolistic competition. Where this is not possible, law and regulation ideally force an industry's performance to mimic the competitive ideal. The remainder of this chapter is devoted to examining antitrust policies.

Antitrust Policy

The previous three chapters set the stage for antitrust policy. The rationale for vigorous antitrust actions is fairly simple. Pure competitors adjust output until the last unit sold provides benefits just equal to production costs. That is, marginal social benefits equal marginal social costs ($MSB = MSC$), so that the market operates in an economically efficient manner. When firms exercise monopoly power, the price of the last unit sold tends to exceed both its cost and the competitive price. Because the price (marginal social benefit) charged by a firm exceeds marginal social cost, there is economic inefficiency. Therefore, competitive markets are more allocatively efficient than those controlled by firms with monopoly power. Moreover, consistent monopoly profit may result in concentrations of wealth and economic power that are not compatible with most social and political ideas of equity.

This analysis may seem straightforward, but there is considerable disagreement as to whether large firms are inherently bad. One legal point of view is that monopoly is bad *per se*. The idea of a benevolent monopoly is discarded in favor of the argument that abuse invariably flows from substantial monopoly power. A natural conclusion from this point of view is to stamp out monopoly power through forced *divestiture,* the breaking up of large corporations into numerous independent small companies. For example, AT&T was recently forced to divest itself of all its local operating companies.

The Argument for Bigness

Defenders of modern corporate giantism argue that large corporations are made necessary by capital-intensive and highly complex modern technology. Many also contend that large enterprises are necessary to comply with the maze of federal, state, and local regulations governing modern business practice. Small firms have difficulty acquiring the capital needed to sustain these endeavors.

Different presidential administrations have interpreted antitrust laws quite differently, but public policy has generally presumed that monopoly power is socially undesirable and should be curtailed. This presumption is based primarily on the economic theory you have learned in the last few chapters. The goals of antitrust policy are to outlaw monopolization of markets and to prohibit specific misconduct associated with monopoly power. We need an overview of our major antitrust laws before evaluating the success of antitrust in the United States.

The Antitrust Laws

The thrust of each of the five major U.S. antitrust laws is to limit monopoly power or to prohibit undesirable business practices. All were passed in response to perceived business abuses—allegations against Standard Oil, the railroads, and others. At one point in our history, there was strong political support for a constitutional amendment to outlaw monopolies.

The Sherman Act   Against this background, the Sherman Antitrust Act was enacted in 1890.

The two major provisions of the **Sherman Antitrust Act** *are:*
Section 1: *Every contract, combination in the form of trust or otherwise, or conspiracy, in*

restraint of trade or commerce among the several States, or with foreign nations, is hereby declared to be illegal.

Section 2: *Every person who shall monopolize, or attempt to monopolize, or combine or conspire with any other person or persons, to monopolize any part of the trade or commerce among several States, or with foreign nations, shall be deemed guilty of a felony . . . .*

Both sections then go on to spell out the penalties for violation of the law. Corporations may be fined up to $1 million; individuals may be fined up to $100,000 for each offense, or they can be imprisoned for up to three years, or both, at the discretion of the court.[4]

Enforcement of Section 2 has been especially challenging. Proving "monopolization" calls for determining the relevant market. This requires scrutiny of both the nature of the market (geographic characteristics) and the nature of the product itself (substitutability from the vantage points of both consumers and other potential producers). Once these questions are settled, the court must determine what constitutes a monopoly in terms of percentage of the market. Must the firm control 100 percent of a market to be guilty of monopolization? Should a 90 percent market share be illegal? 80 percent? 70 percent? Section 2 also prohibits "attempts to monopolize." What conduct is intended to produce a monopoly? It seems ironic from today's perspective, but early court cases often focused on union strike activities as violations of the Sherman Act. These cases and other ambiguities in the Sherman Act led to passage of more specific antitrust laws.

The Clayton Act   The Sherman Act was amended by the Clayton Act in 1914, which spelled out particular offenses more precisely and introduced into law the phrase "where the effect [of various practices] may be to substantially lessen competition or tend to create a monopoly."

According to the **Clayton Act:**
Section 2: *It shall be unlawful for any person engaged in commerce . . . to discriminate in price between different purchasers of commodities of like grade and quality . . . .*
Section 3: *It shall be unlawful for any person engaged in commerce . . . to lease or make a sale or contract for sale of goods, wares, merchandise, machinery, supplies or other commodities . . . or fix a price charged therefor, or discount from or rebate upon such price, on the condition, agreement or understanding that the lessee or purchaser thereof shall not use or deal in the goods . . . , or other commodities of a competitor or competitors of the lessor or seller . . . .*
Section 4: [*This section is quite technical and prohibits mergers where the effect is to substantially lessen competition or tend to create a monopoly.*]
Section 8: [*This section focuses on interlocking directorates, prohibiting any individual from being a director of two or more competing corporations if any of the companies has capital in excess of $1 million.*]

Many qualifications and specific standards have been enumerated by the courts in enforcing the price discrimination section (Section 2). For example, price discrimination is permitted if a defendant can show that is does not reduce competition (e.g., discounts for senior citizens to movies and supersaver fares on airlines). Moreover, price discrimination is permitted for intangible properties or services, or where differences in costs account for different prices.

Business has taxed the courts' ingenuity in dealing with various schemes such as tie-in sales and restrictive agreements under Section 3. (For a long time, IBM only leased its computers and would not permit its equipment to be attached to equipment of other manufacturers. A. B. Dick tied sales of ink to its mimeograph machines.) Business continually devises new schemes to get around Section 3, which are subsequently attacked under the Clayton Act by the government.

The Federal Trade Commission Act   The **Federal Trade Commission (FTC) Act** of 1914 created a commission, the FTC, to investigate and challenge any "unfair methods of competition . . . , and unfair or

---

4. The Sherman Antitrust Act was originally passed in 1890. The fine for violating the act was raised from $5,000 to $50,000 in 1955 and then to $100,000 for individuals and $1,000,000 for corporations in 1976. The 1976 amendments also made Sherman Act violations (previously misdemeanors) into felonies and raised the maximum prison term from one year to three years.

deceptive acts or practices in or affecting commerce." The act did not define "unfair practices," leaving the interpretation of the statute and the determination of what practices are unfair or deceptive up to the FTC, subject to review by the courts. Courts' reviews have been very restrictive and limited the effectiveness of the FTC for decades. Today, the FTC focuses largely on false and misleading advertising. These efforts, together with other investigations of fraud and unfair or deceptive business tactics, help to protect consumers. More recently, the FTC has turned its attention to restrictive state and local regulations and licensing practices that provide little benefit to consumers. The FTC's vigor in challenging perceived unfair business practices ebbs and flows with the political tides of the various presidential administrations, but in large measure the FTC remains the consumer's watchdog.

The Robinson-Patman Act   Section 2 of the Clayton Act was amended by the **Robinson-Patman Act** in 1936. This act was designed to limit price discrimination in the form of special promotional allowances. Discounts were permitted only where justified by differences in costs or when introduced as "good faith" efforts to meet competition. Because quantity discounts have been attacked under the Robinson-Patman Act, many economists have criticized the law as a

protector of small firms from competition rather than a guarantor of competition. There are enormous differences between protecting competitors from failure and promoting competition.

The Celler-Kefauver Antimerger Act   The Clayton Act prohibited the acquisition of a firm's stock by a competitor. The Supreme Court, however, distinguished between acquisition of stock and acquisition of assets (plant, equipment, and so on). If one firm acquired the assets of another, even through illegal acquisition of voting stock, the merger was allowed. This was the path to numerous mergers during the 1930s and 1940s. In 1950, the Celler-Kefauver Antimerger Act attempted to close this loophole in the law.

The **Celler-Kefauver Antimerger Act** made it illegal to acquire either the stock or assets of a competitor. Additionally, the act erected special hurdles for mergers if there was a trend toward concentration in an industry. If two relatively small firms tried to merge to improve their competitive position, the Celler-Kefauver Act (as interpreted) would prohibit such a merger even if this might improve competition (see the Von's Grocery case in Focus 1). Until recently, this act virtually eliminated horizontal and vertical mergers among major corporations. The five major acts and their general contents are shown in Table 4.

TABLE 4   *Summary of Antitrust Laws*

Statute and Year of Enactment	Major Provisions
Sherman Antitrust Act (1890)	Prohibits contracts, combinations, and conspiracies in restraint of trade and forbids monopolization or attempts to monopolize.
Clayton Act (1914)	Prohibits certain forms of price discrimination, contracts that prevent buyers from dealing with sellers' competitors, acquisition of one corporation's shares by another if the effect will be to substantially lessen competition, and interlocking directorates between competing corporations.
Federal Trade Commission Act (1914)	Established the FTC to investigate unfair and deceptive business practices.
Robinson-Patman Act (1936)	Amended the Clayton Act (Section 2) to prohibit discounts and other special price concessions. Price discrimination is permissible only where it is: 1. based on differences in cost. 2. a good faith effort to meet competition. 3. based on differences in marketability of product.
Celler-Kefauver Antimerger Act (1950)	Amended Section 7 of the Clayton Act to plug the loopholes that permitted merger via acquisition of assets. In addition, the law prohibited mergers where there was a trend toward concentration.

Von's Grocery—The Numbers, Ma'am, Just the Numbers!

The belief that competitive performance requires a competitive industrial structure was once a hallmark of antitrust policy. Nowhere was this as evident as in the *United States* v. *Von's Grocery Company* (1966) case. Von's Grocery Company of Los Angeles had acquired a direct competitor, Shopping Bag Food Stores. The merger combined the third and sixth largest local grocery chains, for a combined market share of 7.5 percent. The number of owner-operated single grocery stores had declined from 5,365 in 1950 to 3,590 in 1963. Over the same period, the number of chains nearly doubled.

In finding that the merger violated Section 7 of the Clayton Act, the Court noted: "It is enough for us that Congress feared that a market marked at the same time by both a continuous decline in the number of small businesses and a large number of mergers would slowly but inevitably gravitate from a market of many small competitors to one dominated by one or a few giants, and competition would thereby be destroyed. Congress passed the Celler-Kefauver Act to prevent such a destruction of competition."

The Court simply counted heads and totally ignored the competitive changes that were taking effect. A vigorous dissent by one judge argued that "local competition is vigorous to a fault, not only among chain stores themselves but also between chain stores and single-store operators." Over three-quarters of the acquisitions between 1961 and 1964 (including Von's) were "market extensions, involving neither the elimination of direct competitors in the Los Angeles market nor increased concentration of the market."

This dissent also characterized the majority's opinion as "nothing more than a requiem for the so-called 'Mom and Pop' grocery stores—the bakery and butcher shops, the vegetable and fish markets—that are now economically and technologically obsolete in many parts of the country."

Exemptions from Antitrust Laws

The language of the Sherman Antitrust Act states that every combination in restraint of trade is in violation of the law. As this act was interpreted by the courts, political pressures and economic realities arose, causing various groups to be exempted.

Agricultural Cooperatives The Clayton Act exempted agricultural associations so that nonprofit cooperatives could be formed without violating the antitrust laws, although some constraints try to prevent cooperatives from setting their prices "unduly" high.

Labor Unions National policy favors the right of workers to unionize and bargain collectively. The Sherman Antitrust Act, however, originally was used to stifle union activity. Sections 6 and 20 of the Clayton Act exempted collective bargaining by workers from antitrust actions.

Sports Organizations Curiously, the courts have almost totally exempted professional baseball and have provided specialized exemptions for other amateur and professional sports organizations from antitrust actions on the strange doctrine that they are not in interstate commerce because sporting events are "entertainment, not business." Thus, the NFL, NBA,

NCAA, AAU, and a variety of other associations in our multibillion-dollar sports industry are reasonably free to collude against their employees, potentially competitive organizations, or each other. These exemptions are, however, increasingly under attack in the courts.

Export Industries   The Webb-Pomerene Act of 1918 largely exempts from antitrust actions those associations that focus on export trade. Many nations encourage cartel formation for purposes of international trade. The Webb-Pomerene Act enables U.S. companies to engage in joint ventures when competing with foreign cartels. Export trade associations may legally act somewhat like cartels for American firms, but only in their international operations.

Regulated Industries   The next chapter discusses how detailed regulation replaces market forces in some industries. Normally, the tighter public regulation, the greater the exemption from antitrust laws. Because regulatory agencies presumably express the public interest, exemption from antitrust laws seems sensible to allow the public to realize any gains from cooperation among regulated firms.

The Antitrust Laws in Practice

The complexity of modern business raises numerous issues for public policy. Current antitrust enforcement is based on the Sherman Act, as amended, but Sections 1 and 2 are rather broadly written. What are the meanings of *monopolize* and *attempts to monopolize?* What behavior is permitted, and what is prohibited? And how will oligopolists be treated? How will firms know if they can merge without the threat of legal action from the federal government? All these questions raise important issues for antitrust enforcement.

Monopolization and Monopoly Power

A literal interpretation of Section 1 of the Sherman Act would ban most major transactions. The Sherman Act was vague about what was legal and what was not, leaving that decision to the courts. Nor does Section 2

clearly specify what constitutes a monopoly. To make matters worse, the courts historically have been a bit schizophrenic in interpreting the Sherman Act.

The "Rule of Reason"   In two early cases involving Standard Oil and the American Tobacco Company, the Supreme Court decided that trusts (monopolies) could either be "good" or "bad" and that the Sherman Act only outlaws "bad" restraints on trade.

> These landmark cases established what has been called the **rule of reason**, which developed standards to distinguish good and bad trusts.

Both Standard Oil and American Tobacco were judged "bad" trusts and were subjected to *divestiture;* they were split into several firms.

Where a firm could show that its conduct was based on sound business practice and was a logical consequence of its general practice, some obviously anticompetitive practices (refusals to deal and tie-in sales) were permitted. Whether the courts would allow certain "reasonable" conduct depended on such things as the percentage of the market affected, expected duration of the practice, relative strengths of the parties involved, and the size and nature of the relevant market.

The Per Se Doctrine   In the 1945 case of *U.S. v. Aluminum Co. of America (Alcoa)*, the Supreme Court hinted at a new approach to monopolization, known as the per se doctrine. The Court reasoned that the Sherman Act does not condone "good" trusts and forbid "bad" trusts; it prohibits all monopolization and restraints on trade. Whether or not a firm abused its power or obtained its monopoly by reasonable methods was irrelevant. The fact of monopoly was sufficient. In this case, Alcoa was forced to sell some assets to other firms to enhance competition in the industry.

> Under the **per se doctrine**, certain contracts, combinations, or conspiracies seem inherently so contrary to competition that they are held to be illegal per se.

The government needs only to show that such agreements were reached; whether or not competition has been harmed is immaterial. Among *per se* violations are (*a*) price-fixing agreements that in any way stabilize prices for a particular good, (*b*) schemes that divide customers or markets into territories, (*c*) agreements between competitors to refuse to deal with certain suppliers or customers, and (*d*) "tie-in sales," where a dominant seller forces a buyer to purchase peripheral products in order to purchase the desired good.

After the *per se* approach was adopted, the courts also began trying to address what constitutes a monopoly by looking at such factors as the number, size, and strength of the firms in the market, the nature of technology, and any economies of scale.

Antitrust Policy in Oligopoly Markets

Monopoly power hinders allocative efficiency and may create inequity, regardless of whether this power is exercized by a monopolist or shared among firms in an oligopoly. The Sherman Antitrust Act, however, outlaws *monopolies* and *attempts to monopolize*. To what extent do oligopolies represent "attempts to monopolize"? The previous chapter suggested that stability in pricing might be one hallmark of oligopoly. When oligopolistic prices change, we would predict that all prices in the industry will change simultaneously and by roughly similar amounts due to the close relationships among the firms in the industry.

Conscious Parallelism of Action   Noncollusive oligopolistic interaction may cause identical behavior that is as effective in restraining trade as an overt cartel agreement among firms, but there are no witnesses or documents to prove conspiracy. The dilemma is clear—parallel oligopolistic actions lead to socially undesirable economic effects, but the parallel action results from oligopolistic interdependence; the Sherman Antitrust Act requires formal proof of active conspiracy.

The FTC developed the idea of conscious parallelism of action to deal with this problem. In several landmark cases, the Supreme Court inferred conspiracy from parallel action by competitors.

> **Conscious parallelism of action** *is an inference of "attempts to monopolize" from like changes in prices and outputs by competitors.*

This approach lasted for several decades but was eventually overturned. The courts now must examine the totality of conduct rather than look only at parallel action; identical behavior is not illegal by itself. The courts recognize that parallel business policies may be either the result of independent judgment, a symptom of competition, or the result predicted by our models of noncompetitive markets. (Pure competition yields simultaneous price adjustments—a trait shared with many oligopoly models.) Today, findings of monopolization require clearer evidence of conspiracy.

Shared Monopoly   A different antitrust approach to oligopoly was introduced during the Carter administration in an action by the FTC against the four leading producers of breakfast cereals: Kellogg, General Mills, General Foods, and Quaker Oats. The FTC and Justice Department charged that the breakfast cereal market is effectively a **shared monopoly** because these four firms allegedly used their market power to exclude competitors and earn monopoly profits.

This antitrust action was controversial because of the novel approach used by the FTC and the Justice Department. Both charged the cereal industry with excessive brand proliferation as the major barrier to entry. When a new firm attempts to enter the industry, these four companies introduce and heavily advertise versions of the challenger's cereal. The result, according to the FTC, was monopolization of supermarket shelf space by the "big four," throttling potential competition.

In effect, the FTC accused these cereal makers of following the joint- profit maximization approach discussed in the previous chapter. The four manufacturers argued that they were being harassed for being too successful and for taking advantage of economies of scale in advertising, marketing, and management. The FTC charged that the firms had a tacit agreement not to cut price to compete, but rather, to use nonprice competition (games, puzzles, or prizes) to maintain a stable pricing structure.

This particular antitrust approach, not yet accepted by the courts, may never develop beyond an embryonic stage because cases against cereal makers and tobacco firms were abandoned during the Reagan administration. If the shared monopoly doctrine is ever resurrected, similar arguments might be used to attack the largest firms in industries where concentration and nonprice competition are apparent.

Merger Policy

Some antitrust efforts are intended to squelch monopoly power in its infancy. Strong antimerger policies evolved over the years, but many were abandoned in the early 1980s. The **Hart-Scott-Rodino Antitrust Improvement Act** of 1976 permits the Department of Justice to require (*a*) any individual or business to furnish information relevant to an investigation, especially if they are suspected violators of the law; and (*b*) premerger notification by firms. The latter provision forces firms to wait 30–50 days after notifying the government before consummating any merger. During the waiting period, the Department of Justice can evaluate the legality of proposed mergers and, if the Department concludes that a merger would violate the antitrust laws, it can immediately go to court to stop the merger. The advantage of this approach is that courts can review a proposed merger without having to consider the difficulties encountered in the dissolution of a merged company.

In 1982, the Justice Department announced merger guidelines to improve the predictability of federal merger policy. After noting that numerical standards must be tempered by judgment, the Department categorized mergers according to (*a*) the level of the Herfindahl-Hirschman index in the industry and (*b*) the change in the index that would occur because of the merger. (This change can be calculated simply by multiplying the percentage shares of the two firms and doubling the answer.[5]) The following guidelines then indicate the likelihood of a challenge to a horizontal merger based on the postmerger *HHI*:

1. *HHI* < 1,000: Unconcentrated Industries

The Justice Department is unlikely to challenge any such merger.

2. 1,000 < *HHI* < 1,800: Moderate Concentration

If the change in the *HHI* is less than 100 points, the Department will probably not challenge the merger. The more the change exceeds 100 points, the more likely a challenge will be mounted.

3. *HHI* > 1,800: Highly Concentrated Industries

These mergers raise concerns about competition, and questions will be resolved in favor of challenging the merger. Increases in the *HHI* of less than 50 points will probably go unchallenged, but mergers raising the *HHI* more than 100 points will generally be challenged. Changes in the *HHI* between 50 and 100 points will be resolved by assessing other factors in the market.

The other factors the Department considers include such things as (*a*) whether or not one of the merging firms is a dominant leader in the industry, (*b*) ease of entry into the market, (*c*) ease and profitability of collusion. Where one of the merging firms is the industry leader (35 percent or greater and is twice as large as the second largest firm) market power will be enhanced and the merger will be challenged. Where entry is easy enough that existing competitors could not succeed in raising prices, mergers will go unchallenged. Mergers in homogenous product markets will be scrutinized more closely than those where the products are heterogeneous or "sold subject to complex configuration options or customized production."

Horizontal mergers that might have generated economies of scale or other benefits were once prevented by rigid enforcement of antimerger laws, as typified by the Von's Grocery decision. The Reagan administration took the position that, "Although they sometimes harm competition, mergers generally play an important role in a free enterprise economy. They can penalize ineffective management and facilitate the efficient flow of investment capital and the redeployment of existing productive assets. While challenging competitively harmful mergers, the Department seeks to avoid unnecessary interference with that larger universe of mergers that are either competitively beneficial or neutral."[6]

---

5. The Justice Department noted, " . . . in calculating the *HHI* before the merger, the market shares of the merging firms are squared individually. Thus, $a^2 + b^2$. After the merger, the sum of those shares would be squared. Thus, $(a + b)^2$, which equals $a^2 + 2ab + b^2$. The increase in the *HHI* therefore is represented by $2ab$."

6. Merger guidelines issued by the U.S. Department of Justice, June 14, 1982.

The Future of Antitrust Policy

The complexity and size of modern business have parallels in the complexity and costliness of modern antitrust actions, which may turn into multimillion-dollar affairs. For example, seemingly continuous litigation against IBM was abandoned during the Reagan administration. It had absorbed thousands of hours by hundreds of lawyers, 104,000 pages of transcripts, 726 court days, and many millions of dollars during the 1950s, 1960s, and 1970s. A similarly enormous case against American Telephone and Telegraph was finally settled out of court in 1982.

Major market structures often seem so far removed from the model of pure competition that many economists and policymakers advocate vigorous antitrust initiatives to cure the economic problems posed by monopoly power. Antitrust laws have been on the books for almost a century, however, with little perceptible effect on our industrial structure. Indeed, huge waves of mergers closely followed the Sherman Act (1890), the Clayton Act (1914), and the Celler-Kefauver Antimerger Act (1950). A few of the corporate giants of past years have been dismembered because of antitrust actions (Standard Oil, American Tobacco, and Alcoa), but most (General Motors, DuPont, General Electric, IBM) have escaped the antitrust hatchet largely intact. Most antitrust litigation has been initiated by small companies having complaints about the low pricing policies of their competitors. Most antitrust battles have turned on narrow interpretations of legal technicalities, with the courts frequently trying to protect competitors instead of competition. George Stigler, after reviewing international data, found little evidence that market concentration differs between countries that have strong antitrust laws and those that do not.

The magnitude of antitrust actions seems to depend primarily on the political climate. President Theodore Roosevelt gained a reputation as a "trust buster" at the turn of the century, but attacking monopoly power has been on a back burner in most administrations. Former President Carter initiated a few new antitrust actions, but these were abandoned during the Reagan administration.

Some reasons for early antitrust activities may have diminished over time. Our economy is increasingly open, so that competition from foreign producers makes more of our domestic markets contestable. The tendency for adventurous conglomerate firms to engage in "hit-and-run" entry and exit whenever profits differ among markets is another powerful competitive force. The continuing trend towards ever greater concentration of assets in the hands of the few hundred largest American companies, however, is very discomforting to people disturbed by the potential political aspects of concentrations of economic power. They consider it unfortunate that antitrust policies leave conglomerate mergers untouched.

CHAPTER REVIEW: KEY POINTS

1. *Monopoly power* exists whenever a firm can set the price of its output. (Monopoly power and monopoly are not synonymous.) As monopoly power grows, the gap between price (P) and marginal cost (MC) widens. The *Lerner index of monopoly power* (*LMP*) uses this fact to measure monopoly power as $(P - MC)/P$. Estimating MC with accounting data is difficult, however, and using average costs as a proxy for MC may overstate monopoly power.

2. Market concentration ratios provide some evidence of monopolization or oligopolistic power. *Concentration ratios* are the percentages of total sales, output, or employment in an industry controlled by a small number of the largest firms in the industry. Concentration ratios for the Big 4, Big 8, Big 20, and Big 50 are computed for many industries.

3. Major difficulties are encountered in defining an industry. The existence of *close consumption substitutes* is one consideration; the ease with which potential competitors might enter an industry (*contestability*) is another. The Department of Commerce lumps firms into Standard Industrial Classifications (SICs) to try to solve this problem, but with only mixed success.

4. The *Herfindahl-Hirschman Index* (*HHI*) is the sum of squared market shares (ΣS_i^2). Squaring places

more emphasis on big firms. The Justice Department now uses the *HHI* as a guide to the permissibility of mergers.

5. *Concentration* varies substantially between industries. Nearly 100 percent of all cigarettes produced and sold in the United States are produced by fewer than eight companies, and the eight largest printing companies produce about one-tenth of all printing. Roughly 70 percent of all manufacturing assets, however, are controlled by the 200 largest American corporations. The numbers on concentration within industries grew dramatically from 1890 to 1929, but have only crept up slowly since.

6. Big firms might be justified by enormous capital requirements or substantial economies of scale. In those instances, proper public policy may take the form of regulation (dealt with in the next chapter). The major thrust of public policy where no such justifications for bigness exist has been to encourage competition through *antitrust actions*. The current level of concentration is testimony to the apparent failure of this policy.

7. One reason for merger is to increase the scope of a firm's operations so that economies of scale in information, marketing, advertising, production, or financial management may be exploited. A second reason, which is far more important for public policy, is that merger may eliminate business rivals and facilitate increases in economic concentration and monopoly power. Increases in monopoly power that result from merger may be reflected rapidly in higher prices for the merged companies' stock. This creates *promotional profit* for current stockholders.

8. The first major wave of mergers in the United States lasted roughly from 1890 until 1914, and was dominated by *horizontal* mergers—the absorption of firms' competitors.

9. Most horizontal mergers were outlawed with the passage of the *Clayton Antitrust Act,* so a wave of *vertical* mergers, lasting from 1914 until the 1929 stock market crash resulted in further economic concentration. Vertical mergers unite suppliers of raw materials or intermediate goods with processors or other firms further along the production chain.

10. Merger activity died during the Great Depression, but revived in the mid-1950s. Since most vertical mergers were prohibited by the Celler-Kefauver Antimerger Act, companies that were very dissimilar were merged into *conglomerates.* Merger activities slowed down during the 1970s but re-emerged strongly during the 1980s.

11. The *Big Five Antitrust Laws* are summarized in Table 4.

12. Agricultural cooperatives, athletic organizations, labor unions, export trade associations, and regulated industries are largely exempt from antitrust action.

13. In applying the *Sherman Antitrust Act,* the Court has historically taken two different approaches. The rule of reason approach prohibits bad monopolies and permits reasonable restraints on trade, while the *per se doctrine* forbids all monopolies regardless of conduct.

14. Merger policy is now based on various factors, but if the post-merger *HHI* exceeds 1,800, the Department of Justice is likely to challenge the merger.

PROBLEMS

1. Compute values for the Lerner Index of Monopoly Power (*LMP*) in the following situations. Rank these firms according to the amounts of monopoly power your answers suggest.
   - **a.** Alpha Inc.   Price = $100
     Marginal Cost = $100
   - **b.** Beta Corp.   Price = $0.60
     Marginal Cost = $1.20
   - **c.** Gamma Unl. Price = $12
     Marginal Cost = $10
   - **d.** Delta Inc.   Price = $5
     Marginal Cost = $3

2. Compute Herfindahl-Hirschman Indexes (*HHI*) for the following industries and indicate which of any possible mergers within each industry might be challenged under current Department of Justice antitrust guidelines.
   - **a.** Ten firms all share equally in total sales of silver eating utensils.
   - **b.** Percentages of total sales of automatic garage door openers are divided as follows: Macron = 40%, Contrails = 30%, Vulcan = 20%, and ten small firms each sell 1% of the total market.
   - **c.** The three largest tobacco companies respectively sell 51%, 29%, and 16% of all tobacco. There are eight other tobacco firms, each accounting for 1/2% of industry sales.

QUESTIONS FOR THOUGHT AND DISCUSSION

1. It has been argued that the emergence of large firms that wield sizable monopoly power represents an inevitable outcome of an unencumbered competitive process. Do you agree or disagree? Explain why.

2. According to standard theory, the major economic problem posed by the exercise of monopoly power is economic inefficiency. Studies that have attempted to measure the "welfare loss" caused by monopoly have, however, yielded tiny estimates of loss. No serious empirical study suggests that more than 1–2 percent of GNP is lost because of monopoly power, with most estimates being much less than one percent.[7] Is antitrust a waste of the tax payers' resources if these estimates are correct? Are there other socially important reasons to limit industrial concentration? If so, what are they?

3. When the Oakland Raiders moved to Los Angeles in 1982 they touched a vital nerve of the National Football League. This move, which was subsequently upheld by the courts, weakened the NFL's influence over the movement of franchises and threatened to undercut the pooling of network television revenues (60 percent of NFL income). The NFL is now lobbying Congress for a blanket antitrust exemption. Do you think professional sports should be exempt from antitrust laws? Should owners of professional teams be permitted to move their teams at their discretion? Critics of the NFL argue that the league "is more interested in limiting the number of teams and ensuring profits for the existing 28 owners." Do you agree?

4. The U.S. Department of Justice and the Federal Trade Commission are responsible for ensuring that industrial performance closely approximates the performance of the competitive ideal. Would it be feasible or even beneficial for these federal watchdogs to use the antitrust laws to impose competitive structures on all industries that are highly concentrated? Why?

5. In some concentrated industries, most notably cigarettes and breakfast cereals, the largest firms continually introduce new brands so fast that entry into the industry by smaller firms may be virtually impossible. Should these barriers to entry be permitted? Would consumers lose if existing firms were required to reduce the numbers of brands they market? Explain.

6. A decade ago, the computer industry was dominated by a few companies. Today, competition is fierce. What accounts for the change—government antitrust action? Is the same thing likely to occur in steel, aluminum, and other basic industries? Why?

7. In 1982, the Justice Department proposed to attack a horizontal merger if, after defining the relevant product market for the merged firm, a hypothesized price increase of 5 percent could be expected to be sustained for over a year. Is this a reasonable measure of increased concentration from a merger? Why?

8. Government antitrust actions have been notoriously large and expensive (the IBM and AT&T cases are examples). The typical *private* antitrust case involves about $50,000 in legal fees for each side, about thirty hours of top executives' time, and is usually completed within two years. Because private antitrust actions are relatively inexpensive, some have argued that the law should be liberalized to permit more private antitrust suits and curtail the federal government's role. Do you think this is a workable solution to the mounting costs of federal antitrust litigation? What problems might this pose?

---

7. The first such study (Arnold Harberger, "Monopoly and Resource Allocation," *American Economic Review* 44 (May 1954) :77–87) estimated this loss at only 1/10 of 1 percent of our GNP.

Aspen Skiing Company v. Aspen Highlands Skiing Corporation (1985)

Firms with monopoly power are convenient targets for private antitrust suits from smaller rivals. Is a company with considerable monopoly power under an obligation to cooperate with its smaller business competitors or to enter into a joint operating agreement? Or must it refuse to deal with competitors? This recent Supreme Court decision examines these issues.

Aspen is a destination ski resort with a reputation for "super powder," "a wide range of runs," and an "active night life," including "some of the best restaurants in North America."

Between 1958 and 1964, three independent companies operated the Ajax, Highlands, and Buttermilk mountains. A fourth mountain, Snowmass, opened in 1967. In the early years, each company offered its own day or half-day tickets for use of its mountain. In 1962, however, the three competitors also introduced an interchangeable ticket. The 6-day, all-Aspen ticket provided convenience to the vast majority of skiers who visited the resort for weekly periods, but preferred to remain flexible about what mountain they might ski each day during the visit. It also emphasized the unusual variety of ski mountains available in Aspen.

As initially designed, the all-Aspen ticket program consisted of booklets containing six coupons, each redeemable for a daily lift ticket at Ajax, Highlands, or Buttermilk. The price of the booklet was often discounted from the price of six daily tickets, but all six coupons had to be used within a limited period of time— seven days, for example. The revenues from the sale of the 3-area coupon books were distributed in accordance with the number of coupons collected at each mountain.

In 1964, Buttermilk was purchased by Aspen Skiing Co. (Ski Co.), and, in 1967, Ski Co. opened Snowmass. In the 1971–72 season, the coupon booklets were discontinued and an "around the neck" all-Aspen ticket was developed. This refinement on the interchangeable ticket was advantageous to the skier, who no longer found it necessary to visit the ticket window every morning before gaining access to the slopes.

Ski Co. and Highlands used random sample surveys to allocate the revenues from the 4-area, 6-day ticket. Highlands' share of the revenues from the ticket was 17.5% in 1973–74, 18.5% in 1974–75, 16.8% in 1975–76 and 13.2% in 1976–77. During these four seasons, Ski Co. did not offer its own three-area, multi-day ticket in competition with the all-Aspen ticket. By 1977, multi-area tickets accounted for nearly 35% of the total market.

In the 1970s the management of Ski Co. increasingly expressed their dislike for the all-Aspen ticket. They complained that a coupon method of monitoring usage was administratively cumbersome. They doubted the accuracy of the survey and decried the "appearance, deportment, [and] attitude" of the college students who were conducting it. In addition, Ski Co.'s president had expressed the view that the 4-area ticket was siphoning off revenues that could be recaptured by Ski Co. if the ticket was discontinued. In 1978, Ski Co. offered Highlands a 4-area ticket provided that Highlands would agree to receive a 12.5 fixed percentage of the revenue. Highlands rejected the offer of the fixed percentage.

In its place, Ski Co. offered the 3-area, 6-day ticket featuring only its mountains. In an effort to promote this ticket, Ski Co. embarked on a national advertising campaign that strongly implied to people who were unfamiliar with Aspen that Ajax, Buttermilk, and Snowmass were the only ski mountains in the area.

Highlands finally developed an "Adventure Pack," which consisted of a 3-day pass at Highlands and three vouchers, each equal to the price of a daily lift ticket at a Ski Co. mountain. The vouchers were guaranteed by funds on deposit in an Aspen bank, and were redeemed by Aspen merchants at full value. Ski Co., however, refused to accept them. Later, Highlands redesigned the Adventure Pack to contain American Express Traveler's Checks instead of vouchers. Ski Co. accepted these in exchange for daily lift tickets.

Without a convenient all-Aspen ticket, Highlands basically "becomes a day ski area in a destination resort." Highland's share of the market declined steadily.

In 1979, Highlands filed a complaint alleging that Ski Co. had monopolized the market for downhill skiing services at Aspen in violation of Section 2 of the Sherman Act.

Although Ski Co.'s pattern of conduct may not have been "bold, relentless, and predatory," the record in this case comfortably supports an inference that the monopolist made a deliberate effort to discourage its customers from doing business with its smaller rival. The sale of its 3-area, 6-day ticket, particularly when it was discounted below the daily ticket price, deterred the ticket holders from skiing at Highlands. The refusal to accept the Adventure Pack coupons in exchange for daily tickets was apparently motivated entirely by a decision to avoid providing any benefit to Highlands, even though accepting the coupons would have entailed no cost to Ski Co. itself, would have provided it with immediate benefits, and would have satisfied its potential customers. Thus the evidence supports an inference that Ski Co. was not motivated by efficiency concerns and that it was willing to sacrifice short-run benefits and consumer good will in exchange for a perceived long-run impact on its smaller rival.

Questions

1. This case seems to suggest that if a firm has monopoly power and no valid business reason to refuse to deal with a competitor, it must do so or face triple damages under the Sherman Antitrust Act. Do you agree with this rule?

2. Suppose the four mountains in Aspen were owned by four separate firms, but one mountain was vastly superior to the others for skiing. Assume further that the firm owning the superior mountain refused to enter into a four-mountain, 6-day package with the other firms. Do you think this case would require cooperation or joint marketing of the four mountains?

3. Suppose that Aspen Skiing Company and Aspen Highlands Skiing Corporation decided to merge. What would happen to the *HHI?* Do you think the Justice Department would permit the merger? How are this case, Von's Grocery, and the current merger guidelines related? Is there a significant difference between the joint marketing arrangement required in this case and merger of the two firms?

4. Do these two firms have incentives to enter into price competition? In effect, has the Court ordered and immunized joint-profit maximization under the guise of protecting consumer convenience?

5. Should the Court have only considered the Aspen ski market as the relevant market? Is there competition from other ski resorts in Colorado and the West?

6. Is the effect of this case to eliminate "making a higher profit and making life harder for your competitors" as valid business reasons? Is the Court correct when it states that Ski Co.'s acceptance of Adventure Pack coupons entailed no cost to Ski Co. itself?

CHAPTER 27

The Role of Government Regulation

That life grows ever more complex is a cliché. Complex societies are also regulated societies. At one time, you could count on your fingers the regulations governing most American industries. Today, you would need the appendages in a bushel basket of centipedes. Business regulation is a massive task for government regulators, for the firms they oversee, and for hordes of lawyers and consultants from both sides. Concerns about pollution and the environment; consumer and occupational safety and health; discrimination against women and minority groups; and a host of other social, economic, and political problems all contribute to the rising tide of business regulation. But business activity is not alone in being regulated.

A vast body of law governs private behavior. Consumer protection laws most obviously affect firms, but regulation also broadly restricts the options available to consumers. Laws mandate school attendance until your mid-teens, prohibit self-prescription of penicillin or heroin, require you to stop at red lights, forbid you to walk your dog without a leash and a shovel, ... Focus 1 indicates that even the food that you eat, in this case, hamburgers, do not escape regulation.

Many observers of American business charge that private activity is being suffocated by government intervention. Instead of providing a chicken for every pot, government's finger is in every pie. Extensive regulation is blamed for reducing supplies and driving up production costs. Critics argue that bureaucratic red tape and silly rules stifle productivity and account for much of the recent lag in our international competitiveness.

Have It Their Way

Your Hamburger: 41,000 Regulations

PICTOGRAM ®

The hamburger, staple of the quick, inexpensive meal, is the subject of 41,000 federal and state regulations, many of those stemming from 200 laws and 111,000 precedent-setting court cases.

These rules, cited in a three-volume study by Colorado State University, touch on everything involved in meat production—grazing practices of cattle, conditions in slaughterhouses and methods used to process meat for sale to supermarkets, restaurants and fast-food outlets. Together, they add an estimated 8 to 11 cents per pound to the cost of hamburger.

The chart on this page gives just a sampling of the rules and regulations governing the burger you buy at the corner sandwich stand.

Pesticides—No more than 5 parts of the pesticide DDT per million parts of fat in the meat.

Bun—Enriched bun must contain at least 1.8 milligrams of thiamine, 1.1 milligrams of riboflavin and at least 8 but not more than 12.5 milligrams of iron.

Content—It must be fresh or frozen chopped beef and not contain added water, binders or extenders.

Growth promoters—Use of growth-stimulating drugs must end two weeks before slaughter.

Fat—No more than 30 percent fat content.

Lettuce—Must be fresh, not soft, overgrown, burst or "ribby."

Pickle—Slices must be between ⅛ and ⅜ inches thick.

Tomato—Must be mature but not overripe or soft.

Cheese—Must contain at least 50 percent milk fat and, if made with milk that is not pasteurized, must be cured for 60 or more days at a temperature of at least 35 degrees Fahrenheit.

Ketchup—To be considered Grade A fancy, it must flow no more than 9 centimeters in 30 seconds at 69 degrees Fahrenheit.

Mayonnaise—May be seasoned or flavored as long as the substances do not color it to look like egg yolk.

Inspections—As many as six inspections under Federal Meat Inspection Act can occur as meat is checked before and after slaughter and at boning, grinding, fabrication and packaging stages.

Source: Reprinted from U.S.News & World Report *issue of Feb. 11, 1980. Copyright, 1980, U.S.News & World Report.*

Broad and growing regulation is advocated by critics of a laissez-faire approach who view competitive forces as weak and misinformation, inequity, and instability as pervasive. One possible goal is for government to strive for results paralleling those of an idealized world of pure competition. In this chapter, we will examine (*a*) the nature and extent of regulation, (*b*) some reasons for regulation, (*c*) cases for and against consumer protection, and (*d*) some practical problems of regulation.

The Growth of Government Regulation

A reaction of many victims of a raw deal is, "There ought to be a law to . . . (prevent people from being "cheated" this way)." This is one reason why hundreds of government agencies now regulate business. Figure 1 surveys the growth of American regulatory agencies. Except for a few muckrakers and social reformers, most people once favored moderate laissez-faire capitalism. The Great Depression dislodged widespread belief in the free market system like a blow from a sledge hammer.

Many regulatory programs introduced in the 1930s were intended to quell disruptions caused by business cycles. New laws tightened government's reins over banking, public utilities, securities transactions, and labor contracts; family farmers were supported, mortgage loans were guaranteed, and our welfare system was expanded. The shock of the Great Depression may have permanently altered the role most Americans want for their government.

The 1940s and the 1950s, on the other hand, were almost barren of new regulatory agencies. Then, in the 1960s and 1970s, a new wave of regulation erupted. As Figure 1 illustrates, regulatory agencies more than doubled from 1960 to 1980, with the 1970s alone accounting for over half of all regulatory agencies. This surge of new regulatory agencies was not a consequence of economic upheaval; paradoxically, it occurred during a period when real disposable personal income rose by over 40 percent—one of the more prosperous periods in our history. Why did regulation explode in this period?

One explanation for regulatory growth is the complexity of today's products. Sophisticated technology may have made the simple rules of the past obsolete. Kenneth Boulding argues that just as an astronaut in a space capsule must follow a far stricter regimen than

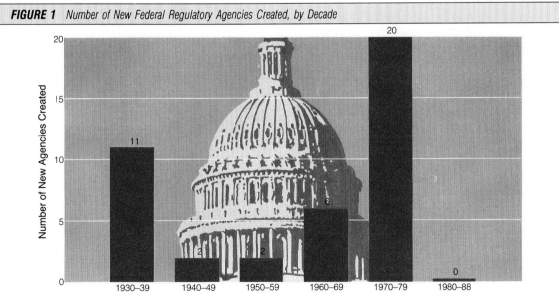

FIGURE 1 *Number of New Federal Regulatory Agencies Created, by Decade*

The power of the gederal government to regulate commerce is established in the Constitution. This power was exercised little before the 1930s, but the 1960s and 1970s were an "Age of Regulation."

Source: Reprinted from September 3, 1979 issue of *Business Week* by special permission, copyright © 1979 by McGraw-Hill, Inc. Data from the Center for the Study of American Business. Updated by authors.

a cowboy on the prairie, so too must a space-age economy be controlled more tightly than the simpler economy of an earlier era.

Robert Heilbroner, another prominent economist, has divided typical government relationships with industry into three phases. Its first role is as *promoter;* its second, as *regulator;* and, finally, it acts as a *guarantor.* He cites railroads as an example. Government actively promoted rail transport with right-of-way land grants and other subsidies late in the nineteenth century. Then railroads were closely regulated during the first half of this century. Finally, government now guarantees the railroads' existence. Much of the rail system was effectively nationalized into Amtrak and Conrail in the 1960s and 1970s. Similar scenarios have been played out in the nuclear, petroleum, and automobile industries. (A government loan guarantee rescued Chrysler in the early 1980s; the U.S. auto industry would probably have shrivelled without recent import restrictions against foreign cars.)

Heilbroner's theory might extend to a fourth phase—*deregulation.* Many people seem tired of today's regulatory maze. The 1980 election of Ronald Reagan signaled an abrupt halt to the creation of new regulatory agencies. He and his political allies found the voting public responsive when they argued that a multitude of complex and contradictory policies served no useful or valid purposes.

Is it possible to reverse the upward trend of regulation? Perhaps, but most proposals to deregulate business have encountered fierce opposition. Surprisingly, regulated industries themselves have spear-headed much of this resistance. Long-term adjustments to rules create vested interests that generate tremendous political pressure to resist reform proposals. For example, consumer groups and the liquor industry joined to vigorously resist a Reagan administration proposal to thoroughly deregulate alcoholic beverage production.

It seems paradoxical that most individual regulations are fervently supported by large groups of people even though public opinion polls suggest that most people perceive total regulation to be excessive. Before we can judge whether our society is over-regulated, we need a sense of how profoundly regulation shapes the U.S. economy.

The Extent of Government Regulation

Don't worry about the government running out of three-letter acronyms to identify federal agencies. There are 26^3 ($= 17,576$) possible three-letter combinations. The alphabet soup of regulatory bodies includes such well-known agencies as the IRS, FAA, FTC, and the SEC. Table 1 lists some major federal regulatory agencies and describes their functions. A frequent charge is that the costs of bureaucratic rules governing business escalate every year.

Direct Costs of Regulation

Critics argue that rules and red tape drive up business costs and the cost of living. A 1981 study of federal economic regulation provides some insight into its cost.[1] Two types of *direct costs* were considered:

1. *Administrative costs.* These include the salaries of government workers, inspectors, office supplies, and other "overhead" expenses.
2. *Compliance costs.* These are costs incurred primarily by the private sector, but also by state and local governments, in the process of complying with federal regulations.

The authors of the study, Murray Weidenbaum and Robert DeFina, found that compliance costs in total were almost 20 times the administrative costs. Based on their analysis, nearly $200 billion is now required annually to meet federal regulations, which is equivalent to:

1. roughly 4 percent of the Gross National Product.
2. nearly $1,000 per person living in the United States.
3. 18 percent of the federal budget.
4. roughly twice the amount that the federal government spends on health.
5. two thirds of the amount devoted to national defense.
6. over one third of private investment in new plant and equipment.

---

1. M. Weidenbaum and R. DeFina, *The Rising Cost of Government Regulation* (St. Louis: Center for the Study of American Business, 31 Jan. 1981).

TABLE 1 *Some Major Federal Regulatory Agencies*

Agency	Areas of Concern and Major Regulatory Function(s)
	Product Markets
Antitrust Division of the Justice Dept.	Promotes competition by enforcing federal antitrust laws.
Federal Communications Commission	Regulates broadcasting, telephone, and other communication services.
Federal Maritime Commission	Regulates foreign and domestic ocean commerce.
Federal Trade Commission	Protects consumers from unfair trade practices, false advertising, and overly restrictive licensing.
Interstate Commerce Commission	Regulates interstate surface transportation, including trucking, railroads, and water carriers.
	Labor Markets
Equal Employment Opportunity Commission	Investigates complaints of discrimination based on race, religion, sex, or age in hiring, promotion, firing, wages, testing, and all other conditions of employment.
National Labor Relations Board	Regulates and enforces collective bargaining agreements between companies and unions, and certifies elections of bargaining representatives.
	Financial Markets
Commodity Futures Trading Commission	Regulates futures trading on eleven U.S. futures exchanges.
Comptroller of the Currency	Supervises operations of over 4,700 national banks.
Federal Deposit Insurance Corporation	Examines, insures, and regulates banks.
Federal Home Loan Bank Board	Supervises and regulates savings institutions that specialize in financing of residential real estate.
Federal Reserve Board	Regulates banks and all financial institutions that offer draftable (checking) accounts.
Securities & Exchange Commission	Regulates all public securities markets to promote full disclosure.
	Energy and Environment
Corps of Engineers	Oversees construction along rivers, harbors, and waterways.
Environmental Protection Agency	Develops and enforces environmental standards for air, water, toxic waste, and noise.
Department of Energy	Oversees national energy policy.
Nuclear Regulatory Commission	Licenses and regulates civilian nuclear power facilities to protect public health and safety and the environment.
	Health and Safety
Consumer Product Safety Commission	Requires reporting of product defects and redesign and labeling to reduce unreasonable risks of injury from consumer products.
Federal Aviation Administration	Regulates aviation industry.
Food & Drug Administration	Protects against impure and unsafe foods, drugs and cosmetics, and other potential hazards.
Occupational Safety & Health Administration	Regulates workplace safety and health conditions.
National Highway Traffic Safety Administration	Regulates motor vehicle safety through safety standards, uniform national speed limit, and protects consumers from vehicles with reset odometers.

Source: U.S. Office of the Federal Register, *The United States Government Manual* 1986/1987.

The $200 billion estimate probably underestimates true direct costs because nearly 20 major regulatory agencies were not included in the study due to lack of data at that time.

One conclusion of this study is that regulatory activities absorb 5 to 10 percent of our annual national income. These data on costs are only one side of the regulatory equation; a balanced evaluation would require estimates of the benefits of government regulation. Even so, these numbers should be useful when Congress evaluates proposals for deregulation or more regulation.

Indirect Costs of Regulation

Governmental budget outlays have swollen as public demands for various regulatory programs have grown. The costs of government go far beyond the national budget, however, because many programs with laudable objectives often generate indirect costs through their effects on workers, consumers, and other participants on the economic stage.

Consider the effects of a program like unemployment compensation. Many workers effectively receive a paid vacation if they are laid off. Unemployment compensation is largely untaxed and is often as much as 80 percent of a worker's take-home wage. Thus, this income security program creates incentives for some people to quit their jobs at the public's expense.

Similarly, government farm programs, intended to protect family farmers, instead enrich many large corporate farms. The higher food prices consumers pay are largely overlooked when government costs are analyzed. These programs also create incredible surpluses of some farm goods. Every man, woman, and child in America would need to eat a box of cornflakes every day for a year to eliminate the corn now stored at government expense.

Our tax structure is also distortive and costly. For example, many firms offer a variety of tax-free fringe benefits to their employees because, were these benefits paid in cash, the employees' income taxes would rise. The result is that some employee benefits are disguised as legitimate business expenses. Thus, many employees drive company cars that are newer and grander than they would buy themselves, join country clubs that they would not join if the company were not paying their dues, and indulge in more elaborate lunches than they would eat if they were paying their own tabs.

Finally, business executives are always looking over their shoulders at what government might say about a strategic business decision, and may not do what is necessary to improve economic efficiency, innovate new products, or provide the best service possible for consumers. We have estimates of the direct costs of regulatory compliance, but how about the indirect costs of having talented people who look for loopholes around taxes or regulations instead of improving a firm's products?

These *indirect costs* of government regulation are incurred whenever people adjust to government policies in ways not intended by policymakers. It may be that the complexity of laws and regulations is made necessary because many people find ways to avoid very simple rules. Thus, the complicated lives we lead as we try to adhere to a maze of bureaucratic rules are among the indirect costs of government. But costs are only one part of the picture. We will now examine some possible benefits of regulation.

Why Is Business Regulated?

This must seem at first glance to be a simple-minded question. Market systems have many shortcomings. In previous chapters, you saw how monopoly power causes economic inefficiency and apparent inequity. Fraud, unsafe working conditions, and other maladies seem common in our market economy.

> The **public interest theory of regulation** *is the idea that people need protection from business abuses. This theory assumes that regulation serves the public's interest by restricting harmful business activities.*

This rationale for regulation went unchallenged for years. When regulation has not operated in the public interest, a standard interpretation is that these imperfections are simply consequences of imperfect people doing their jobs as regulators in imperfect ways. Only recently has this explanation for regulatory peccadilloes been questioned.

After decades of studying the American economy, Nobel Prize winner George Stigler identified numerous instances where regulation failed to guard public

BIOGRAPHY

George Stigler 1911–

The politicians who invited George Stigler to a White House dinner after his Nobel prize was awarded in 1982 were dismayed when Stigler, during a press conference, described the economy as in a depression, not a recession. His friends were not surprised. Stigler's record of advocating laissez-faire policies is matched by a reputation for being a straightshooter who calls them as he sees them.

The University of Chicago's "school" of economic thought has been known for its opposition to activist government policies throughout this century. Tall and lanky George Stigler shared stewardship over this tradition with his short, fellow Nobel-prize-winning friend, Milton Friedman, for almost half a century. Friedman is best known for his work in macroeconomics and monetary theory, while Stigler has been a pioneer in the study of modern microeconomics.

Stigler's research has been testimony to the notion that genius often consists of an ability to see old ideas in new ways. He received his Ph.D. in 1938 from the University of Chicago and spent most of his career there, with occasional side tours to Minnesota, Columbia, and the London School of Economics. He has extended the frontiers of economic study in many areas, including industrial organization, the economics of information, and the sources and effects of government regulation. A hallmark of his work has been rigorous hypothesis testing to ascertain which economic theories seem supported by real world data.

Stigler fundamentally disagrees with those who view the market system as inherently defective because few markets conform to the assumptions of pure or perfect competition. Stigler has found that industries characterized by monopolistic competition or oligopoly act much more competitively, with respect to price, than most models of imperfect competition predict. In particular, he rejects the sticky prices assumed in the kinked-demand curve model. Empirical work that found no relationship between price responsiveness and market structure led him to urge abandonment of kinked demand models.

Stigler was among the first to consider information as an economic good that consumers and firms alike pursue until its marginal benefits and marginal costs are equal. Stigler's seminal 1961 article fueled an explosion of research effort that helped launch the economics of information as a major and growing subdiscipline of economics. He was also the first major modern economist to perceive that regulation is often instigated by the regulated. His extended studies of antitrust policies and regulation have made him extremely skeptical that much government economic activity is in the public interest.

Another focus of his interest has been the sociology of economics as a field of study. His essays on the development of economic theory and methodology are a staple of economists' reading lists. When Stigler challenged his grandson to name Adam Smith's best friend, the youngster is said to have responded, "You, Grandpa." (Most likely correct answer: David Hume.) Nevertheless, the boy's answer accurately reflected Stigler's lasting enthusiasm for the ideas of the eighteenth-century Scottish moral philosopher and economist.

interests. He asked an obvious question: If the public interests are not being served, whose are? His answer turned previous theory on its head.

> The **industry interest theory of regulation** *is the idea that regulation is often tailored to serve the interests of regulated industries instead of those of the general public.*

The traditional public interest theory of regulation combined with Stigler's industry (private) interest theory still leaves one other possibility.

> The **public choice theory of regulation** *emphasizes that bureaucrats produce complex regulations so that their power and budgets will grow.*

This perspective is an extension of Stigler's industry interest theory. Public choice models frequently link special interest laws and regulations with the interests of the bureaucrats who administer them. A detailed discussion of this view is left for our chapter on public choice. In this chapter we will examine the traditional rationale for regulation—the public interest theory—before reviewing Stigler's alternative interpretation.

The Public Interest Theory of Regulation

The public interest theory of regulation centers on some possible failures of the market system: externalities, monopoly power, and imperfect information. Problems of monopoly power and externalities are the foundations for much of business regulation. The idea that imperfect information adversely affects market solutions is used most to rationalize regulation of labor markets and consumer protection.

Regulating Natural Monopolies

One goal of antitrust policy is to lessen monopoly power. Antitrust actions to break up huge firms may, however, cause inefficiency. If market demand is low relative to economies of scale then, at most, a few firms can achieve the lowest possible production costs. Ensuring survival of many small firms would require preventing them from competing and would inefficiently raise costs.

> A **natural monopoly** *occurs if substantial economies of scale will allow only a single firm to simultaneously service market demand and achieve the lowest possible average production costs.*

Railroads, electricity generation, and highways are natural monopolies. Government provides highways, but most natural monopolies are privately owned. These industries are typified by high fixed costs and huge economies of scale. Requiring many small firms to compete is unsustainable and inefficient; the public would be denied the lower costs and prices available if economies of scale were exploited. But how can policymakers prevent a natural monopoly from profiting by artificially restricting output and raising prices?

The dilemma posed by a natural monopoly is diagrammed in Figure 2, which depicts a market where economies of scale are such that only one firm can operate efficiently. If two firms in the industry each produced Q_m, average total costs for each firm would be AC_m. Since $2Q_M = Q_0$, the prices (P_0) these two firms could charge would fall far below AC_m because of limited demand. Consumers would ultimately gain little by having two firms competing with each other, however, because each business would lose money continuously until one went bankrupt. If more than two firms entered the industry, average total costs would be even higher. Unfortunately, if consumers bought from an unregulated monopoly, output would be restricted to Q_m and sold at a price of P_m, possibly exceeding the price associated with some competition. Price exceeds marginal cost in this monopoly solution, so there is economic inefficiency.

The public interest is clearly better served if only one firm exploits these economies of scale and then prices appropriately. If a regulated unit price is restricted to P_r, the firm could realize normal profits and consumers would pay a lower price than the unregulated price P_m. However, socially optimal pricing and output requires that $P = MC$, the desirable resource allocation that results from pure competition. Could a regulator reasonably require that the last unit Q_0 be sold at a price of P_0 so that efficiency is realized? If a price of P_0 is charged for every

FIGURE 2 *The Dilemma of the Natural Monopolist*

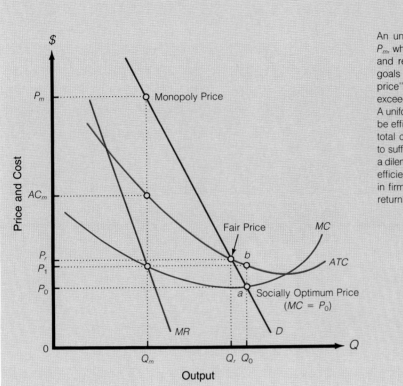

An unregulated monopolist will charge P_m, which is far above marginal cost (MC) and results in severe problems for the goals of efficiency and equity. The "fair price" P_r will just cover costs, but still exceeds MC and so results in inefficiency. A uniform socially optimal price, P_0, would be efficient but would not cover average total cost (P_1). No firm would be willing to suffer losses consistently, which poses a dilemma for society. How can we secure efficiency and still ensure that investors in firms of this type receive fair rates of return?

unit of output, the firm will receive revenue equal to area $0P_0aQ_0$, which is inadequate to cover total costs equal to area $0P_1bQ_0$. No firm would be willing to stay in business if regulations forced such constant losses.

Block Pricing A technique called block pricing has been developed to efficiently generate sufficient revenues to cover all costs, including a normal rate of return.

> *In a **block pricing** system, there is an initial minimum fee charged all users, but the more you use of the regulated monopolist's product, the lower the price for extra units.*

For example, block pricing is used to set rates for electric companies. You pay a hookup fee and then a minimum monthly charge. As you use more and

more electricity, your total bill rises but the rate per extra kilowatt hour declines. Figure 3 replicates the cost and demand data in Figure 2 but shows that with block pricing, revenues (the entire shaded area) can cover costs (the entire crosshatched area). Because the price of the last unit equals its production cost in this example, marginal social benefit equals marginal social cost and this market operates efficiently. Notice that block pricing uses price discrimination to yield efficiency. Block pricing is commonly used for public utilities (natural gas, electric, and telephone services), for railroads and other forms of regulated transportation, and for pipelines.

Rate Making This diagram may seem relatively simple, but utility regulation is a complex process that absorbs the efforts of thousands of people. In practice, **rate making** (setting utility prices) re-

FIGURE 3 How Block Pricing Permits Revenues to Cover Costs and Facilitates Efficiency (MSB = MSC)

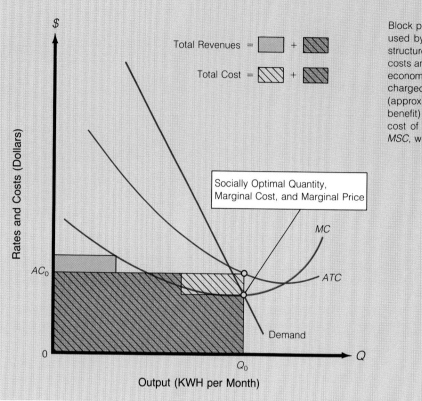

Total Revenues = ▨ + ▨

Total Cost = ▨ + ▨

Block pricing, a form of discrimination used by regulatory bodies to set rate structures, permits a firm to cover its costs and, at the same time, facilitates economic efficiency. The price charged for the last unit of output (approximately the marginal social benefit) just equals the marginal social cost of production. Because *MSB = MSC*, we have economic efficiency.

Socially Optimal Quantity, Marginal Cost, and Marginal Price

MC

ATC

AC_0

Demand

Rates and Costs (Dollars)

Q_0

Output (KWH per Month)

quires that the agency select a base period for calculations (usually the preceding year). It then sums all the firm's operating costs, including depreciation and taxes. A reasonable accounting profit, derived from multiplying the rate base by the percentage rate of profit allowed, is added to operating costs.

> The **rate base** *is the value of capital to which the profit rate applies. The regulator adjusts* **rate structures** *so that total revenue covers all operating costs, including a normal profit.*

There are invariably disagreements over such things as (*a*) items to be included in the rate base and their appropriate values, (*b*) a fair rate of return, (*c*) allowable costs, and (*d*) how to structure rates. If all "costs" are allowed, a utility would have few incentives to be efficient. Executive limousines, private jets, resort homes, and similar luxuries would all become "costs." On the other hand, rates must be high enough to protect the financial health of the utility for

it to attract investors. Finally, the regulatory commission must continually monitor the quality of service.

Control over pricing is the standard approach to caging monopoly power when economies of scale yield natural monopolies. Externalities are another problem that has been used to justify regulation. Direct regulation, however, generally has been used rather than the price system.

Externalities and Direct Regulation

Externalities exist whenever some activity confers benefits or costs on a party not a direct participant in the activity. Pollution is one example of negative externalities that harm groups who do not consume the product.

Some forms of passenger protection in autos carry externalities. Others do not. Such safety equipment as seat belts and air bags protect only a car's occupants and could be sold just like mag wheels, AM-FM radios, and so on. Drivers and their passengers are the primary beneficiaries of this equipment. It directly protects the individual buying it, and externalities are negligible.[2]

Shock-absorbing bumpers are examples of safety equipment that carry externalities. The buyer gains, but other drivers do also. Damage to both cars is reduced when a car with a shock-absorbing bumper collides with another car. External benefits are conferred on nonbuyers of shock-absorbing bumpers, but payments for such external benefits are almost impossible to collect. Thus, private purchases of shock-absorbing bumpers will be less than socially optimal. Consequently, the "public interest" now requires that manufacturers provide such mechanisms on cars. This is an example of a positive externality in which regulation requires a particular type of good. Inoculations against communicable diseases and education requirements are also examples of activities embodying positive externalities.

Negative externalities, many of which we know as pollution, spread costs beyond the transaction in question. When one firm discharges noxious waste into a stream, people who use the stream for recreation pay part of the costs, whether or not they consume the product that generates pollution. No single firm will adequately control its waste voluntarily if cleaning up imposes costs not borne by its competitors. Competitors will undercut price premiums that cover the higher costs of nonpolluting firms. Government intervention may be necessary to compensate for these third-party costs. Direct regulation generally limits some forms of pollution quantitatively and forbids other, more dangerous pollutants. We leave a detailed discussion of externalities and alternative environmental policies to a later chapter.

Imperfect Information

The market operates properly when relatively good information is shared by both buyers and sellers. Sellers commonly, however, can reasonably be assumed to have better information than consumers. This raises the issue of *adverse selection* discussed in our chapter on consumer behavior. Adverse selection occurs when one side (e.g., buyers) agrees to a contract only because they lack information possessed by the other side (e.g., sellers). For example, consumers do not have staffs of safety engineers to assess automobiles or other high-technology equipment. A knowledgeable seller would have incentives to disguise a lack of automotive safety if a problem were discovered after production was under way. The Ford Pinto case is a notorious example.[3] Firms also commonly have better information than workers about on-the-job safety.

One possible remedy is for government to provide information to the public. Various private organizations also evaluate products. For example, *Consumer Reports, Road and Track,* and *Motor Trend* are all sources of information about car performance and safety. Even if information is readily available, however, some people argue that the public lacks the expertise to assess it. As a result, government experts often specify whether a given product can be sold or a given work practice can continue.

Many people believe that imperfect information justifies regulation to monitor e.g., product safety, fraudulent sales practices, the contents of foods and drugs, toy safety, and occupational safety and health. Product traits other than imperfect information, externalities, or declining costs that tend to foster regulation include (*a*) goods considered vital to consumers, (*b*) goods for which supplies or demands fluctuate significantly, (*c*) products that are hooked directly to the consumer's property by such things as wires or pipes, and (*d*) goods that are reasonably homogeneous. Each of these areas either arouses public concern or makes regulation easy to implement. The high risks of financial investments in securities and commodities and the potential for fraud have led to extensive regulation of this area, as illustrated in Focus 2.

The preceding public interest rationales represent traditional reasons for economic regulation. George Stigler recently introduced a fundamental change in the way many economists view much of economic regulation.

---

2. This argument ignores the effect on insurance rates of added injuries to occupants who do not wear protective restraints, and also assumes that the harm to the passenger consists only of medical costs.

3. Ford was acquitted of criminal charges involving the dangerous placement of gas tanks in its Pinto. Nevertheless, Ford lost millions of dollars in suits brought by people maimed when rear-ended Pintos exploded into fiery coffins.

An Alternative View of Regulation

The state—the machinery and power of the state— is a potential resource or threat to every industry in the society. With its power to prohibit or compel, to take or give money, the state can and does selectively help or hurt a vast number of industries.

—*George J. Stigler* (1971)[4]

The public interest view of regulation prevailed until the early 1970s. If the public interest approach is correct, we would expect regulation primarily in highly concentrated industries (to regulate monopoly power), in industries with significant economies of scale, or in those exhibiting substantial externalities. But many regulations in such areas as taxi service, air transportation, trucking, and some professional licensing arrangements (barbering, for example) find little support in the public interest rationale.

Does Business Benefit from Regulation?

The Constitution gives Congress the power "to regulate commerce among the several states." The government can tax, forcibly alter the allocation of resources, or change the economic decisions of households and firms without their consent. The state can use these great powers to raise or lower profitability in any industry through four major mechanisms:

1. direct subsidies to the industry, special tax breaks or punitive taxes, or advantageous or harmful operating regulations.
2. restriction or encouragement of entry or exit.
3. subsidies, taxes, or regulatory limitations on complementary or substitute products.
4. direct price-fixing policies (price floors or ceilings).

All four mechanisms have altered profitability in various industries. The merchant marine is heavily subsidized, as is education. Entry restrictions were effective in the airline industry, where the Civil Aeronautics Board (CAB) did not license a single new trunk line during the forty years after its establishment in 1938. Another example is regulation of trucking by the Interstate Commerce Commission (ICC). In the 1960s and 1970s, applications for new truck lines averaged over 5,000 annually, while the number of firms in operation continually shrank.[5] Law and medicine, too, are professions that have benefited greatly from restrictions on entry.

Government policies also affect an industry's substitutes and complements. Laws prohibiting margarine sales or banning yellow food dyes that allowed it to mimic butter's appearance were enacted in the 1950s when the dairy industry fought to hold its market for butter. The trucking industry vigorously supported development of the interstate highway system. Naturally, railroads opposed its development. Construction unions have successfully opposed reforms to local building codes that block labor-saving technology. The consequence is that many building codes require outdated, labor-intensive construction techniques that drive costs up but provide employment for union workers. Direct price fixing is found in milk and cheese price supports and in many farm and tobacco subsidy programs.

Few of these regulations can be considered in the public interest. Some students of this subject maintain that regulation should promote the public welfare, but fails only because of incompetent management. Other economists argue that agencies, once formed, have been captured by the industry they were created to monitor. Regulators need expertise to regulate, and what better source for this expertise than from within the industry itself? An industry's experts know its problems and possible solutions. But regulators are constantly confronted by the industry's experts and frequently become persuaded by industry arguments. This partially explains why regulations often favor the industry rather than the public, leading to great dissatisfaction on the part of many observers and advocates of regulation.

An Economic Model of Regulation

George Stigler concludes that public interest theories fail to explain most regulations because they assume that business opposes regulation. Assuming, instead, that firms or industries seek regulations that serve their private interests yields implications that are vast-

---

4. George J. Stigler, "The Theory of Economic Regulation," *The Bell Journal of Economic & Management Science* (Spring 1971).

5. *Ibid.*

Options, Rules, and Efficiency

Recent changes in the securities market have been nothing short of revolutionary. The range of choices available to investors, hedgers, and speculators has grown immensely. Nowhere is this more evident than in the options market. An option is the right to buy or sell a specific stock (the underlying stock) at a certain price for a limited period of time. A *call option* gives the owner the right to buy the stock, while a *put option* gives the owner the right to sell the stock. The price at which the stock may be bought or sold is known as the *exercise* (or *striking*) price. Options typically exist for only 3, 6, or 9 months, and so carry an *expiration date*.

On April 26, 1973, the Chicago Board of Trade's Options Exchange (CBOE) initiated standardized trading in options. Options previously had been traded in over-the-counter markets that required brokers to match buyers and sellers, with different option prices and expiration dates spread all over the calendar. The CBOE made options trading more efficient by (*a*) creating a clearing house to execute options contracts, (*b*)

establishing a market to standardize prices, and (*c*) specifying that expiration dates could fall on only certain days of the month. These reforms made it easier to calculate the values of options and keep track of them. Before 1973, less than 500 thousand options traded annually; over 200 million are now traded on the CBOE.

Option prices are influenced by such factors as the (*a*) price and volatility of the underlying stock, (*b*) striking price, (*c*) time remaining to expiration, (*d*) interest rate, and (*e*) dividend rate of the underlying stock. The price of the underlying stock is probably most important. A call option is *in the money* if the stock price is above the striking price. The prices of in-the-money options tend to vary dollar-for-dollar with changes in prices of the underlying stock.

Options allow leveraged speculation, but can also be used to hedge and reduce risk. For example, suppose you owned 100 shares of Apple Computer. Assume the market price is $20 and the 6-month call option with a striking price of $23 is selling for $4. You

could sell a "covered call" (your call is covered by the 100 shares you own) and get $400 now. You are, in effect, selling your stock for $24 per share if the stock's price rises above $23, and you receive $400 to offset losses if the stock price falls. You have thus reduced your "downside" risk by selling the option. However, you have also limited your "upside" reward potential as a trade-off to the reduced risk. As you might expect, option trading is far more sophisticated than our simple transaction suggests. The important point is that as financial instruments, options can be used to balance risk in an investment portfolio.

The market was limited before the CBOE introduced standardized options; even large financial institutions steered clear of puts and calls. The financial regulations established by the CBOE converted what had been a relatively exotic financial instrument into a popular asset in many portfolios. Rules and regulations can, as this example illustrates, enhance efficiency in some markets.

|||||||||||||||||||||||||||||||||||||||||||||||||||||||||||||||||||||||||||||||||||||||||||||||||||||

ly different from those based on public interest theories. Stigler's *industry interest* theory views government as the supplier of regulatory services to firms in an industry. These services are paid for by lobbying, campaign contributions, or other compensation to policymakers who favor the regulations that established firms want.

The major benefit of regulation to an industry is probably entry restriction. All firms seek monopoly power and abhor "cutthroat" competition; many heads of major firms try to form cartels. Cheating by members, however, causes unregulated cartels to disintegrate. One way to stabilize a cartel is through regulation of entry and prices.

A paradox of American law is that cartels are outlawed in some instances and implemented through law in others. Thus, railroads supported passage of the Interstate Commerce Act, airlines supported the establishment of the Civil Aeronautics Board in 1938, and so on. Virtually all regulated industries mount major political offensives against proposed deregulation. The conviction of Teamster's Union officials in 1982 for trying to bribe a member of Congress to oppose trucking deregulation makes this point all too clear.

Occupational licensing is an obvious use of the political process to improve the economic conditions of special interest groups. A license is a barrier to entry into a profession, and is typically required for barbers, dog groomers, lawyers, plumbers, realtors, doctors, and travel agents. You can be jailed or fined if you operate without a license. The call for licensing is often clothed in public interest rhetoric so the public will not object to its pockets being picked. As the supply of new potential entrants into a profession grows to take advantage of higher earnings, entry restrictions evolve that impose ever higher qualifications on new applicants. Higher standards frequently bar would-be members of a profession with credentials far superior to those of "grandfathered" long-term practitioners. Of course, this is done to increase professional quality for the public.

Stigler's theory may explain much of regulation. The voice of business is not the only input into the regulatory process, however, and, in many cases, firms in different industries have conflicting interests. Real concerns about social well-being permeate both the political process and administrative agencies, and genuine public interest considerations may prevail.

In summary, rationales for government intervention in business activities emerge from several sources. No single explanation covers all government regulation in America. Some regulation is due to externalities associated with the products of a given industry. Other controls are based on economies of scale in production, information problems, or the nature of the product itself. Some regulation is the result of an industry's ability to promote its self-interest through regulation. Finally, some regulation serves the interests of the bureaucrats charged with administering the law; they gain power and larger budgets by expanding the scope and complexity of regulation. Each of these explanations seems appropriate to some specific cases, but the overseeing of business is only part of the regulatory landscape. The activities of consumers are also shaped by governmental regulation.

Consumer Protection

Consumption is the sole end and purpose of all production; and the interest of the producer ought to be attended to only so far as it may be necessary for promoting that of the consumer. The maxim is so perfectly self-evident that it would be absurd to attempt to prove it.[6]
—*Adam Smith* (1776)

Consumer protection is considered separately from business regulation because, even though firms are normally the entities directly regulated, consumers ultimately bear the brunt or gain the fruits of these rules. Who is really regulated is unclear. Is the lawn mower industry regulated because it can sell only lawn mowers equipped with elaborate protective devices, or are consumers regulated because they are denied the opportunity to purchase a mower (presumably at lower cost) without elaborate safety mechanisms?

If, as Adam Smith suggested, business exists for the sole purpose of serving consumers' needs, then **consumer protection** legislation may be a wasted effort; competition will make firms fail if they serve consumers inadequately. But most people perceive fraud and other business abuses to be widespread. Unfortunately, as in so many areas of economics, no single approach addresses all the complex issues of consumer protection. Consider some arguments for and against consumer protection legislation.

Arguments Favoring Consumer Protection

Consumers are presumed to be sovereign in capitalistic economies, using their money to "vote" for the goods they want. We generally assume that consumers are capable of making reasoned choices to max-

---

6. Adam Smith, *The Wealth of Nations.*

imize their own welfare. In an economy dominated by numerous buyers and sellers, this assumption has considerable merit; competition often works very well. Consequently, the prevailing approach in this country for many years was characterized by the doctrine of **caveat emptor:** "Let the buyer beware." Under this doctrine, consumers alone bear the consequences for the use, misuse, safety, and overall quality of their purchases. Buyers bear the burden of proof when suing sellers for fraud or deception; the seller is presumed not liable unless proven guilty of fraud or some similar violation of law.

A landmark case in 1916 overturned the basic assumption of *caveat emptor.* In *MacPherson* v. *Buick Motor Company,* Buick was held liable for injuries to MacPherson when a wheel made of defective wood collapsed. The Court concluded that manufacturers are liable if their output was negligently produced. The field of product liability law grew from this case, and *caveat emptor* faded into the sunset. Experts in the field now often refer to the doctrine of **caveat venditor:** "Let the seller beware." Product liability has evolved into a complex legal field, but generally the pendulum has swung far in the direction of protecting consumers. With this legal coat of armor protecting the consumer, further regulation might seem unnecessary.

There are, however, other reasons to protect consumers. As we noted earlier, whenever externalities are associated with the consumption of a product, the private market may not "internalize" these benefits or costs properly. The result is that too little is produced if externalities are positive, too much if externalities are negative. If lawn mowers without guards cause damage to third parties (via noise or damage to property), these costs will be borne by society and not just by lawn mower owners. There will be more than an optimal number of hazardous and noisy lawn mowers.

The concept of *caveat emptor* implicitly assumes that consumers and producers share similar knowledge regarding the safety and effectiveness of a product. This parity in knowledge may have been reasonably true when we were a nation of farmers and shopkeepers and technology was simple, but it can hardly be the case with today's complex array of products. This "progress" is the reason for requiring content labels on packaged foods and drugs, for "truth in lending" legislation, and so on. Even with government requirements that producers reveal certain information, many products are so complicated that most consumers find it impossible to detect basic flaws. The time required for consumers to become technically knowledgeable about such things as automobiles and electronic equipment is obviously prohibitive. Consumers cannot make "expert" evaluations of the usefulness, safety, and performance characteristics of many highly complex products.

The problems of **moral hazard** and **adverse selection** also are used to justify consumer protection. Moral hazard occurs when some parties (e.g., sellers) have incentives not to fulfill their duties under a contract. If you pay in advance for aluminum siding for your house, the firm that made the sale has an incentive to skip town. With adverse selection, differences in the information possessed prior to a contract yield the problem that one party may mistakenly agree to terms that would be unacceptable if the information were shared. For example, a professional team might trade a football player with a disguised drug problem, knowing that he would be unlikely to make the squad of his new team.

Under either *caveat emptor* or *caveat venditor,* people may buy or sell goods subject to legal recourse. The government, however, flatly prohibits production, sales, or purchase of some goods. Heroin, cyclamates, and flammable children's clothing are examples. In these cases, consumers are considered unable to properly assess information that is available. Curiously, some goods only suspected of being harmful, such as food colorings, are prohibited, while harmful substances like tobacco or alcohol are permitted.

Sophisticated marketing often entices consumers, but verifying the claims of most advertisers is almost futile without purchase and consumption. Failure of any high-priced good can be devastating to a consumer. Producers generally possess information on rates of product failure and are often accused of building obsolescence into the designs of some products. How can consumers protect themselves? Reasonable certainty regarding quality and safety is provided by regulation. This certainty can be shared costlessly by consumers. This public good aspect of consumer certainty is another strong argument for government intervention. For example, if medicine is uniformly of high quality because of regulation, your sense of security when taking a drug does not reduce my sense of security in taking the same medicine.

Arguments Against Consumer Protection

Opponents of consumer protection regulation point to the abridgment of economic freedom associated with reducing the range of products available to consumers. Competition alone, they argue, will force business to respond to consumer needs. Most concede, however, that markets do not always operate perfectly. Any good may either exceed or fall short of expectations. No manufacturer is able to make any good totally risk free or perfect. Modern production techniques may limit defects, but imperfections always remain.

Consumers desiring safer products might obtain them by paying the higher prices necessary to cover the higher costs. Individuals differ in their willingness to incur risk, which should be reflected in the types of products they consume. Consumer protection rules tend to make products quite similar, destroying diversity, one major benefit of the market system.

Opponents of consumer protection legislation also argue that the poor are hurt most by this form of government intervention. Poor people have very limited budgets, so they may have to buy goods of inferior quality if they are to consume at all. If regulation eliminates lower quality products, the poor may be effectively prohibited from consuming some kinds of goods. Wealthier groups can afford the added costs and generally buy higher quality goods in any event. For example, compulsory auto safety equipment drives up the relative prices of economy cars far more than those of luxury cars, which often have safety equipment as standard features—and even then, many people fail to wear seat belts. As a result, the rich are relatively less affected by consumer product safety legislation, while lower income groups bear its brunt.

Finally, opponents argue that safer products may not reduce accidents to the extent predicted. Some studies of the effects of auto safety devices and their impact on the overall accident and injury rate have produced startling results. Sam Peltzman concludes in one such study that the enhanced safety of the vehicle leads to changes in the behavior of drivers.[7] He argues that, housed in safer vehicles, some drivers become more reckless, causing more accidents, higher insurance rates, less safe highways, and increased pedestrian deaths. Traffic fatalities continue to rise in spite of mandatory safety equipment and lower speed limits. The evidence is incomplete, however, and considerable research remains before conclusive results can be obtained.

Consumer protection may be warranted when product externalities exist, when products are so technologically sophisticated that sellers have superior information about product quality, or when the price of a good is so high and purchases are so infrequent that a single loss to a consumer would spell disaster. Alternatively, consumer protection reduces freedom, may inhibit quick responses to consumer demands, reduces product choice, and may not accomplish the desired goal of safer products. These and other regulatory problems make the practical aspects of regulation challenging.

Practical Problems of Regulation

Some thorny problems confronting regulators who try to protect the public are the topic of this section. We also take a quick look at some areas of consumer protection. Finally, we provide an overall evaluation of public regulation.

Public Utility Regulation

Utility companies must be able to attract funds from sales of stocks and bonds, so when public utility commissions set rate structures, they normally target rates of return in the 8–12 percent range. Short-run

---

7. Sam Peltzman, "The Effects of Automobile Safety Regulation," *Journal of Political Economy,* 1975: 667.

changes in fuel costs, demand, or efficiency can cause a firm to earn more or less than the target rate. If a firm repeatedly experiences losses or earns in excess of the target return, the regulatory commission usually adjusts rates so that the firm's profit rate returns to normal. Regulation in practice is a complex process. When people are not especially concerned about their utility bills, these regulated monopolies may be able to operate inefficiently and still squeeze favorable rate structures from regulators. When higher costs focus the public eye on utility bills, as has occurred recently, however, popular outcry may prevent utility companies from charging rates that are high enough to cover their costs.

Some economists perceive little evidence that consumers have gained from regulation and argue that regulation of utilities especially has failed to perform the tasks identified by theory. The process of overseeing tends to become rigid and unresponsive to changing conditions over time. In fact, many of these economists suggest that unregulated monopolies might outperform their regulated cousins. The debate over the quality of public utility regulation persists, and rate setting agencies are looking for ways to improve their performance. While reform is often suggested, it seems improbable that any major changes will be implemented in the near future.

Other Regulations in Practice

Consumer regulations are diverse and varied, but they can be separated into a few categories. First, the earliest consumer protection statutes dealt with protecting the consumer from food, drugs, or cosmetics that were mislabeled, misbranded, or adulterated. A second group of laws protects consumers from unfair competition and false or misleading advertising. A third category deals with product safety. This category took on special importance when the Consumer Product Safety Commission was established in 1972. In the labor market, several agencies protect workers from hazardous working conditions, discrimination based on sex or race, and abuses by management or unions of their fundamental rights to collective representation. Another broad category of regulation hems in the financial and banking industry.

Evaluation of Public Regulation

In recent years, numerous politicians have pledged to reduce the level of government intervention in the private sector. The news media have carried numerous horror stories about over-regulation. Deregulation of airline fares in 1978 caused airline ticket prices to fall dramatically and led to a boom in air travel. The case of airline ticket prices became a shining example of the benefits consumers gain once government price fixing is removed. Banking and other financial institutions began a phased-in deregulation in 1980. In addition, congressional proposals for further deregulation in trucking, railroads, and several other industries are on the drawing board.

There seems to be a consensus that some regulation is necessary. But when has regulation gone too far? The president of Dow Chemical Company contends that one third of the millions Dow spends on environmental, transportation, health and safety, and other forms of regulation is wasted. He cited a case where Dow spent $60,000 per plant to lower all railings from 42 inches to roughly 32 inches to meet Occupational Safety and Health Administration (OSHA) requirements. This was done even though Dow's studies had concluded that the 42-inch railings were considerably safer.[8]

As this case and the study by Murray Weidenbaum and Robert DeFina suggest, regulation is not free. In the neighborhood of $200–400 billion is devoted to regulatory activity. Big government may create problems just as enormous as those posed by big business or big labor.

Deregulation and Reregulation

Ronald Reagan's election in 1980 resulted in the enactment of several federal deregulation proposals formulated during the Carter administration, most notably the **deregulation** of trucking, airlines, and banking. The growth of competition in these industries pushed prices down sharply. The economic

---

8. *Business Week*, 4 April 1977, 50.

pressures generated from airline deregulation led to many changes in the industry, including Continental Airline's use of the federal bankruptcy statute to void its union contracts and two-tier wage agreements where new and old employees were subject to different wage ladders.

Regulation often involves a complex combination of price and entry restrictions that can lead to higher prices and less service. Moreover, the competition among regulated firms tends to ignore pricing and be especially focused on advertising, product quality, or new product development. Regulation is often a compromise among conflicting public interest, industry interest, and bureaucratic objectives, which makes the results of deregulation somewhat unpredictable. Deregulation of AT&T taught us that deregulating the provision of a good or service often involves submarkets that may be quite different from each other. Deregulation that works well in one submarket may be less successful in another.

An example of apparent failure occurred when Seattle deregulated its cabs.[9] In the past, local transit unions viewed taxis as threats to their negotiated wages. Taxis also threatened Seattle's municipally owned transit system and it implemented taxi regulation. The predictable results were higher fares, lower taxi usage, slower response time, and high medallion (license) values. Taxis became popular targets for deregulation.

The Seattle taxi market consists of two submarkets: radio-dispatched cabs (roughly 60 percent of the market) and cabs waiting in line for customers at airports, railroad stations, or hotels. Seattle adopted rules by 1980 permitting free entry of taxis and allowed cabs to alter fares as often as every three months by filing a simple rate change. Deregulation was expected to undo all the negative effects blamed on full-scale regulation. In the radio-dispatched submarket, deregulation apparently lived up to expectations. Average fares declined and response time improved.

In the other submarket, however, deregulation produced unique problems. First, long lines of independent taxis developed bottlenecks. Some drivers left their cabs to hustle customers, others blocked driveways or competed violently for customers. At the airport, waiting cabs were confined to a holding area and called up to the terminal as needed. This system restricted price competition since many passengers were visitors and did not know the going price for a cab, were on expense accounts, or were intimidated by having only one cab available. The result was a significant disparity in taxi rates going to and from the airport ($25 to downtown versus $16 from downtown to the airport). The quality of cabs and cabbies also deteriorated and taxis often refused short hauls. These problems caused Seattle to re-examine the issue and eventually adopt a maximum fare scheme based on the median rate for all taxis. As you might expect, the maximum rate soon became the standard charge.

Deregulation of taxis in Seattle, after minor modifications, has probably been favorable, but the experience illustrates how adjustment to deregulation can be unnecessarily costly. Deregulation may not be as simple as its proponents claim. No one expects to see regulation eliminated, but perhaps its efficiency will improve. This reappraisal will probably focus on ways to bring business into the process in a responsible manner. Some regulations that work against the public interest may be eliminated.

Every attempt at deregulation appears to be more than offset as new regulations are added to the books. For example, regulation increasingly governs smoking in public places, consumer protection laws for consumer software purchases, and the use of "junk bonds" in corporate finance. The future might bring under the regulatory umbrella such wide ranging issues as biogenetic research, euthanasia, no-drive days to reduce pollution, sexually transmitted diseases, and liquor promotions such as happy-hours and two-fers.

Deregulation generally stimulates competition, a fact that many people find discomforting. For example, almost every major airline crash generates calls for reregulation of the airlines. A study released by the FAA in 1988, however, indicates that airline safety has actually improved since U.S. skyways were deregulated. The number of passenger fatalities per 100 million miles flown dropped steadily during 1977–87. In spite of such evidence, however, many people in the airline industry would like to see regulation re-imposed.

In this chapter we have provided some ideas about why political pressures for regulation never

---

9. Richard O. Zerbe, Jr., "Seattle Taxis: Deregulation Hits a Pothole," *Regulation* (November/December 1983): 43–48.

end. One lesson is to be wary of advocates of regulation who attempt to persuade legislators that certain laws or rules are in the public interest. Self-interest is a strong incentive to develop persuasive arguments that may bamboozle the general public.

Although many government activities do serve the public interest, the specifics of many of the government policies addressed in the next part of this book are similarly shaped by special-interest groups.

CHAPTER REVIEW: KEY POINTS

1. The *public interest* theory of regulation focuses on some possible failures of the price system, including poor information, fraud, externalities, and monopoly power. Laissez-faire markets will not provide the socially optimal quantity of a product with externalities, so direct regulation is commonly used in an attempt to protect the public interest.

2. A *natural monopoly* involves substantial economies of scale, rendering direct competition impractical. Society has turned to regulation to prevent natural monopolies from reaping enormous profits and to move them towards socially efficient levels of output. The public interest may be served by requiring the firm to use *block pricing,* which uses price discrimination both to achieve efficiency and to equate total revenues from sales of the service with total costs of production, including a normal accounting profit.

3. The *industry interest* view of regulation expressed by George Stigler suggests that industries can gain from regulation, and therefore "demand" regulation from the government. As Stigler has noted, the state can, and often does, change the profitability of an industry through four main mechanisms (*a*) direct taxes or subsidies, (*b*) restrictions on entry, (*c*) impacts on an industry's complementary or substitute products, and (*d*) direct price-fixing policies.

4. Stigler views the government as the supplier of regulatory services to various industries. The costs of obtaining favorable regulation include campaign contributions and lobbying expenses.

5. The bulk of regulatory agencies in this country were created during three decades. The first great surge occurred during the 1930s, when policymakers attempted to buffer the violent swings in the business cycle on our economic system. Well over half of all regulatory agencies, however, came into existence in the 1960s and 1970s. It is not obvious why regulation increased so dramatically during a period of relative prosperity and high economic growth.

6. The law of product liability has evolved from an approach of *caveat emptor*—"Let the buyer beware"—to one of *caveat venditor*—"Let the seller

beware." Direct mandates or prohibition of some transactions are also increasingly common. For example, new cars are required to have specific safety equipment; some new drugs are banned. *Caveat emptor* is most appropriate when both producers and consumers have roughly equal access to knowledge about the product. Today, however, producers commonly have considerably more information about complex products than do consumers. It would be prohibitively costly for consumers to detect design and manufacturing flaws in most goods. In addition, modern corporations may use their massive financial and market power to manipulate consumers. Advertising claims are difficult for consumers to verify. Thus, government regulation is seen by many as the only practical solution to the problem of misrepresentation.

7. Opponents of *consumer protection* regulations argue that unregulated competition will force producers to respond to consumer needs, albeit imperfectly. Those individuals who want safer products will pay for them, and those willing to incur more risk will not. Furthermore, opponents argue that the poor are hurt most by consumer protection, which removes inferior but cheaper products from the market. For many of the poor, consumption opportunities are limited already, and removing the inferior (usually cheaper) products from the market may force them out of the market entirely.

8. Regulating public utilities is considerably more difficult than simple theory would suggest. Major problems arise in determining the *rate base,* a *"fair" rate of return,* and allowable costs. Regulatory agencies face a difficult task in balancing the interests of consumers and utility investors.

9. Regulation is increasingly attacked as misguided and "nit-picky." Various deregulation schemes have been implemented in the 1980s. The next decade will probably bring continued re-appraisal of the government's role as regulator, but whether this will translate into further reductions in regulation is highly speculative.

PROBLEM

1. Assume the demand and costs curves depicted below accurately portray a natural monopoly. What would be the total annual profits earned by this monopolist? At what price and output level would society's wel- fare be maximized? What would be the regulatory price? At this price, what would be the monopolist's annual profit?

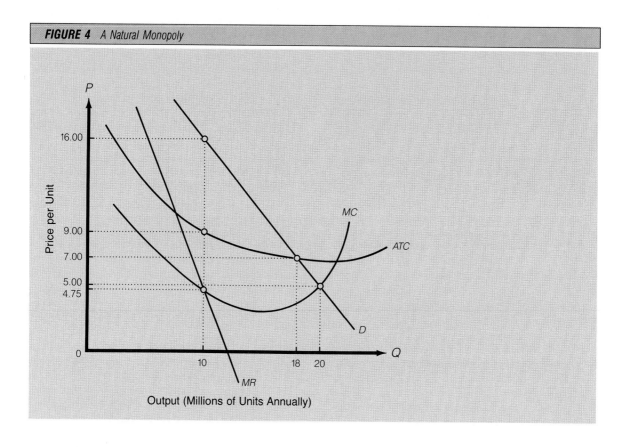

FIGURE 4 *A Natural Monopoly*

Output (Millions of Units Annually)

QUESTIONS FOR THOUGHT AND DISCUSSION

1. The Occupational Safety and Health Act (OSHA) requires that workplaces be made as safe as possible (or more so, according to some critics), with little or no regard for costs. How would you expect OSHA regulations to affect the prices of goods previously produced under hazardous conditions relative to the prices of those that have always been produced in safe work environments? What would you expect to happen to wages in previously hazardous industries? In previously safe industries? What will happen to real wages economywide? To health insurance rates? Should it matter for the purposes of OSHA regulation whether the risks of particular occupations are well known or not? If so, why?

2. Under what circumstances should specific goods (for example, flammable clothing, saccharine, heroin, or marijuana) be prohibited? Under what circumstances should producers be liable for harmful or defective products? When, if ever, should the government provide information about consumer products instead of levying regulatory actions limiting or requiring access to goods (such as prescription drugs or automotive safety equipment, respectively)? When should consumers bear the consequences of faulty goods?

3. Suppose you were a Food and Drug Administration (FDA) official charged with licensing new drugs. There are two types of errors to which you might fall prey (*a*) you might license a harmful drug, or (*b*) you might keep a very beneficial drug off the market. What do you think is the nature of the trade-off between these types of errors? Which of these two types of errors would you wish to minimize if your goal is (*a*) to maximize your prospects for job security or promotion, (*b*) to maximize the public welfare? Are there natural checks in the marketplace if you make the first type of error? If you make the second type of error? What are the probable effects on research and development activities of pharmaceutical companies if you minimize the licensing of harmful drugs? If you minimize keeping good drugs off the market? In which direction do you think you would lean if you were a typical FDA official?

4. Some economists have developed proposals that they suggest will eliminate the need for public utility regulation, infuse an element of competition into situations of natural monopoly, ensure economic efficiency, and eliminate the problems of income distribution posed by monopoly power. The proposals take two forms. First, government licenses to provide such services as electricity, gas, or telephones could be sold to the highest dollar bidder. The proceeds from this license auction could then be rebated to the utility's customers. Alternatively, these monopoly licenses could be awarded to the firm that bids the lowest rate structure. Do you think these proposals provide economic efficiency? Equity? What problems could arise with implementation of these schemes?

5. Two surveys in 1986 revealed that, "a 2–to–1 majority of Americans believe the breakup of American Telephone and Telegraph was a bad idea, and few think telephone service has improved since the breakup. . . ." Twenty percent of those surveyed indicated they had considered canceling telephone service because of increased costs. Do you agree that things are worse since the breakup? Is this another case of the government "fixing something that wasn't broken"? What did the government hope to gain by splitting AT&T into eight separate companies? Are the current problems simply short-term corrections for a long history of monopoly?

6. In 1981, the Reagan administration proposed almost total deregulation of the alcoholic beverage industry. Not only were consumer groups appalled by the proposal, but, paradoxically, the industry was appalled as well. The industry, it seemed, did not want "government off of its back." The industry went so far as to argue that the Federal Bureau of Alcohol, Tobacco, and Firearms is "a very lean, highly efficient organization . . . [providing] a very high return for its tax dollar. . . ." Why would the industry oppose deregulation? Are the tangled vines of federal regulation better than fifty sets of state regulations? Would consumers gain by deregulation of the alcoholic beverage industry?

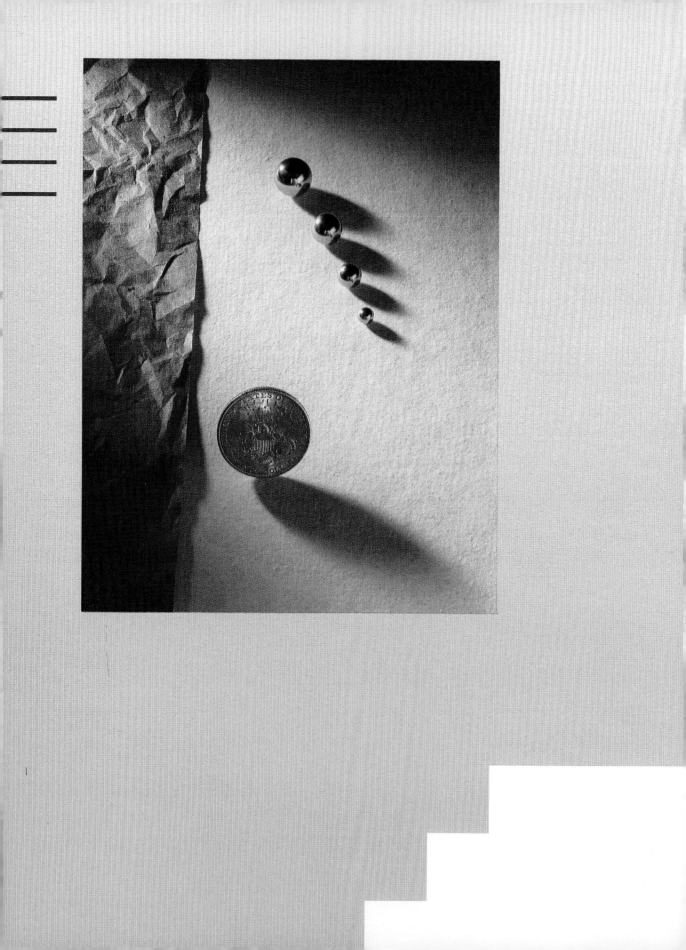

Production and
Markets for Resources

PART 8

We investigated markets for consumer goods in the previous part of this book, focusing on how household demands interact with production costs to determine prices and outputs. Most production costs are ultimately payments to the suppliers of labor, land, capital, or entrepreneurial talent; demands and supplies of these resources meet in markets that share many characteristics of markets for consumer goods. Just as markets for consumer goods range from purely competitive to monopolistic, resource markets range from situations of diffused power (competitive big city markets for secretaries) to single sellers (Bruce Springsteen) or buyers (the U.S. Marine Corps).

In chapter 28, we develop a competitive approach to resource markets called *marginal productivity theory*. As the chapter unfolds, this foundation for resource demands is blended with a theory of factor supplies to explain resource prices and allocations in competitive markets. We focus on competitive labor markets, but the forces of marginal productivity are exerted in competitive markets for all resources.

The use of economic power to alter wage structures and employment by large firms and such organizations as unions and employer associations are the subject of chapter 29. Naturally, unions try to use their economic clout to raise wages, while firms try to maximize their profits by holding wages and other production costs in check.

Discussions of how markets for land, capital, and entrepreneurship determine rates of rent, interest, and economic profit await you in chapter 30, which concludes with an overview of how marginal productivity operates to distribute total income among the owners of different resources.

CHAPTER 28

Wages and Employment in Competitive Labor Markets

In this chapter, we investigate some forces at work in all resource markets but focus on competitive labor markets. First, we explore firms' demands for labor when both labor markets and output markets are competitive. The choices people make about employment is our second area of concern; these choices underpin labor supplies. We then look at *human capital theory,* which provides insights into how people acquire specialized skills to enhance their individual employment opportunities. The resulting differences in workers influence both the demand side and the supply side of labor markets. Our final topics in this chapter are the effects in competitive labor markets of such government policies as minimum wage laws and the application of a comparable worth doctrine.

Derived Demands for Resources

Resource markets seem, on the surface, quite similar to markets for consumer goods, but there is a basic difference. Most resources satisfy human wants only indirectly; producing things people want requires combining labor, capital, land, and entrepreneurial talent. Thus, people's *direct* demands for consumer goods create *derived demands* for resources. These derived demands are based on the productive contributions of the resources to final consumer goods. In a sense, supplies of most resources are also derived in that resource owners seek income so that they can demand goods and services.

*The ultimate demands of consumers for goods yield **derived demands** for the resources that produce those goods.*

This is why job opportunities for computer programmers, technicians, and electronics engineers soar when industrial technology advances. Conversely, demands for teachers collapsed when the post-World War II baby boom went bust and school enrollments dropped. A resurgence of demand for teachers in the 1980s accompanied the enrollment of the offspring of 1950s baby boomers.

The demand for final goods is one dimension of the demand for labor; the other is labor productivity, which depends on technology and the prices and availability of other resources. But how do profit seeking firms translate these influences into a hiring decision? Recall that firms maximize profit by expanding output until marginal revenue equals marginal cost ($MR = MC$). A parallel condition specifies how firms maximize profits in labor markets: they hire additional labor and thus produce and sell more output until the last unit of labor adds as much to revenue as it adds to costs. This principle is the cornerstone for resource acquisitions in all resource markets.

The Demand For Labor

Assume again that you own and operate a gold mine in Colorado, and that labor is the only variable input; other influences on production are fixed. The law of diminishing marginal returns means that beyond some point, extra workers add less and less to total production. For simplicity, the possibility that specialization might initially yield increasing returns is ignored in the operating data listed in Table 1. The mine yields 3 ounces of gold per week if you hire only one miner. Employing a second miner raises total output to 5 ounces per week, for a gain of 2 ounces per week. This is labor's *marginal physical product* (MPP_L); it is listed in column 3 for up to 10 workers.

Marginal Revenue Product

Computing the marginal revenue product requires calculating the extra revenue from the gold each additional miner produces.

Marginal revenue product (MRP) *is the extra sales revenue from the output (ΔPq) generated by an extra resource unit (ΔL).*

TABLE 1 *Data for Western Gold Mine*

(1) Number of Workers L	(2) Total Oz. of Gold Produced per Week q	(3) Marginal Physical Product of Labor MPP_L	(4) Price of Gold per Oz. $P = MR$	(5) Value of the Marginal Product of Labor $VMP = MRP$
1	3.0	3.0	$500	$1,500
2	5.0	2.0	500	1,000
3	6.8	1.8	500	900
4	8.4	1.6	500	800
5	9.8	1.4	500	700
6	11.0	1.2	500	600
7	12.0	1.0	500	500
8	12.8	.8	500	400
9	13.4	.6	500	300
10	13.8	.4	500	200

Note: This table assumes that other factors are fixed and that gold is sold in a competitive market.

Regardless of market structure, all firms base hiring decisions about all factors of production on the resources' *MRP*s, which can be calculated as either $\Delta Pq/\Delta L$ or $MR \times MPP$ (marginal revenue times marginal physical product). A resource's *MRP* reflects its value to a firm, which is not always the same as the value of that resource to the society as a whole.

Value of the Marginal Product

How socially valuable is a resource? We showed earlier that a good's price approximates its marginal social benefit ($P \cong MSB$). Similarly, a resource's marginal social benefit is the value of that resource's marginal product, and is calculated as $P \times MPP$.

> *The social value of the output produced by the marginal worker is known as the* **value of the marginal product (VMP).**

In competition $P = MR$, so the marginal revenue product ($MRP = MR \times MPP_L$) and the value of the marginal product are identical ($VMP = MRP$).

Highly competitive international markets set the price of gold, which in Table 1 is assumed to be $500 per ounce (column 4). The value of the marginal product in column 5 is computed by multiplying columns 3 and 4. A pure competitor's demand for labor is based on the value of the marginal product of labor. Note that *VMP* is influenced by both labor productivity (*MPP*) and the demand for the product (*P*). Labor's *VMP* curve in your gold mine is illustrated in Figure 1; this is your short-run demand curve for labor.

Marginal Factor Cost

The number of miners you will hire to maximize profits depends on what you have to pay them.

> *The extra cost of hiring an additional unit of a resource is its* **marginal factor cost (MFC).**

Marginal factor costs are identical to wage rates (w) in purely competitive labor markets because the wage rate a firm must pay is fixed by impersonal market forces. All payments for labor (e.g., salaries, such fringe benefits as health insurance and paid vacations) are covered by the term *wages.*

The profit-maximizing rule for output decisions (expand until $MR = MC$) leads to the idea that more resources will be hired as long as the extra funds

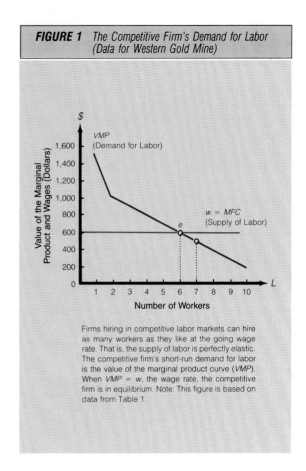

FIGURE 1 The Competitive Firm's Demand for Labor (Data for Western Gold Mine)

Firms hiring in competitive labor markets can hire as many workers as they like at the going wage rate. That is, the supply of labor is perfectly elastic. The competitive firm's short-run demand for labor is the value of the marginal product curve (*VMP*). When *VMP* = *w*, the wage rate, the competitive firm is in equilibrium. Note: This figure is based on data from Table 1.

brought in by a resource (its *MRP*) are at least as great as the money taken away (its *MFC*). Thus, hire more of any input whenever $MRP \geq MFC$. For purely competitive firms operating in competitive labor markets, this translates into a rule: hire until the *VMP* of the last worker employed equals that worker's marginal factor cost. Competitively set wage rates equal marginal factor cost, so profit maximization requires that $VMP = w$.

Mining gold is hard, dirty work, so assume that a purely competitive labor market dictates that each miner be paid $600 weekly. At this wage, you hire six miners (point *e*) because the value of the marginal product of the sixth worker is also $600. You would not hire a seventh because the extra $500 in revenue to you is less than the $600 cost of hiring. You would hire a seventh miner only if weekly wages were $500, an eighth miner at $400, and so on. But if wages rose to $700 weekly, the sixth miner, who generates only $600 in marginal revenue product, would be fired.

The conclusion of this analysis is that, all else equal, the value of the marginal product curve is the competitive firm's demand curve for labor. Just as changes in commodity prices cause movements along demand curves for goods, changes in wages cause movements along demand curves for labor. And, by way of summary, the *VMP* curve is based on the demand for output as reflected in its price (*P*) and by the production technology used (MPP_L).

Shifts in Demands for Labor

The competitive demand curve for labor ($VMP = P \times MPP_L$) may shift if there are changes in the (*a*) prices of output, (*b*) prices of other resources, (*c*) production technology, or (*d*) inherent productivity of workers.

Output Prices   Many people view gold as a very secure asset. If political turmoil and economic uncertainty became widespread, the worldwide demand for gold might skyrocket. If gold rose to $1,000 per ounce, the demand for miners' labor (*VMP*) would increase from D_0 to D_1 in Figure 2. Although the amount of gold each miner produces is unaffected, each level of output has doubled in value because the price of gold doubled, so *VMP* rises; profit-maximizing employment rises from six to nine miners (point *f*) at the $600 weekly wage.

If the gold market then collapsed and gold fell to $100 per ounce, your demand for miners would decline to D_2. You would close the mine, since the *VMP* of no worker ever exceeds $300 per week but each miner's wage is $600. Not only must you pay the fixed costs of owning the mine, but you would lose an additional $300 per week even if you retained only one employee. You are clearly better off to shut down and lose only your fixed costs any time the price of gold falls below $200 per ounce. (*VMP* of the first miner is $600 when gold is $200 per ounce.)

Prices of Other Resources   Changes in the prices of other resources, and, consequently, in their utilization, can also shift demands for labor. Resources are frequently complementary. For example, miners' productivity will tend to rise if lower capital costs induce you to invest in new capital equipment. Replacing dull or broken picks and shovels with newer tools allows miners to process and recover more

gold. Rising marginal physical products of labor would raise their *VMP*s and your demand for labor. Similarly, higher capital costs and reductions in capital per worker might decrease your demand for miners' services. In addition to their complementarity, however, resources are also substitutes for one another. For example, declines in capital costs or huge wage hikes could cause miners to be replaced by machinery.

Technological Change   Technological changes may boost the demand for labor in a very direct way. If newly invented machinery increased every miner's productivity, you would hire more miners. But technological changes do not boost the demand for labor. New excavation equipment might enable machinery to replace some miners. The process of replacing human labor with machinery is known as **automation.** During the 1960s, some social analysts feared that growing automation would structurally disemploy a growing pool of workers. These fears have

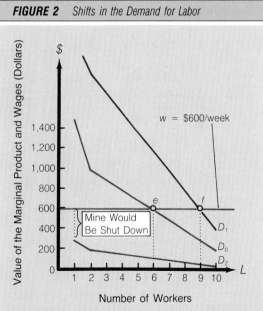

FIGURE 2   *Shifts in the Demand for Labor*

The value of the marginal product of labor equals the output price times the marginal physical product of labor (*VMP* = *P* × *MPP*). Thus, changes in the price of output will shift the *VMP* curve, which is the competitive firm's short-run demand for labor.

proven groundless because producing, repairing, and operating automatic machinery requires labor.

Automation may cause temporary but traumatic dislocations of workers, even if falling demands for labor in some markets are offset by growing demands in other occupations. Some forecasters predict that industrial robots will increasingly take over routine assembly line work, and that employment will shift primarily towards service industries. Many auto workers lost their assembly line jobs when "robots" were introduced in the early 1980s, compounding the high unemployment in Detroit and other "motor cities" caused by slack sales worldwide during 1979–83. In the long run, however, this automation may have saved more jobs than it destroyed. Without domestic automation, the growing comparative advantages of foreign automakers threatened the survival of the entire American auto industry and all its jobs.

The Quality of Labor   Demands for labor rise when people work harder or acquire more productive skills. Education or on-the-job training can enhance labor productivity. Conversely, if, on average, miners quit working as diligently, their *VMP*s and your demand for their labor would fall.

Elasticity of Demand for Labor

We have seen that the demand for labor is a derived demand and that employment varies inversely with the wage rate. But how much do wage changes affect employment?

The responsiveness of the amount of labor demanded (∆L) to a change in wages (∆w) is measured by the **elasticity of demand for labor,** *which is roughly:*[1]

$$e_L = \%\Delta L/\%\Delta w.$$

The elasticity of demand for labor is directly related to (*a*) the elasticity of demand for output, (*b*) labor's share of total costs, (*c*) the ease of substitution between labor and other resources, and (*d*) the time allowed for adjustments to changes in wages.

---

1. Precise computation of e_L requires using midpoint-based formulas as described in our chapter on elasticity.

The Elasticity of Demand for the Final Product
The more elastic the demand for a final output, the harder it is for a firm to raise prices to cover higher labor costs. A wage hike will lower the quantity of labor demanded substantially when higher wages cannot easily be passed on to consumers because the demand for the good is very elastic. Alternatively, if falling wages cause production costs and prices to drop, sales and employment will rise; the greater the elasticity of demand for the product, the more sales and employment rise. Thus, the more elastic (*inelastic*) the demand for the product, the more elastic (*inelastic*) the demand for labor.

Labor's Share of Total Cost   A given wage change's effect on employment is positively related to wages as a proportion of total costs. For example, if wages are only 10 percent of total cost, a 20 percent wage hike raises total costs (and price) by roughly 2 percent. But if wages are 80 percent of total costs, a 20 percent wage hike exerts pressure for a 16 percent rise in price. For the same rise in wages, employment will be less affected in the first instance because smaller increases in output prices will cover the higher wage costs. Thus, the demand for labor is more elastic the greater labor's share of total cost.

The Ease of Factor Substitution   The easier it is to substitute one resource for another, the greater the elasticities of demand for both resources. For example, if it is easy to switch from coal to oil or natural gas in generating electricity, then small changes in the relative prices of these fuels yield huge changes in the primary fuel used, and utility companies' demands for each fuel will be very elastic. Similarly, the demand for labor is very elastic if workers are easily replaced by machines, and vice versa, but the demand for labor tends to be more inelastic the more difficult it is to substitute other resources for labor.

Time   Longer periods allow firms to adjust more completely to changing wages. Resource substitutions are easier and technological change also becomes more feasible. For example, soaring wage rates for coal miners during 1945–65 stimulated automation and more efficient excavating techniques. Thus, the elasticity of demand for labor grows as the time horizon expands to allow more latitude about both technologies and resources.

The Supply of Labor

You should now have some ideas about ways that productivity and output prices shape resource demands and about some determinants of the elasticities of resource demands. We have assumed that a firm can hire all the labor it wants at a fixed wage, but demand is only one dimension of any resource market. Understanding labor markets requires us to examine supply as well.

> The **supply of labor** depicts the amount people are willing to work per time period at alternative wage rates.

Labor supplies for individual markets and the economy as a whole are determined by the:

1. population size and labor force participation rates.
2. preferences of individuals about leisure versus income from work.
3. rates and structures of wages.
4. education, training, and skills of potential workers.

All these influences on labor supplies are considered next, although our lengthy discussion of education and training is postponed until after we consider labor market equilibrium.

Population and Labor Force Participation

Almost 60 percent of our population participates in the labor force, but labor force participation varies by age, gender, and other characteristics. Recent labor force participation by age and gender is shown in Figure 3. People aged 20 to 54 predictably are the most likely to work outside their homes.

> A **labor force participation rate** is the percentage of a given population that is in the work force.

Social forces are reflected in changes in participation rates. Only 37 percent of women over 20 were in the work force in the 1950s. Today, over half work for pay. The rate for men has fallen over this same period from 86 percent to roughly 75 percent. Explaining

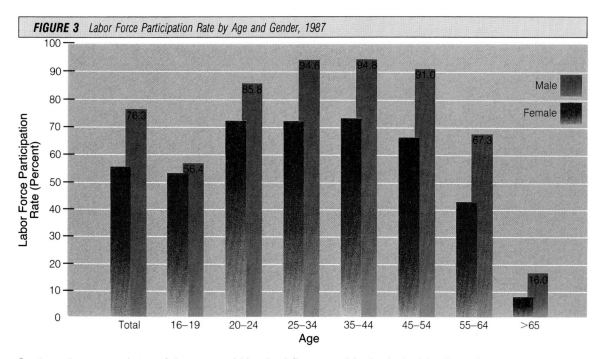

FIGURE 3 Labor Force Participation Rate by Age and Gender, 1987

Gender and age are only two of the many variables that influence participation in the labor force. Others include education, spouse's income or other family income, race, and number and age of children in the family.

Source: *Statistical Abstract of the United States,* 1987, p. 377; *Economic Report of the President,* 1987.

variations in labor force participation requires us to probe some influences on individual labor supply decisions.

Individual Supplies of Labor

Suppose you were offered a job at $10 per hour and could set your own work schedule. Even if you are a full-time student, you might reduce your course load a bit to take advantage of such an offer. Assume that you decide to work 20 hours a week. If the offer were raised to $25 per hour, you might drop out of school altogether and work 40 or 50 hours per week. This means that your labor supply curve is positively sloped between wages of $10 and $25, as shown by curve *ab* in Figure 4.

Let's really get outrageous. If you were offered $100 per hour, would you work more than 50 hours weekly? Unlikely. At a very high wage, you might feel that you were making plenty of money with only 20 hours of work weekly. Two thousand dollars is a tidy sum, and if you work long hours, you might not have time to enjoy the fruits of your labor. Thus, in Figure 4 we show a *backward-bending* supply of labor for all wages above $25 per hour.

Why are individual labor supplies often negatively sloped at high wage rates? The key to answering this question is understanding that changes in wage rates alter the price of **leisure**—a good that is negatively related to the amount of labor supplied. You have less leisure time the more you work.

Recall the income and substitution effects that we explored as separate aspects of people's responses to price changes for a good. The **substitution effect** of a higher wage is to reduce your consumption of leisure activities relative to work because the higher your wage, the more income you surrender when you take off from work. As your wage rises, you tend to work more and consume less leisure time because the opportunity cost of free time has risen. There is, however, an offsetting **income effect:** The demand for leisure, as for any normal good, rises with income. Thus, your higher income causes you to want to "buy" more leisure by working less.

The income and substitution effects operate in opposite directions when the wage rate changes. At low wages, the substitution effect is generally more powerful than the income effect because total income is so low. Thus, a higher wage rate leads to the provision of more work because people tend to substitute work (and the potential for greater consumption) for leisure. When the substitution effect is greater than the income effect, the labor supply curve is positively sloped. When your wages and total income are very high, however, the income effect tends to dominate the substitution effect in your labor decision. This results in a backward-bending supply curve for your labor similar to the curve *bc* in Figure 4.

A change in the wages of any member of a household may affect the labor supply decisions of other members. For example, if a primary worker's earnings failed to keep pace with inflation, other family members might enter the labor market to maintain its standard of living. Another possibility is that a wage hike for a primary breadwinner may induce other members to cut back their work effort as the family unit consumes more "household services" from other family members. (Some economists ar-

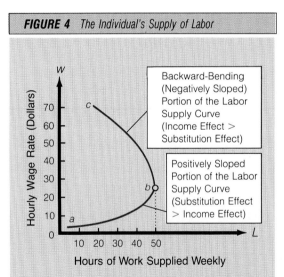

FIGURE 4 The Individual's Supply of Labor

Backward-Bending (Negatively Sloped) Portion of the Labor Supply Curve (Income Effect > Substitution Effect)

Positively Sloped Portion of the Labor Supply Curve (Substitution Effect > Income Effect)

Hours of Work Supplied Weekly

As the wage rate rises, it becomes increasingly costly not to work; therefore, the *substitution effect* induces people to increase the hours they work and reduce leisure. On the other hand, higher wages make greater incomes possible, and this *income effect* will cause people to want more leisure time to enjoy their income. If the substitution effect is more powerful than the income effect, the supply of labor is positively sloped. This tends to be the case when wages are low. However, at high wage rates, the income effect may overpower the substitution effect, in which case the supply of labor is backward bending.

gue that this effect is especially powerful if the entire income of a family is subject to a high tax rate.) If market wages rise for other household members, families may substitute in the opposite direction.

Social roles, customs, and numerous other nonfinancial considerations also influence labor decisions. For example, the birth of a child may temporarily keep its mother at home. Desires for education or training also affect the timing and duration of individual participation in the labor force.

Supplies of Labor to Firms or Industries

Even if all individual supplies of labor were backward bending, the supply of labor facing any firm or industry would still be perfectly elastic or positively sloped. The explanation for this seeming paradox is actually very simple.

Suppose that the Ace Corporation, a major accounting firm in a large city, raises its wage offers slightly. No matter how content accountants happen to be, some will overcome job change inertia and leave their current jobs to take Ace's offer. More pay for the same work sounds pretty good, and the more Ace is willing to pay, the greater will be the number of accountants available to meet Ace's labor requirements. Ace, an individual firm, is clearly faced with a positively sloped supply curve of accountants, even if the total labor supply of current accountants is backward bending. But how about the supply of workers facing the accounting industry? If wages for all accountants doubled, might backward-bending supplies of labor for all current accountants mean that less accounting gets done? NO!

One reason is that some workers with accounting skills who are not presently using them would respond to higher pay by moving back into this line of work. Many young people seeking a remunerative career might also view accounting more favorably. These young people, plus established workers in areas with skills closely related to accounting (such as bookkeepers or financial planners), would view the jump in accountants' wages as a strong incentive to acquire more training in that field. This occurred during the 1970s, and business colleges were flooded with accounting majors. The amount of accountants' services available gradually rose in response to higher wages. The same happens in any industry with growing needs for any type of labor. Higher wages are magnets that attract extra labor services in the long run, even if individual workers may have backward-bending labor supply curves.

In summary, individual supplies of labor are normally positively sloped, but may bend backwards at relatively high wage rates. Even if individual labor supply curves are negatively sloped, however, the supplies of labor facing firms or industries will be positively related to wage rates. The demand for labor depends on labor productivity, technology, the demand for the final product, and the levels of other productive resources employed. We are now in a position to merge labor market supplies and demands to see how equilibrium wages and employment are determined.

Labor Market Equilibrium

A standard plot of some stories that were very popular earlier in this century: Horatio Alger, a poor young country bumpkin, comes to the sinful "Big City." Through righteous thoughts and modest exertion, he wins fame, fortune, and the hand of a fair damsel. Unfortunately, righteousness, wishful thinking, or modest exertion seldom secure a high income. The Horatio Alger legend may occasionally come true, but marginal productivity theory probably more accurately reflects how labor markets will affect your future well-being.

Wages and Employment

Figure 5 depicts the interaction of labor supplies and demands for both an individual firm and all firms hiring from a given labor market. The market demand for labor, D_L, is only roughly the sum of individual firms' demands.[2] The market supply of labor is

---

2. In deriving the market demand curves for consumer goods, we horizontally sum individual demands. In competitive factor markets, such summations of *VMP* curves are only a first approximation. Assume wages fell. Each firm in an industry would demand more labor and produce more output, but this added output could be sold only at lower prices. When the price of the good fell, each firm's *VMP* would shift to the left and less labor would be demanded, as you saw in the gold mine example. This effect reduces the market elasticity of the demand for labor, partially offsetting the employment effect of lower wages. Simple summation does not consider the effects of changes in factor costs on product prices. We leave an expanded discussion of this point to advanced classes.

FIGURE 5 Equilibrium in the Competitive Labor Market

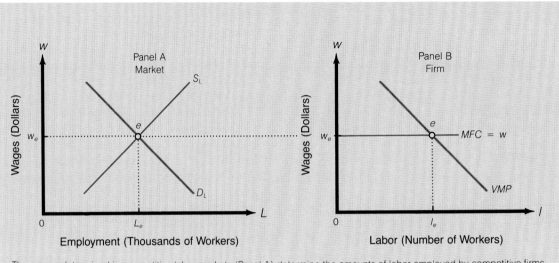

The wages determined in competitive labor markets (Panel A) determine the amounts of labor employed by competitive firms (Panel B), which expand their hiring until the value of the marginal product equals the wage rate ($VMP = MRP = MFC = w$).

precisely the sum of individual labor supplies and is denoted S_L. The interactions of labor supply and demand determine the equilibrium wage (w_e) and employment (L_e).

Equilibrium processes resemble those in purely competitive markets for goods. If current wages are below equilibrium, shortages of labor create a tight job market, and employers will bid wages up in attempts to fill vacancies. During 1974–84, wages rose sharply for anyone with expertise in petroleum or computers. "Head hunters" from employment agencies contacted some people every week or so to see if they were interested in changing jobs. Eventually, however, wages move towards equilibrium.

Wages above equilibrium create labor surpluses and unemployment. The unemployed will ultimately bid wages down as they try to secure jobs, but this can be a painful and time-consuming process. The sharp drop in oil prices during 1985–87 imposed pressure downwards on the incomes of oil workers and depressed local economies in Texas, Oklahoma, and Louisiana that had relied on oil revenues. (Other parts of the country, of course, experienced stronger growth because of declines in energy costs.)

Every firm that hires from a competitive labor market faces a labor supply curve that is horizontal at the existing market wage (w_e), and can hire as much labor as it wishes at that wage. Purely competitive firms hire only until the value of the marginal product of labor ($VMP = MRP$) equals marginal factor cost, which is the wage rate ($MFC = w$). In Figure 5, L_e workers are hired at a wage of w_e (point e in Panel A). Thus, the market clears when

$$VMP = MRP = MFC = w_e,$$

and anyone qualified and willing to work at the prevailing wage is employed; at the same wage, firms hire exactly as much labor as they choose. Purely competitive markets for capital, land, or entrepreneurial skills, which are explored two chapters hence, operate in a similar fashion.

Labor Market Efficiency

Adam Smith's "invisible hand" receives high marks for efficiency in purely competitive product markets. The demand curve for any good reflects society's marginal benefits, and its supply curve reflects society's marginal opportunity costs. Resources are efficiently allocated where the demands and supplies for goods meet, and these allocations reflect societal wants given the prevailing income distribution.

Competitive resource markets are similarly efficient. The demand for labor reflects society's demands for the goods labor produces because the *VMP* curve roughly portrays society's *marginal benefit* curve from employment. The labor supply curve facing an industry reflects the *marginal costs* to society of employing labor in that industry, because that labor might also be at leisure or employed in other industries. This is diagrammed in Figure 6.

Society receives what it pays for when competitive labor markets are in equilibrium (point *e*) because the marginal benefits and marginal costs of employment are equal. Suppose employment were only at L_0. The marginal social benefits from additional employment and production equal w_1 (point *a*), while marginal costs are only w_0 (point *b*). A net social gain equal to distance *ab* can be realized by shifting another unit of labor into this industry. Thus, employment level L_0 is below the socially optimal level of employment in this industry. Conversely, if employment were L_1, the net loss to society from employment of the last worker would be distance *cd*.

Society's resources are allocated efficiently only when marginal benefits and costs are equal, a result achieved in competitive labor markets because marginal benefits and costs are reflected, respectively, in the demand and supply for labor. J. B. Clark, the first internationally prominent American economist, was the developer of the $VMP = w$ rule for efficiency in labor markets. His ideas still dominate analyses of resource markets.

Supply and demand analysis normally assumes that each unit of the item considered is identical. Human labor, however, is far more variegated than long-stemmed roses, bulldozers, or parcels of land. Some variations among people are innate and some are accidental, but many are cultivated to amplify differences in human productivity.

Human Capital

People are not born with the same potential, intelligence, or strength, but inherited differences are magnified or offset by acquired skills that make us more productive. Sharpening our productive talents or acquiring new skills is called investment in human capital.

> **Human capital** *represents improvements made to the labor embodied in human beings.*

Most of us spend years in school or in on-the-job training (*OJT*) preparing ourselves to be better and more productive workers. Self-improvement fanatics may spend most of their lives acquiring human capital. We bring to our training or education certain natural aptitudes and strengths. Our abilities to perform certain tasks are honed as we invest in human capital.

Investment in Education

Education is a lifelong process.

—Anonymous

Investment in new machinery or other physical capital requires sacrifices of potential current consumption so that higher levels of future income and consumption can be realized. Acquiring new skills through education requires similar sacrifices. The

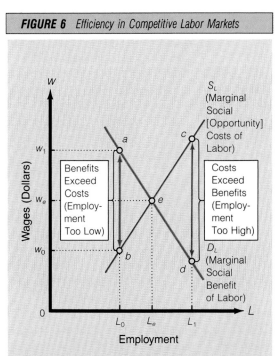

FIGURE 6 *Efficiency in Competitive Labor Markets*

In a competitive world, labor markets operate efficiently. Demands for labor reflect the marginal social benefits from particular employment, and labor supplies reflect the marginal social costs of employment. In equilibrium, $MSB_L = MSC_L$, and there is efficiency.

BIOGRAPHY

J. B. Clark
(1847–1938)

John Bates Clark was the leading American economic theorist at the turn of the century. His position in American economics was similar to that of Alfred Marshall in British economics. Although Clark did not have the advantage of the vigorous intellectual stimulation Marshall received at Cambridge, he was still an important innovator in economic theory.

Clark's complete writings were intended to restructure the classical theories of value and distribution, but his most enduring contribution to economics is found in *The Distribution of Wealth* (1899), which set forth the *marginal productivity theory of income distribution.* Clark sought to prove that every unit of labor and capital is paid precisely the value it adds to total product—its marginal productivity. His model hinges on resource mobility, pure competition, and the law of diminishing returns.

Labor and capital are each interchangeable, according to Clark, so that each worker or piece of capital is, in a sense, the last one. He reasoned that, although tasks within a firm differ in importance, if a worker engaged in an important task were removed, the remaining work would be assigned so that all essential tasks would be done, leaving the least important tasks undone. This means that no single unit of labor is more important than any other.

Firms operate in a region of their production functions where diminishing marginal returns cause each worker added to a work force to increase total product by an amount smaller than did the previous worker. Competition provides an incentive for the employer to add workers as long as the last one hired contributes at least as much to total revenue as the cost of employing that worker. Because every worker is the marginal worker, and because the *last* worker hired adds to the employer's gross income the same amount as the wage rate in a competitive labor market, all workers are paid the values of their marginal products.

Properly understood, Clark's marginal productivity theory is a rebuttal to Marx's charge that competitive capitalism systematically robs labor because workers contribute more to total product than the wages they receive. Clark maintained, on the contrary, that the payment to capital is also determined by its marginal productivity and that there is no "surplus value" expropriated from labor as alleged by Marx. Whatever amount of labor is employed, capital so shapes itself that each unit of equivalent labor is working with the same amount of capital. Thus, the product of every unit of capital is also equivalent to every other; when every unit is paid the value of its contribution to total product, there is no surplus to be expropriated. In short, each factor receives a payment determined by the product of its own final increment, and the reward to capital, no less than the reward to labor, is a necessary payment for its productivity.

Early economists were even more prone to take positions on normative issues than economists today, many of whom pride themselves on their scientific objectivity (if such a thing is possible). Clark tried to use his positive findings to "prove" that payments of income according to contribution (marginal productivity) are inherently equitable. The fact that this idea is as controversial today as when he first pronounced and published his "proof" is testimony that normative issues cannot be resolved scientifically.

time and money you are sacrificing to go to college are examples.

College is partially a consumption experience for many students, offering football games, parties, and other social opportunities. Love of learning may also play a role, but most students perceive earning a degree as one step towards a higher income stream and access to "the good life." If you view your education primarily as an investment that should increase your future income, it is important to select your major carefully since some majors may merely make you a scholarly short-order cook.

Decisions about investing in human capital involve balancing higher lifetime earnings against the costs of acquiring more valuable skills. As a college student, you must pay for tuition, books, and other out-of-pocket expenses, and you have less time for employment during your student years. Moreover, your first job as a new college graduate may not yield the wage you might have earned had you gone directly from high school into the labor market and had four years of work experience. After a few years on the job, however, your income will probably exceed that of most high-school graduates who went directly into the labor market.

Figure 7 graphs typical out-of-pocket costs and income forgone against lifetime earnings from a college degree. The dark line in the figure reflects a typical earnings profile for college graduates over their working lives, while the lighter line indicates average relative earnings for high-school graduates who do not go to college. Area A represents out-of-pocket expenses, B is forgone earnings, and C is the gross returns to average college graduates. As long as your area C is sufficiently larger than $A + B$ to cover a normal rate of return, you can benefit by investing in your education. (We detail this type of calculation two chapters hence.)

Your own prosperity depends on returns from your education, but society as a whole also shares in both the costs (through taxes) and benefits of much training and education. Education tends to make life more predictable and pleasant for everyone. For example, we all benefit from widespread literacy. Can you imagine the traffic snarls if most drivers could not read traffic signs? We also benefit by having well-educated voters. Moreover, well-educated people tend to eventually receive higher incomes, pay more taxes, and commit proportionally fewer crimes. Finally, more productive workers expand average stan-

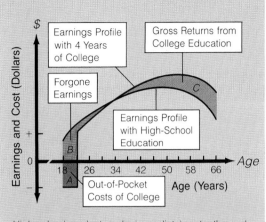

FIGURE 7 *The Individual's Investment in Education*

High-school graduates who immediately enter the work force will not incur the costs of education borne by their college bound peers (*A*) and will initially have higher incomes (*B*). However, typical college educated people eventually surpass the incomes of those who do not extend their formal education (*C*).

dards of living by the extra output their higher productivity provides.

These are only a few of the benefits shared by educated people with society as a whole. These collective benefits may justify some sharing of education costs through taxes. The share of gains going to others declines, however, as we progress through the education system. Things we learn in grade school make us semicivilized. High school civilizes us even more, on average if not in every case. But most benefits derived from college are personal, either in the form of consumption now or higher income later.

Marginal productivity theory suggests that you will receive more income to the extent that a degree makes you more productive. The onset of diminishing returns, however, implies that more education eventually yields successively smaller additions to your lifetime income. These reflections are supported by the private rate of return estimates developed by numerous economists over the last few years. Rates of return decline as individuals become more educated. For example, the personal rate of return from completing the last year of high school (9–11 to 12 years) is roughly 16 percent, while the average return from a college degree is around 12 percent.

One cautionary note: These returns reflect only private earnings and do not include the social bene-

Credentialism

Some critics of modern employment practices think that college degrees are artificial barriers to entry into many occupations. They believe that incompetent practitioners of many professions are protected from competition by people who might be extremely able but who lack the formal education required, either legally or by standard practice, to secure a job. IBM would hire neither Steve Jobs nor Steve Wozniak (the founders of Apple Computers) as computer engineers; neither has a college degree. Today, GE would not hire its founder, Thomas Edison, as a scientist; he lacked even a grade school education. Abe Lincoln could not practice law in most states today; he apprenticed as an attorney but never attended college. Socrates, Aristotle, Plato, and most of your professors lack the credentials now required to teach high school courses in the United States.

According to these critics, there are many people who could successfully do jobs not currently open to them because they lack the necessary degrees. Moreover, acquiring the degrees would waste their time, because degree programs allegedly fail to teach virtually anything required by many jobs. Do you think a management trainee in a department store should be compelled to have a degree? Many chain stores have such requirements. Degrees are no guarantee of competence, nor does the lack of formal education mean that someone is incompetent.

---

fits and personal gratification derived from extended education. For example, the public benefits from the works of Einstein, Keynes, or most Nobel prize winners probably could not have been produced by people with only high-school educations.

Formal education is one way to acquire human capital, but, as Focus 1 indicates, some critics believe formal education to be vastly over-rated as a predictor of individual productivity. Proficiency in some occupations is enhanced little by schooling, but grows immensely with experience and on-the-job training.

Training and Work Experience

Economists distinguish between general and specific training. *General training* increases a worker's marginal productivity equally for many firms. For example, general training on a computer raises a worker's potential productivity with many firms, and acting lessons may open up many roles to an actor. *Specific training*, on the other hand, only increases the productivity of the worker where currently employed. For example, convicts learning to make license plates primarily increase their productivity for prison work, or actors rehearsing specific lines only perform better in certain roles.

A firm will invest in a worker's human capital only if it expects the employee to stay on the job long enough for the firm to recoup at least a normal return on its investment. How can a company that invests large sums to train electronics technicians ensure that they will not quit before the firm recovers its investment? Other firms are willing to pay the going wage for trained electronic technicians. Firms will not provide much general training unless the trainees bear the costs, typically by accepting wages lower than the values of their marginal products. Apprenticeship programs are prime examples: apprentices pay for their general training by accepting wages far below those paid to fully trained workers.

The military uses a different approach. It guarantees substantial general training but requires recruits to legally commit to several years of service. This partially explains why the military harshly penalizes AWOL personnel or deserters. (Private employers cannot copy the military's example because slavery is illegal.)

While much of a technician's training is general, some portion normally represents specific training. The expertise gained when a technician works only on one company's product often cannot be transferred to other firms; that training is specific to that employer. Firms can ignore competition for such services because these job-specific skills lack value to other firms.

Firms consequently absorb the costs of specific training and share in the returns. Military weapons training or knowledge about a particular cost accounting system within a given firm or about a specific delivery route are examples. A firm tries to pay specifically trained workers more than its competitors would but less than the values of their marginal products. These slight wage premiums reduce worker turnover and ensure that, on average, firms secure returns on their investments in specific training.

Turnover and quit rates among a firm's employees are related to the levels of specific training and wage premiums it pays its workers. Firms have strong incentives to retain employees who have substantial specific training. Higher wages are one way to reduce quit rates, but firms employ many nonwage incentives as well. Many career employees do not pressure their employers for big raises during prosperous periods; in turn, these firms offer job security by not laying off such workers when business conditions soften. This behavior is known as an *implicit labor contract*. Seniority rules and pension plans that tie benefits to longevity with a firm also cut turnover and enable firms to recoup their human capital investments.

Unfortunately, their shorter remaining work lives may automatically exclude some older workers from job openings that require substantial specific training. This is one example of ways that market outcomes sometimes seem inequitable and, occasionally, even cruel. These cases often result in attempts to legislate more socially acceptable employment policies. The remainder of this chapter points to the likelihood that such policies will fail if markets are competitive. In the next chapter, we deal with lack of competition in labor markets—situations where policies have greater chances for success.

Government Regulation of Labor Markets

Many labor markets are far from competitive. Some imperfections originate in the private sector (unions or employment discrimination) but some also emerge from government policies. Labor markets are governed by many legal restrictions, ranging from limits on the employment of youngsters to health and safety regulations to minimum-wage laws. Table 2 summarizes the thrust of major U.S. labor laws. Many economists believe that some laws create inefficiency and inequity and are inconsistent with their stated objectives. Minimum-wage laws, for example, may hurt far more workers than they help, with young workers and members of minorities being especially harmed.

Minimum Wages and Unemployment

When Thomas Edison was in the midst of a long string of experiments to develop a practical light bulb, he was asked whether he was making any progress. He replied, "Why certainly. I've learned a thousand ways you can't make a light bulb."[3] Similarly, our society has tried numerous remedies for teenage unemployment, but teenage unemployment rates, especially among minorities, continue to rise. Edison eventually developed a good light bulb, but he kept track of things that did not work. Teenage unemployment continues to grow, perhaps in part because the problem may be aggravated by misguided policies.

Minimum-wage laws are presumably intended to alleviate poverty by ensuring workers a living

---

3. This anecdote is related by Steven P. Zell in "The Problem of Rising Teenage Unemployment: A Reappraisal," *Economic Review* (March 1978), Federal Reserve of Kansas City, March 1978.

TABLE 2 *Major Labor Laws and Regulations*

Labor Law or Regulation	Purpose	Administrative Agency

Wages & Hours of Work
Fair Labor Standards Act, 1938
(both state and federal)
	Controls such matters as:
	  a. child labor
	  b. hours of work, particularly for minors
	  c. minimum wages
		Department of Labor

Equal Pay Act, 1963	Prohibits employers from discriminating on the basis of race, age, or sex in paying wages for equal work performed (equal pay for equal work)	Department of Labor
Workers' Compensation Acts (state statutes) Similar federal statutes are: Federal Employees' Liability Act (railway workers) Jones Act (maritime workers) Longshoremen's and Harbor Workers' Compensation Act (dock workers)	Provides a system to pay workers or their families in the event the worker is killed, injured, or incurs an occupational disease while employed	State workers' compensation agencies (usually entitled "Industrial Commission")
Occupational Safety and Health Act, 1970	Requires each employer to furnish each employee a place of work free from recognized hazards likely to cause injury or death	Department of Labor (Occupational Safety and Health Administration)
Unemployment Compensation (state statutes and the Social Security Act of 1935)	Provides for payments for temporary periods to workers unemployed through no fault of their own	State Unemployment Compensation Boards
Equal Employment Opportunity (Civil Rights Act of 1964 and Equal Employment Opportunity Act of 1972)	Designed to eliminate job discrimination against employees, applicants, or union members based on race, color, religion, sex, age, or national origin	Equal Employment Opportunity Commission (files civil action in Federal District Court) Office of Federal Contract Compliance
Social Security Act of 1935	Provides income at retirement (age 62–65), disability and death benefits, hospital and medical insurance (Medicare) to people over 65	
Pension Reform Act, 1974	Regulates funding requirements, coverage, termination insurance coverage, and management of trusts	Internal Revenue Service, Department of Labor, and Pension Benefit Guaranty Corporation
Collective Bargaining National Labor Relations Act, 1935 (Wagner Act, amended by Taft-Hartley Act in 1947)	Complex act regulating all phases of collective bargaining. Act defines various unfair union and management labor practices, provides for elections of representatives, provides for right to strike, gives states the opportunity to enact state "right-to-work laws," etc.	National Labor Relations Board (NLRB)
Union Administration Labor-Management Reporting and Disclosure Act, 1959 (Landrum-Griffin Act)	Provides for an elaborate system of regulation of union internal activities. Mandates such things as (a) a "Bill of Rights" for union members, (b) elaborate information reporting by union bylaws, etc., (c) yearly financial reports, and (d) democratic election of officers	Department of Labor

wage, but this goal is realized only if inexperienced and unskilled workers can find work. Figure 8 shows the effect of imposing a minimum wage of $3.35 an hour in a competitive labor market for unskilled workers where the equilibrium hourly wage is $2.50 and equilibrium employment is 7 million workers. As Panel A illustrates, when a legal floor on wages is imposed at $3.35 hourly, 2 million unskilled workers are laid off. Another million enter the job market at this higher wage, so 3 million out of 8 million are now unemployed, and the unemployment rate among the unskilled rises from 0 to 37.5 percent.

These unemployed workers filter through the economy in several ways. First, the million that entered the market will look for jobs elsewhere, but since wages are less elsewhere, most will drop back out of the market. The two million disemployed workers will look for work in labor markets not cov-

ered by the minimum wage law, shown in Panel B. The result is that the labor supply in this uncovered market shifts to the right by 2 million workers; wages decline to $2.30 per hour; a million workers find work, and a million do not. This model illustrates that legal wage floors create surpluses of workers and unemployment just as surely as price floors for goods cause surpluses of goods.

Minimum-wage laws have been identified as causes of growing teenage unemployment. In the eight years before 1955, when minimum wages first crept over $1.00 per hour, the teenage unemployment rate hovered around 10 percent; in the twelve years after 1974, when the minimum wage rose above the $2.00 mark, teenage unemployment averaged over 18 percent. (Inflation in this era would have decreased the disemployment effect, but this was roughly offset by the growing proportion of the

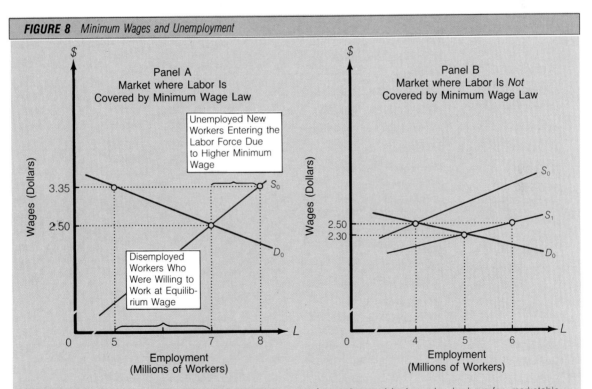

FIGURE 8 *Minimum Wages and Unemployment*

Minimum-wage laws may cause the involuntary unemployment of many impoverished people who have few marketable skills. This result may prove especially harmful for young people who are denied work experiences that would enhance their future employability.

As workers are disemployed in the markets covered by minimum wages (Panel A), they move to uncovered markets (Panel B) and receive lower wages. Not all workers are absorbed by the uncovered market, however, and many remain unemployed.

labor force covered by minimum-wage laws, which increases the disemployment effect.)

A hidden side effect of legal wage floors is that these laws may foster discrimination. In the words of one specialist in this area, Walter B. Williams:

> Aside from causing unemployment for some, the minimum wage law encourages racial discrimination. If an employer must pay a minimum of $2.90 an hour no matter whom he hires, he may as well hire someone whose color he likes. Economists would explain this by saying that the minimum wage law prevents the worker from offering a "compensating difference" for less preferred characteristics. The same principle applies to groceries. Less preferred chuck steak can compete with more preferred filet mignon only by offering a compensating difference—a lower price. If we had a minimum price law for steak of, say, $4.00 per pound, sales of chuck would fall relative to sales of filet. Because uniform minimum price laws encourage people to discriminate against goods and services they perceive as less valuable, chuck steak would be "unemployed."[4]

---

4. Walter B. Williams, "Minimum Wage, Maximum Folly," *The Smith-Kline Forum for a Healthier America*, no. 6 (September 1979).

Indeed, Panel A of Figure 9 shows that between 1948 and 1955, black teenagers had lower average unemployment than whites; since 1956, black teenagers have lost steadily and now suffer twice the unemployment rate experienced by white teenagers. Panel B suggests that many black teenagers may be so discouraged that decreasing numbers participate in the labor market, while participation rates among white teenagers have grown slightly over time. Small wonder that Milton Friedman, a Nobel prize economist, called minimum-wage laws "the most anti-Negro legislation ever passed."

Sex Discrimination and Comparable Worth

The slogan "equal pay for equal work" has become law. History is replete with cases where women and members of minority groups were denied equal access to jobs or paid less than some Caucasian males received for the same work. Some women workers would like to extend this law to raise wages in the occupations into which most women were once

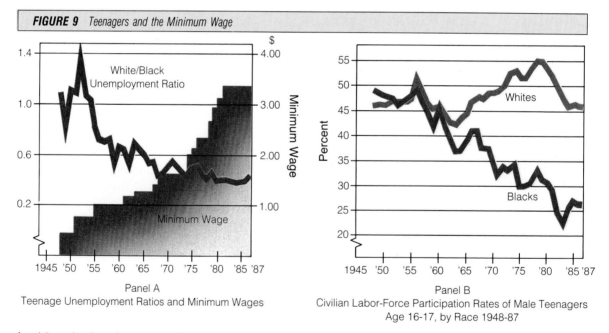

FIGURE 9 *Teenagers and the Minimum Wage*

Panel A
Teenage Unemployment Ratios and Minimum Wages

Panel B
Civilian Labor-Force Participation Rates of Male Teenagers Age 16-17, by Race 1948-87

As minimum legal wages have risen (Panel A), black male teenagers apparently have lost jobs to white male teenagers. As a result, many black teenagers have dropped out of the labor market (Panel B).

Sources: Age group 16–17, *Handbook of Labor Statistics*, 1978; age group 18–19, *Economic Report of the President*, 1987.

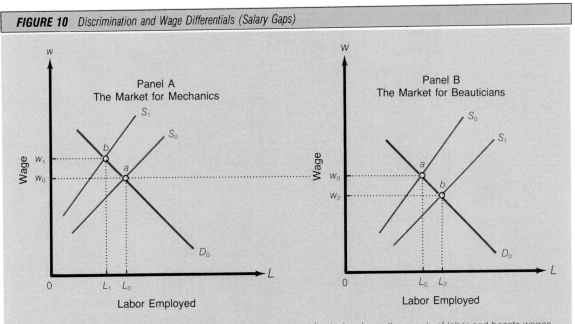

FIGURE 10 Discrimination and Wage Differentials (Salary Gaps)

Excluding women from certain occupations (e.g., work as auto mechanics) reduces the supply of labor and boosts wages in these markets, as shown in Panel A. At the same time, however, labor supplies are swollen and wages are relatively depressed in the occupations into which women are channeled (e.g., cosmetology), as indicated in Panel B.

channeled—nursing, teaching, and clerical work. They argue that holders of these jobs are systematically underpaid. For example, nurses are typically far more educated and bear more responsibility than hospital janitors. Advocates of the **comparable worth** doctrine are aghast that janitors tend to be paid more. Such apparent discrepancies in pay relative to the value of a job must be the result of sex discrimination, according to their reasoning. In fact, a recent study by the AFL-CIO concluded that "women's work pays best if it's done by a man."[5]

Figure 10 illustrates how discrimination can create pay differentials between men and women. Begin by assuming a lack of any discrimination and that the occupations of auto mechanic and beautician require comparable training and effort. Both occupations would have salaries of w_0 and each market would employ L_0 units of labor with roughly equal proportions of men and women.

Now assume that work as a mechanic or in many similar occupations becomes closed to women, while cosmetology and a few other jobs remain open to all. The supply of mechanics will shrink by almost half as women are excluded, while a few male beauticians become mechanics when mechanics' wages rise. Most women previously employed in such work as auto mechanics will move into such occupations as beautician. Supply curves shift to S_1 in Figure 10, reflecting fewer auto mechanics and more beauticians. The result is an occupational wage differential of $w_1 - w_2$.

Remedies to compel "equal pay for *comparable* work" are now being sought in the courts, state legislatures, and the Congress. More than a dozen states now require employers (both public and private) to pay equally for "comparable" work, and numerous others have bills pending in their state legislatures.[6] Even in states where comparable worth is not the law,

5. *Salaried and Professional Women: Relevant Statistics,* compiled by the AFL-CIO's Department for Professional Employees, Jan. 1988.

6. "Comparable Worth: It's Already Happening," *Business Week,* 28 April, 1986, 52–56.

many firms have initiated job evaluation programs to ensure internal equity.

The salary gap that comparable worth is expected to close is not invariant between occupations. Data from the 1984 Census of Population indicates that salary gaps vary by occupation and age.[7] For elementary school teachers and computer programers, the average salary gap is between 80 and 95 percent, while that for lawyers and managers is between 60 and 63 percent. But, as Table 3 illustrates, younger women are faring much better in recent years. This is a reflection of better education and training, and the growing number of young women majoring in business, computer science, law, medicine, and engineering.

Until recently, unequal access to remunerative employment did push many women into occupations that pay relatively little, but the question remains of whether a law requiring "equal pay for comparable work" will achieve the goals of its advocates. The first problem with implementing this approach is ascertaining how much particular jobs should pay. The markets to which this doctrine would apply tend to be quite competitive, but we presumably cannot rely on market wage solutions. This means that officials from some government agency will need to consider the qualities of each job: skill requirements, how pleasant the work environment is, and the relative risks to workers are only a few of the many factors that would need to be considered. Weighing education and classroom teaching duties against hot, sweaty, and dangerous work on a construction crew, for example, is unavoidably subjective. The slow and costly process of unraveling such complex issues would be unlikely to satisfy many people.

Suppose that all these problems were resolved. The basic problem remains that the supplies of nurses, teachers, and clerical workers have been relatively large in the competitive markets for these skills, depressing the equilibrium wages for these jobs. New legal requirements raising wages to above the equilibrium pay for holders of jobs that have historically been "women's work" will, unfortunately, have effects similar to those of a legal minimum wage. Many women currently employed in these oc-

TABLE 3 Male/Female Salary Gap 1975–1986		
	Average Annual Earnings of Women as a Percentage of Men	
Age	**1975**	**1986**
18–24	76	86
25–34	65	74
35–44	52	60
45–54	53	54
55–64	55	54

Source: U.S. Bureau of the Census, cited in "The Truth About the Salary Gap(s)," *Working Women*, January 1988, pp. 61–62.

cupations would lose their jobs, and there would be surpluses of secretaries, teachers, and nurses. These surpluses would be translated into unemployment.

One reason that excessive unemployment in these occupations would rise is because employers would have strong incentives to find substitutes as higher salaries were legally mandated. For example, office work would become even more automated. Receptionist slots would be pared to the bone. Electronic filing systems would be simplified to reduce requirements for some clerical work. Business correspondence would become more standardized to minimize the need for individualized letters, and firms would rely even more heavily on negotiations by telephone. Nurses would find more of their tasks taken over by orderlies or technicians. Schools would be pressured to raise student/teacher ratios in attempts to contain costs.

Thus, the comparable worth approach might be like some policies we described in chapter 4: many members of the groups targeted for help may be harmed in unforeseen ways. Fortunately, this problem may cure itself as time elapses and women increasingly shun traditional "women's careers" to become doctors, lawyers, pilots, architects, or engineers.

Our discussions of minimum-wage laws and comparable worth have assumed that the labor markets for unskilled workers and traditional "women's work" are highly competitive. The past few chapters have emphasized that competitive markets for either consumer goods or productive resources tend to be efficient, and that government policy is likely to be counterproductive. In the next chapter, we will inves-

---

7. "The Truth About The Salary Gap(s)," *Working Women*, Jan. 1988, 61–62.

tigate the effects of inadequate competition in the workplace. You will see that lack of competition tends to cause inefficiency and, perhaps, inequity. These flaws of the market system may be remediable through appropriate government action. The trick, of course, is to design and implement efficient and equitable policies. Wishful thinking or good intentions are not enough.

CHAPTER REVIEW: KEY POINTS

1. The demand for any resource is related to the (*a*) amounts of other factors employed, (*b*) production technology used, and (*c*) demand for the product. Because the demand for labor (or any factor) hinges on the demand for final products, it is a *derived demand*.

2. *Marginal revenue product* (MRP) is the firm's revenues generated by hiring the marginal unit of some input. In pure competition, this is the same as *VMP*. Labor (or any factor) will be employed up to the point where the additional revenue competitive firms receive (*value of the marginal product*, or *VMP*) just equals the cost of an additional unit of the resource (*marginal factor cost*, or *MFC*). In competitive labor markets, the marginal factor cost (*MFC*) equals the *wage rate* (*w*), so pure competition in all markets means that

$$VMP = MRP = MFC = w.$$

3. Increases (*decreases*) in the demand for the product, in labor productivity, or in the amounts of other resources used will normally increase (*decrease*) the *VMP* and demand for labor. Technological changes may either increase or decrease labor demands. *Automation* is the replacement of workers by new technologies.

4. The *elasticity of demand for labor* is directly related to the (*a*) *elasticity of demand for the final product*, (*b*) *labor's share of total costs* represented by the wage bill, (*c*) ease of factor *substitution*, and (*d*) time for *adjustment*.

5. The supply of labor depends on (*a*) wage rates and structures, (*b*) labor force participation, (*c*) the number of hours people are willing to work, and (*d*) the education, training, and skills of workers.

6. Workers experience both *income* and *substitution effects* when wage rates change. Increased wages cause labor to substitute work for leisure because work expands consumption opportunities and leisure is more costly. Higher wages mean, however, that for a given amount of labor effort, workers will earn more income, and, if leisure is a normal good, they will want to consume more leisure and work less. If the substitution effect is larger than the income effect, supplies are positively sloped. Backward-bending labor supplies result when income effects dominate substitution effects.

7. While the individual's labor supply curve may be backward bending, the supply of labor to any industry will always be positively sloped. Industry supplies and demands for labor establish the *equilibrium wage* as each firm hires additional units of labor until the value of the marginal product equals the market wage rate.

8. Competitive demand curves for labor represent the marginal benefits society receives from additional employment, and supply curves reflect the marginal cost to society of using those resources. Employing labor to the point where $D_L = S_L$ is efficient because society's benefits from additional employment equals its costs. More or less employment than where $D_L = S_L$ yields inefficient resource allocations since society gets more (*or less*) than it desires in an opportunity cost sense.

9. Labor quality improves through investments in *human capital* that include formal education and on-the-job training. Education benefits both the individual and society at large. Training is classified as either general or specific: *General training* enhances a worker's productivity equally for many firms, while *specific training* only increases the worker's productivity for the current employer.

10. Turnover and quit rates are negatively related to the levels of specific training workers have received and to the wage premiums paid them. Firms that invest heavily in their employees have strong incentives to retain them and do so (*a*) by paying higher wages than other firms will offer, and (*b*) through special rules based on seniority or pension provisions that reward longevity with the firm.

11. *Minimum-wage laws* intensify the unemployment of unskilled workers (especially teenagers) and may foster discrimination. Widespread implementation of a *comparable worth* doctrine would require bureaucratic comparisons of jobs to determine wages, and might stimulate disemployment of many workers in the competitive occupations into which women have historically been channeled.

PROBLEMS

1. Assume the following relationship holds for labor employed and lawns mowed per 10 hour day for your "Zippy" lawn mowing service.

Labor	Lawns Mowed/Day
1	18
2	34
3	48
4	60
5	70
6	78
7	84
8	88
9	90

a. Compute the Marginal Physical Product of Labor for each additional unit of labor employed.

b. During the months of April and May you receive an average of $15 per lawn mowed, and labor costs $150 per worker per day. How many workers will you employ during these months?

c. Fierce competition from teenagers during June through August drops prices to $10 per lawn. If wages were stuck at $150 per day, how many employees would you lay off each summer? How much of a wage cut would your employees have to take to remain employed during June through August?

2. Your sports paraphernalia plant is facing labor cost increases of twenty percent because a new defense plant in your community is attracting workers and tightening the local labor market. You currently employ fifty workers and your elasticity of demand for labor is 1.10. How many workers will you continue to employ after the wage increases have taken effect?

QUESTIONS FOR THOUGHT AND DISCUSSION

1. Marginal productivity theory suggests that people are paid according to the productive contributions of their resources, including labor. But such things as seniority rules clearly create situations where some people who are paid less are more productive than some people who are paid more. Do you think that the forces of marginal productivity generate a strong tendency for payment to be roughly proportional to contribution? Why or why not?

2. Some successful people like to brag that they started with nothing and owe "nothing to nobody." Marginal productivity theory suggests that technology and the amount of capital and the number of people we work with are powerful influences on our productivity and income. How are "rugged individualists" who believe they have "done it on their own" both supported and rebutted by marginal productivity theory?

3. Some 1930s radicals held that pay should be determined by how vital a job is to society. For example, people who maintain traffic lights or collect trash would be paid more than Hollywood stars or the promoters of such fads as Pictograms. Do you think this argument has merit? Why, or why not?

4. Some highly intelligent, well-educated people work very hard and receive little in return. Is a Ph.D. in music who practices constantly and becomes the world's 211th best oboe player entitled to more pay than a waiter? Does capitalism undervalue artistry or esoteric knowledge? If so, how should we determine appropriate incomes for people whom the market system spurns?

5. Distinguishing between labor and human capital can be extremely difficult. Are there any tasks that can be accomplished by raw labor untempered by some education or experience? If so, what are they?

6. In his book *Inequality*, Christopher Jencks argues that public education may lead to a meritocracy in which incomes differ greatly not because of inheritances of wealth but because of genetic differences. Does income often depend more on who you are than what you can do? Do you think public education facilitates social stability by providing nonviolent avenues for poor children to channel their energies toward becoming rich and powerful adults? Is a meritocracy fairer than an aristocracy based on birth?

7. Firms cannot predict exactly how productive or honest any prospective employee will be once hired. What are shortcomings of each of the following devices some employers use to screen job applicants (*a*) Grades, diplomas, or degrees, (*b*) letters of recommendation, (*c*) on-the-job training or work experience with other employers, (*d*) impressions from interviews, (*e*) tests of aptitudes, skills, or personality, or (*f*) lie detector examinations. Which devices do you think are most effective? Which do you think are too heavily weighted by many employers? Which other mechanisms are (or should be) used to screen job applicants? What are their advantages? Shortcomings?

8. Several studies, after adjusting for other individual characteristics, suggest that short men are paid less than tall men, and that short men are less likely to be promoted. Other studies suggest that attractive people tend to receive higher pay and quicker promotions than those who are considered either plain or beautiful. Are these results consistent with marginal productivity theory? Do you think these studies are correct? If so, what do you think accounts for these and similar findings?

Wayne R. Metz v. Transit Mix, Inc. (1987)

Metz worked for Transit Mix (Transit) as manager of its plant in Indiana. During the three years prior to Metz's discharge, Transit experienced financial problems attributed to the decline in the local construction business. In November 1983, Transit Mix closed its plant and laid off Metz. At that time, Transit had not decided whether it would close the Indiana facility permanently or only for the winter.

In February 1984, Transit sent the assistant manager of another plant (Burzloff) to inspect the Indiana plant and make any necessary repairs. Burzloff obtained permission to take orders from the plant's regular customers while he was there. Burzloff later requested that he be allowed to manage the facility. Transit approved this request and in April 1984 discharged Metz.

At the time of his layoff, Metz had an annual salary of $26,000, or about $15.75 an hour. He was among the highest paid of Transit employees and having worked for Transit twenty-seven years, was its second most senior employee. Burzloff was 43 and had worked for Transit for seventeen years when he replaced the 54-year-old Metz as manager. Burzloff's salary as manager was about $8.05 an hour.

The Age Discrimination in Employment Act, 29 U.S.D.A. Sec. 621–634 (ADEA) prohibits employers from discriminating against employees on the basis of age. Its objective in part is to promote employment of older workers on the basis of their abilities rather than their age. Proving intentional discrimination is often difficult, so a plaintiff may do so by presenting either direct or indirect evidence of discrimination.

In order to permit recovery for an ADEA claim through indirect means, the plaintiff must first establish a *prima facie* case of employment discrimination. This analysis requires only that a plaintiff show that he or she: 1) belongs to the protected class (age 40 or older); 2) was qualified for his or her position; 3) was terminated; and 4) was replaced by a younger person. After the plaintiff has established a *prima facie* case, the defendant employer then has the burden of presenting evidence that the plaintiff's discharge was a result of "some legitimate, nondiscriminatory reason." If the defendant meets this burden, the burden shifts to the plaintiff to prove that the reasons proffered by the employer for the discharge were merely a pretext for discrimination.

The ADEA has consistently been interpreted to prohibit an employer from replacing higher paid employees with lower paid employees to save money. Cost-cutting is not a legitimate, nondiscriminatory reason for discharging an older employee while retaining younger, lower paid employees.

Metz's salary reflected his twenty-seven years of service to Transit. When Transit decided that the company's poor performance no longer justified the salary that the company had given Metz, Transit replaced Metz because of that salary without first asking Metz to take a pay cut.

We are, of course, aware that employers must control costs to remain competitive and that this imperative of survival will inevitably create tensions with prohibitions against age discrimination. We think it would be unwise, however, to translate this imperative into a rule that an older employee can be fired and replaced by an equally proficient younger employee merely because the older employee happens to be earning more money at the moment.

EASTERBROOK, Circuit Judge, dissenting.

The earlier court found that Transit was not going to pay $26,000 to a manager at the Indiana plant because the plant did not do enough business to support such a salary. We have held before, that a firm may layoff or fire employees of any age when economic conditions make that prudent. "Economic conditions" implies a comparison of the employees' wages with their product; a plant that is unprofitable when the average wage is $20 per hour may be a bonanza for the firm when the average wage is $10. If Transit had said: "We are losing money in Indiana, in part because of your high salary, so we are closing that plant," Metz could not have complained.

Metz's victory today is Pyrrhic—not for him but for older employees in general. The court tells employers to keep their plants closed. Throw overpaid employees out of work because their salaries are high but don't you dare hire anyone else at a lower salary to do the work. If that rule were widely followed, the Metzes of the world would be no better off, and the Burzloffs (also in the protected age group) would be worse off. They would be denied advancement, and other employees whom the Burzloffs would manage would never be hired. If Congress wants such a stultifying result, if Congress wants to hurt older workers, so be it. But judges should not go out of their way to injure protected groups.

The customary response is that no one is protected by the ADEA unless qualified for the job. An older employee whose skills have diminished is not qualified. Yet there are degrees of skill; an employee is not "qualified" one day and "unqualified" the next. In business the question is not "is Jones qualified?" but "can Jones do the job well enough to cover his wage?" A welder good enough to work on simple sheet metal at $10 per hour may be unqualified for a welding job, paying $30 per hour, in a nuclear plant or on a bridge where lives depend on the quality of the joint and other, better welders compete for the position. There is no "qualified welder" in the abstract, and there is no "qualified manager of a cement plant" either. To say that someone is "qualified" to manage the Knox plant is to say that he can handle the manufacture and

sale of concrete well enough that he adds to the value of the enterprise at least the cost of his salary. If he cannot do this, he is unqualified for the particular job at the particular time. It is therefore not possible to divorce the ability to do a job from the wage demanded. If the ADEA allows employers to make decisions based on performance—surely it does, even though performance is systematically related to age—then it also allows employers to make decisions based on the interaction of performance and wage. If the wage is too high for the performance, the employer may act.

If we apply this court's analysis rigorously to decisions based on wages, we will require some fundamental changes in the operation of American business. A firm may not close a plant or curtail its operations on the basis of high wage costs. A firm may not give lower paid employees a wage increase without doing the same for higher paid employees if wage discrimination is age discrimination. In times of corporate austerity, firms may freeze or reduce the salaries of their managers and other well paid employees; no more, because that is age discrimination.

Would an employer, bent on slashing costs, find older employees' wages the most attractive target? This is a question about the profile of an employer's wage bill by the age of its employees. The wage-age profile is a cross-sectional analysis (data obtained from a snapshot of everyone's wages at an instant of time). Census data from 1984 gives median hourly wages as follows:

Ages	Hourly Wage
16–19	$3.64
20–24	$4.94
25–29	$6.52
30–34	$7.23
35–39	$7.37
40–44	$7.17
45–49	$7.23
50–54	$7.20
55–59	$6.85
60–64	$6.45
65–69	$4.95
70+	$4.38

Note: Median covers all races and both sexes.

Source: Department of Labor, Bureau of Labor Statistics, Monthly Labor Review 22 (Feb. 1986).

No evidence in this case shows that the wage-age profile at Transit has an upward slope. It is not appropriate to take judicial notice of a wage-age profile that creates a problem—especially when the Court is "noticing" something that is not true.

A growing literature on education, training, employment, and other aspects of human capital suggests that there may be times when employers will pay wages that do not represent the employees' marginal products. For example, while receiving firm-specific training the employee may receive a wage exceeding his product; this is how the firm finances the training (for which the employee will not pay, because it has no use outside the firm). Later the firm will recoup its investment by paying less than the marginal product. Other firms that give their employees access to trade secrets or put them in positions of trust may try to cement the employees' loyalty (or honesty) with "golden hand-cuffs"—wages in excess of the employee's marginal product, a form of special compensation the employee forfeits if he leaves the firm. Still other firms may pay employees slightly less than their marginal product early in their careers, knowing that as each employee's productivity declines at the end of his career, the firm will be paying more than marginal product (thus paying the employee his due over the life cycle). This gives employees strong reasons to stick with their firms and be more productive throughout their careers, which in turn yields society the benefit of everyone's abilities.

Questions

1. This case outlines the general approach taken by our courts in analyzing cases where plaintiffs allege discrimination on the basis of race, sex, age, national origin, or handicap. Does this burden shifting "prima facie" approach seem reasonable to you?
2. Will this decision lead to lay-off provisions where only persons in the nonprotected classes will be laid off?
3. This case interprets the ADEA to prohibit an employer from replacing highly paid older workers with lower paid younger employees. Since a large portion of the work force is between 40 and 65, does this rule essentially restrict employers to replacing workers between the age of 40 and 65 with workers who are older?
4. The majority opinion argues that Transit replaced Metz without first asking him to take a salary cut. Do you think the court would have found age discrimination existed if Transit had asked Metz to accept a salary equal to a younger employee to keep his job?
5. What options does the court leave to firms to remain competitive if highly paid (overpaid?) employees cannot be replaced with lower paid people?

CHAPTER 29

Labor Markets: Monopoly Power, Monopsony Power, and Labor Unions

Product markets range from pure competition to pure monopoly. Resource markets run a similar gamut. The preceding chapter focused on competitive labor markets. In this chapter, we study problems posed by inadequate competition in resource markets. Economic concentration causes three basic problems in resource markets (*a*) firms with monopoly power restrict output and, thus, demand fewer resources than if product markets were purely competitive; (*b*) resource buyers with clout may reduce quantities demanded to hold resource prices down; and (*c*) resource sellers with monopoly power may boost resource prices by restricting the quantity available.

Labor markets are especially plagued by noncompetitive influences: distortive regulations abound, and powerful unions restrict supplies to drive wages up, while powerful employers flex their economic muscle to depress wages. In this chapter, our first theme is the effects of deviations from competition in labor markets. We will address problems posed from

the demand side when employers exercise substantial power, either as sellers of goods or as buyers of labor. Then we'll look at problems of concentrated power from the supply side, among sellers of labor —primarily, labor unions. Finally, we survey the history and current status of American unionism.

Monopolies' Diminished Demands for Labor

You already know that firms with monopoly power raise prices and restrict output to maximize profit. The result for resource markets is that fewer resources are employed than if markets were competitive.

Suppose that gold output began to trickle off in your Colorado gold mine, but one day you discovered a rich vein of tantalite ore. Tantalum is crucial in lining tanks that hold liquids, as an alloy in tungsten-carbide cutting tools, and in certain electronics applications. Tantalum is quite rare, so assume that you gain substantial monopoly power. Relevant portions of the demand for tantalum and your production function are listed in Table 1.

Tantalum output for various numbers of miners parallels that for gold production, but the demand curve for tantalum slopes downward, reflecting your monopoly power. For example (from columns 2 and 3 of Table 1), if you sell 50 pounds per week, you can charge $90 per pound. Raising output to 110 pounds, however, requires a price cut to $50 per pound.

Recall that monopoly power depresses marginal revenue below price because added output is salable only if prices are cut for all units produced. You must now decide (*a*) what price to charge and how much to produce to maximize profits, and (*b*) how many workers to hire to get the job done. The answer to question (*a*) automatically answers question (*b*) because it takes a specific number of workers to produce the most profitable level of output.

Any firm maximizes profit by hiring until the revenue generated by the last worker hired (*MRP*) equals the wage outlays associated with hiring the last worker (*MFC*). If all markets are purely competitive, this translates into the rule that the value of the marginal product ($VMP = P \times MPP = MRP$) equals the wage rate ($MFC = w$), so that $VMP = MRP = MFC = w$. The rule that maximum profits are obtained when $VMP = w$ works only for a pure competitor operating in a competitive labor market. The more general rule

for profit maximization is that $MRP = MFC$. Monopoly power causes the value of the marginal product to exceed the marginal revenue product and reduces the amount of labor hired.

Let's apply this approach to your mine. Column 3 of Table 1 shows that hiring more workers raises tantalum output but lowers its price. The marginal revenue from each extra pound of tantalum mined by extra workers (column 5) is below its price. Thus, each extra miner adds $MR \times MPP$ to your dollar sales volume (column 7—the marginal revenue product, *MRP*, of labor), and this is less than the value of the marginal product (column 8—$P \times MPP$). For example, the third miner raises tantalum output by 18 pounds (from 50 to 68 pounds per week), but its price falls from $90 to $80 per pound. The $10 price cut on the first 50 pounds of tantalum causes your revenue from hiring the third miner to be only $940 (column 7) instead of the $1,440 (18 × $80) realized from selling the tantalum produced by the third miner (column 8).

Thus, because monopoly power causes the price of output to exceed its marginal revenue, labor's value of the marginal product ($VMP = P \times MPP$) is greater than its marginal revenue product ($MRP = MR \times MPP$). The maximum profit rule requires that the marginal revenue product equals the marginal factor cost ($MRP = MFC$). Profit is maximized for your tantalum mine when

$$VMP > MRP = MFC = w.$$

TABLE 1 *Data for Tantalum Production*

Production Function						**Demand for Labor**	
(1)	(2)	(3)	(4)	(5)	(6)	(7)	(8)
Number of Workers *L*	Pounds of Tantalum Produced per Week *q*	Price of Tantalum per Pound *P*	Total Revenue *TR* (*P × q*)	Marginal Revenue *MR* (Δ*TR*/Δ*q*)	Marginal Physical Product of Labor *MPP* (Δ*q*/Δ*L*)	Marginal Revenue Product of Labor *MRP* (*MR × MPP*)	Value of the Marginal Product of Labor *VMP* (*P × MPP*)
1	30	$100	$3,000	$100.00	30	$3,000	$3,000
2	50	90	4,500	75.00	20	1,500	1,800
3	68	80	5,440	55.22	18	940	1,440
4	84	70	5,880	27.50	16	440	1,120
5	98	60	5,880	0	14	0	840
6	110	50	5,500	−31.67	12	−380	600
7	120	40	4,800	−70.00	10	−700	400

FIGURE 1 Equilibrium Level of Employment for the Tantalum Monopolist

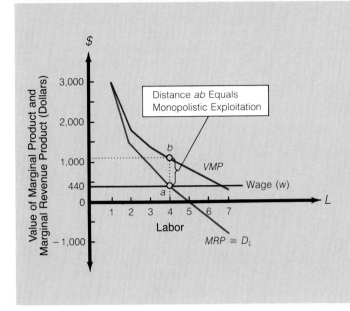

The value of the marginal product ($VMP = P \times MPP$) is the amount of revenue a competitive firm gains when it hires its last worker. The revenue gained from hiring the marginal worker is lower for a firm with monopoly power, because $P > MR$. Hence, the marginal revenue product ($MR \times MPP$) is less than the value of the marginal product. Monopolistic exploitation is the difference between VMP and w (distance ab). Note: The VMP and MRP shown are drawn from Table 1.

The revenue the last worker adds (MRP) equals the cost of hiring (MFC), which in this case is the competitive wage rate w, but this wage rate is below the value of the marginal product. Your monopoly power allows you to pay workers less than the marginal social value of their output, and forces us to distinguish between the VMPs and MRPs of labor. $MRP = MR \times MPP$, so marginal revenue product also equals the change in total revenue realized by hiring one more unit of labor ($MRP = \Delta TR/\Delta L$). Both MRP and VMP (columns 7 and 8 from Table 1) are diagrammed in Figure 1.

Suppose that you now hire labor from a competitive market at $440 weekly. To equate the MRP with the $440 wage, you would hire four workers (point a). Note that at point a, $MRP = MFC$ ($MRP = \$440 = MFC$). The fifth worker adds nothing to total revenue ($MRP = 0$) but would cost $440 per week—clearly a losing proposition.

Exploitation   Resource suppliers who are paid less than the values of their marginal products are said to be exploited.[1]

---

1. *Exploitation* sounds like a very judgmental term, but it is the standard language of this analysis. The early work in this area was done by Marxist economists. This does not invalidate their analysis, but it does explain this inflammatory terminology.

If monopoly power causes the value of the marginal product of labor to exceed the wage rate, the difference is known as **monopolistic exploitation.**

The fourth worker's VMP is $1,120 (point b), which is far above the fourth worker's MRP and wage of $440. The difference between the VMP and w (line ab, or $680) is called *the rate of monopolistic exploitation* of labor. Another source of exploitation arises if firms exert economic clout as resource buyers.

Monopsony in a Labor Market

No single firm's hiring noticeably affects wages in a purely competitive labor market. For example, in large cities the prevailing wages of secretaries, sales clerks, and delivery people are unaffected by any one firm's hiring. Contrast such markets with small towns where a textile mill or coal mine dominates employment. Sole buyers of a good or resource are known as monopsonists.

A buyer has **monopsony power** *if restricting the amount of a good or resource purchased reduces the price the buyer must pay.*

TABLE 2 *Supply of Labor Data for a Firm with Monopsony Power*

(1) Labor L	(2) Weekly Wage w	(3) Total Labor Cost TC_L $(w \times L)$	(4) Marginal Factor (Labor) Cost MFC $(\Delta TC_L / \Delta L)$
1	$250	$ 250	$ 250
2	300	600	350
3	380	1,140	540
4	485	1,940	800
5	550	2,750	810
6	600	3,600	850
7	700	4,900	1,300
8	800	6,400	1,500

A labor monopsonist is the sole employer in a specific labor market and faces the entire labor supply. Thus, its hiring decision determines the wage rate. A labor market in which a monopsonist pays all workers equally is outlined in Table 2. Hiring three workers requires the monopsonist to pay a wage rate of only $380 per week to this community's three most eager beavers. We will assume that wage discrimination is impossible to simplify this analysis. Thus, employing four local workers forces the monopsonist to raise its wage offer to $485 to attract the next, slightly less eager beaver to work, and necessitates a raise of $105 each to the preceding three workers.

The important result is that monopsony power raises marginal factor cost (*MFC*) above the wage rate. If this firm hires three workers at $380 per week, its labor costs are $1,140; these costs rise to $1,940 if the firm employs four workers at $485. Hiring a fourth worker without wage discrimination requires giving raises to $485 per week to the original three workers, which boosts total labor costs by $800, not $485. Such wage hikes cause the *MFC* to exceed the wage rate for each employment level. The *MFC* shown in column 4 of Table 2 is the change in total labor costs from hiring one extra worker. How does the excess of this *MFC* over the wage rate affect this firm's hiring? Figure 2 shows the labor supply and its *MFC* to this monopsonist.

A monopsonist's marginal factor cost curve is above the labor supply curve just as a monopolist's marginal revenue curve is below the demand curve it faces. The value of the marginal product from our

gold mine of previous chapters is also shown, so Figure 2 depicts a monopsony selling a competitive output and *VMP* = *MRP*. This firm maximizes profit by hiring labor until the *MRP* = *MFC* at $800 (point *a* in Figure 2), but only pays $485 each to the four workers willing to work for that weekly wage (point *b*). Thus, *VMP* = *MRP* = *MFC* > 0.

Monopsonistic Exploitation   A labor monopsonist hires fewer workers and pays lower wages than a firm hiring in a competitive labor market. If this firm faced a $600 wage from a competitive labor market, it would hire six workers (point *c*). Thus, the monopsonist pays workers less than a competitive employer would. Absent its monopsony power, this firm would hire four workers at a competitive wage of $800 (point *a*). Monopsony power enables it to hire four workers for a $485 wage, far below the values of their marginal product (*VMP* = $800). The difference ($315) is termed monopsonistic exploitation of labor.

> **Monopsonistic exploitation** *occurs when a firm is the sole buyer of labor in a given market and is equal to the difference between the value of the marginal product of labor and its wage rate.*

Few pure monopsonists exist, although some big firms located in small communities may dominate local labor markets and exercise substantial monopsony power. A more common type of monopsonistic exploitation occurs when firms control individual employees sufficiently to wage discriminate.

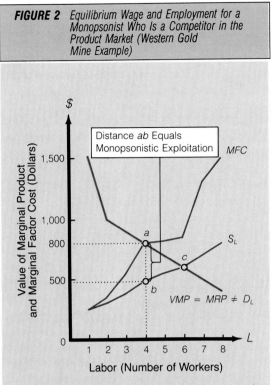

FIGURE 2 Equilibrium Wage and Employment for a Monopsonist Who Is a Competitor in the Product Market (Western Gold Mine Example)

Distance *ab* Equals Monopsonistic Exploitation

If the supply of labor facing a firm is positively sloped, then the wage increases that must be granted to all workers cause the marginal factor cost (MFC) curve to lie above the supply curve. This analysis perhaps naively assumes that wage discrimination is not possible.

Wage Discrimination

Have you ever worked for a company that discouraged workers from sharing information about wages or salaries? Many firms that do not have standard pay scales treat salary information as confidential. This is a common practice when a firm practices wage discrimination.

> **Wage discrimination** *occurs when different workers receive pay that is inconsistent with their individual marginal productivities.*

This is possible only if a firm has some monopsony power, just as price discrimination for goods requires a firm to possess monopoly power. This type of monopsony power may be exercised whenever any employee views a particular firm as offering special advantages such as location, job security, or opportunities for promotion.

In an earlier chapter, our discussion showed that price discrimination may remedy some of the economic inefficiency that occurs when firms exercise monopoly power. Wage discrimination may similarly cure some of the economic inefficiency caused by monopsony power. For example, if the monopsonist shown in Table 2 and Figure 2 could perfectly wage discriminate, it would hire six workers (exactly the same as by a competitive firm) rather than the four it hires as a nondiscriminating monopsonist. However, it would respectively pay the first through sixth workers weekly wages of only $250, $300, $380, $485, $550, and $600—the total weekly wage bill would be only $2,565, instead of the $3,600 that would be paid weekly by a purely competitive employer. The $1,035 difference represents monopsonistic exploitation. Although this wage discrimination does facilitate efficiency, it is widely viewed as inequitable.

Women may suffer especially from wage discrimination because many employers traditionally view women's work decisions as secondary to their husbands' career moves. Reasonable job security for women has been bait to facilitate wage discrimination. The resulting potential for exploitation is a powerful argument for "equal pay for equal work" laws, which may promote equity without hindering efficiency. A problem with extending this reasoning to the doctrine of comparable worth is that most employers in the highly competitive labor markets that would be covered by "comparable worth" have little monopsony power.

Employers who treat salary information as confidential argue that publicizing wage differentials just leads to bickering about which employee deserves what. Under this system, employees have little incentive to reveal their own pay, but seek information about the pay of others. If you learned that someone made less than you did, you would probably be silent if their work was comparable to yours. If, however, someone with a comparable job made more than you, you might use the information to negotiate a raise. It is easy to understand why many workers join employers in a conspiracy of silence when salary information is confidential. Although secrecy may reduce quibbling about salaries when pay scales are not standardized, the major advantage for employers is that confidentiality facilitates wage discrimination and monopsonistic exploitation.

Minimum-Wage Laws and Monopsony Power The effects of minimum-wage laws in competitive labor markets are summarized in Panel A of Figure 3. The prevailing wage is $3.25 before the minimum wage is introduced into the competitive market, and 70 units of labor are employed (point *a*). When a $4.00 minimum-wage law is imposed, employment falls to 58 (point *b*), and unemployment increases to 40 units of labor (98 minus 58); more people want to work at the higher wage (point *c*).

The effect of a minimum wage may be quite different if firms exert monopsony power. Before enactment of a minimum wage in Panel B, fewer workers are employed (50) at a lower wage ($2.75) by the monopsonist (point *g*) than by a comparable competitive firm (point *a*). Introducing the minimum wage alters the monopsonist's *MFC* by forcing the firm to pay at least $4.00 per hour, at which it can hire up to 98 workers. Average wages must rise to attract more than 98 workers, so the firm's *MFC* curve becomes *becdf*, and profit-maximizing employment is 58 workers at $4.00 per hour.

The result that minimum-wage hikes may boost both employment and wages in monopsonistic mar-

kets is often cited as a possible benefit of these laws. Critics rebut this analysis with studies showing that the biggest effect of higher minimum-wage laws is disemployment in competitive labor markets for unskilled workers and teenagers. Lower employment is also likely if firms practiced systematic wage discrimination before a minimum wage was enacted. (We showed how wage discrimination raises employment by monopsonistic firms. Minimum-wage laws may eliminate this effect.) Thus, Panel A probably correctly suggests that minimum wages foster unemployment. Several European countries have reduced teenage unemployment with lower minimum wages for teenagers than for adults. President Reagan's 1983 proposal to drop the minimum wage for teenagers to $1.67 (half the adult minimum) was defeated.

A Summary of Imperfect Competition by Employers

Precise translation of the *MRP = MFC* rule into equilibrium wage and employment levels depends on a firm's product and labor markets, as summarized in Figure 4. When product and labor markets are both competitive (Panel A), the firm hires until *VMP = w*,

FIGURE 3 *Effects of Minimum-Wage Laws in Competitive and Monopsony Markets*

A minimum-wage law will cause unskilled workers to experience unemployment if the labor market is competitive (Panel A). It is theoretically possible, but unlikely, for a minimum wage to increase employment if there is substantial monopsony power in the labor market (Panel B).

FIGURE 4 *Summary of Wage and Employment Equilibria*

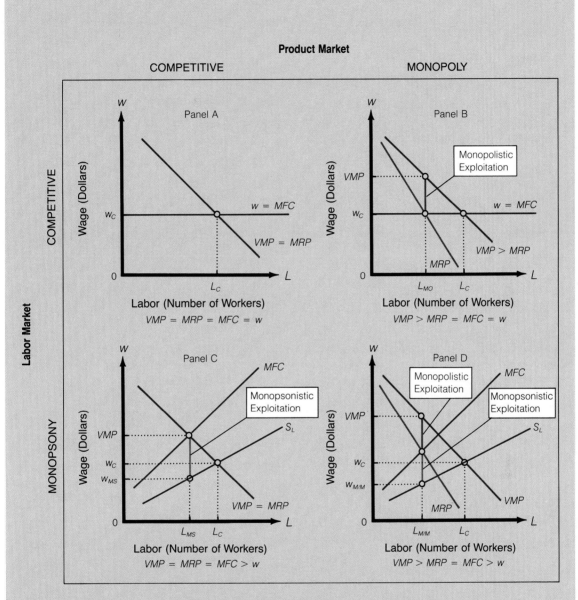

Product Market

COMPETITIVE   MONOPOLY

Labor Market

COMPETITIVE

MONOPSONY

Panel A

$VMP = MRP = MFC = w$

Panel B

$VMP > MRP = MFC = w$

Panel C

$VMP = MRP = MFC > w$

Panel D

$VMP > MRP = MFC > w$

The marginal value of labor to society is the VMP curve; the marginal social cost of labor is the competitively determined wage (w). In a competitive world (Panel A), there is no exploitation of labor, and economic efficiency exists because the marginal benefit to society of a specific employment just equals marginal social cost ($VMP = w$, so $MSB = MSC$). Monopolistic exploitation (Panel B) is accompanied by inefficiency because $VMP > MRP$ implies that the marginal social benefit exceeds the monopolist's marginal private benefit from hiring extra workers ($MSB > MPB$), so $MSB > MSC$. Monopsonistic exploitation (Panel C) is a situation where the monopsonists' marginal private costs are greater than the marginal social costs of employment ($MFC > MSC = w$), so again there is inefficiency. Panel D illustrates the case where the factors leading to inefficiency because of monopoly and monopsony power are combined.

which is efficient. Panel B shows that when a monopolistic seller hires from a competitive labor market, workers are paid less than the values of their marginal products and fewer workers are hired than under competitive conditions. A monopsony labor market combined with a competitive product market is depicted in Panel C. Firms with monopsony power also hire fewer workers at lower wages than would pure competitors. Last, Panel D illustrates equilibrium employment and wages when a labor monopsonist has monopoly power in the product market. Not surprisingly, the monopsonist/monopolist tends to hire fewer workers at lower wages than in any other market structure and is most exploitative—the difference $VMP - w$ is greatest.

You have seen how imperfect competition by employers may distort labor markets. We will now examine the supply side and labor unions.

Unions and Collective Bargaining

Corporate managers represent the interests of the shareholders who own these firms. In the same way, **labor unions** represent the interests of many workers and negotiate work contracts for their members. Major labor contracts cover thousands of workers. The relationships between firm managers and union leaders are often mixtures of public hostility and private symbiosis. Just as oligopolists act strategically when they try to cope with their interdependence in setting prices and output, negotiations by labor unions and management at times resembles a card tournament—or war. Several models have been developed to characterize this process.

Bilateral Monopoly

One early model of collective bargaining was called bilateral monopoly.

> **Bilateral monopoly** *assumes that a union is the sole agent for a firm's labor (a monopoly on the labor [supply] side), while the firm is the sole employer of union labor (a monopsony on the hiring [demand] side).*

The monopsonist employer depicted in Figure 5 would prefer to hire L_e units of labor at a wage rate of

FIGURE 5 *Bilateral Monopoly in Labor Markets*

An early model of collective bargaining, known as *bilateral monopoly*, assumed that employers with monopsony power must deal with unions that have monopoly power as suppliers of labor. When a buyer with monopsony power confronts a seller with monopoly power, price and quantity are determined by which side is the better negotiator or has more power.

w_e. The union, on the other hand, would want the L_e units of labor to be paid at least w_u. Given the marginal revenue product (*MRP*) *curve shown, wage rate* w_u is the maximum that the firm would be willing to pay for L_e units of labor.

The wage limits for bargaining range from w_u to w_e, but this model fails to predict exactly what the wage settlement will be. Moreover, we assumed that the union seeks the highest wage consistent with full employment of its L_e members. The powers that control a union may have other goals, such as maximum wages for workers with seniority or job security for union officials. For these reasons, the bilateral monopoly model does little to explain the bargaining process and is useful only in specifying some general limits to bargaining. About all we can say at this point is that the negotiated wage tends to be closer to the wage desired by the party (union or management) with the greatest power or bargaining savvy.

Union Strategies to Raise Wages

Demands for labor are downward sloping so that wage hikes reduce the quantity of labor demanded and, thus, normally eliminate some jobs. This is one trade-off that union negotiators must weigh; disemployment may be an especially heavy threat if an industry is largely nonunion. Giant national unions try to protect their members by organizing entire industries. In cases of purely local labor markets (construction, for example), only local workers must be unionized to protect union jobs from nonunion competition. A union can choose from several strategies to raise wages once an industry is organized. Consider Figure 6. Without unionization, firms' demands for labor would be D_{L0} and the supply of labor, S_{L0}, with resulting employment of L_e workers at a wage of w_e (point a).

Restricting the Labor Supply

A first union strategy might be to try to shrink labor to this industry by shifting the labor supply curve leftward to S_{L1}, raising the union wage to w_u (point b). The union movement predictably has supported policies such as child labor laws, restrictive immigration policies, compulsory retirement plans, laws to "protect" women from hard or hazardous work, and shorter work weeks. Most craft unions require lengthy apprenticeship programs to restrict competition from other workers. Some unions charge high initiation fees or simply limit new memberships to shift the supply of union labor to the left.

Rationing Work

Where unions control the entire work force for an industry, they may simply set the wage at w_u through bargaining. This creates a huge labor surplus and substantial unemployment or underemployment. The union then uses a *hiring hall* to spread the work available to its members. Rules to allocate jobs range from "first come, first served" to strict "seniority."

Stimulating the Demand for Union Labor

If the union can negotiate a wage of w_u and then raise the demand for its members' labor to D_{L1}, they suffer only minor unemployment at point c. Examples of this approach include using political clout to obtain local building codes that require labor-intensive construction technologies or lobbying for quotas to limit foreign competition for union members' services.

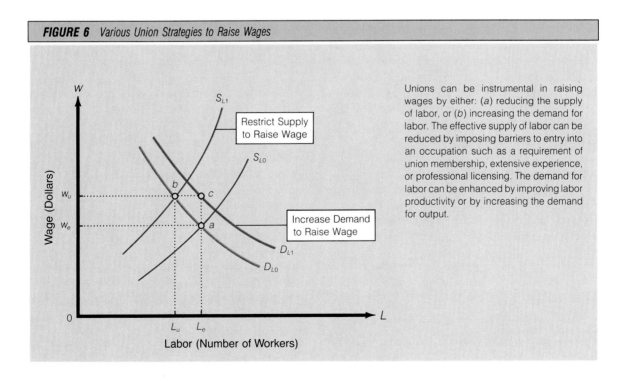

FIGURE 6 *Various Union Strategies to Raise Wages*

Unions can be instrumental in raising wages by either: (*a*) reducing the supply of labor, or (*b*) increasing the demand for labor. The effective supply of labor can be reduced by imposing barriers to entry into an occupation such as a requirement of union membership, extensive experience, or professional licensing. The demand for labor can be enhanced by improving labor productivity or by increasing the demand for output.

Unions may also work with management to increase worker productivity.

Featherbedding refers to work rules that artificially boost the number of workers required for certain tasks. It has been a union strategy to maintain or expand demands for labor in several industries—railroads, printing, and shipping (dock workers). For example, long after coal engines were replaced by diesel, railroad unions insisted that trains carry firemen who rode along even though there were no coal fires to tend.[2] For years, New York musicians had a union contract requiring standby orchestras for every event at which out-of-state musicians played.

Wage Setting and the Duration of Strikes

Bilateral monopoly models identify a range of wages within which union and management will agree but fail to specify the final wage. Moreover, these models ignore **strikes.** John Hicks, a Nobel prize winner, developed a more versatile model of collective bargaining, adapted in Figure 7.[3] The employer willingly offers a wage of w_0 without a strike, but the union insists on a wage of w_1, a difference so great that a strike begins at time zero (0).

Strikers ride a financial and emotional roller coaster. After the euphoria of a brief vacation, reality begins to knock at the workers' doors. Backlogs of do-it-yourself projects are finished, and boredom sets in as the strike drags on. As unemployment checks and union benefits run out, strikers begin to exhaust their past savings and worry about paying their bills. The hardships of long-term idleness cause union wage demands to trickle down along the union resistance curve graphed in Figure 7.

Over the same period, management grows more willing to pay the higher wages traced out as the employer's concession curve. Strikes are seldom surprises, so most firms are able to meet easily foreseen customer orders out of stockpiled inventories. Managers often form skeletal work crews during a strike,

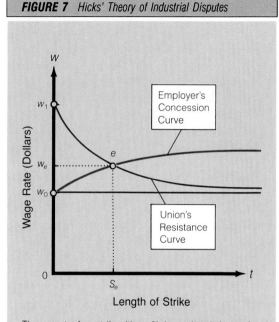

FIGURE 7 Hicks' Theory of Industrial Disputes

The onset of a strike (time 0) is a signal that union workers demand much higher wages than management is willing to pay. As time elapses, workers become willing to settle for less as their financial reserves evaporate, and management is increasingly willing to raise its wage offers as its inventories decline and stockholders and customers apply pressure to settle. Declining wage demands and rising wage offers intersect to signal the end of this particular strike at time S_e.

but eventually inventories shrink and managers become exhausted; the operation grinds towards a halt, raising their willingness to pay higher wages. The intersection (point e) of the employer's concession curve and the union resistance curve marks the end of this strike. The final wage settlement is at w_e, and the expected duration of this strike is S_e. As you can see, this simple model offers considerable insight into labor negotiations.

We have examined some aspects of imperfect labor markets from both the demand side—monopsony and monopoly—and the supply side—labor unions. This provides a background for a broader look at labor market institutions that shape economic activity in the United States, including a brief history of the American labor union movement and some effects of unionism.

---

2. Some states had laws requiring firemen on each train. Such a requirement was a part of the Arizona State Constitution until 1964.

3. J. R. Hicks, *The Theory of Wages* (London: The Macmillan & Company, 1932), Chapter VII.

Labor Unions

Unions traditionally have been organized around a particular craft or industry. Plumbers, machinists, air traffic controllers, and other workers organized on the basis of particular skills rely on *craft unions* to bargain with management. *Industrial unions,* on the other hand, organize all the workers in such industries as mining, steel, autos, and rubber. The current membership of some of today's largest unions is shown in Table 3.

Until their merger, the *American Federation of Labor (AFL)* consisted only of craft unions and competed with the *Congress of Industrial Organizations (CIO),* which covered only industrial unions. *Jurisdictional strikes* often erupted when both attempted to organize the same workers. For example, conflicts in chemical plants sometimes became violent between the CIO's Oil, Chemical, and Atomic Workers Union and AFL craft unions representing electricians or machinists. A treaty between AFL and CIO unions was finally consummated with their 1955 merger into the AFL-CIO.

Today, jurisdictional fights exist primarily between AFL-CIO unions and such independents as the Longshoremen or the Teamsters. These disputes focus on which union will represent given workers and what goals to pursue. Job security and higher wages involve trade-offs. For example, the United Mine Workers Union traditionally sought rapid wage hikes despite the resulting mass substitution of capital for labor and consequent disemployment of many union members. Other unions prize job security and so temper their demands for higher wages.

Union Security

Unions try to ensure job security for their members in part because union leaders seek security themselves. Special clauses in many union contracts are designed to strengthen the hands of union leaders as sole bargaining agents for their members. The strongest protection a union can have is a closed shop agreement with management.

> A **closed shop** *requires union membership as a prerequisite for employment.*

The Taft-Hartley Act of 1947 outlawed this form of union security. Open shops are at the opposite pole from closed shops.

> *In an* **open shop** *the firm employs workers without considering union membership.*

Unions legally must negotiate for all workers in an organized firm, but dues or membership are at the option of each worker. Thus, the open shop may permit nonunion free riders. Unions cannot control nonmembers, so firms can thwart strikes with nonunion workers (called *scabs* by union members), yet these nonunion workers receive all benefits accorded union workers.

The union shop is similar to a closed shop.

> *In a* **union shop** *employers may hire either union or nonunion labor, but new employees must join the union within a specified period to keep their jobs.*

Under a union shop arrangement, workers can be expelled from union membership only for nonpayment of dues. This protects workers from being expelled (with loss of their jobs) for infractions such as disagreeing with the union leadership or violating union policies.

Besides abolishing closed shops, the Taft-Hartley Act allowed state *right-to-work laws* outlawing the union shop. Nineteen states have passed such laws. Unions responded with *agency shop* agreements that require all employees to pay union dues. This arrangement has been defended as preventing non-

TABLE 3 *Some of Our Union Giants*	
Union	**1986 Membership**
AFL-CIO (TOTAL)	13,100,000
Food and Commercial Workers	1,300,000
United Steelworkers	832,800
State and County Employees	956,000
Electrical Workers	920,000
United Automobile Workers	986,000
Independent	
Teamsters	2,000,000

Source: *Statistical Abstract of the United States,* 1988.

union workers from free riding; all workers represented by a union should share the costs of collective bargaining. Unions also exert control over workers through *check-off provisions* in contracts, which require firms to deduct dues from paychecks. These provisions make it easier for unions to collect dues and retain members. The Taft-Hartley Act prohibits firms from deducting union dues unless authorized by a majority of workers, but roughly 80 percent of union contracts now have check-off provisions.

Unions did not develop overnight. The path to modern collective bargaining was paved with strife between union organizers and business owners and managers who do not want to share power with labor. The next section briefly examines the history of union development in this country.

The American Union Movement

A forerunner of modern unions was the Carpenters' Society of Philadelphia, established in 1724, which bargained for wage increases and organized charity work. Interestingly, members who disclosed wages to nonmembers were fined.[4] The first true union was the Federal Society of Cordwainers (shoemakers), formed in 1794. Its sole purpose was to negotiate higher wages. During the early 1800s, numerous unions emerged and then faded away, but within a century, unions had become fixtures on the national scene.

Until the Great Depression, business firms commonly fought union organizers with discharges, violence, and *yellow-dog contracts,* by which workers agreed not to join any union. Employers also circulated *blacklists* of union sympathizers and other "troublemakers." Finally, unions faced considerable legal adversity. Judges sympathetic to business owners issued *injunctions* (or restraining orders) against numerous union acts, including strikes or boycotts. If a union violated an injunction, its leaders could be held in contempt of court and jailed.

In the Danbury Hatters' case in 1908, the Supreme Court declared unions to be combinations in restraint of trade, violating the Sherman Antitrust Act.[5] The United Hatters of North America had tried to organize the Loewe Hat Company of Danbury, Connecticut. After a series of strikes failed, the union announced a national boycott of Loewe's products. The Court ruled that this boycott caused Loewe a loss of $80,000 and applied the Sherman Act's triple damage clause to the union. This case, more than any other, forced unions into the political arena. The Clayton Act (1914) reflected union lobbying and largely exempted labor activity from the provisions of the Sherman Act. Today, union weapons such as strikes and boycotts are legal.

Union growth during the 1920s was hampered when firms aggressively resisted union organizing efforts. Unions were labeled un-American, and yellow-dog contracts were standard operating procedure. Violent strikes, notably the Boston Police strike of 1919, fostered anti-union sentiment. Demands for the services of skilled workers from craft unions fell as mass production spread. Prosperity also aggravated declines in union membership because booming wages and job security left industrial workers content.

The Great Depression softened the mood of the country toward unionism. Believing they were on the brink of disaster, many workers collectively acted to buffer the chaos of the business cycle, and total union membership tripled between 1933 and 1940. Organizing drives were aided by passage of the Wagner Act in 1935. This prolabor legislation guaranteed the right to organize unions and made it an unfair labor practice for a firm to refuse to negotiate with a union supported by a majority of its workers.

The percentage of trade union membership within the labor force continued to grow through the 1940s, but the Wagner Act was widely viewed as too biased in favor of unions. Dissatisfaction with what were felt to be labor abuses during organizing campaigns resulted in passage of the Taft-Hartley Act (1947), which outlawed secondary boycotts (refusals by union members of one firm to handle any intermediate products produced by other firms that were being struck) and jurisdictional strikes (where the only issue was which union would represent workers), and which also permitted states to pass right-to-work laws forbidding union shops.

Although many people fear that unions are growing increasingly powerful, their influence is probably waning. Union membership faltered in the 1950s, and again through the 1980s, as shown in Figure 8. A major problem facing union organizers is the grow-

4. William Miernyk, *The Economics of Labor and Collective Bargaining* (Lexington, MA: Heath, 1965), 14.

5. *Loewe v. Lawlor,* 208 U.S. 274 (1908).

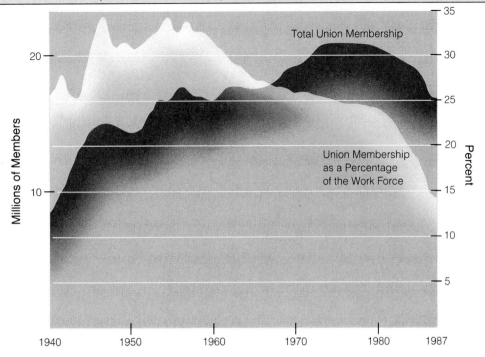

Total union membership has been falling in recent years, but, because the labor force has grown substantially, union membership as a percentage of the work force has been declining even faster.

Source: Bureau of Labor Statistics, *Employment and Earnings,* January, 1988.

ing importance of white-collar workers, who tend to be less enthusiastic about union membership. Some of the chronology of the union movement is detailed in Table 4. With this brief history in mind, we now turn our attention to effects of unions that extend beyond the unionized sectors of the economy.

Economic Effects of Labor Unions

[U]nions . . . receive more credit and at the same time more blame than they deserve.
— *Gary Becker*[6]

In addition to concerns about the political power of large unions, opponents of unions worry about three possible economic effects of unions (*a*) distorted wage structures, (*b*) inflationary pressure, and (*c*) disruption caused by strikes.

6. G. S. Becker, "It's Time to Scrap a Few Outmoded Labor Laws," *Business Week,* 7 March 1988, 18.

Union-Nonunion Wage Differentials   Most people believe that unions can raise their members' wages substantially over nonunion wages. Figure 9 illustrates how a **union-nonunion wage differential** can develop. Assume that markets for union (*U*) and nonunion (*NU*) workers are initially identical, with 20 million workers employed in each sector at a wage of w_e. Total employment equals 40 million. The markets for union and nonunion workers are illustrated in Panels A and B, respectively.

If negotiation raised union members' wages to w_1, 5 million (20 million − 15 million) union workers would be disemployed. After all, one cost of higher wages is less employment. As these workers abandon the job market or seek nonunion jobs, the supply of union labor falls to S_1. Nonunion wages drop to allow the absorption of some of the 5 million disemployed union workers. The nonunion wage would shrink to w_2 as the nonunion labor supply swells to S_2, amplifying the wage differential. Note that total employment falls a bit because some people disemployed

TABLE 4 Important Events in American Labor History

1778— Journeymen printers of New York City united to demand increases in wages, but their organization disintegrated after the increase was granted.

1786— Philadelphia printers gained a minimum wage of $6 a week in the nation's earliest authenticated strike.

1806— The Philadelphia Journeymen Cordwainers went bankrupt after members were found guilty of conspiracy following a strike for higher wages.

1834— The National Trades Union formed as the first national labor federation, but failed to survive the financial panic of 1837.

1842— In *Commonwealth* v. *Hunt*, the Massachusetts Court held labor unions to be legal organizations. Massachusetts and Connecticut laws prohibited children from working more than 10 hours a day.

1862— The "Molly Maguires," a secret society of Irish coal miners, were charged with acts of terrorism against mine bosses; 14 of their leaders were imprisoned and 10 were executed.

1869— The Knights of Labor organized, gaining 700,000 followers by winning railroad strikes and advocating the 8-hour day.

1884— A Bureau of Labor was formed in the Department of Interior, growing into the Department of Labor in 1913.

1886— One policeman was killed and several were wounded in the Chicago Haymarket riot arousing public opinion against unionism and radicalism and retarding the drive for the 8-hour day. The American Federation of Labor (AFL) was founded.

1890— The United Mine Workers first organized in Columbus, Ohio.

1894— The American Railway Union struck the Pullman Co., but was defeated by injunctions and by Federal troops. Eugene V. Debs and several other leaders were imprisoned.

1908— The United Hatters' boycott of D. E. Loewe and Co. was held to be in restraint of trade under the Sherman Antitrust Act.

1912— Massachusetts passed a minimum wage for women and minors.

1914— The Clayton Act limited the use of injunctions in labor disputes and legalized picketing and other union activities.

1917— A strike by copper miners from the Industrial Workers of the World (IWW) was ended when an Arizona sheriff deported 1,200 "wobbly" strikers. Union efforts to organize workers signing "yellow-dog" contracts were held to be unlawful (*Hitchman Coal* v. *Mitchell*).

1921— The Supreme Court held that nothing in the Clayton Act legalized secondary boycotts (*Duplex* v. *Deering*).

1933— Frances Perkins became Secretary of Labor, the first woman named to the Cabinet.

1935— The National Labor Relations (Wagner) Act established nationally the right of workers to organize unions.
The Social Security Act was approved August 14.
The Congress of Industrial Organizations (CIO) was formed to foster industrial unionism.

1937— General Motors agreed to recognize the United Automobile Workers and U.S. Steel recognized the Steel Workers Organizing Committee as the bargaining agents for their members.

1946— The Employment Act of 1946 committed the Government to promote maximum employment, production, and purchasing power.

1947— The Taft-Hartley Act forbade closed shops and secondary boycotts, and permitted states to pass "right-to-work" laws eliminating union shops.

1949— An amendment to the Fair Labor Standards Act (1938) directly limited child labor for the first time.

1953— The Supreme Court upheld the right of the International Typographical Union (AFL) to compel a newspaper to pay for setting unused type, and of the American Federation of Musicians (AFL) to demand that a local "standby" orchestra be employed when a traveling orchestra was hired. The Court said that neither practice violated the "featherbedding" ban in the Taft-Hartley Act.

1955— Merger of the American Federation of Labor and Congress of Industrial Organizations (AFL-CIO) brought under one roof unions representing approximately 16 million workers—over 85 percent of all union members in the United States.

1959— The Labor-Management Reporting and Disclosure (Landrum-Griffin) Act specified as illegal certain improper activities by labor or management.

1962— The Manpower Development and Training Act required the Federal Government to "deal with . . . unemployment resulting from automation and technological changes."
Federal employees' unions were granted the right to bargain collectively with government agencies.

1963— The Equal Pay Act of 1963 prohibited wage differentials based on sex for workers covered by the Fair Labor Standards Act.

1964— The Civil Rights Act of 1964 barred employment discrimination on the basis of race, color, religion, sex, or national origin.

1965— "Medicare" first provided partial coverage for those over 65 for most medical expenses.

1968— The Age Discrimination in Employment Act made it illegal to discharge, refuse to hire, or otherwise discriminate against persons aged 40 to 65.

1970— The first mass work stoppage in the 195-year history of the Post Office Department involved nearly one third of all postal employees, virtually paralyzing mail service.
The Occupational Safety and Health Act established safety and health standards in the nation's workplaces.

1974— The Social Security Act for the first time provided for automatic cost-of-living adjustments.

1975— Interns and residents backed by the AMA struck 22 hospitals in New York.

1981— Air traffic controllers represented by PATCO illegally struck and many of these federal employees were fired.

1982— Union membership falls below 20 percent of the labor force for the first time since the Great Depression.

1988— The United Automobile Workers and General Motors attempt a new form of labor-management relations known as "jointness" and industrial democracy.

---

from the union sector will be unwilling to work at this depressed nonunion wage rate.

Two surveys by H. Gregg Lewis (1963 and 1986, respectively), summarized more than 200 studies of the relative wage effects of unions during the period 1920–1979. Lewis placed the average wage gap in the 15–20 percent range, varying from a Depression-era high of almost 50 percent to a low of 2 percent fol-

lowing World War II.[7] Lewis's work suggests that wage gaps are greatest during economic downturns and least during periods of economic prosperity. He estimates that during 1967–79, the average wage gap

---

7. H. G. Lewis, *Unionism and Relative Wages in the United States: An Empirical Inquiry*, 1963, Chapter V and *Union Relative Wage Effects: A Survey*, 1986, (both from Chicago: The University of Chicago Press).

FIGURE 9 *Union and Nonunion Wage Differentials*

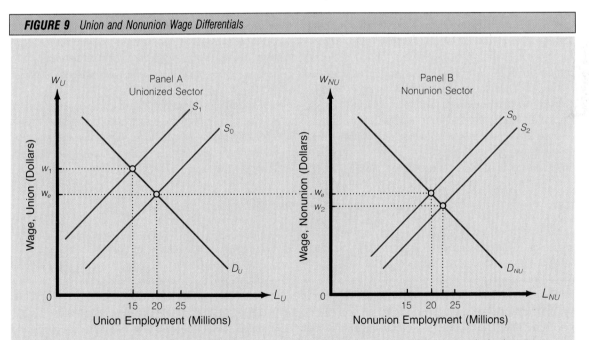

Restricting the supply of labor may cause union wages to rise (Panel A), but flows of labor into the nonunionized sector may cause nonunion wages to fall (Panel B). Thus, unions probably change the distribution but not the average level of wages.

was 15 percent. The sharp decline in unionization during the 1980s, however, may mean that union-nonunion wage gaps have been falling. Lewis noted that this wage gap varies substantially, however, and appears to be affected by geographic region, the type of job, and such characteristics of typical workers as marital status, race, health, and age. This gap widens as an industry becomes relatively more unionized and narrows when unemployment in an industry grows, or if most firms in an industry are larger, or when typical workers are relatively more educated.

Many people think that unions have boosted the wages of most workers. If this were true, then union-ism would increase labor's share of national income. Numerous studies indicate that this has not occurred historically, nor is labor relatively better paid in countries that are more unionized when compared with countries where unions are less important. You should remember, also, that union wage differentials are created in part by depressing the wages of workers in nonunionized sectors of the economy.

Unions and Inflation

Some opponents of unions rant and rave that curing inflation requires controlling "those *#@&$%&! unions." Inflation is blamed on unions on the theory that, through collective bargaining or strikes, they artificially boost wages. Firms then pass these higher costs forward by charging higher prices, stimulating unions to demand higher wages to offset their members' losses due to inflation, and so on. This high-wage/higher-price/higher-wage spiral is thought by many to be the principal cause of inflation in the United States.

Critics of this analysis point out that unions represent under 20 percent of all workers and argue that union wage hikes can only raise prices modestly. If union labor absorbs 20 percent of all production costs and unions negotiate 10 percent wage hikes, output prices need only rise by 2 percent on the average. Moreover, they might point to Figure 9 and argue that union wage hikes are largely offset by the resulting reductions in nonunion wages. Blaming rapid inflation on unions is ludicrous in the eyes of these critics.

One rebuttal is that this analysis ignores union strength in such key industries as steel, automobiles, chemicals, and crucial inputs for other sectors of the economy. Higher wage costs and prices for major intermediate goods ripple through the economy as upward price pressures on all outputs. Union wages are, moreover, standards for many nonunion firms that match collective bargaining agreements to avoid unionization of their workers. Finally, if higher wages create massive unemployment and the federal government responds with expansionary macroeconomic policies, there is a classic supply-side inflation cycle. The debate surrounding the impact of union wage increases on inflation will probably continue for as long as unions exist.

Losses from Strikes

Unions are blamed for innumerable economic woes. One question that arises is: If unions represent only one worker in five, how can they cause rapid inflation, economic chaos from strikes, and other social ills? Economists lack consensus about unions, but most believe their impact is exaggerated. Strikes and the closed-door collective bargaining process make juicy material for the media. Publicity often makes union organizing and bargaining look like bloody battles. Collective bargaining is a frustrating process, but it works most of the time. Only about 2–4 percent of all negotiations result in strikes, and most of these last less than two weeks, as Figure 10 illustrates.

Most strikes occur because the bargaining parties fail to agree about wage issues. The other major causes of strikes are union organization and security; administration of such things as work rules, overtime questions, or safety; interunion and intraunion matters (union rivalry, assignment of work between competing unions, sympathy strikes); and job security disputes.

Strikes may have significant costs beyond the income lost by the strikers. When Teamsters stage a nationwide shut-down, businesses incur higher costs in getting their products to customers. Some sales may be lost because of inability to meet delivery deadlines. After a strike is settled, most firms recoup through increased shipments, and all that is suffered is delay. But this is not always the case. Strikes by farmworkers may leave crops rotting on the ground. Consumer goods, homes, and capital equipment go up in smoke when fire fighters strike. Strikes that reduce supplies cause consumers to bear the costs as higher prices and lower consumption.

Collective bargaining between union and management is now an accepted way to set wage rates and working conditions. Strikes and economic disruption are the prices we pay for this social institution, which has recently expanded to the government sector.

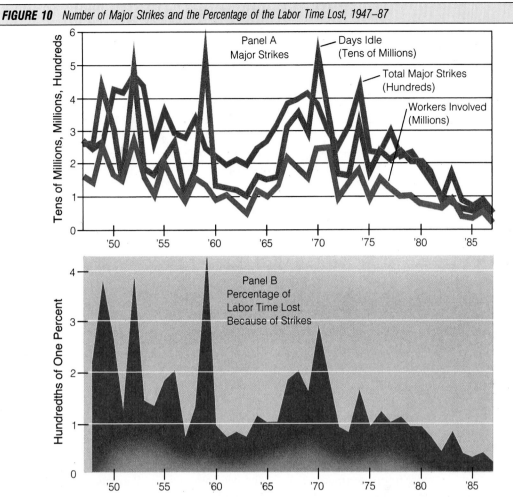

FIGURE 10 Number of Major Strikes and the Percentage of the Labor Time Lost, 1947–87

Only a small percentage of the work force is on strike during any given year, and most of these strikes last only a short period. Although some of the numbers in Panel A seem large, Panel B indicates that well under 1 percent of labor time is lost because of strikes.

Source: U.S. Department of Labor, Bureau of Labor Statistics, *Current Wage Developments,* February, 1988.

Public Employee Unions

The National Labor Relations Act gave private sector employees the right to organize and compels management to bargain in good faith with the workers' elected representatives, but it originally exempted government workers. Public sector unions were almost nonexistent until 1962, when then President Kennedy issued an executive order granting federal Civil Service employees the right to organize—public employee unions spread across the land. Strikes and wage negotiations were prohibited, but unions now bargain about federal policies governing such issues as promotions, discharges, transfers, or leaves of absence. Unless state or local legislation recognizes their public employee unions, however, the rules of the game are often remnants left over from the nineteenth century.

The public has traditionally opposed strikes by public employees, especially teachers, nurses, fire fighters, and police officers. Statutes generally forbid strikes by public employees and substitute binding arbitration as a means of resolving conflicts. Nonetheless, strikes do occur. Figure 11 indicates that public sector unions and strike activity grew for two decades after Kennedy signed the executive order authorizing public unions.

Public employees mix collective bargaining with old-fashioned politics to pressure elected officials into meeting their demands. Authority often is split

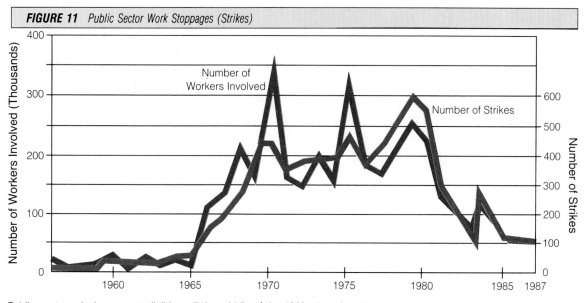

FIGURE 11 Public Sector Work Stoppages (Strikes)

Public sector unionism was negligible until the middle of the 1960s, but since then, strikes by fire fighters, police officers, and teachers have all become increasingly common.

Source: U.S. Department of Labor, *Handbook of Labor Statistics*, 1988. Updated by authors.

between executive and legislative branches, posing major problems for public sector negotiations. One organization may have authority to negotiate, while another must approve pay hikes via government budgets. Public employees often exert pressures to raise wages (or their shares of the budget) by having officials discontinue some other service.

Public sector bargaining may continue to grow as taxpayers demand ever more from government and, therefore, more from government employees. A case where public union militance backfired was the air traffic controllers union (PATCO), which violated court orders not to strike in 1981. Strikers lost their jobs, and their union was abolished. The conflict between taxpayer demands for lower taxes and increased services on the one hand and public employ-

ee demands expressed through their unions on the other will remain troublesome for government at all levels over the next few years.

This chapter has explored the effects on wages and employment when concentrated economic power is wielded in labor markets by resource buyers (monopoly power and monopsony) or resource seller—primarily, unions. The markets for land, entrepreneurship, and capital examined in the next chapter tend to be far more competitive, but you may find a few cases where some of the analysis of this chapter seems to apply. More normally, markets for nonlabor resources tend to operate according to the marginal productivity theory introduced in the previous chapter, but each does so in its own unique way.

CHAPTER REVIEW: KEY POINTS

1. The *marginal revenue product* (*MRP*) curve for a firm selling in an imperfectly competitive product market will be below the *value of the marginal product of labor* (*VMP*) curve. All firms will hire labor until the marginal revenue product equals the *marginal factor cost* (*MFC*) of labor. Because

MRP < *VMP* for employees of firms with monopoly power, they are paid less than the values of their marginal products. This difference is called *monopolistic exploitation.*

2. A *monopsonist* is the sole buyer of a particular resource or good. Labor monopsonists face an entire market supply of labor and, if all workers are paid equally, their marginal factor cost curve will lie above the labor supply curve. Relative to pure competitors, labor monopsonists pay lower wages and hire fewer workers. In addition, labor will be paid less than the value of its marginal product, a difference referred to as *monopsonistic exploitation.*

3. When competitive conditions prevail in both resource and product markets, the firm hires labor until $VMP = MRP = MFC = w$. When monopoly prevails in the product market but the monopoly firm hires labor under competitive conditions, labor is hired up to the point where $VMP > MRP = MFC = w$. Given a competitive product market and monopsony power in the labor market, a firm will maximize profits by hiring labor until $VMP = MRP = MFC > w$. Finally, when a firm has both monopoly and monopsony power, labor is hired up to the point where $VMP > MRP = MFC > w$. Any difference between VMP and w represents *exploitation,* a term borrowed from Marxist jargon.

4. A minimum wage legally set above the equilibrium wage in competitive labor markets will raise unemployment. It is possible, but unlikely, that minimum wages might increase employment and wages simultaneously, but only where there is substantial monopsonistic exploitation of unskilled workers and wage discrimination is not practiced, an unlikely combination. A union wage hike might have the same effect. The markets where minimum-wage hikes raise existing wages are typically rather competitive. Thus, increased unemployment is the normal result when minimum wages are increased.

5. *Bilateral monopoly,* a very early model of collective bargaining, describes the limits to the wage bargaining process but provides little predictive power. Sir John Hicks's bargaining model predicts both final wage settlements and the duration of strikes.

6. *Labor unions* have typically employed three methods to increase the wages of their members (*a*) reductions of the supply of workers to an industry; (*b*) establishing higher wages and then parceling the available work to members; and (*c*) policies designed to increase demands for union labor.

7. Unions have traditionally organized into craft or industrial unions. Craft unions were the bulwark of the *American Federation of Labor* (*AFL*); industrial unions comprised the *Congress of Industrial Organizations* (*CIO*). Frequent jurisdictional disputes over which organization would represent particular workers caused the two to merge into the AFL-CIO in 1955.

8. Unions and their leaders use several kinds of agreements with organized firms to protect their prerog-

atives as sole bargaining agents for workers. *Closed shops* require workers to be union members as a precondition for employment. At the other end of the spectrum, *open shops* permit union and nonunion members to work side by side. This arrangement is quite unsatisfactory to unions since nonmembers receive the benefits of collective bargaining but need not pay union dues. *Union shops* are compromises between closed and open shops. The employer can hire union or nonunion workers, but an employee must join the union within some specified period (usually thirty days) to retain the job. The Taft-Hartley Act of 1947 outlawed the closed shop and permitted individual states to pass right-to-work laws forbidding union shops. In many of these states, *agency shops* have been created to protect unions from free riders. Workers may choose not to belong to the union but must pay dues.

9. Unionism developed in a hostile environment. The Great Depression shifted public policy in favor of collective bargaining. As trade unionism grew, many felt that unions became corrupt and too powerful, and tighter organizing and financial reporting constraints were imposed on labor organizations. The union movement was relatively stable from roughly 1950 until 1980, but has declined as a percentage of the total labor force in the 1980s. The labor force increasingly consists of white-collar workers who are reluctant to join unions.

10. *Wage differentials* between union and nonunion workers average roughly 10–15 percent. Some people blame inflation on excessive union wage demands. Large wage hikes in key industries may set the pattern for other industries. Higher wages may raise unemployment and induce public officials to pursue expansionary macroeconomic policies, further intensifying inflationary pressures. Since organized labor represents less than one sixth of the work force, it is unlikely that unionism explains much inflation.

11. A small percentage of collective bargaining negotiations end in *strikes,* and most are short. Strikes often impose costs on individuals and firms that are not direct parties to labor negotiations. Strikes may cause shortages, shipping delays, or losses of perishable products.

12. Public sector unions have been growing in recent years. Public employee unions frequently mix politics and collective bargaining to win their demands. Public officials negotiating contracts are seldom those who are responsible for developing government budgets; thus, they may have only weak incentives to resist union wage demands.

PROBLEMS

1. Use this information about output and the demand for dehydrated water to answer the following questions:

Labor	Output	Price
0	0	—
1	60	200
2	100	180
3	136	160
4	168	140
5	196	120
6	220	100
7	240	80

   a. Compute and graph Marginal Revenue Product and the Value of the Marginal Product of labor.
   b. If labor is purchased from a competitive market and wage rates are $400 per unit, how many units of labor will you employ?
   c. Given the employment equilibrium in (b), what is the extent of your monopolistic exploitation?

2. Suppose that all of your competitors for the services of professional water dehydrators go bankrupt and you become a monopsonist facing the following labor supply schedule:

Labor	Wage Rate
0	—
1	200
2	300
3	400
4	800
5	1,200
6	1,500
7	1,800

   a. How many workers will you employ now that you are a monopsonist?
   b. What is the extent of both monopolistic and monopsonistic exploitation in this instance?

QUESTIONS FOR THOUGHT AND DISCUSSION

1. Some economists insist that there are so many "greedy capitalists" that exploitation and wage discrimination are impossible. How might competitive drives for profits ensure that everyone is paid "what they're worth"? How do we account for wage differentials between sexes and races? If vigorous competition leads to payment of the value of the marginal product?

2. Many firms view salary information as confidential. Can you cite reasons for this practice other than wage discrimination? Do you believe these other reasons are valid?

3. If most firms in certain highly competitive industries (e.g., textiles) monopolistically exploit their employees and wage discriminate, what would happen to employment if they were forced to quit these practices? Would their current workers be better off? Why or why not?

4. Some people think that wage structures are compressed relative to workers' productivities. In other words, people with high incomes tend to be under-paid relative to their productivity, while those at the bottom of the pay scale are overpaid relative to their productive contribution. Do you think these critics are correct? If so, what does this suggest about the extent of competition in labor markets? If you think that reality is the opposite of this idea, what features of the labor market cause overpayment of people with relatively high salaries and underpayment of people with relatively low wage incomes?

5. The standard model of monopsony leads to substantial underemployment relative to competition and opens up the possibility that minimum-wage laws may expand employment. Can you use logic paralleling the discussion of price discrimination from our chapter on monopoly to show that perfect wage discrimination will cause a monopsonist to hire the same amount of labor as would be employed in a purely competitive labor market? What are the implications of this analysis for economic efficiency? Equity? Do you think that firms having monopsony power also typically have the ability to

wage discriminate? Which do you think more common, monopsony power or the ability to wage discriminate by paying workers in inverse proportion to their desperation for employment?

6. Some economists argue that by permitting collective bargaining, we condone monopoly despite Sherman Antitrust Act prohibitions of monopolies. Is there anything inherently more palatable about labor monopolies than about product monopolies? By encouraging unions to expand through various laws protecting collective bargaining, are we creating what John Kenneth Galbraith has called "countervailing power," where big unions bargaining for workers offset the effects of concentrated industry? Is there any reason to suspect the two forces, big labor and big business, will not combine like OPEC to gouge the little consumer? What forces, if any, keep this from happening?

7. Between 1980 and 1988, union membership had declined to less than 15 percent of the labor force. What do you think accounts for the reduction in union membership during this period? Do you foresee labor unions recovering from this decline, or will it continue? Why do you think so?

8. Right-to-work laws presently exist in nineteen states. Since they outlaw the union shop, how can unions in these states protect themselves from free riders? What arguments can you make in favor of right-to-work laws? Against? More than one student of labor relations actions has commented that the name *right-to-work* was a stroke of genius; that without it few people would vote for the legislation. Are right-to-work laws appropriately named? Why or why not?

9. The Taft-Hartley Act outlaws the closed shop, yet, in some industries or occupations it is virtually impossible to find employment unless you belong to a union. Are these unions doing something illegal? How do you explain this apparent contradiction between the law and reality? Why would employers agree to hire only union members if they did not have to?

10. Some economists argue that the most effective union to date is the American Medical Association. Do you agree? Does the AMA operate like a labor union? In what ways? Name some other professional societies that perform the same functions as unions for their members. Should these associations be subjected to the same democratic standards and financial reporting standards that are applied to unions? How do you think medical doctors would feel if the AMA changed its name to United Medical Doctors of America, Amalgamated Brotherhood of Medical Doctors, or some similar moniker?

National Labor Relations Board v. Bildisco & Bildisco (1984)

On April 14, 1980, Bildisco and Bildisco (Bildisco), in the business of distributing building supplies, filed a voluntary petition in bankruptcy for reorganization under Chapter 11 of the Bankruptcy Code. Bildisco was subsequently authorized by the Bankruptcy Court to operate the business as debtor-in-possession.

At the time of the filing of the petition in bankruptcy, approximately 40 to 45 percent of Bildisco's labor force was represented by Local 408 of the International Brotherhood of Teamsters, Chauffeurs, Warehousemen and Helpers of America (Union). Bildisco has negotiated a 3-year collective-bargaining agreement with the Union that was to expire on April 30, 1982, and which expressly provided that it was binding on the parties and their successors even though bankruptcy should supervene. Beginning in January 1980, Bildisco failed to meet some of its obligations under the collective-bargaining agreement, including the payment of health and pension benefits and the remittance to the Union of dues collected under the agreement. In May 1980, Bildisco refused to pay wage increases called for in the collective-bargaining agreement.

In December 1980, Bildisco requested permission from the Bankruptcy Court, to reject the collective-bargaining agreement. Bildisco testified that rejection would save the company approximately $100,000 in 1981. On January 15, 1981, the Bankruptcy Court granted Bildisco permission to reject the collective-bargaining agreement.

During midsummer 1980, the Union filed unfair labor practice charges with the National Labor Relations Board (Board). The Board found that Bildisco had violated the National Labor Relations Act (NLRA), by unilaterally changing the terms of the collective-bargaining agreement and by refusing to negotiate with the Union. Bildisco was ordered to make the pension, health, and welfare contributions and to remit dues to the Union, all as required under the collective-bargaining agreement. The Board petitioned the Court of Appeals to enforce its order.

The Court of Appeals held that a collective-bargaining agreement is a contract subject to rejection by a debtor-in-possession under the Bankruptcy Code. The authority of the debtor-in-possession to seek rejection of the collective-bargaining agreement was not qualified by the restrictions of the NLRA, which established detailed guidelines for mid-term modification of collective-bargaining agreements because in the court's view, the debtor-in-possession was a "new entity" not bound by the labor agreement. The Court of Appeals concluded, however, that given the favored status Congress has accorded collective-bargaining agreements, a debtor-in-possession had to meet a more stringent test than the usual "business judgment" rule to obtain rejection. The Court of Appeals required the debtor-in-possession to show not only that the collective-bargaining agreement is burdensome to the estate, but also that the equities balance in favor of rejection.

The Court of Appeals refused to enforce the Board's order, rejecting the Board's conclusion that Bildisco, as debtor-in-possession, was the alter ego of the employer, not a "new entity" not bound by the debtor's prior collective-bargaining agreement.

Our determination that a debtor-in-possession does not commit an unfair labor practice by failing to comply with the collective-bargaining agreement does not undermine the policy of the NLRA, for that policy, as we have noted, is to protect the process of labor negotiations, not to impose particular results on the parties. Nevertheless, it is important to note that the debtor-in-possession is not relieved of all obligations under the NLRA simply by filing a petition for bankruptcy. A debtor-in-possession is an "employer" within the terms of the NLRA, and is obligated to bargain collectively with the employees' certified representative over the terms of a new contract pending rejection of the existing contract or following formal approval or rejection by the Bankruptcy Court.

Accordingly, the judgment of the Court of Appeals is Affirmed.

Questions

1. Has the Supreme Court provided a convenient method by which companies can "bust" a union using the bankruptcy laws?

2. The Court suggests that collective bargaining agreements can be voided by a bankruptcy court if the "equities balance in favor of rejection." What factors do you think the Court would look at to determine if this qualification is met?

3. What alternatives are open to the union to prevent rejection of the contract?

4. If the Court had sided with the NRLB (Board), what incentive would there be for unions to negotiate with firms facing bankruptcy?

CHAPTER 30

economic rent
nominal interest rates
real interest rates
economic profit
innovation
risk
uncertainty
capitalization
present value
rates of return

Rent, Interest, Profits, and Capitalization

Market forces shape land rents, interest on capital, and the profits of entrepreneurs much as they determine workers' wages. The derived demands for all these resources are based on the prices of output and each resource's marginal contribution in producing the goods consumers want. Producing the goods people want most requires altering materials so that they become more valuable in form, space, time, or possession. Market prices direct these transformations.

Resources are also altered to make them more valuable. For example, acquiring human capital is a way to make an individual's labor more valuable. Most workers try to learn skills that will increase their wage incomes. Similarly, the drive to increase their incomes cause the owners of nonlabor resources to mold their assets to accomplish economic tasks. Investment in capital, for example, can take innumerable forms; whether new capital will be new punch presses, buildings, measuring instruments, bulldoz-

ers, hand tools, or industrial robots depends on the form of capital its owners expect to be most profitable. Entrepreneurs try to develop special expertise in forms of production that they expect to become most profitable, and land owners plant or sculpt their acreage or build shopping malls on it so that their land is most valuably used.

You may be surprised to learn that the markets for capital, land, and entrepreneurial talents tend to be even more competitive than labor markets. Mobility is a key. Workers tend to be bounded geographically and by habit, but investors compete in international markets—rapidly channeling financial capital between investments when even slight differentials arise in rates of return; economic capital follows soon thereafter. Entrepreneurs also respond quickly to the slightest whiff of a profit opportunity. Although land cannot move geographically, flows of other resources when higher resource payments beckon make land mobile between uses if not spaces.

As you proceed through this chapter, keep in mind that markets for capital, entrepreneurship, and land are all relatively competitive and tend to conform to the principles of marginal productivity theory discussed earlier.

Resource Ratios and Productivity

We indicated earlier that the amounts of other resources used in a production process are major determinants of labor productivity. For example, even unskilled workers in the United States work with much more capital and consequently produce far more than their counterparts in, say, India. Thus, American trash collectors each process more garbage than Indian trash collectors because Americans use more trucks, crushers, and other equipment. The relatively high amount of capital per worker in industrialized countries is a major reason that workers in advanced nations enjoy higher wages on average than those paid to workers in less developed economies.

The flip side of this is that capital productivity rises as the number of workers per machine grows. Large amounts of capital per worker in the United States mean that the amount of labor per unit of capital is low relative to less developed countries such as India. Thus, while output per worker is high in the United States relative to India, output per unit of capital is probably higher in India. In the United States, hand shovels are often idle on big construction projects; in India, a shovel typically is more productive and might be used for three shifts every day.

Figure 1 indicates that as capital per worker (K/L) grows, the average physical product of labor (Q/L, or output per worker) grows, but the average physical product of capital (Q/K, or output per unit of capital) falls. Similar relationships hold for marginal physical products (MPPs) and factor payments. The upshot of this is that labor productivity and wages tend to be higher the greater the capital-to-labor ratio, while interest payments and the productivity of capital tend to be higher the lower the capital-to-labor ratio.

The concept described here holds for virtually all resource ratios: (a) capital is more productive and highly paid the greater the amounts of labor, entre-

FIGURE 1 Outputs per Unit of Input Depend on Capital-to-Labor Ratios

More capital per worker raises wages and worker productivity (whether measured by APP_L or MPP_L), while low amounts of capital per worker causes capital to be more productive, but workers to be less productive. Recall that the average physical product of labor (APP_L) equals output per unit of labor (Q/L), and that the average physical product of capital (APP_K) equals output per unit of capital (Q/K).

preneurial talent, or land working with capital; (b) entrepreneurs will be more productive and highly remunerated the fewer the entrepreneurs attempting to use other given resources; and (c) land will be more productive and draw higher rents the more capital and labor are used to work the land. For example, relative to vast desolate ranches on which a few cowhands try to keep track of a few scattered cattle, small flower farms covered with greenhouses and automatic watering equipment that use large amounts of hand gardening produce much more valuable output per acre.

Although the general principles of marginal productivity govern labor, land, capital, and entrepreneurial talent, each market has unique characteristics. You have already explored some specifics of labor markets in the last two chapters, so we will now examine these other markets.

Economic Rents

When you hear the word rent, you probably think of payments to landlords, the price you pay for the temporary use of a videotape, or a truck or trailer at the local "Rent-All." As seems too often true, economists have taken a perfectly good word, rent, and attached their own special meaning to it.

> **Economic rent** *is realized whenever the owner of any resource is paid more than the minimum amount necessary to elicit the quantity supplied of that productive resource.*

Thus, economic rent is a broad concept that applies to parts of many payments to resource owners.

Economic rents may have little to do with apartment leases or similar "rental" values. For example, many rock musicians often spend years "paying their dues"—working for peanuts in smoke-filled bars and generally hustling just to get by. If they hit it big and begin to pull down seven figures annually, there is an enormous difference between their superstar incomes and the small amounts for which they were once willing to play music. Economists view such differences as economic rents. Land is about the only resource, however, that generates "pure" economic rents.

Pure Land Rents

Land has the unique characteristic that its supply is absolutely fixed. The amount of land available to society cannot change even if payments to landowners ranged from zero to infinity; its supply is perfectly inelastic at Q_s in Figure 2. If demand is D_0, rent per acre will be τ_0 and total rent is area $0Q_s a\tau_0$. If the price of output produced on this land rose or a technological advance enhanced land's physical productivity, raising the derived demand for land to D_1, rent per acre would rise to τ_1, yielding total rent equal to the area $0Q_s b\tau_1$. What will the rent for raw land be if demand is D_2? Zero, and some land will be idle. All payments received for the fixed supply of land are pure rents determined solely by the strength of demand.

The clearest examples of pure economic rents are payments for the use of unimproved land. Note that when people construct dikes or drain swamps, they create capital, not new land. (Recall that any improvement that increases the productivity of natural resources is classified as capital.) Consequently, the supply of land is perfectly inelastic. Changes in demand will result in proportional changes in the economic rents for land. The demand and rental rates for different parcels of land differ according to their location and their physical characteristics.

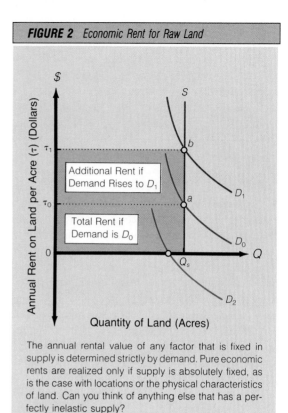

FIGURE 2 *Economic Rent for Raw Land*

The annual rental value of any factor that is fixed in supply is determined strictly by demand. Pure economic rents are realized only if supply is absolutely fixed, as is the case with locations or the physical characteristics of land. Can you think of anything else that has a perfectly inelastic supply?

Location Rents   Why is a vacant square block in Manhattan worth more than an acre of prime Kansas wheat land? Transportation costs are a major reason. Looked at from a different perspective, the customer populations differ, causing different values. One facet of *location rents* is that if a seller can locate so that customers bear lower transportation costs than are incurred in buying from a competitor, the advantageously located seller can charge more for a product.

Suppose that you owned an isolated Kansas farm and replicated a chunk of downtown Manhattan on the north forty, including a hamburger stand. If you cut the price charge at the New York hamburger stand by half and put on an advertising campaign worthy of Ronald McDonald, your sales would fall far short of those by your New York rival. The reason is that for the average hamburger buyer, the total cost of a hamburger (including transportation costs) would be far less at the New York stand than at yours. New Yorkers would become regular customers only if you charged such a low price for hamburgers that transportation costs were overcome. Fat chance!

Another facet of location rents is that a firm is able to pay lower prices for inputs if it locates so that its input suppliers (workers, for example) gain from lower transportation costs than would be incurred from selling to a competing firm. When being in busi-ness at a particular location gives a firm the ability to charge more or to pay less, the owner of the location will become aware of these advantages and charge rents sufficiently high that only normal profits are received by the firm.

For example, suppose you leased a building in a rundown area of Chicago and established a fancy French restaurant. Then suppose that a huge luxury hotel unexpectedly located in the next block—busi-ness would boom and you might profit substantially in the short run. When your lease was up, however, your landlord would raise your rent to exploit the increased profitability of the location. Economic rents of this type are known as *location* or *site rents* and are illustrated in Figure 3.

FIGURE 3 *Value of an Acre of Land, Depending upon Location*

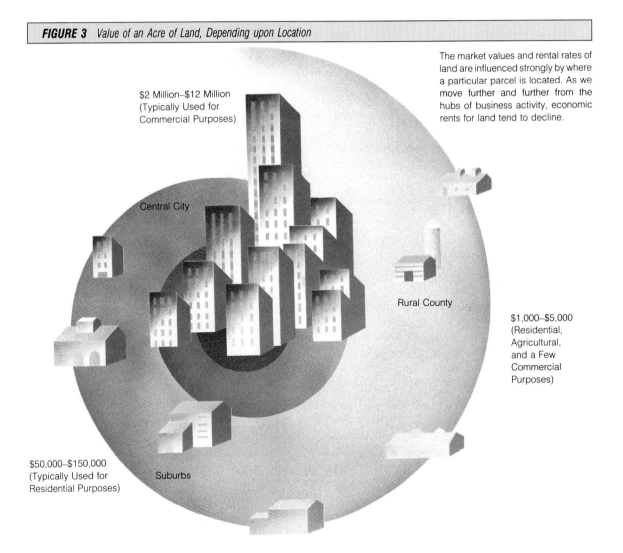

$2 Million–$12 Million
(Typically Used for
Commercial Purposes)

Central City

Rural County

$1,000–$5,000
(Residential,
Agricultural,
and a Few
Commercial
Purposes)

$50,000–$150,000
(Typically Used for
Residential Purposes)

Suburbs

The market values and rental rates of land are influenced strongly by where a particular parcel is located. As we move further and further from the hubs of business activity, economic rents for land tend to decline.

Rents from Physical Characteristics   Marginal productivities and the rental rates of parcels of land reflect differences in fertility or the values of minerals they bear. Some land is not used at all. Windswept deserts and arctic tundra are examples of land so barren and remote that its marginal productivity is effectively zero.

David Ricardo, who originated the theory of pure rent, observed that marginal (barely useful) land commands zero rent whenever equally productive parcels are vacant. For example, you could always live "rent free" at an oasis in the Sahara if at least one comparable oasis were vacant. If the owner tried to charge any positive rent, you would move to a vacant oasis. The production cost saved by using more productive land versus marginal land equals the rental value per period of the more productive land.

Competition for the cost reducing qualities of particular land permits a landowner to charge rent that reflects the productivity differences between the superior land and the marginal (zero rent) land. Ricardo viewed land rent as an **unearned surplus** because the fixed supply of land would be available even at a zero price. Henry George gained fame by arguing that this unearned surplus to landowners could be taxed without creating economic inefficiency. (See his Biography.)

Rents to Other Resources

The concept of economic rent orginated with David Ricardo's analysis of corn and the land used to produce it. Economic rents are received, however, whenever a resource owner is paid more than the minimum amount necessary to induce a given quantity of the resource. Thus, many owners of scarce resources or talents earn economic rents. The economic rents received when resource supply curves are imperfectly elastic are illustrated in Figure 4, which portrays a positively sloped labor supply curve for professional wrestlers. Equilibrium occurs at point *e* when 450 wrestlers work for annual incomes averaging $80,000, but only very reluctant wrestlers (those making up the labor supply near point *e*) are paid the bare minimums necessary for their services. Other wrestlers would work for less and so receive economic rents as surpluses above their minimum acceptance wages. Total rents to wrestlers equal the shaded area above the supply curve but below the wage rate.

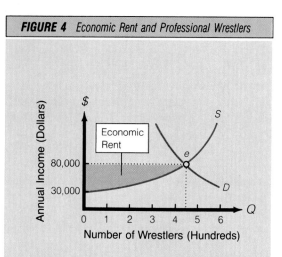

FIGURE 4   *Economic Rent and Professional Wrestlers*

Economic rents are realized whenever the supplier of a productive factor receives more than the minimum necessary to make the factor available to the market. Thus, the area above the supply curve but below the price line represents economic rents. This is sometimes called the *supplier's surplus.* In markets for output, such areas represent *producer surplus,* which is the flip side of consumer surplus. Recall that consumer surplus is the area below a demand curve but above the price line. It is the difference between what a buyer would willingly pay for a specific quantity of a good and the amount actually paid because goods can be bought at a uniform price.

Rents and Efficiency

Economic rent is the surplus received by a resource owner whenever income exceeds the opportunity cost of providing the resource to society as a whole. Economic rents are fairly common because most productive resources are at least partially fixed; their supplies are not perfectly elastic for the entire economy. It is this "fixity" that generates economic rents.

The displeasure of people who view the income distribution as unfair is generally aimed at high incomes received from interest, profit, or rent. Upon hearing about multimillion-dollar-a-year sports figures or movie stars, they may express sentiments such as "No one is worth more than $_____ ($1,000,000?) annually." Do economic rents serve any purpose beyond the enrichment of the owners of

BIOGRAPHY

Henry George (1839–97)

FIGURE 5 *Effect of a Tax on Land: Landowners Bear the Burden*

Tax per Acre

Rent per Acre Net of the Tax

Annual Rent per Acre of Land (τ Dollars)

Quantity of Land (Acres)

Landowners alone bear the full burdens of land taxes because the total amount competitive renters will pay for the use of land is determined strictly by its productivity. If landlords attempt to shift a land tax forward in the form of higher rental rates, there will be surplus land available and pressures for reductions in rents. The rental rate for land is always "all the market will bear."

High birth rates and the arrival of millions of immigrants caused rapid growth of the nineteenth-century American economy. Fertile frontier lands were homesteaded and urban land values boomed. Henry George and his followers believed landowners unjustly reaped major benefits from economic growth, which George perceived as rightfully belonging to society in general. In *Progress and Poverty* (1879), George proposed a **single tax** on land equal to the surplus that landowners were receiving and thought these revenues could finance all government spending. His reasoning is illustrated in Figure 5.

Equilibrium economic rent per acre before the land tax is τ_0 (point *a*). A tax equal to half of annual rent would cut the net rent per acre to landowners to τ_T. They cannot change the supply of land to drive its rental rate up. Attempts to raise rents would fail because surpluses of vacant land would develop. The rent that can be charged land users is strictly demand determined, so landowners cannot avoid the full burden of a pure land tax.

How would a land tax affect allocation? If untaxed land were used optimally, the most profitable uses would remain so after imposing the tax. (If you're able to keep half of all rent, 50 percent of the *highest* possible economic rent is the best you can do.) Thus, land taxes seem allocatively neutral.

The central thrust of George's economics is that land rent can be taxed heavily without distorting production incentives. George felt that "nothing short of making land common property can permanently relieve poverty and check the tendency of wages to the starvation point." He proposed to do this not by directly nationalizing land, but by the roundabout method of taking away the unearned income that proprietors enjoyed from land rents.

Land nationalization schemes were common in George's day, but he generally opposed government intervention and proposed leaving land titles in individual ownership, merely taxing all land at 100 percent of its rental value. This levy should be, according to George, a single tax to replace all other taxes. *Progress and Poverty* became the best-selling work on economics of the period and the bible of the single-tax movement.

A single tax on land sounds appealing, but it suffers from several flaws (*a*) potential revenue would probably not cover today's total government spending; (*b*) administration would be complex because distinguishing the values of land from its improvements—clearing, irrigation, buildings—is quite difficult; (*c*) rent does provide resource owners with incentives to find users who most highly value the resources; and (*d*) land is not the only resource that generates economic rents. A single tax on land rent would impose the full burden of paying for government on landowners. This seems unfair from the vantage point of current landowners.

George's single-tax movement reached its apex in his 1886 race for mayor of New York City. Running as the candidate of the United Labor Party, George finished second but there was wide speculation that he might have won an honest ballot count. Henry George died during another run at the mayor's office in 1897, but nevertheless left his imprint on economic reform movements at home and abroad.

land or specialized talents? If not, these surpluses can be completely taxed by government with no net loss to society. But both the short- and long-run consequences of taxing economic rents might actually cause inefficient allocations of resources.

Short-Run Allocation

Even in the short run, the drive to maximize economic rent creates incentives for resource owners to use their productive resources in the most valuable ways possible and to maintain them properly. Suppose that you own a city block that will potentially rent for $1 million annually. If this rent were taxed 100 percent, would you have any incentive to seek the highest bidder so that the land would be put to its most valuable use? NO!

Henry George argued that land would be used efficiently even if a 50 percent tax on rent were imposed because "half of something is better than half of nothing." But what if the tax were 99.99 percent? The $100 received if you found the $1 million bidder for the use of your land would be unlikely to overcome transaction costs. You might simply let your land lie idle. But what if the site tax were only 80 percent? Or 30 percent? Any tax rate, however low, reduces the incentive to put the land to its most valuable use.

Some movie stars, opera singers, novelists, and athletes realize incomes that seem outrageous. Much of such income is economic rent, so why not impose 100 percent taxes on annual incomes over $1,000,000? This question is partially answered if you ponder how you would react were you in this position. For example, you might immigrate to avoid confiscatory taxes. High income tax rates explain why many English actors and rock stars have become Swiss or American citizens.

If immigration seems unattractive, why bother to be worth more than $1,000,000 annually? Established actors might study their lines less diligently or do fewer films. Might opera singers begin to smoke, or fail to avoid colds or laryngitis? Would successful authors write as much? Would sports superstars play as hard or often? Would they willingly play in industrial towns, or might most gravitate to sunny resort areas? Some might still strive to excel out of personal pride, but, after a certain point, we suspect that cold, hard cash motivates most people whose specialized skills earn large economic rents.

In summary, rents are important even in the short run because they are incentives to maintain rent generating resources and because they are important in ensuring that those who most highly value scarce resources are able to use them.

Long-Run Allocation

Many resources that draw economic rents because they are semifixed for the economy as a whole in the short run are far from fixed over the long haul. Prospects of high income motivate people to invest in assets that subsequently command economic rent. Today's opportunity costs become tomorrow's fixed costs as resources jell into fixed assets. For example, medical students undergo years of expensive training in hopes of high economic rents once their M.D. degrees are in hand. Investors in buildings or capital equipment draw economic rents over the useful lives of these assets.

Would tomorrow's superstar athletes have as much incentive to polish their skills if the economic rents enjoyed by basketball's Michael Jordan, tennis's Steffi Graf, or football's John Elway were taxed away? NO! Would the lawyers of the next generation be as skilled as F. Lee Bailey or Richard "Racehorse" Haynes if the incomes of top attorneys were limited because they are economic rents? From whence would come future Luciano Pavarottis, Danielle Steeles, or Bill Cosbys? The long-run effects of taxing all economic rent would be disastrous because there would be few incentives to invest in oneself or in capital equipment; the entire economy would stagnate.

It should come as no surprise that the annual rental value of any resource is tied closely to its selling price, which is the wealth associated with owning a resource or other asset. Before we discuss capitalization, which is the process of translating rents or other flows of income into wealth, you need an understanding of interest and profits, which also may be capitalized through the process described near the end of this chapter.

Interest

You may have deposits in a bank account that draws interest. Why does the bank pay you interest? The answer seems obvious: because the bank can make loans at higher interest rates than it pays depositors. Most loans, however, are made to business investors who buy economic capital—machines, buildings, and other enhancements to the productivity of natural resources. Thus, interest is ultimately a payment to providers of economic capital. Interest payments are somewhat roundabout in advanced economies, being spread among those who own capital directly and others whose saving and financial investment make it possible for society to accumulate economic capital.

Interest Rates

We will focus on interest payments to holders of financial capital to simplify our analysis. Similar reasoning applies to direct owners of economic capital.

> **Nominal interest rates** *are the percentage monetary premiums paid per time period for the use of money.*

The ultimate lenders are those who save by spending less than their income. If you pay a dime annually for each dollar you owe on a car loan, the annual interest rate is 10 percent. (The people you truly owe are depositors in the lending institution.)

There are many nominal interest rates at any time because of differences in borrowers and debt instruments—car loans, mortgages, government or corporate bonds, and so on. These "IOUs" are a large component of our financial capital. Interest rates vary among these financial instruments because of:

1. *Risk.* Different borrowers have different probabilities of defaulting on their loans. Naturally, higher "risk premiums" in the interest rate are charged the greater the risk of default.
2. *Maturity.* The time until a loan is repaid also varies. Interest rates are generally higher the longer it will take to retire a loan.
3. *Liquidity.* Better developed markets for specific debt instruments drive interest rates down because the transaction costs incurred in buying or selling such IOUs will be lower. Competition among lenders to grant certain types of loans facilitates liquidity.

Interest rates commonly range from a government-subsidized 5 percent annually to a loan shark's 5 percent weekly. References to the rate of interest normally mean the nominal interest rate charged annually on long-term (20–30-year) riskless loans. Interest rates on negotiable long-term government bonds or those charged to "prime" borrowers are reasonable approximations of this concept.

Real interest rates differ from the nominal interest rates if the price level changes.

> The **real interest rate** *is the percentage of purchasing power annually paid by borrowers to lenders.*

Real interest is crucial for the decisions of both borrowers and lenders, and can be computed by subtracting the percentage annual rate of inflation from nominal interest rates. For example, 14 percent nominal interest yields only 6 percent real interest when annual inflation is 8 percent.

Interest income is a payment to providers of economic capital. In chapter 2, you learned that saving makes new capital supplies available; thus, the ultimate capital suppliers in our economy are savers. Just what factors determine the interest rate? After adjusting for inflation, the real interest rate depends on:

1. *The premiums savers require to delay gratification.* Most of us want goods now rather than later, unless we are rewarded for waiting. If 10 percent more goods are required to get us to wait a year to consume some income, the real interest rate tends towards 10 percent.
2. *The premiums for sacrificing liquidity.* Less liquid assets generate higher rates of return, or we would all hold cash.
3. *The productivity of new capital,* which produces extra goods for future use. If new capital reproduces 12 percent of its value in new goods each year, the interest rate tends towards 12 percent.

Over the long run, these three factors are reflected in the demands and supplies of loanable funds.

Markets for Financial Capital

We need to review certain aspects of capital markets before we consider the market for loanable funds. Firms construct buildings, buy machinery, or purposely increase inventories only if they expect to profit by doing so. Firms can finance these investments with funds from (*a*) retained earnings; (*b*) sales of the company's stock; or (*c*) sales of bonds or loans from financial institutions. Naturally, the depositors (savers) are the real lenders. The third approach is called *debt capital.* For simplicity, we will focus on debt capital in the remainder of this section. The thrust of our analysis would not change if we separately considered each form of financial capital. Keep in mind that financial capital is merely a tool used to secure economic (physical) capital.

Demands for Loanable Funds   Investors demand funds for a variety of investments, each of which is expected to yield profits to the business borrower. Just as the demand for labor depends on labor's marginal productivity, the demand for capital depends on its marginal productivity. Capital's marginal productivity (its *MRP*) as a percentage of expenditures on capital is known as the *rate of return on investment* (*r*). Like the demands for other resources, the demand for capital is a derived demand.

The demand for capital goods generates demand for *loanable funds* to finance new investment. In Figure 6, this demand for **loanable funds** is expressed in terms of rates of return and real interest rates. One explanation for the negative slope of demand curves for capital and loanable funds is that greater investment causes more and more capital to be used with fixed amounts of land and labor. The *law of diminishing marginal returns* then causes successive doses of capital to be decreasingly productive.

An alternative approach is to recognize that firms rank potential investment projects from the highest expected rate of return to the lowest. Assuming that funds from retained earnings or new stock offerings are insufficient, these projects underpin the demand for loanable funds shown in Figure 6. Only a few projects will yield a 20 percent rate of return or greater ($1 billion worth in Figure 6). As the rate of return requirement falls, firms find that more projects are advantageous. If interest costs fall to 10 percent, $4 billion worth of projects are profitable (point *b*); $8 billion in new investments generate rates of return of at least 5 percent (point *c*).

Investors do most of the borrowing in this country, but consumers and all levels of government also borrow substantially. Consumer purchases of homes and automobiles fall sharply when interest rates rise, as we saw during the economic slump of the early 1980s. Although the federal government's borrowing seems unaffected by interest rates, state and local governments borrow more to finance schools, parks, and roads when their interest costs are less. Thus, when consumer, investor, and government demands for loanable funds are combined, the market demand curve slopes downward. As with all other markets, however, demand is only half of the story.

Supplies of Loanable Funds   The costs of new buildings or machinery are obviously important in determining the level of business investment. Because the supply curves for capital goods are positively sloped, the costs and prices of investment goods tend to rise during prosperity as demand for investment goods increases, choking off short-term surges in investment. Conversely, declines in the costs of investment goods during economic downturns slow the fall of investment spending.

The major cost of investment, however, is the interest rate. Investors' opportunity costs climb when interest rates rise. Those who have money may make loans instead of buying investment goods. If they must borrow to invest, then a hike in the interest rate makes investment less attractive. Refer back to Figure 6. If the interest rate is 5 percent, then $8 billion in investments have expected rates of return of more than 5 percent and would be profitable; less than a 5 percent rate of return implies that investment is not profitable. As the rate of interest rises, the quantity of loanable funds demanded falls because fewer projects appear profitable.

FIGURE 6   *The Demand Curve for Debt Capital (Loanable Funds)*

The diminishing rate of return to investment in new capital is mirrored in the downward slope of the demand curve for loanable funds. Investors use most of the funds available for borrowing.

The supply of loanable funds is positively related to the price received. The ultimate lenders (savers who supply loanable funds) receive interest for the use of their funds. The major alternative for saver/lenders is current consumption, but a few, who value liquidity highly or who expect a financial crash, may hoard their savings. High interest rates confront individuals with high opportunity costs of current consumption (or hoarding), and many save (providing funds to the capital market) and use their future wealth (amount saved plus interest) for consumption at a later time.

Equilibrium Interest Rates Equilibrium in the financial capital market is illustrated in Figure 7. The initial demand for funds D_0, reflects the rates of return expected by business (plus consumer or government borrowing). It is negatively sloped because investments become less profitable as interest rates rise. The initial supply curve S_0 is positively sloped because household saving grows as interest rates paid savers rise—the opportunity costs of current consumption rise.

The rate of return on new investment equals the interest rate in equilibrium, which occurs at the intersection of the demand (D_0) and supply (S_0) curves in Figure 7. The initial equilibrium rate of return and interest rate will be 8 percent and the quantity of investment loans will equal Q_0. Suppose that expected returns on new capital investments rise so that the demand for loanable funds increases to D_1. Equilibrium interest and investment loans would rise to 10 percent and Q_1, respectively. Trace the effects of the following changes on interest rates and the amounts of investment loans:

1. Households decide to delay consumption and save more.
2. Investors become more optimistic.
3. Families decide that times are sufficiently secure that they can reduce their holdings of currency or other highly liquid assets.

When families increase the rate at which they postpone consumption, the loanable funds available for investment rise and interest rates fall. When investors grow more optimistic, expected rates of return, interest rates, and financial investments all rise. If households feel more secure, they reduce the liquidity of their assets by increasing their financial investments in stocks and bonds, and interest rates fall.

FIGURE 7 The Market for Loanable Funds

An increase in saving will increase the supply of loanable funds and decrease the interest rate. Reduced anxiety about the future tends to expand both the demand for and the supply of loanable funds.

Economic Profit

Most people misunderstand the role of profit in a market economy and substantially overestimate the shares of profit out of sales dollars, national income, and as a return on invested capital. Earlier, you learned that accounting profit is the difference between a firm's total revenues and its explicit costs, which are payments for the use of resources not owned by the firm. Only after subtracting implicit costs (the opportunity costs of resources that the owners provide for a firm's operations) from accounting profit do we have pure economic profit, which is a surplus over opportunity cost and so is a form of pure rent to the firm's owners.

> **Economic profit** is the excess of revenues over the opportunity costs of all resources employed.

In a purely competitive but unchanging economy in which the future was certain and transaction costs were zero, economic profit would always be zero and the implicit payments necessary to maintain owner-provided resources would absorb all accounting profits. In reality, transaction costs are significant, and continuous changes make the future uncertain. Many of these changes are wrought by entrepreneurial quests for profits. Moreover, monopoly power is commonplace. This leads to the major sources of pure economic profits (*a*) monopoly power, (*b*) innovation, and (*c*) uncertainty.

Monopoly Profit

Monopoly power enables some firms to generate total revenue far in excess of the opportunity costs of the resources used. But can a monopolist continually enjoy economic profit? Transaction costs, uncertainty, and entry barriers create short-run profit opportunities. *Monopoly profit* may persist into the long run if barriers prevent entry by competitors, but profits will stimulate resource flows that eliminate monopoly profit in *contestable* markets. If so, profit will have served its function by signalling where society desired greater production. If barriers preclude entry in the long run, economy-wide efficiency will not occur, but monopoly profit encourages least-cost production.

The capitalization process we will describe in a moment suggests that predictable monopoly profit is realized only by people who own a firm when it secures a monopoly position. These profits will be capitalized in the long run into a higher market value for ownership of the monopoly and thus a higher opportunity cost, so that subsequent buyers of ownership shares can expect only normal profits.

Rewards for Innovation

Another explanation for profit is innovation.

Innovation *involves the development and implementation of a new product or production process or the opening of a new market.*

If your firm is among the first to introduce a successful product or try a more efficient technology, you will reap economic profits. Economic profits are eroded by competition as imitators follow in the footsteps of successful innovators. Thomas Edison, for example, became rich when he established General Electric as the outlet for his genius, but General Elec-

tric now faces hordes of competitors and realizes only normal profits. More recently, the invention and development of the Polaroid camera by Edwin Land resulted in immense profits for him and his family.

The innovation theory of profits was first expressed by Joseph Schumpeter as an explanation for the business cycle. When a significant innovation was made, many entrepreneurs would attempt to capitalize on the profit opportunities, and their collective investments would fuel an economic boom. Once the advantages from the innovation were fully absorbed, investment would decline, pushing the economy into a downturn to await another major innovation.

Risk Bearing and Uncertainty

Crystal balls or computer programs that precisely forecast the future are not available, but we can estimate the probability of many future events and try to exploit potential gains while guarding against misfortune. If the likelihood of some potential occurrence is fairly predictable, many people will adjust in similar ways so that only normal rates of return can be expected. Buying insurance is one adjustment against life's possible hazards, or you might *self-insure* by taking your chances. Some aspects of the future, however, seem totally unpredictable. You may be rewarded by unexpected profit for bearing the risk of just being in a line of business if fortune smiles, or you may get clobbered if disaster unexpectedly strikes your industry.

The economist Frank Knight first distinguished risk from uncertainty.[1]

Risk *exists when the probability of a given event can be estimated.*

For example, if a firm can reliably predict that, on average, a production process will yield 3 defective units out of 100, it can adjust for these risks by considering "losses due to defects" as a normal cost of doing business. Similarly, the probabilities of fire, certain accidents, or the death of a key executive can be predicted fairly reliably, and insurance is available. Again, these risks will be reflected in production costs and output prices.

---

1. Frank H. Knight, *Risk, Uncertainty, and Profit* (Boston: Houghton-Mifflin Co., 1921).

Uncertainty, on the other hand, forces entrepreneurs to weigh imperfect information and base their decisions on subjective judgements.

> **Uncertainty** *occurs when a potential occurrence is so unpredictable that forecasts are unavoidably pure guesswork.*

Profits, to Frank Knight, are rewards for bearing uncertainty. Entrepreneurs undertake investments with the expectation of generating sufficient revenues to cover all costs, including allowances for all risks, but the unfolding of time may yield events beyond any entrepreneur's wildest expectations or fears. Uncertainty, in Knight's view, makes it impossible to anticipate economic profits or losses.

The Economic Role of Profits

Uncertainty, innovation, and monopoly power are the major sources of economic profit. But what function do profits perform? Economic profits are powerful signals that prices exceed average production costs and indicate that social welfare will be improved if resources are shifted from unprofitable to profitable sectors of the economy. Conversely, industry-wide economic losses are signals that too many resources are devoted to production of a particular good and could beneficially be shifted elsewhere.

Profits are also a stimulus for efficiency. Entrepreneurs' desires for profits will cause costs to be cut wherever possible, freeing resources for other uses. Competition forces profits down to normal levels as imitators mimic the activities of successful firms, whether success is derived from being in a certain product line or using a more efficient technology. Competition also punishes those who fail to produce efficiently by inflicting economic losses on relatively high-cost firms.

Profits also reward the entrepreneurs who innovate new products and technologies in an uncertain business environment (see Focus 1). The drive for entrepreneurial profit propels society along a path of economic growth and progress.

Flows of predictable rents, interest, or profits are translated into wealth through the process of capitalization whenever the resources that generate the income flows can be sold. In the next section, we examine the mechanics of how competition for income streams determines the market values of income-generating assets.

Capitalizing Income Streams

Suppose that you manage a rock group called "Nuclear Winter," currently being booked as a warm-up act for more popular bands. The group's third album suddenly goes platinum and phones begin to ring. Promoters want "Winter" to headline upcoming concerts, but it is solidly booked for the next six months at $5,000 per appearance.

Who will benefit from the group's popularity during the next six months? Promoters who contracted with your band prior to its hit album will realize economic profits by selling out their concert dates even if they increase ticket prices. How long will these economic profits (which could also be considered rents) continue to be received by individual concert promoters?

Being a smart promoter yourself, you will quit booking "Winter" as an opening act and will raise its fee when you negotiate future contracts so that individual concert promoters earn only normal profits. This *capitalizes* the rents from the group's special skills. The fee now reflects the higher ticket prices and attendance for each performance. If you held exclusive rights to book the group, you could sell the contract for a fat profit.

> **Capitalization** *is a process whereby future income streams are transformed into the current value or wealth, resulting in the elimination of economic profits.*

A similar capitalization process occurs in farming. If grain prices soar because, say, the Soviet Union suffers a drought and makes huge purchases in world markets, farmers temporarily enjoy economic profits. What happens to the price of farmland when this happens? It rises because the expected profits are capitalized into higher land values. Even farmers who own their land find the opportunity cost of holding it rising, squeezing out the economic profit derived from farming. Their higher wealth naturally would keep them from mourning their fates too loudly.

Investors prefer more income to less, and they want it sooner rather than later. Thus, the capitalized value of an income stream will be larger (*a*) the greater the income stream, and (*b*) the more quickly income is realized. Truly understanding these relationships requires knowing how to calculate present values and rates of return.

So You Want to Be an Entrepreneur . . . ?

Work provides many people with the primary meaning for their lives. Surveys indicate that most college students want interesting, secure, and remunerative careers. Many also express desires for jobs that reward hard work with rapid advancement or that contribute to social well-being. Finding "the right job" may entail a little job hopping, but most people eventually spend most of their lives employed by one large company. With luck, it will have a good pension plan.

Several studies suggest that successful entrepreneurs typically march to the beat of their own drummer. Many seemed misfits early in their careers, losing a series of jobs because they refused to be the team players favored by many employers. Most equated compromise with losing and would do almost anything at any time to get their own way.

People afflicted with personalities that make it difficult for them to get along in large organizations often express desires to "be my own boss," but few who go off on their own ever enjoy much success. Indeed, most who eventually succeed do so only after a series of failures. It is hard to overstate how devastating bankruptcy can be, especially to entrepreneurs who have staked their dreams on the success or failure of an enterprise.

What separates highly successful entrepreneurs from most small proprietors or heads of giant corporations? Several characteristics are commonly shared by successful entrepreneurs:

1. *Vision and timing.* Entrepreneurs need the ability to see opportunities where others see only problems. This often requires being in the right place at the right time. Different people interpret the same complex of facts differently. Successful entrepreneurship seems to involve organizing information so that solutions to problems become obvious. The solution may involve reducing production cost, improving the quality of an existing good, or innovating a totally new good.
2. *Conviction and action.* Once entrepreneurs find a key to solving a problem, they act on their convictions. Some people may see solutions to problems, but want security and the conventional "good life" and so lack the faith to pursue their idea to its conclusion. Highly successful entrepreneurs have a very different goal; they want to leave their mark on the world.
3. *Bearing of risk and uncertainty.* Successful entrepreneurs typically have such faith in their business plans that they will risk vast capital

and time to accomplish their goals. This often requires rejecting the financial security that most people seek.
4. *Workaholism.* Most people want high income from a job that allows leisure time every evening and on weekends and regular vacations. A 40-hour, 9-to-5 job is not a goal of most successful entrepreneurs, some of whom put in over 100 hours per week for decades.

G. L. S. Shackle, a prominent economist, describes enterprise as "action in pursuit of the imagined, deemed possible."[2] Entrepreneurs imagine alternative uses of resources, and by organizing resources to correspond to their individual visions, they alter the course of history. If this brief discussion has not squelched any desire you might have to be an entrepreneur because of a wish to shape human history, then you need to watch for opportunities to provide things that people want, be willing to absorb risk, and work extraordinarily hard. Then pray for luck.

---

2. G. L. S. Shackle, Forward to *The Entrepreneur,* by Robert F. Hebért and Albert N. Link (New York: Praeger Publishers, 1982).

Present Values

Economic investment generates additional salable output over the future, yielding an income stream to the investor. The income stream per time period as a percentage of the dollar outlay for a capital good is called the **rate of return.** Determining whether an investment will be profitable requires calculating its present value, which is the value today of all expected future receipts of income.

> The **present value** of an asset is the discounted value today of the expected income stream associated with the asset.

Suppose you were offered a guaranteed right to $100 payable one year from today and that your savings account earned 6 percent interest annually. What is the most you would be willing to pay for this IOU? Certainly less than $100. You can calculate the amount at which you will do equally well with your money in either the savings account or this IOU by answering the following question: How much money would I have to put in the bank at a 6 percent interest rate per year so that when the interest earned in one year is added to the original amount, the total equals $100? This problem boils down to $1.06(PV) = \$100$, where PV stands for present value. If you divide both sides of this equation by 1.06 and then solve for $PV = \$100/1.06$, you have the answer. Similar questions can be answered for any interest rate, any time period, or any amount of money using the following formula:

Present Value

$$PV = \frac{Y_1}{(1+i)^1} + \frac{Y_2}{(1+i)^2}$$

$$+ \ldots + \frac{Y_n}{(1+i)^n} \qquad \textbf{Equation 1}$$

$$= \sum_{t=1}^{n} \frac{Y_t}{(1+i)^t}$$

where:

Y_t = payment expected at time t.
i = annual interest rate or discount rate.
t = time period.
n = the number of periods when payments are expected.
Σ = an arithmetic operator meaning "sum across."

A numerical example should help you see how the formula works. If you use a 6 percent interest rate to discount $100 payable one year from today, the $PV = \$100/1.06$, which equals $94.34. This amount in a savings account paying 6 percent interest would yield $\$94.34 \times (.06) = \$5.66$; at the end of the year your principal plus interest would total to $94.34 + $5.66, which is $100. If you had to wait two years for the $100, what is the most you would pay, assuming the interest rate is 6 percent? The answer is $89, because $\$100/[1 + .06]^2 = \$89$. Naturally, an IOU paying $100 next year plus $100 two years hence would be worth $\$94.34 + \$89.00 = \$183.34$.

The present value formula in Equation 1 may appear formidable, but there is a shortcut in calculating present values if the annual income expected from an asset is fixed into the indefinite future at a constant, Y_t. Such assets, known as *perpetuities,* are computed with the following equation:

Present Value for Perpetuities

$$PV = \frac{Y_t}{i} \qquad \textbf{Equation 2}$$

Thus, if a parcel of land is expected to generate annual rent of $10,000 forever and the interest rate is 10 percent (.10), the present value of the land is $100,000. If a government bond promises to pay $1,000 annually forever to its owner and the interest rate is 8 percent, the bond is worth $12,500. Bonds of this type, called *consols,* are issued by the Bank of England.

Rates of Return

While present value calculations are very important to financial analysts, investors are more often interested in rate of return analysis. If you are majoring in accounting or finance or are just interested in investment analysis, you should pay special attention to both present value and rate of return formulas—you will undoubtedly see them again.

> The **rate of return** is the annual return to an asset expressed as a percentage of the price of the asset.

Investors usually have some idea as to the income stream they might expect from an investment. We can determine the rate of return (r) by solving the following formula:

Rate-of-Return Calculation

$$P = \sum_{t=0}^{n} \frac{Y_t}{(1+r)^t} \qquad \text{Equation 3}$$

where P equals the price of the investment good, r equals the annual rate of return, and all other variables are as defined above. Since we know price (P) and expected income in each time period (Y_t), the only unknown is r, the rate of return. For example, if an asset selling for $100 today will pay $110 a year from today, the rate of return is 10 percent. A $112 payment yields a rate of return of 12 percent. Thus, the larger the expected income in each time period, the greater the rate of return for a given price.

Comparing Present Values and Rates of Return

How are present value and rate of return calculations related to each other and to the capitalization process? If the present value is at least as great as the price ($PV \geq P$), then the expected rate of return is at least as great as the interest rate ($r \geq i$), and you will invest because the asset appears profitable. You will not invest if the price of an asset exceeds your estimate of present value because the expected rate of return will be less than the market rate of interest.

Generally, we know the price (P), the going interest rate (i), and the income expected each year (Y_t) from an investment when we evaluate it.

Break-Even Investments

$$PV = \sum_{t=0}^{n} \frac{Y_t}{(1+r)^t} \qquad \text{Equation 4}$$

When Equation 4 holds, the investment is a *break-even* proposition. For example, if an investor could expect $224 a year hence and the interest rate were 12 percent, a current price of $200 would make an investment strictly a break-even proposition. Your assessment of the present value of an asset, however, may be either higher or lower than the price asked. Similarly, you may estimate the rate of return either above or below the market interest rate.

Present value calculations solve for the current worth of an income stream by discounting expected future income with the market rate of interest, both of which we know. Rate of return analysis also assumes we know how much income to expect in the future and when it will be received, but solves for an unknown *implicit* interest rate (r), while using the known current price to arrive at a solution.

Capitalization and Competition

There is tremendous competition for profits. If you are an astute investor, there will probably be several other astute people who would assess a given investment much as you do. If present value appears to exceed price substantially, there may be bidding wars that rapidly drive the price toward present value. Even if you do manage to pick up what you view as a bargain, you certainly would not then sell it for less than its present value to you.

Thus, the equilibrium price of any asset is its present value. Moreover, after adjusting for risk, competition causes the rate of return expected from any asset to equal the market rate of interest. The process that discounts expected future income by the interest rate to arrive at present value and price is *capitalization.*

How might you use your knowledge of the capitalization process? Assume you own 1,000 shares of a wildcat oil company earning $1 per share per year. If market conditions required a 10 percent rate of return, shares of stock would sell for $10. What if the firm hit a gusher expected to triple its annual earnings? Stock shares would quickly rise to roughly $30 after the gusher was announced. What rate of return would be expected by people who bought stock after this discovery? Roughly 10 percent, just as before. Similar capitalization processes determine most resource prices. Thus, capitalization makes huge profits possible for the people who set up sports franchises and watch them succeed, while people who subsequently buy pieces of paper called "franchises" for millions of dollars can expect only normal returns.

One possible road to riches requires finding assets for which the current owners have underestimated future earning power. You can then purchase these assets relatively cheaply. When the true earning capacity of the assets becomes known, you can become rich by selling the assets for considerably more.

Insider Information and Capitalization

The Securities and Exchange Commission (SEC) enforces laws that forbid trading securities on the basis of insider information—knowledge that is not available to the general public about events that affect securities prices; e.g., unexpected profits or losses, lawsuits, new product development, or plans for mergers or takeovers. Insiders presumably could get a jump allowing them to profit by buying or selling before information concerning profits was available to the public. The judge's ruling in the following case illustrates a typical case of insider trading.

SEC v. Materia (1984)

Our era aptly has been styled the "age of information." Francis Bacon recognized nearly 400 years ago that "knowledge is power," but only in the last generation has it risen to the equivalent of the coin of the realm. Nowhere is this commodity more valuable or volatile than in the world of high finance, where facts are worth fortunes while secrets may be rendered worthless once revealed.

Anthony Materia was employed by a printer of financial documents, including many concerning proposed tender [merger] offers. Because even a hint of an upcoming tender offer may send the price of the target company's stock soaring, the identity of a target is zealously guarded. It is customary, therefore, for offerors (or their law firms) to omit information that might identify a merger target until the last possible moment. Code names are used, blanks are left unfilled until the eve of publication, and misinformation may even be included in early drafts. In sum, a quick reading of preliminary paperwork would not reveal this confidential information.

In his job as a "copyholder," Materia read clients' drafts aloud to a proofreader, who ensured that page proofs conformed to the copy received from the client. Despite scrupulous efforts to keep confidential information secret, Materia divined the identities of at least four tender offer targets between December 1980 and September 1982. He purchased stock within hours of each discovery, and within days—after the offer had been made public—he sold his holdings at substantial gains.

Determined to combat securities fraud, Congress enacted comprehensive yet open-ended statutes capable of adaptation and refinement. In recent years, developments in capital formation and novel means of effecting corporate combinations have spawned a new genre of confidential information. Courts are increasingly called upon to address a myriad of issues regarding the use of such data. We do not believe the drafters of the Securities Exchange Act of 1934—envisaging as they did an open and honest market—would have countenanced the activities engaged in by Anthony Materia.

Questions

1. Will insider trading speed up the process of capitalizing changes in expected profits caused by an event that constitutes the insider information?

2. Most foreign stock exchanges do not forbid trading on insider information. Does trading securities on the basis of insider information merely determine who gains when stock prices rise or fall to reflect capitalization of expected changes in a firm's profitability? Or does insider trading, instead, provide opportunities for fraud, or unfair profits to the traders?

One roadblock that makes this a difficult avenue to wealth, however, is vigorous competition from many other bright people who are also looking for bargains. At times, attempts to discover bargains lead people who acquire *insider information* about financial securities to break the law, as we describe in Focus 2. Profit is likely for anyone who acts on information about events that will affect the values of assets in predictable ways—but only if they act before that information is widely publicized.

The Marginal Productivity Theory of Income Distribution _____

In our chapter on production and costs, we showed that least-cost production by profit-maximizing firms forces them to use combinations of resources so that the marginal products of particular resources are proportional to resource prices. This concept translates into the *principle of equal marginal productivities per dollar:*

$$\frac{MPP_L}{w} = \frac{MPP_K}{r} = \ldots$$

This is one application of the law of equal marginal advantage to production. Multiplying all *MPP*s by the price (*P*) of output reveals that competitive firms must operate so that the values of the marginal products of all resources are proportional to their prices:

$$\frac{VMP_L}{w} = \frac{VMP_K}{r} = \ldots$$

But resource prices are equal to marginal factor costs if resource markets are competitive, and the market compels competitive firms to pay resource owners incomes equal to the resources' *VMP*s, so:

$$\frac{VMP_L}{MFC_L} = \frac{VMP_K}{MFC_K} = \ldots = 1.$$

This suggests that a competitive market system tends to divide income according to the productive contribution of each individual's resources. Of course, product or resource markets are seldom purely competitive, but this brief review does point out some tendencies for distributions of income.

This marginal productivity theory of income distribution cannot even hint, however, at the most equitable income distribution. We address this normative question late in the next part of this book. We have now discussed markets for goods and resources, touching upon certain government policies along the way. The next part of the book explores in greater detail the microeconomic role of government in a market system. We will address various types of inefficiency and inequity whose causes range from inherent problems with market solutions to failures inherent in government decision making.

CHAPTER REVIEW: KEY POINTS

1. *Economic rent* exists whenever resource owners receive more than the minimum required for them to supply given amounts of the resource.
2. Land has a unique economic characteristic—it is fixed in supply. Thus, its supply curve is perfectly inelastic, and all payments for the use of land are pure rent. Land rents vary by location and particular physical characteristics.
3. Land is not the only resource that generates economic rents. Other factors that are supplied at prices above the minimum amounts required to elicit their availability also generate economic rents.
4. "Single taxers" inspired by Henry George propose a 100 percent tax on land rent as a single tax to finance all government spending. They argue that taxing this unearned surplus would not distort the allocation of land, and thus would not hinder economic efficiency. The *single-tax proposal* suffers from (*a*) inability to finance the entire public sector, (*b*) administrative problems in distinguishing land values arising out of improvements made by own-

ers from rent as an unearned surplus, and (*c*) reduced incentives for landowners to put their land to the best possible uses if rent is taxed away.
5. Economic rent promotes economic efficiency by providing resource owners with incentives to put their assets to the most valuable uses.
6. *Nominal interest* rates are the percentage annual premiums paid for the use of borrowed funds. Interest rates on financial instruments vary according to (*a*) risk, (*b*) maturity, and (*c*) liquidity. The interest rate normally means the rate on a long-term riskless bond.
7. In the long run, *real* (purchasing power) *interest rates* depend on (*a*) premiums required to induce savers to delay consumption, (*b*) desires for liquidity, and (*c*) the productivity of capital investments. These factors determine interest rates through the supply and demand for *loanable funds*. Government macroeconomic policies also influence loanable funds markets.
8. *Pure economic profits* are the residual after adjusting accounting profits for the opportunity cost of

resources provided by a firm's owners. Profit may arise from *monopoly power,* bearing business *uncertainty,* or *innovation.*

9. Profits channel resources to their most productive uses in a market economy and stimulate progress as entrepreneurs innovate and endure business uncertainty to secure profits. Profits induce efficiency; competitive firms that do not produce at the lowest possible cost will suffer economic losses.

10. *Present values* are the sums of the discounted values of future income that may be expected from owning an asset. The present value of an asset and its price will be identical in equilibrium. If the present value exceeds price, then the asset is a profitable investment because the expected rate of return exceeds the interest rate. *Capitalization* is the process whereby prices gravitate toward present values of assets.

PROBLEMS

1. Assume the federal government issues a bond that pays $1,000 per year forever. If the general level of interest rates are 10 percent, what will be the price of the bond when issued? After the bond is issued, if interest rates rise to 20 percent, what will happen to the price of the bond? What happens if interest rates fall to 5 percent?

2. Big cash winners on TV game shows or in magazine subscription contests commonly are paid in installments over a period of years. Suppose you won $100,000 in a state lottery, receiving $20,000 today and $20,000 at the end of each of the next four years. If the interest rate is 10 percent, what is the present value of your winnings? Are there other reasons to believe that the values of prizes are overstated? What would you guess is the average percentage of overstatement?

QUESTIONS FOR THOUGHT AND DISCUSSION

1. Land taxes may not cause gross misallocations of land, but property taxes are widely perceived as dissuading owners from improving land in an optimal fashion. High property taxes are also blamed for the deterioration of the urban cores of large cities. How elastic is the supply of improvements to land vis-à-vis the supply elasticity of land per se? How might land values be distinguished from improvements if land taxes replaced property taxes?

2. Economic rents and economic profits are both "surpluses" in excess of opportunity costs from the vantage point of society as a whole. They are unnecessary to secure resources socially. Rent on the land used by any firm is a true opportunity cost to that firm, however, while economic profits are not. Can you reconcile the idea that rents are often opportunity costs to the individual user, but not to society?

3. The Soviet Union, following Marx's theory that interest is a mechanism capitalists use to exploit workers, rejects using an interest rate to discount the future benefits from investment projects. Explain how ignoring interest rates might cause saving to flow into less than socially optimal investments.

4. Accounting profits generally exceed economic profits because accountants may fail to consider implicit costs. Can you think of activities that might generate "implicit revenues" so that economic profits would exceed accounting profits? Might this explain how firms in some competitive lines of business continually generate accounting losses but continue to operate?

5. Some people who start a successful enterprise encounter major difficulties in managing their companies once the firm is on its feet. For example, Steve Wozniak and Steven Jobs built Apple Computers from a tiny operation housed in a garage into a billion-dollar concern between 1976 and 1981, but professional managers and stockholders banded together and ousted both from leadership of the company by 1985. What are the differences in the personalities required to be innovative entrepreneurs and professional managers? Is it likely that one person can embody both sets of attributes? Can you cite other cases in which people who were strong "starters" were weak "finishers"? Where a strong starter established a series of successful companies, but was never able to maintain control once success was enjoyed? Where strong starters proved quite capable of effective management once an enterprise was successful?

FMC Corporation v. Ivan F. Boesky (1987)

This civil suit followed criminal convictions for insider trading of all the individuals mentioned. As you read about this case, try to figure out who was hurt by their behavior.

In 1985, FMC [Ford] management embarked on a plan to "restructure" the corporation. FMC hired Goldman Sachs & Co. (Goldman) as financial advisor. FMC management considered a leveraged buy-out, but later decided in favor of "recapitalization" to decrease the proportionate equity interest of public shareholders and increase the equity held by management. Between December 1985 and May 1986 FMC and Goldman worked out details of the plan.

On February 21, 1986, Goldman outlined the proposed recapitalization in a letter to FMC's board. The proposal called for an exchange of old FMC shares for newly issued FMC stock. The public shareholders would receive one share of New FMC stock plus $70 in cash in exchange for each share of old FMC stock. Management would receive 5.667 shares of New FMC stock in exchange for each share of old stock. When Goldman announced the plan, it also issued its opinion stating that the terms were fair to public shareholders.

In reaching its fairness opinion, Goldman estimated that each share of old FMC stock had a value of $85—the price at which the stock was then trad-ing on the New York Stock Exchange ("NYSE"). Goldman also expected that each share of New FMC stock would have a market value of $15 after the recapitalization.

In the meantime, unknown to FMC, confidential information about the potential recapitalization was leaked to outsiders. Brown, a Goldman vice-president, disclosed the information to defendant Ira Sokolow, a Lehman vice-president, who then passed it on to defendant Dennis Levine, who in turn disclosed the information to defendant Ivan Boesky. Armed with inside tips about the recapitalization, Boesky bought 95,300 shares of FMC common stock. When Boesky began trading on February 18, 1986, FMC stock opened on the NYSE at $71.25 per share. On February 20, 1986, the day before Boesky's purchases ceased, the stock closed at $80.25 per share. During these three days approximately 707,000 shares of FMC stock traded on the NYSE. Boesky's purchases accounted for 13% of all FMC shares traded.

On mid-morning of February 21, 1986, the price of FMC's stock had climbed to $83.00 per share. FMC requested that trading in its stock be temporarily suspended; it then made public the possibility of recapitalization. Trading in the stock then resumed. At the close of trading that day, the price of the stock stood at $85.625. The next day FMC's board approved the recapitalization plan and announced its terms to the public. By then, Boesky had begun to sell the 95,300 shares he purchased during February 18–21.

After the announcement of the recapitalization, FMC stock continued to rise. Therefore; Goldman urged FMC to review the cash portion of the deal. Because of the price rise, Goldman believed that a cash payment of $70 would no longer be fair to public shareholders. Unbeknownst to FMC, Brown told Sokolow and Levine that the cash portion was under review. Levine then told Boesky. With this leaked information, Boesky bought about 1,922,000 shares of FMC stock between March 12, 1986 and April 4, 1986—more than 50% of the total volume of trading in FMC stock during this period. FMC's complaint alleges that, because of Boesky's purchases, the price of FMC stock rose sharply to an artificial and distorted price level.

On April 7, 1986, Goldman informed FMC's board that because of the high market price of FMC stock, Goldman might withdraw its February 21 fairness opinion. The trading price of FMC stock continued to rise, reaching $97 per share on April 25. Goldman consequently threatened to withdraw the fairness opinion unless FMC either increased from $70 to $80 the cash payment to public shareholders, or decreased the number of shares of New FMC stock to be given to management shareholders. FMC's board opted for the $10 cash increase to public shareholders. Goldman also revised its estimate of the post-recapitalization market value of New FMC stock. The new estimate was $17.14 per share.

While the FMC board considered this new plan, the trading price of its stock continued to rise. Thus, on April 26, 1986, FMC's board agreed with Goldman and publicly announced that it would increase $70 to $80 the cash portion to be paid to public shareholders. As a result of this cash increase, the revised recapitalization plan called for an additional $220 million to go to the public shareholders. Goldman issued an opinion stating that the new plan was fair to public shareholders. On May 2, 1986, FMC distributed a joint proxy statement/prospectus to the shareholders for the annual meeting to be held on May 22, 1986. At the meeting, the shareholders approved the plan and FMC executed it on May 28, 1986.

Meanwhile, on April 28, 1986, the first day of trading after the announcement of the increase in the cash to be paid to public shareholders, Boesky began to sell FMC stock. By May, 1986, he had sold enough shares to realize a profit in excess of $20 million.

FMC alleges that as a result of Boesky's illegal conduct it paid $220 million more for the publicly held shares of FMC stock than it would have paid absent that conduct. It also claims that Boesky's actions resulted in an increase in the debt and other costs FMC incurred in its recapitalization. Further, Goldman received more than $17.5 million in fees and expenses; FMC contends these fees should be refunded.

The defendants assert that plaintiff has suffered no injury, and therefore, cannot, consistent with Article III of the Constitution, seek relief under any of the legal theories set forth in the complaint.

The assets of FMC are owned by FMC's shareholders. Therefore, any judgment in favor of FMC will inure to the benefit of those shareholders. Yet these same shareholders would thus receive the alleged $220 million twice, once in the recapitalization, and again as beneficial owners of any judgment collected by FMC from defendants. Or to use the metaphor of one defendant, FMC here asks that it be allowed to shift corporate assets from the left pocket to the right pocket, and then to refill the left pocket by a recovery from the defendants.

Moreover, it is difficult to articulate FMC's injury when all shareholders benefited from the transaction, and creditors of FMC were unharmed. The management shareholders obtained an increased equity interest, and the public shareholders received a cash distribution (perhaps made greater by Boesky's conduct) while retaining a significant equity interest in the corporation. The management shareholders can perhaps complain because their "purchase" of some of the equity held by public shareholders cost the corporation $220 million more than it would have absent the conduct of Boesky. But FMC makes no claim that management suffered an injury.

Questions

1. In early 1986, Goldman estimated that the "fair" value of FMC's stock was $85. Was it just a coincidence that the stock was then trading at $85?

2. The original purpose of the "reorganization" was to "reduce the proportionate equity interest of public shareholders and increase the equity held by management." What does this mean? What was the effect of Boesky's efforts? Who, besides Boesky, benefited from his activities?

3. Many foreign stock exchanges allow insider trading, but publicize warnings to investors that the buyer of stock should beware. What advantages, if any, are there to this approach? Would such a rule facilitate the capitalization of information?

4. When rumors of some impending event push stock prices up before any announcement, have securities laws probably been broken?

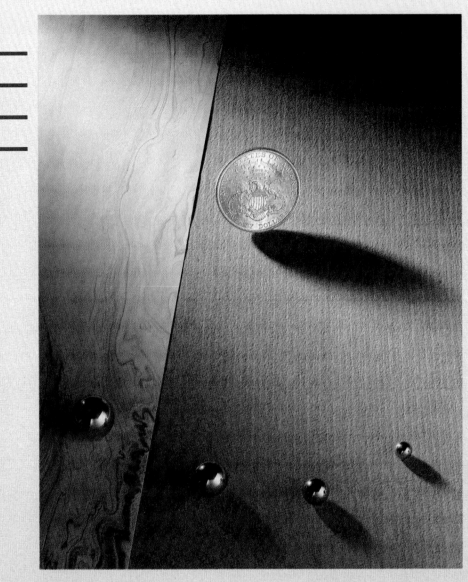

Microeconomic theory provides an array of tools that aid our analyses of problems that confront policymakers at all levels of government. We have used such tools as elasticity, marginalism, diminishing returns, and the law of equal marginal advantage to investigate problems that arise for public policy in such areas as regulation, antitrust, and labor relations. But this barely scratches the surface of the kinds of government policy-making into which microeconomics can offer valuable insights. Other areas include (*a*) crime and punishment, (*b*) defense, (*c*) education, (*d*) energy, (*e*) health, (*f*) science and technology, and (*g*) urban problems. Looking at all possible problem areas would require a book twice as long as this one and a course twice as long as the one in which you are enrolled—exhausting your pocketbooks and the patience of your professors and our publishers. You will have opportunities to study many of these topics if you take further courses in economics.

The major topics discussed in this part of the book begin with a framework for examining policies. First, in chapter 31, we develop a normative theory of the public sector by investigating areas in which the market may fail to allocate resources acceptably. *Market failures* identify economic functions that government may be better suited to fulfill. Then, we survey the structure of American taxes, measuring both current taxes and proposed tax reforms against principles of efficiency and equity. In chapter 32, we focus on *public choice,* an approach that views political behavior from an economic perspective. This area of study provides clues about *government failure*—just as the market may fail at times, public policies are frequently less than ideal. In chapter 33, we examine questions of resource management and environmental quality. The problems of agriculture are our major concerns in chapter 34. Finally, in chapter 35, we address the problem of poverty and issues surrounding the redistribution of income. Applying microeconomic tools to these areas should familiarize you with how to use economic reasoning when you want to investigate any of a multitude of problems.

CHAPTER 31

market failures
externalities
public goods
benefit principle of
    taxation
ability-to-pay principle of
    taxation
vertical equity
horizontal equity
excess burden of a tax
neutral tax
value-added taxes (VATs)

Market Failures and Public Microeconomics

This chapter addresses economic functions that may be appropriate for government in a market economy. Private markets operate under rules set by government, but public policy is typically more extensive when the marketplace is perceived to fail. We will look at different types of *market failure* and the government corrections appropriate for certain failures. Some normative principles of taxation are also a concern: Who should pay for government, and how? Then we survey the strengths and weaknesses of several taxes to assess how well our current system conforms to normative principles of taxation. In the next chapter, we use economic analysis to explore political decision making and *government failure*. There, you will find answers to many questions you may develop about why public policy so often deviates from the ideals we describe in this chapter.

A Normative Framework for Government

Economic problems are ideally resolved equitably and efficiently. Markets are, however, often subject to instability, inequity, and inefficiency. Agriculture and the stock market represent recent examples of instability, while, for many, the homeless illustrate the inequities inherent in markets. Inefficiency may occur in private markets if the transacting parties do not pay the full costs (pollution) or receive the full benefits (national defense) or because the private sector will not provide the product at all (social insurance).

Market failures *identify economic functions that government may be better suited to fulfill.*

They can be categorized as problems of (*a*) *distribution,* (*b*) *stabilization,* or (*c*) *allocation.* People exert political pressure for redistributions of income or wealth when they perceive inequity; instability is a problem when inflation or unemployment are excessive; and misallocation, when resources are not used efficiently.

Richard Musgrave, a specialist in public finance (the study of the economics of government), has argued that muddled thinking and misguided policies arise from attempts to resolve different problem areas simultaneously.[1] He proposed a three-part budget framework to clarify and resolve market failures by first classifying them as problems of allocation, distribution, or stabilization. Each area would be dealt with separately by using the best tools available, with any side effects then being treated by the best cures for them. Thus, the allocation branch would try to cure inefficient resource allocations while assuming that any resulting inequity or instability will be remedied by the distribution or stabilization branches of government.

Suppose, for example, that prisons would be largely self-supporting and more efficient if more inmates worked in prison industries, but that this might cause a loss of jobs in the private firms currently producing competing goods. The allocation branch would ignore this potential disemployment because full employment is the responsibility of the stabilization branch. We will briefly consider Musgrave's proposed distribution and stabilization branches of government before looking at problems with market allocations.

The Distribution Branch

The **distribution** branch of government would concentrate on achieving equity—an unavoidably normative issue—and would rely on taxes and transfer payments. Only taxes collected from people whom policymakers deem to have "too much" could be given as transfers to those perceived to have "too little." The distribution budget would balance at all times. Musgrave assumes that poor people are adequate money managers so that no direct allocations of

goods are required; poverty would be cured with cash grants, and there would be no food stamps, public housing, or Medicaid. We will deal later with some normative and practical problems encountered in redistributing income.

The Stabilization Branch

Market systems may be unstable; cyclical swings in employment and the price level can impose widespread hardships. Musgrave's **stabilization** branch of government would concentrate on achieving full employment, price-level stability, and economic growth. Since the Great Depression of the 1930s, our federal government has used a mix of macroeconomic policies to try to achieve these goals.

The budget of the stabilization branch would be the only part of the total budget ever out of balance, and it would rely solely on positive or negative taxes.[2] When rising prices posed a problem, the stabilization branch would run a budget surplus by imposing positive taxes to siphon away some private purchasing power. The resulting dip in demand would dampen inflationary pressures. If the economy suffered from recession, negative stabilization taxes (driving the budget into deficit) would increase the purchasing power of consumers and investors. Increases in disposable income would stimulate demand, bolstering output and employment. The stabilization budget balances during stable and prosperous periods.

Stabilization is a macroeconomic concern, and redistribution is treated later in this book. Consequently, we will ignore these topics for now and will concentrate on government allocations of goods and services.

The Allocation Branch

The **allocation** branch of government would provide goods that would be provided inadequately, if at all, if left to private decision making. The allocation branch should divert resources from private use to the public sector as long as the marginal benefits exceed the benefits society would receive were the

---

1. Richard A. Musgrave, *The Theory of Public Finance* (New York: McGraw-Hill, 1959), especially chapters 1–3.

2. Note that Musgrave's stabilization budget conducts a Keynesian style of fiscal policy but relies on variations in taxes alone, eschewing changes in government spending as a stabilization tool.

resources used for private goods. The values of the private goods forgone are the opportunity costs of the goods provided by government.

For example, spending on national defense has been a major issue of the 1980s. In an efficient economy, more spending for national defense involves a trade-off because resources must be bid away from competing uses. One possible way to acquire more resources for defense is to cut funding for social programs. For example, when former President Reagan sought more defense spending (his "Star Wars" proposal), he proposed cuts in government outlays for agriculture, transportation, education, housing, welfare, and other areas. Alternatively, national defense might grow at the expense of private consumption or investment.

This allocation process can be seen in Figure 1, which depicts marginal social benefits and costs assumed for Star Wars satellites. For any fewer than 89 satellites, society gains on balance by producing more. But society's marginal benefit in deterring war from the ninetieth satellite is less than its marginal cost, so putting it in orbit would be inefficient.

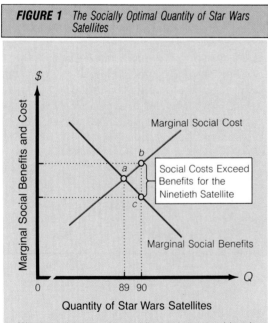

FIGURE 1 *The Socially Optimal Quantity of Star Wars Satellites*

$

Marginal Social Benefits and Cost

Marginal Social Cost

b
a
Social Costs Exceed
Benefits for the
Ninetieth Satellite
c

Marginal Social Benefits

0   89 90   Q

Quantity of Star Wars Satellites

Whether private goods or public goods are considered, economic efficiency requires that marginal social cost equals marginal social benefit ($MSC = MSB$).

There are, however, numerous difficulties with this approach. If contractors compete vigorously for tightly specified government contracts, market prices will reflect the marginal social costs of resources. But where the number of potential contractors is limited or the product cannot easily be specified, costs may be excessive. Another problem arises if policymakers' decisions fail to mirror voters' preferences and benefits. (These problems are treated in the next chapter.) Moreover, forecasting marginal social benefits is often a guessing game, especially for projects expected to yield benefits over a long time horizon or that embody significant externalities. In spite of such difficulties, however, modern *cost/benefit* techniques can provide reasonable estimates of marginal social benefits and costs in many cases.

Ideally, only Musgrave's allocation branch of government would directly alter resource allocations. The stabilization and distribution branches would affect allocation indirectly and only by their influence on the size or distribution of national income. Taxes collected from the beneficiaries of governmentally provided goods would exactly pay for such goods, and the allocation branch would run a balanced budget.[3]

This proposed division of budgeting into three branches—allocation, distribution, and stabilization—aids clear thinking, but in actual budget making, straightforward solutions to certain issues may be opposed because of their side effects. For example, a sales tax might be efficient, but groups concerned about equity may oppose it because of its alleged regressivity. As a result, policymakers are often forced to choose one goal at the cost of another. Before looking at such trade-offs, we need to consider the kinds of market failures that cause most people to look to government for a cure.

Market Failure: Allocation _____

Competitive markets allocate production and consumption for most goods so that marginal social benefits equal marginal social costs. Allocative market failure occurs when marginal social benefits and

---

3. People would not be faced with separate tax bills from the allocation, distribution, and stabilization branches of government. These budgets would be consolidated so that each taxpayer would pay only the net taxes due or receive a net transfer payment.

costs diverge. In such cases, government may be used to provide the socially optimal quantities of some goods and to limit economic bads. (Some cynics argue that this is unlikely because government bureaucracies are hopelessly inefficient, but only philosophical anarchists argue that government provision of certain goods never improves efficiency.)

Musgrave's budget format suggests that government should directly allocate resources only when private suppliers fail to provide certain goods in accord with consumer preferences. Why might the private sector inadequately service consumers? After all, if consumers strongly desire a particular good, won't they willingly pay a price high enough to buy it? Unfortunately, the market system is destined to provide too much or too little of some goods in some very predictable areas. Inadequate competition, externalities, and public goods (e.g., national defense or a system of justice) are the three main reasons why the private sector fails to achieve efficiency because, in unchecked market equilibria, marginal social benefits (MSB) will diverge from marginal social costs (MSC).

Monopoly Power

Firms that exercise monopoly power charge higher prices and produce less than the socially preferred output (the amount produced were markets purely competitive). Long-run average cost curves that decline over a wide range of output relative to the market may make competition inefficient and create pressures for natural monopoly. Antitrust actions may curb monopoly power and promote competition, or regulation can steer the behavior of natural monopolists into a more efficient mode.

Externalities

Exchanges occur only when all parties *directly* involved in transactions expect to gain. The marketplace works best when only these parties are affected. Competition maximizes individual welfare and the general interests of society through specialization and exchange; the marginal social benefits of transactions are equated with their marginal social costs, given the current income distribution. But certain technical characteristics may cause inefficient market solutions for some goods. For example, pollution and obnoxious billboards might be even more prevalent if the market operated unchecked. Riding in a car would be even more dangerous if drivers continually negotiated for the right-of-way, and big city traffic might suffer terminal gridlock. Lack of regulations requiring immunization might allow epidemics of deadly diseases to sweep through the population. (You may have heard of "Typhoid Mary," a restaurant worker who infected thousands of people in her day.)

This type of market failure arises because people not directly engaged in certain transactions are affected.

Externalities *occur when private calculations of benefits or costs differ from the benefits or costs to society because third parties gain or lose from a transaction.*

Market prices and quantities tend to ignore the preferences of these third parties, so market solutions may not yield maximum social welfare.

The case of garbage removal from the Slob family's property is shown in Figure 2. Suppose that this family is immune to informal social pressures to maintain their property. When the Slobs decide how frequently to have trash hauled away, they ignore the diseases their neighbors might contract, declines in the values of adjacent property, or obnoxious odors from their trash. Unless the Slobs are compelled to consider these external costs, they will choose point *a,* leaving Q_0 garbage around their house at a private cost of P_0 per unit. Society might just legally require them to have all their trash hauled off. This attitude, however, ignores the benefits that the Slobs (or even ourselves) derive from being able to let the garbage pile up temporarily instead of having it removed at all points in time. After all, the Slobs are members of society. What we would like to do is make sure that they consider the effects on their neighbors from leaving trash lying around.

The demand curve D reflects the Slob family's gain from littering its own property, cleaning up only occasionally rather than being fastidious at all times. The MSC curve in Figure 2 reflects the losses from litter suffered by both the Slobs and their neighbors, with the MC curve reflecting the Slobs' marginal private cost. Suppose that the Slobs have the legal right to accumulate trash. In this case, the vertical distance between the two cost curves represents the amount neighbors would be willing to pay the Slobs to reduce the accumulation of trash to a level of Q_1, the

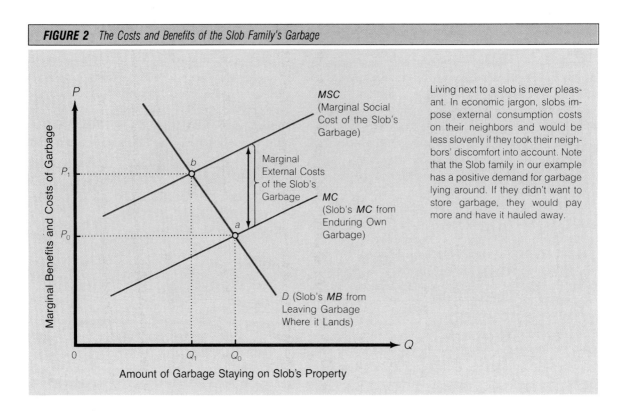

FIGURE 2 The Costs and Benefits of the Slob Family's Garbage

Living next to a slob is never pleasant. In economic jargon, slobs impose external consumption costs on their neighbors and would be less slovenly if they took their neighbors' discomfort into account. Note that the Slob family in our example has a positive demand for garbage lying around. If they didn't want to store garbage, they would pay more and have it hauled away.

socially optimal level. If neighbors could legally limit the Slobs' debris, this vertical distance is the price the neighbors would charge to allow the Slobs to accumulate garbage. Note that the optimal amount of trash is not zero. After all, we all have a little garbage on hand at all times, don't we? No one's home is perfectly immaculate, even on the days when garbage is collected.

How to deal with externalities is addressed in detail in our chapter on environmental quality. It is time to examine the market failure that seems to require the most of government—the public goods problem.

Public Goods

You can solve the problem of wanting more shoes with a trip to a shoe store. But suppose that you want more public parks or a stronger national defense. If you voluntarily send a check to the National Park Service or the Department of Defense, even if they spent your money wisely you would not have appreciably better access to parks or be noticeably better defended. The problem is that these are examples of public goods.

*A **public good** can be enjoyed by numerous individuals at the same time (nonrivalry); once a public good is available, denying access to a consumer is prohibitively expensive (nonexclusion).*

The absence of any identifiable effect causes people to limit their voluntary contributions for public goods. Voluntary funding, if any, tends to fall far short of that needed for optimal provision of such goods.

Rivalry and Nonrivalry Consumption exhausts a *rival good* so that no one else can consume the same unit of it. You cannot eat a peanut butter sandwich if I eat it first; for you to eat peanut butter, it must be in a different sandwich. I cannot use your raincoat if you are wearing it. Peanut butter and raincoats are rival goods. We can, however, enjoy the same TV program without rivalry. When your television set receives signals, it does not affect the signals to mine. A police patrol can simultaneously protect both you and your neighbor from burglary. Police protection and television broadcasts are examples of *nonrival goods*.

Exclusion and Nonexclusion

Restaurants do not have to serve you unless you wear a shirt and shoes. A theater can require you to buy a ticket before seeing a film. Movies and meals are *exclusive goods*. But if a Star Wars satellite protects you from attacks by foreign enemies, your neighbor is automatically protected. Fencing a national park might be both expensive and in conflict with its purpose. These are *nonexclusive goods*. Nonexclusion occurs whenever it is prohibitively expensive to prevent people from enjoying a good.

Product Characteristics and Market Failure

Rival/nonrival and exclusive/nonexclusive relationships are combined in goods in several different ways. Table 1 summarizes these possibilities.

Pure Private Goods

Goods that are both rival and exclusive are *pure private goods* and tend to be efficiently provided by the marketplace. Most goods, from abalone to zithers, are pure private goods.

Excess Capacity

A combination of nonrivalness and exclusiveness generally entails excess capacity. Theaters with empty seats or unsold tickets for airline flights offer examples of nonrival goods, but you can be excluded from flying or enjoying movies. Unless significant economies of scale cause excess capacity and are so significant that monopoly power is a problem, competitive markets normally provide these goods efficiently.

Rival/Nonexclusion

The market fails whenever the costs of excluding a person who does not pay for a good are prohibitive relative to the value of that good. A nonexclusive but rival good is typically overused, if it is provided at all. If I enjoy scenery but also value the roadside as a garbage site, I may toss beer cans out my window as I drive down the highway. The resultant eyesore and the costs of cleaning up my litter are borne by taxpayers at large; my personal costs are trivial. (Most anti-litter laws are only weakly enforced.)

Abuse of the environment becomes rampant when both nonexclusion and rivalness for resource usage are present. In England, everyone once had access to certain property that was held in common, but the "commons" were often treated as though no one owned them. Individuals had little incentive to maintain common property, and it was typically overused and run down.

TABLE 1 *Rivalness and Exclusion*

	Rival	Nonrival
Exclusive	*Pure private goods* will be efficiently provided by the marketplace: Beer Candy bars Automobiles Records	Excess capacity situations. The private market will provide, but government regulation may be used to attain efficiency if economies of scale are significant: Movies Airline flights Rapid transit trips Cable TV
Nonexclusive	Pollution. Regulation is normally used to resolve: Air, water, or noise pollution Litter Assignment of property rights is sometimes used.	*Pure public goods*. There will be less than efficient amounts provided unless government steps in: National defense Flood-control projects Weather forecasts Infectious disease control

Pure Public Goods A *pure public good* is both nonexclusive and nonrival. Weather forecasts on TV may simultaneously benefit you and me in making plans for picnics; preventing weather information from spreading is difficult. If a private meteorologist tried to sell forecasts and you subscribed for this information, the meteorologist could do little to prevent you from passing it along. Hence, the U.S. Weather Service is the major source of weather forecasting.

Providing for Public Goods

Goods that are both nonexclusive and nonrival differ markedly from private goods. It should not be a surprise that total social demands for public goods requires a different construction than market demands for private goods.

Private Demands Versus Public Demands

Recall that market demands for private goods are the *horizontal* summations of individual demand curves—we add together the quantities demanded at each price. This is shown for lobsters, a *private good,* in Panel A of Figure 3. The total demand curve for a *public good,* however, is the *vertical summation* of individual demand curves, as illustrated in Panel B. We all gain by having an extra police patrol cruising our neighborhood at night, so our demand for this additional surveillance reflects the dollar amount we would pay *collectively* for it. The total demand curve for a public good is constructed by adding the funds we each would willingly pay for each possible level of the good.

Optimal Public Goods

After we calculate total demands for public goods, how do we determine how much to provide? Panel B of Figure 3 illustrates Alan's (*A*) and Beth's (*B*) individual demands for police patrols, together with their total demand curve. Note that we assume that both individuals willingly reveal their true preferences for police patrols. The total demand is the vertical summation of Alan's and Beth's demands. We assume that the costs of patrolling are $6 per patrol, but Alan and Beth differ in their revealed benefits from each patrol. If three patrols are provided each night, Alan

FIGURE 3 Market Demands for Private and Public Goods

We all face the same prices for private goods but buy different amounts, so the market demand is the *horizontal* sum of individual demands (Panel A). We all consume the same public goods but value them differently, so the total demand for public goods requires *vertically* summing individual demands (Panel B). Revenue adequate for optimal amounts of a public good are generated if each person pays his or her marginal benefit (in dollars) times the amount provided. In this case, three patrols nightly at $6 per patrol could be secured if *B* paid $6 and *A* paid $12. But both *A* and *B* will try to be "free riders." Thus we use involuntary taxes to pay for public goods.

values each patrol at $2, while Beth values each at $4. The $6 cost per patrol could be covered if each paid in proportion to their gains [($2 × 3) + ($4 × 3)].

Contrast this with the optimal provision of private goods as depicted in Panel A; each individual pays the same price per unit, but each consumes a different quantity of lobsters. Alan consumes 35 pounds of lobsters annually at $2 per pound, while Beth is satisfied with 25 pounds at that price.

The preceding solution to public goods assumes that individuals willingly reveal their preferences. Further, it suggests that we could pay for these public goods by taxing individuals in proportion to "benefits received." This benefit approach, however, is not the only way to levy taxes.

The Microeconomics of Taxation

Taxes are the price we pay for civilization.
— *Oliver Wendell Holmes, Jr.*

We have outlined some areas in which government plays a role in a market economy. Regulation may be important at times, but governmental provision of goods normally requires the government to spend money. Budget outlays can be funded by borrowing, but most government spending is financed by taxes. Many Americans complain loudly about the taxes we pay. As Table 2 shows, however, most foreigners living in developed economies pay far more.

Equity in Taxation

Even the most rabid anarchist benefits from some government programs. The central questions are:

1. How great are the total benefits from government programs?
2. How are these benefits distributed?
3. How much should individuals pay for publicly provided goods?

The Benefit Principle

The benefit principle of taxation is an ancient normative doctrine that taxes should be in proportion to the benefits people receive from government.

TABLE 2 *Taxes as a Percentage of Gross Domestic Product*

Country	1965	1987
Sweden	35.8%	48.8%
France	35.0	44.9
Austria	34.7	42.3
Italy	27.2	41.0
England	30.6	37.6
Canada	25.9	35.3
Portugal	18.5	34.9
Greece	20.6	32.4
Australia	24.7	32.8
Switzerland	20.7	32.1
United States	26.2	30.3
Japan	18.4	28.7
Spain	14.7	26.0

Sources: *CIA World Factbook*, 1987, 1988 and *Handbook of Economic Statistics*, 1987, 1988. Calculations by authors.

The **benefit principle of taxation** *taxes people in proportion to the marginal benefits they receive from a governmentally provided good.*

This principle conforms to the gut feeling most of us have that you should pay for what you get. In the police patrol example, tax revenues just adequate for optimal amounts of this public good can be secured by levying taxes so that citizens share costs in proportion to their marginal benefits.

Taxation according to marginal benefits is, unfortunately, impractical for most pure public goods. The public sector provides an incredible array of goods, and the costs of collecting and processing the information required for appropriately different taxes is prohibitive. Individuals cannot be excluded from enjoying the benefits whether they paid taxes or not. These characteristics of public goods lead to the *free-rider* problem.

Free Riders   Few people would reveal their preferences for public goods if they were taxed accordingly. This is especially true for projects (e.g., national defense) that benefit masses of people, most of whom are unknown to any given taxpayer.

Suppose that taxes were based strictly on your reported benefits from a public good. Some people might assert that they want little or none of it. Extremely crafty types might even try to get tax credits by asserting that the good harms them. Once other people agree to buy a public good, free riders can enjoy it costlessly. If many people attempt to free ride, the public good may not be available at all. Any privately marketed public good would be available in less than optimal quantities because of the free-rider problem.

User Charges   General tax revenues are used to pay for most goods provided through the public sector, but the benefit approach to allocating public goods has been the basis for user charges that relate taxes to expected benefits. When a governmentally provided good has the exclusive characteristics of a private good, benefits can be approximated and users can be charged accordingly. Examples include bus fares and entry fees for public museums, zoos, parks, or toll roads. Gasoline taxes are also roughly proportional to benefits; owners of heavy trucks or drivers of huge gas hogs pay more gas taxes than drivers of fuel-efficient compact cars, but they also put more wear and tear on the highways that gasoline taxes support.

Although the benefit principle of taxation is often inapplicable because individuals' preferences for public goods are concealed, general tax revenues are often used to fund activities where user charges could be easily applied. For example, should vegetarians pay for meat inspections? User charges imposed on meat packers would be shifted forward to meat buyers. Similarly, federal tests of new medicines could be billed to the pharmaceutical companies that want to market them. If airports, air traffic controllers, and airplane safety inspectors were paid for by plane owners, these tax burdens would not be borne by people who benefit little from air transport.

Political and practical difficulties, however, are only two of the drawbacks of benefit taxes. Benefit taxation may conflict with principles of taxation that are based on other concerns about equity.

The Ability-to-Pay Principle

An alternative to the benefit principle of taxation is the idea that taxes should be proportional to one's ability to pay.

> The **ability-to-pay principle** *suggests that the "fairest" tax is one based on your financial ability to support government activities.*

The benefit and ability-to-pay principles, though apparently incompatible, may lead to similar policies. Rich people may benefit more than poor people from such public goods as national defense or police and fire protection because rich people stand to lose more from disasters. Thus, both principles may support the idea that the rich should pay more taxes than the poor.

Vertical Equity   Richard Musgrave labels as vertical equity the idea that a rich individual should pay more taxes than a poor one for each to bear the same burden in supporting government.

> **Vertical equity** *asserts that some people inevitably are in a better position to pay higher taxes and should do so.*

Implementing vertical equity in any tax system involves deciding who should pay higher rates and then writing tax laws that actually collect this amount from the correct people. Wealth and income are normally viewed as good measures of one's ability to pay taxes. Progressive taxation is, however, unnecessary for vertical equity; even regressive tax systems might satisfy this equity principle as long as the rich paid more in absolute terms.

Horizontal Equity   The Fourteenth Amendment to our Constitution (the Equal Protection clause) states ". . . nor shall any State deprive any person of life, liberty, or property, without due process of law; nor deny to any person within its jurisdiction the *equal* protection of the laws." This fundamental concept that "equals must be treated equally" has become known as horizontal equity.

> **Horizontal equity** *requires that individuals who are equal in all important respects be treated equally.*

Implementing a horizontally equitable tax system first requires specifying what constitutes equal circumstances (income, wealth, age, or marital status?). Then we must determine what equal treatment means. Does equal treatment mean equal tax rates or equal tax payments over your lifetime? Our tax system needs to be both horizontally and vertically equitable. Horizontal equity dictates that equals should pay equal taxes; vertical equity that "unequals" should be treated unequally.

Efficiency in Taxation _____

Most economists share the concerns of people who are irritated by apparent inequity in the tax system, but focus instead on areas where greater precision is possible. Specialists in public finance are especially disturbed by excess burdens, most of which are caused by the non-neutral effects of taxation.

Excess Burdens

The total burden of a tax can be measured by the amount of money that would have to be paid the individual on whom the burden falls to make that person just as well off with the tax as without it.

> The **excess burden of a tax** is the difference between the total burden and the tax revenue collected by government.

In his *Wealth of Nations*, Adam Smith suggested that efficiency in taxation requires taxes to be certain (unavoidable), convenient, and that collection costs should be minimized relative to the tax yield. In addition to administration costs and taxpayer compliance costs, taxes impose excess burdens if they distort the prices faced by consumers, workers, savers, investors, or business decision makers. Excess burdens arise when people are made worse off than the taxes actually collected from them. For example, if the government imposes a tax that ultimately collects $100 from you but warps your decisions, the tax may burden you by far more than $100. This distortion does not help the government, and collecting the tax imposes an excess burden on you.

In 1985, Kyoto, Japan began taxing visitors to Buddhist temples. The tax was strongly opposed by most temple priests who claimed the tax violated their religious principles. The priests decided initially to let visitors in free rather than pay the tax but eventually closed the temple doors to visitors. The city was unable to collect any revenue, but tourists suffered (an excess burden). Finally, after negotiations with the priests broke down, the city decided to eliminate the tax.

Supply and demand analysis can allow us to scrutinize excess burdens. In Figure 4, S_0 and D_0 reflect the nontaxed supply and demand for quarts of milk. For simplicity, we assume constant production costs at P_0 per quart.

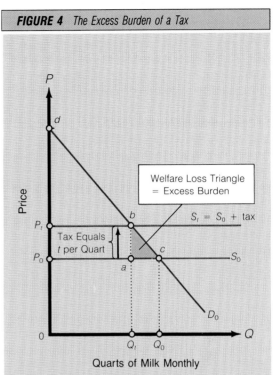

FIGURE 4 *The Excess Burden of a Tax*

Only under ideal circumstances will the losses of consumer surplus and economic rent (or producer surplus) due to a tax be fully offset by tax revenues. In the case shown here, the full burden of the tax is borne by consumers, who lose surplus $P_0 P_t bc$ while government gains revenue of $P_0 P_t ba$. There is a "deadweight" welfare loss of abc.

Suppose a tax of t per quart is imposed on milk. This "tax wedge" shifts the supply curve to S_t from the buyer's perspective. As buyers and sellers adjust to this tax, consumers watch the price of a quart of milk rise from P_0 to P_t, while the amount sold falls from Q_0 to Q_t. At Q_t quarts of milk monthly, the difference between the price paid by the buyer (P_t) and the price received by the seller (P_0) exactly equals tax t. Prior to the tax, consumers paid $0P_0 c Q_0$ for Q_0 quarts of milk but would have willingly paid $0dcQ_0$. Thus, they enjoyed a consumer surplus of $P_0 dc$. The rise in the consumers' price to P_t causes a loss of consumer surplus of the area below the consumer demand curve but above the original price (P_0) and below the new price (P_t). The consumer surplus lost equals the trapezoid $P_0 P_t bc$.

Government, however, gains monthly tax revenues of t per bottle for Q_t quarts of milk, a total of area P_0P_tba, which it can use to meet taxpayers' wants. Therefore, the total loss of consumer surplus minus the gains to government equals area abc (which is $P_0P_tbc - P_0P_tba$). The shaded triangle abc (sometimes called the *welfare-loss triangle*) represents a *deadweight loss* to society from this tax; it is the excess burden of the tax. These losses, however, may be more than offset by gains in consumer surplus from the goods government buys with the tax revenues. Of course, if government spending is inefficient, the "welfare-loss triangle" may understate the total loss to consumers. Government ideally minimizes the welfare-loss triangles incurred in securing any given total of tax revenues.

Neutrality

The neutrality principle combines and extends Adam Smith's certainty, convenience, and economy principles. Ideally, the costs of transferring purchasing power from private hands into the public purse are minimized.

> A **neutral tax** *distorts neither consumer buying patterns nor the production methods used by firms. Its total burden just equals the tax revenue collected—there are no excess burdens.*

The crucial idea behind *tax neutrality* is that the tax directly causes only income effects, not substitution effects.[4] That is, a neutral tax does not induce changes in behavior to avoid the tax; behavior changes only because of lost purchasing power. This requires that taxes be unavoidable.

No action by taxpayers (perhaps at the behest of their lawyers) should enable them to avoid payment, and the only impact on taxpayers should be declines in their purchasing power. For example, tax structures should not encourage fringe benefits in work contracts instead of direct wage payments or financial investment in tax-free municipal bonds rather than capital equipment. Nor should it encourage consumption of housing instead of groceries or automobiles. (Our tax system has done all these things.) Taxes that directly alter the relative benefits and costs facing consumers or business decision makers are non-neutral and inefficient. A neutral tax will be more certain, convenient, and economical than a non-neutral tax.

All taxes, unfortunately, are non-neutral. Most taxes cause substitution effects by directly altering relative prices, thereby changing the behavior of consumers and firms. As a result, taxes are often evaluated by their relative neutrality. Because all taxes are somewhat flawed, economists normally try to specify which are the most nearly neutral (those with the smallest excess burdens) and least inequitable in generating governmental revenues.

Evaluating the Current Tax System

The best taxes are old taxes.
—A Legislator's Proverb

Just how efficient and equitable are the important taxes now used by our federal, state, and local governments? Current sources of taxes are indicated in Figure 5.

Personal Income Taxes

One flaw of progressive personal income taxes is that rising marginal tax rates may discourage investment, work effort, and other attempts to make income. Another is that progressive tax systems historically have been ambiguous and rife with loopholes. These factors erode the tax base and cause legislators to raise tax rates. For example, if erosion of the base causes a tax rate of 50 percent to be applied to only half of potential untaxed income, then the rate could be dropped to 25 percent if all income were taxed.

And what is income, anyway? Many advocates of tax reform favor a comprehensive definition of income; your taxable income would be your total annual consumption spending plus the change in your net wealth over the period. For example, if you spent $8,000 during the year on consumer goods and if the value of your house increased by $5,000 but you lost $2,000 in the stock market, your total income would be $11,000 ($8,000 + $5,000 − $2,000 = $11,000). An income tax structure without loopholes, but at much lower than present rates, could be applied.

---

4. You may want to review the discussion of income and substitution effects from the chapter on consumer choice.

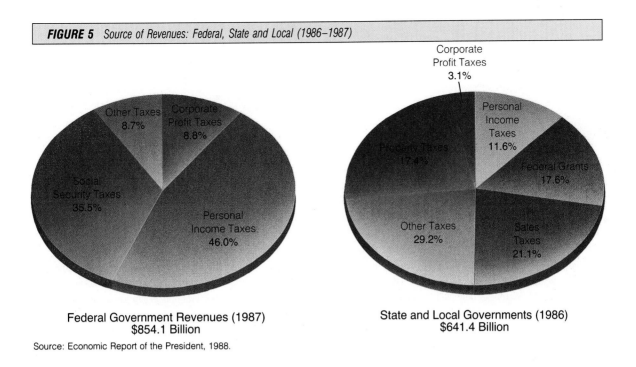

FIGURE 5 Source of Revenues: Federal, State and Local (1986–1987)

Federal Government Revenues (1987)
$854.1 Billion

State and Local Governments (1986)
$641.4 Billion

Source: Economic Report of the President, 1988.

Taxes are a powerful modifier of economic behavior. The Internal Revenue Code has been extremely complex, creating opportunities for individuals and corporations to use tax loopholes to legally avoid tax liabilities. Tax *avoidance* is legal, but high marginal rates have also provided huge incentives for tax *evasion,* which means illegal nonpayment of taxes. These possibilities violate all of Adam Smith's principles of certainty, convenience, and economy.

At first glance, our four-step progressive income tax system might seem an example of an ability-to-pay tax, but it is still riddled with enough loopholes that this impression is clouded. A family with a wage and salary income of $20,000 may pay more taxes than a similar family with particular investment income of $30,000. The principles of vertical and horizontal equity are not completely met by the current income tax system. Several studies indicate, however, that even after allowing for the heavier exploitation of loopholes by high-income families than by low-income families, the incidence of our income tax is, on average, mildly progressive. Not all loopholes are designed only for the rich. Moreover, the idea that loopholes offer huge advantages for those who use them is quite exaggerated, as Focus 1 indicates.

The income tax has often been far from neutral. Exemptions, deductions, tax credits, oil depletion al-lowances, and other loopholes have abounded, and many people changed their behavior to take advantage of these special treatments. Competition for tax loopholes causes overinvestment in tax sheltered areas. For example, much of the 1970s explosion in housing prices may have resulted from surges in demands as middle-class taxpayers bought homes to take advantage of the deductibility of interest payments and the nonreportability of increases in the values of their homes.

You know how complicated computing your federal tax liability can be if you have ever filed a Form 1040 (the long form). State income tax computations are sometimes even more complex. Most economists favor eliminating almost all exemptions, credits, and deductions except for necessary business expenses. Then tax rates could be lowered substantially and still yield the same tax revenues. This eliminates much of the vertical and horizontal inequity in income taxes and substantially reduces the economic inefficiency caused by preferential tax treatments for some sources of income.

For all the flaws of our income tax system, there seems to be widespread support for income taxation with some degree of progressivity. Few Americans favor abolishing the Sixteenth Amendment, which authorized income taxes. The major bone of conten-

Tax Loopholes: Private Benefits and Public Costs

Most people perceive tax loopholes as mechanisms that allow rich people to escape their fair shares of the national tax burden. But do the rich really gain much from loopholes? Contrary to the implications of tidbits that frequently appear in the media (e.g., columns reporting that "Daddy Warbucks only paid $314.83 in taxes last year on his billion dollar income"), few people gain very much by using tax loopholes. Here is an example to show why.

Assume that most investors were in a 50 percent tax bracket, and that all investment markets were initially in equilibrium and could be expected to yield after-tax rates of return equal to 10 percent. Now suppose that the Turkey Farmers Association persuaded Congress to declare that frozen turkeys were vital to the national defense and that income from turkey farming should be exempted from all federal taxes.

This raises the after-tax rate of return from turkeys to 20 percent, and many investors could be expected to try to take advantage of this loophole. As money flowed into turkey farms, however, the resulting sharp drop in turkey prices would be paralleled by a decline in the rate of return from turkey farming. Simultaneously, other investment areas would decline because of outflows of resources towards turkey farming. In these nonfavored areas, the prices of goods would rise, and this would be

paralleled by increases in rates of return for them. The law of equal marginal advantage implies that the final equilibrium would entail equal after-tax rates of return from all investments, including turkey farming.

Those who used this loophole would gain very little from it. Such loopholes ultimately only shift resources towards tax-sheltered areas, which means that fewer resources are used in less favored industries than market forces alone indicate are optimal. Overall, tax loopholes reduce government revenues, but loophole users' gains are trivial. The distorted structure of national output reflects loopholes instead of consumer preferences.

If loopholes ultimately provide so little gain to those who use them, then why do proposals to plug loopholes arouse such outrage? The answer is that closing a loophole can impose huge losses on people who currently use them. For example, many people have bought expensive houses because interest on mortgages is deductible from taxable income. This deductibility has artificially raised the demand for houses and pushed up real estate prices. Were this deduction eliminated, current homeowners would lose, not only because of higher taxes, but because housing prices might plummet as well.

Who gains from loopholes? In large measure, the gainers are those who ac-

quire specialized resources before favorable tax laws are enacted. They can become wealthy when the values of tax-sheltered areas are capitalized. Another group that gains are the tax attorneys, CPAs, and "financial planners" who advise people who want to avoid taxes. But even this group gains very little because most are competent people who would have been successful in other areas had tax loopholes never existed.

Tax reform historically has meant providing relief to groups that seem overburdened because of loopholes enjoyed by too many other groups. This has caused incredible complexity in the tax codes as loopholes have piled on top of loopholes over time—a situation only partially remedied by the Tax Reform Act of 1986.

tion is how to simplify income taxes and make them fairer.

The Reagan administration made tax reform a top priority, but most observers were skeptical—they had heard similar campaign promises for decades. Nevertheless, the 1986 Tax Reform Act (TRA) represented the most complete revamping of our tax system in decades. Income taxes were eliminated for most low-income families, and the act replaced the 15 tax brackets under the old system (ranging from 11 to 50 percent) with two brackets—15 and 28 percent. A "temporary" 5 percent surcharge applies to certain high-income taxpayers, placing them in a 33 percent bracket for a portion of their income. This "yuppie tax" covers taxable income (depending on filing status) ranging from roughly $43,000 to $171,000. This surcharge turns the nominal two-bracket income tax into a four-bracket system. Table 3 details the 1988 tax rates for various filing categories.

The 1986 tax law was not intended to lower most people's taxes. It was intended to be *revenue neutral,* which means that as much tax revenue was expected as under the old system. Its major advantages were consistency and, supposedly, simplicity. Unfortunately, achieving simplicity was delayed because of adjustment clauses that caused filing your income taxes to be an even more complicated process during transition to the new tax system.

Major loopholes were closed, allowing both individual and corporate tax rates to be cut sharply. *Consistency* (loophole closure) was expected to rebuild public confidence so that people in similar circumstances would pay similar taxes (horizontal equity), and that people with high incomes pay their "fair share" (vertical equity). *Simplicity* makes it less necessary to keep detailed breakdowns of personal finances. (Some studies indicate that such accounting absorbs resources equal to 1–2 percent of personal income.)

Most income is now taxed more uniformly, regardless of source. For example, capital gains from stock or real estate investments historically were taxed at around half the investor's normal marginal rate. This preferential treatment was dropped. Deductions were also dropped for most (*a*) medical expenses, (*b*) state and local sales taxes, (*c*) casualty losses, (*d*) interest on consumer loans, and (*e*) deposits into Individual Retirement Accounts. Tax credits and income averaging were also curtailed. These reforms and the lower tax rates they permitted sharply reduced the "tax planning" that dominated many private financial decisions under the old law. Private decision making was refocused towards real values of investments instead of a frantic search for loopholes.

The new law did, however, largely retain the deductibility of real estate interest and property taxes, the two major "middle-class" loopholes. Pressure from state and local governments also caused interest income from state and municipal bonds to remain tax exempt. Nevertheless, most public finance experts perceived the 1986 TRA as a major step in the direction of efficiency and equity.

TABLE 3 Personal Income Tax Rates on Taxable Income (1988)				
Rates	**Joint Return with Two Exemptions**	**Single Taxpayer with One Exemption**	**Head of Household with Two Exemptions**	**Married Filing Separately with One Exemption**
15%	$0–29,750	$0–17,850	$0–23,900	$0–14,875
28	29,750–71,900	17,850–43,150	23,900–61,650	14,875–35,950
33*	71,900–171,090*	43,150–100,480*	61,650–145,630	35,950–124,220
28	Over 171,090	Over 100,480	Over 145,630	Over 124,220

*The 15 percent rate is phased out for high income taxpayers by placing a 5 percent surcharge (33 percent bracket) on certain amounts reflected in this table. As noted, the marginal rate above such amounts drops back to 28 percent.

Source: Internal Revenue Service, 1988.

Payroll Taxes

You may be surprised to learn that the *Social Security* tax may soon be the single largest source of federal revenues. Social Security taxes, unemployment compensation, and workmen's disability taxes are *payroll taxes*. That is, they are based primarily on the payrolls that firms pay.

Try this multiple-choice question: The Social Security tax is borne by (*a*) workers, (*b*) employers, (*c*) consumers, (*d*) a 50/50 split between workers and employers, (*e*) a 50/50 split between workers and consumers.

One pervasive tax myth is the idea that the Social Security tax is split 50/50 by employers and employees. This is the legal incidence of the tax, which in 1988 required employers and employees each to pay 7.51 percent of the first $45,000 in wage income. Table 4 shows how this tax has changed over the years. (Of course, firms cannot pay taxes; only people can. To make this myth consistent, the firm's share is presumably forward-shifted in higher prices to customers.) The simple fact is that the full tax is probably borne by workers. Here is an example to show why.

Suppose that you work for XYZ Corporation and your marginal revenue product is $2,500 monthly. If there are no other employment expenses such as taxes to consider, competition forces XYZ to pay you $2,500 monthly. Now suppose you insist that XYZ send $150 monthly to your Aunt Mary. The firm, however, will not retain your services unless you agree to

allow them to deduct it from your check; if the law dictates that they send checks for $150 to the widowed aunts of all employees, they will cut wages correspondingly. It makes no sense to keep an employee who is worth only $2,500 if total employment costs exceed $2,500 monthly. Likewise, if money also must be sent to Uncle Sam because you are employed, you will bear this full burden: Your gross salary will be reduced by the amount of the tax.

Some critics describe Social Security as a welfare system of payments from the poor to the rich; Social Security has been "pay-as-you-go" for decades. Thus, taxes on current workers cover Social Security payments to retirees. Even the influx of baby boomers into the labor market has not eased the growing tax burden as the ranks of older Americans have swollen. The burdens on workers born between 1960 and the year 2000 may become horrendous when baby boomers begin to reach age 62 in 2008.

Many critics question any system that allows one generation to systematically extract transfer payments from another, or which permits a 65-year-old retiree who draws $100,000 in investment income to receive welfare payments from 18-year-old dishwashers who work for minimum wages. Our Social Security system allows precisely these sorts of things to occur. A recent study of Social Security and racial demographics points out an additional inequity.[5] White work-

---

5. National Center for Policy Analysis, *Social Security and Race*, No. 128, June 1987.

Year	Maximum Covered Base ($)	Tax Rate[a] (Percentage)	Maximum Amount of Tax[a]
1934	2,000	2.0	$ 40
1970	7,800	9.6	748
1975	14,100	11.7	1,650
1980	25,900	12.3	3,176
1985	39,600	14.1	5,584
1988	45,000	15.02	6,759

TABLE 4 Social Security Tax Hikes

Source: *Statistical Abstract of the United States*, 1988.
[a]Half of these rates and amounts are legally levied on employers; the other half is legally borne by employees.

ers tend to live longer than black workers. The consequences, according to this study, are that:

1. A white male entering the labor market today can expect to receive 74 percent more Social Security retirement benefits and 47 percent more Medicare benefits than a black male earning the same wage.
2. A white working couple can expect to receive about 35 percent more retirement and Medicare benefits than a black working couple that has the same lifetime earnings pattern.

Thus, black workers may be subsidizing the retirement of white workers, something totally unintended by Congress.

Among many reform proposals are (*a*) raising the minimum age for retirement benefits, (*b*) eliminating benefits to the wealthy, (*c*) having all revenues come from general revenues, and (*d*) replacing Social Security with a "negative income tax" plan. Pressure will mount to modify the system as the population of older people continues to grow, raising the payroll tax burden.

Sales and Excise Taxes

Sales taxes are percentage taxes that are broadly levied on dollar sales volumes; *excise taxes* are per unit taxes levied on specific goods. Most sales taxes are collected by state and local governments. If sales taxes cover all goods, they are reasonably neutral and efficient. Sales taxes are not neutral, however, to the extent that they exempt items such as food, housing, or labor services. They distort relative prices and economic behavior. Excise taxes are selective, being commonly applied to items like telephone calls, electric service, gasoline, and tires. Some excise taxes, called *sin taxes* (e.g., on cigarettes and liquor), are especially popular ways to raise revenues. Again, price distortions create economic inefficiency.

Sales and excise taxes are widely attacked as regressive under the reasoning that the percentages of income devoted to purchases of taxed goods is higher for the poor than for the rich. Those who attack the regressivity of sales taxes commonly advocate soaking "rich" corporations. This strategy may be a mistake, as the following analysis indicates.

Corporate Income Taxes

Corporate accounting profits are taxed at the rates shown in Table 5. There is an unsettled debate about whether any changes in these rates are immediately forward-shifted to consumers as higher prices, or whether the tax burden falls on stockholders in the short run. In the long run consumers bear much of this tax burden because *corporate income taxes* apply to accounting profits, which are largely normal profits, not economic profits. The corporate income tax raises costs and ultimately prices because normal accounting profits are a long-run production cost. Moreover, even a tax on pure profits may be ultimately borne in part by consumers because overall investment in our economy is dampened; the reduced capital stock drives up prices.

The tax is distortive to the extent that it is forward-shifted; that is, the prices of goods manufactured primarily by corporations are raised relative to the prices of goods most often produced by unincorporated firms. A sad bit of irony is that if, relative to rich people, poor people devote larger shares of their incomes to the mass-produced goods supplied by corporations, it may be that the burden of the tax is regressive. People who think that corporate income taxes "soak the rich" are probably wrong.

If the tax is backward-shifted, people will be reluctant to invest in corporations. (Firms cannot truly pay taxes; only people can—in this case, stockholders.) The corporate sector will shrink relative to noncorporate firms until after-tax rates of return are equalized. There is also the issue of "double taxation of dividends." After the corporate income tax has been

TABLE 5 Corporate Tax Rates	
Taxable Income	**Rate (Percentage)**
$0–50,000	15%
50,001–75,000	25
75,001–100,000	34
100,001–335,000	39
Over 335,000	34

Source: Internal Revenue Service, 1988.

paid, dividends to stockholders are taxed at their individual income tax rates.

The inefficiency and inequity of the corporate income tax combine to make it extremely unpopular among most economists. One proposed reform is to eliminate corporate income taxes and allocate corporate profits to stockholders, who would then pay normal personal income taxes on their shares of corporate profits. Economists from across the political spectrum differ little in their dislike of the corporate income tax, but politicians almost universally favor it because their constituents often see the tax as a way for the "little guy" to get even with Big Business.[6]

Property Taxes

The supply of land is perfectly inelastic. Thus, *land taxes* are relatively neutral—a tax on pure land rent has almost no effect on rental rates for land relative to other resources or goods. People often mistakenly apply this reasoning to property taxes, which are, however, among the least popular levies of all.

A *property tax* is based on the value of landholdings *plus* capital improvements. The supply of land is perfectly inelastic, but improvements are very elastically supplied in the long run. Suppose you own prime land in an area with high property taxes. If you put a new building on it, you will pay higher taxes. Thus, the property tax is a disincentive to development. Similarly, if you are a slum landlord with tenants whose poverty limits the rents you can charge, will you repair or modernize your buildings if your tax bill jumps substantially as a consequence? NO! Many students of the urban scene attribute part of the decay of central cities to high property taxes.

Inheritance and Gift Taxes

Federal **inheritance taxes** are presented in Table 6. There is an impression of progressivity, but keep in mind that the first $600,000 is tax exempt. You might think that inheritance taxes could be avoided if you just gave your heirs the money. There is, however, a federal *gift tax* to plug that loophole.

---

6. Former President Reagan casually proposed eliminating corporate income taxation in 1983, but adverse reactions from other politicians and the media quickly squelched the idea.

TABLE 6 Marginal Tax Rates for Federal Estate and Gift Taxes (1988)

Taxable Net Estate or Gift ($ Thousands)	Marginal Tax Rates
$ 0– 10	18%
10– 20	20%
20– 40	22%
40– 60	24%
60– 80	26%
80– 100	28%
100– 150	30%
150– 250	32%
250– 500	34%
500– 750	37%
750–1,000	39%
1,000–1,250	41%
1,250–1,500	43%
1,500–2,000	45%
2,000–2,500	49%
Over 2,500	50%

Source: Internal Revenue Service, 1988.

Very wealthy individuals avoid the inheritance tax in other ways. For one thing, they can establish trusts that delay disbursements of estates until long after a person's death. For example, if you had assets of $200 million, you might leave the money to your grandchildren with funds being paid out only when they reached age 35, allowing your children to live on the interest in the interim. This is only one of many loopholes that make the inheritance tax an "optional tax" in the words of some experts. One proposed reform of the income/inheritance tax systems is to merge them. That is, any inheritances or gifts would simply be treated as taxable income.

Tax Reform Proposals

Rankings of the fairness of various taxes yield similar responses from the general public and tax experts. Virtually no taxes are thought fair. Our overview suggests that badly flawed taxes have historically outweighed equitable and efficient taxes. Contrary to the legislator's proverb, most old taxes are *not* good taxes. Widespread discontent has led to some major reform proposals to bring our tax system into closer harmony with sound principles of taxation: fairness or equity, economic neutrality, and simplification.

Value-Added Taxes (VATs)

Our tax system has distorted incentives, stifled economic performance, and been so loaded with loopholes that, perhaps, large parts of it should be abandoned. Social Security and corporate income taxes are among possible targets for abolition. But what might replace revenues generated by these taxes? A favorite contender is the value-added tax.

> **Value-added taxes (VATs)** *resemble sales taxes but apply only to differences between sales and a firm's purchases from other firms.*

Thus, a *VAT* is a fixed percentage of a firm's payments for resources and is not applied to intermediate products the firm purchases from other firms.

A major virtue of the *VAT* is that it is reasonably neutral. Another is that tax evasion is extremely difficult, which partially accounts for its use in much of Europe. A drawback is that *VATs* are largely hidden; final customers may be unaware of the *VAT* embodied in the price of a product. A normative objection is that, like sales taxes, *VATs* may be somewhat regressive. Finally, *VATs* require more cumbersome accounting than sales taxes since *VATs* must be paid at several levels of output. Nonetheless, value-added taxes are probably more efficient and less inequitable than corporate income taxes, Social Security, or a number of other levies in the government's tool box.

Flat Rate Taxes

Many critics claim that attempts to make income taxes highly progressive are self-defeating. They argue, first, that high marginal tax rates at the upper end of the income spectrum discourage investment and so, in the long run, actually hold down the incomes of most "working stiffs"—those whose productivity would be enhanced were they working with more capital. The obsolescence of British manufacturing and the comparatively slow growth of British wages are cited as examples of this problem. A second difficulty is that high marginal tax rates increase the payoff from lobbying for new loopholes. These loopholes reduce the true progressivity of a tax system to a mere shadow of the nominal rates. Few high income individuals fail to exploit loopholes. In the words of Barry Bracewell-Milnes: "An economy breathes through its tax loopholes" when high marginal tax rates prevail. Progressivity has been combined with complex loopholes so that even tax experts have often been uncertain as to how much they owed. A third problem is that high marginal tax rates are incentives for illegal tax evasion.

One proposed answer for all these problems is the *flat rate tax.* Some analysts have suggested that a flat income tax of roughly 20 percent without any exemptions or deductions would (*a*) generate more revenue than the current tax system, (*b*) eliminate most tax evasion, (*c*) cut the amount of paperwork required from firms and households, and (*d*) cure the ulcers and headaches common around April 15 of each year. Critics of this proposal, however, fear that a flat income tax system would be an inequitable retreat from society's fight against poverty.

Consumption Taxes

Other critics argue that the major flaw in our income tax system is that, in a shortsighted quest for greater equality, income taxes kill the goose that lays the golden eggs. These critics view disparities in consumption levels, not income, as the root of social inequity. They argue that resource use (*consumption*) is more appropriate as a measure of ability to pay than are potential claims to resources (*income*). Another drawback to taxing income is the severe disincentive to save and invest. The critics' solution is to allow all saving as a deduction from taxes, effectively replacing income taxes with a tax on consumption alone.

A *consumption tax* could be as progressive as any income tax system, so problems of regressivity are not necessarily raised. Moreover, according to the advocates of this approach, the resulting increase in saving and investment would greatly enhance labor productivity, and technological breakthroughs would allow substantial economic growth.

We have looked at the types of government activities that can be rationalized as proper cures for market failures, and have examined various tax structures. Questions about why government spending and taxes so frequently depart from the ideal have been addressed only peripherally, however. Many of these questions are answered when we look at political dimensions of policy-making. The next chapter examines political behavior from an economic perspective.

CHAPTER REVIEW: KEY POINTS

1. Some market solutions may be inefficient; others are inequitable in the minds of many people. It has become conventional to categorize *market failures* as problems of either *allocation, distribution,* or *stabilization.* Attacking problems individually according to this division would permit the use of the best policy tool to solve any problem. Any side effects then may be addressed with appropriate measures. This three-branch distinction is useful for planning, but is tempered by politics in actual budgeting situations.

2. Musgrave's *distribution* branch would secure taxes from those who have "too much," and would provide higher incomes for the needy via a negative income tax of some sort. This budget would be continuously balanced.

3. The *stabilization* branch would run deficits through tax cuts to buffer recessions, and surpluses to dampen inflationary pressures. This would be the only part of the government budget ever out of balance.

4. The *allocation* branch would provide public goods that the market will not provide efficiently because of economies of scale in production or because of nonrivalry and nonexclusion in consumption. *Nonrivalry* means that a good is not used up when any individual enjoys it; a beautiful sunset is an example. *Nonexclusion* means that it is prohibitively expensive to deny access to a good. Note, however, that public provision does not require public production. Private firms often produce goods that government then distributes.

5. A good that is both nonrival and nonexclusive is a *pure public good.* Public goods will be less than optimally provided by the market system, if provided at all, because of attempts to *free ride.* A rival but nonexclusive good embodies *externalities* that often hinder the efficiency of market solutions. Pollution may be the problem if externalities are negative (costly); underproduction may result if externalities are positive (beneficial).

6. The *benefit principle of taxation* suggests that people should pay taxes in proportion to the marginal benefits they receive from a governmentally provided good. Ideally, Musgrave's allocation branch would run a balanced budget based on the benefit principle.

7. The demand for a pure public good is the *vertical summation* of individual demand curves since all can enjoy the good simultaneously, while demands for private goods are summed horizontally. Adequate revenue for optimal quantities of public goods is generated if people pay taxes equal to their marginal benefits multiplied by the amount of public good provided.

8. The *ability-to-pay principle of taxation* requires taxes in proportion to people's income, wealth, or possibly, their consumption. This principle is closely related to the idea that government policies should move the income distribution closer to equality than the market distribution of income.

9. The principle of *horizontal equity* suggests that equals should pay equal taxes; *vertical equity* requires higher taxes on the wealthy than on the poor.

10. If the loss to a taxpayer exceeds the government revenue gained, there is an *excess burden* of taxation. *Neutral taxes* impose only income, not substitution, effects and impose no excess burdens on taxpayers.

11. The *personal income tax* system is nominally progressive, but various loopholes make it somewhat inefficient and inequitable.

12. *Social Security taxes* are the second largest and fastest growing source of federal revenues. They and other *payroll taxes* may be borne primarily by workers. Moreover, they are regressive, typically declining proportionately as personal income rises.

13. *Sales taxes* are reasonably efficient but, like income taxes, are marred by numerous exemptions. Many *excise taxes* apply to "sin" or "wasteful luxuries." Unless they are based on a benefit principle of taxation (for example, public zoo ticket fees or gasoline taxes), they tend to cause inefficiency and be regressive. (Poor people smoke and drink as much, by volume, as rich people.)

14. The *corporate income tax* discriminates against the corporate form of business and against the goods produced primarily by corporations. In the long run, most of this tax is probably forward-shifted to consumers. Thus, in the minds of most experts, this tax tends to be both inefficient and inequitable.

15. *Property taxes* provide disincentives for improvement and are blamed by some for the deterioration of central cities.

16. *Inheritance* and *gift taxes* have high and progressive rates, but can be avoided because these tax laws are riddled with loopholes.

17. A *value-added tax* (*VAT*) is similar to a sales tax in that it is forward-shifted. *VATs* only apply to the value added by each firm. *VATs, flat rate taxes,* and progressive *consumption taxes* (not income) have been proposed as replacements for corporate income taxes or Social Security taxes.

PROBLEMS

Table 7 reflects the astounding coincidence that Mathew's demands for streetlights (a public good) and dry cleaning (a private good) happen to be identical, and that Rachel's demands for lights and cleaning are also identical.

1. Use graph paper to construct individual and market demands for dry cleaning if these two people comprise the market. Assume that their individual demand curves are straight lines.

2. Now graph their individual and collective demands for streetlights.

3. What are the individual price elasticities of demand for dry cleaning if the price of this purely competitive private service is $2? How much would each person purchase per month? What is the market elasticity of demand for dry cleaning if the price is $2? If a dry cleaning monopoly faced a constant $2 average total cost and marginal cost, how much would it charge per item? How much dry cleaning would each individual have done at this price?

TABLE 7 Quantities of Both Goods Wanted Each Month at These Prices

Price	Mathew	Rachel
$8	0	6
$7	3	7
$6	6	8
$5	9	9
$4	12	10
$3	15	11
$2	18	12
$1	21	13

4. Suppose that maintenance and replacement cost averages $6 per streetlight. What number of streetlights would be optimal? If Mathew and Rachel are each charged for streetlights in proportion to their respective marginal benefits, how will the total cost of streetlights be shared?

QUESTIONS FOR THOUGHT AND DISCUSSION

1. Richard A. Musgrave classifies all market failures as problems of either allocation, distribution, or stabilization, and he suggests that government can remedy each through appropriate policy. Are there any economic problems that fall outside these categories? If so, what are they? Do you think that Musgrave is correct in arguing that each problem should be addressed with the tool that is best for alleviating it alone, and that undesirable side effects should be treated by separate policies? Why or why not?

2. Some casual surveys conducted by the authors revealed that a substantial majority of students favor reducing the size and scope of government and taxation. Then we presented students with a list of current and proposed areas of government action and asked whether specific programs should be (*a*) eliminated, (*b*) reduced somewhat, (*c*) maintained at about current levels, or (*d*) expanded. The overall response to this detailed survey led inescapably to the conclusion that students want more government, not less. When asked how to reconcile these responses, the most common argument from students is that they want more services to be more efficiently provided so that taxes can be reduced. A cynical colleague commented that trying to make government more efficient is a bit like trying to teach pigs to sing—it just frustrates you and annoys the pigs. Other than the call for greater efficiency in government, can you reconcile favoring less government but, overall, wanting more extensive public services?

3. Consider such shared social institutions as public officials, our justice system and the rule of law, and regulations such as traffic laws. In what senses are these public goods? Does government regulation that attempts to ensure the qualities or safety of certain products provide some security to consumers? If so, is this security a public good? Why or why not?

4. Many people quietly support the sentiments of "tax resisters" who defiantly refuse to pay income taxes. If tax resistance becomes even more widespread, what will happen to the tax burdens of those who conscientiously pay every bit of their legal tax liabilities each year? What are the effects (psychological and otherwise) on someone who pays taxes honestly when someone else admits cheating and then says that "everybody does it?" Do honest taxpayers subsidize tax cheats?

5. What problems might arise if value-added taxes (VATs) were used to replace the revenues lost from reducing or eliminating Social Security or corporate income taxes? What benefits would result from implementing value-added taxes? Would it matter whether the VAT applied only to consumer goods and services or to both consumption and investment goods?

6. An increasingly popular proposal is to entirely replace the current tax system with a single, flat rate income tax. What are the virtues of this proposal? The drawbacks? The advocates of this approach have managed to tilt recent tax legislation in their favor. How much have recent changes in income tax rates reduced the nominal progressivity of our tax structure? Have some loopholes been eliminated recently so that the actual progressivity of taxes has been affected less? If so, what loopholes have been plugged? Which loopholes remain in place? (Answering this question may require some library research.)

7. Discuss the proposition that inheritance taxes should be eliminated, and that an inheritance should be treated just like regular income for purposes of income taxation.

8. Can you use indifference curves to show that general percentage taxes are more efficient than taxes that apply only to a few commodities? (This is difficult.)

CHAPTER 32

Public Choice

The previous chapter outlined some causes of market failure and described ideal corrections for these failures. Many people assume that government can infallibly cure market flaws, but government policies are often marred by inefficiency and inequity, causing most students to wonder, "Why does policy seem so inconsistent with economic analysis?" The answer is that no allocative mechanism works well in all situations.

There are shortcomings with markets, queuing, brute force, chance, merit, tradition, . . . , and government. The trick is to use the best mechanism for the task at hand. This involves trade-offs. Choosing government to remedy perceived market failures, for example, may mean that the flexibility of response found in markets is lost. Government policy-making cannot be divorced from such realities as lobbying by special interest groups, the desires of incumbents to be reelected, or bureaucratic inertia.

Public choice *analysis examines political behavior from an economic perspective.*

Public choice practitioners believe that the motives behind people's behavior in the political arena differ little from those behind their performance in the private sector. Economists suspect that equal proportions of saints and greedy sinners are found among workers, voters, union leaders, bureaucrats, professors, business tycoons, or politicians.

Our first topic in this chapter is private political behavior: Why do so few people vote, and why do so many seem oblivious to political issues? Then we investigate alternative voting systems: Is majority rule superior to unanimity or point voting in reflecting voters' preferences? Our next broad area is political competition—government as a mechanism through which politicians and special interest groups compete for scarce resources. Finally, we look at government bureaucracy, focusing on ways that individuals may serve their private interests when they lack profit motives for efficiency.

Private Citizens and Politics _____

Consumers vote their dollars for the things they want in private transactions, but have different numbers of dollar votes. In modern democracies, adult citizens (except convicted felons) have equal rights to vote, so their opinions theoretically carry equal weight. Then why do so many people seem indifferent about politics?

Rational Voter Apathy

An election year cliché is that "every vote counts." If people were always rational and if the outcome of every election hung on every vote and was crucial for everyone, then all eligible citizens would vote. We would not hear TV commentators lamenting voter apathy after every election. Fewer than 10 percent of adult citizens even bother to go to the polls in most local elections. Even in hotly contested national elections, a 60 percent turnout is unusually high. Many people evidently conclude that the personal benefits of voting are outweighed by the personal costs. The following is one explanation for why many people judge that voting is not worth the effort.

Suppose that opinion polls indicate that 70 million people plan to vote in the 1992 presidential election and that voters are split 50/50 between the Republican and Democratic candidates. This split maximizes the probability that your vote would matter if presidents were elected by popular vote. What is the probability that a single vote would change the outcome of this election? The probability of an exact 50/50 split of the vote is identical with the probability of flipping a coin 70 million times and obtaining exactly 35 million heads and 35 million tails—infinitesimal. Even if only 1,000 people voted, the probability that you might be the tie breaker if you were the 1,001st voter is less than 3 percent. The probability that any single voter will be the tie breaker is, of course, much lower the larger the number of votes.

The transaction costs of voting are not trivial when you consider the time and resources used to register, walk or drive to the polls, wait in line, learn about candidates and issues, and so on. This raises the question of why so many people do vote. Although the

costs of voting are low, the probability of one vote swinging any important election is nearly zero. Some people argue that, "If you don't vote, you have no right to complain," but there is no law or religious commandment to that effect.

Why Many People Do Vote   The preceding analysis makes it seem almost irrational to vote. Actually, it illustrates why so many people don't bother to vote. But why do some elections draw as much as 70 percent of those eligible to vote? Some people may vote because political campaigns resemble spectator sports: the stakes are generally higher, but voting is a bit like cheering for your favorite football team or buying a ticket to a game. Others believe that voting is a way to support democratic institutions. The most likely motive for voters is that they derive pleasure from thinking of themselves as good citizens, or that failing to vote makes them feel guilty.

Apathetic nonvoters who contend that individual votes "don't matter" are statistically correct. If you think about it a minute, you will probably conclude that it is fortunate that many people don't vote. Voting is most likely among people with intense political preferences, and least likely among people who are reasonably indifferent about politics. It seems more democratic that people who care the most should have the most influence on government.

Rational Political Ignorance

Better the devil you know than the devil you don't know.

                                    —*Unknown*

Can you remember the names of even five people who were on the ballot during the last election? How much did you know about the candidates' positions on tax reform? Automobile pollution standards? Trade with the Soviet Union? Support for agriculture? If you are typical, your answers to these and similar questions are, "Not much."

> **Rational ignorance** *occurs when people decide that the marginal costs of more information exceed its marginal benefits.*

Information is costly. The future is uncertain. Therefore, consumers and producers operate with only imperfect information about markets. They are, to some degree, *rationally ignorant*. Similarly, voters rely on information that is far from perfect. The personal payoff from having in-depth knowledge about all the candidates and issues decided in any important election is trivial, and generally far less than the benefits of information about market choices. For example, textile import quotas now cost consumers billions of dollars annually. If your share is only $5 to $10 and the probability of influencing an election with your vote is negligible, then the time and effort required to learn about candidates' positions on import quotas so that you can vote wisely may be much greater than the personal benefits from a more informed vote. There are, however, significant personal benefits in knowing about the qualities and prices of clothing you buy.

Election results share many attributes of public goods—your president is my president, we share the same sets of laws, and so on. Thus, we should not be surprised that many voters select candidates on the basis of charisma, a flashing smile and a shock of wavy hair, or an impression that a certain candidate is sober, (faithful?), dependable, or reflective. Small wonder that every major political campaign abounds with public relations flacks. Most of the time, the procedure followed when decisions are made by votes is that the majority rules. This is not, however, the only possibility.

Systems of Voting

Feudal kings or queens once dictated most government policies. Even today, over half of the world's 5 billion people live in countries controlled by dictators. Although single votes have little direct influence on elections, those of us fortunate enough to live in democracies can vote to collectively determine who will make policies for us. This raises the question of how accurately voters' preferences are reflected by different voting systems.

Majority Rule

Any group of a dozen or more people (even noneconomists) will find it difficult to agree on anything. Group decisions tend to be middle-of-the-road compromises that are inconsistent with any individual's preferences. Whenever we vote and use a simple **majority rule,** we can be almost certain of losses by members on the minority side of the vote. Majority voting may even result in economic inefficiency, since the minority's losses may outweigh all gains to the side able to swing a majority of votes.

Potential Inefficiencies   Majority voting can yield efficient results but the example in Table 1 points out the possibility of inefficiency. In this case, Proposal X is defeated even though its benefits outweigh the costs by $300, but Proposal Y is adopted even though its costs ($2,000) exceed the benefits ($1,700) by $300.

Notice that if potential gainers from Proposal X shared their gains with the potential losers, all could gain from its passage; if potential losers from Proposal Y compensated the potential gainers, all could gain from its defeat. Thus, passage of Proposal X and defeat of Proposal Y would both be efficient moves. Majority rule voting yields inefficient results for both proposals, however, because it is illegal to pay money

TABLE 1 *Inefficient Outcomes under a Simple Majority Rule*

A Beneficial Proposal (X) is Defeated					An Excessively Costly Proposal (Y) is Adopted				
			Votes					Votes	
Individual	Benefits	Tax Cost	Aye	Nay	Individual	Benefits	Tax Cost	Aye	Nay
A	$ 700	$ 400	X		A	$ 425	$ 400	X	
B	600	400	X		B	575	400	X	
C	350	400		X	C	450	400	X	
D	375	400		X	D	150	400		X
E	275	400		X	E	100	400		X
Total	$2,300	$2,000	2	3	Total	$1,700	$2,000	3	2

for people's votes. (This is one reason for secret ballots.) Markets for votes might shrink the inefficiency inherent in many voting situations, but a market approach to voting is widely viewed as unethical or inequitable.

The basic problem is that *intensities of preference* are easily registered in the marketplace but not under a majority rule. You can buy more or fewer anchovy pizzas, but even if you passionately care who is elected dogcatcher, your vote counts no more than that of someone who simply likes a candidate's name and casts a vote that offsets yours.

Potential Inconsistencies Majority rule voting may also yield inconsistent results, especially if sequential elections (e.g., party primaries) are used to narrow choices. It is, for example, common for analysts to claim that Republican Smith could beat any Democrat in a presidential election, but that he has no chance because loyal Republicans will nominate Republican Jones, who cannot beat any Democrat. An easy illustration of this point considers a three-party system, as reflected in Table 2. Assume that the voters are roughly divided into thirds between the Tory, Whig, and Populist parties, and that the ultimate winner must receive over 50 percent of the vote. If no one receives a clear majority, then there is a runoff election between the top two candidates.

Suppose that Tory voters despise Populists and will vote for Whigs if there are no Tories in a runoff election. Whig voters, however, vote for Populist Party candidates over Tory candidates in runoff elec-

tions. To complete this circle, Populist voters will support Tory over Whig candidates. Table 2 shows the potential results if no candidate receives a clear majority in an initial election. Tory candidates win against Whigs in runoff elections, who would win against Populists, who, in turn, would beat the Tories.

Some analysts believe that the possible inconsistencies apparent in these results of majority rule voting may also foment instability, with parties taking turns being in power. This is known as the *voting cycle* phenomenon. The resulting flip-flops in policies create chaos for long range planning by private decision makers—consumers, workers, or investors. Unstable policies would be less of a problem if changes required unanimous votes.

Unanimity

Some decisions are deemed so important that society requires more than a simple majority vote; minority opinions are weighed more heavily in determining critical social policies. A constitutional amendment requires either a constitutional convention called by three-fourths of all state legislatures or their ratification of an amendment approved by two-thirds of the members of both the U.S. Senate and the House of Representatives. Similar congressional votes are required to override a presidential veto. A jury trying a criminal case must reach a unanimous verdict in most states or the case may be retried. In such situations, requiring **unanimity** or near unanimity limits

TABLE 2 Potential Inconsistencies in Voting			
	Parties in Runoff		
	Tory Versus Whig	**Whig Versus Populist**	**Populist Versus Tory**
Tory voter preferences	Tory	Whig	Tory
Whig voter preferences	Whig	Whig	Populist
Populist voter preferences	Tory	Populist	Populist
Winner	**Tory**	**Whig**	**Populist**

TABLE 3 *The Results from Table 1 if Determined by Ideal Point Voting**

	Proposal X					Proposal Y			
			Votes					**Votes**	
Individual	**Benefits**	**Tax Cost**	**Aye**	**Nay**	**Individual**	**Benefits**	**Tax Cost**	**Aye**	**Nay**
A	$ 700	$ 400	92		A	$ 425	$ 400	8	
B	600	400	53		B	575	400	47	
C	350	400		50	C	450	400	50	
D	330	400		9	D	150	400		91
E	320	400		20	E	100	400		80
Total	$2,300	$2,000	145	79	Total	$1,700	$2,000	105	171

*Ideal point voting would mean that all voters would apportion their votes based on net benefits (benefits − costs). For example, Individual A's net benefits from proposal X are $300 ($700 − $400); net benefits for proposal Y are $25 ($425 − $400). Thus, Individual A's voting pattern would be 92 votes ($\frac{\$300}{\$325} \times 100$) for proposal X and 8 votes ($\frac{\$25}{\$325} \times 100$) for proposal Y.

exploitation of a minority. Moreover, any legal changes under pure unanimity rules presumably would benefit everyone or they would never be adopted. Thus, any changes would clearly be moves toward economic efficiency.

One difficulty with requiring unanimity is that individuals who, on balance, are relatively unaffected by some proposal could withhold their votes to "blackmail" the potential gainers from the proposed change. In a sense, requiring unanimity gives everyone the power to say, "It's my ball, so we play by my rules or we don't play." Although some people might negotiate disproportionate gains for themselves simply because of their political leverage, no voter would ever expect to lose from any unanimous vote.

A far more serious problem is that a unanimity rule is biased in favor of the existing situation. Unanimity might operate well if an overwhelming majority view the current situation as equitable, but it totally blocks political remedies for inequity, leaving only informal negotiation, violence, or the market as avenues open for people to pursue what they perceive as justice. For example, a unanimity requirement precludes any redistribution of income or wealth other than one that is strictly voluntary. A final flaw is that even though a unanimity rule protects the existing rights of minorities, it also provides only crude indications of the intensity of people's preferences.

Point Voting

One proposal to reflect the intensities of preferences better than any "one person, one vote" rule is the use of point voting.

> **Point voting** *assigns equal numbers of points to all voters, which they can allocate among various issues as they see fit.*

Voters ideally would allocate their points in proportion to their intensities of preference: that is, in proportion to their net expected gains or losses from given proposals. Thus, if individuals A, B, C, D, and E each have 100 points to allocate between the proposals in Table 1, they would ideally vote as in Table 3. Proposal X passes and Proposal Y fails; these results reverse the inefficient results under simple majority rule voting. Since Proposal X yields net benefits while Proposal Y's costs exceed its benefits, these ideal "point voting" results are preferable to the results of a simple majority rule.

A major flaw in point voting is that people might skew their voting points towards issues that they expected to be close, figuring that others would ensure the passage or failure of issues not expected to be close. For example, suppose that you favored more spending on both national defense and medical research. If you expected a landslide vote on a national defense proposal but a close vote on medical research, you would probably place all your votes for medical research. Point voting systems are flawed when people try to forecast the outcomes of elections and then vote strategically instead of voting their true preferences. Election results would conform neither to the majority's will nor to reasonable benefit/cost decision making.

Regardless of which voting system is used, most people view government as failing if election results do not reflect voters' preferences. Elections are critical for candidates and for private interests who want to shape government policy. We will now consider forces that shape political campaigns and the policies of those who manage to get themselves elected.

Politicians and Parties

Politics is the art of compromise.

—Unknown

Some people seek political office to mold policy to their ideals, hoping to make this a better world. Others want prestige and revel in the exercise of power. The first step on the path to election is to project an image voters will support when they mark their ballots. One obstacle is that no one can be all things to all people. To the extent that politicians establish positions on the issues, they can be sure of offending some voters in some ways.

"Lumpiness" in Voting

I voted for the lesser of two evils.

—Unknown

When consumers operate in the marketplace, their purchases can be fine-tuned to closely match their tastes and preferences. Even with such "lumpy" purchases as automobiles, you can buy a slightly bigger or smaller car, more or fewer options, keep it longer than your neighbor does, or trade it in sooner. Such fine gradations are not available in politics.

Even if you understand two candidates' campaign platforms, you may favor Madison's stands on education and welfare spending, but prefer Monroe's views on international relations. Voting is a *lumpy decision,* somewhat akin to tie-in sales contracts that require you to buy some things you do not want to get the things you desire. Casting your vote involves trade-

offs because you cannot vote for a set of positions different from those taken by one of the candidates.

This is one reason that most public figures either state their positions on controversial issues in inoffensive terms or they waffle—avoiding direct answers to barbed questions aimed at them by reporters or their political opponents. Rational ignorance among voters and the complexity of most issues are two other reasons that politicians frequently side-step taking a stand. A fourth is that most serious political candidates strive for a moderate image.

The Median Voter Model

Differences among candidates are often more form than substance. It seems that all favor a strong national defense, adequate welfare for the "truly" needy, a balanced budget, and low taxes—positions become as predictable as calls to support "motherhood, apple pie, and the flag." Why do party platforms and political speeches so often seem like carbon copies of one another?

> The **median voter model** *suggests that the median voter must be captured to achieve a majority vote, and attempts to explain why political parties and candidates often seem interchangeable.*

The median voter model partially explains similarities among political parties and candidates. In Figure 1, we assume that the preferences and voting patterns of individuals can be ranked very simply and are normally distributed along a continuum from the extreme left (revolutionary communism, perhaps) to the extreme right (fascism?). Point M is in the precise center of this spectrum and identifies the median voter—exactly half of all voters lie to the left, with the other half being to the right of this position.

Suppose that two candidates are running for an office. The median voter can provide the margin of victory if the winner must receive 50 percent plus 1 vote. Thus, the candidate who adopts positions on the issues closest to point M will capture the median vote and win the election. Regardless of their initial positions (say, L and R, respectively), both candidates find that shifting their positions slightly toward point M boosts their standings in public opinion polls. Figure 1 also uses a slightly right-wing candidate to illustrate

FIGURE 1 How Voter Distributions Push Candidates and Parties Toward the Middle

Votes Lost if Candidate at Point R Moves to Point R_1

Votes Gained by Candidate at R Moving to M

Left-Wing Positions   L   M   R R_1 Right-Wing Positions

The "bell-shaped" curve is based on the assumption that voters are normally distributed from left-wing to right-wing political positions. A right-wing candidate at point R gains by moving toward the political center at point M, but is likely to lose substantial support from a move from R to the more extreme R_1. These losses of votes will be maximized if this candidate's opponent moves to a position just to the left of the candidate's position. The respective potential losses and gains pressure right-wing candidates and parties to move toward middle-of-the-road positions. Naturally, similar pressures would cause a serious left-wing candidate to shift toward the political center at point M.

how movements toward the extremes lose votes, while shifts to the center gain votes. The same would be true of a left-wing candidate. As the candidates each try to maximize their expected votes, each creeps toward point M. Ultimately, their positions may be almost indistinguishable.

You might think that a new third candidate could win this race by entering at, say, point L, leaving the original candidates to split the votes from halfway between points L and M all the way to the extreme right. But this third candidate would also find that moving toward point M increases support by voters. This suggests that, ultimately, virtually all serious candidates for election gravitate toward point M. Similar forces are at work in elections ranging from that for president of your local PTA to the U.S. presidency, pressuring not only political candidates, but political

parties as well, to gradually adopt middle-of-the-road policies.

The dynamic world of politics is grossly oversimplified in this median voter model; otherwise, there would be no differences between candidates or party platforms. Among other reasons, differences exist because:

1. Voters' opinions on the numerous issues in any election cannot be simply described from left to right, and their opinions are only loosely correlated. For example, there may be no predictable connections between people's opinions on welfare, the environment, international trade, and law and order issues.

2. Voter distributions change according to circumstances so that it is impossible for politicians to know exactly where the median voter is on any controversial issue at any point in time.

3. Some politicians do have strong personal beliefs about some issues.

In spite of these qualifications, the median voter model explains the middle-of-the road clustering of politicians and parties, which ignores the preferences of vast numbers of less moderate voters. It also hints at reasons for the dominance of the two-party system.

Two-Party Systems

Shifts in the distribution of voters' preferences over time also helps explain *voting cycles*—why political control tends to swing between two parties in most democratic countries. Normally, one party locates slightly to the left of center, with the other being slightly right of center. Each then advertises itself as "the party of the future" and hopes that circumstances will move more voters in its direction.

The two parties, being reasonably comfortable with each other, then compete through expensive campaigns. A typical congressional campaign now requires a war chest of over $1 million; recently, a U.S. Senate candidate from New York allegedly spent $14 million campaigning for a job that pays less than $100,000 annually—*and lost*. Campaign spending on television spots alone now exceeds $100 million in presidential election years. Such barriers frustrate third-party challenges to either dominant party. Another technique to bar entry is to make it difficult for a third party to get on the ballot. For example, the dominant parties may support laws requiring that petitions be signed by huge numbers of voters before the third party can be on the ballot if it did not receive more than 5 percent of the votes in a prior election.

Third parties tend to be launched from the extremes of the political spectrum and to be based on single issues. If a third party began to attract more voters than either dominant party expected, the closest major party normally adopts the third-party position on that issue. If leaders of a third party seriously want political power, they tend to become more moderate and the party is eventually absorbed by the closest major party. Thus, mature democracies tend to operate under the control of two major parties. Third parties rarely displace major parties, and then only when a major party fails to respond to changes in voter preferences.

Political Allocation

Two things you never want to see made are hot dogs and the law.

—Unknown

Rational political ignorance, low voter turnouts, lumpiness in voting for a candidate, and the tendency for parties and politicians to cluster around middle-of-the-road positions are among the reasons that government policies only weakly mirror voter preferences. Lobbying and protracted negotiations among elected representatives are among the mechanisms that result in budgets and laws intended to balance the desires of *special interest groups,* including those of voters. These mechanisms sometimes provide pressures for policies to more closely conform to voter preferences, but at other times exacerbate problems inherent in political allocations of resources and incomes.

Logrolling

Economists favor most forms of voluntary exchange because both sides expect to gain or no trade occurs.

> *Legislators commonly trade votes to obtain passage of proposals they favor, a process known as* **logrolling.**

For example, one legislator might want more funding to clean up the environment, while another seeks higher agricultural price supports. Trading votes may enable both to get what they want. Logrolling may also be beneficial by allowing legislators to register their *intensities of preference.* Votes about matters upon which a legislator is reasonably indifferent are traded for votes on proposed legislation about which the lawmaker has strong feelings. This process can aid in the attainment of efficiency by allowing strongly held minority views to overcome weak opposition by the majority.

Economists recognize, however, that some exchanges may not be socially beneficial. An extreme case would be an agreement wherein you trade part of your loot from a bank robbery for my services as a lookout and getaway driver. Society's problem is that we are not the only people affected by this transaction—the losses of our victims must be considered. Less dramatic but similarly damaging trades can take place through logrolling that results in pork barrel legislation.

> **Pork barrel legislation** *is legislation funded by general tax revenues from taxpayers everywhere but which primarily benefits people in a narrower geographic area.*

Many federal projects generate benefits that are primarily local. For example, Arizonans make up about 1 percent of our population and pay about 1 percent of federal taxes. Even if a canal system to convey water into dry parts of Arizona would cost $2 billion but generate benefits of only $1 billion, Arizona's senators and representatives would be pressured by their constituents to favor federal funds to build it. Arizonans would pay only 1 percent of the costs, but they would receive most of the benefits—a good deal for Arizonans, but a crummy deal for other voters.

Most pork barrel legislation is packaged with other pieces of pork and then tied to laws that are national in scope. Presidents cannot selectively veto parts of a law, and so must either accept or veto the entire package. Logrolling by lawmakers sympathetic to the goals of special interests is only one mechanism that interest groups use to secure policies they favor. Some special interests focus on control over the life patterns of other citizens.

Merit Goods and Bads

Some goods are deemed so socially important that government intervenes even though the marketplace would resolve consumer wants efficiently. This occurs when a democratic majority, some elite group, or a petty dictatory decides that certain things are desirable and that others are undesirable, regardless of consumer preferences. Thus, welfare programs often provide goods rather than cash because of a sense that the preferences of the poor are inappropriate (i.e., they might spend it on booze). The Surgeon General requires warnings on cigarette packages because some smokers may not have heard about tobacco's dangers. Similarly, primary education is compulsory because "ignorant" parents may not value it adequately for their children. Compulsory education, low-income housing, and food stamps are examples of merit goods.

> The label **merit goods** *refers to activities that would probably be handled efficiently by markets, but not in accord with the wishes of a special interest group that is able to enact policies more in keeping with its elitist perspective. Bans against certain drugs or X-rated movies are examples of sanctions against* **merit bads.**

Possible rationales for intellectually or morally elite groups to overrule individual preferences include arguments that:

1. ignorance, uncertainty, or the "evil" inherent in the human soul may cause people to act improperly.
2. consumers are gullible and easily misled by advertising.
3. market information is asymmetric—suppliers know more about their products than their customers do, and tend to keep negative information secret.
4. income redistribution is most effective when the poor are provided the things they need instead of money.

This last point is especially elitist in that welfare givers perceive welfare recipients as inherently incompetent. (Are the poor in dire straits because they lack income or because they are stupid?)

It is worth pointing out that special interests can gain financially by promulgating policies based on merit good arguments. For example, the food stamp program boosts the demand for food. Thus, agricultural interests favor food stamps instead of cash grants to the poor, but they argue that the poor would simply waste money that should be spent on food. We will not deal further with merit goods, leaving it to you to ascertain whether consumer sovereignty or elitist judgments should dominate in situations where people's choices significantly affect only themselves.

Special Interests

Majority rule voting tends to slight minority interests, but vigorous political action can enable determined minorities to impose policies that are weakly opposed by the majority of voters. For example, opinion polls consistently indicate that most Americans favor more restrictions on private firearms. Yet, for decades, the National Rifle Association has led a successful movement to prevent national gun registration and other curbs. Why? Typical voters care relatively little about gun control and are rationally ignorant of most candidates' positions on this issue. Thus, gun fanciers whose votes and campaign contributions may be based on this issue alone make most politicians leery of pushing gun control. The Equal Rights Amendment also had wide (but weak) popular support, and lost because of opposition by a large and vocal minority. Similarly, people with strong feelings about abortion, prayer in schools, or protecting our steel industry from foreign competition may have disproportionately strong voices in determining certain social policies.

Voting is not the only way for special interests to accomplish their political goals. Money talks, and big money talks loudly. A well financed minority may contribute sufficient campaign funds to affect who gets elected and to shade some politicians' positions on certain issues. Alternatively, campaign volunteers can beat the bushes to get other voters to support specific candidates. Money and bodies also may be turned out to propagandize for important minority issues. And then logrolling comes into play when politicians try to pass legislation favored by the interest groups that back them, including pork barrel projects for the folks in their home districts.

As we indicated earlier, one way that a democracy reflects intense preferences is for a minority to exert vigorous pressure and attain the policies it favors. Much legislation enacted to benefit interest groups, however, may bear inefficiently high levels of social cost.

Rent-Seeking

People are self-interested and try to manipulate allocative mechanisms to enrich themselves. In competitive markets, this normally entails trying to produce goods better or at lower costs. This boosts society's production and potential consumption. Government can be similarly beneficial by setting rules to correct market failures, but economic legislation and regulation often seem tailored for special interest groups. One problem with this is that the gains to special interest groups are often less than the costs to the general public. Indeed, inefficiency in collective decision making arises primarily because costs are spread across a relatively anonymous, heterogeneous, and poorly informed public, while the benefits accrue to small cohesive groups.

> **Rent-seeking** *is the term applied to attempts by interest groups to manipulate public policy where the interest group's gains would be overshadowed by losses to the larger public.*

(Recall that economic rent is any income received in excess of the minimum required to secure the resources that people make available.) Figure 2 uses overly restrictive licensing of taxicabs to show why rent-seeking behavior is economically inefficient and reduces social well-being.

Suppose that the taxi market is initially in a competitive equilibrium, with supply S_0 being perfectly elastic at price P_0 and that demand is D_0. Consumer surplus equals triangle P_0ad, and cab companies cover all their costs, including a normal return on their investment. If major taxi operators thought that regulators could be persuaded to restrict competition, they could follow a rent-seeking strategy. They might cite horror stories to prove that some unwary tourists were gouged by unethical drivers as evidence of the evils of "cutthroat" competition. Suppose that taxi licenses were restricted to Q_1, and granted only to solid, reputable companies. Cab fares would rise to P_1, shrinking consumer surplus to P_1ab. The loss of

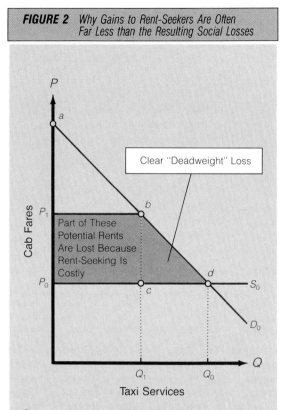

Suppose that rent-seeking cab companies persuade taxi regulators to follow overly restrictive licensing policies. If taxi services fall from Q_0 to Q_1, cab fares will rise from P_0 to P_1 and consumer surplus will shrink from P_0ad to P_1ab. There is a clear "deadweight" loss equal to cbd. Moreover, those who retain their cab licenses will not gain rents (profits) equal to P_0P_1bc. Some of the potential rents will be dissipated because of costs incurred in securing these political restrictions on market entry.

consumer surplus equals the trapezoid P_0P_1bd. You might think that the "deadweight loss" to society would equal triangle cbd, and that taxi companies would reap economic rent equal to P_0P_1bc.

Rent-seeking, however, also absorbs resources directly. Interest groups incur costs when seeking favorable laws or regulations, and devote resources to mold public policies as long as the expected marginal gains exceed their expected marginal costs. Consultants, lawyers, and professional lobbyists might be hired by the parties on all sides of an issue; time and money may be absorbed by hearings in front of regulatory boards or legislative committees.

In some cases, unethical lawmakers or regulators who recognize the potential gains may demand bribes for favorable policies. None of these costs are incurred productively. The net result of rent-seeking behavior is a continuing social loss for as long as inefficient policies are in place, plus losses equal to the costs incurred by interest groups to secure favorable laws or regulations or to oppose unfavorable ones.

We have now discussed voting procedures, political campaigning, and the legislative process from a public choice perspective. Once laws are made, they must be administered. This brings us to the topic of government bureaucracy, which falls under the executive branch of government.

Bureaucracy

A government could print a good edition of Shakespeare's works, but it could not get them written.
—Alfred Marshall

Whether private or public, large organizations must develop extensive sets of formal operating rules or the coordination of tasks becomes impossible. The resulting mountains of red tape causes many people to view bureaucracy as almost synonymous with mindless inefficiency and getting the runaround.

Bureaucracy *commonly refers to any large task-oriented organization.*

The federal government is by far our largest employer. State and local governments also hire their share of workers, as shown in Table 4. Most government employees work in the agencies, or *bureaus,* that implement the laws passed by legislatures. Relatively few government employees are elected to office or appointed by elected officials; most are either civil servants or military personnel.

Many government bureaucrats work hard because they believe deeply in the mission of their agency. Economic theory suggests, however, that the best starting point for analysis of behavior is the assumption of self-interest. Anyone who has worked in a large organization knows that opportunities for raises and promotions are closely tied to the organization's fortunes; prosperity and growth yield larger personnel budgets in both public and private bureaucracies. Thus, we can expect career employees of any large organization to push for growth and to fight budget cuts.

TABLE 4 *Government Employment*

	Millions of Government Employees		
	1970	**1975**	**1987**
Federal			
Military	3.1	2.1	2.2
Civilian		2.7	2.9
State		3.2	4.0
Local		8.8	10.1

Source: Bureau of Labor Statistics, *Monthly Labor Review,* February 1988.

Government bureaucracies tend to have even worse reputations than business bureaucracies. Major differences between public and private bureaucracies emerge because their incentive structures differ. Most divisions of private firms serve as profit centers, and their growth tends to depend on serving more customers better and at lower cost. There are few direct ways to measure the efficiency of most government bureaus, which rely on tax revenues to cover their costs. Legislators tend to consider whether a public service is provided adequately. If not, the standard solution is to boost funding. Thus, paradoxically, less efficiency may cause growth of a bureau's budget. The opposite trend occurs in the private sector.

Have you noticed that it is often easier to buy auto insurance than to get a license for a new car? That the time absorbed in buying $100 worth of groceries is often less than the time spent waiting in a line at the Post Office to buy a roll of stamps? Rewards for efficiency are few in government bureaucracies and may cause relative inefficiency, with two results (*a*) services may be supplied to the public at the convenience of government employees rather than vice versa, and (*b*) government tends to pay relatively high prices for the things it buys. You may have read about the Department of Defense paying outrageous prices for hammers, coffee pots, or similar items. Focus 1 details some reasons for the occurrence of such apparent waste. The basic problem, however, probably originates with the warped incentive structures common in many government bureaus. The tendency for *empire-building* is only one of many types of bureaucratic behavior that emerge from inefficient incentive structures.

Government Contracts

Most government contracts are awarded to the lowest bidder, but recent military contracts for new weapons systems have uniformly been plagued by mammoth "cost overruns," which means that taxpayers have ended up paying much more than the original contract specified. Why? Many people think that recent media reports hint at an answer: in 1985, the Department of Defense (DOD) paid $400 for $17 hammers, $56 for $0.08 Allen wrenches, and $27 for screws that hardware stores sell for less than a dime. The prices of custom-built items for aircraft were even more startling: $600 armrests and toilet covers, $400 ashtrays, and $17,000 coffee pots. The U.S. Army finally abandoned the Sergeant York battle tank after sinking almost $8 billion into the project; it just would not do the job for which it was intended.

Critics cite examples of this sort to indict defense contractors for price-gouging and the military bureaucrats who administered these contracts for flagrant incompetence. If the basic problems were this simple, the solution would be incredibly straightforward: prosecute dishonest contractors and deny them future contracts, and hire more competent people to administer military procurement. Although this might help, the ultimate solution (if there is one) is not this simple. Nor are such problems

unique to the military. Government office buildings, flood control projects, highways, and nuclear power plants also often entail sloppy work and huge cost overruns. Some defense contracts require delivery of weapons systems years into the future, and inflation may drive up costs. Contract specifications are often vague because designs are still on the drawing board. Bids on such projects cannot be ironclad. Still other problems lurk in bureaucratic behavior.

C. Northcote Parkinson, an English writer, developed some "laws" of bureaucracy, one of which is "work expands to absorb the time available." As a project unfolds, specifications tend to grow excessively complex, which can be extremely costly. This occurs because many bureaucrats try to stay (or look) busy. One easy way to stay busy is to constantly write directives that detail the work of people you supervise. The 1985 DOD recipe for fruitcake is an unintentionally comic example—it took 18 pages. The recipe for a modern aircraft carrier runs hundreds of thousands of pages. If the ratio of overspecification for fruitcake holds for U.S. Navy ships, the excess costs from this problem alone sums to billions of dollars.

Another problem is that contractors and contract administrators may share interests that violate the public interest. For example, many retired generals and

admirals ultimately go to work for defense contractors. If you were about to retire as a high-ranking military officer, might you be "understanding" about exorbitant costs incurred by a contractor in accommodating your design changes—especially if that firm was a major employer of someone with your expertise?

We can only touch on some problems of government procurement; a detailed discussion would take volumes. DOD contract foibles have been on display recently, but many government contracts seem executed at much higher costs than private contracts would be. The ultimate problem is inadequate incentives for efficiency. The costs of the resulting inefficiencies are borne by taxpayers.

Empire-Building

It is a commonplace observation that work expands so as to fill the time available for its completion. . . . Politicians and taxpayers have assumed with occasional phases of doubt that a rising total in the number of civil servants must reflect a growing volume of work to be done. Cynics, in questioning this belief, have imagined that the multiplication of officials must have left some of them idle or all of them able to work for shorter hours. But this is a matter in which faith and doubt seem equally misplaced. The fact is that the number of the officials and the quantity of the work to be done are not related to each other at all.

—C. Northcote Parkinson[1]

In large organizations, a manager's status and salary tend to be positively related to the numbers and levels of employees supervised and the amounts of money for which the manager is responsible. This provides managers at all levels with incentives to acquire as many employees as possible. This is known as *empire-building*. In business, this usually requires showing that your division has extraordinary profit potential. In government bureaus, however, it normally requires emphasizing to legislators the enormity of the problem that your agency is supposed to cure. Thus, law enforcement officials predictably talk about the increasing harm from anarchy in the streets and organized crime, educators discuss teacher shortages and the growing demands placed on our schools, admirals and generals talk about unrest in the Middle East and the aggressiveness of communist revolutionaries, agriculture officials talk about the plight of the family farm—the ways that bureaucrats try to build the demands for their services seem endless.

The Growth of Government

Part of the problem is that few experts in any field ever conclude that their area will be of less concern in the foreseeable future. Thus, there are few credible witnesses to dispute claims that society needs to devote more resources in any number of directions.

The result is that legislators, many of whom might want to slash taxes, are inundated with well-documented requests for more funding for a variety of programs.

Pressing social problems seem to beget new programs that acquire lives of their own, even if the original problem fades away. Trying to identify areas to cut is often an exercise in frustration. Interest groups (including bureaucrats) become accustomed to programs that benefit them and always want more rather than less. Attempts to cut any spending category provoke intense lobbying about the budget. One common strategy used by bureau chiefs to combat proposed budget cuts is to assert that any cuts threaten a bureau's most popular services. This strategy usually arouses loud support from the bureau's clients. This was one tactic used by some opponents of attempts to cut social spending in the early 1980s. Former President Reagan's supporters viewed cutting the *growth* of spending as a victory. The final result of the political processes described in this chapter? Government grows and grows, with no end in sight.

Self-Corrections in Politics and Markets

We have discussed how the market operates and how it may fail. This part of the book focuses on the tasks of government in a market economy and why the government may fail to accomplish these tasks appropriately. Most economic issues can be placed on a continuum that stretches from, on one end, problems efficiently resolved in markets to, at the other extreme, issues that seem to require collective action. Whether a particular issue is best resolved in markets or through government is sometimes murky in the broad middle of this continuum. The answer may depend largely on the relative speed and precision with which these allocative mechanisms correct errors or adjust to changing circumstances.

On average, markets tend to respond quickly and efficiently to changes in consumer wants or mistakes made by business decision makers. For example, if markets fail to synchronize the plans of the buyers and sellers of a pure private good (thermal under-

---

1. C. Northcote Parkinson, "Parkinson's Law," *The Economist*, November 1955.

TABLE 5 Market Failures Versus Political Failures

Market Failure	Political Failure
1. Uncertainty about the future.	1. Uncertainty about the future.
2. Rational ignorance about consuming and investing.	2. Rational political ignorance.
3. Free riders for public goods.	3. Nonvoting because of public good aspects of voting.
4. Externalities and pollution.	4. "Tie-in sales" aspects of voting and inability to "fine-tune" spending patterns to voter preferences. All voting systems fail to reflect intensities of preference.
5. Monopoly power.	5. Disproportionate political power for special interests.
6. Inequity in the distributions of income and wealth.	6. Majorities may inefficiently or inequitably vote against interests of minorities.
7. Fosters greediness and unhealthy competitiveness.	7. Fosters bureaucracy and empire-building.

wear or beef tacos, for example), price adjustments tend to cure the resulting shortages or surpluses rather quickly. On the other hand, markets may never adequately provide such public goods as national defense, so these goods are provided through government.

Political adjustments are inherently slow in a democracy, however. When an elected official becomes extremely unpopular, voters must normally wait for the next election to "throw the rascal out"; coups or assassinations are undemocratic. If a legislature enacts a disastrous policy, it may take years to accom-

plish the required legal change. Once on the books, laws, regulations, and spending programs are hard to remove. Even though political solutions may be slow and inexact, government policy may be superior to private decision making when markets fail because of concentrated economic power, nonrivalry, nonexclusion, or inequity. Table 5 summarizes some failings of both the marketplace and government as allocative mechanisms. In the next two chapters, we examine public policies to control externalities and to redress what many people perceive as inequity in the distribution of income that results from market forces.

CHAPTER REVIEW: KEY POINTS

1. No allocative mechanism works ideally under all circumstances. Just as the market fails in some instances, there are forces within all political systems that prevent government from smoothly reflecting the preferences of the people governed. The application of economic analysis to political behavior is known as *public choice*.

2. The probability that one vote will swing a major election is close to infinitesimal. Because the personal payoffs from voting are small, many people do not vote, nor do most find it personally worthwhile to inform themselves on a broad range of social issues. This is known as *rational political igno-*

rance, and tends to be more prevalent than the lack of information confronted when people make market decisions.

3. All voting systems are flawed in that economic efficiency may be lost through political decision making. *Majority rule* voting tends to impose losses on those taking minority positions; this is inefficient if their losses exceed the majority's gains. Majority rule may also lead to inconsistent or unstable political choices.

4. A *unanimity* rule ensures that all changes in laws are efficient because everyone must expect to gain before acquiescing to a change. People who are reasonably indifferent about a policy change, however, might require excessive compensation for agreeing to the change from those who stand to gain much from the change. This would make changes in policies a very cumbersome and time-consuming process. Moreover, a unanimity rule assumes that the initial situation is equitable, which may be untrue in some cases.

5. *Point voting* would allow voters to indicate their preferences by allocating votes in proportion to how strongly they felt about some issues relative to others. This system is flawed, however, by the potential for strategic behavior; people might not vote their preferences per se, tending instead to weigh their votes according to how they expect others to vote.

6. Voting is a *lumpy* process; we cannot pick and choose among the political stances taken by the candidates for an office. The market permits us to fine-tune our decisions, but we generally can choose only a single candidate or platform when we vote.

7. Attempts to maximize their chances for election cause candidates and political parties to try to attract the *median voter,* whose vote tends to determine the outcomes of elections. Rational ignorance among voters causes many candidates to avoid taking stands on issues while attempting to project a moderate image. Political competition for the support of the median voter causes candidates and par-ties to cluster around *middle-of-the-road* positions, and creates pressures for a *two-party system.*

8. *Logrolling* occurs when lawmakers trade votes. This allows legislators to register the intensities of their preferences because they trade votes about which they care little for votes about things which they feel relatively strongly. Logrolling can, however, result in inefficient amounts of *pork barrel legislation,* which occurs when projects that have primarily local benefits are paid for by a broader taxpaying public.

9. *Special interest groups* may be overrepresented because of low voter turnouts, widespread rational political ignorance, and intense lobbying. Intensities of preference, however, may be better reflected in political decisions because of this overrepresentation.

10. *Rent-seeking* involves attempts by special interest groups to manipulate government policies for private gain even though the social costs of special laws or regulations would exceed the expected benefits to the interest group that seeks economic rents.

11. The efficiency of most government *bureaucracies* is hard to measure, and the absence of a profit motive reduces incentives for efficiency in the public sector. Managerial salaries and "perqs" are often tied to the numbers of employees supervised and the size of the agency budget, which leads to *empire-building* and further growth of government.

QUESTIONS FOR THOUGHT AND DISCUSSION

1. The market system and government are both allocative mechanisms. What are some advantages and disadvantages of each? In what areas now dominated by market forces should government assume a greater role, if any? In what areas should government allow market forces greater latitude? Why?

2. Since World War II, government transfer payments as percentages of national income have grown sharply, and federal spending on goods and services has fallen relative to state and local spending. What might be some explanations for these changes in patterns of government outlays?

3. Voting is optional in the United States, but it is illegal not to vote in some countries. Do you think mak-ing voting compulsory would reduce political apathy? How would compulsory voting affect the behavior of politicians? Would government policies be more or less in accord with voter preferences? Why?

4. Medical doctors are sometimes accused of building the demands for their services by exaggerating minor health problems and heightening the concerns of their patients. How might high-level government bureaucrats enhance the sizes and powers of their agencies through similar processes? What political institutions would they need to manipulate? Can you cite any cases where this type of thing seems to have occurred?

5. One proposal to alter the current federal budgeting system is to allow taxpayers to specify the percentages of their income taxes to be allocated to each government budget category. Proponents of this unequal "point voting" system argue that this would eliminate lobbying by special interests for government programs requiring expenditures of tax revenues and would result in budgets more closely attuned to taxpayers' desires. Do you think these arguments have merit? Can you mount other arguments for this proposal? Should the preferences of those who pay a lot of taxes be given more weight than the preferences of those who pay fewer taxes or no taxes? What would you expect the effects to be on income redistribution programs were this proposal adopted? How might strategic behavior cause the budget to fail to truly reflect even taxpayers' preferences?

6. Which of the following voting systems best preserves the rights of minorities (*a*) plurality, (*b*) majority, or (*c*) unanimity? Why?

7. Votes generally fail to reflect the intensity of people's preferences about issues. What mechanisms in the U.S. political system enable people to sway policies about which they feel strongly? Do you think these mechanisms improve the efficiency of policy-making?

8. It is illegal to buy votes in the United States. Can you explain why this ban on the sale of votes is economically inefficient? Would it be desirable to make it legal for people to sell their votes? Why or why not?

9. At times, several positions are filled through a single election. For example, the top three (or five, or seven) vote getters might be elected to a school board or as county commissioners. Why do some voters cast their ballots for fewer than the number of candidates who will gain office, even if they have preferences among those for whom they don't vote?

10. To what extent do you think that private bureaucrats are insulated from pressures for efficiency? Is this a serious problem?

property rights
externalities
moral suasion
pollution rights
bubble concept
offset policy

CHAPTER 33

Externalities and Environmental Economics

"Three Billion Years Plus a Few Minutes"

ooze

cohesion, opulence

twinges, space, undulations

slithering, boring, hatching, germination

increase, complexity, blooming, coordination, cooperation

predation, parasitism, migration, competition, adaptation, selection

crowding, starvation, disease, populations, diversity, camouflage, mimicry

specialization, reduction, exclusion, conversion, blight, drought

pressure, defeat, decline, smoke, decimation

explosion, abuse, ignorance, teeming

contamination, residual, choking

silence, stillness

ooze

—William T. Barry

"Three Billion Years Plus a Few Minutes" by William T. Barry in *Reflection*.
Reprinted by permission of the author.

William Barry eloquently describes the fragility of our existence. Over 5 billion people now inhabit the earth and, at 1.7 percent annual population growth, we should number 6 billion by the year 2000. Our environment's capacity to sustain life is already strained at the seams in places. As we try to stretch this capacity through technological advances and more extensive resource use, environmental decay and resource depletion rear their ugly heads. Problems like acid rain, nuclear waste, and pollution encircle the globe.

Developed economies in Europe, North America, Japan, and the Soviet Union contain one-third of world population but use roughly four-fifths of all resources. Fresh raw materials that enter advanced production-consumption systems ultimately decompose to heat and waste. Some resources seem about to vanish, so attaining a uniformly high quality of life may require either massive recycling or technological advances based on resources that are now unusable. Enhanced environmental quality will require sacrifice. Cleaning up raises costs and prices, lowers production and national income, and foments social and economic disruption.

The Evolution of Property Rights

One view of environmental decay suggests that the fundamental problem is the absence of clearly defined property rights.

> **Private property rights** *assign individuals rights to control certain resources or assets including rights to charge for their use.*

Property rights generally develop in stages (*a*) common access/nonscarcity, (*b*) common access-scarcity/tragedy of the commons, (*c*) agency restrictions, and (*d*) fee-simple property rights. The evolution of environmental quality in the United States is a textbook case of the development of property rights to a scarce resource and of government intervention in this activity.

Common access resources are available on a first-come, first-served basis. Scarcity is not a problem until growth of population and production create overutilization. These resources are then quickly depleted, or become congested or polluted. Examples are such things as litter or the massacre of bison and extinction of passenger pigeons.

General environmental use is now beyond this stage. In most cases, the greater productivity derived by restricted resource use causes common use policies to be abandoned. The enclosure movement in England and range wars between cattle ranchers and sheepherders in the Old American West offer examples of conflicts during transitions from common use to limited use. Often, though not always, we move on to specify fee-simple property rights.

Fee-simple property rights allow the owner to use the property in any fashion, including sale or destruction, as long as the physical property of others is unaffected—physical characteristics are legally protected, not value. Most of the time, evolution from common access/nonscarcity of a resource to scarcity-overuse leads to a system of property rights. Fee-simple property rights are basic for the attainment of economic efficiency in a competitive market economy. Occasions when complete systems of fee-simple property rights seem impractical often lead to market failure.

The two most common reasons for property rights not to develop are that certain types of property rights might be (*a*) very costly to define and enforce; and (*b*) traded in ways that hinder the value of property owned by others. When definition and enforcement seem so costly that reliance on property rights is precluded, public control or legal conventions tend to govern allocation. Stop lights, nontransferable hunting licenses, pro rata shares of common pool oil leases, and technological restrictions on ocean fishing are all cases where a system of fee-simple property rights appears so costly that reasonably efficient alternatives to markets have developed.

Political intervention is also common when one person's actions reduce the value of another's property. If your job pays $10 an hour and I offer to do the same job for $5 an hour, the value of your labor is reduced. Thus, we restrict access to some labor markets through, e.g., immigration policies or child labor laws. If you sell fresh milk for $2 a gallon and I offer to sell it for $1 a gallon, the value of your milk is reduced. Thus, transactions in many commodity markets are controlled. There are almost countless examples of government restrictions on the sale of goods that might impair the *value* (but not the physical characteristics) of the property rights of others. Allocative systems that protect pecuniary interests and not merely the physical rights of others tend to be inefficient; production costs are generally excessive.

Property Rights and Environmental Quality

Environmental decay occurs when shared resources—clean air and water, scenic beauty, or peace and quiet—are abused. Smog, foul water, litter, and the noise levels near airports are evidence that overuse of common property may not always lead to efficient social institutions such as full sets of property rights.

A continuing debate rages about how much purity to seek and what techniques to use. At one extreme, some critics view economic analysis as irrelevant and "greedy capitalism" as the root cause of environmental decay. Their position tends to be, "Forbid all pollution." At the opposite pole are those who believe that fully specified property rights harmonize economic activity. These people believe that if individuals are assigned full rights to control specific resources, a market economy will naturally achieve a healthy ecological equilibrium. We will examine both extreme views and some intermediate positions as well; but first, let us re-address externalities—the origin of many environmental problems. A starting point is recognition that externalities may be either beneficial or harmful.

Externalities

Competition tends to maximize both individual welfare and the public interest if only the parties *directly* involved in transactions are affected; marginal social benefits tend to equal marginal social costs. But if external parties are harmed or helped, market prices and quantities usually fail to account for their preferences and social welfare may not be efficiently served.

> **Externalities** *occur when private calculations of benefits or costs differ from the benefits or costs to society—they are present whenever third parties gain or lose from an activity.*

Externalities may emerge from either consumption or production.

External Benefits

Some *external benefits* originate in production. For example, a utility company might dam a river to generate electricity, and nearby residents may gain a recreation area in the process. Or construction of a large manufacturing plant in a community may induce other firms to locate nearby to profit from a resulting economic boom. Or a pharmaceutical company might develop knowledge to prevent or cure some deadly disease. Legal monopolies on knowledge are prohibited, however, so it would be unable to prevent a competitor from using the new knowledge. (Only specific techniques that are uniquely embedded in some commodity or piece of equipment are patentable.)

External benefits occur not only in production, as the previous examples show, but in consumption as well. If you landscape your yard, your neighbors may benefit without sharing in your expenses. Their property values rise, and they gain through more attractive scenery, sweet-smelling flowers, and the like. If you

and your family are inoculated against a contagious disease, your neighbors benefit because their chances of contracting the disease decline. If you study economics and political science in your spare time, you may enjoy a happier and more productive life. But if, at the same time, you become a more informed voter and better citizen, these gains are shared with the rest of the people in this country. These are just a few of the possible external benefits from some forms of consumption.

Without compensation for those who generate external benefits, activities that embody positive externalities may be at less than optimal levels. For example, applied research may be profitable for a private firm because specific applications are patentable, but basic research is seldom pursued privately because the broad benefits from new knowledge cannot be marketed by the researchers. Similarly, education yields gains to children, but others also gain if better educated people tend to be better informed voters and more productive citizens. If education were strictly private, it might be overpriced and far fewer people would extend their schooling. People would quit buying education as soon as another unit of learning cost more than they expected it to be worth to them. They would not consider any gains to their neighbors when deciding how far to pursue their educations.

From the consumption side, suppose that planting flowering trees in your yard boosts both your personal satisfaction and the value of your property. Your demand for flowering trees is shown in Figure 1 as demand curve D_p. You can purchase all the trees that you desire for P_0 and will plant Q_0 trees. Your neighbors may enjoy the trees nearly as much as you do, and the values of their property may be enhanced by your trees.

Demand curve D_s incorporates your private demand plus the social benefits to your neighbors from your flowering trees. The marginal social benefits of your actions are the sum of any private benefits to you plus any external benefits enjoyed by other people. Getting them to pay for these benefits is, unfortunately, very difficult.

Maximum social welfare occurs when marginal social benefits and costs are equal, so the optimal quantity of planted trees would be Q_s. But you may not plant Q_s trees unless you are compensated for your investment beyond Q_0. This can be accom-

FIGURE 1 Positive Consumption Externalities

Positive consumption externalities cause private market demands (D_p) to understate the marginal benefits to society (D_s) of a good. Consequently, without government intervention (for example, a subsidy), there will be underproduction and consumption of the good. A subsidy of bc per tree would be necessary to induce consumers to plant the socially optimal level of trees.

plished if the government subsidizes tree planting by bc dollars per tree. Without compensation covering the external benefits to your neighbors, you all will miss an opportunity to gain with no one losing. The reason is that in your private decision making, you tend to weigh your private costs and benefits much more heavily than any external benefits.

One cure for potential underproduction is communal arrangements, which may be either implicit or explicit. Implicit agreements occur when neighbors encourage each other to improve their properties through such things as informal and friendly competition—who has the nicest house, the prettiest lawn, and so on. Implicit agreements tend to work best when only a few people are involved. Explicit agreements (community covenants or zoning) are more common when larger numbers must cooperate—all residents of some subdivisions may be required to have so many square feet of living space, or they are restricted from painting their homes other than approved colors, or each agrees to spend a certain

amount on landscaping, and so on. In general, as the number of people affected by an externality grows, restrictions on behavior tend to become more formal and less flexible.

External Costs

Pollution is the common term for a wide range of negative externalities and can arise from either consumption or production. Water pollution flows primarily from production processes; air and noise pollution result about equally from both. For example, both industrial wastes and the residues from washing dishes flow into our sewer systems and then into our water supplies. Automobiles, smokestack industries, and coal-fired electric generation all contribute to the smog that engulfs many major cities and results in corrosive acid rain that falls on even the most remote regions of our world. External costs are generated in many forms of production. Examples include noise pollution near airports, unsightly billboards and junkyards, or factories that belch noxious smoke.

Suppose that farmers use pesticide sprays on their artichoke crops and then irrigate their fields, washing some pesticide onto adjacent properties and into nearby streams because enforceable property rights to water are absent. If this pesticide works its way up the ecological chain—harming both your fishing and health—then you, who may never eat artichokes, partially bear the cost of artichoke production. Assume all farmers exude external costs of $2 per pound of artichokes when using chemical sprays. In Figure 2, the supply curve S_0 is based on farmers' costs, but the marginal social cost is MSC, which is $2 higher.

Suppose that artichoke farmers (and ultimately, their customers) are now taxed $2 per pound if harmful pesticides are used; this covers all social costs of production. The price initially rises from $5 to $6 per pound, and annual output falls to 60,000 tons annually. The reason the price rises and the quantity falls is straightforward. There is a $2 vertical shift of supply from S_0 to MSC when farmers' private costs rise $2 per pound. Farmers previously grew 100,000 tons for private costs of $5 per pound. Private costs are now $2 per pound more for each level of output as long as harmful sprays are used.

Unfortunately for artichoke growers, consumers would not continue to buy 100,000 tons if the price were to climb to $7 per pound. The higher production costs will cause marginal farmers to fail, and consumers will reduce their artichoke consumption to 60,000 tons annually as the price rises to $6 per pound. Equilibrium moves from point *a* to point *b* in the short run, but farmers will look for ways to avoid this $2 pollution charge. Suppose that in the long run they discover nonpolluting organic sprays costing $1 more than inorganic sprays. When they use the organic sprays to avoid the $2 tax, the supply of artichokes will rise from *MSC* to S_1.

What is the final socially optimal output in Figure 2? The answer is 80,000 tons of artichokes at a price of $5.50 per pound (point *c*). At this price, consumers buy and farmers sell what they want, and society's resources are used efficiently. A competitive market system fails to achieve such results if large numbers of people are harmed or large numbers of people pollute. What can we conclude from this analysis? First, external costs cause the private market to provide too much of a product because full costs are not borne by customers. That is, the social costs of production (which equal total private costs plus any external costs) are not charged to consumers. If the full costs are paid by consumers, less is produced and consumed. When a pollution charge is imposed, producers will seek ways to clean up their acts while reducing total costs, which now include any external costs.

Could any lone individual reduce pesticide pollution? You might pay farmers to stop or sue for damages. But the latter solution often involves transaction costs (attorney fees, etc.) that exceed the damage done. For example, individually suing all air polluters in Los Angeles would be very costly relative to the potential personal recompense for the harm done. People may seek legal remedies, however, when damages are extreme. The key is to force each firm to *internalize* (fully consider) the costs of pollution imposed on innocent third parties. If each buyer of a good pays full production costs, including environmental damages, then externalities are internalized, yielding optimal amounts of production and consumption.

FIGURE 2 *Internalizing Pollution Costs: Market Equilibrium with External Costs (Diseconomies) in Production*

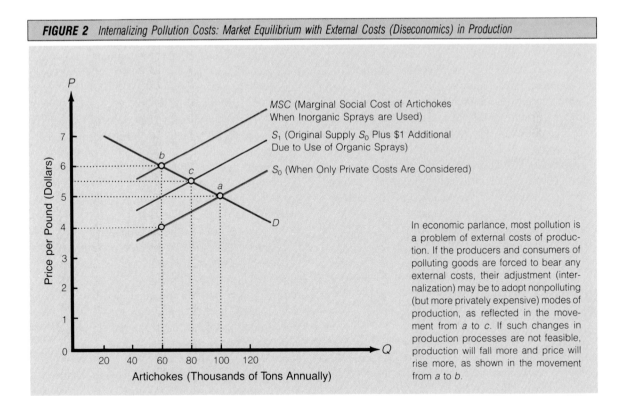

In economic parlance, most pollution is a problem of external costs of production. If the producers and consumers of polluting goods are forced to bear any external costs, their adjustment (internalization) may be to adopt nonpolluting (but more privately expensive) modes of production, as reflected in the movement from *a* to *c*. If such changes in production processes are not feasible, production will fall more and price will rise more, as shown in the movement from *a* to *b*.

Consider such problems as drunk and reckless drivers, loud neighbors who party until dawn, violent criminals, or litterbugs. These are market failures in the sense that consumption-based external costs are imposed on other people. Similar annoyances and dangers might be even more common in a strictly laissez-faire society. Many analysts, however, view these events as examples of government failure because a basic task of government in a market economy is to protect broad legal rights to property, which may include rights to peaceful and tidy neighborhoods and safe streets. Society has tried to control natural tendencies towards overproduction of external "bads" through zoning, social regulation, or other legal sanctions.

Summary: External Benefits and Costs

Unrestricted private markets produce too much (*too little*) of a good when external costs (*benefits*) are present. Externalities are a common market failure because people tend to weigh their private costs and benefits far more heavily than the costs borne or benefits received by outsiders. People maximize their personal welfare by equating the marginal private benefit (*MB*) from an action with its marginal private costs (*MC*). This is normally quite rational because trying to identify and negotiate with all third parties may be prohibitively costly. Thus, market demands mirror marginal private benefits while market supplies reflect marginal private costs.

Society tries to compel decision makers to internalize externalities by assigning certain legal rights to specific groups, through tax incentives or subsidies, or via outright mandates or prohibition. Pollutants are the most notable examples of negative externalities. Ideally, firms will internalize any pollution costs so that consumers ultimately pay full production costs—private plus external (social) costs. Growing amounts of pollution have created a variety of public policies to deal with this problem.

Pollution as a Public Bad; Abatement as a Public Good

A public good, once produced, benefits many people, none of whom can be excluded from enjoying its use. *Pollution abatement* (control) generally fits this definition. Everyone in Los Angeles could enjoy a clearer view of the horizon if smog were eliminated. Thus, environmental quality is a public good. The public good and externality aspects of pollution and its control suggest that government might steer production and consumption toward optimal levels. Optimal output levels require marginal social benefits and costs to be equated. This occurs when all pollution costs are internalized; if they are borne by the consumers and producers of goods whose production or use generates pollution, users and makers will weigh these costs and their decisions will be both personally and socially efficient.

Is Optimal Pollution Zero?

Zero pollution sounds nice, but your first question should be: What would it cost? If perfect purity were costless, we would all demand an immediate end to pollution—but the costs of 100 percent purity are prohibitive. There are trade-offs between environmental quality on the one hand and, on the other, goods required for even modest standards of living. What is optimal pollution? Figure 3 provides an answer using cost-benefit analysis, which compares the costs and benefits of an activity—in this particular case, **pollution abatement.**

Panel A of Figure 3 depicts the total benefits and costs from pollution abatement. The total benefit curve reflects the fact that an increasingly clean environment yields decreasingly valuable additional benefits as we approach 100 percent abatement. This is reflected in a downward sloping marginal social benefit (*MSB*) curve in Panel B. Society's marginal benefit is the sum of all benefits to individuals from each reduction in pollution. Our "output" from pollution abatement translates into a given percentage reduction in pollution. Hence, as we move out along the horizontal axis, more abatement is achieved and the environment becomes cleaner.

The total cost of pollution abatement in Panel A rises as we expand efforts to reduce pollution. In Panel B, the positively sloped marginal social cost (*MSC*) of reducing pollution reflects diminishing marginal returns and increasing marginal costs. More ambitious attempts to reduce pollution entail ever greater sacrifices of resources. Maximizing social welfare requires achieving $MSB = MSC$ (in this example, at points *e* and *f*). To extend abatement beyond the optimal level of pollution ($0f$) would waste resources because further reductions in pollution cost more than they are worth.

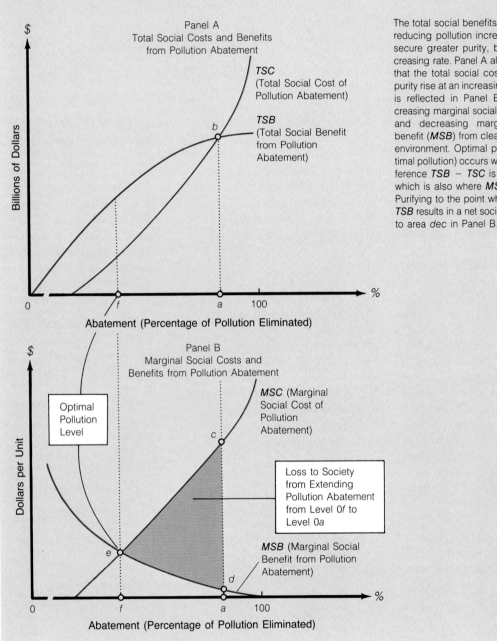

FIGURE 3 *Determining the Optimal Level of Pollution*

Panel A
Total Social Costs and Benefits from Pollution Abatement

TSC (Total Social Cost of Pollution Abatement)

TSB (Total Social Benefit from Pollution Abatement)

b

$

Billions of Dollars

0   *f*   *a*   100   %

Abatement (Percentage of Pollution Eliminated)

The total social benefits (*TSB*) from reducing pollution increases as we secure greater purity, but at a decreasing rate. Panel A also indicates that the total social costs (*TSC*) of purity rise at an increasing rate. This is reflected in Panel B in the increasing marginal social cost (*MSC*) and decreasing marginal social benefit (*MSB*) from cleaning up the environment. Optimal purity (or optimal pollution) occurs where the difference *TSB* − *TSC* is maximized, which is also where *MSC* = *MSB*. Purifying to the point where *TSC* = *TSB* results in a net social loss equal to area *dec* in Panel B.

Panel B
Marginal Social Costs and Benefits from Pollution Abatement

MSC (Marginal Social Cost of Pollution Abatement)

Optimal Pollution Level

c

Loss to Society from Extending Pollution Abatement from Level 0*f* to Level 0*a*

MSB (Marginal Social Benefit from Pollution Abatement)

e

d

$

Dollars per Unit

0   *f*   *a*   100   %

Abatement (Percentage of Pollution Eliminated)

This analysis contradicts the widely held notion that society should completely eliminate pollution regardless of costs. To push pollution control until the total benefits equaled the total costs (point *b* in Panel A) would mean that the last bit of cleanup effort would cost society *ac* (in Panel B), while yielding additional benefits of only *ad*. Society, by cleaning up beyond the optimal level of 0*f* percent to 0*a* percent receives additional benefits of *feda* but uses additional resources worth *feca* to complete the job. The

Should We Export Pollution?

The aroma of Charles Dickens' London was a pungent mix of barnyard, fish market, and refinery. Basic transportation for almost 3 million Londoners was provided by over 200,000 horses; wood and coal fires heated homes and energized industry; and raw sewage and kitchen slops flowed down open gutters into the Thames River.

London's atmosphere is now much more agreeable. One reason is that environmental quality is a luxury good. Thus, London, Rome, or New York are cleaner than Bombay, Mexico City, or Hong Kong. High per capita income yields rules that banish dirtier forms of production. People living in less prosperous regions are less picky; they welcome even unpleasant industries that will provide jobs and income. For example, destitute local communities in the United States may lobby legislators to locate prisons nearby; some poor areas have been competing to be sites for radioactive waste dumps.

Political leaders whose major priorities are growth and development for their countries have frequently tolerated relatively lax safety and environmental standards to stimulate production or to attract industry. It is not surprising that the two most catastrophic industrial accidents ever recorded occurred in (a) Bhopal, India, when hundreds died and thousands were left as invalids after a toxic industrial gas was released, and (b) the Soviet Union, during the "meltdown" of a nuclear power plant at Chernobyl.

Environmental and safety standards tend to be lower in less developed countries. This suggests that environmental quality in the United States and other advanced economies would improve if we import goods that entail substantial pollution from poorer countries that seem more willing to tolerate wastes. Laws to forbid importing goods that were not produced under environmental regulations as stringent as those in the United States have, however, been proposed by several groups on a variety of grounds:

1. Environmentalists who are concerned that our entire planet is being polluted see exporting pollution as a shortsighted solution that will only delay and worsen an ultimate reckoning with the problem of environmental decay.
2. Exporting dirty and dangerous industries is perceived as an immoral way to exploit the poverty of the less developed nations.
3. Domestic industries (and their workers) which must meet strict U.S. environmental standards contend that allowing foreign competition that does not face similar standards is unfair.

The ultimate question is whether developed countries that, because of their prosperity, demand high levels of environmental quality have any right to prohibit less prosperous countries from producing goods that entail substantial pollution. It may be that the comparative advantages of less advanced countries are strongly shaped by high levels of tolerance for environmental degradation.

result is a waste of resources equal in value to the shaded area *dec*.

Another implication is that optimal pollution levels will vary for different regions of the country depending on their respective benefits and costs. Regions particularly vulnerable to acid rain, may for example, want to impose stronger emissions standards than other regions not facing these problems. Densely populated urban areas faced with severe auto pollution may choose to impose travel restrictions (no drive days, commuter lanes) or subsidize mass transit. Focus 1 indicates that trade-offs between production and environmental quality may also affect the locations of certain industries.

Alternative Solutions to Environmental Pollution

Nearly everyone recognizes that environmental decay must be controlled. That is where agreement ends. Extreme conservationists argue for a pristine environment and feel that the social benefits from reducing pollution are overwhelming. To them, only technological limits should be allowed to constrain abatement; economic analysis is irrelevant. Others argue for looser environmental standards and oppose many current regulations and standards as too stringent and costly.

Various methods are available to reduce pollution. These methods can be classified according to their degree of intervention in the market process. The least interventionist is *moral suasion,* followed by various market techniques, then tax and subsidy incentives, and finally, outright government regulation and prohibition. We will examine each of these approaches.

Moral Suasion

Moral suasion lacks legal authority—its goals are to persuade offenders to voluntarily reduce offensive practices and to sensitize people to a problem.

Moral suasion *is social pressure to persuade people or institutions to act in some particular manner.*

For example, "Don't Be a Litterbug" campaigns reduce the trash on public highways, and public hostility has severely limited the areas where smokers indulge their habits. Adverse publicity or consumer boycotts of a polluter's products may persuade a polluter to desist. Moral suasion has limited power, however, because many goods are marketed nationally, public relations campaigns are expensive, and voluntary boycotts ask people to act against their own financial interests. Early in the environmental movement, adverse publicity and threats of boycotts were the only methods available.

Effluent Charges and Subsidies

Many economists have suggested using tax penalties or *effluent charges* to curb environmental decay. This is a modified use of market forces to achieve optimal resource allocations when externalities are present. The government sets the fee (charge) on pollution or the reward for reducing pollution, and polluters are allowed to adjust without overt coercion.

Effluent Charges   The effluent charge approach is illustrated in Figure 4. Again, suppose that a group of polluting manufacturers is located on a public lake

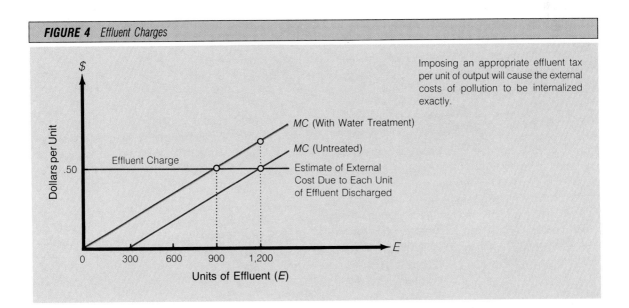

FIGURE 4 *Effluent Charges*

Imposing an appropriate effluent tax per unit of output will cause the external costs of pollution to be internalized exactly.

that could also be used for recreation and fishing. Water pollution reduces the enjoyment derived from boating, skiing, fishing, and picnics.

Assume also that the community leaders estimate that the external cost per unit of effluent is $0.50 when only optimal pollution occurs. To attain the optimal level of discharge into the lake, the community charges the firms $0.50 per unit of discharge. Because the *MC* curve shows that the firms' costs of reducing pollution is less than the effluent charge, pollution will fall by 300 units. The firms will not remove more since the removal cost exceeds the charge; this is the cost to society of putting up with extra pollution.

Subsidizing Abatement

The government might use subsidies (the opposite of taxes) to encourage pollution abatement. Federal grants to pay for pollution control equipment have been used extensively to subsidize cleanups of state or local government sewage facilities. These sewer systems are now required to charge for their services as a condition for receiving these federal funds.

Subsidies to private firms that reduce pollution ultimately are subsidies to these firms' customers, but they are unlikely to be effective unless the subsidies make purification profitable. Subsidies to encourage private pollution abatement could take such forms as grants to pay for equipment, tax credits, or rapid depreciation allowances. Substantial political opposition to subsidizing private pollution abatement has, however, sharply limited such subsidies.

Effective pollution control programs force firms to internalize any external social costs so that waste-spilling companies or their customers pay full (private plus social) costs. Direct regulation is often used, but tends to be a sledgehammer approach.

Market Solutions

Many economists argue that the environmental problem could be easily solved if appropriate property rights were assigned to individuals or groups. Much private property is owned only in a limited way. For example, you may own a car, but there are numerous restrictions on how it can be used. Similar limits apply to ownership of land and buildings, guns, or ham radio equipment.

Lawsuits for Damages

An extensive body of common law has developed to resolve conflicts between property owners. If *property rights* were assigned to protect you from being damaged by pollution, then you could sue harmful polluters. Lawsuits may work fairly well when pollution can be traced directly to a given polluter and the damage can be shown to be caused by that party's effluent. (The Atlas Chemical Company case at the end of the chapter shows how courts approach problems caused by pollution.) But suppose that a firm were given the right to pollute. Your only remedy might be to pay the firm to reduce pollution—if it were worth it to you.

One critical question is: Who has the right to use the environment? This was a crucial issue in the 1879 case of *Sturges* v. *Bridgman*.[1] Sturges, a doctor whose office was next to that of Bridgman, a confectioner, added an examination room next to the confectioner's kitchen. Noisy equipment kept the doctor from examining patients with a stethoscope in the new room, so the doctor sued to prevent the confectioner from operating the equipment. An injunction was granted on the grounds that the machinery imposed external costs on the doctor. (Consider the possibility, however, that this injunction imposed external costs on the candy maker who previously had the right to operate noisy equipment.)

Either private and public lawsuits to protect the environment have some advantages. First, victims of pollutants may be compensated for their losses—they are not with other enforcement methods. Second, successful lawsuits expand legal precedents and alert other polluters to new liability limits, encouraging these firms to adopt cost-justified precautions to avoid future damage claims.

Using the courts to enforce rights to pollute or to be protected from pollution have several disadvantages. First, legal procedures are slow and costly. (Cases tried today have been initiated, on average, two years earlier.) Furthermore, such solutions may not be available if the damaged individual lacks the resources to bring a suit. These solutions alone may leave society saddled with excessive waste. A slightly

---

1. U.S. Supreme Court Case 11 Ch. D. 852 (1879). For a detailed analysis of this case, see Ronald Coase, "The Problem of Social Costs," *Journal of Law and Economics* Vol. III (Chicago: University of Chicago Press, October 1960).

different problem is that where there are numerous polluters and "pollutees," it may be difficult to determine who harmed whom and to what degree. Lawsuits would face almost insurmountable difficulties in solving problems of fouled air in crowded industrial areas.

Legal remedies work best where the number of polluters is small and their victims are few and easily identified. But residents near the Love Canal in New York and in Times Beach, Missouri, experienced at first hand the horrors pollution can produce. Fearful for their own health and that of their children, beset by plummeting property values and a mass of red tape when they sought restitution, the victims of these famous incidents learned how hard it can be to correct the harm done by even easily identified polluters.

Assigning Pollution Rights

A second approach that makes use of the marketplace is for the public sector to sell licenses to discharge wastes.

Pollution rights *are licenses to individuals (firms) to discharge a given level of waste products into the environment.*

Ronald Coase, a prominent economist, has shown that optimal pollution is identical no matter who is assigned the rights, polluter or harmed party, as long as those affected are easily identified, have roughly the same bargaining power (income), and can bargain without cost.[2] This process is diagrammed in Figure 5. The demand for *pollution rights, D_0,* is downward sloping. Pollution would be Q_0 if it were unrestricted and costless. This is the amount of pollution when the environment can be used freely as a garbage dump.

Assume that the community decides to permit only Q_e pollution. Pollution quotas might be auctioned. Business demands to pollute reflect the contribution of pollution to the revenues and profits of the firm. In this view, the environment is just another productive resource. A firm willing to pay only P_a for each right to pollute (point *a*) undoubtedly can clean up its act for P_a or less per unit of effluent. Business

FIGURE 5 *A Market for Pollution "Rights"*

When the right to pollute is strictly limited but for sale on the open market, the demand D_0 for pollution rights depends on the marginal productivity of the environment as a receptacle for industrial waste. Such a market will operate in much the same fashion as markets for other factors of production.

would be willing to pay P_e each for Q_e pollution rights. If purity lovers would be hurt more than P_e by each unit of pollution, they could buy and retain the pollution rights. In this way, the initial sale of these rights would generate revenue for the community. If an auction were held and Q_e rights were sold, then excessive pollution ($Q_0 - Q_e$) would be eliminated.

Assume that the Q_e pollution rights are sold to a group of firms on a lake. What if other firms want to locate on the lake? They could buy rights from the owners of existing pollution rights. This might require buying an especially dirty plant, shutting it down, and transferring the pollution rights to a new plant. Alternatively, a new firm could pay existing firms to install more anti-pollution equipment. Both techniques shift the demand for the right to contaminate from D_0 to D_1 in Figure 5. The value of pollution rights rises, but not the level of waste. Consumers of goods entailing pollution pay full production

2. Coase, R. H., "The Problems of Social Cost," *The Journal of Law and Economics*, Vol. III (Chicago: University of Chicago Press, 1960).

costs as the higher cost of polluting is shifted forward.

This approach has several advantages. First, polluters have strong incentives to clean up. Little administration other than monitoring is required. Also, if the government decides later to reduce pollution, it can repurchase existing rights—or it might sell even more rights as a source of revenue. This approach may be a cheap and attractive alternative to direct regulation, and works especially well in a relatively enclosed environment, like a lake under the control of local authorities. But when spillovers are more pervasive, administration is more difficult. Another major flaw is that some voters and politicians seem to equate pollution with sin and are outraged at the idea of allowing economic reasoning to dominate what is, for them, a moral issue.

Regulations and Prohibition

One politically popular method for reducing environmental damage is direct regulation. Complete prohibition may be desirable in the case of extremely dangerous materials; e.g., highly radioactive wastes. When total bans on certain pollutants are too costly relative to the benefits, the government has often tried to limit noxious wastes through regulations and standards.

Regulation is costly to administer and provides firms no incentives to reduce pollution once a standard is met. Every stringent rule provokes imaginative attempts to discover loopholes around it. This typically results in an incredibly complex patchwork of directives to prevent cheating or avoidance. In some instances, there may be no acceptable alternatives to direct regulation. We need to recognize, however, that the quality of life depends at least as much on production and economic growth as it does on purity, and that there are trade-offs between these goals.

Are Any Abatement Policies Optimal?

Each policy discussed so far has its particular advantages and disadvantages, as summarized in Table 1. None is the "best" for all situations. As in other areas of government policy, "best" depends upon specific social goals and the nature of particular problems.

Where pollution occurs in a closed environment (a lake) and few people are involved, market approaches tend to be viable. Polluters and pollutees might simply be allowed to bargain with each other until they reach a solution. Effluent charges or subsidy schemes may also work efficiently. But where aspects of public goods arise, these approaches break down. Standards and regulations may be appropriate if a problem is widespread and diverse. With extremely hazardous substances, complete prohibition may make the most sense. Different policies are inevitably needed to solve different problems.

This section has provided guidelines for analyzing the complex issue of environmental protection. Securing adequate energy supplies and bolstering economic growth are increasingly balanced against environmental protection and the quality of life as we move towards the twenty-first century. The history of environmental protection in the United States suggests that the Environmental Protection Agency increasingly relies on market solutions to environmental deterioration, although regulation remains a major weapon.

Environmental Policy in the United States

We have examined various techniques to reduce pollution. As we noted earlier, political lags and other difficulties mean that sound economic policies are embraced only slowly, if at all, and transitions are often quite rough. Environmental protection in accord with modern economic analysis generally faces substantial obstacles, both technical and political.

Pollution Control in the United States

By the late 1960s, it was increasingly obvious that the United States had moved into the second phase of property rights: the tragedy of the commons. Environmental degradation was widespread, no longer affecting only isolated cities like Gary, Indiana, or Pittsburgh (which, incidentally, made great strides toward improved air quality). With the passage of environmental legislation for both water and air, Congress more formally delineated our rights to use the environment.

Longstanding arguments about environmental regulation are often rancorous. Environmentalists of-

TABLE 1 Summary and Evaluation of the Various Environmental Policy Options

Policy Option	Advantages	Disadvantages
Moral suasion	Least disruptive to market processes. Educates and sensitizes people to nature of environmental problems. Permits individual choice.	Ineffective in reducing pollution levels.
Market solutions (lawsuits and pollution "rights")	Requires little government intervention. Reduces pollution to a given level depending upon the policy established. Relatively easy to administer. Private lawsuits enable individuals harmed to recover.	Sometimes hard to develop "good" estimates of external costs for particular pollutants and polluters. "License" to pollute is politically unpopular. It may be difficult to prove in a lawsuit who damaged whom. Lawsuits can be costly and expensive. Typically require a "closed" environment to administer effectively.
Tax penalties and subsidies (effluent charges, output taxes, and subsidies)	Relatively easy to administer. Largest polluters have greatest incentives to reduce pollution. Generates revenue to further clean up environment.	Sometimes difficult to estimate appropriate charge or tax. Monitoring compliance can be expensive, especially when large numbers of polluters are involved. Output taxes provide few incentives to clean up pollution or adopt cleaner technology.
Direct regulation	Can be used to keep extremely harmful pollution below dangerous levels. Standards can preserve horizontal equity of the program. Politically most popular.	Once standard is met, polluter has no incentive to reduce pollution below standard (important if standard is above the socially optimal level). Administrative regulation often quite complex and cumbersome. Most interventionist in scope. Large bureaucracy is created to administer program. Does not generate its own revenue. Can become captive agency of particular special-interest groups.

ten react to any environmental deterioration with moral indignation and are accused of largely ignoring the costs of purity. Cost-benefit calculations are shunned in favor of hard-and-fast regulations requiring greater purity. On the other hand, environmentalists commonly complain that bureaucrats fail to aggressively combat pollution. For example, turmoil at the EPA in 1983 reflected outrage that regulators were "selling out" to polluting industries. This rhetoric has been counterbalanced: many firms confronted with the costs of cleaning up have been very

vocal opponents of Environmental Protection Agency (EPA) regulation, criticizing what they see as the ineptitude of environmental managers and politicians. In spite of this furor, there appears to be a smooth and predictable development of environmental policy.

The first step in the movement away from common, unrestricted use of the environment required identifying exactly what created problems such as air pollution. Smog was first noticed in the 1940s as a haze against the foothills behind Pasadena, California, slightly east of Los Angeles. Although smog was first thought to be a passing thing, pressure gradually mounted to clean the persistent brown cloud. The initial impetus for controlling the impure air came from the banking community, which feared default of Los Angeles municipal bonds. The problem was that no one could identify the nature of smog—where it came from or what its effects might be.

When the EPA was first charged with responsibility for improving environmental quality, the only practical solution it perceived was to mandate cleanup by all polluters. Pollution abatement was originally treated on a case by case basis, but uniform mandates quickly seemed necessary on two grounds. First, the EPA set mandatory guidelines because such policies were thought to be easy to monitor. Second, uniform standards constitute equal legal treatment of the affected parties and are nondiscriminatory constitutionally, even though they may dictate unequal burdens of pollution control.

During this period of uniform pollution control, society learned more about pollution and how to measure it, paving the way for pollution rights to emerge as a marketable good. At the same time, political obstacles shaped mandatory rules and standards. Special interest groups lobbied to have rules written to benefit them. Surprisingly, special interest groups have, as often as not, pressed for increased environmental purity. In other words, it is a mistake to think that regulations harm all firms. Some are harmed and some are not. Big steelmakers like rules that drive their smaller competitors out of business. The demise of small firms promotes environmental quality. Firms in polluted regions want pollution control requirements to be as burdensome on firms in cleaner areas. This also enhances environmental protection. In most cases, however, special interest pressures have caused inefficient regulation.

In spite of special interest groups, there has been a steady movement toward more convenient and transferable environmental property rights. In the late 1970s, the EPA began allowing the bubble concept to be implemented in many situations. The "bubble" is a performance standard imposed for the area surrounding a plant or a group of adjacent plants, as opposed to the standards which were originally imposed on each specific source within a plant.

The **bubble concept** *allows firms to transfer pollution rights between individual sources within a plant while at the same time maintaining some standard overall level of environmental quality.*

There is a continuing evolution from the bubble concept to pollution rights that are marketable between plants. The gains from exchange that exist within a plant are also available between plants.

Marketable permits to pollute now exist in a rudimentary form. The EPA now allows an offset policy.

An **offset policy** *permits, for air quality, a new firm to enter an overpolluted area if it induces other businesses to reduce their emissions. Air quality must show a net improvement, and the new firm must meet the individual standards imposed on the others.*

What this means is that a new entrant can bargain with existing firms, either paying them to shut down or to employ more pollution control measures. For example, in California a firm was permitted to build a 40,000 barrel per day oil terminal when it spent $250,000 for an offset created when a local chemical plant closed.[3] Such offsets are now advertised for sale in the *Wall Street Journal.*

Although market solutions have crept into the regulatory postures of agencies like the EPA, there are still many inefficiencies that exist only to enhance the wealth of special interests. For instance, the bubble concept applies only to old "grandfathered" plants, not new ones. The new-versus-old disparity in environmental quality controls is a recurrent theme. Another example of special interest effects is that the net improvement in the environment necessary to qualify an offset as legal is a political football that is often kicked from one end of the field to the other. Firms with offsets for sale commonly try to influence regulators to require great improvements in environmental quality before allowing a new firm to enter a blighted area; this drives up the value of existing rights to pollute.

---

3. Tom Tietenberg, *Environmental and Natural Resource Economics,* 2/e (Glenview, IL: Scott, Foresman/Little, Brown, 1988), p. 351.

The Future of Environmental Protection

One obvious prediction is that we will increasingly enjoy improved environmental quality. As the EPA and the other regulatory agencies become more adept at their jobs, pollution control will cost less and a substitution effect will cause society to demand more purity. Increases in the level of national income will also cause a rising demand for environmental quality because it appears to be a luxury good.

Markets for pollution permits will probably never be as unregulated as those for cars or land. Certain restrictions will be maintained in order to enhance the wealth of special interest groups. Even the market for land is regulated. Zoning laws and other legal requirements exist to protect the value of certain locations vis-à-vis others. It should not be surprising to find this same effect in air pollution rights. Finally, it seems unlikely that pollution taxes will ever be a widespread method of allocating the environment for the disposal of waste. In contrast, both uniform standards and marketable pollution permits endow the regulated firms with this value. It is unlikely that the political process will take this value from them.

To summarize the economics of environmental quality, first we must recognize that the environment is a scarce resource that has competing uses. Second, the political process weighs the cost of property rights definition and enforcement—and the profitability to special interest groups from property rights restrictions—against the inherent efficiency of private property ownership. Our experience in the environmental arena chronicles the changing equilibrium of these forces. As property rights become more completely defined and easily enforced, society is increasingly likely to use private property assignments to allocate the use of our environment.

CHAPTER REVIEW: KEY POINTS

1. Positive *externalities* occur when an activity confers benefits on external third parties. Too few of such activities are undertaken because decision makers tend to ignore the external benefits.

2. Pollution situations in which damaged third parties are uncompensated, and hence unconsidered, are examples of negative externalities. Negative externalities impose costs on third parties. Too many activities generating negative externalities are undertaken because decision makers weigh the costs imposed on others too lightly.

3. Environmental quality is a public good, and controlling environmental pollution is costly. There are trade-offs between protecting the environment and producing goods that generate pollution, so the *optimal pollution* level generally is not zero.

4. *Pollution abatement* may occur through negotiation, *moral suasion* (jawboning and bad publicity), lawsuits initiated by damaged parties, controls (government ceilings on pollution levels), the use of *effluent charges,* or government subsidies for pollution control. No single solution applies to all situations of negative externalities; they must generally be resolved on a case by case basis.

5. The four stages in the development of property rights are (*a*) common access nonscarcity, (*b*) common access-scarcity/tragedy of the commons, (*c*) agency restrictions, and (*d*) fee-simple property rights. The term *fee-simple property rights* means that you can do anything you want with your property so long as you do no physical damage to the property of others.

6. Pollution rights might be auctioned and then made transferable. The Environmental Protection Agency initially relied heavily on direct regulation through pollution ceilings, but is increasingly using *property rights* solutions to control environmental decay.

7. The *bubble concept* sets a pollution performance standard for a plant. A firm can transfer rights to pollute within or between plants inside the "bubble" as long as the standard is met.

8. The *offset policy* allows new firms that wish to produce in a polluted area to operate if they can induce existing firms to reduce air pollutants to "offset" the newcomer's emissions.

QUESTIONS FOR THOUGHT AND DISCUSSION

1. Some analysts insist that external costs are so inherently bilateral that it is hard to determine who is the polluter and who is the pollutee. If a polluter is the one who imposes costs on others, then, when regulation secures greater purity, the people who benefit are the polluters because they impose "cleanup" costs on the factory and its customers. In this view, whether the factory should pay for pollution abatement or whether those who desire purity should "bribe" the firm to install pollution abatement equipment is entirely arbitrary. Moreover, the government need not interfere because, in this view, the parties will privately bargain until an optimal solution is reached. What problems do you see with this approach to environmental quality?

2. What motivates some business firms to argue for stringent uniform standards of allowable pollution nationwide? Do you think it is efficient to require the same standards of firms in metropolitan areas as in isolated areas? If not, which firms should be forced to meet higher standards? Why?

3. Suppose that you are deeply concerned about the welfare of poor people in this country. If you have access to a "magic button" that, when activated, will eliminate all pollution in the United States, should you push the button? Curiously, the answer may be

NO! You will need to draw upon material from the last few chapters to explain why you might not. Now suppose that a second "magic button" would eliminate all urban street crime. Should you push this button? Why or why not?

4. Technological optimists believe that research and development will advance with sufficient speed so that pollution, the energy crisis, and the rapid depletion of nonrenewable resources will be overcome through normal operations of the marketplace. Technological pessimists fear that the advance of technology will only hasten environmental decay and the depletion of resources. To them, only stringent government regulation will forestall stripping the planet of resources and irremediably poisoning our environment. Into which camp do you fall? Why?

5. If your property or person is harmed by pollution, you can sue for damages. What are some of the shortcomings of using the civil courts to resolve the dangers posed by pollutants?

6. Nearly every large city contains neighborhoods whose residents complain loudly about noise from aircraft at a nearby airport. If the airport has been in existence for a long period, is forcing it to relocate an appropriate remedy? Would this be fair? Why or why not?

Atlas Chemical Industries, Inc. v. M. P. Anderson (1974)

Newspapers regularly report situations where the EPA has ordered a firm or industry to stop polluting or to reduce its pollution to "acceptable standards." The following case illustrates another approach to solving some of our environmental problems. It involves a lawsuit by a private individual for damages to his property arising from industrial discharge of harmful matter.

In 1922, Atlas Chemical Industries, Inc., (Atlas), built an activated-carbon processing plant at Marshall, Texas. This plant has been in continuous operation and converts lignite into activated carbon by a process using acids and large quantities of water to wash the lignite. Since 1922, the wash water containing lignite, carbon, and other waste elements has been continuously discharged into Darco Creek. Because of the lignite, carbon, and other constituents, the wash water has an inky black color and tends to leave a black deposit when the solids settle out. Until 1974, when acid-neutralization facilities were installed at the plant, the wash water had an acid content.

Over the years, the creek waters on M. P. Anderson's land have become black, and a black sediment has built up in the creek bottom and creek waters and regularly deposited on sixty acres of M. P. Anderson's land as a result of frequent flooding. Due to the Atlas effluent, the creek waters have been rendered useless, and grass and vegetation in the area of the stream have been destroyed.

In common law actions for damages resulting from this intentional discharge of pollutants, the doctrine of strict liability, as in the classic law of nuisance and trespass, shall apply. In order to prove a *prima facie* case [a case supported by sufficient evidence to warrant submission to a jury] in such pollution litigation, the plaintiff will be required to prove by a preponderance of the evidence the following:

a. That plaintiff has property rights and/or privileges in respect to the use or enjoyment of water, air, land, or other property or interests invaded or interfered with by defendant; and

b. That the defendant has committed an act or acts of commission or omission which

1. endangers or destroys the life of a living thing or being; or
2. gives offense to persons of ordinary sensibilities; or
3. obstructs reasonable and comfortable use of the property; or
4. is a substantial invasion of the public or private use and enjoyment of property; or
5. creates an unreasonable risk or danger to a person, land, or other personal property; or
6. constitutes the alteration of the physical, thermal, chemical, or biological quality of, or the contamination of, any water in this state that renders the water harmful, detrimental, or injurious to humans, animal life, vegetation, or property; or to public health, safety, or welfare; or impairs the usefulness of enjoyment of water for any lawful or reasonable purpose; and

c. That the conduct of the defendant or his act or acts of omission or commission are or were the legal or producing cause of the invasion, injuries, or damages; and

d. That the invasion, or the commission of the acts or the omission of the act or acts is or was intentional. The intentional act, omission, or invasion may be one in which the defendant perpetrates the invasion or interference; or is substantially certain to result from his conduct; and

e. The amount of plaintiff damages.

We believe the public policy of this state to be that however laudable an industry may be, its owners or managers are still subject to the rule that its property cannot be used to inflict injury to the property of its neighbors. To allow industry to inflict injury to the property of its neighbors without just compensation amounts to adverse condemnation, which is not permitted under our law. We know of no acceptable rule of jurisprudence which permits those engaged in important and desirable enterprises to injure with impunity those who are engaged in enterprises of lesser significance. The costs of injuries resulting from pollution must be internalized by the industry as a cost of production and borne by consumers or shareholders or both and not by the injured individual.

During the Industrial Revolution in this country, the law shifted to accommodate economic growth and those who invested therein and was changed to the detriment of isolated individuals who have collectively come to bear the cost of such growth. In recent years, however, the U.S. Congress and the state legislature have recognized that we literally cannot live with the pollution caused by industrial waste and have passed various statutes, rules, and regulations controlling the disposal and emission of pollutants. It is as if we have allowed a monster (pollution) to be created which will either devour or destroy us all. "[P]ollution is waste. We can't get rid of waste by moving it from here to there. We already are at the stage where 'there' is getting so full that it's backing up to 'here'." No longer can we permit industrial development and pollution at the expense of individuals. The social utility of allowing uncontrollable pollution without compensation for the injury caused thereby is no longer tolerable. Neither the benefit of pollution-causing activity to the community nor the comparative investments of plaintiff or de-fendant will be factors considered in determining whether there is a compensable injury. Citizens who are injured should be allowed to maintain an action for an interference which is unreasonable and offensive to persons of ordinary sensibilities. During this century, the course of law has been to incorporate economic growth and the protection of important production, which quickly became the paramount value in the resolution of conflicting interests in pollution litigation. "But in this age of environmental concern it is clear that this value warrants no greater emphasis than others. Thus, it is time for the reassessment of the law to the end of redressing its imbalance, a time for reflection on where responses to legitimate needs in another time carry the law."

Judgement for M. P. Anderson in the sum of $61,375.

Questions

1. Will this decision enhance the allocation of resources in Texas?
2. What did the court mean by the phrase "the costs of injuries resulting from pollution must be internalized by the industry"? Do you agree with that statement? Why or why not?

3. What are some of the costs of such a decision?
4. Do you expect there to be a large number of private suits for pollution damage in Texas? Do you agree with the requirements for a *prima facie* case?
5. Texas has a Water Quality Board to supervise and regulate the quality of water in the state. If Atlas met the standards required by the Texas Water Quality Board, would you have decided for Atlas instead of Anderson? Why?
6. The award to Anderson in this lawsuit was for past damage to his land. If Atlas Chemical Industries, Inc. continues to discharge effluents that harm Anderson's land, should he be permitted to sue again? What limits would you set on recoverable damages?
7. How could Atlas avoid damages in the future? Do any of these approaches internalize the harm to the firm?

CHAPTER 34

The Economics of Agriculture

Farming conjures images of a simpler and more rewarding lifestyle. The hectic pace of modern life causes many suburbanites, who find watching their gardens grow a deeply satisfying, almost mystical experience, to long for land of their own. This nostalgia, which largely ignores the hardships farmers confront, might be explained by the ability of many of us to trace our roots back to the land. Two centuries ago, 19 of 20 Americans relied on agriculture for income; today only 1 American in 40 remains on the farm, but economic pressures for farmers to leave their land have not abated.

The major objectives of this chapter are to (*a*) survey the farm problem, (*b*) identify its causes, (*c*) evaluate past and present U.S. agricultural policies, and (*d*) note some possible future directions for agricultural policy.

The Farm Problem

Agriculture, our largest single industry, is often cited as the prime example of pure competition, but government is heavily involved in farming. The tiny minority of Americans who are farmers is an even smaller proportion of all farmers on Earth, but they easily feed all of us and generate surpluses for export to help feed a hungry world. This agricultural abundance contrasts sharply with the low and erratic farm incomes shown in Figure 1. Subsidies to agriculture soar and add billions of dollars to the federal deficit, but pressures mount that will drive even more farmers into urban labor markets. Movie and recording stars perform at benefits for farmers unable to pay their mortgages, yet the U.S. farm belt has among the

FIGURE 1 Per Capita Farm Income Versus Non-farm Income (Thousands of Dollars per Capita and Relative Percentage)

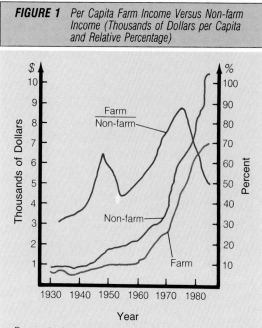

Per capita income in agriculture is generally less than in the rest of the economy, and tends to be far more erratic as well.

FIGURE 2 Leaving the American Family Farm, 1910–1985 (Millions of Households)

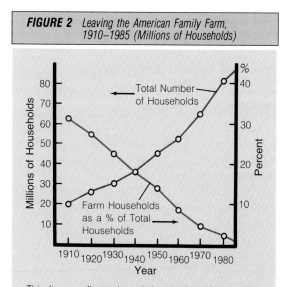

This figure reflects the relative decline of agriculture as a way of American family life throughout this century, and the absolute decline since 1940.
Sources: Statistical History of the United States, Bureau of the Census, Series A350-352, Economic Report of the President and Statistical Abstract of the United States, 1988.

most fertile land anywhere and our farm technology is unsurpassed. Unravelling the paradoxes in American agriculture requires applying microeconomic tools to a bewildering mix of historical forces and meandering public policies.

Low and Unstable Farm Income

The woes of American family farmers have been widely chronicled, but they are far from new. Figure 1 illustrates the basic problem. For more than two centuries, average farm income has been both unstable and considerably lower than for non-farmers. From a modern peak of roughly 90 percent in 1973, farm income had fallen to about half of average urban income by the early 1980s. A common adjustment for many farmers has been to find temporary or part-time employment elsewhere; non-farm earnings at times provide roughly half of the annual income of roughly half of all farmers. An even more significant adjustment to the enduring pressures of low and erratic income has been the exodus of farmers or their children from rural areas, as shown in Figure 2.

Credit Problems

The farm belt has recently been plagued by yet another problem. Farming was moderately prosperous in the early 1970s, when many people viewed land as a good hedge against inflation. This induced many farmers to go deeply in debt as they tried to expand their landholdings and invest heavily in new machinery and buildings. Consequently, land prices rose sharply. Then, during 1980–1986, commodity prices and farm revenues fell and the real market value of farm land dropped by roughly 30 percent. Figure 3 reflects the resulting hikes in most farmers' debt-to-equity ratios. Rising real interest rates added to farmers' woes and many found it impossible to service their mortgage payments, so auctioneers' gavels signalled a wave of farm foreclosures during 1984–86. Failure rates in many farming communities, especially in the Midwest, rose to the highest rates since the 1930s. A few foreclosures provoked violence when neighboring farmers tried to unite in resistance.

Less well publicized but almost as frequent were failures of farm community banks, which accounted for nearly half of all bank failures during 1984–86.

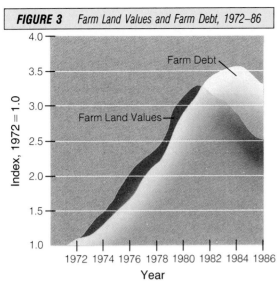

FIGURE 3 *Farm Land Values and Farm Debt, 1972–86*

Index, 1972 = 1.0

Year

Modest agricultural prosperity combined with inflation to drive rural land prices up sharply during the 1970s. Farm debt escalated as well, in part to finance new equipment but primarily for land acquisitions by farmers who vieed low real interest rates as opportunities to expand. When rising interest rates and weak agricultural prices drove land prices down during 1980–1986, many farmers went even deeper in debt just trying to keep their heads above water. This was often a losing battle, and farm forclosures became a frequent tragedy.

Sources: Michael T. Belongia and R. Alton Gilbert, "The Farm Credit Crisis: Will It Hurt the Whole Economy?," *Federal Reserve Bank of St. Louis Review*, December 1985, p. 6 and *Statistical Abstract of the United States*, 1986.

These failures left many rural areas without convenient sources of credit, adding yet another problem to be surmounted by farmers.[1]

Competition and the Marginal Producer

Even a whiff of potential profit causes competitive firms that are currently suffering losses to hold on, and attracts new firms that may rely on resources that are ill-suited to specific forms of production. Humans make decisions at the margin, so some marginal firms that teeter on the brink of failure exist in all

competitive industries. For example, were a price floor on Alaskan bananas set sufficiently high ($40 a pound?), there would almost certainly be an Alaskan banana industry and struggling Alaskan banana growers who would argue for higher price supports. Our farm problem resembles this far-fetched example because marginal family farmers are most threatened with extinction. Note, however, that a marginal farmer may not be on marginal land. If a farmer using good land fails (e.g., is "marginal" because of credit problems), the land tends to be taken over by another farmer.

Now that you have an overview of the farm problem and some of its consequences, a brief look at the nature and structure of the agriculture industry is needed so that we can extend our analysis.

The Industrial Structure of Agriculture

Farms range from labor-intensive small plots that grow exotic flowers, fruits, vegetables, or poultry, to huge wheat farms densely covered with grain, to arid and isolated ranches that stretch from horizon to horizon, barely supporting 5 or 10 cattle per section.

Number and Sizes of Farm Properties

Identifying the typical farm sometimes seems a futile exercise. Variations in the scale of U.S. farming operations are indicated in Table 1. Although the average

TABLE 1 *Number of Farms and Land in Farms, 1985 (Thousands)*

Size	Number	Percent
Under 50 acres	579	29.8%
50–179 acres	639	32.9%
180–499 acres	450	23.1%
500–1,000 acres	163	8.4%
over 1,000 acres	114	5.8%
Total	1,945	

Source: *Statistical Abstract*, 1987, and *Bureau of Census*, 1982.

[1]Charles Calomiris, Glenn Hubbard, and James Stock, "The Farm Debt Crisis and Public Policy," *Brookings Papers on Economic Activity*, (Washington, D.C.: The Brookings Institution), vol 2, 1986, pp. 441–79.

(mean) farm covers more than 400 acres, over 60 percent cover fewer than 180 acres and account for less than one-eighth of total agricultural acreage. Most of these are the "family" farms that have been the primary focus of the media and policymakers. At the other extreme, roughly 1 farm in 7 exceeds 500 acres. These larger farms tend to be corporate, and collectively control about 70 percent of total acreage.

This summary of the structure of agriculture raises questions about the value of farm property. The distinction between farmers' incomes and their wealth is often overlooked in surveys of the farm problem. Persistently low farm income should cause the market value of farm property to be relatively low. That farm land remains comparatively high in the face of low incomes has led to a cliché that "farming is a way to live poor and die rich."

Farm Income and Wealth

Farm land and improvements approached $700 billion in total value in 1985, averaging $360,000 per farm—and only 16 percent of this value was mortgaged. Thus, average farm owners were worth about $300,000 in real estate alone, ignoring machinery and livestock. While farm incomes typically lag behind those in urban areas, the average farm owner is wealthier than the average non-farmer. Averages (means) can be misleading, however; most farmers own less than the 429 "average" acreage, and an acre in Idaho is worth far less than one in Iowa or California.

Larger farms account for a disproportionate share of total farm wealth, leaving many farmers quite poor when compared to average urban families. Tenant farmers or sharecroppers, who pay 35–40 percent of their revenues to landowners, tend to be poor. Figure 3 indicates, moreover, that farm land values declined during 1980–1985 and farm mortgages rose to record levels. This mirrored the turmoil in agriculture in recent years; land prices fell because of declining commodity prices, thus leaving many farmers strapped with heavy debt burdens incurred in the 1970s when their futures had looked considerably brighter.

Causes of the Farm Problem

Politicians have done the most to encourage the production of food in all countries where the main medical problem is obesity, and the most to discourage it in all countries where starvation remains a threat.
—The Economist

Famine is a recurring problem in many less developed countries; cheap and abundant food supplies are a prerequisite for healthy economic growth. In the United States and parts of Europe, however, this goal has been largely met, leading to a very different set of problems. Excessive agricultural production and depressed prices have brought problems for most American farmers and have led to conflicting policies (*a*) U.S. agricultural output has been restricted by programs that directly subsidize farmers, and (*b*) the prices of farm goods have been artificially maintained above the levels that would have resulted from unhindered market forces, creating incentives to expand already excessive levels of production.

The problems that farmers face stem largely from three factors:

1. rapid growth in agricultural productivity,
2. low price and income elasticities of demand for farm products, and,
3. the relative immobility of agricultural resources.

Growth in Agricultural Productivity

Modern machinery, new strains of seed, selective animal breeding, extensive irrigation, and custom blended fertilizers are among the technological advances that have swollen U.S. agricultural yields while substantially shrinking rural labor requirements. Productivity growth in agriculture, illustrated in Figure 4, has exceeded that for any other major industry. These productivity gains have not been confined to any single agricultural commodity, but apply across the board. You might expect income to rise whenever you produce more. Explosive growth of agricultural output has not, however, greatly increased farm revenues because total food consumption is relatively insensitive to both its own price and consumer income.

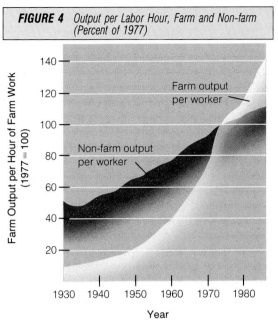

FIGURE 4 Output per Labor Hour, Farm and Non-farm (Percent of 1977)

Agricultural productivity growth has exceeded the growth rates in manufacturing and services for centuries. Recent advances in agricultural technologies have created almost irresistible pressures for even more farm families to leave the land. The steepness of these curves reflect productivity advances; average farmers now produce 16 times as much as in 1930, while typical non-farm workers produce only about 2.5 times more than in 1930.

Source: *Statistical Abstract of the United States*, 1988.

Demand Elasticities for Farm Products

Farm products, like other goods, conform to the law of demand: quantity demanded is lower at higher prices and vice versa. The demand for agricultural products, however, exhibits two characteristics that have created problems for the farmer: it is both relatively price inelastic and grows only slowly over time. That demand is relatively price inelastic means that quantities adjust little when prices change. When goods are "necessities," the amounts people consume tend not to be significantly influenced by their prices. This implies that the proportion of income spent on these goods will grow if prices rise, or fall if prices decline.

The price elasticity of demand for various agricultural goods is shown in Table 2. The absence of good substitutes for all farm commodities taken together causes their collective demands to be relatively inelastic: between .2 and .5. Taken singly, some farm products have relatively elastic demands because there are many other farm products that are close substitutes for them, e.g., apples, pears, peaches, and oranges, or pork, beef, and lamb. If the price of apples, for example, increases drastically, people simply substitute in the direction of oranges or some other fruit.

Substitution is also more difficult when the demand for the primary food or fiber is derived from that for some processed product. Cotton, wheat, and hops are good examples. These commodities account for only a fraction of input costs in the finished product (e.g., cloth, bread, and beer, respectively). Thus, a change in price will not heavily affect the final price and hence the quantity demanded. The important point about the relatively inelastic demand for farm products is that when technological advances sharply boost agricultural outputs, consumers require substantial price cuts before they will buy the added production. This is a "Catch 22" for farmers. If only one farmer becomes more productive and harvests a bigger crop, that farmer benefits. But when all farmers become more productive, they all lose because the inelastic demand causes prices and farm revenues to plummet.

Most agricultural products are also relatively income inelastic; Column C of Table 2 reveals that several major farm outputs are even inferior goods. This means that farmers tend not to share in general prosperity because, even if our economy grows rapidly, the demand for farm output grows at a much slower pace. Total demand for farm goods is roughly proportional to population, but U.S. population growth is far below that of our agricultural productivity.

The combined effects of low price and income elasticities and rapid productivity gains are illustrated in Figure 5. Assume the market is in initial equilibrium at point e_0 and equilibrium price and output are P_0 and Q_0, respectively. As the economy grows, farm demand also grows, but not as fast as the general economy. Thus, demand only shifts to D_1. During the same time, rising productivity shifts supply out to S_1. The end result is that farm prices and incomes plummet, while output rises to equilibrium point e_1.

TABLE 2 *Some Price and Income Elasticities of Demand*

	Price Elasticities (A)	Price Elasticities (B)	Income Elasticity (C)
Cotton (at farm)	0.1		
Wheat (at farm)	0.02–0.2		
Flour (retail)		0.80	−0.36
Corn (at farm)	0.03–0.5	0.50	
Apples (retail)	1.3		
Peaches (retail)	1.5		
Citrus (retail)	0.8		
Oranges		0.66	
Potatoes (retail)		0.11	
Starchy roots			−0.20
Beef (retail)	0.8–1.1	0.64	
Cattle (at farm)		0.68	
Pork (retail)	0.7–1.0		
Hogs (at farm)		0.46	
Pig products			−0.20
Lamb (retail)	1.8–2.3	1.78	
Chicken (retail)	1.1–1.2	0.78	
All meat products (retail)	0.4–0.6		
Milk		0.35	−0.50
Eggs (retail)	0.3–0.4	0.32	0.37
Butter (retail)	0.3–1.4	0.65	0.42
Margarine (retail)	0.3–0.8		−0.20
Sugar		0.24	
All Food (retail)	0.2–0.5		

Sources: (A) USDA, 1959 (B) P. George and G. King, *Consumer Demand for Food Commodities in the United States with Projections for 1980*, Giannini Foundation, 1971 (C) Heinz Kohler, *Intermediate Microeconomics*, 2/e (Glenview, Il: Scott, Foresman and Co., 1986).

FIGURE 5 *Why the Trend in Farm Revenues Is Down*

When rapid growth in agricultural supplies (S_0 to S_1) is accompanied by only modest growth of the demands for agricultural goods (D_0 to D_1), the result is a sharp drop in farm revenues and financial catastrophe for many farmers. The relative price inelasticity of demand causes farm revenue to fall, so area $0P_0e_0Q_0$ is much larger than area $0P_1e_1Q_1$.

Immobility of Farm Resources

Most American farmers have adopted modern technology and large scale farming has grown dramatically, but agriculture remains primarily a family business; workers on most farms belong to a single family, with fewer than one-third being hired hands. This makes it difficult for most farmers to layoff employees during periods of slack demand. Demands for most farm outputs fail to keep pace with growth in the overall economy, hastening the painful process of reallocating resources away from farming; many children abandon family traditions after generations in farming, or entire families surrender to pressures to move on. Depressed agricultural markets do not necessarily weaken farmers' personal incentives to adopt more efficient technology. Techniques that lower costs and increase the output from a given acreage appear even more attractive to individual farmers when markets are weak, so that farm modernization and mechanization is not slowed by agricultural gluts. Surpluses of farm products have resulted in declines in the amounts of farm labor utilized rather than reductions in all resources used in agriculture.

Arguments for Aid to Agriculture

Don't complain about farmers when your mouth is full.

—A bumper sticker

Many arguments have been advanced for aiding the farmer—most of them by farmers. These arguments for aid to farmers are, in the eyes of farmers, not pleas for welfare payments; rather, they are warranted by the unique positions and merits of farmers:

1. Working the land with your hands is widely viewed as a more real experience than the abstract work done by city folks. This leads to a perception of the family farm as a primary source of desirable social values, and thus, as something worth preserving.

2. Most farmers view agriculture as confronting extraordinary hardships that are not paralleled in other industries. Droughts, floods, blight, and insect infestations are cited as examples of hazards unique to agriculture.

3. Farmers argue that much of American economic growth over the past 200 years can be traced to the freeing up of resources made possible because of productivity gains in agriculture, and further, that a plentiful and relatively cheap food supply has increased the health, longevity, and productivity of our labor force. Thus, according to farmers, positive spillovers from agriculture to a well nourished population justifies public aid to farmers.

4. Agriculture is highly competitive; millions of farmers cannot individually control their output prices. Farmers contrast this to situations where firms possess much more control over the price and the total industry supply of their products. If General Motors raises its prices, it will lose some, but not all, of its customers, given people's preferences for various makes of cars. (And Ford and Chrysler will probably also boost prices.) But if one wheat farmer tries to charge more than the current market price, who will buy? Since most goods and services bought by farmers (oil and gas, machinery, rail transportation, etc.) are produced by firms with some degree of control over prices, farmers lack leverage and end up with a low and shrinking share of national income.

5. Finally, national economic policies are frequently adopted that unintentionally harm farmers. Many farmers believe that they are used as pawns when the government prohibits, e.g., exports of wheat to the USSR or South Africa, because the administration hopes to force concessions by foreign governments. They also feel victimized by federal deficits and "tight" money policies that drive interest rates up, or by macroeconomic policies that raise the exchange rate of the dollar, severely limiting agricultural exports.

Traditional Farm Programs

Congress has yielded to these arguments and tried numerous programs to aid the farmer. The principal thrust of these programs has been to restrict farm production in order to raise prices and incomes. These programs can be classified into:

1. crop limitation programs,
2. purchase-loan price-support programs to boost farm prices, and
3. purchase-and-resale subsidy programs.

To understand these programs, you need to understand the concept of agricultural "parity." Parity conventionally stresses attempts to achieve fairness by placing bargaining parties on an equal footing. Agricultural parity refers to something a bit different.

The Concept of Parity

In the rich and mainly industrial countries farmers are paid too much, so they produce too much. In the poor and mainly agricultural countries farmers are paid too little, so they produce too little.

—The Economist

The concept of parity pricing was first introduced into law with the Agricultural Adjustment Act of 1933. The basic goal is to maintain the real purchasing power of the prices farmers receive for each unit of output. Thus, if during a 1909–14 base period, a farmer could buy a certain amount of consumer goods with the revenue from one bushel of wheat, "parity" suggests that the same relationship should prevail in 1990. Thus, parity requires the relationship between per unit farm prices and the prices farmers typically pay to remain constant. At times, Congress has paid lip service to the parity concept in setting agricultural policies, although this relationship has been relatively erratic, as Figure 6 indicates.

FIGURE 6 *Parity Pricing*

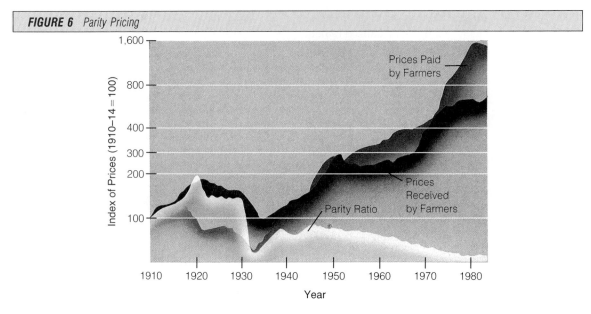

The idea that agricultural prices should maintain "parity" with other prices is an attempt to put a straightjacket on changes in relative prices as signals of society's changing priorities. Policy has only erratically been based on this concept.

Most neutral analysts are skeptical about the idea that parity pricing is equivalent to fairness because rapid productivity gains have slashed the amounts of inputs used per unit of farm output, and so average production costs have declined even when input costs have not. Nevertheless, the parity concept was a cornerstone of farm policy from 1933 through the 1960s. Many farmers adopted "100 percent parity" as a rallying cry during the early 1980s when they sought more help from Washington and wanted price floors raised. Until the early 1970s, Congress generally maintained parity prices in the 70–90 percent range, although during World War II, price floors averaged 106 percent of the parity formula. More recently, however, only dairy farming has fallen under the parity concept.

Crop Limitation Programs

Progams intended to limit supply are based on the reasoning that a smaller output would command a higher price. Because the demand for farm output is price inelastic, then total farm revenue rises when smaller crops are sold at higher prices. Since less will be produced, total costs will be somewhat less, and therefore profits (net farm income) will rise. This analysis is shown graphically in Figure 7. The crop limitation program reduces total output from Q_0 to Q_1, causing prices to rise from P_0 to P_1.

Crop limitation programs raise a fundamental question: Whose crops will be limited? One approach is to restrict the amounts of particular commodities that each farmer can sell. Farmers who produce more than their quotas get angry when they cannot market their total crop at the inflated market price, but allowing them to do so would drive the market price down. One technique has been for government control boards (primarily at the state level) to allow only these quotas to be sold at the high price they initially set, with lower prices for any remainder. Dairy farmers, for example, typically are assigned quotas for fluid milk that can be sold at a relatively high price. A dairy can sell more than this quota, but only by accepting a lower price for milk that can legally only be made into cheese, ice cream, butter, or other processed milk products. (Is it either efficient or equitable for drinkers of whole milk to subsidize eaters of cottage cheese? This is effectively what happens.) At times, torrents of surplus products have caused farmers not to harvest their crops. At other times, state agricultural control boards have burned or dumped oranges, potatoes, and milk into empty fields. Such policies are not unique to the United States. For example, thousands of tons of Brazilian coffee have been dumped in the ocean over the past half century.

Another approach is for government to allot acreage. Only farmers with "allotment" rights are allowed to grow certain crops, and only specified amounts of land can be cultivated. Does this mean that if wheat farmers are allowed to plant, say, only half the land previously used to grow wheat, that wheat production will fall by half? NO! Wheat farmers will continue to cultivate their best land; only the worst half will not be planted with wheat. Moreover, the resulting high price for wheat stimulates more intensive cultivation (e.g., more fertilizer and more thorough harvesting).

Allotment programs for grain, peanuts, soybeans, sugar beets, and cotton have frequently caused more crops to be grown with less total acreage. And, of course, the total amounts of crops grown bear, on average, higher production costs than were farmers allowed to use all their land. While not as flagrant as destroying harvested crops, these programs are also extremely inefficient. Dissatisfaction with various crop limitation programs led farmers to advocate a slightly different approach.

FIGURE 7 Crop Limitation

Reducing supply boosts revenue whenever demand is relatively inelastic. If crop limitations reduce supply from S_0 to S_1, farm revenues grow by $P_0 P_1 e_1 a$ minus $Q_1 a e_0 Q_0$.

Purchase-Loan Price-Support Program

Under a purchase-loan price-support program, the government guarantees farmers a higher price than would have prevailed in the market. These artificially higher prices are enforced through either outright government purchase of the surplus at the price floor, or it may be kept off the market by using a government loan program. Under a *storage and loan* program, farmers store their output and obtain loans equal to the price floor, known as the "support" price. If the market price is lower than this support price, the farmer does not repay the loan and surrenders title to the crop to the government. But if the market price exceeds the support price, farmers pay off their loans and sell their output on the market at a higher price. For the farmer, this is a "heads I win, tails you lose" proposition. The support price was linked to the parity price until the 1970s, when the parity concept was largely abandoned.

The nature of these programs is diagrammed in Figure 8. Equilibrium e_0 would prevail without government intervention and yield price P_0 to the farmer. Since this is below the support price (P_1), the government must shift total demand (private + public demand) to D_1 to accommodate the current year's crop at the support price. Because only Q_1 could be sold to private individuals at support price P_1, the government must purchase quantity $Q_0 - Q_1$. What is to be done with this surplus? Our government has provided these surplus commodities as foreign aid to developing nations, as the principal ingredient of the school lunch program, and as commodity supplements to the needy in the United States. Even so, farm surpluses have often filled silos and overflowed into mothballed ships or been dumped into mountains of grain along railroad sidings. Sometimes these surpluses simply rot.

Note that these programs cause total farm income to rise by $(P_1 - P_0) \times Q_0$ and that we pay $P_1 \times Q_1$ for food as consumers and $P_1 \times (Q_0 - Q_1)$ for surpluses as taxpayers. Do the gains to farmers offset the losses experienced by the rest of us? NO! The reduction in food consumed ($Q_0 - Q_1$) had value to us (as consumers) equal to area $Q_1 g e_0 Q_0$. This reduction in consumption is a loss to us without being a gain to the farmer. (We buy food and then are forced not to consume it, except for the parts that are used for school lunch programs, foreign aid, and supplements

FIGURE 8 Using Loan Guarantees to Bolster Farm Prices

Purchase-loan price-support programs may boost farm incomes, but in an extraordinarily inefficient way. Resources are used to produce food and fiber that no one ever uses. At the margin, farmers' costs rise so that their net income is not enhanced by this program; any predictable flows of cash are capitalized in higher prices for the land that produces the subsidized goods. **Note:** We have simplified this graph and that in the next figure by assuming that supply is fixed. The results would not be substantially different were we to allow supply to be somewhat elastic in the relevant period.

guaranteed support price, P_1, and total farm production is Q_0. Now, instead of storing the surplus necessary to achieve the support price, the commodity is sold to consumers at the equilibrium price P_0. The farmer receives price supports from the Department of Agriculture equal to the difference in prices ($P_1 - P_0$) times the amounts of the commodity produced. This program is essentially the same as the purchase-loan-storage program except that government sells the commodity on the open market for what it will bring rather than dumping it abroad or letting it rot.

This program has the advantage over the other two of lower prices to consumers so that consumers are not clobbered by a double-edged sword of higher prices and higher taxes to support farm incomes. While this program was economically more efficient than the other programs, it had one major flaw politically—direct payments to farmers permitted the public to see the extent to which certain farmers were benefitting. Payments to individual farms and/or corporations exceeding $1,000,000 per year were not uncommon. Getting paid not to produce while simul-

for the poverty stricken, e.g., cheese giveaways.) The area $Q_1ge_0Q_0$ is a net social welfare loss from these programs.

The general effect of the program is clear—higher prices and incomes to the farmer, and higher prices to the consumer but less food. In addition to the inefficiency of this system of redistribution of income from consumers to farmers, there is the additional cost of storage that must be borne by taxpayers.

Purchase-and-Resale Subsidy Programs

Direct purchase-and-resale subsidies are the most complicated of all farm programs. They generally involve paying a higher price than a free market would dictate to the farmer, and then reselling food to consumers at whatever price the market allows. Figure 9 depicts such a program. Again the farmer is

FIGURE 9 A Purchase-and-Resale Subsidy Program

Purchase and resale subsidy programs are more efficient than farm programs that remove produced goods from the market. There is still a welfare loss triangle equal to abe_0 in this figure, however, because consumers value the extra goods produced as a consequence of this subsidy less than the costs incurred for the extra production.

taneously receiving large subsidies became a political scandal. The result was restrictions by Congress on the total subsidies or payments any individual or corporation could receive. After a brief stop at $55,000, the subsidy ceiling was reduced to $20,000 in the 1973 Agriculture and Consumer Protection Act.

Who Benefited from Traditional Farm Programs?

The bulk of farm subsidies have been paid to fewer than one fifth of all farmers. The realization by Congress of such an unequal distribution of farm subsidies and the dramatic increases in farm prices in the early 1970s led to a reappraisal of past policies and a new farm bill in 1973. This Act set the future course of farm policy. This new policy, along with declining farm prices, has brought about the confrontation between farmers and the administration we read about so much in the news.

Agricultural Policies of the 1970s and 1980s

Traditional farm policies served the farmer relatively well until the early 1970s, when agricultural exports began to surge because of:

1. a 1972 decision by the Soviet Union to fill its domestic shortfall through imports from the U.S.,
2. rising demands for livestock resulting from increased consumer incomes,
3. poor agricultural harvests in several nations, and
4. a sharp depreciation of the dollar in international currency markets.

Boom Years in the Early 1970s

In the early 1970s, international commodity prices rose rapidly because of bad weather conditions and sparse harvests throughout much of the world. American farmers prospered, encouraging expansion and entry into the competitive agriculture industry. By 1973, most organizations representing farmers urged the government to allow food production to expand to meet both domestic and expanded export markets.

The focus of policy shifted from concerns about overproduction and low farm income to avoiding possible shortages, inflation from high farm prices, and using agricultural exports to reverse persistent deficits in our balance of payments. Farmers were anxious to cash in on booming demands for food and fiber and did not want outdated policies—primarily crop restriction programs—to hold them back. Former Secretary of Agriculture Earl Butz led the charge to accommodate farmers' wishes.

Agriculture and Consumer Protection Act of 1973
As a result Congress enacted the Agriculture and Consumer Protection Act of 1973 that embodied a four-year program with the following basic features:

1. *Target prices:* The previous price supports based upon parity were replaced with target prices established by law. These target prices represented guaranteed minimum price floors on basic agricultural commodities, and were established considerably below the peak farm prices of 1973 but generally above the support prices of previous years. When market prices were above these target prices, the government left agriculture to the free market. When prices fell below the target, direct payments to the farmer were based on normal yields and acreage.

2. *Agricultural production:* Although the previous crop limitation programs were extended, the Agriculture Department largely refrained from imposing crop limits and generally encouraged aggressive expansion by farmers.

3. *Subsidy ceilings:* As indicated earlier, the 1973 Act limited payments to $20,000 per individual farmer for all commodity programs combined. The 1973 Agriculture and Consumer Protection Act along with adverse domestic and global weather conditions provided the farmer with record or near record incomes. Per capita income for the farm population (including farmers' non-farm earnings) actually exceeded that of the non-farm population in 1973.

Predictably, this agriculture bonanza was not shared equally among farmers. Most small farmers gained little ground during this period, but rural prosperity created by record prices and farm incomes throughout 1973–76 added to strong inflationary pressures then being experienced in the economy. This made agriculture a hot political issue that precipitated consumer boycotts of many grocery store chains and some types of food, along with export embargoes on other agricultural products.

The agricultural prosperity during the 1970s (shown in Figure 10) yielded many secondary benefits for farmers. High incomes generated rapid capitalization of farm land, so that farmers who owned their farms experienced huge gains in their wealth. Capital gains to farmers were nearly twice as great as the record total net farm income of this period. The result of this prosperity was reflected in farmers' balance sheets. Proprietors' equity almost doubled during 1970–1976, and farm mortgages fell from roughly 17 percent to 15 percent of the total value of farm land. The greatest enrichment of farmers during this period resulted from the skyrocketing price of farmland. Although propelled by rapid general inflation, farmland rose even faster than other prices. From less than $200 per acre in 1970, average acreage rose to over $700 by 1980.

Many farmers viewed this prosperity as a signal to expand, and invested heavily in more, bigger, and better machinery and bought more high-priced acre-

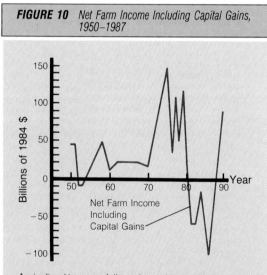

FIGURE 10 *Net Farm Income Including Capital Gains, 1950–1987*

Agricultural incomes follow a boom-bust cycle that makes farming sometimes seem a bit like playing Russian roulette. Note that inclusion of capital gains to farmers makes the erratic income streams shown in Figure 1 even more volatile. Source: Calomiris, *BPEA*, p. 446.

Source: Calomiris, *BPEA*, p. 446.

age to cultivate. Some land that had previously lain fallow was planted and harvested. Many non-farmers entered agriculture, expecting the prosperity to continue. The result was that both long-time farmers and new entrants into farming went deeply in debt in the hope of making fortunes. Unfortunately for most of those who followed this strategy, getting rich in farming is the exception rather than the rule.

Recent Rural Hardships

The substantial gains in farm incomes and wealth recorded in the 1970s occurred in an era of relatively little government intervention. You might think that farmers would consequently favor a hands-off policy. Nothing could be further from the truth.

Although the domestic demand for farm products has remained relatively strong, two factors combined to cause farm income to fall sharply: the erosion of export markets and a worldwide rapid growth of agricultural harvests. By 1977, the dollar had depreciated to a record low on international money markets. This stimulated foreign demands for our farm exports. Then, when the dollar rose back towards peak levels in the early 1980s and foreign crop failures were reversed, exports of U.S. agricultural products fell sharply. Several countries that had been major net importers of food products became net exporters during this period, e.g., China and Indonesia. Exports were also curtailed a bit by embargoes against some foreign governments (e.g., to protest the USSR's invasion of Afghanistan).

Even more significant were the bountiful harvests in American agriculture, which have swollen supplies and caused farm prices to fall substantially relative to production costs. The market prices of agricultural land also dropped, reflecting general gloom among farmers. From a peak of $823 in 1982, the average price per acre of farmland collapsed to $679 by 1985, precipitating a wave of farm foreclosures and bankruptcies throughout rural America. These slippages enflamed many farmers into calling for 100 percent parity, a return to older agricultural policies, and threats of strikes if their demands were not met.

Target prices and the acreage set-asides reestablished by the Food and Agriculture Act of 1977 have not provided major windfalls to farmers. These programs only postponed financial disasters that were brewing in the late 1970s. Target prices allowed market prices to achieve equilibrium levels and, if they were deemed too low, direct subsidies were paid to farmers who participated in the program. Even this program, however, left many farmers very unhappy. The reason? The prosperity of the early 1970s encouraged many people (primarily farmers' children) to enter the farming industry, while existing farmers expanded their operations by paying premium prices for land and machinery. When the future of any industry appears bright, many participants are willing to go deeply in debt so that they will share in the pie. High interest rates were more than offset by inflation during most of 1975–79 and so did not discourage a flood of new financial investments in agriculture. Inflation began declining faster than interest rates fell during the early 1980s and, simultaneously, farm income began declining. Consequently, land prices softened and many farmers found that their property was worth less than they had paid for it and, in some cases, less than its mortgaged value. Foreclosures were met with militant resistance by such organizations as the American Agriculture Movement.

Many observers of the business scene view this sequence of events as a simple reflection of the market at work. Overly optimistic business forecasts cause firms (including farmers) to bite off more than they can chew. The inevitable result is that many will be forced into bankruptcy. The power of farmers as a voting bloc is on the wane. Nevertheless, the importance of agriculture to the American economy means that it is unlikely that the U.S. will revert to a less interventionist approach to the farm problem.

New Directions for Farm Policy

Targeted income maintenance may be required to save particular groups of farms [that are] deemed socially valuable.
—Calomiris, Hubbard, and Stock

If the intention of policymakers is to "save the family farm" rather than to enrich large, corporate farmers, then it is inefficiently costly for agricultural policies to continue to rely on unfocused price supports, acreage reduction programs, export subsidies, and other broad gauge government transfer programs. These traditional approaches may be like trying to use a water pitcher to bail out the Titanic. A more narrowly focused federal emphasis on ensuring that small farmers have access to credit markets (i.e., something like an expanded FHA loan guarantee program for small farmers) is one possibility. Another alternative is for the government to use a needs test in dispensing its transfers. Poor farm families alone would be subsidized.

One problem with this approach, however, is farmers' insistence that they seek, not welfare payments, but rather, just compensation for their contributions to society. Another problem is that explicitly setting welfare payments at higher levels for family farmers than for other impoverished Americans is politically unpalatable. If so, it may be the case that the only long-run cure for small and inefficient family farmers is to allow them to go out of business. There are no easy answers to the dilemmas confronted in redesigning agricultural policies.

CHAPTER REVIEW: KEY POINTS

1. The major problem for farmers is that income from agriculture has been relatively low and erratic for generations. No other sector of the economy has as consistently experienced tremendous productivity growth, so these low incomes are largely market signals that our society desires shifts of resources from agriculture into other forms of economic activity.

2. The demand for all farm products lumped together tends to be relatively price and income inelastic. Thus, much lower prices are required to clear markets when agricultural supplies grow significantly, and the widespread adoption of more productive agricultural technologies tends to drive farmers' revenues down sharply.

3. Farming is our largest industry, and it is among our most competitive. There are strong political pressures for the federal government to support farmers, however, for at least two reasons (*a*) many non-farmers have great empathy for farming as a way of life, and (*b*) although a small minority, farmers have been active for a century in making their problems known to lawmakers.

4. The strong tendency for people to make decisions at the margin means that there will always be high-cost marginal producers who will be wiped out by slight reversals in the markets where they operate. No policy can prevent this from happening. The principal thrust of agricultural policy has been to restrict farm production to raise prices and farm revenues. These farm programs can be classified into (*a*) crop restriction programs, (*b*) purchase-loan price-support programs to boost farm prices, and (*c*) purchase-and-resale subsidy programs.

5. *Parity pricing* is based on the notion that the prices of farm products should not change relative to the prices farmers pay. A policy of 100 percent parity would enrich farmers who experience productivity gains and would freeze the incentives for efficient reallocations that are imbedded in relative price changes.

6. Most policies intended to preserve the family farm have largely benefited large farming operations, many of which are corporate.

PROBLEMS

1. Although demands for farm products tend to be relatively price and income inelastic, these demands tend to be roughly proportional to population. What does this imply about the coefficient of the population elasticity of these demands?

2. Suppose that both the short-run price elasticity of demand for wheat and its income elasticity are .3, and that its population demand elasticity is 1.0. If 120 million tons of wheat were sold in 1989 at a price of $6 per bushel, what will happen to its price if, between 1989 and 1990, population grows 2 percent, income grows 3 percent, and that good weather and the growth of agricultural productivity causes the amount of wheat marketed to rise to 140 million bushels?

QUESTIONS FOR THOUGHT AND DISCUSSION

1. Suppose that you were an extraordinarily efficient farmer who owned prime agricultural acreage. Would your income necessarily rise if government guarantees a price for some of your crops that is high enough to allow less efficient farmers to survive if it, simultaneously, restricts your output through an acreage allotment program? Why or why not?

2. Rapid growth of agricultural productivity over the centuries has meant that the proportion of population required in agriculture to feed the rest of us has consistently declined. Can you think of mechanisms other than relatively low farm incomes that would have accomplished the movement from rural areas into the urban work force indicated by this technological change?

3. If the value of the dollar on international currency markets is relatively high, U.S. agricultural exports tend to be constricted, as occured during 1980 through 1984. When the dollar falls sharply, however, U.S. agricultural exports rise sharply, as they did during 1986 through 1988. Should the federal government buffer farmers against swings in their incomes that occur because of volatility in the international value of the dollar? Why or why not?

4. Richard McDougal, president of the American Cattlemen's Association, testified before the House Agriculture Committee that:

"Unfortunately for us, the best cure for low prices is low prices. That is, low prices bring about needed supply adjustments. . . . Similarly, the best cure for high prices is high prices. That is, high prices and profits bring supply increases, which then moderate prices to consumers."

Do you agree with this statement? Explain.
Mr. McDougal went on to testify:

"Production of agricultural commodities is inherently cyclical . . . hundreds of thousands of individual producers make production decisions, in response to cost-and-price relationships . . . . Just as cattlemen overresponded to favorable returns in the late 1960s and early 1970s, wheat producers overresponded to . . . [high] prices in 1975."

Does this analysis seem basically correct to you? What would be the impact on the livestock industry of very high grain prices? Should we guarantee high prices to one group at the expense of others? Consider the trade-off between equity and efficiency.

U.S.A. v. Paul J. Johnson (1957)

Our Constitution was written to prevent tyranny in many areas of personal freedom (the Bill of Rights, etc.), but the federal government, under its constitutional authority to regulate commerce, often restricts economic freedom. The Agricultural Adjustment Act (1938) was intended to stabilize agriculture and improve the incomes of relatively poor farmers. Not all farmers benefited, however, as this case illustrates.

Paul Johnson is an Arkansas farmer. During 1956, wheat production was controlled under the Agricultural Adjustment Act of 1938. Johnson, without having a wheat acreage allotment, planted 50.5 acres to a mixed crop of wheat and singletary peas; the mixed crop was harvested, and the wheat was separated from the peas and fed to Johnson's hogs. The government contends that Johnson produced a farm marketing excess subject to a statutory penalty at the rate of 45 percent of the parity price of wheat, which amounted to $1.07 per bushel, or a total of $269.64, the amount sued for.

Johnson admits that he planted a mix of wheat and singletary peas and fed the wheat to his hogs. He earnestly contends that this should not subject him to a penalty, however, because his crop was what he calls "hog wheat," as contrasted to what he calls "flour wheat." That is, it was low grade wheat never intended to be milled into flour,

and that Congress never intended to restrict the growing of such wheat.

It is now well-settled (in other cases) that wheat produced on excess acreage is subject to penalty even though it is never marketed, but is consumed on the farm by feeding it to livestock or otherwise; the reason is that such wheat overhangs the market as a price depressant, and, further, that such wheat supplies a need that would otherwise be met by purchases and thus competes with wheat in commerce. Johnson argues that in those cases, the courts were not concerned with "hog wheat," which is unsuitable for milling or marketing and so cannot affect interstate commerce. Thus, the heart of this argument lies in his distinction between "flour wheat" and "hog wheat." In addition to contending that he produced no wheat, Johnson alleges that he did not apply for or receive any payments under the wheat program.

Granting that Johnson's argument is ingenious, neither the statute nor the regulations distinguish, as far as penalty is concerned, between different kinds of wheat based on differences in grade, quality, or suitability for milling. As to the allegation that he did not apply for government payments, liability does not depend upon participation in the wheat program or upon having received government benefits; the penalty applies to all producers whether they participate in the program or not, and regardless of whether or not they receive benefits.

Paul Johnson may well think it unfair and an unreasonable restraint upon his liberty to be subject to a penalty for planting on his own land a mixture of wheat and singletary peas and then feeding the wheat to his own hogs. But it is unfortunately true in this country, as elsewhere, that losses of liberty in greater or lesser degrees frequently march hand-in-hand with government subsidies in any field, whether industry, commerce, agriculture, or education; and, as Johnson will learn as a result of this litigation, such losses are not confined to those who personally benefit from the programs involved.

Let a judgement in favor of the United States be entered.

Questions

1. Can you cite other instances where government subsidies with restrictions on actions to some individuals result in losses of freedom to others? . . . losses of wealth or income?

2. Are there any limits to government's ability to mandate, forbid, or prosecute certain individual activities? How does the military draft apply? Marijuana laws? The 55 MPH speed limit?

3. Admittedly, Paul Johnson has lost some "freedom" in this instance. What has been gained and by whom? Are the "gains" sufficient to offset the "losses"? Who decides these questions, and with what criteria?

CHAPTER 35

Redistribution of Income and Wealth

Most Americans wake up knowing that we will have full bellies and roofs to sleep under that night. But haunting images of starving children regularly appear on television. About half of the world's people suffer from malnutrition and live in squalor. Not surprisingly, poor people tend to be less healthy and die younger than those who command more resources. In the United States, slum dwellers and derelicts consume much less than prosperous suburbanites, and the incomes of migrant farm workers fall far below the national average. Overseas, the opulence enjoyed by some wealthy people contrasts even more starkly with the lives of the impoverished.

Why is the relative prosperity that most Americans, Japanese, and Western Europeans enjoy so rare elsewhere? Why are some people poor, while others consume conspicuously and extravagantly? Do prosperous people have a duty to share with the less fortunate? If voluntary sharing seems inadequate, should government redistribute income and wealth? These are among the questions addressed in this chapter.

We will first discuss whether "money can buy happiness"—*redistribution* is a potential cure for poor people's misery only if financial resources can secure happiness. We then present some alternative ethical criteria that address redistributing income and wealth. Finally, we identify influences on present distribution patterns, describe current American welfare programs, and look at proposed reforms for what some people call "the welfare mess."

Prosperity and Happiness

Would most of us like more wealth than we have? Almost certainly. Jeremy Bentham, the utilitarian philosopher, offered two important propositions about wealth and utility. The first is reasonably well accepted: All else equal, more income or wealth makes people happier. Bentham's second proposition is more controversial: On the average, additional income means more to the poor than to the rich. That is, income itself may be subject to the law of diminishing marginal utility. We will deal with these issues in turn.

Does Money Buy Happiness?

We do not mean this question literally, of course, but rather: Are the rich happier than the poor? Many religious people reject this idea, believing that the only truly satisfying path is grounded in their particular faith. Many soap operas, pulp magazines, and bad novels suggest that the price of being rich is a life of pain and suffering. (Most of us would gladly risk such misery.)

Numerous surveys indicate that, on average, health and longevity are positively related to income and wealth. Prosperous people also tend to rate themselves happier than people who are not, as the study reported in Figure 1 shows. In a survey, people were asked how happy they were. The responses shown in Panel A were assigned weights of +2 for "very happy," +1 for "pretty happy," and zero for "not too happy," leading to the *utility score* in Panel B. Utility scores climb as income rises, supporting Bentham's idea that higher income yields greater happiness, although there is a possibility of reverse causation—cheerful people may get better jobs and do better financially.

Do Extra Dollars Mean More to the Poor than to the Rich?

A positive answer to this question suggests that *if* we ignore the effects on production and investment, society might gain through redistributions of income and wealth from the rich to the poor. This is a big "if." Small wonder that it is among the most controversial propositions in economics.

This issue cannot be settled objectively because there is no scientific way to compare people's levels of satisfaction. People favoring greater income equality might argue that extra dollars are most valuable to the poor because necessities generate more *utils* (imaginary measures of satisfaction introduced in an earlier chapter) than such luxuries as the mink coats or golf clubs purchased by the rich. Defenders of current distributions could respond that income must mean more to the well-to-do because most work hard for their incomes.

Advocates of redistribution might then assert that (*a*) the poor lack the resources possessed by people with high incomes, (*b*) discrimination denies equal

FIGURE 1 Income and Happiness

In Panel A, the percentage of people who rate themselves "pretty happy" seems unaffected by income. The response "very happy," however, is far more common for people with higher incomes, and relatively few of them are "not too happy." Many low-income people consider themselves "not too happy," while few are "very happy." This suggests that general satisfaction with life is positively related to income, as shown in Panel B.
Source: Drawn from a survey of Illinois residents, reported in N. M. Bradburn and D. Caplovitz, *Report on Happiness* (Chicago: Aldine, 1965).

opportunities to many poor people, or even (*c*) the disutility associated with work is relatively higher for the poor because they lack access to pleasant and remunerative jobs. Defenders of the status quo might then argue that wealthy people save and invest much larger proportions of their high incomes and that without these investments, the poor would be even worse off. This debate spins in circles, but it is impossible to scientifically ascertain the best income distribution. This does not mean, however, that it is a waste of effort to try to understand these normative issues.

Ethical Criteria for Distribution ___

When wealth is centralized, the people are dispersed. When wealth is distributed, the people are brought together.
>—*The Analects of Confucius, Book 14*

Controversies over who should have what predate the written word. Distribution has been thought unfair by most "have nots" in all societies, and by many conscience stricken "haves" as well. At least three schools of thought offer competing answers about how to distribute income fairly.

One view is that income should be based on contribution; a second, that income should be distributed according to need; and a third, that income should be distributed equally. Distributions in all modern economies are based on a blend of these criteria. Those whose contributions are valued more tend to receive higher incomes so that they will have incentives to contribute. Many people with special needs receive tailored attention from private or public charities. Finally, progressive income taxes and welfare payments are among the mechanisms intended to make incomes more equal. The ethical bases of these criteria differ markedly.

The Contribution Standard

. . . he that will not work shall not eat.
>—*John Smith*
>*The General Historie of Virginia, 1624*

We've already discussed how markets determine income payments to resource suppliers. Competition distributes income in proportion to the values of the marginal products and amounts of resources people supply. Marginal productivity theory provides roots for the *contribution standard,* whose advocates believe that rewarding contribution is both equitable and efficient. The contribution standard encourages

work effort, investment, and attempts to profit by serving other people's demands.

The **contribution standard** *is the idea that income should be distributed according to the productivity of one's resources.*

An implicit assumption is that markets accurately gauge productivity. Thus, who gets how much is fairly determined by an impersonal market system, without the favoritism inherent in centralized decision making.

Income differences generated by a contribution standard are not a disadvantage, according to its champions, in part because people with high incomes save proportionally more, facilitating investment and economic growth. This yields gains to both the rich and the poor; it is a cliché that "A rising tide lifts all boats." Moreover, inequality is equitable if it results from smarter or harder work, longer hours, or saving and investing.

For example, should a cab driver who works a 60-hour week subsidize one who works 30 hours? Should a factory worker who draws interest from savings squeezed from a slim paycheck share the interest with others who spend everything they make? Advocates of the contribution standard answer NO to such questions, asserting that it is compatible with capitalism, sets efficient incentives for production and economic growth, and maximizes individual freedom. Moreover, a contribution standard uses "carrots" (income) to reward productivity instead of the "sticks" (punishment for sloth) common under other systems.

Opponents of the contribution standard, however, wonder how well markets measure productivity. They argue further that the very young, the very old, and the handicapped among us must share in our income if our society is to be fair and humane.

The Needs Standard

From each according to ability, to each according to needs.
>—*Louis Blanc*

Some people lack the skills or the physical or mental attributes to be very productive. Others inherit great wealth and, by resource ownership alone, claim to be productive. Citing such perceived inequities, many opponents of the contribution standard favor distributing "to each according to needs."[1]

*The **needs standard** is the idea that income should be distributed in accord with need.*

This famous Marxist slogan is difficult to implement, however, and poses severe problems for production incentives. How do you determine a person's needs? Distributing primarily according to a *needs standard* requires a bureaucratic assessment of people's needs. Why would anyone bother to work if distribution were strictly by need? Is it proper to replace economic incentives with the coercive force of government?

These and other problems with distributing according to needs were discussed in more depth in chapter 2. Trade-offs between efficiency and equity, however, can be heart wrenching. Most people agree that at least the basic needs of those who cannot provide for themselves must be accommodated because we should not allow orphans, the aged, the severely handicapped, or society's misfits to starve. Whether capable but lazy people should be guaranteed the necessities of life is a separate issue.

The Equality Standard

Dividing income equally avoids the great disparities in income that occur under the contribution standard and dispenses with the immense bureaucracy required for a needs standard.

*The **equality standard** is the idea that income should be distributed equally among the population.*

All that an equality standard requires is accurate national income accounting and a census of population: divide national income by population, then mail each family a check for its share. Moreover, there is an economic rationale that an equal distribution of income generates the maximum economic welfare possible in a society under certain conditions.

Suppose you were the utilitarian ruler of a country and were intent on maximizing social happiness. You have the right to divide a given national income to accomplish this goal. You suspect that some of your subjects would be reasonably happy with very little, while others would gain great happiness from higher monetary incomes. You, unfortunately, cannot measure any individual's gain in happiness from a higher money income, nor can you objectively compare happiness between individuals. If you try to find out who would gain the most from more than an equal share, most people will exaggerate their needs and some may lie to you. If you are convinced that each person gains from higher income but that, on average, the poor gain more than the rich, then the expected happiness of the community will be maximized if you simply divide all income equally.

Like distribution according to needs, however, equal sharing of income erodes personal incentives for productivity. One ideal of socialism is to replace the selfish individuals assumed in conventional economic theory with people filled with desire to work for the betterment of all humanity. Attempts to educate masses of people into altruistic modes of behavior have uniformly failed, however, and enforced production quotas replaced income incentives for production in such countries as the Soviet Union and China. The failure of this approach has caused a new generation of leaders in both countries to experiment with more personal systems of rewards.

1. An interesting historical note is that Marx viewed distribution according to need as an objective to be implemented only after a "dictatorship of the proletariat" gave way to "pure communism." According to Marx, the most glaring inequity of capitalism is that workers are paid less than the values of their *average* products because exploitative capitalists steal any production in excess of subsistence wages. Thus, Marx was an advocate of a productivity standard, were productivity defined by averages rather than marginal products. After Marx's death, John Bates Clark developed marginal productivity theory and the argument that payments to owners of their resources' marginal products would absorb all production. It would be interesting, were it possible, to know what Marx's own reaction would have been to Clark's rebuttal of the exploitation doctrine.

Inequality and Inequity

Life is unfair.

—*John F. Kennedy (1960)*

If differences are perceived as inequitable, then evidence that Kennedy was right abounds. People differ in natural ability, inheritance, opportunity, in the times and places they were born, in age, race, sex, and religion. Most of all, they differ in luck. Some face discrimination, some are maimed or die in car wrecks or wars, and some are homely, demented, or physically or mentally impaired. Others are attractive, healthy, bright, buy winning lottery tickets, or are born with silver spoons in their mouths.

Some inequities may be remedied through government policies or social reforms. The inequity of slavery ended with the Civil War, and discrimination by religion, race, or sex is now illegal in education, housing, and employment. Other apparent inequities may never be cured. It is impossible, for example, for a genius to transfer IQ points to someone less intellectually gifted, or for a world-class sprinter to give speed to us slowpokes.

No society will ever achieve a consensus that everyone is treated fairly because equity is unavoidably subjective. Suppose that everyone agreed with the idea of *horizontal equity*: equals should be treated equally. Even this would do little to resolve equity in a world where every person is somewhat unique. Advocates of the contribution standard argue that inequality of income or wealth is frequently justified by differences in the productivity of individuals' resources. Yet difficulties in specifying equity when people and circumstances differ have caused critics of a contribution standard to focus on inequality as evidence of inequity.

Just how unequal is income distribution in the United States? Table 1 shows pretax and pretransfer distributions of income since 1935. Although changes

proceed only at a snail's pace, notice that the share of the middle 60 percent of recipients is now over half of all income. Moreover, because taxes are mildly progressive while transfers tend to be regressive, Table 1 understates the share of net income received by people at the bottom and overstates the share of people at the top. Before we explore how much tax and transfer policies reduce inequality, we need to introduce a device for comparing distributions of income or wealth.

Lorenz Curves

It is hard to see changes in the income distribution and the extent of inequality from Table 1. Lorenz curves, developed by a German statistician, allow visual comparisons between distributions across time and between countries.

A **Lorenz curve** *shows the cumulative percentage distribution of income or wealth in a society.*

On the axes of the Lorenz curve in Figure 2 are the cumulative percentages of families and family incomes before taxes and transfers. Data (e.g., from Table 1) are sequentially summed to form the cumulative distribution listed below the figure. For example, if the bottom 20 percent and the second lowest 20 percent of the population, respectively, receive 5 percent and 12 percent of all income, then the lowest

Family Group	Percent of Total Income					
	1935	1950	1960	1970	1980	1987
Lowest 20 percent	4.1	4.5	4.8	5.4	5.3	4.9
Second 20 percent	9.1	12.0	12.2	12.2	11.6	11.1
Middle 20 percent	14.1	17.4	17.8	17.6	17.5	17.0
Fourth 20 percent	20.9	23.4	24.0	23.8	24.0	24.3
Highest 20 percent	51.7	42.7	41.3	40.9	41.6	42.8
Top 5 percent	N/A	17.3	15.9	15.6	15.3	15.9
Total	100.0	100.0	100.0	100.0	100.0	100.0

TABLE 1 The Distribution of Income Before Taxes and Transfers, 1935–84

Source: *Statistical Abstract of the United States*, 1986, 1988, and U.S. Bureau of the Census, *Money Income of Households, Families, and Persons in the United States* (Washington: U.S. Government Printing Office), 1986; 1987 estimates by authors.
Note: Numbers may not add up to 100 due to rounding.

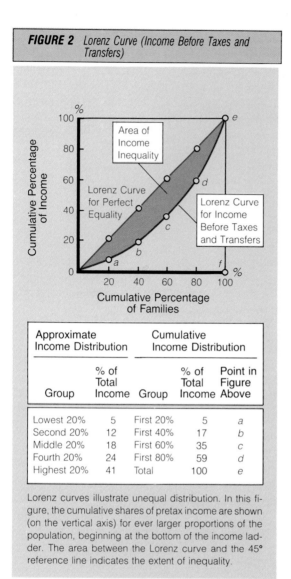

FIGURE 2 Lorenz Curve (Income Before Taxes and Transfers)

Approximate Income Distribution		Cumulative Income Distribution		
Group	% of Total Income	Group	% of Total Income	Point in Figure Above
Lowest 20%	5	First 20%	5	a
Second 20%	12	First 40%	17	b
Middle 20%	18	First 60%	35	c
Fourth 20%	24	First 80%	59	d
Highest 20%	41	Total	100	e

Lorenz curves illustrate unequal distribution. In this figure, the cumulative shares of pretax income are shown (on the vertical axis) for ever larger proportions of the population, beginning at the bottom of the income ladder. The area between the Lorenz curve and the 45° reference line indicates the extent of inequality.

40 percent of the population receives 17 percent of total income. And if the middle 20 percent gets 18 percent of total income, then the lowest 60 percent of the population receives 35 percent (5 + 12 + 18 = 35). And so on.

If the Lorenz curve were a diagonal like the straight line 0e, then income would be distributed evenly—each fifth of the population would receive one-fifth of income. If one family had all income while the rest of us had nothing, the Lorenz curve would be identical to the bottom and right-hand axes—line 0fe. The Lorenz curve for the United States is the curved line. The shaded area reflects

inequality; the larger this area, the more unequal the income distribution.

Note, however, that lifetime earnings patterns prevent continuously equal income distributions. Younger families typically earn less than more established families, primarily because of differences in work experience and past saving. Even if every family had identical lifetime incomes, inequality would exist at every point in time because of typical age/earnings profiles.

The Changing Distribution of Income

How much has income inequality been reduced in the United States? Table 1 suggests that the pretax distribution of income has changed little since 1950. But high income families pay more taxes and receive fewer transfer payments, on average, than those with less income. Figure 3 shows pretax income distributions for 1929 and 1984, along with a dashed Lorenz curve for 1972 (the only year for which data are available) reflecting the greater equality of net income that results after taxes and transfer payments.

The state of economic development is a powerful influence on the relative distribution of income, with more advanced countries tending to have greater income equality regardless of the economic system. For example, several studies indicate that distribution is more equal in such capitalist countries as the United States, Japan, and West Germany than in such avowedly socialist countries as Cuba, Iraq, Ethiopia, or Nicaragua. The shift towards greater equality in the United States shown by the pretax Lorenz curves for 1929 and 1984 largely reflects the growing prosperity of the middle class over the past 50 years. Most transfer and tax policies designed to reduce inequality are of more recent vintage, having been distilled during the social ferment of the 1960s.

Income inequality has generated many hotly debated proposals for redistribution. But redistributing income raises such questions as: Should society provide welfare to a rich person who suffers severe but temporary business losses? Should a welfare recipient who wins $10,000 in a lottery be cut from the welfare rolls for a year or two? Such paradoxes for income redistribution schemes have given rise to other controversial proposals that concentrate on redistributing wealth because, as the preceding questions suggest, income and prosperity are only roughly correlated.

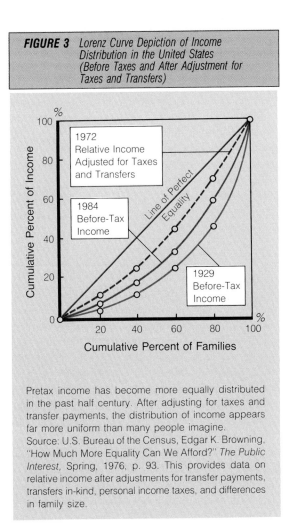

FIGURE 3 *Lorenz Curve Depiction of Income Distribution in the United States (Before Taxes and After Adjustment for Taxes and Transfers)*

1972
Relative Income
Adjusted for Taxes
and Transfers

Line of Perfect
Equality

1984
Before-Tax
Income

1929
Before-Tax
Income

Cumulative Percent of Income

Cumulative Percent of Families

Pretax income has become more equally distributed in the past half century. After adjusting for taxes and transfer payments, the distribution of income appears far more uniform than many people imagine.
Source: U.S. Bureau of the Census, Edgar K. Browning, "How Much More Equality Can We Afford?" *The Public Interest,* Spring, 1976, p. 93. This provides data on relative income after adjustments for transfer payments, transfers in-kind, personal income taxes, and differences in family size.

The Distribution of Wealth

Wealth is the sum of assets—financial and economic capital—minus liabilities. Median household wealth in 1988 was nearly $37,000.[2] Household assets include such items as stocks, mutual fund shares, real estate, motor vehicles and so on. Do poor people occasionally have high incomes? Do wealthy people sometimes experience low incomes? The surprising answer to both questions is YES. Wealth is cumulative unspent income and is a stock variable, while income

___
2. U.S. Bureau of the Census, *Household Wealth and Asset Ownership: 1984* (Washington: U.S. Government Printing Office, 1986). Updated by authors.

is a flow variable.[3] Wealth tends to generate income, but some high-income people don't save and never achieve wealth; you may have read about high rolling financiers or big lottery winners declaring bankruptcy. On the other hand, some wealthy people occasionally have low-income years. This is common for retirees. Most welfare programs are intended for people plagued by both little wealth and low income.

If you thought the income distribution was skewed towards the top, look at the wealth distribution in Figure 4. A 1986 Bureau of the Census study

___
3. *Stock variables* are timeless, while *flow variables* lack meaning without a time period. A millionaire's assets exceed debts by at least $1 million, and time is irrelevant. It matters greatly, however, whether you make $100 hourly or weekly.

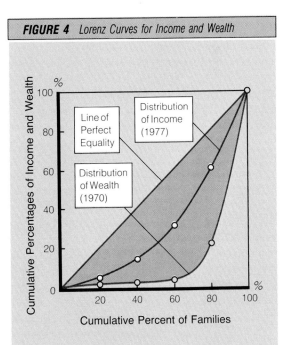

FIGURE 4 *Lorenz Curves for Income and Wealth*

Line of
Perfect
Equality

Distribution
of Income
(1977)

Distribution
of Wealth
(1970)

Cumulative Percentages of Income and Wealth

Cumulative Percent of Families

Measured wealth is much less equally distributed than income. Critics of these statistics argue, however, that this difference only considers nonhuman wealth. Because human capital is much more evenly distributed across the population, its inclusion would presumably cause the distributions of income and wealth to be virtually identical. Can you use arguments developed in our earlier discussion of capitalization processes to argue that the distributions of income and wealth must be identical in equilibrium?

indicates that the lowest fifth of households had under 0.5 percent of assets, while the top 12 percent held 38 percent of wealth.[4] White families average 12 times as much wealth as blacks, and 8 times as much as Hispanics. Only 2 percent of minority families were classified as wealthy, while 14 percent of whites were in the richest bracket. The wealthy tend to be professional or self-employed and in stable homes. The poor tend to be uneducated and in broken homes. The major determinant of wealth, however, seems to be age. Typical heads of wealthy families are older than 55, while young families are often poor. Time allows you to acquire wealth—another good reason to prefer growing older to its alternative.

Determinants of Distribution

Now that you have seen snapshots of the distributions of income and wealth, we need to explore why some people are rich and some are poor. Many rich people inherit fortunes. (The most valuable talent anyone could have might be aptitude at parent selection.) Productive assets generate income with no labor efforts by their owners, so heirs to fortunes generally land in high income brackets. Rent, interest, and corporate profit account for only about one-fifth of all income, but the bulk flows to the top 2 percent of the populace.

Income differentials also arise because, contrary to slogans and wishful thinking, we are not all created equal. Some of us are born with talents that especially suit us for remunerative careers. This is most obvious in entertainment or professional sports. Frustration will be your only reward if you cannot carry a tune but try to sing professionally or stand less than 6′8″ tall and pursue a career as a center in the National Basketball Association. Levels of energy, motivation, amiability, and insight also separate individuals. Some people make choices that seem to destine them to poverty. Perpetual students in esoteric disciplines, most artists, actors, and musicians, and some ministers select occupations for psychic income, not material rewards. Discrimination based on race, sex, age, ethnic background, height, or general appear-ance also causes differences in the options available to otherwise equally gifted individuals.

Occupational restrictions may also keep qualified people out of some jobs. For example, doctors are the highest paid professionals, on average, but medical practice requires specialized education and the slots available in medical schools are limited. Some people step into management of a family business, while others bounce from job to job for years before settling into one that suits them. Finally, luck may play a major role in who gets a high paying job and who doesn't—although some people seem to manufacture their own luck.

Poverty in America _____

Many people view poverty as evidence of the inequity of capitalism. In their minds, any economy generating over $5 trillion in output should not allow the squalor and deprivation seen in our urban ghettos and many rural communities. Critics of this position note that the poor in the United States are not nearly as destitute as the down and out in India, North Africa, or other less developed regions. Defenders of our current distribution also point out that the "poor" in this country often have televisions, refrigerators, and numerous other items that are considered luxuries in most other countries. Focus 1 points out that poverty is far from an absolute concept; our views of poverty depend on average standards of living in a society.

What Does Poor Mean?

Identifying the poor requires a definition of poverty. The 20 percent of our population with the lowest income is sometimes viewed as impoverished, but such an approach makes poverty incurable. Other definitions rely on estimates of the costs for families of various sizes and compositions of a "minimum" diet needed for life—soybeans, liver, lard, and other basic products. Such bland menus contain adequate nutrients, but would quickly bore anyone. One attempt to identify what it means to be poor relies on "the poverty line."

> The **poverty line** is an index estimating the costs of securing the minimal requirements for food, shelter, fuel, clothing, and transportation.

---

4. All studies of wealth, including this one, ignore human capital. In equilibrium, wealth and income are proportional if human capital is included in wealth.

Poverty: A Relative Concept

Friend: *How's your spouse?*
Economist: *Relative to what?*
—*An Unknown Pundit*

This quip reflects a tendency among economists to measure almost everything relative to some alternative. *Poverty*, which is a "lack of wealth or material comfort," is no exception. People might agree that anyone without the physical means to sustain normal life is absolutely impoverished, but beyond that definition, poverty seems a relative concept that is determined by time and place. For example, many Americans below our official "poverty line" have amenities enjoyed only by the wealthy in less developed countries and seem prosperous relative to beggars and slum dwellers in some countries. And consider how standards of living have changed over the centuries.

The average lifespan of Europeans who survived childhood 1,000 years ago was less than 45 years. People in developed economies now typically live into their 70s because of advances in nutrition and medicine. Polio, cholera, small pox, diphtheria, and leprosy are now extinct or quite rare in developed econ-

omies. Canning and refrigeration make it possible to store food for long periods, and the growth of commerce has enriched diets throughout the world. Even the nobility of medieval times did not have access to things that many Americans who are classified as poverty-stricken take for granted: aspirin, fast-food restaurants, telephones, running water, automobiles, electric lighting, indoor plumbing, garbage collection, paved roads, public education and transportation, antibiotics, grocery stores, "painless" dentistry, television, and heating systems for their homes—this list could be extended for several pages.

Some Americans at society's bottom rungs—bag ladies and derelicts—do lead miserable lives, but food stamps and transfer payments make "life on the dole" at least physically tolerable in most advanced economies. Suppose that you had to choose between (*a*) the physical comforts of a typical U.S. family relying on welfare for all its income in 1988, and (*b*) the standard of living enjoyed by noble members of King Arthur's court. If you ignore the trappings

of power enjoyed by feudal nobility, we suspect that you would be reluctant to trade the range of choices available to most poor Americans for life in a damp and drafty castle.

This does not mean that poor Americans have a soft life. There is no doubt that the most destitute people in our society are often homeless, cold, and hungry. Our point, instead, is that poverty is determined by cultural norms, of which material comforts are only one dimension. Wealth and income ultimately provide their holders with freedom, power, and deference from others. Poor people have relatively less power and fewer choices over their lives. And, to paraphrase Rodney Dangerfield, they "don't get no respect."

This index is adjusted for family size, sex and age of the family head, number of minor children, and whether residence is rural or urban. Poverty thresholds in 1988 for various families are presented in Table 2. The poverty threshold for an average family of four is now nearly $12,000 in annual income.

Although historically one family in eight has been impoverished on average, there is tremendous turnover among the poor. During a typical decade, more than 90 percent of the poor population changes; some people fall into poverty, replacing others who move above the poverty line. In spite of policies

TABLE 2 Poverty Cutoff Levels by Size of Family and Sex of Head of Household, 1988	
Size of Family	**Poverty Threshold**
1 person	$ 5,867
Under 65 years	6,001
Over 65 years	5,532
2 persons	7,502
Head under 65 years	7,758
Head over 65 years	6,977
3 persons	9,198
4 persons	11,790
5 persons	13,955
6 persons	15,767
7 persons	17,870
8 persons	19,861
9 or more persons	23,693

Source: U.S. Bureau of the Census, *Poverty in the United States: 1985* (Washington: U.S. Government Printing Office), 1987. Updated by authors.

designed to reduce inequality, roughly 1–2 percent of all people remain destitute year after year.

Private charity alleviates some poverty, but many people see government aid as the only real remedy for poor people's misery. The attack on poverty has been two-pronged, stressing job opportunities where practical and income maintenance programs for those who cannot or will not work. Rapid economic growth during the 1960s may have provided the biggest boost to standards of living for those at the bottom of the economic ladder; Figure 5 indicates that the percentage of families below the poverty line dropped after President Johnson launched a "War on Poverty" in 1964. Federal funding for most federal welfare programs has grown continuously ever since, but roughly 30 million people remained below the poverty line in 1987; poverty rates among black families have consistently been almost three times greater than for white families.

A sharp jump in unemployment combined with reductions in the growth of social spending during the early 1980s may have worsened the plight of many people at the bottom of the income scale. This precipitated pressures for more federal funding from many who are concerned about poverty, but these pressures were offset somewhat by opponents of welfare spending. Some opposition may emerge from prosperous taxpayers who are unwilling to share, but a growing chorus of critics is skeptical that poverty can be cured by "throwing money at it." Their view, elaborated in Focus 2, is that recent welfare programs have yielded limited gains to some poor people, but reduce work incentives among both taxpayers and welfare recipients and foster among many recipients an unhealthy dependence on government.

Some analysts divide the impoverished into *involuntary* and *voluntary* categories. Involuntary poverty occurs among people who cannot provide for themselves; those who voluntarily choose to be impoverished could earn adequate income but prefer to rely on welfare programs. One recent study suggests that by 1983, welfare programs were so generous that each additional $4,000 spent on welfare caused one additional family to voluntarily fall into poverty.[5] How might higher welfare spending cause people to accept lower total income? Do you know workers who hate their jobs and would cheerfully quit working if society freely gave them half their current income? Similar choices may explain why increasing numbers of people choose to be poor.

Continuing debates between the advocates and opponents of welfare programs are mirrored in swings in social policies. Knowledge of some characteristics of typical poor families should help you understand why there are people who live on the ragged edge throughout their lives.

Profiles of Poverty

F. Scott Fitzgerald once said "The rich are different from you and me." Ernest Hemingway replied, "Yes, they are different. They have more money." This exchange can be turned upside down. Are the poor inherently different from the rich, or do they simply lack money?

Numerous studies indicate that certain personal characteristics are closely related to poverty. Some characteristics are not matters of choice: blacks, Hispanics, Native Americans, and new immigrants tend to be poverty stricken more often than other popula-

---

5. "The New Structural Poverty: A Quantitative Analysis," by L. Gallaway, R. Vedder, and T. Foster, in *War on Poverty—Victory or Defeat?*, Hearings before the Joint Economic Committee, June 20, 1985. (Washington: U.S. Government Printing Office, 1986).

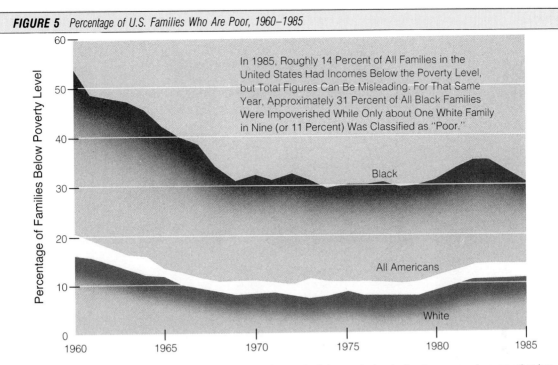

FIGURE 5 *Percentage of U.S. Families Who Are Poor, 1960–1985*

In 1985, Roughly 14 Percent of All Families in the United States Had Incomes Below the Poverty Level, but Total Figures Can Be Misleading. For That Same Year, Approximately 31 Percent of All Black Families Were Impoverished While Only about One White Family in Nine (or 11 Percent) Was Classified as "Poor."

(y-axis: Percentage of Families Below Poverty Level; x-axis: 1960, 1965, 1970, 1975, 1980, 1985; regions labeled Black, All Americans, White)

Social programs developed in the 1960s probably account for much of the gradual reduction in measured poverty that has occurred. The economic slumps of 1974–75, 1980, and 1982–83 were periods when the percentage of those living below the poverty line increased. The number of people living in poverty is substantially less when you include in-kind government transfers as income. Finally, the data in this figure indicates that black families on average are almost three times as likely to be poor as are their white counterparts.

Source: U.S. Department of Commerce, Bureau of the Census, *Current Population Reports,* P-60, No. 158 and No. 156, April 1987.

tion groups. The poor have relatively less education and labor participation, greater rates of illness and physical or mental disability, relatively more children, and heads of household who are female or very young or very old, as reflected in Figure 6.

The most important determinant of income is the relationship of the family (or individual) to the labor market. Income opportunities are crucial if people are to be able to cure their own poverty. If jobs are the key, then government policies to maintain full employment might reduce poverty by providing job opportunities for the less fortunate. But high employment alone will not solve the problem of poverty. Unless discrimination is a barrier, job openings are generally won by those who are most willing and qualified to work. Many poor people lack the experience, training, and education a good job requires. Moreover, there are regional pockets of unemployment and poverty caused by the decline of some industries: Appalachian coal mining from the 1920s

into the 1970s is an example. Centers for such "smokestack" industries as steel and autos experienced similar problems in the early 1980s, although these industries began to recover during 1986–88.

Alternative Views of Poverty

Some critics of welfare programs cite evidence that the poor tend to commit more crimes and be less able, less motivated, less mobile, more reproductive, and less educated than the general population. To these critics, the high incidence of poverty among certain racial or ethnic groups reflects failings of the cultural norms of these groups. There are, after all, prosperous members of every group. The success stories of many recent immigrants, especially from Vietnam and Cuba, are cited as evidence that protracted welfare is unnecessary. To these critics, the basic problem is failure to conform to the work ethic that has enabled other members of these same

FIGURE 6 *Family Characteristics by Income Level, 1984*

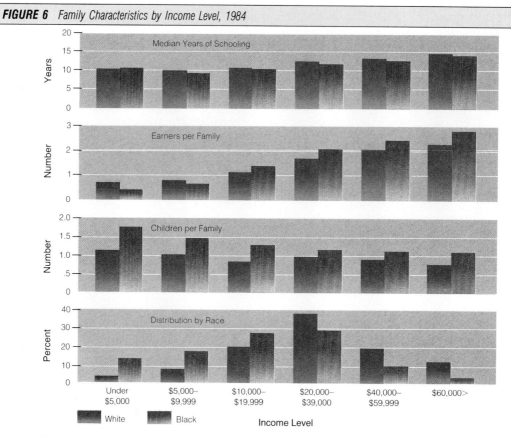

Caucasian families with few children and more than one highly educated worker bringing home the bacon tend to have the highest incomes. Black families with numerous children, few workers, and low levels of education are commonly caught in the trap of poverty.

Source: U.S. Department of Commerce, Bureau of the Census, *Current Population Reports*, P-60, No. 156, April 1987.

groups to succeed. These critics argue that many poor people are responsible for much of their own misery and that most welfare payments waste taxpayers' money because they reinforce the bad choices made by most of those who wind up poor.

A counterargument is that blaming the poor for their problems is misguided: that poor youngsters are obvious victims of poverty, and that immobility, nonparticipation in the labor force, and lack of education often reflect lack of opportunity or outright discrimination. Moreover, many of the aged poor have been poor all their lives, many large families were poor before they became large, and so on. If members of certain groups are denied equal chances to participate in the economy, those who lack skills or suffer from discrimination will remain poor. Studies

suggest that racial discrimination may have accounted for as much as 40 percent of poverty in the 1960s, but more recent studies yield substantially lower estimates, an indication that discrimination may be abating.[6]

---

6. See J. Haworth, J. Gwartney, and C. Haworth, "Earnings, Productivity, and Changes in Employment Discrimination During the 1960s," *American Economic Review*, March 1975, pp. 158–68, and J. Long, "Earnings, Productivity, and Changes in Employment Discrimination During the 1960s: Additional Evidence," *American Economic Review*, March 1977, pp. 225–27. Thomas Sowell in *Ethnic America* (Basic Books, 1981) provides estimates that discrimination accounted for only about 10 percent of black/white wage differentials by the late 1970s. For a look at employee benefits and discrimination see B. F. Kiker and Sherrie Rhine, "Fringe Benefits and the Earnings Equation," *Journal of Human Resources*, March 1987, pp. 126–37.

Progress and Poverty Programs

Annual spending on social programs grew from $29.5 billion to $484.5 billion between 1960 and 1985, but the number of people living below the poverty line actually grew over this period. Architects of the "War on Poverty," begun in 1964, often assigned responsibility to the broad society for poor people's woes and saw welfare programs as compensation for social injustice. Many people maintain similar attitudes today and advocate further expansion of these programs to remedy poverty. Some recent critics of our welfare system paradoxically blame much of current poverty on attitudes and programs instituted during the 1960s. Prominent among these critics are Thomas Sowell, an economist, and Charles Murray, a political scientist.

In his 1984 book *Losing Ground*, Murray cites evidence of deterioration in the quality of life among many groups that seem stuck at the bottom. Between 1960 and 1965, black students' academic aptitude test scores rose from 68 percent to 79 percent of the average scores of whites; 1965 was the peak year for both groups. The average scores of black students on these tests had fallen to less than half of white norms by 1980. Annual rates of violent crime rose from 161 to 581 per 100,000 population between 1960 and 1980. One black child in 5 was born to an unmarried mother in the 1950s;

roughly half of all black infants today are illegitimate, and rates of white illegitimacy rose from less than 1 in 50 to over 1 in 10. Six out of 7 white families include a married couple; the rate for black families has fallen sharply, to only 3 out of 5.

The basic problem, according to these recent critics, is that the rhetoric supporting many welfare programs implies that the poor bear no responsibility for alleviating their own poverty and that no stigma should be attached to being on welfare. This point of view means that the poor should not be expected to do anything for themselves; it is society's responsibility to lift people out of poverty.

These critics contend that such attitudes cause many poor people to feel like victims who cannot deal with their own problems, and who psychically cannot claim responsibility for their accomplishments. They become trapped in a culture of poverty. Few avenues of escape are open through which to gain any sense of personal pride. The result is that some welfare families may remain on welfare for generations—suspended in a childish state of dependence on a system that is encouraged by social workers.

What solutions are available? Few critics of the current welfare system favor abandonment of all welfare programs. Cutting all public assistance to

zero would flood the nation's streets with many more millions of destitute and desperate people. Instead, most of these critics propose that programs be restructured to provide more incentives for poor people to work, to keep their families together, and to diligently pursue their education and on-the-job training. Most of all, welfare programs should seek to instill in poor people a sense that they control their own destinies. In the words of Murray, "The lesson is not that we can do no good at all, but that we must pick our shots."

Economic Discrimination

Most of us agree that it is wrong to discriminate on the basis of sex, race, or other characteristics irrelevant to economic contribution or personal worth.

Economic discrimination *occurs when equivalent resources (labor) receive different payments (wages) even though their potential productive contributions are identical.*

There are many reasons for discrimination in labor markets. *Personal discrimination,* or *bigotry,* may play a major role, whether it is an employer's bigotry or the fear of bigotry from potential customers or other workers.[7] This may partially account for the lower average wages of women and members of some minority groups. On the other hand, managers' friends and relatives and some Caucasian males may receive preferential treatment.

Economic discrimination in labor markets takes several forms. Members of certain groups may suffer because:

1. *Wage discrimination* causes them to be paid less than members of other groups for equal work.
2. *Employment discrimination* excludes them from certain jobs.
3. *Occupational discrimination* bars them from certain occupations.
4. *Human capital discrimination* denies equal access to education or on-the-job training.
5. Outright *bigotry* fosters inequitable housing conditions, higher prices, and reduced medical care, for example.

Although bigotry stimulates the other four types of discrimination, it is not necessarily their only cause. Different groups, for example, may have different cultural norms about the values of education or hard work. Another problem is that different types of discrimination tend to reinforce each other. For example, low prospective wages yield reduced incentives for investment in human capital, ultimately widening income differences.

The battle against discrimination predates the American Revolution. From the time of Lincoln's Emancipation Proclamation through the present, we have slowly marched toward an era in which government enforces a variety of civil rights legislation ensuring equal access to such things as education, housing, and employment opportunities.

Legal controversy has marked almost all policies intended to achieve equal opportunity: busing children to integrate our schools, and *affirmative action* plans imposed to overcome past occupational, wage, and employment discrimination. Although the path to equal opportunity has been rocky, there has been major progress on the civil rights front in the past few decades. Disagreements continue, however, about the extent to which discrimination accounts for income differentials between groups, what kinds of discrimination are involved, and what policies will best remedy its effects.[8] One approach emphasizes welfare programs to compensate the victims of such earlier social policies as segregation or slavery, although extensive welfare programs are also advocated on other grounds.

Public Policies to Eliminate Poverty

Just who is "on welfare"? Who should receive welfare? How much? Such questions are meaningless without a definition of welfare.

Welfare *is received by anyone for whom the ratio of the personal benefits received (B) from government programs relative to the taxes paid (T) are greater than for average taxpayers.*

Thus, a person is on welfare if $B_i/T_i > B_0/T_0$, where B_i and T_i are the individual's benefits and taxes and B_0 and T_0 are the total benefits and taxes in the community or society. This can also be written as $B_i/B_0 > T_i/T_0$. For example, people are on welfare if they receive 2 percent of the total benefits from government programs ($B_i/B_0 = 0.02$) but only pay 1 percent

---

7. Discrimination may occur because of customs or language. See Kevin Lang, "A Language Theory of Discrimination," *Quarterly Journal of Economics,* June 1986, pp. 363–82.

8. Thomas Sowell, for one (in his *Ethnic America*), has argued that affirmative action has been more hindrance than help to members of minority groups. For example, he suggests that other people who encounter minorities in professional positions or high-level jobs commonly assume that these individuals gained their status not from competency, but to "fill some quota." A prospective employer may, thus, discount the previous experience of minority applicants who might otherwise be perfect for particular jobs and who would get these jobs were it not for the presumption that their previous experience was based solely on affirmative action requirements.

of the taxes used to support government $(T_i/T_0 = 0.01)$.

Our welfare system is an amalgam of many programs. In fact, people who are quite wealthy may be "on welfare." For example, some wealthy recipients contributed far less to Social Security than they received after they reached retirement age. Most welfare recipients are, however, in low income groups. One major program provides aid for dependent children.

Aid to Families with Dependent Children

Aid to Families with Dependent Children (AFDC) is federally mandated but administered by state and local governments. Explosive growth in AFDC rolls over the past two decades has been attributed to (*a*)

relaxed requirements that increased the number of eligible families, (*b*) reductions in the social stigma from being on welfare, (*c*) work *disincentives* and pressures to dissolve families inherent in AFDC payment structures, and (*d*) payment differentials that cause the poor to flock into areas where welfare benefits are the most generous. The rapid growth in enrollment has created widespread concern that the AFDC system is out of control.

Panel A in Figure 7 illustrates the work disincentive effects of the original AFDC programs. Assume that if a given family has no earnings, the AFDC grant is $3,000 annually (point *a* in Panel A). If the family earns up to an additional $3,000, the basic grant remains the same (point *b*). When the family's earnings exceed $3,000, however, AFDC grants are reduced dollar-for-dollar, so this poor family gains nothing by earning between $3,000 and $6,000 yearly

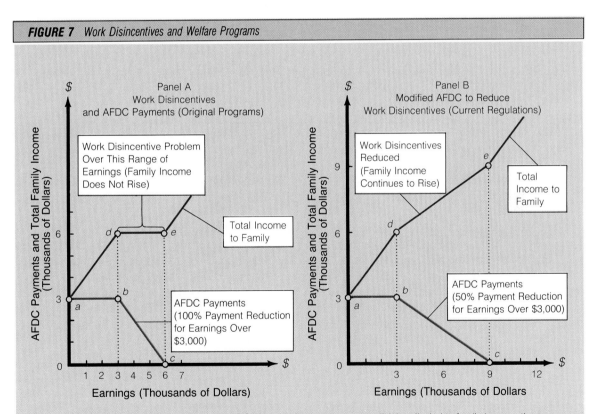

FIGURE 7 Work Disincentives and Welfare Programs

Can your take-home income fall if you earn more? When welfare programs are disjointedly tied to family income, the answer is yes. This incentive not to work is gradually being remedied, but Panel A reflects that this was a severe problem in the early 1970s. Under current regulations, the poor may face a marginal tax rate of 50 percent or more on additional income from employment, as shown in Panel B. While this still acts as a disincentive to work, it is much less severe than in the early 1970s when the adjusted marginal tax rate was often more than 100 percent for the working poor.

(points *d* to *e*). Even worse, extra income is taxed and there may be losses of *in-kind subsidies* (Medicaid, food stamps, or public housing subsidies). This opens up the possibility that a welfare family's spendable income could fall faster than its earnings grew.

Poor families were often penalized for working, so many followed the path of least resistance. AFDC benefits are especially skimpy if families include an able-bodied male, which has pressured many males to abandon their wives and kids. Panel A shows that a 100 percent payment reduction on earned income over $3,000 is equivalent to a 100 percent marginal tax rate on earned income. Families do not gain from higher earnings if the entire increase goes to the government. These disincentives in AFDC and similar programs have contributed to the "welfare mess," as it has been labeled by the media.

In the late 1970s, modest reforms of AFDC rules were aimed at cutting the 100 percent or higher implicit tax rate faced by many poor families, but further changes during 1981–83 reversed some of these reforms. Average "marginal tax rates" on AFDC benefits are now estimated at around 50 percent. Today's regulations are less distortive than earlier programs in this respect. Panel B of Figure 7 shows how lower implicit tax rates allow greater work incentives. As earnings exceed $3,000, benefits fall at a rate of only $.50 per $1, not dollar-for-dollar. Labor earnings now raise welfare families' spendable income; this was a rarity under the early system.

AFDC, unemployment compensation, and Social Security are among the many welfare programs that dispense cash grants. Other systems attempt to aid the poor through in-kind subsidies, including public housing, food stamps, Medicare and Medicaid, and various education, training, and rehabilitation programs. In-kind subsidies generally entail relatively high administrative costs and implicitly assume that recipients are incompetent to manage money were it given directly to them. Most economists are skeptical of this reasoning, and view in-kind payments as inefficient. For example, it costs taxpayers roughly $1.12 to give a poor family a food stamp with a face value of $1. The $1 food coupon is worth less than $1 to most recipients because it cannot be used for purchases other than food. Cash grant programs will typically provide benefits to poor people that are closer to their costs to taxpayers. Thus, in-kind transfers are relatively inefficient forms of welfare.

Another problem area is that many government transfer programs are based on criteria other than poverty. If farmers, the elderly, families headed by single women, the members of certain minority groups, or the disabled tend to be poor, it does not follow that separate programs are required for each group. Programs to aid the blind, the infirm, the aged, or members of minority groups do not exclude the wealthy blind, the wealthy handicapped, the wealthy aged, or wealthy minorities. Similarly, there are affluent farmers, bankers, and TV station owners who are welfare recipients by our definition of welfare. They benefit from special subsidies or regulations bearing no relation to the taxes they pay.

Welfare Reform

Transfer payments of various types have been the fastest growing component of government spending in the United States since World War II. A number of reforms have been proposed. Some are intended to cut the growth of transfer payments; other reforms would redistribute more income to the poor.

Workfare

The hardship of the Great Depression resulted in a national system of *unemployment compensation* administered by state agencies. Unfortunately, the side effects may be as undesirable as the broken families and idleness generated by AFDC. Sporadic employment patterns are encouraged, some income goes unreported, and some people who are not truly interested in work during some periods claim to be looking for jobs—causing unemployment statistics to be overstated and misdirecting macroeconomic policymaking. Some who believe that the welfare system as a whole encourages idleness advocate workfare to replace welfare. Workfare would require able-bodied people who seek unemployment compensation or other public assistance to do jobs for the local government units that dole out such benefits.

Consolidation

The current welfare system is mired in excessive regulations and paperwork, and income maintenance programs are fragmented among AFDC, unemployment compensation, food stamps, Medicaid, public housing, Social Security, and private charity. Ridding welfare programs of the work disincentives embedded in current policies is one major task of welfare reform; another is placing the welfare system under a single administrative umbrella, reducing duplication and costs. Some major programs are not based on income and thus benefit people who are not poor. There may be substantial gains from consolidation—both for taxpayers and for impoverished recipients. For these reasons, many economists favor a negative income tax approach to replace existing programs. Overall, we want the truly poor to get more aid, but where possible, we wish to preserve incentives for them to earn income on their own.

Family Allowance Plans

Many European nations and most British Commonwealth countries now have family allowance plans (*FAP*s).

> *Transfer payments from* **family allowance plans** *are based on the number of minor children in a family and are generally adequate to feed and clothe each child.*

Family allowance plans provide basic income floors, but the incomes from these plans are then taxed as normal income and the progressivity of income taxes shrinks the *FAP* subsidy as a family's income rises.

Poverty seems especially harmful to children, so Family Allowance Plans were proposed by the Nixon, Ford, and Carter administrations. A family allowance plan would be easier and cheaper to administer than the current welfare system. It would provide greater incentives for work than the many welfare programs that now confront the poor with very high implicit marginal tax rates; poor people's net incomes would always rise if they worked. Finally, it would eliminate situations where some poor people are technically ineligible for welfare but pay taxes to provide welfare to people who are better off. (For example, an impoverished family headed by a low-wage working male may pay taxes to provide AFDC for a family without a working head of household. Average AFDC payments often exceed the family income of the working male.) Insufficient income for a given family unit, including children, would be the sole criterion for net (after-tax) receipts of welfare.

Negative Income Taxes

Negative income taxes (*NITs*) are variants of family allowance plans.

> **Negative income tax** *plans attempt to balance the goals of equity and efficiency, and begin with an income floor. The level of assistance is reduced as additional income is earned by the family, but less than dollar for dollar.*

A typical *NIT* plan is diagrammed in Figure 8. The basic *NIT* floor on family income in this example is $6,000 and, as the family earns an additional dollar in income, *NIT* benefits are reduced by $0.40. Thus, the negative income tax rate is 40 percent. When the family earns $15,000 on its own, *NIT* benefits are zero [$6,000 − ($15,000 × $0.40) = $0]. Beyond $15,000, the family pays positive taxes like everyone else. Most economists envision these plans replacing all other income assistance plans. They would be administered through the Internal Revenue Service.

Conflicts Within NITs Negative income taxes would be simple to administer and would eliminate the need to dovetail numerous programs but, like any form of income assistance, *NITs* must balance equity and efficiency. This entails setting support levels that preserve work incentives, provide equitable income floors, and minimize administrative costs. Equity considerations might dictate high support flows, while efficient work incentives require low negative marginal tax rates. The cost of a program escalates when these attributes are combined. For example, in Figure 8, if poverty levels for average families were considered to be $6,000, then the plan as diagrammed would subsidize both the poor and some nonpoor; families with earnings between $6,000 and $15,000 continue to receive subsidies.

High basic floors, low negative income tax rates, and low break-even income levels cannot coexist because, mathematically:

$$\frac{\text{break-even}}{\text{level of income}} = \frac{\text{basic income floor}}{\text{negative income tax rate}}.$$

Thus, the break-even level of income rises when the income floor rises or the negative income tax rate falls. Tax revenues fall and the total cost of the program rises. Reduced disincentives for work may,

FIGURE 8 *Negative Income Taxes*

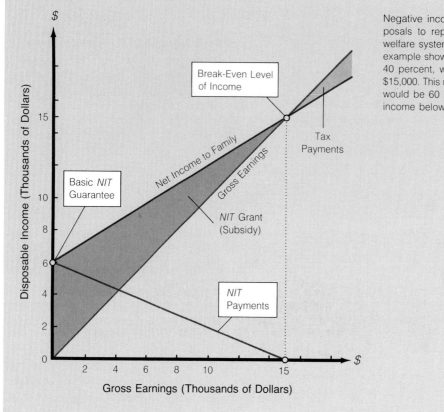

Disposable Income (Thousands of Dollars)

Break-Even Level of Income

Basic *NIT* Guarantee

Net Income to Family

Gross Earnings

NIT Grant (Subsidy)

Tax Payments

NIT Payments

Gross Earnings (Thousands of Dollars)

Negative income taxes (*NIT*s) are proposals to replace most of the current welfare system with cash grants. In the example shown, the marginal tax rate is 40 percent, with break-even income of $15,000. This means that welfare receipts would be 60 percent of any shortfall of income below $15,000 annually.

however, cut costs by making many of the poor less reliant on the public dole. Moreover, if an *NIT* plan replaced the current hodgepodge of welfare programs, administrative costs should fall—allowing higher income floors and/or reductions in taxes.

There are other criticisms of *NIT* proposals, however. Some argue that *NIT* plans are too inflexible to solve many specific problems facing the poor. For example, older people may be unable to respond to work incentives, while youngsters need special care and assistance that parents may not provide. Others argue that in-kind services should supplement income assistance because many families may not wisely use the funds provided under an *NIT* plan. Proponents argue that an *NIT* package could provide both

sufficient work incentives and an adequate income floor while replacing a bureaucratic, erratic, and expensive system with a consistent program.

In this chapter, we have looked at ethical criteria for the distribution of income and have shown that economic analysis can offer insights into solutions for issues that have a high normative content. For example, economic analysis can address such questions as whether reasonable welfare payments will lift more people out of poverty than are induced to become impoverished. Statistical studies of such issues are still relatively primitive. As we conclude this part of the book, we hope that you can see how microeconomic analysis can facilitate clear thinking about an enormous variety of public policies.

CHAPTER REVIEW: KEY POINTS

1. *Lorenz curves* are one way to portray inequality. Lorenz curves for income are graphical representations of the cumulative percentages of income received by given cumulative percentages of families. If the Lorenz curve is a straight-line diagonal, the income distribution is perfectly equal. Deviations from this diagonal reflect inequality in distribution.

2. Tracing the pretax and pretransfer *income distribution* since 1935 gives the appearance of little change, although the share of middle-class families has grown. When taxes and transfers are considered, however, the U.S. income distribution has become markedly more equal since the early 1930s.

3. The Social Security Administration has developed income indices that define *poverty lines* for various family sizes, ages, and locations.

4. The causes of *poverty* are many and varied. Relative to middle- or upper-class families, the poor tend to have less education, few earners, and more children. These characteristics of the poor are not necessarily the causes of poverty. *Discrimination* may be an important factor. Persistent discrimination reduces incentives to invest in education and other marketable skills. Discrimination is often cited as the primary reason that a relatively large proportion of black families are in the lower income categories.

5. The major government program to fight poverty is *Aid to Families with Dependent Children* (AFDC). A floor on family income is established, but as the family earns additional income, reductions of AFDC benefits often pose extreme *disincentives* for work. Given the large number of different programs designed to help the poor, $1 increases in earned income sometimes result in more than $1 of lost benefits.

6. *Negative income tax plans* (*NITs*) have been suggested as solutions to the "welfare mess." Negative income tax proposals provide a floor on income; as additional income is earned, benefits are reduced but by less than the additional income earned. *NIT* proposals contain two essential elements: a basic floor income and a negative income tax rate. Increases in the floor or reductions in the negative tax rate increase the costs of the program. Equity considerations indicate needs for higher floors, while efficiency considerations point to needs for lower negative tax rates. Both goals cannot be satisfied with any one negative income tax plan.

7. Opponents of *NIT* proposals argue that guaranteed income floors will not solve all the problems of the poor. Proponents argue that providing sufficient income will solve the major problems. In general, *NIT* plans consolidate numerous programs under one administrative roof and might allow either reduced costs or increased benefits.

PROBLEMS

1. Using the income distribution data for three populations listed in Table 3, plot the Lorenz curve for each country. Which country has the most unequal distribution of income? The most equal?

2. Which of the following Negative Income Tax plans has the highest break-even level of income?
   a. Basic income floor of $6,000; a negative income tax rate of 50 percent.
   b. Basic income floor of $8,000; a negative income tax rate of 60 percent.
   c. Basic income floor of $4,500; a negative income tax rate of 30 percent.

TABLE 3 Income Distribution Data for Three Populations

Family Group	Countries		
	A	B	C
Lowest 20 percent	10	12	18
Second 20 percent	15	15	19
Middle 20 percent	20	20	20
Fourth 20 percent	25	23	21
Highest 20 percent	30	30	22

QUESTIONS FOR THOUGHT AND DISCUSSION

1. Should society extend welfare to the less fortunate? Should the circumstances causing their poverty be considered? If so, how? Should cash grants be emphasized, or should society directly provide (*a*) housing, (*b*) medical care, or (*c*) food stamps. Why?

2. Should we seek equality of opportunity or equality of result?

3. In what sense are income and wealth exactly proportional in equilibrium? (You may need to review the capitalization process discussed in a previous chapter to answer this question.)

4. Society devotes increasing amounts of resources to medical care for critical and sometimes incurable diseases or injuries. It is not unusual, for example, for the medical expenses of a very premature infant to exceed $1 million, and even if it survives, the long-term consequences for the child are often tragic. Many parents cannot afford such outlays, and hospitals often simply treat these costs as overhead costs to be borne by other patients. Is this use of society's resources appropriate? What are some possible opportunity costs? Is this equitable? Why or why not?

5. Family assistance plans and negative income taxes presume that the poor lack money but not the skills to manage it. Administrative costs of these programs would be relatively low. Food stamp programs, Medicaid, and the provision of social workers seem predicated on the idea that poor people would not spend money properly if it were given to them. These programs bear high administrative costs. Do you think the poor are better off if their spending is closely supervised? If so, up to what proportion of government outlays for welfare could be spent for administrators and red tape before it would be better just to give money to the poor?

6. Suppose that you were in charge of an overcrowded lifeboat filled with the survivors of a shipwreck. Unless some passengers leave the boat, all will perish. Would it be fair for you to allocate the spaces available to the highest bidders? Would this be efficient? If not, would it be fairer or more efficient were a few affluent passengers able to persuade a sufficient number of poorer people to relinquish their space by offering contracts guaranteeing prosperity for the volunteers' families? If not, what other allocative mechanism would be fairer or more efficient? Why?

7. In John Rawls' *A Theory of Justice* (Harvard, 1971), he proposes the following mental exercise as an approach for deciding how society might be made fairer. Suppose you were given a computer with a data bank containing every economic mechanism ever tried and every theory ever proposed to answer the questions of What?, How?, For whom?, and When? You also have the advice of any social philosopher, living or dead. Your task is to design a just society, and you must address many issues, including distributing wealth and income. Your final overall plan will be instituted worldwide. The hook is that your position in the world will then be decided randomly—providing a powerful incentive for you to consider the final positions of all people. What are some changes you would make to current social institutions?

8. In *Anarchy, State, and Utopia* (New York: Basic Books, 1974), Rawls' colleague, Robert Nozick, argues that over time individuals acquire inalienable rights. His *entitlement theory of justice* is an ethical argument for the adage that "Possession is nine-tenths of the law." In Nozick's view, you are entitled to your property unless it can be proven that you, or the people who transferred it to you, unethically acquired it. He concludes that government redistributions of wealth or income are ethically wrong because they violate people's basic rights to choose how their property will be used. In his words, "There is no justified sacrifice of some of us for others." Do you think that historical events ethically justify the degree of inequality that now exists? Why or why not?

Global Economics

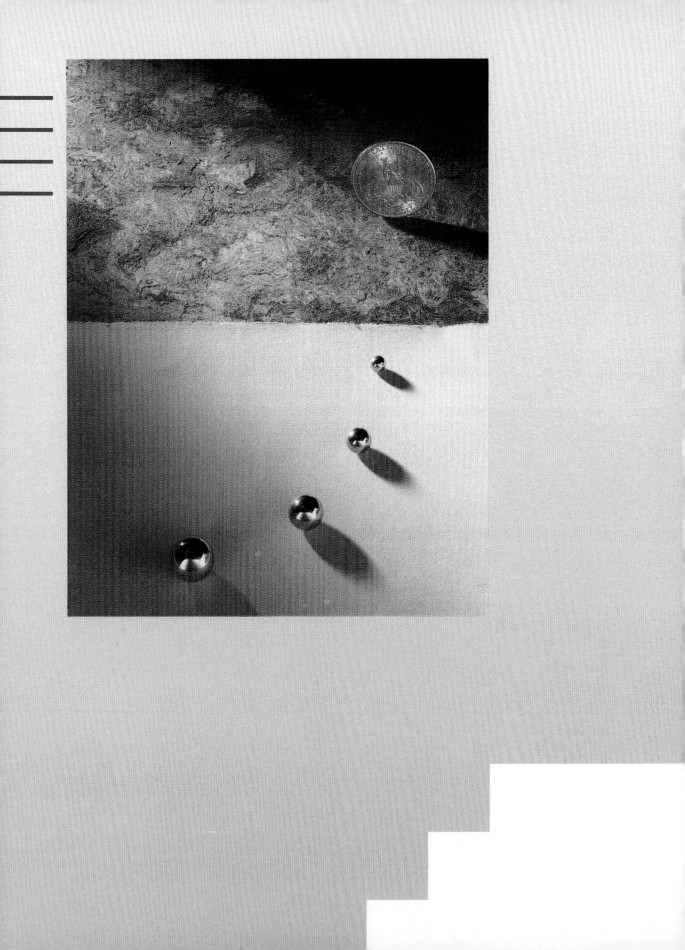

The International Economy

PART 10

International trade is growing faster than domestic production and income in most nations throughout the world, including the United States. This book has largely focused on a *closed* economy up to this point, although we frequently referred to issues and examples drawn from the international scene. In this section we open up the economy and consider how international trade and finance affect standards of living everywhere.

People in many countries sing the protectionist's song—"restrict imports of 'cheap' foreign goods." This was one campaign theme during the 1988 presidential election. How almost everyone ultimately gains from trade and why it is foolish to restrict most forms of international trade are among the major topics we address in chapter 36.

The last vestiges of an international gold standard collapsed in the early 1970s, provoking many who are concerned with the problem of international payments to advise its readoption. The advantages and disadvantages of the different means available to pay for imports and be paid for exports are at the heart of our discussion in chapter 37.

Finally, the last chapter of this book examines various philosophies that underlie alternative economic systems and how these philosophies have been put into practice. Everyone in our modern world should know something about how other economies operate, and their advantages and disadvantages.

CHAPTER 36

International Trade

Specialized production and exchange yield enormous benefits. The gain to both Hawaiians and Texans from trading sugar for oil is an obvious example. Similar advantages arise from transactions whether the people with whom we deal are American or foreigners. The exchange of goods and services across national boundaries is called **international trade.** Trade is generally a positive sum game; both sides expect to gain or they do not trade. International transactions are more complex than domestic trade, however, because of differences in currencies and national policies.

In this chapter, we discuss the nature of international trade and some advantages and possible disadvantages of commerce between traders separated by international borders. We will also evaluate some arguments against free trade, and consider the effects of policies that restrict trade.

The Size and Scope of Trade

International trade subtly affects our daily lives in ways most Americans don't even notice. We drink coffee from South America, cocoa from Ghana, or tea from India; wear Swiss watches and clothes made in China; watch televisions made in Japan; and burn gasoline refined from Saudi Arabian oil in Hyundais, Yugos, or Toyotas. Most of our shoes, the graphite in our pencils, and even the elastic in our underwear come from abroad.

Year after year, international trade grows in importance throughout the world. Among industrialized nations, international trade as a percentage of GNP ranges from 8 to 12 percent in the United States to roughly 30 percent in Great Britain. In absolute terms, the sheer size of the United States makes it the single most important international trader; our exports and imports each exceeded $500 billion in 1988. Statistics that indicate the importance of international trade in some of the world's major trading nations are displayed in Figure 1. Generally, however, international trade is even more crucial to small countries than to large ones.

Foreign countries are markets for our production, so U.S. exports are one source of Aggregate Demand. Imports add to our Aggregate Supply; they are sources of consumption and investment goods. At the same time, however, they detract from Aggregate Demand, making marketing more difficult for the domestic producers who compete with imports. Con-

sequently, macroeconomic policy must consider the impact of international trade on domestic inflation, unemployment, economic growth, and the level of GNP.

Why do Nations Trade?

The United States contains vast amounts of fertile land, immense supplies of raw materials, an unmatched stock of capital equipment, and a highly skilled work force. Our GNP is more than twice that of our nearest competitor, but exports and imports

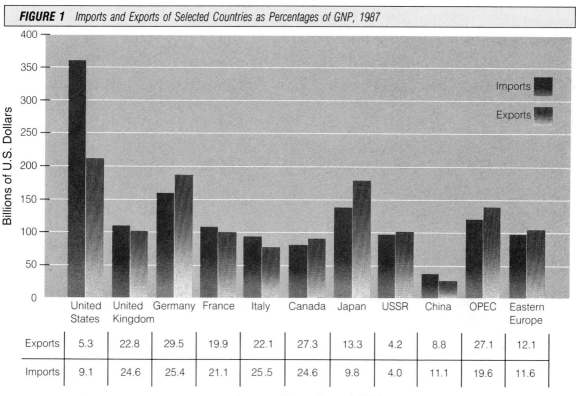

FIGURE 1 Imports and Exports of Selected Countries as Percentages of GNP, 1987

	United States	United Kingdom	Germany	France	Italy	Canada	Japan	USSR	China	OPEC	Eastern Europe
Exports	5.3	22.8	29.5	19.9	22.1	27.3	13.3	4.2	8.8	27.1	12.1
Imports	9.1	24.6	25.4	21.1	25.5	24.6	9.8	4.0	11.1	19.6	11.6

Average Percentage of GNP

Although the United States is a major trader, trade is less important to us as a percentage of GNP than it is to any other developed nation. Curiously, Japan is not as heavily dependent on trade as some might think. Highly specialized countries, such as OPEC member nations, are heavily dependent on trade. The major communist powers are not major traders.

Source: *Economic Report of the President,* 1988.

each average 8–12 percent of our GNP. Why do Americans bother to trade with the rest of the world?

One reason for foreign trade is that some technologies or natural resources are inadequate for domestic consumption and investment. This is why we import Bolivian tin and export farm equipment and computers to Bolivia. Even when self-sufficiency is possible, foreign trade often will be advantageous. Figure 2 indicates the composition of U.S. foreign trade and Figure 3 reveals which countries are our principal trading partners.

Economic efficiency requires achieving the lowest possible opportunity cost for all types of production. If the opportunity costs of producing everything everywhere are minimized, the total value of global production is maximized. This requires international trade, which is a way for consumers to get goods at lower cost without having to travel to where they are produced, and for resource owners (e.g., labor) to receive higher income without having to relocate to wherever their products are most advantageously consumed.

The Concept of Absolute Advantage

The notion of *absolute advantage* emerges from differences in the abilities of individuals and nations to produce goods from given resources. For example, one Saudi Arabian worker can get more oil out of 10 acres of Saudi Arabian land than one Georgian working the same size plot in Georgia. The Georgian, however, might be able to raise more peanuts per acre than the Saudi Arabian. In this case, the Saudi Arabian has an absolute advantage in oil production, while the Georgian has an absolute advantage in peanut growing. Obviously, each would gain from specialized production and trade. This notion led Adam

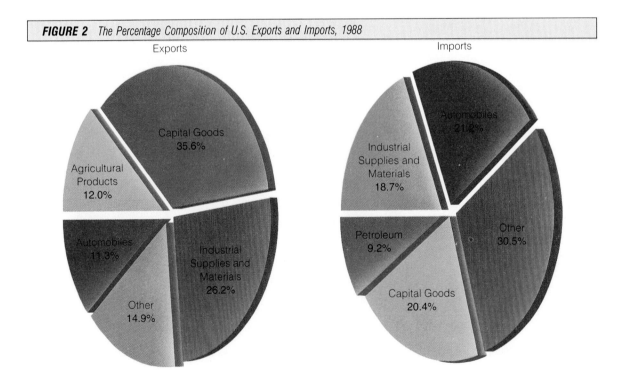

FIGURE 2 The Percentage Composition of U.S. Exports and Imports, 1988

Exports

- Capital Goods 35.6%
- Agricultural Products 12.0%
- Automobiles 11.3%
- Industrial Supplies and Materials 26.2%
- Other 14.9%

Imports

- Automobiles 21.2%
- Industrial Supplies and Materials 18.7%
- Petroleum 9.2%
- Other 30.5%
- Capital Goods 20.4%

The composition of our exports appears roughly balanced, except for net imports of fuels and minerals and net exports of machinery and agricultural products. Each of these broad categories, however, disguises a rich diversity of imports and exports.

Source: *Economic Report of the President,* 1988.

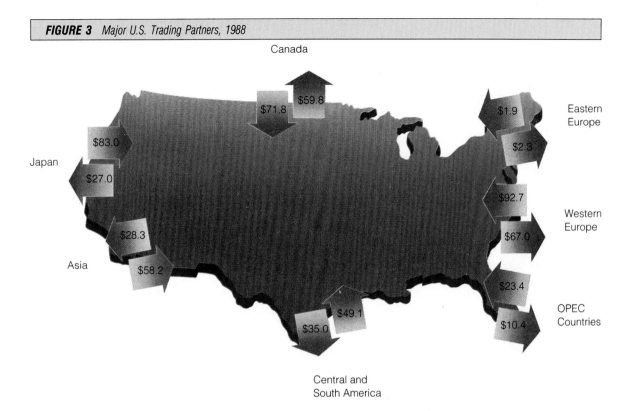

FIGURE 3 *Major U.S. Trading Partners, 1988*

Canada

$71.8 $59.8

Eastern Europe
$1.9
$2.3

Japan
$83.0
$27.0

Western Europe
$92.7
$67.0

Asia
$28.3
$58.2

OPEC Countries
$23.4
$10.4

Central and South America
$49.1
$35.0

We have recently run deficits with most of our major trading partners, especially Japan and the OPEC countries.
Note: All figures presented here are in billions of U.S. dollars.

Source: *Economic Report of the President,* 1988.

Smith and other early economists to attempt to state a broad economic principle.

> The **"principle" of absolute advantage** *asserts that nations gain by producing goods that require fewer domestic resources and exchanging their surpluses for goods produced abroad with fewer resources.*

This approach is incomplete, however, because it ignores the gains that may be available through trade when one party has an absolute advantage in producing almost all goods (or, in a simple model, each of two goods).

The Law of Comparative Advantage

Suppose that typical American workers can produce either four decorated screens (for use as room dividers) or eight electric drills monthly, while Chinese workers can average only two hand-painted screens

or one drill. The "absolute advantage" approach offers no reason why Americans might gain from trade. The law of comparative advantage was developed by David Ricardo (1772–1823) and shows how trade can enrich people in both countries, even though American workers have absolute advantages in both goods.

Table 1 helps illustrate this key concept in international trade. Without trade, two drills are sacrificed to produce each decorated screen in the United States, while in China, each screen costs only half of a drill. Imagine that you could costlessly move between these countries and that you initially had one screen. You could begin by trading it for two U.S. drills and then trade the drills for four Chinese screens, for which you would receive eight U.S. drills, and so on. Successively trading American drills for Chinese screens, and vice versa, would enable you to grow rich.

TABLE 1 *Outputs per Worker and Their Costs*

| Country | Electric Drills per Worker | Painted Screens per Worker | Pre-trade Costs | | Free Trade Costs |
			Drills per Screen	Screens per Drill	
United States	8	4	2	1/2	1:1
China	1	2	1/2	2	1:1

China increasingly would specialize in screen painting and the United States, in drill production. As long as the costs of screens relative to drills did not change (price ratios of 2:1 in the United States and 1:2 in China), no one in either country would lose and you would gain. This specialization and exchange is an example of how trade can increase economic efficiency; you have gained and no one has lost because of trade. Our example is a bit misleading, however, because the prices of drills relative to screens were constant in both the United States or China. Moreover, international trade is very competitive, so it is unlikely that you could get rich as an arbitrager.

Arbitrage and Trade   You encountered *arbitrage* in chapter 4—the process of buying at a lower price in one market and selling at a higher price in another, where both prices are known to the arbitrager and the price differential exceeds transaction costs. Whenever differentials in relative prices between markets exceed the transaction costs associated with intermarket transfers of goods, arbitragers risklessly profit by buying low and selling high. This process boosts demand in the market with the lower price, driving that price up, and raises supply in the market with the higher price, sending it down. Hence, arbitrage pressures relative prices toward equality in all markets. In our example, the relative price of drills to screens might go from 2:1 in the United States and 1:2 in China to say, 1:1 in both countries. Americans import "cheap" Chinese screens while the Chinese import "cheap" U.S. drills.

Competition between arbitragers tends to keep the economic profits of traders near zero, so most of your gains actually would have been split between Americans and Chinese. U.S. drill makers and screen consumers would gain as the price of drills relative to screens rose. (The U.S. price of screens falls.) Simi-larly, Chinese screen makers and drill buyers would gain as the prices of screens relative to drills rose. Using similar examples, David Ricardo generalized this concept in 1817.

> *According to the* **law of comparative advantage,** *mutually beneficial trade can always take place between countries whose pre-trade relative opportunity costs and price structures differ.*

In our example, however, U.S. producers and Chinese consumers of screens might appear to lose, and so might U.S. consumers and Chinese producers of drills. In a moment we will show that even they normally gain from trade.

The Terms of Trade   Comparative advantage suggests that mutually beneficial trade can take place whenever relative production costs differ between nations. The phrase "terms of trade" refers to the prices of exported goods relative to imported goods:

$$\text{terms of trade} = \frac{\text{prices of exports}}{\text{prices of imports}}.$$

In our example, drills initially cost only half a screen in the United States but two screens in China, while screens cost two drills in the United States but only half a drill in China; the terms of trade settled at a 1:1 price ratio in both countries. Intuitively, terms of trade should end up between the relative pre-trade production costs of the goods in the two countries.

Gains from Trade

Most gains from trade are obviously distributed between Chinese and American households. People everywhere gain from trade in several ways.

BIOGRAPHY

DAVID RICARDO
(1772–1823)

David Ricardo's genius was illustrated in the practical world of affairs as well as in the realm of ideas. Disinherited by his wealthy Jewish father for marrying a Quakeress at the age of 21, Ricardo and his bride joined the Unitarian church, which at the time was viewed as a radical sect.

Ricardo successfully pursued a business career as stockjobber and then as loan contractor, and when he was 42, his accumulated wealth permitted him to retire from business. Bored with the idle life, he turned his attention to politics and intellectual pursuits. After a hesitant beginning as a writer on economic subjects, Ricardo etched his name on the pages of history by publishing a treatise, *On the Principles of Political Economy and Taxation.* He was not an accomplished writer, having a heavy handed, obscure, and abstract style. Nevertheless, the force of his logic almost immediately attracted a close knit band of gifted if dogmatic disciples.

Ricardo's appeal was based on his ability to cast a wide assortment of serious problems into simple analytical models that considered only a few strategic variables, but that yielded sweeping conclusions of a very practical nature. One example of Ricardo's penetrating insight concerns the doctrine of comparative costs. Earlier economists had taught that it pays a country to concentrate on the production of those goods it can produce more cheaply than any other country and to import those goods it can obtain at less cost than it would cost to produce them at home. Ricardo developed the following not-so-obvious implication of this doctrine: Under free trade, not all goods are necessarily produced in countries where their absolute cost of production is lowest. He demonstrated that it could pay a country to import something, even though it could produce the same product with fewer resources at home. Ricardo's demonstration rests on the idea of relative efficiency, or comparative costs.

Ricardo's principle is developed in greater detail in the present chapter, but it is important to note that the core of all free trade arguments harks back to this Ricardian concept. Ricardo's discussion of land rent and his analysis of taxation were also pathbreaking works that place modern economists forever in his debt.

Uniqueness Gains

Nature fails to provide local sources of some goods in certain regions around the world. For example, diamonds, chromium, tin, petroleum, bauxite, and other minerals are not distributed smoothly across the earth's surface. Goods that cannot be produced without these natural resources would not be available at all to many of the world's people without international trade.

> The **uniqueness gains** *from trade arise from trading for goods that are simply not available from local sources.*

Uniqueness gains also characterize trade for certain foods, fibers, and animal products, such as spices, bananas, coffee, cocoa, tobacco, and frozen fish.

Gains from Scale

Adam Smith was the first economist to note that specialization is limited by the size of the market. Moving beyond domestic markets into international markets facilitates specialization that, in turn, allows expanded production. This occurs, in part, because least-cost production for some goods requires output levels that exceed market demands within a single country.

Gains from scale *occur when access to export markets stimulates production of larger amounts of goods at lower average costs.*

For example, Haiti would not, by itself, support an aluminum mill with sufficient capacity to produce at efficiently low costs. Nor is there sufficient demand for VCRs in Switzerland alone to allow efficient production. Gains from scale include product diversity that allows demands to be served that are skimpy in even the largest countries. Not even the U.S. market is large enough alone to justify low-cost research, development, and production of medicines to treat extremely exotic diseases.

Short-Run Specialization Gains

People gain even if they could produce imported goods because, through specialization, the purchasing power of their incomes rises. Access to export markets raises the values of what people produce. Even those who do not work directly on exported goods ultimately have higher incomes because competition in resource markets grows. Moreover, they are able to buy goods at lower opportunity costs than if they relied solely on domestic production.

> **Short-run specialization gains** *from trade arise from producing and selling goods in which you have a comparative advantage, and buying goods from others who can produce at lower cost.*

In a moment we will show that these short-run gains from trade alone generally outweigh losses that arise because some people who compete with imports suffer disruptions to their lives and temporary losses of income.

Long-Run Dynamic Gains

The purchasing power of national income grows quickly when imports are expanded, but the long-run effects of trade may be even more important than this immediate growth.

> **Long-run dynamic gains** *occur when trade accelerates economic growth and development.*

This growth occurs when (*a*) trade spreads technological advances and (*b*) the higher income from trade fosters new capital formation. The dynamic gains from trade are especially apparent in the rapid development of such economies as Japan, Taiwan, South Korea, Singapore, Hong Kong, and China.

The Spread of Technology   Trade spreads technology that would be known only locally if each country operated in isolation. Technological advances tend to feed on each other—one researcher's discovery is improved upon by another, who stimulates a third, *ad infinitum.* Imagine how primitive life would be if every national group had to rediscover the wheel, electricity, and the advantages of indoor plumbing.

Capital Formation   Dynamic gains also arise because trade boosts the value of national output, making it easier for people to save and invest. In less developed nations, higher income can enable people to move beyond bare subsistence; their saving allows new capital formation that can provide a way to break out of the vicious circle of poverty.

International Political Stability

International trade also stimulates smoother international relations. To the extent that trade raises our standards of living, it also makes us more dependent upon the people of other nations, and they on us.

> **Political gains** *from trade arise when economic interdependency facilitates international political stability.*

Economic interdependency provides powerful incentives for peaceful solutions to disagreements. Trade raises the potential losses from war and thus, reduces the likelihood of armed conflict.

Net Gains from Specialization

Some types of gains from trade seem obvious. We turn now to demonstrating those gains that may seem the least clear. Exchange confers *net* gains to the participants; even in the short run the gains from specialization and trade generally exceed any losses. Comparative advantage is a key to identifying the net gains from specialization and trade.

In our example where Chinese screens were traded for American drills, a merchant profited by buying where prices were relatively low and selling where they were higher; these gains were not shared between Americans and Chinese. Here is a simple short-run model showing that there are generally net gains from trade, and suggesting who shares in them. We consider only two countries, but the logic still holds if we consider any country vis-à-vis the rest of the world, or a host of goods instead of only two. In fact, the net gains available from trade rise as the number of traded goods rises and as the number of traders grows.

We will begin with the following assumptions:

1. Production-possibilities curves for both China and the United States are characterized by constant opportunity costs, but technologies differ between the two countries;

2. only two goods (drills and painted screens) are produced and traded;

3. goods, but not resources, can move freely between countries, while resources can move freely only between domestic industries; and

4. all prices are perfectly flexible.

These simplifying assumptions may seem unrealistic, but they are used only to illustrate a point; most can be relaxed without changing the basic analysis.

Let us begin with aggregate production relationships for the United States and China similar to those outlined in Table 1. We will assume that workers in the United States can produce 400 million screens or 800 million drills annually, or any combination in between, maintaining constant opportunity costs of two screens per drill. Similarly, Chinese workers are able to produce 400 million drills or 800 million screens annually because we assume China's labor force is four times as large as ours.

Constant production costs yield linear production-possibilities frontiers (*PPFs*) like those shown as solid lines in Figure 4. These frontiers can also be

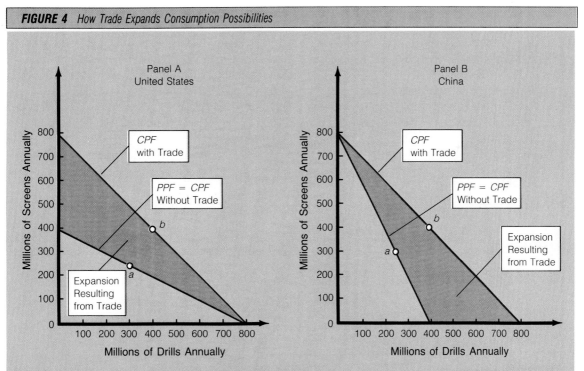

FIGURE 4 How Trade Expands Consumption Possibilities

Prior to trade, a country's sustainable consumption possibilities are limited by its production-possibilities frontier. When trade commences, both trading partners experience net gains from trade because, by specializing in those goods they produce at lowest relative cost and by importing those things that they find costly to make themselves, they can each consume more of *all* goods. Thus, their consumption possibilities expand beyond their production possibilities, just as we gain individually by trading with others instead of relying strictly on what we personally produce.

thought of as *consumption-possibilities frontiers* (*CPF*s) since, without trade, neither country could sustain consumption beyond these boundaries. Suppose that both countries are originally producing and consuming at point *a* in both panels of Figure 4, which graphically reflects column 1 of Table 2. Finally, assume that the final trading ratio is 1:1; one drill trades for one screen.

The United States will specialize in the good with the lowest domestic costs, drills, with annual production at 800 million units. Each drill now may be traded for a screen, so a total of up to 800 million drills plus screens might be consumed. The American *CPF* expands as shown in Panel A of Figure 4. Symmetrically, China will specialize in screen production (800 million annually), and by trading screens for drills, can expand its consumption to any combination of screens and drills along the line *CPF* in Panel B.

A simplifying assumption reflected in Figure 4 and Table 2 is that after trade commences, each country consumes at point *b* in both panels. Table 2 outlines the specific gains from trade to each country. In the United States annual consumption of drills rises by 100 million units and consumption of screens rises by 150 million units. Similar gains are realized by China.

Note that people in both nations can consume more of both goods. This possibility exists with any specialization and exchange, whether inside a country or internationally. At a local level, an example is the homebuilder whose family has a nicer house than if the family had to produce its own food, clothing,

and all other amenities of life, in addition to its own home.

Moving toward free trade resembles economic growth created by rapid technological advances. We can consume more even though no more resources are available than previously; even in the short run, both countries' gains from free trade typically outweigh any losses. Gains from trade are positively related to the diversity in comparative advantages among the trading groups.

The final terms of trade are 1:1 in our example, although they need not fall precisely at the midpoint of no-trade prices. All prices are shaped by both demand and supply. The production-possibilities frontiers we used address only the supply side, but explicitly considering demand would not change our conclusion that trade confers net gains on both trading parties.

Short-Run Gainers and Potential Losers

You may lose if the price of your output falls relative to the prices of the things you buy. Thus, economists talk about an "adverse change in the terms of trade" whenever export prices fall relative to import prices. For example, an adverse change in the U. S. terms of trade occurred when the price of imported oil skyrocketed in the early 1970s, while vigorous international competition precluded similar hikes in our export prices.

Whenever trade expands, changes in the relative prices of imports and exports benefit some people

TABLE 2 *Specialization Gains from Trade*

Country ——— Commodity	(1) Output and Consumption Before Trade (Millions)	(2) Production After Trade Commences (Millions)	(3) Exports (−) Imports (+) (Millions) Terms of Trade Are 1:1	(4) Consumption After Trade (Millions) (2) + (3)	(5) Gains from Trade (Millions) (4) − (1)
United States					
Drills	300	800	−400	400	100
Screens	250	0	+400	400	150
China					
Drills	250	0	+400	400	150
Screens	300	800	−400	400	100

FIGURE 5 International Excess Demands and Supplies

Panel A shows that at screen prices below $80, the United States has excess demands. Panel C indicates that China has excess supplies of screens at prices above $40. When American excess demands confront China's excess supplies in international markets (Panel B), imports and exports must be equal, and a price is determined that will prevail in both markets. (Excess supplies are the horizontal distances from demand to supply curves; excess demands are the horizontal distances from supply curves to demand curves.)

and harm others, even though, on balance, the gains exceed any losses. Some individuals may suffer adverse changes in their individual "terms of trade" if trade exposes their output to competition from foreigners whose production costs are lower.

A simple demand and supply model of the international screen market will enable you to see why some people dislike certain aspects of trade. We will abandon the confines of our "constant cost" model. For simplicity, we also assume that the dollar is the world currency; the complications of a multicurrency world are the subject of international finance.

Figure 5 depicts market demands and supplies for screens in the United States (Panel A) and in China (Panel C). Without trade, U. S. screen prices would be $80 (or 2 drills). At every price below $80, there is an excess demand (*XD*) for screens in the United States. Domestic producers are willing to supply fewer screens than American buyers would purchase. This excess demand (the horizontal distance between the supply and demand curves) is graphed as XD_a in the

center panel of Figure 5 and indicates how many screens would be imported at various prices.

In China screens would cost only $40 each (or half a drill) without the American market in which to sell. At prices exceeding $40, Chinese screen painters are willing to sell more screens than Chinese consumers are willing and able to buy. This excess supply (*XS*) or surplus, (the horizontal distance between the supply and demand curves) is graphed as XS_c in the center panel of Figure 5, and indicates how many Chinese screens would be available for export at various prices greater than $40.

Equilibrium between our willingness to import and China's willingness to export occurs when our excess demand equals their excess supply. With free trade, screens will sell for $60 in both the United States and China; annual Chinese production will rise to 11 million screens, but U. S. production will drop by 1 million screens. Moreover, Chinese purchases of screens decline by 1 million, while American screen buying rises by 2 million annually.

Individual Gainers and Losers

Who gains from trade? Chinese screen makers sell more screens at higher prices. American screen buyers also gain; the price of a screen in the United States has dropped from $80 to $60, and purchases have risen. Now, for possible short-run losers: American screen makers may lose when the price falls to $60 (from $80), and Chinese screen buyers may lose as the price rises to $60. Screen ownership in China could decline because of the higher price, but higher Chinese income would tend to boost their purchases of screens. The net effect is uncertain. American screen output falls, but note that world screen production has risen by 1 million units. Even former U. S. screen makers tend to gain when they move into production of drills—goods in which the United States possesses a comparative advantage.

Because Americans are buying $180 million worth of screens from China ($60 × 3 million), we will have "balanced trade" if we export $180 million worth of drills to China. We could build figures for the drill market similar to Figure 5 and would conclude that trade causes drill prices to fall in China, while drill prices rise in the United States; employment and output of the Chinese drill industry declines, but less than the U. S. drill industry grows. There will be more of both drills and screens after trade commences.

Table 3 summarizes the gainers and possible short-term losers from trading drills for screens, and vice versa. You should keep in mind, however, that this analysis only looks at short-run *specialization* gains and losses and that it only balances one import against one export. In a world of countless imports and exports, even those whose income falls because of lower-priced import competition for the good they produce also gain when they buy imports—including goods they personally produce—at lower prices.

For example, the income of textile workers may fall because of competition from imported clothing, but they gain when they buy low-priced imports of oil, cars, VCRs, . . . , *and* clothes. When the uniqueness, scale, dynamic, and political gains from trade are considered as well, it is hard to imagine anyone who ultimately loses from international trade.

Can we be fairly sure that gains to the four groups of winners more than offset the losses to the four groups of potential losers? We can. The previous section shows how the total value of production and consumption rises in both countries. Worldwide production of each good rises as trade expands. Because both countries' consumption-possibilities frontiers expand, the gainers in each country could (but seldom do) compensate the losers from trade so that every man, woman, and child in both countries gains. (If I gain $50 from a transaction that causes you to lose $20, we are both ahead if I share my gain by giving you $25.)

Trade Adjustment Assistance

Most successful movements to restrict trade have been launched by groups who lose because they operate at comparative disadvantages when forced to compete with foreign producers. They are effective politically because they are strongly opposed to importing certain goods. Suppose that 100,000 people would lose $10,000 apiece annually if restrictions on textiles imports were eliminated (a total of $1 bil-

TABLE 3 *Gainers from Specialization and Potential Short-Run Losers from Trade*		
Country	**Gainers**	**Possible Losers**
United States	Drill sellers Screen buyers	Drill buyers Screen sellers
China	Drill buyers Screen sellers	Drill sellers Screen buyers

lion), while 200 million other Americans will shell out an average of an extra $10 a year for clothing (a total of $2 billion) if textile imports continue to be restricted. You have 100,000 people who will vote for or against politicians based largely on their platforms on textile quotas, and 200 million people who are, for the most part, oblivious to their personal losses and of politicians' positions on trade.

Let us see why trade restrictions are inefficient and what might be done to ensure that everyone gains from free trade. In our example, if the 200 million consumers each contributed $6 annually to a relief fund for the 100,000 textile workers, each textile worker could receive $12,000 annually. If we set up the relief fund only with the precondition that textiles be freely imported, textile workers would gain ($2,000 each) and so would textile consumers ($4 each annually). Clearly, this would be a move in the direction of economic efficiency; everyone gains, and no one loses.

Examples like this caused recent trade acts to include clauses for *trade adjustment assistance,* intended to provide retraining and financial assistance for workers displaced because of liberalized international trade. It is, unfortunately, very difficult to identify who loses from lower trade barriers. Congress has failed to provide much funding for this program, which was among the first programs on the chopping block in the early 1980s when politicians sought to reduce government spending and balance the federal budget. The result has been a period of rising sentiment for trade restrictions. Support for higher trade barriers is voiced by many unions and managers of industries threatened by foreign competition.

Arguments Against Free Trade

Goods tend to be produced at minimum opportunity cost and then traded by their producers for other goods that are subjectively more valuable to them. Thus, free trade tends to maximize the value of the world's production. Then why is free trade the exception instead of the general practice? The answer lies in arguments *against* free trade, and *for* import barriers against foreign goods. Some arguments are par-

tially valid, but others verge on the irrational. All too commonly, irrational arguments prove persuasive or semi-valid charges against free trade are applied incorrectly. It is also unfortunate that most trade barriers protect domestic industries in incredibly inefficient ways. We will begin by examining the weakest arguments for trade barriers and then work up the ladder to more telling thrusts against free trade.

Nationalism

Nationalistic "Buy American" campaigns (or pleas to shop at local merchants instead of going to a big town, etc.) entail asking or requiring people to act against their own interests. Policymakers who yield to such chauvinistic arguments deny us the gains from exchange in order to e.g., subsidize domestic producers or hold down foreigners' incomes. At times, such policies may generate psychic income by, e.g., defending "cultural identity" or "our national heritage," but most trade restrictions are actually contrary to our national interests because they diminish our own economic power.

The Exploitation Doctrine

Some people perceive trade as a zero sum game. They reason that if one trader gains, the other must lose. Thus, if we gain, we must be exploiting our trading partner. Such reasoning may hold for poker or roulette, but the gains from trade we just described indicate that people on both sides of an exchange gain. Transactions do not occur without expectations of gain. The belief that people in less developed countries lose absolutely and so are exploited when they trade with people in developed countries is clearly wrong.

A more sophisticated argument is that trade results in "relative oppression." That is, the stronger party's gains far outweigh benefits to the weaker trader. This argument is normally wrong because the gains from trade are generally greatest to small countries; the less your trade affects the terms of trade offered by your trading partners, the greater your ability to exploit differences in the relative opportunity costs of production. For example, Monaco, a very small country, relies very heavily on trade and would be far less prosperous if it did not operate in the world market. The United States and Germany, on the other hand, have wide internal markets as well as a rich mix of resources. These giants rely less on international trade than countries like Monaco or Switzerland. Imagine how destitute Kuwait might be without trade. Its natural resources consist largely of sand, oil, and more sand. Through trade, the Kuwaiti per capita income now exceeds that of most Americans.

Retaliation

Many countries restrict imports from the United States, so why shouldn't we retaliate with barriers against their exports? This argument is often directed at Japan, which severely restricts imports of U.S. machinery and agricultural goods. One problem is that this notion ignores the harm done to U.S. consumers by retaliatory policies. When we restrict imports, we reduce the amounts of goods available to Americans and domestic prices rise.

Nevertheless, in some situations, our threat to retaliate against foreign governments' trade barriers can tip international negotiations so that their markets are opened to American exports. Just as workers' rights to strike must be exercised occasionally for the threat of a strike to have weight in union negotiations with management, the threat of retaliation against foreign trade barriers may be viable only if we occasionally do retaliate.

But retaliation is an effective negotiating tool only if it causes other countries to adopt freer trade policies, just as a strike harms union workers if it fails to yield a better work contract. And just as a permanent strike would harm workers, we normally compound the damage done by foreign trade restrictions if we retaliate with policies that are maintained in the long run. We may harm foreign producers, but we harm ourselves as well. In fact, some analysts argue that the worldwide depression of the 1930s was substantially worsened because of escalating retaliation by many major trading nations, and fear that a major trade war would cause another global depression.

Anti-Dumping

The accusation that foreign producers compete unfairly by "dumping" is raised almost every time an American producer is undersold.

Dumping *occurs when a country exports at lower prices than those charged within the exporting country.*

Dumping might result from international price discrimination, which is a policy of charging desperate (domestic) buyers more than less desperate (foreign) buyers. In such a case, customers in the country "dumped on" are the beneficiaries of the discriminatory policy. Alternatively, a foreign government might attempt to create jobs by subsidizing exports. (Japan is commonly accused of such policies.) Finally, there may be "predatory" dumping, which means that a seller tries to establish a worldwide monopoly by driving competitors out of the market. Presumably, prices could then be raised to yield monopoly profits.

There is scant evidence of dumping, however, and if it does occur the customers who buy at lower prices are major beneficiaries. Congress has enacted laws against foreign producers dumping in U. S. markets. Should our government protect Americans from low prices? Dumping is legally inferred whenever imports are sold below cost. In one case, Mexican tomato growers were barred from U.S. markets because they were selling below cost. The sad fact was that a bumper crop had depressed the price so much that tomatoes sold below cost in Mexico. Banning U. S. imports simply compounded the losses of Mexican tomato growers.

Infant Industries

Although loud clamoring for protection is now heard from "senile" industries, a slightly more valid but still misleading argument for trade restrictions is protection of **infant industries.** Shortly after the American Revolution, Alexander Hamilton argued that British industrial superiority only reflected a head start over American economic development and that protection of infant industries from low-cost British competition was necessary for U.S. industrialization.

Figure 6 shows what happens if production costs decline as industrialization proceeds. If the world price is P_w for some commodity and average production costs follow path AC_0 over time, eventually declining to P_w, then in the long run a protected infant industry will mature, be competitive in the world market, and not require a protective tariff. Notice, however, that if consumers buy constant

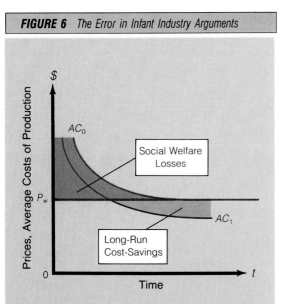

FIGURE 6 *The Error in Infant Industry Arguments*

The infant industry argument suggests that protection should be used so that immature industries can become competitive in the world market. However, tariffs or quotas designed to buffer infant industries from foreign competition will cause losses of social welfare (the orange area) unless they are offset by extraordinarily low costs (the blue area) in the long run. Of course, if such cost savings are possible, there is no need for protection because profit-seekers will invest in this industry anyway.

quantities of the protected good in each period, they lose an amount equal to the orange area below AC_0 and above P_w. This loss is inefficient because these burdens are not offset by lower costs after the industry is established.

A path like AC_1 is necessary for the efficient establishment of a new industry. The discounted value of the long run lower costs (shaded blue) must exceed the initial losses (orange). Of course, if entrepreneurs perceive that in the long run they will achieve average production costs that are below world prices, they will build the new industry without protection. Even if the infant industry argument is occasionally semi-valid, it would be better to subsidize the industry than to protect it with trade barriers.

The infant industry argument contains only the barest kernel of logic and is largely invalid, but it has been used by many less developed countries to justify protectionist policies; the almost uniform result is inefficient production and little or no growth in per

capita income. For example, protection of a government-subsidized Indian automobile plant was rationalized by an infant industry argument in the 1970s. Directed by Sanjay Gandhi, the current Prime Minister's older brother, the factory ultimately produced only a few vehicles that resembled cheap Fiats, but average production cost exceeded that for a luxury Mercedes Benz. This high price tag illustrates how ignoring comparative advantages can lead to financial disaster. Indians would have been far better off if their government had focused on production that used labor (its abundant factor) more intensively and capital (its scarce resource) less.

Trade and Payments Deficits

Anxiety about deficits in balances of trade or payments is, in part, a throwback to a theory called *mercantilism*. Mercantilists argued that a country grows stronger by exporting more than it imports, drawing the balances in gold. Adam Smith discredited this theory by pointing out that, not money, but real goods and resources are the true wealth of a nation.

Nevertheless, there may be times when concerns about trade or payments imbalances are legitimate. Some people advocate tariffs or quotas to reduce these deficits. The resulting misallocations are seldom worth any improvement in the balance of payments. When we run a trade deficit and there are net outflows of funds that "weaken the dollar," it is usually better to allow natural market adjustments to rectify the imbalance.

Moreover, there is the threat that other countries will retaliate if we impose trade barriers to solve imbalances of trade or payments. Finally, shouldn't we be happy that foreigners are willing to sell us more than we sell them—if they are willing to take dirty green paper for the difference? Just as decapitation will cure the common cold, trade barriers may cure deficits in the balances of trade or payments, but better remedies are available.

Job Destruction

The view that imports reduce domestic employment is based on simpleminded logic: we will produce goods ourselves if we don't import them. One obvious fallacy: If imports reduce employment, exports expand it. In fact, one major study suggests that even more jobs are created in export industries than are lost because of imports.

Another problem is that import barriers invite retaliation that destroy jobs in export industries. In fact, trade barriers frequently trade good jobs for bad jobs. When imports threaten an industry's survival, the marketplace is signaling that the industry is relatively inefficient and may be "senile." Trade barriers sustain comparatively inefficient industries and retard more efficient growth. Resources will ultimately be better paid if they are moved into areas in which they have comparative advantages.

If maintaining employment in certain industries is a national priority for some reason, there is still the question of whether trade barriers are the right tools to use. In general, trade barriers are incredibly inefficient ways to promote employment. The prices of the goods protected by import barriers rise far more than the incomes of protected workers. Several studies indicate that (voluntary?) limits on auto exports from Japan boosted U.S. carmakers' share of domestic sales by 6–8 percent, but raised American car prices by an average of $400–$600, while Japanese import prices rose between $2,000 and $3,800 apiece.[1] The result was that each American auto worker's job that was saved because of trade restrictions cost U.S. car buyers between $100,000 and $241,000. Table 4 presents a set of estimates of the costs of saving jobs through trade barriers.

These numbers may seem astounding, but trade barriers cause American consumers to lose in many ways, most of which are hidden.

1. Consumers subsidize U.S. industries and resource suppliers (e.g., workers) who lack comparative advantages in areas protected by trade barriers.

2. Non-tariff barriers subsidize efficient foreign suppliers, substantially worsening our balance of payments. These trade barriers effectively enable foreign producers to exercise monopoly power. The result is enrichment of foreign firms to the tune of billions of dollars each year.

To illustrate how inefficient trade barriers are as a way to protect jobs, consider how costly it might be to guarantee jobs for 1,000 American diamond miners. The United States has a few sparse diamond fields. Barriers that caused mediocre diamonds to cost $20,000 per carat might stimulate domestic diamond mining in some regions. South Africa and the Soviet

Union, however, would secure enormous profits in selling in the U.S. market. The high costs of trade barriers suggest that other policies to protect workers' incomes would be more efficient. For example, Table 4 suggests that for most protected industries, one-time trade adjustment assistance of $40,000 per worker displaced by freer trade would have been a bargain.

Harmful Income Redistribution

The United States is commonly perceived as having relatively less labor but more capital than the rest of the world. A model of trade known as the *Heckscher-Ohlin* theory suggests that goods that require heavy doses of a country's abundant resources will be exported, and that goods intensive in a country's scarcest resources will be imported. A corollary of this theory is that owners of resources that are more plentiful nationally than worldwide garner all short-run specialization gains from trade, while owners of resources that are relatively abundant internationally but scarce domestically suffer short-run losses from the specialization caused by freer trade.

This approach has been interpreted as suggesting that trade provides American capital owners with more potential customers while U.S. workers face stiffer competition from low-wage foreign labor. Thus, American wages are driven down by trade while returns to capital rise; the net specialization gains from trade are received exclusively by capital owners. Capital owners could more than compensate workers for income shrinkage caused by trade, but our institutions are not geared for such transfers (e.g., failure to fund trade adjustment assistance). Hence, working class people suffer while the rich get richer.

This theory may help explain some of the American labor movement's support for trade barriers. If we are truly concerned about income inequality, however, we should not ignore the gains to poor foreign workers when their products are exported, nor should we forget the uniqueness, scale, dynamic, and political benefits of trade.

The Heckscher-Ohlin model has often been misapplied by ignoring some major sources of U.S. comparative advantage. A partial rebuttal to the idea that capitalists gain from trade while American labor loses is that, more than other types of resources, the United States has relative abundances of rich farm land and

---

1. Robert W. Crandall, "Import Quotas and the Automobile Industry: The Costs of Protectionism," *The Brookings Review,* Summer 1984, 62–74.

TABLE 4 Annual Cost for Protecting U.S. Jobs from Foreign Competition—1979–85

Industry	Annual Total Costs ($ Billions)	Annual Cost per Job Saved ($ Thousands)
Automobiles	5.8	105–241
Book manufacturing	0.5	100
Dairy products	5.5	220
Fishing (tuna)	N/A	240
Glassware	0.2	200
Maritime	3.0	270
Shoes	N/A	30–46
Steel	6.8	114–750
Sugar	0.9	60
Textiles and apparel	27.0	40–45

Sources: G. Hufbauer, et al., *Trade Protection in the United States: 31 Case Studies* (Washington, D.C.: Institute for International Economics, 1986), Federal Trade Commission studies cited by Phil Gramm, "New Protection = Old Sophistry," *Wall Street Journal*, 4 Oct. 1985, 21.

labor that is adept with sophisticated technology. These resources are relatively scarce in the rest of the world, so American agricultural incomes and the incomes of highly skilled workers are enhanced by international trade. The post-World War II industrialization of Western Europe and Japan has shifted this country's gains from trade away from capitalists toward highly skilled workers and farmers. Less developed countries have also benefited enormously from increased competition among modern industrial powers for raw materials.

Exploiting Monopoly/Monopsony Power

A country that is a major importer or exporter of a good can flex its economic muscles through trade restrictions to drive prices up or down. For example, a country having monopoly power might be able to impose an export tariff that would be borne in part by "foreign devils." If so, it is conceivable that the citizens of the exporting country would gain.

The monopolistic or monopsonistic unit may gain tremendously by manipulating its output or purchases and consequently, prices, but only by imposing even greater losses on its customers or suppliers. For example, the Organization of Petroleum Exporting Countries (OPEC) jacked up oil prices by over 1,000 percent during the 1970s by agreeing to raise prices and restrict the outputs of member countries. They prospered for a period—but at the cost of worldwide economic recession that was especially hard on less developed countries. Brazil and Colombia, somewhat less successfully, combined to raise coffee prices, but only at considerable cost to coffee drinkers.

It would be naive to expect altruism to deter countries from exercising economic clout. A country's leaders should be leery of muscling around its trading partners, nevertheless, because abuse of monopoly/monopsony power invites retaliation and raises the specter of a disastrous trade war.

Diversity

Volatile demands or supplies can be devastating if a country specializes in only a few major outputs. Colombia's reliance on coffee is one example. Droughts, floods, or coffee blight can easily wipe out a year's income, or large harvests in Brazil might severely depress world prices. Diversification is one way of spreading the risk, just as farmers rotate their crops to "rest the soil" and spread their risks.

Protection of developing industries may encourage diversity, but at some cost in efficiency. These efficiency losses might be thought of as insurance premiums, but diversification could be encouraged at far less cost by production subsidies. On rare occasions diversification may be a valid goal for narrowly specialized countries, but not in the U.S. and other richly varied economies. Even small countries' diversification policies have often been so misdirected that opportunities for development were lost.

National Defense

Domestic access to certain products is crucial for our national defense, so we might want to protect such industries as aircraft or weapons from foreign competition. This argument is often misused and results in perverse policies. For example, the idea that we should not depend on foreign oil has been used for the past century to justify "Drain America First" policies that actually increased our long run dependence on foreign oil suppliers.

We have only discussed import barriers to this point. National defense may provide more legitimate reasons for bans on exports of critical products and materials. Sales of scrap metal to Japan prior to World War II were clearly short-sighted. It would be equally foolish to allow terrorists or the Mafia to buy atomic weapons on a free market basis.

One final note: one major gain from trade is that it causes specialization and mutual interdependence. This raises the price of conflict and provides incentives to avoid war. Freer trade tends to promote peace and international harmony and reduce the need for national defense.

Trade Barriers _____

A number of mechanisms are used as barriers to free trade, but the most important are tariffs and quotas. Each can be imposed on either imports or exports, but restrictions on imports are far more common than export barriers.

Tariffs

In the United States, tariffs on exports are forbidden by the Constitution.

> A **tariff** *is a special tax that applies only to goods traded internationally.*

Import tariffs raise the domestic prices of goods and stimulate domestic production. The United States is a major trader in most goods, so U. S. tariffs also tend to drive down the incomes of foreign producers.

Suppose that we have a tariff on imported steel of $25 per ton, that the international price is $100 a ton, and that U.S. demands and supplies of steel are as depicted in Figure 7. Without a tariff, the United States imports 60 million tons of steel and domestic production is 100 million tons annually. The $25 per ton tariff allows American steelmakers to boost production to 120 million tons, but cuts domestic steel usage by 20 million tons (to 140 million) while imports fall 40 million tons. Government collects revenues from the tariff equal to the shaded area *abfe,* or $500 million ($25 × 20 million).

Non-Tariff Barriers

International negotiations to reduce trade barriers (e.g., *GATT,* the General Agreement on Trade and Tariffs) have tended to focus on tariffs. The result is growth of non-tariff barriers to restrict free trade. For example, rigid U. S. regulatory standards have been used to limit automobile imports and drive up their prices. You might think this is appropriate, but a hint that safety or environmental standards are not always the real issue arises from the fact that Japanese standards drive up the prices of U. S. car exports to Japan even more. Both U. S. and Japanese car makers have lobbied for regulations that are disadvantageous to foreign producers.

Quotas are the most common non-tariff barriers to trade.

> **Quotas** *limit the quantities of goods that may be imported or exported over a given time.*

Both quotas and tariffs inefficiently raise the prices of imported goods so that potential gains from trade are not fully realized, but the side effects of quotas make them especially harmful. Let us investigate why.

Suppose the $25 tariff in Figure 7 is replaced by an import quota of 20 million tons annually—the domestic price remains at $125 per ton, but government would collect no revenues. Importers who secured import licenses would collectively pick off profits of $500 million—20 million tons of steel costing $100 per ton could be sold for $125 a ton. These potential profits make import licenses very valuable and provide inducements for bribery and corruption.

Voluntary Export Restrictions In its international negotiations, the United States has traditionally been a cheerleader for freer international trade. Our actual policies, however, have been a bit schizophrenic. Fear of a trade war coupled with international treaties

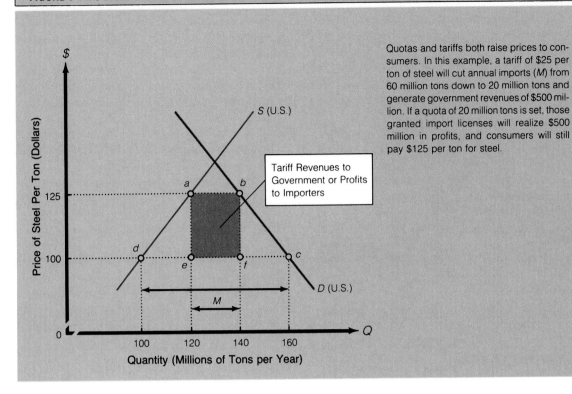

FIGURE 7 The Effects of Quotas and Tariffs

Quotas and tariffs both raise prices to consumers. In this example, a tariff of $25 per ton of steel will cut annual imports (*M*) from 60 million tons down to 20 million tons and generate government revenues of $500 million. If a quota of 20 million tons is set, those granted import licenses will realize $500 million in profits, and consumers will still pay $125 per ton for steel.

Tariff Revenues to Government or Profits to Importers

(instigated by the United States) to reduce tariffs have made it difficult for American policymakers to bow to political pressures for protectionism by raising tariffs. This has diverted most industries that want protection from imports into lobbying for *voluntary export restrictions* (*VER*s). Our government threatens foreign industries with high import barriers unless they restrict exports. *VER*s are "voluntary" only in the sense that you "voluntarily" give to a robber who points a gun at you and gives you a choice between "Your money or your life."

Japan imposed quotas on textile exports to the United States in the 1970s, and on its auto exports in the 1980s. We indicated earlier that restrictions on auto imports from Japan saved American auto workers' jobs at a cost of from $100,000 to $241,000 each. Curiously, the Japanese auto industry gained. The preceding analysis of quotas shows how. Limits on Japanese auto exports raised the prices they received for their cars and boosted their profits by billions of dollars. These profits would have been converted

into U. S. tax revenues if tariffs had been used instead of quotas.

The Japanese reaction to this *VER* illustrates how regulation provokes unanticipated adjustments that may defeat its stated purpose. The goal of the *VER* was to protect American jobs and reduce the U.S. trade deficit but it only limited the number of Japanese exports—not their value. Consequently, Japanese carmakers focused on exporting more luxurious vehicles—Acuras, Nissan 300ZXs, Mazda 929s, and Toyota Supras and Land Cruisers. Thus, some of the import pressure on economy cars was shifted to another market segment. But Yugos and Korean Hyundais and Daihatsus were not subject to quotas, so they partially replaced the low-end Japanese exports in American garages. Even voluntary quotas have unpredictable results.

Another problem is that rigid quotas fail to accommodate changes in demand. Growth in demand can be met by imports with a tariff system, but not under import quotas. Finally, relative to tariffs, quotas retard the incentives of foreign producers to do research and innovation. Conclusion: From the perspective of the citizen/taxpayer, tariffs are preferable to quotas. However, either mechanism causes economic inefficiency.

A Final Argument for Freer Trade

Perfect government policies might, in an ideal world, achieve any feasible set of goals we chose. Optimal trade barriers could efficiently exploit our own monopoly/monopsony power and counter that exercised by foreigners. Ideal barriers might also be constructed to protect American jobs, incomes, and infant industries, bolster our national defense, rectify trade and payments imbalances, and offset unfair practices by foreign governments.

In the real world, however, most trade barriers are enacted because of pressures from special interests. These barriers depress our national income, stimulate foreign retaliation and hostility against the United States, endanger jobs in export industries, and shrink competition for domestic firms that exercise monopoly power. Nor has growth of non-tariff barriers to trade prevented enormous and growing trade and payments deficits.

A major reason that U. S. trade policies are so far from ideal is that specific trade barriers strongly affect the incomes of members of special interest groups who are willing to work hard in the political arena for their passage. But members of the general public are politically apathetic about, e.g., import quotas on shoes, because their individual well-being is affected relatively little. The result is mounting pressure for protectionism that will inefficiently benefit the few at much higher cost to the broad public.

International trade is a major source of economic development. At the same time, consumer demands grow and broaden as their incomes grow, so trade tends to expand as the world economy grows. In this chapter we have explored the gains from trade and exposed the fallacies behind most arguments against free trade. We hope you will remember these discussions when people debate trade policies.

CHAPTER REVIEW: KEY POINTS

1. International trade is important to people throughout the world. The smaller and less diversified an economy is, the greater is the importance of its international trade.
2. The *law of comparative advantage* suggests that there will be net gains to all trading parties whenever their pre-trade relative opportunity costs and price structures differ between goods.
3. A country's *consumption-possibilities frontier* (*CPF*) expands beyond its *production-possibilities frontier* (*PPF*) with the onset of trade, or with the removal of trade restrictions.
4. The *terms of trade* are the prices of exports relative to the costs of imports. An *adverse change* in the terms of trade lowers the country's *CPF,* while a *favorable change* in the terms of trade expands it.
5. Gains from trade arise because international transactions (*a*) provide unique goods that would not otherwise be available, (*b*) allow highly specialized industries to exploit economies of scale, (*c*) speed the spread of technology and facilitate capital accumulation, (*d*) encourage peaceful international relations, and (*e*) facilitate specialization according to comparative advantage.
6. Domestic producers of imported goods may suffer short term losses from trade, as do domestic consumers of exported goods. Their losses, however, are overshadowed by the specialization gains to the consumers of imports and the producers of exports. The gainers could always use parts of their gains to compensate the losers so that, on balance, no one loses. Moreover, *uniqueness, scale, dynamic,* and *political gains* from trade make it unlikely that anyone loses from trade in the long run.
7. Even the most valid of the arguments against free trade are substantially overworked. The arguments that are semi-valid include the ideas that (*a*) the income redistributions from trade are undesirable; (*b*) desirable diversity within a narrow economy is hampered by free trade; (*c*) national defense re-

quires restrictions to avoid dependence on foreign sources, and (more validly) export restrictions to keep certain technologies out of the hands of potential enemies; and (*d*) major exporters of a commodity can exercise monopolistic power by restricting exports, while important consuming nations can exercise monopsonistic power through import restrictions.

8. Any exercise of international monopoly/monopsony power invites retaliation and causes worldwide economic inefficiency. Those who lose because of trade restrictions will lose far more than is gained by the "winners."

9. If trade is to be restricted, *tariffs* are preferable to *quotas* because of the higher tax revenues and the smaller incentives for bribery and corruption.

10. *Trade adjustment assistance* is one way that the gainers from trade might compensate the losers so that all would gain. The difficulty of identifying the losers and the failure to fund this program adequately have resulted in mounting pressures for trade restrictions.

PROBLEMS

1. Suppose that workers in Java can each produce 10 tons of sugar or 200 shirts per year, while Cubans can each produce either 15 tons of sugar or 45 shirts annually. There are 10 million workers on each island.
   a. Use graph paper to draw *PPF*s for each country.
   b. What are the prices of these goods in each country without trade? Will the final terms of trade settle between these relative prices?
   c. Show graphically what happens to the *CPF*s of these islands if they begin trading and the terms of trade settle at the exact midpoint of the initial price ratios without trade.

   d. Identify the groups that unambiguously realize short-run specialization gains from trade, and the groups that might lose from trade.

2. Suppose that England is abundantly endowed with capital but has a relative scarcity of labor, while India has abundant labor but sparse capital. Assume that tea production requires intensive labor inputs while woolens are produced with relatively more capital. According to the Heckscher-Ohlin theory of trade, which goods will be imported and which exported in each country? Which resource owners gain from trade, and which lose?

QUESTIONS FOR THOUGHT AND DISCUSSION

1. How do a nation's endowments of labor, natural resources, and capital shape the kinds of outputs in which it has comparative advantages? What influence might weather have? Can you think of other determinants of a country's areas of comparative advantage?

2. One critic of U. S. policies argues that " . . . either we allow Mexican goods freer access to American markets or we allow Mexicans to immigrate into the United States more freely or we must send billions of dollars in foreign aid to Mexico to prevent a revolution that adopts anti-American policies." How does this argument mesh with ideas from this chapter?

3. Restrictions on oil imports on the grounds of national security undoubtedly led to greater domestic exploitation. Because petroleum is a depletable re-

source, this may account for our current increased, rather than decreased, dependence on "unreliable foreign sources." What are alternatives to import restrictions as ways to assure the availability of oil in the event of a national emergency? Would these mechanisms work as well to assure availability for goods other than nonrenewable resources?

4. Should American consumers pay higher prices because of trade barriers to protect the jobs of workers in "senile" industries? Do such policies in effect "protect consumers from lower prices"? What limits do you think there should be on free trade internationally? Are there valid reasons for protectionist policies?

5. The American steel, auto, and television receiver industries were all in bad shape even before the

economy began to slump in the early 1980s. Plant closings in these industries led to calls for tariffs and quotas on steel, autos, and televisions. Do restrictions on trade make more sense in a slumping economy than in one that is prosperous? What are some disadvantages to using trade restrictions to bolster declining industries or a stagnant economy?

6. The Heckscher-Ohlin model of international trade has been extended to "prove" that international transactions tend to "equalize" factor payments (e.g., the purchasing power of wages and rates of return to capital). Since World War II, rapid growth in labor incomes in Japan and Western Europe relative to that in the United States seems to support this theory. Can you explain what mechanisms tend to equalize resource payments?

7. Most models of international trade assume that goods move across international borders, but that people and capital do not. Can you use the principles you have learned in this chapter to explain immigration patterns and international capital flows?

CHAPTER 37

International Finance

The previous chapter addressed aspects of international trade but left unanswered questions about *international finance*, which addresses such issues as (*a*) the macroeconomic consequences of flows of funds to finance international transactions, and (*b*) how these transactions are funded when some traders are based in countries that use francs or pesos, for example, while their trading partners are accustomed to dealing in yen or dollars. You may have heard about deficits or surpluses in balances of payments, which are accounts that summarize international flows of money. The nature of balance of payments accounts and some macroeconomic consequences of payments imbalances are our first topics in this chapter.

How prices are set when traders use different currencies is our second concern. A key to this puzzle is provided by looking at the ways that the relative val-

ues of currencies—their *exchange rates*—can be determined. Exchange rates are extremely important prices because they translate *all* wages and prices in one country's currency into their values in another country's currency. This completes the framework you need to interpret recent changes in conventions for international payments. Our final task in this chapter is an overview of influences on the international value of the dollar during the past few years.

Balances of Payments and Trade

Most Americans react with a "What? Me worry?" shrug and then a yawn when Dan Rather, Tom Brokaw, or Peter Jennings announce the latest deficit in our *balance of payments*. The U.S. has run persistent international trade deficits and balance of payments deficits in the 1980s. Most individuals find it difficult to identify the personal effects of these deficits. Trade deficits or surpluses provide starting points for understanding international finance.

There is no special reason for inflows of dollars from sales of U.S. exports to match the outflows of dollars for our purchases of imports.

If the dollar value of merchandise imports exceeds that for exports of U.S. merchandise, then the U.S. experiences a **balance of trade deficit.** *But if the dollar value of our merchandise exports exceeds the dollar value of imports, there is a* **balance of trade surplus.**

Naturally, trade deficits in some countries are exactly balanced by trade surpluses in other countries—one country's imports are another's exports.

Balance of Payments Accounts

Accounting for international transactions in merchandise and services is the first step in building our balance of payments accounts.

Our **balance of payments account** *summarizes flows of payments between the U.S. and foreigners with whom Americans deal.*

Transactions that cause Americans to send funds abroad drive this account towards a deficit; transactions that bring funds into the United States moves the balance of payments towards a surplus.

A **deficit** *occurs in our balance of payments whenever money outflows from the U.S. exceed the country's monetary inflows. A* **surplus** *occurs in periods when money inflows exceed outflows.*

Table 1 outlines the U.S. balance of payments account, which covers two major categories: the current account and the capital account. The *current account* deals with both transfers and trade in goods and services. The *capital account* records transactions in such items as stocks, bonds, or real estate. These accounts are balanced by changes in the holdings of foreign currencies or net outflows of U.S. money—items (9) and (10) in this table.

The Current Account Only merchandise shipments are considered when computing the balance of trade, but dollar-for-dollar, international transfers and sales of services have roughly equivalent macroeconomic effects. Transfer payments include such items as cash gifts and grants between individuals in separate countries.

Many people intuitively believe that international trade occurs only in merchandise, not services. Nevertheless, a French tourist who exchanges francs for dollars and then gets a haircut in a Chicago barber shop before returning to Paris is effectively importing that haircut, and the barber is, perhaps unknowingly, an exporter. Foreign students in your class who pay their tuitions after exchanging their national currencies for dollars are "importing" education to their countries. How many of your professors do you think recognize that they are partially "exporting" their lectures?

The Capital Account Foreign investments are a major cause of outflows of financial capital. Deposits to a Swiss bank account or purchases of stock on the Hong Kong exchange by Americans also cause outflows of funds. Similarly, if a Japanese firm builds an auto assembly plant in the United States, or buys a U.S. Treasury bond, funds flow into the United States.

The statistical discrepancy in these accounts is large. This occurs because many transactions cannot be identified by type. For example, it is almost impossible to trace funds exchanged in such illicit transactions as drug smuggling (dollars for cocaine), nor is it easy to tell what foreign tourists buy after they exchange their money for dollars. Data for foreign purchases of U.S. financial securities are also often not accounted for separately.

After we sum all the transactions that draw money into the United States and subtract all transactions that send funds abroad, we have the balance of payments surplus ($+$) or deficit ($-$), which is an overall measure of net international transactions.

Imbalances of Payments

One consequence of the enormous federal budget deficits of recent years has been persistent balance of payments deficits in the 1980s, a topic addressed in

TABLE 1 *The United States Balance of Payments (1987 Billions of Dollars)*

	Receipts (+)	Payments (−)	Balance
Current Account			
(1) Merchandise Exports	+251		
(2) Merchandise Imports		−410	
Trade Balance			−159
(3) Net Investment Income	+ 14		
(4) Net Services		− 3	
(5) Net Unilateral Transfers		− 13	
Current Account Balance			−161
(1 + 2 + 3 + 4 + 5)			
Capital Account			
(6) Capital Outflows		− 64	
(7) Capital Inflows	+203		
(8) Statistical Discrepancy		− 17	
Official Reserves Transactions Balance			+122
(1 + 2 + 3 + 4 + 5 + 6 + 7 + 8)			
Method of Financing			
(9) Increases in U.S. Official Reserve Assets (−)		− 9	
(10) Increase in Foreign Official Assets (+)	+ 48		
Total Financing of Surplus			+ 39
Sum of 1 through 10			0

Source: *Survey of Current Business,* March 1988.

chapter 15. We showed that if net private domestic saving $(S - I)$ was inadequate to cover any government deficit $(G - T)$, then the budget deficit will be financed by foreigners: $S + T - I - G = X - M$. Our domestic saving and taxes have been inadequate to cover domestic investment and government outlays in recent years $(S + T < I + G)$, so the United States has run large deficits in its current account $(X - M < 0)$.

The countries that we trade with run surpluses in their balances of trade (their current accounts) to cover their purchases of U.S. financial capital (Treasury bonds, corporate stocks and bonds, or real estate). Foreign financial investment in the United States is one way that Americans have been able to "live beyond" their current incomes in recent years. Reversing the deficits in our current account would require domestic saving or taxes to grow, or government outlays to shrink—a difficult set of choices that specialists in international economics call the *absorption* problem. Unless Americans are willing to save more, pay more taxes, or cut back on domestic investment, we must rely on inflows of foreign financial capital.

One way to attract foreign capital is to make investments in U.S. assets attractive. International movements of funds are controlled by the forces of supply and demand operating through international money markets. The relative strengths of supplies and demands for a country's money are reflected in the relative prices of national currencies—their exchange rates.

Exchange Rates

Most international transactions require the currency of the buyer to be exchangeable for the currency of the seller. For example, Americans generally want dollars when they sell to foreign customers. This requires foreigners who buy from Americans to acquire U.S. dollars to consummate these transactions.[1] They express their demands for dollars by supplying their own currencies. Similarly, we demand foreign goods, make loans to foreigners, or invest abroad by supplying dollars, which translates into demands for foreign currencies. The relative demands and supplies of various currencies determine their relative prices, which are called exchange rates.

Suppose you buy a pound of Brazilian coffee. Your grocer will accept U.S. dollars to pay the coffee wholesaler, who probably pays dollars to the importer. But most Brazilian coffee growers do not ultimately want dollars from the importer; they want Brazilian cruzados to pay their workers and suppliers. This means that dollars must be exchanged for cruzados. Thus, your coffee purchase is ultimately translated into a demand for cruzados in international money markets and, simultaneously, into a supply of dollars.

The price of one currency (cruzados) in terms of another (dollars) is called the **exchange rate.**

If $1 can be exchanged for 500 cruzados, then the cruzados is priced at $.002—one-fifth of a cent—and the Brazilian exchange rate is 500. It takes 500 cruzados for a Brazilian to buy a dollar's worth of U.S. merchandise. Note that these exchange rates are reciprocals of each other—if $1 = 500 cruzados, then a cruzados = 1/500th of a dollar.

Exchange rates among currencies translate all prices (including wages and interest rates) in a single currency into their values in other currencies. If a low exchange rate of the dollar for the yen makes investment in the United States look attractive to Japanese investors, Japanese financial capital will tend to flow into the United States. Huge federal budget deficits in the 1980s have created pressures for U.S. reliance on foreign capital. Our need to attract this foreign capital

has, in turn, caused the international value of the dollar to fall sharply during 1985-1988.

If the dollar recovers so that it will buy more yen in future years, the Japanese who have invested in U.S. assets will receive more yen when they exchange their dollar incomes; their investments will be even more profitable than expected. But Japanese investors will be out of luck if the dollar falls further on international markets. What looks like a good foreign investment if exchange rates are stable may be a spectacular gem if the foreign currency's exchange rate rises, or a miserable dog if it falls. There are two basic ways that an exchange rate may rise—*appreciation* or *revaluation*, and two ways that an exchange rate can fall—*depreciation* or *devaluation*.

Currency Appreciation and Depreciation

Exchange rates are like other prices in that changes in supplies and demands cause exchange rates to fluctuate unless governments control them. Table 2 shows exchange rates in 1988 of a number of currencies for the U.S. dollar.

There is **appreciation** *of a nation's currency if market forces cause foreign currencies to become cheaper.*

TABLE 2 *Foreign Exchange Rates*

	U.S. $ value		Foreign units per U.S. $	
	July 26	July 25	July 26	July 25
England [pound]	1.7185	1.7340	.5819	.5767
Canada [dollar]	.8247	.8295	1.2125	1.2055
Argentina [austral]	.080321	.082169	12.4500	12.1700
Australia [dollar]	.8040	.8110	1.2438	1.2330
Austria[Austral]	.0767	.0773	13.0350	12.9340
Belgium [franc]	.0259	.0260	38.65	38.46
Brazil [cruzado]	.0043	.0044	230.68	227.73
Denmark [krone]	.1420	.1431	7.0420	6.9890
Finland [mark]	.2278	.2294	4.3890	4.3600
France [franc]	.1599	.1611	6.2550	6.2055
W Germany [mark]	.5388	.5436	1.8560	1.8395
Greece [drachma]	.0067	.0068	148.45	147.15
Holland [guilder]	.4773	.4815	2.0950	2.0770
India [rupe	.0775	.0755	12.90	13.25
Ireland [R] [pound]	1.4490	1.4615	.6901	.6842
Israel [shekel]	.6135	.6150	1.6300	1.6260
Italy [lire]	.000729	.000735	1371	1361
Japan [yen]	.007561	.007587	132.25	131.80
Mexico [peso] f	.000429	.000429	2330	2330
Norway [krone]	.1486	.1495	6.7310	6.6900
Portugal [escudo]	.0067	.0067	150.00	149.600
Saudi Arabia [riyal]	.2666	.2666	3.7510	3.7515
So Africa [rand]	.4107	.4142	2.4350	2.4145
Spain [peseta]	.008150	.008217	122.700	121.70
Sweden [krona]	.1571	.1581	6.3660	6.3255
Switzerland [franc]	.6472	.6538	1.5450	1.5295
f-floating rate.				

---

1. The U.S. dollar has historically been so universally convertible that foreigners often require dollar payments when they sell to other foreigners. OPEC, for example, has stated its oil prices in dollars. Thus, if Kuwaitis sell oil to the Czechs, they may be reluctant to accept Czechoslovakian korunas, requiring dollars instead. This creates an international transactions demand for dollars; few other currencies are used internationally as mediums of exchange, and none as commonly as the dollar. More about this in a moment.

For example, if the cruzado's price fell from $.002 to $.001, a dollar would buy twice as many cruzados and thus, has appreciated.

Depreciation *of the domestic currency (e.g., dollars in the United States) means that foreign currencies have grown in value.*

A depreciated dollar buys fewer cruzados (and less coffee) than previously.

Revaluation and Devaluation

Supply and demand have largely determined exchange rates since 1973. Before then, treaties were widely used to set exchange rates. At times, however, these international agreements were undone by powerful market forces.

When fixed exchange rates are adjusted, the currency that appreciates is **revalued,** *and the depreciating currency is* **devalued.**

In an earlier era, many currencies were based on a *gold standard* by which a fixed amount of money exchanged for a certain amount of gold. Gold standards automatically yield fixed international exchange rates.

Even today, some exchange rates are fixed and occasionally must be altered. For example, exchange rates among European Common Market currencies are fixed, and tend to "float" in unison vis-à-vis other currencies. When the French economy suffered from high inflation and a flight of capital during 1983, however, the French franc was *devalued* relative to the German deutsche mark, the British pound, the Dutch guilder, and all other Common Market currencies. The franc also *depreciated* relative to major currencies external to the Common Market. Realizing how market forces affect exchange rates is fundamental to understanding how the international economy operates.

Demands and Supplies of Currencies

Foreign money is collectively known as *foreign exchange.* Demands for foreign exchange resemble domestic demands for money. Although most demands for foreign exchange are based on international transactions, some key currencies (primarily the dollar) are demanded for precautionary reasons, or because they are viewed as stable assets. (The transactions, precautionary, and asset demands for money were discussed in chapter 14.) For the moment, however, we will focus on the transactions demand for foreign exchange.

For simplicity, assume that the only two currencies are American dollars ($) and German deutsche marks (*DM*s). Our demand for deutsche marks is mirrored in our willingness to supply dollars. To see this, consider point *a* in both panels of Figure 1, which shows that if the exchange rate is one-for-one, we are willing to supply one billion dollars for one billion deutsche marks. When we can get *DM*2 for $1 (point *b* in Panel A), we are willing to supply $2 billion dollars to get *DM*4 billion (each DM costs $0.50 at point *b* in Panel B). And so on. Comparing the matched points between Panels A and B will confirm that any information found in one is duplicated in the other.

Changes in exchange rates cause movements along international supply and demand curves for a currency, paralleling the way that price changes cause changes in quantities demanded or supplied along supply and demand curves for goods. And, just as we assume certain influences constant to construct standard demand curves, isolating the effects of exchange rates on the quantity of dollars demanded to build the German demand curve for dollars requires holding constant (*a*) the prices of substitutes (foreign goods are the relevant substitutes); (*b*) foreign incomes; (*c*) foreign tastes and preferences; (*d*) expectations about exchange rate changes and relative inflation rates in both countries; and (*e*) the dollar prices of U.S. goods. Symmetrically, we hold U. S. incomes, prices, preferences, expectations, and foreign prices in *DM*s constant when drawing the U. S. supply curve of dollars. Changing any of these numerous variables shifts the demand or supply of dollars.

We hold the dollar prices of American goods constant in the United States and the *DM* prices of German goods constant in Germany, but dollar prices of imports from Germany and the *DM* prices of our exports will change proportionally if exchange rates

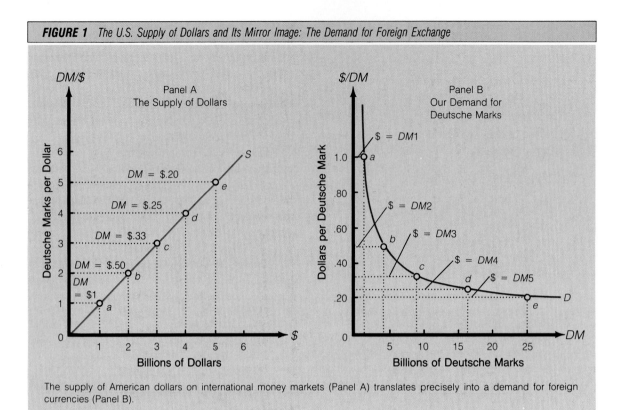

FIGURE 1 *The U.S. Supply of Dollars and Its Mirror Image: The Demand for Foreign Exchange*

The supply of American dollars on international money markets (Panel A) translates precisely into a demand for foreign currencies (Panel B).

fluctuate. This is the key to why the demand and supply curves of dollars (or *DM*s) slope down and up, respectively.[2]

The Supply of Currencies

The supply of dollars, shown in Panel A of Figure 1, is based on offers by Americans to buy foreign currencies, which we then use to buy foreign goods and services or to invest abroad. This supply curve slopes upward because if foreign currency becomes more expensive, it costs more dollars to buy foreign goods and services. Many previous American buyers of imports may drop out of the market or shift to substi-

tutes (movements such as $e \rightarrow d \rightarrow c \rightarrow b \rightarrow a$). Conversely, if our exchange rate rises and we can buy more *DM* per dollar, we will be willing to supply greater quantities of dollars. This supply curve will shift if there are changes in American incomes or tastes, or in the prices of the foreign goods we import.

The Demand for Currencies

Our transaction demand for deutsche marks in Panel B of Figure 1 is really a demand by Americans to buy German consumer goods and to invest overseas. We measure the price of the *DM* in terms of dollars. Like most demand curves, this demand curve slopes down from left to right. If *DM*s become more expensive in terms of dollars, the dollar prices of German goods and investments rise and Americans will buy fewer German goods and invest less abroad; instead, Amer-

---

2. Technically, this requires that international demands and supplies of goods be elastic, conditions that we assume are met throughout our exposition in this chapter.

icans will buy more American goods and invest more domestically. This means that they will demand fewer *DM*s. When *DM*s are cheaper, Americans will buy more of them because imports from Germany will be cheaper, as will dollar investments in Germany.

Equilibrium Exchange Rates

The supply curve of dollars is actually a "flipped over" demand curve for foreign currencies, as shown in Panel B of Figure 1. (Remember that exchange rates are the reciprocals of each other.) We offer (supply) dollars in order to buy foreign exchange, and ultimately, foreign goods. The demand curve for dollars is similarly a "flipped over" supply curve of the foreign currency.

This means that we can look at the same market with either set of curves. That is, our demand for foreign currency (Panel B) mirrors our supply of dollars (Panel A); foreign demands for dollars (Panel A) are the supplies of foreign currencies (Panel B). We only need to look at one market in order to know precisely what is happening in the other. Henceforth, we will only look at the dollar market; no additional information is gained by looking at the markets for *DM*s (used here to represent all foreign currencies).

Interactions between these supply and demand curves determine equilibrium exchange rates and quantities of dollars and foreign currencies. In Figure 2, the equilibrium price of German *DM*s is $0.50. This is the same as saying that the equilibrium price of the dollar is *DM*2. If the exchange rates of the dollar and

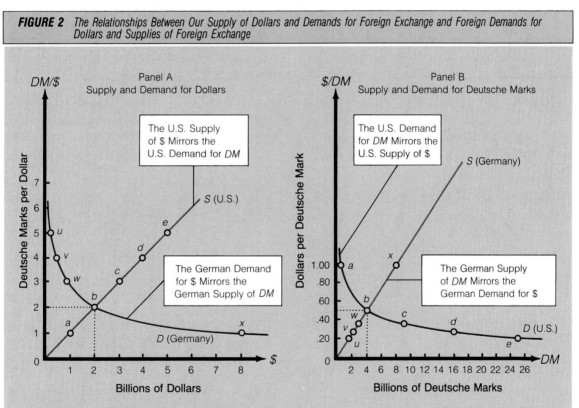

FIGURE 2 The Relationships Between Our Supply of Dollars and Demands for Foreign Exchange and Foreign Demands for Dollars and Supplies of Foreign Exchange

The markets for dollars (Panel A) and deutsche marks (Panel B) embody identical information. Our supply of dollars is a demand for deutsche marks, and the demand for dollars is expressed by the supply of deutsche marks. Thus, we only need to look at the market for one currency in order to know precisely the state of the market for the other currency.

deutsche mark are in equilibrium, this does not necessarily mean that the values of international transactions are offsetting so that there are no net flows of foreign exchange between countries.

Foreign Demands for Dollars

Among the reasons that the United States has been able to run huge and persistent deficits in its balances of payments are our size, importance in world trade, and history of political and economic stability. This has created transactions, precautionary, and asset demands for the dollar as a unique international money, so that it is used for many international transactions even if no Americans are involved.

Transactions Demands Foreigners have transactions demands for dollars not only so that they can buy U.S. goods or invest in the United States, but also to transact with each other. For example, if Saudi Arabia exports oil to Brazil, it is unlikely that Brazilians will be able to pay for the oil with Saudi riyals, and the Saudis may be unwilling to accept Brazilian cruzados. Use of the dollar solves this dilemma—Saudis will take dollars in exchange for their oil. The international acceptability of dollars causes Brazilians, Saudis, and other foreigners to seek dollars even if they have no intention of buying from U.S. companies.

Precautionary and Asset Demands Rich foreigners who fear revolutions or chaos in their own countries may acquire dollars for precautionary reasons. This was evident when Ferdinand Marcos fled the Philippines; he and his entourage carried suitcases filled with dollars, and were reputed to have had vast dollar accounts in Swiss banks. Foreign economic instability may also be a source of asset demands for dollars. For example, Israelis or South Americans may use dollar-denominated securities to hedge against rapid inflations in their own countries.

The point is that persistent deficits in the U.S. balance of payments may not be a sign of disequilibrium. Foreigners may want dollars more than they want the U.S. goods that the dollars would buy. We have become the world's banker, which means that we supply dollars the way other countries supply cars

or cameras. In a sense, dollars may be the major U.S. export, and Americans gain substantially by the payments deficit. The production cost of dollars is trivial, and the U.S. economy gains tremendous *seignorage* (profit from printing money) in the process of supplying international money.

There are occasions, however, when imbalances of payments signal disequilibrium. We need to examine the ways that foreign exchange markets can bring international supplies and demands of a currency into balance.

Curing Exchange Rate Disequilibria

Suppose that the exchange rate of the dollar for the *DM* is artificially held below equilibrium at, say, $0.25 per *DM* (*DM*4 per dollar) as shown in Figure 3—relative to equilibrium, German *DM*s are too cheap and dollars are too expensive. Situations like this offer one explanation for imbalances of international payments. In this example, there is a *surplus* of dollars on international markets, and the United States will experience a *deficit* of payments. Germany runs a compensating balance of payments *surplus*; if we constructed a graph depicting the *DM* market, it would show a *shortage* of *DM*s internationally. Be sure that you understand how surpluses of a currency imply that the issuing country experiences a balance of payments deficit, while a currency shortage implies a surplus in a country's balance of payments. This jargon is sometimes confusing.

Regardless of the cause of deficits or surpluses in a country's balance of payments, there are four basic ways of dealing with these imbalances. We can (*a*) allow changes in exchange rates, (*b*) adopt controls to ration foreign exchange, (*c*) follow macroeconomic policies to shift the supply or demand curves for foreign exchange, or (*d*) allow flows of money from deficit to surplus countries.

Each of these mechanisms has been widely used in some regions during some periods. Most payments, whether domestic or international, were made in currencies denominated in gold until World War I.

An economic surplus of dollars leads to a deficit in the U.S. balance of payments. This implies that there is an offsetting economic shortage of deutsche marks and that Germany will experience a balance of payments surplus.

Fixed amounts of each currency exchanges for a given amount of gold under an ideal **gold standard** *so that all exchange rates are also fixed.*

A gold standard makes exchanging one currency for any other easy because all their values in terms of gold are fixed. An ounce of gold exchanges for an ounce of gold. But the supply of gold did not keep pace with the volume of transactions in rapidly growing economies, so countries everywhere in the world abandoned the gold standard and turned to *fiat* (paper) money.

The worldwide abandonment of gold-denominated money and movement to fiat currencies raises the question: What are the appropriate exchange rates between currencies? One answer to this question is given if governments intervene through *fixed exchange rate* agreements (price controls) or through other regulations intended to stabilize exchange rates. Alternatively, it can be left to supply and demand. Since 1973, although some countries have linked their exchange rates to those of other countries (e.g., currencies in the European Common Market), most exchange rates have been *flexible*—governed largely by the forces of the marketplace.

Flexible (Floating) Exchange Rates

In Figure 4, there would be no deficits or surpluses if the *DM* rose to $0.50, which means $1 is only worth *DM*2 instead of *DM*4. As the price of the dollar fell and the price of foreign exchange rose, we would export more and import less, restoring equilibrium. This solution is called flexible (or *floating*) exchange rates and has been the dominant system used for over a decade.

A system of **flexible exchange rates** *allows the relative prices of currencies to be set by market forces.*

FIGURE 4 *Flexible Exchange Rates: A Market Solution to Balance of Payments Deficits*

If exchange rates are flexible, an economic surplus of dollars will cause the dollar to depreciate until the quantity of dollars demanded equals the amount supplied. Symmetrically, the deutsche mark will appreciate until equilibrium is reached. American balance of payments deficits and German balance of payments surpluses will be reduced or eliminated.

Thus, international supplies and demands for various currencies have largely determined exchange rates since 1973.

One major objection to flexible exchange rates is that too much uncertainty may enter the sphere of international transactions because of exchange risk.

Exchange risk *arises because sellers lose if they agree to accept the buyers' national currency and it depreciates, while buyers lose if they agree to pay in the sellers' national currency and it appreciates.*

Uncertainty is encountered because buyers and sellers in international trade would each like the value of future payments stated in their own currencies and might otherwise suffer losses.

Suppose, for example, that you were an importer of German cameras, and you contracted to buy 1,000 cameras to be delivered and paid for 120 days from today. If the contract specified payment in *DM*s and the *DM* appreciated in the next four months, you would wind up paying more dollars for the deutsche marks due than you had expected. On the other

hand, if dollar payments were specified and the *DM* appreciated, the exporter would receive fewer *DM*s than expected. This exchange risk is a potent argument against flexible exchange rates.

Defenders of flexibility counter this objection by pointing out that importers and exporters can insure against exchange risk by dealing in forward markets that match future inflows against future outflows of dollars.

In **forward markets** *for currencies, sellers can contract to receive the currency desired in exchange for the currency received from buyers, or a buyer can contract to secure the currency desired by the seller.*

This insurance against exchange risk, however, involves transaction costs that are absent if exchange rates are absolutely fixed. An even more critical failing is that forward (futures) markets exist for only a few currencies, and even these are available for only limited future periods, as Table 2 illustrates. Critics also charge that flexible exchange rates encourage destabilizing speculation but, per our discussion in chapter 4, it is unlikely that speculation is destabilizing in the long run.

Although flexible exchange rates adjust for surpluses and deficits automatically and have many of the desirable characteristics associated with market solutions, many governments reject flexible exchange rates, trying to resolve problems with international payments in other ways.

Macroeconomic Corrections

A balance of payments deficit will evaporate if the supply and demand curves shown in Figure 5 shift to intersect at an equilibrium exchange rate (price) of *DM*4 instead of *DM*2. The burden of curing deficits or surpluses in this way falls on macroeconomic adjustments.

Imbalances of payments caused by disequilibrium may be cured through **macroadjustments** *to Aggregate Demand that change nominal GNP (PQ).*

One option is for the deficit country to follow contractionary fiscal policies; domestic Aggregate Demand, including the demand for imported goods, will shrink. Another possibility is to reduce the mon-

FIGURE 5 *Using Macroeconomic Adjustments to Eliminate Deficits*

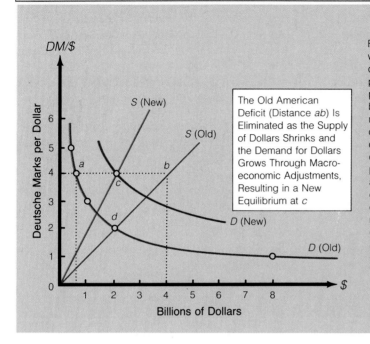

The Old American Deficit (Distance *ab*) Is Eliminated as the Supply of Dollars Shrinks and the Demand for Dollars Grows Through Macroeconomic Adjustments, Resulting in a New Equilibrium at *c*

Flows of funds from imbalances of payments will cause Aggregate Demand to grow in surplus countries. If all countries are close to full employment, the prices of domestic goods in surplus countries will rise, making imports better buys. The resulting growth in imports will be reflected in rising demands for the currencies of deficit countries. At the same time, monetary outflows will dampen Aggregate Demand in deficit countries. There will be decreases in the prices of domestic goods relative to imports, and the international supplies of deficit countries' currencies will decline as imports fall. Thus, the exchange rate remains stable, with all adjustments coming in the form of higher prices in countries that initially experienced surpluses and lower prices in deficit countries. This solution poses no special problem if prices are perfectly flexible. If prices are rigid downward, however, macroeconomic adjustments may impose severe hardships.

ey supply when a balance of payments deficit (a foreign exchange shortage) poses a problem. The resulting recessionary fall in output and/or deflation of domestic prices will cause us to import less. Either contractionary monetary or fiscal policies reduce the international supply of dollars shown in Figure 5.

Contractionary macroeconomic policies also induce lower prices for American exports and encourage foreigners to buy more from us. The supply of foreign currency (*DM*s) grows along with foreigners' demands for dollars in Figure 5. (Remember that the supply curve of *DM*s mirrors the demand for dollars.) The original deficit in payments (distance *ab*) is eliminated as the economy moves from disequilibrium in the balance of payments (point *d*) to equilibrium (point *c*).

Some experts argue that deficits pose few problems; after all, deficit countries actually export money, which has a very low production cost, and receive goods and services embodying much higher production costs. These analysts recommend that the balance of payments surpluses in some countries be cured with expansionary macroeconomic policies, causing domestic prices to rise in surplus countries

and the prices of their imports to fall; their surpluses of receipts from international trade would therefore be eliminated.

These sorts of *macroadjustments* are automatic under a gold standard, which was the policy of most developed countries in the half century preceding World War I. Payments deficits reduced a country's supply of gold money; surpluses increased it. But because corrections brought about through macropolicy require deflation and stimulate unemployment in countries experiencing a deficit, they tend to be unpopular with the people who live in those countries. Nor do most leaders of countries having excessive surpluses in their balances of payments welcome the suggestion that expansionary or inflationary macroeconomic policies are in order.

Several foreign finance ministers, for example, urged the American government to follow contractionary policies in the 1960s and 1970s to cure our chronic balance of payments deficits. We offered counterproposals that their governments should pursue expansionary policies to cure their chronic surpluses, and they predictably ignored us. An interesting about-face occurred when contractionary U.S.

monetary policies in the early 1980s dampened U.S. inflation and bolstered the international value of the dollar—foreign governments urged the Reagan administration to follow more expansionary policies to fight the worldwide recession that was at least partially attributable to our counterinflationary policies. A foreign diplomat compared dealing with the United States to " . . . sharing a bed with an elephant; you must be careful when you nudge the beast to get it to roll over."

Exchange Controls

We might ration foreign exchange to eliminate deficits. At $0.25 per *DM*, only *DM*2 billion (at point *a* in Figure 6, worth $500 million) are available to Americans, but they would like to buy *DM*16 billions ($4 billion at point *b*) worth of German goods. The U.S.

government could allocate the available *DM*2 billion among would-be importers through licenses, or it could restrict certain imports by using quotas or tariffs. Many Americans wanting to tour Germany or buy German cameras or VWs would have to do without.

Such techniques are called exchange controls and are used in most underdeveloped countries today.

Under a system of **exchange controls,** *a government limits access to foreign exchange to favored industries or individuals and makes it illegal to exchange foreign for domestic currencies except through that government's banks at official exchange rates.*

Exchange controls are extremely inefficient and share many of the failings of quotas (described in the preceding chapter). Controls must be exercised

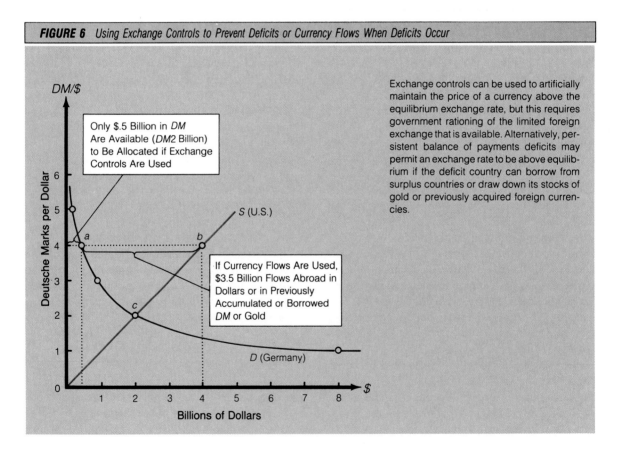

FIGURE 6 *Using Exchange Controls to Prevent Deficits or Currency Flows When Deficits Occur*

Only $.5 Billion in *DM* Are Available (*DM*2 Billion) to Be Allocated if Exchange Controls Are Used

S (U.S.)

If Currency Flows Are Used, $3.5 Billion Flows Abroad in Dollars or in Previously Accumulated or Borrowed *DM* or Gold

D (Germany)

Exchange controls can be used to artificially maintain the price of a currency above the equilibrium exchange rate, but this requires government rationing of the limited foreign exchange that is available. Alternatively, persistent balance of payments deficits may permit an exchange rate to be above equilibrium if the deficit country can borrow from surplus countries or draw down its stocks of gold or previously acquired foreign currencies.

through some government agency, and they create powerful incentives for smuggling, bribery, graft, black marketeering, and general corruption.

Fixed Exchange Rates

Our earlier discussions of price controls indicated that if prices are fixed above their equilibrium values, there will be surpluses; while if the price of a good is held below its equilibrium value, there will be a shortage of that good. The same results hold for international currency markets.

If we have accumulated reserves of foreign exchange, or if we can beg, borrow, or steal reserves of foreign currencies from our friends and allies, we can rely on international flows of currencies or debt as the fourth and final solution to a balance of payments deficit.

Currency *or* **debt flows** *can accommodate imbalances of international payments.*

In Figure 6, $0.5 billion dollars (*DM*2 billion) of our annual foreign exchange needs are met by regular inflows of foreign currency. How can we accommodate our remaining $3.5 billion (*DM*14 billion) outflow of funds? One system requires an international agreement to "fix" exchange rates.

In 1944, the Bretton Woods Agreement was struck, establishing the International Monetary Fund and a system of fixed exchange rates. (The International Monetary Fund lingers on, but the fixed exchange rate died of natural causes in 1973.) Under the Bretton Woods Agreement, most nations "pegged" the value of their currency to the dollar, which the United States agreed to redeem for gold at $35 per ounce. Because the values of all major currencies were pegged to the dollar (and thus, to gold), these currencies were "fixed" relative to each other as well.

The U.S. Treasury used some of the gold it had acquired over the previous century to pay parts of chronic deficits experienced from 1951 to 1973. Most of these deficits, however, were absorbed by foreign central banks when our trading partners bought the surplus dollars. Our theoretical willingness to redeem at least some dollars for gold and the willingness of our trading partners to absorb surplus dollars was a key to the fixed exchange rate system of this period.

A system of **fixed exchange rates** *requires governments to establish and maintain constant relative values for their currencies.*

Figure 7 shows how foreign governments (e.g., Germany) can ensure that our currency will never fall below certain values if they buy the dollars sent out as our balance of payments deficits. Similarly, we can set floors for the values of their currencies if we buy their money when they run deficits. In our example, the German government can supply *DM*s or other currencies "on loan" to the United States and take the excess dollars off the market. This enables the two countries to maintain *fixed exchange rates.*

Persistent U.S. deficits will cause growing piles of American dollars to accumulate in German banks. The widespread acceptability of the dollar may enable Germans to use U.S. currency to pay for their imports, but then these dollars wind up consuming space in other foreign central banks. There is a limit to the amount of dollars foreign governments will absorb. After a saturation point is reached, surplus dollars will return via the capital account of the U.S. balance of payments when foreigners begin buying Treasury bonds or corporate securities, U.S. firms, U.S. real estate, or they may simply invest and establish production facilities in the United States.

Fixed exchange rates pose no special problems as long as exchange rates reflect the relative supplies and demands of currencies. In other words, fixed exchange rates do not cause any special problem as long as their values are the same as flexible exchange rates would be. Even if fixed exchange rates are initially in equilibrium, however, differences in macroeconomic policies or rates of economic growth between countries, or changes in tastes or technologies will cause the relative supplies and demands of currencies to change. Shortages and surpluses emerge amid persistent disequilibria in balances of payments whenever fixed exchange rates fail to reflect the true demands and supplies of currencies.

In summary, there are four basic ways to deal with surpluses or deficits in balances of payments— change the price (float), ration (control), shift the curves (macroadjustments), or allow currency flows. Similar solutions apply equally to surpluses or shortages of wheat, gasoline, teachers, or skateboards. You

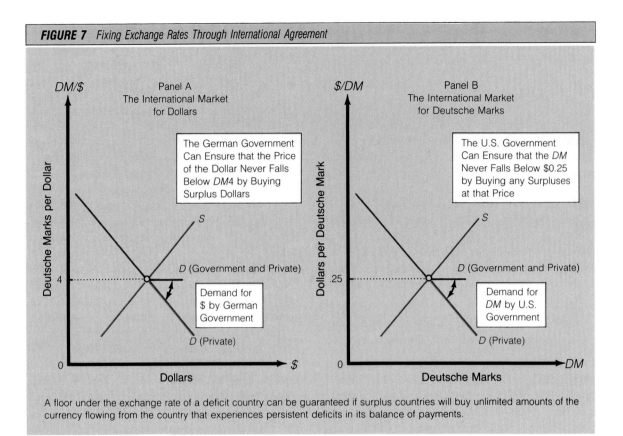

FIGURE 7 Fixing Exchange Rates Through International Agreement

Panel A
The International Market
for Dollars

DM/$

Deutsche Marks per Dollar

The German Government
Can Ensure that the Price
of the Dollar Never Falls
Below *DM*4 by Buying
Surplus Dollars

S

4

D (Government and Private)

Demand for
$ by German
Government

D (Private)

0

Dollars

$

Panel B
The International Market
for Deutsche Marks

$/DM

Dollars per Deutsche Mark

The U.S. Government
Can Ensure that the *DM*
Never Falls Below $0.25
by Buying any Surpluses
at that Price

S

.25

D (Government and Private)

Demand for
DM by U.S.
Government

D (Private)

0

Deutsche Marks

DM

A floor under the exchange rate of a deficit country can be guaranteed if surplus countries will buy unlimited amounts of the currency flowing from the country that experiences persistent deficits in its balance of payments.

can add a lot of frills, but this simple supply and demand analysis is what the complex world of international finance is really all about.

The Dirty Float: 1973 to ?

Most exchange rates have been flexible since 1973, but with some government intervention. In most markets for goods and services, surpluses or shortages are cured by price changes, a process detailed in chapter 3. Floating systems allow exchange rates to vary, so it would seem that U.S. balance of payments deficits (surpluses of dollars) should be cured automatically if they are signs of disequilibrium. But if imbalances of payments should vanish automatically, then why have U.S. payments deficits been so persistent?

We indicated earlier that one part of the answer is that foreigners have often wanted American dollars even more than they wanted American goods. This suggests that our consistent deficits in international payments may be signs of economic and political health. Parts of U.S. deficits may be true symptoms of international imbalances, however, because governments everywhere have constantly intervened in foreign exchange markets.

Explaining Persistent U.S. Payments Deficits

If a country runs large and persistent deficits, foreign banks will accumulate substantial amounts of that country's currency because foreign suppliers will exchange the payments they receive for their own money. Why have foreign private and central banks permitted the United States to run persistent balance of payments deficits?

The answer to this question is multifaceted. First, between 1946 and 1971, the dollar was the only major currency redeemable for gold, at least for purposes of international payments. Foreign central banks could present $35 to the U.S. Treasury and demand one ounce of gold. It was illegal for Americans who were not jewelers, coin collectors, or dentists to own gold bullion, bars, or coins during this period. Any American gold not used industrially or in teeth or jewelry was used to back the dollar for international transactions.

The end of World War II saw the United States as the only major country with its manufacturing capacity intact. We supplied much of the world's needs and generally demanded payment in gold because most other currencies were either unstable or worthless. Hence, as we entered the 1950s, the United States had substantial gold on hand. The dollar was a nearly perfect substitute for gold for purposes of international payments because it was redeemable for gold.

This meant that our money was often viewed as at least as valuable as the American goods that might be bought with it by, say, the Italians; people in other countries would cheerfully accept dollars when they would not accept lire in payment for Italian purchases. In a sense, the convertibility of U.S. dollars into gold (under a "partial reserve system" much like that used by commercial banks) enabled the United States to create "international money."

International trade in the post–World War II period grew far more rapidly than the quantity of gold available for international payments. The acceptability of the U.S. dollar as an international *key currency* made it possible for the U.S. Treasury and the FED to accommodate increasing world demands for an international medium of exchange by simply printing money. Americans gained through *seignorage* (differences between money's face value and its production cost) from this ability to print international money because we were able to export less than the total value of the goods we imported. In a sense, we consumed more than we produced. The difference was made up by the dollars we printed that circulated among foreign countries, seldom being redeemed for American output or resources. The international acceptability of the dollar has been the major reason that the United States was able to run persistent and large deficits between 1951 and the present.

The relative prices of most currencies in international exchange markets presumably have been set by supply and demand since 1973. We may still run deficits under a floating exchange rate system, however, if foreigners commonly demand our dollars instead of American goods and services. Even so, foreign demand for dollars as insurance or as an internationally accepted means of payment do not completely explain the magnitudes of the U.S. balance of payments deficits throughout the 1970s.

The central banks and treasuries of a number of countries accumulated dollars during the 1970s to prevent the exchange rate of the dollar from falling even further or more rapidly than it did; the "float" has been a dirty float. Why would foreign governments (for example, Japan) wish to maintain high prices for imports from the United States and concomitant low prices for Japanese products exported to Americans? Part of the answer is that employment and growth in the Japanese and some other economies are heavily dependent on their export industries. In addition, the Japanese farmers and manufacturers who compete with imports from the United States are very powerful politically.

When the Japanese central bank buys and holds the dollars paid for Japanese exports, the effect is the same as a tariff on their imports and a subsidy on their exports. This Japanese policy of acquiring growing amounts of dollars has resulted in subsidies to American consumers by Japanese consumers. Until Japanese taxpayers and voters catch on, we may continue to gain at their expense.[3] Curiously, our government pressured the Japanese government to adopt policies to eliminate the U.S. trade deficit with Japan. Can you figure out why?

In sum, the United States has been able to run balance of payments deficits fairly consistently for over three decades because:

1. Until the early 1970s, the international monetary system (under the Bretton Woods Agreement) used fixed exchange rates that were adjusted only to cure a "fundamental disequilibrium." It was

---

3. This support for the dollar can be viewed as a hidden subsidy that Japan, and more especially, Germany, used to induce the United States to provide defense services. Tens of thousands of American soldiers are stationed in Germany.

advantageous to many of our trading partners to maintain the primacy of the dollar until inflationary pressures from the Vietnam era and the emergence of other sound national currencies led to the downfall of fixed exchange rates, which had required a sound dollar as a foundation.

2. There has been a strong demand for the dollar for use as an international medium of exchange.

3. Dollar holdings have been viewed as "insurance" in politically or economically unstable countries.

4. Such countries as Japan and West Germany have supported the dollar at artificially high exchange rates in order to boost American demand for their exports. These policies have increased employment and economic growth in these countries.[4]

The Dance of the Dollar _____

The dollar was indisputably the world's key currency from the end of World War II until the mid-1960s. Then the exchange value of the dollar declined rela-

---

4. Throughout the 1970s, our government urged foreign governments to run budget deficits, increase their money supplies, and reduce trade barriers against American products, among other measures.

tive to most major currencies during the 1970s, hitting its low in 1978. The dollar then recovered steadily until late 1985, as Figure 8 demonstrates. But why did the dollar fall during the 1970s? Why was it so strong in the early 1980s? And why did it weaken again after 1985? There are a number of explanations, all of them at least partially correct.

We know that the price of anything will fall if supply grows relative to demand, and vice versa. Some explanations for the fall of the dollar during the 1970s focus on reduced desires by foreigners to hold dollars; others focus on increased supplies of dollars in international markets. Although growing supplies and falling demands for the dollar (or vice versa) are interrelated, we will deal first with factors that alter international demands for dollars.

Inflation and Exchange Rates

There was substantial inflation during the 1970s not only in the United States, but throughout the world. When our inflation abated in the early 1980s, the dollar surged upward in international exchange markets until 1985.

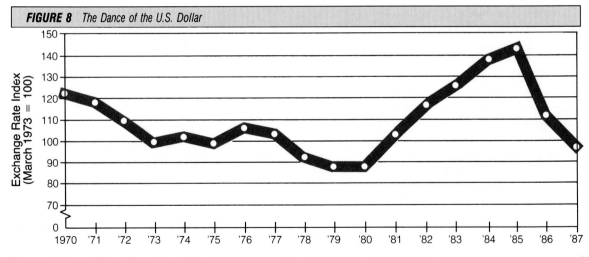

FIGURE 8 *The Dance of the U.S. Dollar*

The overall depreciation of the dollar relative to the average of other major currencies during the 1970s reflected the maturation of other currencies, the declining prestige of the United States, problems with inflation, the deterioration of our terms of trade as the prices of imports grew faster than the prices of our exports (for example, oil imports versus machinery exports), rising concern about the future of the dollar and of the American economy, and a host of other problems. The dollar's strong recovery as the 1980s began signaled a reversal of this downward spiral.

Source: *Economic Report of the President*, 1988.

Relative Inflation When prices increase faster in the United States than elsewhere, we buy more imports and supply more dollars internationally, but the demands for our exports and dollars fall. This line of reasoning leads to a classical explanation for falling exchange rates—relatively rapid inflation in the United States during the 1970s reduced foreign demands for dollars. Coupled with an increased supply of dollars, we have one part of the explanation for declining exchange rates. Then, as American inflation abated in the early 1980s, the recovery of the dollar became stronger. Thus, relative inflation causes depreciation of a currency, while less than the average international rate of inflation causes exchange rate appreciation.

Expectations There was an international perception during the 1970s that more than any other major industrialized country, the United States was committed to expansionary, and consequently, inflationary policies. Increased income, whether real or inflated, causes higher demands for imports. If other countries are not expected to follow similarly expansionary policies, there are growing pressures for balance of payments deficits.[5]

U.S. inflation throughout the 1970s probably generated international expectations of continued inflationary policies and relative inflation in this country. Such expectations led foreigners to treat dollars as hot potatoes; their dollar holdings fell dramatically at times between 1974 and 1980.

Whenever international money managers have expected the United States to experience both continued relative inflation and substantial balance of trade deficits, there has been downward pressure on the dollar. When U.S. monetary growth began to slow in 1979, the dollar began its recovery. An American recession during 1981–83 spread to the rest of the world as it choked off our demands for imports and constricted the international supply of dollars. High U.S. interest rates also attracted short-term financial investments by foreigners, further strengthening the

dollar. It seems ironic that recessions bolster the dollar, but they do.

By 1985, the exchange rate of the dollar was so high that foreign finance ministers and American policymakers were alarmed. They agreed to follow policies to depreciate the dollar. Accordingly, foreign central banks sold dollars on international markets, increasing the supply to private financiers. Fear that the United States might begin following more expansionary macroeconomic policies caused many private financial institutions to be leery of holding many dollars. Coupled with record deficits in the U.S. balances of payments and trade that caused the international supply of dollars to swell, the dollar drifted down during 1985–88.

Budget Deficits and Anemic Saving

We previously discussed (in chapter 15 and earlier in the current chapter) the way that federal budget deficits and inadequate private domestic saving create pressure for borrowing from foreigners, which may take the form of foreign investments in the United States. (If $S + T < I + G$, then $X < M$.) But foreigners will invest in the United States only if this appears more profitable than investment elsewhere. If the exchange rate of the dollar appreciates, foreign investors gain, but depreciation of the dollar would cause them to lose. One way for foreigners to feel that investment in the U.S. is secure is for the exchange rate of the dollar to be so low that they think it likely that it will only rise.

Persistent federal budget deficits (our last surplus was experienced in 1969) create pressures for capital flows into the United States to offset current account deficits. But capital tends to flow into countries where, after adjustment for both normal business risks and exchange rate risk, the expected rate of return is the highest. Federal deficits pushed down the dollar in the late 1970s, and again during 1985 through 1988.

Portfolio Adjustments

For some time after World War II, the U.S. dollar and gold were viewed as the only stable international mediums of exchange. The world's supply of gold grew more slowly than the volume of international

---

5. This action reduces the exchange rate of the dollar, and by increasing the prices of our imports and decreasing the prices of U.S. exports, eliminates the deficits.

transactions. Consequently, institutions like central banks and international corporations were happy to use the dollars made available by our balance of payments deficits to meet their transactions demands for money and desires for liquid assets.

Economic instability in the United States beginning during the Vietnam conflict led to diminished confidence in the dollar. During the same period, numerous industrialized economies throughout the world matured or reached full recovery from World War II; their currencies became attractive parts of the liquid portfolios of many countries' central banks, competing with the dollar as a reserve asset. The growing availability of good substitutes for dollars led financial institutions around the world to diversify, holding smaller proportions of their assets in dollars.

When the dollar began to depreciate a little during the mid-1970s, it fell off the pedestal that had caused so many countries to hold dollars. The huge proportion of international reserves held by foreign central banks in U.S. currency caused the "dollar overhang" to collapse. For example, in 1977 alone almost 60 percent of the dollars held by OPEC countries were exchanged for other currencies, intensifying pressure for the dollar to fall.

Several countries attempted in the late 1970s to price their exports (e.g., OPEC oil) on an index of such strong foreign currencies as the Swiss franc and German deutsche mark. These experiments temporarily weakened the dollar because it was less demanded for international transactions, but ultimately failed, forcing renewed reliance on the dollar as the world's key currency and further bolstering the dollar's recovery in the early 1980s.

Oil and the Balance of Trade

During the 1970s our cumulative payments deficit added almost 30 percent to the total amount of dollars held abroad. Substantial parts of payment deficits over this period were attributable to oil imports. The international price of oil grew sharply when OPEC exercised its muscles during 1973–81. Because American production technology is extremely energy intensive, higher oil prices only slowly reduced our oil imports. The dollar value of oil imports grew dramatically during the 1970s, worsening our balance of payments deficit. This—and our own increasing preferences for Japanese electronics, cameras, and

cars—pushed down the exchange rate of the dollar. But by the early 1980s, our imports of crude oil were declining and the dollar began showing considerable strength in international financial markets.

The Monetarist Explanation

All the factors we have offered provide bits and pieces of a solution to the temporary decline of the dollar. Predictably, some monetarists attribute the slide of the dollar to too rapid growth in the U.S. money supply (and declining rates of monetary growth were credited with its recovery). We will use the deutsche mark (*DM*) to explain the monetarist mechanism. The reasoning goes that if the supply of dollars grows relative to the demand for dollars faster than the supply of *DM*s grows relative to the demand for them, then the dollar will depreciate relative to the deutsche mark.

The problem with this approach is that while it is unquestionably true, it has little explanatory value. In fact, in recent years the U.S. money supply grew less rapidly than the money supplies of virtually any other major country, yet the dollar danced downward relative to almost every major currency. Monetarists were unable to explain the declining demand for the dollar, other than by vague references to inflation; then the dollar's recovery was attributed to diminishing inflation.

In summary, among possible explanations for the decline of the dollar during the 1970s were:

1. relative inflation of the dollar;
2. expectations that inflation in the U.S. would remain higher than elsewhere;
3. expected continuation of trade deficits;
4. persistent and growing federal budget deficits;
5. adjustments of international portfolios against the dollar;
6. modest depreciation caused the dollar to lose its "halo";
7. larger trade deficits caused by high oil prices;
8. too rapid monetary growth in the U.S.

The recovery of the dollar in the 1980s apparently occurred because of reversals of a number of these factors. Each explanation seems logically plausible, yet none alone is a satisfactory explanation for the swings in the exchange rate of the dollar, and some are even contrary to the evidence.

CHAPTER REVIEW: KEY POINTS

1. Since we have no world currency, we must establish the value of each national currency in terms of all others. The *exchange rate* is the value of one currency in terms of another.

2. *Balance of payments* accounts record the flows of money into and out of a country and provide information about trade relationships among countries.

3. *Flexible,* or *floating,* systems of *exchange rates* permit the values of currencies to be set by market forces. If a country experiences a balance of payments *surplus* (*deficit*) under such a system, it is an indication that the country's citizens or government (*foreigners*) desire foreign (*domestic*) currencies.

4. A *fixed* exchange rate system imposes price ceilings and floors on currencies, often resulting in persistent disequilibria in balances of payments.

5. Explanations for the decline of the dollar in the 1970s range from relative inflation to expectations of continued inflation and payments deficits to federal budget deficits to the emergence of other strong international currencies to the cartelization of oil to too rapid monetary growth. Opposite trends then strengthened the dollar until 1985. Each of these explanations bears the germ of truth, but none alone is adequate to explain the dance of the dollar.

PROBLEM

1. Calculate all possible exchange rates if a U.S. dollar ($) will buy 2 Deutsche marks (*DM*), ½ of a British pound (£), 6 French francs (*F*), or 120 Japanese yen (*Y*).

QUESTIONS FOR THOUGHT AND DISCUSSION

1. One popular myth is that surpluses in the balances of trade and payments are good omens, while deficits are symptoms that a country may be suffering from economic anemia. Yet persistent U.S. balance of payments deficits during the past three decades may have been unavoidable simply because of the relative vigor of the American economy. How is this so? How have Americans gained from the trade deficit? From the payments deficit? How have they lost from these deficits? On balance, have the gains outweighed the losses?

2. Conventional theories of international finance suggest that imbalances of payments are signs of disequilibrium. A recent theory called "global monetarism," however, hypothesizes (among other things) that surpluses can be expected when people in some countries want more money more than they want more goods, while people in other countries have "too much" money, and willingly trade some of their money for imports. How might persistent surpluses or deficits occur in equilibrium?

3. Global monetarists also favor fixed exchange rates, arguing that flexible rates make no more sense than reducing the price of the quarter relative to the penny if there are surpluses of quarters and shortages of pennies. What are the major differences, if any, between these situations? Do these economists have a point? What mechanisms are available to accommodate deficits or surpluses under fixed exchange rates? What are the implications of fixed exchange rates for the independence of macroeconomic policies?

4. After the dollar declined in the 1970s, foreign tourists found the United States an excellent place to shop for bargains. The United States quit being such a haven

for foreign shoppers when the dollar recovered in the early 1980s. Then the decline of the dollar during 1985–88 drew tourists to the United States, and foreign investment in the United States soared. Similarly, when the Mexican peso depreciated severely in 1982–83, many Americans scurried to Mexico for bargains. Why do such bargains for foreigners sometimes emerge when a currency depreciates or is devalued? What does the existence of such bargains suggest about whether these currencies are temporarily overvalued or undervalued? What does your answer suggest about the way balances of payments might change for these countries in the very near future?

5. Under what circumstances might depreciation or devaluation of a currency cause deficits in a country's balance of payments to worsen? How is your answer related to elasticities of demands and supplies for exports and imports? Why is any worsening of payments deficits likely to be strictly a short-term problem?

6. Recent growth of foreign investment in the United States alarms many Americans. There are calls to sharply limit foreign holdings of U.S. assets, but in periods when U.S. investment abroad has been vigorous, there are complaints that we are exporting jobs to low-wage countries. Can you offer arguments that justify both special limits on U.S. investment by foreigners and on foreign investments by Americans? Or should investors be allowed to place their capital wherever they think it will yield the largest profit?

libertarianism

anarcho-syndicalism

utopian socialism

Fabian socialism

Christian socialism

communism (Marxism)

dialectical materialism

class warfare

central planning

indicative planning

welfare state

small is beautiful

CHAPTER 38

Capitalism and Its Alternatives

Many mechanisms, including markets, can be used to allocate resources and distribute goods. How different economic systems operate is the focus of this chapter. We begin with an overview of capitalism and libertarians, its strongest defenders. Anarcho-syndicalism, our second topic, shares with libertarianism a distaste for government, but is less enamored of capitalism. Then we survey several types of socialism, including Marxism. After a birds-eye view of how different social philosophies are expressed in contemporary economies, the chapter concludes with discussions of possible limits to economic growth and "Buddhist economics"—the idea that the ultimate solution to economic want is spiritual rather than physical. When you finish this chapter, you should have a sense of the spectrum of mechanisms that people use to deal with scarcity.

Perspectives on Capitalism

Although market higgling and haggling predate written history, the first systematic description of capitalism was in Adam Smith's *Wealth of Nations* (1776). This pathbreaking book spawned countless studies of market economies. Most developed economies rely heavily on the market system, but markets play only minor roles in the lives of two thirds of the world's population. In some countries, primitive economic conditions limit market transactions; in others, leaders who oppose capitalism have outlawed most market activities.

Critics of capitalism claim that only greed and other base motives are nurtured by competition, which permeates everything from schools to athletics to business. They identify growing corporate power as an inevitable outcome of capitalistic competition. Giant multinational corporations flourish, dominating world trade. The arguments for the superior efficiency of capitalism assume vigorous competition among many small firms, a situation that exists in only a few sectors of most modern market economies.

Modern capitalism, according to its critics, is corrupt, unstable, inefficient, exploitative, dehumanizing, and outmoded. These critics view capitalism as pitting wealthy elites against the starving and powerless, and predict that it will soon "be swept into the dustbin of history." Capitalism's advocates naturally believe that these critics are wrong and cite many virtues of the price system, the two most important being freedom and efficiency.

Libertarianism

Power corrupts, and absolute power tends to corrupt absolutely.
—*Lord Acton*

Libertarians join anarchists in a dislike of bureaucracy and government. Anarchists see giant corporations and big government as twin threats to freedom and as exploiters of labor. Libertarians focus more narrowly on problems posed by government. In the libertarian view, corporate abuses would evaporate if government did not suppress competitive behavior and foster concentrated economic power.

> **Libertarians,** *the modern champions of laissez-faire capitalism, prize freedom as the most important social value, and advocate replacing government with the market system wherever possible.*

Libertarians see other goals as empty without freedom and constantly look for areas where government can be eliminated. Among the government activities that libertarians believe could and should be left to private choice are:

1. the military draft;
2. laws controlling prescription drugs, narcotics, consensual sex between private individuals, and pornography;
3. laws giving parents controls over teenagers;
4. regulation of utility companies;
5. discretionary monetary and fiscal policies;
6. public parks, roads, and highways;
7. mandatory automotive safety equipment;
8. wage and price controls;
9. usury laws;
10. social security;
11. education;
12. welfare;
13. the postal service;
14. radio and television broadcasting; and
15. professional licensing.

Libertarians view most government action as hindering freedom and advocate markets as efficient and equitable cures for almost all social problems. They would restrict government to protecting private property rights and enforcing contracts. That government has never been so limited explains why some libertarians call pure capitalism "the unknown ideal." But libertarians cannot claim a monopoly in their opposition to government.

Anarcho-Syndicalism

There's no government like no government.
—*An Anarchist Slogan*

One group of capitalism's foes perceive corporate giants and government as parasites that exploit the working class. This group consists of anarchists, who would retain private property rights, and syndicalists, who seek collective worker-ownership of nonhuman resources. Hatred of government is the glue that binds anarchism to syndicalism. Both groups are convinced that a ruling elite always controls government. Under industrial capitalism, capitalists and professional managers control government; under centrally planned socialism, government is in the grip of an enormous bureaucracy. Anarchists and syndicalists believe that governments monopolize and institutionalize violence through imperialistic wars and police brutality. Hence, both groups would do away with the twin evils of corporate capitalism and the state.

Anarchism

Anarchists are popularly stereotyped as wild-eyed bomb-throwers, but a little research reveals that their philosophy derives from the view that without government, worldwide violence and exploitation would be reduced.

Philosophical **anarchism** *counts on cooperation among people to ensure social harmony in the absence of government or law.*

Anarchists are not necessarily opposed to the market system, but view modern capitalism as a system in which professional corporate managers and government officials are in cahoots to exploit workers. Corporations exist only because of government recognition. In an idealized anarchy, the rights to what individuals produce could not be "stolen" by capitalists who rely on government to legitimize their exploitation of workers. Most anarchists would recognize private property rights and disavow social ownership of anything. In this position, anarchism is closer to libertarianism than to socialism.

But how might government be eradicated? Answers to this question range from pacifism to bloody revolution. William Godfrey, an English clergyman, and the Russian Prince Kropotkin thought that if we all just ignored government, it would dry up and blow away. The image of anarchists as bomb throwers originated with Mikhail Bakunin, who convinced his followers that random violence could precipitate the collapse of governments and capitalism. Instead, widespread fear of violence brought anarchism a lasting disrepute when his followers began throwing bombs a century ago.

Syndicalism

Many of the socialist reformers described in the next section have faith that their goals can be achieved peacefully through the ballot box. Syndicalists disagree, viewing the state as an oppressive vehicle manipulated by power hungry plutocrats. Syndicalism was the brainchild of the French philosopher Georges Sorel (1847–1922), who viewed stupid wars, corruption, and gross mismanagement as inevitable consequences of government.

Syndicalism *echoes anarchism in demanding the abolition of both the state and corporate capitalism. Syndicalism resembles socialism in that private ownership of nonhuman resources would be abolished; each industry would be owned by its workers and run by elected worker committees. Society would be reorganized into* **syndicates,** *which are, effectively, industrywide trade unions.*

Thus, there would be an auto syndicate, a steel syndicate, an electronics syndicate, and so on. Syndicates would replace government and control the workplace, but would leave people alone in all other matters.

Syndicalism arrived in the United States in 1905 with the founding of the Industrial Workers of the World (IWW) by Daniel Deleon, Eugene V. Debs, and "Big Bill" Haywood, all of whom are legends in the history of American radicalism. Debs collected over a million votes as the Socialist candidate for president during World War I, even though he had been jailed for sedition by then President Woodrow Wilson.

IWW members, known as *wobblies,* grew in numbers to more than 100,000 before World War I. They intended to overthrow capitalism by locking out managers and seizing factories. The IWW was especially powerful among Western miners, railroad workers, and merchant seamen, who participated in more than 150 violent strikes before succumbing to internal strife arising from the lack of a coherent vision of what to do "after the revolution."

Today, syndicalist ideas find expression in Western Europe and North America in "profit sharing" plans and in union demands for voices in managerial decisions. In Eastern Europe, the trend towards decentralized socialism is somewhat syndicalist, Yugoslavia being especially distinguished by "worker-management." *Solidarity,* the organization led by Lech Walesa that has given fits to the Polish government throughout the 1980s, has syndicalist goals.

Evolutionary Socialism

There may be more species of birds than of socialists, but not many.

The unifying theme of **socialism** *is the call for social ownership of all nonhuman factors of production—capital and natural resources.*

This does not necessarily mean that under socialism you would not own your own toothbrush. Ideally, it does mean that land, factories, and all major capital equipment would be held in trust by government so that everyone could share equitably in national income.

Within the socialist camp, there are schisms about the best path to socialism, how far social ownership should extend, and which groups should make social and economic decisions. Some socialists believe that socialism will evolve democratically through the ballot box. Others insist capitalists control political processes, leaving violent revolution as the only way to institute socialist goals. The most conspicuous of these are *communists,* who have tried to adapt the ideas of Karl Marx to the more complex circumstances of the twentieth century. Much of the world's population now finds itself governed by Marxists of one breed or another. Before we explore Marxism, we will briefly outline other forms of socialism.

Utopian Socialism

Dreamers who have sought to improve our imperfect world are scattered across the pages of history. Sir Thomas More (1478–1535), a saint and martyr of the Catholic Church who served as an advisor to England's Henry VIII, was one such dreamer. More's famous book, *Utopia,* borrowed a Greek word meaning "no place." Today, *utopian* commonly refers to unrealistic ideals. More blamed poverty, waste, and avarice on private property, and proposed the creation of "Utopia," where everyone would share everything.

> **Utopian socialism** *is the idea that if all property were owned collectively, greed would vanish, social policies would be democratic, and opportunities for cultural enrichment and personal growth would abound.*

People would work for the common good in jobs of their choice. Prices would be superfluous because there would be as much joy from giving as from receiving; supplying and demanding would be equally satisfying.

More's ideas were largely ignored until early in the nineteenth century, when social ferment and the prospect of revolution swept Europe. Utopian socialism bloomed. Prominent utopians of this period included the French philosopher Charles Fourier (1772–1837) and the philanthropist Robert Owen (1771–1858). Owen, though born into poverty, became wealthy as a Scottish cotton mill owner while still in his twenties. Infatuated with the utopian vision, he financed several self-contained, communally-owned villages in Scotland and the United States. Neat rows of houses, free education, better working conditions, and wages in proportion to hours worked attracted thousands of people to this grand experiment. But all utopian communities of this period were (predictably?) poorly managed and uniformly failed.

It seems ironic that many of Owen's dreams have been integrated into public policies in most mixed economies in Western Europe and North America. Free public education, socialized medicine in much of Europe and medical insurance in the United States, healthier working conditions, and substantial parts of our current welfare system are the offspring of the ideas of the utopian socialists.

Fabian Socialism

Founded in England in 1884, the **Fabian Society** abandoned the ideal of small communities, urging instead nationalization of heavy industry and municipal ownership of public utilities. Otherwise, their agenda echoed reforms proposed by utopian socialists: laws forbidding child labor, limiting working hours for women, providing free education and medical care, redistributing wealth, guaranteeing the right to vote, and ensuring a safe workplace.

The early Fabians included several young intellectuals who later gained prominence: author and playwright George Bernard Shaw, science fiction writer H. G. Wells, economist and historian G. D. H. Cole, and Sidney and Beatrice Webb, a married team of economists. This small band grew and, as it collected members who were active in the British union movement, evolved into the present British Labour party.

Christian Socialism

It is easier for a camel to pass through a needle's eye than for a rich man to enter the Kingdom of Heaven.
—The Gospel of Matthew

Many conservative theologians interpret Christianity as supporting the status quo. The sanctity of private property and the idea that kings rule by "divine right" are among the gospels preached by some orthodox clerics. These clerics cite the scripture to "render unto Caesar that which is Caesar's and unto God that which is God's," to justify existing distributions of wealth, status, and power. In this view, social struggle is a diversion from spiritual development.

The "social gospel" movement, started over a century ago by a group of French Catholic priests who borrowed many of the ideas of Thomas More, reflects a very different view.

Charity, good works, and peaceful social reforms are at the core of **Christian Socialism.**

Repudiating the violence advocated by revolutionary socialists, Christian socialism stresses the dignity of work and favors labor unions. It resembles Fabian socialism in its goals, even though most Fabians were atheists or agnostics.

Pope Leo XIII and Pope Pius XI affirmed Catholicism's support for the "social gospel." Pope John Paul II followed in this tradition when he denounced revolution but urged labor reforms and supported the Polish "Solidarity" movement. Protestant theologians who were Christian socialists included Paul Tillich and Reinhold Niebuhr. The "social gospel" remains a powerful force within the World Council of Churches, as a mainspring of the ecumenical movement, and in church related social programs.

An offshoot of this movement is the "liberation theology" espoused by radical South American priests who advocate violent revolution to overthrow repressive governments. This philosophy blends Christianity with elements of Marxism, but it is opposed by more conventional Christian socialists, while most Marxists view liberation theology as a refusal to recognize reality.

Marxism: Revolutionary Socialism

The history of . . . society is the history of class struggles.
—Karl Marx

Few people have left footprints on history comparable to those of Karl Marx. In the century following his death, more than one-third of humanity has come to be governed by professed Marxists.

A central tenet of **Marxism** *is the idea that capitalism will be replaced by socialism only after a violent revolution.*

History as Economic Dialectics

Marx extended economic analysis far beyond the realms studied by most economists. Marxists believe that all of history can be interpreted as resolutions to *contradictions* emerging from the competing interests of people in different economic classes. These interpretations are rooted in *dialectical* analysis, a method originated by the German idealist philosopher, Georg Hegel.

According to Hegelian dialectics, every concept or **thesis** has meaning only when pitted against its opposite, or **antithesis.** Thus, the idea of *long* means nothing unless contrasted with its antithesis, the idea of *short,* and *rich* means nothing without *poor.* Interactions between a thesis and its antithesis yield a **synthesis,** which advances our understanding of an ever-changing reality. Thus, the notions of long and short synthesize into the concept of *distance,* and rich and poor yield the concepts of *income* and *wealth.* These syntheses advance our understanding of the world and of the human condition. Hegel believed that historical changes were dominated by dialectical changes in ideas that yielded more accurate perception.

Marx rejected as irrelevant the Hegelian focus on ideas, instead insisting that history unfolds through dialectical processes among economic interests—the material world holds the keys to historical change. This is why Marxism is sometimes called **dialectical materialism.** If cause and effect relationships embedded in the dialectical process never change, then precise explanations of the past permit perfect predictions about the future.

Marx believed he had discovered the fundamental laws of history in the perception that all social and cultural changes are determined by juxtaposing thesis and antithesis in the ways we produce, exchange, distribute, and consume goods. These "contradictions" (from the Marxist jargon) are rooted in conflicts between different socio-economic groups, or classes.

According to Marxists, **class warfare** *is an inevitable step in the historical process that facilitates economic progress.*

For example, the Marxist view of the Industrial Revolution is that it pitted an aggressive new class of manufacturers against vested agricultural interests throughout Europe, but especially in England. The ascendance of industrialization led to entirely new government policies, including a resurgence of British imperialism. Laws were adopted that evicted most peasants from their land so that they were forced to work in factories. Exploited workers were then pitted against industrial magnates, whom they would eventually displace during a short but bloody revolution.

BIOGRAPHY

Karl Marx (1818–83)

Marx was a genius . . . the rest of us were talented at best.
—*Friedrich Engels*

During the twentieth century, the ideas of Karl Marx have had a larger impact on human history than have those of nearly any other social philosopher. Marx's thoughts have left indelible marks in a number of academic disciplines, including philosophy, education, psychology, history, and economics. Nevertheless, his major work, *Das Kapital,* must be seen for what he meant it to be, a critical analysis of capitalism as an economic system. Although Marx's was clearly the dominant contribution, virtually all his work was done in collaboration with his friend, Friedrich Engels. Curiously, Engels lived comfortably on his income from owning and managing a factory.

Scholars disagree on the extent to which events in Marx's life colored his thoughts on society, but two characteristics of Marx's personality and experience are prominent. One is that adversity often came his way. For example, although Marx received a Ph.D. in philosophy from the University of Jena, no university would hire him to teach. His inflammatory rhetoric and close association with political radicals deprived him of a stable income and led to his expulsion from Germany. Exile was to play an important role in his life. Later, Marx was also forced by the governments of Belgium and France to leave those countries.

He finally settled his family in England, which was far too tolerant of individual freedoms to expel him. He sporadically tried to eke out a living as a journalist, serving for a time as a foreign correspondent to the *New York Herald-Tribune.* (Would the course of history have been different if the newspaper had ever given Marx a raise?)

Had it not been for occasional doles from Engels, the entire Marx household might have starved. As it was, they were destitute.

Another factor in Marx's experience was ambivalence. Some have attributed this trait to his parents' conversion to Christianity from Judaism, more for social convenience than from conviction. During adulthood, Marx's dual commitment to scholarly understanding and political action created constant difficulties for him. He knew that his passion for reading and studying interfered with his political activism. At the same time, his political zeal crept into his scholarship, so that his writings contained frequent partisan outbursts and scathing condemnations of class interests.

Despite these characteristics, or perhaps because of them, Marx left a lasting mark on the world. His originality as a social thinker lies in an ambitious attempt to synthesize all social knowledge since the time of Aristotle. Marx wanted to achieve a better understanding of the conditions of human development so that the process by which humanity moves to the highest stage of development might be accelerated. His vision of this ultimate society, dimly sketched, was that of a communist system based on rational planning, cooperative production, and equality of distribution. Above all, it was to be a society liberated from all political and bureaucratic hierarchies.

Those societies that we call Marxist today score very poorly on this last point, but for Marx the "withering away of the state" was critical. Perhaps the tendency of his followers to compromise on this matter was what led Marx to declare on his deathbed, "I am not a Marxist."

Marx viewed this sequence as inevitable. In dialectical terms, thesis (feudal agricultural interests) met antithesis (industrial entrepreneurs—the *bourgeoisie*), leading to synthesis (the triumph of industrialization) within which there was a contradiction (wretchedness of the working masses). This synthesis became the new thesis (industrial capitalism), which, in confronting its antithesis (workers, known as *proletarians,* resent exploitation), leads to a new synthesis (the *dictatorship of the proletariat*).

In Marxist analysis, each stage of economic development is necessary, and collapses only when it reaches maximum efficiency, paralleling the larvae-pupae-cocoon-adult maturation of a butterfly. Thus, Marxists declare that "capitalism contains the seeds of its own destruction." But why should the chain of events leading to the overthrow of capitalism be inevitable? Answering this question requires digging a bit deeper into Marxist doctrine.

Wages and Value

What makes something valuable? Most modern economists use market supplies and demands to explain the relative prices of goods. Marxists view this approach as superficial and argue that a good's value is proportional to the labor socially necessary for its production. For example, if golf balls require twice the labor needed to produce ballpoint pens, then balls are worth twice as much as pens. This *labor theory of value* was the standard explanation of prices from the time of John Locke until late in the nineteenth century.

But what is "socially necessary labor," and what about the roles land and capital play in production? Marx defined *socially necessary labor* to include not only direct labor time, but also the labor used to construct factories and to produce the equipment used in production. Marxists view all commodities and capital as *embodied* labor. Thus, production that uses up capital simply transforms the labor embodied in capital into a different form of congealed labor.

Interestingly, Marxists perceive only "hands-on" working time as labor. Service workers and pencil pushers are not regarded as providing real labor. (Adam Smith had similar reservations about managers and service workers.) Nor is all hands-on work socially necessary. For example, if you make mud pies that no one wants, your labor is not socially necessary. The labor theory of value is basically a supply approach, but by specifying that only "socially necessary labor" counts, Marxists bring demand in through the back door.

If prices are proportional to the amounts of direct and embodied labor in products, what determines wages? Karl Marx relied on the *subsistence theory of wages* developed by earlier thinkers to answer this question. This theory holds that wages will barely be adequate for biological needs, with minor adjustments to meet the social and customary needs of workers. Unlike most classical economists, Marx believed that unemployment, not population pressures, forces wages toward subsistence levels. When workers produce more than is required to meet a payroll, capitalists are able to exploit workers by paying them less than the value of their production. These differences are termed *surplus values* in the Marxist idiom. Marxists view all payments of interest, rent, and profits as surplus value.

Surplus Value and Capital Accumulation

According to Marxist dogma, people in mature industrial societies are divided into two basic classes: *capitalists* and workers. Workers, also known as the *proletariat,* own nothing but their own labor. Capitalists control working conditions and hours. A "reserve army of the unemployed" will take the jobs of workers unwilling to accept the working conditions laid down by capitalists. Competition from this surplus labor compels workers to accept subsistence wages. By setting longer working hours than those necessary to cover the subsistence wage, capitalists "appropriate" surplus values from workers. For example, if a worker can produce the subsistence wage in 5 hours but is forced to work 10 hours, a capitalist employer can appropriate surplus value equal to 5 hours of labor time.

Workers are unable to save because they only receive subsistence wages. Capitalists, however, receive more than is necessary for their subsistence and convert most of this "stolen" surplus value into the embodied labor known as capital. This exploitation enables capitalists to accumulate capital to protect their privileged positions and to avoid exploitation themselves. (Big fish eat little fish.) Because capital accumulation facilitates economic growth, capitalism is viewed as a necessary stage of development. Once society has accumulated sufficient capital, however, the capitalist "robber barons" are dinosaurs on their way to extinction.

Class Warfare

The proletarians have nothing to lose but their chains. They have a world to win. Workingmen of all countries unite!
—Karl Marx and Friedrich Engels
The Communist Manifesto, (*1848*)

Marxists view ever greater capital accumulation as an inevitable result of competition among capitalists for surplus values. Marx believed that capitalism was plagued by a number of contradictions. Concentrated wealth creates one contradiction. Who will buy the goods produced with growing stocks of congealed labor? Workers can afford little from their subsistence wages, while capitalists spend far less than the surplus values they appropriate as their incomes. This leads to "underconsumption" and declining rates of profit. In Marxist theory, this contradiction yields capitalist business cycles.

Marxists believe that capitalism is dynamically unstable. This means that each cyclical decline will be worse than the previous one, while successive economic booms accelerate at unsustainable rates. This occurs, according to Marx, because some capitalists will be wiped out during each depression and will be forced to join the proletariat. Thus, capital will be controlled by a shrinking pool of entrepreneurs. The final stage predicted by Marxists, *monopolistic finance capital,* involves an incredible concentration of economic power held by financial trusts. During this stage, imperialist wars rage among capitalist nations. Finally, massive unemployment will trigger short but violent revolutions during which workers will seize control over the resources stolen from them over many generations.

Marxist Predictions

The works of Marx and his collaborator, Engels, were written over a century ago. At that time, the evils of the factory system seemed blatant, and the aroma of revolution wafted throughout Europe. Marx and Engels were far from alone in predicting revolutions to overthrow the existing order. Their "dialectical materialism" did, however, generate several specific predictions about the road to revolution:

1. ever-greater unemployment and immiseration of workers;
2. declining rates of profit;
3. explosive business cycles;
4. rising concentrations of economic power;
5. increasingly aggressive imperialistic policies; and
6. bloody revolutions as capitalistic economies reach maturity.

Mature capitalism would fall to communism like rotten fruit. Class struggles would end when the proletariat overthrew capitalists and their middle-class lackeys, the *petit bourgeoisie.* A short "dictatorship of the proletariat" would follow, during which workers would share the full values of production (subsistence wages plus surplus values). Then, government would wither away, as outdated as an adult's baby tooth. Communism would evolve as the final synthesis, characterized by a classless society in which people would live and work under the condition "from each according to ability, to each according to needs." And everyone would live happily ever after. In the end, the communist ideal resembles More's *Utopia.*

Most Marxist predictions seem way off target. Unemployment rates vary over the business cycle but there is no discernible upward trend over the past century, even though growing percentages of the world's people have moved into the industrial labor force. The purchasing power of wages has risen rapidly over time. Are industrial workers increasingly miserable when most have color televisions and paid vacations? As Joan Robinson, a modern Marxist, noted, " 'You have nothing to lose but the prospect of a suburban home and a motor car' would not have been much of a slogan for a revolutionary movement."

Average rates of profit have varied widely over the past century, but there are no discernible long-run trends. Sporadic booms and busts have plagued capitalism, but with decreasing severity during the past half century. Marx was, however, almost alone in correctly predicting greater industrial concentration. Economic power did become more concentrated from 1850 to 1930, but more recent evidence of increased industrial concentration is hard to glean from the data.

Increased roles for government, including the development of the modern welfare state, apparently have placed a safety net under the living standards of the poor, dampened business cycles, and diminished the growth of concentration. Most of the evils of capitalism identified by Marxists have been at least partially cured by the growing role of government in the market system. Marx's assertion that "the state is nothing but the organized collective power of the ruling classes" is almost certainly wrong.

Perhaps the most telling rebuttal of Marxist predictions is that communist revolutions have bypassed most industrialized capitalist nations, occurring instead in feudal agricultural economies. The Soviet Union, China, Cuba, Vietnam, Campuchea, Nicaragua, and other underdeveloped countries have "gone communist." Czechoslovakia and East Germany were industrialized before falling to Marxism, but were conquered or destabilized by wars. Imperialistic wars started by capitalist nations largely ended around the turn of the last century.

Significant imperialism originates mainly from the Soviet Union (the USSR's 1979 offensive in Afghanistan is one example) and Cuba (the Angolan and Ethiopian revolutions were executed in part by Cuban troops). Marxists have pointed to the Vietnam War as evidence of American imperialism, but economic motives for our involvement are hard to find. Marx, referring to Czarist Russia in 1867, asserted: "The policy of Russia is changeless. . . . Its methods . . . may change, but the polar star of its policy—world domination—is a fixed star." It is ironic that one of Marx's few correct prophecies concerns the first country to follow the Marxist path.

One famous Marxist slogan is: "Religion is the opiate of the masses." Paul Samuelson, a Nobel prize winner, has paraphrased this as: "Marxism is the opiate of the Marxists." No matter how brutal some socialist regimens are (for example, the Soviet Union under Stalin or Cambodia under Pol Pot) or how poorly Marxian predictions conform to the world, many Marxists persist in believing that humanity would be better off under worldwide communism.

Have ideal societies been implemented when Marxists have gained control? Marx and Engels wrote thousands of pages on the ultimate collapse of capitalism, but less than a hundred pages hint at specific mechanisms to replace markets. When communist revolutions succeeded in feudal rather than industrialized countries, the new leaders were on their own. Alternatives to markets as ways to answer What? How? and for Whom? had to be invented.

The next section examines the economies of six countries with varying combinations of central planning and market decision making: the USSR, China, France, Sweden, Yugoslavia, and Great Britain.

Alternative Economic Systems

The conditions under which men produce and exchange vary from country to country, and within each country again from generation to generation. Political economy, therefore, cannot be the same for all countries and all historical epochs.

—*Friedrich Engels*

Resource ownership under socialism and capitalism alike implies the right to receive the income generated by the resources and to decide how resources will be used. Ownership is collective in socialist economies, with government acting as trustee over capital and land. Conversely, both ownership of most resources and decision making are largely private in capitalist economies.

Even if ownership is primarily private, however, the government allocates most resources in all wartime economies and under Fascist regimes (Hitler, Mussolini, et al.). Alternatively, ownership may be collective but controlled at industry or local levels, where small groups perform entrepreneurial functions; e.g., syndicalism or decentralized socialism. All these alternative systems have been tried during some period of history.

Central Planning

Most of American business detests the idea of central planning. Ironically, central planning resembles planning within many corporate giants, and central planning bureaucracies are similar to corporate hierarchies.

Central planning *occurs when the government sets wages and prices and specifies output quotas in a detailed way.*

Planning in business firms is geared to maximize profit, but if a government directly controls resources and ignores profits, how does it determine what, how, and for whom to produce? Central planning is the major alternative to a market system. In large, diversified economies, coordinating production and distribution is incredibly difficult, but this has not prevented central planning in the USSR, China, and some of their satellites.

The Soviet Experience   The October Revolution of 1917 was led by Vladimir Ilyich Ulyanov (widely known as Lenin). Under Bolshevik communism, the Soviet economy floundered until the first *Five Year Plan* in 1929 under Iosif Djugashvili (known as Stalin). The Soviet economy averaged annual growth estimated at 4–6 percent between 1929 and 1970, which is especially remarkable when the destruction of Soviet industry during World War II is taken into account. Although Soviet economic growth has faltered in recent years, the economic distortions common under central planning make this early growth even more impressive.

Central planning requires detailed targets for every sector of the economy. After production quotas are set, the Soviet central planning agency, *Gosplan,* must channel some outputs to other industries. For example, coal and iron ore are required for the steel industry to meet its quota. Chaotic coordination was common prior to computers. Even today, production processes often sit idle while waiting for necessary intermediate goods.

Once the central plan is set, responsibility for meeting quotas is left to "enterprise managers" whose income now depends heavily on achieving these quotas. Production quotas are set in specific terms such as product mix, weight, number of units, value, and so on, which are called *success indicators.* Each indicator unfortunately leads to a different type of distortion.

Suppose that you were in charge of nail production and your quota was set in tons of nails. What would be the easiest way to beat your quota? By weight, heavy spikes are easier to produce than small nails. Naturally, if your quota were set in numbers of nails, you would produce lots of tacks. Length? Long skinny nails. Value? Only high priced steel would become nails.

The result is that consumers' needs are poorly met, and most intermediate goods are of inferior quality. Gold filigreed sewing machines that did not work resulted when quotas were set in terms of value. Similarly, quotas for square feet of housing generate warped floors and cracked walls, and required units of clothing invite sloppy sewing on shoddy material. Former Premier Kruschev cited a case where the chandelier quota was expressed in tons. You can imagine what happened. Many failures of central planning occupy warehouse space for years and finally become landfill.

Forecasts that Soviet production would surpass that of the United States by the year 2000 have not been taken seriously since roughly 1970. Central planning's glory years of growth during 1929–65 degenerated to unmet Five Year Plans and general stagnation during the past two decades. Then, Premier Gorbachev's ascendance in 1985 brought a new generation to power. Under the banners of *perestroika* (social and economic reform) and *glasnost* (openness), these younger leaders express increasing willingness to experiment with market forces. Gorbachev and his followers hope a streamlined and efficient economy will permit achieving the primary Marxist goal of greater equity.

Why is the severe misalllocation of central planning relatively rare in market economies? The answer is fairly simple. Managers of capitalist enterprises know that profits require production to be cost efficient and to consist of goods that consumers demand. Otherwise, firms will go bankrupt.

Why have the Soviets historically relied on central planning? Ideology provides part of the answer. Traditional Marxists view the market system as intolerable and central planning as necessary. Another part of the answer is that top planning bureaucrats are reluctant to surrender their political power. But the strongest explanation is that the Soviet Union grew in spite of the inefficiencies that emerge from planning. Table 1 compares the historical growth of the Soviet economy with growth in other major countries.

Why did growth defy the handicap of central planning? Most prices and wages are set within Gosplan.

TABLE 1 *Per Capita GNP for Selected Countries (in Billions of 1985 U.S. Dollars)*

Per Capita GNP, 1985 U.S. Dollars

United States	$16,710
Sweden	10,600
France	9,280
United Kingdom	7,860
USSR	7,400
Yugoslavia	5,600
China	340

Per Capita GNP Growth for Selected Countries

	1961–65	1966–70	1971–75	1976–80	1981–85
United States	3.1	1.9	1.2	2.3	1.4
Sweden	4.5	3.5	2.2	1.0	1.6
France	4.5	4.5	3.2	2.8	.7
United Kingdom	2.5	2.0	2.0	1.7	1.3
USSR	3.1	3.9	2.1	1.4	1.1
Yugoslavia	N/A	N/A	3.5	4.8	.4
China	N/A	5.5	3.3	4.7	8.0

Source: CIA, *Handbook of Economic Statistics*, 1986.

Setting high prices for consumer goods and holding wages down enabled planners to divert vast output to the military and into investment in heavy industry. It seems paradoxical that the surplus values extracted from workers have probably been larger under central planning than in most capitalist economies. During earlier Five Year Plans, massive investment depressed the living standards of most Soviet citizens.

Soviet consumers now enjoy slightly larger pieces of a much larger pie because of these earlier sacrifices, but there are invariably shortages of many goods and surpluses of others because the forces of supply and demand are largely ignored. Moreover, the real costs of most goods far exceed their ruble prices because of time spent acquiring information about availability and then waiting; even high prices and low wages have not curtailed the long lines for goods in which most Soviet adults have spent almost 10 percent of their lives.

The *convergence hypothesis,* first stated in the 1960s by a Soviet economist named Lieberman, suggests that capitalist economies will become increasingly socialistic, while centralized socialism increasingly will rely on market forces. Growing regulation in the United States is cited as evidence of the con-

vergence hypothesis. Soviet *kholkhoz* (private) markets in which most meat and vegetables are traded are increasingly important. In 1988, Premier Gorbachev announced plans to allow greater experimentation with agricultural cooperatives as replacements for state collective farms.

Contrary to Lieberman's hypothesis, however, there is also evidence of divergence. Recent federal deregulation of U.S. business has been paralled in the USSR by crackdowns on "economic crime," which means illegally buying or selling things ranging from blue jeans to cars to industrial machinery. Without the grease of underground capitalism, the Soviet economy might grind to a halt. Our underground economy is probably tiny compared with Soviet underground markets, which have allowed a large number of ruble millionaires to buy their ways into the privileged lifestyles of their country's ruling class.

Marx's dream of a "withering away of the state" turned into the Stalinist nightmare of a rigid bureaucracy controlled by a small clique. Premier Gorbachev is trying to institute sweeping reforms but had achieved only cosmetic changes by 1988. Roberto Michels, an early sociologist, may have explained why with an idea he termed *the iron law of oligarchy.* He observed that British and Italian union leaders jealously guarded their power, that their attempts to retain power commonly required vertical hierarchies of underlings, and that leaders' successors were much like themselves. He theorized that virtually all organizations from local PTAs to the United Nations follow this pattern. Certainly the Soviet leadership has followed this pattern until recently, with one generation of high-living bureaucrats being succeeded by another. Whether the latest generation of Soviet reformers will change this pattern remains to be seen.

The Chinese Experience

When Mao Tse-tung led the Communists to victory in 1949 he imposed a stable but oppressive government on China, which had known little except political turmoil, oppression, and famine for centuries. China's new leaders initially viewed the USSR as a model and imported a host of Soviet policies, including central planning. Even after an ideological schism in the 1950s evolved into general hostility between the two countries, the Peoples' Republic of China remained a strong command economy. In many ways, there was less economic freedom in China than in the USSR. For example, Soviet workers typically had more choices than Chinese workers about their employment.

Mao insisted that "the new man in China" dutifully and selflessly work for the common good rather than personal advancement. He abhorred the use of material incentives to encourage work effort and was hostile towards technical experts and professional managers. Consequently, communal leaders and factory managers were frequently chosen because of loyalty to Maoist principles instead of ability to do the job. According to Mao, the "new Chinese man" should be able to perform every type of work and all work is equally valuable. Thus, China often compounded the inefficiency of central planning with failures to benefit from a specialized work force.

The People's Republic compiled an enviable growth record in spite of these problems, although there were severe downturns when Mao instituted "The Great Leap Forward" from 1958 to 1960 and "The Great Proletarian Cultural Revolution" from 1966 to 1969. During these periods, experts who had managed to get the economy going were purged. These disruptions caused great losses of Chinese production and income.

China has averaged 3–6 percent annual growth since the death of Mao and the ouster of his cohorts. A major reason is that experts and skilled professional managers eventually regained power after each purge. Deng Xiaoping, a practical leader determined to modernize China, began opening the Chinese economy up to market determination of prices and outputs in the 1980s. Central planning is gradually giving way to a decentralized form of socialism, with stress on worker cooperatives. China is also experimenting with allowing ambitious entrepreneurs to open their own small firms.

Although China still officially follows egalitarian policies, party leaders obviously live far more comfortably than the Chinese masses. Lavish parties to entertain visiting foreign dignitaries hint at this luxury. Even so, the distribution of income and wealth may be a bit more equal in China than in capitalist economies or in the Soviet Union. Chinese communism has also nearly eradicated the once common evils of illiteracy, child prostitution, begging, and starvation. Medical care is widely available where once it was unknown. The Chinese are not litterbugs. Unlike many other underdeveloped countries, China is quite sanitary. But the revolution extracted massive costs in human life over a thirty year period, and restrictions on individual freedom are only slowly being phased out.

After Marco Polo visited the court of Kublai Khan, he described China to fifteenth century Europeans as cruel and mysterious. China remains a mystery to Western economists because Chinese statistics are even more misleading and less available than Soviet statistics. As the nation becomes more modernized and open, better information about the Chinese economy should become available.

Decentralized Socialism, Indicative Planning, and Welfare States

Modified capitalism and centrally planned socialism, as practiced respectively in the United States and the Soviet Union, delineate a range of economic systems that leaves a vast middle ground. Private ownership of productive resources may be blended with substantial planning and extensive welfare systems, or social ownership of resources may be combined with market determinations of what is produced and how production occurs. There is actually more economic planning in France, a nominally capitalist country, than in such avowedly Marxist countries as Yugoslavia or Rumania.

France and "Indicative Planning"

Although the French economy is primarily capitalistic, it uses planning far more than other modern Western economies.

> In a system of **indicative planning,** *leaders of government, industry, and labor unions meet regularly to exchange information and to negotiate targets for industrial production.*

The French use this process to try to avoid specific shortages, surpluses, and production "bottlenecks." For example, if housing is expected to boom, the lumber and brick industries are alerted, and construction unions are asked to step up their apprenticeship programs. A bumper crop of superior wines might cue officials to negotiate for reduced foreign tariffs on French exports.

The French government also has tight controls on investment. By setting up plans to coordinate economic activities, it normally secures voluntary compliance to the overall plan. When specific unions or industries fail to comply, however, the government has shown little reluctance about using sanctions and price controls. Government is very significant in the French economy, collecting 2 francs in taxes out of every 5 francs of GNP.

Planning initially expanded under the administration of Francois Mitterand, elected in 1981. Mitterand nationalized banking as well as some heavy industry. Although the French economy performed very well for a period after the inception of indicative planning, with fairly consistent growth and negligible unemployment from the mid-1950s until the mid-1970s, it faltered even more than most other European economies in the early 1980s. This resulted in a return to greater reliance on markets during 1984–88.

Sweden's Welfare State

Sweden is a typical Scandinavian economy. Severe poverty has been eliminated because the welfare system covers every Swede from the cradle to the grave.

> In modern **welfare states,** *productive resources are largely privately owned, but high taxes and a massive welfare system mean that income is distributed across the society.*

Thus, the Swedish economy has been called "welfare capitalism."

Worker productivity in Sweden is unsurpassed, and per capita income now rivals that in the United States, in spite of reduced incentives that many people consider vital to hard work. Only about 5 percent of Swedish enterprises are government operated. More than 90 percent of all businesses are private; roughly 5 percent operate as producer or consumer cooperatives.

Many Americans view themselves as very heavily taxed, with 30 percent of gross domestic product absorbed by taxes. In Sweden, taxes are nearly half of the country's GNP, the highest tax take of any industrialized capitalist economy. The surprisingly simple tax system relies heavily on a very progressive income tax structure to foot the bill for most social programs.

Swedish prosperity is unquestionably aided by the fact that the nation has avoided major wars for more than a century and that it allocates few resources to national defense. A long history of industrialization has fostered a well developed work ethic. Collective bargaining is widespread, and negotiations between unions and management have been peaceful.

Worker Management in Yugoslavia

Like many Eastern European countries, Yugoslavia emerged from World War II as a Soviet satellite. Its strong man, Marshall Josip Broz, known as Tito, had an independent streak. Breaking with the USSR in 1950, Yugoslavia abandoned rigid central planning and adopted a system uniquely its own.

This system is very close to syndicalism. Yugoslavia's economy combines social ownership of resources with market determinations of prices and outputs and enterprise management by worker councils. Moderate "indicative planning" is used, with substantial attempts to coordinate the economy through meetings between workers' councils and government officials.

Yugoslavia has experimented with several mechanisms (including price controls) to achieve stable economic growth, but a syndicalist-like fear of "state bureaucratism" has stunted the growth of government. In keeping with classical Marxism, Yugoslavs believe that the onset of socialism should precipitate a "withering away" of the state. In their minds, this erosion cannot begin too soon. Consequently, most economic activity is conducted by 566 small communes, or self-contained government units.

Most economic policies have been adopted in a pragmatic fashion rather than on the basis of pure Marxist theory. Some policies have worked well; others have proved disastrous. Consequently, Yugoslavia has experienced economic swings similar to those in many Western economies that have followed "stop-go" economic policies.

Although still far from a wealthy country, Yugoslavia has developed substantially since World War II, averaging roughly 4 percent annual growth. Whether this syndicalist path will continue will depend on whether the Yugoslavs are able to stay out of the Soviet orbit. Still, the past success of worker management in Yugoslavia has prompted interest in this concept in such diverse economies as the Peoples' Republic of China and Great Britain.

Has the Sun Set on Britain?
Rudyard Kipling's famous line, "The sun never sets on the British Empire," was true when he wrote it at the turn of the century. Since World War I, however, the British Empire's colonies have evolved into only a very loose confederation, and there are now at least a dozen countries that exceed Great Britain as a world power. Mighty civilizations have risen and fallen before, but why did the world's first industrial giant fall by the wayside? Some observers attribute Britain's decline to World War I. Others point to a lack of coherent and consistent economic policy.

Just as the Middle East has spawned many important religions, Great Britain is the birthplace of most of the world's economic systems. Utopian and Fabian socialism, the welfare state, the roots of capitalist ideology, and Keynesian demand management policies all found British soil to be a fertile breeding ground. Marx researched most of the three volumes of *Das Kapital* in the British Museum.

The decline of Britain may have resulted from erratic policies that meandered among the ideas expressed by a variety of economic prophets. From John Locke's writings about private property until World War I, Britain was among the most capitalistic of countries. Then Fabian socialism gave birth to Labour governments that nationalized much of British industry.

Militant unionism and an unwillingness to promote new investment have rendered British industry obsolete. Britain has been reluctant to allow entrepreneurs to pursue the most profitable investments available; instead, political pressures have channeled investment spending towards senile industries. The extensive and expensive British welfare system appears to have caused serious problems for work incentives, while high tax rates and threats of nationalization have dampened new investment and technological innovations.

Highly progressive tax rates, especially on investment income, have stymied entrepreneurship and left English workers using antique technology. But wealth is apparent on London streets. This paradox is explained by the fact that many wealthy English people choose to squander their money on furs and Rolls Royces rather than engage in risky investments from which taxes prohibit much of a rate of return.

Just as the Roman Empire dissolved and Italy emerged, the British Empire has devolved into England. Italy and England have followed similar paths in terms of economic power and international influence. Whether England's downward spiral is halted may be contingent on how well Prime Minister Thatcher succeeds in her announced plans to resurrect the marketplace. Following the supply-side path initiated in the United States by former President Reagan, she is attempting to slash income taxes and stimulate private investment.

Is Small Both Beautiful and Necessary?

Scarcity exists when people want more than is available. There are two basic ways to deal with the problem of scarcity. The first, emphasized in all of the economies we have described and by most economists of both capitalist and socialist persuasions, is to stretch resources as much as possible by maximizing production to try to accommodate human desires. The second approach is to try to reduce human wants to levels consistent with the resources at hand. Those who advocate this second path are opposed to both capitalist and socialist visions of the proper economic system.

One set of critics attack vast material production as an improper goal that leads us away from fulfilling our spiritual needs. These critics focus on inner peace and living in harmony with nature as more appropriate goals. According to them, "small is beautiful." Religious leaders who preach that materialism pits individual against individual and against the divine will are legion. The teachings of E. F. Schumacher, who developed what he calls *Buddhist economics,* are representative of this view.

Other critics of capitalism accept material production as desirable but argue that unchecked capitalism devours depletable resources and will leave nothing for future generations. These critics argue that there are natural *limits to growth* and view environmental despoliation as part of the price we pay for excessive economic development. They fear the onset of a new Dark Age in which human society will have "run out" of everything, and believe that if "small is beautiful," small is also necessary to our survival.

Buddhist Economics

Minimizing human wants is the central thrust of many idealists and religious people who recognize that people have fundamental material needs but who consider color televisions, flashy clothes, and sporty cars as distractions that impede spiritual development. Thus, things that many of us consider necessary for "the good life" are perceived as actually getting in the way of the good life favored by these idealists. Such critics believe that most of our material demands are foisted on us by capitalists who use the demands for their products to cajole people into working forty hours a week or more.

Under a capitalistic system, income, status, and worth depend on work, so we create work by creating artificial demands. Although many religions require their priests to take vows of poverty, certain aspects of Buddhism contain the most elaborate stric-

tures, which assert that the path to nirvana (enlightenment) requires only minimal material comforts. These critics think that socialists have bought the line, "more means better," although the socialist stress on replacing competition with cooperation is at least partly in keeping with the religious values underlying the Buddhist approach.

In a best selling book, *Small Is Beautiful: Economics As If People Mattered,* E. F. Schumacher elaborated the economic ideas of Mohandas Gandhi, who led India to independence from Britain after World War II.[1] Schumacher has referred to these ideas as "Buddhist economics," although they also draw from Hindu teachings.

> *The idea that* **"small is beautiful"** *stresses curbing material want as the key to dealing with scarcity, and emphasizes local self-sufficiency, and small scale, labor-intensive technology.*

Gandhi rejected mass production and the sophisticated technology used in modern industrial states. He recognized that production in isolated villages is inevitably lower than in densely populated cities in which crowds of people work on hectic assembly lines, but felt the benefits of the simple life were well worth the production forgone. Gandhi's philosophy is akin to Buddhism in its emphasis on the spiritual enrichment to human life available, in this case, by avoiding industrialization.

Limits to Growth

In the minds of critics who argue that economic growth must be controlled, the energy crisis of the 1970s and widespread pollution are coupled with computer forecasts that excessive desires for consumer "goodies" will soon deplete the natural resources of "Spaceship Earth." These critics, which include such prominent economists as Kenneth Boulding, argue that capitalism encourages people in developed economies to seek ever higher consumption. In their view, this "cowboy" mentality promotes a disregard for the pollution generated by heavy

---

1. E. F. Schumacher, *Small Is Beautiful: Economics As If People Mattered* (New York: Harper and Row, 1973).

industry and "anti-Earth gas guzzlers" and depletes the minerals, timber, and other resources necessary to sustain future generations.

They point out that known reserves of petroleum, coal, metallic ores, and other finite raw materials are insufficient to allow consumption by the populations of less developed countries to grow to the standards of living enjoyed by people in North America and Western Europe. Moreover, their projections suggest that even without economic growth, if raw materials continue to be depleted at current rates, most will be gone within two or three generations. Their solutions? Get natural, rid ourselves of plastic-oriented mindsets, and just generally scale everything down.

Defenders of capitalism and growth try to rebut these arguments by suggesting that technological advances will permit continued growth, and that automatic changes in relative prices will force us to use natural resources more efficiently as they become scarcer. Moreover, they suggest that we will learn to use raw materials presently seen as worthless as our technology advances. Those who advocate limits to growth are generally pessimistic that technology will bail us out of the difficulties they foresee.

CHAPTER REVIEW: KEY POINTS

1. *Libertarianism* is a philosophy that rejects almost all but the simplest government activities. It strongly advocates laissez-faire capitalism.

2. *Anarchy* is the absence of government. *Syndicalism* is a system in which an industry's workers own the means of production, which are controlled by democratically elected worker councils. Syndicates are effectively trade unions that own their industries.

3. *Socialism* entails eliminating private ownership of nonhuman productive resources, which would be owned collectively.

4. *Marxism* is based on *dialectical materialism,* which suggests that the course of human history is determined by clashes between an economic *thesis* and its *antithesis* that yield a *synthesis,* or progression, for human life.

5. Marxism postulates conflicts between economic classes that emerge from the theft by capitalists of *surplus values,* which are the excesses of production over subsistence wages. These surplus values are translated into accumulations of capital.

6. Marx predicted (*a*) growing wretchedness and unemployment of the working class, (*b*) ever-greater concentrations of capital, (*c*) declining rates of profit, (*d*) explosive business cycles, (*e*) increasingly aggressive imperialistic policies, and (*f*) bloody revolutions as capitalist economies reached full maturity. In most respects, except for the (now slowing) concentration of capital, these predictions seem erroneous.

7. The Soviet Union and the People's Republic of China have used *central planning* extensively, and have managed very high growth rates in their command economies by forcing consumption down in order to raise social saving and investment. These economies have been plagued with inefficiency; great loss of freedom has been just one cost of their rapid economic development. China and the USSR both seem increasingly willing to let market forces operate now that pragmatic new leaders are at the helm.

8. *Indicative planning* is used in France to coordinate the activities of industries, unions, and government. Although not as bureaucratic as Soviet central planning, the French government has used strong legal and economic sanctions to ensure compliance with its plans.

9. Northern European nations such as Sweden have extensive welfare programs financed by heavy tax rates. Industry is largely in private hands, and labor productivity is as high as anywhere in the world.

10. *Worker management* of industry has been used in Yugoslavia, which has rejected Soviet-style central planning in favor of indicative planning. The results of this experiment in syndicalism have been mixed, but have attracted attention.

11. Perhaps the most radical criticisms of capitalism and all economies based on material production assume that the proper solution to scarcity is to curtail our material wants and to simplify the economy as much as possible, even if it requires large losses of production. Somewhat less radical critics argue that there are *limits to growth,* and that we must all learn to live with less.

QUESTIONS FOR THOUGHT AND DISCUSSION

1. People work not only to receive wages and salaries, but also for self-respect, the applause of their peers, and the respect of their neighbors. Many business firms confer impressive sounding titles on their employees, or recognize long service with the proverbial gold watch. Worker heroes in the Soviet Union are awarded "Stakhanovite" medals if they consistently exceed their production quotas. "Self criticism" and plaudits dished out in group therapy sessions shaped the personalities and work habits of Mao's "new man" in China. These are a few of the many techniques that have been tried in attempts to mold or reduce greed as motivation for work. Do you think human beings are inherently self-interested, or are we only conditioned to be greedy? If conditioning explains our greed, are the techniques we have described likely to be successful in reducing or channeling self-interested behavior? Can you think of other techniques that would reduce avaricious behavior? Do you think it would be better if we were all less greedy? Why or why not? How do your answers to these questions relate to the economic system you think operates most efficiently and most compatibly with human welfare?

2. Suppose you were the president of an extremely impoverished country. After reading this chapter, would you choose socialism, capitalism, or some other system as the best path to accomplish economic growth and development? Why?

3. The role of government would be extremely limited if a libertarian became president and if libertarians were elected to majorities in Congress. Assuming that they did not all resign as a means of reducing government, what are some of the institutions or regulations that libertarians would eliminate or modify?

Epilogue

Where do you go from here? A few of you may regret having taken economics; others may feel that the time it took to prepare for this course was well spent, but you have no intention of extending your formal training in economics. Still others may choose to take three or four more courses in this field. We can promise those of you who fit into any of these categories that you will encounter economic concepts repeatedly, regardless of the path your life takes.

But this epilogue is really addressed to those few students who find the analytical methods we use and the problems we tackle so intriguing that you are considering a career as an economist. We are grateful that there are so few of you; otherwise, the supply of economists might be so great that those of us who love economic reasoning would not be able to live comfortably while doing the work we like best. John Maynard Keynes once issued a challenge to aspiring economists that we would like to echo:

> *The study of economics does not seem to require any specialized gifts of an unusual order. Is it not, intellectually regarded, a very easy subject compared with the higher branches of philosophy and pure science? Yet good, or even competent economists are the rarest of birds. An easy subject, at which few excel! The paradox finds its explanation, perhaps, in that the master economist must possess a rare combination of gifts. He must be a mathematician, historian, statesman, philosopher—in some degree. He must understand symbols and speak in words. He must contemplate the particular in terms of the general, and touch abstract and concrete in the same flight of thought. He must study the present in the light of the past for the purposes of the future. No part of man's nature or institutions must lie entirely outside his regard. He must be purposeful and disinterested in a simultaneous mood; as aloof and incorruptible as an artist, yet sometimes as near the earth as a politician.*
>
> —*J. M. Keynes (1924)*

Everyone who wishes to be an economist would do well to pursue the lofty goals implicit in Keynes's description.

Glossary
Name Index
Subject Index

GLOSSARY

Ability to Pay Principle The idea that the rich should pay more taxes than the poor (*See also* Benefit Principle of Taxation.)

Absolute Advantage The early idea that nations should produce the goods for which fewer resources are absorbed than in other countries and exchange their surpluses for goods produced with fewer resources elsewhere; replaced by the Law of Comparative Advantage.

Absolute Price The monetary price of a good. (*See also* Relative Price.)

Administration Lag The period that passes before discretionary changes in macroeconomic policy can be implemented; monetary policy can be implemented quickly through the actions of the FED and its Federal Open Market Committee; fiscal policies entail long administration lags because discretionary changes in taxes or government expenditures require changing the law.

Administrative Costs of Regulation Include the salaries of government workers, inspectors, office supplies, etc. (*See also* Compliance Costs of Government Regulation.)

Adverse Selection Occurs when a party to a contract has been deceived about the qualities it expects to receive from a transaction.

Aggregate Demand Curve The negative relationship that exists between the general price level (P) and the quantity demanded (Q) of total national output.

Aggregate Expenditures The sum of consumption, investment, government purchases, and net exports ($C + I + G + [X - M]$).

Aggregate Expenditures Curve The relationship between Aggregate Expenditures and income; positively sloped because income induces spending. Sometimes known as a Keynesian cross diagram.

Aggregate Supply Curve A positive relationship between real national production (Q) and the absolute price level (P).

Aid to Families with Dependent Children (AFDC) A major program designed to alleviate poverty; originally this program was characterized by a payment structure which provided overwhelming incentives for recipients not to work.

Allocative Mechanisms Alternative modes for a society to use in deciding how inputs will be allocated among competing ends and how incomes and production will be distributed.

Anarchism The idea that government should be eliminated, leaving people largely free to do as they pleased. Anarchists believe that social harmony would evolve naturally through cooperative efforts. Most philosophical anarchists recognize the importance of private property rights and, hence, completely disavow social ownership.

Appreciation of a Currency When the exchange rate (price) of a currency increases as measured by its exchange rates with other currencies.

Arbitrage The risklessly profitable process of buying a good at a lower price in one market and selling the same good at a higher price in another market; forces relative prices of the same good toward equality in all markets.

Artificial Barriers to Entry Significant barriers to entry that are not caused by natural market forces. These barriers are erected by government or by existing firms to exclude competition.

Asset Demand for Money Exists because people (*a*) perceive money as riskless relative to alternative assets, (*b*) confront transaction costs in acquiring other assets that exceed their expected rate of return, and (*c*) expect the prices of alternative assets to fall in the near future.

Automatic (Built-in) Stabilizers Government tax and spending mechanisms that automatically drive the federal budget into deficit when the economy slumps or into a surplus when the economy suffers from inflationary pressures; tends to stabilize economic activity.

Automation Technological advances that replace human labor by machinery.

Autonomous Expenditure Spending unrelated to income; occurs at zero income. Investment, government purchases, net exports, and part of consumer spending are all treated as autonomous in very simple Keynesian models.

Autonomous Spending Multiplier The number which, when multiplied by the sum of the autonomous components of Keynesian Aggregate Spending, yields equilibrium income; in very simple Keynesian models, this multiplier equals the reciprocal of the marginal propensity to save.

Average Fixed Cost (*AFC*) Total fixed cost (*tfc*) per unit of output (*q*); *tfc/q* graphs as a rectangular hyperbola.

Average Physical Product of Labor (*APP$_L$*) Production per worker; equals total output (*q*) divided by labor (*L*); *q/L*.

Average Propensity to Consume (*apc*) The proportion of disposable income that is consumed; *apc* = C/Y_d.

Average Propensity to Save (*aps*) The proportion of disposable income saved; *aps* = S/Y_d.

Average Revenue Revenue per unit of output; synonym for price in the absence of price discrimination; equals total revenue (*TR*) divided by output: *TR/q*.

Average Revenue Product Revenue per unit of an input; is computed by dividing a given total revenue (*TR*) by the amounts of given resources (e.g., workers (*L*)) generating this revenue (e.g., *TR/L*).

Average Total Cost (*ATC*) Total cost incurred per unit of output; often termed *average cost* or *unit cost;* *ATC* = *AVC* + *afc*.

Average Variable Costs (*AVC*) Variable cost per unit of output; equals *TVC/q*. (*See also* Variable Costs).

Bad, Economic Anything the consumption of which decreases human happiness.

Balance of Payments A record of the payments between a country and the countries with which it trades. Balance of payments deficits occur when a country's payments of money to foreigners exceed its receipts from foreigners. A balance of payments surplus occurs when a country's receipts from foreigners exceed its payments to foreigners.

Balance of Trade (Deficit, Surplus) The relationship between a country's annual exports and imports. A deficit in the balance of trade exists when the dollar value of a country's imports exceeds the dollar value of its exports. A surplus in the balance of trade exists when the dollar value of a country's exports exceeds the dollar value of its imports. Differs from balance of payments because foreign investment flows and loans, etc., affect payments.

Barrier to Entry A significant obstacle of some sort that either discourages or prevents the entry of firms into an industry.

Barter Trading goods for other goods rather than money.

Basic Economic Problem A problem of scarcity, which means that fewer goods are freely available than people want to consume.

Basic Economic Questions *What* economic goods will be produced, *when* and *how* will resources be used for which types of production, and *who* will be allowed to use the goods?

Benefit Principle of Taxation The idea that individuals should be taxed in proportion to the marginal benefits that they receive from governmentally provided commodities and services. (*See also* Ability to Pay Principle).

Bilateral Monopoly Occurs when a monopoly supplier confronts a monopsonistic buyer.

Black Market Transactions that violate legal price ceilings.

Blacklisting Circulation by employers of lists to bar hiring of union organizers or other "troublemakers."

Block Pricing Price discrimination for utility rates.

Board of Governors The governing body of the Federal Reserve System. Six regular board members are appointed to staggered 14-year terms of office; the Chair is appointed to a 4-year term.

Bonds Promises by government or corporations to pay certain amounts of money by specific future dates.

Break-Even Point The rate of output at which total revenue equals total cost.

Bretton Woods Agreement (1944) Established both the International Monetary Fund and a fixed exchange rate system with the dollar as the world's key currency. Other nations agreed to peg their currencies to the dollar.

Budget Deficits or **Surpluses** Occur, respectively, when government outlays exceed or fall below government revenues.

Budget Line A line showing various combinations of goods which cost the same amount as the consumer's income.

Bureaucracy A large organization with many employees, called bureaucrats; tends to be governed by many rules and regulations, called red tape.

Business Cycles Alternating periods of expansion and contraction in economic activity.

Business Firms Centers of production, they sell goods in output markets and buy services in resource markets.

Buyers' Market Occurs when the prevailing market price lies above the equilibrium price, resulting in a surplus.

Capital All physical improvements made to natural resources that facilitate production, including buildings and all machinery and equipment.

Capital Deepening When the percentage growth of the capital stock exceeds the growth rate of the labor force; real per capita output normally rises.

Capital Widening When the labor force and capital stock experience similiar percentage rates of growth.

Capitalism An economic system based on private property rights and emphasizing private, as opposed to governmental or collective, decision making. (*See also* Laissez-Faire, Socialism.)

Capitalization The process whereby income streams are transformed into wealth, resulting in the elimination of economic profits.

Cartel An organization of firms that jointly make decisions about prices and production for the entire group, usually attempts to charge monopoly prices and limit production to monopoly rates of output. OPEC is an example.

Caveat Emptor An ancient legal doctrine which suggests that buyers are the best judges of whether or not they receive full value from the goods they purchase, and that buyers should bear the consequences of their own decisions: it means "let the buyer beware."

Caveat Venditor A legal doctrine reflected in prohibitions against fraud and in sellers' legal liability for damages if unknown dangers lurk in a product; a Latin phrase meaning "let the seller beware."

Celler-Kefauver Antimerger Act (1950) This act made it illegal for major firms to acquire the stock or assets of their competitors.

Central Bank An institution whose function it is to make a nation's financial system operate as smoothly as possible; serves as the government's banker.

Central Planning or **Centralized Decision Making** Major economic decisions are made by some central authority, as in the Soviet Union.

Christian Socialism Emphasizes the virtues and dignity of work and advocates labor unionization; rejects the violent means to overthrow capitalism advocated by radical socialists and communists.

Circular Flow Model Depicts how households and business firms interact. Households are centers for wealth holding and consumption, and they buy goods from the firms that produce them; firms buy resources from households in order to produce.

Classical Theory A systematic study of the functioning of a market economy which concluded that, in the long run, the economy would always attain full employment at equilibrium GNP, assuming the validity of Say's Law and flexible wages, prices, and interest rates.

Clayton Act (1914) This act specified particular offenses more precisely than did the Sherman Act (1890); the Clayton Act forbade price discrimination and interlocking directorates, exempted collective bargaining from antitrust actions, and exempted agricultural associations so that nonprofit corporations could be formed without violating antitrust laws.

Closed Shop A firm that has agreed to hire only union members; these agreements are illegal under the Taft-Hartley Act.

Coincident Indicators Data series that tend to reach their high points or low points approximately at the same time as aggregate economic activity reaches its high points and low points.

Collective Bargaining The process by which workers who are members of a labor union negotiate with an employer to set wages, hours, and working conditions.

Command Economy These economic systems resolve the basic economic questions through central planning; allocations of inputs and distributions of goods are coordinated by a bureaucracy.

Commodity Any tangible produced good that may be owned.

Commodity Money Has substantial value independently of what it will buy. Gold and silver coins are examples.

Common Stock Ownership shares in a corporation.

Communism An idealized classless society in which all people would live and work under the condition "from each according to ability, to each according to needs"; under communism, all nonhuman property would be owned collectively.

Comparable Worth The idea that jobs typically filled by women should generate wages equal to those paid to men with comparable skills.

Comparative Advantage, Law of The idea that mutually beneficial trade can always take place between two countries (or individuals) whose pre-trade costs and price structures differ.

Competition A process driving price close to opportunity cost. Pure competition requires (*a*) numerous potential buyers and sellers; (*b*) homogeneous outputs or inputs, precluding nonprice competition; (*c*) each buyer and seller to be small relative to the market so that no single decision will influence the price of the item or service; and (*d*) an absence of long run barriers to entry or to exit. (*See also* Contestable Markets Theory.)

Complementary Goods Goods that are consumed together, such as tennis racquets and tennis balls; a negative cross-price elasticity of demand exists between complementary goods.

Compliance Costs of Government Regulation Costs incurred mainly by the private sector (and also by state and local governments) in the process of complying with regulations. (*See also* Administrative Costs of Regulation.)

Concentration Ratio The percentage of some aspect of market power (e.g., sales) wielded by the leading four or eight firms in an industry.

Conglomerate A firm that operates in several different industries.

Constant Cost Industry The long-run industry supply curve is horizontal; constant per unit production costs are incurred for every output level because the supplies of all the resources used are perfectly price elastic.

Consumer Equilibrium (the Cardinal Utility Approach) A consumer maximizes total utility when the last cents spent on each good yield the same number of utils of satisfaction; no reallocation of spending will increase total utility.

Consumer Equilibrium (the Indifference Curve Approach) Consumers maximize satisfaction upon reaching tangency between their budget constraint lines and the highest attainable indifference curves.

Consumer Price Index (*CPI*) A statistical comparison, over time, in the prices of goods bought by typical urban consumers; the base year equals 100, with subsequent changes in the price level reflecting inflation (over 100) or deflation (under 100).

Consumer Surplus A gain to consumers arising from differences between the amounts of money they would willingly pay to consume goods and the amounts that they must pay in order to consume the good; the area below their demand curves but above the price line.

Consumption Spending by households for goods used to gratify human wants; the major component of Aggregate Demand.

Contestable Markets Theory Suggests that all advantages of pure competition as a market structure are realized if freedom of entry and exit exists, and that the number of firms currently in a market is less important for efficiency than the threat of potential new entrants. (*See also* Competition.)

Contraction (Recession) A decline in economic activity; unemployment and inventories rise unexpectedly.

Contribution Standard The idea that income should be distributed according to the productivity of one's resources.

Corporation An organization formed under state law that is considered a legal person distinct and separate from its owners.

Cost-Push Inflation Upward price level movements that originate on the supply side of the economy; cost-push cycles of inflation generate clockwise adjustment paths of inflation versus real output.

Costs of Unemployment, Economic Include the opportunity costs of the output unemployed workers could have produced were they employed.

Credit A promise to pay at some future date is exchanged for money.

Cross Elasticity of Demand A measure of the responsiveness of the quantity demanded of one good to changes in the price of another; computed by dividing the percentage change in quantity demanded of a good by the percentage change in price of another good: $\%\Delta Q_x/\%\Delta P_y$; positive for substitute goods, but negative for complementary goods.

Crowding-Out Hypothesis The idea that increases in governmental spending inevitably cause reductions in private consumption or investment.

Crude Quantity Theory of Money A monetary theory that the price level is exactly proportional to the nominal money supply (*M*).

Currency Coins and paper money.

Cyclical Deficit The difference between government revenues and outlays that emerges because the macroeconomy is operating below its potential. (*See also* Structural Deficit.)

Cyclical Unemployment Unemployment that results from a recession.

Decentralized Decision Making When most decisions about what to produce, when and how to produce, and who gets to use output are determined in private markets.

Decentralized Socialism Economic systems characterized by social ownership of resources, but which rely on markets to resolve the economic problem by setting equilibrium prices and quantities.

Decrease in Demand An entire demand curve shifting downward and to the left; occurs only if one or more of the nonprice determinants of demand change. Less will be purchased at each possible price.

Decrease in Supply The entire supply curve shifts to the left; occurs only if one of the nonprice determinants of supply changes so that less will be available at each possible price.

Decreasing Cost Industry An industry for which the long-run supply curve is negatively sloped, reflecting declines in per unit costs as production in the industry increases.

Deflating The use of a price index to adjust monetary values for changes that occur to the price level over time.

Deflationary Gap (*See also* Recessionary Gap.)

Demand Purchases of a good that people are actually willing and able to make, given the prices and choices available to them.

Demand Curve A graph of the maximum quantities of a good that people are willing to purchase at various market prices.

Demand Deposits Funds kept in a financial institution that by law must be available upon the depositor's demand; checking accounts.

Demand, Law of The quantity demanded of an economic good varies inversely with its price.

Demand Price The highest price that buyers are willing and able to pay for a specific amount of a good or resource. Also known as subjective price. (*See also* Supply Price.)

Demand Schedule A table reflecting the maximum quantities of a given good or resource that will be purchased at various market prices.

Demand-Side or **Demand-Pull Inflation** Hikes in the general price level that originate on the demand side of the economy; caused by either excessively rapid increases in the rate of growth of the nominal money supply or upward shifts in autonomous real expenditure schedules; demand-pull inflation generates a counterclockwise adjustment path of inflation versus real output.

Depreciation The amount of capital used up during a period. Also known as the capital consumption allowance.

Depreciation of a Currency A decrease in the value of one currency measured in terms of its exchange rates with other currencies.

Depression A sharp and sustained decline in business activity.

Derived Demand The demand for a resource that exists because of its productivity; resource demands are derived from demands for output.

Devaluation of a Currency Occurs when exchange rates are either "pegged" or fixed under a gold standard and some government decides to decrease the gold content of its currency; not synonymous with depreciation of currency.

Development, Economic Qualitative changes in an economic system; economic development occurs when there are improvements in either the quality of life or the quality of goods, or both.

Dialectical Materialism Karl Marx's explanation of historical change; all massive social and cultural changes are determined by contradictions that exist in the ways that societies produce, exchange, distribute, and consume goods; for the most part, these contradictions are embedded in conflicts that exist between the different classes in society.

Diminishing Marginal Returns, Law of When additional equal units of a variable input are applied to fixed inputs, a point is inevitably reached where total output increases at a diminishing rate; diminishing marginal returns are pervasive even in the long run because it is virtually impossible to vary all of the influences on production both proportionally and simultaneously.

Diminishing Marginal Utility, Principle of Consumption of successive units of a good eventually causes an additional unit of the good to yield less extra satisfaction than that of the preceding unit.

Diminishing Returns, Law of The further any activity is extended, the more difficult (and costly) it is to extend it further.

Dirty Float Occurs when governments intervene in a "floating" foreign exchange market to stabilize exchange rates.

Discount Rate (d) The interest rate that the FED charges member banks when they borrow money from FED "discount windows."

Discretionary Fiscal Policy Deliberate changes in government spending and tax policies for economic stabilization purposes.

Discrimination, Economic Occurs when equivalent units of a resource receive different rates of remuneration even though their potential marginal contributions to total output are the same.

Diseconomies of Scale A firm's average costs rise as output rises.

Disequilibrium When the forces for change in a system are not in balance.

Disincentives Penalties that discourage an activity; often applied to government policies that discourage productive activities.

Disinflation A significant decrease in the rate of inflation, this normally creates pressures for recessions.

Disposable Personal Income (DPI) The after-tax income households receive in a given year; equals consumption plus saving ($C + S$).

Dissaving Negative saving; occurs when desired consumption exceeds income; families go in debt or draw down past savings to afford their purchases.

Distortion Costs of Inflation Losses from distorted decisions caused when inflation warps relative prices and reduces certainty.

Distribution Branch The government arm in Musgrave's framework that would ensure equity; would tax and transfer to attain proper income distribution.

Divestiture When court orders require large corporations to break down into smaller independent companies.

Division of Labor Specialization of labor by task, e.g., when one person designs a computer program, another writes the computer code, a third "debugs" the program, a fourth writes the user manual, a fifth copies the program to diskettes, a sixth packages and ships the programs, and so on.

Double Coincidence of Wants A requirement of barter that you must locate someone who has what you want and who wants what you have to trade.

Dumping When a country sells an export for less than the price charged domestically for the same good; might result from international price discrimination, which is a policy of charging desperate domestic buyers more than indifferent foreign buyers; predatory dumping occurs when a country tries to drive competitors out of a market to establish a monopoly.

Durable Goods Consumer goods that are useful for more than one year.

Economic Growth Quantitative change in an economic system; occurs when a society acquires greater productive capacity that can be used for consumption or investment.

Economic Incidence of a Tax The final burden of a tax; that is, who actually pays the tax through lower purchasing power.

Economic (Capital) Investment Purchases of new output that can be used for further production. The four basic types of new capital are (a) new business structures; (b) new residential structures; (c) new machinery and equipment; and (d) inventory accumulation.

Economic Profits The excess of revenues over the opportunity costs of the resources employed; these profits are a reward to an entrepreneur if they exceed the minimum necessary to continue the firm's existence and are a premium for risk bearing and innovating.

Economic Rent Surpluses reaped by owners of a resource if it is paid more than the minimum necessary to elicit the supply of the resource.

Economics The study of how individuals and societies allocate their limited resources in attempts to satisfy their unlimited wants.

Economies of Scale When long-run average costs fall as output rises.

Economies of Scope Cost savings realized because certain types of production are complementary.

Efficiency, Economic Occurs when the opportunity cost of some specific amount of a good is at its lowest possible value, and when maximum production from given resources and costs is achieved; implies that gains to anyone entail losses to someone else.

Efficient Markets Theory The idea that all possible gains that are foreseeable will be exploited by private individuals.

Elasticity The sensitivity of one variable relative to some other variable. (*See also* Income Elasticity of Demand, Price Elasticity of Demand (or Supply).)

Eminent Domain Government's legal right to acquire property without the previous owner agreeing to the price government pays.

Empire Building Exaggerating the difficulty of the mission of a bureaucracy so that the budget of the agency will be expanded.

Employment Act of 1946 Established the Council of Economic Advisors and set priorities of full employment with price level stability, but provided few directives to the executive branch about how to achieve such goals.

Employment Discrimination Occurs when particular groups suffer more unemployment than do other groups.

Entrepreneurship The organizing function which combines the services provided by other resources so that goods are produced.

Entry and Exit into an Industry If there are no barriers to entry and exit, entry into an industry by outside competitors or exit of existing firms will continue until economic profits are zero; positive profits will attract new entrants, while economic losses will cause exit from an industry. Potential entry is crucial for competition and the key to "contestable" markets theory.

Equal Distribution of Income Standard One ethical criterion for distributing income and wealth; assumes that an extra dollar means more to the poor than to the rich, and ignores the disincentives for production that occur when incomes are independent of productivity.

Equal Marginal Advantage, Law of Efficiency requires similar resources to be used in equally advantageous ways. In consumption, this means that the last cent spent on any good must generate the same satisfaction as the last cent spent on any other good. In production, the last cent spent on any resource must yield the same production as the last cent spent on any other resource.

Equal Marginal Productivities per Dollar, Principle of The last few cents spent on any resource must yield the same additional output as the last few cents spent on any other resource. This is a requirement for least cost production and maximum profit.

Equal Marginal Utilities per Dollar, Principle of The last few cents spent on any good yield identical amounts of satisfaction or utility; algebraically, this requires $MU_1/P_1 = MU_2/P_2 = \ldots = MU_m/P_m$, where the subscripts 1 through $m-1$ denote commodities and m denotes money.

Equation of Exchange $MV = PQ$ Where M denotes the nominal money supply, V denotes the income velocity of money, P denotes an index for the general price level, and Q denotes real output; a tautology, since it is true by definition.

Equilibrium Exists when the pressures that bring about change in the market system are in balance. Macroeconomic equilibrium—when desired demand expenditure equals actual income or output. Micro-

economic equilibrium—when the quantities of a good or resource demanded and supplied are equal.

Equilibrium (Market-Clearing) Price The market price that clears the market.

Equilibrium Quantity The quantity of a good marketed at the equilibrium price.

Equity Fairness, a normative concept; value judgments are inherent in specifying what is fair.

Escalator Clauses Contractual obligations specifying that future payments of money will be adjusted for price level changes.

Excess Burdens of a Tax The amounts by which the total burden of a tax exceeds government revenue yielded by the tax.

Excess Demand The amount by which the quantity demanded exceeds the quantity supplied when the prevailing market price lies below the market-clearing price; normally associated with shortages.

Excess Reserves (XR) The amounts by which banks' legal (total) reserves exceed their required reserves.

Excess Supply The amount by which the quantity supplied exceeds the quantity demanded when the prevailing market price lies above the market-clearing price; normally associated with surpluses.

Exchange Controls Legal limits on the ability to buy or sell foreign currencies; frequently stimulate black markets for foreign money.

Exchange Rate The value of one currency expressed in terms of another currency, or some combination of other currencies.

Excise Tax A per unit tax that is levied on a specific good.

Exclusive Good A good is exclusive if individuals can be excluded from access to the good at a relatively low cost; if these people do not pay, they may be excluded from consuming the good.

Expansion (Recovery) The phase of the business cycle when economic activity begins to increase; employment rises, and inventories fall unexpectedly.

Expected Rate of Inflation The percentage annual rate at which economic transactors expect the general price level to rise.

Expenditure Approach to Estimating GNP GNP equals the sum of personal consumption, investment, government purchases of commodities and services, and net exports: $GNP = C + I + G + (X - M)$.

Explicit Costs Outlays of money to individuals or firms that are external to the producer; some examples are wages paid employees, rent payments, utility bills, and purchases of intermediate goods.

Exploitation Payment of wages that are less than the value of the marginal product of labor. May result from an employer's monopsony power as a hirer of labor, or because a firm has monopoly power.

Exports Goods manufactured in this country and purchased by foreigners.

External Supply Shocks These shocks, which originate outside the economy, shift the Aggregate Supply curve to the left; rising production costs create pressures for supply-side (cost-push) inflation and increasing unemployment.

Externalities Market failures that occur whenever some activity affects economic transactors who are not directly involved in the activity. Pollution is an example of a negative externality; education generates positive externalities to the extent that all of society gains from being a part of a more educated populace. External costs and benefits are largely ignored by individual decision makers.

Fabian Socialism This socialist theory advocates nationalizing only heavy industry; all other property would be privately owned, although extensive welfare programs would ensure that people's needs were met.

Family Allowance Plan (*FAP*) Many European countries now have family allowance plans that are based on the number of minor children in each family; these payments are usually adequate to feed and to clothe each child in the family and are made regardless of a family's level of income.

Featherbedding The employment of workers who are not in productive jobs; normally a result of union pressure or inefficient government regulation.

Federal Funds Market A privately operated network that enables banks to borrow or lend large amounts of money for very short periods.

Federal Open Market Committee (FOMC) The policy-making body within the Federal Reserve System.

Federal Reserve System (FED) Central bank of the United States; created by Congress in 1913 to buffer financial crises by acting as a bankers' bank and lender of last resort; the FED's primary role is conducting monetary policy.

Federal Trade Commission (FTC) Act (1914) Created the FTC and empowered it to challenge any "unfair methods of competition . . . , and unfair or deceptive acts or practices in or affecting commerce."

Fiat Money Money that is worthless as a commodity and which has value only because of its use as a medium of exchange.

Final Goods Goods bought by the consumers or investors who ultimately use them.

Financial Capital Securities; paper claims to goods or resources.

Financial Intermediation The process by which household saving is made available through financial institutions to those desiring to spend in excess of their income (especially investors).

Financial Investment Paper documents representing financial claims on assets; created when purchases of stocks, bonds, and real estate are made.

Fine-Tuning Government attempts to make the economy function as smoothly as possible by frequently changing both monetary and fiscal policies to offset even minor fluctuations in economic activity.

Firm An entity that operates one or more plants and which buys productive resources from households.

Fiscal Drag A tendency to generate budget surpluses in a growing economy, assuming that government spending and tax rates remain unchanged; arising because of our progressive income tax, fiscal drag retards growth of Aggregate Demand.

Fiscal Policy Policies for government spending or setting tax rates or revenues to either stimulate or contract economic activity; intended to offset cyclical fluctuations in economic activity.

Fisher Effect Adjustments of nominal interest rates as borrowers and lenders compensate for expected inflation in order to secure some equilibrium "real" rate of interest.

Fixed Costs The total of all costs not related to the level of production; fixed costs are also known as historical, sunk, or overhead costs, and are irrelevant for rational decision making.

Fixed Exchange Rates A system in which international agreements set the values of all currencies in terms of one another; the exchange rates of currencies are not allowed to respond to changes in the relative supplies and demands for the currencies; balance of payments surpluses and deficits occur in a fixed exchange rate system when equilibrium exchange rates differ from the fixed (pegged) exchange rates and can be eliminated only through adjustments of Aggregate Demands or Aggregate Supplies.

Flexible (Floating) Exchange Rates The major alternative to a system of fixed exchange rates; under this exchange rate system, markets for individual currencies determine their equilibrium and actual exchange rates.

Flexible Wages, Prices, and Interest Rates According to classical theory, full employment was guaranteed by the existence of perfectly flexible wages, prices, and interest rates (*See also* Say's Law.)

Flow Variable An economic variable that is only meaningful if measured over a period of time; income and production are examples.

Foreign Exchange A stock of foreign currencies held as an asset.

Forward (Futures) Markets Markets in which contracts to deliver currencies or products at some future date are bought and sold.

Fractional Reserve Banking System A banking system in which banks are legally required to hold only a fraction of their demand deposit liabilities in the form of reserves.

Free Enterprise System Agreements to trade are made by private buyers and sellers; ownership of resources is private, not social.

Free Good A good for which the quantity demanded fails to exceed the quantity available at a price of zero.

Free-Rider Problem Encountered in the consumption of public goods; refers to the lack of incentives for people to reveal their true preferences for public goods once these goods are provided; nonexclusive goods can be consumed at a zero price by those who contribute nothing to cover their production costs.

Frictional Unemployment Unemployment that exists because no one possesses perfect knowledge concerning job opportunities, nor free mobility between places of employment; lends a certain flexibility to the economy.

Functional Distribution of Income A breakdown of total income into the proportions paid to owners of various types of resources.

Functional Finance The view that balance in the economy is important and that imbalance in the federal budget is not important.

Future Goods Investments (postponed consumption) that raise productive capacity.

Gains from Scale Cost savings realized because international trade enables firms to become larger because they serve larger markets.

Gains from Specialization of Labor The extra output yielded when workers combine different types of expertise to perform a particular task.

Gains from Trade Improvements in human welfare because trading parties gain by acquiring (*a*) unique goods that they could not produce, (*b*) goods at lower costs than could be yielded by own-production, (*c*) transfers of technology, (*d*) greater income that, through higher saving, stimulates investment, (*e*) gains from economies of scale made possible by larger markets, and (*f*) calmer relations with other people because of mutual interdependence.

Game Theory A technique that requires assessing the potential gains and losses from all possible strategies by all participants in some activity so that the most likely combinations of choices and outcomes can be ascertained.

General Equilibrium Analysis A method of analysis which not only looks at the direct effects of some variables on others, but also at indirect effects and feedbacks among the economic variables.

General Training Training that increases the productivity of a worker equally for numerous possible places of employment.

GNP (Implicit Price) Deflator A price index composed largely of components from the *CPI* and *PPI;* used to adjust nominal GNP for changes in the price level.

GNP Gap The amount by which current GNP is below potential GNP.

Gold Standard Money may be exchanged at a fixed rate for gold; e.g., until 1933, one ounce of gold could be bought from the U.S. Treasury for $35, or sold to it for $35.

Good, Economic Anything which satisfies a human want and, in so doing, increases human happiness.

Gresham's Law Bad money drives out good.

Gross National Product (GNP) The value of all production that takes place annually.

Herfindahl-Hirschman Index (*HHI*) The sum of the squares of the market shares of the firms in an industry; *HHI*s are now used as a guideline for antitrust actions.

Hoarding Holding money in idle cash balances; money that is hoarded is not spent on consumption or investment; causes velocity to fall.

Horizontal Combination A firm which has numerous plants producing identical or similar products.

Household Income Used for consumption, saving, or taxes.

Households Individual or family units that provide input services, and that are the ultimate storehouses of wealth; they purchase goods in the output markets, and they sell resources in input markets.

Human Capital Improvements made in the labor embodied in human beings; people invest in human capital so that their labor services become both more productive and more highly paid.

Human Capital Discrimination Reduces access by certain groups to schooling, on-the-job training, or to human capital investments.

Humphrey-Hawkins (Full Employment and Balanced Growth) Act (1978) Augments the Employment Act of 1946 by (*a*) identifying specific economic priorities; (*b*) directing the president to establish goals based on those priorities; and (*c*) creating procedures to improve the coordination and development of economic policy between the president, the Congress, and the Federal Reserve System.

Hyperinflation or **Galloping Inflation** Increases in the price level at rates exceeding 50 percent per month.

Idle Cash Balances Money that is hoarded.

Impact Lag The period that passes before newly implemented changes in policy have an impact on economic activity; the impact lag of tax policy is short relative to that of monetary policy.

Implicit Costs The opportunity costs of all resources that a firm's owner makes available for production without direct outlays of money; examples are the values of the entrepreneur's funds, labor, and land tied up in the firm.

Imports Goods produced in foreign countries and consumed or invested domestically.

Income Approach to Estimating GNP GNP is the sum of personal consumption, total savings, and total taxes ($GNP = C + S + T$). It is also the sum of incomes received: wages, rent, interest, and profit ($w + r + i + \pi$).

Income Effect Changes in consumption patterns arising because price changes also change the purchasing power of money incomes; may be positive, negative, or zero.

Income Elasticity of Demand A measure of the responsiveness of the quantity demanded of a good to changes in real income; computed by dividing the percentage change in the quantity demanded of a good by the percentage change in real income: $\%\Delta q_{xd}$ / $\%\Delta Y$. (*See also* Elasticity, Price Elasticity of Demand (or Supply).)

Income Velocity (V) of Money $V = PQ/M$; the number of times annually that the average unit of money changes hands during the process of purchasing GNP (PQ).

Incomes Policies Measures intended to curb inflation without reducing Aggregate Demand expenditures; these policies include jawboning, wage and price guidelines, and wage and price controls.

Increase in Demand When the entire demand curve shifts upward and to the right; more will be purchased at every price; occurs only if one of the nonprice determinants of demand changes.

Increase in Supply When the entire supply curve shifts rightwards; buyers will be offered more at every price; occurs only if a nonprice determinant of supply changes; causes equilibrium price to decrease.

Increasing Cost Industry An industry whose long-run supply curve is an upward sloping line; higher costs per unit are incurred as production in the industry increases.

Index Numbers Numbers used to make relative comparisons of a specific variable between time periods.

Indicative Planning France, whose economy is primarily capitalistic, uses indicative planning which entails trying to coordinate economic activity by setting production targets for major industries.

Indifference Curve A line connecting the various combinations of two goods that yield the same total utility; the consumer is indifferent among the various bundles of goods along an indifference curve.

Indirect Business Taxes Taxes that are viewed by business firms as production costs; are not part of National Income since they are not resource payments. Examples are sales and excise taxes.

Induced Expenditures Expenditures that depend on income.

Industrial Policy Government uses subsidies, tax breaks, and protection from foreign competition to support "target industries" that have high productivity, strong "linkages," or future importance.

Industry All firms that compete in some market.

Industry Interest Theory of Regulation Regulation of industry serves not the public interest, but instead serves the interests of the regulated industries.

Infant Industry Argument for Tariffs The notion that emerging industries need to be protected from more efficient, established, foreign competitors.

Inferior Good A good for which the income elasticity of demand is negative; the demand for this type of economic good varies inversely with real income; technically, a good for which the income effect of a price change is negative.

Inflation Upward movements of the absolute price level.

Inflationary Gap The amount by which autonomous expenditures exceed those necessary for full employment income or output.

Informative Advertising Accurate information provided to consumers so that good economic choices can be made at lowered transaction costs; not a waste of resources.

In-Kind Transfers Welfare paid, not as cash, but rather as, e.g., food stamps, educational grants, or housing allowances.

Innovation In the 1930s, Joseph Schumpeter argued that progress in capitalist systems is driven by major innovations, including (a) the introduction of a new good, or new quality in a familiar product; (b) the introduction of new technology; (c) the opening of a new market; (d) the discovery of a major source of raw materials; and (e) the reorganization of a major industry.

Inputs Things used in the production process, such as labor and raw or semifinished materials.

Interest Payments per period for capital services.

Intermediate Goods Semiprocessed goods used in the production of other economic goods.

International Trade Exchanges of goods across national boundaries; facilitates efficient use of the world's scarce resources.

Investment Additions to the economy's real capital stock, i.e., all final purchases of capital equipment (machinery, tools, etc.), all residential or commercial construction, and changes in inventories.

Invisible Hand Automatic market adjustments toward equilibrium.

Involuntary Saving Occurs when government policies decrease consumption in order to stimulate capital accumulation; governments can force individuals to save a portion of their income through taxation, inflationary financing of government expenditures, or by setting low wages and high prices.

Jawboning Oratory used by policymakers to persuade people or institutions to act against their individual interests; especially common as an exhortation to hold prices below equilibrium levels.

Joint Profit Maximization A cartel of oligopolistic firms tries to share the profits that a monopoly would make if it controlled the industry.

Key Currency An international medium of exchange; use of the U.S. dollar as an international medium of exchange was a major reason that the U.S. has been able to run persistently large balance of payments deficits since 1951.

Keynes Effect The initial decreases (increases) in both the nominal interest rate and the real interest rate brought about by an increase (decrease) in the rate of growth of the nominal money supply.

Keynesian Aggregate Demand Total spending on domestically produced goods during a given year: $C + I + G + (X - M)$.

Keynesian Aggregate Supply The net value of all new goods and services available for purchase in a country during a given year.

Keynesian Fiscal Policy Policies designed to combat the problems associated with inadequate Aggregate Demand which plagued economies throughout the world during the 1930s.

Keynesian Government Growth Ratchet The tendency for government to grow because policymakers cut taxes and expand spending during economic downturns but do not raise taxes or cut spending during inflationary episodes.

Keynesian Investment Schedule The idea that investment demand is insensitive to movements of the interest rate, but that it is very sensitive to changes in expectations.

Keynesian Liquidity Preference The idea that the demand for money is extremely sensitive to interest rate movements and may even become horizontal at very low interest rates.

Keynesian Model A framework used to describe how output responds to changes in Aggregate Demand; generally ignores price level changes.

Keynesian Monetary Transmission Mechanism The idea that changes in the nominal money supply affect consumer spending only indirectly; money $\rightarrow$ interest rate $\rightarrow$ investment $\rightarrow$ income represents the chain of events emanating from a change in the money supply rate of growth.

Keynesian Theory Specifies that macroeconomic adjustments involve changes in quantities below full employment and that price level changes only become the major adjustment mechanism when Aggregate Demand grows at full employment.

Keynes's Fundamental Psychological Law of Consumption Consumption expenditures increase as income rises, but by a smaller amount.

Kinked Demand Curve Model of Oligopoly An oligopolistic pricing model that explains noncollusive oligopolistic behavior and predicts stickiness or rigidity of prices in oligopolistic industries.

Labor Labor services are typically measured in terms of the total amount of time worked during a given interval.

Labor Force Participation Rate (LFPR) The proportion of a population in the labor force; computed by dividing the labor force by the total population.

Labor Theory of Value The idea that the value of anything is exactly proportional to the labor time socially necessary for its production; this approach was the standard economic explanation of price until late in the 1800s and is still an article of faith among Marxists.

Labor Union A worker organization that negotiates labor contracts with firms' managers to set wages and the conditions of work.

Laffer Curve A figure illustrating the idea that very high tax rates may so discourage productive efforts that fewer tax revenues are collected than if tax rates were substantially lower.

Lagging Indicators Data series that reach their respective high points and low points after the economy has peaked or troughed.

Laissez-Faire This philosophy embraces the notion that a market system operates most efficiently when government minimizes its activity in the economy; according to this philosophy, governments should provide national defense and police protection, specify property rights, and enforce contracts drawn up between economic agents—and little or nothing else. (*See also* Capitalism, Socialism.)

Land Includes all material resources, such as unimproved land, minerals, water, air, timber, wildlife, and fertility of the soil.

Leading Indicators Data series that reach their respective high points and low points before business cycle peaks and troughs.

Legal Barriers to Entry Governmentally erected barriers to entry into an industry; these barriers maintain monopoly power by legally prohibiting or limiting competition from other firms; barriers include patents, copyrights, and licensing or bonding restrictions.

Legal Incidence of a Tax Falls on the party who legally must pay the tax to government, but the economic burdens may be shifted to others.

Legal Reserves Total bank reserves; the sum of bankers' required reserves and excess reserves.

Lerner Index of Monopoly Power (LMP) An estimate of monopoly power using the percent by which price of output exceeds marginal cost; monopoly power is then measured as: $(P - MC)/P$.

Libertarianism A philosophy based on the notion that individual freedom is the most important social goal; libertarianism emphasizes the inherently coercive nature of government, and urges reliance on the free market system to resolve nearly every human problem.

Limit Pricing Occurs when firms that possess monopoly power set a profitable price that is low enough to discourage potential entrants.

Liquidity How easy (costless) it is to turn an asset into cash; the transaction costs entailed with the purchase or sale of an asset is directly related to its illiquidity.

Liquidity Preference The total demand for money in a Keynesian model; derived by summing the transactions, precautionary, and asset (speculative) demands for money.

Liquidity Trap The horizontal portion of the Keynesian liquidity preference curve; occurs only when economic transactors choose to hold all increases in the nominal money supply in idle cash balances; it is doubtful if perfect liquidity traps have ever existed.

Logrolling When legislators trade votes.

Long Run (LR) A period of sufficient duration for all feasible resource adjustments to any event to be completed.

Long Run Average Cost Curve (LRAC) A curve showing the minimum average costs of producing each level of output after adjusting all resource inputs, including the size of the plant.

Long Wave Theory of Business Cycles A theory of long (50–60 year) waves in economic activity was developed in the 1920s by a Russian economist named Kondratieff.

Lorenz Curve A Lorenz curve shows the degree of inequality that exists in distributions of income or wealth in a particular society.

$M1$ = currency + demand deposits in commercial banks + all interest paying checkable accounts.

$M2 = M1$ + time deposits.

$M3 = M2$ + long-term deposits (Certificates of Deposit or CDs).

Macroeconomic Equilibrium Occurs when Aggregate Supply and Aggregate Demand are equal; when this occurs, the economy is stationary.

Macroeconomics The branch of economics concerned with aggregate variables such as the levels of total economic activity, unemployment, inflation, the balance of payments, economic growth and development, the money supply, and the federal budget.

Majority Rule When the winning side of a vote must capture 50 percent plus one vote.

Malthusian Prognosis Reverend Thomas Malthus, an early nineteenth century English economist, promulgated the dismal notion that all workers were doomed to live a subsistence existence; in formulating his forecast, Malthus neglected to consider the favorable impact of technological advances on the world's ability to produce food.

Mandatory Wage and Price Controls Price ceilings that carry legal penalties for noncompliance; instituted primarily during wars.

Margin Requirements A FED tool that sets the legal minimum percentage down payments required for purchases of stock.

Marginal Cost = Marginal Revenue (mc = mr) A condition required for maximum profits. Typically, $mr > mc$ for units prior to the $mr = mc$ level of output, so extra output boosts profit or cuts losses. Higher output levels entail $mr < mc$ and would not be produced.

Marginal Cost (mc) The change in total cost associated with producing an additional unit of output; computed by dividing the change in total cost

(ΔTC) by the change in output (Δq): $mc = \Delta TC/\Delta q = \Delta TVC/\Delta q$.

Marginal Factor Cost (*MFC*) The additional cost incurred in purchasing the services of an additional unit of a productive input; computed by dividing the change in total cost of production (ΔTC) by the change in input (ΔN): that is, $\Delta TC/\Delta N$; also computed by dividing the change in total variable costs of production (ΔTVC) by the change in input (ΔN): that is, $\Delta TVC/\Delta N$.

Marginal Physical Product of Labor (*MPP$_L$*) The additional output produced by an additional unit of labor; computed by dividing the change in total output (Δq) by the change in labor (ΔL):$\Delta q/\Delta L$.

Marginal Propensity to Consume (*mpc*) The change in saving brought about by a small change in disposable income *(mpc = $\Delta C/\Delta Y_d$)*.

Marginal Propensity to Save (*mps*) The change in saving brought about by a small change in disposable income *(mps = $\Delta S/\Delta Y_d$)*.

Marginal Revenue (*mr*) The additional revenue associated with selling an additional unit of output; computed by dividing the change in total revenue by the change in output: $mr = \Delta TR/\Delta q$.

Marginal Revenue Product (*mrp*) The additional total revenue generated by an additional unit of a variable input; computed by dividing the change in total revenue (ΔTR) by the change in input (ΔN): that is $\Delta TR/\Delta N$; or by multiplying marginal revenue by the marginal physical product of a unit of input: that is, $mr \times MPP_n$.

Marginal Social Benefits (*msb*) Computed by summing the marginal private benefits and the marginal external benefits, if any, from consuming additional units of commodities or services.

Marginal Social Costs The sum of marginal private costs and any marginal external costs incurred in producing additional units of a good.

Marginal Utility (*MU*) The added utility or satisfaction derived by a consumer from the consumption of an additional unit of a good.

Market Mechanism that enables buyers and sellers to strike bargains and to transact.

Market Demand Curve A graphic representation totalling all individual demand curves; it is derived for most goods by horizontally summing all individual demand curves.

Market Economies Systems that rely on market interaction of supplies and demands to resolve scarcity; the price system is used to coordinate the diverse plans of consumers and producers.

Market Equilibrium When neither shortages nor surpluses exist because, at the prevailing price, the quantities demanded and supplied are equal.

Market Failure When the market resolution of an economic problem is inefficient, inequitable, or unstable.

Market Period An interval too short to allow changes in decisions about amounts of output, so that only prices may be varied.

Market Price The price that is confronted in the market whether we buy or not.

Market Supply Curve A figure derived by horizontally summing all individual supply curves.

Market System (*See also* Capitalism, Free Enterprise System.)

Marginalism The idea that decisions are based on the effects of small changes from a current situation.

Maximizing Behavior *Homo sapiens* are perceived as human calculators who strive to maximize pleasure and to minimize pain.

Measure of (Net) Economic Welfare (MEW) A welfare measure obtained after deducting from GNP items that do not contribute to economic welfare and adding items that do, but which are not counted in GNP.

Measure of Value and Unit of Account The function performed by money as a common denominator through which the relative prices of goods are stated; reduces the information costs associated with exchange.

Median Voter Model Suggests that the median voter must be captured to achieve a majority of the vote, and attempts to explain why political parties and candidates tend to be so similar, and why two parties tend to dominate electoral processes.

Medium of Exchange The most important service that money provides; refers to standard items used to execute transactions.

Menu (Repricing) Costs of Inflation The costs in time and effort incurred in redesigning rate schedules and repricing goods.

Mercantilism A discredited economic doctrine that fostered imperialism and advocated surpluses in a country's balance of trade.

Merger The joining of two or more firms into a single firm.

Merit Goods or **Bads** Rival and exclusive goods that some elite deems either so desirable or undesirable that government intervenes, even though markets could satisfy consumer wants efficiently.

Microeconomics The branch of economics that focuses on individual decision making, the allocation of resources, and how prices, production, and the distribution of income are determined.

Middlemen Business firms that convey goods from the ultimate producer to the ultimate user. Middleman operations are only profitable if they reduce transaction costs.

Mixed Economies Societies in which some allocations rely on the market system while others rely on government or some other allocative mechanism.

Model The structure of a theory.

Monetarism The idea that erratic monetary growth in the money supply is the major cause of macroeconomic instability.

Monetarist Monetary Transmission Mechanism The idea that changes in the nominal money supply affect private spending directly; an increase in the money supply yields a proportional rise in nominal GNP: $MS \longrightarrow (C + I) \longrightarrow Y$ is the causal chain emanating from a change in the monetary growth rate.

Monetary Base or **High-Powered Money (MB)** The total of bank reserves plus currency held by the non-banking public.

Monetary Growth Rule The idea that the economy will be relatively stable if the money supply is set to grow at a low fixed percentage rate regardless of short-run economic conditions.

Money Illusion Decision makers suffer from money illusion if their decisions are based on movements of the monetary values of economic variables rather than on the real values of the variables.

Money Multiplier (m_p, m_a) Potentially equals the reciprocal of the reserve-requirement ratio ($m_p = 1/rr$) —the number which, when multiplied by a change in total reserves, yields the potential change in the money supply. Actually, $m_a = MS/MB$ because of currency holdings of the public, excess reserves, and other leakages.

Monopolistic Competition An industry in which many firms sell slightly differentiated goods and there is freedom of entry or exit; monopolistic competition resembles pure competition, but goods are heterogeneous and each firm possesses a bit of monopoly power.

Monopoly The lone seller of a good that has no close substitutes.

Monopoly Power Possessed whenever a seller can force prices up by restricting output.

Monopsonist The sole buyer of a particular good or resource.

Monopsony Power Possessed whenever a buyer can force prices down by restricting purchases.

Moral Hazard Occurs when a contract creates an incentive for opportunistic behavior that raises the costs or lowers the benefits to the other party.

Moral Suasion (*See also* Jawboning.)

Multiplier Effect The total change in spending that results when new autonomous spending boosts income which, in turn, is spent, creating more income, and so on. (*See also* Autonomous Spending Multiplier.)

National Banks Banks chartered by the Comptroller of the Currency and that must be members of the Federal Reserve System.

National Debt The value of government bonds in the hands of the public or foreigners.

National Income (NI) A measure of economic activity computed by summing all resource incomes; equals the sum of wages and salaries, rents, interest, and corporate and noncorporate incomes.

Natural Barriers to Entry Significant barriers to entry that result from the nature of the good or from the cost structure inherent in its production.

Natural Monopoly A market in which only one seller can most efficiently produce an economic good; the production process is characterized by tremendously large fixed costs and relatively small variable costs; emerges where the market demand is small relative to the economies of scale.

Natural Rate Theory The notion that the economy is inherently stable and that unemployment and real interest will coincide with their natural rates in the long run; according to this theory, traditional Keynesian policy goals are unattainable because attempts to drive down unemployment or real interest rates more than can be reconciled with people's preferences are self-defeating in the long run.

Negative Externality When a market transaction imposes costs on third parties not directly involved in any aspect of the exchange.

Negative Income Taxes (NIT) Negative income tax plans represent attempts to reconcile equity and efficiency considerations in resolving the problems posed by income inequality and poverty; the negative income tax plan maintains incentives for recipients to work to earn additional income.

Net Investment Gross investment minus depreciation; represents net additions to an economy's capital stock or productive capacity.

Net National Product (NNP) The net value of commodities and services produced in the economy after adjusting for the fact that we have used up productive capacity; equals GNP minus depreciation; also equals National Income (NI) plus indirect business taxes.

Neutral Tax Imposition of a neutral tax distorts neither consumer buying patterns nor the methods used by firms in the conduct of their business; in other words, the imposition of a neutral tax does not distort relative prices by inducing substitution effects.

New Classical Macroeconomics Modern theories that extend classical theories of competitive markets, normally resulting in underpinnings for laissez-faire macroeconomic policies.

Nominal Rate of Interest The average annual percentage monetary premium paid to use money.

Nominal Values The current dollar values of economic variables.

Nondiscretionary Fiscal Policy (*See also* Automatic Stabilizers.)

Nondurable Goods Goods that are used up in less than one year.

Noneconomic Costs of Unemployment Include the psychological trauma of being unemployed and the social unrest unemployment engenders.

Nonexclusive Good A good is nonexclusive if a person can enjoy it without paying for the right to consume; the result when it is relatively expensive to prevent individuals from consuming a good.

Nonrival Good A good is nonrival if consumption of the good by an individual does not prevent consumption of the same unit of that good by other individuals.

Normal Good Any good with a positive income elasticity of demand.

Normal Profits A normal production cost; income that entrepreneurs must receive to make production worthwhile to them.

Normative Economics Deals with values and addresses what should be rather than what is.

Occam's Razor The "principle of parsimony," which suggests that the simplest workable theories are also the best and most useful.

Occupational Discrimination Exclusion of certain groups from particular occupations.

Oligopoly A market in which several large firms control most of an industry's output. The few firms that comprise the industry must each consider other firms' reactions before setting its policies; mutually interdependent behavior is the unique characteristic of oligopoly; the importance of predictability leads to cooperation between firms. Pure oligopolies produce homogeneous outputs, while impure oligopolies produce slightly differentiated outputs.

Open-Market Operations When the FED's Open Market Committee buys and sells U.S. bonds; these operations determine the size of the money supply by varying the reserves in the banking system.

Open Shop A firm that employs workers without considering union membership.

Opportunity Cost The value of the next best opportunity to a good or to some activity.

Opportunity Cost of Money Keynesians view the true price of money as the interest rate, since the closest alternatives to money as an asset are stocks, bonds, and other assets that pay interest. Monetarists argue, instead, that the true price of money is the reciprocal of the absolute price level—the purchasing power of money—since money is a substitute for all other goods and assets.

Outputs Transformed materials; the results of production.

Paradox of Thrift The possibility suggested by Keynes that an increase in planned saving at all income levels (depicted by an upward shift of the saving function) may cause equilibrium income or output to decrease, and could result in less saving rather than more.

Parity The idea that government subsidies should be used to ensure that agricultural goods' prices are stable relative to other prices.

Partial Equilibrium Analysis A method of economic analysis which looks at the direct effects of some chosen variables on others, assuming other influences constant.

Partnership An unincorporated firm formed by two or more persons.

Patents Legal barriers to entry that extend to their holders a renewable right to produce an economic good for 17 years and that prohibits the production of the good by other firms; intended to promote research and development of new goods and technologies.

Peak (Boom) The phase of the business cycle when a preponderance of measures of economic activity are at their high points.

Per Capita Income A crude measure of economic well-being computed by dividing National Income by the population.

Perfectly Price Elastic Demand or **Supply Curves** Horizontal lines at the current market price; perfectly price elastic demand or supply curves have a price elasticity of infinity at every point.

Permanent Income (Wealth) The average income expected over one's lifetime; according to Milton Friedman, permanent income explains a person's patterns of consumption and money holdings.

Perpetuity A bond that will pay a fixed amount of money each year until it is purchased by the government that issued it.

Personal Discrimination Bigotry; generates inequitable housing conditions, higher prices for comparable goods, reduced medical care, and other problems.

Persuasive Advertising Designed to persuade or to mislead consumers rather than to inform them; entails a waste of resources.

Phillips Curve An inverse statistical relationship between the rate of change of the general price level and the rate of unemployment; in 1959, A. W. Phillips, an English economist, reported findings to provide an empirical foundation for the idea that policymakers faced a permanent trade-off between unemployment and inflation; during the 1970s, the Phillips curve proved highly unstable.

Planned Injections Equal Planned Withdrawals A condition necessary for macroeconomic equilibrium. Injections include all forms of autonomous spending; withdrawals represent such dilutions from spending streams as saving or taxation.

Planned or **Intended Investment** The amount of investment that business firms desire to make at each income level, assuming that business expectations remain unchanged.

Planned or **Intended Saving** The amounts of saving desired at each income level, assuming that savers' expectations remain constant.

Plant A production facility with a specific location, it may be involved in processing, fabrication, assembly, wholesale, or retail.

Plurality When the outcome of an election is determined by which side gets the most votes; a majority is unnecessary.

Point Voting When each voter can spread a certain number of votes among various electoral issues in accord with the voter's intensity of preferences.

Political Business Cycles Swings in economic activity that occur when macroeconomic policies are manipulated to improve incumbents' chances of reelection. The economy booms before elections, and stagnates after them.

Pollution In economic jargon, a negative externality.

Pollution Abatement Programs Techniques used to reduce pollution.

Pork Barrel Legislation Legislation that yields benefits that are primarily local, but where funding is by the national government.

Positive Economics Value-free descriptions of and predictions about relationships among economic variables.

Positive Externality Occurs when a market activity bestows benefits on economic transactors who are not direct parties to the activity.

Potential GNP What an economy could produce at high rates of utilization of all resources; full employment GNP approximates potential GNP.

Precautionary Demand for Money The amount of money that economic transactors desire to hold to cover unexpected expenses; is positively related to income or wealth.

Present Value The present value of any asset is the value today of the expected income stream associated with the asset, discounted by the interest rate; the demand price of the asset.

Pre-trade Costs The rate of exchange that exists domestically between two goods prior to international trade; also referred to as the domestic terms of trade; given by the slope at each point along the production-possibility frontier.

Price Ceiling A maximum legal price set at the behest of buyers.

Price Discrimination Occurs when essentially the same good is sold at different prices, and price differentials do not reflect different production costs; perfect price discrimination absorbs all potential consumer surplus derived from consuming a good.

Price Elasticity of Demand (or Supply) Measures of the responsiveness of the quantity demanded (supplied) of a good to changes in the price of the good; computed by dividing percentage changes in quantities demanded (supplied) of a good by the percentage changes in its price: $\%\Delta q_{xd}/\%\Delta P_x$ (or $\%\Delta q_{xs}/\%\Delta P_x$). (*See also* Elasticity, Income Elasticity of Demand.)

Price Floor A minimum legal price set at the behest of sellers.

Price Taker or **Quantity Adjuster** A competitive buyer or seller whose actions do not affect prices; they can choose only among quantities.

Private Debt Debts owed by consumers or business firms.

Private Ownership System An economy in which most resources are privately owned.

Product Differentiation When consumers perceive differences in competing goods; real differences in similar products may be related to their durability, styling, or other physical characteristics; imaginary differences result from advertising or the imaginations of consumers; firms use product differentiation in attempts both to shift the demands for their products to the right and to decrease the price elasticity of the demands for their goods.

Production Occurs when materials are transformed in ways that make them more valuable.

Production Function The technical relationship that exists between inputs and outputs; allows all inputs to vary as different rates of production are achieved; not synonymous with total product curve.

Production-Possibility Frontier (*PPF*) A curve showing the various combinations of goods that an economy could produce, assuming a fixed technology and full employment and efficient resource utilization.

Profit The excess of a firm's total revenues over total cost; accounting profits consider only the explicit costs incurred by a firm; economists view total costs in terms of opportunity costs, which include both explicit and implicit costs; is a return to entrepreneurship for bearing uncertainty and innovating.

Progressive Taxes Tax rates which vary directly with income, so that the proportion of income devoted to taxes rises as income rises.

Promotional Profits The increases in the values of stock controlled by individuals who engineer a merger.

Property Rights Legal rights that people possess over property; the broadest of property rights are fee-simple property rights that allow individuals (*a*) to use goods in any manner so long as other people's property rights are not violated; (*b*) to exchange these property rights for others; and (*c*) to deny the use of their goods to others.

Property Tax A tax based on the value of capital improvements and land.

Proportional Taxes Tax rates that do not vary with income; the same percentage of income is collected in taxes regardless of the income level.

Proprietors Individuals in business for themselves.

Psychic Income Value of nonmonetary satisfaction gained from an activity.

Psychological Theories of the Business Cycle Focus on the herd instincts of human beings coupled with prolonged periods of optimism and pessimism.

Public Choice Economic interpretations of political behavior.

Public Debt Created when the government spends more than it collects in tax revenue; the government increases the public debt when it sells bonds to the public to finance a deficit.

Public Finance Microeconomic study of government taxing and spending.

Public Good A public good is a good which can be consumed by more than one individual at a time (nonrivalry) and whose consumption cannot be denied a consumer who desires it (nonexclusion) once the good is provided.

Public Interest Theory of Regulation This theory suggests that government should control unethical business practices and regulate businesses plagued by such market failures as (*a*) externalities, or (*b*) mo-

nopoly power derived from economies of scale.

Public Ownership System A system in which the government owns nonhuman resources and acts as collective trustee for its citizens.

Pure Private Good A pure private good is both rival and exclusive; the marketplace is well suited for providing pure private goods efficiently. A pure public good is both nonrival and nonexclusive; the government may need to provide pure public goods to improve efficiency.

Quantity Demanded The amount of a good purchased at a given price.

Quantity Supplied The amount of a good supplied at a given price.

Quantity Theory of Money The idea that the dominant determinant of the price level is the money supply. An extreme version attributes all inflation to excessive monetary growth.

Queuing Allocating goods or resources on a first come/first served basis. This tends to result in queues (lining up for access).

Quota A quantitative restriction on trade, the imposition of quotas raises the prices of imported goods and causes failure to fully realize potential gains from international trade.

Rate Base The value of a regulated firm's capital stock to which an acceptable, or fair, rate of return applies.

Rate of Return The annualized average size of the income stream per time period as a percentage of the dollar outlay for an investment.

Rational Expectations The notion that markets operate so efficiently that policy goals will not be achieved, even in the short run, unless the timing and the effects of demand-management policies come as surprises to the public.

Rational Ignorance Decision makers will search for information only as long as the expected benefit exceeds the expected cost and, thus, may choose to be rationally ignorant of much information.

Real Rate of Interest The annual percentage premium of purchasing power paid by a borrower to a lender for the use of money; the amount of extra goods, expressed in percentage terms, that can be enjoyed if consumption is delayed; computed by adjusting the nominal interest rate for the rate of general price change.

Real Values The current dollar value of economic variables after adjustment for price level changes.

Recession Modern name for a depression.

Recessionary Gap A deficiency in autonomous expenditure that, if filled, would be multiplied so that full employment output was achieved.

Recognition Lag Arises because policymakers' perceptions about current economic conditions are clouded, and time and effort are required to gather, compile, process, and interpret data to gain some feeling for any widespread changes in economic activity; applies equally to both monetary and fiscal policies.

Regressive Taxes Tax rates which vary inversely with income, so that tax payments decline relative to income as income rises.

Regulation Q Empowered the FED to limit the interest rates paid on time deposits in commercial banks; now phased out.

Reindustrialization (*See also* Industrial Policy.)

Relative Price Price of a good in terms of another good. (*See also* Absolute Price.)

Rent Payments per time period for the services of land. (*See also* Economic Rent.)

Rent-Seeking Attempts by special interest groups to shape public policies to their advantage, even though such policies may impose excessive costs on the general public.

Required Reserves (*RR*) The reserves that banks are legally required to hold against their deposits.

Reserve-Requirement Ratio (*rr*) The fraction of its deposit liabilities that a bank must hold in reserves.

Reserves The amounts of money held in a bank's vault or on deposit at the FED to meet reserve requirements or withdrawals of deposits.

Resources Land, labor, capital, and entrepreneurship.

Ricardian Equivalence The idea that people will adjust so that whether government spending is financed by taxes or bonds is irrelevant.

Risk The likelihood of an event for which a probability can reasonably be estimated. (*See also* Uncertainty.)

Rival Good A good is rival if consumption of a unit of the good by one individual exhausts that particular unit so that another individual cannot consume it.

Robinson-Patman Act (1936) Amended Section 2 of the Clayton Act; this act was designed to limit price discrimination; however, it permitted discounts if they could be justified by differences in costs of production or if they were introduced as "good faith" efforts to meet competition.

Rule of Reason The rule of reason approach to the Sherman Act, permitted certain restrictive business practices of a firm despite their anticompetitive effects if the firm could show that its conduct was based on sound business practice and was secondary to its primary business practices.

Rule of 72 The time required for some variable to double is calculated by dividing its percentage annual growth rate into 72. This approach adjusts for compounding (e.g., interest on interest).

Sales Tax A percentage tax that is typically levied on the sales value of most commodities and/or services.

Saving The change in one's total wealth over some period of time.

Say's Law "Supply creates its own demand"; that is, the very act of producing a product creates an equivalent amount of demand, since people do not work for the sake of work alone; named after the classical economist, Jean Baptiste Say.

Scarce Good A good for which the quantity demanded exceeds the amount available at a zero dollar price.

Scarcity Occurs because resources are limited and cannot satisfy all of our unlimited wants.

Seasonal Unemployment Unemployment that varies with the seasons.

Seignorage The profits made by governments when they coin or print money.

Sellers' Market When the prevailing market price lies below the equilibrium price, resulting in a shortage.

Services Intangible economic goods.

Sherman Antitrust Act (1890) Our first antitrust law; specifies that "every contract, combination in the form of trust or otherwise, or conspiracy, in restraint of trade or commerce among the several States, or with foreign nations, is hereby declared illegal"; and, according to the second section, "every person who shall monopolize, or attempt to monopolize . . . shall be deemed guilty of a felony."

Shifted Backward A tax is shifted backward when its economic incidence falls on owners of resources supplied to the firm.

Shifted Forward A tax is said to be shifted forward when the economic incidence of the tax falls on the consumer.

Shortage Occurs if some people cannot buy all of an economic good for which they are willing to pay the going price.

Short Run (*SR*) An analytic period of time in which at least one resource is fixed so that firms can neither enter nor leave the marketplace—a firm can shut its plant down, but it cannot leave the industry.

Shutdown Point The price/output combination at which total revenue just equals total variable costs; in the short run, the firm must at least cover the variable costs of production; if it cannot, then it will shut down and minimize its losses by incurring only fixed costs.

Socialism A system characterized by collective ownership of property and government allocation of resources. (*See also* Capitalism, Laissez-Faire.)

Socially Necessary Labor The Marxist concept that includes not only direct labor time, but also the labor time used to construct factories and to produce capital equipment; Marxists view all commodities and capital as congealed labor.

Special Interest Groups Groups that can gain from public policies that may not be in accord with the interests of other groups or society as a whole.

Specialization When different resources (e.g., people's labor) are used to produce different goods. This is most advantageous when resources are allocated so that every good is produced at the lowest possible opportunity cost.

Specific Training Training that a firm provides a worker that only increases the productivity of the worker for that firm.

Speculative Demand for Money Inversely related to the interest rate; refers to the amount of money that economic transactors desire to hold at alternative interest rates for the purpose of speculating against movements in the prices of stocks or bonds.

Speculators Middlemen who buy a good in the hope of selling it at a higher price at a later point in time. Profitable speculation tends to reduce price volatility and the risks to others of doing business.

Spillovers (Externalities) When benefits or costs are bestowed upon third parties who are not part of a transaction; produce false price signals and lead to nonoptimal decisions.

Stabilization Branch This branch of government in Musgrave's framework would be responsible for achieving full employment, price stability, and economic growth.

Stagflation The simultaneous occurrence of high rates of inflation and high rates of unemployment; stagflation, or inflationary recession, occurs during both demand-induced and supply-induced cycles of inflation when Aggregate Supply declines relative to Aggregate Demand.

Standard Industry Classification (SIC) Codes Categories developed by the Bureau of Census to classify industries.

Standard of Deferred Payment Money performs this function by being acceptable in the payment of contractual obligations involving future payments.

State Banks Banks that are chartered by state governments; they have the option of becoming members of the Federal Reserve System.

Statutory (Legal) Incidence of a Tax Falls on the party responsible for paying the tax, but a tax's economic incidence may be shifted.

Stock Variable An economic variable that can be measured holding time constant.

Store of Value Money is a store of value in that, except for inflation, it is a relatively riskless way of holding wealth.

Structural Deficit The budget shortfall that would result because of the design of current government tax and outlay programs, were the economy operating at its capacity. (*See also* Cyclical Deficit.)

Structural Unemployment Unemployment that arises because workers do not possess the skills required for existing job opportunities.

Subsistence Theory of Wages The theory that classical economists used to explain how wage rates were determined; this theory suggests that wages would be sufficient to meet the biological needs of workers, with only minor adjustments to meet the social and customary needs of workers.

Substitute Goods Goods that are substituted one for another in consumption; positive cross price-elasticities of demand exist between substitute goods.

Substitution Effect The change in the pattern of consumption brought about by a change in the relative price structure; the substitution effect of a price change is always negative, for consumers will always substitute cheaper goods for more expensive goods; the substitution effect is generally so powerful that it serves as the theoretical underpinning for the law of demand.

Superior Good A good for which the income elasticity of demand is greater than one; that is, the demand for this kind of economic good is very sensitive to real income changes.

Supply The amounts of goods or resources that producers or owners are willing to sell in the market under various conditions.

Supply Curve A graph representing the maximum quantities of a good or resource that producers or owners are willing to supply at various market prices.

Supply, Law of The quantity of an economic good supplied varies directly with its price.

Supply Price The lowest price at which sellers are willing to make a specific quantity of a good available. (*See also* Demand Price.)

Supply-Side Economics A reemphasis on the importance of the effects of government policies on Aggregate Supply; this rebuts the Keynesian emphasis on Aggregate Expenditures.

Surplus, or Excess Supply The excess of the quantity supplied over the quantity demanded at a given price.

Surplus Value The difference between the total value of what workers produce and what workers are paid for their labor services; surplus value is expropriated by the capitalists, according to Marxists; surplus value is the sum of rent, interest, and profits.

Survival Principle The idea that the most efficient firms in an industry are those that remain viable over time; the optimal size of firms is indicated by the size of the firm that survives in an industry over time.

Syndicalism A revolutionary sociopolitical theory that advocates the overthrow of government and the reorganization of society into syndicates, which are effectively industrywide trade unions.

Taft-Hartley Act (1947) This legislation amended the Wagner Act and made certain union labor practices unfair, outlawed the closed shop, and permitted individual states to pass "right-to-work" laws that ban union shops.

Tariff A tax on internationally traded goods; the imposition of tariffs raises the prices of imported goods and prevents full realization of potential gains from international trade.

Technological Change Occurs when given resources produce more output, or when a given amount of output can be produced with fewer inputs; refers to greater efficiency in market processes, improved knowledge concerning the use of inputs in production, the advent of completely new production processes, improvements in the quality of human and nonhuman resources, and new inventions and innovations. The idea of progress is tightly bound up in the process of technological change.

Terms of Trade The prices of exported goods relative to imported goods after international trade has commenced.

Theory A testable hypothesis concerning the way in which observable facts are related.

Tie-In Sales Attempts by firms to exploit their market power by using tie-in sales agreements that require customers to buy another product as a condition for buying the monopolized good.

Total Burdens of a Tax The amounts of money that individuals would have to be paid to make them just as well off with the tax as without.

Total Cost All costs to the firm of producing a given rate of output; computed by multiplying the quantity of a good produced by the per unit cost of producing the good.

Total Product Curve The technical relationship that exists between production and various levels of one input, assuming that other resources are held constant.

Total Revenue The dollar value of a firm's sales; computed by multiplying the quantity of a good sold by its per unit price ($P \times Q$).

Total Revenue Minus Total Cost ($TR - TC$) The profit-maximizing firm will produce that rate of output at which total revenue exceeds total cost by the greatest amount.

Trade Adjustment Assistance Provides retraining and financial assistance for workers disemployed because of liberalized international trade.

Transaction Costs The costs associated with gathering information about products and transporting goods and people geographically or between markets.

Transactions Demand for Money The amount of money that economic transactors desire to hold in order to execute expected transactions; is positively related to income and wealth.

Transfer Payments Transfers of income from one set of households to another set through such programs as welfare payments, Social Security, and food stamps.

Trap of Underdevelopment Less developed countries typically remain underdeveloped for the following reasons (*a*) high rates of population growth that result in low per capita incomes; (*b*) negligible capital accumulation because of low saving rates fostered by low per capita incomes; (*c*) consumers buy rather primitive goods; and (*d*) low labor productivity.

Trough (Depression) Phase of the business cycle when most measures of economic activity are at their low point.

Unanimity A requirement that all voters agree before new policies are implemented.

Uncertainty When a reasonable estimate cannot be made of the probability that some event will occur. (*See also* Risk.)

Unemployment A condition that occurs when an individual wants work but is without a job.

Unintended Inventory Changes A balancing item for the economy, these changes in inventories resolve any differences between the planned saving and planned investment functions and ensure that actual saving and actual investment are equal at all times.

Union Shop A firm that will hire nonunion workers, but joining the union is a requirement for continued employment.

Uniqueness Gains Gains that arise because exchange allows traders to secure goods not available from local sources in reasonable quantities at reasonable prices.

Usury Law A legal ceiling on the interest rates that lenders may charge borrowers.

Util An imaginary unit of measurement of satisfaction.

Utilitarianism A philosophy developed in England during the 1800s by Jeremy Bentham, an eccentric English philosopher and social reformer; this school of thought embraced the notion that satisfactions or utilities of individuals could be measured, and it sought "the greatest happiness for the greatest number."

Utopian Socialism All property would be collectively owned and all decisions would be democratic.

Value Added The excess of a firm's revenues over the amount it pays to other firms for intermediate goods; used to calculate GNP and, in much of Europe, as a major base for taxes.

Value-Added Approach to Estimating GNP GNP equals the sum of the values added to economic goods at each level of production.

Value of Money The purchasing power of money, which is determined by the interaction of the supply of and demand for money.

Value of the Marginal Product (VMP) The value of the output produced by an additional unit of a variable input; computed by multiplying the price of output (P_x) by the marginal physical product of a unit of input (MPP_N): that is, $VMP = (P_x) \times (MPP_N)$.

Variable Costs Costs that vary with the level of production; variable costs are also known as direct costs or prime costs, and are the only costs that rational decision makers consider.

Vertical Combination A firm having different plants producing products at different production levels within an industry.

Voluntary Saving The voluntary decisions of individuals to defer consumption until some future date.

Voluntary Unemployment The frictional unemployment that exists when everyone who wants to work at the prevailing wage rate has a job or can find one rapidly.

Wage-Price Controls Legal restrictions most often used to keep prices from coinciding with their equilibrium levels.

Wage Discrimination Occurs when members of a particular group are paid less than are members of other groups for doing equal work.

Wages Payments per time period for labor services.

Wagner Act (1935) Guaranteed labor the right to organize independent unions and made a company's refusal to negotiate with an elected union an unfair labor practice.

Webb-Pomerene Act (1918) Exempts export trade associations from antitrust litigation.

Yellow-Dog Contracts Contracts that were widely used by business firms during the antiunion years to prevent the formation of labor unions by their employees; as a condition of employment, workers were forced to sign a yellow-dog contract, which was an agreement not to join a labor organization.

Zero Economic Profit The long-run equilibrium state of pure competition. All opportunity costs are covered by revenues, but there will be no net resource movements because no better opportunities exist elsewhere.

NAME INDEX

Ackley, Gardner, 361
Acton, Lord, 792
Arrow, Kenneth, 36fn*

Bain, Joe, 528
Bakunin, Mikhail, 793
Barry, William T., 693
Batra, Raveendra, 152
Bauer, P. T., 396
Baumol, William, 512fn
Bazelon, David, 221
Becker, Gary S., 623fn
Behr, Michael, 417fn
Bentham, Jeremy, 423, 425–26
Blanc, Louis, 729
Boulding, Kenneth, 461, 805
Bush, George, 213, 319

Cacy, J. A., 360fn
Cagan, Phillip, 114
Carlyle, Thomas, 58, 385
Chamberlin, E. H., 523–24
Clark, John Bates, 596, 730fn
Clark, John Maurice, 4
Coase, Ronald H., 702fn, 703fn
Coleman, John S., 284
Confucius, 729
Coolidge, Calvin, 85
Cournot, A. A., 503

DeFina, Robert, 566fn
Denison, Edward S., 391
Dukakis, Michael, 213, 219

Edison, Thomas A., 498, 644
Edwards, Edgar O., 393fn
Einstein, Albert, 8
Eisner, Robert, 296fn
Elliott, Donald, 9fn
Emerson, Ralph Waldo, 71
Engels, Friedrich, 796–98

Fisher, Irving, 257, 343–45
Ford Henry, 450, 498
Foster, T., 736fn
Fourier, Charles, 794
Friedman, Milton, 96, 267–68

Galbraith, John Kenneth, 88
Gallaway, Lowell, 736fn
Galles, Gary, 435fn
Gandhi, Mohandas, 805
Garwood, Joe, 9fn
Geis, Irving, 24
George, Henry, 639
George, P., 716
Gordon, Robert J., 320fn
Gwartney, James, 738fn

Harberger, Arnold, 560
Haworth, C., 738fn
Haworth, J., 738fn
Hayek, Friedrich A., 354
Hazlitt, Henry, 17
Hebert, Robert, 646fn
Hegel, Georg, 795
Heilbroner, Robert, 566
Hicks, John R., 620
Holmes, Oliver Wendell, 663
Hotelling, Harold, 542
Huff, Darrell, 24

Jefferson, Thomas, 40

Kalecki, Michael, 362
Kemp, Jack, 235fn
Kenney, Robert M., 525
Keynes, John Maynard, 8, 220, 808
King, G., 716
Kipling, Rudyard, 804
Knight, Frank H., 644
Kohler, Heinz, 716
Kondratieff, N. D., 151
Kuznets, Simon, 129

Laffer, Arthur, 207, 211
Lerner, Abba P., 281fn
Lewis, H. G., 625fn
Lincoln, Abe, 343
Link, Albert N., 646fn
Locke, John, 38
Long, J., 738fn

Malthus, Rev. Thomas, 148, 384
Marshall, Alfred, 480
Marx, Karl, 149, 391, 795–800
Michels, Roberto, 801
Miernyk, William, 622fn
Mitchell, Wesley C., 143
More, St. Thomas, 794
Morgenstern, Oskar, 133, 537
Musgrave, Richard A., 657

Nader, Ralph, 88
Nordhaus, William, 135
Nozick, Robert, 746
Nurkse, Ragnar, 393fn

Okun, Arthur, 11fn
Orwell, George, 35
Owen, Robert, 794

---

*Some names recur so frequently in this book (e.g., Adam Smith, John Maynard Keynes, and Milton Friedman) that not all references to them in the text are cited here.

Panzar, J., 512fn
Pareto, Vilfredo, 496
Parkinson, C. Northcote, 689
Peltzman, Sam, 578
Phillips, A. W., 328
Plaut, Steven, 440fn

Quirk, James P., 18

Rawls, John, 746
Ricardo, David, 282, 638, 755
Robbins, Lionel C., 3
Robinson, Joan, 523–24
Rostow, W. W., 392

Samuelson, Paul A., 799
Sargent, Thomas, 349fn
Say, Jean Baptiste, 153

Scherer, F. M., 549fn
Schiavo Campo, Salvatore, 9fn
Schumacher, E. F., 805
Schumpeter, Joseph A., 149–50, 644
Shackle, G. L. S., 646fn
Shaw, George Bernard, 10, 794
Simon, Carl, 136fn
Smith, Adam, 5, 60, 64, 65, 543
Smith, John, 729
Sorel, Georges, 793
Sowell, Thomas, 738fn, 740
Stern, Gary H., 289fn
Steward, Frances, 394fn
Stigler, George, 531, 534, 536, 569
Stocking, George, 515fn
Stockman, David, 208fn

Terkel, Studs, 107fn
Thomas, Dana L., 155, 156fn
Tufte, I. E., 362fn
Turner, Robert, 123

Veblen, Thorstein, 433, 434
Vetter, Richard, 736fn
Viner, Jacob, 8
von Mises, Ludwig, 354
von Neumann, Jon, 537

Walras, Leon, 496–97
Watkins, M. W., 515fn
Webster, Daniel, 253
Weidenbaum, Murray, 566fn
Whitworth, Regan, 9fn
Williams, Walter B., 602fn
Willig, R., 512fn
Witte, Ann D., 136fn

Youngman, Henny, 253

Zell, Steven P., 599fn
Zerbe, Richard O., 580fn

SUBJECT INDEX

Quadrants, 19
Quantity adjusters, 473, 474 (*See* Price taker)
Quantity adjustment (macroeconomics), 181
Quantity demanded, 50
Quantity theory of money, 155, 257–62, 268
Queuing, 35, 800
Quota, 766, 800
  in international trade, 766–67
  in production, 800

Racial discrimination, (*See* Discrimination)
Raiders, corporate, 88, 532–33
Random selection, 35
Rate base, 572
Rate of interest, (*See* Interest rates)
Rate of return, 153, 169, 171, 641–42, 647–49
Rate structure of utilities, 572
Rational expectations, 346–50
Rational ignorance, 94, 433, 678
  political, 678
Rational self-interest, 4–5
Real rate of interest, 341–45, 641
Recessionary gap, 191
Recessions, 143
  policymakers' natural dislike for, 364
  to discipline labor, 364
  to reduce inflationary pressures, 363–64
Recognition lag, 355, 357
Recovery (business cycle), 143
Redistribution of income, Chapter 35
  and inflation, 118–19
Regressive tax, 94, 664, 671
Regulation, 91, Chapter 27
  administrative costs, 566
  compliance costs, 566–68
  and consumers, 436–37, 576–78
  and deregulation, 579–80
  direct costs of, 566–68
  does business benefit from?, 574
  economic model of, 574–76
  and externalities, 572–73, 704
  and imperfect information, 435–36, 573
  indirect costs of, 568
  of labor markets, 599–604
  of natural monopolies, 511, 570–72

of pollution, 572–73, 704
rise of government, 565–66
why business is regulated, 568–70
Reindustrialization, 367
Relative price, 44, 221
Rent, economic, 4, 636–40
  allocation function of, 640
  on land, 4, 636–39
  in national income accounting, 127, 129
  to other resources, 638–40
  and profits, 643, 645
Rent-seeking, 686
Repricing (menu) costs of inflation, 117
Required reserves (banking), 239
Reserve requirement, 239–40, 244
Reserves, excess (banking), 230, 239–40
Resources, 4, Chapters 28–30
  altering, 4, 446
  demand for, 586–90, 611–17, 635, 650
  least cost combination of, 458–62, 469–71, 650
  ratios and productivity, 635
Retained (corporate) earnings, (*See* Undistributed corporate profits)
Retaliation (international trade), 762
Revaluation of a currency, 775
Ricardian equivalence, 282
"Rights" to pollute, 694, 703, 706
Right-to-work laws, 621
Risk, 4, 82, 644
Risk aversion, 246
Risk avoidance and money, 256
Rival good, 91, 660
Robinson-Patman Act of 1932, 553
Rule of Reason, 555
Rule of 72, 381–82
Rules vs. discretion, 249, 274–75, 370–71

Sales tax, 93–94, 671
Saving, 31
  and capital formation, 385–86, 643
  in classical theory, 153
  involuntary, 388–89
  voluntary, 387–88
  (*See* Consumption schedule)
Saving schedule, 165–67
Savings and Loan Associations, 246
Say's Law, 153, 159

Scale, gains from trade, 756
Scarcity, 3
Seasonal unemployment, 104
Securities, 4, 86, 243–44, 641–43
Securities markets, 246
Seignorage, 223
  international, 778, 785
Self-insurance, 644
Self-interest, 5
Services, 84, 424
Sherman Antitrust Act of 1890, 551, 553–56, 558
Shifting of taxes, (*See* Incidence of taxes)
Short run, 57, 58, 446, 476, 756
Shortages, 60
  and price ceilings, 73–74, 366–67
Short-run period of production, 447
Shutdown point, 484–85
Single tax movement, 639
Slope of a line, 22
"Small is beautiful," 805
Social costs of inflation, 117
Social costs of unemployment, 107
Social goods, (*See* Public goods)
Social Security system, 298–99, 770–81
Socialism, 40, 793
  Christian, 795
  evolutionary, 793–95
  Fabian, 794
  Marxist, 795–99
  Utopian, 794
Sole proprietorship, 86
Soviet Union, 800–802
Special interest groups, 685–86
Specialization, 13
Specialization gains from trade, 756–60
Specific training, 598
Speculative demand for money, 255
Speculator, 71
Spillovers, (*See* Externalities)
Stabilization branch, 657
Stabilization policies (lags in), 353–58
Stagflation, 306, 312, 331
Standard of deferred payment (money), 221
Standard unit of account (money), 220–21
Stock, 86
Stock market crash of 1929, 155–56, 243
Store of value (money), 220
Strikes, 620, 626–27

Unions, (*See* Labor unions)
Uniqueness gains from trade, 755
Unlimited liability, 86
Usury laws, 250
Util, 425
Utilitarianism, 425
Utility analysis, 425–32
Utility, regulation of companies, 570–72, 578
Utopian socialism, 794

Value-added taxes (*VAT*), 673
Value-added technique for estimating GNP, 130
Value judgments, 10
Value of the marginal product (*VMP*), 588, 612, 614, 617
Variable costs, 451
Velocity of money, 258–59, 263–64
Vertical equity, 664
Vertical integration, 86
Vertical mergers, 549–50
Vertical summation, (*See* Public goods)
Vietnam and inflation, 33–34
Voluntary Export Restrictions (*VER*s), 766–67
Voluntary poverty, 736
Voluntary saving, 387–88 (*See* Consumption, Saving)

Voluntary unemployment, 102
Voting, 678–83
apathy, 678
lumpiness, 36–37, 682
majority rules, 679–80
median voter model, 682–83
point system, 681
and political business cycles, 361–62
tie-in sales aspects of, 682
unanimity, 680

Wage and price controls, 73–75, 315, 364–67
Wage determination
in competitive markets, 593–94
in noncompetitive markets, Chapter 29
Wage differentials, 604, 625–26
Wage discrimination, 615
Wage price policies, 364–67
freeze, 365–66
Wages, 4, 84
differentials in, 604, 625–26
and labor markets, Chapters 28–29
minimum, 75, 599–602
money versus real, 312–13, 335–36
in national income accounting, 127–28
and productivity, 329, 588, 589, 594, 650

subsistence, 797
and unions, 625
Wagner Act, 600, 622
War Against Poverty, 33
Wealth, 647–49, 733
distribution of, 733
and money demand, 267
Wealth effect on Aggregate Demand, 307–9
Webb Pomerene Act of 1918, 555
Wedges, 72
Welfare loss triangle, 665
Welfare programs, 739–42 (*See* Transfer payments)
proposals for reform, 742–44
Welfare state, 803
Wobblies (IWW), 793
Worker management (Yugoslavia), 803
Workfare, 742
World trade, (*See* International trade)
World War II and production possibilities, 33

Yellow dog contracts, 622
Yugoslavia, economic growth, 803

Zero economic profit, 488
Zero sum game, 538

Year	Personal Consumption Expenditures ($ Billions)	Gross Private Domestic Investment ($ Billions)	Government Purchases of Goods and Services ($ Billions)	Net Exports of Goods and Services ($ Billions)	Gross National Product ($ Billions)	National Income ($ Billions)	Personal Income ($ Billions)	Consumer Personal Savings ($ Billions)
1929	77.3	16.7	8.9	1.1	103.9	84.7	84.3	2.6
1930	69.9	10.3	9.2		90.4	75.4	77.0	1.4
1931	60.5	5.6	9.2		75.8	59.7	65.9	0.7
1932	48.6	1.0	8.1		58.0	42.8	50.2	−1.6
1933	45.8	1.6	8.3	0.4	56.0	39.4	46.3	−0.9
1934	51.3	3.3	9.8		65.1	49.5	54.0	0.4
1935	55.7	6.4	10.0		72.2	57.2	60.4	2.1
1936	61.9	8.5	12.0		82.5	65.0	68.6	3.6
1937	66.5	11.8	11.9		90.4	73.6	74.1	3.8
1938	63.9	6.5	13.0		84.7	67.4	68.3	0.7
1939	67.0	9.5	13.6	1.2	91.3	71.2	72.1	1.8
1940	71.0	13.4	14.2	1.8	100.4	79.6	77.6	3.0
1941	80.8	18.3	25.0	1.5	125.5	102.8	95.2	10.0
1942	88.6	10.3	59.9	0.2	159.0	136.2	122.4	27.0
1943	99.5	6.2	88.9	−1.9	192.7	169.7	150.7	32.7
1944	108.2	7.7	97.1	−1.7	211.4	182.6	164.5	36.5
1945	119.6	11.3	83.0	−0.5	213.4	181.6	170.0	28.7
1946	143.9	31.5	29.1	7.8	212.4	180.7	177.6	13.6
1947	161.9	35.0	26.4	11.9	235.2	196.6	190.2	5.2
1948	174.9	47.1	32.6	7.0	261.6	221.5	209.2	11.1
1949	178.3	36.5	39.0	6.5	260.4	215.2	206.4	7.4
1950	192.1	55.1	38.8	2.2	288.3	239.8	228.1	12.6
1951	208.1	60.5	60.4	4.5	333.4	277.3	256.5	16.6
1952	219.1	53.5	75.8	3.2	351.6	291.6	273.8	17.4
1953	232.6	54.9	82.8	1.3	371.6	306.6	290.5	18.4
1954	239.8	54.1	76.0	2.6	372.5	306.3	293.0	16.4
1955	257.9	69.7	75.3	3.0	405.9	336.3	314.2	16.0
1956	270.6	72.7	79.7	5.3	428.2	356.3	337.2	21.3
1957	285.3	71.1	87.3	7.3	451.0	372.8	356.3	22.7
1958	294.6	63.6	95.4	3.3	456.8	375.0	367.1	24.3
1959	316.3	80.2	97.9	1.5	495.8	409.2	390.7	21.8
1960	330.7	78.2	100.6	5.9	515.3	424.9	409.4	20.8
1961	341.1	77.1	108.4	7.2	533.8	439.0	426.0	24.9
1962	361.9	87.6	118.2	6.9	574.6	473.3	453.2	25.9
1963	381.7	93.1	123.8	8.2	606.9	500.3	476.3	24.6
1964	409.3	99.6	130.0	10.9	649.8	537.6	510.2	31.5
1965	440.7	116.2	138.6	9.7	705.1	585.2	552.0	34.3
1966	477.3	128.6	158.6	7.5	772.0	642.0	600.8	36.0
1967	503.6	125.7	179.7	7.4	816.4	677.7	644.5	45.1
1968	552.5	137.0	197.7	5.5	892.7	739.1	707.2	42.5
1969	597.9	153.2	207.3	5.6	963.9	798.1	772.9	42.2
1970	640.0	148.8	218.2	8.5	1,015.5	832.6	831.8	57.7
1971	691.6	172.5	232.4	6.3	1,102.7	898.1	894.0	66.3
1972	757.6	202.0	250.0	3.2	1,212.8	994.1	891.6	61.4
1973	837.2	238.8	266.5	16.8	1,359.3	1,122.7	1,101.7	89.0
1974	916.5	240.8	299.1	16.3	1,472.8	1,203.5	1,210.1	96.7
1975	1,012.8	219.6	335.0	31.1	1,598.4	1,289.1	1,313.4	104.6
1976	1,129.3	277.7	356.9	18.8	1,782.8	1,441.4	1,451.4	95.8
1977	1,257.2	344.1	387.3	1.9	1,990.5	1,617.8	1,607.5	90.7
1978	1,403.5	416.8	425.2	4.1	2,249.7	1,838.2	1,812.4	110.2
1979	1,566.8	454.8	467.8	18.8	2,508.2	2,047.3	2,034.0	118.1
1980	1,732.6	437.0	530.3	32.1	2,732.0	2,203.5	2,258.5	136.9
1981	1,915.1	515.5	588.1	33.9	3,052.6	2,443.5	2,520.9	159.4
1982	2,050.7	447.3	641.7	26.3	3,166.0	2,518.4	2,670.8	153.9
1983	2,234.5	502.3	675.0	−6.1	3,405.7	2,719.5	2,838.6	130.6
1984	2,430.5	664.8	735.9	−58.9	3,772.2	3,028.6	3,108.7	164.1
1985	2,629.4	641.6	818.6	−79.2	4,010.3	3,229.9	3,327.0	127.1
1986	2,799.8	671.0	869.7	−105.5	4,235.0	3,422.9	3,534.3	130.6
1987	2,966.0	716.4		−119.9	4,486.2	3,635.9	3,745.8	120.2

Source: Economic Report of the President, 1988.
Note: 1987 data preliminary.